JFC

Michael W. Foley
Mark McCulley

SAMS

Unleashed

Trademarks

All terms mentioned in this book that are known to be trademarks or service marks have been appropriately capitalized. Sams cannot attest to the accuracy of this information. Use of a term in this book should not be regarded as affecting the validity of any trademark or service mark.

Warning and Disclaimer

Every effort has been made to make this book as complete and as accurate as possible, but no warranty or fitness is implied. The information provided is on an "as is" basis. The authors and the publisher shall have neither liability or responsibility to any person or entity with respect to any loss or damages arising from the information contained in this book or from the use of the CD-ROM or programs accompanying it.

EXECUTIVE EDITOR
Tim Ryan

ACQUISITIONS EDITOR
Tim Ryan

DEVELOPMENT EDITOR
Tim Ryan

MANAGING EDITOR
Patrick Kanouse

PROJECT EDITOR
Rebecca Mounts

COPY EDITOR
Pat Kinyon

INDEXER
Erika Millen

PROOFREADER
Gene Redding

TECHNICAL EDITOR
Jeff Perkins

SOFTWARE DEVELOPMENT SPECIALIST
Adam Swetnam

INTERIOR DESIGN
Gary Adair

COVER DESIGN
Aren Howell

LAYOUT TECHNICIANS
Brandon Allen
Timothy Osborn
Staci Somers
Mark Walchle

Contents at a Glance

Contents

APPENDIXES

B `com.foley.chart` PACKAGE SOURCE CODE   1185

C `com.foley.utility` SOURCE CODE   1237

About the Author

Dr. Michael W. Foley has been designing and developing Java applications since the release of the first Java Developer's Kit. He has also been using the JFC since the first beta releases of the toolkit were released for review. He architected and led the development of the JFC-based user interface for the System Management Arts (SMARTS) InCharge server. Foley has collaborated on other Java programming books and has written many technical papers. Foley was previously president of his own consulting company. He holds a Ph.D. in electrical engineering, and his research consisted of object-oriented design and analysis of simulation applications of electrical power distribution systems.

Mark McCulley works in the field of software engineering both as a programmer and as a technical writer. In a previous career, he designed CPUs and memory systems for microcomputers. Always on the lookout for easier and better ways to do things, he began learning Java in early 1997. Mark is especially interested in music and multimedia software and created the first commercially available MIDI sequencer for the Atari ST computer in 1986.

Dedication

To Molly, you make it all worthwhile.

—Mike Foley

To my father, Charles R. McCulley, Jr., who first introduced me to computers. Remember when you took me to the office on Saturdays and let me play with the adding machines? It's not a coincidence that I turned out to be an engineer...

—Mark McCulley

Acknowledgments

I would like to thank Christine Doerr and John Ellison for teaching me all that I know about writing. You were great mentors and I sure miss working with you. Thanks also to the staff at Macmillan for giving me the opportunity to work on this project and for turning the manuscript into a real book. And last but not least, a heartfelt thanks to Jan, Tamara, Jenny, and Ian for bringing joy and purpose to my life.

Tell Us What You Think!

As the reader of this book, *you* are our most important critic and commentator. We value your opinion and want to know what we're doing right, what we could do better, what areas you'd like to see us publish in, and any other words of wisdom you're willing to pass our way.

As the Executive Editor for the Java team at Macmillan Computer Publishing, I welcome your comments. You can fax, email, or write me directly to let me know what you did or didn't like about this book—as well as what we can do to make our books stronger.

Please note that I cannot help you with technical problems related to the topic of this book, and that due to the high volume of mail I receive, I might not be able to reply to every message.

When you write, please be sure to include this book's title and author as well as your name and phone or fax number. I will carefully review your comments and share them with the author and editors who worked on the book.

Fax: 317-817-7070

Email: java@mcp.com

Mail: Tim Ryan
         Executive Editor
         Java
         Macmillan Computer Publishing
         201 West 103rd Street
         Indianapolis, IN 46290 USA

Introduction

The Java Foundation Classes (JFC) provide a rich collection of user interface classes. The most visible aspect of the JFC is the Swing component toolkit. The Swing component toolkit is a graphical user interface (GUI) toolkit consisting of lightweight components. It contains replacement components for the AWT visual components (such as menus, toolbars, dialog boxes, and so on) that are used to build GUIs. It also contains complex components such as trees and tables that do not have AWT equivalents.

The Swing components are JavaBean compliant. This allows the components to be integrated easily in component design tools. It also allows the Swing components to be integrated easily with other JavaBean-compliant toolkits.

The Swing component toolkit is designed and built using the Model View Controller (MVC) architecture. In this architecture, the data to be displayed is contained in the model, the component displaying the data in the model is the view, and the controller mutates the data. The model sends messages to listeners, typically views, when it changes. The views then update themselves to reflect the current state of the model. The separation of the model from the view allows multiple views to simultaneously display the same data. The Swing visual components act as both the view and the controller, simplifying the architecture.

The Swing visual components employ a pluggable look-and-feel. Each visual component consists of two or more instances. One or more classes define the API for the component, and another set of classes acts as the user interface for the component. The collection of user interface classes is known as a look-and-feel. The JFC contains standard look-and-feel implementations for most popular computer systems and a generic look-and-feel. This allows a program designed and implemented by using Swing components to execute without modification on any kind of computer and to always look and feel just like a program written specifically for the particular computer on which it is running. Conversely, it can also be implemented to always look the same, regardless of what type of computer on which it is running.

The fact that the Swing component toolkit is built on the MVC and pluggable look-and-feel architecture makes the toolkit more complex than traditional user interface toolkits. The visual components contain convenience methods to hide this complexity for casual usage. However, when using the toolkit for serious development, the architecture must be understood. When it is understood, the benefits far outweigh the extra effort required to learn and use its capabilities.

As large and complex a body of work as the Swing component toolkit is, it is only a portion of the JFC. The JFC also contains Java 2D, Drag and Drop (DND), and the Accessibility API. Java 2D is a set of classes for advanced 2D graphics and imaging. DND provides a technology that enables data transfer across Java and native applications, across Java applications, and within a single Java application. The Accessibility API is an interface that enables the use of assistive technologies such as screen magnifiers and audible text readers. These technologies are designed to help people with disabilities interact and communicate more easily and efficiently with JFC components. The Swing components are the primary focus of this book; however, DND and the Accessibility API are also discussed. Java 2D is not addressed in this book.

Who This Book Is Written For

This book is written for developers who are writing JFC-based applications or applets. The book assumes the reader is familiar with the Java language, particularly the AWT. After the first part of the book, each chapter presents one or more component or concept in its entirety. This allows these chapters to be read out of order if desired. You can read the chapter presenting the component you currently are working with and return to earlier chapters when desired.

What This Book Covers

This book consists of six sections. Each section contains multiple chapters that describe related JFC concepts. Multiple example applications are used to demonstrate the strengths and weaknesses of the topic being presented. The JFC is a new toolkit. The vast majority of the components are well designed and implemented. However, there are still some rough edges. These are pointed out so you know what to avoid when creating JFC applications.

Part I, "JFC Architecture," introduces the Swing component toolkit. The MVC architecture and common design patterns used throughout the toolkit are presented. The JComponent class, which serves as the root of the visual components in the Swing toolkit, is included.

In Part II, "JFC Components," you will learn about the basic Swing components. By the end of this section, you will be able to create complete applications or applets containing menus and toolbars. You will learn how to use the Swing components that replace their AWT equivalents. You will be able to create graphical user interfaces consisting of buttons, labels, lists, textual components, and trees and tables. Each component is demonstrated in multiple example applications, providing many hints to get the most out of these components.

In Part III, "Container Components," you will see the container components that are part of the Swing component toolkit. You will learn how to create complex user interfaces using tabbed panes and split panes. You will see how any Swing component can be placed in a scroll pane. You will also see how internal frames can be used to create frames within frames. The internal frame and its support classes provide a framework for building multidocument user interfaces. Each container class is presented with working applications that demonstrate a typical usage of the container. The components from Part II of the book are often used in these examples.

Part IV, "Dialog Boxes," presents the dialog box support contained in the JFC. The JFC contains a rich collection of preconfigured dialog boxes. The `JOptionPane` class allows you to present the user with a message, informational, question, or arbitrary dialog box with a single line of code. There are also more complex preconfigured dialog boxes. The file chooser and color chooser dialog boxes allow a file or color to be chosen. Once again, the implementation of these dialog boxes can be achieved in one or two lines of application code. Numerous examples for the use of each dialog box are presented.

As many preconfigured dialog boxes as the JFC contains, you will often need to build custom dialog boxes. The support for arbitrary dialog boxes contained in the JFC for modal and non-modal dialog boxes is also presented in Part IV of this book.

In Part V, "Extending JFC Components," you will learn how to extend Swing components as well as create completely new components. The pluggable architecture is dissected. The responsibilities it imposes on a component to work within the architecture are fully discussed and demonstrated. Various methods for customizing Swing components are discussed. The properties contained in the `UIManager` are presented. Modifying these properties provides an easy technique for altering the look for a class of component. How to replace the user interface object of existing Swing components to change the look or the feel of the component is also covered. Taking this method to its extreme, a complete look-and-feel implementation is developed.

In this part of the book, you will also learn how to create a new component that supports the pluggable look-and-feel and MVC architectures. These techniques are demonstrated by the development of a chart component that uses the same data model as the Swing table component. The component is used in an application where a single data model is shared between a table and a chart. When data in the table is edited, the chart dynamically updates to reflect the change.

Part VI, "Advanced JFC Concepts," presents numerous advanced JFC programming techniques. In this part of the book, you will learn about the Accessibility API and Drag and Drop. You will also learn about the undo/redo support built into the JFC. The ToolTip and focus managers are presented in this part of the book. You will learn how custom cursors can be used in the JFC. You will also see how the UIManager serves as the focal point for the pluggable look-and-feel architecture introduced in Part V.

Each component and concept presented is supported by one or more working example applications. As complete and educational as these examples are, they do not demonstrate every API for each class in the JFC. To fill in the gaps, a reference section is contained at the end of the book. This section gives the complete API for each Swing class.

After reading this book and going through the examples, you will have the tools required to build complete arbitrary and complex JFC applications and applets. When you arrive at this point, you will truly appreciate the power and elegance of the architecture on which the JFC is built.

JFC Architecture

PART
I

Introduction to JFC

CHAPTER 1

IN THIS CHAPTER

In Java 1.0, user interfaces were created by using the Abstract Window Toolkit (AWT). The AWT provides a set of primitive user interface components. These include such elements as buttons, labels, and text fields; higher-level user-interface components such as lists and choice boxes; classes for creating frames and dialog boxes; and classes to support menus that may be attached to a frame. The AWT also contains an applet entry point.

The original AWT was a peer-based toolkit, meaning that each component created a peer that was implemented in native code for the platform on which the Java Virtual Machine (JVM) was executing. The peer in turn created a window in which the component was displayed. This process of requiring each interface component to create its own window makes the AWT classes difficult to port and proved taxing on system resources. It also led to a problem common among toolkits that target multiple platforms: the least common denominator problem. Toolkits that only support components available on all the targeted platforms lead to an inferior component set that doesn't meet the needs of serious application development.

The AWT also contains classes that are not directly user-interface components. These typically are support classes, including a rich set of AWT Layout Manager classes and geometry classes.

In Java 1.1, extensions of AWT components can be lightweight. A lightweight component is created by extending the AWT `Component` or `Container` class directly. With the introduction of lightweight components, the door was opened for pure Java lightweight component toolkits. Eliminating the requirement for native peers circumvents the least common denominator problem and means that the single Java implementation of a component can be used for all targeted platforms.

The JFC 1.2 Extension

To address the shortcomings of the AWT, the Java Foundation Classes (JFC) were developed. The development of the JFC was unique. JavaSoft provided developers early access releases of the toolkit knowing that the application program interface (API) was subject to change. The developers were asked to use the toolkit and provide feedback on the usability aspects of API for the toolkit. This process was repeated many times before the first official release, known as JFC 1.1 and Swing 1.0.

JFC 1.2 is an extension of the AWT, not a replacement for it. The JFC visual components extend the AWT `Container` class. Thus the methods contained in the `Component` and `Container` classes that AWT programmers are familiar with are still valid for JFC visual classes. This fact also ensures that classes written at the component or container abstraction level will work with JFC classes. A classic example of this is layout managers. A layout manager may be set for any container and arranges components. Since JFC classes extend these classes, layout managers will continue to work as they did with AWT classes.

The AWT user-interface classes are now superseded by classes provided by the JFC. The support classes often play just as important a part in JFC applications as they did in AWT-based applications. AWT support classes, those that do not create a native window, are not replaced by JFC classes.

JFC 1.2 consists of five major packages:

- Swing
- Pluggable Look-and-Feel (PL&F)
- Drag and Drop
- Accessibility
- 2D

WHY THE NAME "SWING"?

Swing is the unofficial name of the Java GUI classes contained in the JFC. The story is that Swing got its name at the 1997 JavaOne convention in San Francisco. A planned demonstration of the new component set was to be set to music. A Swing team member, Georges Saab, voiced the observation that swing music was enjoying a comeback. He went on to suggest that swing would make a nice code name for the project. The slogan potential was not lost on the room full of engineers, including the very famous one provided by Duke Ellington in a popular song, "It Don't Mean a Thing if It Ain't Got That Swing." Thus the name Swing was adopted. The early releases of the component library were released under the code name Swing. Even though Swing components were officially added to JFC 1.1, the name Swing has persisted. This has led to the often quoted statement from the JFC project leader Rick Levenson, "It's spelled 'J', 'F', 'C', but it's pronounced Swing." The name Swing is also used for the package name of the JFC classes.

Swing

Swing components allow for efficient graphical user interface (GUI) development. Swing components are a collection of lightweight visual components. They contain replacements for the basic heavyweight AWT components as well as complex user-interface components such as trees and tables.

Swing components contain a pluggable look-and-feel, abbreviated as PL&F or plaf. This allows the same application to run with a native look-and-feel on different platforms. For example, when running on a Windows platform, the application will look like an application written specifically for the Windows-based computer. The same application, when run on an Apple Macintosh computer, looks like it was written specifically for the Macintosh. When the application is run on a UNIX workstation, it looks like a UNIX application, and so on for any platform to which the JVM has been ported.

Another use of the PL&F is to have an application behave the same on any platform on which it is executed. The JFC contains operating system–neutral look-and-feels that allow an application to present the same look-and-feel independent of the operating system where it executes. This capability can reduce the learning curve for users of applications running in a heterogeneous computer environment.

As a developer, you are not limited to the PL&F shipped with the JFC. You can develop your own look-and-feel that can be used by any JFC application. An organization may want to develop its own to give applications a consistent look-and-feel for use on all its hardware platforms.

Unlike their AWT equivalents, Swing components do not contain peers. Swing components are 100% pure Java and were designed to allow for mixing AWT heavyweight and Swing lightweight components in an application. However, in practice this has proven problematic. Whenever possible you should use all Swing components and components derived from them.

The major difference between lightweight and heavyweight components is that a lightweight component can have transparent pixels while a heavyweight component is always opaque. By taking advantage of transparent pixels, a lightweight component can appear to be non-rectangular, while a heavyweight component must always be rectangular. A mouse event occurring in a lightweight component falls through to its parent component, while a mouse event in a heavyweight component does not propagate through to its parent component. When a lightweight component overlaps a heavyweight component, the heavyweight component is always drawn on top of the lightweight component, regardless of the relative z-order of the two components.

The Swing components are JavaBean compliant. This allows the components to be used easily in a Bean-aware application building program. The Swing release contains `BeanInfo` classes for the Swing UI (user interface) components to aid in using Swing in builder applications.

With all these great new features provided by the JFC, it may be asked if the AWT is required at all. The answer is yes, it is. This is because Swing is an extension for the AWT, not a replacement. The root of the majority of the Swing hierarchy is the JComponent class. This class is an extension of the AWT Container class. Thus the necessity of the AWT classes, even when using Swing components. This is demonstrated in Figure 1.1. This figure shows that Swing is built on the base AWT classes, but not on the AWT UI component classes. For example, the AWT button or label classes are not extended.

FIGURE 1.1

The Swing architecture.

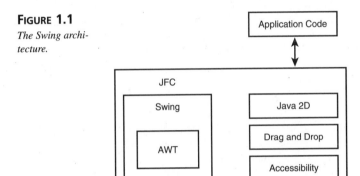

When there are equivalent classes in each toolkit for a particular UI component, the Swing version should be used. For example, the AWT provides an implementation of a button in the Button class. Swing also provides an implementation for a button in the JButton class. The JButton class should be used in JFC applications. This allows the PL&F to be changed and the button to be drawn by using the current PL&F. The JFC contains many complex components, such as a tree and table, that simply are not available in the AWT.

Swing components comprise a large percentage of the JFC release and are the major focus of this book. However they are not the only innovations contained in the JFC. The JFC contains the Java 2D classes. These classes provide an API for advanced two-dimensional graphic rendering in Java: many different paint styles, APIs for defining complex shapes, coordinate transformations, and more. The Drag and Drop API provides data transfer between Java and native applications as well as within a single Java application. The Accessibility APIs are provided to aid people with disabilities while interacting with JFC components. Unlike Swing, however, these portions of the JFC are not 100% pure Java implementations. The AWT components are to be enhanced to support these new features in the 1.2 release of the JDK.

Packages

The Swing component toolkit consists of over 250 pure Java classes and 75 interfaces contained in more than 10 packages. They are used to build lightweight user interfaces. Swing consists of non–user-interface (non-UI) classes as well as the more familiar user-interface (UI) classes. The non-UI classes provide services and other operations for the UI classes. They do not display anything on screen. Examples of non-UI Swing classes are the events fired by Swing components and the Swing data model classes. The UI classes, such as buttons and labels, create visible components that applications can display on screen, and they can be combined to create a complete graphical user interface. The Swing UI components descend from the JComponent class, and all begin with the capital letter J.

Swing packages that are typically used by developers when building GUIs are listed, and briefly explained, in the following sections.

WHERE SHOULD THE SWING PACKAGES LIVE?

As was mentioned earlier in the chapter, Swing was released to developers for feedback during design and development of the toolkit. There were two versions of the toolkit for review: one that ran with the released 1.1 version of the JDK, and another that ran with the 1.2 beta version of the JDK. The root of the toolkit for the 1.1 JDK was contained in the com.sun.java.swing package. Support classes were located in sub-packages to this base package. The root of the toolkit for the 1.2 beta JDK was java.awt.swing. Due to security restrictions browsers can not download from the network core Java classes, that is, classes whose package name begins with java. The com.sun.java.swing package name allowed 1.1-enabled browsers to download the Swing packages from the server.

When the 1.2 beta4 version of the JDK was released, it was also announced that the Swing packages were not to be part of the java.awt.swing package, but would remain in the 1.1 JDK-compatible com.sun.java.swing package. In JDK Release Candidate 1, the package name changed to javax.swing. The rational for this decision was that many developers had developed applications using the 1.1 names, and changing to the 1.2 package name would be complicated. This decision has been very controversial. Until this point, classes contained in com.sun packages have been undocumented and not guaranteed to be available on all platforms. Developers have raised the concern that the Swing packages will not be available on all platforms. However, JavaSoft has guaranteed that Swing is part of the core Java release and will be available on all platforms, including browsers.

This author agrees with the concerns expressed by many developers after the package name announcement. The core Java packages should follow a consistent naming convention. The reason cited for not changing the name is insufficient. Changing package names for the Swing packages in a large project would have been painful; however, this would have been a one-time change, and developers were told of the intention to change the package names from the beginning. Now developers are going to have to live with the pain of a non-standard named package for the foreseeable future.

The Swing Package: `javax.swing`

This is the largest of the Swing packages consisting of approximately 100 classes and 25 interfaces. The majority of the UI classes (the "J" classes) are contained in this package. The exceptions are `JTableHeader`, implemented in the `javax.swing.table` package, and `JTextComponent`, implemented in the `javax.swing.text` package. Both of these packages are described shortly. Also contained in this package are high-level choice components. This type of component allows the user to visually choose a value from a fixed set of possible values—choosing a color, for example. The components in this package are the primary focus of this book (see Figure 1.2). Examples of their use are given throughout.

FIGURE 1.2

Examples of the basic Swing components in the Windows PL&F.

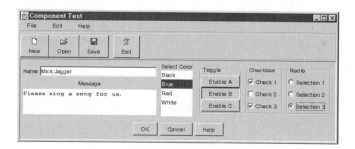

The Basic Package: `javax.swing.plaf.basic`

The Basic package contains classes that define the default look-and-feel of Swing components. By extending these classes, components with a customized PL&F can be developed. This is the second largest package in terms of the number of classes, containing approximately 40 classes. The high number of classes should give a feel for the amount of work required to develop a complete PL&F.

The Border Package: `javax.swing.border`

The Border package contains the `Border` interface and nine classes that implement this interface. Typically classes in this package are not instantiated directly; instead, instances are obtained via methods in the `BorderFactory` class contained in the `javax.swing` package. However, the constants defined in the classes in this package are often used when obtaining borders from the factory. Classes in this package can be extended to create a specialized border. The Border package and the borders contained in the JFC are presented in Chapter 5, "Basic Components."

The Event Package: `javax.swing.event`

The Event package defines events specific to Swing components. The events defined in this package fill roles similar to those defined in the `java.awt.event` package. There are approximately 25 Swing-specific events. The events themselves and their associated `Listener` interfaces are defined in this package. Swing events are used by the various data models contained in the JFC. The events are presented with the classes that fire the particular event.

The Multipackage: `javax.swing.plaf.multi`

The Multipackage consists of multiplexing UI classes. These allow Swing components to have UIs provided by multiple user-interface factories.

The Pluggable Look-and-Feel Package: `javax.swing.plaf`

The PL&F package consists of classes that provide Swing components with pluggable look-and-feel capabilities. If a custom PL&F is being developed and the classes in the `javax.swing.plaf.basic` package cannot be extended, the abstract classes contained in this package can be used as a starting point. The JFC is shipped with three PL&Fs: the Windows PL&F contained in the `com.sun.java.swing.plaf.windows` package (see Figure 1.2), the Motif PL&F contained in the `com.sun.java.swing.plaf.motif` package (see Figure 1.3), and the Metal platform-neutral PL&F contained in the `javax.swing.plaf.metal` package (see Figure 1.4). The Macintosh PL&F contained in the `com.sun.java.swing.plaf.mac` package is available separately.

FIGURE 1.3

The Motif PL&F.

FIGURE 1.4

The Metal PL&F.

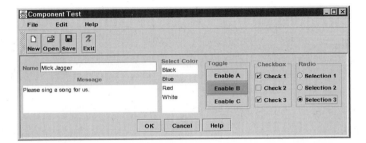

The Table Package: `javax.swing.table`

The Table package contains classes and interfaces specific to the Swing table component, `JTable`. It contains the `TableColumnModel` and `TableModel` interfaces, as well as interfaces that define rendering and editing components for a table. There are also default implementations of each of these interfaces in this package. Simple tables can be created and used without knowledge of the interfaces or classes in this package. To utilize the full capabilities of the `JTable` component, however, the classes and interfaces contained in this package must be understood. An example of a Swing table is shown in Figure 1.5. A complete description of the `JTable` component and the support classes contained in this package is presented in Chapter 12, "Table Component."

FIGURE 1.5

The Swing table component.

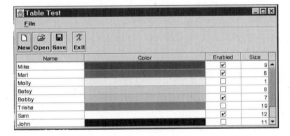

The Text Package: `javax.swing.text`

The Text package contains classes and interfaces for the rich set of text manipulation components contained in the Swing toolkit. These include the various document and document support interfaces, as well as default implementations of these interfaces. The Text package also contains two child packages, the `javax.swing.text.html` package for HTML content and the `javax.swing.text.rtf` package for rich text format content. A complete overview of the text features in the JFC is presented in Chapter 7, "Text Components."

The Tree Package: `javax.swing.tree`

This package contains classes that are used with the Swing tree component, JTree (see Figure 1.6). The TreeModel and various node interfaces are defined in this package, as well as default implementations of each interface. The JTree component may be used to create simple trees without knowledge of the interfaces and classes contained in this package. To take full advantage of the JTree component, the interfaces and classes in this package must be understood. A complete description of the JTree component and its supporting classes contained in this package is presented in Chapter 11, "Tree Component."

FIGURE 1.6

The Swing tree component.

The Undo Package: `javax.swing.undo`

The Undo package contains the interfaces and classes required to implement the undo functionality in JFC applications. This allows for an application to easily add Undo and Redo functionality. A complete description of the Undo and Redo features of the JFC is presented in Chapter 28, "Undo and Redo."

Drag and Drop

The JFC drag-and-drop capabilities allow the transfer of data between Java applications, as well as Java to native applications. A component may be a drag source, a drop target, or both. As is common with well-written Java toolkits, interfaces define the methods required to be a drag source or drop target. Implementing these interfaces allows the component to participate in a drag operation.

An unusual aspect of drag-and-drop in the Java environment is flavor maps. A flavor map is a mapping between the device-dependent data type and the Java device-independent data type. This allows a Java application to transfer data with a native application without requiring the Java application to know the specifics about the native data types.

The Drag and Drop Package: `java.awt.dnd`

This package consists of four interfaces and fourteen classes that define drag-and-drop operations. There is an interface that a drag source and a drop target must implement, as well as an interface for the data flavors that can be transferred. A complete drag-and-drop example is given in Chapter 34, "Drag and Drop."

Accessibility

The Java Accessibility API provides the framework for JFC applications to interact with assistive technologies. A properly written JFC application can be executed by assistive technologies such as Braille terminals and screen readers just as easily as it is run on conventional computers.

The Accessibility Package: `javax.accessibility`

The Accessibility package consists of eight interfaces and five classes. It contains the `Accessible` interface that is the main interface for the JFC Accessibility package. Any accessible component must implement this interface. The Accessibility package is presented in Chapter 33, "Accessibility."

Summary

The Java Foundation Classes provide a lightweight extension to the original AWT toolkit contained in the Java Virtual Machine. The user-interface portion of the JFC was developed under the codename Swing. The name has stuck, and these packages are still known as the Swing packages. Although these packages consist of over 250 classes and 75 interfaces, learning how to use the JFC is not an insurmountable task. These classes are divided into user interface (UI) classes, known as the J classes, and non-user interface (non-UI) classes. The UI classes contain a visual representation that can be used to interact with the user. The combination of instances of these classes is used to develop a complete graphical user interface. The non-UI classes provide support for the UI classes. Examples of non-UI classes include the Swing `Event` class and the model classes. These classes will be explored and their use demonstrated in the remainder of this book.

MVC Architecture

CHAPTER 2

The design of the JFC is built upon a variant of the Model View Controller (MVC) architecture. This is not a new architecture for software applications, but it is new to the Java graphical user interface toolkit. MVC is a well-understood architecture that has been used in other programming languages for years. The JFC makes extensive use of a couple of design patterns. Understanding the architecture and these patterns will enhance your ability to build robust JFC applications.

The JFC can be used like a typical graphical user interface toolkit: create and arrange a display's buttons, lists, and so on. If the user interacts with the display, the data is queried from the view and stored elsewhere in the application. Similarly, if the application's data changes, the program queries the data and updates the view components. In this scenario, the view contains its own copy of the data it displays. The application is responsible for keeping the view's data in sync with its internal data representation.

The JFC can be used in this dumb toolkit mode, but by doing so you ignore a much more powerful underlying technology called the Model View Controller (MVC) architecture. In MVC, the application data is contained in the model, one or more views are used to present the data to the user, and controls are used to interact with the data in the model.

The remainder of this chapter describes the MVC architecture, as well as a few other design patterns common in the JFC.

The MVC Architecture

The Model View Controller architecture consists of three types of classes. The model consists of the application data classes. The view consists of the application presentation. The controller classes define how user interaction is handled in the application. The MVC architecture decouples these functional components, allowing for easier reuse of code than in a traditional user interface toolkit.

Some communication mechanisms must be provided with the decoupled functional entities in the MVC architecture. In the JFC, a subscribe-and-publish paradigm is employed. Under this paradigm, objects express interest in a data source by subscribing. When the data source changes state, a notification is published to the subscribed object. Multiple objects can subscribe to the same data source at the same time. Similarly, an object can subscribe to multiple data sources. An object unsubscribes from a data source when it is no longer interested in it. After unsubscribing, the data source will not send additional events to the subscriber. The controller objects are used to mutate the data sources. The mutation is typically accomplished by calling a method on the data model.

The MVC example shown in Figure 2.1 shows that the views have subscribed to the model data source. A source of input causes the first controller object to send a message that changes the data contained in the model. After the model has changed its state, it publishes a change message to each of the views that have previously subscribed with the model. In this example, the entities that subscribe to the model are shown as views.

FIGURE 2.1
MVC communication example.

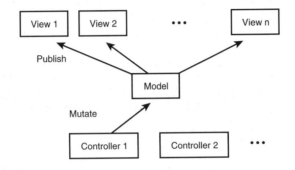

However, any type of object can subscribe to receive data change messages. For example an object that logs changes to a file could subscribe to the data model. It is important to understand that the order in which subscribers are notified is undefined. This gives models the flexibility to serve subscribers in any way convenient for that model. It also prohibits designing views that require notifications in a specified order from a single model. If notification order is required, subscribers must daisy chain themselves and forward the notification in the proper order. This situation is depicted in Figure 2.2. Daisy chaining subscribers complicates each subscriber. It must be capable of accepting subscription requests and publishing messages when they are received.

FIGURE 2.2
Daisy-chained subscribers.

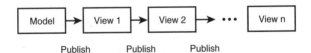

Combined View and Control in JFC

The JFC has taken some liberties in its implementation of the MVC architecture. In the JFC, the visual components double as both views and controllers. The justification for this design is that the visual components interact with the user, and it is burdensome to force that component to send a message to a controller that forwards the control message to the model. This simplification of the architecture leads to more efficient components, but does limit flexibility.

The JFC defines a read-only view of the data by defining interfaces for each type of data model. Default implementations for each model interface are also provided. This allows a view to display the contents of any data source that implements the model interface.

Defining the data model as an interface allows the JFC to be more efficient than conventional component toolkits. In a conventional toolkit, the data is copied into the component for display. This requires multiple copies of the same data to be present in the application. For example, to populate an AWT `List` component, code similar to the following can be used.

```
String[] fruits = { "Apple", "Banana", "Orange", "Pear" };
List list = new List();
for( int i = 0; i < fruits.length; i++
    list.add( fruits(i));
```

As seen in this example, the application stores the data to be presented in the `List` component in an array. The `List` component itself creates additional storage for the data it displays. Thus there are two copies of the data structure, one in the application and another in the `List` component. If the application's data array changes, the `List` will not reflect the change unless the application explicitly updates it with the new data. This forces the application not only to manage the data, but also to keep all views of the data current. This example also suffers the inefficiency of the time taken to add each item to the list. The `add` method of the `List` class is synchronized, which, at the time of this writing, is still a costly operation in Java.

When using the JFC, your class containing the data could implement the `ListModel` interface. The `ListModel` interface provides methods for the view to query the size of the model and retrieve items from the model. The previous example for a `List` visual component would look like the following in the JFC:

```
class TestListModel extends AbstractListModel {
    String[] fruits = { "Apple", "Banana", "Orange", "Pear" };

    public int getSize() {
        return( fruits.length );
    }

    public Object getElementAt(int index) {
        return( fruits[ index ] );
    }
}

// Some view needing to display the fruits list.
ListModel model = new TestListModel();
JList list = new JList( model );
```

This example takes advantage of one of the default model implementations: the `AbstractListModel` class. Methods to add and remove subscription listeners are inherited from the superclass. The concrete model class only needs to define the methods to return the actual data. The model interfaces, as well as their associated abstract and default implementations, will be presented later in this book as each component is presented.

For such a trivial example, creating a class to contain the data may seem like overkill, and probably is. When the data consists of thousands of items, however, the JFC architecture shines. The data source can implement multiple model interfaces, allowing many view components to present the data with various visual representations. Finally, multiple visual components can be developed to read the same model. This allows the data to implement fewer model interfaces and still be presented with many different visual representations.

When evaluating a toolkit, performance measures such as "How long does it take to add ten thousand items to a list?" are often considered. These types of measurements for properly written JFC applications are irrelevant. The reason for this is that ten thousand items are never added to a list. Instead, the data source implements the `ListModel` interface and is immediately available for display. The difference in these two architectures is demonstrated in the following example:

```java
package com.foley.test;

import java.awt.*;

import javax.swing.*;

/**
 * A simple example to time adding items to an AWT List and
 * JFC JList components.
 *
 * @author Mike Foley
 **/
public class TestList {

    /**
     * Application entry point.
     * The arguments are not used.
     *
     * @param args Command line arguments passed to the application.
     **/
    public static void main( String[] args ) {

        //
        // Time adding Strings to an AWT List component.
        //
        long d = System.currentTimeMillis();
        List awtList = new List();
        for( int i = 0; i < 10000; i++ ) {
            awtList.add( "Item " + i );
        }
```

```
System.out.println( "AWT time: " +
    ( System.currentTimeMillis() - d ) );

//
// Time creating a ListModel and adding it to
// a JList component.
//
d = System.currentTimeMillis();
ListModel model = new AbstractListModel() {
    public int getSize() { return( 10000 ); }
    public Object getElementAt( int index )
        { return( "Item " + index ); }
};
JList jfcList = new JList( model );
System.out.println( "JFC time: " +
    (System.currentTimeMillis() - d ) );
    }
}
```

When running this example on a 300MHz Pentium II processor computer with 128MB of RAM, the AWT `List` creation averaged a whopping 1.65 seconds while the JFC `JList` creation averaged approximately 0.015 seconds. The `JList` was two orders of magnitude faster. This obviously is a jaded example because the objects for the `JList` are lazily created when requested by the view. However, it approximates many real-world programming examples when the data to be displayed is already in a data structure in memory or can be lazily evaluated when, and if, requested. The JFC architecture gives the application developer the flexibility to store and/or evaluate data in the best way for your particular application. It does not force an assumed structure on the data.

It should be pointed out that the JFC contains convenience methods for handling simple examples such as that shown previously. The most likely manner in which this example would be coded using the JFC is as follows:

```
String[] fruits = { "Apple", "Banana", "Orange", "Pear" };
JList list = new JList( fruits );
```

In this example, the `JList` class creates an anonymous inner class that implements the `ListModel` interface. This model, which is hidden from the caller, wraps the array given in the `JList` constructor. The inner class is used by the list component as the data model.

The previous discussion illustrates the power of the JFC toolkit. It can be used as a light-weight viewing engine for any data source, or, using default models and convenience methods, it can be used like a traditional widget toolkit. Most production applications will exhibit examples of both uses of the JFC toolkit.

The JFC provides the `Action` interface to embody elements of application behavior. The JFC provides many `Action`-aware components that allow an action to be easily tied to a keystroke, menu item, or toolbar. If an application or applet is developed with actions that define behavior, the actions may be thought of as the controllers in the MVC architecture. The Action interface will be presented in detail in Chapter 4, "JFC Programming Techniques," and examples of Action-aware components will be presented throughout this book.

Factory Design Pattern

The version of the MVC design pattern implemented in the JFC may be the most visible pattern used, but there are others sprinkled throughout. The parameterized factory design pattern creates an instance of a class depending on the parameter given to the factory. This pattern is easily implemented in Java and is used to hide specific class details from a Client class.

The parameterized factory pattern can be implemented in Java by exposing an interface that defines the behavior of classes in a package. Then one or more static creation functions are provided for clients to obtain instances of classes in the package. Parameters passed to one of the construction methods determine which class in the package is instantiated. The Client class interacts with the Concrete class returned from the factory creation method through the public methods defined in the package's public interface(s).

Parameterized Factory Pattern Example

The following example demonstrates the parameterized factory design pattern. The example implements a Reporter package that writes messages to either the console or a file. An application uses a factory method to obtain a reference to a Reporter. The client code interacts with the Reporter through the methods defined in the Reporter interface shown here.

```
package com.foley.reporter;

import java.io.IOException;


/**
 * The Reporter interface. All types of
 * Reporters must implement this interface. A client
 * gets a handle to a Reporter using the ReporterFactory
 * class.
 *
 * @see ReporterFactory
 * @author Mike Foley
 **/
public interface Reporter {
```

```
/**
 * Method to write a message to the reporting system.
 * A newline is added after the message is written.
 *
 * @param message The message to be written.
 **/
public void writeln( String message ) throws IOException;

/**
 * Existing Reporter types.
 **/
static final ReporterType CONSOLE = new ReporterType();
static final ReporterType FILE = new ReporterType();


/**
 * Type safe class for reporters.
 **/
final class ReporterType {
}

} // Reporter
```

In this simple example, the Reporter only defines one method, writeln. Also of interest in the Reporter interface are the type-safe constants of defined Reporter types. These types are used in the ReporterFactory as well as by clients to specify the type of Reporter desired.

The ReporterFactory, shown next, is used by clients to obtain a handle on a Reporter of the desired type. The static getReporter method is passed one of the type-safe constants defined in the Reporter interface. This value is tested, and the proper Reporter type is returned to the caller. Using the type-safe constants in the getReporter method allows the compiler to detect improper type requests. This would not be possible if an int was used for the Reporter type.

The ReporterFactory lazily creates a single Reporter instance of the proper type when it is requested. Clients requesting the Reporter share the single instance of the requested type. However, this implementation detail is hidden from the client. If a separate FileReporter is desired for each client, this change may be implemented in the factory without altering client code.

```
package com.foley.reporter;

import java.io.IOException;


/**
 * A factory class to retrieve a Reporter of the specified
```

```
 * type. If additional Reporter types are added to the system,
 * the factory method must be updated to construct the new types.
 *
 * @author Mike Foley
 **/
public class ReporterFactory extends Object {

    /**
     * The shared Reporter instances.
     * These are lazily created when requested.
     **/
    private static ConsoleReporter consoleReporter;
    private static FileReporter fileReporter;


    /**
     * Method to obtain a Reporter.
     *
     * @param type The type of Reporter desired.
     * @return The Reporter of the specified type.
     * @exception IOException If the Reporter can not be initialized.
     **/
    public static Reporter getReporter( Reporter.ReporterType type )
        throws IOException {

        if( type == Reporter.CONSOLE ) {

            //
            // Return the console reporter instance.
            // If this doesn't yet exist, create it.
            //
            if( consoleReporter == null )
                consoleReporter = new ConsoleReporter();
            return( consoleReporter );

        } else if( type == Reporter.FILE ) {

            //
            // Return the file reporter instance.
            // If this doesn't yet exist, create it.
            //
            if( fileReporter == null )
                fileReporter = new FileReporter();
            return( fileReporter );

        }

        throw( new RuntimeException(
                "A new Reporter type must have been added." ) );
```

```
    } // getReporter

} // ReporterFactory
```

The two concrete `Reporter` types are shown next. Each class implements the `Reporter` interface, allowing them to be returned by the `ReporterFactory`. In the `writeln` method, the `ConsoleReporter` simply calls the `System.out.println` method to echo the message to the console. The `FileReporter` is slightly more complex, as a `File` is created in the constructor. The file is written to in the `writeln` method.

```java
package com.foley.reporter;


/**
 * A Reporter that writes to the console.
 *
 * @author Mike Foley
 **/
class ConsoleReporter implements Reporter {

    /**
     * writeln, from Reporter
     *
     * Method to write a message to the reporting system.
     * Write the message to the console.
     *
     * @param message The message to be written.
     **/
    public synchronized void writeln( String message ) {
        System.out.println( message );
    }

} // ConsoleReporter


package com.foley.reporter;

import java.io.File;
import java.io.DataOutputStream;
import java.io.FileOutputStream;
import java.io.IOException;


/**
 * A Reporter that writes to a file. The file
 * written to is hard coded to 'Reporter.txt'
 * in the current directory.
 *
 * @author Mike Foley
```

```
**/
class FileReporter implements Reporter {

    /**
     * The file and stream to Report to.
     **/
    File outputFile;
    DataOutputStream outputStream;


    /**
     * Construct a FileReporter.
     *
     * @exception IOException If the file can not be opened for writing.
     **/
    FileReporter() throws IOException {

        outputFile = new File( "Reporter.txt" );
        outputStream = new DataOutputStream(
                        new FileOutputStream( outputFile ) );

    }


    /**
     * writeln, from Reporter
     *
     * Method to write a message to the reporting system.
     * Write the message to the Reporter file.
     *
     * @param message The message to be written.
     * @exception IOException If the message can not be written.
     **/
    public synchronized void writeln( String message )
        throws IOException {
        outputStream.writeBytes( message + "\n" );
    }

} // FileReporter
```

The classes presented to this point are all contained in the Reporter package. Combined, they implement a parameterized factory. The last example in this section contains an application to obtain a handle to a Reporter and write messages to it. The application requires a single parameter—the type of Reporter to create. After testing the command line argument, the Reporter of the requested type is obtained from the ReporterFactory. Notice the use of the type-safe constant when requesting the Reporter. A few messages are written with the desired Reporter.

The test application is in a different package than the Reporter itself. This is common for parameterized factories. The package interface and factory are public. However, the

2

MVC
ARCHITECTURE

Concrete classes that implement the package interface are not `public`. Thus, the only methods of these classes exposed to clients are those that are defined in the package interface, `Reporter` in this example.

```java
package com.foley.test;

import java.io.IOException;

import com.foley.reporter.Reporter;
import com.foley.reporter.ReporterFactory;


/**
 * A simple class to test the Reporter package.
 *
 * @author Mike Foley
 **/
public class TestReporter extends Object {

    /**
     * Create a Reporter of the given type, and echo
     * a few lines of text to it. The type is determined
     * by the program argument as follows:
     *
     *      file        FileReporter
     *      console     ConsoleReporter
     *
     **/
    public static void main( String[] args ) {

        //
        // Ensure we have an argument.
        //
        if( args.length != 1 ) {
            usage();
            System.exit( -1 );
        }

        //
        // Create the proper Reporter.
        //
        Reporter reporter = null;
        try {
            if( args[0].toLowerCase().equals( "file" ) ) {
                reporter = ReporterFactory.getReporter( Reporter.FILE );
            } else if( args[0].toLowerCase().equals( "console" ) ) {
                reporter = ReporterFactory.getReporter(Reporter.CONSOLE);
            } else {
                usage();
                System.exit( -2 );
            }
```

```
        reporter.writeln( "This is a simple test of the Reporter" );
        reporter.writeln(
                "It will be written to a file, or the console" );

    } catch( IOException io ) {
        System.out.println( "Reporter system error." );
        io.printStackTrace();
        System.exit( -3 );
    }
} // main


/**
 * Write a simple usage message to the console.
 **/
private static void usage() {
    System.out.println( "usage:\tTestReporter reporterType" );
    System.out.println( "\twhere reporterType is console or file" );
} // usage

} // TestReporter
```

An example of the parameterized factory pattern in the JFC is the Border package. The Border package defines a `Border` interface that specifies the methods all borders must implement. The `BorderFactory` class contains public static methods for obtaining a handle to concrete borders that can be used for the calling class's components.

The Border package in the JFC is not a pure parameterized factory pattern. It allows the classes in the Border package to be instantiated directly. However, this is discouraged. The reason for this is more practical than just the desire for design purity. In some situations, borders may be shared among clients. If the `BorderFactory` is used to obtain a reference to the desired border, the factory can share borders when appropriate. The current implementation of the `BorderFactory` class shares `Bevel` and `Etched` borders that use the default colors. In the JFC, the `BorderFactory` lives in the Swing package instead of the Border package.

A complete reference to borders and the `BorderFactory` is given in Chapter 5, "Basic Components." Borders are also used in examples throughout this book.

Singleton Pattern

The singleton pattern is a design pattern used to ensure that only one instance of a class is instantiated. This single instance is shared by any classes requiring its services.

The singleton pattern can be implemented in Java by using a protected, or `private`, constructor for a class and a `public` access method to obtain a handle to the single instance of the class. This is demonstrated with the following simple example:

```
public class MySingleTon extends Object {

    /**
     * The reference to the one and only instance
     * of the mySingleTon class.
     **/
    private static MySingleTon mySingleTon = null;

    /**
     * Protected constructor ensures that this class,
     * or subclasses, are the only entities
     * that can create instances of the class.
     **/
    protected MySingleTon() {
    }

    /**
     * Public access method.
     * Lazily create the shared instance of this class.
     * @return the shared instance of this class.
     **/
    public static MySingleTon getMySingleTon() {
        if( mySingleTon == null ) {
            mySingleTon = new MySingleTon();
        }

        return( mySingleTon );
    }

    // Public service methods for this class
    // would follow.
    //
    public void doSomething() {
    }
}
```

In this example, the constructor method is protected. This prevents multiple instances of the class from being created, but still allows the class to be extended. If the class were final, the constructor would be `private`. A static `public` access method is provided that allows clients to retrieve a handle to the shared instance of the class. In this example, the instance is lazily evaluated. The shared instance will not be created until it is requested. If the shared instance must be created at all times, the static initializer method called when the class is loaded could be used to create the shared instance. As in any other class, `public` methods are provided to operate on the singleton instance.

Clients use the singleton instance by first calling the static access method to obtain the reference to the instance. Then methods can be called on that instance, just as if it had been created with the new operator. The following example shows how a client may use the MySingleTon class:

```
MySingleTon mySingleTon = MySingleTon.getMySingleTon();
//
// Call methods on mySingleTon
//
mySingleTon.doSomething();
```

The JFC contains many examples of singleton classes. Most of them are service-type classes. One such example is the ToolTipManager class. The single instance is retrieved via the sharedInstance static method. The ToolTipManager class is discussed in Chapter 25, "ToolTips and Debug Graphics."

Summary

This chapter introduced the architecture on which the JFC is built. The JFC is built on a modified Model View Controller architecture. The view and controllers are combined into a single object in the JFC. This simplification requires less messaging between objects. Specifically, the views do not need to message controllers, who in turn message the model in response to user gestures. Instead, the view messages the model directly. This simplification reduces messaging at the cost of reducing flexibility in the design and reuse of controller objects.

The factory and singleton design patterns were introduced in this chapter. These design patterns are used throughout the JFC. Having an understanding of these patterns will enable you to obtain a deeper understanding of the JFC, and it will allow your code to build on the JFC architecture and not simply use the toolkit.

JComponent

CHAPTER 3

The JComponent class is the root of the visual component class hierarchy in the JFC. The visual components are known as the "J" classes. This is because each of the class names begins with the letter J. As such, the functionality contained in the JComponent class is available to all the visual components contained in the JFC. The JComponent class turns into a repository of functionality required for all visual components. This includes keystroke handling, accessibility support, borders, and much more. This common functionality makes the JComponent class a large and complex one that must be thoroughly understood to take full advantage of the JFC toolkit. A hint of the complexity and sheer size of the JComponent class is the approximately 30 javadoc pages for the class that accompany the JFC toolkit.

This chapter will dissect the JComponent class, looking at each segment of its functionality individually. Specifically, you will see the following:

- The visual class hierarchy
- Pluggable look-and-feel support in JComponent
- Keystroke handling in JComponent
- The Border property
- Scrolling support
- Accessibility support
- Internationalization support

Top of the JFC Visual Component Hierarchy

The JComponent class sits atop the hierarchy of the visual classes contained in the JFC. This hierarchy is shown in Figure 3.1. Its position in the hierarchy implies that its functionality is common to all visual components in the JFC toolkit. This makes understanding the JComponent class critical to taking full advantage of the JFC toolkit.

The JComponent class is an abstract class that extends the AWT Container class. The Container class extends the AWT Component class. In the AWT, there is a distinction between components that are containers and those that are not. For example, the AWT Label class extends Component. As such, other components cannot be added to instances of the Label class. However, the AWT Panel class extends the Container class, which does allow components to be added to it. Thus, the position in the class hierarchy defines if a class can act as a container or not. With the JComponent class extending the Component class, this distinction doesn't exist in the JFC. Thus, every JComponent is a container, even though many are not designed to be used as such. This forces those classes to carry the extra baggage of being a container, even though it is not used. This is an unfortunate consequence of the JFC being layered on top of the AWT. Most, if not all, of the functionality contained in the JComponent class would be better suited in the Component class.

FIGURE 3.1

JFC visual component class hierarchy.

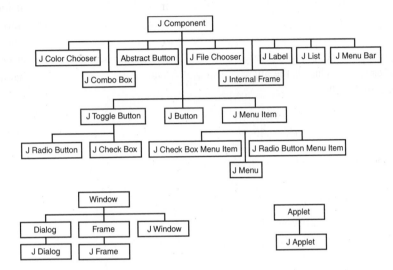

Client Properties

A client property is a piece of information that can be attached to an instance of any JFC visual component. The property consists of a name-value pair. The name is a key that uniquely identifies the value for a particular instance. Internally, client properties are implemented as a Dictionary, specifically an instance of the HashTable class. Client properties are used internally by the JFC in many situations. For example, a component's ToolTip, keyboard bindings, and the next focus component are all stored as client properties on a component.

Client properties are not limited to use within the JFC itself. Components that extend JFC visual components can store data in client properties as well as arbitrary code that creates and uses instances of JFC visual components. The former will be discussed in Part V of this book, "Extending JFC Components," while the later will be discussed here.

An arbitrary Object can be associated with a JFC visual component instance by using the putClientProperty method contained in the JComponent class. When the property is placed on the component, a key is associated with the object. The client property can be obtained later via the getClientProperty method and the key used when adding the property. A simple example of using a client property is shown in the following:

```
JButton button = new JButton( "Help" );
button.putClientProperty( "SpecialColor", Color.blue );
Color myColor = ( Color )button.getClientProperty( "SpecialColor" );
```

This example adds a client property with the String key "SpecialColor" to an instance of the JButton class. In this example, a string is used as the key, but an arbitrary object can be used as the key. The property in the example is a Color but, like the key, the property can be of any type. If the property value is null in the putClientProperty call, the property is removed from the instance. However, null cannot be used as the key. If this occurs, a NullPointerException is thrown. The getClientProperty method returns the object associated with the given key for the instance. If there has not been an object associated with the key, null is returned. Any number of client properties can be added to a component. However, each property must have a unique key.

When a client property is set, a PropertyChange event is fired by the component that contains the property. The name of the property change event is the value returned from the toString method key used to store the client property. This provides a very versatile mechanism for attaching data to a visual component and allowing other objects to listen for changes in this property.

ToolTip Support

ToolTips are the pop-up windows common in modern user interfaces that present the user with a short informative message when the mouse rests over the component. ToolTips are also known as *flyover* help. The JComponent class contains a client property for ToolTips. The ToolTip is stored as a client property rather than a member variable to save space. All JComponent instances do not contain ToolTips, so allocating a reference to a string in every instance is obsessive.

The setToolTipText method can be used to set the ToolTip for a J component. The following is a simple example for adding a ToolTip to a JButton instance:

```
JButton button = new JButton( "Help" );
button.setToolTipText( "Open the on-line help for this window" );
```

When the setToolTipText method is called with a non-null string, the component is registered with the ToolTip manager to enable ToolTips. If the string is null, the component is removed from the ToolTip manager. The ToolTip manager and its options are described in Chapter 25, "ToolTips and Debug Graphics."

The current value of the `ToolTip` property can be queried with the `getToolTipText` method. This method returns the current `String` value of the `ToolTip` client property or `null` if a ToolTip hasn't been registered for the component.

There are many situations when the ToolTip for a component is not static. Instead, it depends on the current state of the component or where the mouse is located in the component. When creating components that extend the `JComponent` class, the `getToolTipText` method that requires a `MouseEvent` as its parameter can be overridden. In this method, the component determines the ToolTip for the current state of the component and for the mouse event. The `String` ToolTip is returned from this method and used as the ToolTip. The component can also specify where the ToolTip is to be displayed. The `JComponent` class contains the `getToolTipLocation` method. The ToolTip manager calls this method before displaying a ToolTip for the component. If the method returns `null` as the default implementation in `JComponent`, the ToolTip manager determines the location for the ToolTip. However, this method can be overridden to return a `Point` that the ToolTip manager will use as the location for the ToolTip.

Border Property

The `JComponent` class contains a `Border` property. This property refers to a class that implements the `Border` interface. When a border has been specified for a component, the component handles painting the border.

Having a `Border` property in the `JComponent` class provides an easy mechanism for adding a border to any `JComponent` instance. Moreover, since a `JComponent` is a `Container`, it provides an easy mechanism for adding a border to a group of components. For example, Figure 3.2 shows the results of running the following code:

```
JPanel panel = new JPanel();
panel.setLayout( new GridLayout( 3, 2 ) );
JLabel label = new JLabel( "First Name" );
panel.add( label );
JTextField firstNameText = new JTextField();
panel.add( firstNameText );
label = new JLabel( "Last Name" );
panel.add( label );
JTextField lastNameText = new JTextField();
panel.add( lastNameText );
label = new JLabel( "Age" );
panel.add( label );
JTextField ageText = new JTextField();
panel.add( ageText );
panel.setBorder( BorderFactory.createTitledBorder( "Age Data" ) );
```

FIGURE 3.2

Border around multiple compo-nents.

In the figure, a titled border is placed around a JPanel instance that contains labels and text fields. A border is added to a component by using the setBorder method contained in the JComponent class. The Border property is a bound property of a JComponent with the name border. Unfortunately, at the time of this writing, the property names are hard coded in the JComponent class rather than defining constants with the property name. The complete list of bound properties defined in the JComponent class is presented in Table 3.1 later in this chapter. Setting the border will invalidate the component. Similarly, the current border can be queried by using the getBorder method. In the example, only one component contains a border; however, any number of components can contain a border to achieve the desired visual effect.

A complete description of creating and using borders is presented in Chapter 5, "Basic Components."

The Border property has another roll in the JComponent class. When a border has been set for a JComponent instance, the size of the border is used as the insets property for that component. Recall that JComponent extends the AWT Container class, so even JFC classes that aren't typically used as containers have the insets property. When the getInsets method of the JComponent class is called, it first checks if the border has been set. If so, the border's Insets are returned to the caller. If not, the Insets from the getInsets method of its parent class, Container, are returned.

Size Preferences

AWT components contain the trio of methods getPreferredSize, getMinimumSize, and getMaximumSize to aid layout managers when they are arranging containers. In these methods, the component is to determine the requested size based on its current state. For example, the JLabel class determines its preferred size based on its font and text that needs to be displayed. By default the JComponent class behaves the same as the AWT Component class for size calculations. However, JComponent adds the setPreferredSize, setMinimumSize, and setMaximumSize methods for setting the sizes. If one of the sizes has been explicitly set via one of these methods, the associated "get" method returns that size, rather than computing the size based on state. Thus the value specified in the "set" method takes precedence over a calculated value.

After having learned from the AWT that hard-coding component sizes is bad and that the preferred technique is to dynamically determine size based on font, screen resolution, and so on, why has the JFC changed the rules? The truth of the matter is that the rules have not changed. Everything you have learned about dynamically determining a component's size still applies. However, the JFC gives you the flexibility to alter the sizing behavior of a component that the layout manager will use. For example, you may want a certain label to always occupy at least the left 25 percent of a container, regardless of the text it contains. This functionality can be achieved easily by using the setMinumumSize method of the label. Also, some classes of components, such as a JViewPort, don't have natural minimum, maximum, or preferred sizes. You may want to set these sizes to achieve the desired layout of a container.

After a size has been explicitly set by using one of the "set" methods, setting the size to null will restore default behavior. This allows size overriding to be turned on and off via any of the setter methods.

Each of the three sizes is a bound property in the JComponent class. A complete list of bound properties defined in the JComponent class is presented in Table 3.1 later in this chapter.

Keystroke Handling

The JComponent class provides a wealth of keystroke handling functionality. These methods provide a much higher level interface than processing individual keystroke events in a subclass of JComponent. You are also able to set which action is executed for a keystroke that occurs in a JComponent without having to subclass the component.

3

JComponent

The registerKeyboardAction method is used to bind a KeyStroke to an ActionListener. When the KeyStroke is detected, the actionPerformed method of the ActionListener is called. Registering a keyboard action for a component enables keyboard events for that component. Internally, the JComponent class stores a Hashtable of registered keyboard actions as a client property. One of three conditions can be specified when binding the KeyStroke with the ActionListener.

The first, WHEN_FOCUSED, requires that the KeyStroke event occur in the component when it has the keyboard focus for the action to be invoked. The second, WHEN_ANCESTOR_OF_FOCUSED_COMPONENT, will invoke the action if the component is the ancestor of the component with the focus or is itself the focus component. This condition is useful for registering keystroke actions on a dialog box for dialog box default behavior. For example, the Escape key could be mapped to the cancel action in the content pane of a JDialog instance. Then, when this key is typed in any JComponent in the dialog box, the cancel action would be invoked. The last condition, WHEN_IN_FOCUSED_WINDOW, will invoke the action if the component is in the same window as the component where the KeyStroke was entered. This is convenient when you do not want to register the keystrokes at the top of a containment hierarchy. The same effect can be achieved by having a cancel button that registers the close action to the escape KeyStroke with the WHEN_IN_FOCUSED_WINDOW condition. In this situation, when the escape key is pressed in any JComponent in the dialog box, the cancel button's close action would be invoked. Let's look at an example of each of these cases.

The first example, shown next, registers a keyboard action to the ageText JTextField component shown in Figure 3.2. This code will cause the textActionListener's actionPerformed method to be called whenever the Escape key is entered in the ageText component and only in the ageText component.

```
ActionListener textActionListener = new ActionListener () {
    public void actionPerformed( ActionEvent event ) {
        System.out.println( "textActionListener " + event );
    }
};

ageText.registerKeyboardAction( textActionListener,
                    KeyStroke.getKeyStroke( KeyEvent.VK_ESCAPE, 0
),
                    JComponent.WHEN_FOCUSED );
```

This code example introduces two new classes; KeyStroke and KeyEvent. The KeyStroke class is part of the JFC, and the KeyEvent class is part of the AWT. A complete discussion of the KeyEvent class is beyond the scope of this book. However, it is sufficient to say that the KeyEvent class contains virtual bindings for keystrokes. These are defined with constants defined in the class. Each virtual key constant begins with the

VK_ preface. Using the constants defined in the KeyEvent class will ensure that your application is not dependent on a particular keystroke mapping. The previous example uses the VK_ESCAPE constant that, as its name implies, represents the Escape key.

The second class introduced in the previous example is the JFC KeyStroke class. This class encapsulates a key being typed on the keyboard and is the subject of the next section.

Changing the condition in the registerKeyboardAction method from WHEN_FOCUS to WHEN_IN_FOCUSED_WINDOW, shown next, will cause the textActionListener to get called when the Escape key is entered in any of the JTextField instances in the panel. If there were more components in the same window as the ageText component, the Escape key being typed in any of those components would cause the textActionListener to be invoked.

```
ageText.registerKeyboardAction( textActionListener,
                KeyStroke.getKeyStroke( KeyEvent.VK_ESCAPE, 0 ),
                JComponent.WHEN_IN_FOCUSED_WINDOW );
```

A similar effect can be obtained by changing the WHEN_IN_FOCUSED_WINDOW condition to WHEN_ANCESTOR_OF_FOCUSED_COMPONENT and registering the keyboard action with the JPanel instance instead of the ageText JTextField instance.

```
panel.registerKeyboardAction( textActionListener,
                KeyStroke.getKeyStroke( KeyEvent.VK_ESCAPE,
0 ),

JComponent.WHEN_ANCESTOR_OF_FOCUSED_COMPONENT );
```

Because the three JTextField instances in this example are children of the JPanel instance, the textActionListener is invoked when the Escape key is entered in any of the instances. Unlike the previous example, if there were other panels that were siblings to this panel, the textActionListener would not be invoked if the Escape key was entered in the sibling panels. However, if the other components were also children of the panel, the textActionListener would be invoked.

It is interesting to notice that the source of the event delivered to the ActionListener is the component on which the keyboard action is registered. This may or may not be the component where the event originated. For instance, in the previous example the source of the event is the JPanel instance, not the JTextField instance where the keystroke was typed.

There is an overloaded version of the registerKeyboardAction method that contains a String parameter. This method's signature is shown next. When this version of the

3

JComponent

method is used, the String parameter is specified as the action command in the ActionEvent delivered to the ActionListener when the KeyStroke is received.

```
public void registerKeyboardAction(ActionListener anAction, String
aCommand,
                          KeyStroke aKeyStroke, int aCondition )
```

If a keyboard action is registered on a component that exactly matches an existing keyboard action registered for that component, the new action replaces the old action. The KeyStroke must exactly match the existing KeyStroke, including modifiers.

A keyboard action can be removed from a component by using the unregisterKeyboardAction method. This method requires one parameter, the KeyStroke that fires the action. If there is not an action registered for the KeyStroke instance specified in the unregisterKeyboardAction call, the method does nothing. All registered keyboard actions can be removed from an instance of a JComponent by using the resetKeyboardActions method. This method clears the Hashtable used internally to store registered KeyStrokes.

The keystrokes registered on a JComponent instance can be queried with the getRegisteredKeyStrokes method. This method returns an array of KeyStroke instances. As mentioned earlier in this section, the keyboard actions are stored in a Hashtable client property in the JComponent class. Thus the Hashtable is enumerated and its elements are stored in an array before being returned to the caller. If there are no keyboard actions registered for the instance, an empty array (an array of length 0) is returned.

The condition for a KeyStroke can be queried by using the getConditionForKeyStroke method. This method takes the KeyStroke to be checked as a parameter and returns the condition specified for that KeyStroke, or UNDEFINED_CONDITION if the KeyStroke has not been registered for the JComponent.

The action that will be invoked when a KeyStroke is received in a JComponent instance can be queried with the getActionForKeyStroke method. This method takes a KeyStroke instance and returns the ActionListener whose actionPerformed method will be called when the KeyStroke with proper modifiers is entered. If an action is not registered for the given KeyStroke, null is returned.

The KeyStroke Class

A KeyStroke instance contains its key character, key code, modifiers, and a flag for key pressed or released state. The key character is the character representation of the KeyStroke instance. The key code is the integer code defined in the KeyEvent class. The modifier field represents any modifier for the KeyStroke. Common modifiers are the Ctrl and Alt keys. The final field represents if the KeyStroke instance is a key pressed or key released keystroke.

The application does not create KeyStroke instances. Instead, the KeyStroke class caches instances, and the application obtains a handle to a KeyStroke instance with one of the overloaded getKeyStroke methods. These methods are public static methods, allowing them to be called from any other class. There are currently five variants of the getKeyStrokeMethod, shown next.

```
public static KeyStroke getKeyStroke(char keyChar)
public static KeyStroke getKeyStroke(char keyChar, boolean onKeyRelease)
public static KeyStroke getKeyStroke(int keyCode, int modifiers, boolean
onKeyRelease)
public static KeyStroke getKeyStroke(int keyCode, int modifiers)
public static KeyStroke getKeyStroke(String representation)
```

These access methods match nicely to the attributes within a KeyStroke instance. The possible modifiers for variants that take a modifier are java.awt.Event.SHIFT_MASK, java.awt.Event.CTRL_MASK, java.awt.Event.META_MASK, java.awt.Event.ALT_MASK. A KeyStroke without a modifier is specified by using 0 for the modifier. The modifiers can be logically ORed together to specify multiple modifiers. For example, to obtain the KeyStroke for the popular command Ctrl+Alt+Delete KeyStroke would be as follows:

```
KeyStroke.getKeyStroke( KeyEvent.VK_DELETE, CTRL_MASK ¦ ALT_MASK ),
```

At the time of this writing, the getKeyStroke method taking a String parameter is not implemented.

The KeyStroke class defines a convenience method, getKeyStrokeForEvent, that will extract the KeyStroke from a KeyEvent. The following is the method's signature:

```
public static KeyStroke getKeyStrokeForEvent(KeyEvent anEvent)
```

Once a KeyStroke instance is in hand, access methods defined in the KeyStroke class can be used to query the instance's attributes. These methods are:

```
public char getKeyChar()
public int getKeyCode()
public int getModifiers()
public boolean isOnKeyRelease()
```

You should notice that there are no corresponding setter methods for the attributes. KeyStroke instances are immutable. This allows the instances to be cached and shared. If the instances were not immutable, one method could change the KeyStroke that is shared between many methods in an application. This of course could have disastrous consequences.

Scrolling Support

The JFC provides traditional scrolling of any component by using the `JScrollPane` and `JViewport` classes. Once the component is placed in a viewport contained in a scroll pane, scrollbars can be used to translate the view of the component. The `JComponent` class also supports autoscrolling. When the `JComponent` instance has autoscrolling enabled, the component will scroll when the mouse is dragged in the component. Thus, with autoscrolling enabled, the user of the application can scroll the component by dragging the mouse from within the component. With autoscrolling enabled, the scrollbars are not required; however, they can be used as normal.

The `setAutoscrolls` method is used to enable or disable autoscrolling for a `JComponent` instance. This method takes one `boolean` parameter. Passing `true` enables autoscrolling, and `false` disables autoscrolling. The `getAutoscrolls` method is used to query the current state of autoscrolling. Notice that the method is `getAutoscrolls` and not `isAutoscrolling` as you might have expected. Also, autoscrolling is not a bound property in the `JComponent` class.

The autoscrolling feature gives the `JComponent` developer a tremendous amount of power from within the toolkit itself. A complete autoscrolling example will be presented in Chapter 15, "Scrolling Components."

When a `JComponent` is contained in a `JViewport` instance contained in a `JScrollPane` instance, the `scrollRectToVisible` method can be used to programmatically display any portion of the component in the viewport. This method climbs the `JComponent` instance's lineage until the viewport containing the instance is found. Once the viewport is found, the `scrollRectToVisible` of the viewport is called. The `scrollRectToVisible` takes one parameter, an AWT `Rectangle` instance. The coordinates of the rectangle are translated as the search up the parent hierarchy is performed.

Focus Transversal Support

The JFC contains a default focus manager that will determine which component will obtain the focus when a focus transversal request is made. The default focus manager will determine the next component to receive input focus and transfer focus to that component. The default search algorithm is a top-to-bottom, left-to-right search. The search algorithm can be modified by altering the focus manager itself, or by having the components in the view contain hints for the focus manager. The focus manager is discussed in detain in Chapter 26, "Focus Managers."

The JComponent class contains the setNextFocusableComponent method to set the component that should receive the input focus after the component whose property was set. This method takes a single component as an argument that is stored in a client property in the JComponent. Calling this method with a null parameter will clear the property. The focus manager calls the getNextFocusableComponent method to retrieve the component that should receive the focus next. If this method returns null, the focus manager determines the next component to receive focus by itself. This is a public method, so it can be called by classes other than the focus manager if required.

The default focus transversal order for the JTextField instances shown in Figure 3.2 can be reversed by using the code shown next. This example demonstrates that care must be taken when setting the next focus component. It is very easy to create a focus transversal order that isn't expected by the user. This will make your application difficult to use.

```
firstNameText.setNextFocusableComponent( ageText );
lastNameText.setNextFocusableComponent( firstNameText );
ageText.setNextFocusableComponent( lastNameText );
```

> **CAUTION**
>
> A bug in the DefaultFocusManager that is used by the JFC throws an array out-of-bounds exception when a next focus component has been set by using the setNextFocusableComponent method.

The isFocusTraversable method can be called to determine if a JComponent instance can acquire the input focus. Subclasses may need to override this method to return true if they can obtain the input focus. The default implementation in the JComponent class will only return true if a registered KeyStroke action has the WHEN_FOCUSED condition. Subclasses may also need to override the isFocusCycleRoot method. When this method returns true, it tells the focus manager that this component contains its own focus cycle. This will keep the focus cycling within this component and not departing to other components on the next focus component event. The default implementation of this method returns false. A JComponent instance can manage its own focus by returning true from the isManagingFocus method. When this is the case, the focus manager will ignore focus transversal events in that component. It is the responsibility of the component to handle these events properly. The default implementation of this method in the JComponent class returns false.

A component can ask the focus manager for the input focus or to give focus to a component by calling the requestFocus method. However, the component must have the requestFocuesEnabled property set to true for this method to succeed. The

setRequestFocusEnabled method can be used to enable or disable the
requestFocusEnabled property. Its default value is true, allowing the focus to be
requested for the component. The current state of this property can be queried by using
the isRequestFocusEnabled method. The requestFocusEnabled property is not bound.
It should be noted that setting this property to false does not disable the component
from receiving the focus, only from receiving it programmatically via the requestFocus
method. As was shown earlier, the isFocusTraversable method can be used to disable a
component from receiving the input focus. The hasFocus method can be used to determine if a component currently has the input focus. The requestDefaultFocus can be
called on a container to give the input focus to the component that is the default for that
container. For example, the default focus component on a dialog box can be the OK
button.

Property Listener Support

The JFC visual components are compliant with the JavaBeans specification. The
JComponent class contains the methods for manipulating property change listeners and
convenience methods for sending notifications to the listeners. Recall that a property
change listener can register with an object and be notified when a bound property in
that object changes. There are two types of property change listeners:
PropertyChangeListener and VetoableChangeListener. A PropertyChangeListener
simply receives notifications when properties change in the object that the listener registered with. A VetoableChangeListener can take a more active role in the changing of
the property. When a vetoable listener receives a change notification, it may throw a
PropertyVetoException to abort the property change in the object to which it was listening. A complete description of the property change protocol is beyond the scope of
this book but can be obtained from the JavaBeans specification.

Since the JComponent class is the root of the visual component hierarchy in the JFC
toolkit, it makes sense for this class to contain the methods to add and remove property
change listeners. The JComponent class contains the required add and remove methods
that are compliant with the JavaBeans specification. The signatures for these methods
are as follows:

```
public void addPropertyChangeListener(
➥    java.beans.PropertyChangeListener listener)
public void removePropertyChangeListener(
➥    java.beans.PropertyChangeListener listener)
public void addVetoableChangeListener(
➥    java.beans.VetoableChangeListener listener)
public void removeVetoableChangeListener(
➥    java.beans.VetoableChangeListener listener)
```

The bound properties in JComponent are presented in Table 3.1. You will immediately see that all of the property names are not defined as constants in this class or any other class or interface. This forces you to embed the String property name somewhere in your code, either where you use the property or in a constant that you define. This is incredibly poor programming practice whose example should not be followed in your code. As developers, I think we should expect more from a core toolkit such as the JFC. The JComponent properties are not vetoable. The concrete subclass of the JComponent class that your code is listening for property change events from may define additional properties as well as those defined in the JComponent class. You are guaranteed that all the "J" visual components contain these bound properties.

TABLE 3.1   BOUND PROPERTIES DEFINED IN THE JComponent CLASS

Property Name	Setter Method	Getter Method
UI	setUI	not available
PreferredSize	setPreferredSize	getPreferredSize
MaximumSize	setMaximumSize	getMaximumSize
MinimumSize	setMinimumSize	getMinimumSize
Border	setBorder	getBorder
Opaque	setOpaque	isOpaque
Ancestor	addNotify	getParent
Ancestor	removeNotify	getParent
property key name	putClientProperty	getClientProperty

3

JComponent

NOTE

The property change support contained in the JComponent class is to migrate to the AWT Component class in a future release of the JDK.

The add and remove families of methods are public methods that are used by clients of the component. The JComponent class also defines a family of protected methods that fire the property change events. These methods simplify property management for subclasses of the JComponent class. The convenience methods are listed next. Notice how there are firePropertyChange methods that take intrinsic types as parameters. These fire methods create the objects of the corresponding type for the caller before firing the actual event. It is interesting to notice that the corresponding methods are not provided for firing vetoable events.

```
firePropertyChange(String propertyName, Object oldValue, Object newValue)
firePropertyChange(String propertyName, byte oldValue, byte newValue)
firePropertyChange(String propertyName, char oldValue, char newValue)
firePropertyChange(String propertyName, short oldValue, short newValue)
firePropertyChange(String propertyName, int oldValue, int newValue)
firePropertyChange(String propertyName, long oldValue, long newValue)
firePropertyChange(String propertyName, float oldValue, float newValue)
firePropertyChange(String propertyName, double oldValue, double newValue)
firePropertyChange(String propertyName, boolean oldValue, boolean
newValue)

fireVetoableChange(String propertyName, Object oldValue, Object newValue)
```

You will see these methods again in Part V of this book when you are creating your own JComponent subclasses.

Pluggable Look-and-Feel Support

The JComponent class is where the pluggable look-and-feel support is located. The JComponent class defines the methods that subclasses must override if they support the pluggable look-and-feel architecture. The UIManager uses these methods to determine the user interface class for instances. They are typically used when an instance is created to initialize the user interface and when the look-and-feel changes for the application. The UIManager is discussed in Chapter 30, "Pluggable Look-and-Feel."

The getUIClassID method returns the String class name for the look-and-feel class for the component. This String is actually a key into the look-and-feel user interface table contained in the UIManager. The value associated with this key will determine the user interface class for the component. A complete reference to how the user-interface object is created for a component is presented in Part V of this book. When the component's look-and-feel needs changing, the public updateUI method is called. This method must query the UIManager for the current user interface for the class and then set the user interface for itself. The updateUI method is nearly identical in all JComponent sub-classes. A typical example, from the JLabel class, is shown next. The update method is required to allow a type-safe setUI method.

```
public void updateUI() {
    setUI((LabelUI)UIManager.getUI(this));
    invalidate();
}
```

Subclasses of JComponent override the setUI method and change the user interface parameter to the specific type required for that component. The subclass then calls its parent's setUI method. This allows the setUI method to be type safe while still allowing the functionality to be encapsulated in the JComponent class. The following is the setUI method in the JLabel class:

```
public void setUI(LabelUI ui) {
    super.setUI(ui);
}
```

The setUI method contained in the JComponent class is shown next. It takes a ComponentUI instance as a parameter. The other user interface classes must extend this class for the user interface methods in the JFC to work. This method un-installs the current user interface and then installs the new user interface. As we saw in the previous section, the user interface is a bound property.

```
protected void setUI(ComponentUI newUI) {
    /* We do not check that the UI instance is different
     * before allowing the switch in order to enable the
     * same UI instance *with different default settings*
     * to be installed.
     */
    if (ui != null) {
        ui.uninstallUI(this);
    }
    ComponentUI oldUI = ui;
    ui = newUI;
    if (ui != null) {
        ui.installUI(this);
    }
    invalidate();
    firePropertyChange("UI", oldUI, ui);
}
```

These methods will be demonstrated further in Part V of this book.

Miscellaneous Features

Until now, this chapter has presented major functional units contained in the JComponent class. The JComponent class also contains some smaller units of functionality that are explored in this section.

Accessibility Support

The JComponent class contains an accessibleContext property. This property can be queried with the getAccessibleContext method. The JComponent class provides the framework for supporting accessibility but does not implement the functionality. The JComponent class cannot do this; it doesn't have the required information to do so. Instead, subclasses provide the information and work in the framework defined in

JComponent. Also, JComponent doesn't implement the Accessible interface. Subclasses that add the required knowledge to allow the accessibleContext defined in JComponent to have meaning should implement this interface. Accessibility is discussed further in Chapter 33, "Accessibility."

Parent Changes

The JComponent class overrides the addNotify and removeNotify methods contained in the java.awt.Component class. These methods are called when the parent of a JComponent subclass is set or removed for the instance. The parent class' methods are still called, but both these methods fire a property change event with the name of ancestor. Thus, a bound property named ancestor has been added for JFC components that are fired when the familiar addNotify and removeNotify methods are called. This property is to be moved into the Component class in a future version of the JDK.

Debug Graphics

The JComponent class introduces the concept of debug graphics. When debug graphics are enabled, a component paints itself slowly, allowing the component developer to easily see how the component is painting itself. Debug graphics are enabled or disabled for a component via the setDebugGraphicsOptions method. The current state of these options can be queried with the getDebugGraphicsOptions method. A complete description of using debug graphics and available options is presented in Chapter 25.

Double Buffering

A serious problem with the AWT is poor painting performance. Many component developers reduced this problem by double buffering their components. When a component is double buffered, it paints to an offscreen buffer and then updates the display in a single operation. Even though this makes the painting of a component slower than painting directly to the screen, it appears better to the user because the display update is done very quickly. The user does not see the raw painting operation, only the result when the display is updated.

Double buffering was such a common painting optimization that it was built into the JFC. Having double buffering contained in the toolkit allows for further optimizations to be made. When a component is double buffered, its children are also double buffered using the same buffer. When each component managed its double buffering, multiple offscreen images were created—one for each component. The JFC optimizes the buffer creation to a single buffer for the top-level component. This single buffer is shared by all the components contained in that component. This saves a significant amount of memory.

The setDoubleBuffered method is used to enable double buffering for a component that extends JComponent. This method takes a single boolean parameter specifying the state for double buffering. The isDoubleBuffered method can be used to determine if a component is currently double buffered. While these methods are contained in the JComponent class, they rarely need to be called by application code. The content pane of JFC top-level components has double buffering enabled. As will be shown in Chapter 8, "Frame Windows," the content pane is the parent in most JFC component hierarchies. Thus, the components added to the content pane are double buffered, even if their setDoubleBuffered method is not explicitly called.

Efficiency Methods

Creating unnecessary temporary objects can cause significant performance problems in a Java application. The AWT Component class creates objects and returns them to the caller in its getBounds, getSize, and getLocation methods. In many applications, the object returned from these methods is a temporary object. To avoid the creation of the object, new versions of these methods have been added to the JComponent class. The new version takes an instance of the class that is returned from the method. The parameter object is altered to contain the values from the component, and it is also returned from the method. The old and new techniques for using getBounds are shown next. This will be more efficient if the getBounds method is called for multiple components because the same Rectangle instance can be shared for all the calls.

```
//
// Original JDK 1.1 getBounds technique
// This caused a Rectangle to be created in
// the getBounds method.
//
Rectangle bounds = component.getBounds();

//
// New JDK 1.2 getBounds technique
//
Rectangle bounds = new Rectangle();
component.getBounds( bounds );
```

Another common programming technique is to call the getSize method and then use the height and width properties from the returned Rectangle. The JComponent class defines the getWidth and getHeight methods that return these properties directly without creating a Rectangle instance. Similarly, there are the getX and getY methods to return the x and y coordinates without creating a Point instance, as would be done if the getLocation method were called. An example of the old and new techniques for the getSize method is shown next.

3

JComponent

```
//
// JDK 1.1 getSize technique.
// This caused two Rectangle instances to be created.
//
int width = component.getSize().width;
int height = component.getSize().height;

//
// New JDK 1.2 technique
int width = component.getWidth();
int height = component.getHeight();
```

> **NOTE**
>
> Identical versions of the methods described in this section contained in the
> JComponent class have also been added to the Component class. Because the
> JComponent class is a descendent of the Component class, this is an obvious dupli-
> cation of code. The methods should be removed from the JComponent class.
> However, wherever they reside, these methods should be used to increase the
> performance of your components and applications.

Summary

This chapter has taken a long look at the JComponent class. This class serves as the root
of the visual component hierarchy contained in the JFC. As such, it has become a dump-
ing ground for functionality required by all the visual components.

You looked at how client properties are an efficient place to store data that may or may
not be present for a given component. You saw that all JComponent instances may contain a ToolTip and a border. You saw how a single method call is all it takes to enable
double buffering for a component. The JComponent class contains methods for handling
keystrokes and automatic scrolling. Using the family of focus methods contained in the
JComponent class, hints can be given to the focus manager for how focus transversal
should occur. A component can also be specified to not be able to acquire the input focus
programmatically or not at all. You were also introduced to the look-and-feel support
contained in the JComponent class. This support is the foundation of the pluggable look-
and-feel architecture contained in the JFC.

As much material as this chapter covered about the JComponent class, it is not complete.
There is more functionality that is used primarily by subclasses. This additional functionality is presented in Part V of this book.

JFC Programming Techniques

CHAPTER 4

In This Chapter

Writing applications and applets using the JFC toolkit isn't that different than using any other toolkit written in Java. However, there are some issues that must be understood when designing a JFC-based application. The first is that the Swing component toolkit is not thread safe. Code that alters the state of Swing components must be executed in the event-dispatch thread. Therefore, if your application contains multiple threads that need to report information to the user, special programming techniques must be used.

The Swing toolkit optimizes painting through the use of a repaint manager. Understanding this class, and creating your own repaint manager if necessary, can enhance the performance and visual appearance of Swing applications.

The `Action` interface is provided in the Swing toolkit to allow a single bit of functionality to be easily added to multiple user interface controls. The `Action` interface is an extension of the `ActionListener` interface contained in the AWT. As such, an `Action` can be used anywhere an `ActionListener` can be used. However, as we will see later in this book, `Action`s are integrated with menus and toolbars in the JFC.

This chapter discusses some of the unique programming techniques required to design and write complete JFC applications and applets. You will learn

- How to write thread-safe JFC code
- How to use the `RepaintManager`
- How to encapsulate bits of application functionality in an `Action`

Thread Safety Requirements of JFC

JFC requires that Swing components be accessed by only one thread at a time. The normal thread of execution is the application's event-dispatch thread. JavaSoft documentation states the following:

> Once a Swing component has been realized, all code that might affect or depend on the state of that component should be executed in the event-dispatch thread.

While this requirement may seem onerous at first glance, you won't often need to access components from other threads, and when you do, the `SwingUtilities` class provides an easy mechanism to execute code on the event-dispatch thread.

Components are considered to be *realized* as soon as their `setVisible`, `show`, or `pack` methods are called. Components are also considered realized when they are added to a container that is realized.

The event-dispatch thread is the application's main thread of execution. All event listeners are called on this thread, so you normally don't need to be concerned about thread safety. If you are creating threads, however, you must ensure that their execution is thread safe when accessing Swing components.

Exceptions to the Rule

There are a few exceptions to the requirement of not accessing Swing components on threads other than the event-dispatch thread. The `repaint`, `revalidate`, and `invalidate` methods are thread safe and can be called by any thread, including timer threads. These methods use different techniques to obtain thread safety. The `repaint` and `revalidate` methods use the repaint manager to post a message to the event-dispatch thread to call `paint` and `validate`, respectively. If multiple `repaint` or `revalidate` messages are in the queue when they are to be dispatched, the repaint manager will attempt to collapse the multiple events into a single event call. The `invalidate` method uses the more traditional approach to thread safety: It obtains a lock on the component and marks it as invalid. In addition to these methods, all of the methods to add and remove event listeners are guaranteed to be thread safe.

`main` Entry Point Considerations

The code in an application's `main` entry point is not executed in the event-dispatch thread. To be absolutely safe, you should not place any GUI code after the first call to either the `setVisible`, `show`, or `pack` method. JavaSoft documentation says the following code is typically safe, even though the `show` method follows the `pack` method.

```
public class MyApplication {
    public static void main(String[] args) {
        JFrame frame = new JFrame("MyApplication");
        // add JFC components here
        frame.pack();                      // realizes components
        frame.show();
        // No more GUI calls!
    }
}
```

This is because it's unlikely that a `paint` call will reach the frame before the `show` method call returns. After the `show` call, the GUI event dispatching moves from the main thread to the event-dispatching thread. All subsequent calls that alter JFC components must be in the event-dispatch thread.

4

JFC
PROGRAMMING
TECHNIQUES

Using `invokeLater` and `invokeAndWait`

There are situations where you will need to access Swing user interface components on threads other than the event-dispatch thread. The following list gives some examples of such situations.

- When you must perform a long initialization sequence at startup time.

  The initialization cannot occur in the event-dispatching thread because repainting and event dispatching would be blocked for the duration of the initialization. However, the initialization code does need to update GUI components to indicate the progress of the initialization.

- When you must update the user interface as the result of a non-AWT event.

  Programs, such as servers that can receive requests from other programs, may need to update GUI components in response to external requests that are not executing in the event-dispatch thread.

When you need to access Swing component methods that are not guaranteed to be thread safe from threads other than the event-dispatch thread, you can use the `invokeLater` and `invokeAndWait` methods in the `SwingUtilities` class. These methods allow code to be run on the event-dispatch thread. `SwingUtilities` also provides the `isEventDispatchThread` to allow you to determine at runtime if code is running in the event-dispatch thread.

```
public static void invokeLater(Runnable code);
public static boolean isEventDispatchThread();
public static void invokeAndWait(Runnable code);
```

The `invokeLater` and `invokeAndWait` methods take a `Runnable` object and execute it on the application's event-dispatch thread. The following fragment shows how you can use an anonymous inner class as a `Runnable` object to contain code to be executed by `invokeLater`.

```
Runnable Update = new Runnable() {
    public void run() {
        // Put your code here
    }
};
SwingUtilities.invokeLater(Update);
```

Note that the `Runnable` interface contains a single method, `run`. The code in the `run` method is the code that is executed when the runnable object is invoked.

4

JFC
PROGRAMMING
TECHNIQUES

> **NOTE**
>
> The `invokeAndWait` method is similar to the `invokeLater` method except that it waits until the `Runnable` object is executed before returning. You can use `invokeAndWait` the same way you use `invokeLater` to ensure that your access of Swing components is thread safe.

Timers

JFC timers utilize timer listeners to serve as callbacks for periodic or one-shot timer objects. All timer listeners are executed in a single system thread to reduce the usage of system resources.

The system timer thread executes timer action events in the event-dispatch thread—you don't need to use `invokeLater` and `invokeAndWait` to access Swing components in timer listeners. A complete description of timers in the JFC is presented in Chapter 31, "Timers."

The Repaint Manager

All Swing components and any custom components based on `JComponent` utilize a repaint manager to manage screen repaint and double buffering operations. The repaint manager keeps track of invalid components and dirty regions and batches these operations so that they can be processed simultaneously on the event-dispatch thread. Repaint operations are done through the use of an offscreen buffer to ensure smooth repaints. JFC maintains one repaint manager instance per thread group.

Any JFC application can take advantage of the services of the repaint manager simply by using the component `repaint` and `revalidate` methods. The only reason for most applications to directly access the repaint manager is to disable double buffering for performance, debugging, or other reasons. However, the repaint manager is designed to be extensible for applications that want to plug in their own repaint batching or double buffering solutions.

The `RepaintManager` Class

The repaint manager is represented by the `RepaintManager` class. Listing 4.1 gives the class signature of this class.

LISTING 4.1   RepaintManager CLASS SIGNATURE

```
public class RepaintManager extends Object
{
  // Public constructors
    public RepaintManager();
  // Public class methods
    public static RepaintManager currentManager(JComponent component);
    public static void setCurrentManager(RepaintManager manager);
  // Public instance methods
    public void addDirtyRegion(JComponent component component,
                               int x, int y,
                               int width, int height);
    public synchronized void addInvalidComponent(JComponent component);
    public Rectangle getDirtyRegion(JComponent component);
    public Dimension getDoubleBufferMaximumSize();
    public Image getOffscreenBuffer(Component component,
                                    int desiredWidth,
                                    int desiredHeight);
    public boolean isCompletelyDirty(JComponent component);
    public boolean isDoubleBufferingEnabled();
    public void markCompletelyClean(JComponent component);
    public void markCompletelyDirty(JComponent component);
    public void paintDirtyRegions();
    public synchronized void
                    removeInvalidComponent(JComponent component);
    public void setDoubleBufferingEnabled(boolean enable);
    public void setDoubleBufferMaximumSize(Dimension size);
    public synchronized String toString();
    public void validateInvalidComponents();
}
```

There is a public constructor for RepaintManager, but you would use it only if you were writing your own custom repaint manager and wanted to subclass the JFC repaint manager. JFC maintains a single repaint manager instance for each thread group (application). You can access the current repaint manager by calling a static class method, currentManager. The following line of code illustrates how to get the current repaint manager and use it to disable double buffering.

```
RepaintManager.currentManager(this).setDoubleBufferingEnabled(false);
```

Note that the currentManager method takes a component as an argument. This construction is an artifact from an early version of the JFC—the component argument is currently not used by the currentManager method. However, it's a good idea to provide a non-null component for this parameter because future versions of the JFC may depend on it.

The repaint manager provides the addDirtyRegion, getDirtyRegion, isCompletelyDirty, markCompletelyClean, markCompletelyDirty, and paintDirtyRegions methods for managing component repaint operations. The JComponent class and the repaint manager itself use these methods—applications do not normally call these methods directly. Likewise, the addInvalidComponent, removeInvalidComponent, and validateInvalidComponents methods are for managing component revalidations. Applications also don't normally call these methods directly.

The repaint manager provides the getDoubleBufferMaximumSize, isDoubleBufferingEnabled, setDoubleBufferingEnabled, and setDoubleBufferMaximumSize methods for applications to manage double buffering— the use of these methods is discussed in the "Using the Repaint Manager to Manage Double Buffering" section later in this chapter. The getOffscreenBuffer method is used only by the JComponent class—applications do not normally need to access the repaint manager's offscreen buffer.

Using the Repaint Manager to Manage Repaint and Revalidation Operations

The internal operation of the repaint manager is closely integrated with the various painting and layout validation methods in the JComponent class. When you call a component's revalidate method, the repaint manager adds the component to a list of components that require revalidation. It then queues a component work request (if one is not already queued) to be executed on the event-dispatch thread. Likewise, when you call a component's repaint method, the repaint manager adds the region to be painted to a list of dirty regions and, if necessary, queues a component work request. When the component work request is executed, it validates the invalid components, paints the dirty regions to an offscreen buffer, and then copies the contents of the offscreen buffer to the display. Figure 4.1 illustrates the role of the repaint manager in executing component repaint and revalidate requests.

If you use the revalidate and repaint methods, your application will automatically take advantage of the services of the repaint manager. Be sure to use the new revalidate method in place of the older invalidate/validate method pair.

Using the Repaint Manager to Manage Double Buffering

Double buffering is a screen drawing technique that performs multiple drawing operations to an offscreen buffer and then copies this buffer to the screen. The result is that a number of separate drawing operations will appear as a single smooth screen transition. This technique is essential for applications that do animation. The tradeoff for using double buffering is a slight decrease in graphics performance and increased memory usage to support the offscreen buffer.

FIGURE 4.1

Repaint manager operation.

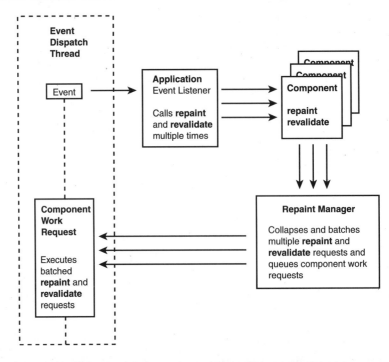

NOTE

The repaint manager performs double buffering on a per-component basis—it does not render multiple unrelated components to the offscreen buffer before copying the buffer to the display. The repaint manager does render all of a component's children to the offscreen buffer before copying the buffer to the display.

All Swing components are designed to support double buffering. There are two `JComponent` methods, `setDoubleBuffered` and `isDoubleBuffered`, that you can use to control double buffering at the component level. By default, double buffering is disabled for most components. The only components that are double buffered by default are the `JPanel`, `JPopupMenu`, and `JRootPane` components.

> **NOTE**
>
> The fact that most Swing components do not have double buffering enabled by default is somewhat misleading. If any ancestor of a component has double buffering enabled, the repaint manager will double buffer the child component. All children of a double buffered component are, in effect, double buffered themselves. Since JRootPane is the root of most containment hierarchies, it's safe to say that all Swing components in a JFC application are double buffered.

Enabling and Disabling Double Buffering

The repaint manager provides global control for double buffering for all components owned by a thread group (application). The setDoubleBufferingEnabled method enables and disables double buffering. The isDoubleBufferingEnabled method returns a Boolean indicating whether double buffering is currently enabled or disabled. By default, the repaint manager enables double buffering. The following line of code illustrates how to enable double buffering with the repaint manager.

```
RepaintManager.currentManager(this).setDoubleBufferingEnabled(true);
```

In addition to setDoubleBufferingEnabled, the repaint manager also includes the isDoubleBufferingEnabled method to determine if double buffering is enabled for the application. By default, the repaint manager enables double buffering.

> **NOTE**
>
> You must disable double buffering for the "flash graphics" option to operate properly with debug graphics. See Chapter 25, "ToolTips and Debug Graphics," for more information on using debug graphics.

Setting the Offscreen Buffer Size

Each repaint manager instance maintains a single offscreen buffer. Since there is only one repaint manager instance per application, all components in the application share the same buffer.

The repaint manager provides the getDoubleBufferMaximumSize and setDoubleBufferMaximumSize methods to get and set the maximum size of the offscreen buffer. Note that buffer size is not specified in bytes but is specified as a Dimension. The

4

JFC PROGRAMMING TECHNIQUES

buffer itself is an Image, not just a block of memory. The default size of the buffer is the screen size of the display on which the application is running.

Actions

In the JFC toolkit, an Action encapsulates a bit of application functionality and information to identify the functionality. Standard identification information contained in an Action can be a string to be used in a menu or a ToolTip for the Action, as well as an Icon to be used in a toolbar. However, an Action is not limited to only containing this data. The Action interface defines the putValue and getValue methods for adding and retrieving any piece of information by using a key. The data is stored in the Action in a data structure conforming to the java.util.Dictionary class.

Creating a class that implements the Action interface allows a single bit of functionality to be easily added to multiple user interface controls. The Action interface is an extension of the ActionListener interface contained in the AWT. As such, a class that implements the Action interface can be used anywhere an ActionListener can be used. However, as we will see later in this book, Actions are integrated with menus and toolbars in the JFC. This integration allows Actions to be added directly to menus and toolbars. This integration allows applications built with Actions encapsulating functionality to easily create menu and keyboard interfaces.

The Action interface is presented in the following code. As can be seen, constants are defined for the keys used when adding the standard descriptions to an Action. The setEnabled method can be used to enable or disable the Action, similar to how a Component can be enabled or disabled. Finally, the interface defines methods for adding and removing property change listeners. An Action-aware control listens for PropertyChangeEvents fired by the Action and updates its state accordingly. For example, when an Action is added to a menu or toolbar and the Action is disabled, the menu and toolbar will display the control associated with the Action as disabled.

```java
public interface Action extends ActionListener {
    /**
     * Useful constants that can be used as the storage-retrieval key
     * when setting or getting one of this object's properties (text
     * or icon).
     */
    public static final String DEFAULT = "Default";
    public static final String NAME = "Name";
    public static final String SHORT_DESCRIPTION = "ShortDescription";
    public static final String LONG_DESCRIPTION = "LongDescription";
    public static final String SMALL_ICON = "SmallIcon";

    /**
```

```
   * Puts/gets one of this object's properties
   * using the associated key.  If the value has
   * changed, a PropertyChangeEvent will be sent
   * to listeners.
   */
  public Object getValue(String key);
  public void putValue(String key, Object value);

  /**
   * Sets/tests the enabled state of the Action. When enabled,
   * any component associated with this object is active and
   * able to fire this object's <code>actionPerformed</code> method.
   */
  public void setEnabled(boolean b);
  public boolean isEnabled();

  /**
   * Add or remove a PropertyChange listener. Containers and attached
   * components use these methods to register interest in this Action
   * object. When its enabled state or other property changes,
   * the registered listeners are informed of the change.
   */
  public void addPropertyChangeListener(
              PropertyChangeListener listener);
  public void removePropertyChangeListener(
              PropertyChangeListener listener);

}
```

To ease the burden of writing Actions, the AbstractAction class is provided by the JFC. The AbstractAction class, as its name implies, is an abstract class. It manages property change listeners and fires PropertyChangeEvents when a value is changed in the Action, or when the enabled state of the Action changes. An annoying characteristic of the AbstractAction implementation is that a null value cannot be added to the Action by using the putValue method. If this is attempted, a NullPointerException is thrown. Classes that extend the AbstactAction class must provide an implementation for the actionPerformed method. This is where the functionality contained in the Action lives.

Perhaps the most trivial Action that can be written is shown next. This is an Action that does nothing. From the NoOpAction class, it is seen how easily an Action can be written. When the AbstractAction class is extended, the subclass must simply provide an actionPerformed method. The NoOpAction class also supplies a name for the Action in its constructor. The AbstractAction class provides the implementation for the methods defined in the Action interface. The only method left to implement is the method defined in the ActionListener interface, actionPerformed.

4

JFC PROGRAMMING TECHNIQUES

```
package com.foley.utility;

import java.awt.event.*;

import javax.swing.*;


/**
 * Class NoOpAction
 * <p>
 * An action which does nothing.
 * <p>
 * @author Mike Foley
 * @version 1.2
 **/
public class NoOpAction extends AbstractAction {

    /**
     * The default name used in a menu.
     **/
    private static final String DEFAULT_NAME = "NoOp";


    public NoOpAction() {
        super( DEFAULT_NAME );
    } // NoOpAction

    /**
     * actionPerformed, from ActionListener
     * <p>
     * Do nothing.
     * <p>
     * @param event The event causing the action to fire.
     **/
    public void actionPerformed( ActionEvent event ) {
    } // actionPerformed

} // NoOpAction
```

The NoOpAction class shows that writing an Action is not any more difficult that writing an ActionListener. However, an Action provides a great deal more functionality than a simple ActionListener. To demonstrate, let's look at a more useful Action. The ExitAction is shown in the following code. When invoked, this Action shuts down the Java Virtual Machine. The class contains a static initializer to load the default Icon associated with the Action. The class contains many constructors to allow the Action to be customized at construction time. The setValue method can be used to customize an existing instance of the ExitAction class. The name given in the constructor is the name used for the Action in a menu. The Icon specified in the constructor would be used if the `Action` is added to a toolbar. The `actionPerformed` method is called to invoke the `Action`, in this case, exiting the application. In Chapter 9, "Menus and Toolbars," as well as in examples throughout this book, it will be seen how to add this `Action` to a menu and toolbar.

```
package com.foley.utility;

import java.awt.event.ActionListener;
import java.awt.event.ActionEvent;

import javax.swing.AbstractAction;
import javax.swing.Icon;


/**
 * Class ExitAction
 * <p>
 * An action which shuts down the Java virtual machine.
 * <p>
 * @author Mike Foley
 * @version 1.2
 **/
public class ExitAction extends AbstractAction {

    /**
     * The default name and Icon for the Action.
     **/
    private static final String DEFAULT_NAME = "Exit";
    private static final String DEFAULT_ICON_NAME = "exit.gif";
    private static Icon DEFAULT_ICON;

    /**
     * ExitAction, default constructor.
     * Create the Action with the default name and Icon.
     **/
    public ExitAction() {
        this( DEFAULT_NAME, DEFAULT_ICON );
    } // ExitAction

    /**
     * ExitAction, constructor.
     * Create the Action with the given name and
     * default Icon.
     *
     * @param name The name for the Action.
     **/
    public ExitAction( String name ) {
        this( name, DEFAULT_ICON );
    } // ExitAction
```

```
/**
 * ExitAction, constructor.
 * Create the Action with the given name and
 * Icon.
 *
 * @param name The name for the Action.
 * @param icon The small icon for the Action.
 **/
public ExitAction( String name, Icon icon ) {
        super( name, icon );
} // ExitAction

/**
 * putValue, overridden from AbstractAction.
 * Guard against null values being added to the Action.
 *
 * @param key The key for the value.
 * @param value The value to be added to the Action.
 **/
public void putValue( String key, Object value ) {
    if( value != null )
        super.putValue( key, value );
}

/**
 * actionPerformed, from ActionListener
 * <p>
 * Perform the action.  Exit the JVM.
 * <p>
 * @param event The event causing the action to fire.
 **/
public void actionPerformed( ActionEvent event ) {
    System.exit(0);
} // actionPerformed

/**
 * static initialization. Load the default Icon.
 **/
static {
    try {
        DEFAULT_ICON = ImageLoader.loadIcon( DEFAULT_ICON_NAME );
    } catch( InterruptedException ie ) {
        System.err.println( "Could not load ExitAction default Icon"
);
    }
}

} // ExitAction
```

Using `Action` classes to encapsulate the functionality of a control, or the application itself, makes it easier to create user interfaces. This programming technique also allows the user interface and the program's functionality to be kept separate. This makes it easier to modify the user interface without altering the application's functional classes.

Actions to Set the Look-and-Feel

Swing components are shown in the various look-and-feel implementations provided with the JFC throughout this book. The following action is used to set the look-and-feel for an application. When invoked, the SetLookAndFeelAction will update the look-and-feel to that named by the lookAndFeelName parameter specified for the action. It will also update the UI of components registered in the framesToUpdate vector and the component that is the source of the ActionEvent that invoked that action. The methods that actually change the look-and-feel and update the component tree are presented in Chapter 30, "Pluggable Look-and-Feel," and Chapter 33, "Accessibility." There are also extensions of the SetLookAndFeelAction that are initialized for the standard look-and-feel implementations that are shipped with the JFC. The name of one of these actions embeds the name of the look-and-feel that it will activate. For example, the action to set the MS Windows look-and-feel is named SetWindowsLookAndFeelAction. Each of these actions is part of the com.foley.utility package shown in Appendix C, "com.foley.utility Source Code."

```
package com.foley.utility;

import java.awt.*;
import java.awt.event.*;
import java.util.*;

import javax.swing.*;


/**
 * Class SetLookAndFeelAction
 * <p>
 * An action which sets the look and feel to the given look
 * and feel class name.
 * <p>
 * @author Mike Foley
 * @version 1.2
 **/
public class SetLookAndFeelAction extends AbstractAction {

    /**
     * The default name used in a menu.
     **/
    private static final String DEFAULT_NAME = "Set Look and Feel";

    /**
```

```
 * The key into our property table of the name of the
 * class containing the look and feel.
 **/
private static final String LOOKANDFEELNAME_KEY
                    = "LookAndFeelNameKey";


/**
 * The key into our property table for the collection of
 * Frames to update when this action is invoked.
 **/
private static final String FRAMESTOUPDAT_KEY
                    = "FramesToUpdateKey";


/**
 * Initialize the Action with the given name and L&F name.
 * <p>
 * @param name The name for the Action.
 * @param lookAndFeelName The look and feel class name.
 **/
public SetLookAndFeelAction( String name, String lookAndFeelName ) {
    this( name, null, lookAndFeelName, null );
} // SetLookAndFeelAction


/**
 * Initialize the Action with the given name and L&F name.
 * <p>
 * @param name The name for the Action.
 * @param icon The Icon for the Action.
 * @param lookAndFeelName The look and feel class name.
 * @param framesToUpdate Each Component in this array will have its
 *                       component tree udpated when this action is
 *                       invoked.
 **/
public SetLookAndFeelAction( String name, Icon icon,
                        String lookAndFeelName,
                        Vector framesToUpdate ) {
    super( name );

    if( lookAndFeelName == null )
        throw new RuntimeException(
            "Look-and-feel name may not be null." );

    if( icon != null )
        putValue( SMALL_ICON, icon );
    putValue( LOOKANDFEELNAME_KEY, lookAndFeelName );
    if( framesToUpdate != null )
        putValue( FRAMESTOUPDAT_KEY, framesToUpdate );

} // SetLookAndFeelAction
```

```java
/**
 * actionPerformed, from ActionListener
 * <p>
 * Perform the action.  Set the look and feel
 * to that defined by the look-and-feel attribute.
 * Update the source frame, and frames in the
 * frames Vector.
 * <p>
 * @param event The event causing the action to fire.
 **/
public void actionPerformed( ActionEvent event ) {

    try {
        String lookAndFeelName = ( String )getValue(
                                    LOOKANDFEELNAME_KEY );
        UIManager.setLookAndFeel( lookAndFeelName );

        //
        // Update component tree for the source of the event.
        //
        Object o = event.getSource();
        if( o instanceof Component ) {
            Frame frame = JOptionPane.getFrameForComponent(
                            ( Component )o );
            SwingUtilities.updateComponentTreeUI( frame );
        }


        //
        // See if there are any registered frames to update.
        //
        Vector framesToUpdate = ( Vector )getValue(
                                    FRAMESTOUPDAT_KEY );
        if( framesToUpdate != null ) {
            for( Enumeration e = framesToUpdate.elements();
                            e.hasMoreElements(); ) {
                Object f = e.nextElement();
                if( f instanceof Component ) {
                    Frame frame = JOptionPane.getFrameForComponent(
                                    ( Component )f );
                    SwingUtilities.updateComponentTreeUI( frame );
                }
            }
        }
    } catch( ClassNotFoundException cnf ) {
        throw new RuntimeException( cnf.getLocalizedMessage() );
    } catch( InstantiationException ie ) {
        throw new RuntimeException( ie.getLocalizedMessage() );
    } catch( UnsupportedLookAndFeelException ulf ) {
        throw new RuntimeException( ulf.getLocalizedMessage() );
    } catch( IllegalAccessException ia ) {
        throw new RuntimeException( ia.getLocalizedMessage() );
    } // catch
```

4

JFC PROGRAMMING TECHNIQUES

```
    } // actionPerformed

} // SetLookAndFeelAction
```

Summary

To fully understand and exploit the power of the JFC, some programming techniques need to be understood. This chapter addressed some of those issues. It was seen that the JFC is a single-threaded toolkit. Due to the multithreaded nature of Java, this may have come as a surprise to many programmers. The JFC developers decided that most user interface code was inherently single threaded. Thus the extra complexity and perfor-mance penalty for making the Swing toolkit multithreaded were not worth the effort. This decision is being hotly debated, and probably will be for as long as the toolkit is used. However, the fact is that this version of the toolkit is single threaded and using it in a multithreaded application requires special programming techniques. These techniques where discussed in this chapter. For most types of updates of a Swing component from a thread other than the event-dispatch thread, the invokeLater or invokeAndWait method must be used. These methods place a Runnable object in the event-dispatch thread's queue. This ensures that when the Runnable object's run() method is invoked, it will be in the event-dispatch thread.

For reccurring operations, the JFC provides the Timer class that will fire an ActionEvent in the event-dispatch thread. Thus the listener's actionPerformed method is free to update Swing components.

This chapter investigated the RepaintManager contained in the JFC. Understanding this class, or even providing your own implementation of a RepaintManager, can enhance the efficiency of painting JFC applications.

Finally, this chapter investigated Actions. It was shown how an Action could be used to encapsulate a piece of application functionality and store data associated with that func-tionality. The associated data can consist of a String used in a menu representation of the Action or an Icon to represent the Action on a toolbar, to name a few of the stan-dard data items contained in an Action. Designing applications that contain Actions allows the user interface to be separated from the functionality of the application. This gives the programmer more flexibility when creating the user interface for the applica-tion. It also allows the user interface and the application's functionality to change inde-pendently of one another.

JFC Components

IN THIS PART

Basic Components

CHAPTER 5

When building a user interface, there is a need for basic user interface components. This chapter presents the basic components supplied with the JFC.

In this chapter you will learn how to use:

- Separators
- Borders
- Icons
- Labels

Separator

Perhaps the simplest component in the JFC is the `JSeparator` class. The `JSeparator` displays an etched line that is typically used to divide areas in a panel (see Figure 5.1). This class is commonly used in menus but can be used in any container.

Creating a separator is a simple task. Simply call the constructor of the class—it doesn't take any parameters. This is shown in the following code fragment. The separator can then be added to a container. Many of the examples in the remainder of this book will show the `JSeparator` class in action.

```
JSeparator separator = new JSeparator();
```

FIGURE 5.1

A JSeparator.

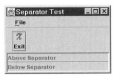

Borders

Borders are often used to group components that perform a related function. The JFC makes this particularly easy because the `JComponent` class provides a property for a border. This means that any `JComponent`, both simple components and complex containers, can have a border. Also, borders can be nested to create any visual appearance desired.

The `Border` Interface

The methods that define a JFC border are contained in the `Border` interface. These methods are shown in the next code example. Any component can implement this interface and be used as a border for a `JComponent`. However, as you will see in the remainder of this section, the JFC provides a rich set of standard borders. Due to the stock borders, implementing the `Border` interface is rarely required.

```
public interface Border
{
    /**
     * Paints the border for the specified component with the specified
     * position and size.
     * @param c the component for which this border is being painted
     * @param g the paint graphics
     * @param x the x position of the painted border
     * @param y the y position of the painted border
     * @param width the width of the painted border
     * @param height the height of the painted border
     */
void paintBorder( Component c, Graphics g,
                     int x, int y, int width, int height );

    /**
     * Returns the insets of the border.
     * @param c the component for which this border insets value applies
     */
    Insets getBorderInsets(Component c);

    /**
     * Returns whether or not the border is opaque.  If the border
     * is opaque, it is responsible for filling in it's own
     * background when painting.
     */
    boolean isBorderOpaque();
}
```

The Border Package

The borders that are part of the JFC are contained in the `javax.swing.border` package. This package consists of the `Border` interface itself, an abstract border class that serves as the parent to the eight concrete borders, and the concrete border classes. The border class hierarchy is shown in Figure 5.2.

FIGURE 5.2

The Border package class hierarchy.

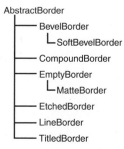

AbstractBorder
- BevelBorder
  - SoftBevelBorder
- CompoundBorder
- EmptyBorder
  - MatteBorder
- EtchedBorder
- LineBorder
- TitledBorder

An instance of a concrete border can be created and set for any JComponent. The following code shows how to create a SoftBevelBorder instance. The remaining borders will be presented in the BorderFactory section later in this chapter. The next section shows how to add the border to a JComponent.

```
Border border = new SoftBevelBorder( BevelBorder.LOWERED );
```

Adding a Border to any JComponent

The setBorder method in JComponent is provided for setting the border. Because this method is in JComponent, any JFC component, or any component derived from a JFC component, can contain a border. This means that both simple components, such as JLabel instances, and container components, such as JPanel instances, can contain a border. This makes it extremely easy to add borders to group-related components in a panel. This is a powerful feature of the JFC. An example of the setBorder method will be shown in the next section.

The getBorder method can be used to query the current border surrounding a JComponent. The returned border can then be altered for the current situation. This method will return null if the component doesn't currently have a border.

The BorderFactory

Instances of the borders in the Border package can be instantiated directly, as shown in a previous section. However, the JFC borders are designed to be shared among components. To facilitate sharing borders, a factory has been built to retrieve borders. The BorderFactory consists of a collection of static methods used to obtain a handle to a border. The BorderFactor lives in the javax.swing package, even though the borders themselves live in the javax.swing.border package. These methods follow the naming pattern create*Type*Border, where *Type* is one of the border classes in the javax.swing.border package. There is a create method that corresponds to each public constructor in the border classes. Each of the borders that can be retrieved via the BorderFactory is discussed in the following sections.

LineBorder

The static BorderFactory method createLineBorder will return an instance of a LineBorder. As its name implies, a simple line represents a line border. The color of the border must be specified. Optionally, a thickness for the border can be specified. If the thickness is omitted, a border with a thickness of one pixel is returned. The following application demonstrates how to obtain a blue LineBorder with a thickness of five pixels and set it for a JLabel component. This label and its border are shown in Figure 5.3.

FIGURE 5.3

A simple `LineBorder` *around a* `JLabel`.

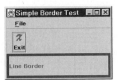

```
package com.foley.test;

import java.awt.*;

import javax.swing.*;
import javax.swing.border.*;

import com.foley.utility.ApplicationFrame;


/**
 * An application that displays a border
 * around a label in a frame.
 *
 * @author Mike Foley
 **/
public class SimpleBorderTest extends JFrame {

    /**
     * Application entry point.
     * Create the frame, and display it.
     *
     * @param args Command line parameter. Not used.
     **/
    public static void main( String args[] ) {

ApplicationFrame frame =
                    new ApplicationFrame( "Simple Border Test" );

        //
        // Create a label and add the border around the label.
```

5

BASIC COMPONENTS

```
//
JLabel label = new JLabel( "Line Border" );
Border border = BorderFactory.createLineBorder( Color.blue, 5 );
label.setBorder( border );

frame.getContentPane().add( label, BorderLayout.CENTER );

frame.pack();
frame.setVisible( true );

   } // main

} // SimpleBorderTest
```

BevelBorder

The static `BorderFactory` method `createBevelBorder` returns an instance of the `BevelBorder` class. A `BevelBorder` can be used to give a component a raised or sunken look. The next code fragment shows how to obtain a reference to a `BevelBorder`. As the example shows, the `RAISED` or `LOWERED` constant defined in the `BevelBorder` class is used to set the border type. These borders are then added to instances of the `JLabel` class. The resulting components are shown in Figure 5.4.

FIGURE 5.4

Beveled borders.

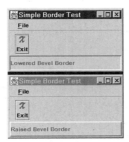

```
JLabel label = new JLabel( "Lowered Bevel Border" );
Border border = BorderFactory.createBevelBorder( BevelBorder.LOWERED );
label.setBorder( border );

JLabel label = new JLabel( "Raised Bevel Border" );
Border border = BorderFactory.createBevelBorder( BevelBorder.RAISED );
label.setBorder( border );
```

The convenience methods `createRaisedBevelBorder` and `createLoweredBevelBorder` are provided in `BorderFactory` to create a raised or lowered bevel border without requiring a parameter. By using these method, the previous code could be expressed as follows:

```
JLabel label = new JLabel( "Lowered Bevel Border" );
Border border = BorderFactory.createLoweredBevelBorder();
label.setBorder( border );

JLabel label = new JLabel( "Raised Bevel Border" );
Border border = BorderFactory.createRaisedBevelBorder();
label.setBorder( border );
```

These bevel borders use the colors specified by the look-and-feel currently in use. The colors contained in the `BevelBorder` can be specified in the `createBevelBorderMethod`. You have two options when specifying colors. You can specify the highlight and shadow colors and let the border determine the inner and outer shades for each border. Or you can specify all four colors that the border uses to paint itself. These colors are the `highlightOuter`, `highlightInner`, `shadowOuter`, and `shadowInner`. An example of using the methods in the `BorderFactory` to obtain a `BevelBorder` with an arbitrary color scheme is presented next. Care should be taken when using these methods because it is very easy to create unattractive borders. The various look-and-feels have different color schemes, making this task even more difficult.

```
Border border = BorderFactory.createBevelBorder(
                    BevelBorder.RAISED, Color.blue, Color.red );
Border border = BorderFactory.createBevelBorder(
                    BevelBorder.LOWERED, Color.blue, Color.red,
                    Color.yellow, Color.gray );
```

EtchedBorder

The static `BorderFactory` method `createEtchedBorder` returns an instance of the `EtchedBorder` class. Obtaining an etched border from the `BorderFactory` is demonstrated in the following code. This border, after being added to a `JLabel`, is shown in Figure 5.5.

```
JLabel label = new JLabel( "Etched Border" );
Border border = BorderFactory.createEtchedBorder();
label.setBorder( border );
```

FIGURE 5.5

EtchedBorder
around a JLabel.

The highlight and shadow color used in the etched border can be specified while obtaining an etched border from the `BorderFactory`, as in the following:

```
Border border = BorderFactory.createEtchedBorder(
                    highlightColor, shadowColor )
```

EmptyBorder

The static `BorderFactory` method `createEmptyBorder` returns an instance of the `EtchedBorder` class. As the name implies, and empty border is a border that is not painted. The first question that comes to mind is, why would such a border be desired? The answer is that empty borders have replaced `Insets` from the AWT as the desired mechanism for adding space around a component.

The `BorderFactory` contains two static overloaded methods to obtain a handle on an `EmptyBorder`. The more interesting of the two `createEmptyBorder` methods is the version that takes parameters. The amount of space taken by the border on each side of the bordered component can be specified by using this method. Notice that the space on each side is individually specified in the same order as when creating an `Insets` instance. This allows a non-symmetric border, if desired. A picture of an `EmptyBorder` is not presented, because it is difficult to see.

```
Border border = BorderFactory.createEmptyBorder();
Border iBorder = BorderFactory.createEmptyBorder(
                      top, left, bottom, right );
```

MatteBorder

The static `BorderFactory` method `createMatteBorder` returns an instance of the `MatteBorder` class. The method to obtain a matte border is similar to the method to obtain an empty border. This is because the matte border extends the `EmptyBorder` class. In addition to the border size parameters, a color or icon can be specified when creating a matte border.

When a color is specified, the border looks suspiciously like a line border. The fundamental difference between the two borders is that the line border is the same thickness on each side of the bordered component. The matte border can be a different size on each side of the component. The following line of code retrieves a blue matte border with a thickness of five pixels from the `BorderFactory` (see Figure 5.6).

```
JLabel label = new JLabel( "Matte Border" );
Border border = BorderFactory.createMatteBorder(
                      5, 5, 5, 5, Color.blue );
label.setBorder( border );
```

FIGURE 5.6

A matte border.

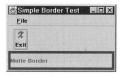

When given an `Icon`, the matte border paints the `Icon` in the border. The `Icon` is repeated as often as necessary to fill the border. The following line of code creates a matte border by using the `Icon` named `checker`. A simple red and white checked pattern icon was used to create the checkered matte border in Figure 5.7. From these figures, it can be seen how the icon image is repeated over and over to fill the border.

```
//
// Assume the checker.gif image is in the current directory.
//
ImageIcon checker = new ImageIcon( "checker.gif" );
JLabel label = new JLabel( "Matte Border" );
Border border = BorderFactory.createMatteBorder( 4, 4, 4, 4, checker );
label.setBorder( border );
```

FIGURE 5.7

A checkered matte border created by repeating a checker icon.

CompoundBorder

In the previous sections, you looked at the simple borders contained in the JFC. Borders can be combined to create an endless variety of compound borders. The `BorderFactory` static method `createCompoundBorder` returns an instance of a compound border. A compound border consists of two borders, one nested inside the other. A typical use of a compound border is to add space between a decorative border and the component.

In the examples given in the previous sections, you saw that the label's text approaches the border. This is awkward in appearance. Using a compound border can alleviate this problem. An empty border with the desired margin can be placed inside the decorative border. The following line of code creates such a border. The first parameter is the outer border, and the second is the inner border (see Figure 5.8). In the figure it is easy to see how the empty border provides a margin between the label's text and the matte border.

```
//
// Assume the checker.gif image is in the current
// directory.
//
ImageIcon checker = new ImageIcon( "checker.gif" );
JLabel label = new JLabel( "Matte Border" );
Border border = BorderFactory.createCompoundBorder(
            BorderFactory.createMatteBorder( 4, 4, 4, 4, checker ),
            BorderFactory.createEmptyBorder( 4, 4, 4, 4 ) );
label.setBorder( border );
```

FIGURE 5.8

A compound matte and empty border.

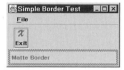

Compound borders can be nested to add additional visual appeal. This is accomplished by creating a CompoundBorder as shown earlier, and then using this border as the outside border in another CompoundBorder. This nesting can be performed to an arbitrary depth. The following code fragment creates a border consisting of a matte border surrounded by bevel borders. This creates a sunken matte border (see Figure 5.9).

```
//
// Assume the checker.gif image is in the current
// directory.
//
ImageIcon checker = new ImageIcon( "checker.gif" );
JLabel label = new JLabel( "Sunken Matte Border" );
Border border = BorderFactory.createCompoundBorder(
          BorderFactory.createBevelBorder( BevelBorder.LOWERED ),
          BorderFactory.createMatteBorder( 4, 4, 4, 4, checker ) );
border = BorderFactory.createCompoundBorder(
          border,
          BorderFactory.createBevelBorder( BevelBorder.RAISED ) );
border = BorderFactory.createCompoundBorder(
          border,
          BorderFactory.createEmptyBorder( 2, 2, 2, 2 ) );
label.setBorder( border );
```

FIGURE 5.9

Double nested CompoundBorder.

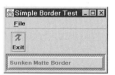

Restraint must be shown when using multiple compound borders. It's easy to get carried away and create unattractive ones.

A nice use of the compound border is when a matte border is not desired on each side of the component. The matte border and an empty border can be combined to provide this functionality, while keeping the border symmetric around the component.

Adding a Title to a Border

It is often desirable to add a title to the border surrounding the components when grouping components. The BorderFactory method createTitledBorder returns an instance of a TitledBorder. This type of border can be used to add a title to any border. The text, font, position, and color of the border can be specified while obtaining the border or altered later by calling methods contained in the `TitledBorder` class.

The title can be placed above or below the bordered component. It can also be placed above, below, or through the border. The positioning of the border is determined by two parameters that can be specified when obtaining the titled border, or through methods in the `TitledBorder` class. The properties for positioning the border are `titlePosition` and `titleJustification`. These constants are defined in the `TitledBorder` class, not in the `SwingConstants` class. The JFC is somewhat inconsistent about which constants are defined where. It is unfortunate that these constants weren't shared with others that convey the same meaning in the `SwingConstants` class. Figure 5.10 demonstrates the available constants and how the title is positioned for each combination of the positioning constants.

The following code fragment obtains the handle to a `TitledBorder` from the `BorderFactory`. The word "Title" will be centered above the border. Figure 5.10 shows all the possible combinations of title positioning around a `JLabel`. Notice how the `TitledBorder` class requires a reference to the border that is getting the title, an etched border in the example below.

```
Border etched = BorderFactory.createEtchedBorder();Border border =
BorderFactory.createTitledBorder(
                    etched, "Title",
                    TitledBorder.CENTER,
                    TitledBorder.ABOVE_TOP );
```

Figure 5.10

Positions for a border's title.

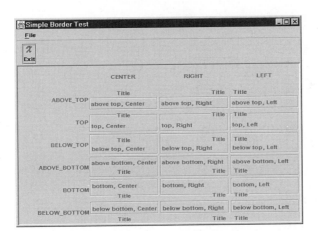

Creating Your Own Border

As was described earlier in this chapter, `Border` is an interface. This allows any class to implement this interface and be set as the border to any instance of a `JComponent` extension.

This section presents three classes, two of which can be used as borders. The third class is an abstract base class for the two concrete `Border` classes. These borders use the Java threading mechanism to create an animated border. The first class is an abstract class named `AnimatedBorder`. This class extends the JFC `EmptyBorder` class. The `EmptyBorder` class manages the real estate where the border paints. This is done with the `Insets` for the border. `EmptyBorder` extends the `AbstractBorder` class. Many borders that you will create will extend `AbstractBorder`, as do most of the JFC borders.

The `AnimatedBorder` class is presented in Listing 5.1. Its primary duty is to manage the thread used to create the animation. It contains one bound property that determines how often the animation occurs. To support the bound property, the class contains the required methods for managing `PropertyChangeListeners`.

The run method is very simple. It sleeps the amount of time specified by the `sleepTime` property and then forces the border to be painted. Classes that extend `AnimatedBorder` perform the actual animation in their `paintBorder` method. Recall that `paintBorder` is one of the methods defined in the `Border` interface. This ensures that all borders will contain the `paintBorder` method.

LISTING 5.1 THE `AnimatedBorder` CLASS

```
package com.foley.borders;

import java.awt.Insets;
import java.awt.Component;
import java.awt.Graphics;
import java.awt.Color;

import java.beans.PropertyChangeSupport;
import java.beans.PropertyChangeListener;

import javax.swing.JComponent;

import javax.swing.border.Border;
import javax.swing.border.EmptyBorder;


/**
 * AnimatedBorder is an abstract class that can be
 * extended to create animated borders.  This class
```

```
 * manages the animation thread.  It forces the border
 * to be redrawn each animation cycle.  It is the
 * responsibility of the child class to track
 * which animation cycle they are drawing.
 *
 * @author Mike Foley
 * @see Border
 **/
public abstract class AnimatedBorder extends EmptyBorder
    implements Runnable {

    /**
     * The component this Border borders.
     **/
    private JComponent c;

    /**
     * The delay between border paints.
     **/
    private int sleepTime = 250;

    /**
     * Support for property change listeners, and bound
     * property names.
     **/
protected PropertyChangeSupport changes =
                                 new PropertyChangeSupport(this);
    public static final String SLEEP_TIME_PROPERTY = "SleepTimeProperty";


    /**
     * Constructor
     * Create an Insets structure and call our working constructor.
     *
     * @param c The component we border.
     * @param top The top border width.
     * @param left The left border width.
     * @param bottom The bottom border width.
     * @param right The right border width.
     **/
    public AnimatedBorder( JComponent c, int top, int left,
                         int bottom, int right ) {
        this( c, new Insets( top, left, bottom, right ) );
    }


    /**
     * Constructor.
     * Store a reference to the component we border.
     * Create, and start, the thread which performs
```

continues

LISTING 5.1   CONTINUED

```java
 * the animation.
 *
 * @param c The component we border.
 * @param insets The border size.
 **/
public AnimatedBorder( JComponent c, Insets insets ) {
    super( insets );
    this.c = c;
    Thread animator = new Thread( this );
    animator.start();
}


/**
 * Set the sleep time.  This is the cycle time
 * between animations.
 * This is a bound property.
 *
 * @param sleepTime The new animation cycle time.
 **/
public void setSleepTime( int sleepTime ) {

    Integer old = new Integer( this.sleepTime );
    this.sleepTime = sleepTime;

    changes.firePropertyChange( SLEEP_TIME_PROPERTY,
                   old, new Integer( this.sleepTime ) );

} // setSleepTime


/**
 * @return The current cycle time.
 **/
public int getSleepTime() {
    return( this.sleepTime );
}


/**
 * @return The component we border.
 **/
public JComponent getBorderedComponent() {
    return( c );
}


/**
 * The animation thread.
```

```
    * Sleep the specified amount of time, then
    * repaint the bordered component.  This is an
    * expensive way to force the border to redraw.
    * If the animated borders are placed around
    * complex components, this can be an issue.
    **/
   public void run() {

       while( true ) {

           try {
               Thread.sleep( sleepTime );

               //
               // Repaint is thread safe for Swing components.
               c.repaint();
           } catch( InterruptedException ie ) {
               // Don't care if interrupted.
           }
       }
   } // run


   /**
    * Add the given listener to those receiving property change
    * notifications.
    *
    * @param l the PropertyChangeListener
    * @see #removePropertyChangeListener
    **/
   public void addPropertyChangeListener( PropertyChangeListener l ) {
       changes.addPropertyChangeListener( l );
   } // addPropertyChangeListener


   /**
    * Remove the given listener from those receiving property change
    * notifications.
    *
    * @param l the PropertyChangeListener
    * @see #addPropertyChangeListener
    **/
public void removePropertyChangeListener(PropertyChangeListener l) {
       changes.removePropertyChangeListener( l );
   } // removePropertyChangeListener

} // AnimatedBorder
```

The first concrete extension of the AnimatedBorder class is the ColorAnimatedBorder.

This class paints a matte type border in a different color each animation cycle. This can be used to smoothly fade in or out a border color, or to grab attention by starkly varying the border color. The array of colors is created in the constructor. Each time the border is painted, the next color in the array is used for the color of the border.

The constructor calls the `makeColors` method, which creates the array of colors cycled through during the animation. This class could be extended, and overriding the `makeColors` method to create a different array of colors gives any color effect desired. The complete source listing for the `ColorAnimatedBorder` is given in Listing 5.2.

LISTING 5.2   THE `ColorAnimatedBorder` CLASS

```
package com.foley.borders;

import java.awt.Insets;
import java.awt.Component;
import java.awt.Graphics;
import java.awt.Color;

import javax.swing.JComponent;

import javax.swing.border.Border;
import javax.swing.border.EmptyBorder;


/**
 * ColorAnimatedBorder is a concrete AnimatedBorder.  It
 * paints the border a different color each animation cycle.
 *
 * @see AnimatedBorder
 * @see Border
 * @author Mike Foley
 **/
public class ColorAnimatedBorder extends AnimatedBorder {

    /**
     * The colors used for the border.  The elements in this
     * array are stepped through, and drawn each cycle.
     **/
    protected Color[] colors = null;

    /**
     * The index of the next color to use when drawing the border.
     **/
    private int currentColorIndex = 0;


    /**
     * Constructor.
```

```
 * Create insets from the raw parameter and call our
 * constructor taking Insets to do the work.
 *
 * @param c The component we border.
 * @param top The top border width.
 * @param left The left border width.
 * @param bottom The bottom border width.
 * @param right The right border width.
 **/
public ColorAnimatedBorder( JComponent c, int top, int left,
                            int bottom, int right ) {
    this( c, new Insets( top, left, bottom, right ) );
}


/**
 * Constructor.
 * Make the colors used to paint the border.
 *
 * @param c The component we border.
 * @param insets The border size.
 **/
public ColorAnimatedBorder( JComponent c, Insets insets ) {
    super( c, insets );
    colors = makeColors();
}


/**
 * Make an array of colors that are stepped through during
 * the paintBorder methods.
 * If a great number of colors (thousands) are to be animated,
 * it may better to create one color each paint cycle, and let the
 * GC free the colors when no longer needed.
 **/
protected void makeColors() {
    Color[] colors = new Color[ 20 ];
    int step = 12;

    for( int i = 0; i < colors.length; i++ ) {
        colors[ i ] = new Color( 100, 100, i * step );
    }

    return( colors );

} // makeColors


/**
 * Paint the border.
```

continues

LISTING 5.2   CONTINUED

```
       * Get the color at the current color index.  Then update the index.
       * The index is wrapped, so that the array of colors repeat every
       * length of the array.
       *
       * @param c The bordered component.
     * @param g The graphics to paint with.
       * @param x The X location of the bordered component.
       * @param y The Y location of the bordered component.
       * @param width The width of the bordered component.
       * @param height The height of the bordered component.
       **/
      public void paintBorder( Component c, Graphics g, int x,
                               int y, int width, int height ) {

          //
          // Save the current color so we can restore at end of method.
          //
          Color oldColor = g.getColor();

          g.translate( x, y );

          //
          // Set the color to paint with.  Increment the color index.
          // Wrap if needed.
          //
          Color color = colors[ currentColorIndex++ ];
          currentColorIndex %= colors.length;

          //
          // Get our size.
          //
          Insets insets = getBorderInsets( c );

          //
          // Paint the border.
          //
          g.setColor( color );
          g.fillRect( 0, 0, width - insets.right, insets.top );
          g.fillRect( 0, insets.top, insets.left, height - insets.top );
      g.fillRect( insets.left, height - insets.bottom,
                      width - insets.left, insets.bottom );
      g.fillRect( width - insets.right, 0,
                      insets.right, height - insets.bottom );

          //
          // Restore the Graphics object's state.
          //
          g.translate( -x, -y );
          g.setColor( oldColor );
```

```
    } // paintBorder

} // ColorAnimatedBorder
```

The second child of the `AnimatedBorder` class is the `ChaserLightsBorder` class. This class provides a border that mimics chaser lights. The lights are drawn as simple circles whose diameters are the border width. A single pixel is placed between each light. By changing the direction property, the chasing direction can be altered. The on and off color of the lights can be specified by setting bound properties. The number of "on" lights between the "off" chaser light is also a bound property. Setting this property to 2 turns every other light on. The complete source listing for the `ChaserLightsBorder` class is given in Listing 5.3.

LISTING 5.3   THE `ChaserLightsBorder` CLASS

```java
package com.foley.borders;

import java.awt.Insets;
import java.awt.Component;
import java.awt.Graphics;
import java.awt.Color;

import javax.swing.JComponent;

import javax.swing.border.Border;
import javax.swing.border.EmptyBorder;


/**
 * ChaserLightsBorder is a concrete AnimatedBorder.  It
 * paints the border as a chase light.
 *
 * @see AnimatedBorder
 * @see Border
 * @author Mike Foley
 **/
public class ChaserLightsBorder extends AnimatedBorder {

    /**
     * The index of the next 'light' to be out
     * when drawing the border.
     **/
    private int currentLightIndex = 0;

    /**
     * The number of 'lights' to be on in a row
```

continues

LISTING 5.3   CONTINUED

```
    **/
    private int onLightCount = 5;

    /**
     * The first off light index for this cycle.
     **/
    private int firstOffLightIndex = 0;

    /**
     * The color to draw on 'lights'
     **/
    private Color onLightColor = Color.yellow;

    /**
     * The color to draw off 'lights'
     **/
    private Color offLightColor = Color.white;

    /**
     * The direction of light travel.  True = forward.
     **/
    private boolean direction = true;

    /**
     * Bound property names.
     **/
    public static final String DIRECTION_PROPERTY = "DirectionProperty";
    public static final String ONLIGHTCOLOR_PROPERTY =
                                        "OnLightColorProperty";
    public static final String OFFLIGHTCOLOR_PROPERTY =
                                        "OffLightColorProperty";


    /**
     * Constructor.
     * Create insets from the raw parameter and call our
     * constructor taking Insets to do the work.
     *
     * @param c The component we border.
     * @param top The top border width.
     * @param left The left border width.
     * @param bottom The bottom border width.
     * @param right The right border width.
     **/
    public ChaserLightsBorder( JComponent c, int top, int left,
                        int bottom, int right ) {
        this( c, new Insets( top, left, bottom, right ) );
    }
```

```
/**
 * Constructor.
 * Call our super.  We don't do any additional processing.
 *
 * @param c The component we border.
 * @param insets The border size.
 **/
public ChaserLightsBorder( JComponent c, Insets insets ) {
    super( c, insets );
}


/**
 * Set the on light count of the chaser lights.
 * This value is one greater than the number of lights
 * on before the off light.  A value of two will give
 * every other light being off.  A value of one will give
 * all lights on, not very good.
 *
 * This is a bound property.
 *
 * @param onLightCount The new on light count.
 **/
public void setOnLightCount( int onLightCount ) {

    if( onLightCount < 1 )
throw new IllegalArgumentException(
                    "Negative or zero onLightCount given" );

    Integer old = new Integer( this.onLightCount );
    this.onLightCount = onLightCount;

    changes.firePropertyChange( ONLIGHTCOUNT_PROPERTY,
                        old, new Integer( this.onLightCount ) );
} // setOnLightCount


/**
* @return The number of lights - 1 in a row between the off light.
 **/
public int getOnLightCount() {
    return( this.onLightCount );
}


/**
 * Set the direction of the chaser lights.  True means
 * forward.
 * This is a bound property.
 *
 * @param direction The new direction of the chaser lights.
```

continues

LISTING 5.3   CONTINUED

```
     **/
    public void setDirection( boolean direction ) {

        Boolean old = new Boolean( this.direction );
        this.direction = direction;

        changes.firePropertyChange( DIRECTION_PROPERTY,
                            old, new Boolean( this.direction ) );
    } // setDirection


    /**
     * @return The direction the chaser lights are going.
     **/
    public boolean getDirection() {
        return( this.direction );
    }


    /**
     * Set the color for 'on' lights.
     * This is a bound property.
     *
     * @param onLightColor The new color for 'on' lights.
     **/
    public void setOnLightColor( Color onLightColor ) {

        Color old = this.onLightColor;
        this.onLightColor = onLightColor;

        changes.firePropertyChange( ONLIGHTCOLOR_PROPERTY,
                            old, this.onLightColor );

    } // setOnLightColor


    /**
     * @return The color for 'on' lights.
     **/
    public Color getOnLightColor() {
        return( this.onLightColor );
    }


    /**
     * Set the color for 'off' lights.
     * This is a bound property.
     *
     * @param offLightColor The new color for 'off' lights.
```

```
 **/
public void setOffLightColor( Color offLightColor ) {

    Color old = this.offLightColor;
    this.offLightColor = offLightColor;

    changes.firePropertyChange( OFFLIGHTCOLOR_PROPERTY,
                        old, this.offLightColor );

} // setOffLightColor


/**
 * @return The color for 'off' lights.
 **/
public Color getOffLightColor() {
    return( this.offLightColor );
}


/**
 * Paint the border.
 * Get the color at the current color index.  Then update the index.
 * The index is wrapped, so that the array of colors repeat every
 * length of the array.
 *
 * @param c The bordered component.
 * @param g The graphics to paint with.
 * @param x The X location of the bordered component.
 * @param y The Y location of the bordered component.
 * @param width The width of the bordered component.
 * @param height The height of the bordered component.
 **/
public void paintBorder( Component c, Graphics g, int x,
                        int y, int width, int height ) {

    //
    // Save the current color so we can restore at end of method.
    //
    Color oldColor = g.getColor();

    g.translate( x, y );

    //
    // Get our size.
    //
    Insets insets = getBorderInsets( c );

    //
    // Paint the border.
```

continues

LISTING 5.3   CONTINUED

```
// Set the current light index.  Start at 0.
//
currentLightIndex = 0;

//
// Top
int xpos = 0;
int ypos = 0;
if( 0 < insets.top ) {
    do {
        setGraphicsColor( g );
        g.fillOval( xpos, ypos, insets.top, insets.top );
        xpos += insets.top + 1;
    } while( xpos < width );
}

//
// Right
xpos = width - insets.right;
ypos = insets.top;
if( 0 < insets.right ) {
    do {
        setGraphicsColor( g );
        g.fillOval( xpos, ypos, insets.right, insets.right );
        ypos += insets.right + 1;
    } while( ypos < height - 2 * insets.bottom );
}

//
// Bottom
xpos = width - insets.right;
ypos = height - insets.bottom;
if( 0 < insets.bottom ) {
    do {
        setGraphicsColor( g );
        g.fillOval( xpos, ypos, insets.bottom, insets.bottom );
        xpos -= insets.bottom + 1;
    } while( 0 < xpos );
}

//
// Left
xpos = 0;
ypos = height - 2 * insets.bottom;
if( 0 < insets.left ) {
    do {
        setGraphicsColor( g );
        g.fillOval( xpos, ypos, insets.left, insets.left );
        ypos -= insets.left + 1;
```

```
            } while( 0 < ypos - insets.top );
        }


        //
        // Update the light off index.  If going forward, increment
        // else decrement.  Wrap the index as required.
        //
        if( direction ) {
            firstOffLightIndex += 1;
            firstOffLightIndex %= onLightCount;
        } else {
            firstOffLightIndex -= 1;
            if( firstOffLightIndex < 0 )
                firstOffLightIndex = onLightCount - 1;
        }


        //
        // Restore the Graphics object's state.
        //
        g.translate( -x, -y );
        g.setColor( oldColor );

    } // paintBorder


    /**
     * Set the color to draw the next light with.
     * We update the currentLight Index.  This index
     * must be reset each cycle.
     *
     * @param g The graphics used to paint.
     **/
    private void setGraphicsColor( Graphics g ) {

        if( currentLightIndex % onLightCount == firstOffLightIndex ) {
            g.setColor( offLightColor );
        } else {
            g.setColor( onLightColor );
        }

        //
        // Update the currentLightIndex, wrap if required
        //
        currentLightIndex += 1;

    }

} // ChaserLightsBorder
```

Very interesting visual effects can be created by using animated borders. However, creating a thread for each border makes the cost of these borders rather high. If multiple animated borders are to be used in an application or applet, a single thread should be used to control the animation in all of the animated borders.

A Complete but Gaudy Border Example

The previous sections provided code fragments demonstrating how to create the various types of borders contained in the JFC. This section applies those ideas in a complete example application. The application is a somewhat silly JFrame extension that displays many types of bordered components in its display area. Listing 5.4 is the complete listing for the BorderTest application. The results of running the application are shown in Figure 5.11. The ImageLoader class, used to load Icons for the borders, is presented in the next section. ExitAction, used in the frame's menu, was presented in Chapter 4, "JFC Programming Techniques."

FIGURE 5.11

The complete BorderTest *application.*

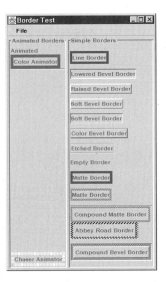

LISTING 5.4   BorderTest APPLICATION

```
package com.foley.test;

import java.awt.*;

import javax.swing.*;
import javax.swing.border.*;

import com.foley.borders.*;
```

```
import com.foley.utility.ExitAction;
import com.foley.utility.ImageLoader;


/**
 * An application that displays many borders
 * in its frame.
 *
 * @author Mike Foley
 **/
public class BorderTest extends JFrame {

    public static BorderTest frame;

    private Icon checker;
    private Icon abbey;
    private Icon stop;
    public static Image bullseye;
    public static Image bullseye2;

    /**
     * BorderTest, null constructor.
     **/
    public BorderTest() {
        this( null );
    } // BorderTest


    /**
     * BorderTest, constructor.
     *
     * @param title The title for the frame.
     **/
    public BorderTest( String title ) {
        super( title );
    } // BorderTest


    /**
     * frameInit, from JFrame
     *
     * Create the contrent for this frame.
     **/
    protected void frameInit() {

        //
        // Let our super create the content and associated panes.
        //
        super.frameInit();
```

continues

LISTING 5.4   CONTINUED

```java
        try {
            //
            // Load the images used.
            //
            checker = ImageLoader.loadIcon( "checker.gif" );
            abbey = ImageLoader.loadIcon( "abbey.gif" );
            stop = ImageLoader.loadIcon( "stop.gif" );
        } catch( InterruptedException ie ) {
            System.err.println( "Could not load images" );
            System.exit( -1 );
        }

        JMenuBar menubar = createMenu();
        setJMenuBar( menubar );

        Container content = getContentPane();

        JPanel borders = createBorderPanel();
        JPanel animatedPanel = createAnimatedBorderPanel();

        //
        // Add the border panels to the content.
        //
        borders.setBorder( BorderFactory.createTitledBorder(
    ➥BorderFactory.createBevelBorder( BevelBorder.LOWERED ),
                        "Simple Borders" ) );
        content.add( borders, BorderLayout.EAST );

        animatedPanel.setBorder( BorderFactory.createTitledBorder(
                            BorderFactory.createLoweredBevelBorder(),
                            "Animated Borders" ) );
        content.add( animatedPanel, BorderLayout.WEST );

    } // frameInit


    /**
     * Create the menu for the frame.
     *
     * @return The menu for the frame.
     **/
    protected JMenuBar createMenu() {

        JMenuBar menubar = new JMenuBar();

        JMenu file = new JMenu( "File" );
        file.add( new ExitAction() );
        menubar.add( file );
```

```
        return( menubar );

    } // createMenu


    /**
     * Create a panel containing many 'simple' borders.
     *
     * @return A panel containing many borders around labels.
     **/
    protected JPanel createBorderPanel() {

        JPanel simpleBorders = new JPanel();
        simpleBorders.setLayout( new BoxLayout(
simpleBorders, BoxLayout.Y_AXIS ) );

        int strutHeight = 10;
        simpleBorders.add( Box.createVerticalStrut( strutHeight ) );

        JLabel lineBorder = new JLabel( "Line Border" );
        Border border = BorderFactory.createLineBorder( Color.blue, 5 );
        lineBorder.setBorder( border );
        simpleBorders.add( lineBorder );

        simpleBorders.add( Box.createVerticalStrut( strutHeight ) );

        JLabel lowBevelBorder = new JLabel( "Lowered Bevel Border" );
        border = BorderFactory.createBevelBorder( BevelBorder.LOWERED );
        lowBevelBorder.setBorder( border );
        simpleBorders.add( lowBevelBorder );

        simpleBorders.add( Box.createVerticalStrut( strutHeight ) );

        JLabel raisedBevelBorder = new JLabel( "Raised Bevel Border" );
        border = BorderFactory.createBevelBorder( BevelBorder.RAISED );
        raisedBevelBorder.setBorder( border );
        simpleBorders.add( raisedBevelBorder );

        simpleBorders.add( Box.createVerticalStrut( strutHeight ) );

        JLabel softBevelBorder = new JLabel( "Soft Bevel Border" );
        border = new SoftBevelBorder( BevelBorder.RAISED );
        softBevelBorder.setBorder( border );
        simpleBorders.add( softBevelBorder );

        simpleBorders.add( Box.createVerticalStrut( strutHeight ) );

        softBevelBorder = new JLabel( "Soft Bevel Border" );
        border = new SoftBevelBorder( BevelBorder.LOWERED );
        softBevelBorder.setBorder( border );
```

continues

5

BASIC COMPONENTS

LISTING 5.4   CONTINUED

```
            simpleBorders.add( softBevelBorder );

            simpleBorders.add( Box.createVerticalStrut( strutHeight ) );

            JLabel ourcolorBevelBorder = new JLabel( "Color Bevel Border" );
            border = BorderFactory.createBevelBorder( BevelBorder.LOWERED,
                                    Color.blue, Color.red,
                                    Color.yellow, Color.gray );
            ourcolorBevelBorder.setBorder( border );
            simpleBorders.add( ourcolorBevelBorder );

            simpleBorders.add( Box.createVerticalStrut( strutHeight ) );

            JLabel etchedBorder = new JLabel( "Etched Border" );
            border = BorderFactory.createEtchedBorder();
            etchedBorder.setBorder( border );
            simpleBorders.add( etchedBorder );

            simpleBorders.add( Box.createVerticalStrut( strutHeight ) );

            JLabel emptyBorder = new JLabel( "Empty Border" );
            border = BorderFactory.createEmptyBorder();
            emptyBorder.setBorder( border );
            simpleBorders.add( emptyBorder );

            simpleBorders.add( Box.createVerticalStrut( strutHeight ) );

            JLabel matteBorder = new JLabel( "Matte Border" );
            border = BorderFactory.createMatteBorder(5, 5, 5, 5, Color.blue);
            matteBorder.setBorder( border );
            simpleBorders.add( matteBorder );

            simpleBorders.add( Box.createVerticalStrut( strutHeight ) );

            JLabel checkerBorder = new JLabel( "Matte Border" );
            border = BorderFactory.createMatteBorder( 4, 4, 4, 4, checker );
            checkerBorder.setBorder( border );
            simpleBorders.add( checkerBorder );

            simpleBorders.add( Box.createVerticalStrut( strutHeight ) );

            simpleBorders.add( new JSeparator() );

            JLabel compondBorder = new JLabel( "Compound Matte Border" );
            border = BorderFactory.createCompoundBorder(
                BorderFactory.createMatteBorder( 4, 4, 4, 4, checker ),
                BorderFactory.createEmptyBorder( 4, 4, 4, 4 ) );
            compondBorder.setBorder( border );
            simpleBorders.add( compondBorder );
```

```
        JLabel abbeyBorder = new JLabel( "Abbey Road Border" );
        border = BorderFactory.createCompoundBorder(
            BorderFactory.createMatteBorder( 4, 6, 4, 6, abbey ),
            BorderFactory.createEmptyBorder( 4, 4, 5, 4 ) );
        abbeyBorder.setBorder( border );
        simpleBorders.add( abbeyBorder );

        simpleBorders.add( Box.createVerticalStrut( strutHeight ) );

        compondBorder = new JLabel( "Compound Bevel Border" );
        border = BorderFactory.createCompoundBorder(
            BorderFactory.createBevelBorder( BevelBorder.LOWERED ),
            BorderFactory.createMatteBorder( 4, 4, 4, 4, checker ) );
        border = BorderFactory.createCompoundBorder(
            border,
            BorderFactory.createBevelBorder( BevelBorder.RAISED ) );
        border = BorderFactory.createCompoundBorder(
            border,
            BorderFactory.createEmptyBorder( 2, 2, 2, 2 ) );

        compondBorder.setBorder( border );
        simpleBorders.add( compondBorder );

        simpleBorders.add( Box.createVerticalStrut( strutHeight ) );

        return( simpleBorders );
    }

/**
 * Create a panel containing many animated borders.
 *
 * @return A panel containing many animated borders.
 **/
protected JPanel createAnimatedBorderPanel() {

        JPanel animatedPanel = new JPanel();
        animatedPanel.add( new JLabel( "Animated" ) );
        animatedPanel.setLayout(
                new BoxLayout( animatedPanel, BoxLayout.Y_AXIS ) );
        JLabel animated = new JLabel( "Color Animator" );
        animated.setBorder(
                new ColorAnimatedBorder( animated, 6, 6, 6, 6 ) );
        animatedPanel.add( animated );
        animatedPanel.add( new JSeparator() );
        animated = new JLabel( "Chaser Animator" );
        animated.setBorder(
                new ChaserLightsBorder( animated, 6, 6, 6, 6 ) );
        animatedPanel.add( animated );

        return( animatedPanel );
```

continues

5

BASIC
COMPONENTS

LISTING 5.4   CONTINUED

```
    }

    /**
     * Application entry point.
     * Create the frame, and display it.
     *
     * @param args Command line parameter. Not used.
     **/
    public static void main( String[] args ) {

        JFrame frame = new BorderTest( "Border Test" );
        frame.pack();
        frame.setVisible( true );
    } // main

} // BorderTest
```

Icons

In the AWT, bitmap graphics were drawn by using the Image class. In the JFC, components that use bitmap graphics require a class that implements the Icon interface. Thus, in the JFC, icons replace images for component decorations. However, the methods typically used to load or create a bitmap are the Toolkit image methods, which still return an image. To aid in this conversion, the JFC provides the ImageIcon class.

Icon Interface

The Icon interface defines the methods that define an icon. Any class can implement this interface and be used wherever an icon is wanted.

The methods defined in the Icon interface are used to query the size of the icon and to do the actual icon rendering. The following shows these methods in the Icon interface.

```
public interface Icon
{
    public abstract void paintIcon(Component c, Graphics g, int x, int y)
    public abstract int getIconWidth();
    public abstract int getIconHeight();
}
```

ImageIcon Class

The ImageIcon class is the Icon workhorse class in the JFC. This class contains constructors to create an icon from a file, URL, byte array, or an Image. The image can be set after creation to a new `Image` instance. The class also contains a method to obtain the image from the class. This provides a conversion between images and icons. A description can be specified with the image.

Listing 5.5 presents a utility class that can be used to load images and create icons. Since the `ImageIcon` class implements the `Icon` interface, it can be used for creating icons. The `ImageLoader` class extends `Component`. This allows it to be an `ImageObserver` during image loading. The class contains two static methods for image manipulation. The first, `loadImage`, attempts to load an image contained in the named resource. The method tries to get a URL to the resource. This allows the method to find images in JAR files as well as from a file system. If the resource is found, a `MediaTracker` is used to load the image. The method waits for the image to load, so the calling code can use the image immediately. The `loadImage` method returns an image.

The second static method, `loadIcon`, returns an icon. This method is used more in JFC programming. The `loadIcon` method calls the `loadImage` method to load the requested image. If the image is successfully loaded, an `ImageIcon` is created from the image. Because `ImageIcon` implements `Icon`, returning the `ImageIcon` is, in effect, returning an icon. The `ImageLoader` class is used in the border example application presented in the last section and shown in Listing 5.4.

If the image is stored in a file and loaded from an application, or if the URL pointing to the image data is already created, the `ImageIcon` class itself can be used to load the image. This is done by passing the filename or URL to the constructor of the `ImageIcon` class. During construction, the `ImageIcon` class will load the image by using a `MediaTracker`. This ensures that the image is available after the constructor has completed.

LISTING 5.5   `ImageLoader` CLASS FOR LOADING IMAGES AND CREATING ICONS

```
/**
 * A class containing static methods which can
 * be used to load Images and Icons. This class will
 * find the named resource in the local file system,
 * or a jar file, specified in the CLASSPATH.
 * <p>
 * @author Mike Foley
 * @version 1.2
 **/
public class ImageLoader extends Component {
    private static ImageLoader imageLoader;

    /**
     * ImageLoader, constructor.
```

continues

Listing 5.5   CONTINUED

```java
 * <p>
 * There should not be any instances of this
 * class created outside the private one used
 * in the class.
 **/
private ImageLoader() {
    super();
}


/**
 * loadImage
 * <p>
 * Load the image with the given name.
 * <p>
 * @param imageName The name of the image to load.
 * @return The Image for the image with the given name.
 * @see #loadIcon
 **/
public static Image loadImage( String imageName )
    throws java.lang.InterruptedException {

    //
    // get the image, and wait for it to be loaded.
    //
    URL url = Object.class.getResource( imageName );

    //
        // If the URL could not be located above, try
        // prepending a '/' to the image's ResourceName. This
        // will cause the search to begin at the top of the
        // CLASSPATH.
        //
      if( url == null )
            url = Object.class.getResource( "/" + imageName );
    if( url == null ) {
RuntimeException e = new RuntimeException(
                                "Image " + imageName + " not found" );
        e.printStackTrace();
        throw e;
    }

    //
    // get the image, and wait for it to be loaded.
    //
    Image image = Toolkit.getDefaultToolkit().getImage( url );
    MediaTracker tracker = new MediaTracker( imageLoader );
    tracker.addImage( image, 0 );
    tracker.waitForID( 0 );
```

```
        return( image );

    } // loadImage


    /**
     * loadIcon
     * <p>
     * Load the Icon with the given name.
     * <p>
     * @param imageName The name of the image to load.
     * @return The Icon for the image with the given name.
     * @see #loadImage
     **/
    public static Icon loadIcon( String imageName )
        throws java.lang.InterruptedException {

        Image image = loadImage( imageName );
        return( new ImageIcon( image ) );

    } // loadIcon


    /**
     * static initialization.
     * <p>
     * Create an instance of this class that can be
     * used as the parameter to the MediaTracker while
     * loading images.
     **/
    static {
        imageLoader = new ImageLoader();
    } // static

} // ImageLoader
```

GrayFilter Class

The GrayFilter class is a utility class used to create grayed out versions of images. This class is an extension of the AWT class RGBImageFilter.

In the JFC, the GrayFilter class is used in components containing icons. If a disabled image is not specified, the component creates an image from the normal image to use when the component is disabled. Calling the static createDisabledImage method contained in this class performs this function.

The following code fragment creates a disabled icon from an image. Notice that the createDisabledImage takes an image and returns an image. As in the previous section, an `ImageIcon` is created from the image and used wherever an icon is required. The `createDisabledImage` method is used internally by Swing components, but can also be used by any class to create grayed out images.

```
Icon disabledIcon = new ImageIcon(
                    GrayFilter.createDisabledImage( myImage ) );
```

Label Components

The JFC contains many components that contain a label. This section presents the simple labeled components. You will learn how to do the following:

- Create labels
- Position the text in labels
- Add images to labels
- Position the text relative to the image

The `JLabel` Class

The `JLabel` class extends `JComponent`. It provides a display area for text, an icon, or both. The `JLabel` class does not respond to input events and cannot obtain the input focus.

The most common use for the `JLabel` class is to display a single line of text. A `JLabel` can be created with a `String` parameter for this purpose as shown in the following:

```
JLabel label = new JLabel( "Text on label" );
```

This label will be left aligned and horizontally centered in its display area. The horizontal alignment can be specified at construction time as shown in the following line of code:

```
JLabel label = new JLabel( "Text on label", SwingConstants.CENTER );
```

This will create a horizontally centered label. Other possible horizontal alignments are `SwingConstants.LEFT`, `SwingConstants.LEADING`, `SwingConstants.RIGHT`, and `SwingConstants.TRAILING`. The horizontal alignment can be set after creation with the `setHorizontalAlignment` method and passing it the desired alignment. The horizontal alignment is a bound property named `horizontalAlignment`. Notice how the `JLabel` class takes advantages of the constants in the `SwingConstants` interface rather than defining the constants in the `JLabel` class itself. This is inconsistent with what you saw in the `TitledBorder` class presented in the previous section. The horizontal alignment can be queried with the `getHorizontalAlignment` method. It is also unfortunate that the property names in `JLabel` are not class constants. Instead, they are hard coded into the source code.

The vertical alignment can be set with `setVerticalAlignment`. Possible alignments are `SwingConstants.TOP`, `SwingConstants.BOTTOM`, and the default, `SwingConstants.CEN-TER`. The vertical alignment can only be set after the label is created. There is not a version of the constructor with a vertical alignment parameter. The vertical alignment is a bound property named `verticalAlignment`. The vertical alignment can be queried using the `getVerticalAlignment` method.

The application presented in Listing 5.6 creates a panel containing `JLabel` instances with the possible combinations for vertical and horizontal text positions. The application simply creates the `JLabel` instances and sets the appropriate properties. The labels are arranged in a 4×4 grid where the first column and top rows are labels for the position of the text. An AWT `GridLayout` layout manager is used for creating the grid. This ensures that each cell is the same size. A strut is used for the 0,0 position in the grid that does not contain a label. The resulting frame is presented in Figure 5.12. As can be seen from the figure, the `JLabel` is very flexible with the text alignment.

FIGURE 5.12

The `LabelTest` *application results.*

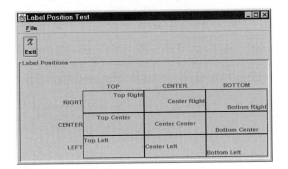

LISTING 5.6 `LabelTest` APPLICATION

```
package com.foley.test;

import java.awt.*;

import javax.swing.*;
import javax.swing.border.*;

import com.foley.utility.ApplicationFrame;


/**
 * An application that displays possible label placement
 * in a frame.
 *
```

continues

LISTING 5.6.   CONTINUED

```java
 * @author Mike Foley
 **/
public class LabelTest extends Object {

    /**
     * Create a panel containing possible label positions.
     *
     * @return A panel containing many titled borders.
     **/
    protected static JPanel createLabelPanel() {

        //
        // Labels
        //
        int strutHeight = 10;
        JPanel labelPanel = new JPanel();
        labelPanel.setLayout( new GridLayout( 4, 4 ) );

        labelPanel.add( Box.createVerticalStrut( strutHeight ) );
        JLabel title = new JLabel( "TOP", SwingConstants.CENTER );
        title.setVerticalAlignment( SwingConstants.BOTTOM );
        labelPanel.add( title );
        title = new JLabel( "CENTER", SwingConstants.CENTER );
        title.setVerticalAlignment( SwingConstants.BOTTOM );
        labelPanel.add( title );
        title = new JLabel( "BOTTOM", SwingConstants.CENTER );
        title.setVerticalAlignment( SwingConstants.BOTTOM );
        labelPanel.add( title );

        title = new JLabel( "RIGHT", SwingConstants.RIGHT );
        labelPanel.add( title );
        title = new JLabel( "Top Right", SwingConstants.RIGHT );
        title.setVerticalAlignment( SwingConstants.TOP );
        title.setBorder( BorderFactory.createLineBorder( Color.black ) );
        labelPanel.add( title );
        title = new JLabel( "Center Right", SwingConstants.RIGHT );
        title.setVerticalAlignment( SwingConstants.CENTER );
        title.setBorder( BorderFactory.createLineBorder( Color.black ) );
        labelPanel.add( title );
        title = new JLabel( "Bottom Right", SwingConstants.RIGHT );
        title.setVerticalAlignment( SwingConstants.BOTTOM );
        labelPanel.add( title );
        title.setBorder( BorderFactory.createLineBorder( Color.black ) );


        title = new JLabel( "CENTER", SwingConstants.RIGHT );
        labelPanel.add( title );
        title = new JLabel( "Top Center", SwingConstants.CENTER );
        title.setVerticalAlignment( SwingConstants.TOP );
```

```java
title.setBorder( BorderFactory.createLineBorder( Color.black ) );
labelPanel.add( title );
title = new JLabel( "Center Center", SwingConstants.CENTER );
title.setVerticalAlignment( SwingConstants.CENTER );
title.setBorder( BorderFactory.createLineBorder( Color.black ) );
labelPanel.add( title );
title = new JLabel( "Bottom Center", SwingConstants.CENTER );
title.setVerticalAlignment( SwingConstants.BOTTOM );
title.setBorder( BorderFactory.createLineBorder( Color.black ) );
labelPanel.add( title );


title = new JLabel( "LEFT", SwingConstants.RIGHT );
labelPanel.add( title );
title = new JLabel( "Top Left", SwingConstants.LEFT );
title.setVerticalAlignment( SwingConstants.TOP );
title.setBorder( BorderFactory.createLineBorder( Color.black ) );
labelPanel.add( title );
title = new JLabel( "Center Left", SwingConstants.LEFT );
title.setVerticalAlignment( SwingConstants.CENTER );
title.setBorder( BorderFactory.createLineBorder( Color.black ) );
labelPanel.add( title );
title = new JLabel( "Bottom Left", SwingConstants.LEFT );
title.setVerticalAlignment( SwingConstants.BOTTOM );
title.setBorder( BorderFactory.createLineBorder( Color.black ) );
labelPanel.add( title );

return( labelPanel );

}


/**
 * Application entry point.
 * Create the frame, and display it.
 *
 * @param args Command line parameter. Not used.
 **/
public static void main( String args[] ) {

    JFrame frame = new ApplicationFrame( "Label Position Test" );

    JPanel labels = createLabelPanel();

    //
    // Add the border panels to the content.
    //
    labels.setBorder( BorderFactory.createTitledBorder(
                BorderFactory.createBevelBorder(BevelBorder.LOWERED),
                "Label Positions" ) );
```

continues

5

BASIC
COMPONENTS

LISTING 5.6   CONTINUED

```
        frame.getContentPane().add( labels, BorderLayout.CENTER );

        frame.pack();
        frame.setVisible( true );

    } // main

} // LabelTest
```

The text displayed in the JLabel can be altered after construction using the setText method. The JLabel text is the bound property named text. The text can be queried with the getText method.

The JLabel class is a descendant of the AWT Component class. JLabel inherits methods for setting the foreground and background colors and the font with which to display the label. However, JLabel, as with all the JFC components, inherits from JComponent. As described in the JComponent chapter, these are lightweight components. Thus, the default behavior of JLabel is to not draw its background. The background of its container is used instead. The side effect of this is that setting the background color of a label has no effect. To force the JLabel class to paint with the background color specified, the label must be made opaque. Calling the setOpaque method with a parameter of true does this. The current opaque setting can be queried with the isOpaque method. The opaque setting for the JLabel is a bound property named opaque. The setFont method is overridden to force the label to be repainted after the font changes. This allows setting the font to behave consistently with setting other label properties that repaint the label after their value changes.

Adding an Image

As was mentioned in the introduction to this section, a JLabel can display an icon as well as a string. The icon can be specified in the JLabel constructor or set later using the setIcon method. The icon is the bound property named icon.

The following code demonstrates creating a JLabel with an icon.

```
JLabel iconLabel = new JLabel( myIcon );
```

As with a JLabel containing a string, the icon's alignment can be specified. The default alignment for the icon-only JLabel is to center the icon both horizontally and vertically in its display space. The same alignment methods presented in the previous section for string-only labels apply to icon labels. For example, the following code fragment will create a JLabel containing an icon in the bottom-right portion of the JLabel's display area.

```
JLabel iconLabel = new JLabel( myIcon, SwingConstants.RIGHT );
iconLabel.setVerticalAlignment( SwingConstants.BOTTOM );
```

A single `JLabel` can contain both an icon and a string. Both the icon and string can be specified at construction, as shown in the following code fragment. Either the string or icon can be specified after creation with the `setIcon` or `setText` method, respectively.

```
JLabel label = new JLabel( "Test", myIcon, SwingConstants.RIGHT );
```

This label will use the default string-to-icon placement, which is to place the string to the right of the icon. A default gap of four pixels is placed between the text and the image. However, the positioning property can be altered with the `setHorizontalTextPosition` method. The possible values—`RIGHT`, `CENTER`, `LEFT`, `LEADING`, and `TRAILING`—are defined in the `SwingConstants` interface. This is a bound property name—`horizontalTextPosition`. The current value of this property can be queried with the `getHorizontalTextPosition` method.

Similarly, the vertical position of the text relative to the icon can be specified with the `setVerticalTextPosition` method. Possible values for this property—`TOP`, `CENTER`, and `BOTTOM`—are defined in the `SwingConstants` interface. The vertical text position is a bound property named `verticalTextPosition`. The current value of this property can be queried with the `getVerticalTextPosition` method.

The gap between the icon and string can be specified with the `setIconTextGap` method. This method will set the distance between the icon and the string to the given number of pixels. The distance between the icon and the string is a bound property named `iconTextGap`. As previously mentioned, the default value for this property is four pixels.

The alignment properties, previously described for a label containing text, move the text and icon as a unit. Setting the `horizontalAlignment` and `verticalAlignment` properties allows the text and icon to be positioned in the label.

The application presented in Listing 5.7 creates a panel containing `JLabel` instances with the various text-to-icon placements specified. This application follows the same general structure as the application in the previous section. The difference is that icons are added to each label, and the text-to-icon placement is specified. The resulting display is shown in Figure 5.13. In this example, the horizontal alignment for each label is `CENTER`.

FIGURE 5.13

The
`LabelAndIconTest`
application result.

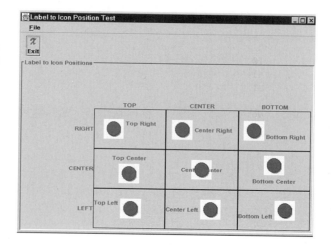

LISTING 5.7   LabelAndIconTest APPLICATION

```
package com.foley.test;

import java.awt.*;

import javax.swing.*;
import javax.swing.border.*;

import com.foley.utility.ApplicationFrame;
import com.foley.utility.ImageLoader;


/**
 * An application that displays possible label placement
 * in its frame.
 *
 * @author Mike Foley
 **/
public class LabelAndIconTest extends Object {

    private static Icon stop;


    /**
     * Create a panel containing possible label positions.
     *
     * @return A panel containing many titled borders.
     **/
    private static JPanel createLabelAndIconPanel() {

        //
```

```
// Labels and icons.
//
int strutHeight = 3;
strutHeight = 10;
JPanel labelAndIcon = new JPanel();
labelAndIcon.setLayout( new GridLayout( 4, 4 ) );

labelAndIcon.add( Box.createVerticalStrut( strutHeight ) );
JLabel title = new JLabel( "TOP", SwingConstants.CENTER );
title.setVerticalAlignment( SwingConstants.BOTTOM );
labelAndIcon.add( title );
title = new JLabel( "CENTER", SwingConstants.CENTER );
title.setVerticalAlignment( SwingConstants.BOTTOM );
labelAndIcon.add( title );
title = new JLabel( "BOTTOM", SwingConstants.CENTER );
title.setVerticalAlignment( SwingConstants.BOTTOM );
labelAndIcon.add( title );

title = new JLabel( "RIGHT", SwingConstants.RIGHT );
labelAndIcon.add( title );
title = new JLabel( "Top Right", stop, SwingConstants.CENTER );
title.setHorizontalTextPosition( SwingConstants.RIGHT );
title.setVerticalTextPosition( SwingConstants.TOP );
title.setBorder( BorderFactory.createLineBorder( Color.black ) );
labelAndIcon.add( title );
title = new JLabel( "Center Right", stop,
                    SwingConstants.CENTER );
title.setHorizontalTextPosition( SwingConstants.RIGHT );
title.setVerticalTextPosition( SwingConstants.CENTER );
title.setBorder( BorderFactory.createLineBorder( Color.black ) );
labelAndIcon.add( title );
title = new JLabel( "Bottom Right", stop,
                    SwingConstants.CENTER );
title.setHorizontalTextPosition( SwingConstants.RIGHT );
title.setVerticalTextPosition( SwingConstants.BOTTOM );
labelAndIcon.add( title );
title.setBorder( BorderFactory.createLineBorder( Color.black ) );


title = new JLabel( "CENTER", SwingConstants.RIGHT );
labelAndIcon.add( title );
title = new JLabel( "Top Center", stop, SwingConstants.CENTER );
title.setHorizontalTextPosition( SwingConstants.CENTER );
title.setVerticalTextPosition( SwingConstants.TOP );
title.setBorder( BorderFactory.createLineBorder( Color.black ) );
labelAndIcon.add( title );
title = new JLabel( "Center Center", stop,
                    SwingConstants.CENTER );
title.setHorizontalTextPosition( SwingConstants.CENTER );
title.setVerticalTextPosition( SwingConstants.CENTER );
```

continues

LISTING 5.7   CONTINUED

```java
            title.setBorder( BorderFactory.createLineBorder( Color.black ) );
            labelAndIcon.add( title );
            title = new JLabel( "Bottom Center", stop,
                                SwingConstants.CENTER );
            title.setHorizontalTextPosition( SwingConstants.CENTER );
            title.setVerticalTextPosition( SwingConstants.BOTTOM );
            title.setBorder( BorderFactory.createLineBorder( Color.black ) );
            labelAndIcon.add( title );


            title = new JLabel( "LEFT", SwingConstants.RIGHT );
            labelAndIcon.add( title );
            title = new JLabel( "Top Left", stop, SwingConstants.LEFT );
            title.setHorizontalTextPosition( SwingConstants.LEFT );
            title.setVerticalTextPosition( SwingConstants.TOP );
            title.setBorder( BorderFactory.createLineBorder( Color.black ) );
            labelAndIcon.add( title );
            title = new JLabel( "Center Left", stop, SwingConstants.LEFT );
            title.setHorizontalTextPosition( SwingConstants.LEFT );
            title.setVerticalTextPosition( SwingConstants.CENTER );
            title.setBorder( BorderFactory.createLineBorder( Color.black ) );
            labelAndIcon.add( title );
            title = new JLabel( "Bottom Left", stop, SwingConstants.LEFT );
            title.setHorizontalTextPosition( SwingConstants.LEFT );
            title.setVerticalTextPosition( SwingConstants.BOTTOM );
            title.setBorder( BorderFactory.createLineBorder( Color.black ) );
            labelAndIcon.add( title );

            return( labelAndIcon );

    }


    /**
     * Application entry point.
     * Create the frame, label panel,
     * and display them.
     *
     * @param args Command line parameter. Not used.
     **/
    public static void main( String args[] ) {

        try {
            //
            // Load the images used.
            //
            stop = ImageLoader.loadIcon( "stop.gif" );
        } catch( InterruptedException ie ) {
            System.err.println( "Error loading images" );
```

```
        System.exit( -1 );
    }

    JFrame frame = new ApplicationFrame(
                    "Label to Icon Position Test" );

    JPanel labels = createLabelAndIconPanel();

    //
    // Add the border panels to the content.
    //
    labels.setBorder( BorderFactory.createTitledBorder(
                    BorderFactory.createBevelBorder(
                                BevelBorder.LOWERED ),
                "Label to Icon Positions" ) );
    frame.getContentPane().add( labels, BorderLayout.CENTER );

    frame.pack();
    frame.setVisible( true );

  } // main

} // LabelAndIconTest
```

A separate icon can be specified for use when the label is disabled. Because an instance of the JLabel class cannot acquire input focus, the exact definition of a disabled label is somewhat vague. However, the JLabel class is a descendant from the AWT Component class, so it can be enabled and disabled with the setEnabled method. If an icon has been specified by using the setDisabledIcon method, this icon will be drawn when the label is disabled. If a disabled icon has not been specified and an icon has been specified, a disabled icon will be created with the GrayFilter class previously described.

When creating user interfaces, a label is often used in conjunction with another component. For example, a label is used to describe the data to be entered into a text field in a form display. The JLabel class contains two methods that work in tandem and specify a mnemonic and an associated component for the label. When the mnemonic is activated, the input focus is requested for the associated component. The setDisplayedMnemonic method is used to set the mnemonic for the label. A character or keycode can be passed to this method. The setLabelFor method specifies the component that is to receive focus when the mnemonic is activated. Both properties must be set with non-null values for this behavior to be active. These are both bound properties, named labelFor and displayedMnemonic, respectively. The current value for the properties can be queried with the getLabelFor and getDisplayedMnemonic methods. In the setLabelFor method, if the associated component is a descendant of the JComponent class, the label sets itself as the labeledBy client property of the component. This allows the component to check if a label has been set for it.

The previous paragraphs presented the bound properties contained in the `JLabel` class. Table 5.1 summarizes these properties. The Swing visual components are JavaBean-compliant, and the property setter and getter methods conform to the Bean property naming convention. There are not constants defined for the property names at the current time. The property names are hard coded in the JFC source code. If you find that a listener is not receiving a property notification when you think it should, make sure you do not have a typo in the property name. The compiler could perform this type of check for you if the names were defined as constants. This is an unfortunate situation that hopefully will be rectified in the future. As you will see in the next chapter, these properties are also available for the buttons contained in the JFC.

TABLE 5.1 `JLabel` Class Bound Properties

Property Name	*Setter Method*	*Getter Method*
Text	setText	getText
Icon	setIcon	getIcon
DisabledIcon	setDisabledIcon	getDisabledIcon
DisplayedMnemonic	setDisplayedMnemonic	getDisplayedMnemonic
Opaque	setOpaque	
IconTextGap	setIconTextGap	getIconTextGap
VerticalAlignment	setVerticalAlignment	getVerticalAlignment
HorizontalAlignment	setHorizontalAlignment	getHorizontalAlignment
HorizontalTextPosition	setHorizontalTextPosition	getHorizontalTextPosition
VerticalTextPosition	setVerticalTextPosition	getVerticalTextPosition
LabelFor	setLabelFor	getLabelFor

Summary

This chapter presented the basic components contained in the JFC. Borders provide a means of grouping other components and adding interesting visuals. The JFC contains the `BorderFactory` class that is used to create a border. The `Icon` interface and `ImageIcon` class were presented for bitmap graphic manipulation. Labels are used in many user interface situations. The `JLabel` class addressed one of the limitations of the AWT, an easy component with which to display images. Instances of the `JLabel` class can contain text and an icon. The methods for placing the text and icon were presented. A label can have a mnemonic and a component associated with it. When the mnemonic is activated, the label will request the input focus for the associated component.

The Button
Hierarchy

CHAPTER 6

The JFC provides many buttons that can be used in your graphical user interfaces. These buttons include a push button, check box, toggle button, and radio button. The various buttons are the first you have encountered thus far that take advantage of the Model View Controller architecture on which the JFC is built. In this chapter, you will learn:

- The button model
- The button hierarchy
- How to create push buttons
- Use an `Action`-aware button
- How to create check boxes
- How to create toggle buttons
- How to create radio buttons

The `ButtonModel` Interface

The `ButtonModel` interface defines the methods that must be implemented by a class that is to behave as a model for a button. This one interface is used for every button defined in the JFC. This allows code written for one type of button to work with any other, provided all interactions are done through the `ButtonModel` interface.

The `ButtonModel` interface is presented in Listing 6.1. The first thing you may notice is that the interface is quite long, containing over twenty methods. There are three types of listeners that can be added and five different Boolean states that can be set and queried. All this for a single button!

The `ButtonModel` interface inherits from the AWT `ItemSelectable` interface. The `ItemSelectable` interface is also shown in the listing. The first interface provides for an `ItemListener` and a method to query the selected objects.

LISTING 6.1   ButtonModel INTERFACE

```
public interface ItemSelectable
{
        // Methods 3
    public abstract void addItemListener(ItemListener);
    public abstract Object[] getSelectedObjects();
    public abstract void removeItemListener(ItemListener);
}


public interface ButtonModel extends ItemSelectable {

    /**
```

```
 * Indicates partial commitment towards pressing the
 * button.
 *
 * @return true if the button is armed, and ready to be pressed
 * @see #setArmed
 */
boolean isArmed();

/**
 * Indicates if the button has been selected. Only needed for
 * certain types of buttons - such as RadioButton or Checkbox.
 *
 * @return true if the button is selected
 */
boolean isSelected();

/**
 * Indicates if the button can be selected or pressed by
 * an input device (such as a mouse pointer). (Checkbox-buttons
 * are selected, regular buttons are "pressed".)
 *
 * @return true if the button is enabled, and therefore
 *          selectable (or pressable)
 */
boolean isEnabled();

/**
 * Indicates if button has been pressed.
 *
 * @return true if the button has been pressed
 */
boolean isPressed();

/**
 * Indicates that the mouse is over the button.
 *
 * @return true if the mouse is over the button
 */
boolean isRollover();

/**
 * Marks the button as "armed". If the mouse button is
 * released while it is over this item, the button's action event
 * fires. If the mouse button is released elsewhere, the
 * event does not fire and the button is disarmed.
 *
 * @param b true to arm the button so it can be selected
 */
public void setArmed(boolean b);
```

continues

LISTING 6.1 CONTINUED

```java
/**
 * Selects or deselects the button.
 *
 * @param b true selects the button,
 *          false deselects the button.
 */
public void setSelected(boolean b);

/**
 * Enables or disables the button.
 *
 * @param b true to enable the button
 * @see #isEnabled
 */
public void setEnabled(boolean b);

/**
 * Sets the button to pressed or unpressed.
 *
 * @param b true to set the button to "pressed"
 * @see #isPressed
 */
public void setPressed(boolean b);

/**
 * Sets or clears the button's rollover state
 *
 * @param b true to turn on rollover
 * @see #isRollover
 */
public void setRollover(boolean b);

/**
 * Sets the keyboard mnemonic (shortcut key or
 * accelerator key) for this button.
 *
 * @param key an int specifying the accelerator key
 */
public void setMnemonic(int key);

/**
 * Gets the keyboard mnemonic for this model
 *
 * @return an int specifying the accelerator key
 * @see #setMnemonic
 */
public int  getMnemonic();

/**
```

```
 * Sets the actionCommand string that gets sent as part of the
 * event when the button is pressed.
 *
 * @param s the String that identifies the generated event
 */
public void setActionCommand(String s);

/**
 * Returns the action command for this button.
 *
 * @return the String that identifies the generated event
 * @see #setActionCommand
 */
public String getActionCommand();

/**
 * Identifies the group this button belongs to —
 * needed for radio buttons, which are mutually
 * exclusive within their group.
 *
 * @param group the ButtonGroup this button belongs to
 */
public void setGroup(ButtonGroup group);

/**
 * Adds an ActionListener to the button.
 *
 * @param l the listener to add
 */
void addActionListener(ActionListener l);

/**
 * Removes an ActionListener from the button.
 *
 * @param l the listener to remove
 */
void removeActionListener(ActionListener l);

/**
 * Adds an ItemListener to the button.
 *
 * @param l the listener to add
 */
void addItemListener(ItemListener l);

/**
 * Removes an ItemListener from the button.
 *
 * @param l the listener to remove
```

continues

LISTING 6.1   CONTINUED

```
  */
void removeItemListener(ItemListener l);

/**
 * Adds a ChangeListener to the button.
 *
 * @param l the listener to add
 */
void addChangeListener(ChangeListener l);

/**
 * Removes a ChangeListener from the button.
 *
 * @param l the listener to remove
 */
void removeChangeListener(ChangeListener l);


}
```

The JFC class `DefaultButtonModel` implements the `ButtonModel` interface and by default it, or a descendant, is used as the model for JFC buttons. The event flow between the `DefaultButtonModel` and possible listeners is shown in Figure 6.1. In the figure, the top label on each arc represents the listener method called to deliver the event whose name appears below the method name.

FIGURE 6.1

`ButtonModel` *event flow.*

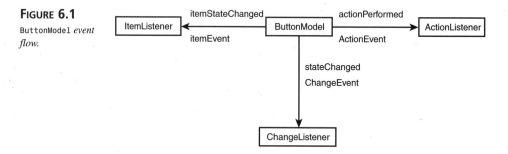

A `ChangeEvent` is sent to listeners whenever a state variable changes. The state variables are the five `boolean` properties and the mnemonic defined in the model interface. The `ChangeEvent` class definition is shown next. As can be seen, the class doesn't add anything to the AWT `EventObject` that it inherits. The only real information that can be obtained from the event is the event's source. It is up to the listener to then query the source to determine what the change was and what action to take. The methods defined in the `ButtonModel` interface can be used to determine the button's state.

```
public class  ChangeEvent
     extends java.util.EventObject
{
          // Constructors 1
     public ChangeEvent(Object);
}
```

An `ItemEvent` is sent when the selected status of the button changes. The following is the class definition of `ItemEvent`. This event, unlike the `ChangeEvent`, carries the item information in the event itself. The `getStateChange` method can be called on the event to see if the item has changed to `SELECTED` or `DESELECTED`. These constants are also defined in the `ItemEvent` class.

```
public class  ItemEvent
     extends java.awt.AWTEvent
{
          // Fields 8
     public static final int DESELECTED;
     public static final int ITEM_FIRST;
     public static final int ITEM_LAST;
     public static final int ITEM_STATE_CHANGED;
     public static final int SELECTED;
     Object item;
     private static final long serialVersionUID;
     int stateChange;

          // Constructors 1
     public ItemEvent(ItemSelectable, int, Object, int);

          // Methods 4
     public Object getItem();
     public ItemSelectable getItemSelectable();
     public int getStateChange();
     public String paramString();
}
```

The final event that a class implementing the `ButtonModel` interface must provide methods for is the `ActionEvent`. An `ActionEvent` is sent when the button is clicked. Programmatically, this looks like the button becoming not pressed while being armed. This implies that the `ActionEvent` is sent from the `setPressed` method in the `DefaultButtonModel` class. The `ActionEvent` definition is shown next. Many clients of a button, or a `ButtonModel`, are only concerned with this one event. An `ActionEvent` contains an `ActionCommand` `String`. Listeners of multiple `ButtonModel` instances often use the `ActionCommand` `String` to determine which button was pressed. By default the `ActionCommand` will be the text shown on the button. However, this can be set with the `setActionCommand` method and queried with the `getActionCommand` method.

```
public class  ActionEvent
     extends java.awt.AWTEvent
{
        // Fields 10
    public static final int ACTION_FIRST;
    public static final int ACTION_LAST;
    public static final int ACTION_PERFORMED;
    public static final int ALT_MASK;
    public static final int CTRL_MASK;
    public static final int META_MASK;
    public static final int SHIFT_MASK;
    String actionCommand;
    int modifiers;
    private static final long serialVersionUID;

        // Constructors 2
    public ActionEvent(Object, int, String);
    public ActionEvent(Object, int, String, int);

        // Methods 3
    public String getActionCommand();
    public int getModifiers();
    public String paramString();
}
```

Examples showing the usage of the listeners for the `ButtonModel` and the associated events will be presented in the next sections.

JFC Button Hierarchy

The JFC doesn't contain a single button, it contains an entire hierarchy of buttons. Each button provides a different look and functionality, but all use the `ButtonModel` interface. The button hierarchy is presented in Figure 6.2. The following sections present the `JButton` and `JToggleButton` and their descendents, but the `JMenuItem` and its descendants will not be presented here. Instead, they are presented in Chapter 9, "Menus and Toolbars."

FIGURE 6.2

The JFC button hierarchy.

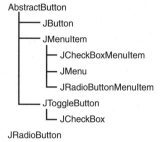

```
AbstractButton
 ├── JButton
 ├── JMenuItem
 │    ├── JCheckBoxMenuItem
 │    ├── JMenu
 │    └── JRadioButtonMenuItem
 └── JToggleButton
      └── JCheckBox
JRadioButton
```

The top of the button hierarchy is the AbstractButton class. Thus the behavior implemented in this class if available to all JFC buttons. The AbstractButton class does not inherit from the JLabel class; however, it defines identical properties for text and icon alignment as well as text-to-icon relative positioning. These are the horizontalAlignment, verticalAlignment, horizontalTextPosition, and verticalTextPosition properties. However, the horizontalTextPosition is a bound property for buttons, even though it was omitted from labels. See Chapter 5, "Basic Components," for a complete description of these properties. This is a situation where multiple inheritance, or delegation, in Java could be argued for. At the very minimum, a properties interface, similar to the SwingConstants interface, could be defined containing the property names for bound properties that convey the same meaning in multiple classes. As it stands today, constants for property names are defined in the AbstractButton class, but hard-coded in the JLabel class.

The AbstractButton class provides for a disabled icon as described in the previous chapter for the JLabel class. However, the AbstractButton class contains many more icons. The other icons allow you to specify the icon when the button is selected, pressed, rolled over, rolled over and selected, or disabled and selected. A total of seven icons can be specified for a single button. The methods to set the various icons and the associated bound property names are presented in Table 6.1, which lists all the bound properties introduced in the AbstractButton class. The rollover icons are used when the mouse is rolling over the button. By default, the rollover icons are not enabled. To enable rollover behavior, the setRolloverEnabled method must be called with a parameter of true. Calling the method with a parameter of false will disable rollover behavior. The rollover behavior is a bound property named rolloverEnabled.

TABLE 6.1 AbstractButton ICON METHODS AND PROPERTY NAMES

Property Name	Setter Method	Getter Method
icon	setIcon	getIcon
disabledIcon	setDisabledIcon	getDisabledIcon
disabledSelected Icon	setDisabledSelected Icon	getDisabled SelectedIcon
pressedIcon	setPressedIcon	getPressedIcon
rolloverIcon	setRolloverIcon	getRolloverIcon
rolloverSelected Icon	setRolloverSelected Icon	getRollover SelectedIcon
selectedIcon	setSelectedIcon	getSelectedIcon

continues

TABLE 6.1 CONTINUED

Property Name	Setter Method	Getter Method
text	setText	getText
margin	setMargin	getMargin
horizontalAlignment	setHorizontal Alignment	getHorizontal Alignment
verticalAlignment Alignment	setVertical Alignment	getVertical
horizontalText Position	setHorizontalText Position	getHorizontal TextPosition
verticalText Position	setVerticalText Position	getVerticalText Position
borderPainted	setBorderPainted	isBorderPainted
focusPainted	setFocusPainted	isFocusPainted
rolloverEnabled	setRollover Enabled	isRollover Enabled
model	setModel	getModel

The model that contains the button's state can be set and queried with the setModel and getModel methods. As was explained in the previous section, calling the setActionCommand defined in the ButtonModel interface specifies the Action command sent as part of the ActionEvent when the button is pressed. The AbstractButton class provides a convenience function, setActionCommand, that gets the current model for the button and calls the model's setActionCommand method. This allows the Action command to be set from the handle to the button. Similarly, the AbstractButton class wraps the setMnemonic method from the ButtonModel interface. The mnemonic provides a keyboard interface for pressing the button. The only Boolean properties from the model that are wrapped by the AbstractButton class are the selected and enabled properties. These are the setSelected and setEnabled methods. The AbstractButton class also wraps the get versions of each of these methods. The wrapper methods allow buttons to be used easily without interacting with the ButtonModel itself.

By default, a button that has the keyboard focus will paint itself with a box around the button's content but inside the border. This gives the user visual feedback that the button has the focus. Calling the setFocusPainted method and passing a parameter of false will stop this behavior. Calling the method with a parameter of true enables the painting of the focus visual feedback on the button. The focusPainted property is a bound property named focusPainted. The state of this property can be queried with the isFocusPainted method. The focus painting behavior can also be altered by the current look-and-feel being used. Similarly, painting the border can be controlled with the setBorderPainted method. When false is passed to this method, a border is not painted around the button. By default, the value of this property is true, allowing the border to be painted.

The AbstractButton class provides the doClick method to allow the button to be pressed programmatically. The onscreen button will actually draw itself pressed and then released, as if a user pressed the button with the mouse. The associated events will also get fired. For example, an ActionEvent will be sent when the doClick method is called.

Simple Buttons: The JButton Class

The most common button class for normal use is the JButton class. The class provides the user interface component for the familiar push button. The JButton class extends the AbstractButton class, thus the functionality discussed in the previous section is available to instances of the JButton class.

The previous section contained the theory of button events and properties contained in the JFC. The JButton is the first concrete button class presented, so look at some examples. Creating a button is a simple matter. The following code fragment creates a button with the text OK. The simple button is shown in Figure 6.3 with the Windows look-and-feel. The dashed line around the button signifies that the button has the keyboard focus. The dashed line is painted because the focusPainted property is set to true by default for this look-and-feel.

```
JButton ok = new JButton( "OK" );
```

FIGURE 6.3

A simple OK
JButton.

Whether or not your current OK button does anything can be thought about like the proverbial tree falling in the woods. If there is no one there to hear it fall, does it make any noise? The current button doesn't have any external listeners, so it doesn't fire any events to your code. However, it is still processing input events and waiting for your listener, so it can fire events. First, add a simple ChangeListener to print the state changes as the button undergoes its normal operation. This code example is shown in Listing 6.2.

LISTING 6.2   OK BUTTON WITH SIMPLE ChangeListener

```java
package com.foley.test;

import java.awt.*;

import javax.swing.*;
import javax.swing.event.*;

import com.foley.utility.ApplicationFrame;


/**
 * An application that prints state changes of a JButton.
 *
 * @author Mike Foley
 **/
public class ButtonEventTest extends Object {

    /**
     * Create a panel containing a button and event listener.
     * The event listener simply dumps the button's state to
     * the console.
     *
     * @return A panel containing a button.
     **/
    static private JPanel createButtonPanel() {

        JPanel buttonPanel = new JPanel();
        JButton ok = new JButton( "OK" );
        buttonPanel.add( ok );

        ButtonModel model = ok.getModel();
        System.out.println( "armed=" + model.isArmed() + " " +
                            "enabled=" + model.isEnabled() + " " +
                            "pressed=" + model.isPressed() + " " +
                            "rollover=" + model.isRollover() + " " +
                            "selected=" + model.isSelected() );
        ok.addChangeListener( new ChangeListener() {
            public void stateChanged( ChangeEvent e ) {
                JButton button = ( JButton )e.getSource();
                ButtonModel b = button.getModel();
                System.out.println( "armed=" + b.isArmed() + " " +
                            "enabled=" + b.isEnabled() + " " +
                            "pressed=" + b.isPressed() + " " +
                            "rollover=" + b.isRollover() + " " +
                            "selected=" + b.isSelected() );
            }
        } );

        return( buttonPanel );
```

```
    }

    /**
     * Application entry point.
     * Create the frame, and display it.
     *
     * @param args Command line parameter. Not used.
     **/
    public static void main( String args[] ) {

        JFrame frame = new ApplicationFrame( "Button Event Test" );

        JPanel buttons = createButtonPanel();

        frame.getContentPane().add( buttons, BorderLayout.CENTER );
        frame.pack();
        frame.setVisible( true );

    } // main

} // ButtonEventTest
```

In this example, an anonymous inner class is used as a change listener. Since the ChangeEvent does not deliver the state of its source with the event, the button's model is obtained from the JButton instance that is the source of the event. You can safely cast the Object returned from the getSource method of the ChangeEvent, because you know the listener is only registered to one object, the OK JButton you created. The output from the change listener when the button is pressed and released is shown in Figure 6.4 (extra lines have been inserted into the output to group related events). The first line is printed immediately after the button has been created. This is the default state of the button. The next two ChangeEvents come after the button is pressed. The first event is from the button being armed, or ready to fire. The second event is from the button becoming pressed. The final event is when the button is released.

FIGURE 6.4

ButtonEventTest *application output.*

```
// Default state of button model.
armed=false enabled=true pressed=false rollover=false
selected=false
// Button armed and pressed. Resulting from mouse down over
button.
armed=true enabled=true pressed=false rollover=false
selected=false
armed=true enabled=true pressed=true rollover=false
selected=false
// Button pressed. Resulting from mouse up over button.
armed=true enabled=true pressed=false rollover=false
selected=false
```

In the results presented here, the `rollover` property is always `false`. This is due to the fact that rollover detection is disabled by default. Adding the following line of code in the `createButtonPanel` method to the current example, after the button has been created, will enable rollover detection.

```
ok.setRolloverEnabled( true );
```

The result of the same experiment with rollover detection enabled is presented in Figure 6.5. The default state of the button hasn't changed. The second and third lines are from events generated when the mouse is passed over the button. The first event is when the mouse enters the button's window, and the second is when it exits. These events make it clear why the property is named `rollover`. The final five events are the sequence when the button is pressed and released, and when the mouse exits the button's window. It is seen that the middle three events are the same as the previous example, except the `rollover` property is `true`. The first and last events are from the mouse entering and exiting the button's window.

FIGURE 6.5

JButton
ChangeEvent*s with*
rollover detection
enabled.

```
// Default state of button model.
armed=false enabled=true pressed=false rollover=false
selected=false

// Mouse rolls over button, no mouse buttons pressed.
armed=false enabled=true pressed=false rollover=true
        selected=falsearmed=false enabled=true
        pressed=false rollover=false selected=false

// Mouse back over button.
armed=false enabled=true pressed=false rollover=true
selected=false

// Button armed and pressed. Resulting from mouse down over
button.
armed=true enabled=true pressed=false rollover=true
selected=false
armed=true enabled=true pressed=true rollover=true
selected=false

// Button pressed. Resulting from mouse up over button.
armed=true enabled=true pressed=false rollover=true
selected=false

// Mouse not over button any longer.
armed=true enabled=true pressed=false rollover=false
selected=false
```

The ChangeListener in this example is illustrative for demonstrating the normal state transitions of the DefaultButtonModel. However, an ActionListener is used more frequently in practice. This listener gets notified whenever the button gets clicked. The following code is used to add an ActionListener to a button. The ActionListener can be added to the createButtonPanel method from the previous example. The ChangeListener can be removed or left in place. The button can have any number and combination of listeners at any given time. The ActionListener simply prints the ActionEvent it receives. The result from clicking the button with this ActionListener is shown in Figure 6.6. The output assumes that the ChangeListener was removed from the button. It shows that the event was of the type ACTION_PERFORMED, the action command was OK, and the JButton was the source of this ActionEvent.

```
JButton ok = new JButton( "OK" );
ok.addActionListener( new ActionListener() {
    public void actionPerformed( ActionEvent e ) {
        System.out.println( "ActionEvent " + e );
    }
} );
```

FIGURE 6.6

Output from the ActionListener.

```
ActionEvent
java.awt.event.ActionEvent[ACTION_PERFORMED,cmd=OK] on
javax.swing.JButton[,356,5,49x25,
layout=javax.swing.OverlayLayout]
```

In this simple example, it is obvious from which button the event came. In many situations, this isn't so clear. For example, the same ActionListener can be listening for events from many action event sources. In this situation, the action command can be used to determine which operation to perform in the listener. Using the action command in the listener also allows multiple action sources to generate the same behavior. As demonstrated in the previous example, the default action command for a button is the text of the button. For all but the most trivial applications, if the action command is going to be used, it should be explicitly set. The primary reason for this is that the action command should not be tied to the text on the button.

When an application is internationalized, the text that appears on the button will be read from a resource bundle. Thus, the text may be different depending on where in the world the application is executed. If the application explicitly sets the action command, it doesn't matter what text appears on the button. Also, if an icon is placed on the button without any text, the action command is undefined. For these reasons, it is preferable to explicitly set the action command if it is going to be used in your application.

```
ResourceBundle bundle = ResourceBundle.getBundle( "LabelResources",
                                    Locale.getDefault() );
```

```
JButton ok = new JButton( bundle.getString( "okButton" ) );
ok.setActionCommand( "ok" );
```

When this code fragment was run in a United States locale, the button shown in Figure 6.3 would be displayed. If the code were run in a German locale, the button shown in Figure 6.7 would be displayed. In the figure, the frame's strings have not been internationalized. The action command reported in an `ActionEvent` is the same in both examples, that being the string OK.

FIGURE 6.7

The OK button in a German locale.

Using Actions with Buttons

As was seen in Chapter 4, "JFC Programming Techniques," the `Action` interface extends the `ActionListener` interface. Thus any class that implements the `Action` interface is an `ActionListener`. This allows an `Action` to be added directly to a button and invoked when the button is pressed. This is demonstrated in the following code fragment:

```
JButton button = new JButton( "OK" );
Action exitAction = new ExitAction();
button.addActionListener( exitAction );
```

However, using code like this to tie an `Action` to a button doesn't take full advantage of `Action`. For example, when an `Action` is disabled, the button should become disabled as well. For this type of integration, the button needs to be `Action`-aware. As you will see in Chapter 9, Swing menus and toolbars are `Action`-aware. Unfortunately, the `JButton` class is not.

To provide an `Action`-aware button, the `JButton` class can be extended to provide the required functionality. The `AButton` class shown in Listing 6.3 is such a class. An instance of the `AButton` class can be used as a substitute for a `JButton` instance anywhere a button is required.

LISTING 6.3   USING THE `AButton` CLASS TO MAKE AN `Action`-AWARE BUTTON

```
package com.foley.utility;

import java.beans.*;

import javax.swing.*;
```

```
/**
 * The AButton class is an Action-aware button.
 * The button will configure itself to the Action set using
 * the setAction method.
 *
 * The class may only be configured for one Action at
 * a time. If a second Action is set using the setAction
 * method, the first Action will be removed. However, other
 * ActionListeners may be added as normal, using the
 * addActionListener method.
 *
 * @author Mike Foley
 **/
public class AButton extends JButton
    implements PropertyChangeListener {

    /**
     * The Action this button is configured for.
     **/
    private Action action;

    /**
     * Bound property names.
     **/
    public static final String ACTION_PROPERTY = "action";


    /**
     * AButton, default constructor.
     * Creates a button with no set text or icon.
     **/
    public AButton() {
        super();
    }

    /**
     * AButton, constructor
     * Creates a button from the given Action.
     *
     * @see setAction
     * @param action The Action to configure this button to.
     **/
    public AButton( Action action ) {
        super();
        setAction( action );
    }


    /**
     * Configure the button for the given Action.
```

continues

LISTING 6.3 CONTINUED

```
 * If the button was already configured for
 * an Action, remove that Action from being
 * a listener to this button.
 * The Action is a bound property.
 *
 * @param action The Action to configure this button to.
 **/
public void setAction( Action action ) {

    Action oldAction = this.action;
    if( oldAction != null ) {
        //
        // Remove the bind between the button and the
        // old action.
        //
        oldAction.removePropertyChangeListener( this );
        removeActionListener( oldAction );
    }

    this.action = action;

    if( action != null ) {

        //
        // Update our appearance to that of the new action.
        //
        setText( ( String )action.getValue( Action.NAME ) );
        setIcon( ( Icon )action.getValue( Action.SMALL_ICON ) );

        setEnabled( action.isEnabled() );

        //
        // Bind ourself to the new Action.
        //
        action.addPropertyChangeListener( this );
        addActionListener( action );

        //
        // Set the text below the Icon.
        //
        setHorizontalTextPosition( JButton.CENTER );
        setVerticalTextPosition( JButton.BOTTOM );

    } else {

        //
        // null Action, set the button's view to 'empty'
        setText( "" );
        setIcon( null );
```

```
        } // else

        //
        // The Action is a bound property.
        //
        firePropertyChange( ACTION_PROPERTY, oldAction, this.action );

    } // setAction


    /**
     * propertyChange, from PropertyChangeListener.
     * Only handle changes from the Action we are configured for.
     *
     * @param event The property change event causing this method call.
     **/
    public void propertyChange( PropertyChangeEvent event ) {
        if( event.getSource() == action ) {

            //
            // Get the name of the changed property, and
            // update ourself accordinly.
            //
            String propertyName = event.getPropertyName();

            if( propertyName.equals( Action.NAME ) ) {
                setText( ( String )event.getNewValue() );
            } else if( propertyName.equals(Action.SMALL_ICON)) {
                setIcon( ( Icon )event.getNewValue() );
                invalidate();
            } else if( propertyName.equals( "enabled" ) ) {
                Boolean enabled = ( Boolean )event.getNewValue();
                setEnabled( enabled.booleanValue() );
            }

            //
            // Update our display.
            //
            repaint();
        }

    } // propertyChange

} // Abutton
```

The ABUTTON class provides a default constructor, as well as a constructor that takes an Action instance. The second constructor passes the given Action instance to the setAction method. This is where the work is done. If the button had been previously configured for a different Action instance, that tie is broken. The button is removed as a

`PropertyChangeListener` for the `Action`, and the `Action` is removed as an `ActionListener` from the button. Then, if the new `Action` is non-null, the button is configured from the new `Action`. The name and icon are retrieved from the new `Action` and set on the button. The default text placement is below the icon on the button. However, this can be changed by using the icon and text placement methods contained in the `JButton` class. The button's enabled state is set to that of `Action`. Finally, the button and action are bound together by adding the `AButton` as a `PropertyChangeListener` to `Action`, and the `Action` as an `ActionListener` to the button. If the new `Action` is null, the button is cleared. Its text and icon are set to empty. The button's `Action` is a bound property of the `AButton` class, so a `PropertyChangeEvent` is fired at the bottom of the `setAction` method.

The other non-constructor method in the `AButton` class is the `propertyChange` method. This method is from the `PropertyChangeListener` interface and must be implemented for the `AButton` class to listen to changes in its bound `Action`. When a `PropertyChangeEvent` is received, the source is checked. The `AButton` class is only interested to changes in its bound `Action`. If the source is the bound `Action`, the changed property is retrieved and the button is updated. After the button has been updated, it is painted to update the display.

A possible limitation to the `AButton` class is that it only manages one `Action` at a time. This is due to the fact that the `JButton` class is designed to display one string and icon at a time. This makes it natural to configure the button for a single `Action`. However, the `AButton` class can still invoke multiple `Actions`. The one `Action` for which the `AButton` is configured is specified with the `setAction` command, or in the constructor. The other `Actions` that are to be invoked when the button is pressed may be added as `ActionListeners` to the button by using the `addActionListener` method.

A simple application to test the `AButton` class is shown in Listing 6.4. It adds an instance of the `AButton` class that is bound to an `ExitAction` to the center of a frame. Pressing the button will exit the application. The resulting frame is shown in Figure 6.8.

LISTING 6.4   APPLICATION TO TEST THE `AButton` CLASS

```
package com.foley.test;

import java.awt.*;

import javax.swing.*;

import com.foley.utility.*;

/**
```

```
 * An application that displays an AButton in a frame.
 *
 * @author Mike Foley
 **/
public class AButtonTest extends Object {


    /**
     * Application entry point.
     * Create the frame, and display it.
     *
     * @param args Command line parameter. Not used.
     **/
    public static void main( String args[] ) {

        JFrame frame = new JFrame( "Action Button Test" );

        //
        // Create the AButton, and add an ExitAction.
        //
        AButton button = new AButton();
        button.setAction( new ExitAction() );

        frame.getContentPane().add( button, BorderLayout.CENTER );
        frame.pack();
        frame.setVisible( true );

    } // main

} // AButtonTest
```

FIGURE 6.8

AButtonTest
application.

JToggleButton

The JToggleButton class provides a two-state button. A two-state button is one that doesn't spring back when released. The first time the button is clicked, it stays in the pressed position. The next time the button is pressed, it returns to the unpressed position. The exact rendering of a pressed button is look-and-feel dependent. A JToggleButton in each position is shown in Figure 6.9 for the Windows look-and-feel, and in Figure 6.10 for the Metal look-and-feel.

Like the JButton class, the JToggleButton class extends the AbstractButton class. The functionality presented for the AbstractButton class is available to instances of the

JToggleButton class. The application in Listing 6.5 shows the creation of a
JToggleButton and adds the ChangeListener and ActionListener used in the previous
example. Running the example application is instructive to see the event flow for a
JToggleButton instance.

LISTING 6.5   JToggleButton WITH A ChangeListener AND ActionListener

```
package com.foley.test;

import java.awt.*;
import java.awt.event.*;

import javax.swing.*;
import javax.swing.event.*;

import com.foley.utility.ApplicationFrame;


/**
 * An application that prints state changes of a JToggleButton.
 *
 * @author Mike Foley
 **/
public class ToggleButtonEventTest extends Object {

    /**
     * Create a panel containing a button and event listener.
     * The event listener simply dumps the button's state to
     * the console.
     *
     * @return A panel containing a button.
     **/
    static private JPanel createButtonPanel() {

        JPanel buttonPanel = new JPanel();

        JToggleButton toggle = new JToggleButton( "Toggle" );
        buttonPanel.add( toggle );

        toggle.addActionListener( new ActionListener() {
            public void actionPerformed( ActionEvent e ) {
                System.out.println( "ActionEvent " + e );
            }
        } );
        toggle.addChangeListener( new ChangeListener() {
            public void stateChanged( ChangeEvent e ) {
                JToggleButton button = ( JToggleButton )e.getSource();
                ButtonModel m = button.getModel();
                System.out.println( "armed=" + m.isArmed() + " " +
                                    "enabled=" + m.isEnabled() + " " +
```

```
                                  "pressed=" + m.isPressed() + " " +
                                  "rollover=" + m.isRollover() + " " +
                                  "selected=" + m.isSelected() );
            }
        } );

        return( buttonPanel );

    }


    /**
     * Application entry point.
     * Create the frame, and display it.
     *
     * @param args Command line parameter. Not used.
     **/
    public static void main( String args[] ) {

        JFrame frame = new ApplicationFrame( "ToggleButton Event Test" );

        JPanel buttons = createButtonPanel();

        frame.getContentPane().add( buttons, BorderLayout.CENTER );

        frame.pack();
        frame.setVisible( true );

    } // main

} // ToggleButtonEventTest
```

FIGURE 6.9

JToggleButton
*using the Windows
look-and-feel.*

FIGURE 6.10

JToggleButton
*using the Metal
look-and-feel.*

In the application, the same ChangeListener and ActionListener that were presented in the last section for the JButton examples were added to an instance of a JToggleButton. The results of executing this example are presented in Figure 6.11. The first line represents the default state of the JToggleButton. With the exception of the button being armed, this is the same as the default state of the JButton. One ChangeEvent is delivered when the mouse button is pressed the first time. This is from the pressed property changing to true. The next two ChangeEvents are delivered when the mouse is released. The first is from the button being selected, and the second from the pressed state returning to false. This property is a bit misleading. The button is drawn pressed, but the pressed property is false. This is because the pressed property refers to the mouse button, not the JToggleButton. The selected property is the property that represents the drawn state of the JToggleButton. Finally, an ActionEvent is delivered.

FIGURE 6.11
 	
ChangeListener
and
ActionListener
results.
	``
	// Default state, button 'up'
	armed=true enabled=true pressed=false rollover=false
	selected=false
	
	// Mouse button pressed
	armed=true enabled=true pressed=true rollover=false
	selected=false
	
	// Mouse released
	armed=true enabled=true pressed=true rollover=false
	selected=true
	armed=true enabled=true pressed=false rollover=false
	selected=true
	ActionEvent
	java.awt.event.ActionEvent[ACTION_PERFORMED,cmd=Toggle]
	on javax.swing.JToggleButton
	[,381,5,71x25,layout=javax.swing.OverlayLayout]
	
	// Button pressed when button 'down'
	armed=true enabled=true pressed=true rollover=false
	selected=true
	
	// Button released
	armed=true enabled=true pressed=true rollover=false
	selected=false
	armed=true enabled=true pressed=false rollover=false
	selected=false
	ActionEvent
	java.awt.event.ActionEvent[ACTION_PERFORMED,cmd=Toggle] on
	javax.swing.JToggleButton[
	➥,381,5,71x25,layout=javax.swing.OverlayLayout]
	``

The second group of events is delivered as a result of the button being pressed. That is when the toggle button transitions from being selected to not being selected. Visually this is the transition from the button being pressed to not being pressed. The first ChangeEvent is delivered when the mouse button is pressed, and the pressed property transitions to `true`. The next two `ChangeEvent`s are delivered when the button is released. The first is when the toggle button is no longer selected (it is not drawn pressed), and the second is to show that the mouse button is no longer pressed. Once again, an `ActionEvent` is delivered. For a `JToggleButton`, an `ActionEvent` is generated for the button being both selected and unselected.

Check Boxes

The `JCheckBox` class extends the `JToggleButton` class. It provides a different visual appearance to the same features as the `JToggleButton`. When a `JCheckBox` is selected, it is drawn checked instead of pressed as the `JToggleButton` is. Also, the `JCheckBox` doesn't go up and down as the other buttons you've seen. The application in Listing 6.6 shows how to create a `JCheckBox`. The resulting boxes are shown in Figure 6.12. In the `createCheckBoxPanel` method, an instance of the `JCheckBox` class can be set to checked by setting the selected property to `true`. By default, the check box will not be checked.

LISTING 6.6   JCheckBox

```
package com.foley.test;

import java.awt.*;

import javax.swing.*;

import com.foley.utility.*;


/**
 * An application that displays a couple of JCheckBox
 * instances.
 *
 * @author Mike Foley
 **/
public class CheckBoxTest extends Object {

    /**
     * Create a panel containing a couple of check boxes.
     *
     * @return A panel containing a button.
     **/
    static private JComponent createCheckBoxPanel() {

        JBox checkBoxPanel = JBox.createVerticalJBox();
```

continues

LISTING 6.6   CONTINUED

```
        JCheckBox check1 = new JCheckBox( "Option 1" );
        checkBoxPanel.add( check1 );
        JCheckBox check2 = new JCheckBox( "Option 2" );
        check2.setSelected( true );
        checkBoxPanel.add( check2 );

        return( checkBoxPanel );

    }


    /**
     * Application entry point.
     * Create the frame, and display it.
     *
     * @param args Command line parameter. Not used.
     **/
    public static void main( String args[] ) {

        JFrame frame = new ApplicationFrame( "CheckBox Test" );

        JComponent buttons = createCheckBoxPanel();

        buttons.setBorder( BorderFactory.createLoweredBevelBorder() );

        frame.getContentPane().add( buttons, BorderLayout.CENTER );

        frame.pack();
        frame.setVisible( true );

    } // main

} // CheckBoxTest
```

FIGURE 6.12

*JCheckBox
instances.*

As was previously stated, the JCheckBox class extends the JToggleButton class. The JCheckBox class does not alter events fired from those defined in the JToggleButton class. Thus, the event flow described in the previous section for the JToggleButton is the same as the event flow for the JCheckBox class. The listeners from the example in that section can be added to one or both of the JCheckBox instances in this example to print the event flow.

Radio Buttons

The `JRadioButton` class extends the `JToggleButton` class. It provides a different visual representation than that given by the `JToggleButton`. The following application shows how instances of the `JRadioButton` class are created. The resulting frame containing the radio buttons is shown in Figure 6.13. The `JRadioButton` instances are created in the `createRadioPanel` method. The first two buttons are left in their default state, not selected. The third button is selected by passing the `setSelected` method a parameter of `true`. In this application, more than one of the radio buttons can be selected at the same time. The next section describes how to enforce the typical radio button behavior of only one button in a group being selected at the same time.

LISTING 6.7   JRadioButton TEST APPLICATION

```
package com.foley.test;

import java.awt.*;

import javax.swing.*;

import com.foley.utility.*;


/**
 * An application that displays a few of JRadioButtons
 * instances.
 *
 * @author Mike Foley
 **/
public class RadioButtonTest extends Object {

    /**
     * Create a panel containing a few of radio buttons.
     *
     * @return A panel containing a button.
     **/
    static private JComponent createRadioPanel() {

        JBox radioButtonPanel = JBox.createVerticalJBox();

        JRadioButton radio1 = new JRadioButton( "Option 1" );
        radioButtonPanel.add( radio1 );
        JRadioButton radio2 = new JRadioButton( "Option 2" );
        radioButtonPanel.add( radio2 );
        JRadioButton radio3 = new JRadioButton( "Option 3" );
```

continues

LISTING 6.7   CONTINUED

```
        radio3.setSelected( true );
        radioButtonPanel.add( radio3 );

        return( radioButtonPanel );

    }


    /**
     * Application entry point.
     * Create the frame, and display it.
     *
     * @param args Command line parameter. Not used.
     **/
    public static void main( String args[] ) {

        JFrame frame = new ApplicationFrame( "Radion Button Test" );

        JComponent buttons = createRadioPanel();

        buttons.setBorder( BorderFactory.createLoweredBevelBorder() );

        frame.getContentPane().add( buttons, BorderLayout.CENTER );

        frame.pack();
        frame.setVisible( true );

    } // main

} // RadioButtonTest
```

FIGURE 6.13

Instances of the
JRadioButton
class.

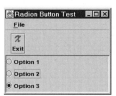

Once again, because the JRadioButton class extends the JToggleButton class, it does not alter events fired from those defined in the JToggleButton class. Thus, the event flow described in the JToggleButton section is the same as the event flow from the JCheckBox class.

Radio Button Groups

The most common usage of JRadioButton instances is to place them into a
ButtonGroup. The ButtonGroup ensures that only one button is selected at any given
time. The following example takes the JRadioButtons from the previous example and
places them in a ButtonGroup. Calling the setSelected method will set the selected
state of the given ButtonModel to the given state. This method takes a ButtonModel, not
the button itself. The getSelection method is used to query the currently selected
ButtonModel. It is interesting to note that the names of these methods are not symmetric.
The name of the getSelection method was the symmetric name, getSelected for many
beta releases of the JFC. The resulting radio buttons will appear the same as they did in
the last example and are shown in Figure 6.13.

Buttons can be removed from a ButtonGroup instance by using the remove method contained in the ButtonGroup class. An Enumeration containing the current set of buttons in
the group can be obtained with the getElements method. With the exception of the
remove method, these methods are demonstrated in Listing 6.8.

LISTING 6.8   ButtonGroup EXAMPLE APPLICATION

```
package com.foley.test;

import java.awt.*;
import java.util.Enumeration;

import javax.swing.*;

import com.foley.utility.*;


/**
 * An application that creates and displays a
 * ButtonGroup.
 *
 * @author Mike Foley
 **/
public class ButtonGroupTest extends JFrame {

    /**
     * Create a panel containing a ButtonGroup
     * consisting of a couple of RadioButtons.
     *
     * @return A panel containing a button group.
     **/
    static private JComponent createButtonGroupPanel() {
```

continues

LISTING 6.8   CONTINUED

```java
        JBox radioPanel = JBox.createVerticalJBox();
        ButtonGroup group = new ButtonGroup();
        JRadioButton radio1 = new JRadioButton( "Option 1" );
        radioPanel.add( radio1 );
        group.add( radio1 );
        JRadioButton radio2 = new JRadioButton( "Option 2" );
        radioPanel.add( radio2 );
        group.add( radio2 );
        JRadioButton radio3 = new JRadioButton( "Option 3" );
        radioPanel.add( radio3 );
        group.add( radio3 );

        // Select the third radio button.
        group.setSelected( radio3.getModel(), true );

        // Get the selected button's model.
        ButtonModel model = group.getSelection();

        // Enumerate the buttons in the group
        for( Enumeration e = group.getElements(); e.hasMoreElements();) {
            System.out.println( e.nextElement() );
        }

        return( radioPanel );
    }


    /**
     * Application entry point.
     * Create the frame, and display it.
     *
     * @param args Command line parameter. Not used.
     **/
    public static void main( String args[] ) {

        JFrame frame = new ApplicationFrame( "Button Group Test" );

        JComponent buttons = createButtonGroupPanel();
        buttons.setBorder( BorderFactory.createLoweredBevelBorder() );

        frame.getContentPane().add( buttons, BorderLayout.CENTER );

        frame.pack();
        frame.setVisible( true );

    } // main

} // ButtonGroupTest
```

Adding the JRadioButtons to the ButtonGroup does not change the events fired from the buttons. However, when a new button is selected, a ChangeEvent will be delivered to listeners of the previously selected button.

JRadioButton instances are the most common class of buttons added to a ButtonGroup instance. However the add and remove methods in the ButtonGroup class take instances of the AbstractButton class. This means that any of the buttons presented in this chapter can be added to a ButtonGroup. It is unfortunate that an interface was not used to specify this parameter rather than AbstractButton. Then any class that implemented the interface could be added to a ButtonGroup. The ButtonModel interface could have been used for this purpose. Instances of JToggleButton and JCheckBox probably lend themselves to being placed in a ButtonGroup more than do instances of the JButton class.

Summary

This chapter presented the button hierarchy contained in the JFC. Buttons are a fundamental user interface component. The JFC provides a hierarchy of buttons that should address most user interface needs. Even though the JFC buttons and JLabel class are siblings in the JFC class hierarchy, they both contain the same functionality for text and icon manipulation. The classes in the button hierarchy were the first example of the Model View Controller architecture encountered thus far in this book. The ButtonModel interface was examined, as well as the AbstractButton class that implements this interface. The AbstractButton class is the root of the JFC button hierarchy. The events the JFC buttons fire were also examined.

An omission in the JFC is that buttons are not Action-aware components. However, you saw that making an Action-aware button is a simple matter. The AButton class that can configure itself for a single Action at a time was presented. The class listens to changes in the Action to keep the button in sync with the Action. When the button is pressed, the Action is invoked.

Text Components

CHAPTER 7

Textual components in JFC come in two flavors: API-compatible replacements for the AWT `TextField` and `TextArea` classes, as well as a new generation of components that raise the level of text manipulation components provided in Java. Each text component allows text to be copied from or to the Clipboard.

In this chapter, you will learn how to use

- The `JTextField` Class
- The `JTextArea` Class
- The `JPasswordField`
- The `JTextPane` Class
- The `JEditorPane` Class
- The Document Model

The `JTextField` Class

The `JTextField` class provides a lightweight, near API-equivalent replacement for the AWT `TextField` class. A `JTextField` instance contains a single line of text that the user can edit. The `JTextField` class does not provide the `setEchoChar` and `getEchoChar` methods available in the `TextField` class. Instead, the `JPasswordField` class is provided for entering secure information. The `JPasswordField` class is the topic of the next section.

The initial text and column width of the text field can be specified in its constructor. Calling the default constructor will create an empty text field. The `setText` method can be used to replace the existing text in the component. Passing `null` or an empty string to this method will clear the text field. The `setColumns` method updates the column width of the text field. The `getColumns` method returns the current value of this property. When the text field is empty, the `getText` method will return an empty string, not `null`.

The alignment of the text in a `JTextField` instance can be specified with the `setHorizontalAlignment` method. The parameters for this method are the familiar `LEFT`, `RIGHT`, and `CENTER` constants defined in the `SwingConstants` interface that you saw earlier in this book when specifying the text alignment on labels and buttons. The current value of this property can be queried with the `getHorizontalAlignment` method. The horizontal alignment is the only bound property introduced by the `JTextField` class. The name of the property is the hard-coded string `horizontalAlignment` defined in the `JTextField` class.

If the Enter key is struck in a text field, an `ActionEvent` is sent to all registered listeners. Calling the `setActionCommand` method will specify the `ActionCommand` for the event. If the `ActionCommand` has not been set, the text in the text field is used. Modifying the `Keymap` for the text field can disable firing an `ActionCommand` from `JTextField` instances. The `Keymap` for textual components will be discussed later in this chapter.

The most common usage of the `JTextField` class is to obtain a small amount of text from the user. The `TextFieldTest` application shown in Listing 7.1 presents a simple example of a `JTextField` in a frame. It demonstrates reading and setting the contents in a `JTextField` instance as well as receiving `ActionEvents` from the component. When the Enter key is clicked in the text field, the contents of the text field are printed to the console and then cleared. The resulting window is shown in Figure 7.1.

FIGURE 7.1

The `TextFieldTest` *application.*

LISTING 7.1 THE `TextField` APPLICATION

```
package com.foley.test;

import java.awt.*;
import java.awt.event.*;

import javax.swing.*;

import com.foley.utility.ApplicationFrame;


/**
 * An application that displays a JTextField instance
 * in its frame.
 *
 * @author Mike Foley
 **/
public class TextFieldTest extends Object {

    /**
     * Application entry point.
     * Create a frame, the text field and display it.
     * Add an ActionListener to the text field that
     * echos the contents of the field when an
     * ActionEvent is received.
     *
     * @param args Command line parameter. Not used.
     **/
    public static void main( String args[] ) {
```

continues

LISTING 7.1 CONTINUED

```java
JFrame frame = new ApplicationFrame( "TextField Test" );

JTextField textField = new JTextField( "Initial Data", 24 );
textField.setActionCommand( "TestText" );

//
// Add the ActionListener.
//
textField.addActionListener( new ActionListener() {
    public void actionPerformed( ActionEvent event ) {
        System.out.println( "ActionCommand = " +
                            event.getActionCommand() );
        JTextField source = ( JTextField )event.getSource();
        System.out.println( "Text =" + source.getText() );
        source.setText( null );
        System.out.println();
    }
} );

textField.setBorder( BorderFactory.createLoweredBevelBorder() );
frame.getContentPane().add( textField, BorderLayout.CENTER );

frame.pack();
frame.setVisible( true );

} // main

} // TextFieldTest
```

The JTextField class delegates tracking of the columns that are visible in the text field to a BoundedRangeModel instance. This is of most importance when the entire text contained in the text field is not visible. The minimum, maximum, value, and extent properties of the model define the portion of the text visible in the text field. The getHorizontalVisibility method returns the BoundedRangeModel used for the text field. Adjusting the value property in the model sets the first character visible in the text field. The JTextField class contains the setScrollOffset and getScrollOffset convenience methods that set and query the value property of the model directly. Once again, the value property only affects text fields that contain a string that is too long to fit in its display area. Furthermore, the setScrollOffset method does not have any effect until this is the case.

> **NOTE**
>
> The `JTextField` class handles strings that do not fit in its display area very poorly. When the user enters an additional character, the existing text as well as the new character are pushed to the left of the insertion position; the insertion position does not move. Typically the text to the right of the insertion position is scrolled right and the insertion position moves right one character. This condition is exacerbated when the insert position is in the first column. In this state, the newly entered text is not visible because it is pushed left out of view, making it appear to the user that the character he or she typed was not accepted by the control.
>
> Another odd behavior is that the control tries to display the last character in the text field. This often causes the insertion location to shift left, possibly to the first column, while the user is typing. This is very confusing for the user.

The `JPasswordField` Class

The `JPasswordField` class is an extension of the `JTextField` class that provides a control for entering text but does not display the originally entered text. Instead, an arbitrary character is echoed in the Password field. The echo character can be requested. However, if the look-and-feel implementation contains a custom graphical technique to display input characters, this request might not be honored.

The constructors for the `JPasswordField` class are identical to those contained in the `JTextField` class. These create a Password field with the default echo character, the asterisk * character. The `setEchoChar` method specifies the character to echo in the Password field when the user enters a character. This is to give feedback that a character was in fact received. Passing this method the value of `0` resets the echo character to its default value. The `echoCharIsSet` method returns `true` if the echo character has been set and `false` otherwise. The `getEchoChar` returns the current value of this property. For an unexplained reason, the echo character is not a bound property of the `JPasswordField` class.

When an echo character other than an asterisk is used in a `JPasswordField` instance, the Password field does not display the alternate echo character properly. The width of an asterisk is used to advance the cursor, even when it is not the echo character. This bug makes using arbitrary echo characters unfeasible at this time. This can be seen in Figure 7.2 when a - is used as the echo character in a `JPasswordField` instance.

For security reasons, the `copy` and `cut` methods are disabled in the `JPasswordField` class. If either of these actions is attempted, a beep is sounded and the action is not performed.

The getText method is not used to query the text in a Password field. Instead, the getPassword method is used. Once again, this is for security reasons. The getPassword method returns an array of characters, rather than a String instance. For security reasons, it is suggested that each character in the array be overwritten when the calling method is done with the password.

The PasswordFieldTest application shown in Listing 7.2 presents an application that displays a JPasswordField instance in a frame that resembles a login dialog box. The resulting frame is shown in Figure 7.2.

FIGURE 7.2

The
PasswordFieldTest
application.

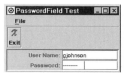

LISTING 7.2 THE PasswordFieldTest APPLICATION

```
package com.foley.test;

import java.awt.*;
import java.awt.event.*;

import javax.swing.*;

import com.foley.utility.ApplicationFrame;


/**
 * An application that displays a JPasswordField instance
 * in its frame.
 *
 * @author Mike Foley
 **/
public class PasswordFieldTest extends Object {

    /**
     * Application entry point.
     * Create a frame and a login type display.
     *
     * @param args Command line parameter. Not used.
     **/
    public static void main( String args[] ) {

        JFrame frame = new ApplicationFrame( "PasswordField Test" );

        JPanel panel = new JPanel();
```

7

```java
panel.setLayout( new GridLayout( 2, 2 ) );

JLabel nameLabel = new JLabel( "User Name: ",
                                SwingConstants.RIGHT );
JLabel passwordLabel = new JLabel( "Password: ",
                                SwingConstants.RIGHT );
JTextField userNameTextField = new JTextField( 12 );
JPasswordField passwordPasswordField = new JPasswordField( 12 );
passwordPasswordField.setEchoChar( '-' );

panel.add( nameLabel );
panel.add( userNameTextField );
panel.add( passwordLabel );
panel.add( passwordPasswordField );

//
// Add the ActionListener.
//
passwordPasswordField.addActionListener( new ActionListener() {
    public void actionPerformed( ActionEvent event ) {
        System.out.println( "ActionCommand = " +
                            event.getActionCommand() );
        JPasswordField source =
                    ( JPasswordField )event.getSource();
        char[] password = source.getPassword();
        for( int i = 0; i < password.length; i++ ) {
            System.out.print( password[i] );
            password[i] = ( char )0;
        }
        source.setText( null );
        System.out.println();
        System.out.println();
    }
} );

panel.setBorder( BorderFactory.createLoweredBevelBorder() );
frame.getContentPane().add( panel, BorderLayout.CENTER );

frame.pack();
frame.setVisible( true );

} // main

} // PasswordFieldTest
```

As can be seen in Figure 7.2, the `PasswordFieldTest` application uses a - character as its echo character. An `ActionListener` is registered with the Password field to be notified when the Enter key is pressed. The `ActionListener` calls the `getPassword` method to query the password and then prints each character to the console. As suggested, each character in the password array is cleared after it is used. The Password field control must be reset after clearing the characters in its password array. If this is not done, the view will still show the echoed characters from the previous password. However, calling getPassword will not return those characters. Calling the setText method with a null parameter after the password has been processed performs this.

The PasswordFieldTest application prints the ActionCommand in its ActionListener method. The JPasswordField inherits the ActionCommand processing from the JTextFieldClass. This sets the ActionCommand to the contents of the text field (the password in this case) if it hasn't explicitly been set by the application by using the setActionCommand method. This is a security hole in the current JPasswordField implementation. To avoid this security hole, your applications should always explicitly set the ActionCommand by calling the setActionCommand method for each JPasswordField used in the application.

The JTextArea Class

The JTextArea class is a lightweight textual component that supports multiple lines of plain text. It is meant to be a replacement for the AWT TextArea class and contains almost the entire API contained in the TextArea class. A fundamental difference in the two classes is that the TextArea class manages scrolling internally while the JTextArea class implements the Scrollable interface. This allows a JTextArea instance to be placed into a JScrollPane instance when scrolling is required. It can be used directly when scrolling is not desired.

Configuring a JTextArea Instance

The JTextArea class contains many constructors, ranging from the default constructor to a version where the number of rows and columns and initial text for the text area can be specified, with many variants in between. As with all the textual components, specifying the number of rows and columns is used during the calculation of the preferred size of the component. Depending on the layout manager used in the text area's parent container, this value may or may not affect the size of the component.

The number of rows and columns in the text area can be altered after construction by using the setColumns and setRows methods. The current value of these properties can be queried with the getColumns and getRows methods. It is odd, but neither of these properties is bound in the JTextArea class. These properties may very well be of interest to a PropertyChangeListener listener, but the current implementation does not fire a propertyChangeEvent when either property changes.

The TextAreaTest application is shown in Listing 7.3. This is a simple application that displays a JTextArea instance in a frame. This application will be expanded to show additional capabilities of the JTextArea class throughout this section. The window created from Listing 7.3 is shown in Figure 7.3.

FIGURE 7.3

The TextAreaTest *application window.*

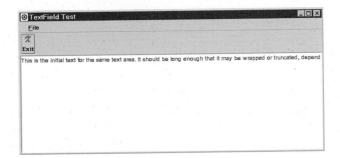

LISTING 7.3 THE TextAreaTest APPLICATION

```
package com.foley.test;

import java.awt.*;

import javax.swing.*;

import com.foley.utility.ApplicationFrame;


/**
 * An application that displays a JTextArea instance
 * in its frame.
 *
 * @author Mike Foley
 **/
public class TextAreaTest extends Object {

    /**
     * Application entry point.
     * Create a frame, the text area and display it.
     * @param args Command line parameter. Not used.
     **/
    public static void main( String args[] ) {

        String data = "This is the initial text for the " +
                      "same text area. It should be long " +
                      "enough that it may be wrapped or truncated, " +
                      "depending on the JTextArea instance's settings.";


        JFrame frame = new ApplicationFrame( "TextField Test" );
```

continues

LISTING 7.3 CONTINUED

```
        JTextArea textArea = new JTextArea( data, 12, 30 );

        textArea.setBorder( BorderFactory.createLoweredBevelBorder() );
        frame.getContentPane().add( textArea, BorderLayout.CENTER );

        frame.pack();
        frame.setVisible( true );

    } // main

} // TextAreaTest
```

Figure 7.3 demonstrates the default behavior when a line is longer than the width of the text area. The text area truncates the line unless line wrapping is enabled. Passing the setLineWrap method a parameter of true will enable line wrapping. Once wrapping is enabled, the setWrapStyleWord method is used to specify whether wrapping is performed at word or character boundaries. Passing true to this method wraps lines at word boundaries; false will enable wrapping at character boundaries. The getLineWrap and getWrapStyleWord methods return the current value of each of these properties. Both these properties are bound in the JTextArea class. Table 7.1 presents the complete list of bound properties added in the JTextArea class.

TABLE 7.1 NON-INHERITED BOUND PROPERTIES OF THE JTextArea CLASS

Property Name	Setter Method	Getter Method
tabSize	setTabSize	getTabSize
lineWrap	getLineWrap	setLineWrap
wrapStyleWord	setWrapStyleWord	getWrapStyleWord

Adding the following lines to the TextAreaTest application enables line wrapping at word boundaries. The resulting window is shown in Figure 7.4.

```
textArea.setLineWrap( true );
textArea.setWrapStyleWord( true );
```

Instead of enabling line wrapping in a text area, the text area can be placed in a scroll pane instance. In this situation, instead of wrapping the text to make it visible in the text area, a scrollbar is displayed when a line is longer than the width of the text area. This can be used to alter the visible text in the text area. A complete description of the JScrollPane class is presented in Chapter 15, "Scrolling Components." The line of code adding the text area to the frame can be changed as shown to place the text area into a scroll pane. The resulting window is shown in Figure 7.5.

```
frame.getContentPane().add(
➥        new JScrollPane( textArea ), BorderLayout.CENTER );
```

FIGURE 7.4

*Line wrapping
enabled at word
boundaries.*

FIGURE 7.5

JTextArea *in a*
JScrollPane.

Figure 7.5 demonstrates the interaction between a scroll pane and a text area when line wrapping is disabled. The single line of text is not wrapped, and the user must scroll to see the text. If there are more lines of text than are visible in the text area, a vertical scrollbar is displayed to allow scrolling up and down. Scrolling can be used in conjunction with line wrapping. In this case, lines are wrapped at the edge of the text area, so the horizontal scrollbar is not required. However, if there is more text than can be displayed in the text area, a vertical scrollbar is displayed. This is shown in Figure 7.6. The text area shown in this figure has line wrapping enabled at word boundaries and is placed in a scroll pane.

FIGURE 7.6

JTextArea *in a*
JScrollPane *with
word wrapping
enabled.*

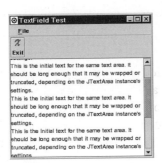

The other bound property defined in the JTextArea class is the tab size. The default value for this property is eight spaces. It can be set and queried with the setTabSize and getTabSize methods, respectively.

Manipulating Text in a JTextArea Instance

The initial text in a JTextArea instance may be specified when constructing the text area. The text may be replaced later using the setText method. It can be queried with the getText method. This behavior is the same as seen earlier in the chapter for the single line JTextField class.

The JTextArea class contains methods to programmatically insert, append, and replace text. The append method appends the given String instance to the end of existing text in the text area. The insert method inserts the given String instance at the given column offset in the text area. Columns are numbered from 0 in a text area, so to insert a string at the beginning of a text area, the following code fragment would be used:

```
textArea.insert( 'Text to insert', 0 );
```

The replaceRange method can be used to replace a range of text with a new String instance. The new string does not have to be the same length as the text to be replaced. Indeed, passing an empty string has the effect of deleting the text in the given range.

The number of lines in a text area can be queried with the getLineCount method. The line displaying a given offset in the text area can be queried with the getLineOfOffset method. Methods that perform the opposite calculations are getLineStartOffset and getLineEndOffset. These two methods take a line number as a parameter and return the offset of the first and last characters of that line in the text area.

Document Model

Up to this point, the Swing text manipulation components behaved similarly to their AWT equivalents. However, the JFC textual model goes well beyond what was provided by the AWT. Even though you have not seen it yet, the textual components are displaying the data contained in a complex data model.

The data model used for JFC textual components is defined in the swing.text package. The data model allows styles to be added to the text. This allows multiple fonts, point sizes, and colors to appear in the same component. Images can also be added to a document model.

The components presented earlier in this chapter view a document model. However, they are not capable of rendering all the capabilities that can be expressed in the model. For this capability to be realized, two textual components were introduced in the JFC: JTextPane and JEditorPane. These classes are discussed in the next sections.

The Document interface defines the text data model. Methods are defined for adding and removing listeners in the document. A document can consist of more than simple characters. Elements can be inserted into the document to "mark up" the text. Typical elements are to turn bold or italic fonts on and off. An element can have an arbitrary set of attributes associated with it. The set of currently active elements defines how the text in the document will be rendered in the view.

The JTextComponent class serves as the root of the textual class hierarchy in the JFC. It manages the caret, commands, and keymaps. The caret is a pluggable object in the JTextComponent class. The setCaret method is provided to change the caret used for the text component. The getCaret method can be used to query the current caret. The caret is a bound property in the JTextComponent class. The complete list of bound properties introduced in the JTextComponent class is presented in Table 7.2. With the exception of the FOCUS_ACCELERATOR_KEY property, the property names are hard coded in the JTextComponent class.

TABLE 7.2 Non-Inherited Bound Properties of the JTextComponent Class

Property Name	Setter Method	Getter Method
document	setDocument	getDocument
margin	setMargin	getMargin
caret	setCaret	getCaret
highlighter	setHighlighter	getHighlighter
keymap	setKeymap	getKeymap
caretColor	setCaretColor	getCaretColor
selectionColor	setSelectionColor	getSelectionColor
selectedTextColor	setSelectedTextColor	getSelectedTextColor
disabledTextColor	setDisabledTextColor	getDisabledTextColor
FOCUS_ACCELERATOR_KEY	setFocusAccelerator	getFocusAccelerator
editable	setEditable	isEditable

The JTextComponent supports a set of built-in commands. Each command implements the Action interface. As you saw in Chapter 6, "The Button Hierarchy," it is easy to add an action to a button. As you will see in Chapter 9, "Menus and Toolbars," it is just as easy to add an action to menus and toolbars. The getActions method can be called to

query the set of actions supported by a text component. The ShowTextActions application shown in Listing 7.4 queries the actions registered for a JTextArea instance and
displays the name of each action in the text area itself. Unfortunately, descriptions are
not specified for the text actions, so these cannot be displayed. The application is shown
in Figure 7.7.

FIGURE 7.7

The ShowTextActions
application.

LISTING 7.4 THE ShowTextActions APPLICATION

```
package com.foley.test;

import java.awt.*;

import javax.swing.*;

import com.foley.utility.ApplicationFrame;


/**
 * An application that displays the Actions
 * in a JTextArea instance.
 *
 * @author Mike Foley
 **/
public class ShowTextActions extends Object {

    /**
     * Application entry point.
     * Create a frame, the text area and display it.
     * @param args Command line parameter. Not used.
     **/
```

```
public static void main( String args[] ) {

    JFrame frame = new ApplicationFrame( "ShowTextActions" );

    JTextArea textArea = new JTextArea( 12, 30 );

    Action[] actions = textArea.getActions();
    for( int i = 0; i < actions.length; i++ ) {
        textArea.append(
                actions[i].getValue( Action.NAME ).toString() );
        textArea.append( "\n" );
    }

    frame.getContentPane().add( new JScrollPane( textArea ),
                        BorderLayout.CENTER );

    frame.pack();
    frame.setVisible( true );

} // main

} // ShowTextActions
```

The default actions shown by the ShowTextActions application are defined in the DefaultEditorKit class. In that class, constants are defined for each of the action names displayed in the application. These constants can be used by applications, rather than hard coding the action name.

The JTextComponent class provides the keymap property that maps keystrokes to actions. The getKeymap and setKeymap methods are provided to query and set the keymap for a given text component. The keymap property is a bound property. The class also maintains a list of named keymaps. A named keymap can be added by calling the static addKeymap method. The static getKeymap method will return the keymap associated with the string name passed to the method. This method will return null if a keymap hasn't been added with the given name. The loadKeymap method is a convenience method that loads the given KeyBinding array into the given keymap instance. If there already is a binding associated with an action in the keymap, it will be replaced with the new binding. The KeyBinding class shown in Listing 7.5 is defined in the JTextComponent class. The class simply maps a Keystroke instance to an action name.

LISTING 7.5 THE KeyBinding CLASS

```
/**
 * Binding record for creating key bindings.
 */
public static class KeyBinding {
```

continues

LISTING 7.5 CONTINUED

```
    /**
     * The key.
     */
    public KeyStroke key;

    /**
     * The name of the action for the key.
     */
    public String actionName;

    /**
     * Creates a new key binding.
     *
     * @param key the key
     * @param actionName the name of the action for the key
     */
    public KeyBinding(KeyStroke key, String actionName) {
        this.key = key;
        this.actionName = actionName;
    }
}
```

The Keymap interface shown in Listing 7.6 defines the responsibilities of a class that can be used as a keymap. The JTextComponent class defines a class named DefaultKeymap that it loads with the name DEFAULT_KEYMAP. This keymap will be shared by all text components created by an application.

LISTING 7.6 THE Keymap INTERFACE

```
public interface Keymap {

    /**
     * Fetches the name of the set of key-bindings.
     *
     * @return the name
     */
    public String getName();

    /**
     * Fetches the default action to fire if a
     * key is typed (i.e. a KEY_TYPED KeyEvent is received)
     * and there is no binding for it.  Typically this
     * would be some action that inserts text so that
     * the keymap doesn't require an action for each
     * possible key.
     *
```

```
 * @return the default action
 */
public Action getDefaultAction();

/**
 * Set the default action to fire if a key is typed.
 *
 * @param a the action
 */
public void setDefaultAction(Action a);

/**
 * Fetches the action appropriate for the given symbolic
 * event sequence.  This is used by JTextController to
 * determine how to interpret key sequences.  If the
 * binding is not resolved locally, an attempt is made
 * to resolve through the parent keymap, if one is set.
 *
 * @param key the key sequence
 * @returns  the action associated with the key
 *   sequence if one is defined, otherwise null
 */
public Action getAction(KeyStroke key);

/**
 * Fetches all of the keystrokes in this map that
 * are bound to some action.
 *
 * @return the list of keystrokes
 */
public KeyStroke[] getBoundKeyStrokes();

/**
 * Fetches all of the actions defined in this keymap.
 *
 * @return the list of actions
 */
public Action[] getBoundActions();

/**
 * Fetches the keystrokes that will result in
 * the given action.
 *
 * @param a the action
 * @return the list of keystrokes
 */
public KeyStroke[] getKeyStrokesForAction(Action a);

/**
 * Determines if the given key sequence is locally defined.
```

continues

LISTING 7.6 CONTINUED

```
 *
 * @param key the key sequence
 * @return true if the key sequence is locally defined else false
 */
public boolean isLocallyDefined(KeyStroke key);

/**
 * Adds a binding to the keymap.
 *
 * @param key the key sequence
 * @param a the action
 */
public void addActionForKeyStroke(KeyStroke key, Action a);

/**
 * Removes a binding from the keymap.
 *
 * @param keys the key sequence
 */
public void removeKeyStrokeBinding(KeyStroke keys);

/**
 * Removes all bindings from the keymap.
 */
public void removeBindings();

/**
 * Fetches the parent keymap used to resolve key-bindings.
 *
 * @return the keymap
 */
public Keymap getResolveParent();

/**
 * Sets the parent keymap, which will be used to
 * resolve key-bindings.
 *
 * @param parent the parent keymap
 */
public void setResolveParent(Keymap parent);


}
```

The default keymap is loaded in the JTextComponent class with the following code.

```
static final KeyBinding[] defaultBindings = {
    new KeyBinding(KeyStroke.getKeyStroke(KeyEvent.VK_BACK_SPACE, 0),
                DefaultEditorKit.deletePrevCharAction),
    new KeyBinding(KeyStroke.getKeyStroke(KeyEvent.VK_DELETE, 0),
                DefaultEditorKit.deleteNextCharAction),
```

```
        new KeyBinding(KeyStroke.getKeyStroke(KeyEvent.VK_RIGHT, 0),
                    DefaultEditorKit.forwardAction),
        new KeyBinding(KeyStroke.getKeyStroke(KeyEvent.VK_LEFT, 0),
                    DefaultEditorKit.backwardAction)
};

static {
    try {
        keymapTable = new Hashtable(17);
        Keymap binding = addKeymap(DEFAULT_KEYMAP, null);
        binding.setDefaultAction(
                new DefaultEditorKit.DefaultKeyTypedAction());
        EditorKit kit = new DefaultEditorKit();
        loadKeymap(binding, defaultBindings, kit.getActions());
    } catch (Throwable e) {
        e.printStackTrace();
        keymapTable = new Hashtable(17);
    }
}
```

From the `defaultBindings` table, you can see that the default keymap only contains mappings for four simple actions as well as the default action. The look-and-feel for the application can add additional bindings to the keymap.

Input Filtering

A common requirement in textual components is to limit the type of text that can be entered into the component. For example, in a form where a person's age is entered, only a positive integer value is allowed. When using an AWT text component, this functionality was typically achieved by overriding the keyboard-input method and only passing valid keystrokes to the text component.

This approach also can be taken with JFC text components; however, it is not the preferred method. Instead, a custom document class that only accepts valid values can be created and set for the text component. This technique has many advantages over keystroke filtering. First, it works for text pasted into the component as well as text entered via the keyboard. Second, the custom document class can be used for any class that expects a document model. Finally, it allows the data manipulation code to be removed from the view code.

The `TextFilterDocument` class shown in Listing 7.7 is an extension to the `PlainDocument` class. The `insertString` method is overridden. This method is called whenever text is to be added to the document. The `TextFilterDocument` class only allows the characters 0–9 to be added to the document. This policy is enforced in the `insertString` method. When a string is to be inserted into the document, each character is tested. If any character is not a digit, a beep is sounded and the text is not added to the model. If each character is a digit, the `PlainDocument` class's version of the `insertString` method is called with the same parameters as those given to the method.

LISTING 7.7 THE `TextFilterDocument` CLASS

```java
package com.foley.utility;

import java.awt.Toolkit;

import javax.swing.text.*;


/**
 * Document to only allow numbers.
 * <p>
 * @author Mike Foley
 **/
public class TextFilterDocument extends PlainDocument {

    /**
     * Valid number strings.
     **/
    public static final String NUMBERS = "0123456789";


    /**
     * TextFilterDocument, constructor
     **/
    public TextFilterDocument()
{
        super();
}


    /**
     * A String is being inserted into the Document.
     * Ensure that all characters are in NUMBERS.
     *
     * @param offset Where the new string goes.
     * @param string The String to be inserted after check.
     * @param attributeSet Attributes for the new string.
     **/
    public void insertString( int offset, String string,
                              AttributeSet attributeSet )
        throws BadLocationException {

        //
        // If nothing to insert, do nothing.
        //
```

```
        if( string == null )
            return;

        //
        // Ensure each character in the string is a number.
        //
        for( int i = 0; i < string.length(); i++ ) {
            if( NUMBERS.indexOf( string.valueOf(
                string.charAt(i) ) ) == -1 ) {

                //
                // Not a number, don't insert the string.
                // Beep to let the user know something is wrong.
                //
                Toolkit.getDefaultToolkit().beep();
                return;
            }
        }

        //
        // Let our parent do the real work.
        //
        super.insertString( offset, string, attributeSet );

    } // insertString

} // TextFilterDocument
```

The `TextFilterDocument` class can be used as the model in a `JTextField` instance by using the following line of code.

```
JTextField integerTextField = new JTextField( new TextFilterDocument() );
```

If a character other than 0–9 is entered in `integerTextField`, a beep is sounded and the character is not displayed in the component. This technique can be extended to form more complex textual filters.

The `JEditorPane` Class

The `JEditorPane` class is a textual component that can be configured to edit different content types. The `EditorKit` currently being used by the Editor pane defines the content type understood by the component. The `setEditorKit` and `getEditorKit` methods can be used to set and query the current editor kit. The editor kit is the only new bound property defined in the `JEditorPane` class. The JFC provides editor kits for plain, HTML, and RTF text. Example usage of each of these content types is given in this section.

Text Content, the `JTextPane` Class

The JTextPane class extends the JEditorPane class. It is capable of displaying styled text contained in a Document model. The class configures itself with a StyledEditorKit instance as its editor kit. Passing a StyledDocument to the class's constructor also can create an instance of the class. The setDocument method is overridden to ensure that the document being set for the JTextPane instance is a StyledDocument instance. If this is not the case, an IllegalArgumentException is thrown.

The remaining methods in the JTextPane class are convenience methods that pass the message to the StyledDocument or StyledEditorKit. The JTextPane class allows components and icons to be added as well as text. These are added by calling the insertComponent and insertIcon methods, respectively.

The ShowTextPaneActions application shown in Listing 7.8 is a modified version of the ShowTextActions presented in Listing 7.4. Instead of showing the actions available for a JTextArea instance in a text area, the actions available for a JTextPane instance are shown in a text pane. The resulting application is shown in Figure 7.8.

FIGURE 7.8

The ShowTextPane Actions *application.*

LISTING 7.8 THE ShowTextPaneActions APPLICATION

```
package com.foley.test;

import java.awt.*;

import javax.swing.*;
import javax.swing.text.*;

import com.foley.utility.ApplicationFrame;
```

```
/**
 * An application that displays the Actions
 * in a JTextPane instance.
 *
 * @author Mike Foley
 **/
public class ShowTextPaneActions extends Object {

    /**
     * Application entry point.
     * Create a frame, the text pane and display it.
     * @param args Command line parameter. Not used.
     **/
    public static void main( String args[] ) {


        JFrame frame = new ApplicationFrame( "ShowTextPaneActions" );

        JTextPane textPane = new JTextPane();
        StyledDocument document = textPane.getStyledDocument();
        Action[] actions = textPane.getActions();
        for( int i = 0; i < actions.length; i++ ) {
            try {
                document.insertString( document.getLength(),
                            actions[i].getValue( Action.NAME ).toString(),
                            null );
                document.insertString( document.getLength(),
                            "\t", null );
                document.insertString( document.getLength(),
                            actions[i].toString(), null );
                document.insertString( document.getLength(),
                            "\n", null );
            } catch( BadLocationException bl ) {
                System.err.println( bl );
            }
        }

        frame.getContentPane().add( new JScrollPane( textPane ),
                                BorderLayout.CENTER );

        frame.pack();
        frame.setVisible( true );

    } // main

} // ShowTextPaneActions
```

The ShowTextPaneActions application is almost identical to the ShowTextActions application. However, in this version of the application, the action itself is also printed to the text pane. In the figure you can also see that the `JTextPane` class wraps lines that are too long to display in the width of the component.

Styled Text

In the `ShowTextPaneActions` application, a text pane is being used to display the actions. This allows styles to be added to the text. The third parameter to the `insertString` method is the `AttributeSet` to be applied to the text. Passing `null` for this parameter uses the current attributes in effect where the text is inserted. If an attribute set is specified, the text will be formatted by using the format defined by the given attribute set. The `main` method from the `ShowTextActions` application can be modified as shown in Listing 7.9 to add styles to the text added to the text pane. The resulting application is shown in Figure 7.9.

LISTING 7.9 STYLES ADDED TO THE `ShowTextPaneActions` APPLICATION

```
/**
 * Application entry point.
 * Create a frame, the text pane and display it.
 * Use styled text in the text pane.
 * @param args Command line parameter. Not used.
 **/
public static void main( String args[] ) {

    JFrame frame = new ApplicationFrame( "ShowTextPaneActions" );

    MutableAttributeSet bold = new SimpleAttributeSet();
    StyleConstants.setFontFamily( bold, "Times" );
    StyleConstants.setBold( bold, true );
    StyleConstants.setFontSize( bold, 12 );

    MutableAttributeSet normal = new SimpleAttributeSet();
    StyleConstants.setFontFamily( normal, "Courier" );
    StyleConstants.setBold( normal, false );
    StyleConstants.setFontSize( normal, 8 );

    JTextPane textPane = new JTextPane();

    StyledDocument document = textPane.getStyledDocument();
    Action[] actions = textPane.getActions();
    for( int i = 0; i < actions.length; i++ ) {
        try {
            document.insertString( document.getLength(),
                    actions[i].getValue( Action.NAME ).toString(),
                    bold );
            document.insertString( document.getLength(),
                    "\t", bold );
```

```
        document.insertString( document.getLength(),
                actions[i].toString(), normal );
        document.insertString( document.getLength(),
                "\n", normal );
    } catch( BadLocationException bl ) {
        System.err.println( bl );
    }
}


frame.getContentPane().add( new JScrollPane( textPane ),
BorderLayout.CENTER );

    frame.pack();
    frame.setVisible( true );

} // main
```

FIGURE 7.9

Styled text in the ShowTextPane Actions *application.*

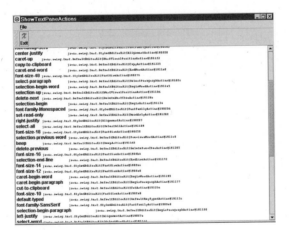

The AttributeSet interface defines an immutable view of an attribute set. Each attribute in the set is a name/value pair. The MutableAttributeSet interface extends the AttributeSet interface and provides method to add and remove attributes from the set. The SimpleAttributeSet class implements the MutableAttributeSet interface. As such, it can be used to specify a style in the text pane. The StyleConstants class contains methods that add attributes to a MutableAttributeSet with well-known names. Each method in the class is static. In the previous example, the font was made bold with the following line of code:

```
StyleConstants.setBold( bold, true );
```

The StyleConstants class adds an attribute to the given MutableAttributeSet with the name FontConstants.Bold and a value of Boolean.TRUE. The FontConstants class is defined in the `StyleConstants` class and defines constants and methods for setting and querying the constants for such well-known attributes as font family, font size, bold, italic, and underlined. When using the `StyleConstants` class, the `FontConstants` class usage is hidden from the calling code.

Adding Icons and Components

The `JTextPane` class allows icons and components to be embedded in its content. The `insertComponent` and `insertIcon` methods are provided for this purpose. These methods are convenience methods that set the given icon or component in the current attribute set and replace the text at the current position with an empty string. Since the icon or component is in the attribute set at that location, it is drawn in the view.

The `TextPaneIcons` application shown in Listing 7.10 demonstrates the usage of these two methods. The resulting window is shown in Figure 7.10.

FIGURE 7.10

The `TextPaneIcons`
application.

LISTING 7.10 THE `TextPaneIcons` APPLICATION

```
package com.foley.test;

import java.awt.*;
import java.awt.event.*;
import java.util.Hashtable;

import javax.swing.*;
import javax.swing.text.*;

import com.foley.utility.ApplicationFrame;
```

```
/**
 * An application that displays the icons
 * and labels in a JTextPane instance.
 *
 * @author Mike Foley
 **/
public class TextPaneIcons extends Panel {

    /**
     * The Actions available in a Hashtable.
     * This allows an Action to be looked-up
     * by name.
     **/
    Hashtable commands;


    /**
     * TextPaneIcons, constructor.
     * <p>
     * Create the text panel. This is a panel
     * with a JTextPane in the center region, and
     * buttons in the south.
     **/
    public TextPaneIcons() {

        setLayout( new BorderLayout() );

        JTextPane textPane = new JTextPane();
        commands = createCommands( textPane );

        add( new JScrollPane( textPane ), BorderLayout.CENTER );

        add( createButtons(), BorderLayout.SOUTH );

    } // TextPaneIcons


    /**
     * Create the buttons for the application.
     * <p>
     * @return A Component containing the buttons for the application.
     **/
    protected Component createButtons() {

        JPanel buttons = new JPanel();
        buttons.setLayout( new BoxLayout( buttons, BoxLayout.X_AXIS ) );

        JButton b;
```

continues

LISTING 7.10 CONTINUED

```java
        b = new JButton( "Icon" );
        b.addActionListener( new AddIconAction( "logo.gif" ) );
        buttons.add( b );

        b = new JButton( "Label" );
        b.addActionListener( new AddLabelAction( "Hello" ) );
        buttons.add( b );

        b = new JButton( "Clear" );
        b.addActionListener( new ClearAction() );
        buttons.add( b );

        b = new JButton( "Copy" );
        b.addActionListener( getAction( DefaultEditorKit.cutAction ) );
        buttons.add( b );

        b = new JButton( "Copy" );
        b.addActionListener( getAction( DefaultEditorKit.copyAction ) );
        buttons.add( b );

        b = new JButton( "Paste" );
        b.addActionListener( getAction( DefaultEditorKit.pasteAction ) );
        buttons.add( b );

        return( buttons );
    }


    /**
     * Create a Hashtable of the Actions registered for
     * the given JTextComponent. The key for each element
     * is the action's name, and the value is the action
     * itself.
     * <p>
     * @return A Hashtable of Actions.
     **/
    protected Hashtable createCommands( JTextComponent textComponent ) {

        Hashtable commands = new Hashtable();

    Action[] actions = textComponent.getActions();
        for (int i = 0; i < actions.length; i++) {
            Action a = actions[i];
            commands.put( a.getValue( Action.NAME ), a );
        }
        return( commands );
    }


    /**
```

```
 * Look up the Action associated with the given name.
 * Null will be returned if there is not an Action for
 * the given name.
 * <p>
 * @return The Action associated with the given name.
 **/
protected Action getAction( String name ) {
 return( ( Action )commands.get( name ) );
}


/**
 * Application entry point.
 * Create a frame, the text pane and display it.
 * Create buttons along the bottom of the
 * window for editing in the text pane.
 * @param args Command line parameter. Not used.
 **/
public static void main( String args[] ) {

    JFrame frame = new ApplicationFrame( "TextPane Icons" );

    frame.getContentPane().add( new TextPaneIcons(),
                             BorderLayout.CENTER );

    frame.pack();
    frame.setVisible( true );

} // main


/**
 * An action that clears the text component.
 **/
class ClearAction extends TextAction {

    ClearAction() {
        super( "Clear" );
        putValue( Action.SHORT_DESCRIPTION,
            "Clear the text in the target" );
    }

    /**
     * Perform the action. If a text component can
     * be obtained from the event, clear it. If not,
     * beep.
     * <p>
     * @param event The event causing us to be called.
     **/
    public void actionPerformed( ActionEvent event ) {
```

continues

LISTING 7.10 CONTINUED

```java
                JTextComponent target = getTextComponent( event );
                if( target != null ) {
                    try {
                        Document document = target.getDocument();
                        document.remove( 0, document.getLength() );
                    } catch( BadLocationException ble ) {
                        System.err.println( ble );
                    }
                } else {
                    Toolkit.getDefaultToolkit().beep();
                }
            }
        }


/**
 * An action that adds an Icon to
 * the target text pane when invoked.
 **/
class AddIconAction extends TextAction {

    /**
     * The name of the icon to be
     * added to the text pane.
     **/
    private String iconName;

    /**
     * AddIconAction, constructor.
     * <p>
     * @param iconName The name of the image to be added
     *                 to the text pane
     **/
    public AddIconAction( String iconName ) {
        super( "Clear" );
        putValue( Action.SHORT_DESCRIPTION,
            "Insert an icon into the target" );
        this.iconName = iconName;
    }

    /**
     * Perform the action. If a textpane component can
     * be obtained from the event, add the icon. If not,
     * beep.
     * <p>
     * @param event The event causing us to be called.
     **/
    public void actionPerformed( ActionEvent event ) {
        JTextComponent target = getTextComponent( event );
        if( target instanceof JTextPane && iconName != null ) {
            Icon icon = new ImageIcon( iconName );
```

```
            ( ( JTextPane )target ).insertIcon( icon );
        } else {
            Toolkit.getDefaultToolkit().beep();
        }
    }

} // AddIconAction

/**
 * An action that adds a JLabel instance to
 * the target text pane when invoked.
 **/
class AddLabelAction extends TextAction {

    /**
     * The label for the JLabel instances
     * added to the text pane.
     **/
    private String labelText;

    /**
     * AddLabelAction, constructor.
     * <p>
     * @param labelText The text for the label added to the text pane
     **/
    public AddLabelAction( String labelText ) {
        super( "AddLabel" );
        putValue( Action.SHORT_DESCRIPTION,
            "Insert a label into the target" );
        this.labelText = labelText;
    }

    /**
     * Perform the action. If a textpane component can
     * be obtained from the event, add the label. If not,
     * beep.
     * <p>
     * @param event The event causing us to be called.
     **/
    public void actionPerformed( ActionEvent event ) {
        JTextComponent target = getTextComponent( event );
        if( target instanceof JTextPane && labelText != null ) {
            JLabel label = new JLabel( labelText );
            label.setOpaque( true );
            ( ( JTextPane )target ).insertComponent( label );
        } else {
            Toolkit.getDefaultToolkit().beep();
        }
    }

} // AddLabelAction

} // TextPaneIcons
```

New actions are created for clearing the text pane, inserting an icon, and inserting a component. These actions, as well as a few of the standard actions in the `DefaultEditorKit` class, are added to buttons placed to the bottom of the text pane. When the button labeled Icon is clicked, a new icon is inserted into the text pane at the caret location. Similarly, when the button labeled Label is pressed, a `JLabel` instance is inserted into the text pane. In each action, a new icon or label is created. This is because the same icon or label cannot be added to the text pane multiple times. These actions extend the `TextAction` class. This class is located in the `swing.text` package and extends the `AbstractAction` class.

The `TextAction` class contains the `getTextComponent` method that will find the `JTextComponent` associated with the given event. It will return `null` if a `JTextComponent` is not found. Using this method allows the text actions to not be bound to a single text component. This allows a single instance of each text action to be used with any number of text components.

HTML Content

The `HTMLEditorKit` is defined in the `swing.text.html` package. This editor kit understands HTML content. When an instance of this class is used as the editor kit in a `JEditorPane` instance, HTML content can be viewed in the component. The easiest way to achieve this configuration is to pass an editor pane a URL pointing to a reference containing HTML content.

The `TextPaneContent` application shown in Listing 7.11 creates a URL from the first argument passed to the application on the command line. The `setPage` method of the `JEditorPane` class is passed this URL. If the content type of the URL is HTML, the editor pane creates an `HTMLEditorKit` and sets it for the editor pane. The content is then displayed in the editor pane. Nothing else needs to be done by the programmer. Also, because the parameter to the `setPage` method is a URL, the content doesn't need to reside locally. The `getPage` method can be used to query the current page displayed in the editor pane. The `TextPaneContent` application is shown in Figure 7.11.

If the document associated with the editor pane is a descendant of the `AbstractDocument` class, the page specified in the `setPage` method may be loaded asynchronously. Setting the asynchronous load priority property of the document to a value greater than or equal to zero enables asynchronous loading of the page. Setting this property to a negative number forces synchronous loading of the page. The `setAsynchronousLoadPriority` method contained in the `AbstractDocument` class may be used to specify this property. The `getAsynchronousLoadPriority` may be used to query the current value of this unbound property.

FIGURE 7.11

The
TextPaneContent
application.

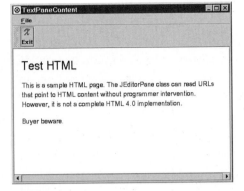

LISTING 7.11 THE TextPaneContent **APPLICATION**

```
package com.foley.test;

import java.awt.*;

import java.net.*;
import java.io.IOException;

import javax.swing.*;
import javax.swing.text.*;

import com.foley.utility.ApplicationFrame;


/**
 * An application that displays the given URL
 * in a text pane.
 *
 * @author Mike Foley
 **/
public class TextPaneContent extends Object {

    /**
     * Application entry point.
     * Create a frame, the text pane and display it.
     * Load the content of the URL passed as the
     * arguement to the application.
     * <p>
     * @param args A URL to load into the text pane.
     **/
    public static void main( String args[] ) {

        //
        // Ensure there is a parameter.
```

continues

LISTING 7.11   CONTINUED

```
            //
            if( args.length < 1 ) {
                System.err.println( "The URL of the content to load must " +
                                    "be passed as the first argument to " +
                                    "the application." );
                System.exit( -1 );
            }

            //
            // See if a URL can be made from the argument.
            //
            URL content = null;
            try {
                content = new URL( args[0] );
            } catch( MalformedURLException me ) {
                System.err.println( "Could not create a URL from the " +
                                    "parameter passed to the application.\n"
                                    + args[0] );
                System.exit( -2 );
            }
            JFrame frame = new ApplicationFrame( "TextPaneContent" );

            JEditorPane editorPane = new JEditorPane();

            try {
                editorPane.setPage( content );
            } catch( IOException io ) {
                System.err.println( "Could not load content from the URL\n" +
                                    content );
                System.exit( -3 );
            }
            frame.getContentPane().add( new JScrollPane( editorPane ),
                                BorderLayout.CENTER );
            frame.pack();
            frame.setVisible( true );

        } // main

} // TextPaneContent
```

> **NOTE**
>
> The JEditorPane shows tremendous promise for handling HTML content.
> However, the current editor kit implementation isn't complete. The editor pane
> throws an exception when keystrokes are pressed in the component. These
> problems limit the usage of the HTML editor kit to only displaying simple HTML
> content.

RTF Content

The RTFEditorKit is defined in the swing.text.rtf package. This editor kit understands rich text format (RTF) content. When an instance of this class is used as the editor kit in a JEditorPane instance, RTF content can be viewed in the component.

The TextPaneContent application presented in the previous section will display a URL containing RTF content as well as HTML content. This is because the JEditorPane class will create an RTFEditorKit and set it for the editor pane when a URL with RTF content is set for the editor. Once again, nothing else needs to be done by the programmer. The TextPaneContent application loaded with RTF content is shown in Figure 7.12.

FIGURE 7.12

RTF content in the
TextPaneContent
application.

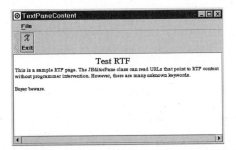

> **NOTE**
>
> The JEditorPane class's handling of RTF content suffers some of the same shortcomings as its handling of HTML content. The current editor kit implementation doesn't recognize many RTF keywords. Once again, the usage of the RTF editor kit is limited to only displaying simple RTF content.

Content Handling Methods

The JEditorPane also recognizes plain text content. In this case, a plain text editor kit is created and set for the editor pane. These content types are registered during the static initialization of the JEditorPane class. The code that performs this operation is shown next. The registerEditorKitForContentType method is called for each content type that the editor pane has editor kits. The registerEditorKitForContentType method manages a hashtable where the content type is the key and the name of the class to be used as the editor kit for that content type is the value.

The createEditorKitForContentType method can be used to create an editor for one of the known content types. This method takes the String content type as a parameter and returns the editor kit it creates. It returns `null` if the type has not been registered or if any other error occurs. The `JEditorPane` class does not contain a method to query the known content types.

```
registerEditorKitForContentType("text/plain",
    " javax.swing.JEditorPane$PlainEditorKit");
registerEditorKitForContentType("text/html",
    " javax.swing.text.html.HTMLEditorKit");
registerEditorKitForContentType("text/rtf",
    " javax.swing.text.rtf.RTFEditorKit");
registerEditorKitForContentType("application/rtf",
    " javax.swing.text.rtf.RTFEditorKit");
```

If you create an editor kit that you want to handle a content type, it must be registered by using the `registerEditorKitForContentType` method, just as the `JEditorPane` class does for text, HTML, and RTF content. Similarly, if you write a better version of the HTML or RTF editor pane, that class needs to be registered with the `JEditorPane` class for it to be used instead of the version shipped with the JFC.

The content type can be explicitly set for an editor pane. Calling the `setContentType` method and passing it the name of the content type to set for the editor creates the proper editor kit and sets it for the editor pane. If an unknown content type is passed to this method, it silently fails. The `getContentType` method returns the name of content currently being viewed in the editor.

Summary

The text components in the JFC contain basic components that provide lightweight replacements for the AWT textual components. However, these components are built by using the Model View Controller architecture that is common to most JFC components. The model is defined by the `Document` interface. This interface provides a more detailed representation than the `JTextArea` or `JTextField` class can render. To address this deficit, the `JTextPane` and `JEditorPane` classes are provided. These classes are able to render the marked-up text represented in the document model.

The concept of an editor kit has been defined to encapsulate a particular textual content. By creating an editor kit, any type of content can be handled in the document. Editor kits are provided that understand HTML and RTF data formats.

The combination of the `Document` interface, the `JEditorPane` class, and the editor kits provides a substantial enhancement over the textual components provided in the AWT. Using these components with the editor kits provided is a relatively easy task. However, to add custom functionality to an editor kit or to create an editor kit requires a far deeper understanding of the text package. This chapter gives an introduction to the deeper understanding required to achieve this functionality, as well as providing examples of using the editor kits provided by the JFC.

Frame Windows

CHAPTER

8

A frame is a top level window that typically contains a title, various window decorations such as a border, and minimize and maximize buttons. The JFC provides the `JFrame` class for use as a top level frame. In this chapter you will learn:

- How to use the `JFrame` class
- See the various panels created in a `JFrame` instance
- How to create an applet by using JFC components
- How to create a Splash Window by using the `JWindow` class

The JFrame Class

The JFC `JFrame` class is an extension to the AWT `Frame` class. An instance of the `JFrame` class is a heavyweight component. It creates a top-level window that can be positioned and sized independently of other windows. The `JFrame` instance is managed by the system window manager. The window manager typically adds window decorations to the frame. The decorations can allow the user to interactively resize the window, position the window, and iconify the window.

Creating and displaying an instance of the `JFrame` class is a simple matter. The following code snippet creates a frame with the title of `Frame Test`. The second line sets the frame's visibility to `true`, which has the effect of displaying the frame. Passing the `setVisible` method a value of `false` will hide a currently displayed window. The frame created when using the Windows look-and-feel is shown in Figure 8.1.

```
JFrame frame = new JFrame( "Frame Test" );
frame.setVisible( true );
```

Figure 8.1

Simple frame.

The simple frame created in Figure 8.1 is resizable. It contains the default Java icon on the far left of the titlebar, the specified title in the center of the titlebar, the minimize and maximize buttons, as well as a close button to the far right of the titlebar. These are the default window decorations for the Microsoft Windows look-and-feel. As simple as this frame is, there are many useful operations available. Most of these are inherited from the AWT `Frame` and `Window` classes. The most common of these methods will be presented here, but a complete description of the AWT classes is beyond the scope of this book.

The icon can be changed to any image by using the setIconImage method. The current image can be queried with the getIconImage method. The title of the frame can be queried and set after construction by calling the setTitle and getTitle methods, respectively.

The frame's resizable state can be set with the setResizable method. This method takes a boolean parameter that specifies whether the frame should be resizable or not. The current value of this property can be queried with the isResizable method.

It is often desirable to have the cursor set for every component in a frame. Since the JFrame class is a descendent of the AWT Component class, the cursor can be set for an instance of a JFrame. Setting the cursor for the frame will have the effect of setting the cursor for each component contained in that frame which has not explicitly set its own cursor. The setCursor method can be used to set the cursor to any cursor defined in the AWT Cursor class. How to create a custom cursor is described in Chapter 27, "Custom Cursors." The cursor will be set for the center of the frame. The window manager sets the cursor for the frame's titlebar and border.

The following example listing, Listing 8.1, gives a complete application that creates a frame and configures it by using some of the methods presented in the previous paragraphs. The resulting frame contains an image in its titlebar, cannot be resized, and uses the cross-hair cursor defined in the AWT Cursor class. The resulting active and non-active frames are shown in Figure 8.2. Notice how setting the resizable property of the frame to false removes the icon and full-screen window decorations from the upper-right of the titlebar.

LISTING 8.1   THE FrameTest APPLICATION

```
package com.foley.test;

import java.awt.*;
import javax.swing.*;


/**
 * An application that displays a frame that
 * may not be resized; has an image, and a cross
 * hair cursor.
 *
 * @author Mike Foley
 **/
public class FrameTest extends Object {
```

continues

8

FRAME WINDOWS

LISTING 8.1   CONTINUED

```java
/**
 * Application entry point.
 * Create the frame, and display it.
 *
 * @param args Command line parameter. Not used.
 **/
public static void main( String args[] ) {

    try {
        UIManager.setLookAndFeel(
            "com.sun.java.swing.plaf.windows.WindowsLookAndFeel" );
    } catch( Exception ex ) {
        System.err.println( "Exception: " +
                            ex.getLocalizedMessage() );
    }

    JFrame frame = new JFrame();

    //
    // Assume .gif is in current directory.
    //
    frame.setIconImage(
        ( new ImageIcon( "bullseye.gif" ) ).getImage() );

    frame.setTitle( "Test Frame" );
    frame.setResizable( false );
    frame.setSize( 200, 200 );
    frame.setCursor(
        Cursor.getPredefinedCursor( Cursor.CROSSHAIR_CURSOR ) );

    frame.setVisible( true );

} // main

} // FrameTest
```

FIGURE 8.2

Non-resizable frame.

The `JFrame` class is a descendant of the AWT `Window` class. It will generate the `WindowEvents` defined for that class. The `WindowEvent` class is presented in Listing 8.2. These events are delivered by calling the methods in the `WindowListener` interface shown in Listing 8.3.

LISTING 8.2   THE WindowEvent CLASS

```
public class  WindowEvent
    extends java.awt.event.ComponentEvent
{
        // Fields 10
    public static final int WINDOW_ACTIVATED;
    public static final int WINDOW_CLOSED;
    public static final int WINDOW_CLOSING;
    public static final int WINDOW_DEACTIVATED;
    public static final int WINDOW_DEICONIFIED;
    public static final int WINDOW_FIRST;
    public static final int WINDOW_ICONIFIED;
    public static final int WINDOW_LAST;
    public static final int WINDOW_OPENED;
    private static final long serialVersionUID;

        // Constructors 1
    public WindowEvent(Window, int);

        // Methods 2
    public Window getWindow();
    public String paramString();
}
```

LISTING 8.3   THE WindowListener INTERFACE

```
public interface  WindowListener
    extends java.util.EventListener
{
        // Methods 7
    public abstract void windowActivated(WindowEvent);
    public abstract void windowClosed(WindowEvent);
    public abstract void windowClosing(WindowEvent);
    public abstract void windowDeactivated(WindowEvent);
    public abstract void windowDeiconified(WindowEvent);
    public abstract void windowIconified(WindowEvent);
    public abstract void windowOpened(WindowEvent);
}
```

8

FRAME WINDOWS

To demonstrate some of the methods described previously, they are added to the simple frame created at the beginning of this section. Listing 8.4 contains a new example JFrame. This time, the default JFrame constructor is called. The title is set in the WindowListener instance added to the frame, so it doesn't need to be specified at construction time. The setIconImage method is called in the WindowListener when the frame is iconified or de-iconified. This method sets the frame's icon to the given image. The setIconImage method is contained in the AWT Frame method and inherited by JFrame. This explains why an image is passed to this method rather than an icon as in most JFC methods. The desired size of the window is set to 200×200 pixels. The cursor is set to the hand cursor, which is one of the predefined cursors defined in the AWT Cursor class. Finally, the frame is displayed by calling setVisible with the parameter of true.

LISTING 8.4   ADDING A WindowListener TO THE JFrame

```
package com.foley.test;

import java.awt.*;
import java.awt.event.*;
import javax.swing.*;


/**
 * An application that displays a frame that
 * may not be resized; has an image, and a cross
 * hair cursor.
 *
 * @author Mike Foley
 **/
public class FrameTest extends Object {

    /**
     * Application entry point.
     * Create the frame, and display it.
     *
     * @param args Command line parameter. Not used.
     **/
    public static void main( String args[] ) {

        try {
            UIManager.setLookAndFeel(
                "com.sun.java.swing.plaf.windows.WindowsLookAndFeel" );
        } catch( Exception ex ) {
            System.err.println( "Exception: " + ex.getLocalizedMessage()
);
        }

        //
        // Assume .gif is in current directory.
        //
        final Image bullseye =
                ( new ImageIcon( "bullseye.gif" ) ).getImage();
        final Image bullseye2 =
                ( new ImageIcon( "bullseye2.gif" ) ).getImage();

        final JFrame frame = new JFrame();
```

```
        frame.setIconImage( bullseye );

        frame.setSize( 200, 200 );
        frame.setCursor(
            Cursor.getPredefinedCursor( Cursor.HAND_CURSOR ) );

        frame.setVisible( true );

        frame.addWindowListener( new WindowListener() {
            public void windowActivated( WindowEvent e ) {
                frame.setTitle( "Active" );
                System.out.println( "windowActivated " + e );
            }
            public void windowClosed( WindowEvent e ) {
                System.out.println( "windowClosed " + e );
            }
            public void windowClosing( WindowEvent e ) {
                System.out.println( "windowClosing " + e );
            }
            public void windowDeactivated( WindowEvent e ) {
                frame.setTitle( "Not Active" );
                System.out.println( "windowDeactivated " + e );
            }
            public void windowDeiconified( WindowEvent e ) {
                frame.setIconImage( bullseye );
                System.out.println( "windowDeiconified " + e );
            }
            public void windowIconified( WindowEvent e ) {
                frame.setIconImage( bullseye2 );
                System.out.println( "windowIconified " + e );
            }
            public void windowOpened( WindowEvent e ) {
                System.out.println( "windowOpened " + e );
            }
        } );

    } // main

} // FrameTest
```

A WindowListener is added to the frame to capture WindowEvents. The WindowListener is a very simple class that prints each event when it is received. It also sets the frame's title in the windowActivated and windowDeactivated methods. The icon is set in the windowIconified and windowDeiconified methods. This WindowListener can be used to determine the order in which WindowEvents are delivered to an instance of the JFrame class. The instance created by executing this code is shown in Figure 8.3. The console printout from running the application and interacting with the frame is shown in Figure 8.4. In this figure, comments have been added to clarify what operation was taking place before the WindowEvents were delivered to the WindowListener instance.

FIGURE 8.3

Enhanced frame.

FIGURE 8.4

Results from enhanced frame interaction.

```
// frame displayed and activated.
windowOpened java.awt.event.WindowEvent[WINDOW_OPENED]
on frame1
windowActivated
java.awt.event.WindowEvent[WINDOW_ACTIVATED] on frame1

// another frame is activated.
windowDeactivated
java.awt.event.WindowEvent[WINDOW_DEACTIVATED] on frame1

// frame is activated, and iconified
windowActivated
java.awt.event.WindowEvent[WINDOW_ACTIVATED] on frame1
windowIconified
java.awt.event.WindowEvent[WINDOW_ICONIFIED] on frame1
windowDeactivated
java.awt.event.WindowEvent[WINDOW_DEACTIVATED] on frame1

// frame is restored
windowActivated
java.awt.event.WindowEvent[WINDOW_ACTIVATED] on frame1
windowDeiconified
java.awt.event.WindowEvent[WINDOW_DEICONIFIED] on frame1
windowActivated
java.awt.event.WindowEvent[WINDOW_ACTIVATED] on frame1

// frame closed
windowClosing java.awt.event.WindowEvent[WINDOW_CLOSING]
on frame1
windowDeactivated
java.awt.event.WindowEvent[WINDOW_DEACTIVATED] on frame1
```

NOTE

This example showed how to catch window events when the frame is iconified and deiconified. An application can set the iconified state of a frame by passing the Frame.ICONIFIED or Frame.NORMAL constant as the parameter to the setState method inherited from the AWT Frame class. The current state of this property may be queried by calling the getState method.

The previous example demonstrates many features of a frame, but to this point nothing has been displayed in the frame. The next section describes how to use the features of the JFrame class to display components in the frame.

Panels Created by `JFrame`

The previous discussion of `JFrame` methods was focused on the methods inherited from AWT classes. This section is the first that discusses the enhancements introduced by the `JFrame` class. Differences from the AWT `Frame` class will also be presented.

To add content to an AWT `Frame`, the `add` method is used. The AWT `Frame` comes configured with a `BorderLayout`. To add a `JLabel` as the only component in an AWT `Frame`, the following code snippet would be used.

```
Frame f = new Frame();
f.add( new JLabel( "Test Label" ), BorderLayout.CENTER );
```

This is not the technique to use when adding components to an instance of the `JFrame` class. The `JFrame` instance comes configured with a single child, an instance of the `JRootPane` class. The `JRootPane` creates a hierarchy of children, of which components are added to the `contentPane`. The `JRootPane` is described in detail in the next section. When using an instance of the `JFrame` class, the last example would be changed to the following:

```
JFrame f = new JFrame();
f.getContentPane().add( new JLabel( "Test Label" ), BorderLayout.CENTER );
```

As can be seen in the example, the `JLabel` instance is not added to the frame itself. Rather, the `contentPane` is obtained by using the `getContentPane` method that returns an instance of a `Container`. The default `contentPane` is an instance of the `JPanel` class. It is to this pane that the label is added. From the example, it is seen that the `contentPane` comes configured with a `BorderLayout`. If a different layout manager is called for, it should be set on the `contentPane`, not the frame itself. Requiring components to be added to the `contentPane` and layout managers set on the `contentPane` is incompatible with the AWT `Frame` class. This incompatibility is a common source of programming errors. To aid in finding this type of programming bug, the `JFrame` class throws an error if a component is added to the frame directly or to a layout manager set for the frame. Extensions of the `JFrame` class can disable this checking by calling the protected `setRootPaneCheckingEnabled` method with a parameter of `false`. Similarly, the `isRootPaneCheckingEnabled` method can be used to query the state of the `rootPaneCheckingEnabled` property. Both of these methods are protected and cannot be called from general-purpose frame clients. The default state for this property is `false`, disabling root pane checking.

8

FRAME WINDOWS

The JFrame class allows the program to specify the action to be taken when the frame is closed via a window decoration or some other method outside the program's control. The AWT Frame doesn't do anything in this circumstance. Thus, if the program wants the frame to close, a WindowListener has to be added to the frame, and the appropriate method implemented to perform this task. The JFrame contains the defaultCloseOperation property that specifies what to do when the frame is closed by using such an operation. The possible values for this property are HIDE_ON_CLOSE, DISPOSE_ON_CLOSE, and DO_NOTHING_ON_CLOSE. The default value, HIDE_ON_CLOSE, hides the window but does not dispose of it. This close option allows the frame to be reused. However, it is the application's responsibility to dispose of the frame when it is no longer needed. The second possible value for the defaultCloseOperation property is DISPOSE_ON_CLOSE. When this value is specified, the window is not only closed, it is also disposed of. The final possible value is DO_NOTHING_ON_CLOSE. As the name implies, this option does nothing when the user initiates a close operation. It is the application's responsibility to perform the correct action. This option is compatible with the AWT Frame close operation. The defaultCloseOperation property is not a bound property.

This is an example of where type-safe constants would be a benefit to the JFC. The parameter to the setDefaultCloseOperation is defined as an int, rather than a defined type. This allows any valid int to be passed to this method, even though there are only three legal values. If a type is defined for the parameter, the compiler can verify that a valid parameter is passed to this method. Furthermore, the JFrame class does not validate the int passed to the method. At a bare minimum, an IllegalArgumentException should be thrown by the setDefaultCloseOperation method if an integer other than one of the constants defined for this property is passed to the method.

The setDefaultCloseOperation method can be used to specify the defaultCloseOperation property. One of the constants described in the previous paragraph is passed as the lone parameter to this method. The current defaultCloseOperation can be queried with the getDefaultCloseOperation method. The following code snippet can be added to the previous frame example to demonstrate the defaultCloseOperation property. Once added, the frame will not be closed if the close button on the frame's titlebar is pressed.

```
frame.setDefaultCloseOperation( JFrame.DO_NOTHING_ON_CLOSE );
System.out.println( frame.getDefaultCloseOperation() );
```

The JRootPane Class

An instance of the JFrame class contains exactly one child, an instance of the JRootPane class. The JRootPane in turn creates and manages multiple children. The hierarchy of instances created by the JRootPane instance is shown in Figure 8.5.

FIGURE 8.5

JRootPane child instances.

The `glassPane` is a `JPanel` instance that is added first to the `rootPane`, but is normally not shown. This allows the `glassPane` to receive all mouse input events and draw on top of all other children contained in the `rootPane` when shown. The `layeredPane` is an instance of the `JLayeredPane` class. This instance manages the `contentPane` and optional `menuBar`. The default `contentPane` is an instance of the `JPanel` class. The `menuBar`, if present, is an instance of the `JMenuBar` class. Both these instances are placed in the `FRAME_CONTENT_LAYER` of the `layeredPane`. The `glassPane`, `layeredPane`, and `contentPane` are guaranteed to be non-null for an unmodified `JFrame` instance.

The `JRootPane` instance creates a private layout manager to manage its children. The `glassPane` is expanded to cover the entire screen space given to the `rootPane`. When the `glassPane` is visible, all of its children components are drawn above other components in the `rootPane` and receive all the mouse events. The `layeredPane` is also sized to fill the entire viewable area given to the `rootPane`. If there is a `menuBar`, the `layeredPane` positions it across the top of its viewable area. The `contentPane` is given the remainder of the viewable area. If other windows are added to the `rootPane`, the custom layout manager ignores them. If an application adds a layout manager to the `rootPane`, it is the responsibility of that layout manager to position the `rootPane`'s standard children.

The `JFrame` class contains methods for querying and setting each of the panes used in the frame. These methods follow the JavaBeans naming convention and are listed in Table 8.1.

TABLE 8.1   `JFrame` PANE METHODS

Setter Method	Getter Method	Affected Pane
setContentPane	getContentPane	contentPane
setGlassPane	getGlassPane	glassPane
setLayeredPane	getLayeredPane	layeredPane
setRootPane	getRootPane	rootPane

The `layeredPane` is responsible for positioning the menu bar. However, the `JFrame` class provides convenient methods for setting and getting the menu bar. These are `setJMenuBar` and `getJMenuBar`, respectively. Using menus in the JFC will be covered extensively in the next chapter.

8

FRAME WINDOWS

A common use for the glassPane is to block input events from the components in the contentPane. This is typically accompanied by displaying the predefined wait cursor. Listing 8.5 presents an application that creates a single button in the frame's contentPane. When clicked, the ActionListener registered for the button sets the wait cursor on the frame's glassPane and displays it. An empty MouseAdapter is added to the glassPane to receive capture mouse events. This has the effect of catching all mouse events before the button receives them. Thus, clicking the button when the wait cursor is displayed will not have any effect. This simple application does not contain an action to remove the glassPane. However, passing the setVisible method the parameter false does this. This will be presented in the next section. The application, after pressing the button, is shown in Figure 8.6.

LISTING 8.5   USING THE glassPane CONTAINED IN THE JFrame CLASS

```
package com.foley.test;

import java.awt.*;
import java.awt.event.*;
import javax.swing.*;


/**
 * An application that displays a frame.
 * It demonstrates the glassPane in the JFrame class.
 *
 * @author Mike Foley
 **/
public class GlassPaneTest extends Object {

    private static JComponent createContent() {
        JPanel content = new JPanel();
        JButton addButton = new JButton( "Add Glass Pane" );
        content.add( addButton );
        addButton.addActionListener( new ActionListener() {
            public void actionPerformed( ActionEvent e ) {
Component root = SwingUtilities.getRoot( ( Component )
➥e.getSource() );
                if( root instanceof JFrame ) {
                    JFrame frame = ( JFrame )root;

                    Component glassPane = frame.getGlassPane();
                    glassPane.addMouseListener( new MouseAdapter() {} );
glassPane.setCursor( Cursor.getPredefinedCursor
➥( Cursor.WAIT_CURSOR ) );
                    glassPane.setVisible( true );
                }
            }
```

```
    } );

    return( content );
}

/**
 * Application entry point.
 * Create the frame, and display it.
 *
 * @param args Command line parameter. Not used.
 **/
public static void main( String args[] ) {

    JFrame frame = new JFrame( "Glass Pane Test" );

    frame.getContentPane().add( createContent(),
                                BorderLayout.CENTER );

    frame.pack();

    frame.setVisible( true );

} // main

} // GlassPaneTest
```

FIGURE 8.6

The
GlassPaneTest
application.

Extending **JFrame** and Overriding the **frameInit** Method

Many applications define an extension to the JFrame class that is used as a frame by that application. The extended frame class is customized for the application. The JFrame class provides hooks to be used by extensions to customize the resulting frame instance. Instead of creating the JRootPane instance in the JFrame constructor, the protected frameInit method is called. This method enables window and keyboard events, sets the background color, and calls the protected createRootPane method. By overriding this method, the rootPane can be modified or entirely replaced. The signatures for these two protected methods are as follows:

```
protected void frameInit();
protected JRootPane createRootPane();
```

The JRootPane instance behaves similarly to the JFrame instance. It doesn't simply create its children in the constructor. Instead, it calls protected create methods. This allows children to alter the behavior of any, or all, of the child panes. These protected methods are defined as follows:

```
protected Component createGlassPane();
protected JLayeredPane createLayeredPane();
protected Container createContentPane();
```

Complete guidelines and examples of extending JFC components are given in Part V, "Extending JFC Components."

The ApplicationFrame class, shown in Listing 8.6, presents an extension of the JFrame class. This class overrides the frameInit method to set the application's icon. In the frameInit method, the super frameInit is first called to create the standard JFrame panes. Only after this call has been completed can the extension use the contentPane, or any of the other panes, normally available in a JFrame instance. The ApplicationFrame class follows the lead of the JFrame itself by not creating the application components; instead, it calls a protected method that performs this task. This allows the ApplicationFrame to be extended to replace the inside of the frame by overriding the createApplicationContent method, but still allows the extension to keep the decorations established by the ApplicationFrame class. In the next chapter, you will see how to add more interesting menus and a complete toolbar. The ApplicationFrame class contains the setWaitCursorVisible method that will show or hide the glassPane, depending on the boolean parameter passed to the method. The wait cursor is set on the glassPane when it is displayed. This provides an easy way to display the wait cursor and block mouse events from components in the contentPane.

LISTING 8.6   THE ApplicationFrame CLASS

```
package com.foley.utility;

import java.awt.*;

import java.awt.event.*;

import java.io.Serializable;

import javax.swing.*;

import javax.swing.border.*;

import javax.swing.event.*;
```

```
/**
 * A toplevel frame. The frame customizes the
 * Icon and content in the frameInit method.
 *
 * @author Mike Foley
 **/
public class ApplicationFrame extends JFrame implements Serializable {

    /**
     * MouserAdapter to consume mouse events on glassPane.
     **/
    private MouseAdapter ourMouseAdapter;


    /**
     * ApplicationFrame, null constructor.
     **/
    public ApplicationFrame() {
        this( null );
    }


    /**
     * ApplicationFrame, constructor.
     *
     * @param title The title for the frame.
     **/
    public ApplicationFrame( String title ) {
        super( title );
    }


    /**
     * Customize the frame for our application.
     **/
    protected void frameInit() {
        //
        // Let the super create the panes.
        super.frameInit();

        ourMouseAdapter = new MouseAdapter() {};

        Image bullseye = new ImageIcon( "bullseye.gif" ).getImage();
        setIconImage( bullseye );

        JMenuBar menuBar = createMenu();
        setJMenuBar( menuBar );

        JToolBar toolBar = createToolBar();
        Container content = getContentPane();
```

continues

LISTING 8.6 CONTINUED

```
        content.add( BorderLayout.NORTH, toolBar );

        createApplicationContent();

    } // frameInit


    /**
     * Create the content for the application
     **/
    protected void createApplicationContent() {
    } // createApplicationContent


    /**
     * Create the menu for the frame.
     *
     * @return the menu for the frame.
     **/
    protected JMenuBar createMenu() {
        JMenuBar menuBar = new JMenuBar();

        JMenu file = new JMenu( "File" );
        file.setMnemonic( KeyEvent.VK_F );

        JMenuItem item;

        item = new JMenuItem( "Exit", exitIcon );
        item.setHorizontalTextPosition( SwingConstants.RIGHT );
        item.setMnemonic( KeyEvent.VK_X );
        item.setAccelerator( KeyStroke.getKeyStroke(
                             KeyEvent.VK_X, Event.CTRL_MASK ) );
        item.addActionListener( new ActionListener() {
            public void actionPerformed( ActionEvent e ) {
                System.exit( 0 );
            }
        } );
        file.add( item );

        menuBar.add( file );
        return( menuBar );

    } // createMenuBar


    /**
     * Create the mouse listener for the frame.
     *
     * @return the MouseListener for the content in the frame.
```

```
    **/
    protected MouseListener createMouseListener() {
        return new ApplicationMouseListener();
    }

    protected JToolBar createToolBar() {
        final JToolBar toolBar = new JToolBar();
        toolBar.setFloatable( false );
        toolBar.add( new ExitAction() );
        return( toolBar );
    }


    /**
     * Show or hide the wait cursor. The wait cursor
     * is set on the glass pane so input mouse events
     * are blocked from other components.
     * <p>
     * @param waitCursorVisible True to show the wait cursor,
     *                          False to hide the wait cursor.
     **/
    public void setWaitCursorVisible( boolean waitCursorVisible ) {
        Component glassPane = getGlassPane();
        if( waitCursorVisible ) {
            //
            // Show the wait cursor.
            //
            glassPane.addMouseListener( ourMouseAdapter );
            glassPane.setCursor(
                    Cursor.getPredefinedCursor( Cursor.WAIT_CURSOR ) );
            glassPane.setVisible( true );
        } else {
            //
            // Hide the wait cursor.
            //
            glassPane.removeMouseListener( ourMouseAdapter );
            glassPane.setCursor(
                Cursor.getPredefinedCursor( Cursor.DEFAULT_CURSOR ) );
            glassPane.setVisible( false );
        }
    }
}

} // ApplicationFrame
```

The ApplicationFrame class can be tested by altering the main method in the FrameTest application given at the start of this chapter. The main method can create an instance of the ApplicationFrame class instead of the JFrame class. The following is a possible version of the new main method:

```
public static void main( String args[] ) {

    //
    // Create an ApplicationFrame instead of a JFrame
    // The return type may still be declared as a JFrame, since
    // ApplicationFrame extends JFrame.
    //
    JFrame frame = new ApplicationFrame( "Test ApplicationFrame" );
    frame.setSize( 200, 200 );
    frame.setVisible( true );

} // main
```

The resulting frame as defined in the `ApplicationFrame` class is shown in Figure 8.7.

FIGURE 8.7

An `ApplicationFrame` *instance.*

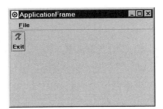

JApplet

The `JApplet` class is an extension of the AWT `Applet` class. This class is the preferred entry point when creating applets that contain JFC components. The structure of the `JApplet` class is the same as the `JFrame` class. It contains one child, an instance of the `JRootPane` class. When adding children or setting the layout manager for the applet, the content pane is used rather than the instance of the `JApplet` class itself. The applet can create instances of the `JFrame` class to be displayed outside the browser if desired.

The `JApplet` itself is configured similarly to the `JFrame` class presented in the previous section. It contains a single child, an instance of the `JRootPane` class. Thus, as with `JFrame` instances, components are not added directly to a `JApplet` instance. Instead, they are added to its `contentPane`. Also, the methods to query the panes in the `JFrame` listed in Table 8.1 are also available in the `JApplet` class.

The `JApplet` class extends the AWT `Applet` class, so the familiar `init`, `destroy`, `start`, and `stop` methods are used for `JApplet` programming. The `SimpleApplet` class is presented in Listing 8.7. This class creates an applet containing the same children components that create a simple form. The `SimpleApplet` class performs its initialization in the `init` method that is overridden from the AWT `Applet` class. This method calls the `createAppletContent` method to perform the actual work. This allows extensions of the `SimpleApplet` class to easily modify the content contained in the applet. In the

createAppletContent method, the contentPane is obtained from the JApplet instance.
This is the pane where applets should add their components.

LISTING 8.7   SimpleApplet CLASS

```
package com.foley.test;

import java.awt.*;
import javax.swing.*;

/**
 * A simple Applet that uses JFC Components.
 **/
public class SimpleApplet extends JApplet {

    public SimpleApplet() {
        super();
    }

    /**
     * Create components for our applet.
     **/
    public void init() {
        //
        // Let the super do its work.
        super.init();

        createAppletContent();

    } // init

    /**
     * Create the content for the applet
     **/
    protected void createAppletContent() {

        Container content = getContentPane();
        content.setLayout( new GridLayout( 4, 2 ) );
        content.add( new JLabel( "Name: ", SwingConstants.RIGHT ) );
        content.add( new JTextField() );
        content.add( new JLabel( "Street: ", SwingConstants.RIGHT ) );
        content.add( new JTextField() );
content.add( new JLabel( "City and State: ",
➥SwingConstants.RIGHT ) );
        content.add( new JTextField() );
        content.add( new JLabel( "zip Code: ", SwingConstants.RIGHT ) );
        content.add( new JTextField() );

    } // createAppletContent

} // SimpleApplet
```

To use the `SimpleApplet` class, an HTML page is required for use in a Java-enabled browser or in the Appletviewer utility program contained in the Java Development Kit. The following is a very simple HTML page for the test applet. The resulting applet as displayed in the Appletviewer is shown in Figure 8.8.

```
<HTML>
<HEAD>
<TITLE> The SimpleApplet Test Page </TITLE>
</HEAD>
<BODY>

The SimpleApplet:

<APPLET CODE="com.foley.test.SimpleApplet.class" WIDTH=400 HEIGHT=70>
</APPLET>
</BODY>
</HTML>
```

FIGURE 8.8

A `SimpleApplet` *instance in a browser.*

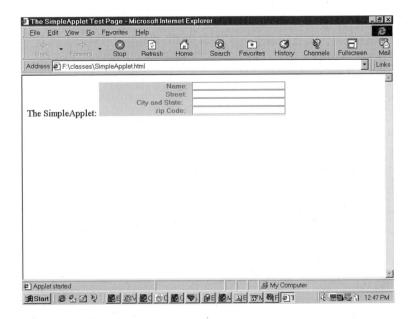

The `JWindow` Class

The `JWindow` class extends the AWT `Window` class. It provides a window that the caller is responsible for managing. Unlike instances of the `JFrame` class, instances of the `JWindow` class do not contain window decorations. The majority of `Component` instances are bound by the frame in which they are contained. The `JWindow` doesn't contain this restriction.

The window can be placed anywhere on the display. Typical uses for `JWindow` instances in the JFC are pop-up menus and ToolTips.

The `JWindow` class structure is the same as the `JFrame` class. It creates a single child that is an instance of the `JRootPane` class. When adding or enumerating the children of the window, the content pane must be used. A handle to the content pane is obtained with the `getContentPane` method. In fact, all the methods listed in Table 8.1 for the `JFrame` class are available for use with the `JWindow` class. See the `JFrame` discussion earlier in this chapter for a complete description of using the panes created by the `JRootPane` class.

A `JWindow` can be used to create a "splash" window. The splash window is displayed quickly after an application begins, and is displayed while it is initializing. It often contains a company logo and copyright notice but not a titlebar, menu, or other window decorations typically found on a frame. The `SplashWindow` class shown next implements such a window. It extends the `JWindow` class, so it will not contain a titlebar or resize borders. This class will display an icon centered on the screen. The class creates a `JLabel` instance for displaying the icon and adds this label to the center of its content pane. The `setVisible` method is extended to center the window on the screen before its parent's `setVisible` method is called to create and display the window.

`Icon` in the `SplashWindow` class is a bound property. Since the `SplashWindow` class is not a descendant of the `JComponent` class, it can not utilize the `PropertyChangeSupport` contained in that class. As such, the `SplashWindow` class manages `PropertyChangeListeners` itself. However, in a future release of the AWT and JFC, the `PropertyChangeSupport` is going to be moved from the `JComponent` class to the AWT `Component` class. At this time, the `PropertyChangeListener` support contained in the `SplashWindow` class can be removed, because the functionality will be inherited from the `Component` class.

```
package com.foley.utility;

import java.awt.*;
import java.beans.*;
import javax.swing.*;


/**
 * A window that contains an image.
 *
 * @author Mike Foley
 **/
public class SplashWindow extends JWindow {

    /**
     * The icon displayed in the window.
```

```
**/
private Icon splashIcon;

/**
 * A label used to display the icon.
 **/
private JLabel iconLabel;

/**
 * Bound property support, and name constants.
 **/
private PropertyChangeSupport changeSupport;
public static final String SPLASHICON_PROPERTY = "SplashIcon";


/**
 * SplashWindow, null constructor.
 **/
public SplashWindow() {
    this( null );
}


/**
 * SplashWindow, constructor.
 *
 * @param splashIcon The icon to view in the window.
 **/
public SplashWindow( Icon splashIcon ) {
    super();
    iconLabel = new JLabel();
    iconLabel.setBorder( BorderFactory.createRaisedBevelBorder() );
    getContentPane().add( iconLabel, BorderLayout.CENTER );
    setSplashIcon( splashIcon );
}


/**
 * Set the image displayed in the window.
 * This is a bound property named SPLASHICON_PROPERTY.
 * If this property is changed when the window is
 * visible, the window is NOT re-centered on the screen.
 *
 * @param splashIcon The icon to draw in the window.
 **/
public void setSplashIcon( Icon splashIcon ) {
    Icon old = this.splashIcon;
    this.splashIcon = splashIcon;
    iconLabel.setIcon( splashIcon );
    pack();
    if( changeSupport != null ) {
```

```
changeSupport.firePropertyChange( SPLASHICON_PROPERTY,
➥old, splashIcon );
        }
    }


    /**
     * Extend the setVisible method to center this window
     * on the screen before being displayed.
     *
     * @param visible True if showing the window, false if hiding.
     **/
    public void setVisible( boolean visible ) {

        if( visible ) {

            //
            // Display the window in the center of the screen.
            //
Dimension screenSize =
➥Toolkit.getDefaultToolkit().getScreenSize();
            Dimension size = getSize();
            int x;
            int y;

            x = screenSize.width / 2 - size.width / 2;
            y = screenSize.height / 2 - size.height / 2;

                setBounds( x, y, size.width, size.height);
        }

        //
        // Let super show or hide the window.
        //
        super.setVisible( visible );
    }


    /**
     * Need to handle PropertyChangeListeners here until this
     * type of code is moved from JComponent to Component.
     **/
    public synchronized void addPropertyChangeListener(
        PropertyChangeListener listener ) {
        if (changeSupport == null) {
            changeSupport = new PropertyChangeSupport(this);
        }
        changeSupport.addPropertyChangeListener(listener);
    }
    public synchronized void removePropertyChangeListener(
        PropertyChangeListener listener ) {
```

```
        if (changeSupport != null) {
            changeSupport.removePropertyChangeListener(listener);
        }
    }
}

} // SplashWindow
```

Listing 8.8 contains a simple application to test the `SplashWindow` class. It simply loads an icon and then creates and displays the `SplashWindow`. The resulting window is shown in Figure 8.9.

FIGURE 8.9

An example of a
`SplashWindow`.

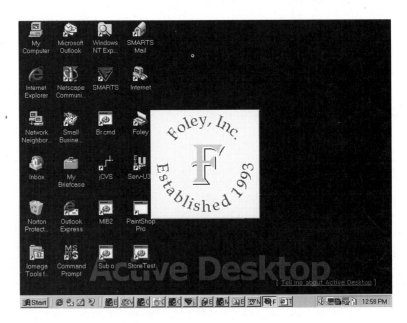

LISTING 8.8 APPLICATION TO TEST THE `SplashWindow`

```
package com.foley.test;

import java.awt.*;
import javax.swing.*;

import com.foley.utility.SplashWindow;
import com.foley.utility.ImageLoader;


/**
 * An application that displays a frame that
 * may not be resized; has an image, and a cross
 * hair cursor.
 *
```

```
 * @author Mike Foley
 **/
public class SplashTest extends Object {

    /**
     * Application entry point.
     * Create the splash window, and display it.
     *
     * @param args Command line parameter. Not used.
     **/
    public static void main( String args[] ) {

        Icon icon = null;

        //
        // Assume the .gif file is local.
        //
        icon = new ImageIcon( "logo.gif" );
SplashWindow splashWindow = new SplashWindow( icon );
        splashWindow.setVisible( true );

    } // main
} // SplashTest
```

Summary

This chapter presented the top-level display components contained in the JFC. The JFrame class provides an independent frame for building displays. Instances of the JFrame class contain window decorations provided by the display system's window manager. The JApplet class provides the entry point for applets developed by using the JFC toolkit. Applets typically provide the entry point to Java classes loaded into a browser. The JWindow class provides an arbitrary window for building displays. This class was extended to create a splash screen. It is similar to the JFrame class; however, window decorations are not displayed on instances of the JWindow class.

Each of the top-level classes contains one child, an instance of the JRootPane class. This instance creates multiple panes for program use. Children are not added directly to the top-level component. Instead, they are added to the content pane. The glassPane can be displayed to catch input events before they are passed to the components in the contentPane. You saw how this feature can be used to display a wait cursor in a JFrame instance.

8

FRAME WINDOWS

Menus and Toolbars

IN THIS CHAPTER

- Creating Menus   *216*
- Types of Menu Items   *228*
- Placing Menus   *247*
- Creating Toolbars   *261*

CHAPTER 9

Menus and toolbars have become an integral tool for launching operations in modern graphical user interfaces. Menus typically contain the full suite of operations supported by the application. Context sensitive pop-up menus are often available over various areas of the application.

Toolbars, also known as buttonbars, often contain only commonly used operations. Each operation is represented by an image on a button. However, many applications now support multiple toolbars, each containing related operations. These can be shown and hidden by the user as required.

JFC menus and toolbars are Action-aware components. This allows Action instances to be added directly to these components.

In this chapter, the JFC components for implementing menus and toolbars are presented. You will learn

- How to create menus
- How to add a menubar to a frame
- How to create pop-up menus
- How to create toolbars

Creating Menus

The JFC provides components for creating menus that can be attached to a frame or used in a pop-up menu. The implementation of a menu is contained in the JMenu class. Instances of the JMenu class contain instances of JMenuItems. A menu item can be textual, it can contain an image, and it can be a radio or toggle button. Cascading menus are implemented by a menu containing another instance of the JMenu class. The cascading effect can be nested to any level desired.

Manipulating Items in Menus

A simple menu can be implemented by creating a JMenu instance and adding items to the menu. This technique is shown in the application that follows. The menu is created with the createMenu method that returns a JMenuBar instance. In this simple example, a single JMenu named File is created. The menu items are added to the menu. For a more complex menu, multiple JMenu instances can be added to the menubar. You will see examples of this later in the chapter. In the frameInit method, the menubar is added to the frame. Adding menus to a frame and using pop-up menus are discussed later in this chapter. The menu resulting from the following code is shown in Figure 9.1 after it has been added to a JFrame instance. The JFrame class was presented in the previous chapter.

```
package com.foley.test;

import java.awt.event.*;
import java.util.*;
import javax.swing.*;

import com.foley.utility.*;

/**
 * An application that creates a menu in a frame.
 *
 * @author Mike Foley
 **/
public class MenuTest extends JFrame {

    public static MenuTest frame;


    /**
     * MenuTest, null constructor.
     **/
    public MenuTest() {
        this( null );
    } // MenuTest


    /**
     * MenuTest, constructor.
     *
     * @param title The title for the frame.
     **/
    public MenuTest( String title ) {
        super( title );
    } // MenuTest


    /**
     * frameInit, from JFrame
     *
     * Create the contrent for this frame.
     **/
    protected void frameInit() {

        //
        // Let our super create the content and associated panes.
        //
        super.frameInit();

        JMenuBar menubar = createMenu();
        setJMenuBar( menubar );
```

```
} // frameInit


/**
 * Create the menu for the frame.
 *
 * @return The menu for the frame.
 **/
protected JMenuBar createMenu() {

    JMenuBar menubar = new JMenuBar();

    JMenu file = new JMenu( "File" );
    file.add( "New" );
    file.add( "Open..." );
    file.add( "Close" );
    file.addSeparator();
    file.add( "Save" );
    file.add( "Save As..." );
    file.addSeparator();
    file.add( "Exit" );

    menubar.add( file );

    return( menubar );

} // createMenu


/**
 * Application entry point.
 * Create the frame, and display it.
 *
 * @param args Command line parameter. Not used.
 **/
public static void main( String args[] ) {

    JFrame frame = new MenuTest( "Menu Test" );
    frame.pack();
    frame.setVisible( true );

} // main

} // MenuTest
```

This menu uses a convenience version of the add method. The items in the menu are created in the add method and given the name of the String instance passed as the parameter. The addSeparator method is used to add an instance of the JSeparator class to the menu. The add and addSeparator methods append the new item to the end of the menu items contained in the menu.

FIGURE 9.1

File menu
attached to a
JFrame.

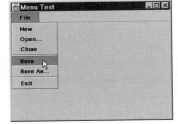

It is often convenient to create the JMenuItem and add the instance to the menu. This
way, the code creating the menu has a handle to the item, allowing easy manipulation of
the item. The JMenuItem class inherits from the AbstractButton class. As such, it will
generate the same events as other buttons. Button events were discussed in Chapter 6,
"The Button Hierarchy." A typical technique for adding functionality to a menu is to add
an ActionListener to each item in the menu. This is shown in the following modified
version of the createMenu method:

```java
/**
 * Create the menu for the frame.
 *
 * @return The menu for the frame.
 **/
protected JMenuBar createMenu() {

    JMenuBar menubar = new JMenuBar();

    JMenu file = new JMenu( "File" );
    file.add( "New" );
    file.add( "Open..." );
    file.add( "Close" );
    file.addSeparator();
    file.add( "Save" );
    file.add( "Save As..." );
    file.addSeparator();

    //
    // Create the menuitem ourself, and add
    // an ActionListener.
    //
    JMenuItem item = new JMenuItem( "Exit" );
    item.addActionListener( new ActionListener() {
        public void actionPerformed( ActionEvent e ) {
            System.exit( 0 );
        }
    } );
    file.add( item );

    menubar.add( file );
```

9

```
        return( menubar );

    } // createMenu
```

In this example, the `JMenuItem` for the Exit menu item is explicitly created. The menu item can also be created with an icon. Since the menu item is an extension of the `AbstractButton` class, it can contain a string, an icon, or both. With the handle of the `JMenuItem`, an `ActionListener` can be added to the item. When the menu item is selected, the `actionPerformed` method will be called. The item is added to the menu by using the version of the `add` method in the `JMenu` class that takes a `JMenuItem` instance as its parameter. As with the previous version of the `add` method, the new item is appended to the list of items in the menu.

There is also a version of the `add` method in the `JMenu` class that takes a `Component` as its parameter. This allows any `Component` instance to be added to a menu. For example, the following version of the `createMenu` method creates another `JMenu` and adds an instance of the `JComboBox` class to the menu. The second menu is also added to the menubar, creating a menu with two items on the frame. The resulting menu is shown in Figure 9.2. Listeners could be added to the `JComboBox` instance to receive events when items in the combo box are selected.

```
    /**
     * Create the menu for the frame.
     *
     * @return The menu for the frame.
     **/
    protected JMenuBar createMenu() {

        JMenuBar menubar = new JMenuBar();

        JMenu file = new JMenu( "File" );
        file.add( "New" );
        file.add( "Open..." );
        file.add( "Close" );
        file.addSeparator();
        file.add( "Save" );
        file.add( "Save As..." );
        file.addSeparator();

        //
        // Create the menuitem ourself, and add
        // an ActionListener.
        //
        JMenuItem item = new JMenuItem( "Exit" );
        item.addActionListener( new ActionListener() {
            public void actionPerformed( ActionEvent e ) {
                System.exit( 0 );
            }
```

```
            } );
            file.add( item );

            menubar.add( file );

            //
            // Add a JComboBox to the menu.
            //
            JMenu combo = new JMenu( "ComboBox" );
            Vector data = new Vector();
            data.addElement( "Apple" );
            data.addElement( "Grape" );
            data.addElement( "Orange" );
            JComboBox comboBox = new JComboBox( data );
            combo.add( comboBox );

            menubar.add( combo );

            return( menubar );

    } // createMenu
```

FIGURE 9.2

Menubar with a
JComboBox
instance.

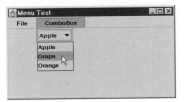

The JMenu class is Action aware. This allows Action instances to be added to a menu by using the version of the add method that takes an Action as its parameter. The JMenu class obtains the name and small icon from the Action instance and uses these to construct a JMenuItem. The Action is added as an ActionListener of the menu item. This ensures that the Action is called when the menu item is selected. A private PropertyChangeListener in the JMenu instance is added to the Action. This listener is notified of changes to the Action. If the Action's name or small icon changes, the PropertyChangeListener will update the menu item to the new values. Also, if the enabled status of the Action changes, the enabled status of the menu item will update to reflect the current enabled state of the Action. Finally, the menu item is added to the menu.

As an example of using an Action instance in a menu, an ExitAction is created and added to a menu. The ExitAction class was presented in Chapter 4, "JFC Programming Techniques." The modified createMenu method is shown in the following code. The

9

**MENUS AND
TOOLBARS**

combo box from the previous section was omitted from this example. In this version of the `createMenu` method, the explicit creation of the menu item and adding the `ActionListener` are not required. This work is performed in the `JMenu` class when the `Action` instance is added to the menu.

```
/**
 * Create the menu for the frame.
 *
 * @return The menu for the frame.
 **/
protected JMenuBar createMenu() {

    JMenuBar menubar = new JMenuBar();

    JMenu file = new JMenu( "File" );
    file.add( "New" );
    file.add( "Open..." );
    file.add( "Close" );
    file.addSeparator();
    file.add( "Save" );
    file.add( "Save As..." );
    file.addSeparator();

    //
    // Add an Action to the menu.
    //
    file.add( new ExitAction() );

    menubar.add( file );

    return( menubar );

} // createMenu
```

An instance of the `ExitAction` is added to a menu using the `add` method of the `JMenu` class. The line of code to add the `Action` is shown next. Figure 9.3 shows the `ExitAction` on the menu. Notice how the name and icon associated with the `Action` are placed on the menu without intervention from the calling code. The `actionPerformed` method in the `ExitAction` instance is called when the menu item is chosen. This of course will exit the application. When applications are designed by using `Action`s to encapsulate application behavior, creating menus is very simple.

```
file.add( new ExitAction() );
```

The various overloaded versions of the `add` method work nicely when creating menus. The items in the menu are appended to the existing items in the menu. Thus the items are displayed in the order they are added to the menu. The `JMenu` class provides other methods to manipulate items in the menu. As data in an application changes state, menu items may need to be added or removed from an application's menu system. To provide this functionality, overloaded `insert` and `remove` methods are provided. There are versions of the `insert` method that correspond to the add methods allowing `String`, `Action`, and `JMenuItem` instances to be passed as parameters.

FIGURE 9.3

`ExitAction` *in the File menu.*

Each of the `insert` methods takes an integer offset as its second parameter. This specifies the position in the menu where the new item is to be inserted. The existing menu items are numbered from zero. For the File menu shown in the examples so far in this chapter, the item list in the menu looks like that shown in Figure 9.4. After the following lines of code are executed to insert the Print menu items, the menu looks as shown in Figure 9.5. This example uses the convenience method `insertSeparator` to insert a `JSeparator` into the menu after the printing-related items.

```
file.insert( "Print Setup...", 7 );
file.insert( new PrintAction(), 8 );
file.insertSeparator( 9 );
```

FIGURE 9.4

Inserting a menu item.

Position	Menu Item
0	New
1	Open
2	Close
3	Separator
4	Save
5	SaveAs
6	Separator
7	Exit ← Items inserted before current item 7

9

MENUS AND TOOLBARS

If a negative position is passed to any of the `insert` methods, an `IllegalArgumentException` is thrown. On the other hand, if an index greater than the number of items in the menu is specified, the item to be inserted is placed at the end of the items in the list. In this case, the `insert` method behaves similarly to the add method.

FIGURE 9.5

Print menu item inserted.

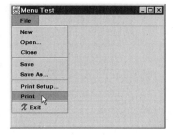

Menu items can be removed by index or by specifying the JMenuItem instance to be removed from the menu. The JMenu class provides the removeAll method to clear all items from the menu. To remove the Save operation–related menu items from the previous examples, the following lines of code could be executed:

```
file.remove( saveMenuItem );
file.remove( 4 );
file.remove( 4 );
```

The first remove call takes a reference to the Save menu item as a parameter. This causes the Save menu item, located at position four, to be removed from the menu. The other items in the list slide down so there is not a gap in the item list after an item has been removed from the menu. The menu item order before and after this menu item has been removed is shown in Figure 9.6. The next call removes the item at position four. This is now the Save As... menu item. Once again, the remaining menu items slide down to fill in the gap left by the removed menu item. The last call once again removes the menu item at position four, which is now a separator.

FIGURE 9.6

Save menu item removed.

Position	Menu Item		Final Order
0	New		New
1	Open		Open
2	Close		Close
3	Separator		Separator
4	~~Save~~ ←	Removed item 4	SaveAs
5	SaveAs		Separator
6	Separator		PrintSetup
7	PrintSetup		Print
8	Print		Separator
9	Separator		Exit
10	Exit		

Similar to the insert method, when a negative index is passed to any of the remove methods, an IllegalArgumentException is thrown. However, unlike the insert methods, when an index greater than the number of items in the menu is passed to a remove method, an ArrayIndexOutOfBoundsException is thrown. This exception seems to be more of a bug than a feature. I would expect that proper error handling for such an index should result in an `IllegalArgumentException` being thrown.

`JMenuItem` Events

The `JMenuItem` class is a descendant of the `AbstractButton` class described in Chapter 6. Instances of the `JMenuItem` class fire the events defined for that class, as well as events from its ancestors. Among these are `ChangeEvent`, `ItemEvent`, and `ActionEvent` defined for buttons. The `JMenuItem` class also fires `MenuKeyEvent` and `MenuDragMouseEvent` instances. A `MenuKeyEvent` is fired when a keystroke has been received by the menu item. The `MenuKeyEvent` class extends the `java.awt.event.KeyEvent` class. The path of the menu item in the menu hierarchy is delivered with the event.

```
public class MenuKeyEvent extends KeyEvent {
    private MenuElement path[];
    private MenuSelectionManager manager;

    public MenuKeyEvent(Component source, int id, long when,
                        int modifiers, int keyCode, char keyChar,
                        MenuElement p[], MenuSelectionManager m) {
        super(source, id, when, modifiers, keyCode, keyChar);
        path = p;
        manager = m;
    }

    public MenuElement[] getPath() {
        return path;
    }

    public MenuSelectionManager getMenuSelectionManager() {
        return manager;
    }
}
```

A `MenuKeyEvent` is delivered in each of the three methods defined in the `MenuKeyListener` interface, shown next. A `MenuKeyListener` is called when a key is pressed and released in a menu. The `menuKeyTyped` method is called after a key press and release in the menu. A `MenuKeyListener` is added to a `JMenuItem` by calling the `addMenuKeyListener` method. It can be removed with the `removeMenuKeyListener` method.

```
public interface MenuKeyListener extends EventListener {
    /**
     * Invoked when a key has been typed.
     * This event occurs when a key press is followed by a key release.
     */
    void menuKeyTyped(MenuKeyEvent e);
```

```
/**
 * Invoked when a key has been pressed.
 */
void menuKeyPressed(MenuKeyEvent e);

/**
 * Invoked when a key has been released.
 */
void menuKeyReleased(MenuKeyEvent e);
}
```

When the mouse is dragged over a JMenuItem instance, it fires MenuDragMouseEvent events to registered listeners. The MenuDrawMouseEvent class is shown next. The MenuDrawMouseEvent class extends the java.awt.event.MouseEvent class. As such, it delivers with it the standard mouse event information such as mouse coordinates and click count. Similarly to the MenuKeyEvent, the path to the menu item where the event occurred is delivered with the event.

```
public class MenuDragMouseEvent extends MouseEvent {
    private MenuElement path[];
    private MenuSelectionManager manager;

    public MenuDragMouseEvent(Component source, int id, long when,
                              int modifiers, int x, int y, int clickCount,
                              boolean popupTrigger, MenuElement p[],
                              MenuSelectionManager m) {
        super( source, id, when, modifiers, x, y,
               clickCount, popupTrigger );
        path = p;
        manager = m;
    }

    public MenuElement[] getPath() {
        return path;
    }

    public MenuSelectionManager getMenuSelectionManager() {
        return manager;
    }
}
```

A MenuDragMouseEvent instance is delivered to MenuDragMouseListener in one of the four methods contained in the MenuDragMouseListener interface shown next. The names of the methods describe which mouse gesture causes the corresponding method to be called. The addMenuDragMouseListener method is called to add a MenuDragMouseListener to a menu item, and the removeMenuDragMouseListener will remove the listener from the menu item.

```
public interface MenuDragMouseListener extends EventListener {
    void menuDragMouseEntered(MenuDragMouseEvent e);
    void menuDragMouseExited(MenuDragMouseEvent e);
    void menuDragMouseDragged(MenuDragMouseEvent e);
    void menuDragMouseReleased(MenuDragMouseEvent e);
}
```

JMenu Events

The JMenu class extends the JMenuItem class. Instances of the JMenu class fire the events defined for that class, as well as events from its ancestors. Among these are ChangeEvent, ItemEvent, ActionEvent (described for buttons in Chapter 6), and the MenuKeyEvent and MenuDragMouseEvent shown in the previous section. The JMenu class also defines the MenuEvent that is delivered to MenuListeners in one of the methods defined in the MenuListener interface. The MenuEvent is shown in the following code listing. As seen in this listing, unlike the events fired from the JMenuItem class, the MenuEvent doesn't deliver additional information from the standard java.util.EventObject. Thus, the only information delivered by the MenuEvent is the source of the event.

```
public class MenuEvent extends EventObject {
    public MenuEvent(Object source) {
        super(source);
    }
}
```

MenuEvents can be delivered to one of the three methods defined in the MenuListener interface. These methods are shown in the following code. The menuSelected method is called when a menu is shown. This method provides a hook allowing the listener to customize the menu before it is displayed. The menuDeselected method is called when the menu is hidden. The current implementation of the JFC does not use the menuCanceled method.

```
public interface MenuListener extends EventListener {
    void menuSelected(MenuEvent e);
    void menuDeselected(MenuEvent e);
    void menuCanceled(MenuEvent e);
}
```

The addMenuListener and removeMenuListener methods are used to add and remove a MenuListener from an instance of the JMenu class.

Types of Menu Items

The examples in the previous section showed JMenu instances that contained instances of the JMenuItem class. JMenuItem instances may be the most common items added to menus, but they are not the only choice. The JFC contains three classes that extend JMenuItem and are designed to be used in menus. These are the JCheckBoxMenuItem and JRadioButtonMenuItem classes, as well as the JMenu class itself. These classes, as well as an in-depth discussion of the JMenuItem class, are presented in this section.

The JMenuItem Class

As was seen in the previous section, instances of the JMenu class often create JMenuItem instances to add to the menu. However, the code constructing the menu can create the JMenuItem itself and add the instance to the menu. The primary reason for doing this is to have a reference to the JMenuItem instance. The instance can then be customized or have event listeners added to it. It should be noted that the add method returns the JMenuItem instance added to the menu when a JMenuItem or Action is passed as a parameter. However, when a String is passed as a parameter, the JMenuItem is not returned from the add method. The reason for this difference is to mimic the API from the AWT Menu class. In this writer's opinion, this is an example where providing a better API for the JMenu class should have been more important than being API compatible with the AWT Menu class.

The JMenuItem class is an extension of the AbstractButton class. Instances of the JMenuItem class can contain text, an icon, or both. The methods for managing the icon position relative to the text for a button, presented in Chapter 6, apply for the JMenuItem class. The previous section showed creating text-only menu items. The following lines of code show how to create a JMenuItem containing only an icon and both text and an icon on the same menu item. When both text and an icon are contained on a menu item, it is customary to have the icon to the left of the text. However, the default placement of the icon is to the right of the text. This requires a call to the setHorizontalTextPosition method to place the icon to the left of the text. The inherited access methods for setting and querying the JMenuItem text String and Icon instances are available to alter these properties after menu creation. As with any button, the menu items' enabled status can be set. In this example, the JMenuItem is disabled. The resulting menu from the previous examples and the menu items in the following version of the createMenu method are shown in Figure 9.7.

```
/**
 * Create the menu for the frame.
 *
 * @return The menu for the frame.
```

```
**/
protected JMenuBar createMenu() {

    Icon saveIcon = null;
    Icon exitIcon = null;

    try {
        //
        // Load the images used.
        //
        saveIcon = ImageLoader.loadIcon( "save.gif" );
        exitIcon = ImageLoader.loadIcon( "exit.gif" );
    } catch( InterruptedException ie ) {
        System.err.println( "Error loading images" );
        System.exit( -1 );
    }

    JMenuBar menubar = new JMenuBar();

    JMenu file = new JMenu( "File" );
    file.add( "New" );
    file.add( "Open..." );
    file.add( "Close" );
    file.addSeparator();

    // Add a save item containing only an Icon
    JMenuItem saveMenuItem = new JMenuItem( saveIcon );
    file.add( saveMenuItem );
    file.add( "Save As..." );
    file.addSeparator();

    // Add an Exit item containing both text and an Icon
    JMenuItem exitMenuItem = new JMenuItem( "Exit", exitIcon );
    exitMenuItem.setHorizontalTextPosition( SwingConstants.RIGHT );
    exitMenuItem.setEnabled( false );
    exitMenuItem.addActionListener( new ActionListener() {
        public void actionPerformed( ActionEvent e ) {
            System.exit( 0 );
        }
    } );
    file.add( exitMenuItem );


    menubar.add( file );

    return( menubar );

} // createMenu
```

FIGURE 9.7

Images and disabled Exit
JMenuItem.

The JMenuItem class allows a mnemonic to be set for the item. The mnemonic corresponds to one of the letters in the menu item's text. When specified, the mnemonic character displays with an underline on the menu item and allows the item to be selected via keyboard input. The JMenu class is an extension of JMenuItem, so a mnemonic can be set on the menu itself. The mnemonic is set with the setMnemonic method and can be queried with the getMnemonic method. The parameter to the setMnemonic method should be one of the constants defined in the java.awt.event.KeyEvent class. This ensures portability in the mnemonic specified. The mnemonic can also be specified at construction time by using the version of the constructor that takes the item's text and mnemonic as parameters. However, there is not a constructor that takes the item's text, icon, and mnemonic as parameters.

Accelerator keystrokes can be assigned to menu items. This allows the item to be selected without traversing the menus. Accelerators provide a shortcut for advanced users of the application. The setAccelerator method can be used to set the accelerator, and the getAccelerator method is used to query the current accelerator in effect for the menu item. The setAccelerator method requires an instance of the KeyStroke class as a parameter. As was shown in Chapter 3, "JComponent," the Keystroke class provides a shared instance of a representation of a key typed on the keyboard. To obtain a shared instance, one of the overloaded static KeyStroke.getKeyStroke methods is used.

The version of the MenuTest application in Listing 9.1 adds mnemonics and accelerators to the File menu used throughout this chapter. In the createMenu method for each menu item, the instance is created, and then the setMnemonic and setAccelerator methods are called to specify those properties. Then the customized menu item is added to the menu. The resulting menu is shown in Figure 9.8. In this example code listing, the Exit menu item is the only item with functionality attached to the item. It will close the application if selected.

FIGURE 9.8

Mnemonics and accelerators added to the File menu.

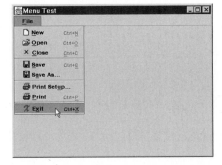

LISTING 9.1   FILE MENU WITH MNEMONICS AND ICONS

```java
package com.foley.test;

import java.awt.*;
import java.awt.event.*;
import java.util.*;

import javax.swing.*;

import com.foley.utility.*;


/**
 * An application that creates a menu in a frame.
 *
 * @author Mike Foley
 **/
public class MenuTest extends JFrame {

    public static MenuTest frame;


    /**
     * MenuTest, null constructor.
     **/
    public MenuTest() {
        this( null );
    } // MenuTest


    /**
     * MenuTest, constructor.
     *
     * @param title The title for the frame.
     **/
    public MenuTest( String title ) {
```

continues

LISTING 9.1   CONTINUED

```java
        super( title );
} // MenuTest


/**
 * frameInit, from JFrame
 *
 * Create the contrent for this frame.
 **/
protected void frameInit() {

    //
    // Let our super create the content and associated panes.
    //
    super.frameInit();

    JMenuBar menubar = createMenu();
    setJMenuBar( menubar );

} // frameInit


/**
 * Create the menu for the frame.
 *
 * @return The menu for the frame.
 **/
protected JMenuBar createMenu() {

    Icon newIcon = null;
    Icon openIcon = null;
    Icon closeIcon = null;
    Icon saveIcon = null;
    Icon saveasIcon = null;
    Icon printIcon = null;
    Icon printsetupIcon = null;
    Icon exitIcon = null;

    try {
        //
        // Load the images used.
        //
        newIcon = ImageLoader.loadIcon( "new.gif" );
        openIcon = ImageLoader.loadIcon( "open.gif" );
        closeIcon = ImageLoader.loadIcon( "close.gif" );
        saveIcon = ImageLoader.loadIcon( "save.gif" );
        saveasIcon = ImageLoader.loadIcon( "saveas.gif" );
        printIcon = ImageLoader.loadIcon( "print.gif" );
        printsetupIcon = ImageLoader.loadIcon( "printsetup.gif" );
```

```
            exitIcon = ImageLoader.loadIcon( "exit.gif" );
    } catch( InterruptedException ie ) {
        System.err.println( "Error loading images" );
        System.exit( -1 );
    }

    JMenuBar menubar = new JMenuBar();

    JMenu file = new JMenu( "File" );
    file.setMnemonic( KeyEvent.VK_F );

    JMenuItem item = new JMenuItem( "New", newIcon );
    item.setHorizontalTextPosition( SwingConstants.RIGHT );
    item.setMnemonic( KeyEvent.VK_N );
item.setAccelerator( KeyStroke.getKeyStroke(
                         KeyEvent.VK_N, Event.CTRL_MASK ) );
    file.add( item );

    item = new JMenuItem( "Open", openIcon );
    item.setHorizontalTextPosition( SwingConstants.RIGHT );
    item.setMnemonic( KeyEvent.VK_O );
item.setAccelerator( KeyStroke.getKeyStroke(
                         KeyEvent.VK_O, Event.CTRL_MASK ) );
    file.add( item );

    item = new JMenuItem( "Close", closeIcon );
    item.setHorizontalTextPosition( SwingConstants.RIGHT );
    item.setMnemonic( KeyEvent.VK_C );
item.setAccelerator( KeyStroke.getKeyStroke(
                         KeyEvent.VK_C, Event.CTRL_MASK ) );
    file.add( item );

    file.addSeparator();

    item = new JMenuItem( "Save", saveIcon );
    item.setHorizontalTextPosition( SwingConstants.RIGHT );
    item.setMnemonic( KeyEvent.VK_S );
item.setAccelerator( KeyStroke.getKeyStroke(
                         KeyEvent.VK_S, Event.CTRL_MASK ) );
    file.add( item );

    item = new JMenuItem( "Save As...", saveasIcon );
    item.setHorizontalTextPosition( SwingConstants.RIGHT );
    item.setMnemonic( KeyEvent.VK_A );
    file.add( item );

    file.addSeparator();

    item = new JMenuItem( "Print Setup...", printsetupIcon );
    item.setHorizontalTextPosition( SwingConstants.RIGHT );
```

9

MENUS AND TOOLBARS

continues

LISTING 9.1   CONTINUED

```java
            item.setMnemonic( KeyEvent.VK_U );
            file.add( item );

            item = new JMenuItem( "Print", printIcon );
            item.setHorizontalTextPosition( SwingConstants.RIGHT );
            item.setMnemonic( KeyEvent.VK_P );
item.setAccelerator( KeyStroke.getKeyStroke(
                            KeyEvent.VK_P, Event.CTRL_MASK ) );
            file.add( item );

            file.addSeparator();

            item = new JMenuItem( "Exit", exitIcon );
            item.setHorizontalTextPosition( SwingConstants.RIGHT );
            item.setMnemonic( KeyEvent.VK_X );
item.setAccelerator( KeyStroke.getKeyStroke(
                            KeyEvent.VK_X, Event.CTRL_MASK ) );
            item.addActionListener( new ActionListener() {
                public void actionPerformed( ActionEvent e ) {
                    System.exit( 0 );
                }
            } );
            file.add( item );

            menubar.add( file );

            return( menubar );

        } // createMenu


        /**
         * Application entry point.
         * Create the frame, and display it.
         *
         * @param args Command line parameter. Not used.
         **/
        public static void main( String args[] ) {

            JFrame frame = new MenuTest( "Menu Test" );
            frame.pack();
            frame.setVisible( true );

        } // main

    } // MenuTest
```

The JMenu Class

The JMenu class itself is an extension of the JMenuItem class. This implies that JMenu instances can be added to other instances of the JMenu class, enabling cascaded menus.

Listing 9.2 shows how to change the New menu item in the createMenu method into a cascaded menu. The additional menu contains menu items for many different New types. The resulting menu is shown in Figure 9.9.

FIGURE 9.9

A cascading File/New menu.

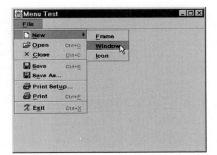

LISTING 9.2   FILE MENU WITH CASCADING NEW MENU

```
/**
 * Create the menu for the frame.
 *
 * @return The menu for the frame.
 **/
protected JMenuBar createMenu() {

    Icon newIcon = null;
    Icon openIcon = null;
    Icon closeIcon = null;
    Icon saveIcon = null;
    Icon saveasIcon = null;
    Icon printIcon = null;
    Icon printsetupIcon = null;
    Icon exitIcon = null;

    try {
        //
        // Load the images used.
        //
        newIcon = ImageLoader.loadIcon( "new.gif" );
        openIcon = ImageLoader.loadIcon( "open.gif" );
        closeIcon = ImageLoader.loadIcon( "close.gif" );
        saveIcon = ImageLoader.loadIcon( "save.gif" );
        saveasIcon = ImageLoader.loadIcon( "saveas.gif" );
```

continues

9

MENUS AND
TOOLBARS

LISTING 9.2 CONTINUED

```
        printIcon = ImageLoader.loadIcon( "print.gif" );
        printsetupIcon = ImageLoader.loadIcon( "printsetup.gif" );
        exitIcon = ImageLoader.loadIcon( "exit.gif" );
    } catch( InterruptedException ie ) {
        System.err.println( "Error loading images" );
        System.exit( -1 );
    }

    JMenuBar menubar = new JMenuBar();

    JMenu file = new JMenu( "File" );
    file.setMnemonic( KeyEvent.VK_F );

    //
    // Change New menu into a cascaded menu.
    //
    JMenu newMenu = new JMenu( "New" );
    newMenu.setMnemonic( KeyEvent.VK_N );
    newMenu.setIcon( newIcon );
    newMenu.setHorizontalTextPosition( SwingConstants.RIGHT );

    JMenuItem item = new JMenuItem( "Frame" );
    item.setHorizontalTextPosition( SwingConstants.RIGHT );
    item.setMnemonic( KeyEvent.VK_F );
    newMenu.add( item );

    item = new JMenuItem( "Window" );
    item.setHorizontalTextPosition( SwingConstants.RIGHT );
    item.setMnemonic( KeyEvent.VK_W );
    newMenu.add( item );

    item = new JMenuItem( "Icon" );
    item.setHorizontalTextPosition( SwingConstants.RIGHT );
    item.setMnemonic( KeyEvent.VK_I );
    newMenu.add( item );

    file.add( newMenu );

    item = new JMenuItem( "Open", openIcon );
    item.setHorizontalTextPosition( SwingConstants.RIGHT );
    item.setMnemonic( KeyEvent.VK_O );
item.setAccelerator( KeyStroke.getKeyStroke(
                        KeyEvent.VK_O, Event.CTRL_MASK ) );
    file.add( item );

    item = new JMenuItem( "Close", closeIcon );
    item.setHorizontalTextPosition( SwingConstants.RIGHT );
    item.setMnemonic( KeyEvent.VK_C );
item.setAccelerator( KeyStroke.getKeyStroke(
```

```
                             KeyEvent.VK_C, Event.CTRL_MASK ) );
        file.add( item );

        file.addSeparator();

        item = new JMenuItem( "Save", saveIcon );
        item.setHorizontalTextPosition( SwingConstants.RIGHT );
        item.setMnemonic( KeyEvent.VK_S );
item.setAccelerator( KeyStroke.getKeyStroke(
                             KeyEvent.VK_S, Event.CTRL_MASK ) );
        file.add( item );

        item = new JMenuItem( "Save As...", saveasIcon );
        item.setHorizontalTextPosition( SwingConstants.RIGHT );
        item.setMnemonic( KeyEvent.VK_A );
        file.add( item );

        file.addSeparator();

        item = new JMenuItem( "Print Setup...", printsetupIcon );
        item.setHorizontalTextPosition( SwingConstants.RIGHT );
        item.setMnemonic( KeyEvent.VK_U );
        file.add( item );

        item = new JMenuItem( "Print", printIcon );
        item.setHorizontalTextPosition( SwingConstants.RIGHT );
        item.setMnemonic( KeyEvent.VK_P );
item.setAccelerator( KeyStroke.getKeyStroke(
                             KeyEvent.VK_P, Event.CTRL_MASK ) );
        file.add( item );

        file.addSeparator();

        item = new JMenuItem( "Exit", exitIcon );
        item.setHorizontalTextPosition( SwingConstants.RIGHT );
        item.setMnemonic( KeyEvent.VK_X );
item.setAccelerator( KeyStroke.getKeyStroke(
                             KeyEvent.VK_X, Event.CTRL_MASK ) );
        item.addActionListener( new ActionListener() {
            public void actionPerformed( ActionEvent e ) {
                System.exit( 0 );
            }
        } );
        file.add( item );

        menubar.add( file );

        return( menubar );

    } // createMenu
```

The `createMenu` method shown here can be placed into any of the sample applications presented earlier in this chapter for testing. Notice how adding a `JMenu` instance to another `JMenu` instance created the cascaded menu. Also notice that the `JMenu` class does not have a constructor that takes an `Icon` instance as a parameter. However, an icon can still be added to the menu by calling the `setIcon` method. This technique could be used to add icons to the menus on the menubar; however, this is not a common practice.

The `JMenu` class provides methods for querying the items contained in the menu. The `getMenuComponentCount` method returns the number of items in the menu. The `getMenuComponent` method returns the component at the specified index. The `getMenuComponents` method returns an array of all the components in the menu. The `getItemCount` method is equivalent to the `getMenuComponentCount` method, and is provided for compatibility with the AWT menus. The `getItem` method is equivalent to the `getMenuComponent` method, except it returns an instance of the `JMenuItem` class. If the component at the specified index is not an instance of the `JMenuItem` class, the `getItem` method returns the `JMenu` itself, (`this`). The rational for this is unknown. The `isMenuComponent` can be used to determine if a component is in the menu's submenu hierarchy.

The `isTopLevelMenu` method returns `true` if the menu is attached to a menubar. The `isPopupMenuVisible` can be used to determine if the menu's pop-up menu is currently visible. The `isSelected` method returns `true` if the menu is currently popped up. The `isSelected` method is similar but slightly different from the `isPopupMenuVisible` method. A menu can be popped up, but the pop-up menu's window may not be visible.

> **NOTE**
>
> The `JMenu` class contains a constructor that takes a `boolean` parameter specifying that the menu be a tear-off menu. This property must be specified at creation time; there is not a `set` method for the property. The `isTearOff` method can be used to query the status of this property. Even though these methods are in the `JMenu` class's API, tear-off menus are not yet implemented in the JFC menu system.

The `JCheckBoxMenuItem` Class

The `JCheckBoxMenuItem` class is an extension of the `JMenuItem` class. As such, the discussion in the previous section applies to the `JCheckBoxMenuItem` class. An instance of the `JCheckBoxMenuItem` represents a menu item that will display selected or unselected. The visual representation is defined by the current look-and-feel. However, it is typical for a check to be placed on a selected check box menu item.

The `setSelected` method is used to select or unselect the menu item. The `getSelected` method queries the current selected state of the item. The `setState` and `getState` methods perform the same functionality as the `setSelected` and `getSelected` methods. These methods are provided for compatibility with other component toolkits. The `setSelected` and `getSelected` pair are the standard methods for selection in menus and buttons in the JFC. These methods should be used instead of the `setState` and `getState` pair. The initial selected state can also be specified in the constructor. If an initial selection state is not specified, the item will not be selected.

The following version of the `createMenu` method adds two `JCheckBoxMenuItem` instances to an Options menu. The first check box is not initially selected, and the second check box corresponding to the Echo menu item is initially selected. Mnemonics and accelerators are set for each check box menu item. Typing the accelerator key performs the same task as selecting the item in the menu. The next time the window is displayed, the check box will reflect that the item had been selected. Notice how the call to the `setHorizontalTextPosition` method is not required to position the icon properly for check box menu items. The default position for an icon is to the left of the text, as is customary for menu items. The resulting menu, when the `createMenu` shown in Listing 9.3 is added to the `MenuTest` application, is shown in Figure 9.10.

FIGURE 9.10.

A menu that contains `JCheckBoxMenuItem` *instances.*

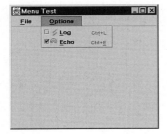

LISTING 9.3   OPTIONS MENU WITH `JCheckBoxMenuItem`

```
/**
 * Create the menu for the frame.
 *
 * @return The menu for the frame.
 **/
protected JMenuBar createMenu() {

    Icon newIcon = null;
    Icon openIcon = null;
    Icon closeIcon = null;
    Icon saveIcon = null;
```

continues

9

MENUS AND
TOOLBARS

LISTING 9.3   CONTINUED

```java
Icon saveasIcon = null;
Icon printIcon = null;
Icon printsetupIcon = null;
Icon exitIcon = null;
Icon logIcon = null;
Icon echoIcon = null;

try {
    //
    // Load the images used.
    //
    newIcon = ImageLoader.loadIcon( "new.gif" );
    openIcon = ImageLoader.loadIcon( "open.gif" );
    closeIcon = ImageLoader.loadIcon( "close.gif" );
    saveIcon = ImageLoader.loadIcon( "save.gif" );
    saveasIcon = ImageLoader.loadIcon( "saveas.gif" );
    printIcon = ImageLoader.loadIcon( "print.gif" );
    printsetupIcon = ImageLoader.loadIcon( "printsetup.gif" );
    exitIcon = ImageLoader.loadIcon( "exit.gif" );
    logIcon = ImageLoader.loadIcon( "log.gif" );
    echoIcon = ImageLoader.loadIcon( "echo.gif" );
} catch( InterruptedException ie ) {
    System.err.println( "Error loading images" );
    System.exit( -1 );
}

JMenuBar menubar = new JMenuBar();

JMenu file = new JMenu( "File" );
file.setMnemonic( KeyEvent.VK_F );

JMenu newMenu = new JMenu( "New" );
newMenu.setMnemonic( KeyEvent.VK_N );

JMenuItem item = new JMenuItem( "Frame" );
item.setHorizontalTextPosition( SwingConstants.RIGHT );
item.setMnemonic( KeyEvent.VK_F );
newMenu.add( item );

item = new JMenuItem( "Window" );
item.setHorizontalTextPosition( SwingConstants.RIGHT );
item.setMnemonic( KeyEvent.VK_W );
newMenu.add( item );

item = new JMenuItem( "Icon" );
item.setHorizontalTextPosition( SwingConstants.RIGHT );
item.setMnemonic( KeyEvent.VK_I );
newMenu.add( item );
```

```
        file.add( newMenu );

        item = new JMenuItem( "Open", openIcon );
        item.setHorizontalTextPosition( SwingConstants.RIGHT );
        item.setMnemonic( KeyEvent.VK_O );
item.setAccelerator( KeyStroke.getKeyStroke(
                        KeyEvent.VK_O, Event.CTRL_MASK ) );
        file.add( item );

        item = new JMenuItem( "Close", closeIcon );
        item.setHorizontalTextPosition( SwingConstants.RIGHT );
        item.setMnemonic( KeyEvent.VK_C );
item.setAccelerator( KeyStroke.getKeyStroke(
                        KeyEvent.VK_C, Event.CTRL_MASK ) );
        file.add( item );

        file.addSeparator();

        item = new JMenuItem( "Save", saveIcon );
        item.setHorizontalTextPosition( SwingConstants.RIGHT );
        item.setMnemonic( KeyEvent.VK_S );
item.setAccelerator( KeyStroke.getKeyStroke(
                        KeyEvent.VK_S, Event.CTRL_MASK ) );
        file.add( item );

        item = new JMenuItem( "Save As...", saveasIcon );
        item.setHorizontalTextPosition( SwingConstants.RIGHT );
        item.setMnemonic( KeyEvent.VK_A );
        file.add( item );

        file.addSeparator();

        item = new JMenuItem( "Print Setup...", printsetupIcon );
        item.setHorizontalTextPosition( SwingConstants.RIGHT );
        item.setMnemonic( KeyEvent.VK_U );
        file.add( item );

        item = new JMenuItem( "Print", printIcon );
        item.setHorizontalTextPosition( SwingConstants.RIGHT );
        item.setMnemonic( KeyEvent.VK_P );
item.setAccelerator( KeyStroke.getKeyStroke(
                        KeyEvent.VK_P, Event.CTRL_MASK ) );
        file.add( item );

        file.addSeparator();

        item = new JMenuItem( "Exit", exitIcon );
        item.setHorizontalTextPosition( SwingConstants.RIGHT );
        item.setMnemonic( KeyEvent.VK_X );
```

continues

9

MENUS AND TOOLBARS

LISTING 9.3   CONTINUED

```
item.setAccelerator( KeyStroke.getKeyStroke(
                          KeyEvent.VK_X, Event.CTRL_MASK ) );
        item.addActionListener( new ActionListener() {
            public void actionPerformed( ActionEvent e ) {
                System.exit( 0 );
            }
        } );
        file.add( item );

        menubar.add( file );

        //
        // Create an options menu containing two
        // CheckBoxMenuItems.
        //
        JMenu options = new JMenu( "Options" );
        options.setMnemonic( KeyEvent.VK_O );

        JCheckBoxMenuItem cbItem = new JCheckBoxMenuItem( "Log", logIcon
);
        cbItem.setMnemonic( KeyEvent.VK_L );
cbItem.setAccelerator( KeyStroke.getKeyStroke(
                          KeyEvent.VK_L, Event.CTRL_MASK ) );
        options.add( cbItem );

        cbItem = new JCheckBoxMenuItem( "Echo", echoIcon, true );
        cbItem.setMnemonic( KeyEvent.VK_E );
cbItem.setAccelerator( KeyStroke.getKeyStroke(
                          KeyEvent.VK_E, Event.CTRL_MASK ) );
        options.add( cbItem );

        menubar.add( options );

        return( menubar );

    } // createMenu
```

The JRadioButtonMenuItem Class

Like the JCheckBoxMenuItem presented in the last section, the JRadioButtonMenuItem class is an extension of the JMenuItem class. As such, the discussion in the JMenuItem section applies to the JRadioButtonMenuItem class. An instance of the JRadioButtonMenuItem represents a menu item that will display selected or unselected. The visual representation is defined by the current look-and-feel. However, it is typical for a filled or empty circle to be placed on the radio button menu item to represent the selected or unselected state of the menu item. It is typical to place the radio buttons into an instance of the ButtonGroup class. The button group ensures that only one of the buttons in the group is selected at a given time. See the "Radio Button Groups" section of Chapter 6 for a complete description of using radio buttons in button groups.

The version of the createMenu method in Listing 9.4 adds a button group for selecting the foreground color to the Options menu from the previous section. A cascading menu is used for the color selection menu. This helps visually separate the radio button menu items from the rest of the menu. Like the JCheckBoxMenuItem, the icon in instances of the JRadioButtonMenuItem class is placed in the standard location—to the left of the text. However, unlike the JCheckBoxMenuItem class, the JRadioButtonMenuItem doesn't contain a constructor allowing the selected state of the button to be specified. A separate call to the setSelected method is required to set the initially selected button in the group. After being configured, each radio button is added to both the menu and the button group.

Although it is customary to use the first letter of the menu item as the mnemonic, this example contains two items with the same first letter. To prevent multiple items from using the same mnemonic, the letter "u" is used for the item named Blue. As we have seen in the previous sections, the setAccelerator method is used to specify the accelerator key combination in the JRadioButtonMenuItem instances. When the createMenu method shown in Listing 9.4 is used in the MenuTest application shown earlier in this chapter, the resulting menu is the one shown in Figure 9.11.

FIGURE 9.11

A menu that contains JRadioButtonMenu Item *instances.*

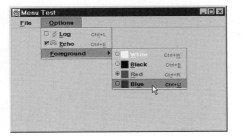

9

MENUS AND TOOLBARS

LISTING 9.4   OPTIONS MENU WITH JRadioButtonMenuItem INSTANCES

```
/**
 * Create the menu for the frame.
 *
 * @return The menu for the frame.
 **/
protected JMenuBar createMenu() {

    Icon newIcon = null;
```

continues

LISTING 9.4   CONTINUED

```java
            Icon openIcon = null;
            Icon closeIcon = null;
            Icon saveIcon = null;
            Icon saveasIcon = null;
            Icon printIcon = null;
            Icon printsetupIcon = null;
            Icon exitIcon = null;
            Icon logIcon = null;
            Icon echoIcon = null;
            Icon whiteIcon = null;
            Icon blackIcon = null;
            Icon redIcon = null;
            Icon blueIcon = null;

            try {
                //
                // Load the images used.
                //
                newIcon = ImageLoader.loadIcon( "new.gif" );
                openIcon = ImageLoader.loadIcon( "open.gif" );
                closeIcon = ImageLoader.loadIcon( "close.gif" );
                saveIcon = ImageLoader.loadIcon( "save.gif" );
                saveasIcon = ImageLoader.loadIcon( "saveas.gif" );
                printIcon = ImageLoader.loadIcon( "print.gif" );
                printsetupIcon = ImageLoader.loadIcon( "printsetup.gif" );
                exitIcon = ImageLoader.loadIcon( "exit.gif" );
                logIcon = ImageLoader.loadIcon( "log.gif" );
                echoIcon = ImageLoader.loadIcon( "echo.gif" );
                whiteIcon = ImageLoader.loadIcon( "white.gif" );
                blackIcon = ImageLoader.loadIcon( "black.gif" );
                redIcon = ImageLoader.loadIcon( "red.gif" );
                blueIcon = ImageLoader.loadIcon( "blue.gif" );
            } catch( InterruptedException ie ) {
                System.err.println( "Error loading images" );
                System.exit( -1 );
            }

            JMenuBar menubar = new JMenuBar();

            JMenu file = new JMenu( "File" );
            file.setMnemonic( KeyEvent.VK_F );

            JMenu newMenu = new JMenu( "New" );
            newMenu.setMnemonic( KeyEvent.VK_N );

            JMenuItem item = new JMenuItem( "Frame" );
            item.setHorizontalTextPosition( SwingConstants.RIGHT );
            item.setMnemonic( KeyEvent.VK_F );
            newMenu.add( item );
```

```
        item = new JMenuItem( "Window" );
        item.setHorizontalTextPosition( SwingConstants.RIGHT );
        item.setMnemonic( KeyEvent.VK_W );
        newMenu.add( item );

        item = new JMenuItem( "Icon" );
        item.setHorizontalTextPosition( SwingConstants.RIGHT );
        item.setMnemonic( KeyEvent.VK_I );
        newMenu.add( item );

        file.add( newMenu );

        item = new JMenuItem( "Open", openIcon );
        item.setHorizontalTextPosition( SwingConstants.RIGHT );
        item.setMnemonic( KeyEvent.VK_O );
item.setAccelerator( KeyStroke.getKeyStroke(
                            KeyEvent.VK_O, Event.CTRL_MASK ) );
        file.add( item );

        item = new JMenuItem( "Close", closeIcon );
        item.setHorizontalTextPosition( SwingConstants.RIGHT );
        item.setMnemonic( KeyEvent.VK_C );
item.setAccelerator( KeyStroke.getKeyStroke(
                            KeyEvent.VK_C, Event.CTRL_MASK ) );
        file.add( item );

        file.addSeparator();

        item = new JMenuItem( "Save", saveIcon );
        item.setHorizontalTextPosition( SwingConstants.RIGHT );
        item.setMnemonic( KeyEvent.VK_S );
item.setAccelerator( KeyStroke.getKeyStroke(
                            KeyEvent.VK_S, Event.CTRL_MASK ) );
        file.add( item );

        item = new JMenuItem( "Save As...", saveasIcon );
        item.setHorizontalTextPosition( SwingConstants.RIGHT );
        item.setMnemonic( KeyEvent.VK_A );
        file.add( item );

        file.addSeparator();

        item = new JMenuItem( "Print Setup...", printsetupIcon );
        item.setHorizontalTextPosition( SwingConstants.RIGHT );
        item.setMnemonic( KeyEvent.VK_U );
        file.add( item );

        item = new JMenuItem( "Print", printIcon );
        item.setHorizontalTextPosition( SwingConstants.RIGHT );
```

continues

9

MENUS AND
TOOLBARS

LISTING 9.4   CONTINUED

```
            item.setMnemonic( KeyEvent.VK_P );
item.setAccelerator( KeyStroke.getKeyStroke(
                            KeyEvent.VK_P, Event.CTRL_MASK ) );
        file.add( item );

        file.addSeparator();

        item = new JMenuItem( "Exit", exitIcon );
        item.setHorizontalTextPosition( SwingConstants.RIGHT );
        item.setMnemonic( KeyEvent.VK_X );
item.setAccelerator( KeyStroke.getKeyStroke(
                            KeyEvent.VK_X, Event.CTRL_MASK ) );
        item.addActionListener( new ActionListener() {
            public void actionPerformed( ActionEvent e ) {
                System.exit( 0 );
            }
        } );
        file.add( item );

        menubar.add( file );

        //
        // Create an options menu containing two
        // CheckBoxMenuItems.
        //
        JMenu options = new JMenu( "Options" );
        options.setMnemonic( KeyEvent.VK_O );

        JCheckBoxMenuItem cbItem = new JCheckBoxMenuItem( "Log", logIcon
);
        cbItem.setMnemonic( KeyEvent.VK_L );
cbItem.setAccelerator( KeyStroke.getKeyStroke(
                            KeyEvent.VK_L, Event.CTRL_MASK ) );
        options.add( cbItem );

        cbItem = new JCheckBoxMenuItem( "Echo", echoIcon, true );
        cbItem.setMnemonic( KeyEvent.VK_E );
cbItem.setAccelerator( KeyStroke.getKeyStroke(
                            KeyEvent.VK_E, Event.CTRL_MASK ) );
        options.add( cbItem );

        JMenu foreground = new JMenu( "Foreground" );
        foreground.setMnemonic( KeyEvent.VK_F );

        ButtonGroup group = new ButtonGroup();

JRadioButtonMenuItem rbItem =
                    new JRadioButtonMenuItem( "White", whiteIcon );
        rbItem.setForeground( Color.white );
```

```
        rbItem.setMnemonic( KeyEvent.VK_W );
        rbItem.setAccelerator( KeyStroke.getKeyStroke(
                        KeyEvent.VK_W, Event.CTRL_MASK ) );
foreground.add( rbItem );
        group.add( rbItem );

        rbItem = new JRadioButtonMenuItem( "Black", blackIcon );
        rbItem.setForeground( Color.black );
        rbItem.setSelected( true );
        rbItem.setMnemonic( KeyEvent.VK_B );
        rbItem.setAccelerator( KeyStroke.getKeyStroke(
                        KeyEvent.VK_B, Event.CTRL_MASK ) );
        foreground.add( rbItem );
        group.add( rbItem );

        rbItem = new JRadioButtonMenuItem( "Red", redIcon );
        rbItem.setForeground( Color.red );
        rbItem.setMnemonic( KeyEvent.VK_R );
        rbItem.setAccelerator( KeyStroke.getKeyStroke(
                    troke.getKeyStroke(
                        RL_MASK ) );
        foreground.add( rbItem );
        group.add( rbItem );

        options.add( foreground );

        menubar.add( options );

        return( menubar );

    } // createMenu
```

Placing Menus

The previous section showed how to create menus and add the various types of menu items supported by the JFC to a menu. The examples showed the resulting menu attached to a frame. In the JFC, a menu can be attached to a frame or used in a pop-up menu. Both of these scenarios will be presented in this section.

Frame Menus

In the JFC, an instance of the JFrame class can contain one menubar that is displayed across the top of the frame, immediately below the title bar. The menubar is an instance of the JMenuBar class. In turn, the menubar can contain one or more menus that are instances of the JMenu class. The menubar is attached to the frame by using the JFrame class's setJMenuBar method. The setMenuBar method inherited from the awt.Frame class is not used for this purpose.

The menu shown in Figure 9.11 was attached to the JFrame class's frameInit method. The menubar is created in the createMenu method called from the frameInit method. The menu is added to the frame by using the setJMenuBar method. Using a separate method to create the menubar allows subclasses to override the menu and change the menu. The menu could also be created in the constructor. However, the frame has multiple constructors and only one frameInit method. This technique is demonstrated in the previous examples in this chapter.

In the JMenuBar class, the add method is used to append the given menu to the list of top-level menus already contained on the menubar. The menus appear on the menubar in the order they are added. The remove method can be used to remove a menu at a given index.

Some look-and-feel implementations of the menubar treat the Help menu differently than other menus. It is customary to have the Help menu the last menu; some look-and-feel implementations place the Help menu to the far right of the menubar. The JMenuBar class provides the setHelpMenu method to specify which menu should be treated as the Help menu. The Help menu can be queried with the getHelpMenu method.

> **NOTE**
>
> The current implementation of the JMenuBar class contains the setHelpMenu and getHelpMenu methods presented in the previous paragraph. However, they are not yet implemented and throw an error if called. An implementation for these methods should be available in a future version of the JMenuBar class.

The current menus contained in the menubar can be queried using the getMenu method. The index of the desired menu is passed to the method. The number of menus contained on a menubar can be determined using the getMenuC method. The getSubElements method can be used to obtain an array of MenuElement instances, one for each menu in the menubar. To iterate through the menus on a menubar, the following code snippet could be used.

```
for( int i = 0; i < menuBar.getMenuCount(); i++ ) {
    JMenu menu = menuBar.getMenu( i );
    // Operate on menu.
    System.out.println( i + ": " + menu );
}
```

A JMenuBar instance delegates selection management to a SingleSelectionModel instance. The model can be queried with the getSelectionModel method and set with the setSelectionModel method. However, the default selection model is sufficient for most applications. The selection model is not a bound property in the JMenuBar class. The setSelected method can be used to set the currently selected component in the menu. This is a convenient method that passes the selection to the SingleSelectionModel instance.

Pop-up Menus

Instances of the JPopupMenu class are used by the JMenu class to display their menus. This use of the class is typically hidden from application developers. However, a developer can create an instance of the JPopupMenu class to provide a menu anywhere desired. These are often used to provide context-sensitive menus that are displayed when the user clicks on a component.

Creating and configuring a pop-up menu is very similar to creating a frame menu. The instance of the JPopupMenu class is created, and then Actions, Components, and JMenuItems can be added or inserted into the pop-up menu. Conspicuously missing from the JPopupMenu class API are methods to remove menu items from the menu. The pop-up menu can contain a label, used like a title. The label can be specified at construction time and set and queried later by using the setLabel and getLabel methods.

A Component contained in the pop-up menu can be obtained by calling the getComponentAtIndex method with the index of the desired Component. Conversely, the index of a Component in the menu can be determined with the getComponentIndex method.

The pop-up menu can be displayed and positioned by using the show method. This method takes an invoker Component in which the pop-up menu is to be displayed, and the x and y coordinates in the invoker's coordinate space. The setVisible method is used to hide the menu and to redisplay it if required. The current visibility of the menu can be determined using the isVisible method. The menu can be moved with the setLocation method. A pop-up menu can be used over a different Component by changing the invoker via the setInvoker method. The current invoker Component can be queried by using the getInvoker method.

The ApplicationMouseListener class is used to listen for the popupTrigger MouseEvent. When it is detected, the pop-up menu is created and displayed. The source of the MouseEvent is used as the invoker Component. The coordinates where the mouse was located at the time of the event are queried from the event and used to position the pop-up menu at the mouse location. It should be noted that the MouseListener needs to check for the pop-up trigger in both the mousePressed and mouseReleased methods. This is because pop-up menus are triggered by different events for different look-and-feels.

```java
package com.foley.utility;

import java.awt.*;
import java.awt.event.*;

import javax.swing.*;


/**
 * Pop up the context sensitive menu when the pop-up
 * trigger event is delivered.
 **/
class ApplicationMouseListener extends MouseAdapter
    implements MouseListener {

    /**
     * See if the mouse event is the pop-up trigger. If so,
     * display the pop-up menu.
     *
     * @param e The mouse event causing this call.
     **/
    public void mouseReleased( MouseEvent e ) {
        if( e.isPopupTrigger() ) {
showPopupMenu( ( Component )e.getSource(),
                            e.getX(), e.getY() );
        }
    }


    /**
     * See if the mouse event is the pop-up trigger. If so,
     * display the pop-up menu.
     *
     * @param e The mouse event causing this call.
     **/
    public void mousePressed( MouseEvent e ) {
        if( e.isPopupTrigger() ) {
showPopupMenu( ( Component )e.getSource(),
                            e.getX(), e.getY() );
        }
    }


    /**
     * Display the pop-up menu using the given invoker, and at the
     * specified location.
     *
     * @param invoker The component used as the menu's invoker.
     * @param x The X coordinate for the pop-up menu.
     * @param y The Y coordinate for the pop-up menu.
     **/
```

```
        private void showPopupMenu( Component invoker, int x, int y ) {
            Icon saveIcon = null;
            Icon saveasIcon = null;
            Icon printIcon = null;
            Icon printsetupIcon = null;

            try {
                //
                // Load the images used.
                //
                saveIcon = ImageLoader.loadIcon( "save.gif" );
                saveasIcon = ImageLoader.loadIcon( "saveas.gif" );
                printIcon = ImageLoader.loadIcon( "print.gif" );
                printsetupIcon = ImageLoader.loadIcon( "printsetup.gif" );
            } catch( InterruptedException ie ) {
                System.err.println( "Error loading images" );
                return;
            }

            JPopupMenu popup = new JPopupMenu( "Title" );

            JMenuItem item = new JMenuItem( "Save", saveIcon );
            item.setHorizontalTextPosition( SwingConstants.RIGHT );
            item.setMnemonic( KeyEvent.VK_S );
            popup.add( item );

            item = new JMenuItem( "Save As...", saveasIcon );
            item.setHorizontalTextPosition( SwingConstants.RIGHT );
            item.setMnemonic( KeyEvent.VK_A );
            popup.add( item );

            popup.addSeparator();

            item = new JMenuItem( "Print Setup...", printsetupIcon );
            item.setHorizontalTextPosition( SwingConstants.RIGHT );
            item.setMnemonic( KeyEvent.VK_U );
            popup.add( item );

            item = new JMenuItem( "Print", printIcon );
            item.setHorizontalTextPosition( SwingConstants.RIGHT );
            item.setMnemonic( KeyEvent.VK_P );
            popup.add( item );

            popup.show( invoker, x, y );

        }

} // ApplicationMouseListener
```

Listing 9.5 demonstrates how the ApplicationMouseListener shown here is registered
with each Component added to the content pane of an ApplicationFrame. This is done

9

**MENUS AND
TOOLBARS**

by using a `ContainerListener` instance. When the `componentAdded` method is called, the `ApplicationMouseListener` instance is registered with the new `Component`. If the `componentRemoved` method is called, the `MouseListener` instance is removed from the `Component` being removed from the content pane. This technique only works for simple containers without deeply nested components. For arbitrary container hierarchies, a more complex `ContainerListener` would be required. The pop-up menu created by this sample code is shown in Figure 9.12.

FIGURE 9.12

A `JPopupMenu`
in the
`ApplicationFrame`.

LISTING 9.5 `MouseListener` ADDED TO ALL Components OF AN `ApplicationFrame`

```
package com.foley.utility;

import java.awt.*;

import java.awt.event.*;

import java.io.Serializable;

import javax.swing.*;

import javax.swing.border.*;

import javax.swing.event.*;


/**
 * A toplevel frame. The frame customizes the
 * Icon and content in the frameInit method.
 *
 * @author Mike Foley
 **/
public class ApplicationFrame extends JFrame implements Serializable {

    private static Icon exitIcon;
    private static Icon closeIcon;
    private static Icon saveIcon;
    private static Icon saveasIcon;
    private static Icon openIcon;
    private static Icon newIcon;
    private static Icon printIcon;
    private static Icon printsetupIcon;
```

```
        private static Icon logIcon;
        private static Icon echoIcon;
        private static Icon whiteIcon;
        private static Icon blackIcon;
        private static Icon redIcon;
        private static Icon blueIcon;

        /**
         * The MouseListener for content components. This will
         * pop up a menu is the popupTrigger is received.
         **/
        private MouseListener mouseListener;


        /**
         * Load images used in the frame.
         **/
        static {
            try {
                closeIcon = ImageLoader.loadIcon( "close.gif" );
                exitIcon = ImageLoader.loadIcon( "exit.gif" );
                saveIcon = ImageLoader.loadIcon( "save.gif" );
                saveasIcon = ImageLoader.loadIcon( "saveas.gif" );
                openIcon = ImageLoader.loadIcon( "open.gif" );
                newIcon = ImageLoader.loadIcon( "new.gif" );
                printIcon = ImageLoader.loadIcon( "print.gif" );
                printsetupIcon = ImageLoader.loadIcon( "printsetup.gif" );
                logIcon = ImageLoader.loadIcon( "log.gif" );
                echoIcon = ImageLoader.loadIcon( "echo.gif" );
                whiteIcon = ImageLoader.loadIcon( "white.gif" );
                blackIcon = ImageLoader.loadIcon( "black.gif" );
                redIcon = ImageLoader.loadIcon( "red.gif" );
                blueIcon = ImageLoader.loadIcon( "blue.gif" );
            } catch( InterruptedException ie ) {
            }

        }


        /**
         * ApplicationFrame, null constructor.
         **/
        public ApplicationFrame() {
            this( null );
        }


        /**
         * ApplicationFrame, constructor.
         *
```

9

MENUS AND TOOLBARS

continues

LISTING 9.5   CONTINUED

```java
     * @param title The title for the frame.
     **/
    public ApplicationFrame( String title ) {
        super( title );
    }


    /**
     * Customize the frame for our application.
     **/
    protected void frameInit() {
        //
        // Let the super create the panes.
        super.frameInit();

        try {
            Image bullseye = ImageLoader.loadImage( "bullseye.gif" );
            setIconImage( bullseye );
        } catch( InterruptedException ie ) {
            System.err.println( "Could not laod image bullseye.gif" );
            ie.printStackTrace();
        }

        JMenuBar menuBar = createMenu();
        setJMenuBar( menuBar );

        createApplicationContent();

    } // frameInit


    /**
     * Create the content for the applictaion
     **/
    protected void createApplicationContent() {

        mouseListener = createMouseListener();
        Container content = getContentPane();
        content.addContainerListener( new ContainerListener() {
            public void componentAdded( ContainerEvent e ) {
                Component c = e.getChild();
                c.addMouseListener( mouseListener );
            }
            public void componentRemoved( ContainerEvent e ) {
                Component c = e.getChild();
                c.removeMouseListener( mouseListener );
            }
        } );
```

```
        JPanel center = new JPanel();
        center.setLayout( new GridLayout( 4, 2 ) );

        center.add( new JLabel( "Name: ", SwingConstants.RIGHT ) );
        center.add( new JTextField() );
        center.add( new JLabel( "Street: ", SwingConstants.RIGHT ) );
        center.add( new JTextField() );
center.add( new JLabel( "City and State: ",
                            SwingConstants.RIGHT ) );
        center.add( new JTextField() );
        center.add( new JLabel( "Zip Code: ", SwingConstants.RIGHT ) );
        center.add( new JTextField() );

center.setBorder( BorderFactory.createBevelBorder(
                                    BevelBorder.LOWERED ) );

        content.add( BorderLayout.CENTER, center );

    } // createApplicationContent


    /**
     * Create the menu for the frame.
     *
     * @return The menu for the frame.
     **/
    protected JMenuBar createMenu() {
        JMenuBar menuBar = new JMenuBar();

        JMenu file = new JMenu( "File" );
        file.setMnemonic( KeyEvent.VK_F );

        JMenu newMenu = new JMenu( "New" );
        newMenu.setMnemonic( KeyEvent.VK_N );

        JMenuItem item = new JMenuItem( "Frame" );
        item.setHorizontalTextPosition( SwingConstants.RIGHT );
        item.setMnemonic( KeyEvent.VK_F );
        newMenu.add( item );

        item = new JMenuItem( "Window" );
        item.setHorizontalTextPosition( SwingConstants.RIGHT );
        item.setMnemonic( KeyEvent.VK_W );
        newMenu.add( item );

        item = new JMenuItem( "Icon" );
        item.setHorizontalTextPosition( SwingConstants.RIGHT );
        item.setMnemonic( KeyEvent.VK_I );
        newMenu.add( item );
```

9

MENUS AND TOOLBARS

continues

LISTING 9.5 CONTINUED

```
        file.add( newMenu );

        item = new JMenuItem( "Open", openIcon );
        item.setHorizontalTextPosition( SwingConstants.RIGHT );
        item.setMnemonic( KeyEvent.VK_O );
item.setAccelerator( KeyStroke.getKeyStroke(
                              KeyEvent.VK_O, Event.CTRL_MASK ) );
        file.add( item );

        item = new JMenuItem( "Close", closeIcon );
        item.setHorizontalTextPosition( SwingConstants.RIGHT );
        item.setMnemonic( KeyEvent.VK_C );
item.setAccelerator( KeyStroke.getKeyStroke(
                              KeyEvent.VK_C, Event.CTRL_MASK ) );
        file.add( item );

        file.addSeparator();

        item = new JMenuItem( "Save", saveIcon );
        item.setHorizontalTextPosition( SwingConstants.RIGHT );
        item.setMnemonic( KeyEvent.VK_S );
item.setAccelerator( KeyStroke.getKeyStroke(
                              KeyEvent.VK_S, Event.CTRL_MASK ) );
        file.add( item );

        item = new JMenuItem( "Save As...", saveasIcon );
        item.setHorizontalTextPosition( SwingConstants.RIGHT );
        item.setMnemonic( KeyEvent.VK_A );
        file.add( item );

        file.addSeparator();

        item = new JMenuItem( "Print Setup...", printsetupIcon );
        item.setHorizontalTextPosition( SwingConstants.RIGHT );
        item.setMnemonic( KeyEvent.VK_U );
        file.add( item );

        item = new JMenuItem( "Print", printIcon );
        item.setHorizontalTextPosition( SwingConstants.RIGHT );
        item.setMnemonic( KeyEvent.VK_P );
item.setAccelerator( KeyStroke.getKeyStroke(
                              KeyEvent.VK_P, Event.CTRL_MASK ) );
        file.add( item );

        file.addSeparator();

        item = new JMenuItem( "Exit", exitIcon );
        item.setHorizontalTextPosition( SwingConstants.RIGHT );
        item.setMnemonic( KeyEvent.VK_X );
```

```
item.setAccelerator( KeyStroke.getKeyStroke(
                          KeyEvent.VK_X, Event.CTRL_MASK ) );
        item.addActionListener( new ActionListener() {
            public void actionPerformed( ActionEvent e ) {
                System.exit( 0 );
            }
        } );
        file.add( item );

        menuBar.add( file );

        JMenu options = new JMenu( "Options" );
        options.setMnemonic( KeyEvent.VK_O );

        JCheckBoxMenuItem cbItem = new JCheckBoxMenuItem( "Log", logIcon
);
        cbItem.setMnemonic( KeyEvent.VK_L );
cbItem.setAccelerator( KeyStroke.getKeyStroke(
                          KeyEvent.VK_L, Event.CTRL_MASK ) );
        options.add( cbItem );

        cbItem = new JCheckBoxMenuItem( "Echo", echoIcon, true );
        cbItem.setMnemonic( KeyEvent.VK_E );
cbItem.setAccelerator( KeyStroke.getKeyStroke(
                          KeyEvent.VK_E, Event.CTRL_MASK ) );
        options.add( cbItem );

        JMenu foreground = new JMenu( "Foreground" );
        foreground.setMnemonic( KeyEvent.VK_F );

        ButtonGroup group = new ButtonGroup();

JRadioButtonMenuItem rbItem =
                    new JRadioButtonMenuItem( "White", whiteIcon );
        rbItem.setForeground( Color.white );
        rbItem.setMnemonic( KeyEvent.VK_W );
        rbItem.setAccelerator( KeyStroke.getKeyStroke(
                          KeyEvent.VK_W, Event.CTRL_MASK ) );
        foreground.add( rbItem );
        group.add( rbItem );

        rbItem = new JRadioButtonMenuItem( "Black", blackIcon );
        rbItem.setForeground( Color.black );
        rbItem.setSelected( true );
        rbItem.setMnemonic( KeyEvent.VK_B );
        rbItem.setAccelerator( KeyStroke.getKeyStroke(
                          KeyEvent.VK_B, Event.CTRL_MASK ) );
        foreground.add( rbItem );
        group.add( rbItem );
```

9

MENUS AND TOOLBARS

continues

LISTING 9.5 CONTINUED

```java
        rbItem = new JRadioButtonMenuItem( "Red", redIcon );
        rbItem.setForeground( Color.red );
        rbItem.setMnemonic( KeyEvent.VK_R );
        rbItem.setAccelerator( KeyStroke.getKeyStroke(
                            KeyEvent.VK_R, Event.CTRL_MASK ) );
        foreground.add( rbItem );
        group.add( rbItem );

        rbItem = new JRadioButtonMenuItem( "Blue", blueIcon );
        rbItem.setForeground( Color.blue );
        rbItem.setMnemonic( KeyEvent.VK_U );
        rbItem.setAccelerator( KeyStroke.getKeyStroke(
                            KeyEvent.VK_U, Event.CTRL_MASK ) );
        foreground.add( rbItem );
        group.add( rbItem );

        options.add( foreground );

        menuBar.add( options );


        return( menuBar );

    } // createMenuBar


    /**
     * Create the mouse listener for the frame.
     *
     * @return The MouseListener for the content in the frame.
     **/
    protected MouseListener createMouseListener() {
        return new ApplicationMouseListener();
    }


    /**
     * Application entry point.
     * Create the frame, and display it.
     *
     * @param args Command line parameter. Not used.
     **/
    public static void main( String[] args ) {

ApplicationFrame frame =
                        new ApplicationFrame( "ApplicationFrame" );
        frame.pack();
        frame.setVisible( true );
```

```
    }

} // ApplicationFrame
```

Pop-up Menu Events

Similar to the way the JMenu class fired MenuEvents to the methods defined in the
MenuListener interface, the JPopupMenu class fires PopupMenuEvents to the methods
defined in the PopupMenuListener interface. A quick comparison of the MenuEvent
shown earlier in this chapter and the PopupMenuEvent shown next reveals that the
PopupMenuEvent is the same as the MenuEvent. Neither delivers information with the
event beyond what is contained in the EventObject class. The reason for the new class is
to distinguish between event types.

```
public class PopupMenuEvent extends EventObject {
    public PopupMenuEvent(Object source) {
        super(source);
    }
}
```

Similarly, comparison of the MenuListener interface, shown earlier in this chapter, and
the PopupMenuListener interface, shown in the following code, reveals semantically
equivalent methods defined in each interface. Unfortunately, the names of the methods
are different. The names in the PopupMenuListener interface are much more descriptive
than the equivalents in the MenuListener interface. The popupMenuWillBecomeVisible
method is called immediately before the pop-up menu is shown. The
popupMenuWillBecomeInvisible is called immediately before the menu is hidden.
Finally, the popupMenuCanceled method is called if the menu was dismissed without an
item being selected.

```
public interface PopupMenuListener extends EventListener {

    /**
     *  This method is called before the pop-up menu becomes visible
     */
    void popupMenuWillBecomeVisible(PopupMenuEvent e);

    /**
     * This method is called before the pop-up menu becomes invisible
     * Note that a JPopupMenu can become invisible any time
     */
    void popupMenuWillBecomeInvisible(PopupMenuEvent e);

    /**
     * This method is called when the pop-up menu is canceled
     */
    void popupMenuCanceled(PopupMenuEvent e);
}
```

9

MENUS AND
TOOLBARS

PopupMenuListeners can be added to pop-up menus created by the JMenu class and pop-up menus created by the application directly. For example, the following code can be used to add a PopupMenuListener to the pop-up menu created by the Options menu in the ApplicationFrame's menu presented in the previous code.

```java
JMenu options = new JMenu( "Options" );
options.setMnemonic( KeyEvent.VK_O );
// Option menu created and added to the menubar.

JPopupMenu optionsPopUpMenu = options.getPopupMenu();
optionsPopUpMenu.addPopupMenuListener( new PopupMenuListener() {
    public void popupMenuWillBecomeVisible(PopupMenuEvent e) {
        System.out.println( "popupMenuWillBecomeVisible" );
    }
    public void popupMenuWillBecomeInvisible(PopupMenuEvent e) {
        System.out.println( "popupMenuWillBecomeInvisible" );
    }
    public void popupMenuCanceled(PopupMenuEvent e) {
        System.out.println( "popupMenuCanceled" );
    }
} );
```

The MenuElement Interface

The MenuElement interface should be implemented by any Component that is added to a JMenu instance. However, as you have seen in the previous section, this requirement is not enforced. This interface is shown in the following:

```java
public interface MenuElement {

    /**
* Process a mouse event. event is a MouseEvent with source being
     * the receiving element's component.
     * path is the path of the receiving element in the menu
     * hierarchy including the receiving element itself.
     * manager is the MenuSelectionManager for the menu hierarchy.
* This method should process the MouseEvent and change the
     * menu selection if necessary
     * by using MenuSelectionManager's API.
* Note: you do not have to forward the event to sub-components.
     * This is done automatically
     * by the MenuSelectionManager.
     */
    public void processMouseEvent( MouseEvent event,MenuElement path[],
                                   MenuSelectionManager manager);


    /**
     *   Process a key event.
     */
```

```
public void processKeyEvent( KeyEvent event, MenuElement path[],
                             MenuSelectionManager manager);

    /**
     * Call by the MenuSelection when the MenuElement is added or remove
     * from the menu selection.
     */
    public void menuSelectionChanged(boolean isIncluded);

    /**
 * This method should return an array containing the
     * sub-elements for the receiving menu element
     */
    public MenuElement[] getSubElements();

    /*
 * This method should return the java.awt.Component
     * used to paint the receiving element.
 * The returned component will be used to convert
     * events and detect if an event is inside
     * a MenuElement's component.
     */
    public Component getComponent();
}
```

The JFC menu items delegate to their UI object the processMouseEvent and processKeyEvent methods. The menuSelectionChanged method is used to inform the Component when it is added or removed from the menu selection. The Component should update its selection state accordingly. The Component returns an array of MenuElement instances that are children of that item from the getSubElements. If the Component doesn't have any children menu items, it should return an array of length 0, not null. The getComponent method returns the Component used to paint the menu. The JMenu and JMenuItem classes return this from the getComponent method.

Creating Toolbars

Many applications contain one or more toolbars. The JFC provides the JToolBar class to facilitate adding toolbars to your application or applet. The JToolBar class implements a floating toolbar that can be dragged off the original frame into its own frame. It can then be redocked onto any side of the original frame. To accomplish this functionality, the JToolBar class is designed to work with a container employing a BorderLayout for Component positioning. To allow the toolbar to be docked on any side of the frame, user components should only occupy the center region of the BorderLayout, leaving the north, south, east, and west regions for the toolbar. The current version of the JFC is designed for a single toolbar in a region. Thus, creating complex toolbars still requires additional user code.

Any component can be added to a toolbar by using the add method. In practice, the most common components contained on a toolbar are instances of the JButton class displaying icons. The JToolBar class is Action aware. This allows Action instances to be added to the toolbar directly. The toolbar will query the Action for its name and small icon and will place these on a JButton instance that is added to the toolbar.

The toolbar instance configures itself with a BoxLayout layout manager oriented along the x axis for horizontally oriented toolbars and along the y axis for vertical toolbars. Components added to the toolbar will be placed to the right of existing components in the toolbar for horizontal toolbars, and below existing components in vertical toolbars. The JToolBar class does not provide any insert methods. However, remove methods are inherited from the AWT Container class. Reordering a toolbar can be performed by removing components and adding them in a different order. The getComponentIndex method will return the index of the given component. This method returns -1 if the component is not found in the toolbar. The inverse of this method, getComponentAtIndex, returns the Component at the given index. This method returns null if the index is larger than the number of components in the toolbar and will throw an ArrayIndexException if the index is negative.

Passing the setOrientation method the constant HORIZONTAL or VERTICAL, defined in the SwingConstants interface, can change the orientation of a toolbar. When the orientation is changed, a new BoxLayout layout manager with the proper axis for the new orientation is created and set for the toolbar. The toolbar is then revalidated and repainted to reflect the new orientation. The current orientation can be queried by using the getOrientation method. The orientation of the toolbar is not a bound property.

The following code creates a toolbar and adds it to the ApplicationFrame presented earlier in this section. The toolbar is created in the protected createToolBar method called from the modified frameInit method shown next. This allows extensions of the ApplicationFrame class to change the default toolbar if desired. The toolbar is added to the north region of the content pane. Recall that the content pane is configured with a BorderLayout by default. Instances of the JButton class are created containing icons and added to the toolbar. The ExitAction is also added to the toolbar. The resulting frame containing the toolbar is shown in Figure 9.13.

```
/**
 * Customize the frame for our application.
 **/
protected void frameInit() {
    //
    // Let the super create the panes.
    super.frameInit();
```

```
    // Create the menu, and add it to the frame
    JMenuBar menuBar = createFrameMenu();
    setJMenuBar( menuBar );

    // Create the toolbar, and add it to the NORTH region
    // of the content pane.
    JToolBar toolBar = createToolBar();
    Container content = getContentPane();
    content.add( BorderLayout.NORTH, toolBar );

    createApplicationContent();

} // frameInit

/**
 * Create the toolbar for the frame.
 * <p>
 * @return The toolbar for the frame.
 **/
protected JToolBar createToolBar() {
    JToolBar toolBar = new JToolBar();

    // Add items to the toolbar.
    toolBar.add( new JButton( newIcon ) );
    toolBar.add( new JButton( openIcon ) );
    toolBar.add( new JButton( saveIcon ) );
    toolBar.add( new JButton( closeIcon ) );
    toolBar.addSeparator();
    toolBar.add( new JButton( printIcon ) );
    toolBar.addSeparator();
    toolBar.add( new ExitAction() );
    return( toolBar );
}
```

FIGURE 9.13

This is a JToolBar
added to the
ApplicationFrame.

The first thing that stands out in Figure 9.13 is that when adding an Action instance to a toolbar, both the name and icon associated with the Action are added to the JButton placed on the toolbar. Thus, if Actions and user-created buttons are added to a toolbar, care must be taken to ensure a consistent look. A better createToolBar method is shown in Listing 9.6. The updated toolbar is shown in Figure 9.14.

9

MENUS AND
TOOLBARS

FIGURE 9.14

A better JToolBar
for the
ApplicationFrame.

LISTING 9.6   TOOLBAR WITH ASSOCIATED ActionS AND ICONS

```
/**
 * Create the toolbar for the frame.
 * <p>
 * @return The toolbar for the frame.
 **/
protected JToolBar createToolBar() {
    JToolBar toolBar = new JToolBar();

    JButton button = new JButton( "New", newIcon );
    button.setHorizontalTextPosition(JButton.CENTER);
    button.setVerticalTextPosition(JButton.BOTTOM);
    toolBar.add( button );

    button = new JButton( "Open", openIcon );
    button.setHorizontalTextPosition(JButton.CENTER);
    button.setVerticalTextPosition(JButton.BOTTOM);
    toolBar.add( button );

    button = new JButton( "Save", saveIcon );
    button.setHorizontalTextPosition(JButton.CENTER);
    button.setVerticalTextPosition(JButton.BOTTOM);
    toolBar.add( button );

    button = new JButton( "Close", closeIcon );
    button.setHorizontalTextPosition(JButton.CENTER);
    button.setVerticalTextPosition(JButton.BOTTOM);
    toolBar.add( button );

    toolBar.addSeparator();

    button = new JButton( "Print", printIcon );
    button.setHorizontalTextPosition(JButton.CENTER);
    button.setVerticalTextPosition(JButton.BOTTOM);
    toolBar.add( button );

    toolBar.addSeparator();

    toolBar.add( new ExitAction() );

    return( toolBar );
}
```

The `addSeparator` method adds space between the buttons on the toolbar. This allows the buttons to be easily grouped by functionality.

The dimpled region to the far left of the toolbar in Figure 9.14 provides a handle that can be dragged to detach the toolbar from the frame. The toolbar can be docked on a different side of the frame or left in its own window. These options are shown in Figures 9.15 and 9.16. This region is specific to the Metal look-and-feel and is not present in the Windows look-and-feel. When using the Windows look-and-feel, the toolbar can be dragged to any region in the frame where a button is not located.

FIGURE 9.15

The `JToolBar` *in its own window.*

FIGURE 9.16

The `JToolBar` *in the south region.*

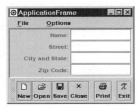

9

MENUS AND TOOLBARS

There are situations where it is not desirable to allow the user to move the toolbar. The toolbar can be fixed in the location set by the application by calling the `JToolBar` `setFloatable` method with a parameter of `false`. The state of the floatable property can be queried with the `isFloatable` method. This property can be changed at runtime to alter whether or not the toolbar is floatable. When the toolbar is not floatable, the dimpled drag region of the toolbar is not displayed in the Metal look-and-feel. This type of toolbar is shown in Figure 9.17. The default setting is to allow the toolbar to float. The `floatable` property is not bound in the `JToolBar` class.

The margin between the toolbar's border and its components can be set with the `setMargin` method. This method takes an `Insets` instance to specify the margin on each side of the toolbar. The `getMargin` method returns an `Insets` instance with the current margins for the toolbar. The `margin` property is bound in the `JToolBar` class with the name of `margin`. This is the only bound property defined in the `JToolBar` class. This property seems redundant. The JToolBar class inherits from the JComponent class. As such, it contains the border property that can be used for the same purpose as the margin property.

FIGURE 9.17

A fixed instance of the JToolBar *class.*

Summary

Menus and toolbars are an important part of a modern graphical user interface. The JFC provides a rich set of APIs for building these user interface components. Menus can contain text and/or icons. Check box and radio button menu items are supported. Any depth of cascading menus can be implemented. A menu can be attached to a frame or popped up anywhere desired.

The JFC provides the JToolBar class for adding toolbars to a frame. The toolbar will float by default. This allows the toolbar to be docked to any side of the frame or placed in its own window. You can specify that the toolbar not be allowed to float. In that case, the user will not be able to drag it off the frame or to a different location.

Both menus and toolbars are Action-aware components. This allows Action instances to be added directly to menus and toolbars. The menu and toolbar will update their visual representations if the name, icon, or enabled status of the Action changes. This provides an easy way to ensure that the menu- and toolbar-enabled statuses are in sync with application actions.

JList, JComboBox, and Bound Controls

IN THIS CHAPTER

The JList and JComboBox classes create components that allow the user to select from a list of choices. The data models for these two classes are very similar. In fact, the ComboBoxModel interface extends the ListModel interface, adding methods to set and query a selected item.

The JList and JComboBox classes introduce you to the rendering portion of the Swing component architecture. When the items in a list or combo box are painted, the component itself doesn't do the painting. Instead, the painting is delegated to a renderer object. A single renderer can paint the entire component.

The JFC contains the BoundedRangeModel interface, which constrains an integer value between a minimum and maximum value. This data model is used by a number of classes in the JFC, most of which are presented in this chapter.

This chapter will introduce a number of new JFC classes and data models. You will learn:

- Rendered drawing
- How to use the JList class
- How to use the JComboBox class
- How to use the BoundedRangeModel interface
- How to use the JScrollBar class
- How to use the JSlider class
- How to use the JProgressBar class

Rubber Stamp Drawing

Complex controls such as lists can contain thousands of items to display. Creating a JLabel, or another component, to display each item in the list would be too resource-intensive to be practical. However, it would be nice to be able to independently configure each item in the list for display.

The JFC solution to this dilemma is to use a rendering component to visualize an item in the list. When the list needs to paint an item, the renderer is moved to the location where the item in the list needs to be displayed, sized correctly, and configured for the current item. Finally, the renderer paints the item. A stock JList instance uses an instance of the DefaultListRenderer class (which itself is an extension of the JLabel class) to visualize its items. However, a custom renderer can be added to the list to achieve any visual effect required. As you progress through this section, you will see that many JFC components employ a rendering component for visualization (the JTree and JTable classes discussed in the next two chapters, to name a few).

The `ListCellRenderer` Interface

The methods that define a rendering entity for instances of the `JList` class are defined in the `ListCellRenderer` interface, shown in Listing 10.1. As such, any class can implement this interface and act as a renderer for a list. In practice, however, the majority of renderers used are extensions of the `JLabel` class and implement the `ListCellRenderer` interface.

The `ListCellRenderer` interface contains a single method: `getListCellRendererComponent`. When this method is called, the renderer must configure the component that will render the value object passed to the method. The list where the item is being drawn is passed to this method. This way, if a renderer needs to know which list it is rendering, it does not need to keep a reference to the list, allowing a single renderer to be shared between any number of lists. The current state of the item in the list is also passed to the `getListCellRendererComponent` method. This allows the renderer to give visually distinct characteristics to selected items and items with the input focus. After the renderer has configured the component, it returns it to the caller.

The renderer should *not* create a new component instance each time the `getListCellRendererComponent` method is called. Instead, one component should be created and reconfigured with the current list item on each call. As previously mentioned, many times the renderer is itself a component. In that case, the renderer configures itself in the `getListCellRendererComponent` method and returns this from the method.

Listing 10.1 The `ListCellRenderer` Interface

```
public interface ListCellRenderer
{
    /**
     * Return a component that has been configured to display the
     * specified value. That component's <code>paint</code> method is
     * then called to "render" the cell.  If it is necessary to compute
     * the dimensions of a list because the list cells do not have a
     * fixed size, this method is called to generate a component on which
 * <code>getPreferredSize</code> can be invoked.
 *
     * @param list The JList we're painting.
     * @param value The value returned by
     *              list.getModel().getElementAt(index).
     * @param index The cells index.
     * @param isSelected True if the specified cell was selected.
     * @param cellHasFocus True if the specified cell has the focus.
     * @return A component whose paint() method will render the
     *          specified value.
```

continues

LISTING 10.1 CONTINUED

```
 *
 * @see JList
 * @see ListSelectionModel
 * @see ListModel
 */
Component getListCellRendererComponent(
    JList list,
    Object value,
    int index,
    boolean isSelected,
    boolean cellHasFocus);
}
```

A Simple `ListCellRenderer`

The `SimpleListCellRenderer` class is shown in Listing 10.2. This class is adapted from the default `ListCellRenderer` used by the `JList` class, but fixes a couple of bugs contained in the default renderer. The `SimpleListCellRenderer` class extends the `JLabel` class. In its constructor, the component is configured to be opaque, forcing the background color to be painted by the renderer. The component's border is created in the constructor, and a reference is kept to the border instance.

The `getListCellRendererComponent` configures the `JLabel` to the current state of the given value. If the list item is selected, the selected colors are queried from the list and set on the label. If not, the normal colors are obtained from the list and set on the label. Similarly, the list's font is queried and set on the label. If the list item is an instance of an icon, it is added to the label and the text is cleared. Otherwise, the `toString` method of the list item is called to get the object's string representation. Finally, the `Border` property is set for the label and the label is returned to the caller.

The `getListCellRendererComponent` method of a renderer has the potential to be called many times. It also has a significant impact on a list's performance. This being the case, the method must be efficient. Avoid unnecessary object creation in this method. Whenever possible, you should reconfigure objects for the current value rather than creating a new instance.

LISTING 10.2 THE `SimpleListCellRenderer` CLASS

```
package com.foley.utility;

import java.awt.*;
import java.io.*;

import javax.swing.*;
```

```java
import javax.swing.border.*;


public class SimpleListCellRenderer extends JLabel
    implements ListCellRenderer, Serializable
{

    protected static Border emptyBorder;

    public SimpleListCellRenderer() {
        super();

            emptyBorder = BorderFactory.createEmptyBorder( 2, 2, 2, 2 );

            //
            // We change the background color, so need to be opaque.
            //
        setOpaque(true);
    }


    public Component getListCellRendererComponent(
        JList list,
        Object value,
        int index,
        boolean isSelected,
        boolean cellHasFocus)
    {

        if( isSelected ) {
            //
            // Draw like any other list when selected.
            //
            setBackground( list.getSelectionBackground() );
            setForeground( list.getSelectionForeground() );
        } else {
            //
            // Paint in the list normal foreground and background colors.
            //
            setBackground( list.getBackground() );
            setForeground( list.getForeground() );
        } // else

        setFont( list.getFont() );

        if( value instanceof Icon ) {
            setIcon( ( Icon )value);
            setText( "" );
        } else {
```

continues

LISTING 10.2 CONTINUED

```
            setIcon( null );
            setText( (value == null ) ? "" : value.toString() );
        } // else

        setBorder( ( cellHasFocus ) ?
                UIManager.getBorder( "List.focusCellHighlightBorder" ) :
emptyBorder );

    return this;
    }

} // SimpleListRenderer
```

The SimpleListRenderer, as well as more exciting list renderers, are demonstrated in the next section covering the JList class.

Using the JList Class

The JList class provides the visual representation for selecting items in a set. In its simplest form, a list can be instantiated with an array or vector of objects. The list will create one item in the list for each element in the vector or array. This technique is demonstrated in the ListTest application for an array in Listing 10.3, which results in the list shown in Figure 10.1. Similarly, the setListData method can be called to replace the data contained in the list to the given array or vector.

LISTING 10.3 THE ListTest APPLICATION

```
package com.foley.test;

import java.awt.*;

import javax.swing.*;
import javax.swing.border.*;

import com.foley.utility.ApplicationFrame;


/**
 * An application that displays JList instances
 * in its frame.
 *
 * @author Mike Foley
 **/
public class ListTest extends Object {

    /**
```

```
 * Application entry point.
 * Create a frame, the list and display it.
 *
 * @param args Command line parameter. Not used.
 **/
public static void main( String args[] ) {

    String[] data = {"Apple", "Orange", "Grape", "Banana" };

    JFrame frame = new ApplicationFrame( "List Test" );

    JList list = new JList( data );

    frame.getContentPane().add( list, BorderLayout.CENTER );

    frame.pack();
    frame.setVisible( true );

} // main

} // ListTest
```

FIGURE 10.1

*A simple list
created from an
array.*

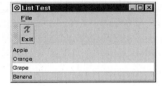

The list in the previous example allows multiple items to be selected in the list. In Figure 10.1, all items are selected except the item Grape. The default look-and-feel behavior is to perform a Ctrl+mouse-click to select items after the first item is selected. The list can be configured to allow the selection of a single item or multiple items. When multiple item selection is allowed, the selection can be specified to allow a continuous range or arbitrary items in the list. The setSelectionMode method can configure the list with the desired selection model.

The constants shown in Table 10.1 are defined in the JList class for the acceptable selection modes. The getSelectionMode method returns the current selection mode of the list.

TABLE 10.1   SELECTION MODES FOR A JList

Selection Mode	Description
SINGLE_SELECTION	A single item can be selected at a time.
SINGLE_INTERVAL_SELECTION	Multiple items in one contiguous interval can be selected at a time.
MULTIPLE_INTERVAL_SELECTION	Multiple items can be selected in an order.

The colors used for displaying selected elements can be set and queried using the setSelectionForeground/getSelectionForeground and setSelectionBackground/getSelectionBackground methods. These properties are bound in the JList class.

After displaying the list, the user's selection will need to be queried at some point. The indexes of the selected items, or the values themselves, can be queried. The getSelectedIndex and getSelectedValue methods return the index or value of the selected item in the list. If multiple selections are allowed, the index of the first selected item, or its value, is returned. If there is not a selected item, the getSelectedIndex method returns -1, while the getSelectedValue method returns null.

When multiple selection is enabled, the set of selected item's indexes or the set of selected values can be queried with the getSelectedIndices or getSelectedValues methods. The getSelectedIndices method returns an array of the indices of the selected items in numerical order, from the lowest index to the highest. Both methods return null if the selection set is empty. If only the range of selected indices is required, the getMinSelectionIndex and getMaxSelectionIndex methods can be used. If there are no items selected, both methods return -1. Also, if only one item is selected, both methods return the same index.

In many lists, there will be more data elements than can be displayed at one time. When this is the case, the list can be added to a JScrollPane. By default, the scroll pane will display scrollbars when it cannot display the entire contents of the list in its viewable area. A complete description of the JScrollPane class and its options is presented in Chapter 15, "Scrolling Components." The main method of the ListTest application can be changed to create a list that scrolls, as shown in Listing 10.4. The setVisibileRowCount method was used to configure the list to display five elements. The getVisibleRowCount method returns the number of elements displayed in the list. The resulting list is shown in Figure 10.2.

LISTING 10.4   PLACING A JList INSTANCE IN A JScrollPane INSTANCE

```
public static void main( String args[] ) {

        String[] data = {"Apple", "Orange", "Grape", "Banana",
                         "Mango", "Pineapple", "Peach", "Pear" };

        JFrame frame = new ApplicationFrame( "List Test" );

        JList list = new JList( data );
        list.setVisibleRowCount( 5 );

        JScrollPane scrollPane = new JScrollPane( list );
        scrollPane.setBorder( BorderFactory.createLoweredBevelBorder() );

        frame.getContentPane().add( scrollPane, BorderLayout.CENTER );

        frame.pack();
        frame.setVisible( true );

    } // main
```

FIGURE 10.2

A JList contained in a JScrollPane.

Once the list is in a scroll pane, you may need to programmatically alter which elements are visible in the viewport. The ensureIndexIsVisible method scrolls the view to force an element at the specified index to be displayed. If the index is already visible, the method doesn't alter the list. The range of indexes currently being displayed can be queried with the getFirstVisibleIndex and getLastVisibleIndex methods.

The bounds of a range of cells in the list can also be queried with the getCellBounds method. The indexes of the first and last rows are passed to the method, and the Rectangle that bounds the rows containing the indices is returned.

Instances of the JList class do not fire high-level mouse events. For example, you may want to fire an ActionEvent when a double-click is detected over a list element. This isn't built into the list, so it has to be programmed by users of the list. To aid in such development, the locationToIndex method is provided. This method takes a Point instance as a parameter to the method and returns the index of the element whose bounds contain that point. If the point isn't over an element in the list, -1 is returned.

A double-click of the left mouse button on an item in a list can be detected with the following mouse listener:

```
list.addMouseListener( new MouseAdapter() {
    public void mouseClicked( MouseEvent e ) {
        if( e.getClickCount() == 2 &&
            !( e.getModifiers() == InputEvent.ALT_MASK ) &&
            !( e.getModifiers() == InputEvent.META_MASK ) ) {
            int index = list.locationToIndex(e.getPoint());
            if( 0 <= index )
                System.out.println("Double-clicked on Item " + index);
        }
    }
} );>
```

The `ListModel` Interface

As you saw in the previous section, the JList class provides convenience methods for creating a list from a vector or array. However, you will often need to present data in a list that is contained in a data structure more complex than a simple array or vector. To do this, the class containing the data can implement the ListModel interface. Then the class can be used as the data model for a JList instance. Listing 10.5 shows this interface. As you can see, implementing the ListModel is very simple. The class must be able to return the size of the list, as well as an element at any given index in the range of 0 through one less than the size of the list. The class implementing the ListModel interface must also manage ListDataListener instances.

LISTING 10.5 THE ListModel INTERFACE

```
public interface ListModel
{
  /**
   * Returns the length of the list.
   */
  int getSize();

  /**
   * Returns the value at the specified index.
   */
  Object getElementAt(int index);

  /**
   * Add a listener to the list that's notified each time a change
   * to the data model occurs.
   * @param l the ListDataListener
   */
  void addListDataListener(ListDataListener l);
```

```
/**
 * Remove a listener from the list that's notified each time a
 * change to the data model occurs.
 * @param l the ListDataListener
 */
void removeListDataListener(ListDataListener l);
}
```

The `ListDataListener` interface and `ListDataEvent` class are shown in Listing 10.6. They are implemented by classes that are interested in changes to a `ListModel`. The `JList` class implements `ListDataListener` to observe changes in its data model. It is the responsibility of the model to fire the appropriate event when the data contained in the model changes. For example, if the list grows or shrinks, the `intervalAdded` or `intervalRemoved` method of listeners must be called so they can update their view.

The `ListDataEvent` class contains the information about which items in the list have changed. The type of the event can be queried with the `getType` method. This method will return one of the three constants defined in the event. However, the type is somewhat redundant because an `INTERVAL_ADDED` type event is the parameter for the `intervalAdded` method, an `INTERVAL_REMOVED` type event is the parameter for the `intervalRemoved` method, and an `INTERVAL_CHANGED` type event is the parameter for the `contentsChanged` method. The two indices that are contained in the event, and returned from the `getIndex0` and `getIndex1` methods, define the range of items that are associated with the event. The range is inclusive of the values returned from the `get` methods.

LISTING 10.6   THE `ListDataListener` INTERFACE

```
public interface ListDataListener extends EventListener {

    /**
     * Sent after the indices in the index0,index1
     * interval have been inserted in the data model.
     * The new interval includes both index0 and index1.
     */
    void intervalAdded(ListDataEvent e);


    /**
     * Sent after the indices in the index0,index1 interval
     * have been removed from the data model.  The interval
     * includes both index0 and index1.
     */
    void intervalRemoved(ListDataEvent e);
```

continues

10

JList, JComboBox, AND BOUND CONTROLS

LISTING 10.6 CONTINUED

```
    /**
     * Sent when the contents of the list have changed in a way
     * that's too complex to characterize with the previous
     * methods.  Index0 and index1 bracket the change.
     */
    void contentsChanged(ListDataEvent e);
}

public class ListDataEvent extends EventObject
{
    public static final int CONTENTS_CHANGED = 0;
    public static final int INTERVAL_ADDED = 1;
    public static final int INTERVAL_REMOVED = 2;

    private int type;
    private int index0;
    private int index1;

    public int getType() { return type; }
    public int getIndex0() { return index0; }
    public int getIndex1() { return index1; }

    public ListDataEvent(Object source,int type,int index0,int index1) {
        super(source);
    this.type = type;
    this.index0 = index0;
    this.index1 = index1;
    }
}
```

To aid in building `ListModel` classes, the `AbstractListModel` class is provided. As its name implies, this is an abstract class. It manages the `ListDataListeners` and contains methods to fire events to those listeners. Extensions of this class must manage the data in the list and implement the `getSize` and `getElementAt` methods. Extending the `AbstractListModel` class allows the model to manage the data in the list without concerning itself with the listeners.

An example of a `ListModel` is shown in Listing 10.7. The `CustomListModel` class extends the `AbstractListModel` class to inherit the `ListDataModelListeners` management functionality contained in the parent class. The `CustomListModel` class is a data model that grows and shrinks over time. It configures a JFC timer to receive notifications every `UPDATE_TIME` milliseconds. In the `actionPerformed` method called by the timer, the model adds or removes an item from the list depending on if the list is currently growing or shrinking. The size of the list is bounded by 0 and the `maxSize` attribute. The `actionPerformed` method fires the appropriate event to notify listeners of the change in the model.

An interesting observation can be made by looking at the `getElementAt` method in the `CustomListModel` class. The class does not contain a data structure, such as an array or vector, for the elements in the list. This is a key concept of the JFC architecture. The model need not contain all the data contained in the model at any given time. It only needs to be capable of returning any element in the model when it's requested. For example, a JFC model can be used as the front end to a database. The database can contain thousands of records, but the JFC model does not need to load the entire table locally when it is created. Indeed, if a record is not requested, the model never needs to retrieve that record. The model can retrieve the records on demand.

In other circumstances, it may make more sense to preload all the data into the model so it's immediately available for display. The architecture of the JFC is flexible enough that the model developer can decide what is best for the current model being implemented.

LISTING 10.7   THE `CustomListModel` CLASS

```
package com.foley.list;

import java.awt.event.*;

import javax.swing.*;
import javax.swing.event.*;


/**
 * CustomListModel is a list data model that grows
 * and shrinks over time. The data elements are calculated
 * 'on demand'.
 *
 * @author Mike Foley
 **/
public class CustomListModel extends AbstractListModel
    implements ActionListener {

    /**
     * The current size of the data model.
     **/
    private int size = 0;

    /**
     * The maximum size that the data model will grow to.
     **/
    private int maxSize = 25;

    /**
     * True if we are growing, false if we are shrinking.
```

continues

LISTING 10.7   CONTINUED

```
  **/
private boolean growing;

/**
 * The timer interval. This determines how
 * often the data in the model changes.
 **/
private static final int UPDATE_TIME = 500;


/**
 * CustomListModel, constructor
 * <p>
 * Initialize the model to a size of 0, and growing.
 * Create a timer and start it.
 **/
public CustomListModel() {
    size = 0;
    growing = true;

    //
    // Create a Timer that will call
    // our actionPerformed method event
    // UPDATE_TIME milliseconds.
    //
    Timer timer = new Timer( UPDATE_TIME, this );
    timer.start();
}


/**
 * getSize, from ListModel.
 * <p>
 * @return The length of the list.
 **/
public int getSize() {
    return( size );
}


/**
 * getElementAt, from ListModel.
 * <p>
 * @return The value at the specified index.
 * @param index The index of the requested element.
 **/
public Object getElementAt( int index ) {
    return( "Model Element: " + index );
}
```

```
/**
 * actionPerformed, from ActionListener.
 * <p>
 * Our timer has expired. If we are growing, increment
 * the size of the model by one. If we have hit the maximum
 * size for the model, change the direction so the next time
 * we are called, we will decrement. Fire an interval added
 * event to notify listeners that a new element is in the model.
 * <p>
 * If we are decrementing, reduce the model size and fire an
 * interval removed event. If the size gets to zero, change the
 * direction so we grow the next time this method is called.
 * <p>
 * @param event The event causing this method to be called.
 **/
public void actionPerformed( ActionEvent event ) {

    if( growing ) {
        //
        // We are getting bigger.
        //
        int origSize = getSize();
        size += 1;
        if( maxSize - 1 <= size ) {
            growing = false;
        }
        fireIntervalAdded( this, origSize, origSize );

    } else {
        //
        // We are getting smaller.
        //
        size -= 1;
        if( size < 1 ) {
            growing = true;
        }
        fireIntervalRemoved( this, size, size );

    }

  } // actionPerformed

} // CustomListModel
```

Listing 10.8 is a test application that works out the CustomListModel class. It creates a frame and places a list as the only component in the frame. An instance of the CustomListModel class is set as the data model for the list. The running application is shown in Figure 10.3.

LISTING 10.8   THE `CustomListModelTest` APPLICATION

```java
package com.foley.test;

import javax.swing.*;

import com.foley.list.CustomListModel;

import com.foley.utility.ApplicationFrame;

/**
 * An application that displays a JList that
 * uses an instance of the CustomListModel data
 * model.
 *
 * @author Mike Foley
 **/
public class CustomListModelTest extends Object {

    /**
     * Application entry point.
     * Create a frame, the list and display it.
     *
     * @param args Command line parameter. Not used.
     **/
    public static void main( String args[] ) {

        JFrame frame = new ApplicationFrame( "CustomListModel Test" );

        CustomListModel model = new CustomListModel();
        JList list = new JList( model );
        list.setPrototypeCellValue( "Model Element: 00000" );

        JScrollPane scrollPane = new JScrollPane( list );
        scrollPane.setBorder( BorderFactory.createLoweredBevelBorder() );

        frame.getContentPane().add( scrollPane );

        frame.pack();
        frame.setVisible( true );

    } // main

} // CustomListModelTest
```

FIGURE 10.3

The
`CustomListModel`
test application.

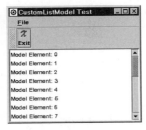

The `CustomListModelTest` application calls the `setPrototypeCellValue` method contained in the `JList` class. An optimization in the `JList` class enables the size of the list cells to be specified once and not dynamically determined for each cell. When the `setPrototypeCellValue` method is called, the list configures its renderer with the value passed to the method. The preferred size of the rendering component is used to set the fixed cell width and height. The fixed cell width and height can also be set directly with the `setFixedCellWidth` and `setFixedCellHeight` methods. Each of these methods has an associated `get` method and is a bound property of the `JList` class. A complete list of bound properties added by the `JList` class is presented in Table 10.2. The bound properties inherited from `JComponent` and beyond are still fired by `JList` instances, of course.

TABLE 10.2 NON-INHERITED BOUND PROPERTIES OF THE JList CLASS

Property Name	Setter Method	Getter Method
prototypeCellValue	setPrototypeCellValue	getPrototypeCellValue
fixedCellWidth	setFixedCellWidth	getFixedCellWidth
fixedCellHeight	setFixedCellHeight	getFixedCellHeight
cellRenderer	setCellRenderer	getCellRenderer
selectionForeground	setSelectionForeground	getSelectionForeground
selectionBackground	setSelectionBackground	getSelectionBackground
visibleRowCount	getVisibleRowCount	setVisibleRowCount
model	setModel	getModel
selectionModel	setSelectionModel	getSelectionModel

The `setPrototypeCellValue` method is a nice optimization contained in the `JList` class. However, it requires a great deal of information about the data model before it can choose the correct prototype value. A typical prototype value is the largest value in the model. This will ensure that every element in the list has adequate space when displayed. This information is typically not available to the list or to the client configuring the list. However, it would be reasonable for the model to know this information. A nice addition

10

**JList,
JComboBox, AND
BOUND CONTROLS**

to the `ListModel` interface would be a `getPrototypeCellValue` method. This would allow the list to be configured to the correct size without guessing what that size is.

The Selection Model

As shown earlier in this chapter, a list supports multiple modes for selecting items in it. However, the selection isn't managed by the list itself. Just as the data is contained in a separate data model, a separate selection model manages selection. The responsibilities of a list section model are defined by the `ListSelectionModel` interface. A class that implements this interface is used to manage selection in the list. The JFC contains the concrete class `DefaultListSelectionModel`, which can be used in a list. In fact, the methods for setting the selection mode and altering the selection set for the list, presented earlier in the chapter, are simple wrapper methods that forward the request to the current selection model.

Implementing the `ListSelectionModel` interface is far less common than implementing the `ListModel` interface. In most cases, the `DefaultListSelectionModel` can be used. However, there are still situations where you want to obtain a handle on a list selection model, such as to allow multiple lists to share a single `ListSelectionModel`. This way, when the selection changes in one list, it will also change in the lists that share the common model.

Listing 10.9 contains a simple application to present the idea of a common `ListSelectionModel`. The `ListSelectionModelTest` application creates two lists that share a single `ListSelectionModel`. When an element in either list is selected or deselected, the corresponding element in the other list is also selected or deselected (Figure 10.4).

LISTING 10.9   THE `ListSelectionModelTest` APPLICATION

```
package com.foley.test;

import java.awt.*;
import javax.swing.*;

import com.foley.utility.ApplicationFrame;


/**
 * An application that displays a few JList instances
 * that share the same ListSelectionModel.
 *
 * @author Mike Foley
 **/
public class ListSelectionModelTest extends Object {
```

```
/**
 * Application entry point.
 * Create a frame, the lists and display it.
 * Set the selection model in each list to be the
 * same.
 *
 * @param args Command line parameter. Not used.
 **/
public static void main( String args[] ) {
    String[] firstNames = { "Mike", "Mari", "Molly",
                            "Betsy", "Bobby" };
    String[] lastNames = { "Jones", "Smith", "Johnson",
                           "White", "Connor" };

    JFrame frame = new ApplicationFrame( "ListSelectionModel Test" );

    JList list1 = new JList( firstNames );
    JList list2 = new JList( lastNames );

    list1.setPrototypeCellValue( "Long First Name" );
    list2.setPrototypeCellValue( "Long Last Name" );

    ListSelectionModel selectionModel = list1.getSelectionModel();
    list2.setSelectionModel( selectionModel );

    JScrollPane scrollPane1 = new JScrollPane( list1 );
    JScrollPane scrollPane2 = new JScrollPane( list2 );

    scrollPane1.setBorder(BorderFactory.createLoweredBevelBorder());
    scrollPane2.setBorder(BorderFactory.createLoweredBevelBorder());

    frame.getContentPane().add( scrollPane1, BorderLayout.WEST );
    frame.getContentPane().add( scrollPane2, BorderLayout.EAST );

    frame.pack();
    frame.setVisible( true );

} // main

} // ListSelectionModelTest
```

FIGURE 10.4

The ListSelection ModelTest *application.*

The `ListSelectionModelTest` application works very nicely because each `ListModel` contains the same number of elements. If the list models contain a different number of elements, a valid selection in one list may not be valid in the other. This can be demonstrated by changing the `lastNames` array to contain only three members, as in the following line of code:

```
String[] lastNames = { "Jones", "Smith", "Johnson" };
```

The new `ListSelectionModelTest` application is shown in Figure 10.5.

FIGURE 10.5

The `ListSelection ModelTest` *application with non-symmetric lists.*

Figure 10.5 shows that if the `JList` instance receives a selection event that is outside the number of elements in the list, it ignores that selected item. This enables views to share a single list model even if the data models are not the same size. It should be mentioned that classes other than `JList` that use a `ListSelectionModel` to manage selections may behave differently.

`ListSelectionListener` and `ListSelectionEvent`

To monitor changes in a class that implements the `ListSelectionModel` interface, the `ListSelectionListener` interface must be implemented. This interface and the `ListSelectionEvent` class are shown in Listing 10.10. When the list selection model changes, the `valueChanged` method of the listener is called. The parameter to this method is an instance of the `ListSelectionEvent` class. This event delivers the range of where a selection change has occurred in the selection model. However, the event does not tell the listener which elements have changed. It is the responsibility of the listener to query the model to determine the new selection state of each element in the range contained in the `ListSelectionEvent`.

The other piece of information contained in a `ListSelectionEvent` is the `valueIsAdjusting` flag. When this is `true`, it tells the listener that there are many events being delivered in rapid succession. If the listener is a graphical component, it may choose not to repaint itself until this flag is `false`. At that time, the rapid series of events will have ended.

LISTING 10.10 THE ListSelectionListener INTERFACE AND ListSelectionEvent CLASS

```java
public interface ListSelectionListener extends EventListener
{
  /**
   * Called whenever the value of the selection changes.
   * @param e the event that characterizes the change.
   */
  void valueChanged(ListSelectionEvent e);
}

public class ListSelectionEvent extends EventObject
{
    private int firstIndex;
    private int lastIndex;
    private boolean isAdjusting;

    /**
     * Represents a change in selection status between firstIndex
     * and lastIndex inclusive (firstIndex is less than or equal to
     * lastIndex).  At least one of the rows within the range will
     * have changed, a good ListSelectionModel implementation will
     * keep the range as small as possible.
     *
     * @param firstIndex The first index that changed.
     * @param lastIndex The last index that changed,
     *                  lastIndex >= firstIndex.
     * @param isAdjusting An indication that this is one of
     *                    a rapid series of events
     */
    public ListSelectionEvent(Object source, int firstIndex,
                         int lastIndex, boolean isAdjusting)
{
    super(source);
    this.firstIndex = firstIndex;
    this.lastIndex = lastIndex;
    this.isAdjusting = isAdjusting;
    }

    /**
     * @return The first row whose selection value may have changed.
     */
    public int getFirstIndex() { return firstIndex; }

    /**
     * @return The last row whose selection value may have changed.
     */
    public int getLastIndex() { return lastIndex; }
```

continues

LISTING **10.10**   CONTINUED

```
/**
 * @return True if this is one of a rapid series of events
 */
public boolean getValueIsAdjusting() { return isAdjusting; }

}
```

JList Class and Model Interactions

In the previous sections, you saw the models that the JList view interacts with. The view-to-model interaction is depicted in Figure 10.6. Arrow 1 is the view initializing from the ListModel. The view adds a listener to the data model so that it will be notified if the model changes. When the user interacts with the view, the selection is changed in the ListSelectionModel. This is shown by arrow 2. The view also listens to the model for selection changes. This allows the selection to be made programmatically and the view to be updated. If the data in the model changes, a change event will be sent to the view, as shown by arrow 3.

FIGURE **10.6**

JList *view and model interaction.*

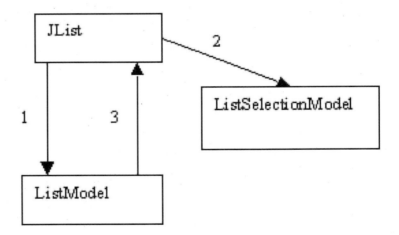

Combo Boxes

A combo box is a visual component similar to a list. It allows a single element in a list to be selected. The selected element is shown in the combo box, as well as a control to expand the combo box into a list. An unexpanded combo box requires less screen real estate than a list. However, the box must be expanded to show the possible choices in the combo box.

Classic Combo Box

The JComboBox class is the JFC visual component that represents a combo box control. Programming with the JComboBox class is similar to the JList class, presented in the previous section. It contains convenience functions for creating a combo box and setting the data displayed using an array or vector. An example of creating a simple combo box is shown in Listing 10.11, and the resulting component is shown in Figure 10.7.

LISTING 10.11 THE ComboBoxTest APPLICATION

```
package com.foley.test;

import java.awt.*;
import java.awt.event.*;

import javax.swing.*;
import javax.swing.border.*;

import com.foley.utility.ApplicationFrame;


/**
 * An application that displays JComboBox instance
 * in its frame.
 *
 * @author Mike Foley
 **/
public class ComboBoxTest extends Object {

    /**
     * Application entry point.
     * Create a frame, the combo box and display it.
     *
     * @param args Command line parameter. Not used.
     **/
    public static void main( String args[] ) {

        String[] data = {"Apple", "Orange", "Grape", "Banana",
                         "Mango", "Pineapple", "Peach", "Pear" };

        JFrame frame = new ApplicationFrame( "Combobox Test" );

        JComboBox combobox = new JComboBox( data );
        combobox.setBorder( BorderFactory.createLoweredBevelBorder() );
        frame.getContentPane().add( combobox, BorderLayout.CENTER );

        frame.pack();
        frame.setVisible( true );
```

continues

LISTING 10.11   CONTINUED

```
    } // main

} // ComboBoxTest
```

FIGURE 10.7

*JComboBox in use:
The first item is
selected (top), the
user clicks the
down-arrow to
display choices
(middle), and the
new item is select-
ed (bottom).*

The first combo box, shown in Figure 10.7, depicts when the control is first displayed. The first item from the data array is selected in the combo box. The second combo box appears after the user clicks on the down-arrow to display the possible choices that can be selected. The third combo box shows that an item has been selected.

You may not want to have an element selected when the combo box is initially displayed. This can be accomplished by passing the setSelectedIndex method a parameter of –1.

The window containing the list of items can be shown or hidden programmatically. The methods hidePopup and showPopup are provided for this purpose. The current visibility of the popup can be determined with the isPopupVisible method. The maximum number of rows displayed in the popup window can be controlled using the setMaximumRowCount method. The current value of this property can be queried with the getMaximumRowCount method. The maximumRowCount property is a bound property of the JComboBox class. The list of bound properties introduced by the JComboBox class is presented in Table 10.3.

The pop-up can be specified as a lightweight or heavyweight component by calling the `setLightWeightPopupEnabled` method. Passing this method `true` enables lightweight popups. Passing it `false` enables peer-based popup components. The default value of this property is `true`, enabling lightweight popups to be used when they will fit in the current window. This is important because if your application mixes lightweight and heavyweight components and a lightweight popup is used, it will be displayed under any heavyweight components in that area. If this is the case, lightweight popups have to be disabled. The `isLightWeightPopupEnabled` method queries the current state of this property. This is not a bound property of the `JComboBox` class.

TABLE 10.3 NON-INHERITED BOUND PROPERTIES OF THE `JComboBox` CLASS

Property Name	*Setter Method*	*Getter Method*
model	setModel	getModel
editable	setEditable	getEditable
maximumRowCount	setMaximumRowCount	getMaximumRowCount
renderer	setRenderer	getRenderer
editor	setEditor	getEditor
enabled	setEnabled	getEnabled

The renderer used by the `JComboBox` class is an instance of the `ListCellRenderer` class. This class was described at the beginning of this chapter. The `editor` property is discussed later in this chapter.

The selected item and its index can be queried with the `getSelectedItem` and `getSelectedIndex` methods, respectively. The `getSelectedObjects` method returns the selected item in an array of length 1, or an empty array if there is no item selected. The selected item can be set programmatically using either the `setSelectedItem` or `setSelectedIndex` method. The `getItemCount` method returns the number of items in the combo box. The `getItemAt` method returns the item at the specified index. What happens when an index that is out of range is passed to the `getItemAt` method is unspecified. It is reasonable to expect some type of `RuntimeException` to be thrown. The `DefaultListModel` class throws an `ArrayIndexOutOfBoundsException` exception in this case.

The `ComboBoxModel`

The data model employed by the `JComboBox` class is an instance of the `ComboBoxModel`. This interface extends the `ListModel` interface. This means that the methods described in the previous section for the `ListModel` class hold for the `ComboBoxModel` class as well. It also means that the same class of listener, `ListDataListener`, can be used for both models. The `ComboBoxModel` adds methods that support a selected item in the list. The selected item is the item shown at the top of the combo box and when the combo box is not expanded. The `ComboBoxModel` interface is shown here:

```
public interface ComboBoxModel extends ListModel {
   /**
    * Set the selected item
    **/
   void setSelectedItem(Object anItem);

   /**
    * Return the selected item
    **/
   Object getSelectedItem();
}
```

The first thing you may notice about the `ComboBoxModel` interface is the inconsistencies with the `ListModel`. The `ComboBoxModel` and the `JComboBox` class call members of the control "items," while the `ListModel` and the `JList` class call the members "elements." This type of inconsistency makes working with these two controls more difficult than it needs be.

For example, a reference to a `JComboBox` instance calls the `getItemAt` method to query a member of the combo box, while a reference to the `ComboBoxModel` calls the `getElementAt` method to query the exact same member. The following code fragment demonstrates this inconsistency. If the `ComboBoxTest` program adds the following line after the creation of the `JComboBox` instance, both of the `println` statements print Banana. This is shown in Figure 10.8.

```
JComboBox combobox = new JComboBox( data );
ComboBoxModel comboBoxModel = combobox.getModel();
Object item3 = combobox.getItemAt( 3 );
Object element3 = comboBoxModel.getElementAt( 3 );
System.out.println( "item: " + item3 );
System.out.println( "element: " + element3 );
```

FIGURE 10.8

Output from a modified `ComboBoxTest` *application.*

```
item: Banana

element: Banana
```

The less obvious question to ask about the `ComboBoxModel` is: Why is it needed? The only feature added by the `ComboBoxModel` is management of a selected item. However, in the previous section you saw the elegant solution of selection state management being delegated to the `ListSelectionModel` by the `JList` class. The `JComboBox` class could have used the exact same solution.

If the name inconsistencies were resolved and the list selection model, in single selection mode, or better still a `SingleSelectionModel` instance, was used by both the `JList` and `JComboBox` classes, there would be no difference to the programmer in basic functionality between one control and the other. Sharing models between different views is a powerful aspect of the MVC architecture. Unfortunately, the JFC missed the mark with these two particular controls.

JComboBox Class and Model Interaction

The default model used by instances of the `JComboBox` class is the `DefaultComboBoxModel` class. It extends the `AbstractListModel` class presented earlier in this chapter. When the selected item is changed, it fires a `ContentsChanged` event with both the start and end indexes set to –1. This obviously breaks the semantics of the `contentsChanged` method contained in the `ListDataListener` interface. For better or worse, this is what is done by the `DefaultComboBoxModel` class.

The `DefaultComboBoxModel` class implements the `MutableComboBoxModel` interface, shown in Listing 10.12. This interface is an extension of the `ComboBoxModel` interface that adds methods to edit the elements in the combo box. The `addElement` method appends the given object to the model. The `insertElementAt` method allows an object to be placed at the given offset into the model. The `removeElement` method removes the given element from the model, and the `removeElementAt` method removes the object at the specified index from the model.

LISTING 10.12 THE `MutableComboBoxModel` INTERFACE

```
public interface MutableComboBoxModel extends ComboBoxModel {
    /**
     * Adds an item to the end of the model.
     */
    public void addElement( Object obj );

    /**
     * Adds an item to the end of the model.
     */
    public void removeElement( Object obj );
```

continues

LISTING **10.12**   CONTINUED

```
/**
 * Adds an item at a specific index
 */
public void insertElementAt( Object obj, int index );

/**
 * Removes an item at a specific index
 */
public void removeElementAt( int index );
}
```

NOTE

The MutableComboBoxModel interface was a late, and very welcome, addition to the JFC. However, where is the MutableListModel interface? An interface that defines methods for changing a list model would allow changes to be made to the model using the API defined in the interface, rather than assuming an implementation for the ListModel interface.

The JComboBox class listens to the ComboBoxModel currently in use. When the selected item changes in the model, the combo box sends an ActionEvent to any ActionListeners of the instance. This allows clients of the JComboBox class to listen for action events from the combo box rather than selection change events from the model.

However, caution must be taken here. If a ComboBoxModel other than the default model is used, the ActionEvent notification may break because the ComboBoxModel does not define an event for the selected item being changed. As mentioned in the previous paragraph, the DefaultComboBoxModel class overloads the semantics of the ContentsChanged event. However, different implementations of the ComboBoxModel interface may not behave the same way. If the JComboBox class does not receive the magic ContentsChanged event, the ActionEvent will not be fired from the JComboBox instance. This would not be a problem if the models clearly defined the event that should be fired when the selected item changes. This is another argument for using a ListSelectionModel, or the restricted single selection variant SingleSelectionModel, for combo boxes.

The command string sent in an ActionEvent can be set and queried with the setActionCommand and getActionCommand methods. For some unknown reason, actionCommand is not a bound property in the JComboBox class.

Editable Combo Box

A combo box can be configured so the user can type an entry into the top portion of the control. This allows the user to enter his choice without selecting from the list. By default, a combo box is not editable. It can be made so by passing `true` to the `setEditable` method. The `isEditable` method returns the current state of the `editable` property. Similarly to how the painting of items in the combo box is delegated to a renderer, editing is delegated to an editor. The editor's responsibilities are defined in the `ComboBoxEditor` interface, shown in Listing 10.13.

LISTING 10.13   THE `ComboBoxEditor` INTERFACE

```
public interface ComboBoxEditor {

  /**
   * Return the component that should be added to the tree hierarchy for
   * this editor
   **/
  public Component getEditorComponent();

  /**
   * Set the item that should be edited. Cancel any editing if necessary
   **/
  public void setItem(Object anObject);

  /**
   * Return the edited item
   **/
  public Object getItem();

  /**
   * Ask the editor to start editing and to select everything
   **/
  public void selectAll();

  /**
   * Add an ActionListener. An action event is generated when
   * the edited item changes
   **/
  public void addActionListener(ActionListener l);

  /**
   * Remove an ActionListener
   **/
  public void removeActionListener(ActionListener l);
}
```

Querying the selected item for an editable combo box is slightly more complex than it is for a non-editable combo box. The methods typically used, getSelectedItem and getSelectedIndex, are the same. However, the user may type any value into the combo box editor, including elements that are not in the list of choices in the ComboBoxModel. In this case, the getSelectedIndex method returns –1. The getSelectedItem method returns exactly what the user entered into the editor, whether this string is in the model or not. This behavior is demonstrated in the EditableComboBox application, shown in Listing 10.14.

LISTING 10.14   THE EditableComboBoxTest APPLICATION

```java
package com.foley.test;

import java.awt.*;
import java.awt.event.*;

import javax.swing.*;
import javax.swing.border.*;

import com.foley.utility.ApplicationFrame;


/**
 * An application that displays an editable JComboBox instance
 * in its frame.
 *
 * @author Mike Foley
 **/
public class EditableComboBoxTest extends Object {

    /**
     * Application entry point.
     * Create a frame, the combo box and display it.
     *
     * @param args Command line parameter. Not used.
     **/
    public static void main( String args[] ) {

        String[] data = {"Apple", "Orange", "Grape", "Banana",
                        "Mango", "Pineapple", "Peach", "Pear" };

        JFrame frame = new ApplicationFrame( "Editable Combobox Test" );

        final JComboBox combobox = new JComboBox( data );
        combobox.setEditable( true );
        combobox.setSelectedIndex( -1 );

        combobox.addActionListener( new ActionListener() {
```

```
                public void actionPerformed( ActionEvent event ) {
                    System.out.println( combobox.getSelectedIndex() +
                                        " " + combobox.getSelectedItem() );
        }
            } );
        combobox.setBorder( BorderFactory.createLoweredBevelBorder() );
        frame.getContentPane().add( combobox, BorderLayout.CENTER );

        frame.pack();
        frame.setVisible( true );

    } // main

} // EditableComboBoxTest
```

In this example, a JComboBox instance is created. The setEditable method is called to enable editing. The setSelectedIndex method is passed the value of –1 to clear the selection in the combo box. This way, there is no value in the combo box when it is first displayed. An ActionListener is added to the combo box to receive notification when the selected item in the combo box changes. When a notification is received, the selected item and its index are printed to the console. The application is shown in Figure 10.9.

FIGURE 10.9

The EditableComboBox Test *application: Before a selection is made (top), after an item has been selected (middle), and after editing (bottom).*

The first panel of Figure 10.9 shows the combo box from the EditableComboBoxTest application before a selection has been made. The editor paints differently than the non-editable combo box shown in Figure 10.7. This gives the user visual feedback that the combo box is in fact editable. The second panel shows the combo box after the item labeled Grape has been selected. The output from the application is shown in Figure 10.10. The first line is the result from `ActionListener` added to the combo box. The item is Grape and its index is 2. The final slide shows the combo box after editing to contain the string Bean. Figure 10.10 shows the result from `ActionListener`. This time, the item is not contained in the `ComboBoxModel`, so its index returned from the `getSelectedIndex` method is –1. The `ActionEvent` is fired when the user presses the Enter key after changing the text, or when the editor loses the input focus.

FIGURE 10.10

Output from the `EditableComboBox` `Test` *application.*

```
 2 Grape

-1 Bean
```

KeySelection Managers

The `JComboBox` class defines an inner interface that manages selection in the combo box with keystrokes. The `KeySelectionManager` interface shown in Listing 10.15 defines a single method, `selectionForKey`. This method returns the index of the element selected by the given character in the given `ComboBoxModel`. It returns –1 if the character does not select an element.

The `JComboBox` class contains the `selectWithKeyChar` method that calls the key selection manager with the given character and selects the element at the index returned from the key selection manager. The `selectWithKeyChar` method returns `true` if an element was selected, `false` otherwise. A `ComboBoxEditor` could use this capability to streamline editing in a combo box by allowing the user to select an element in the model by typing its first character. The `KeySelectionManager` for a combo box can be set with the `setKeySelectionManager` method and queried with the `getKeySelectionManager` method. The `keySelectionManager` is not a bound property.

LISTING 10.15 THE `KeySelectionManager` INTERFACE

```java
public interface KeySelectionManager {
    /** Given <code>aKey</code> and the model, returns the row
     *  that should become selected. Return -1 if no match was
     *  found.
     *
     * @param  aKey  a char value, usually indicating a keyboard key that
     *               was pressed
     * @param aModel a ComboBoxModel — the component's data model,
     *               containing the list of selectable items
     * @return an int equal to the selected row, where 0 is the
```

```
    *           first item and -1 is none.
    */
    int selectionForKey(char aKey,ComboBoxModel aModel);
}
```

Bounded Components

The JFC contains a few components that display information that falls within a numerical range. These components use the `BoundedRangeModel` to manage the range and the current value. Examples of range components in the JFC are scrollbars, sliders, and progress bars. These components and the `BoundedRangeModel` are discussed in this section.

The `BoundedRangeModel` Interface

The `BoundedRangeModel` interface specifies the methods required for the JFC bounded range model. This type of model specifies a constrained integer range with a minimum, maximum, and current value. A listener to the model is defined as a `ChangeListener`. The `ChangeListener` is notified when any of the properties of the model change. The `BoundedRangeModel` contains the `valueIsAdjusting` flag, which allows listeners of the model to optimize their behavior. This flag is set to `true` when many changes are going to occur quickly in the model, and set to `false` when the changes are complete. A typical example of this behavior is when the user drags a scrollbar.

The `BoundedRangeModel` defines the `extent` property. For a view such as a scrollbar, the extent represents the portion of the model that is currently viewed. The `extent` must be non-negative and the current value in the model, and it cannot be greater that the model's maximum value.

The `setRangeProperties` method is defined to allow all the properties defined by the `BoundedRangeModel` to be set with a single method call.

Classes that implement the `BoundedRangeModel` interface should guarantee the following relationship between the model properties:

```
minimum <= value <= value + extent <= maximum
```

Listing 10.16 shows the complete `BoundedRangeModel` interface.

10

JLIST, JCOMBOBOX, AND BOUND CONTROLS

LISTING 10.16   THE BoundedRangeModel INTERFACE

```
public interface BoundedRangeModel
{
    /**
     * Returns the minimum acceptable value.
     *
     * @return the value of the minimum property
     * @see #setMinimum
     */
    int getMinimum();


    /**
     * Sets the model's minimum to <I>newMinimum</I>.    The
     * other three properties may be changed as well, to ensure
     * that:
     * <pre>
     * minimum <= value <= value+extent <= maximum
     * </pre>
     * <p>
     * Notifies any listeners if the model changes.
     *
     * @param newMinimum the model's new minimum
     * @see #getMinimum
     * @see #addChangeListener
     */
    void setMinimum(int newMinimum);


    /**
     * Returns the model's maximum.  Note that the upper
     * limit on the model's value is (maximum - extent).
     *
     * @return the value of the maximum property.
     * @see #setMaximum
     * @see #setExtent
     */
    int getMaximum();


    /**
     * Sets the model's maximum to <I>newMaximum</I>. The other
     * three properties may be changed as well, to ensure that
     * <pre>
     * minimum <= value <= value+extent <= maximum
     * </pre>
     * <p>
     * Notifies any listeners if the model changes.
     *
     * @param newMaximum the model's new maximum
```

```
 * @see #getMaximum
 * @see #addChangeListener
 */
void setMaximum(int newMaximum);


/**
 * Returns the model's current value.  Note that the upper
 * limit on the model's value is <code>maximum - extent</code>
 * and the lower limit is <code>minimum</code>.
 *
 * @return  the model's value
 * @see     #setValue
 */
int getValue();


/**
 * Sets the model's current value to <code>newValue</code>
 * if <code>newValue</code> satisfies the model's contraints.
 * Those constraints are:
 * <pre>
 * minimum <= value <= value+extent <= maximum
 * </pre>
 * Otherwise, if <code>newValue</code> is less than
 * <code>minimum</code> it's set to <code>minimum</code>,
 * if it's greater than <code>maximum</code>
 * then it's set to <code>maximum</code>, and
 * if it's greater than <code>value+extent</code> then it's set to
 * <code>value+extent</code>.
 * <p>
 * When a BoundedRange model is used with a scrollbar the value
 * specifies the origin of the scrollbar knob (aka the "thumb" or
 * "elevator").  The value usually represents the origin of the
 * visible part of the object being scrolled.
 * <p>
 * Notifies any listeners if the model changes.
 *
 * @param newValue the model's new value
 * @see #getValue
 */
void setValue(int newValue);


/**
 * This attribute indicates that any upcoming changes to the value
 * of the model should be considered a single event. This attribute
 * will be set to true at the start of a series of changes to the
 * value, and will be set to false when the value has finished
```

continues

10

**JList,
JComboBox, and
Bound Controls**

Listing 10.16 CONTINUED

```
 * changing.  Normally this allows a listener to only take action
 * when the final value change is committed, instead of having to do
 * updates for all intermediate values.
 * <p>
 * Sliders and scrollbars use this property when a drag is under way.
 *
 * @param b true if the upcoming changes to the value property are
 *             part of a series
 * @see #getValueIsAdjusting
 */
void setValueIsAdjusting(boolean b);


/**
 * Returns true if the current changes to the value property are part
 * of a series.
 *
 * @return the valueIsAdjustingProperty.
 * @see #setValueIsAdjusting
 */
boolean getValueIsAdjusting();


/**
 * Returns the model's extent, the length of the inner range that
 * begins at the model's value.
 *
 * @return  the value of the model's extent property
 * @see      #setExtent
 * @see      #setValue
 */
int getExtent();


/**
 * Sets the model's extent.  The <I>newExtent</I> is forced to
 * be greater than or equal to zero and less than or equal to
 * maximum - value.
 * <p>
 * When a BoundedRange model is used with a scrollbar the extent
 * defines the length of the scrollbar knob (aka the "thumb" or
 * "elevator").  The extent usually represents how much of the
 * object being scrolled is visible.
 * <p>
 * Notifies any listeners if the model changes.
 *
 * @param  newExtent the model's new extent
 * @see #getExtent
 * @see #setValue
```

```
    */
    void setExtent(int newExtent);


    /**
     * This method sets all of the model's data with a single method
     * call. The method results in a single change event being generated.
     * This is convenient when you need to adjust all the model data
     * simultaneously and do not want individual change events to occur.
     *
     * @see #setValue
     * @see #setExtent
     * @see #setMinimum
     * @see #setMaximum
     * @see #setValueIsAdjusting
     */
    void setRangeProperties( int value, int extent, int min,
                             int max, boolean adjusting );


    /**
     * Adds a ChangeListener to the model's listener list.
     *
     * @param x the ChangeListener to add
     * @see #removeChangeListener
     */
    void addChangeListener(ChangeListener x);


    /**
     * Removes a ChangeListener from the model's listener list.
     *
     * @param x the ChangeListener to remove
     * @see #addChangeListener
     */
    void removeChangeListener(ChangeListener x);

}
```

Change Event and Listener Interface

The ChangeListener interface defines the responsibilities of listeners to a BoundedRangeModel instance. This interface is shown below. The listener must implement one method, the stateChanged method. This method is called when any of the properties in the bounded range model change. The parameter to the stateChanged method is a ChangeEvent instance. This event is also shown below:

```
public interface ChangeListener extends EventListener {
    void stateChanged(ChangeEvent e);
```

```
}
public class ChangeEvent extends EventObject {
    public ChangeEvent(Object source) {
        super(source);
    }
}
```

As you can see from the ChangeEvent class, it does not deliver any information specific to BoundedRangeModel. Thus, the listener must query the source of the event from the ChangeEvent and query the model for its current state. Example usages of the ChangeListener interface and ChangeEvent class are presented in the next section.

The JSlider Control

The JSlider class implements a control that allows the user to select a value from a bounded range. A pointer is drawn, which the user can slide to select the desired value. The JSlider class employs a BoundedRangeModel to manage its range and the current value. A JSlider instance can be created and displayed using the SliderTest application, shown in Listing 10.17. The resulting slider is shown in Figure 10.11.

LISTING 10.17   THE SliderTest APPLICATION

```
package com.foley.test;

import java.awt.*;
import java.awt.event.*;

import javax.swing.*;
import javax.swing.border.*;

import com.foley.utility.ApplicationFrame;


/**
 * An application that displays a JSlider instance
 * in its frame.
 *
 * @author Mike Foley
 **/
public class SliderTest extends Object {

    /**
     * Application entry point.
     * Create a frame, the list and display it.
     *
     * @param args Command line parameter. Not used.
     **/
```

```
    public static void main( String args[] ) {

        JFrame frame = new ApplicationFrame( "Slider Test" );

        JSlider slider = new JSlider();

        slider.setBorder( BorderFactory.createLoweredBevelBorder() );
        frame.getContentPane().add( slider, BorderLayout.CENTER );

        frame.pack();
        frame.setVisible( true );

    } // main

} // SliderTest
```

FIGURE 10.11

The SliderTest *application.*

Calling the default constructor of the JSlider class creates a slider with a range from 0 to 100 and an initial value of 50. However, from looking at the slider in Figure 10.11, there is no way of knowing this. The slider can be configured to display the range and various tick mark options. The JSlider class also contains wrapper methods for the BoundedRangeModel methods. This allows the model's properties to be set by calling methods on the slider itself rather than the model, if the developer is so inclined.

The setOrientation method can be called for the slider to display vertically or horizontally. This method takes an integer parameter that must be one of the two orientation constants defined in the SwingConstants interface. These constants are HORIZONTAL and VERTICAL. An IllegalArgumentException is thrown if a parameter other than one of these two is passed to the method. The JSlider class implements the SwingConstants interface, so the constant can be specified as SwingConstants.VERTICAL or JSlider.VERTICAL.

The JSlider class also contains a constructor that takes the orientation, minimum, maximum, and initial value for the slider.

Calling the setInverted method with a parameter of true can be called to invert the slider. An inverted horizontal slider contains its maximum value to the left and its minimum value to the right, and a vertical slider contains its maximum value on the top and its minimum value on the bottom. The getInverted method will return the current state of the inverted property, which is a bound property of the JSlider class. The complete list of bound properties added by the JSlider is shown in Table 10.4.

TABLE 10.4   NON-INHERITED BOUND PROPERTIES OF THE JSlider CLASS

Property Name	Setter Method	Getter Method
model	setModel	getModel
orientation	setOrientation	getOrientation
labelTable	setLabelTable	getLabelTable
inverted	setInverted	getInverted
majorTickSpacing	setMajorTickSpacing	getMajorTickSpacing
minorTickSpacing	setMinorTickSpacing	getMinorTickSpacing
snapToTicks	setSnapToTicks	getSnapToTicks
paintTicks	setPaintTicks	getPaintTicks
paintTrack	setPaintTrack	getPaintTrack
paintLabels	setPaintLabels	getPaintLabels

Controlling Tick Marks

The JSlider class can be configured to display both major and minor tick marks. The setMajorTickSpacing and setMinorTickSpacing methods specify the tick mark spacing. The parameter is the number of units between tick marks. The number of tick marks drawn depends on the range of the slider and the spacing parameter. A major tick mark is drawn at the minimum value, and at every major tick mark spacing interval after that until the slider's maximum is reached. The equation for where tick marks are drawn is as follows:

```
TickLocation = minimum + n * spacing
Where n = 0,1, range/spacing
```

The same logic is used for the minor tick marks, except that the minor tick spacing parameter is used. Also, if both a minor and major tick mark land on the same value, the major tick mark is drawn.

Finally, the setPaintTicks method must be called with a parameter of true to have the slider paint the tick marks. The following code can be used in the SliderTest application to create and configure the slider to contain tick marks:

```
JSlider slider = new JSlider();
slider.setMajorTickSpacing( 20 );
slider.setMinorTickSpacing( 5 );
slider.setPaintTicks( true );
```

The resulting slider is shown in Figure 10.12.

FIGURE 10.12

*A JSlider with
tick marks.*

The default range for the slider, 0-100, is still being used. Thus, with a major tick mark spacing of 20, major ticks appear at 0, 20, 40, 60, 80, and 100. Similarly, with the minor tick spacing set to 5, minor ticks are expected at 5, 10, 15, 25, 30, and so on, up to 95. Notice that minor ticks are not expected at 0, 20, and so on, where the major ticks are located.

The slider shown in Figure 10.12 allows the value to fall on any integer value from 0 to 100. Sometimes you want to allow values to be selected only where the tick marks are displayed. This can be achieved by passing `true` to the `setSnapToTicks` method. Passing `false` to this method allows any value to be selected again.

Controlling Labels

In the previous section, tick marks were added to the slider to indicate where a selected value lies in the range of possible values. However, the range still is not shown on the slider. Labels can be added to the slider by passing `true` to the `setPaintLabels` method. If the following line is added to the previous version of the `SliderTest` application, the slider will look as shown in Figure 10.13.

```
slider.setPaintLabels( true );
```

FIGURE 10.13

*Labels added to a
slider.*

Figure 10.13 shows that a label has been added for each major tick mark. For labels to be drawn, the major tick mark spacing must be specified. However, the tick marks need not be painted. The labels in Figure 10.13 could be painted without the tick marks with the following slider configuration:

```
JSlider slider = new JSlider();
slider.setMajorTickSpacing( 20 );
slider.setPaintLabels( true );
```

If the values in the slider are to represent percentages, currency, or some other type of formatted number, you want the labels on the slider to show the number's type. This can be achieved in a couple of different ways. One approach is to subclass the JSlider class and create the properly formatted labels. Another approach is to set the labels using the setLabelTable method. The approach taken depends on the current requirements.

For a one-shot formatted slider where the major tick mark spacing and range are not going to change, setting the label table may be appropriate. However, for a general-purpose slider where the major tick spacing and range need to be flexible, extending the JSlider class may be more appropriate. In the next sections we'll look at each alternative.

Setting the Label Table

The label table in the JSlider class is an AWT dictionary that contains a mapping from an integer to a component. The slider uses the components in the dictionary as the labels for the slider. There must be a label component for every Integer value associated with each major tick mark.

To configure a percent slider with labels that correspond to the major tick spacings, use the code in Listing 10.18. The resulting slider is shown in Figure 10.14.

LISTING 10.18   THE PercentSliderTest APPLICATION

```
package com.foley.test;

import java.awt.*;
import java.awt.event.*;
import java.util.Hashtable;
import java.text.NumberFormat;

import javax.swing.*;
import javax.swing.border.*;

import com.foley.utility.ApplicationFrame;


/**
 * An application that displays a JSlider instance
 * in its frame.
 *
 * @author Mike Foley
 **/
public class PercentSliderTest extends Object {

    /**
     * Application entry point.
```

```
 * Create a frame, the list and display it.
 *
 * @param args Command line parameter. Not used.
 **/
public static void main( String args[] ) {

    JFrame frame = new ApplicationFrame( "Percent Slider Test" );
    NumberFormat percent = NumberFormat.getPercentInstance();

    Hashtable table = new Hashtable();
    for( int i = 0; i <= 100; i += 20 ) {
        JLabel l = new JLabel(
                   percent.format( ( double )i / 100.0 ) );
        table.put( new Integer( i ), l );
    }
    JSlider slider = new JSlider();
    slider.setMajorTickSpacing( 20 );
    slider.setMinorTickSpacing( 5 );
    slider.setPaintTicks( true );
    slider.setPaintLabels( true );
    slider.setLabelTable( table );
    slider.setBorder( BorderFactory.createLoweredBevelBorder() );
    frame.getContentPane().add( slider, BorderLayout.CENTER );

    frame.pack();
    frame.setVisible( true );

} // main

} // PercentSliderTest
```

FIGURE 10.14

The PercentSlider Test *application.*

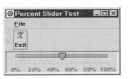

In the PercentSliderTest application, the label table is created with the percent number formatter. One JLabel instance is created for each major tick on the slider. This creates a nice slider, but it is not very versatile. If the major tick spacing parameter is changed, so must the label table. For formatted sliders whose range or major tick spacing is subject to change, extending the JSlider class provides a better solution.

Extending JSlider

The previous section showed how to configure the label table for a slider. This was adequate for one-shot configurations. However, to create a general-purpose formatted text slider, an extension to the JSlider class is called for. Luckily, the JSlider class provides the necessary hooks to make this an easy task. The JSlider class calls the createStandardLabels method to create the labels displayed in the slider. Our extension can override this method to create the formatted labels.

Listing 10.19 shows the PercentSlider class, which extends the JSlider class. Its public API is identical to the JSlider class, with the exception of the setLabelTable method. This method is not available in the PercentSlider class. This is because creating the label table for the class is the primary purpose of the PercentSlider class. Allowing users to set this table could remove the percent signs on the labels. Another enhancement of the PercentSlider is that the labels are created whenever the major tick spacing changes. This allows an existing percent slider to be reconfigured. The current implementation of the JSlider class does not allow this—once the labels are created, they are used for the duration of the class's lifetime, unless the user explicitly sets or re-creates the table.

LISTING 10.19   THE PercentSlider CLASS

```
package com.foley.utility;

import java.text.NumberFormat;
import java.util.Hashtable;

import javax.swing.*;


/**
 * The PercentSlider class is a slider that formats its
 * labels using the % sign.
 * <p>
 * @author Mike Foley
 **/
public class PercentSlider extends JSlider
{
    /**
     * PercentSlider, constructor
     * <p>
     * Configure the slider for normal percent range,
     * 0-100 and a current value of 0. The default major
     * tick spacing is set to 25 and minor tick spacing
     * to 5. Both labels and ticks are painted.
     * <p>
     * These values may be changed by the client using the
     * public API.
     *
     * @see JSlider
     **/
```

```
public PercentSlider() {
    setMinimum( 0 );
    setMaximum( 100 );
    setValue( 0 );
    setMajorTickSpacing( 25 );
    setMinorTickSpacing( 5 );
    setPaintTicks( true );
    setPaintLabels( true );

}


/**
 * Create labels for the slider. Format each label
 * to contain a percent sign. A label is created
 * for each value from:
 * <p>
 *       start + x * increment
 * <p>
 * until the maximum value is reached.
 * <p>
 * @param increment The delta between labels.
 * @param start The value of the first label.
 * @return The table of labels for the slider.
 **/
public Hashtable createStandardLabels( int increment, int start ) {
    if ( start > getMaximum() || start < getMinimum() ) {
        throw new IllegalArgumentException(
                    "Slider label start point out of range." );
    }

    NumberFormat percent = NumberFormat.getPercentInstance();

    Hashtable table = new Hashtable();

    for ( int i = start; i <= getMaximum(); i += increment ) {
        JLabel l = new JLabel(
                    percent.format( ( double )i / 100.0 ) );
        table.put( new Integer( i ), l );
    }

    return table;
}


/**
 * The label table is created by this class. Do not
 * allow it to be set from the outside.
 * <p>
```

continues

LISTING 10.19   CONTINUED

```
        * @exception RuntimeException If this method is called.
        **/
       public void setLabelTable() {
           throw new RuntimeException(
                       "Cannot set the label table for the PercentSlider" );
       }


       /**
        * setMajorTickSpacing
        * <p>
        * This method in the JSlider class does not create
        * labels if the label table has been created once.
        * This may cause the labels to be drawn in areas that
        * do not correspond to the major ticks. This is fixed
        * here by creating the label table whenever a new
        * major tick spacing is specified.
        * <p>
        * @param n The new major tick spacing.
        **/
       public void setMajorTickSpacing( int n ) {
           if( getMajorTickSpacing() != n )
               setLabelTable( createStandardLabels( n ) );
           super.setMajorTickSpacing( n );
       }
} // PercentSlider
```

The `PercentSliderTest` application can be modified to display an instance of the `PercentSlider` class. The following code can be used instead of the code to create and configure the `JSlider`. The modified `PercentSliderTest` application produces a slider that looks identical to the previous version of the application, shown in Figure 10.14.

```
JSlider percentSlider = new PercentSlider();
percentSlider.setBorder( BorderFactory.createLoweredBevelBorder() );
frame.getContentPane().add( percentSlider, BorderLayout.CENTER );
```

Painting the `JSlider`'s Track

For some types of controls, such as a volume control, you don't want to paint the slider's track. The `paintTrack` property controls this behavior. Passing the `setPaintTrack` method `false` will stop the slider from painting the track. As you have seen from the previous examples in this chapter, the default value for this property is `true`. The `getPaintTrack` method can query the current setting of this property. The `paintTrack` property is bound in the `JSlider` class.

Adding the following line of code to the `PercentSliderTest` application, shown in the previous section, will disable the track from being drawn in the slider:

```
slider.setPaintTrack( false );
```

The resulting slider is shown in Figure 10.15.

FIGURE 10.15
A trackless slider
in the
`PercentSliderTest`
application.

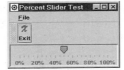

Displaying the `JSlider`'s Value

Up to this point, you have displayed and configured `JSlider` instances, displayed tick marks, and displayed labels for the range of the slider. However, you have not been able to display the current value of the slider. Most of the time, this is useful. It is very rare that a slider is used to alter a value without showing the user the current value selected in the slider. Unfortunately, there is no `setPaintValue` method in the `JSlider` class. Thus, to show the current value of the slider, you must do some work.

The `JSlider` class again could be extended to display the current value somewhere in its space. However, this is not the approach you'll take here. Instead, a panel is created that contains the slider and a label for the current value. The panel will be a mediator between the slider and label. It will listen for change events from the slider and update the label when such events are received.

The `SliderValuePanel` class is shown in Listing 10.20. In its constructor, the slider and label are created. The slider is configured to paint tick marks and labels. A `JLabel` is created to display the current value in the slider. The class registers itself as a `ChangeListener` to the slider so that it's notified when the value in the slider changes. The `stateChanged` method being called performs this function. This method queries the current value of the slider and writes that value in the label. The panel is configured with a `BorderLayout` manager. The slider is placed in the center region and the label in the south.

LISTING 10.20   THE `SliderValuePanel` CLASS

```
package com.foley.utility;

import java.awt.*;

import javax.swing.*;
import javax.swing.event.*;
```

continues

LISTING 10.20   CONTINUED

```java
/**
 * The SliderValuePanel class is a panel that contains a
 * slider and a label to display the current value in the slider.
 * <p>
 * The current implementation requires the user to get the slider
 * to configure it. Wrapper methods for the BoundedRangeModel
 * method should be provided.
 * <p>
 * @author Mike Foley
 **/
public class SliderValuePanel extends JPanel
     implements ChangeListener {

    /**
     * Components in the panel.
     **/
    private JSlider slider;
    private JLabel label;

    /**
     * The String that the current value is appended to.
     **/
    private static final String labelBase = "Current Value: ";


    /**
     * SliderValuePanel, constructor
     * <p>
     * Create the JSlider instance and JLabel instance
     * and arrange them in the panel.
     **/
    public SliderValuePanel() {
        super();

        setLayout( new BorderLayout() );

        slider = new JSlider();
        slider.setMajorTickSpacing( 20 );
        slider.setMinorTickSpacing( 5 );
        slider.setPaintTicks( true );
        slider.setPaintLabels( true );

        label = new JLabel( labelBase + slider.getValue() );

        add( slider, BorderLayout.CENTER );
        add( label, BorderLayout.SOUTH );

        slider.addChangeListener( this );
    }
```

```
    /**
     * Return the slider in this panel. This allows
     * clients to get a handle to the slider and configure
     * it.
     * <p>
     * @return The slider in this panel.
     **/
    public JSlider getSlider() {
        return( slider );
    }


    /**
     * stateChanged, from ChangeListener
     * <p>
     * The slider in the panel value has changed.
     * Update the label's text.
     * <p>
     * @param event The event causing this method to be called.
**/
    public void stateChanged( ChangeEvent event ) {
        label.setText( labelBase + slider.getValue() );
    }

} // SliderValuePanel
```

The SliderValuePanel easily could be enhanced so that the position of the label relative to the slider would be a property of the panel, rather than hard coded as it currently is. It would also be useful to allow the slider to be set. This would allow enhanced sliders, such as the PercentSlider presented earlier in the chapter, to be used with the SliderValuePanel class. A final enhancement would be to change the label to a JTextField so the user could enter the desired value directly. This would require the panel to listen to changes in the textfield and update the slider after the user entered a new value.

The SliderValuePanelTest application, shown in Listing 10.21, is used to test the SliderValuePanel class. This application creates the SliderValuePanel instance and adds it to a frame for display. The resulting window is shown in Figure 10.16. When this application is executed, the slider can be dragged, and the label will update as the slider moves to display the current value in the slider.

LISTING 10.21   THE `SliderValuePanelTest` APPLICATION

```java
package com.foley.test;

import java.awt.*;

import javax.swing.*;
import javax.swing.border.*;

import com.foley.utility.ApplicationFrame;
import com.foley.utility.SliderValuePanel;


/**
 * An application that displays a SliderValuePanelTest instance
 * in its frame.
 *
 * @author Mike Foley
 **/
public class SliderValuePanelTest extends Object {

    /**
     * Application entry point.
     * Create a frame, the list and display it.
     *
     * @param args Command line parameter. Not used.
     **/
    public static void main( String args[] ) {

        JFrame frame = new ApplicationFrame( "SliderValuePanel Test" );

        SliderValuePanel sliderValuePanel = new SliderValuePanel();
        sliderValuePanel.setBorder(
                    BorderFactory.createLoweredBevelBorder() );

        frame.getContentPane().add( sliderValuePanel,
                            BorderLayout.CENTER );

        frame.pack();
        frame.setVisible( true );

    } // main

} // SliderValuePanelTest
```

FIGURE 10.16

The `SliderValuePanel` `Test` *application.*

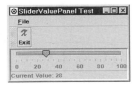

The `JScrollBar` Class

The `JScrollBar` class is used internally by JFC classes. However, it can be instantiated and used directly by user classes as well. Like the `JSlider` class, the `JScrollBar` class employs a `BoundedRangeModel` to manage its range and current value. In fact, as you saw during the discussion of the `BoundedRangeModel` interface, some of its properties are designed with a scrollbar in mind. The `extent` property comes to mind.

The `JScrollBar` class contains a wrapper method for the properties of `BoundedRangeModel`. These methods are convenience methods that forward their parameters to the model. The `JScrollBar` class also implements the `java.awt.Adjustable` interface. As such, it must contain the methods defined in that interface. The bound properties introduced by the `JScrollBar` class are presented in Table 10.5.

TABLE 10.5 NON-INHERITED BOUND PROPERTIES OF THE `JScrollBar` CLASS

Property Name	Setter Method	Getter Method
orientation	setOrientation	getOrientation
model	setModel	getModel
unitIncrement	setUnitIncrement	getUnitIncrement
blockIncrement	setBlockIncrement	getBlockIncrement

Note that the constants used as the parameters for the `setOrientation` method of the `JScrollBar` class are defined in the AWT `Adjustable` interface that `JScrollBar` implements. Earlier in this chapter, you saw constants with the exact same names and purposes used in the `JSlider` class defined in the `SwingConstants` class. Having constants with identical names and meanings in multiple locations is a dangerous habit. Luckily, the constants are defined with the same values so they can be used interchangeably. We can only hope that as AWT and JFC mature, this type of overlap will be eliminated.

You saw the `JScrollBar` class in action earlier in this chapter in the `JList` class. You will also see it in later chapters when the `JScrollPane` class is explored.

The `JProgressBar` Class

The `JProgressBar` class provides a class that can show the progress of an operation. A progress bar is commonly seen at the bottom of a frame when a lengthy operation is under way. It is updated periodically to indicate the status of the operation.

The `JProgressBar` class tracks the minimum, maximum, and current values in a `BoundedRangeModel` instance. The class contains the familiar convenience methods for setting and getting the model's minimum, maximum, and current values. The default values for these properties define a range from 0 to 100, and an initial value of 0. These properties are not bound to the `JProgressBar` class; interested parties must listen to the model to be notified when these properties change.

> **NOTE**
>
> There are no bound properties defined in the `JProgressBar` class. If the model changes for the progress bar and a listener was listening to the old model, it will be unaware of the change. The listener will no longer receive change events from the model that controls the progress bar that it is interested in.
>
> To avoid this type of error, the `JProgressBar` class allows a `ChangeListener` to be added to it directly, rather than to its `BoundedRangeModel`. The progress bar listens for changes in the model and forwards all `ChangeEvents` from the model to its registered listeners.

The orientation of the progress bar can be specified with the `setOrientation` method. Legal values for the orientation property are the constants `HORIZONTAL` and `VERTICAL`, defined in the `SwingConstants` interface. The `JProgressBar` class implements this interface, so the constant can be specified as either `SwingConstants.HORIZONTAL` or `JProgressBar.HORIZONTAL`. The `getOrientation` method returns the current value of this property. The `orientation` property is not bound in the `JProgressBar` class.

The `ProgressBarTest` application, shown in Listing 10.22, creates a `JProgressBar` instance and adds it to a frame. The application uses the default range for the progress bar and sets its value to 25. The resulting progress bar is shown in Figure 10.17.

LISTING 10.22   THE `ProgressBarTest` APPLICATION

```
package com.foley.test;

import java.awt.*;

import javax.swing.*;

import com.foley.utility.ApplicationFrame;


/**
 * An application that displays a JProgressBar instance
 * in its frame.
 *
 * @author Mike Foley
```

```
**/
public class ProgressBarTest extends Object {

    /**
     * Application entry point.
     * Create a frame, the progress bar and display it.
     *
     * @param args Command line parameter. Not used.
     **/
    public static void main( String args[] ) {

        JFrame frame = new ApplicationFrame( "ProgressBar Test" );

        JProgressBar progressBar = new JProgressBar();
        progressBar.setValue( 25 );

        frame.getContentPane().add( progressBar, BorderLayout.CENTER );

        frame.pack();
        frame.setVisible( true );

    } // main

} // ProgressBarTest
```

FIGURE 10.17

The
ProgressBarTest
application.

Unlike what you saw with the JSlider class earlier in this chapter, the JProgressBar class contains a property for displaying the current value in the progress bar. Passing true to the setStringPainted method will paint the current value in the progress bar as a percentage of the model's range. By default, the string is not painted. The string painted in the progress bar can be specified by calling the setString method. This method can be repeatedly called as the progress is incremented, if desired. Each time it's called, the new string will be painted in the progress bar. If a string has been specified for the progress bar using this method, it is painted in the progress bar rather than calculating the completion percentage. The displayed string can be queried with the getString method. After a string has been specified, passing null to the setString method will restore the default behavior.

The isStringPainted method can be called to query the current state of the stringPainted property. The default behavior of the getString method calls the getPercentComplete method. This method returns a double that represents the percentage of the value in range defined in the progress bar's model. The value is between 0.0 and 1.0.

Adding the following line of code to the `ProgressBarTest` application will cause the string to be painted as a percentage of the model's range. The resulting progress bar is shown in Figure 10.18.

```
progressBar.setStringPainted( true );
```

FIGURE 10.18

A string displayed in the `JProgressBar`.

Passing `false` to the `setBorderPainted` method will hide the border around the progress bar. The `isBorderPainted` method will query the current state of the `borderPainted` property. The default behavior is to paint the border around the progress bar.

Summary

This chapter covered a lot of material. The `ListModel` and `ListSelectionModel` were presented, as well as how the `JList` class uses these two models. You also learned how to use the `JList` class to present the user with a choice of options.

The `JComboBox` class and its associated models, `ComboBoxModel` and `MutableComboBoxModel`, were presented. This class was compared and contrasted with the `JList` class and its models, and the inconsistencies between these classes were explained. Unfortunately, these inconsistencies make programming the two classes overly complex.

The `BoundedRangeModel` was presented, as well as three classes that use this model. You learned about the `JSlider` class. An extension to the class was presented to demonstrate how typed labels can be used in a slider. The `JScrollBar` class was introduced, which will be used more extensively in Chapter 15 when scroll panes are presented. Finally, you learned about the `JProgressBar` class, which provides a component that displays the value in its `BoundedRange` model as a percentage of the model's range.

Tree Component

IN THIS CHAPTER

The JTree class is an implementation of a control that allows you to view data in a hierarchical structure. The AWT did not have a component comparable to the JTree class. Perhaps the most familiar example of a tree component in use is in a file manager type application. The file system's directory structure is organized as a tree, so the view is a natural fit.

The JTree class provides convenience methods for easy tree configuration. A tree can be configured to allow editing of the nodes in the tree. The TreeModel interface is available for creating custom data models to be viewed in the tree component. By using these techniques, the JTree class can be configured to meet almost any need for a tree component.

In this chapter, you will learn

- How to create and use the JTree class
- About the TreeModel interface
- About the TreeNode and MutableTreeNode interfaces
- How to create and use a renderer for a tree
- How to use an editor with a tree

Using the JTree Component

The visual control in the JFC for displaying hierarchical data structures is the JTree class. The tree consists of multiple nodes that can be expanded and collapsed to display more or less detail of the underlying data model. The top node in the tree is known as the root node. A node that does not contain any children nodes is known as a leaf node.

The simplest example of a JTree instance is presented in Listing 11.1. The default JTree constructor is called, and the tree is displayed. An instance of the ApplicationFrame class, presented in Chapter 8, "Frame Windows," is used to display the tree. The resulting tree after being expanded is shown in Figure 11.1.

LISTING 11.1   THE SimpleTreeTest APPLICATION

```
package com.foley.test;

import java.awt.*;

import javax.swing.*;
import javax.swing.border.*;

import com.foley.utility.ApplicationFrame;
```

```
/**
 * An application that displays a JTree instance
 * in its frame.
 *
 * @author Mike Foley
 **/
public class SimpleTreeTest extends Object {

    /**
     * Application entry point.
     * Create a frame and the tree and display them.
     *
     * @param args Command line parameter. Not used.
     **/
    public static void main( String args[] ) {

        JFrame frame = new ApplicationFrame( "SimpleTreeTest Test" );

        JTree tree = new JTree();
        tree.setBorder( BorderFactory.createLoweredBevelBorder() );

        frame.getContentPane().add( tree, BorderLayout.CENTER );

        frame.pack();
        frame.setVisible( true );

    } // main

} // SimpleTreeTest
```

FIGURE 11.1

The default JTree *instance.*

The tree shown in Figure 11.1 uses the default tree model contained in the JTree class. The model is created in the protected getDefaultTreeModel method. JTree extensions can override this method to contain a different default model. It is seen in the figure that the root node of the tree is shown by default. Icons are associated with each node in the tree. The default icons are look-and-feel specific but tend to be of the file management type like those shown for the Metal look-and-feel in Figure 11.1. Notice that the leaf icon is different than that of non-leaf nodes. The control to the left of the icon, a dot in this figure, can be used to expand and collapse the node. This application also demonstrates that the default tree needs some data to display.

NOTE

Figure 11.1 shows a JTree instance when the Metal look-and-feel is being used. The horizontal lines above each node that is a child of the root node is specific to this look-and-feel. In fact, Metal defines a client property for the JTree class. When the JTree.lineStyle property is set to one of the three known values—Angled, None, and the default Horizontal—the look-and-feel draws the lines appropriately. The property strings are case sensitive. This property is ignored in the other standard look-and-feel implementations. The Angled option, shown in Figure 11.2, is the line style familiar with most tree users.

FIGURE 11.2

Angled lines in the default JTree instance.

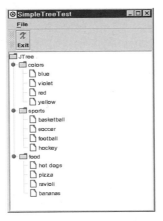

The JTree class contains versions of the constructor that take an instance of an array, Hashtable, or Vector as a parameter. You can modify the SimpleTreeTest application to create a tree instance from one of these collection classes by instantiating the JTree instance with one of the following blocks of code shown in Listing 11.2. (For the Vector and Hashtable initialization, the java.util.Vector or java.util.Hashtable package must be imported at the top of the application.) The resulting trees are shown in Figure 11.3.

LISTING 11.2   INITIALIZING A TREE FROM A COLLECTION

```
// Test using an array.
String[] data = { "Mike", "Mari", "Molly" };
JTree tree = new JTree( data );

// Test using a Vector.
Vector data = new Vector();
data.addElement( "Mike" );
data.addElement( "Mari" );
data.addElement( "Molly" );
JTree tree = new JTree( data );

// Test using a Hashtable.
Hashtable data = new Hashtable();
data.put( "Mike", new Integer(0) );
data.put( "Mari", new Integer(1) );
data.put( "Molly", new Integer(2) );
JTree tree = new JTree( data );
```

FIGURE 11.3

JTree *initializa-
tion from the stan-
dard JDK 1.1 col-
lections.*

Figure 11.3 shows that the tree does not show the root node when initialized from a collection. You can force the root node to be displayed by passing true to the
setRootVisible method. The root visibility status is a bound property in the JTree
class. The complete list of bound properties introduced in the JTree class is presented in
Table 11.1. The nodes in the tree created from the Hashtable are in a different order than
the other two trees, and the data is not in a tree hierarchy. This is because the collection
passed to the constructor does not contain hierarchical information. Having the collection
contain other collections as members can rectify this situation. The following code shows
this for the Vector class (see Figure 11.4), but a similar approach can be used for other

collection types. The type of collection can be mixed also. For example, a vector can contain hashtables as its elements.

```
Vector data = new Vector();
Vector names = new Vector();
names.addElement( "Mike" );
names.addElement( "Mari" );
names.addElement( "Molly" );

data.addElement( names );
JTree tree = new JTree( data );
```

FIGURE 11.4

Vector-created tree.

In Figure 11.4, you can see that the data is displayed as a tree, but somewhat clumsily. The default tree implementation calls the `toString` method of the `Object` class for each node. This probably is not the desired string for a `Vector`, `Hashtable`, or array. The `toString` method in the `Vector` class is final, so an anonymous extension to the `Vector` class that overrides the `toString` method cannot be used. Later in this chapter you will see how the `JTree` class can be extended and how a custom rendering class can be used to overcome this situation. Even though the basic collections can be used to populate the tree, simply put, they are the wrong data structure for a tree. Fortunately, the JFC defines the `TreeModel` and `TreeNode` interfaces that are the correct data structure for a tree. When a collection is used to initialize a tree, a tree model is created by traversing the collection and creating parent nodes for each collection found and leaf nodes for other types of objects. These interfaces and the classes that implement them in the JFC are the subject of the next section.

TABLE 11.1 BOUND PROPERTIES INTRODUCED IN THE JTree CLASS

Property Name	Setter Method	Getter Method
CELL_RENDERER_PROPERTY	setCellRenderer	getCellRenderer
EDITABLE_PROPERTY	setEditable	isEditable
TREE_MODEL_PROPERTY	setModel	getModel

Property Name	Setter Method	Getter Method
ROOT_VISIBLE_PROPERTY	setRootVisible	isRootVisible
SHOWS_ROOT_HANDLES_PROPERTY	setShowsRoot Handles	getShowsRoot Handles
ROW_HEIGHT_PROPERTY	setRowHeight	getRowHeight
LARGE_MODEL_PROPERTY	setLargeModel	isLargeModel
INVOKES_STOP_CELL _EDITING_PROPERTY	setInvokesStop CellEditing	getInvokesStop CellEditing
SCROLLS_ON_EXPAND_PROPERTY	setScrollsOn Expand	getScrollsOn Expand
SELECTION_MODEL_PROPERTY	setSelection Model	getSelection Model
VISIBLE_ROW_COUNT_PROPERTY	setVisibleRow Count	getVisibleRow Count

The JTree class defines three selection modes. SINGLE_TREE_SELECTION mode allows the selection of only one path at a given time. The CONTIGUOUS_TREE_SELECTION mode allows multiple contiguous paths to be simultaneously selected. The DISCONTIGUOUS_TREE_SELECTION mode allows any paths to be simultaneously selected. The DISCONTIGUOUS_TREE_SELECTION mode is the default selection mode for a JTree instance. The selection mode is defined and enforced by the tree's selection model discussed in the next section.

The swing.tree Package

The interfaces that define the tree's data model and the nodes contained in that model are defined in the javax.swing.tree package. The classes that implement these interfaces and are used internally by the JFC are located in this package also. The classes and interfaces are available for you to use in your applications as well. This section describes the interfaces and classes that are typically encountered when building tree views in the JFC.

TreeModel Interface

The TreeModel interface contained in the swing.tree package defines the data model used by the JTree class (see Listing 11.3). By examining the interface, you can see that the model consists primarily as a reference to the tree's root node. The other methods are convenience methods to hide implementation details from the view. For example, the

number of children can be determined for any node in the tree by passing the
getChildCount method to the node whose child count is desired. How to find the node
in the tree data structure is hidden from the caller.

LISTING 11.3 THE TreeModel INTERFACE

```
public interface TreeModel
{

    /**
     * Returns the root of the tree. Returns null only if the tree has
     * no nodes.
     *
     * @return   the root of the tree
     */
    public Object getRoot();


    /**
     * Returns the child of <I>parent</I> at index <I>index</I> in the
     * parent's child array.  <I>parent</I> must be a node previously
     * obtained from this data source.
     *
     * @param   parent a node in the tree, obtained from this data source
     * @return   the child of <I>parent</I> at index <I>index</I>
     */
    public Object getChild(Object parent, int index);


    /**
     * Returns the number of children of <I>parent</I>.  Returns 0 if the
     * node is a leaf or if it has no children.  <I>parent</I> must be a
     * node previously obtained from this data source.
     *
   * @param  parent   a node in the tree, obtained from this data source
     * @return the number of children of the node <I>parent</I>
     */
    public int getChildCount(Object parent);


    /**
     * Returns true if <I>node</I> is a leaf.  It is possible for this
     * method to return false even if <I>node</I> has no children.  A
     * directory in a file system, for example, may contain no files;
     * the node representing the directory is not a leaf, but it also
     * has no children.
     *
     * @param   node a node in the tree, obtained from this data source
     * @return   true if <I>node</I> is a leaf
```

```
         */
        public boolean isLeaf(Object node);

        /**
         * Messaged when the user has altered the value for the item
         * identified by <I>path</I> to <I>newValue</I>. If <I>newValue</I>
         * signifies a truly new value the model should post a
         * treeNodesChanged event.
         *
         * @param path path to the node that the user has altered.
         * @param newValue the new value from the TreeCellEditor.
         */
        public void valueForPathChanged(TreePath path, Object newValue);

        /**
         * Returns the index of child in parent.
         */
        public int getIndexOfChild(Object parent, Object child);

        /**
         * Adds a listener for the TreeModelEvent posted after the tree
         * changes.
         *
         * @see     #removeTreeModelListener
         * @param   l       the listener to add
         */
        void addTreeModelListener(TreeModelListener l);

        /**
         * Removes a listener previously added with
         * <B>addTreeModelListener()</B>.
         *
         * @see     #addTreeModelListener
         * @param   l       the listener to remove
         */
        void removeTreeModelListener(TreeModelListener l);

}
```

The `DefaultTreeModel` class is a complete implementation of the `TreeModel` interface. It is used internally by the `JTree` class as the `TreeModel` when a `TreeModel` is not explicitly set. The `DefaultTreeModel` class requires a `TreeNode` in its constructor. This node is used as the root of the tree. The `swing.tree` package defines interfaces for two types of tree nodes, a mutable and immutable variant. These interfaces are described in the next section.

Tree Nodes

The JFC tree data structure defines two interfaces for tree nodes. The first, TreeNode, defines a static node. Once constructed and placed into a tree, this type of node cannot change its position in the tree or its children structure. The second interface is the MutableTreeNode interface. This type of node can be relocated in a tree, moved from one tree to another, and have its children structure change dynamically. These two interfaces are shown in Listing 11.4.

LISTING 11.4 THE TreeNode AND MutableTreeNode INTERFACES

```
public interface TreeNode
{
    /**
     * Returns the child <code>TreeNode</code> at index
     * <code>childIndex</code>.
     */
    TreeNode getChildAt(int childIndex);

    /**
     * Returns the number of children <code>TreeNode</code>s the receiver
     * contains.
     */
    int getChildCount();

    /**
     * Returns the parent <code>TreeNode</code> of the receiver.
     */
    TreeNode getParent();

    /**
     * Returns the index of <code>node</code> in the receiver's children.
     * If the receiver does not contain <code>node</code>, -1 will be
     * returned.
     */
    int getIndex(TreeNode node);

    /**
     * Returns true if the receiver allows children.
     */
    boolean getAllowsChildren();

    /**
     * Returns true if the receiver is a leaf.
     */
    boolean isLeaf();

    /**
```

```
 * Returns the children of the receiver as an Enumeration.
 */
Enumeration children();
}

public interface MutableTreeNode extends TreeNode
{
/**
 * Adds <code>child</code> to the receiver at <code>index</code>.
 * <code>child</code> will be messaged with <code>setParent</code>.
 */
void insert(MutableTreeNode child, int index);

/**
 * Removes the child at <code>index</code> from the receiver.
 */
void remove(int index);

/**
 * Removes <code>node</code> from the receiver.
 * <code>setParent</code> will be messaged on <code>node</code>.

 */
void remove(MutableTreeNode node);

/**
 * Resets the user object of the receiver to <code>object</code>.
 */
void setUserObject(Object object);

/**
 * Removes the receiver from its parent.
 */
void removeFromParent();

/**
 * Sets the parent of the receiver to <code>newParent</code>.
 */
void setParent(MutableTreeNode newParent);
}
```

The TreeNode interface defines a node that does not change its structure, or its location in the tree, for its lifetime. This type of node can still have children; it simply cannot dynamically add or remove children. The TreeNode class must be capable of returning its parent node in tree from the getParent method. However, the interface does not define a method for setting the parent. Thus, a class that implements TreeNode should take a reference to its parent in its constructor. The remainder of the methods defined in the TreeNode interface manages the node's children. However, the interface doesn't contain methods to create the children's structure. Like the parent reference, the children can be specified in an implementation class's constructor.

The MutableTreeNode interface extends the TreeNode interface. It adds methods to allow the node to change its location in the tree and the number of children it contains. The removeFromParent and setParent methods allow the node to be moved in the tree while leaving the node's children unaltered. The insert and remove methods allow the children of the node to be dynamically added and removed. The final method defined in the MutableTreeNode interface, setUserObject, is a bit strange. The user object concept is sound; it allows the node to contain a reference to one object that is not interpreted by the node and that the application can use as it sees fit without having to keep another data structure mapping the user objects to the tree nodes. However, there is not a method to get the user object, so the application is out of luck trying to query the user object from the node.

Classes that implement the TreeNode interface can benefit from the user object reference just as much as those that implement the MutableTreeNode interface. To keep the TreeNode interface non-mutable, it should contain the getUserObject method and require the binding to be done at construction time. This would be similar to what is done with the parent reference at this time.

This apparent oddity can be explained by the fact that the JFC contains only one class that implements the node interfaces, the DefaultMutableTreeNode class. As its name implies, it implements the MutableTreeNode interface. This class defines a getUserObject method. It looks as though not containing this method in the TreeNode interface was an oversight by the JFC development team. It is unfortunate, though, because it forces a great deal of code to assume an implementation of the MutableTreeNode class, rather than the much more desirable condition of working at the interface level.

Internally, the DefaultMutableTreeNode class is the workhorse node class in the JFC. It is the lone tree node implementation in the tree package. It implements the MutableTreeNode interface. As such, it serves as a general-purpose tree node that can be dynamically altered in any way desired. Looking at the documentation for the DefaultMutableTreeNode class shows that its public API is far richer than that found in the MutableTreeNode interface. However, using the extra methods not defined in the interface ties your code to that implementation of the MutableTreeNode interface and makes it more difficult to incorporate new tree node implementations later.

When a DefaultMutableTreeNode instance has a non-null user object, its toString method is called when the toString method is called for the node. This allows the text in the tree to display the user object's toString text. This class contains the getUserObject method that is not defined in either of the tree node interfaces.

The `DefaultMutableTreeNode` class contains many methods for querying the children and structure of the node. Many of these methods are generally applicable to a tree node and rely on the fact that the node is mutable. For example, the `getLeafCount` method returns the number of leaf instances that are descendants from the current node. This method is valid for non-mutable nodes as well as mutable nodes. It would have been desirable to split the rich API contained in the `DefaultMutableTreeNode` into two classes: a non-mutable version containing the static structure methods, and a mutable node that contains the mutation methods.

Tree Paths

A path in the tree data structure defines a linear path from the root of the tree to a node. The node may or may not be a leaf in the tree. Perhaps the easiest way to think of a path is to start at a node and keep following its parent, its parent's parent, and so on until the root of the tree is reached. Reversing this lineage defines a tree path.

The `swing.tree` package contains the `TreePath` class that defines the path from the root of the tree to a node in the tree. The `TreePath` class's constructor takes an array of node objects that define the path. The class does not validate the path passed to the method. You will see the `TreePath` class used in `JTree` methods for expanding the tree. Paths are used extensively in the tree's selection model, which is the subject of the next section.

Tree Selection Model

As you have seen earlier with the `ListModel` interface and `JList` class, the `TreeModel` interface and `JTree` class delegate selection management to a separate selection model, the `TreeSelectionModel`. The `TreeSelectionModel` is an interface that defines the selection model for a JFC tree. Looking at the interface that is shown in Listing 11.5, you see that it contains 27 method signatures, making it one of the biggest interfaces in the JFC.

The `TreeSelectionModel` defines three selection modes for a tree. The `SINGLE_TREE_SELECTION` mode allows only one path to be selected at a given time. The `CONTIGUOUS_TREE_SELECTION` mode allows multiple contiguous paths to be simultaneously selected. The `DISCONTIGUOUS_TREE_SELECTION` mode allows any paths to be simultaneously selected. The `setSelectionMode` and `getSelectionMode` methods are used to alter and query the selection mode property. The remainder of the methods contained in the interface are used to alter the selected path set. The semantics of each selection method are not defined for each selection mode. For example, the `setSelectionPaths` method takes an array of `TreePath` instances as its lone parameter. If the selection mode is single selection and this array contains more than one path, which path is selected is not defined in the `TreeSelectionModel` interface. It is up to the class that implements

the interface to decide the behavior. The DefaultTreeSelectionModel class that is provided in the JFC only selects the first path in this case. However, an application should
not assume this behavior from other classes that implement the TreeSelectionModel
interface. For instance, another implementation can select the last path in the array.

LISTING 11.5   THE TreeSelectionModel INTERFACE

```
public interface TreeSelectionModel
{
    /** Selection can only contain one path at a time. */
    public static int            SINGLE_TREE_SELECTION = 1;

    /** Selection can only be contiguous. This will only be enforced if
     * a RowMapper instance is provided. */
    public static int            CONTIGUOUS_TREE_SELECTION = 2;

/** Selection can contain any number of items that are not
     * necessarily contiguous. */
    public static int            DISCONTIGUOUS_TREE_SELECTION = 4;

    /**
 * Sets the selection model, which must be one of
     * SINGLE_TREE_SELECTION, CONTIGUOUS_TREE_SELECTION or
     * DISCONTIGUOUS_TREE_SELECTION.
     */
    void setSelectionMode(int mode);

    /**
     * Returns the selection mode.
     */
    int getSelectionMode();

    /**
     * Sets the selection to path.  If this represents a change, then
     * the TreeSelectionListeners are notified.
     *
     * @param path new path to select
     */
    void setSelectionPath(TreePath path);

    /**
     * Sets the selection to the paths.  If this represents a
     * change the TreeSelectionListeners are notified.
     *
     * @param paths new selection.
     */
    void setSelectionPaths(TreePath[] paths);

    /**
     * Adds path to the current selection.  If path is not currently
```

```
    * in the selection the TreeSelectionListeners are notified.
    *
    * @param path the new path to add to the current selection.
    */
  void addSelectionPath(TreePath path);

  /**
   * Adds paths to the current selection.  If any of the paths in
* paths are not currently in the selection the
   * TreeSelectionListeners are notified.
   *
   * @param path the new path to add to the current selection.
   */
  void addSelectionPaths(TreePath[] paths);

  /**
   * Removes path from the selection.  If path is in the selection
   * The TreeSelectionListeners are notified.
   *
   * @param path the path to remove from the selection.
   */
  void removeSelectionPath(TreePath path);

  /**
   * Removes paths from the selection.  If any of the paths in paths
   * are in the selection the TreeSelectionListeners are notified.
   *
   * @param path the path to remove from the selection.
   */
  void removeSelectionPaths(TreePath[] paths);

  /**
   * Returns the first path in the selection.
   */
  TreePath getSelectionPath();

  /**
   * Returns the paths in the selection.
   */
  TreePath[] getSelectionPaths();

  /**
   * Returns the number of paths that are selected.
   */
  int getSelectionCount();

  /**
   * Returns true if the path, path, is in the current selection.
   */
  boolean isPathSelected(TreePath path);
```

continues

LISTING 11.5 CONTINUED

```java
/**
  * Returns true if the selection is currently empty.
  */
boolean isSelectionEmpty();

/**
  * Empties the current selection.  If this represents a change in
  * the current selection, the selection listeners are notified.
  */
void clearSelection();

/**
  * Sets the RowMapper instance.  This instance is used to determine
  * what row corresponds to what path.
  */
void setRowMapper(RowMapper newMapper);

/**
  * Returns the RowMapper instance that is able to map a path to a
  * row.
  */
RowMapper getRowMapper();

/**
  * Returns all of the currently selected rows.
  */
int[] getSelectionRows();

/**
  * Gets the first selected row.
  */
int getMinSelectionRow();

/**
  * Gets the last selected row.
  */
int getMaxSelectionRow();

/**
  * Returns true if the row identified by row is selected.
  */
boolean isRowSelected(int row);

/**
  * Updates what rows are selected.  This can be externally called in
  * case the location of the paths change, but not the actual paths.
  * You do not normally need to call this.
  */
void resetRowSelection();
```

```
/**
 * Returns the lead selection index. That is the last index that was
 * added.
 */
int getLeadSelectionRow();

/**
 * Returns the last path that was added.
 */
TreePath getLeadSelectionPath();

/**
 * Add a PropertyChangeListener to the listener list.
 * The listener is registered for all properties.
 * <p>
 * A PropertyChangeEvent will get fired in response to an
 * explicit setFont, setBackground, or SetForeground on the
 * current component.  Note that if the current component is
 * inheriting its foreground, background, or font from its
 * container, then no event will be fired in response to a
 * change in the inherited property.
 *
 * @param listener  The PropertyChangeListener to be added
 */
void addPropertyChangeListener(PropertyChangeListener listener);

/**
 * Remove a PropertyChangeListener from the listener list.
 * This removes a PropertyChangeListener that was registered
 * for all properties.
 *
 * @param listener  The PropertyChangeListener to be removed
 */
void removePropertyChangeListener(PropertyChangeListener listener);

/**
  * Adds x to the list of listeners that are notified each time the
  * selection changes.
  *
  * @param x the new listener to be added.
  */
void addTreeSelectionListener(TreeSelectionListener x);

/**
  * Removes x from the list of listeners that are notified each time
  * the selection changes.
  *
  * @param x the listener to remove.
  */
void removeTreeSelectionListener(TreeSelectionListener x);
}
```

The `DefaultTreeSelectionModel` class in the `swing.tree` package implements the `TreeSelectionModel` interface and is used by instances of the `JTree` class for selection management unless the selection model is explicitly set to a different class. The class contains one bound property, the `SELECTION_MODE_PROPERTY`. (The `SELECTION_MODE_PROPERTY` constant is defined in the `DefaultTreeSelectionModel` class.) This property change event is fired when the selection mode changes in the model.

Rendering and Editing

You saw in Chapter 10, "JList, JComboBox, and Bound Controls," how the `JList` class delegates drawing of its elements to a rendering object. The `JTree` class employs the same strategy. The `TreeCellRenderer` interface defines the methods that must be implemented by a renderer that can be used with a `JTree` instance. This interface contains a single method, `getTreeCellRendererComponent`. When called, the implementing class must return a `Component` configured properly for rendering the value passed to the method. Listing 11.6 shows the `TreeCellRenderer` interface.

LISTING 11.6   THE `TreeCellRenderer` INTERFACE

```
public interface TreeCellRenderer {

    /**
     * Sets the value of the current tree cell to <code>value</code>.
     * If <code>selected</code> is true, the cell will be drawn as if
     * selected. If <code>expanded</code> is true the node is currently
     * expanded and if <code>leaf</code> is true the node represents a
     * leaf and if <code>hasFocus</code> is true the node currently has
     * focus. <code>tree</code> is the JTree the receiver is being
     * configured for.
     * Returns the Component that the renderer uses to draw the value.
     *
 * @return      Component that the renderer uses to draw the value.
     */
    Component getTreeCellRendererComponent(JTree tree, Object value,
                    boolean selected, boolean expanded,
                    boolean leaf, int row, boolean hasFocus);

}
```

The `JTree` instance also allows editing in place. The gesture that begins editing is look-and-feel specific, but a single click will start editing for the standard look-and-feel implementations contained in the JFC. The strategy for editing is analogous to that used for rendering. One cell editor is used for the entire tree. It is moved to the proper location and sized to the required size when editing begins. The editor manages the editing process. When the editing is complete, the data in the editor is copied to the data model.

The `TreeCellEditor` interface defines a single method: `getTreeCellEditorComponent`. However, the interface extends the `CellEditor` interface. This interface is contained in the `java.awt.swing` package. The `CellEditor` interface defines the methods used to mediate the editing and data transfer between the model and the editor. You will see this interface again in the next Chapter 12, "Table Component." The interface that defines the editor for the table component also extends the `CellEditor` interface. Listing 11.7 shows the `CellEditor` and `TreeCellEditor` interfaces.

LISTING 11.7   THE `CellEditor` AND `TreeCellEditor` INTERFACES

```
public interface CellEditor {

    /** Returns the value contained in the editor**/
    public Object getCellEditorValue();

    /**
     * Ask the editor if it can start editing using <I>anEvent</I>.
     * <I>anEvent</I> is in the invoking component coordinate system.
     * The editor cannot assume the Component returned by
     * getCellEditorComponent() is installed.  This method is intended
     * for the use of client to avoid the cost of setting up and
     * installing the editor component if editing is not possible.
     * If editing can be started this method returns true.
     *
 * @param anEvent      the event the editor should use to consider
     *                 whether to begin editing or not.
     * @return true if editing can be started.
     * @see #shouldSelectCell()
     */
    public boolean isCellEditable(EventObject anEvent);

    /**
     * Tell the editor to start editing using <I>anEvent</I>.  It is
     * up to the editor if it wants to start editing in different states
     * depending on the exact type of <I>anEvent</I>.  For example, with
     * a text field editor, if the event is a mouse event the editor
     * might start editing with the cursor at the clicked point.  If
     * the event is a keyboard event, it might want to replace the value
     * of the text field with that first key, etc.  <I>anEvent</I>
     * is in the invoking component's coordinate system.  A null value
     * is a valid parameter for <I>anEvent</I>, and it is up to the
     * editor to determine what is the default starting state.  For
     * example, a text field editor might want to select all the text and
     * start editing if <I>anEvent</I> is null.  The editor can assume
```

continues

LISTING 11.7   CONTINUED

```
 * the Component returned by getCellEditorComponent() is properly
 * installed in the client's Component hierarchy before this method is
 * called. <p>
 *
 * The return value of shouldSelectCell() is a boolean indicating
 * whether the editing cell should be selected or not.  Typically,
 * the return value is true, because is most cases the editing cell
 * should be selected.  However, it is useful to return false to keep
 * the selection from changing for some types of edits.  eg. A table
 * that contains a column of check boxes, the user might want
 * to change those check boxes without altering the selection.
 * (See Netscape Communicator for just such an example.)  Of course,
 * it is up to the client of the editor to use the return value, but
 * it doesn't need to if it doesn't want to.
 *
* @param anEvent the event the editor should use to start
 *                      editing.
 * @return true if the editor would like the editing cell to be
 *                  selected
 * @see #isCellEditable()
 */
    public boolean shouldSelectCell(EventObject anEvent);

    /**
     * Tell the editor to stop editing and accept any partially edited
     * value as the value of the editor.  The editor returns false if
     * editing was not stopped, useful for editors that validate and
     * cannot accept invalid entries.
     *
* @return      true if editing was stopped
     */
    public boolean stopCellEditing();

    /**
     * Tell the editor to cancel editing and not accept any partially
     * edited value.
     */
    public void cancelCellEditing();

    /**
     * Add a listener to the list that's notified when the editor starts,
     * stops, or cancels editing.
     *
* @param l the CellEditorListener
     */
    public void addCellEditorListener(CellEditorListener l);

    /**
     * Remove a listener from the list that's notified
```

```
     *
     * @param  l                 the CellEditorListener
     */
    public void removeCellEditorListener(CellEditorListener l);
}


public interface TreeCellEditor extends CellEditor
{
    /**
     * Sets an initial <I>value</I> for the editor.  This will cause
* the editor to stop editing and lose any partially edited value
     * if the editor is editing when this method is called. <p>
     *
     * Returns the component that should be added to the client's
     * Component hierarchy.  Once installed in the client's hierarchy
     * this component will then be able to draw and receive user input.
     *
* @param table the JTree that is asking the editor to edit
     *               This parameter can be null.
     * @param value the value of the cell to be edited.
     * @param isSelected true is the cell to be rendered with
     *                     selection highlighting
     * @param expanded true if the node is expanded
     * @param leaf true if the node is a leaf node
     * @param row the row index of the node being edited
     * @return the component for editing
     */
    Component getTreeCellEditorComponent(JTree tree, Object value,
                    boolean isSelected, booleanexpanded,
                    boolean leaf, int row);
}
```

Pulling It All Together: A Complete JTree Example

The previous sections have presented the interfaces and classes that are required to take full advantage of the JTree class. This section will present an example that uses these classes to create a complete tree example application.

The TreeTest application in Listing 11.8 creates a JTree instance and displays it in an ApplicationFrame. The resulting application is shown in Figure 11.5. The tree's data model is created in the createTreeModel method. An instance of the DefaultMutableTreeNode class is created for each node in the tree. The user object for the node is passed to the constructor. In this example, the user object is the String that represents the name of the node. However, any Object can be used as the user object. By default, the toString method on the user object is called to query the String that represents the node in the tree.

The structure of the tree is determined by calling the add method on the parent node and passing the child node as the parameter to this method. The child node must be an instance that implements the MutableTreeNode interface. The add method works similarly to the add methods you saw for menus in Chapter 9, "Menus and Toolbars." The new node is placed as the last child of the parent node. When the parent is expanded, the children are shown in the order they were added to the node. The add method it is not defined in the MutableTreeNode interface, but is part of the DefaultMutableTreeNode class's public API.

The placement of a node added to its parent can be specified if added by using the insert method. This method requires the index where the child is added into the parent node. The createTreeModel method finishes by creating an instance of the DefaultTreeModel class. The root node for the tree is passed to the constructor to bind the model to the tree nodes.

The visual components are instantiated and arranged in the createTreePanel method. A split pane is created for the center of the application. The JSplitPane class is presented in Chapter 16, "Split Pane." An instance of the JTree class is created by using the model returned from the createTreeModel method as its data model. This tree is added as the left component in the split pane. A JTextArea is created and added to the right region of the split pane. The selected nodes in the tree will be displayed in this area. A panel with a BorderLayout is created, and the split pane is added as the center region of this panel. A panel containing buttons is placed in the south region of this panel. One button expands the selected node in the tree and all its children. The other button clears the text in the JTextArea instance. Finally, a TreeSelectionListener is added to the tree. This will enable the valueChanged method to be called whenever the selection in the tree changes. The panel containing the split pane and button panel is returned from the createTreePanel method and set as the content pane of the ApplicationFrame instance.

LISTING 11.8   THE TreeTest APPLICATION

```
package com.foley.test;

import java.awt.*;
import java.awt.event.*;
import java.util.*;

import javax.swing.*;
import javax.swing.event.*;
import javax.swing.tree.*;
import javax.swing.border.*;
```

```java
import com.foley.utility.ApplicationFrame;


/**
 * An application that displays a JTree.
 *
 * @author Mike Foley
 **/
public class TreeTest
    implements ActionListener, TreeSelectionListener {

    /**
     * The tree used in the center of the display.
     **/
    JTree tree;

    /**
     * The component where the selected path is displayed.
     **/
    JTextArea textArea;

    /**
     * The text contained in the JTextArea initially and after a clear.
     **/
    private static final String INITIAL_TEXT = "Selected Path Events\n";

    /**
     * Create the tree test component.
     * The display is a tree in the center of a BorderLayout.
     * The EAST region contains a JTextArea where selected
     * paths are displayed.
     * The bottom region contains buttons.
     * <p>
     * @return The component containing the tree.
     **/
    public JComponent createTreePanel() {

        JSplitPane treePanel = new JSplitPane();

        tree = new JTree( createTreeModel() );
        tree.setEditable( true );
        tree.setCellEditor( new TreeLeafEditor( tree ) );
        tree.addTreeSelectionListener( this );
        tree.setBorder( BorderFactory.createLoweredBevelBorder() );

        treePanel.setLeftComponent( new JScrollPane( tree ) );

        JPanel buttonPanel = new JPanel();
        JButton expand = new JButton( "Expand Selected" );
```

continues

LISTING 11.8 CONTINUED

```java
        expand.addActionListener( this );
        JButton clear = new JButton( "Clear Path Display" );
        clear.addActionListener( new ActionListener() {
            public void actionPerformed( ActionEvent event ) {
                textArea.setText( INITIAL_TEXT );
            }
        } );
        buttonPanel.add( expand );
        buttonPanel.add( clear );

        textArea = new JTextArea( INITIAL_TEXT, 16, 50 );
        textArea.setBackground( expand.getBackground() );
        textArea.setBorder( null );
        textArea.setBorder( BorderFactory.createEmptyBorder(4,4,4,4) );
        treePanel.setRightComponent( new JScrollPane( textArea ) );

        JPanel totalPanel = new JPanel();
        totalPanel.setLayout( new BorderLayout() );
        totalPanel.add( treePanel, BorderLayout.CENTER );
        totalPanel.add( buttonPanel, BorderLayout.SOUTH );
        totalPanel.setBorder( BorderFactory.createLoweredBevelBorder() );

        return( totalPanel );

    }


    /**
     * Create the data model used in the tree contained
     * in the application.
     * <p>
     * @return The data model for the tree.
     **/
    protected TreeModel createTreeModel() {
        DefaultMutableTreeNode root =
                    new DefaultMutableTreeNode( "Music Collection" );

        DefaultMutableTreeNode albums =
                    new DefaultMutableTreeNode( "Albums" );
        DefaultMutableTreeNode cds = new DefaultMutableTreeNode( "CDs" );
        DefaultMutableTreeNode tapes =
                    new DefaultMutableTreeNode( "Tapes" );

        root.add( albums );
        root.add( cds );
        root.add( tapes );

        DefaultMutableTreeNode stonesAlbums =
                new DefaultMutableTreeNode( "Rolling Stones" );
        albums.add( stonesAlbums );
```

```
        stonesAlbums.add( new DefaultMutableTreeNode( "Hot Rocks" ) );
        stonesAlbums.add(
            new DefaultMutableTreeNode( "Black and Blue" ) );
        stonesAlbums.add(
            new DefaultMutableTreeNode( "Sticky Finger" ) );

        DefaultMutableTreeNode c1 =
            new DefaultMutableTreeNode( "Classical" );
        DefaultMutableTreeNode c2 =
            new DefaultMutableTreeNode( "Best Rock of the 60s" );
        DefaultMutableTreeNode c3 =
            new DefaultMutableTreeNode( "70s Disco Favorites" );
        DefaultMutableTreeNode c4 =
            new DefaultMutableTreeNode( "Broadway Hits" );
        DefaultMutableTreeNode c5 =
            new DefaultMutableTreeNode( "Country's Best?" );

    cds.add( c1 );
    cds.add( c2 );
    cds.add( c3 );
    cds.add( c4 );
    cds.add( c5 );

        DefaultMutableTreeNode s1 =
            new DefaultMutableTreeNode( "Rolling Stones" );
        DefaultMutableTreeNode s2 =
            new DefaultMutableTreeNode( "Beatles" );
        DefaultMutableTreeNode s3 =
            new DefaultMutableTreeNode( "The Who" );

    c1.add( new DefaultMutableTreeNode( "Beethoven's Fifth" ) );

    c2.add( s1 );
    c2.add( s2 );
    c2.add( s3 );

    s1.add( new DefaultMutableTreeNode( "Gimmie Shelter" ) );
    s1.add( new DefaultMutableTreeNode( "Some Girls" ) );
    s1.add( new DefaultMutableTreeNode( "Emotional Rescue" ) );
s2.add( new DefaultMutableTreeNode( "White Album" ) );
    s2.add( new DefaultMutableTreeNode( "Abby Road" ) );
    s2.add( new DefaultMutableTreeNode( "Let it be" ) );

    s3.add( new DefaultMutableTreeNode( "Tommy" ) );
    s3.add( new DefaultMutableTreeNode( "The Who" ) );

    c3.add( new DefaultMutableTreeNode( "Saturday Night Fever" ) );
    c3.add( new DefaultMutableTreeNode( "Earth Wind and Fire" ) );

    c4.add( new DefaultMutableTreeNode( "Cats Soundtrack" ) );
```

continues

LISTING 11.8   CONTINUED

```java
        c5.add( new DefaultMutableTreeNode( "Unknown" ) );

        return( new DefaultTreeModel( root ) );

    } // createTreeModel


    /**
     * actionEvent, from ActionListener.
     * <p>
     * The expand button was pressed. Expand the selected paths
     * in the tree.
     * <p>
     * @param event The actionEvent causing this method call.
     **/
    public void actionPerformed( ActionEvent event ) {
        TreePath[] paths = tree.getSelectionPaths();
        if( paths != null ) {
            for( int i = 0; i < paths.length; i++ ) {
                expandPath( paths[i] );
            }
        }
    }


    /**
     * valueChanged, from TreeSelectionListener.
     * <p>
     * The selected state in the tree changed. Show the
     * selected path in the text area.
     * <p>
     * @param event The event causing this method to be called.
     **/
    public void valueChanged( TreeSelectionEvent event ) {

        TreePath[] paths = event.getPaths();

        for( int i = 0; i < paths.length; i++ ) {
            //
            // Display the path and state.
            //
            Object[] path = paths[i].getPath();
            textArea.append( event.isAddedPath( paths[i] ) ?
                            "ADDED: " : "REMOVED: " );
            textArea.append( paths[i] + "\n" );
            for( int j = 0; j < path.length; j++ ) {
                textArea.append( "\t" + path[j] + "\n" );
            }
            if( event.isAddedPath( paths[i] ) ) {
```

```
                Object pathObject = paths[i].getLastPathComponent();

                //
                // This test is unfortunate. The MutableTreeNode
                // interface does not have a getUserObject method, so
                // we must test for a specific implementation.
                //
                if( pathObject instanceof DefaultMutableTreeNode ) {
                    Object userObject =
                ( ( DefaultMutableTreeNode )pathObject ).getUserObject();
                        textArea.append("User Object: " + userObject + "\n");
                }
            }
        }
        textArea.append( "------------------------------------\n" );

    }


    /**
     * Expand the node at the end of the given path.
     * This requires expanding all children nodes of the
     * path recursively until the entire subtree has been
     * expanded.
     **/
    private void expandPath( TreePath path ) {
        Object o = path.getLastPathComponent();
        if( o instanceof TreeNode ) {
            for( Enumeration e = ( ( TreeNode )o ).children();
            e.hasMoreElements(); ) {
                TreeNode node = ( TreeNode )e.nextElement();
                expandChildren( node );
            }
        }
    }


    /**
     * Expand all the children of the given node.
     * <p>
     * @param expandNode The root of the subtree to expand.
     **/
    private void expandChildren( TreeNode expandNode ) {

        if( expandNode.isLeaf() ) {

            Stack nodes = new Stack();

            //
            // Push the parents of the current node
```

continues

LISTING 11.8 CONTINUED

```
                    // until the root of the tree is reached.
                    //
                    TreeNode node = expandNode;
                    nodes.push( node );
                    while( ( node = node.getParent() ) != null )
                        nodes.push( node );

                    //
                    // Create a path to the node passed into this
                    // method by popping each element from the stack.
                    //
                    TreeNode[] path = new TreeNode[ nodes.size() ];
                    for( int i = 0; i < path.length; i++ )
                        path[i] = ( TreeNode )nodes.pop();
                    TreePath treePath = new TreePath( path );

                    //
                    // Expand the path.
                    //
                    tree.makeVisible( treePath );

                } else {

                    //
                    // Expand the children of the
                    // node passed to the method.
                    //
                    for( Enumeration e = expandNode.children();
                        e.hasMoreElements(); ) {
                            expandChildren(
                    ( DefaultMutableTreeNode )e.nextElement() );
                    }

                } // else

            } // expandChildren


    /**
     * Application entry point.
     * Create the frame, and place a tree into it.
     *
     * @param args Command line parameter. Not used.
     **/
    public static void main( String args[] ) {

        TreeTest treeTest = new TreeTest();
        JFrame frame = new ApplicationFrame( "Tree Test" );
        frame.getContentPane().add( treeTest.createTreePanel(),
                            BorderLayout.CENTER );
```

```
        frame.pack();
        frame.setVisible( true );

    } // main

} // TreeTest
```

FIGURE **11.5**

The TreeTest
application.

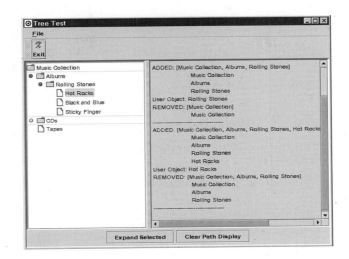

The TreeTest class implements the TreeSelectionListener interface and is added as a listener to the tree contained in the center of the application. This enables the valueChanged method to be called whenever the selection in the tree changes. Unlike some of the other events in the JFC, the TreeSelectionEvent instance delivered to this method contains the information about the change in the selected path set for the tree. In this application, the paths contained in the event are written to the JTextArea instance in the right region of the display. The array of changed TreePaths is queried from the event with the getPaths method. For each path, the isAddedPath method can be called to determine if the path was added or removed from the tree's selection set. The method returns true for new paths and false for paths that were selected but are no longer selected. Each path is written to the text area. The final piece of information obtained in the valueChanged method is the user object for the node. This points to an unfortunate flaw in the MutableTreeNode interface. It does not contain a getUserObject method. This forces the valueChanged method to test for the DefaultMutableTreeNode class, making this code unusable for other classes that implement the MutableTreeNode interface. This is a serious flaw in the JFC tree and greatly reduces the ability to write reusable code.

A setEditable method is passed a parameter of true to allow the tree to be edited in place. When a tree is made editable, any node in the tree can be edited. The gesture that starts the edit is look-and-feel specific. However, the single-click gesture is used in the current JFC look-and-feel implementations. For the TestTree, it is desirable to allow only leaf nodes to be editable. A custom cell editor provides this functionality for the tree. The setCellEditor method specifies an instance of the TreeLeafEditor class shown in Listing 11.9. This will be used as the editor for the tree. This class is an extension of the DefaultCellEditor class. It overrides the isCellEditable method. This method demonstrates how a TreePath to a node can be queried from a tree for given x and y coordinates. By using the isLeaf method, the cell editor then checks if the hit node is a leaf node and only returns true if it is. The tree with the TreeLeafEditor activated is shown in Figure 11.6.

LISTING 11.9 THE TreeLeafEditor CLASS

```
package com.foley.utility;

import java.awt.event.*;
import java.util.*;

import javax.swing.*;
import javax.swing.tree.*;


/**
 * A tree editor that only allows editing of leaf nodes.
 * <p>
 * @author Mike Foley
 **/
public class TreeLeafEditor extends DefaultCellEditor {

    /**
     * The tree we are editing.
     **/
    JTree tree;

    public TreeLeafEditor( JTree tree ) {
        super( new JTextField() );
        this.tree = tree;
    }


    /**
     * The cell is only editable if it is a leaf node and
     * the number of mouse clicks is equal to the value
     * returned from the getClickCountToStart method.
     * <p>
```

```
   * @param event The event to test for cell editablity.
   * @return True if the cell is editable given the current event.
   * @see getClickCountToStart
   **/
  public boolean isCellEditable( EventObject event ) {

      if( event instanceof MouseEvent ) {
          MouseEvent mouseEvent = ( MouseEvent )event;
          if( mouseEvent.getClickCount() == getClickCountToStart() ) {
TreePath hitPath = tree.getPathForLocation(
                                           mouseEvent.getX(),
                                           mouseEvent.getY() );
              Object hitObject = hitPath.getLastPathComponent();
              if( hitObject instanceof TreeNode )
                  return( ( ( TreeNode )hitObject ).isLeaf() );
          }
      }
      return( false );
  }

} // TreeLeafEditor
```

FIGURE 11.6

*Node being edited
in the* TreeTest
application.

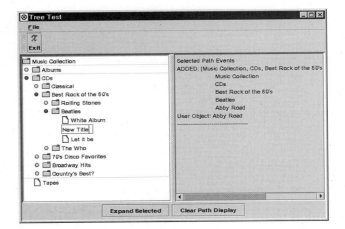

The application creates a button that causes a selected node in the tree to totally expand the sub-tree for which it serves as the root. Thus, if this button is hit when the root of the tree is selected, the entire tree is expanded displaying all the leaf nodes contained in the tree. The expansion is performed in the expandChildren method that requires a TreeNode parameter. The TreeNode passed to the method serves as the root node of the sub-tree that is expanded. The method works by checking to see if the node passed to it is a leaf. If so, a path to the node is created and expanded in the tree. If the node is not a leaf, the makeVisible method found in the JTree class is called for each child of the node. This logic is repeated for each child of the original node, and its children, and so on, until the entire sub-tree data structure has been traversed. It is important to understand that only the leaf nodes need to be expanded. This is because the path to the leaf contains its parent. Thus, if all leaves are expanded, the entire sub-tree has been expanded. You will find yourself writing many recursive methods, such as the expandChild method, when traversing the nodes in a tree.

Setting Global Icons

The TreeTest application presented in the previous section displayed a tree containing information about a music library. The tree structure presented the data in a nicely structured visual. However, the file system icons used in the tree make the component somewhat less than ideal. Fortunately, the JFC provides a couple of techniques that can be used to specify the icons that are used in the tree. If the icons are to be changed for each tree that is going to be used in the application, changing the user interface properties for the tree icons is most appropriate. If you need each tree in your application to have custom icons, or the icon is based on the node's contents rather than its position in the tree, a custom TreeCellRenderer is appropriate. This section demonstrates the former technique. A custom cell renderer will be shown in the next section.

The current look-and-feel determines the default icons used in the tree. However, the application can override the default values by changing properties in the UIManager. A complete description of the UIManager is presented in Chapter 30, "Pluggable Look-and-Feel." For this discussion, it is sufficient to understand that the UIManager contains a Dictionary that maps user interface properties to their value. These values are queried by the component and used in its display. For the JTree component, there are properties for the various icons displayed in the tree. The list of properties is presented in Table 11.2.

TABLE 11.2   ICON PROPERTIES FOR THE JTree CLASS

Property Name	Usage
Tree.openIcon	When a non-leaf node is expanded
Tree.closedIcon	When a non-leaf node is collapsed
Tree.leafIcon	For a leaf node
Tree.expandedIcon	Icon for the expanded control
Tree.collapsedIcon	Icon for the collapsed control

The main method for the TreeTest application can be modified, as shown in Listing 11.10, to register the icons desired for your application with the UIManager. Then any

`JTree` instance created in the application will use the new icons. The modified tree containing the custom images is shown in Figure 11.7.

LISTING 11.10   REGISTERING CUSTOM IMAGES IN THE `TreeTest` APPLICATION

```
public static void main( String args[] ) {

        Icon albumIcon = new ImageIcon( "album.gif" );
        Icon albumsIcon = new ImageIcon( "albums.gif" );
        Icon expandedIcon = new ImageIcon( "TreeExpanded.gif" );
        Icon collapsedIcon = new ImageIcon( "TreeCollapsed.gif" );
        UIDefaults defaults = UIManager.getDefaults();
        defaults.put( "Tree.openIcon", openIcon );
        defaults.put( "Tree.closedIcon", closedIcon );
        defaults.put( "Tree.leafIcon", leafIcon );
        defaults.put( "Tree.expandedIcon", expandedIcon );
        defaults.put( "Tree.collapsedIcon", collapsedIcon );

        TreeTest treeTest = new TreeTest();
        JFrame frame = new ApplicationFrame( "Tree Test" );
        frame.getContentPane().add( treeTest.createTreePanel(),
                                    BorderLayout.CENTER );
        frame.pack();
        frame.setVisible( true );

    } // main
```

FIGURE 11.7
*Custom icons in
the* `TreeTest`
application.

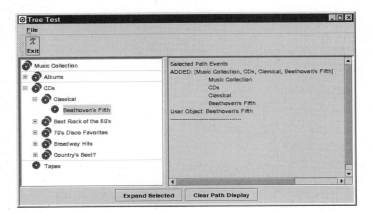

Using a Custom Tree Renderer

The example in the previous section showed how to globally replace a tree's icon in an application. This technique will suffice for many applications; but when complete control over a tree's icons is required, a custom renderer for the tree must be provided. If the

granularity for specifying icons in a tree described in the previous section suffices, a
DefaultTreeCellRenderer instance can be customized and set for the tree. The
DefaultTreeCellRenderer class contains methods for setting the opened, closed, and
leaf icons, as well as methods for setting the text color and font. If this level of customization meets your requirements, there is no need to create your own renderer class.

When you need different icons for nodes that are at the same level in the hierarchy, a
custom renderer class will have to be written. You saw earlier in this chapter that a renderer for a JTree instance must implement the TreeCellRenderer interface. The
AlbumTreeRenderer class, shown in Listing 11.11, extends the JLabel class and implements the TreeCellRenderer interface. In the class's constructor, it sets its opaque property to true. This is required in renderers that paint the background color of the cell. The
AlbumTreeRenderer needs to paint the background color to show selected items in the
tree. The renderer is bound to the tree by adding the following line of code in the
createTreePanel method of the TreeTest application after the tree has been created:

```
tree.setCellRenderer( new AlbumTreeRenderer() );
```

For a renderer to display different icons for different nodes, it requires information about
the nodes. This can be achieved by using many techniques. The method presented here is
if the user object in a node is an instance of the AlbumCollectionItem class, its getIcon
method is called to obtain the icon for the node. To make the renderer a bit more generic,
an interface can define the getIcon method, and this would be checked for instead of the
AlbumCollectionItem class in the renderer.

LISTING 11.11   THE AlbumTreeRenderer CLASS

```
package com.foley.utility;

import java.awt.Component;

import javax.swing.*;
import javax.swing.tree.*;


/**
 * A tree renderer that knows about the record
 * collection tree.
 * <p>
 * @author Mike Foley
 **/
public class AlbumTreeRenderer extends JLabel
    implements TreeCellRenderer, AlbumTypes {

    /**
     * AlbumTreeRenderer, Constructor.
```

```
 * <p>
 * The renderer must be opaque so the background
 * color is painted.
 **/
public AlbumTreeRenderer() {
    setFont( UIManager.getFont( "Tree.font" ) ) ;
    setOpaque( true );
}


/**
 * Configures the renderer based on the passed in components.
 * Text for the cell is obtained from the toString() method of
 * the value parameter.
 * <p>
 * Foreground and background colors are obtained from the
 * UIManager.
 * <p>
 * If the value is a DefaultMutableTreeNode, and its user object
 * is an AlbumCollectionItem, the icon is obtained from the item
 * and set for the cell.
 **/
public Component getTreeCellRendererComponent( JTree tree,
                           Object value,
                           boolean selected,
                           boolean expanded,
                           boolean leaf,
                           int row,
                           boolean hasFocus ) {

        //
        // Set the text for the cell.
        //
    if( value != null )
        setText( value.toString() );
    else
        setText( "" );

        //
        // Set the colors for the cell.
        //
    if( selected ) {
setBackground( UIManager.getColor(
                "Tree.selectionBackground" ) );
        setForeground( UIManager.getColor(
                "Tree.selectionForeground" ) );
    } else {
        setBackground( UIManager.getColor( "Tree.textBackground" ) );
        setForeground( UIManager.getColor( "Tree.textForeground" ) );
```

continues

Listing **11.11**   CONTINUED

```
        } // else

        //
        // The type of the node is stored in the user object
        // in the mutable tree node.
        //
        setIcon( null );
        if( value instanceof DefaultMutableTreeNode ) {
DefaultMutableTreeNode node = ( DefaultMutableTreeNode )value;
            Object o = node.getUserObject();
            if( o instanceof AlbumCollectionItem ) {
                AlbumCollectionItem albumItem = ( AlbumCollectionItem )o;
                setIcon( albumItem.getIcon() );
            }
        }

        return( this );
    }

} // AlbumTreeRenderer
```

The createTreeModel method in the TreeTest application must be updated to specify
AlbumCollectionItem instances as the user object for each node in the tree where an
icon is desired. In the original tree model, the user object for each node was a String
containing the name of the node. This is changed to an AlbumCollectionItem instance
with the same name and an appropriate icon. Examples of this change for the top of the
tree are shown in the following code fragment:

```
DefaultMutableTreeNode albums = new DefaultMutableTreeNode(
                    new AlbumCollectionItem( "Albums", albumsIcon ) );
DefaultMutableTreeNode cds = new DefaultMutableTreeNode(
                    new AlbumCollectionItem( "CDs", cdsIcon ) );
DefaultMutableTreeNode tapes = new DefaultMutableTreeNode(
                    new AlbumCollectionItem( "Tapes", tapesIcon ) );
```

The AlbumCollectionItem class is very simple. It binds the String name and icon
together. Since the DefaultMutableTreeNode class calls the toString method of its user
object when its toString method is called, the AlbumCollectionItem class returns its
name in its toString method. This will ensure that the name is displayed properly in the
tree. The icon specified in the constructor is returned from the getIcon method. The
complete class is shown in Listing 11.12.

LISTING 11.12 THE `AlbumCollectionItem` CLASS

```java
package com.foley.utility;

import javax.swing.*;


/**
 * The AlbumCollectionItem class binds a name
 * and icon together.
 * <p>
 * @author Mike Foley
 **/
public class AlbumCollectionItem {
    String name;
    Icon icon;

    /**
     * AlbumCollectionItem, Constructor
     * <p>
     * @param name The name of this item.
     * @param icon The icon for this item.
     **/
    public AlbumCollectionItem( String name, Icon icon ) {
        this.name = name;
        this.icon = icon;
    }

    /**
     * @return The name of this item.
     **/
    public String getName() {
        return( name );
    }

    /**
     * @return The icon associated with this item.
     **/
    public Icon getIcon() {
        return( icon );
    }

    /**
     * @return The String representation of this item.
     **/
    public String toString() {
        return( name );
    }

} // AlbumCollectionItem
```

The new tree created with the custom renderer is shown in Figure 11.8. Notice how different icons are used for siblings in the tree. To achieve this effect, a custom renderer is required. The renderer could further customize the tree by changing fonts and colors for each node.

FIGURE 11.8

A custom cell renderer in the TreeTest *application.*

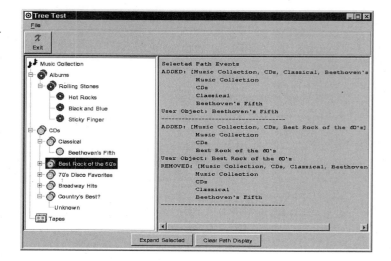

Summary

The JTree component is a complex control that provides tremendous capabilities. To take full advantage of these capabilities, a substantial number of classes and interfaces must be understood. This chapter presented the convenience methods in the JTree class that allow a tree to be constructed by using standard JDK collection classes such as Vectors and Hashtables. You saw that using these data structures does not take full advantage of the JTree class. To fully utilize the power of the JTree class, the TreeModel and TreeNode interfaces must be understood and incorporated into the tree's design. The JFC contains implementations of these interfaces, as well as the MutableTreeNode interface, that allow building of a complex tree data structure and displaying it with relative ease.

An example application containing a tree component was presented. The icons used in the tree were customized to icons supplied by the application. You also saw how the JTree class allows for customization of renderers and editors. The renderer can be used to customize the display of a node for the tree.

Table Component

CHAPTER 12

IN THIS CHAPTER

The `JTable` component is the most complex visual component in the JFC toolkit. During the review phases of the toolkit, the `JTable` class underwent the most API changes before they were stabilized to those contained in the current `JTable` class. To effectively use the `JTable` class in your applications, you must understand what the component is and is not designed to do. First, it is not a spreadsheet. However, you could have it view a spreadsheet data model. The `JTable` class is designed to be a high performance view of tabular data. The data is contained in a data model separate from the view. The columns in the table can be in a different order than they are in the data model. Not all columns in the data model need be displayed in the table. The table can be configured to allow selection of rows, columns, both rows and columns, or single cells.

This chapter will lead you through the complexities of using the `JTable` class. You will start with simply displaying tabular data in a table and continue to highly customize the table's appearance.

You will learn how to

- Display tabular data in a table
- Use the `TableModel` interface and other support classes and interfaces in the Table package
- Control selection in a table
- Add renderers and editors to a table
- Customize the table's headers

Table Elements

The `JTable` class delegates a great deal of functionality to support classes located in the `swing.table` package. A typical table is shown in Figure 12.1. In this figure, the various delegates are shown. The headers are displayed in an instance of the `JTableHeader` class. Each column is an instance of the `TableColumn` class that is managed by an instance of the `TableColumnModel` class. Selection is delegated to one or more `ListSelectionModel` instances. Finally, the data displayed in the table is encapsulated in a `TableModel`. A `TableCellEditor` is shown editing color values in the figure. A `TableCellRenderer` is used to paint the cells that are not being edited. Using and customizing these classes are the subjects of the remainder of this chapter.

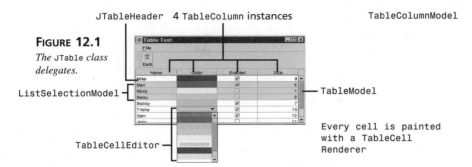

JTableHeader 4 TableColumn instances   TableColumnModel

FIGURE 12.1
The JTable class delegates.

ListSelectionModel

TableCellEditor

TableModel

Every cell is painted with a TableCell Renderer

A Simple Table

The JTable and its associated classes and interfaces provide a wealth of features and customization possibilities. However, sometimes you just want to present tabular data in a table. The JTable class contains methods for easily performing simple tasks as well as the complex issues covered later in this chapter.

The JTable class contains a pair of constructors for creating a table from simple Java collections. The first takes a two-dimensional array as its first parameter, the second takes a Vector of Vectors. As its second parameter, each method requires that the column names for the table be stored in the same class of collection as the data. The SimpleTableTest application shown in Listing 12.1 creates a table by passing a Vector containing the data for the table and another Vector containing the column names to the JTable constructor. The table created by the application is shown in Figure 12.2.

The Vector containing the data is a Vector of Vectors. Each Vector contained by the wrapping vector represents one row in the table. The default technique to view each object in the table is to call its toString method. This is appropriate for many types of objects, but not all. For example, columns two and three in this table could be better represented by using the actual color for column two and a check box for column three. Later in this chapter you will see how this can be accomplished by setting renderers for the table.

FIGURE 12.2
The SimpleTableTest application.

LISTING 12.1 THE SimpleTableTest APPLICATION

```
package com.foley.test;

import java.awt.*;

import java.util.Vector;

import javax.swing.*;
import javax.swing.border.*;

import com.foley.utility.ApplicationFrame;


/**
 * An application that displays a JTable instance
 * in its frame.
 *
 * @author Mike Foley
 **/
public class SimpleTableTest extends Object {

    /**
     * Application entry point.
     * Create a frame, the table and display it.
     *
     * @param args Command line parameter. Not used.
     **/
    public static void main( String args[] ) {

        JFrame frame = new ApplicationFrame( "SimpleTableTest Vector" );
        Vector data = new Vector();
        Vector row = new Vector();
        row.addElement( "Mike" );
        row.addElement( Color.blue );
        row.addElement( new Boolean( true ) );
        data.addElement( row );

        row = new Vector();
        row.addElement( "Mari" );
        row.addElement( Color.red );
        row.addElement( new Boolean( true ) );
        data.addElement( row );

        row = new Vector();
        row.addElement( "Molly" );
        row.addElement( Color.yellow );
        row.addElement( new Boolean( false ) );
        data.addElement( row );

        Vector columnNames = new Vector();
```

```
        columnNames.addElement( "Name" );
        columnNames.addElement( "Color" );
        columnNames.addElement( "Boolean" );
        JTable table = new JTable( data, columnNames );

        table.setBorder( BorderFactory.createLoweredBevelBorder() );

        frame.getContentPane().add( table, BorderLayout.CENTER );

        frame.pack();
        frame.setVisible( true );

    } // main

} // SimpleTableTest
```

The `SimpleTableTest` application creates a bare-bones table. It doesn't display the column names, and the column width is too small for the second column. To create a more pleasing table, more than just the constructor needs to be called.

The table header can be queried from the table by calling the `getTableHeader` method and arranged anywhere you want. Typically, the header is shown above the data. The following code creates the table and displays its header above the table. The resulting table is shown in Figure 12.3.

```
JTable table = new JTable( data, columnNames );
JTableHeader tableHeader = table.getTableHeader();

JPanel tablePanel = new JPanel();
tablePanel.setBorder( BorderFactory.createLoweredBevelBorder() );
tablePanel.setLayout( new BorderLayout() );
tablePanel.add( tableHeader, BorderLayout.NORTH );
tablePanel.add( table, BorderLayout.CENTER );

frame.getContentPane().add( tablePanel, BorderLayout.CENTER );
```

FIGURE 12.3

A table with the header displayed.

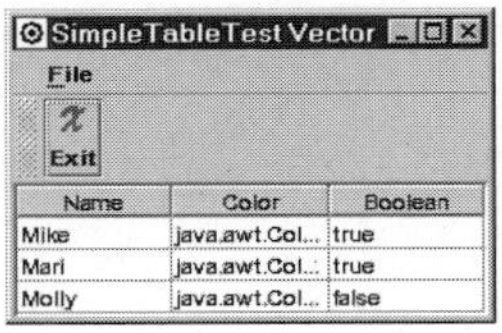

The header is an instance of the `JTableHeader` class contained in the `java.awt.swing.table` package. It allows the area between two columns to be dragged to resize the columns. The column name itself can be dragged to change the order of the columns in the table. (This is the default behavior of the `JTableHeader` class; later you will see how to change this.)

If this code seems like a lot of work to display the columns for a table, you are correct; it is. The JTable class contains specialized code for handling the typical configuration of a table, that being the table placed in a scroll pane. (The JScrollPane class is discussed in Chapter 15, "Scrolling Components.") The JTable class detects when it is added to a JScrollPane and configures itself appropriately. The configuration is performed in the protected configureEnclosingScrollPane method. This protected method allows extensions to the JTable class to alter a table's configuration when it is added to a JScrollPane instance. The earlier example can be simplified to the following code that creates the table shown in Figure 12.4.

```
JTable table = new JTable( data, columnNames );
frame.getContentPane().add( new JScrollPane( table ),
                              BorderLayout.CENTER );
```

FIGURE 12.4

Simplified JTable *construction.*

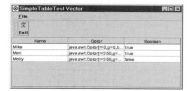

After the table has been placed in a JScrollPane, its scrolling behavior is specified in the JTable class. The JTable class implements the Scrollable interface. This interface is discussed in Chapter 15. The JTable class returns false from the getScrollableTracksViewportWidth and getScrollableTracksViewportHeight methods to signify that the table width and height are not determined by the scroll pane's viewport size. The JTable class returns the height of a row for the vertical unit scrolling increment and one pixel for the horizontal unit scroll increment. It would be an improvement if the horizontal scrolling increment could be set to the width of the column being scrolled out of view. The block scrolling size is set to both the horizontal and vertical viewport size. This enables one "page" of the table to be scrolled in block mode. The preferred size for the viewport can be set by using the setPreferredScrollableViewportSize method. This value is used by the viewport to set its size.

Passing false to the setShowGrid method will hide the grid displayed in the table. Also, you can show only the vertical or horizontal portion of the grid with the setShow-HorizontalLines and setShowVerticalLines methods. Passing true or false to these methods will show or hide the lines in the table. If the table in the SimpleTableTest application is created as follows, only the horizontal lines in the table will be displayed. This is seen in Figure 12.5. The color of the grid can be set with the setGridColor method. The `getGridColor` method returns the current value of the grid. Neither the display state or color of the grid are bound properties in the `JTable` class.

```
JTable table = new JTable( data, columnNames );
table.setShowGrid( false );
table.setShowHorizontalLines( true );
table.setGridColor( Color.blue );
frame.getContentPane().add( new JScrollPane( table ),
                              BorderLayout.CENTER );
```

FIGURE 12.5

A table with blue horizontal grid-lines.

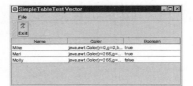

Table Selection Models

The `SimpleTableTest` application was presented in the previous section. This application created a `JTable` instance that used the default table selection model row selection. However, the `JTable` class supports many selection modes. The table delegates both column and row selection to a class that implements the `ListSelectionModel` interface. Internally, this class is the `DefaultListSelectionModel` class that was presented in Chapter 10, "JList, JComboBox, and Bound Controls." Thus, the selection modes for rows and columns in a table are the same as rows in a list. These are single selection mode, contiguous selection mode, and non-contiguous selection mode. The table can also be configured to allow only cells to be selected instead of entire rows or columns.

The selection mode can be set by querying the selection model from the table and setting the desired mode directly, or by calling convenience methods provided by the `JTable` class that update the selection models themselves.

You'll start by looking at the convenience functions provided by the `JTable` class. The easiest methods to use for configuring selection are `setRowSelectionAllowed` and `setColumnSelectionAllowed`. Passing `true` to either of these methods enables the selection, and `false` disables it. Passing `false` to both these methods will enable cell selection. The `setSelectionMode` method is used to set the type of selection allowed. The selection mode is defined in the `ListSelectionModel` interface described in Chapter 10. Possible modes that can be passed to this method are
`ListSelectionModel.SINGLE_SELECTION`, `ListSelectionModel.SINGLE_INTERVAL_ SELECTION`, and `ListSelectionModel.MULTIPLE_INTERVAL_SELECTION`. For a complete description of these modes, see Chapter 10.

Calling the setSelectionMode method contained in the JTable class sets the new mode for both the row and column selection model. If you require a different selection mode for rows and columns, the mode must be set on the selection model itself. The row selection model can be obtained by calling the getSelectionModel method contained in the JTable class. To obtain a handle to the column selection model, you must go through the column model. The column model is obtained via the getColumnModel method. With the column model in hand, its getSelectionModel method can be called to obtain the column selection model. Then the setSelectionMode method of the model can be called.

The foreground and background colors of selected cells can be specified by using the setSelectionForeground and setSelectionBackground methods, respectfully. There are corresponding "get" versions of these methods to obtain the current value of the property. The selectionForeground and selectionBackground properties are the only bound properties contained in the JTable class. At first glance this may seem odd for such a large class. However, as you will see later in this chapter, the JTable class delegates much of its functionality to support classes that contain bound properties or defines dedicated listener interfaces and events to notify observers of changes.

With that said, there are properties in the JTable class that should be bound but are not. The gridColor property immediately comes to mind. The bound properties for the JTable class are shown in Table 12.1. Notice that the property names are hard-coded strings in the JTable class. Use caution when testing for these property names in your source code.

TABLE 12.1 BOUND PROPERTIES OF THE JTable CLASS

Property Name	*Setter Method*	*Getter Method*
selectionBackground	setSelection Background	getselection Background
selectionForeground	setSelection Foreground	getselection Foreground

The previous paragraph explained how to set the selection mode for a JTable instance. After the mode is set, it may be necessary to set or query the selection set in the table. The methods presented in Chapter 10 for the ListSelectionModel can be used for setting and getting the set of selected rows or columns from the row or column list selection model. The JTable class also provides convenience functions for many of these methods. This allows the selected rows and columns to be queried directly from the table.

The setRowSelectionInterval can be used to select rows in an inclusive range defined by the two integer parameters passed to the method. Rows can be inserted into the selection set by using addRowSelectionInterval. This method also takes two parameters to define the inclusive range of rows to add to the selected row set. The selection mode must support the rows added to the set or all rows cannot be selected.

The setColumnSelectionInterval and addColumnSelectionInterval methods provide analogous functionality for columns. Rows or columns can be removed from the selection set with the removeRowSelectionInterval and the removeColumnSelectionInterval methods. Both these methods also take two integer parameters that define the inclusive range of rows or columns to be removed from the selection set. To remove a single row from the selected set, both parameters would be the same: the row to be deselected.

The clearSelection method clears both the row and column selection set. The selectAll method checks the current selection, and, if a row is selected, all rows are selected. Also, if a column is selected, all columns are selected. If both are selected when this method is called, all rows and columns are selected.

The number of selected rows can be determined with the getSelectedRowCount method. The getSelectedRows method returns an array of the indices of all selected rows or an empty array if there are not any selected rows. The getSelectedRow method returns the index of the last selected row, or -1 if no rows are selected. The equivalent methods for querying column selection status are getSelectedColumnCount, getSelectedColumns, and getSelectedColumn. The table provides the isRowSelected, isColumnSelected, and isCellSelected method to easily test if a row, column, or cell is selected.

The ListSelectionModel for rows or columns can be set directly. This allows for custom selection models, or, as was shown in Chapter 10 for the JList class, for sharing selection models. A ListSelectionModel can be shared between lists and tables. For rows, the ListSelectionModel is set by using the setSelectionModel method. To set the selection model for columns, the column model must first be obtained from the table, and then the selection model set on the column model. This can be done with the following code fragment:

```
ListSelectionModel mySelectionModel;
// mySelectionModel created and initialized.
table.getColumnModel().setSelectionModel( mySelectionModel );
```

Column Creation and Resizing Modes

You can configure JTable instances to automatically create columns whenever its data model is set or changes structure. Passing true to the setAutoCreateColumnsFromModel method enables this capability. The columns are created in the `createDefault ColumnsFromModel` method. This method creates an instance of the `TableColumn` class for each column in the model and adds it to the table. The `TableColumn` class is discussed further in the next section. The current value of this property can be queried by using the `getAutoCreateColumnsFromModel` method. If this property is `false`, it is the table's client's responsibility to create and add columns to the table. `createDefaultColumnsFromModel` is a public method that can be called by clients.

Column headers allow columns to be resized by dragging on the border between two columns. (Columns can be configured to not be resizable, or have minimum and maximum sizes. This will be shown in the next section.) As the user drags to set a column's width, the behavior of other columns is defined by the `autoResizeMode` property. The `setAutoResizeMode` sets the property to one of the three legal values shown in Table 12.2. These values are integer constants defined in the `JTable` class.

TABLE 12.2   COLUMN RESIZE MODES

Mode Constant	*Behavior*
`AUTO_RESIZE_OFF`	Do nothing
`AUTO_RESIZE_LAST_COLUMN`	Space goes to last column
`AUTO_RESIZE_ALL_COLUMNS`	Space distributed between all columns

When the `autoResizeMode` property is set to `AUTO_RESIZE_OFF` when a column is resized, the other columns move to allow the column to expand or contract, but do not change size. In this mode, the width of the table changes as the column size changes. When the mode is `AUTO_RESIZE_LAST_COLUMN`, the last column expands or contracts an amount equal to the space removed or added to the column being resized. When the mode is `AUTO_RESIZE_ALL_COLUMNS`, space given or taken from the column being resized is evenly distributed to all other columns in the table. The last two modes do not change the width of the table as a column is resized. The default mode for this property is `AUTO_RESIZE_ALL_COLUMNS`.

You can specify the space between rows and columns with the `setIntercellSpacing` method. This method takes a `Dimension` as its single parameter. As such, the row spacing can be specified using the `Dimension`'s `width` property and the column spacing with its `height` property. The current spacing can be queried by using the `getInterCellSpacing`. The width and height of the returned dimension are set to the row and column spacing, respectively.

12

Models and Support Classes Used by the `JTable` Class

The previous section described how to create tables from Java data types. These data types may not be the best representation for the data contained in your application. To allow data stored in any representation, the `TableModel` interface is defined. Classes containing data that you want to display in a table can implement this interface and then be used as the data model for one or more tables. The order of the columns in the table need not match the order of the columns in the data model. Moreover, the table need not display all the columns in the data model. To enable this type of functionality, the table model interface and table support classes must be understood. These are contained in the `javax.swing.table` package.

The `TableModel` Interface and Support Classes

The `TableModel` interface, shown in Listing 12.2, defines the methods that a class must implement to be used as the data source for a table. The methods `getRowCount` and `getColumnCount` define the size of the data structure. The data querying and setting methods, `getValueAt` and `setValueAt`, take integer parameters for the row and column of the data. These methods return and take an `Object` parameter, allowing any class of data to be stored in the data model. Moreover, each column in the model can contain a different class of `Object`. The `getColumnName` method returns the `String` name for the column. This is used in the table header, if displayed.

The `getColumnClass` method returns the class of object stored in that column of data. The `JTable` class uses this information to select appropriate editors and renderers for the table. The model must return `true` from the `isCellEditable` method for editing to be allowed. Finally, the class that implements the `TableModel` interface must manage `TableModelListeners`. As with all JFC models, it is the model's responsibility to fire the appropriate event if the data in the model changes. For the `TableModel`, this is a `TableModelEvent`.

LISTING 12.2   THE TableModel INTERFACE

```
public interface TableModel
{
    /**
     * Returns the number of records managed by the data source object. A
     * <B>JTable</B> uses this method to determine how many rows it
     * should create and display.  This method should be quick, as it
```

continues

LISTING 12.2 CONTINUED

```
 * is called by <B>JTable</B> quite frequently.
 *
 * @return the number or rows in the model
 * @see #getColumnCount()
 */
public int getRowCount();

/**
 * Returns the number of columns managed by the data source object. A
 * <B>JTable</B> uses this method to determine how many columns it
 * should create and display on initialization.
 *
 * @return the number or columns in the model
 * @see #getRowCount()
 */
public int getColumnCount();

/**
 * Returns the name of the column at <i>columnIndex</i>.  This is
 * used to initialize the table's column header name.  Note, this
 * name does not need to be unique.  Two columns on a table can have
 * the same name.
 *
 * @param   columnIndex    the index of column
 * @return   the name of the column
 */
public String getColumnName(int columnIndex);

/**
 * Returns the lowest common denominator Class in the column.  This
 * is used by the table to set up a default renderer and editor for
 * the column.
 *
 * @return the common ancestor class of the object values in
 *          the model.
 */
public Class getColumnClass(int columnIndex);

/**
 * Returns true if the cell at <I>rowIndex</I> and <I>columnIndex</I>
 * is editable.  Otherwise, setValueAt() on the cell will not change
 * the value of that cell.
 *
 * @param rowIndex the row whose value is to be looked up
 * @param columnIndex the column whose value is to be looked up
 * @return true if the cell is editable.
 * @see #setValueAt()
 */
public boolean isCellEditable(int rowIndex, int columnIndex);
```

```
    /**
     * Returns an attribute value for the cell at <I>columnIndex</I>
     * and <I>rowIndex</I>.
     *
     * @param rowIndex the row whose value is to be looked up
     * @param columnIndex the column whose value is to be looked up
     * @return the value Object at the specified cell
     */
    public Object getValueAt(int rowIndex, int columnIndex);

    /**
     * Sets an attribute value for the record in the cell at
     * <I>columnIndex</I> and <I>rowIndex</I>.  <I>aValue</I> is
     * the new value.
     *
     * @param aValue the new value
     * @param rowIndex the row whose value is to be changed
     * @param columnIndex the column whose value is to be changed
     * @see #getValueAt()
     * @see #isCellEditable()
     */
    public void setValueAt(Object aValue, int rowIndex, int columnIndex);

    /**
     * Add a listener to the list that's notified each time a change
     * to the data model occurs.
     *
     * @param l the TableModelListener
     */
    public void addTableModelListener(TableModelListener l);

    /**
     * Remove a listener from the list that's notified each time a
     * change to the data model occurs.
     *
     * @param l the TableModelListener
     */
    public void removeTableModelListener(TableModelListener l);
}
```

To aid developers creating classes that implement the TableModel interface, the javax.swing.table package contains the AbstractTableModel class. This abstract class manages TableModelListener instances and contains convenience methods for firing TableModelEvents. Classes that extend the AbstractTableModel class must provide implementations for the getRowCount, getColumnCount, and getValueAt methods. This provides the view with a read-only view of the data in the model. The AbstractTableModel class provides default implementation for the isCellEditable and setValueAt methods. The isCellEditable method returns false for all row and column values passed to it. This creates a read-only table allowing the setValueAt method to be empty. The getColumnClass method simply returns the Object class. The getColumnName method labels columns similar to a spreadsheet. Column names are A, B, and so on.

To provide an editable TableModel implementation, the isCellEditable and setValueAt methods must also be overridden. To allow different editors and renderers for different classes of data, the getColumnClass method must be overridden as well. At this point, the extension to AbstractTableModel has nearly implemented the TableModel interface, so it may be asked, "Why extend AbstractTableModel at all?" The extension inherits the TableModelListener management functions, but more significantly, it inherits the fire methods provided by the AbstractTableModel class. These methods allow the model to easily fire TableModelEvents to listeners. The fire methods are shown in Table 12.3.

TABLE 12.3   AbstractTableModel CLASSES FIRE METHODS

Method Name	*Purpose of Event*
FireTableCellUpdated (int row, int column)	Notify all listeners that the value of the cell at (row, column) has been updated.
fireTableChanged(TableModel Event e)	Forward the given notification event to all TableModel Listeners that registered themselves as listeners for this table model.
fireTableDataChanged()	Notify all listeners that all cell values in the table's rows may have changed.
fireTableRowsDeleted(int firstRow, int lastRow)	Notify all listeners that rows in the (inclusive) range [firstRow, lastRow] have been deleted.
fireTableRowsInserted(int firstRow, int lastRow)	Notify all listeners that rows in the (inclusive) range [firstRow, lastRow] have been inserted.
fireTableRowsUpdated(int firstRow, int lastRow)	Notify all listeners that rows in the (inclusive) range [firstRow, lastRow] have been updated.
fireTableStructureChanged()	Notify all listeners that the table's structure has changed.

The TableModelListener interface, shown in Listing 12.3, must be implemented to receive events from the table model. As can be seen from the listing, this is a simple interface. It defines one method, tableChanged. This is called when the table model being listened to changes. The TableModelEvent instance passed as the parameter to this method contains the information as to what type of change occurred. The

TableModelEvent class is also shown in Listing 12.3. This class defines constants that define the type of change that occur in the model. Possible types for the event are INSERT, DELETE, and UPDATE. After the type of event has been determined by using the getType method, the range of effected rows can be obtained with the getFirstRow and getLastRow methods. The affected column can be obtained from the getColumn method. The constant ALL_COLUMNS is defined to signify that all columns in the table are involved with the event.

The TableModelEvent also contains special case conditions. If an ALL_COLUMNS UPDATE event is received with a last row of Integer.MAX_VALUE, this means that the entire table's row data has changed and the view should reread this information from the model. If an ALL_COLUMNS UPDATE event is received for the HEADER_ROW, the structure of the table has changed. The view must reinitialize its columns and refresh the view. These magic event types add a level of complexity to the TableModelEvent that in this author's opinion was unnecessary. Adding a couple of additional event types, or extending the TableModelListener interface for these special cases, would have made the event flow between the TableModel and its listeners much more clear and alleviated a significant amount of special case code in the listener.

LISTING 12.3   THE TableModelListener INTERFACE AND TableModelEvent CLASS

```
public interface TableModelListener extends java.util.EventListener
{
    /**
     * This fine grain notification tells listeners the exact range
     * of cells, rows, or columns that changed.
     */
    public void tableChanged(TableModelEvent e);
}


public class TableModelEvent extends java.util.EventObject
{
    public static final int INSERT =  1;
    public static final int UPDATE =  0;
    public static final int DELETE = -1;

    public static final int HEADER_ROW = -1;

    public static final int ALL_COLUMNS = -1;

//
//   Instance Variables
//
```

continues

LISTING 12.3 CONTINUED

```
protected int        type;
protected int     firstRow;
protected int     lastRow;
protected int     column;

//
// Constructors
//

    /**
     * All row data in the table has changed. Listeners should discard
     * any state that was based on the rows and requery the TableModel
     * to get the new row count and all the appropriate values.
     * The JTable will repaint the entire visible region on receiving
     * this event, querying the model for the cell values that are
     * visible. The structure of the table i.e. the column names, types,
     * and order have not changed.
     */
    public TableModelEvent(TableModel source) {
        // Use Integer.MAX_VALUE instead of getRowCount() in
        // case rows were deleted.
        this(source, 0, Integer.MAX_VALUE, ALL_COLUMNS, UPDATE);
    }

    /**
     * This row of data has been updated.
     * To denote the arrival of a completely new table with a different
     * structure use <code>HEADER_ROW</code> as the value for the
     * <I>row</I>. When the JTable receives this event and its
     * <I>autoCreateColumnsFromModel</I> flag is set it discards any
     * TableColumns that it had and reallocates default ones in the
     * order they appear in the model. This is the same as calling
     * <code>setModel(TableModel)</code> on the JTable.
     */
    public TableModelEvent(TableModel source, int row) {
        this(source, row, row, ALL_COLUMNS, UPDATE);
    }

    /**
     * The data in rows [<I>firstRow</I>, <I>lastRow</I>] have been
     * updated.
     */
    public TableModelEvent(TableModel source, int firstRow, int lastRow) {
        this(source, firstRow, lastRow, ALL_COLUMNS, UPDATE);
    }

    /**
     * The cells in column <I>column</I> in the range
     * [<I>firstRow</I>, <I>lastRow</I>] have been updated.
```

```
   */
public TableModelEvent( TableModel source, int firstRow,
                        int lastRow, int column ) {
    this(source, firstRow, lastRow, column, UPDATE);
}


/**
 * The cells from (firstRow, column) to (lastRow, column) have been
 * changed. The <I>column</I> refers to the column index of the cell
 * in the model's coordinate system. When <I>column</I> is ALL_
 * COLUMNS, all cells in the specified range of rows are
 * considered changed.
 *   <p>
 * The <I>type</I> should be one of: INSERT, UPDATE, and DELETE.
 */
public TableModelEvent( TableModel source, int firstRow, int lastRow,
                        int column, int type) {
    super(source);
    this.firstRow = firstRow;
    this.lastRow = lastRow;
    this.column = column;
    this.type = type;
}
```

```
//
// Querying Methods
//

/** Returns the first row that changed.  HEADER_ROW means the meta
 * data, i.e. names, types, and order of the columns.
 */
public int getFirstRow() { return firstRow; };

/** Returns the last row that changed. */
public int getLastRow() { return lastRow; };

/**
 *  Returns the column for the event.  If the return
 *  value is ALL_COLUMNS; it means every column in the specified
 *  rows changed.
 */
public int getColumn() { return column; };

/**
 *  Returns the type of event - one of: INSERT, UPDATE, and DELETE.
 */
public int getType() { return type; }
}
```

12

The `TableColumnModel` Interface and Associated Classes

The `JTable` class delegates column information to a column model. The required methods for a column model class are defined in the `TableColumnModel` interface shown in Listing 12.4. The `TableColumnModel` interface is another long interface that typically will not be implemented by developers. The `DefaultTableColumnModel` class is provided for use in `JTable` instances. However, the flexibility to replace the `DefaultTableColumnModel` is available, if required, as long as the replacement column model class implements this interface. This is a good design pattern for Java development. The view class interfaces to model classes through interfaces, and a default implementation of that class is provided. This allows for the view to be easily used with default behavior and still allow that behavior to be overridden or extended by providing custom classes that implement the model interface.

LISTING 12.4 THE `TableColumnModel` INTERFACE

```
public interface TableColumnModel
{
//
// Modifying the model
//

    /**
     * Appends <I>aColumn</I> to the end of the receiver's tableColumns
     * array. This method also posts the columnAdded() event to its
     * listeners.
     *
     * @param    aColumn          The <B>TableColumn</B> to be added
     * @see      #removeColumn()
     */
    public void addColumn(TableColumn aColumn);

    /**
     * Deletes the <B>TableColumn</B> <I>column</I> from the
     * receiver's table column's array.  This method will do nothing if
     * <I>column</I> is not in the table's column's list.
     * This method also posts the columnRemoved() event to its
     * listeners.
     *
     * @param    column           The <B>TableColumn</B> to be removed
     * @see      #addColumn()
     */
    public void removeColumn(TableColumn column);

    /**
```

```
 * Moves the column and heading at <I>columnIndex</I> to
 * <I>newIndex</I>. The old column at <I>columnIndex</I> will now be
 * found at <I>newIndex</I>. The column that used to be at
 * <I>newIndex</I> is shifted left or right to make room.
 * This will not move any columns if <I>columnIndex</I> equals
 * <I>newIndex</I>. This method also posts the columnMoved()
 * event to its listeners.
 *
 * @param columnIndex the index of column to be moved
 * @param newIndex New index to move the column
 * @exception IllegalArgumentException if <I>column</I> or
 *                                     <I>newIndex</I>
 *                                     are not in the valid range
 */
public void moveColumn(int columnIndex, int newIndex);

/**
 * Sets the <B>TableColumn's</B> column margin to <I>newMargin</I>.
 * This method also posts the columnMarginChanged() event to its
 * listeners.
 *
 * @param    newMargin                the width margin of the column
 * @see      #getColumnMargin()
 */
public void setColumnMargin(int newMargin);

//
// Querying the model
//

/** Returns the number of columns in the model */
public int getColumnCount();

/** Returns an Enumeration of all the columns in the model */
public Enumeration getColumns();

/**
 * Returns the index of the first column in the receiver's
 * column's array whose identifier is equal to <I>identifier</I>,
 * when compared using <I>equals()</I>.
 *
 * @return the index of the first table column in the receiver's
 *         tableColumns array whose identifier is equal to
 *         <I>identifier</I>, when compared using equals().
 * @param  identifier  the identifier object
 * @exception IllegalArgumentException if <I>identifier</I>
 *            is null or no TableColumn has this identifier
 * @see #getColumn()
 */
```

continues

LISTING 12.4   CONTINUED

```java
    public int getColumnIndex(Object columnIdentifier);

    /**
     * Returns the <B>TableColumn</B> object for the column at
     * <I>columnIndex</I>
     *
     * @return the TableColumn object for the column at
     *          <I>columnIndex</I>
     * @param  columnIndex      the index of the column desired
     */
    public TableColumn getColumn(int columnIndex);

    /** Returns the width margin between each column */
    public int getColumnMargin();

    /**
     * Returns the index of the column that lies on the <I>xPosition</I>,
     * or -1 if it lies outside the any of the column's bounds.
     *
     * @return  the index of the column or -1 if no column is found
     */
    public int getColumnIndexAtX(int xPosition);

    /** Returns the total width of all the columns. */
    public int getTotalColumnWidth();

//
// Selection
//

    /**
     * Sets whether the columns in this model can be selected.
     * @see #getColumnSelectionAllowed()
     */
    public void setColumnSelectionAllowed(boolean flag);

    /**
     * @return true if columns can be selected.
     * @see #setColumnSelectionAllowed()
     */
    public boolean getColumnSelectionAllowed();

    /**
     * @return the indices of all selected columns, or an empty int array
     *          if no column is selected.
     */
    public int[] getSelectedColumns();

    /**
```

```
 * @return the number of selected columns.  0 if no columns are
 *         selected.
 */
public int getSelectedColumnCount();

public void setSelectionModel(ListSelectionModel newModel);

public ListSelectionModel getSelectionModel();

//
// Listener
//

    public void addColumnModelListener(TableColumnModelListener x);
    public void removeColumnModelListener(TableColumnModelListener x);
}
```

12

TABLE COMPONENT

Looking at the `TableColumnModel` interface, you can see that methods are provided to query the state of the column model. This includes the number of columns in the model, the margin for each column, the total column width, the index of a column, the column at an index, and an `Enumeration` of all columns. The table's column structure can be changed dynamically. Methods are provided to add and remove columns as well as to move columns.

As you saw earlier in this chapter, the `TableColumnModel` contains a `ListSelectionListener` to manage column selection. The model defines methods for setting and getting the selection model, as well as convenience methods for manipulating column selection status and querying the selection set.

Finally, you see that `TableColumnModelListeners` can be registered with the model. This allows views or other interested classes to be notified when the column model changes. Calling one of the methods defined in the `TableColumnModelListener` interface shown in Listing 12.5 performs the notification. Each method in the interface delivers an instance of the `TableColumnModelEvent`, also shown in the listing. It is interesting to note the different styles of listener interfaces and events between the `TableModelListener`/`TableModelEvent` pair presented earlier in this section and the `TableColumnModelListener`/`TableColumnModelEvent` pair shown here. The `TableModelListener` defines a single method, and the event delivered provides the type information. The `TableColumnModelListener` interface defines multiple methods, one for each type of change in the column model, and the event simply provides the index of effected column. The first style makes implementing the interface easier, but requires a more complex method to decode and handle the event. The second style requires more work to implement the interface, but the purpose of each method is clearly defined. Both styles of listener/event pairs are valid, but one would expect the same style to be used with such closely related models.

LISTING 12.5 THE `TableColumnModelListener` AND `TableColumnModelEvent` CLASSES

```java
public interface TableColumnModelListener extends java.util.EventListener
{
    /** Tells listeners that a column was added to the model. */
    public void columnAdded(TableColumnModelEvent e);

    /** Tells listeners that a column was removed from the model. */
    public void columnRemoved(TableColumnModelEvent e);

    /** Tells listeners that a column was repositioned. */
    public void columnMoved(TableColumnModelEvent e);

    /** Tells listeners that a column was moved due to a margin change.*/
    public void columnMarginChanged(ChangeEvent e);

    /**
     * Tells listeners that the selection model of the
     * TableColumnModel changed.
     */
    public void columnSelectionChanged(ListSelectionEvent e);
}


public class TableColumnModelEvent extends java.util.EventObject
{
//
//   Instance Variables
//

    /** The index of the column from where it was moved or removed */
    protected int      fromIndex;

    /** The index of the column to where it was moved or added from */
    protected int      toIndex;

//
// Constructors
//

    public TableColumnModelEvent(TableColumnModel source,
        int from, int to) {
        super(source);
        fromIndex = from;
        toIndex = to;
    }

//
// Querying Methods
//
```

```
    /** Returns the fromIndex.  Valid for removed or moved events */
    public int getFromIndex() { return fromIndex; };

    /** Returns the toIndex.  Valid for add and moved events */
    public int getToIndex() { return toIndex; };
}
```

The `TableColumnModel` consists of a set of `TableColumn` instances. When a column is retrieved from the model, it is an instance of the `TableColumn` class. This class encapsulates the information about the appearance of a column in the table. It contains attributes for the column width, minimum and maximum width, and whether it is resizable or not. The minimum and maximum values are enforced when the user is resizing the column by dragging its border. This class also can contain a renderer and editor. This allows each column in the table to use its own renderer and editor. Later in this chapter, you will see how it is possible to set a renderer and editor for a given type for the entire table. Setting the value on the column overrides the value set for the table. This gives the developer total control over how the data in a column is displayed and edited. The column header's renderer can also be set. A `PropertyChangeListener` can be registered with the `TableColumn` instance to be notified of changes to these properties. Table 12.4 contains a complete list of bound properties contained in the `TableColumn` class. The constants used for the property names are defined in the `TableColumn` class.

TABLE 12.4 BOUND PROPERTIES OF THE `TableColumn` CLASS

Property Name	Setter Method	Getter Method
HEADER_RENDERER _PROPERTY	setHeaderRenderer	getHeaderRenderer
HEADER_VALUE _PROPERTY	setHeaderValue	getHeaderValue
CELL_RENDERER _PROPERTY	setCellRenderer	getCellRenderer
COLUMN_WIDTH _PROPERTY	setWidth	getWidth

The order of the columns in the `TableColumnModel` does not have to coincide with the order in the data model. This allows different tables to view the same model data in different orders or different sets of columns from the data model. The methods `convertColumnIndexToModel` and `covertColumnIndexToView` in the `JTable` class can be used to map from the view's coordinate space to the models, and vice versa.

The `columnAtPoint` method can be used to determine which column lies below a point. This is often used for hit detection in mouse listeners added to the table.

The `TableColumn` class goes against the general design of the `JTable` class, that being that the interaction between the various table components is defined in an interface and a default implementation for the interface is provided. However, `TableColumn` is a class. This makes it more difficult to replace with a custom implementation than if `TableColumn` were an interface and the implementation contained in a `DefaultTableColumn` class, as was seen earlier in this chapter for the `TableColumnModel` interface and its default implementation, the `DefaultTableColumnModel` class.

Pulling It All Together: A `JTable` Example

The table presented by the `SimpleTableTest` application did, in fact, present the data passed to the constructor. However, with a little extra effort, the `JTable` component can yield a much nicer display. This section will present a custom data model, renderers, and editors that combine to make a complete table. The example code for each portion of the table will be given as it is presented. The source listing that can be compiled and executed for the example will be presented in its entirety at the end of the section.

The default renderer for the table calls the `toString` method of the `Object` being rendered. For the second and third columns in the `SimpleTableTest` application, a more appropriate rendering would be color coded for column two and a check box for column three. There are multiple ways to accomplish this goal. You can add a custom renderer to the `TableColumn` instance that represents columns two and three in the `ColumnModel`. However, that is not the approach taken here. Instead, a renderer will be registered with the table for each class that requires custom rendering. This allows the same renderer to be shared by multiple columns in a table if they each contain the same class of data.

The first step is to define an extension to the `AbstractTableModel` class that has a more intimate understanding of the data it contains than results from passing a `Vector` or array to the `JTable` class's constructor. The `TableTestModel` class shown in Listing 12.6 is such a class (Figure 12.6 shows the output from this listing). Internally, this class stores its data in a two-dimensional array. The design of the data model is such that the name column is not editable, but the other columns are. This information is obtained by clients of the model via the `isCellEditable` method. If the column index passed to this function is `0`, `false` is returned. `true` is returned for all other columns. The row parameter is not used in this method. The model also protects against the name being set in the `setValueAt` method. If a column index of `0` is passed to this method, a `RuntimeException` is thrown, and the data in the model is not altered. The model returns the proper `Class` for the data stored in each column from the `getColumnClass` method.

This is possible for this data model, because the data in every cell in a column is of the same type. If this is not the case, the getColumnClass method must return a common ancestor of the classes contained in the column. This can be the Object class itself.

The structure of the TableTestModel is static. Thus, the only time the data in the model changes is in the setValueAt method. This method calls the fireTableCellUpdated method inherited from the AbstractTableModel class to notify listeners when a value changes. If this model is shared between multiple tables, edits in one table are displayed in the other tables after the update event is received. The data model can use the other convenience methods inherited from the AbstractTableModel class if rows are added or deleted from the model or other structure changes in the model are allowed.

12

TABLE COMPONENT

Figure 12.6

The TestTableModel *used as a* JTable *data model.*

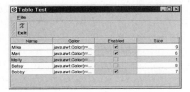

Listing 12.6 The TableTestModel Class

```
/**
 * Table model that returns the Class of the data in
 * a particular column. This allows the table to set
 * renderers for the data.
 **/
class TableTestModel extends AbstractTableModel {

    /**
     * The data in the model.
     **/
    Object[][] data = {
        { "Mike", Color.blue, new Boolean( true ), new Integer(9) },
        { "Mari", Color.red, new Boolean( true ), new Integer(6) },
        { "Molly", Color.yellow, new Boolean( false ), new Integer(1) },
        { "Betsy", Color.orange, new Boolean( false ), new Integer(8) },
        { "Bobby", Color.lightGray, new Boolean( true ), new Integer(7) }
        };

    /**
     * The column names for the model.
     **/
    String[] columnNames = { "Name", "Color", "Enabled", "Size" };

    /**
```

continues

LISTING 12.6   CONTINUED

```java
 * TableTestModel, constructor.
 **/
TableTestModel() {
    super();
}


/**
 * getRowCount, from TableModel.
 *
 * @return The number of rows in the data.
 **/
public int getRowCount() {
    return( data.length );
}


/**
 * getColumnCount, from TableModel.
 *
 * @return The number of columns in the data.
 **/
public int getColumnCount() {
    return( data[0].length );
}

/**
 * getValueAt, from TableModel.
 *
 * @param row The row of the requested data object.
 * @param column The column of the requested data object.
 * @return The object at the specified cell.
 **/
public Object getValueAt( int row, int column ) {
    return( data[ row ][ column ] );
}

/**
 * setValueAt, from TableModel.
 *
 * Set the data value in the given location to the
 * given object.
 *
 * @param value The new data object.
 * @param row The row of the new data object.
 * @param column The column of the new data object.
 **/
public void setValueAt( Object value, int row, int column ) {
    if( column == 0 )
```

```
            throw new RuntimeException(
                    "The Name column is not editable" );

        data[ row ][ column ] = value;
    }


    /**
     * getColumnName, from TableModel.
     *
     * @param column The column index whose name is desired.
     * @return The name of the column with the given index.
     **/
    public String getColumnName( int column ) {
        return( columnNames[ column ] );
    }

    /**
     * getColumnClass, from TableModel.
     *
     * @param column The column index whose Class is desired.
     * @return The Class of the data for the column with the given index.
     **/
    public Class getColumnClass( int column ) {
        return( data[0][ column ].getClass() );
    }


    /**
     * isCellEditable, from TableModel.
     *
     * All columns except the first are editable in this model.
     *
     * @param row The row of the cell whose editability is requested.
     * @param column The column of the cell whose editability
     *                  is requested.
     * @return true if the cell is editable, false otherwise.
     **/
    public boolean isCellEditable( int row, int column ) {
        if( column == 0 ) {
            return( false );
        } else {
            return( true );
        }
    }
}
```

The table created when using an instance of the TestTableModel as the data model for an instance of the JTable class is shown in Figure 12.6. The model can be set for the table by calling the setModel method or by specifying the model in the JTable class's constructor. This is shown in the following line of code.

```
JTable table = new JTable( new TableTestModel() );
```

This model can be added to the SimpleTableTest application, and it is the model used for the TableTest application developed in this section.

You will immediately notice the change in this table shown in Figure 12.6 to those shown earlier in this chapter. When the Boolean class is returned from the getColumnClass method in the TestTableModel method, the JTable class uses a JCheckBox for the cell renderer, and when a Number is returned, the text is right aligned. This magic is enabled in the protected createDefaultRenderers method in the JTable class. This method creates and registers renders for known classes by using the setDefaultRenderer method. The set of renderers registered is shown in Table 12.5.

Extensions of the JTable class can override the createDefaultRenderers method to establish a different set of renderers. Also, the setDefaultRenderer method is public. This allows clients of the JTable class to change the default renderer or add renderers for additional classes of objects. When a renderer is registered for a class, it is used to render all columns in the model that contain that class of data. Thus, registering a renderer for a class is a global setting, while setting the renderer for a TableColumn instance is only valid for that column, even if multiple columns contain that class of data.

If set, the ToolTip for the table is retrieved from the renderer. If the renderer does not have a ToolTip, the tip is retrieved from the table. This allows custom renderers to contain ToolTips specific for the class of data that they render. ToolTips are enabled for JTable instances by default. However, calling the setToolTipText method with a null parameter will cause the table to remove itself from the ToolTipManager.

TABLE 12.5 DEFAULT RENDERERS FOR THE JTable CLASS

Class	Renderer	Positioning
Object	DefaultTableCellRenderer	Left-aligned text
Number	DefaultTableCellRenderer	Right-aligned text
ImageIcon	DefaultTableCellRenderer	Centered Icon
Boolean	CheckBoxRenderer	Centered JCheckBox

The default rendering of the JTable class presents the Boolean instances in the table appropriately. However, as you can see in Figure 12.6, the cell containing the JCheckBox isn't rendered the same as other cells in its row. Also, the Color data still leaves room for improvement. Registering your own renderer for the Color class makes this improvement. A new renderer for the Boolean class that paints the same color as the other cells is also registered. This has the effect of replacing the default Boolean renderer. Listing 12.7

contains the code for the new renderers and registers them with the table. The `Boolean` renderer is a complete class that extends the `JCheckBox` class and implements the `TableCellRenderer` interface. The majority of the class's work is performed in the `getTableCellRendererComponent` method. In this method, the check box is configured for the current state of the cell that will be rendered. The selected state for the check box is set based on the value passed to the method. If the cell is selected, the selected foreground and background colors are queried from the table and set on the check box. Similar processing occurs for an unselected cell. Finally, the check box is returned as the rendering component.

The color renderer is made by creating an anonymous class that extends the `DefaultTableCellRenderer` class and sets its background color in the `setValue` method. The renderer must be made opaque so that it paints its background. This makes the color renderer very simple. However, if you wish to use this technique in multiple tables, it should be made into a standalone class.

The table created using the enhanced renderers is shown in Figure 12.7.

Figure 12.7

Enhanced renderers in the `JTable`.

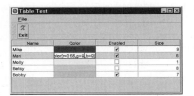

Listing 12.7   Enhanced `Boolean` and `Color` Class `TableCellRenderers`

```
/**
 * The SelectedCheckBoxRenderer class is almost the same as the
 * default check box renderer in the JTable class. However, it
 * paints the cell in the normal table selected colors when it is
 * selected. This avoids the white areas in the table for Boolean
 * columns. Also, if all columns in the table are Boolean, you
 * wouldn't be able to see the selected row using the default renderer!
 *
 * @author Mike Foley
 **/
class SelectedCheckBoxRenderer extends JCheckBox
    implements TableCellRenderer {

    private Border noFocusBorder;
    private Color unselectedForeground;
    private Color unselectedBackground;
```

continues

LISTING 12.7   CONTINUED

```
/**
 * SelectedCheckBoxRenderer, default constructor.
 *
 * We need to be opaque so our background color is painted.
 * Create our border. Keep a reference around so it can be
 * reset when we are not selected.
 * Center the check box to match the position of the Boolean editor.
 **/
public SelectedCheckBoxRenderer() {
    super();
    setOpaque( true );

    noFocusBorder = new EmptyBorder( 1, 2, 1, 2 );
    setBorder( noFocusBorder );

    setHorizontalAlignment( JLabel.CENTER );
}


/**
 * Set the foreground color. Remember the color, so
 * we can reset it when we are not selected.
 *
 * @param c The new foreground color.
 **/
public void setForeground(Color c) {
    super.setForeground(c);
    unselectedForeground = c;
}


/**
 * Set the background color. Remember the color, so
 * we can reset it when we are not selected.
 *
 * @param c The new background color.
 **/
public void setBackground(Color c) {
    super.setBackground(c);
    unselectedBackground = c;
}


/**
 * Clear the foreground and background colors after
 * updating the UI. This will cause the colors to be
 * read from the table property portion of the UI.
 **/
public void updateUI() {
```

```
        super.updateUI();
        setForeground( null );
        setBackground( null );
    }


    /**
     * getTableCellRendererComponent, from TableCellRenderer
     *
     * Configure the check box for the given state.
     *
     **/
    public Component getTableCellRendererComponent( JTable table,
                         Object value, boolean isSelected,
boolean hasFocus, int row, int column ) {

        //
        // Check or uncheck the JCheckBox.
        //
        setSelected((value != null && ((Boolean)value).booleanValue()));

        //
        // If we are selected, paint in the table's selection colors.
        //
        if( isSelected ) {
            super.setForeground( table.getSelectionForeground() );
            super.setBackground( table.getSelectionBackground() );
        } else {
            super.setForeground( ( unselectedForeground != null ) ?
                          unselectedForeground : table.getForeground() );
            super.setBackground( ( unselectedBackground != null ) ?
                          unselectedBackground : table.getBackground() );
        } // else

        //
        // If we have the focus, paint in the focus color for the table
        // and set the focus border.
        // If not, set the no focus border.
        //
        if( hasFocus ) {
            setBorder( UIManager.getBorder(
                    "Table.focusCellHighlightBorder" ) );
            if (table.isCellEditable(row, column)) {
                super.setForeground( UIManager.getColor(
                            "Table.focusCellForeground" ) );
                super.setBackground( UIManager.getColor(
                            "Table.focusCellBackground" ) );
            }
        } else {
```

continues

LISTING 12.7   CONTINUED

```
            setBorder( noFocusBorder );
        }

        return( this );
    }

} // SelectedCheckBoxRenderer


        //
        // Create and register a Color class renderer.
        //
        DefaultTableCellRenderer colorRenderer =
            new DefaultTableCellRenderer() {
            public void setValue( Object value ) {
                setBackground( ( Color )value );
            }
        };

        colorRenderer.setOpaque( true );
        table.setDefaultRenderer( Color.class, colorRenderer );

        table.setDefaultRenderer( Boolean.class,
                            new SelectedCheckBoxRenderer() );
```

> **NOTE**
>
> The SelectedCheckBoxRenderer class shown in Listing 12.7 assumes that the value passed to the getTableCellRendererComponent method is a Boolean. This means that if this class is registered as a renderer in a table for a class that is not a Boolean or a descendent of Boolean, the renderer will throw a ClassCastException when used. Similarly, the color renderer assumes that a Color is passed in its setValue method. If the renderer were used to renderer values other than colors, a ClassCastException would be thrown.

Figure 12.7 also shows the cell containing the color red being edited. You can see that the editor is a JTextField with the text set to the String returned from the toString method of the Color instance. This is obviously undesirable behavior. The solution is to create a cell editor and set it for the Color class.

Similar to what you saw previously for renderers, the JTable class calls the protected createDefaultEditors method to create and register default editors for the table. Table 12.6 lists the classes for which default editors are registered. Extensions to the JTable class can override this method to register a different set of editors for the table. Clients can also register editors by using the `public setDefaultEditor` method.

TABLE 12.6 DEFAULT EDITORS FOR THE JTable CLASS

Class	Renderer	Positioning
Object	DefaultCellEditor	JTextField with left-aligned text
Number	DefaultCellEditor	JTextField with right-aligned text
Boolean	DefaultCellEditor	Centered JCheckBox

The code shown next shows an editor that allows the colors to be chosen in the table. The editor is a `DefaultCellEditor` containing a `JComboBox` that has been configured for the valid colors for the data model. If any color is allowed in the data model, an editor could be created from the `JColorChooser` class. This class is presented in Chapter 19, "Choice Dialog Boxes." The `JComboBox` is also configured with the renderer shown in Listing 12.8. This renderer displays colors similarly to the renderer in the table. The resulting editor is shown in Figure 12.8.

```
JComboBox comboBox = new JComboBox();
comboBox.addItem( Color.black );
comboBox.addItem( Color.gray );
comboBox.addItem( Color.red );
comboBox.addItem( Color.pink );
comboBox.addItem( Color.orange );
comboBox.addItem( Color.yellow );
comboBox.addItem( Color.green );
comboBox.addItem( Color.blue );
comboBox.addItem( Color.cyan );
comboBox.addItem( Color.white );
comboBox.addItem( Color.lightGray );
comboBox.setRenderer( new ColorCellRenderer() );

table.setDefaultEditor( Color.class, new DefaultCellEditor( comboBox ) );
```

FIGURE 12.8
The custom Color *class renderer.*

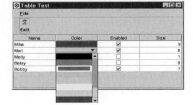

LISTING 12.8 THE ColorCellRenderer CLASS

```
/**
 * ColorCellRenderer is a rendering class that expects
 * Color values. When this is the case, it paints the color
 * as the background of the label. If not, show the String
 * returned from the toString method of the value Object.
 *
 * @author Mike Foley
 **/
class ColorCellRenderer extends JLabel implements ListCellRenderer {

    Border selectedWhiteBorder;
    Border selectedBlackBorder;

    /**
     * ColorCellRenderer, default constructor.
     * We must be opaque so the background is painted.
     **/
    public ColorCellRenderer() {
        setOpaque( true );
        selectedWhiteBorder = BorderFactory.createMatteBorder(
                                     3, 5, 3, 5, Color.white );
        selectedBlackBorder = BorderFactory.createMatteBorder(
                                     3, 5, 3, 5, Color.black );
    }


    /**
     * Configure yourself for the state passed.
     * If the value is a Color, set the background to that
     * color. If not use the toString method of the value
     *
     **/
    public Component getListCellRendererComponent(
        JList list,
        Object value,
        int index,
        boolean isSelected,
        boolean cellHasFocus)
    {

        if( value instanceof Color ) {
            setText( "        " );
            setBackground( ( Color )value );
            if( isSelected ) {
                if( value.equals( Color.white ) )
                    setBorder( selectedBlackBorder );
                else
                    setBorder( selectedWhiteBorder );
            } else {
```

```
                    setBorder( null );
            }
        } else {
            setText( value.toString() );
            if( isSelected ) {
                setBackground( list.getSelectionBackground() );
                setForeground( list.getSelectionForeground() );
            } else {
                setBackground(list.getBackground());
                setForeground(list.getForeground());
            }
        }


        return this;
    }

} // ColorCellRenderer
```

The user gesture to begin editing a cell is look-and-feel specific. It also depends on the editor. For example, an editor built on a `JTextField` requires a double-click to commence editing, while the editor built on the `JCheckBox` for `Boolean` data requires only a single click to edit the cell. This type of inconsistency is annoying to the user and gives editing the table a bad feel. The `editCellAt` method is used to start a cell editing if the cell allows editing.

The default cell editor for `Number` and `Object` instances doesn't have a way to cancel editing. Editing is stopped by pressing the Enter key or selecting a different cell in the table. However, if the cell had been edited, the change is set in the data model. It is desirable to give the user a way to cancel editing without changing the data model. The following cell editor provides this functionality. When the escape key is pressed, editing is canceled without changing the data model. The editor is then registered as the editor for the `Number` class. A similar editor that contains left-aligned text should be registered for the `Object` class if your tables contain any columns that use the `Object` editor. If this editor is going to be used in multiple tables, it should be encapsulated in its own class that can be used as the editor for each table.

```
JTextField textField = new JTextField();
final DefaultCellEditor cancelCellEditor =
➡                        new DefaultCellEditor( textField );
textField.setHorizontalAlignment( SwingConstants.RIGHT );
textField.addKeyListener( new KeyAdapter() {
    public void keyReleased( KeyEvent event ) {
        if( event.getKeyCode() == KeyEvent.VK_ESCAPE )
            cancelCellEditor.cancelCellEditing();
    }
} );
table.setDefaultEditor( Number.class, cancelCellEditor );
```

The renderer for the column's header can be specified also. A common need for this is for multiline headers. The `MutliLineHeaderRenderer` class shown in Listing 12.9 implements a multiline column header renderer. This class extends the `JTextArea` class to provide a multiline textual display region. In the `getTableCellRendererComponent` method, the color and border are set to those defined in the current `JTableHeader` contained in the table. The proper border is obtained from the `UIManager`. This ensures that the multiline header will look the same as default renderers used on other tables. A complete description of obtaining component properties from the `UIManager` is presented in Part V, "Extending JFC Components," and in Chapter 30, "Pluggable Look-and-Feel."

The problem with the current implementation of the `MultiLineHeaderRenderer` class is that it doesn't dynamically obtain multiline data from the header or data model. The current table package is designed for single-line headers. Using multiple line headers requires overriding methods in one of the standard classes or using "known" models. For example, a custom data model can return `String` instances with embedded line-feed characters from its `getColumnName` method. However, if this is done, the header will not display properly using the default column header renderer.

A single instance of the `MultiLineHeaderRenderer` can be shared among all `TableColumn` instances in the `TableColumnModel`. The code fragment to query the columns from the table and set the renderer is shown next. If columns can be dynamically added to the table, a `TableColumnModelListener` would need to be added to the `TableColumnModel` to set the renderer for new columns. The table using the `MultiLineHeaderRenderer` is shown in Figure 12.9.

LISTING 12.9 THE `MultiLineHeaderRenderer` CLASS, AND ADDING IT TO A TABLE

```
//
// Create a multiline renderer, and set it for each column in
// the table.
//
MultiLineHeaderRenderer headerRenderer = new MultiLineHeaderRenderer();
TableColumnModel columnModel = table.getColumnModel();
for( Enumeration e = columnModel.getColumns(); e.hasMoreElements(); ) {
    TableColumn column = ( TableColumn )e.nextElement();
    column.setHeaderRenderer( headerRenderer );
}


/**
 * An example of a multiline table header.
 * To be used effectively, known header value types
 * would need to be specified in an interface that
 * could be tested for here. This would allow useful
 * data to be queried for the additional rows in the header.
```

```
 * This could be done by a specialized table model that
 * returns column headers with breaks in the returned
 * String from the getColumnName method that could be
 * interpreted here.
 **/
class MultiLineHeaderRenderer extends JTextArea
    implements TableCellRenderer, Serializable {

    /**
     * MultiLineHeaderRenderer, default Constructor.
     * Set the number of rows to two. For a production
     * header renderer, the number of rows would probably
     * be determined dynamically depending on the header value.
     **/
    public MultiLineHeaderRenderer() {
        super( 2, 20 );
        setOpaque( true );
    }


    /**
     * Configure in the standard table header colors and border.
     * The multiline string is a bit contrived here. Would need
     * to get a real multiline header from the table model, or
     * values of known types, i.e. interfaces.
     **/
    public Component getTableCellRendererComponent(JTable table,
                        Object value, boolean isSelected,
                        boolean hasFocus, int row, int column) {

        if (table != null) {
            JTableHeader header = table.getTableHeader();
            if (header != null) {
                setForeground(header.getForeground());
                setBackground(header.getBackground());
                setFont(header.getFont());
            }
        }

        setText( (value == null) ? "Column " + column :
                "Column " + column + "\n" + value.toString() );
        setBorder( UIManager.getBorder("TableHeader.cellBorder") );
        return this;
    }
}
```

FIGURE 12.9

Multiline table headers.

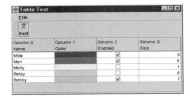

Entire Source Listing of the TableTest Application

The previous portion of this section presented the functional components of the TableTest application. For completeness, the entire source listing is given in Listing 12.10. This includes the renderers, editors, and the data model. The code is contained in a single source file. To allow the renderers or editors to be used in multiple tables, they need to be moved into their own source file.

LISTING 12.10   THE TableTest APPLICATION

```java
package com.foley.test;

import java.awt.*;
import java.io.Serializable;

import java.util.*;

import javax.swing.*;
import javax.swing.border.*;
import javax.swing.table.*;

import com.foley.utility.ApplicationFrame;


/**
 * An application that displays a JTable instance
 * in its frame.
 *
 * @author Mike Foley
 **/
public class TableTest extends Object {

    /**
     * Application entry point.
     * Create a frame and the table and display them.
     *
     * @param args Command line parameter. Not used.
     **/
    public static void main( String args[] ) {
```

```
        JFrame frame = new ApplicationFrame( "TableTest" );

        JTable table = new JTable( new TableTestModel() );

        //
        // Create and register a Color class renderer.
        //
        DefaultTableCellRenderer colorRenderer =
            new DefaultTableCellRenderer() {
            public void setValue( Object value ) {
                setBackground( ( Color )value );
            }
        };

        colorRenderer.setOpaque( true );
        table.setDefaultRenderer( Color.class, colorRenderer );

        //
// Create a combo box with colors available in the table.
// The combo box will be used for the Color cell editor.
// The combo box itself has a custom list renderer.
        //
        JComboBox comboBox = new JComboBox();
        comboBox.addItem( Color.black );
        comboBox.addItem( Color.gray );
        comboBox.addItem( Color.red );
        comboBox.addItem( Color.pink );
        comboBox.addItem( Color.orange );
        comboBox.addItem( Color.yellow );
        comboBox.addItem( Color.green );
        comboBox.addItem( Color.blue );
        comboBox.addItem( Color.cyan );
        comboBox.addItem( Color.white );
        comboBox.addItem( Color.lightGray );
        comboBox.setRenderer( new ColorCellRenderer() );

        table.setDefaultEditor( Color.class,
                            new DefaultCellEditor( comboBox ) );

        table.setDefaultRenderer( Boolean.class,
                            new SelectedCheckBoxRenderer() );

        //
        // Add an editor for the Number class that aborts the edit
        // without changing the data model when the escape key is
        // entered during the edit.
        //
        JTextField textField = new JTextField();
        final DefaultCellEditor cancelCellEditor =
                            new DefaultCellEditor( textField );
```

continues

LISTING 12.10 CONTINUED

```
        textField.setHorizontalAlignment( SwingConstants.RIGHT );
        textField.addKeyListener( new KeyAdapter() {
            public void keyReleased( KeyEvent event ) {
                if( event.getKeyCode() == KeyEvent.VK_ESCAPE )
                    cancelCellEditor.cancelCellEditing();
            }
        } );
        table.setDefaultEditor( Number.class, cancelCellEditor );

        //
        // A single multiline renderer may be shared between all
        // columns in the table. Set the renderer for each column.
        //
        MutliLineHeaderRenderer headerRenderer =
                                new MutliLineHeaderRenderer();
        TableColumnModel columnModel = table.getColumnModel();
        for( Enumeration e = columnModel.getColumns();
                e.hasMoreElements(); ) {
            TableColumn column = ( TableColumn )e.nextElement();
            column.setHeaderRenderer( headerRenderer );
        }

        //
        // Only allow row selection.
        //
        table.setRowSelectionAllowed( true );
        table.setColumnSelectionAllowed( false );

        //
        // Add the table to a scroll pane and add to the content
        // pane of the frame.
        //
        frame.getContentPane().add( new JScrollPane( table ),
                                BorderLayout.CENTER );

        frame.pack();
        frame.setVisible( true );

    } // main

} // TableTest


/**
 * An example of a multiline table header.
 * To be used effectively, known header value types
 * would need to be specified in an interface that
 * could be tested for here. This would allow useful
 * data to be queried for the additional rows in the header.
```

```
 * This could be done by a specialized table model that
 * returns column headers with breaks in the returned
 * String from the getColumnName method that could be
 * interpreted here.
 **/
class MutliLineHeaderRenderer extends JTextArea
     implements TableCellRenderer, Serializable {

    /**
     * MutliLineHeaderRenderer, default Constructor.
     * Set the number of rows to two. For a production
     * header renderer, the number of rows would probably
     * be determined dynamically depending on the header value.
     **/
    public MutliLineHeaderRenderer() {
        super( 2, 20 );
        setOpaque( true );
    }


    /**
     * Configure in the standard table header colors and border.
     * The multiline string is a bit contrived here. Would need
     * to get a real multiline header from the table model, or
     * values of known types, i.e. interfaces.
     **/
    public Component getTableCellRendererComponent(JTable table,
                        Object value, boolean isSelected,
                        boolean hasFocus, int row, int column) {

        if (table != null) {
            JTableHeader header = table.getTableHeader();
            if (header != null) {
                setForeground(header.getForeground());
                setBackground(header.getBackground());
                setFont(header.getFont());
            }
        }

        //
        // Add a second line that is the column number.
        //
        setText( (value == null) ? "Column " + column :
                "Column " + column + "\n" + value.toString() );
        setBorder( UIManager.getBorder("TableHeader.cellBorder") );
        return this;
    }
}
```

continues

LISTING 12.10   CONTINUED

```java
/**
 * ColorCellRenderer is a rendering class that expects
 * Color values. When this is the case, it paints the color
 * as the background of the label. If not, show the String
 * returned from the toString method of the value Object.
 *
 * @author Mike Foley
 **/
class ColorCellRenderer extends JLabel
    implements ListCellRenderer, Serializable {

    Border selectedWhiteBorder;
    Border selectedBlackBorder;

    /**
     * ColorCellRenderer, default constructor.
     * We must be opaque so the background is painted.
     **/
    public ColorCellRenderer() {
        setOpaque( true );
        selectedWhiteBorder = BorderFactory.createMatteBorder(
                                     3, 5, 3, 5, Color.white );
        selectedBlackBorder = BorderFactory.createMatteBorder(
                                     3, 5, 3, 5, Color.black );
    }


    /**
     * Configure yourself for the state passed.
     * If the value is a Color, set the background to that
     * color. If not, use the toString method of the value
     *
     **/
    public Component getListCellRendererComponent(
        JList list,
        Object value,
        int index,
        boolean isSelected,
        boolean cellHasFocus)
    {

        if( value instanceof Color ) {
            setText( "        " );
            setBackground( ( Color )value );
            if( isSelected ) {
                if( value.equals( Color.white ) )
                    setBorder( selectedBlackBorder );
                else
                    setBorder( selectedWhiteBorder );
```

```
                } else {
                    setBorder( null );
                }
            } else {
                setText( value.toString() );
                if( isSelected ) {
                    setBackground( list.getSelectionBackground() );
                    setForeground( list.getSelectionForeground() );
                } else {
                    setBackground(list.getBackground());
                    setForeground(list.getForeground());
                }
            }
        }


        return this;
    }

} // ColorCellRenderer


/**
 * The SelectedCheckBoxRenderer class is almost the same as the
 * default check box renderer in the JTable class. However, it
 * paints the cell in the normal table selected colors when it is
 * selected. This avoids the white areas in the table for Boolean
 * columns. Also, if all columns in the table are Boolean, you
 * wouldn't be able to see the selected row using the default renderer!
 *
 * @author Mike Foley
 **/
class SelectedCheckBoxRenderer extends JCheckBox
        implements TableCellRenderer, Serializable {

    private Border noFocusBorder;
    private Color unselectedForeground;
    private Color unselectedBackground;


    /**
     * SelectedCheckBoxRenderer, default constructor.
     *
     * We need to be opaque so our background color is painted.
     * Create our border. Keep a reference around so it can be
     * reset when we are not selected.
     * Center the check box to match the position of the Boolean editor.
     **/
    public SelectedCheckBoxRenderer() {
        super();
        setOpaque( true );
```

continues

LISTING 12.10   CONTINUED

```
        noFocusBorder = BorderFactory.createEmptyBorder( 1, 2, 1, 2 );
        setBorder( noFocusBorder );

        setHorizontalAlignment( JLabel.CENTER );
    }


    /**
     * Set the foreground color. Remember the color, so
     * we can reset it when we are not selected.
     *
     * @param c The new foreground color.
     **/
    public void setForeground(Color c) {
        super.setForeground(c);
        unselectedForeground = c;
    }


    /**
     * Set the background color. Remember the color, so
     * we can reset it when we are not selected.
     *
     * @param c The new background color.
     **/
    public void setBackground(Color c) {
        super.setBackground(c);
        unselectedBackground = c;
    }


    /**
     * Clear the foreground and background colors after
     * updating the UI. This will cause the colors to be
     * read from the table property portion of the UI.
     **/
    public void updateUI() {
        super.updateUI();
        setForeground( null );
        setBackground( null );
    }


    /**
     * getTableCellRendererComponent, from TableCellRenderer
     *
     * Configure the check box for the given state.
     *
     **/
```

```
    public Component getTableCellRendererComponent(JTable table,
                        Object value, boolean isSelected,
                        boolean hasFocus, int row, int column) {

        //
        // Check or uncheck the JCheckBox.
        //
        setSelected((value != null && ((Boolean)value).booleanValue()));


        //
        // If we are selected, paint in the table's selection colors.
        //
        if( isSelected ) {
            super.setForeground( table.getSelectionForeground() );
            super.setBackground( table.getSelectionBackground() );
        } else {
            super.setForeground( ( unselectedForeground != null ) ?
                            unselectedForeground : table.getForeground()
);
            super.setBackground( ( unselectedBackground != null ) ?
unselectedBackground
                            unselectedBackground :
table.getBackground() );
        } // else

        //
        // If we have the focus, paint in the focus color for the table.
        // and set the focus border.
        // If not, set the no focus border.
        //
        if( hasFocus ) {
            setBorder( UIManager.getBorder(
                        "Table.focusCellHighlightBorder" ) );
            if (table.isCellEditable(row, column)) {
                super.setForeground( UIManager.getColor(
                                "Table.focusCellForeground" ) );
                super.setBackground( UIManager.getColor(
                                "Table.focusCellBackground" ) );
            }
        } else {
            setBorder( noFocusBorder );
        }

        return( this );
    }

} // SelectedCheckBoxRenderer


/**
```

continues

LISTING 12.10 CONTINUED

```
 * Table model that returns the Class of the data in
 * a particular column. This allows the table to set
 * renderers for the data.
 **/
class TableTestModel extends AbstractTableModel
    implements Serializable {

    /**
     * The data in the model.
     **/
    Object[][] data = {
        { "Mike", Color.blue, new Boolean( true ), new Integer(9) },
        { "Mari", Color.red, new Boolean( true ), new Integer(6) },
        { "Molly", Color.yellow, new Boolean( false ), new Integer(1) },
        { "Betsy", Color.orange, new Boolean( false ), new Integer(8) },
        { "Bobby", Color.lightGray, new Boolean( true ), new Integer(7) }
        };

    /**
     * The column names for the model.
     **/
    String[] columnNames = { "Name\nFirst", "Color", "Enabled", "Size" };


    /**
     * TableTestModel, constructor.
     **/
    TableTestModel() {
        super();
    }


    /**
     * getRowCount, from TableModel.
     *
     * @return The number of rows in the data.
     **/
    public int getRowCount() {
        return( data.length );
    }


    /**
     * getColumnCount, from TableModel.
     *
     * @return The number of columns in the data.
     **/
    public int getColumnCount() {
        return( data[0].length );
    }
```

```
/**
 * getValueAt, from TableModel.
 *
 * @param row The row of the requested data object.
 * @param column The column of the requested data object.
 * @return The object at the specified cell.
 **/
public Object getValueAt( int row, int column ) {
    return( data[ row ][ column ] );
}


/**
 * setValueAt, from TableModel.
 *
 * Set the data value in the given location to the
 * given object.
 *
 * @param value The new data object.
 * @param row The row of the new data object.
 * @param column The column of the new data object.
 **/
public void setValueAt( Object value, int row, int column ) {
    if( column == 0 )
        throw new RuntimeException(
                        "The Name column is not editable" );

    data[ row ][ column ] = value;
    fireTableCellUpdated( row, column );
}



/**
 * getColumnName, from TableModel.
 *
 * @param column The column index whose name is desired.
 * @return The name of the column with the given index.
 **/
public String getColumnName( int column ) {
    return( columnNames[ column ] );
}

/**
 * getColumnClass, from TableModel.
 *
 * @param column The column index whose Class is desired.
 * @return The Class of the data for the column with the given index.
 **/
public Class getColumnClass( int column ) {
    return( data[0][ column ].getClass() );
}
```

continues

12

TABLE
COMPONENT

LISTING 12.10   CONTINUED

```
/**
 * isCellEditable, from TableModel.
 *
 * All columns except the first are editable in this model.
 *
 * @param row The row of the cell whose editability is requested.
 * @param column The column of the cell whose editability is
 *                  requested.
 * @return true if the cell is editable, false otherwise.
 **/
public boolean isCellEditable( int row, int column ) {
    if( column == 0 ) {
        return( false );
    } else {
        return( true );
    }
}
}
```

Scrolling a Table

As was seen in Chapter 3, "JComponent," the JComponent class defines the autoscrolls property. In the JComponent class, the default value for this property is defined to be false. However, the JTable class overrides the value for this property and sets it to true. This allows large tables contained in a JScrollPane instance to be scrolled both horizontally and vertically by dragging the mouse in the desired direction. The scrollbars do not need to be used. Currently in the JFC, the JList and JTable classes are the only two classes that take advantage of this functionality.

Summary

The JTable class uses a complex collection of interfaces and classes by delegating much of its functionality to support classes. This requires understanding how interfaces and classes work and how they interact with one another to fully understand how the table component works. The immaturity of these interfaces and classes is apparent in the inconsistency of implementation of interrelated classes and the small number of bound properties in the JTable class. These inconsistencies raise the bar on the learning curve for effectively using the Table package.

This chapter doesn't present every method contained in the JTable class or the classes in the table package. However, the most common methods, and those required for customization, are presented here. The complete API for all these classes is given in the reference section.

The current set of default renderers and editors for the JTable class is very limited. This chapter showed how to create a renderer and an editor for the Color class, as well as enhancing the existing renderers for the Boolean, Number, String, and Object classes. As the JFC matures, you can remain hopeful that a rich collection of renderers and editors will be provided from the toolkit. Obvious omissions other than the Color class are the Date class and editors that verify Numbers.

A complex example was presented that contained a custom data model, custom data renderers, and editors. After understanding this example, you should be equipped with the tools required to create tables of arbitrary complexity.

Container
Components

IN THIS PART

CHAPTER 13

JPanel and Box Classes

The simplest of the JFC container components is the JPanel class. It provides a lightweight replacement for the AWT Panel class. However, the JPanel class extends the JComponent class, not Panel as you may have expected.

The Box class is a container component that contains a BoxLayout for its layout manager. The Box class also contains methods for creating and adding invisible spacing components to the layout. These components give more options when you're laying out the children of the Box container. The Box class breaks form with the rest of the JFC containers. It does not extend the JComponent class; instead, it extends the AWT Container class. This makes Box behave differently than other JFC components. For example, the Box class does not have a border property. If a border is needed around a Box container, it must first be added to a JPanel instance, and the border must be set on the JPanel instance.

In this chapter, you will learn

- How to use the JPanel class.
- How to use the Box class.
- How to add glue, rigid, and strut components to Box.

The JPanel Class

The JPanel class is a lightweight replacement for the AWT Panel class. The primary purpose of the class is to provide a concrete container in the JFC. If you recall from the discussion of the JComponent class in Chapter 3, "JComponent," it is an abstract class. As such, it cannot be instantiated. The JPanel class is provided to give a concrete container class. Being an extension of the JComponent class, it is a container and inherits the features contained in that class.

The JPanel class adds very little functionality to its inherited API. As a matter of fact, its constructors contain most of the useful functionality. The signatures of the four constructors contained in the class are shown below. As with its AWT cousin, the JPanel class is configured with a shared instance of the FlowLayout class. However, you can specify any layout manager desired in the constructor. By default, instances of the JPanel class are double buffered and opaque. As with any JComponent, these properties can be set with public methods:

```
JPanel()
JPanel(boolean isDoubleBuffered)
JPanel(java.awt.LayoutManager layout)
JPanel(java.awt.LayoutManager layout, boolean isDoubleBuffered)
```

Later in this chapter, you will see how the JPanel class can be extended to provide a custom container class.

The Box Class

The Box class is an oddity in the JFC. It provides a lightweight container that is configured with the BoxLayout layout manager. When it's configured to align components along the y-axis, adding components to the Box is like stacking objects in a box (thus the name of this class and the layout manager). The BoxLayout class is a new layout manager that is part of the JFC. The Box class also contains several static methods that create invisible components to help control the layout of the container. What makes the Box class unusual is that it does not extend the JComponent class. This means that the properties contained in that class are not inherited. This includes, but is not limited to, the border property and keyboard handling. To fully understand the Box class, you must first look at the BoxLayout class.

The BoxLayout Class

The BoxLayout class is a layout manager contained in the JFC. Conceptually, it is similar to the FlowLayout layout manager contained in the AWT, in that it lays out a container's components in the order they are added to the container. However, the BoxLayout allows the components to be stacked vertically as well as placed horizontally. The BoxLayout layout manager also does not wrap components.

The orientation of the BoxLayout is specified at construction and cannot be altered thereafter. The constants X_AXIS and Y_AXIS are defined in the BoxLayout class to specify a left-to-right or top-to-bottom component arrangement, respectively. The following lines of code could be used to create a JPanel and configure it with a vertically oriented BoxLayout layout manager:

```
JPanel panel = new JPanel();
BoxLayout boxLayout = new BoxLayout( panel, BoxLayout.Y_AXIS );
panel.setLayout( boxLayout );
```

You will notice in this code fragment that the BoxLayout class requires an AWT Container parameter in its constructor. This is unlike the AWT layout managers, which do not bind themselves to the container they are managing at construction. This reference is used internally by the BoxLayout class to ensure that instances are not shared between multiple container instances. Because the binding is an AWT Container and not a JComponent, the BoxLayout class can be used to manage any container.

The BoxLayout class respects a component's minimum and maximum size properties. When the BoxLayout class is configured to stack components along the y-axis, it tries to size each component to its preferred height. The layout manager will try to size each component to the same width, the largest preferred width in the container. If the container is wider than this width, the components are sized to the container's width if possible.

Listing 13.1 contains a simple application that demonstrates this behavior. Three instances of the JPanel class are added to a panel that is configured with a vertically oriented BoxLayout layout manager. Each panel added to the outer panel is given a different background color to distinguish it from each others. The panel is shown in Figure 13.1 at its original size and then after being enlarged. As shown in the figure, the panels are resized to fill the space of the container. Also, each panel is sized equally, horizontally and vertically.

LISTING 13.1 THE BoxLayoutTest APPLICATION

```java
package com.foley.test;

import java.awt.*;

import javax.swing.*;

import com.foley.utility.ApplicationFrame;


/**
 * An application that displays panels in a
 * panel configured with a BoxLayout layout manager.
 *
 * @author Mike Foley
 **/
public class BoxLayoutTestextends Object {

    /**
     * Application entry point.
     * Create a panel with a BoxLayout layout manager.
     *
     * @param args Command line parameter. Not used.
     **/
    public static void main( String args[] ) {

        JFrame frame = new ApplicationFrame( " BoxLayoutTest" );

        JPanel panel = new JPanel();
        panel.setBorder( BorderFactory.createLoweredBevelBorder() );
        BoxLayout boxLayout = new BoxLayout( panel, BoxLayout.Y_AXIS );
        panel.setLayout( boxLayout );

        //
        // Add three panels to the outer panel.
        // Give each panel a different background color to
        // distinguish them in the window.
        //
        JPanel p = new JPanel();
```

```
            p.setBackground( Color.yellow );
            panel.add( p );

            p = new JPanel();
            p.setBackground( Color.blue );
            panel.add( p );

            p = new JPanel();
            p.setBackground( Color.green );
            panel.add( p );


            frame.getContentPane().add( panel, BorderLayout.CENTER );
            frame.pack();
            frame.setVisible( true );

        } // main

} // BoxLayoutTest
```

FIGURE 13.1

The BoxLayout *manager.*

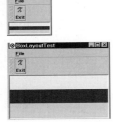

The BoxLayout class respects the minimum and maximum sizes of components while laying out a container. You can verify this by changing the preceding example to set minimum and maximum sizes for the three panels managed by the BoxLayout layout manager, as shown here:

```
JPanel p = new JPanel();
p.setBackground( Color.yellow );
p.setMinimumSize( new Dimension( 200, 10 ) );
p.setMaximumSize( new Dimension( 200, 10 ) );
panel.add( p );

p = new JPanel();
p.setBackground( Color.blue );
p.setMaximumSize( new Dimension( 100, 5 ) );
panel.add( p );

p = new JPanel();
```

```
p.setMinimumSize( new Dimension( 300, 20 ) );
p.setMaximumSize( new Dimension( 400, 30 ) );
p.setBackground( Color.green );
panel.add( p );
```

The resulting panel, after the window has been expanded, is shown in Figure 13.2. As you can see, the maximum size for each of the color panels has not been exceeded.

FIGURE 13.2

Minimum and maximum sizes in the BoxLayout *manager.*

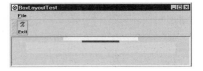

In Figure 13.2, each colored panel is centered in the center panel. The BoxLayout layout manager uses the alignmentX or alignmentY property contained in the AWT Component class to determine where components are located when they don't fill the width of the container for vertical layouts, or the height for horizontal layouts. Each of the alignment properties is a float value that ranges from 0.0 to 1.0. The value 0.0 represents left alignment for vertical layouts and top alignment for horizontal layouts. Similarly, 1.0 represents right alignment for vertical layouts and bottom alignment for horizontal layouts. A value of 0.5 is center alignment for both types of layouts. The constants LEFT_ALIGNMENT, RIGHT_ALIGNMENT, TOP_ALIGNMENT, BOTTOM_ALIGNMENT, and CENTER_ALIGNMENT are defined in the AWT Component class for these common placements.

The JPanel class contains default values for the alignmentX and alignmentY properties of 0.5, which explains why the panels are centered in Figure 13.2. However, other classes may have different default values for these properties. For example, the JLabel class has the alignmentX property set to Component.LEFT_ALIGNMENT. You can verify this by changing the preceding example to create JLabel instances instead of JPanel instances. This is shown below. The opaque property is set to true for each label. This wasn't required for the panels because, as you saw in the previous section, panels are opaque by default:

```
JLabel label = new JLabel( "Label 1" );
label.setOpaque( true );
label.setBackground( Color.yellow );
panel.add( label );

label = new JLabel( "Label 2" );
label.setOpaque( true );
label.setBackground( Color.blue );
panel.add( label );

label = new JLabel( "Label 3" );
```

```
label.setOpaque( true );
label.setBackground( Color.green );
panel.add( label );
```

The resulting window is shown in Figure 13.3. Note that the `JLabel` class returns its preferred size as its minimum and maximum sizes. Once again, other classes may behave differently.

FIGURE 13.3

JLabel *instances in the* BoxLayout *layout manager.*

Understanding how the `alignmentX` and `alignmentY` properties are used by the `BoxLayout` layout manager is difficult without practice. Listing 13.2 contains an application that dynamically alters these properties to show how a `BoxLayout` layout manager uses them when laying out a panel. This application contains three sliders that alter the `alignmentX` or `alignmentY` property of the three `JLabel` instances in its left panel. The application, shown in Figure 13.4, takes a single parameter that specifies the axis by which to configure the `BoxLayout` layout manager. Passing the application `horizontal` configures the layout manager along the x-axis. Specifying `vertical` or no parameter configures the layout manager for the y-axis. Moving the sliders allows you to see how the properties are used by the layout manager.

FIGURE 13.4

Horizontal and vertical BoxLayoutTest *application.*

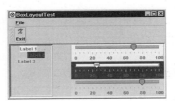

The `BoxLayoutTest` panel itself uses a `BoxLayout` layout manager to configure the label and slider panel. The `glue` component added in the constructor will be discussed in the next section. It is also educational to replace the labels with other types of components to see their default alignment parameters. The `BoxLayoutTest` application demonstrates how relatively complex arrangements can be built by nesting panels.

LISTING 13.2   THE BoxLayoutTest APPLICATION

```
package com.foley.test;

import java.awt.*;

import javax.swing.*;
import javax.swing.event.*;

import com.foley.utility.ApplicationFrame;


/**
 * An application that displays a set of three labels in
 * a panel on the left side of the window. Three sliders
 * are shown on the right. Each sliders controls one of
 * the alignment properties of the corresponding label.
 * If the layout is X or Y oriented determines the property
 * to control.
 * <p>
 * As the sliders are moved, the label panel is revalidated
 * to show the new layout.
 *
 * @author Mike Foley
 **/
public class BoxLayoutTest extends JPanel
    implements ChangeListener {

    /**
     * If true, the layout is horizontal, if false, vertical.
     **/
    private boolean horizontal;

    /**
     * The sliders that control the alignment property.
     **/
    protected JSlider slider1;
    protected JSlider slider2;
    protected JSlider slider3;

    /**
     * The label's who's alignment property is being set.
     **/
    protected JLabel label1;
    protected JLabel label2;
    protected JLabel label3;

    protected JPanel labelPanel;


    /**
     * Create the component is the display.
     * Use a BoxLayout to arrange the nested panels.
```

```
 * This class acts as a mediator between the sliders
 * and the labels.
 **/
public BoxLayoutTest( boolean horizontal ) {

    this.horizontal = horizontal;

    BoxLayout boxLayout = new BoxLayout( this, BoxLayout.X_AXIS );
    setLayout( boxLayout );

    labelPanel = createLabelPanel();
    labelPanel.setBorder( BorderFactory.createLoweredBevelBorder() );
    add( new JScrollPane( labelPanel ) );

    add( Box.createGlue() );

    JPanel sliders = createSliderPanel();
    add( sliders );
}


/**
 * Create the labels used in this demo.
 **/
protected JPanel createLabelPanel() {

    JPanel panel = new JPanel();
    BoxLayout boxLayout;
    if( isHorizontal() )
        boxLayout = new BoxLayout( panel, BoxLayout.X_AXIS );
    else
        boxLayout = new BoxLayout( panel, BoxLayout.Y_AXIS );
    panel.setLayout( boxLayout );

    label1 = new JLabel( "Label 1" );
    label1.setOpaque( true );
    label1.setBackground( Color.yellow );
    panel.add( label1 );

    label2 = new JLabel( "Label 2" );
    label2.setOpaque( true );
    label2.setBackground( Color.blue );
    panel.add( label2 );

    label3 = new JLabel( "Label 3" );
    label3.setOpaque( true );
    label3.setBackground( Color.green );
    panel.add( label3 );

    return( panel );
}
```

13

**JPanel AND Box
CLASSES**

continues

LISTING 13.2   CONTINUED

```java
/**
 * @return True if the alignment is horizontal.
 **/
public boolean isHorizontal() {
    return( horizontal );
}


/**
 * Create the sliders.
 * Each slider contains the range from 0-100 that
 * will be mapped to 0 - 1.0 for the label alignment.
 * <p>
 * This method assumes the labels are already created.
 * Set the slider background to match the label's background
 * that the slider adjust.
 **/
protected JPanel createSliderPanel() {
    JPanel panel = new JPanel();
    BoxLayout boxLayout = new BoxLayout( panel, BoxLayout.Y_AXIS );
    panel.setLayout( boxLayout );

    slider1 = new JSlider();
    slider1.setPaintLabels( true );
    slider1.setPaintTicks( true );
    slider1.setMajorTickSpacing( 20 );
    slider1.setMinorTickSpacing( 5 );
    slider1.setBackground( Color.yellow );
    if( isHorizontal() )
        slider1.setValue( ( int )( label1.getAlignmentY() * 100 ) );
    else
        slider1.setValue( ( int )( label1.getAlignmentX() * 100 ) );
    panel.add( slider1 );
    slider1.addChangeListener( this );

    slider2 = new JSlider();
    slider2.setPaintLabels( true );
    slider2.setPaintTicks( true );
    slider2.setMajorTickSpacing( 20 );
    slider2.setMinorTickSpacing( 5 );
    slider2.setBackground( Color.blue );
    slider2.setForeground( Color.white );
    if( isHorizontal() )
        slider2.setValue( ( int )( label1.getAlignmentY() * 100 ) );
    else
        slider2.setValue( ( int )( label1.getAlignmentX() * 100 ) );
    panel.add( slider2 );
    slider2.addChangeListener( this );

    slider3 = new JSlider();
    slider3.setPaintLabels( true );
```

```
        slider3.setPaintTicks( true );
        slider3.setMajorTickSpacing( 20 );
        slider3.setMinorTickSpacing( 5 );
        slider3.setBackground( Color.green );
        if( isHorizontal() )
            slider3.setValue( ( int )( label1.getAlignmentY() * 100 ) );
        else
            slider3.setValue( ( int )( label1.getAlignmentX() * 100 ) );
        panel.add( slider3 );
        slider3.addChangeListener( this );

        return( panel );
    }


    /**
     * One of the sliders has changed. See which
     * one and update the alignment property of
     * the corresponding label.
     **/
    public void stateChanged( ChangeEvent e ) {
        Object source = e.getSource();
        if( source == slider1 ) {
            int value = slider1.getValue();
            if( isHorizontal() )
                label1.setAlignmentY( ( float )value / ( float )100.0 );
            else
                label1.setAlignmentX( ( float )value / ( float )100.0 );
        } else if( source == slider2 ) {
            int value = slider2.getValue();
            if( isHorizontal() )
                label2.setAlignmentY( ( float )value / ( float )100.0 );
            else
                label2.setAlignmentX( ( float )value / ( float )100.0 );
        } else if( source == slider3 ) {
            int value = slider3.getValue();
            if( isHorizontal() )
                label3.setAlignmentY( ( float )value / ( float )100.0 );
            else
                label3.setAlignmentX( ( float )value / ( float )100.0 );
        }

        //
        // Force the label panel to layout the labels.
        //
        labelPanel.revalidate();
    }


    /**
     * Application entry point.
```

continues

LISTING 13.2   CONTINUED

```
 * Create the panels and display them.
 * <p>
 * The application takes a single parameter,
 * horizontal. If this is not specified, or no
 * parameter is specified, vertical alignment
 * is used. If more parameters are specified, they
 * are ignored.
 * <p>
 * @param args vertical for vertical alignment.
 **/
public static void main( String args[] ) {

    boolean horizontal = false;

    //
    // Parse the single possible parameter.
    //
    if( 0 < args.length ) {
        String param = args[0].toUpperCase();
        if( param.equals( "HORIZONTAL" ) )
            horizontal = true;
    }

    JFrame frame = new ApplicationFrame( " BoxLayoutTest" );

    JPanel panel = new BoxLayoutTest( horizontal );
    panel.setBorder( BorderFactory.createLoweredBevelBorder() );

    frame.getContentPane().add( panel, BorderLayout.CENTER );
    frame.pack();
    frame.setVisible( true );

} // main

} // BoxLayoutTest
```

Invisible Components

The BoxLayout layout manager class places components next to each other in the container being managed. This often causes the container to appear cramped. This is shown in Figure 13.3, where the labels are placed right on top of each other. An empty border could be set on the labels to space the container, or invisible components could be added to the container. The Box class contains static methods that return invisible components, which can be used to help arrange the components in a container. Three types of invisible components are available: rigid, glue, and strut. However, JavaSoft is discouraging the use of struts with the BoxLayout layout manager. From the JavaSoft documentation:

The Box class provides another kind of filler for putting fixed space between components: a vertical or horizontal strut. Unfortunately, struts have unlimited maximum heights and widths (for horizontal and vertical struts, respectively). This means that if you use a horizontal box within a vertical box, the horizontal box can sometimes become too tall. For this reason, we recommend that you use rigid areas instead of struts.

The following two sections give example usage of the rigid and glue invisible components. The strut component is not discussed here. The methods that create these components are static, so they can be used to add invisible components to any container, not just instances of the Box class.

rigid **Components**

A rigid component takes up a defined amount of space and is not resizable. The static createRigidArea method in the Box class takes a Dimension parameter and returns an AWT component the size of the given dimension. Space can be added between the labels from the example application, shown in Figure 13.3, by adding rigid components to the container. The following change to the code, which creates the labels and adds them to the container, demonstrates this technique:

```
//
// Add three labels to the outer panel.
// Give each label a different background color
// and make it opaque to see the color.
//
// Use rigid areas to add some space between the labels.
//
panel.add( Box.createRigidArea( new Dimension( 1, 4 ) ) );

JLabel label = new JLabel( "Label 1" );
label.setOpaque( true );
label.setBackground( Color.yellow );
panel.add( label );

panel.add( Box.createRigidArea( new Dimension( 1, 4 ) ) );

label = new JLabel( "Label 2" );
label.setOpaque( true );
label.setBackground( Color.blue );
panel.add( label );

panel.add( Box.createRigidArea( new Dimension( 1, 4 ) ) );

label = new JLabel( "Label 3" );
label.setOpaque( true );
label.setBackground( Color.green );
panel.add( label );

panel.add( Box.createRigidArea( new Dimension( 1, 4 ) ) );
```

13

**JPanel AND Box
CLASSES**

The resulting container is shown in Figure 13.5.

FIGURE 13.5

`rigid` *components added to a* `BoxLayout`.

glue Components

The example in the previous section used `rigid` components to add space between the labels in the container. This added a fixed area between the labels that did not change. If the container is resized, this may not produce the desired results. For example, Figure 13.6 shows the previous example after it has been expanded. All the extra space from the layout is added to the bottom of the container, and the labels remain fixed at the top of the container.

FIGURE 13.6

Expanded `rigid` *components in the* `BoxLayout` *example.*

An invisible `glue` component will stretch to any size required by the layout manager. In the previous example, if the labels were to remain vertically centered in the container, the first and last `rigid` components could be changed to `glue`. However, a `glue` component's preferred dimensions are zero width and height. Replacing the `rigid` component would remove the space on top of the first label and below the bottom label. This is shown in Figure 13.7. If the initial space above and below the labels is desired, the `glue` can be added along with the `rigid` components. When the container is resized, the labels remain centered in the container. This code is shown below, and the resulting container is shown in Figure 13.8.

FIGURE 13.7

`glue` *augmenting top and bottom* `rigid` *components in a* `BoxLayout`.

FIGURE 13.8

Top and bottom
glue *components*
in addition to
rigid *components*
in a BoxLayout.

```
panel.add( Box.createGlue() );
panel.add( Box.createRigidArea( new Dimension( 1, 4 ) ) );

JLabel label = new JLabel( "Label 1" );
label.setOpaque( true );
label.setBackground( Color.yellow );
panel.add( label );

panel.add( Box.createRigidArea( new Dimension( 1, 4 ) ) );

label = new JLabel( "Label 2" );
label.setOpaque( true );
label.setBackground( Color.blue );
panel.add( label );

panel.add( Box.createRigidArea( new Dimension( 1, 4 ) ) );

label = new JLabel( "Label 3" );
label.setOpaque( true );
label.setBackground( Color.green );
panel.add( label );

panel.add( Box.createRigidArea( new Dimension( 1, 4 ) ) );
panel.add( Box.createGlue() );
```

A glue component could be placed between each label. This would force the BoxLayout
layout manager to evenly distribute extra space between each label in the container. This
code is shown below, and the resulting container is shown in Figure 13.9, both before
and after resizing the frame. As shown in the figure, the rigid components add spacing
to the initial layout, and the glue components force the layout manager to evenly distribute the labels when the panel is larger than its preferred size.

13

JPanel AND Box
CLASSES

FIGURE 13.9

glue *components
in addition to*
rigid *components
in a* BoxLayout.

```
panel.add( Box.createGlue() );
panel.add( Box.createRigidArea( new Dimension( 1, 4 ) ) );

JLabel label = new JLabel( "Label 1" );
label.setOpaque( true );
label.setBackground( Color.yellow );
panel.add( label );

panel.add( Box.createRigidArea( new Dimension( 1, 4 ) ) );
panel.add( Box.createGlue() );

label = new JLabel( "Label 2" );
label.setOpaque( true );
label.setBackground( Color.blue );
panel.add( label );

panel.add( Box.createRigidArea( new Dimension( 1, 4 ) ) );
panel.add( Box.createGlue() );

label = new JLabel( "Label 3" );
label.setOpaque( true );
label.setBackground( Color.green );
panel.add( label );

panel.add( Box.createRigidArea( new Dimension( 1, 4 ) ) );
panel.add( Box.createGlue() );
```

The methods `createVerticalGlue` and `createHorizontalGlue` in the `Box` class create invisible `glue` components that only expand in one direction.

Static Configuration Methods

The Box class contains two static methods that return a Box configured with a BoxLayout along the implied axis. These methods, createHorizontalBox and createVerticalBox, configure the BoxLayout layout manager along the x-axis and y-axis, respectively. Using one of these methods eliminates the need to call the Box constructor with the axis parameter.

The JBox Class

In the previous section, the Box class was presented. It was pointed out that the Box class doesn't extend the JComponent class. As such, it does not inherit the properties or functionality of that class. You also saw how the BoxLayout class provides simple layout management that is sufficient for many containers. Creating your own JBox class can eliminate the shortcomings of the Box class.

The JBox class shown in Listing 13.3 is a replacement for the Box class, which is a descendant of the JComponent class. Because the methods that create invisible components in the Box class are static, they can be used to create invisible components for the JBox class:

LISTING 13.3   THE JBox CLASS

```
package com.foley.utility;

import javax.swing.*;


/**
 * The JBox class is a Box replacement that
 * is a descendent of the JComponent class.
 * It is a JPanel configured with a BoxLayout
 * layout manager.
 * <p>
 * @author Mike Foley
 **/
public class JBox extends JPanel {

    public JBox( int orientation ) {
        BoxLayout boxLayout = new BoxLayout( this, orientation );
        setLayout( boxLayout );
    }

    /**
```

continues

LISTING 13.3   CONTINUED

```
   * Create a JBox configured along its X-axis.
   * <p>
   * @return A JBox configured along its X-axis.
   **/
  public static JBox createHorizontalJBox() {
      return new JBox( BoxLayout.X_AXIS );
  }


  /**
   * Create a JBox configured along its Y-axis.
   * <p>
   * @return A JBox configured along its Y-axis.
   **/
  public static JBox createVerticalJBox() {
      return new JBox( BoxLayout.X_AXIS );
  }

} // JBox
```

Using the JBox Class

The JBox class is an API-compatible replacement for the Box class contained in the JFC. The static, invisible component-creation methods are not duplicated in the JBox class. These methods are static in the Box class, so they can be used with the JBox class, or any other class for that matter. The primary reason for using the JBox class instead of the Box class is to enable the functionality inherited from the JComponent class. For example, a border can be set on a JBox instance, but not on a Box instance.

Listing 13.4 presents the JBoxTest application, which replaces the JPanel instance configured with a BoxLayout layout manager from the previous section with a JBox instance. The static createVerticalJBox method in the JBox class is used to create a box configured with a BoxLayout instance aligned along its vertical axis. Notice how a border is added to the JBox instance itself in the next line. Keystroke management, as shown in Chapter 3, "HTML Tools," could also be added to the JBox instance. The resulting application looks and behaves identically to that shown in Figure 13.9.

LISTING 13.4   THE JBoxTest APPLICATION

```
package com.foley.test;

import java.awt.*;

import javax.swing.*;
```

```java
import com.foley.utility.*;


/**
 * An application that displays a JBox panel.
 * Three labels are added to the panel. They are
 * separated with rigid areas and glue. This spaces
 * the labels in the preferred size of the panel,
 * and evenly spaces the labels in larger sizes.
 * <p>
 * @author Mike Foley
 **/
public class JBoxTest extends Object {

    /**
     * Application entry point.
     * Create the JBox and labels. Add the labels
     * to the jBox, and space them using glue
     * and rigid invisible components.
     * <p>
     * @param args Command line parameter. Not used.
     **/
    public static void main( String args[] ) {

        JFrame frame = new ApplicationFrame( "JBoxTest" );

        JPanel panel = JBox.createVerticalJBox();
        panel.setBorder( BorderFactory.createLoweredBevelBorder() );

        panel.add( Box.createGlue() );
        panel.add( Box.createRigidArea( new Dimension( 1, 4 ) ) );

        JLabel label = new JLabel( "Label 1" );
        label.setOpaque( true );
        label.setBackground( Color.yellow );
        panel.add( label );

        panel.add( Box.createRigidArea( new Dimension( 1, 4 ) ) );
        panel.add( Box.createGlue() );

        label = new JLabel( "Label 2" );
        label.setOpaque( true );
        label.setBackground( Color.blue );
        panel.add( label );

        panel.add( Box.createRigidArea( new Dimension( 1, 4 ) ) );
        panel.add( Box.createGlue() );

        label = new JLabel( "Label 3" );
        label.setOpaque( true );
        label.setBackground( Color.green );
```

continues

LISTING 13.4 CONTINUED

```
        panel.add( label );

        panel.add( Box.createRigidArea( new Dimension( 1, 4 ) ) );
        panel.add( Box.createGlue() );

        frame.getContentPane().add( panel, BorderLayout.CENTER );
        frame.pack();
        frame.setVisible( true );

    } // main

} // JBoxTest
```

Summary

This chapter presented JPanel and Box, two relatively simple container classes contained in the JFC. The JPanel class provides a lightweight container that can be instantiated. It inherits the majority of its functionality from the JComponent class and contains very little additional code.

The Box class is an unusual JFC visual component in that it doesn't inherit from the JComponent class. It's a lightweight extension of the AWT Container class that comes configured with a BoxLayout layout manager. This layout manager is new to the JFC. Its options and usage were also presented in this chapter. (The BoxLayout class can be used with any container, not just the Box class.)

The Box class contains static methods to create invisible components that can add space in a container. Although these methods were presented in containers managed by a BoxLayout layout manager, they can be added to any container. The rigid component is of a fixed size that does not change. A glue component has a zero preferred size, but it can be expanded in one or both directions to fill the component, as required by the layout manager.

The JBox class was created to fill the void of the Box class. It is a descendant of the JComponent class, so it inherits the features contained in that class. This class is more consistent with other JFC visual components than the Box class.

JTabbedPane Class

In This Chapter

The JTabbedPane class provides a visual component that allows multiple panels to be viewed one at a time in a single area. Tabs are provided to change from panel to panel in the main view. Tabbed panels are often used in configuration dialog boxes. Related options are placed on the same panel. The tabs on the tabbed panel represent the complete set of options available for configuration. This allows a great deal of information to be presented to the user in a relatively small amount of screen real estate. Using tabs to switch from panel to panel utilizes the screen space efficiently.

In this chapter you will learn how to

- Create and configure JTabbedPane class instances
- Add and remove panels from instances of the JTabbedPane class
- Dynamically alter the component and tab's title and icon
- Programmatically alter the panel displayed in the tabbed pane

JTabbedPane Class Usage

The JTabbedPane class is a container that allows multiple components to be added but only displays one component at a time. Tabs are located on one of the sides of the displayed component that allow the user to choose which component is currently visible in the center of the tabbed pane.

Creating an instance of the JTabbedPane class is a simple matter. The class contains two constructors: an empty constructor and one that takes a single parameter which specifies where the tabs are located on the panel. You can position the tabs on any side of the tabbed pane. The parameters to define the placement, defined in the SwingConstants class, are TOP, BOTTOM, RIGHT, and LEFT. The JTabbedPaneTest application shown in Listing 14.1 creates a tabbed pane with the tabs on the bottom and displays it in a frame. When using the default constructor, the tabs are placed on the top of the tabbed pane.

Tab placement is a bound property that can be changed after creation. The setTabPlacement method sets the property and invalidates the tabbed panel. The property name is tabPlacement. See Table 14.1 for a complete list of bound properties defined in the JTabbedPane class. You can query the current value of the property by using the provided getTabPlacement method. The number of tabs in a tabbed pane can be queried with the getTabCount method, and the number of rows required to display the tabs can be queried with the getTabRunCount method.

LISTING 14.1 JTabbedPaneTest APPLICATION

```
package com.foley.test;

import java.awt.*;
```

```java
import javax.swing.*;

import com.foley.utility.ApplicationFrame;


/**
 * An application that displays a JTabbedPane in a frame.
 *
 * @author Mike Foley
 **/
public class JTabbedPaneTest extends Object {

    /**
     * Application entry point.
     * Create the frame, and display a tabbed pane in it.
     *
     * @param args Command line parameter. Not used.
     **/
    public static void main( String args[] ) {

        JFrame frame = new ApplicationFrame( "JTabbedPaneTest" );

        JTabbedPane tabbedPane = new JTabbedPane( SwingConstants.BOTTOM );
        tabbedPane.setBorder( BorderFactory.createLoweredBevelBorder() );

        frame.getContentPane().add( tabbedPane, BorderLayout.CENTER );
        frame.pack();
        frame.setVisible( true );

    } // main

} // JtabbedPaneTest
```

TABLE 14.1 NEW BOUND PROPERTIES IN THE JTabbedPane CLASS

Property Name	Setter Method	Getter Method
model	setModel	getModel
tabPlacement	setTabPlacement	getTabPlacement

Adding Components to the JTabbedPane Instance

The frame created by the JTabbedPaneTest application is shown in Figure 14.1. In the figure, you see that an empty tabbed pane is not very interesting. Components must be added to the tabbed pane for the tabs to display. The original API for the JTabbedPane class contained many versions of the addTab and insertTab methods for adding components to the tabbed pane. However, these method names do not follow the JavaBeans standard naming convention for adding components to a container. This caused visual design tools difficulty, because the JTabbedPane class had to be handled with special code. To address this issue, a set of overloaded add methods were added to the JTabbedPane class that map to the appropriate addTab or insertTab method. The add method appends the given component to the existing set of components in the tabbed panel. Using the add method, the tabs will be displayed in the order the components are added to the tabbed pane. When a component is added by using the insertTab method, its placement can be specified. These methods are consistent to the methods you saw in earlier chapters for adding menu items to menus and items to a toolbar.

FIGURE 14.1

The
JTabbedPaneTest
application.

Use the following code to add a component to a tabbed pane:

```
tabbedPane.add( new JLabel( "Tab 1" ) );
```

This version of the add method uses the name of the component for the tab's label in the tabbed pane. It is often desirable to specify the text for the tab's label when adding the component to the tabbed pane. Due to a quirk in the various add method implementations, both of the following lines perform this task:

```
tabbedPane.add( "Tab 1", new JLabel( "Tab 1" ) );
tabbedPane.add( new JLabel( "Tab 2" ), "Tab 2" );
```

This seemingly contradictory code is because the version of the add method that takes an Object constraint as its second parameter tests to see if the Object is an instance of the String class. If so, the add method calls the addTab method with the String constraint used as the tab's name. There is also an add method that takes the position of where the new tab is located. To add the new tab at the start of the tabs, the following line of code can be used. This version of the add method calls the insert method with the specified index.

```
tabbedPane.add( new JLabel( "Tab 3" ), "Tab 3 ", 0 );
```

As was mentioned earlier, each version of the add method calls either the addTab or insertTab method contained in the JTabbedPane class. In fact, each variant of the addTab method calls the insertTab method. The signatures for these methods are shown next. Looking at the signature, you see that an Icon can be added to the tab for a component. The tab can contain an Icon, a String, or both. Also, the ToolTip for a tab can be specified when adding a component to the tabbed pane. However, there is no convenient method to alter the ToolTip after the component has been added to the tabbed pane.

```
addTab( String title, Icon icon, Component component, String tip )
addTab( String title, Icon icon, Component component )
addTab( String title, Component component )
insertTab( String title, Icon icon, Component component,
➥ String tip, int index )
```

Adding Tabs to the JTabbedPaneTest Application

You can use any or all of the previously shown methods to add tabs to the JTabbedPaneTest application. If the following lines of code are added after the tabbed pane is created, the window shown in Figure 14.2 will be created:

```
//
// add some tabs to the tabbed pane instance.
//
tabbedPane.add( new JLabel( "Tab 1" ) );
tabbedPane.add( new JLabel( "Tab 2" ), "Tab 2" );
tabbedPane.add( new JLabel( "Tab 3" ), "Tab 3 ", 0 );
tabbedPane.addTab( "Tab 4", new ImageIcon( "red.gif" ),
                   new JLabel( "Tab 4" ), "This is the tip" );
```

FIGURE 14.2

Tabs added to the
JTabbedPaneTest
application.

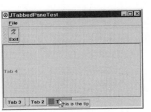

With the exception of the tab labeled Tab 3, the order of the tabs in Figure 14.2 are the order in which they were added to the tabbed pane. The version of the add method used for this tab specified an index of 0 placing that tab first in the tabbed panel. The last tab is the only tab for which a ToolTip and an icon have been specified.

Removing Components from the JTabbedPane Instance

After adding components to an instance of the JTabbedPane class, it may become necessary to remove one or more of the components. The removeTabAt method removes the tab at the given index from the tabbed pane. Indexes in the tabbed pane are zero-based with a range from 0 to one less than the integer returned from the getTabCount method. This method requires that the numerical index of the component be removed. If you have a reference to the component to be removed, the remove method can be called. This method takes the component as its parameter.

You can clear the tabbed pane by calling the removeAll method. This method will clear the tabbed pane and leave it in the same state it was after being created.

Altering Existing Components

Existing components or tabs in a tabbed pane can be altered. To facilitate finding the index of a component, the indexOfComponent method is provided. Similarly, the indexOfTab method determines the index of a tab in the tabbed pane. These methods search the tabbed pane to determine the index of the given component, tag text, or icon. By using these methods, the application does not need to store the index of components or tabs in the tabbed pane. These methods are also useful to determine the index where a new component should be added.

You can replace the tab at a given index with the setComponentAt method. This method takes the index of the component to be replaced and the component. The text or icon on the tab for the given index is not changed. Passing a negative index, or an index greater than the number of tabs in the view, will cause an ArrayIndexOutOfBoundsException to be thrown. You can query the component at the given index by using the getComponentAt method. The text or icon on an existing tab can be updated with the setTitleAt and setIconAt methods respectively. The current value for these properties can be queried with the getTitleAt and getIconAt methods. Once again, specifying an out of bounds index will cause an ArrayIndexOutOfBoundsException to be thrown.

The setForegroundAt and setBackgroundAt methods set the foreground and background colors of the tabs at the given index. Note that these methods alter the colors in the tab but not the component itself. Thus, if you add the following lines of code to the JTabbedPaneTest application, the tabbed pane will look as shown in Figure 14.3. Notice that Tab 2 is selected in the figure.

```
tabbedPane.setForegroundAt( 0, Color.red );
tabbedPane.setForegroundAt( 1, Color.yellow );
tabbedPane.setBackgroundAt( 0, Color.yellow );
tabbedPane.setBackgroundAt( 1, Color.red );
```

FIGURE 14.3

Colored tabs
in the
JTabbedPaneTest
application.

You can query the bounds of a tab with the getBoundsAt method. This method returns a Rectangle containing the size of the tab at the given index. Once again, the size is of the tab itself, not the component in the tabbed pane.

A tab can be enabled and disabled in the tabbed pane. The setEnableAt method changes the enabled state of a tab, and the isEnabledAt method queries the current state of this property. The setDisabledIconAt method sets an icon for a disable tab. If a disabled icon has not been set and the tab contains an icon, a disabled icon is created by using the GrayFilter class as shown in Chapter 5, "Basic Components." The currently defined disabled icon for a tab can be queried with the getDisabledIconAt method.

Displaying Components

The JTabbedPane class employs a SingleSelectionModel instance to track which component is currently displayed in the container. The SingleSelectionModel interface, shown in Listing 14.2, defines a selection model that allows only one item to be selected at a given time. It contains methods for setting and querying the selected index, as well as clearing the selection. A ChangeListener can be added to the model to receive notifications when the selection changes. The ChangeListener interface and its associated ChangeEvent class are discussed in Chapter 6, "The Button Hierarchy."

It is interesting to note that the comment before the clearSlection method states that clearing the selection will set the selected value to -1. This is an implementation detail that should not be assumed by the user of the model. The DefaultSingleSelectionModel class in the JFC does exhibit this behavior, but other implementations of the model may not. The isSelected method is provided to determine if there is currently a selected index in the model. A ChangeListener can be added directly to the tabbed pane itself instead of with the model. The JTabbedPane class listens to the SingleSelectionModel and forwards change messages to all ChangeListeners registered with the JTabbedPane instance.

14

JTabbedPane
CLASS

LISTING 14.2 THE SingleSelectionModel INTERFACE

```
public interface SingleSelectionModel {
    /**
     * @return  the model's selection, or -1 if there is no selection.
     * @see      #setSelectedIndex
     */
    public int getSelectedIndex();

    /**
     * Sets the model's selected index to <I>index</I>.
     *
     * Notifies any listeners if the model changes
     *
     * @see    #getSelectedIndex
     * @see    #addChangeListener
     */
    public void setSelectedIndex(int index);

    /**
     * Clears the selection (to -1).
     */
    public void clearSelection();

    /**
     * Returns true if the selection model currently has a selected value
     */
    public boolean isSelected();

    /**
     * Adds <I>listener</I> as a listener to changes in the model.
     */
    void addChangeListener(ChangeListener listener);

    /**
     * Removes <I>listener</I> as a listener to changes in the model.
     */
    void removeChangeListener(ChangeListener listener);
}
```

You can set the current SingleSelectionModel for the tabbed pane with the setModel method, and query it with the getModel method. Changing the selected index will cause listeners to be notified of the change. The JTabbedPane class contains the setSelectedIndex and getSelectedIndex convenience methods for setting and querying the selected index in the model. These methods simply call the equivalent methods on the current model. The getSelectedComponent method can be used to query the selected component. This method returns null if there is not a selected component. Similarly, you can set the displayed component by using the setSelectedComponent method.

A Complete JTabbedPane Sample Application

Listing 14.3 shows the DynamicTabbedPaneTest application that allows tabs to be dynamically added and removed from the test tabbed pane. The application consists of two view areas: the tabbed pane to the left and the control panel to the right. Upon application initialization, three tabs are added to the tabbed pane. After that, clicking the Add Tab button will add a new tab to the tabbed pane. Clicking the Remove Selected button will remove the selected tab from the tabbed pane. The Select None button will clear the selection in the tabbed pane when chosen. The final component in the control panel displays the selected tab in the tabbed pane. Notice that the selected tab is counted from 0.

Each tab contains a JLabel instance and a JTextField instance. The label displays the number of the tab. Tabs are numbered sequentially from the start of the application beginning with zero. The JTextField instance contains the text of the tab's title. This text can be edited, and will update the tab's title to the string entered in the text field when the enter key is typed in the text field. The initial title for the tab is its number.

The DynamicTabbedPaneTest application is shown in Figure 14.4 after some tabs have been added and removed. The titles of some of the tabs have also been edited. In this example, the location of the tabs is not explicitly set, so the tabs are placed on top of the components, in their default locations.

LISTING 14.3   THE DynamicTabbedPaneTest APPLICATION

```java
package com.foley.test;

import java.awt.*;
import java.awt.event.*;

import javax.swing.*;
import javax.swing.event.*;

import com.foley.utility.JBox;
import com.foley.utility.ApplicationFrame;


/**
 * An application that displays a JTabbedPane in a frame.
 * New tabs may be added to the tab by pressing a button.
 * The title of a tab may be updated by hitting enter in the
 * textField contained in the tab.
 *
 * @author Mike Foley
 **/
public class DynamicTabbedPaneTest extends Object {
```

continues

14

JTabbedPane
CLASS

LISTING 14.3   CONTINUED

```java
private JBox jBox;
private JTabbedPane tabbedPane;
private JLabel selectedLabel;

private int addedTabCount;


/**
 * Create the panel for the test application.
 * This panel contains a JTabbedPane to the left,
 * and some configuration controls to the right.
 **/
public DynamicTabbedPaneTest() {

    //
    // No tabs have been added yet.
    //
    addedTabCount = 0;

    tabbedPane = createTabbedPane();
    tabbedPane.setBorder( BorderFactory.createLoweredBevelBorder()  );

    jBox = JBox.createHorizontalJBox();
    jBox.add( tabbedPane );

    jBox.add( Box.createRigidArea( new Dimension( 10, 10 ) ) );

    JPanel controlPanel = createControlPanel();
    jBox.add( controlPanel );
}


/**
 * Create the tabbed pane used in the application.
 * Add a few interesting tabs.
 * <p>
 * @return The tab pane instance for this application.
 **/
protected JTabbedPane createTabbedPane() {
    JTabbedPane tabbedPane = new JTabbedPane();

    addTab( tabbedPane );
    addTab( tabbedPane );
    addTab( tabbedPane );

    tabbedPane.setForegroundAt( 0, Color.red );
    tabbedPane.setBackgroundAt( 0, Color.yellow );
    tabbedPane.setForegroundAt( 1, Color.yellow );
    tabbedPane.setBackgroundAt( 1, Color.red );
```

```
        return( tabbedPane );
}


/**
 * Create the controls for adding and removing tabs.
 * <p>
 * @return The control panel.
 **/
protected JPanel createControlPanel() {
    JPanel controlPanel = new JPanel();
    BoxLayout boxLayout = new BoxLayout( controlPanel,
                                         BoxLayout.Y_AXIS );

    controlPanel.setLayout( boxLayout );

    JButton addButton = new JButton( "add tab" );
    controlPanel.add( addButton );
    controlPanel.add( Box.createRigidArea( new Dimension(10,10) ) );
    addButton.addActionListener( new ActionListener() {
        public void actionPerformed( ActionEvent event ) {
            addTab( tabbedPane );
            getCenter().repaint();
        }
    } );

    JButton removeButton = new JButton( "remove selected" );
    controlPanel.add( removeButton );
    controlPanel.add( Box.createRigidArea( new Dimension(10,10) ) );
    removeButton.addActionListener( new ActionListener() {
        public void actionPerformed( ActionEvent event ) {
            removeSelectedTab();
        }
    } );

    JButton noneButton = new JButton( "select none" );
    controlPanel.add( noneButton );
    controlPanel.add( Box.createRigidArea( new Dimension(10,10) ) );
    noneButton.addActionListener( new ActionListener() {
        public void actionPerformed( ActionEvent event ) {
            tabbedPane.getModel().clearSelection();
        }
    } );

    selectedLabel = new JLabel();
    setSelectedLabel();
    controlPanel.add( selectedLabel );
    controlPanel.add( Box.createRigidArea( new Dimension(10,10) ) );
    tabbedPane.addChangeListener( new ChangeListener() {
        public void stateChanged( ChangeEvent event ) {
```

14

JTabbedPane
CLASS

continues

LISTING 14.3 CONTINUED

```
                        setSelectedLabel();
                }
        } );
        return( controlPanel );
    }


    /**
     * Update the text on the selectedLabel to the currently
     * selected tab in the tabbedPane.
     **/
    private void setSelectedLabel() {
        if( tabbedPane.getModel().isSelected() )
            selectedLabel.setText( "Selected Index: " +
                                    tabbedPane.getSelectedIndex() );
        else
            selectedLabel.setText( "None Selected" );
    }


    /**
     * Create a JLabel and add it to the tabbed pane.
     * The text of the label matches the tab's text, and
     * is simply the number of tabs created during this
     * run of the application.
     * <p>
     * @return The index of the newly added tab.
     **/
    private int addTab( final JTabbedPane tabbedPane ) {
        String name = "Tab " + addedTabCount;
        final JPanel panel = new JPanel();
        panel.setLayout( new BorderLayout() );

        panel.add( new JLabel( name ), BorderLayout.NORTH );
        final JTextField textField = new JTextField( name );
        textField.addActionListener( new ActionListener() {
            public void actionPerformed( ActionEvent event ) {
                //
                // Update the title of our tab to that entered.
                //
                String newTitle = textField.getText();
                int index = tabbedPane.indexOfComponent( panel );
                tabbedPane.setTitleAt( index, newTitle );
                //
                // validate and paint the tabs to display properly.
                //
                tabbedPane.revalidate();
                tabbedPane.repaint();
            }
```

```
        } );

        panel.add( textField, BorderLayout.SOUTH );

        tabbedPane.add( panel, name );
        tabbedPane.revalidate();

        //
        // Bump the number of tabs added.
        //
        addedTabCount += 1;

        return( tabbedPane.getTabCount() - 1 );
    }


    /**
     * Remove the currently selected tab from the tabbed pane.
     **/
    private void removeSelectedTab() {
        if( tabbedPane.getModel().isSelected() ) {
            int selectedIndex = tabbedPane.getSelectedIndex();
            tabbedPane.removeTabAt( selectedIndex );
            tabbedPane.revalidate();
            getCenter().repaint();
        }
    }


    /**
     * @return The center component in this object.
     **/
    public JComponent getCenter() {
        return( jBox );
    }


    /**
     * Application entry point.
     * Create the frame, and display a tabbed pane in it.
     *
     * @param args Command line parameter. Not used.
     **/
    public static void main( String args[] ) {

        JFrame frame = new ApplicationFrame( "DynamicTabbedPaneTest" );
        JTabbedPaneTest test = new JTabbedPaneTest();

        frame.getContentPane().add( test.getCenter(),
                                    BorderLayout.CENTER );
```

continues

14

JTabbedPane
CLASS

LISTING 14.3   CONTINUED

```
        frame.pack();
        frame.setVisible( true );

    } // main

} // DynamicTabbedPaneTest
```

FIGURE 14.4

The complete
DynamicTabbedPane-
Test *application.*

Summary

The JTabbedPane class provides a container that shows one component in a set of components at a given time. Tabs are provided to allow the user to switch the currently visible component. The tabs can be placed on any side of the component display area. Methods are provided to set the foreground and background colors of the tabs. The component added to the tabbed pane itself controls its colors. The class employs a SingleSelectionModel to track which component is selected. If there is not a component selected, the tabbed pane displays empty.

Methods are provided to dynamically alter the components in the tabbed pane. You can insert a component at any given position or append it to the end of the existing components in the tabbed pane. A component can be removed dynamically from the tabbed pane, or all components can be removed with a single method call. Each of the add and remove types of methods can operate on a given component or index. Methods are also provided to convert from index to component, and vice versa.

Components and tabs already in the tabbed pane can be changed. The component can be replaced, as well as the text and icon in the tab.

To demonstrate the use of the JTabbedPane class, a complete example using many of the methods in the JTabbedPane class was presented. In this application, tabs can be added and removed interactively from the tabbed pane. The title for the tab also can be edited.

Scrolling Components

IN THIS CHAPTER

We have seen the need for scrolling large components earlier in this book when dealing with the JList and JTable classes. Many applications contain data structures or pictures that cannot be displayed completely on the computer's screen. Often this situation is handled by creating a large component displaying the data or picture and allowing the user to scroll the component to see the portion of the component that they want. When creating large lists and tables, we saw how easy it was to enable these components to be scrolled. At that time, however, the scrolling support contained in the JFC was not fully described. These capabilities are described in this chapter.

The JFC provides the JScrollPane class to allow any component to be easily scrolled. The JScrollPane class manages horizontal and vertical scrollbars, column and row header components, corner components, and a viewport. However, all components may not be visible in every scroll pane. The viewport in the scroll pane manages the actual component that is to be scrolled. The horizontal header scrolls right and left as the content scrolls, but not vertically. It is always on top of the data. The column header component behaves similarly, but for columns. It moves up and down with the content but does not move horizontally.

In this chapter, you will learn

- How the JViewport class works
- How the JScrollPane class works
- How to manage the scrollbar policy
- How to add headers to the scroll pane

The JViewport Class

The JViewport class is used by the JScrollPane class to manage the view of the underlying component being displayed in the scroll pane. The JViewport class extends the JComponent class. When a scrollbar contained in the scroll pane is scrolled, it is the viewport that moves. A viewport can be thought of as the viewer on a camcorder. As the camcorder is moved about, different portions of the scenery are visible in the viewer. As the camcorder moves right, additional scenery on the right is visible and scenery to the left is removed from the viewer. A viewport displaying a portion of a large component is shown in Figure 15.1.

The JViewport class contains a single default constructor. The constructor configures the viewport with its layout manager, a ViewportLayout instance by default. However, extensions of the JViewport can change the default layout manager by overriding the createLayoutManager method and returning a different layout manager. Typically,

JViewport instances are not created by user code. Instead, the viewport created by the JScrollPane class is used. This is demonstrated later in this chapter.

Figure 15.1

JViewport instance displaying a portion of a large component.

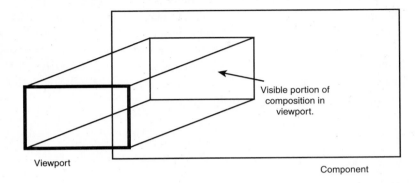

Visible portion of composition in viewport.

Viewport

Component

A JViewport instance manages one child, a descendant of the AWT Component class. The child component can be a container itself and can contain many other components, but the viewport itself has only a single child. The child is set and queried with the setView and getView methods. When the component is set via the setView method, the viewport adds a component listener to the component. If the component is later resized, the viewport notifies listeners that have registered for changes by using the addChangeListener method. A listener is removed with the removeChangeListener method.

A viewport can be configured to create an offscreen image that buffers the visual representation of the visible portion of the child component. This allows the viewport to scroll faster. When the viewport's paint method is called, if the viewport has not been scrolled, the component is drawn to the image that is then copied to the display. If the viewport has been scrolled, the image is moved the appropriate amount and then the exposed portion of the child component is drawn to the image. The complete image is then copied to the display. This allows scrolling to be performed faster by not having to repaint the entire component when a small scroll is performed. The offscreen image is known as a *backing store*. To enable the backing store, true is passed to the setBackingStoreEnabled method. The current state of this attribute can be queried via the isBackingStoreEnabled method.

Whether to use a backing store is a classic tradeoff between time and memory. Using the extra memory for the backing store allows the scrolling to be performed faster. Unfortunately, calling setBackingStoreEnabled with a parameter of false does not free the storage allocated for the backing store image. This means that once the backing store is enabled, the offscreen image will not be garbage collected until the entire viewport is eligible for garbage collection, even though it is no longer used.

When a component is first added to a viewport, its upper-left corner is aligned with the upper-left corner of the viewport. This will not be the case once the component is scrolled. If it is required to determine which portion of the view is visible, the JViewport class provides the getExtentSize and getViewPosition methods to query the size of the visible portion of the component and the position of the component in the upper-left corner of the viewport. The getViewRect method returns an AWT Rectangle instance that combines the information of the previous two calls. These locations as they relate to the underlying component are shown in Figure 15.2. The size of the underlying view can be queried with the getViewSize method. If the viewport does not contain a component, a size of (0,0) is returned. Otherwise the size of the component is returned. If the size has not been explicitly set, the preferred size of the component is returned.

Figure 15.2

JViewport class positioning of a large component.

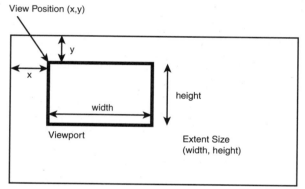

It is also possible to programmatically alter which portion of the underlying component is visible in the viewport. The setViewPosition method defines which point of the component will be located in the upper-left corner of the viewport. The setExtentSize method will define the size of the visible portion of the component. The setViewSize method will set the size of the underlying component. Changing either the view position or the extent size causes the viewport to notify change listeners that a change has occurred. However, the exact nature of the change is not delivered with the change event. The listener must query the viewport for its new state. The view can also be scrolled by using the scrollRectToVisible method. This method ensures that the given rectangle is visible.

ViewportLayout Layout Manager

The default behavior of the JViewport class is to create an instance of the ViewportLayout class to manage its single child component. The ViewportLayout class assumes it is managing a `JViewport` instance, so it is not a general-purpose layout manager. The layout manager can be set to a different layout manager if required. Also, extensions to the `JViewport` class can override the `createLayoutManager` method to return a different class of `LayoutManager` for the viewport.

The `ViewportLayout` layout manager positions components that are smaller than the viewport in the upper-left corner, leaving extra space below or to the right of the component. However, if the origin of the component is displayed and the component is smaller than the viewport in either direction, the component is resized to the size of the viewport in that direction. If both directions are smaller than the viewport, the component will be resized to the viewport's size. If the component implements the `Scrollable` interface and is set to track the viewport's size, the component is sized to the viewport's size.

The `JScrollPane` Class

The JFC class that is typically used for scrolling a component is the `JScrollPane` class. The `JScrollPane` class is an extension of the `JComponent` class and manages a `JViewport` instance, scrollbars, and viewport headings. The `JViewport` class manages the component that is to be scrolled and was described in the previous section. Instances of the `JScrollBar` class, described in Chapter 10, "JList, JComboBox, and Bound Controls," are used for the scrollbars. The heading instances are also of the `JViewport` class. One heading can be specified for the horizontal axis and another for the vertical axis.

The `JScrollPane` class manages a single viewport in the center of its area. The viewport is specified by using the `setViewport` method. Instead of specifying the viewport, the component to be scrolled can be specified by using the `setViewportView` method. In this case, the `JScrollPane` class creates the viewport itself. By default, an instance of the `JViewport` class is used for the viewport. However, extensions to the `JScrollPane` class can override the `createViewport` method to return an extension of the `JViewport` class to be used. The `getViewport` method can be used to query the current viewport in the `JScrollPane` instance. This method will return `null` if there is not a viewport defined in the scroll pane. The viewport is a bound property of the `JScrollPane` class.

Listing 15.1 shows a simple application that displays `JLabel` instances stacked in a box. The version of the `JScrollPane` constructor taking the view component as a parameter is used. The resulting application is shown in Figure 15.3.

LISTING 15.1   THE ScrollPaneTest APPLICATION

```java
package com.foley.test;

import java.awt.*;
import java.awt.event.*;

import javax.swing.*;
import javax.swing.border.*;

import com.foley.utility.ApplicationFrame;
import com.foley.utility.JBox;


/**
 * An application that displays a large component
 * in a JScrollPane.
 *
 * @author Mike Foley
 **/
public class ScrollPaneTest extends Object {

    /**
     * Application entry point.
     * Create a frame, the component, scrollpane and display it.
     *
     * @param args Command line parameter. Not used.
     **/
    public static void main( String args[] ) {

        JFrame frame = new ApplicationFrame( "ScrollPane Test" );

        Font ourFont = new Font( "Helvitica", Font.BOLD, 24 );
        JBox box = JBox.createVerticalJBox();

        JLabel label = new JLabel();
        label.setText( "This is a long message that will not" +
                       " fit on may displays. " +
                       "Better scroll it!" );
        label.setFont( ourFont );
        box.add( label );

        label = new JLabel();
        label.setText( "The JBox contains many labels." );
        label.setFont( ourFont );
        box.add( label );

        label = new JLabel();
        label.setText( "Each label is stacked on top of" +
                       " each other in a JBox container." );
        label.setFont( ourFont );
```

```
        box.add( label );

        label = new JLabel();
        label.setText( "It may be too tall as well as too wide." );
        label.setFont( ourFont );
        box.add( label );

        label = new JLabel();
        label.setText( "Better scroll it!" );
        label.setFont( ourFont );
        label.setAutoscrolls( true );
        box.add( label );

        JScrollPane scrollPane = new JScrollPane( box );

        frame.getContentPane().add( scrollPane, BorderLayout.CENTER );

        frame.pack();
        frame.setVisible( true );

    } // main

} // ScrollPaneTest
```

FIGURE 15.3

The
ScrollPaneTest
application.

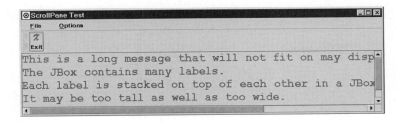

The JScrollPane class overrides the isOpaque method defined in the JComponent class. Recall that this method returns true if the component paints every pixel in its area. The JScrollPane class checks the opaque property of the component being scrolled in its viewport. Only if this property is true, and the component is at least as big as the viewport, does the JScrollPane class return true from the isOpaque method. Thus, the JScrollPane class is only opaque if the component being scrolled is opaque.

The border for a scroll pane can be set by using the standard setBorder method inherited from JComponent. This places a border around the center component as well as any scrollbars, headers, or corners that may be visible. If a border is desired around the viewport only, the setViewportBorder method can be used. This property is a bound property defined for the JScrollPane class. Clients listening for property change events will receive a change of the property name viewportBorder. The current state of this property is queried with the getViewportBorder method. This property, as well as the other bound properties introduced in the JScrollPane class, are presented in Table 15.1.

TABLE 15.1   BOUND PROPERTIES INTRODUCED BY THE JScrollPane CLASS

Property Name	*Setter Method*	*Getter Method*
VerticalScroll BarPolicy	setVerticalScroll BarPolicy	getVerticalScroll BarPolicy
HorizontalScroll BarPolicy	setHorizontalScroll BarPolicy	getHorizontalScroll BarPolicy
viewportBorder	setViewportBorder	getViewportBorder
horizontal\ScrollBar	setHorizontalScrollBar	getHorizontal ScrollBar
verticalScrollBar	setVerticalScrollBar	getVerticalScrollBar
viewport	setViewport	getViewport
rowHeader	setRowHeader	getRowHeader
columnHeader	setColumnHeader	getColumnHeader
LOWER_LEFT_CORNER	setCorner	getCorner
LOWER_RIGHT_CORNER	setCorner	getCorner
UPPER_LEFT_CORNER	setCorner	getCorner
UPPER_RIGHT_CORNER	setCorner	getCorner

The JScrollPane class overrides the isValidateRoot method defined in the JComponent class to return true. This means that child components that call the revalidate method will be validated. This eliminates the need to call invalidate followed immediately by validate, seen in many AWT-based applications. For a full discussion of the revalidate and isValidateRoot methods, see Chapter 3, "JComponent."

ScrollPaneLayout Layout Manager

By default, the JScrollPane class uses an instance of the ScrollPaneLayout class, or one of its descendants, for its layout manager. This class manages the nine potential children of the scroll pane. These are the viewport in the center, the horizontal scrollbar on the bottom, the vertical scrollbar on the right, the column header on the top, the row header on the left, and the four corner components.

The ScrollPaneLayout class sizes the horizontal scrollbar and the column header to their preferred heights and to the width of the scroll pane, less the width of the row header and vertical scrollbar, if either is visible. Similarly, the vertical scrollbar and the row header are sized to their preferred widths and to the height of the scroll pane, less the height of the column header and horizontal scrollbar, if either is visible. The viewport is given the remainder of the scroll pane's size, assuming there is space still available. The corner components are sized to the height and width of their adjacent components if they are visible. For example, the lower-right corner is the height of the horizontal scrollbar and the width of the vertical scrollbar if these components are visible. The corner component is not visible if its adjacent components are not visible. The `ScrollPaneLayout` class will size it to a width and height of zero, making it not visible.

Scrolling Policy

How the `JScrollPane` class displays its scrollbars can be configured. The scrollbars can always be displayed, never displayed, or displayed as required. The "as required" policy will display scrollbars when the center component's size extends beyond the viewport's size and hide them when the component is smaller than this size. The horizontal and vertical scrollbars are hidden and shown independently of each other.

Specifying the scrolling policy for instances of the `JScrollPane` class is done independently for the horizontal and vertical directions. The `setHorizontalScrollBarPolicy` and `setVerticalScrollBarPolicy` methods are used to set the policy for each direction. Both of these methods take a single parameter that is a constant defined in the `ScrollPaneConstants` interface. Allowed values for the `setVerticalScrollBarPolicy` method are `VERTICAL_SCROLLBAR_AS_NEEDED`, `VERTICAL_SCROLLBAR_ALWAYS`, and `VERTICAL_SCROLLBAR_NEVER`. Similarly, for the `setHorizontalScrollBarPolicy` method the defined constants for the scrolling policy are `HORIZONTAL_SCROLLBAR_AS_NEEDED`, `HORIZONTAL_SCROLLBAR_ALWAYS`, and `HORIZONTAL_SCROLLBAR_NEVER`. There are also versions of the `JScrollPane` class's constructor that allow the scrolling policy to be specified. The scrolling policy for each direction can be independently queried by using the `getHorizontalScrollBarPolicy` and getVerticalScrollBarPolicy methods. The default scrolling policy is "as needed" in both directions. The scrolling policy of each direction is a bound property of the `JScrollPane` class.

A handle to each individual scrollbar can be obtained via the `getHorizontalScrollBar` and `getVerticalScrollBar` methods. Once this handle is obtained, the methods in the `JScrollBar` class can be called directly. For example, it is often desirable to set the unit and block increments via the `setUnitIncrement` and `setBlockIncrement` methods defined in the `JScrollBar` class for the scrollbars.

Specifying Row and Column Headings

The methods to set the headings in a scroll pane are named `setRowHeader` and `setColumnHeader`. These names suggest tabular data in the scroll pane, but this does not have to be the case. These methods take an instance of the `JViewport` class and set it as the header in the appropriate direction. When a column header view is set, it scrolls right and left in sync with the main view, but it doesn't scroll up or down. Similarly, a row header view scrolls up and down with the main view, but does not scroll right or left. The current headers can be queried via the `getRowHeader` and `getColumnHeader` methods. Each of these methods returns `null` if a header has not been specified for that axis. Both the `rowHeader` and `columnHeader` properties are bound in the `JScrollPane` class.

As was mentioned in the previous paragraph, the `setRowHeader` and `setColumnHeader` methods require a viewport as their parameter. The `setRowHeaderView` and `setColumnHeaderView` methods allow any component to be specified for the header. These methods will create a viewport if necessary and will set the given component as the view for the viewport. If a column header had been previously specified, it is reused by setting its view property to the component passed as the argument to these methods.

> **NOTE**
>
> Using either of the `setRowHeaderView` or `setColumnHeaderView` methods can cause difficulty when replacing a header. Since the existing viewport is reused, a view header property change event is not fired by the `JScrollPane` class. Since the `JViewport` class does not fire a property change event when its view is changed, there is no way to be informed of this change. This condition is exacerbated by the fact that a property change event is fired if a header has not already been set for the scroll pane. This appears to be a bug rather than a feature.

Header views can be added to the `ScrollPaneTest` application presented earlier in this chapter by adding the following lines of code after the scroll pane has been created. The resulting scroll pane is shown in Figure 15.4.

```
scrollPane.setColumnHeaderView(
            new JLabel( "Column Header", SwingConstants.CENTER )
);scrollPane.setRowHeaderView( new JLabel( "Row Header" ) );
```

Specifying Corner Components

When a `JScrollPane` instance contains headers and scrollbars, there is a gap in the corners of the scroll pane where these components meet. A component can be specified that is placed into each corner with the `setCorner` method. This single method is used to set the component in any of the corners. The first parameter to this method must be one of the corner location constants defined in the `ScrollPaneConstants` interface. The constants are `LOWER_LEFT_CORNER`, `LOWER_RIGHT_CORNER`, `UPPER_LEFT_CORNER`, and `UPPER_RIGHT_CORNER`. Notice that these and the other scrollbar constants are defined in the `ScrollPaneConstants` interface, not the `SwingConstants` interface. The size of the corner component is determined by the available space due to the height and width of the headers and/or scrollbar that the corner is next to. The default scroll pane layout manager ignores the preferred size of the corner component itself. The current component defined for a corner can be queried with the `getCorner` method. The corner being queried is also specified with one of the corner constants defined in the `ScrollPaneConstants` interface. The corner components are bound properties in the `JScrollPane` class.

FIGURE 15.4

*Headers added
to the
ScrollPaneTest
application.*

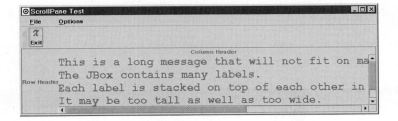

The following lines of code will add corner components to the `ScrollPaneTest` application. Each corner is a different color to make it obvious when each corner is visible. It is instructive to resize the application to display and hide the scrollbars to see when the corners are displayed. Removing one and then the other header and then both headers and executing the application will give all possible cases for corner components being displayed. The resulting scroll pane is shown in Figure 15.5.

```
JLabel lowerLeftCorner = new JLabel();
lowerLeftCorner.setOpaque( true );
lowerLeftCorner.setBackground( Color.blue );
scrollPane.setCorner( ScrollPaneConstants.LOWER_LEFT_CORNER,
                      lowerLeftCorner );

JLabel lowerRightCorner = new JLabel();
lowerRightCorner.setOpaque( true );
lowerRightCorner.setBackground( Color.yellow );
scrollPane.setCorner( ScrollPaneConstants.LOWER_RIGHT_CORNER,
                      lowerRightCorner );

JLabel upperLeftCorner = new JLabel();
upperLeftCorner.setOpaque( true );
upperLeftCorner.setBackground( Color.green );
```

15

**SCROLLING
COMPONENTS**

```
scrollPane.setCorner( ScrollPaneConstants.UPPER_LEFT_CORNER,
                      upperLeftCorner );

JLabel upperRightCorner = new JLabel();
upperRightCorner.setOpaque( true );
upperRightCorner.setBackground( Color.red );
scrollPane.setCorner( ScrollPaneConstants.UPPER_RIGHT_CORNER,
                      upperRightCorner );
```

> **NOTE**
>
> A current bug in the `ScrollPaneLayout` class causes the wrong component to be removed from the layout. Removing the lower-right component will `null` the lower-left component, in effect removing the wrong component from the layout manager.

FIGURE 15.5
Corners added to the `ScrollPaneTest` application.

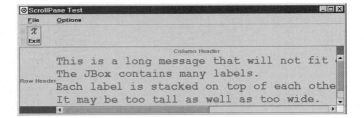

JComponent Scrolling Support

As we saw in Chapter 3, the `JComponent` class contains the `autoscrolls` property that is set with the `setAutoscrolls` method. When this property is `true`, an instance of the `Autoscroller` class is created for the component. This class extends the `MouseAdapter` utility class and overrides the `mouseDragged` method. This method scrolls the component in the viewport when the mouse is dragged.

When you are creating a custom component that will likely be contained in a scrollpane, the class should implement the `Scrollable` interface shown in Listing 15.2. The methods in this interface provide hints for the `scrolling` class. Currently four JFC classes implement this interface. They are the `JTable`, `JTextComponent`, `JTree`, and `JList` classes.

LISTING 15.2   THE Scrollable INTERFACE

```
public interface Scrollable
{
    /**
     * Returns the preferred size of the viewport for a view component.
     * For example the preferred size of a JList component is the size
     * required to accommodate all of the cells in its list, however the
     * value of preferredScrollableViewportSize is the size required for
     * JList.getVisibleRowCount() rows.   A component without any
     * properties that would affect the viewport size should just return
     * getPreferredSize() here.
     *
     * @return The preferredSize of a JViewport whose view is this
     *         Scrollable.
     * @see JViewport#getPreferredSize
     */
    Dimension getPreferredScrollableViewportSize();


    /**
     * Components that display logical rows or columns should compute
     * the scroll increment that will completely expose one new row
     * or column, depending on the value of orientation.  Ideally,
     * components should handle a partially exposed row or column by
     * returning the distance required to completely expose the item.
     * <p>
     * Scrolling containers, like JScrollPane, will use this method
     * each time the user requests a unit scroll.
     *
     * @param visibleRect The view area visible within the viewport
     * @param orientation Either SwingConstants.VERTICAL or
       SwingConstants.HORIZONTAL.
     * @param direction Less than zero to scroll up/left, greater
     *                  than zero for down/right.
     * @return The "unit" increment for scrolling in the specified
     *         direction
     * @see JScrollBar#setUnitIncrement
     */
    int getScrollableUnitIncrement( Rectangle visibleRect,
    ➥int orientation, int direction);


    /**
     * Components that display logical rows or columns should compute
     * the scroll increment that will completely expose one block
     * of rows or columns, depending on the value of orientation.
     * <p>
     * Scrolling containers, like JScrollPane, will use this method
```

continues

LISTING 15.2   CONTINUED

```
    * each time the user requests a block scroll.
    *
    * @param visibleRect The view area visible within the viewport
    * @param orientation Either SwingConstants.VERTICAL or
    *                    SwingConstants.HORIZONTAL.
    * @param direction Less than zero to scroll up/left, greater
    *                  than zero for down/right.
    * @return The "block" increment for scrolling in the
    *         specified direction.
    * @see JScrollBar#setBlockIncrement
    */
   int getScrollableBlockIncrement( Rectangle visibleRect,
                                    int orientation, int direction );


   /**
    * Return true if a viewport should always force the width of this
    * Scrollable to match the width of the viewport.  For example a
    * normal text view that supported line wrapping would return true
    * here, since it would be undesirable for wrapped lines to disappear
    * beyond the right edge of the viewport.  Note that returning true
    * for a Scrollable whose ancestor is a JScrollPane effectively
    * disables horizontal scrolling.
    * <p>
    * Scrolling containers, like JViewport, will use this method each
    * time they are validated.
    *
    * @return True if a viewport should force the Scrollables width
    *         to match its own.
    */
   boolean getScrollableTracksViewportWidth();


   /**
    * Return true if a viewport should always force the height of this
    * Scrollable to match the height of the viewport.  For example a
    * columnar text view that flowed text in left to right columns
    * could effectively disable vertical scrolling by returning
    * true here.
    * <p>
    * Scrolling containers, like JViewport, will use this method each
    * time they are validated.
    *
    * @return True if a viewport should force the Scrollables height
    *         to match its own.
    */
   boolean getScrollableTracksViewportHeight();
}
```

Summary

The JFC provides rich support for scrolling components. The `JScrollPane` class manages a viewport, scrollbars, headers, and corner components. These components work together to allow any component to be scrolled. The `JViewport` class occupies the center region of the scroll pane. The viewport can contain a single child. That child is the component that is scrolled. The viewport acts as a window where a portion of the child component can be seen. As the component is scrolled, different portions of the child component are displayed. A backing store can be used to enhance scrolling. When enabled, an offscreen image is created and used for painting. The scrolling policy can be set to only display the scrollbars when they are needed, to always display the scrollbars, or to never display the scrollbars. The `JScrollPane` class is a validated root container.

Split Pane

CHAPTER 16

Many modern user interfaces allow multiple views to appear in the same frame. The user can drag the divider between the views to allocate the space given to each view. The JFC provides the `JSplitPane` class to manage two components that can be interactively resized by the user. Each split pane manages two components. However, the child components themselves may be instances of the `JSplitPane` class. The nesting of split panes allows an arbitrary number of resizable panes to be available in a single window.

In this chapter, you will learn

- How to use the `JSplitPane` class.
- How to configure the `JSplitPane` divider.
- How to nest `JSplitPane` instances.

The `JSplitPane` Class

The `JSplitPane` class manages two child components that are separated by a divider. When the mouse cursor is over the divider, it changes to the Resize icon. The user can drag the divider to alter the size of the two components. The components can be stacked on top of each other or be placed side-by-side.

The default `JSplitPane` constructor creates a split pane that positions the two managed components side-by-side. The following code fragment creates a split pane and adds two managed components:

```
splitPane = new JSplitPane();
splitPane.setRightComponent( rightComponent );
splitPane.setLeftComponent( leftComponent );
```

The `setRightComponent` and `setLeftComponent` methods specify the two components that the split pane manages. When the components are aligned top-to-bottom, the `setTopComponent` and `setBottomComponent` methods can be used to specify the managed components. If the split pane is configured right-to-left, the `setTopComponent` method specifies the left component and the `setBottomComponent` method specifies the right component. Similarly, if the split pane is configured for top-to-bottom placement, the `setLeftComponent` method specifies the top component and the `setRightComponent` method specifies the bottom component.

The current components in each region in the split pane can be queried with the `getBottomComponent`, `getTopComponent`, `getRightComponent`, and `getLeftComponent` methods. The `getBottomComonent` and `getRightComponent` methods return the same component. Similarly, `getTopComponent` and `getLeftComponent` both return the other component in the split pane. If either of the managed components is `null`, the other component receives the entire area allocated to the split pane, and the user cannot drag the divider. Unfortunately, there is no visual feedback to the user that the divider is disabled. The cursor also still changes to the Resize icon, telling the user that the drag operation should succeed.

The default constructor of the `JSplitPane` class creates two instances of the `JButton` class and adds them as the left and right components in the split pane. Thus, if you create a split pane using the default constructor and don't add any components, you'll get a split pane containing two buttons, as shown in Figure 16.1.

FIGURE 16.1

The `JSplitPane`
*instance resulting
from the default
constructor.*

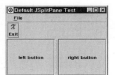

The orientation for the split pane can be specified at construction or changed later with the `setOrientation` method. One of two constants, `VERTICAL_SPLIT` or `HORIZON-TAL_SPLIT`, defined in the `JSplitPane` class, is passed to this method. The parameter specifies the orientation of the managed components, not the divider component. The default orientation is `HORIZONTAL_SPLIT`, which results in a left-to-right component placement. The current orientation can be queried with the `getOrientation` method. The orientation is a bound property of the `JSplitPane` class. The complete list of bound properties introduced in the `JSplitPane` class is shown in Table 16.1. The property names are constants defined in the `JSplitPane` class.

There is a version of the constructor for the `JSplitPane` class in which the orientation and managed components can be specified. An example usage of this constructor is shown next. When a vertical split pane is constructed, the components are specified top and then bottom. When a horizontal split pane is constructed, the components are specified left and then right.

```
splitPane = new JSplitPane( JSplitPane.VERTICAL_SPLIT,
            topComponent, bottomComponent );
splitPane = new JSplitPane( JSplitPane.HORIZONTAL_SPLIT,
            leftComponent, rightComponent );
```

TABLE 16.1   BOUND PROPERTIES DEFINED BY THE `JSplitPane` CLASS

Property Name	Setter Method	Getter Method
DIVIDER_SIZE_PROPERTY	setDividerSize	getDividerSize
ONE_TOUCH_EXPANDABLE_PROPERTY	setOneTouchExpandable	isOneTouchExpandable

continues

TABLE 16.1   CONTINUED

Property Name	Setter Method	Getter Method
LAST_DIVIDER_LOCATION_PROPERTY	setLastDividerLocation	getLastDividerLocation
ORIENTATION_PROPERTY	setOrientation	getOrientation
CONTINUOUS_LAYOUT_PROPERTY	setContinuousLayout	isContinuousLayout

By default, when the user drags the divider, the components in the split pane are not redrawn until the drag operation is complete. However, the setContinuousLayout method can be passed the parameter of true to force the components to be laid out and painted as the user drags the divider. The current value of this property can be queried with the isContinuousLayout method. Be careful about setting the CONTINUOUS_LAYOUT_ PROPERTY to true. For complex components in the split pane, the dragging can become very slow, making your application appear sluggish to the user.

The JSplitPaneTest application is a complete example of the JSplitPane class. It is shown in Listing 16.1. A static main method is provided to execute the application. In the main method, an ApplicationFrame instance is instantiated. Then an instance of the JSplitPaneTest class is constructed and added to the content pane of the frame. Finally, the frame is displayed. In the JSplitPaneTest class' constructor, a JSplitPane instance is created and a table and tabbed pane are added to the right and left sides, respectively. The table and tabbed pane classes were presented in Chapters 11 and 12, and the details of their usage won't be repeated here. The frame containing the split pane created by the JSplitPaneTest application is shown in Figure 16.2.

LISTING 16.1   THE JSplitPaneTest APPLICATION

```
package com.foley.test;

import java.awt.*;
import java.awt.event.*;

import java.io.Serializable;
import javax.swing.*;
import javax.swing.border.*;
import javax.swing.event.*;
import javax.swing.table.*;

import com.foley.utility.JBox;
import com.foley.utility.ApplicationFrame;


/**
 * An application that displays a JSplitPane in a frame.
```

```
 * The components in the split pane are a table and
 * a tabbed pane.
 * <p>
 * @author Mike Foley
 **/
public class JSplitPaneTest extends Object {

    /**
     * The splitPane for the test.
     **/
    JSplitPane splitPane;


    /**
     * JSplitPaneTest, Constructor
     * <p>
     * Create a splitpane and add a table and tabbedpane
     * to the splitpane.
     **/
    public JSplitPaneTest() {
        splitPane = new JSplitPane();
        splitPane.setRightComponent( createTabbedPane() );
        splitPane.setLeftComponent( createTable() );
    }


    /**
     * @return The split pane.
     **/
    public JSplitPane getSplitPane() {
        return( splitPane );
    }


    /**
     * Create the tabbed pane used in the application.
     * Add a few interesting tabs.
     * <p>
     * @return The tab pane instance for this application.
     **/
    protected JTabbedPane createTabbedPane() {
        JTabbedPane tabbedPane = new JTabbedPane();

        addTab( tabbedPane, "Tab1" );
        addTab( tabbedPane, "Tab2" );
        addTab( tabbedPane, "Tab3" );

        tabbedPane.setForegroundAt( 0, Color.red );
        tabbedPane.setBackgroundAt( 0, Color.yellow );
```

continues

LISTING 16.1   CONTINUED

```
        tabbedPane.setForegroundAt( 1, Color.yellow );
        tabbedPane.setBackgroundAt( 1, Color.red );

        return( tabbedPane );
    }


    /**
     * Create a table and place the table in a scrollpane.
     * <p>
     * @return  The scrollpane containing the table.
     **/
    public JComponent createTable() {
        JTable table = new JTable( new TableTestModel() );

        //
        // Create and register a Color class renderer.
        //
        DefaultTableCellRenderer colorRenderer =
            new DefaultTableCellRenderer() {
            public void setValue( Object value ) {
                setBackground( ( Color )value );
            }
        };

        colorRenderer.setOpaque( true );
        table.setDefaultRenderer( Color.class, colorRenderer );
        table.setDefaultRenderer( Boolean.class,
                                  new SelectedCheckBoxRenderer() );

        JScrollPane scrollPane = new JScrollPane( table );
        return( scrollPane );
    }


    /**
     * Create a JLabel and add it to the tabbed pane.
     * The text of the label matches the tab's text, and
     * is simply the number of tabs created during this
     * run of the application.
     **/
    private void addTab( final JTabbedPane tabbedPane, String name ) {
        final JPanel panel = new JPanel();
        panel.setLayout( new BorderLayout() );

        panel.add( new JLabel( name ), BorderLayout.NORTH );
        final JTextField textField = new JTextField( name );

        JBox box = JBox.createHorizontalJBox();
```

```
        box.add( new JLabel( "Tab name: " ) );
        textField.addActionListener( new ActionListener() {
            public void actionPerformed( ActionEvent event ) {
                //
                // Update the title of our tab to that entered.
                //
                String newTitle = textField.getText();
                int index = tabbedPane.indexOfComponent( panel );
                tabbedPane.setTitleAt( index, newTitle );
                //
                // validate and paint the tabs to display properly.
                //
                tabbedPane.revalidate();
                tabbedPane.repaint();
            }
        } );

        box.add( textField );
        panel.add( box, BorderLayout.SOUTH );

        tabbedPane.add( panel, name );
        tabbedPane.revalidate();

    }


    /**
     * Application entry point.
     * Create the frame, and display a splitpane in it.
     *
     * @param args Command line parameter. Not used.
     **/
    public static void main( String args[] ) {

        JFrame frame = new ApplicationFrame( "JSplitPaneTest" );
        JSplitPaneTest test = new JSplitPaneTest();

        frame.getContentPane().add( test.getSplitPane(),
                                    BorderLayout.CENTER );
        frame.pack();
        frame.setVisible( true );

    } // main

} // JSplitPaneTest


/**
 * Table model that returns the Class of the data in
```

continues

LISTING 16.1   CONTINUED

```
 * a particular column. This allows the table to set
 * renderers for the data.
 **/
class TableTestModel extends AbstractTableModel
    implements Serializable {

    /**
     * The data in the model.
     **/
    Object[][] data = {
        { "Mike", Color.blue, new Boolean( true ), new Integer( 9 ) },
        { "Mari", Color.red, new Boolean( true ), new Integer( 6 ) },
        { "Molly", Color.yellow, new Boolean( false ), new Integer( 1 ) },
        { "Betsy", Color.orange, new Boolean( false ), new Integer( 8 ) },
        { "Bobby", Color.lightGray, new Boolean( true ), new Integer( 7 ) },
        { "Trisha", Color.gray, new Boolean( false ), new Integer( 10 ) },
        { "Sam", Color.white, new Boolean( true ), new Integer( 12 ) },
        { "John", Color.black, new Boolean( false ), new Integer( 11 ) } };

    /**
     * The column names for the model.
     **/
    String[] columnNames = { "Name", "Color", "Enabled", "Size" };


    /**
     * TableTestModel, constructor.
     **/
    TableTestModel() {
        super();
    }


    /**
     * getRowCount, from TableModel.
     *
     * @return The number of rows in the data.
     **/
    public int getRowCount() {
        return( data.length );
    }


    /**
     * getColumnCount, from TableModel.
     *
     * @return The number of columns in the data.
     **/
    public int getColumnCount() {
```

```
            return( data[0].length );
    }

    /**
     * getValueAt, from TableModel.
     *
     * @param row The row of the reqeusted data object.
     * @param column The column of the reqeusted data object.
     * @return The object at the specified cell.
     **/
    public Object getValueAt( int row, int column ) {
        return( data[ row ][ column ] );
    }

    /**
     * setValueAt, from TableModel.
     *
     * Set the data value in the given location to the
     * given object.
     *
     * @param value The new data object.
     * @param row The row of the new data object.
     * @param column The column of the new data object.
     **/
    public void setValueAt( Object value, int row, int column ) {
        if( column == 0 )
            throw new RuntimeException(
                        "The Name column is not editable" );

        data[ row ][ column ] = value;
        fireTableCellUpdated( row, column );
    }


    /**
     * getColumnName, from TableModel.
     *
     * @param column The column index whose name is desired.
     * @return The name of the column with the given index.
     **/
    public String getColumnName( int column ) {
        return( columnNames[ column ] );
    }

    /**
     * getColumnClass, from TableModel.
     *
     * @param column The column index whose Class is desired.
     * @return The Class of the data for the column with the given index.
```

continues

LISTING 16.1   CONTINUED

```
    **/
    public Class getColumnClass( int column ) {
        return( data[0][ column ].getClass() );
    }


    /**
     * isCellEditable, from TableModel.
     *
     * All columns except the first are editable in this model.
     *
     * @param row The row of the cell whose editablility is requested.
     * @param column The column of the cell whose state is requested.
     * @return true if the cell is editable, false otherwise.
     **/
    public boolean isCellEditable( int row, int column ) {
        if( column == 0 ) {
            return( false );
        } else {
            return( true );
        }
    }
}


/**
 * ColorCellRenderer is a rendering class that expects
 * Color values. When this is the case, it paints the color
 * as the background of the label. If not, show the String
 * returned from the toString method of the value Object.
 *
 * @author Mike Foley
 **/
class ColorCellRenderer extends JLabel
        implements ListCellRenderer, Serializable {

    Border selectedWhiteBorder;
    Border selectedBlackBorder;

    /**
     * ColorCellRenderer, default constructor.
     * We must be opaque so the background is painted.
     **/
    public ColorCellRenderer() {
        setOpaque( true );
        selectedWhiteBorder = BorderFactory.createMatteBorder(
                                        3, 5, 3, 5, Color.white );
        selectedBlackBorder = BorderFactory.createMatteBorder(
                                        3, 5, 3, 5, Color.black );
    }
```

```
    /**
     * Configure ourself for the state passed.
     * If the value is a Color, set the background to that
     * color. If not use the toString method of the value
     *
     **/
    public Component getListCellRendererComponent(
        JList list,
        Object value,
        int index,
        boolean isSelected,
        boolean cellHasFocus)
    {

        if( value instanceof Color ) {
            setText( "          " );
            setBackground( ( Color )value );
            if( isSelected ) {
                if( value.equals( Color.white ) )
                    setBorder( selectedBlackBorder );
                else
                    setBorder( selectedWhiteBorder );
            } else {
                setBorder( null );
            }
        } else {
            setText( value.toString() );
            if( isSelected ) {
                setBackground( list.getSelectionBackground() );
                setForeground( list.getSelectionForeground() );
            } else {
                setBackground(list.getBackground());
                setForeground(list.getForeground());
            }
        }


        return this;
    }

} // ColorCellRenderer


/**
 * The SelectedCheckBoxRenderer class is almost the same as the
 * default check box renderer in the JTable class. However, it
 * paints the cell in the normal table selected colors when it is
 * selected. This avoids the white areas in the table for Boolean
 * columns. Also, if all columns in the table are Boolean, you
```

continues

LISTING 16.1   CONTINUED

```
 * wouldn't be able to see the selected row using the default
 * renderer!
 *
 * @author Mike Foley
 **/
class SelectedCheckBoxRenderer extends JCheckBox
    implements TableCellRenderer, Serializable {

    private Border noFocusBorder;
    private Color unselectedForeground;
    private Color unselectedBackground;


    /**
     * SelectedCheckBoxRenderer, default constructor.
     *
     * We need to be opaque so our background color is painted.
     * Create our border. Keep a reference around so it can be
     * reset when we are not selected.
     * Center the checkbox to match the position of the Boolean editor.
     **/
    public SelectedCheckBoxRenderer() {
            super();
        setOpaque( true );

        noFocusBorder = BorderFactory.createEmptyBorder( 1, 2, 1, 2 );
        setBorder( noFocusBorder );

        setHorizontalAlignment( JLabel.CENTER );
    }


    /**
     * Set the foreground color. Remember the color, so
     * we can reset it when we are not selected.
     *
     * @param c The new foreground color.
     **/
    public void setForeground(Color c) {
        super.setForeground(c);
        unselectedForeground = c;
    }


    /**
     * Set the background color. Remember the color, so
     * we can reset it when we are not selected.
     *
     * @param c The new background color.
```

```
**/
public void setBackground(Color c) {
    super.setBackground(c);
    unselectedBackground = c;
}


/**
 * Clear the foreground and background colors after
 * updating the UI. This will cause the colors to be
 * read from the table property portion of the UI.
 **/
public void updateUI() {
    super.updateUI();
        setForeground( null );
        setBackground( null );
}


/**
 * getTableCellRendererComponent, from TableCellRenderer
 *
 * Configure the checkbox for the given state.
 *
 **/
public Component getTableCellRendererComponent( JTable table,
                        Object value,
                        boolean isSelected,
                        boolean hasFocus,
                        int row, int column ) {

    //
    // Check or uncheck the JCheckBox.
    //
    setSelected((value != null && ((Boolean)value).booleanValue()));

    //
    // If we are selected, paint in the table's selection colors.
    //
        if( isSelected ) {
            super.setForeground( table.getSelectionForeground() );
            super.setBackground( table.getSelectionBackground() );
        } else {
            super.setForeground( ( unselectedForeground != null ) ?
                    unselectedForeground : table.getForeground() );
            super.setBackground( ( unselectedBackground != null ) ?
                    unselectedBackground : table.getBackground() );
    } // else

    //
```

continues

LISTING 16.1 CONTINUED

```
            // If we have the focus, paint in the focus color for the table.
            // and set the focus border.
            // If not, set the no focus border.
            //
                if( hasFocus ) {
                    setBorder( UIManager.getBorder(
                            "Table.focusCellHighlightBorder" ) );
                    if (table.isCellEditable(row, column)) {
                        super.setForeground( UIManager.getColor(
                                        "Table.focusCellForeground" ) );
                        super.setBackground( UIManager.getColor(
                                        "Table.focusCellBackground" ) );
                    }
                } else {
                    setBorder( noFocusBorder );
                }

            return( this );
        }

} // SelectedCheckBoxRenderer
```

FIGURE 16.2

*The
JSplitPaneTest
application win-
dow.*

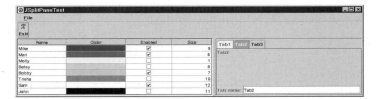

JSplitPane Divider Configuration

In the JSplitPaneTest application, the default configuration for the divider was used.
The size of the slider is look-and-feel dependent. The divider in the Windows look-and-
feel is three pixels wide, in the Java look-and-feel it is eight pixels wide, and in the motif
look-and-feel it is a whopping 18 pixels wide. If the default value of the divider is not
appropriate for your application, you can specify it by using the setDividerSize
method. The current size of the divider can be queried with the getDividerSize method.
As shown in Table 16.1, the divider's size is a bound property of the JSplitPane class.

The divider can be configured with a region that allows either panel to be collapsed by
clicking the mouse over the control. Once collapsed, the panel can be restored to its
original size by clicking on the other arrow in the one-touch control. The
setOneTouchExpandable method activates or deactivates this control. Its current state
can be queried with the isOneTouchExpandable method. The oneTouchExpandable

property is a bound property of the JSplitPane class. Add the following line of code to the JSplitPaneTest constructor to enable one-touch expansion mode in the split pane:

```
splitPane.setOneTouchExpandable( true );
```

The resulting window is shown in Figure 16.3. The one-touch region is the area with the two black arrows at the top of the divider. Clicking the top arrow collapses the left region, and clicking the bottom arrow collapses the right region. Figure 16.4 shows the window after the top arrow has been clicked to collapse the region containing the table. The bottom arrow would be clicked to restore the window to its original layout.

NOTE

When you're using the one-touch control, the default divider size of the Windows and Java look-and-feels makes the control difficult to click. This is more of a factor with the Windows look-and-feel. Increasing the size of the divider to 10 pixels or more gives the controls more space, allowing them to be clicked easier.

FIGURE 16.3

A one-touch control added to JSplitPane...

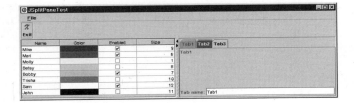

The location of the divider can be specified by the application using the setDividerLocation method. The integer parameter to this method is look-and-feel dependent. However, the current look-and-feel implementations interpret this parameter as a pixel count. It is the x location for a horizontally aligned split pane and the y location for a vertically aligned split pane. The current value of the divider can be queried with the getDividerLocation method.

FIGURE 16.4

...and a collapsed
JSplitPane.

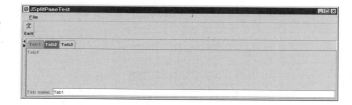

The previous divider location is a bound property of the split pane. When the continuous layout property is `false`, a property change listener will be notified of the last divider location after a drag operation is complete. The name of the property in the `PropertyChangeEvent` is the `String` defined by the `LAST_DIVIDER_LOCATION_PROPERTY` constant in the `JSplitPane` class. If the continuous layout property is `true`, the listener will receive a stream of change events as the user drags the divider. The `getDividerLocation` method can be used to query the current location of the divider in the `propertyChange` method. The `getLastDividerLocation` method can be called to query the divider's previous location. This value is also delivered to listeners by the `PropertyChange` event.

There is a `setLastDividerLocation` method that is used by the look-and-feel implementations to set this property and initiate the `PropertyChangeEvent` being fired. This method is rarely used by user applications.

There is also a variant of the `setDividerLocation` method that takes a `double` as its parameter. The parameter must be between 0.0 and 1.0. It is interpreted as the percentage of the split pane given to the top or left component, depending on the orientation. The remainder of the area is given to the other component. Calling this method will also cause a `LAST_DIVIDER_LOCATION_PROPERTY` `PropertyChangeEvent` to be sent to any `PropertyChangeListeners` listeners registered on the split pane.

The minimum and maximum placement locations for the divider can be queried with the `getMinimumDividerLocation` and `getMaximumDividerLocation` methods. These values cannot be set directly by the application. Instead, they are determined by the preferences of the components managed by the split pane. Component sizing is discussed in the next section.

Controlling Component Sizes

The `JSplitPane` class manages two AWT component children. When either or both of these components are instances of the `JComponent` class, the `JSplitPane` class respects the `minimumSize` property of the child. If this property is set to a nonzero value in the child component, the divider can't move into a position that would make that component smaller than its minimum size. However, if the split pane is contained in the content pane of a JFrame instance, as in the JSplitPaneTest application shown earlier in this chapter, resizing the frame can make a component smaller than its minimum size. This causes the divider to jump to the component's minimum size the next time the user drags it.

When the split pane is smaller than the combined minimum sizes of its managed children, the user cannot drag the divider. Unfortunately, the user doesn't get any visual feedback that this condition has been entered. The cursor still changes to the Resize icon, telling the user that the divider can be dragged. This gives the user the impression that there is something wrong with the application when in fact there is not. To correct this problem, the splitpane should not change the shape of the cursor to the Resize icon when the user is not able to resize the panes.

The components managed by the split pane can be reset to their preferred sizes through the resetToPreferredSize method. The divider will be moved to the appropriate location in the split pane after the components are sized.

A commonly misunderstood aspect of the JSplitPane class is the minimumSize property. If the components managed by the split pane have 0 in the Split dimension, the split pane will give its entire area to one of the components, and the other component will not be seen. This condition is demonstrated by the JSplitPaneTest2 application, shown in Listing 16.2. The resulting window is shown in Figure 16.5. To alleviate this condition, the minimumSize property can be set on the component or the location of the divider can be specified by the application.

LISTING 16.2 THE JSplitPaneTest2 APPLICATION

```
package com.foley.test;

import java.awt.*;

import javax.swing.*;

import com.foley.utility.ApplicationFrame;


/**
 * An application that displays a JSplitPane in a frame.
 * It demonstrates a 0 minimum size of one of the components
 * in the split pane.
 * <p>
 * @author Mike Foley
 **/
public class JSplitPaneTest2 extends Object {
```

continues

LISTING 16.2 CONTINUED

```java
/**
 * The splitPane for the test.
 **/
JSplitPane splitPane;


/**
 * JSplitPaneTest2, Constructor
 * <p>
 * Create a splitpane and add a table and tabbed pane
 * to the splitpane.
 **/
public JSplitPaneTest2() {
    splitPane = new JSplitPane();

    splitPane.setRightComponent(
            new JScrollPane( new JLabel( "Hello" ) ) );

    JComponent left = new JComponent() {};
    splitPane.setLeftComponent( left );

}


/**
 * @return The split pane.
 **/
public JSplitPane getSplitPane() {
    return( splitPane );
}


/**
 * Application entry point.
 * Create the frame, and display a splitpane in it.
 *
 * @param args Command line parameter. Not used.
 **/
public static void main( String args[] ) {

    JFrame frame = new ApplicationFrame( "JSplitPaneTest2" );
    JSplitPaneTest2 test = new JSplitPaneTest2();

    frame.getContentPane().add( test.getSplitPane(),
                                BorderLayout.CENTER );
    frame.pack();
    frame.setVisible( true );

} // main
```

```
} // JSplitPaneTest2
```

FIGURE 16.5

*A JSplitPane with
a 0 minimum size
component.*

Nesting JSplitPane Instances

The JSplitPane class manages two child components at most. However, the child components can themselves be split panes. You can create almost any combination of resizable panes by *nesting* split panes.

The NestedJSplitPaneTest application is shown in Listing 16.3. This application creates a horizontally aligned split pane. A separate, vertically aligned split pane is added as the right and left components in the first split pane. A label is added as the top and bottom components in each of the nested split panes. This creates a window with four regions, as shown in Figure 16.6. Moving the vertical divider alters the size of all four components displayed in the window. Moving either horizontal divider only alters the size of the two components in that nested split pane.

LISTING 16.3   THE NestedJSplitPaneTest APPLICATION

```java
package com.foley.test;

import java.awt.*;

import javax.swing.*;

import com.foley.utility.ApplicationFrame;


/**
 * An application that displays a JSplitPane in a frame.
 * It demonstrates nested split panes.
 * <p>
 * @author Mike Foley
 **/
public class NestedJSplitPaneTest extends Object {

    /**
     * The splitPane for the test.
     **/
```

continues

LISTING 16.3   CONTINUED

```java
    JSplitPane splitPane;


    /**
     * NestedJSplitPaneTest, Constructor
     * <p>
     * Create a splitpane that contains separate split
     * panes as its children.
     **/
    public NestedJSplitPaneTest() {

        JSplitPane right = new JSplitPane( JSplitPane.VERTICAL_SPLIT,
                                    new JLabel( "Top Right" ),
                                    new JLabel( "Bottom Right" ) );
        JSplitPane left = new JSplitPane( JSplitPane.VERTICAL_SPLIT,
                                    new JLabel( "Top Left" ),
                                    new JLabel( "Bottom Left" ) );
        splitPane = new JSplitPane( JSplitPane.HORIZONTAL_SPLIT,
                                    left, right );

    }


    /**
     * @return The split pane.
     **/
    public JSplitPane getSplitPane() {
        return( splitPane );
    }


    /**
     * Application entry point.
     * Create the frame, and display a splitpane in it.
     *
     * @param args Command line parameter. Not used.
     **/
    public static void main( String args[] ) {

        JFrame frame = new ApplicationFrame( "NestedJSplitPane Test" );
        NestedJSplitPaneTest test = new NestedJSplitPaneTest();

        frame.getContentPane().add( test.getSplitPane(),
                                    BorderLayout.CENTER );
        frame.pack();
        frame.setVisible( true );

    } // main

} // NestedJSplitPaneTest
```

FIGURE 16.6

Nested JSplitPane *instances.*

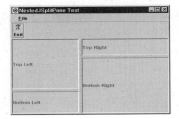

Summary

The JSplitPane class manages two child components that can be placed side-by-side or one on top of the other. A divider visually separates the two components. The default size and look of the divider are look-and-feel specific. The user can drag the divider to alter the size of the two child components contained in the split pane. The split pane respects the minimumSize property of JComponent children. This may restrict the user from resizing the child components to arbitrary sizes.

To overcome the limitation of a split pane managing only two children, split panes can be nested. By specifying one or both children of the split pane as another instance of the JSplitPane class, you can create almost any layout.

CHAPTER 17

Internal Frames

The success of programs like MS Word and Excel popularized the multiple document interface (MDI). This type of interface contains many frame windows contained in a single top-level frame. The internal frames can be sized, dragged, and iconified independently of the other frames. The single top-level frame groups the internal frames. If the top-level frame is iconified, the internal frames are iconified with it. The MDI allows all the views in an application to be contained in a single frame. This interface model is showing its age at this time and is being replaced by variants of the MDI.

The JFC contains the `JInternalFrame` and `JDesktopPane` classes that provide a frame and a frame management pane that can be added to other frames. The internal frames are added to the desktop pane that interfaces with the desktop manager. The `DesktopManager` instance is responsible for managing look-and-feel–specific issues regarding frame decorations, closing, moving, and so on. These classes allow the application developer to create whatever interface he or she requires. A complete MDI interface is not provided in the JFC. Instead, the tools required to build any type of interface are provided.

In this chapter, you will learn

- How to use the `JInternalFrame` class
- How the `JDesktopPane` is used
- How to use the `JInternalFrame` and `JDesktopPane` classes together

The JInternalFrame Class

The `JInternalFrame` class provides a lightweight container sharing most of the features of the `JFrame` class. The fundamental difference between the two classes is that you can add a `JInternalFrame` instance to other frames, and a `JFrame` instance is a top-level window. The `JInternalFrame` class extends the `JComponent` class, while the `JFrame` class extends the AWT `Frame` class.

The discussion of the `JRootPane` class (and the panes it creates) being the single child of a `JFrame` instance presented in Chapter 8, "Frame Windows," is valid for the `JInternalFrame` class and will not be repeated here. However, it is worth repeating that adding components and setting layout managers are performed on the content pane, not the internal frame itself. This technique will be demonstrated throughout this chapter.

A `JInternalFrame` instance appears similar to a top-level frame. It contains a titlebar and a border. The titlebar may contain a title, an icon, minimize and maximize buttons, and a close button. The window decoration is only shown if the internal frame supports the operation. A `JInternalFrame` created with the default constructor will not contain any of these decorations as the default state of an internal frame is not iconifiable, not maximizable, not closable, not resizable, and the title is empty. If the internal frame is resizable, the user can drag on the border to resize the frame. Each of these properties can be set individually with the setResizable, setClosable, setIconifiable, and setMaximizable methods. The current value of each of these properties can be queried with the is version of each method. For example, the isMaximizable method may be used to query the state of the maximizable property. These are not bound properties of the internal frame.

You can specify the title with the setTitle method and query it with the getTitle method. The title is a bound property of the JInternalFrame class. The icon for the internal frame can be set with the setFrameIcon method. The getFrameIcon method can be used to query the current icon associated with the internal frame. The frame icon is also a bound property of the class. The complete list of bound properties introduced in the JInternalFrame class is shown in Table 17.1. The property names are constants defined in the JInternalFrame class.

TABLE 17.1 BOUND PROPERTIES INTRODUCED IN THE JInternalFrame CLASS

Property Name	Setter Method	Getter Method
MENU_BAR_PROPERTY	setMenuBar	getMenuBar
MENU_BAR_PROPERTY	setJMenuBar	getJMenuBar
CONTENT_PANE_PROPERTY	setContentPane	getContentPane
LAYERED_PANE_PROPERTY	setLayeredPane	getLayeredPane
GLASS_PANE_PROPERTY	setGlassPane	getGlassPane
ROOT_PANE_PROPERTY	setRootPane	getRootPane
IS_CLOSED_PROPERTY	setClosed	isClosed
IS_ICON_PROPERTY	setIcon	isIcon
TITLE_PROPERTY	setTitle	getTitle
IS_SELECTED_PROPERTY	setSelected	isSelected
FRAME_ICON_PROPERTY	setFrameIcon	getFrameIcon

NOTE

It seems odd that pane properties are fired from the JInternalFrame class. The setter and getter methods are convenience methods that call the appropriate method of the JRootPane class. If the PropertyChangeEvent were fired from the JRootPane class, it would also be available from the JWindow, JFrame, and JDialog classes that also use the JRootPane class but do not fire a PropertyChangeEvent when one of the panes is changed.

The `InternalFrameTest` application is shown in Listing 17.1. In the `main` method, an `ApplicationFrame` is created and displayed. A `JInternalFrame` instance is created and configured to be resizable, closable, iconifiable, and maximizable. There are also variants of the `JInternalFrame` class constructor that allow these properties to be specified at construction time. The internal frame is then added to the center of the content pane of the application frame. The resulting windows for the Java and Windows look-and-feel are shown in Figure 17.1. The internal frame class Java look-and-feel is very different than the Windows look-and-feel. The icons and resize borders are very unique. The Java look-and-feel also contains the controversial notch under the controls on the right side of the titlebar. Unfortunately, the icons and border cannot be set to match those found on the top-level frame. This is because the Windows window manager defines the look of those controls, and they cannot be altered by the application. This fact makes the Java look-and-feel less appealing for internal frames.

LISTING 17.1   THE `InternalFrameTest` APPLICATION

```
package com.foley.test;

import java.awt.*;
import javax.swing.*;

import com.foley.utility.ApplicationFrame;


/**
 * An application that displays a frame that
 * contains internal frames.
 *
 * @author Mike Foley
 **/
public class InternalFrameTest extends Object {

    /**
     * Application entry point.
     * Create the frame, and display it.
     *
     * @param args Command line parameter. Not used.
     **/
    public static void main( String args[] ) {

        //
        // Un-comment these lines to enable the Windows LAF.
        //
//      try {
//          UIManager.setLookAndFeel(
//              "com.sun.java.swing.plaf.windows.WindowsLookAndFeel" );
```

```
//      } catch( Exception ex ) {
//          System.err.println( "Exception: " +
//              ex.getLocalizedMessage() );
//      }



        JFrame frame = new ApplicationFrame( "Internal Frame Test" );

        JInternalFrame internalFrame =
                    new JInternalFrame( "Internal JLabel" );
        internalFrame.getContentPane().add( new JLabel( "Hello" ) );
        internalFrame.setResizable( true );
        internalFrame.setClosable( true );
        internalFrame.setIconifiable( true );
        internalFrame.setMaximizable( true );
        internalFrame.pack();

        frame.getContentPane().add( internalFrame, BorderLayout.CENTER );

        frame.pack();
        frame.setVisible( true );

    } // main

} // InternalFrameTest
```

FIGURE 17.1

Internal frames in the Java (top) and Windows (bottom) look-and-feels.

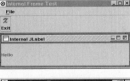

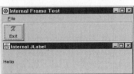

The `InternalFrameTest` application shows that `JInternalFrame` instances can be used like any other component. Although the class is used primarily in an MDI type mode, it can be used with any layout manager. However, current bugs in the `JInternalFrame` class cause `NullPointerException` exceptions to be thrown when the mouse is clicked over the internal frame.

The methods to enable an internal frame to be iconifiable, maximizable, and closable were presented earlier. If these properties are enabled, there are also methods that allow the application to set and query the corresponding states. For example, if the internal frame is closable, the isClosed method can be used to determine if it is currently closed, and the setClosed method can be used to close the internal frame. The dispose method is called when the internal frame is no longer required. The methods for an iconifiable internal frame are isIcon, to determine if the frame is currently iconified, and setIcon, to iconify and restore the internal frame. For the maximizable property, the associated methods are isMaximum and setMaximum.

A Top-Level Internal Frame?

As was pointed out in the previous section, mixing internal frames by using the Java look-and-feel on the MS Windows platform looks odd. The native frame contains the Windows titlebar controls and resize border while the internal frames contain the Java look-and-feel titlebar controls and resize border. A pseudo top-level frame can be created by adding an internal frame to a JWindow instance. An example demonstrating this technique is shown in Listing 17.2. The WindowFrameTest application creates the window shown in Figure 17.2.

LISTING 17.2   THE WindowFrameTest APPLICATION

```
package com.foley.test;

import java.awt.*;
import java.awt.event.*;

import javax.swing.*;

import com.foley.utility.*;


/**
 * An application that displays an internal frame
 * in a JWindow instance. This gives a top-level
 * frame that looks like an internal frame. However,
 * it does not interact with a Window Manager
 * properly.
 *
 * @author Mike Foley
 **/
public class WindowFrameTest extends Object {

    /**
     * Create an internal frame.
     * <p>
     * @return The newly created internal frame.
     **/
```

```java
public static JInternalFrame createInternalFrame() {

    final JInternalFrame internalFrame =
                       new JInternalFrame( "Internal JLabel" );
    JMenuBar menuBar = new JMenuBar();

    JMenu file = new JMenu( "File" );
    file.setMnemonic( KeyEvent.VK_F );

    Action exitAction = new ExitAction();
    file.add( exitAction );

    menuBar.add( file );
    internalFrame.setJMenuBar( menuBar );

    JToolBar toolBar = new JToolBar();
    toolBar.add( exitAction );

    internalFrame.getContentPane().add( toolBar,
                                   BorderLayout.NORTH );

    JComponent content = new JLabel( "Internal Frame Content",
                                 SwingConstants.CENTER );
    content.setBorder( BorderFactory.createLoweredBevelBorder() );
    internalFrame.getContentPane().add(
                       content,
                       BorderLayout.CENTER );
    internalFrame.setResizable( true );
    internalFrame.setClosable( true );
    internalFrame.setIconifiable( true );
    internalFrame.setMaximizable( true );
    internalFrame.pack();

          return( internalFrame );
}


/**
 * Application entry point.
 * Create the window, add an internal frame
 * and display.
 *
 * @param args Command line parameter. Not used.
 **/
public static void main( String args[] ) {

    JWindow window = new JWindow();
    JInternalFrame internalFrame = createInternalFrame();
```

continues

LISTING 17.2   CONTINUED

```
        window.getContentPane().add( internalFrame,
                                     BorderLayout.CENTER );
        window.setLocation( new Point( 200, 100 ) );
        window.setSize( new Dimension( 400, 300 ) );
        window.setVisible( true );

    } // main

} // WindowFrameTest
```

FIGURE 17.2

The
WindowFrameTest
application.

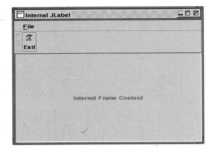

As can be seen in Figure 17.2, the window appears to be a top-level frame that possesses the Java look-and-feel. Unfortunately, the controls on the internal frame do not interact with the system's window manager. This means that pressing the iconify button on the titlebar does not iconify the window. The JFC developers realize the need for a frame that is entirely drawn by JFC classes. This will allow top-level frames, similar to the window created by the WindowFrameTest application, that will interact with the system's window manager. Once this type of frame is part of the JFC, internal frames and top-level frames can be drawn with any desired look.

The JDesktopPane Class

The previous section described many of the options available in the JInternalFrame class. An example was presented where an internal frame was added to the content pane of a JFrame instance. While this is a valid use of an internal frame, the class was designed to be used in conjunction with the JDesktopPane class. When an internal frame is added to a desktop pane, the internal frame behaves as an independent frame in the desktop pane.

The JDesktopPane class extends the JLayeredPane class. It creates a virtual desktop to be used by internal frames. It manages the potential overlap when multiple children are added to a desktop pane. The `JDesktopPane` class provides the link between the internal frames and the `DesktopManager` instance installed by the current look-and-feel. The desktop manager is responsible for performing the operations on the internal frame. For example, when an internal frame is to be iconified, it is the `DesktopManager` that performs the operation. This allows a look-and-feel to specify how these operations are performed.

There are not very many methods in the `JDesktopPane` class that are typically called by application code. The two that are of interest are the `getAllFrames` method and the `getAllFramesInLayer` method. The `getAllFrames` method returns an array of all `JInternalFrame` instances contained in the desktop pane, and the `getAllFramesInLayer` returns an array of the internal frames in a particular layer in the desktop pane. The `getDesktopManager` method will return a reference to the `DesktopManager` associated with the desktop pane.

The `DesktopManager` Interface

The `DesktopManager` interface defines the responsibilities of a desktop manager. A class that implements this interface is set as the desktop manager in a desktop pane when its user interface component is set. This allows a look-and-feel to dictate how the desktop operations are performed. For example, a look-and-feel can choose to place iconified windows along the right edge of the desktop instead of the customary location along the bottom. The `DesktopManager` interface is shown in Listing 17.3.

LISTING 17.3   THE `DesktopManager` INTERFACE

```
public interface DesktopManager
{
    /** If possible, display this frame in an appropriate location.
      * Normally, this is not called, as the creator of the
      * JInternalFrame will add the frame to the appropriate parent.
      */
    void openFrame(JInternalFrame f);

    /**
      * Generally, this call should remove the frame from its parent.
      */
    void closeFrame(JInternalFrame f);

    /**
      * Generally, the frame should be resized to match its
      * parent's bounds.
      */
    void maximizeFrame(JInternalFrame f);
```

continues

LISTING 17.3   CONTINUED

```
/** Generally, this indicates that the frame should be restored to
 * its size and position prior to a maximizeFrame() call.
 */
void minimizeFrame(JInternalFrame f);

/**
 * Generally, remove this frame from its parent and add an
 * iconic representation.
 */
void iconifyFrame(JInternalFrame f);

/**
 * Generally, remove any iconic representation that is present
 * and restore the frame to its original size and location.
 */
void deiconifyFrame(JInternalFrame f);

/**
 * Generally, indicate that this frame has focus. This is usually
 * called after the JInternalFrame's IS_SELECTED_PROPERTY has been
 * set to true.
 */
void activateFrame(JInternalFrame f);

/**
 * Generally, indicate that this frame has lost focus.
 * This is usually called after the JInternalFrame's IS_
 * SELECTED_PROPERTY has been set to false.
 */
void deactivateFrame(JInternalFrame f);

/** This method is normally called when the user has indicated that
 * they will begin dragging a component around. This method should
 * be called prior to any dragFrame() calls to allow the
 * DesktopManager to prepare any necessary state.
 * Normally <b>f</b> will be a JInternalFrame.
 */
void beginDraggingFrame(JComponent f);

/** The user has moved the frame. Calls to this method will be
 * preceded by calls to beginDraggingFrame().
 *  Normally <b>f</b> will be a JInternalFrame.
 */
void dragFrame(JComponent f, int newX, int newY);

/** This method signals the end of the dragging session.
 * Any state maintained by the DesktopManager can be removed
 * here.  Normally <b>f</b> will be a JInternalFrame.
 */
```

```
    void endDraggingFrame(JComponent f);

    /** This method is normally called when the user has indicated that
     * they will begin resizing the frame. This method should be called
     * prior to any resizeFrame() calls to allow the DesktopManager to
     * prepare any necessary state.  Normally <b>f</b> will be a
     * JInternalFrame.
     */
    void beginResizingFrame(JComponent f, int direction);

    /** The user has resized the component. Calls to this method
     * will be preceded by calls to beginResizingFrame().
     *   Normally <b>f</b> will be a JInternalFrame.
     */
    void resizeFrame(JComponent f, int newX, int newY,
                     int newWidth, int newHeight);

    /** This method signals the end of the resize session. Any state
     * maintained by the DesktopManager can be removed here.
     * Normally <b>f</b> will be a JInternalFrame.
     */
    void endResizingFrame(JComponent f);

    /** This is a primitive reshape method.*/
    void setBoundsForFrame(JComponent f, int newX, int newY,
                           int newWidth, int newHeight);
}
```

Integrating JInternalFrame and JDesktopPane Usage

For the JInternalFrame class to shine, it must be used in conjunction with the JDesktopPane class. When an internal frame is added to a desktop pane, it behaves as an independent frame in the desktop pane. It can be dragged, iconified, maximized, and sized independently of other internal frames contained in the desktop pane.

The MDIFrame class shown in Listing 17.4 is an example frame showing how a desktop pane can be added to a JFrame instance. The MDIFrame class is a JFrame extension that configures itself with a JDesktopPane instance in the center region of its content pane. An Action is added to the File menu and to the toolbar that creates and adds an internal frame to the desktop pane when invoked. The internal frame creation method adds a JLabel instance to the content pane of the internal frame. This is for demonstration only. Your application would add its content to the internal frame instance.

LISTING 17.4   THE MDIFrame CLASS

```java
package com.foley.utility;

import java.awt.*;

import java.awt.event.*;

import java.io.Serializable;

import javax.swing.*;

import javax.swing.border.*;

import javax.swing.event.*;


/**
 * A top-level frame. The frame configures itself
 * with a JDesktopPane in its content pane.
 *
 * @author Mike Foley
 **/
public class MDIFrame extends JFrame implements Serializable {

    /**
     * The desktop pane in our content pane.
     **/
    private JDesktopPane desktopPane;


    /**
     * MDIFrame, null constructor.
     **/
    public MDIFrame() {
        this( null );
    }


    /**
     * MDIFrame, constructor.
     *
     * @param title The title for the frame.
     **/
    public MDIFrame( String title ) {
        super( title );
    }


    /**
     * Customize the frame for our application.
```

17

```java
    **/
    protected void frameInit() {
        //
        // Let the super create the panes.
        super.frameInit();

        JMenuBar menuBar = createMenu();
        setJMenuBar( menuBar );

        JToolBar toolBar = createToolBar();
        Container content = getContentPane();
        content.add( toolBar, BorderLayout.NORTH );

        desktopPane = new JDesktopPane();
        desktopPane.setPreferredSize( new Dimension( 400, 300 ) );
        content.add( desktopPane, BorderLayout.CENTER );

    } // frameInit


    /**
     * Create the menu for the frame.
     * <p>
     * @return The menu for the frame.
     **/
    protected JMenuBar createMenu() {
        JMenuBar menuBar = new JMenuBar();

        JMenu file = new JMenu( "File" );
        file.setMnemonic( KeyEvent.VK_F );

        JMenuItem item;

        file.add( new NewInternalFrameAction() );
        file.add( new ExitAction() );

        menuBar.add( file );
        return( menuBar );

    } // createMenuBar


    /**
     * Create the toolbar for this frame.
     * <p>
     * @return The newly created toolbar.
     **/
    protected JToolBar createToolBar() {
        final JToolBar toolBar = new JToolBar();
        toolBar.setFloatable( false );
```

continues

LISTING 17.4   CONTINUED

```java
        toolBar.add( new NewInternalFrameAction() );
        toolBar.add( new ExitAction() );
        return( toolBar );
    }


    /**
     * Create an internal frame.
     * A JLabel is added to its content pane for an example
     * of content in the internal frame. However, any
     * JComponent may be used for content.
     * <p>
     * @return The newly created internal frame.
     **/
    public JInternalFrame createInternalFrame() {

        JInternalFrame internalFrame =
                    new JInternalFrame( "Internal JLabel" );
        internalFrame.getContentPane().add(
                    new JLabel( "Internal Frame Content" ) );
        internalFrame.setResizable( true );
        internalFrame.setClosable( true );
        internalFrame.setIconifiable( true );
        internalFrame.setMaximizable( true );
        internalFrame.pack();

        return( internalFrame );
    }


    /**
     * An Action that creates a new internal frame and
     * adds it to this frame's desktop pane.
     **/
    public class NewInternalFrameAction extends AbstractAction {

        /**
         * NewInternalFrameAction, constructor.
         * Set the name and icon for this action.
         **/
        public NewInternalFrameAction() {
            super( "New", new ImageIcon( "new.gif" ) );
        }

        /**
         * Perform the action, create an internal frame and
         * add it to the desktop pane.
         * <p>
         * @param e The event causing us to be called.
```

```
        **/
      public void actionPerformed( ActionEvent e ) {
          JInternalFrame internalFrame = createInternalFrame();
          desktopPane.add( internalFrame,
                              JLayeredPane.DEFAULT_LAYER );
      }

    } // NewInternalFrameAction

} // MDIFrame
```

The MDITest application presented in Listing 17.5 creates an instance of the MDIFrame
class and displays it using the Windows look-and-feel. The resulting frame, after adding
a few internal frames, is shown in Figure 17.3. Notice that iconified internal frames can
be seen at the bottom of the figure. This demonstrates that the internal frames are in fact
internal. Iconified and maximized internal frames still reside within the enclosing JFrame
instance.

LISTING 17.5 THE MDITest APPLICATION

```
package com.foley.test;

import javax.swing.*;

import com.foley.utility.MDIFrame;


/**
 * An application that displays a frame that
 * contains internal frames in an MDI type
 * interface.
 *
 * @author Mike Foley
 **/
public class MDITest extends Object {

    /**
     * Application entry point.
     * Create the frame, and display it.
     *
     * @param args Command line parameter. Not used.
     **/
    public static void main( String args[] ) {

        try {
            UIManager.setLookAndFeel(
                "com.sun.java.swing.plaf.windows.WindowsLookAndFeel" );
```

continues

LISTING 17.5   CONTINUED

```
        } catch( Exception ex ) {
            System.err.println( "Exception: " +
                        ex.getLocalizedMessage() );
        }

        JFrame frame = new MDIFrame( "MDI Test" );

        frame.pack();
        frame.setVisible( true );

    } // main

} // MDITest
```

FIGURE 17.3

The MDITest *application's frame.*

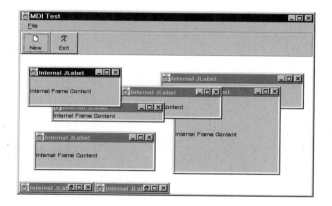

By default, the contents of the internal frame are drawn as the frame is dragged. This feature makes dragging frames sluggish on many computers. To increase responsiveness while dragging frames, the frame may be dragged in outline mode when the default desktop manager is being used. Outline mode is enabled by setting the dragMode client property on the desktop pane to outline. Clearing this property, by setting its value to null, will enable the default drag mode. Unfortunately, both the property name and its one valid value are hard-coded strings in the DefaultDesktopManager class. Setting the dragMode property is demonstrated in the following code fragment.

```
JDesktopPane desktopPane = new
JDesktopPane();desktopPane.putClientProperty( "JDesktopPane.dragMode",
outline" );
```

The MDIFrame class is by no means a complete MDI implementation. It does provide insight as to the JInternalFrame and JDesktopPane usage and how a complete MDI interface could be developed using these classes.

Customizing the `JInternalFrame` Instances

As was mentioned earlier in this chapter, the `JInternalFrame` class can be configured as the `JFrame` class is configured. This includes adding a toolbar and menu to the frame. These items take up valuable screen real estate and are not common on internal frames, but they are supported. The `createInternalFrame` method in the `MDIFrame` class can be changed to add these items. The updated method is shown next. It creates a `JMenuBar` instance and sets it on the internal frame by using the `setJMenuBar` method. A `JToolBar` is also created and added to the north region of the internal frame's content pane. These are the same techniques used with the `JFrame` class. A new `Action` is created that disposes of the internal frame passed in its constructor. The action is added to both the menu and toolbar. The `DisposeInternalFrameAction` is also shown in Listing 17.6. The new version of the `MDIFrame` is shown in Figure 17.4.

LISTING 17.6 MODIFIED METHODS IN THE MDIFrame CLASS

```
/**
 * Create an internal frame.
 * <p>
 * @return The newly created internal frame.
 **/
public JInternalFrame createInternalFrame() {

final JInternalFrame internalFrame =
                        new JInternalFrame( "Internal JLabel" );
    JMenuBar menuBar = new JMenuBar();
    JMenu file = new JMenu( "File" );
    file.setMnemonic( KeyEvent.VK_F );

    Action disposeAction =
            new DisposeInternalFrameAction( internalFrame );
    Action exitAction = new ExitAction();
    file.add( disposeAction );
    file.add( exitAction );

    menuBar.add( file );
    internalFrame.setJMenuBar( menuBar );

    JToolBar toolBar = new JToolBar();
    toolBar.add( disposeAction );
    toolBar.add( exitAction );

    internalFrame.getContentPane().add( toolBar, BorderLayout.NORTH );

    JComponent content = new JLabel( "Internal Frame Content" );
    content.setBorder( BorderFactory.createLoweredBevelBorder() );
    internalFrame.getContentPane().add(
                        content,
```

continues

LISTING 17.6   CONTINUED

```
                          BorderLayout.CENTER );
    internalFrame.setResizable( true );
    internalFrame.setClosable( true );
    internalFrame.setIconifiable( true );
    internalFrame.setMaximizable( true );
    internalFrame.pack();

    return( internalFrame );
}


/**
 * An Action that disposes of an internal frame.
 **/
public class DisposeInternalFrameAction extends AbstractAction {

    /**
     * The internal pane to close.
     **/
    private JInternalFrame internalFrame;


    /**
     * CloseInternalFrameAction, constructor.
     * Set the name and icon for this action.
     * <p>
     * @param internalFrame The internal frame that we dispose of.
     **/
    public DisposeInternalFrameAction( JInternalFrame internalFrame ) {
        super( "Close", new ImageIcon( "close.gif" ) );
        this.internalFrame = internalFrame;
    }

    /**
     * Perform the action, dispose of the internal frame.
     * <p>
     * @param e The event causing us to be called.
     **/
    public void actionPerformed( ActionEvent e ) {
        internalFrame.dispose();
    }

}
```

FIGURE 17.4

A menu and tool-bar added to the internal frame.

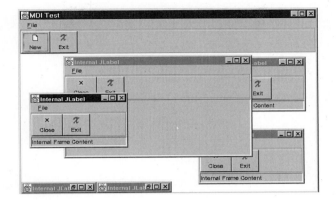

Summary

The JFC provides the `JDesktopPane` and `JInternalFrame` classes that work together to provide a framework for building multiple document interface type user interfaces. The `JInternalFrame` class's API is very similar to that of the `JFrame` class. The `JFrame` class provides a top-level window, while the `JInternalFrame` class provides a frame that can be added to other components. Typical use of the internal frames is for it to be added to a `JDesktopPane` instance. The `JDesktopPane` class extends the `JLayeredPane` class. When an internal frame is added to a desktop pane, it functions as a frame that can be independently sized, moved, iconified, and maximized from other internal frames contained in the desktop pane. The complete reference of the `JInternalFrame` class and the panes it creates were not presented, as they are the same as the `JFrame` class presented in Chapter 8. Once the `JFrame` class and its use is understood, the `JInternalFrame` class is almost completely understood as well.

Sample applications were presented that placed a desktop pane into the content pane of a `JFrame` instance. Multiple internal frames were added to the desktop pane. These applications demonstrated the cooperative nature of the `JDesktopPane` and `JInternalFrame` classes. These two classes are typically used together.

17

INTERNAL FRAMES

Dialog Boxes

JOptionPane

IN THIS CHAPTER

The JOptionPane class is the workhorse class for predefined dialog boxes contained in the JFC. In this chapter, you will learn how to use the JOptionPane class to

- Display message dialog boxes.
- Display and process confirmation dialog boxes.
- Display and process input dialog boxes.
- Display and process selection dialog boxes.
- Display and run Actions.
- Use internal frame versions of the dialog boxes.

The JOptionPane class provides a robust dialog box framework. It contains static methods for displaying simple dialog boxes to display information or prompt the user for input. These methods follow the naming convention showXXXDialog, where XXX is the type of dialog box to display. All JOptionPane dialog boxes are modal, meaning that they will block input to the rest of the application until the user finishes with the dialog box.

A JOptionPane dialog box consists of four regions: the icon, the message area, the input area, and the option button area. Each of these regions might or might not be shown. The exact size and placement of each region is dependent on the look-and-feel being used. Typical placement for these regions is shown on a sample dialog box shown in Figure 18.1.

FIGURE 18.1

JOptionPane *regions.*

The remainder of this chapter describes the myriad of options available in the JOptionPane, and gives examples of their use. This is followed by examples showing the use of each dialog box that can be constructed with the JOptionPane class.

Common JOptionPane Configuration

Convenience methods are provided in the JOptionPane class to display the predefined dialog boxes in the JOptionPane class. These methods conform to the following naming convention:

ShowXXXDialog

where *XXX* is the type of dialog box to display. Possible values for the type are Confirm, Input, Message, and Option. The parameters to the show method are dependent on the type of dialog box. However, many parameters are common to one or more of the dialog boxes. The remainder of this section will present the common parameters used by dialog boxes created in the JOptionPane class.

Parent Component

The first parameter to each of the show methods of the JOptionPane class is an AWT Component descendant used to determine the parent of the dialog box. If the component is not null, the frame of the component is used as the parent frame for the dialog box. The parent's frame is also used for the placement of the dialog box. The exact placement is dependent on the look-and-feel being used. If the parent component is null, a default parent frame will be used. The default frame can be set with the static setRootFrame method. The frame given to this method will be used as the parent for dialog boxes opened with a null parent parameter. Finally, if the root frame has not been set and a null parent is provided, the SwingUtilities getSharedOwnerFrame method is used to get the shared owner frame for the application. See the discussion of the SwingUtilities class in Chapter 32, "Swing Utilities," for a complete description of the shared owner frame.

The JOptionPane contains two static methods that are useful in a wide variety of situations, not just for dialog boxes. The first, named getFrameForComponent, will search the component's lineage to find the Frame for a given component. It will return null if the component doesn't have a Frame in its ancestry. The second method, named getDesktopPaneForComponent, performs a similar function except it looks for a JDesktopPane in the component's lineage. Both these methods are static. As such, they can be invoked from any class where the Frame or JDesktopPane of a component is required.

Message

Each of the predefined dialog boxes in the JOptionPane class takes an Object as a message parameter. The JOptionPane interprets the type of this Object and displays it accordingly. The most common usage for this parameter is a String. When a String is given for the message, it is displayed as is in the dialog box. However, the message parameter of the dialog box is far more powerful than a simple String viewer. If an Icon instance is given for the message, it is wrapped in an instance of the JLabel class and placed in the dialog box. If a Component instance is passed as the message, the Component is used directly. If another type of Object is passed as the message, its toString method will be called, and the returned String will be placed in the dialog box. Finally, an array of Object instances can be passed as the message. In this case, the logic previously described will be applied to each element in the array, and they will be stacked in the message area with lower array indexes on top of higher indexes. This provides a simple mechanism for a multi-line dialog box. An array of String instances can be passed as the message parameter. In this case, the String instances will be displayed in the dialog box one on top of the other.

Message Type

The message type parameter is used to define the category of the dialog box. Possible values for this parameter are ERROR_MESSAGE, INFORMATION_MESSAGE, WARNING_MESSAGE, QUESTION_MESSAGE, and PLAIN_MESSAGE. The look-and-feel currently being used can interpret this parameter to decide which icon to display and modify the dialog accordingly. There might be differing layouts and icons for each message type. The default icons for each message type for a given look-and-feel are shown in Table 18.1. Notice that the PLAIN_MESSAGE message type provides a dialog box that does not contain an icon. Examples of each of the message types will be given in the "Predefined Dialog Boxes" section later in this chapter.

TABLE 18.1   ICONS FOR MESSAGE TYPES

Message Type	Java LAF	Motif LAF	Windows LAF
ERROR_MESSAGE	⊗	⊘	⊗
INFORMATION_MESSAGE	𝒊	i	𝒊
PLAIN_MESSAGE	None	None	None
QUESTION_MESSAGE	?	?	?
WARNING_MESSAGE	!	!	⚠

Option Type

The final common parameter to the show family of methods is the option type. This parameter defines the set of buttons that will appear in the dialog box. The JOptionPane class defines constants for many typical use cases. The available constants, and the buttons shown in the dialog box when each constant is used, are shown in Table 18.2.

TABLE 18.2 OPTION TYPES

Parameter	Buttons
YES_NO_OPTION	Yes and No
YES_NO_CANCEL_OPTION	Yes, No, and Cancel
OK_CANCEL_OPTION	OK and Cancel
DEFAULT_OPTION	OK

> **NOTE**
>
> The text that appears on the buttons in the JOptionPane dialog box has been internationalized. The text is read from a resource file, and may not appear exactly as shown throughout this chapter when used with a JDK configured for a language other than English.

Properties

Instances of the JOptionPane class fire PropertyChangeEvent messages when values of bound properties change. Interested parties can add themselves as a property change listener to be notified when the JOptionPane instance has been modified.

Table 18.3 gives a list of the bound properties contained in the JOptionPane class, and the method used to alter the property.

TABLE 18.3 JOptionPane PROPERTY TYPES

Property	Setter Method	Getter Method
ICON_PROPERTY	setIcon	getIcon
INITIAL_SELECTION_ VALUE_PROPERTY	setInitialSelectionValue	getInitialSelectionValue
INITIAL_VALUE_PROPERTY	setInitialValue	getInitialValue
INPUT_VALUE_PROPERTY	setInputValue	getInputValue
MESSAGE_PROPERTY	setMessage	getMessage
MESSAGE_TYPE_PROPERTY	setMessageType	getMessageType
OPTION_TYPE_PROPERTY	setOptionType	getOptionType
OPTIONS_PROPERTY	setOptions	getOptions
SELECTION_VALUES_PROPERTY	setSelectionValues	getSelectionValues
VALUE_PROPERTY	setValue	getValue
WANTS_INPUT_PROPERTY	setWantsInput	getWantsInput

18

JOptionPane

Predefined Dialog Boxes

The JOptionPane class contains static methods for displaying many predefined dialog boxes. These are the show methods that were discussed earlier in the chapter. Using these methods allows the application to present a dialog box to the user with a single line of code. These methods encompass the most generally used portions of the JOptionPane class. The following sections present each of these methods in detail.

Message and Informational

The JOptionPane class can be used to present an informational dialog box to the user. One of the overloaded variants of the static showMessageDialog method can be used to do this. The complete signature of this method is the following:

```
showMessageDialog(Component, Object, String, int, Icon)
```

The Component and Object parameters are required. The remaining parameters are optional. Default values for the optional parameters display an informational dialog box with a title of "Message" and an OK button. The following application can be used to display the simple dialog box shown in Figure 18.2. The following code provides a vivid example of the power of the JOptionPane class. In a single line, a complete modal dialog box is displayed. This simple application framework can be used for the JOptionPane examples throughout this chapter. The relevant JOptionPane method can be substituted for the one in the main method of the JOptionTest application shown next.

```java
package com.foley.test;

import javax.swing.*;

/**
 * An application that displays a JOptionPane dialog box.
 *
 * @author Mike Foley
 **/
public class JOptionTest extends Object {


    /**
     * Application entry point.
     * Display a dialog box from the JoptionPane class.
     *
     * @param args Command line parameter. Not used.
     **/
    public static void main( String args[] ) {
        JOptionPane.showMessageDialog( null, "Invalid Entry" );
        System.exit(0);
    } // main

} // JOptionTest
```

FIGURE 18.2
Simple informational dialog box.

It is a simple matter to change the style of the dialog box. By specifying the type parameter, the default icon and title for the dialog box can be changed. This provides an easy method to specify the urgency of the dialog box. For example, adding the ERROR_MES-SAGE message constant, the urgency of the dialog box is considered to be greater than the informational dialog box shown in Figure 18.2. The dialog box produced with the following line of code is shown in Figure 18.3. Passing the showMessageDialog a null parent causes the dialog box to be centered on the screen. Passing a non-null parent parameter will cause the dialog box to be centered relative to the frame containing the component passed to the showMessageDialog method. Notice how the given message parameter appears in the center of the dialog box, and the title is used for the title of the dialog box.

```
JOptionPane.showMessageDialog( null, "Invalid Entry", "Error",
JOptionPane.ERROR_MESSAGE );
```

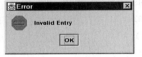

FIGURE 18.3
Error message dialog box.

By changing the type of the dialog, the JOptionPane used a different icon. This gives the user a visual cue for the type of the information being presented.

If the default icons don't meet your requirements, the icon to be placed in the dialog box can be specified. The following modification to the showMessageDialog method call creates a dialog box containing the stop icon (see Figure 18.4):

```
JOptionPane.showMessageDialog( null, "Invalid Entry",
                    "Error", JOptionPane.ERROR_MESSAGE, stop );
```

This example assumes that the icon named stop has been previously loaded. Loading images and creating icons was discussed in Chapter 5, "Basic Components," and will not be repeated here.

FIGURE 18.4
Dialog box with a custom icon.

18

JOptionPane

Yes/No/Cancel

In many situations, you need a dialog box to ask the user for confirmation before performing an action. The JOptionPane class provides the showConfirmDialog method to present the user with a modal dialog box asking for confirmation. A simple invocation of this method is shown next. The dialog box created by this method call is shown in Figure 18.5. In the figure notice that the Yes button is selected by default. Once again, the power of the JOptionPane is shown in this example. One simple line of code produces a modal dialog box requesting user input.

```
JOptionPane.showConfirmDialog( null, "Continue?" );
```

FIGURE 18.5

*Simple confirma-
tion dialog box.*

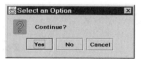

After presenting the dialog box, the thread in which the calling code is executing waits for the user input. This allows the JOptionPane method to return the selection the user makes. The returned value is an integer that can be one of the option constants defined in the JOptionPane class. Client code can check the returned value against these constants and take the appropriate action. This is demonstrated in the version of the JOptionTest application shown in the following code:

```
package com.foley.test;

import javax.swing.*;

/**
 * An application that displays a JOptionPane dialog box.
 *
 * @author Mike Foley
 **/
public class JOptionTest extends Object {

    /**
     * Application entry point.
     * Display a dialog box from the JOptionPane class.
     *
     * @param args Command line parameter. Not used.
     **/
    public static void main( String args[] ) {

        int result = JOptionPane.showConfirmDialog( null,
                                "Continue?",
                                "Confirmation Required",
```

```
                            JOptionPane.YES_NO_OPTION );
        switch( result ) {
            case JOptionPane.YES_OPTION:
            // Yes button was pressed.
            System.out.println( "Yes button" );
            break;

            case JOptionPane.NO_OPTION:
            // No button was pressed.
            System.out.println( "No button" );
            break;

            case JOptionPane.CANCEL_OPTION:
            // Cancel button was pressed.
            // (Not possible with the YES_NO_OPTION parameter.
            System.out.println( "Cancel button" );
            break;

            case JOptionPane.CLOSED_OPTION:
            // Window was closed without a button being pressed.
            System.out.println( "Closed button" );
            break;

        } // switch( result )

        System.exit(0);

    } // main

} // JOptionTest
```

When executed, this code produces the dialog box shown in Figure 18.6. You may notice that the Cancel button is not shown in this confirmation dialog box. This call to the showConfirmDialog method supplied two additional parameters. The first is the title for the dialog box, Confirmation Required in this example. The second additional parameter specifies which buttons to display. In this example, the YES_NO_OPTION was given, specifying that only the Yes and No buttons should be displayed.

FIGURE 18.6
Yes/No dialog box.

Table 18.4 lists the constants that can be given for the type parameter to the showConfirmDialog method. The type parameter determines which buttons are displayed as well as the possible values returned. Each dialog box can return the CLOSED_OPTION constant. This constant is returned if the user closes the dialog box without selecting any

of the buttons in the dialog box. The CLOSED_OPTION will typically be handled in the same way as the NO_OPTION or CANCEL_OPTION.

TABLE 18.4   CONFIRMATION DIALOG BOX CONSTANTS

Parameter Values	Buttons	Possible Return
YES_NO_OPTION	Yes and No	YES_OPTION, NO_OPTION, CLOSED_OPTION
YES_NO_CANCEL_OPTION	Yes, No, Cancel	YES_OPTION, NO_OPTION, CANCEL_OPTION, CLOSED_OPTION
OK_CANCEL_OPTION	OK and Cancel	OK_OPTION, CANCEL_OPTION, CLOSED_OPTION
DEFAULT_OPTION	OK	OK_OPTION, CLOSED_OPTION

An example of a dialog box constructed with the OK_CANCEL_OPTION is presented next. This code can be placed into the last JOptionTest application. The resulting dialog box is shown in Figure 18.7. In this example, an array of strings is given as the message parameter. This creates a multiline dialog box. Notice that the second String is a single character. This creates the blank line in the dialog box. If an empty string is given, the dialog box does not show the blank line.

```
String[] message = new String[3];
message[0] = "Selected objects will be deleted";
// Single space to cause blank line in dialog box.
message[1] = " ";
message[2] = "Do you want to continue?";
int result = JOptionPane.showConfirmDialog( null,
                                            message,
                                            "Confirmation Required",
JOptionPane.OK_CANCEL_OPTION );
```

FIGURE 18.7

OK/Cancel dialog box.

As with all the standard JOptionPane dialog boxes, the showConfirmDialog method has a variant that allows the icon to be specified with the message type parameter, or explicitly by passing an Icon parameter. When the following code is inserted into the JOptionTest application, the dialog box shown in Figure 18.8 is displayed. The ERROR_MESSAGE parameter is passed to the showConfirmDialog method, telling the JOptionPane to use the error Icon defined for the look-and-feel currently in use.

```
String[] message = new String[3];
message[0] = "Connection timed out";
message[1] = " ";
message[2] = "Do you wish to continue?";
int result = JOptionPane.showConfirmDialog( null,
                                            message,
                                            "Line Time Out",
                                            JOptionPane.YES_NO_OPTION,
                                            JOptionPane.ERROR_MESSAGE );
```

FIGURE 18.8

Error confirmation dialog box.

Input Dialog Boxes

There are many situations when a program needs to get input from the user. The JOptionPane class provides the showInputDialog to query the user for simple one-line input requirements. A simple input dialog box can be displayed with the following single line of code. The input dialog box displayed is shown in Figure 18.9. In this example, the dialog box is displayed with the default title, icon, and buttons. The default icon is the icon used with the QUESTION_MESSAGE message type.

```
String reply = JOptionPane.showInputDialog( null, "Enter your name:" );
```

FIGURE 18.9

Simple input dialog box.

Similar to the showConfirmDialog method, the showInputDialog method blocks the calling thread until the user dismisses the dialog box. The showInputDialog method returns a String containing the text entered by the user. If the Cancel button is clicked or the window is closed, a null sString is returned. If the user clicks the "OK" button without entering anything in the text area of the dialog box, an empty String is returned.

18

JOptionPane

This allows the calling code to distinguish between the various actions the user may have performed.

One of the overloaded versions of the `showInputDialog` method takes a title `String`, and message type parameter. A typical example of a warning input dialog box can be displayed with the line of code presented in the main method of the following version of the `JOptionTest` application. After the dialog box is dismissed, the application echoes the user's input to the console. The resulting dialog box is shown in Figure 18.10.

```
package com.foley.test;

import javax.swing.*;

/**
 * An application that displays a JOptionPane dialog box.
 *
 * @author Mike Foley
 **/
public class JOptionTest extends Object {


    /**
     * Application entry point.
     * Display a dialog box from the JOptionPane class.
     *
     * @param args Command line parameter. Not used.
     **/
    public static void main( String args[] ) {

        String reply = JOptionPane.showInputDialog( null,
                              "Enter log name:",
                              "Database Troubles",
                              JOptionPane.WARNING_MESSAGE );
        System.out.println( "User entered: " + reply );

        System.exit(0);

    } // main

} // JOptionTest
```

FIGURE 18.10

Warning input dialog box.

Selection

Perhaps the most interesting variant of the showInputDialog methods takes an array of Object instances and an Object reference as its last two parameters. The array parameter defines a list of choices to be presented to the user. The single Object parameter should be one of the items in the array. This will be the initially selected item in the choice. The presentation of the choice to the user is not defined in the JFC specification. It is left for the look-and-feel implementation. However, each of the look-and-feel implementations contained in the JFC use a JComboBox for presentation.

An example of using an array of Object instances in an input dialog box is presented next. An array of String instances is created and initialized. In the call to showInputDialog, the array is passed as the selection values, and the third item in the array is specified as the initially selected item, the string "Green" in this example. After the user dismisses the dialog box, the test application echoes the user's choice to the console. The dialog box is shown in Figure 18.11. The dialog box created in this example does not contain an icon. This is because the PLAIN_MESSAGE type was specified for the dialog box.

```
package com.foley.test;

import javax.swing.*;

/**
 * An application that displays a JOptionPane dialog box.
 *
 * @author Mike Foley
 **/
public class JOptionTest extends Object {

    /**
     * Application entry point.
     * Display a dialog box from the JOptionPane class.
     *
     * @param args Command line parameter. Not used.
     **/
    public static void main( String args[] ) {

        String[] colors = { "Red", "Yellow", "Green", "Black" };
        Object selected = JOptionPane.showInputDialog( null,
                        "Enter log name:",
                        "Database Troubles",
                        JOptionPane.PLAIN_MESSAGE,
                        null,
                        colors,
                        colors[2] );
```

```
        System.out.println( "User selected: " + selected );

        System.exit(0);

    } // main

} // JOptionTest
```

FIGURE 18.11

*Selection input
dialog box.*

Notice how the return value is an Object. The returned Object is the selected item if the user clicks the "OK" button. If "Cancel" is chosen, or the window is closed, null is returned from the showInputDialog method.

Both the array of selection items and the initially selected items are Objects. This allows any type of Object to be selected in the dialog box. For most types of Objects, the toString method is called to determine what is placed in the choice for the user. However, if the array contains icons, the icon itself is placed in the choice presented to the user.

Providing Custom Options

If the button combinations provided by the predefined option choice constants don't meet the needs of a dialog box, the showOptionDialog method is provided to customize the option buttons contained in the dialog box. This variant of the show dialog method takes an array of Object instances that are used as the options presented to the user. It also takes an Object parameter that is one of the items in the array. This Object is the default option for the dialog box. If the items in the array are Components, they are used directly. An Icon option is placed on a JButton instance and added to the dialog box. Other types of Objects have their toString method called to determine the String that is used for the text on a JButton. The instance of the JButton is then added to the dialog box.

An example of the showOptionDialog method is to create an Abort, Retry, Cancel dialog box. An array of Strings can be used for the options and passed to the showOptionDialog method. The following code creates this dialog box. The dialog box created in this example is shown in Figure 18.12.

```
package com.foley.test;

import javax.swing.*;
```

```
/**
 * An application that displays a JOptionPane dialog box.
 *
 * @author Mike Foley
 **/
public class JOptionTest extends Object {


    /**
     * Application entry point.
     * Display a dialog box from the JOptionPane class.
     *
     * @param args Command line parameter. Not used.
     **/
    public static void main( String args[] ) {

        String[] options = { "Abort", "Retry", "Cancel" };
        int choosen = JOptionPane.showOptionDialog( null,
                            "The device is not ready",
                            "Device Error",
                            JOptionPane.YES_NO_OPTION,
                            JOptionPane.ERROR_MESSAGE,
                            null,
                            options,
                            options[2] );
        //
        // Returned value depends on position of items in option
        // array parameter.  Changing this array forces this switch
        // statement to be changed as well.
        //
        switch( choosen ) {

            case 0:
            // Abort selected
            System.out.println( "Abort choosen" );
            break;

            case 1:
            // Retry selected
            System.out.println( "Retry choosen" );
            break;

            case 2:
            // Cancel selected
            System.out.println( "Cancel choosen" );
            break;

            case JOptionPane.CLOSED_OPTION:
            // User closed the box.  Nothing selected.
            System.out.println( "Dialog Closed" );
```

18

JOptionPane

```
          break;

      } // switch( reply )

        System.exit(0);
  } // main

} // JOptionTest
```

FIGURE 18.12

Abort, Retry, Cancel dialog box.

The integer returned from the dialog box can be used to determine which option the user chose. The returned value is the offset of the selected option in the option array parameter, or the CLOSED_OPTION if the user closed the dialog box without making a selection.

Care must be taken when testing the return value from the showOptionDialog method. Due to the fact that the returned value is the 0-based position of the selected object in the array of options, changing the order of the options in the array forces the code that tests the returned value to be changed. This is suspect in the design of the showOptionDialog method. Any code using this method should contain comments reflecting these details.

Rolling Your Own

The various versions of the static show*XXX*Dialog methods are adequate for a wide variety of dialog boxes. However, they don't solve every situation. For situations where there is not an appropriate canned dialog box, an instance of the JOptionPane class can be created and used as desired. The JOptionPane class contains a multitude of public constructors for this purpose. Most of these map to one or more of the static show*XXX*Dialog methods. In these cases, the show*XXX*Dialog should be used.

If your application contains Actions to perform control operations, it may be desirable to have an action-aware JOptionPane. This dialog box would act similar to the action-aware JMenu and JToolBar classes presented in Chapter 9, "Menus and Toolbars." This functionality can be accomplished by creating the JOptionPane with the proper controls.

The following demonstrates how to make an action-aware JOptionPane dialog box.

```
JButton[] options = new JButton[2];
options[0] = new JButton( "Exit" );
options[0].addActionListener( new ExitAction() );
```

```
options[1] = new JButton( "Cancel" );
options[1].addActionListener( new NoOpAction() );

JOptionPane pane = new JOptionPane( "Exit Application",
JOptionPane.QUESTION_MESSAGE,
JOptionPane.DEFAULT_OPTION,                                    null,
                                   options,
                                   options[1] );
for( int i = 0; i < options.length; i++ )
    options[i].addActionListener( new OptionPaneActionListener( pane ) );
JDialog dialog = pane.createDialog( parent,
                                    "Exit Confirmation" );

dialog.setVisible( true );


class OptionPaneActionListener extends Object
    implements ActionListener {

    /**
     * The JOptionPane which the action source
     * we are listening on lives.
     **/
    JOptionPane optionPane;


    public OptionPaneActionListener( JOptionPane optionPane ) {
        this.optionPane = optionPane;
    } // OptionPaneActionListener

    public void actionPerformed( ActionEvent event ) {
        optionPane.setValue( event.getSource() );
    } // actionPerformed

} // OptionPaneButton
```

In this example, and array of buttons is created, one button for each `action` in the dialog box. The `Action` is added as an `ActionListener` for the button. This will cause the `Action` to be executed when the button is pressed. The array of buttons is passed as the options to the `JOptionPane` constructor. When a `Component` is used as an option to a `JOptionPane`, it is the responsibility of the `Component` to call the `setValue` method of the `JOptionPane` instance when activated. The `value` property is set to the `Component` itself. This allows the caller to determine which option the user chose. The value is a bound property, allowing listeners to receive notifications when the `value` property changes. To perform this function, another `ActionListener` is added to each button. This `ActionListener` is a class dedicated to calling the `setValue` method of the `JOptionPane` it is given at construction time. The call is made when the listener receives an `actionPerformed` message. The value is set to the source of the `ActionEvent`.

18

JOptionPane

After the `ActionListeners` are added, the `createDialog` method of the `JOptionPane` class is called. This method creates a `JDialog` instance with the given title. The `JOptionPane` is added as the center component to the content pane of the dialog box. The `createDialog` method also adds an internal `WindowListener` to the `JDialog` instance. The `WindowListener` catches `WindowClosing` events, and sets the `value` property of the `JOptionPane` to `null` when such an event is received. This allows clients to know when the dialog box was closed without the user choosing an option. The `createDialog` method also adds a property change listener to the `JOptionPane`. When the `INPUT_VALUE_PROPERTY` or `VALUE_PROPERTY` change, the window is closed and disposed of. This is how a custom `Component` calling the `setValue` method closes the dialog box. The custom `Component` does not have to close the dialog box itself.

This example demonstrates the responsibilities of `Components` added to a `JOptionPane`. However, it is clumsy to use. Instead of manually creating the buttons and adding the required listeners, it would be more desirable to pass the `JOptionPane` an array of `Action` instances, and have `JOptionPane` do the work. This is not possible with the current implementation of the `JOptionPane` class. However, it is a simple matter to extend the `JOptionPane` class to provide the desired functionality. The `ActionOptionPane` is such a class (see Listing 18.1). It contains a constructor matching the full function `JOptionPane` constructor and overrides the `setOptions` method. In the constructor, the arguments are passed to the `JOptionPane` constructor, with the exception of the `options` and `initialValue` parameters. These are passed as `null`. This will cause an instance of the `JOptionPane` class to be created and configured with the proper message, message type, option type, and icon. As before, an `ActionListener` is created to call the `setValue` method when an option is selected. Next, the `setOptions` method is called with the original options array. Finally, the initial value is set to the given `Object`.

The overridden `setOptions` method creates a new array of options that it will pass to the `setOptions` method contained in the `JOptionPane` class. Each instance in the given array is checked to see if it is an `Action` instance. When an `Action` is detected, a `JButton` is created with the name of the `Action`. The `Action` is added as an `ActionListener` to the new button to execute the `Action` when the button is clicked. The `ActionListener` created in the constructor is also added to each button. This will call the `setValue` method of the dialog box when the button is pressed. The `JButton` replaces the `Action` in the options array that will be passed to the parent's `setOptions` method. If the `Object` in the options array is not an `Action`, it is not altered. When the processed array is passed to the `setOptions` method in `JOptionPane`, buttons will be added wherever `Action` instances were in the original options array.

LISTING 18.1   ActionOptionPane CLASS

```java
package com.foley.dialogs;

import java.awt.event.*;

import javax.swing.*;


/**
 * An Action aware JOptionPane extension.
 *
 * @author Mike Foley
 **/
public class ActionOptionPane extends JOptionPane {

    private final ActionListener setValueActionListener;

    /**
     * ActionOptionPane, constructor.
     *
     * Let the parent JOptionPane create and configure
     * the dialog. Set the options to the configured dialog
     * box using our version of the setOptions method.
     *
     * @param message The message for the dialog box.
     * @param messageType The type of the message.
     * @param optionType The type for the options.
     * @param icon The icon to use in the dialog box.
     * @param options The options to use for the dialog box.
     * @param initialValue The initally selected option.
     *                      Must be one of the options above.
     * @see JOptionPane
     **/
    public ActionOptionPane( Object message,
                    int messageType,
                    int optionType,
                    Icon icon,
                    Object options[],
                    Object initialValue) {

        super( message, messageType, optionType, icon, null, null );

        setValueActionListener = new ActionListener() {
            public void actionPerformed( ActionEvent event ) {
                setValue( event.getSource() );
            } // actionPerformed
        };

        setOptions( options );
```

continues

LISTING 18.1   CONTINUED

```
            setInitialValue( initialValue );
    }

    /**
     * setOptions, overrided from JOptionPane
     *
     * Scan the list of options, and for each Action create
     * a JButton and add the Action as an ActionListener.
     * Then let the super class, JOptionPane, process the
     * new list of options.
     *
* @param options The options, that become buttons,
                        for the dialog box.
    **/
    public void setOptions( Object[] options) {
        Object[] ourOptions = new Object[ options.length ];
        for( int i = 0; i < options.length; i++ ) {
            if( options[ i ] instanceof Action ) {
                Action action = ( Action )options[ i ];
                JButton button = new JButton(
                            ( String )action.getValue( Action.NAME ) );
                button.addActionListener( setValueActionListener );
                button.addActionListener( action );
                ourOptions[ i ] = button;
            } else {
                ourOptions[ i ] = options[ i ];
            }
        }
        super.setOptions( ourOptions );
    }

} // ActionOptionPane
```

A simple usage of the `ActionOptionPane` dialog class is shown in Listing 18.2. In this example, an exit confirmation dialog box is created and tied to the exit menu item. When the Exit menu item is selected, the resulting dialog box is shown in Figure 18.13. Notice that the returned value of the `ActionOptionPane` dialog box does not have to be checked. This is because the `Action` performs the function when the button is clicked. However, if the button that was clicked is required, it can be queried with the `getValue` method on the created `ActionOptionPane`.

If your application is designed with a rich collection of actions, this is a very convenient method to manage dialog boxes. It also provides an easy visual presentation that allows users to invoke operations.

FIGURE 18.13

Action-aware dialog box.

LISTING 18.2   EXIT DIALOG BOX USING ActionOptionPane

```java
package com.foley.test;

import java.awt.*;
import java.awt.event.*;
import java.util.*;

import javax.swing.*;

import com.foley.dialogs.*;
import com.foley.utility.*;


/**
 * An application that tests the ActionOptionPane dialog.
 *
 * @author Mike Foley
 **/
public class ActionOptionTest extends JFrame {

    public static ActionOptionTest frame;


    /**
     * ActionOptionTest, null constructor.
     **/
    public ActionOptionTest() {
        this( null );
    } // ActionOptionTest


    /**
     * ActionOptionTest, constructor.
     *
     * @param title The title for the frame.
     **/
    public ActionOptionTest( String title ) {
        super( title );
    } // ActionOptionTest
```

continues

18

JOptionPane

LISTING 18.2   CONTINUED

```
/**
 * frameInit, from JFrame
 *
 * Create the contrent for this frame.
 **/
protected void frameInit() {

    //
    // Let our super create the content and associated panes.
    //
    super.frameInit();

    JMenuBar menubar = createMenu();
    setJMenuBar( menubar );

} // frameInit


/**
 * Create the menu for the frame.
 *
 * @return The menu for the frame.
 **/
protected JMenuBar createMenu() {

    //
    // Load the images used.
    //
    Icon exitIcon = new ImageIcon( "exit.gif" );

    JMenuBar menubar = new JMenuBar();

    JMenu file = new JMenu( "File" );

    JMenuItem item = new JMenuItem( "Exit", exitIcon );
    item.setHorizontalTextPosition( SwingConstants.RIGHT );
    item.setMnemonic( KeyEvent.VK_X );
    item.setAccelerator( KeyStroke.getKeyStroke( KeyEvent.VK_X,
Event.CTRL_MASK ) );
    item.addActionListener( new ActionListener() {
        public void actionPerformed( ActionEvent e ) {
            showExitConfirmation( ( Component )e.getSource() );
        }
    } );
    file.add( item );

    menubar.add( file );

    return( menubar );
```

```
    } // createMenu

    /**
     * Display the Action aware exit confirmation dialog.
     *
     * @param parent The parent for the dialog. May be null.
     **/
    private void showExitConfirmation( Component parent ) {

        Action[] actions = new Action[2];
        actions[0] = new ExitAction( "OK" );
        actions[1] = new NoOpAction("Cancel" );
        JOptionPane pane = new ActionOptionPane( "Exit Application",
JOptionPane.QUESTION_MESSAGE,
JOptionPane.DEFAULT_OPTION,
                                        null, actions,
                                        actions[1] );

JDialog dialog = pane.createDialog( parent,
                                        "Exit Confirmation" );
        dialog.setVisible( true );

        //
// The action has been executed.
        // If the button which was pressed is needed,
        // it can be queried with the getValue method.
        //
        Object selected = pane.getValue();

    }


    /**
     * Application entry point.
     * Create the frame, and display it.
     *
     * @param args Command line parameter. Not used.
     **/
    public static void main( String args[] ) {

        JFrame frame = new ActionOptionTest( "ActionOptionPane Test" );
        frame.pack();
        frame.setVisible( true );

    } // main

} // ActionOptionTest
```

continues

18

JOptionPane

LISTING 18.2   CONTINUED

```
package com.foley.utility;

import java.awt.event.*;

import javax.swing.*;


/**
 * Class NoOpAction
 * <p>
 * An action which does nothing.  This is sometimes
 * needed for Action aware components.
 * <p>
 * @author Mike Foley
 * @version 1.2
 **/
public class NoOpAction extends AbstractAction {

    /**
     * The default name used in a menu.
     **/
    private static final String DEFAULT_NAME = "NoOp";


    /**
     * NoOpAction, default constructor.
     * <p>
     * Create the action with the default name.
     **/
    public NoOpAction() {
        this( DEFAULT_NAME, null );
    } // NoOpAction

    /**
     * NoOpAction, constructor.
     * <p>
     * Create the action with the given name.
     * <p>
     * @param name The name for the Action.
     **/
    public NoOpAction( String name ) {
        this( name, null );
    } // NoOpAction


    /**
     * putValue.
     *
     * The AbstractAction class putValue method may not
```

```
 * be passed a null newValue parameter. Filter those
 * call here.
 * @TODO Remove calls to putValue with a null newValue.
 *
 * @param key The key for the value.
 * @param newValue The value for the associated key.
 **/
public void putValue(String key, Object newValue) {
    if( key != null && newValue != null )
        super.putValue( key, newValue );
}

/**
 * actionPerformed, from ActionListener
 * <p>
 * Do nothing.
 * <p>
 * @param event The event causing the action to fire.
 **/
public void actionPerformed( ActionEvent event ) {
} // actionPerformed

} // NoOpAction
```

Internal Frame Versions

Each of the methods presented thus far for displaying a dialog box by using the JOptionPane class creates a dialog box in its own frame. This allows the dialog box to be moved independently from its parent frame. There are also versions of each of these methods that create an internal frame version of the dialog box. A complete guide to internal frames is given in Chapter 17, "Internal Frames."

Table 18.5 shows the list of methods that create frames and the corresponding internal frame version of the methods.

TABLE 18.5   INTERNAL FRAME METHOD NAMES

Frame Version	Internal Frame Version
CreateDialog	CreateInternalFrame
ShowConfirmDialog	ShowInternalConfirmDialog
ShowInputDialog	ShowInternalInputDialog
ShowMessageDialog	ShowInternalMessageDialog
showOptionDialog	ShowInternalOptionDialog

Just as the show*XXX*Dialog methods contain many overloaded variants of each method, there are many overloaded variants of the showInternal*XXX*Dialog methods. The functionality of these methods is the same for the external and internal frame versions. The primary difference is in the presentation of the dialog box. The internal versions of the dialog box cannot extend beyond the frame of their parent component. At the present time, the internally framed dialog boxes cannot be resized. However, there is no apparent reason for this restriction, and it may be lifted in a future version of the internal frame dialog boxes. The internal frame dialog boxes are the entire width of their parent component. This appears to be a bug in these dialog boxes. Unlike the non-internal dialog boxes in the JOptionPane class, the showInternal*XXX*Dialog methods must be passed a non-null parent. This parameter defines the frame where the dialog box will be displayed.

The JInternalOptionTest application shown in Listing 18.3 creates buttons in its content pane. Each button opens a different variant of the internal message dialog box by using the JOptionPane class. The application after being resized larger than its packed size is shown in Figure 18.14. Figure 18.15 shows the application after the Warning Dialog Box button was pressed. The internal dialog box is shown below the buttons in the application. Notice how displaying the internal dialog box also repositioned the buttons. The same undesirable behavior is exhibited when using the Windows look-and-feel. This is shown in Figure 18.16.

The initial implementation of the internal frame dialog boxes contained in the JOptionPane class is of inferior quality to the external frame versions of equivalent dialog boxes. The current implementation throws many exceptions in the user interface classes. The current state of these dialog boxes is unusable in a commercial quality application.

FIGURE 18.14

JInternalOption-Test *application before displaying internal dialog box.*

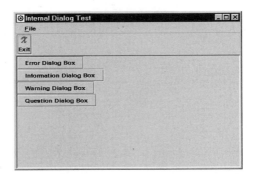

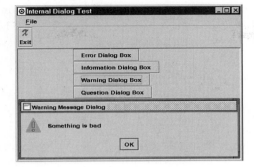

FIGURE 18.15

JInternalOption-
Test *after display-
ing internal warn-
ing dialog box.*

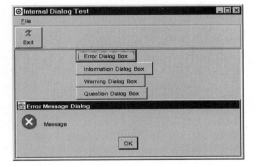

FIGURE 18.16

JInternalOption-
Test *after display-
ing internal error
dialog box using
the Windows look-
and-feel.*

18

JOptionPane

LISTING 18.3 JInternalOptionTest APPLICATION

```java
package com.foley.test;

import java.awt.*;
import java.awt.event.*;

import javax.swing.*;
import com.foley.utility.ApplicationFrame;
import com.foley.utility.JBox;


/**
 * An application that displays an internal
 * JOptionPane dialog box.
 *
 * @author Mike Foley
 **/
public class JInternalOptionTest extends Object {

    private JFrame frame;
```

continues

LISTING 18.3   CONTINUED

```
/**
 * JInternalOptionTest, default Constructor.
 * <p>
 * Create a frame. Add some buttons that display
 * an internal JOptionPane when activated.
 **/
public JInternalOptionTest() {
    frame = new ApplicationFrame( "Internal Dialog Test" );

    JComponent content = createContent();
    content.setBorder( BorderFactory.createLoweredBevelBorder() );
    frame.getContentPane().add( content );

    frame.pack();
    frame.setVisible( true );
}

protected JComponent createContent() {
    JBox box = JBox.createVerticalJBox();

    JButton errorMessageButton = new JButton( "Error Dialog Box" );
    errorMessageButton.addActionListener( new ActionListener() {
        public void actionPerformed( ActionEvent event ) {
            JOptionPane.showInternalMessageDialog( ( Component
)event.getSource(),
                            "Message",
                            "Error Message Dialog",
                            JOptionPane.ERROR_MESSAGE );
        } // actionPerformed
    } );
    box.add( errorMessageButton );

    JButton informationMessageButton = new JButton(
 "Information Dialog Box" );
    informationMessageButton.
addActionListener( new ActionListener() {
        public void actionPerformed( ActionEvent event ) {
Object[] message = { "TEST", "If you have a lot of information",
                            "to display to the user, you may",
                            "give an array of objects to the",
                            "message box.",
                            " ",
"The dialog box will display each object",
                            "on its own line, and size"
                            "the dialog", properly to fit"
                            "each object" };
                JOptionPane.showInternalMessageDialog( ( Component
)event.getSource(),
                            message,
```

```
                                    "Information Message Dialog",
                                    JOptionPane.INFORMATION_MESSAGE );
            } // actionPerformed
        } );
        box.add( informationMessageButton );

JButton warningMessageButton = new JButton( "Warning Dialog Box" );
        warningMessageButton.addActionListener( new ActionListener() {
            public void actionPerformed( ActionEvent event ) {
                JOptionPane.showInternalMessageDialog( ( Component
)event.getSource(),
                                    "Something is bad",
                                    "Warning Message Dialog",
                                    JOptionPane.WARNING_MESSAGE );
            } // actionPerformed
        } );
        box.add( warningMessageButton );

JButton questionMessageButton = new JButton( "Question Dialog Box" );
        questionMessageButton.addActionListener( new ActionListener() {
            public void actionPerformed( ActionEvent event ) {
                Object[] nodes = { "Node1", "Node2", "Node3" };
                JOptionPane.showInternalMessageDialog( ( Component
)event.getSource(),
                                    new JTree( nodes ),
                                    "Question Message Dialog",
                                    JOptionPane.QUESTION_MESSAGE );
            }
        } );
        box.add( questionMessageButton );

        return( box );
    }


    /**
     * Application entry point.
     * Create an instance of the test application.
     *
     * @param args Command line parameter. Not used.
     **/
    public static void main( String args[] ) {

        //
        // Enable this code for the windows L&F.
        // Only valid on the MS Windows platform.
        //
        /*
```

continues

LISTING 18.3   CONTINUED

```
        try {
            UIManager.setLookAndFeel(
"com.sun.java.swing.plaf.windows.WindowsLookAndFeel" );
        } catch( Exception ex ) {
System.err.println( "Exception: " + ex.getLocalizedMessage() );
        }
        */
        new JInternalOptionTest();
    } // main

} // JInternalOptionTest
```

Summary

The JOptionPane class provides a rich set of predefined dialog boxes. The static show*XXX*Dialog methods provide one-line methods for displaying many common dialog boxes. To further simplify application code, the dialog boxes block, enabling the calling code to process the user's response in the code immediately following the show*XXX*Dialog method used to display the dialog box.

In this chapter you have seen how to display message dialog boxes. The message type parameter allows the dialog to convey different levels of severity in the message. You also saw how to query the user for one-line of textual input. The JOptionPane class can be configured to present a set of choices to the user. The dialog box blocks until an option is selected or the user closes the dialog box. You also saw how to extend the JOptionPane class to create an action-aware dialog box.

There are internal versions of each of the pre-defined dialog boxes contained in the JOptionPane class. These dialog boxes are contained in its parent frame and do not extend beyond it. Unfortunately, the internal versions of these dialog boxes are of inferior quality and not usable at this time.

The predefined dialog boxes will suffice for many simple, and not so simple, dialog boxes. However, if one of the predefined dialog boxes doesn't meet your needs, the JOptionPane class also provides for almost unlimited customization.

CHAPTER 19

Choice Dialog Boxes

Using predefined system dialog boxes for choosing data in an application allows for a consistent look-and-feel across all applications. The current version of the JFC contains two such dialog boxes, the `JFileChooser`, and the `JColorChooser`.

In this chapter, you will learn how to

- Use the `JFileChooser` to select a file.
- Add `FileType` filters to a `JFileChooser`.
- Use the `JColorChooser` to select a color.

There are many situations where a choice is required from the user. These choices are often presented to the user in a dialog box. The JFC contains a stock dialog box for choosing a file and choosing a color. In the future, the set of stock chooser dialog boxes will be expanded. There are pending versions of components to choose a date, font, and money. There are also pending versions of preview classes. These classes can preview an image, an audio clip, or a file. Hopefully these classes will be supported in the near future. This chapter provides details and examples of using the stock dialog boxes.

The `JFileChooser` Class

There are many situations where you will want to prompt the user for a filename. The JFC provides a platform-independent `JFileChooser` class to obtain file information. The class contains a control to visually select a file. There is a convenient method to open a modal dialog box containing a file chooser instance. With this dialog box, your application can interact with the dialog box by using the same API for any platform on which it is executing. However, the appearance of the dialog box is dependent on the current look-and-feel being used. The `JFileChooser` class contains predefined modes for creating dialog boxes configured in Save or Open modes. It can also be customized for other file selection purposes.

To create an Open mode file choice dialog box, use the following code fragment.

```
JFileChooser fileChooser = new JFileChooser();
fileChooser.showOpenDialog( parentComponent );
```

The code in this example displays the file dialog box shown in Figure 19.1 for the Microsoft Windows look-and-feel. This is a dialog box familiar to all users of the MS Windows operating system. The same dialog box using the Java look-and-feel is shown in Figure 19.2. It is seen that the dialog boxes are basically the same with different icons. The top of the dialog box allows the user to choose drives and directories. There are buttons to move up a directory, go to the user's home directory, or create a new directory. The last two buttons allow a list or detailed view to be selected. The center of the dialog box displays a list of files and subdirectories contained in the current directory. The bottom of the dialog box displays the currently selected file and the current file filter.

The previous example uses default values for the initial path displayed in the chooser. A string can be given in the JFileChooser's constructor to specify the initial path that is displayed in the dialog box. The setCurrentDirectory method can be used to set the directory after the file chooser has been created. A file reference can be passed to the setSelectedFile method to specify the file initially selected in the file chooser component.

FIGURE 19.1

JFileChooser *default Open mode options MS Windows look-and-feel.*

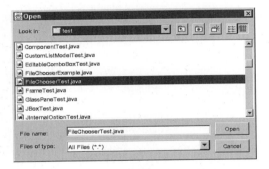

FIGURE 19.2

JFileChooser *default Open mode options Java look-and-feel.*

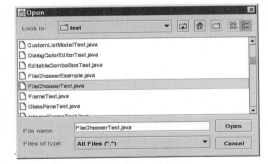

19

CHOICE DIALOG BOXES

Calling the showSaveDialog method instead of the showOpenDialog method will display a Save mode file chooser. The next code demonstrates this. Notice that the parent parameter in the showSaveDialog method box can be null. In this case the dialog box is centered on the display. A null parameter to the showOpenDialog method behaves in the same way.

The resulting dialog box is shown in Figure 19.3. In the figure, it is seen that the Save mode changes the title of the dialog box and the top button's text to Save. The functionality of the dialog box is identical to the Open mode dialog box.

```
JFileChooser fileChooser = new JFileChooser();
fileChooser.showSaveDialog( null );
```

FIGURE 19.3

JFileChooser
*default Save mode
options MS
Windows look-
and-feel.*

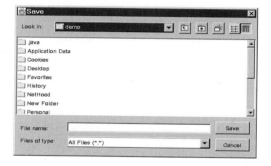

The file chooser dialog boxes you've seen display both files and directories. The dialog box can be configured to display only directories, files, or the default mode of both files and directories. The setFileSelectionMode method takes a single integer parameter to specify the mode. Possible values for the parameter are the constants FILES_ONLY, DIRECTORIES_ONLY, and FILES_AND_DIRECTORIES defined in the JFileChooser class. The getFileSelectionMode returns the current mode of the file chooser. The selection mode must be set before the dialog box is displayed to be effective. Hidden files can be shown or not shown in the file chooser. Passing true to the setFileHidingEnabled method will cause the file view to not show hidden files. The current state of this property may be queried with the isFileHidingEnabled method. The default value for this property is true to not display hidden files. By default, the file chooser allows one file or directory to be selected. Passing true to the setMultipleSelectionEnabled method will enable more than one file or directory to be selected. The current state of this property can be queried with the isMultipleSelectionEnabled method.

Specifying File Filters

By default, the `JFileChooser` dialog box shows all the files in the current directory. File filters can be added to the current set of choices, or a new filter can be specified. A file filter is defined in the `FileFilter` abstract class shown next. Extensions of this class that are to be used as file filters must provide implementation of the two methods defined in this class. The first method, `accept`, returns `true` or `false` depending on whether the given file matches the filter criteria. The second method, `getDescription`, returns the description of the file filter. This is used in the file filter choice box in the file chooser dialog box. The `FileFilter` class should not be a class, it should be an interface. This would give developers more flexibility when creating file filters.

```
public abstract class FileFilter {
    /**
     * Whether the given file is accepted by this filter.
     */
    public abstract boolean accept(File f);

    /**
     * The description of this filter. For example: "JPG and GIF Images"
     * @see FileView#getName
     */
    public abstract String getDescription();
}
```

The `addChoosableFileFilter` method adds the given file filter to the current set of filters. This method can be called repeatedly to add as many file filters as desired. The `setFileFilter` method sets the current file filter for the dialog box. If the `setFileFilter` method is called before any others are added, the filter passed to the method replaces the default filter that matches all files. If the `setFileFilter` method is called after one or more filters have been added, the given filter is set at the active filter in the dialog box. If the given filter was not previously added, it is added during the `setFileFilter` call. The default filter that matches all files is not removed in this case. The `removeChoosableFileFilter` method can be used to remove a filter from the dialog box. The current set of file filters can be queried with the `getChoosableFileFilters` method. The currently active file filter may be queried with the `getFileFilter` method. If there are not any file filters defined in the file chooser, the dialog box matches all files.

The following example demonstrates adding file filters to a `JFileChooser` dialog box. The `ExtensionFileFilter` class matches files whose extensions match one of the extensions registered with the filter. The extension is registered with the `addExtension` method and should not contain a '.' in the string passed to this method. The file extension match is case insensitive. The `ExtensionFileFilter` class extends the `FileFilter` abstract class so it can be used with the `JFileChooser` class. In the example, two

ExtensionFileFilter instances are created and configured, one for .java files, and the other matches both .html and .htm files. The filters are added to the JFileChooser instance before it is displayed. The filters will not be shown in the dialog box if they are added after any of the showDialog method variants are called. The resulting dialog box is shown in Figure 19.4.

```java
package com.foley.test;

import java.io.File;
import java.util.Hashtable;

import javax.swing.*;
import javax.swing.filechooser.*;


/**
 * An application that displays a JFileChooser dialog box.
 *
 * @author Mike Foley
 **/
public class FileChooserTest extends Object {

    /**
     * Application entry point.
     * Display a dialog box from the JOptionPane class.
     *
     * @param args Command line parameter. Not used.
     **/
    public static void main( String args[] ) {

        JFileChooser filechooser = new JFileChooser();

        //
        // Create a filter for Java source files.
        //
        ExtensionFileFilter filter = new ExtensionFileFilter();
        filter.addExtension( "java" );
        filter.setDescription( "Java Source Files" );
        filechooser.addChoosableFileFilter( filter );

        //
        // Create a filter for HTML pages.
        // Match both .html and .htm
        //
        filter = new ExtensionFileFilter();
        filter.addExtension( "html" );
        filter.addExtension( "htm" );
        filter.setDescription( "HTML Pages" );
        filechooser.addChoosableFileFilter( filter );
```

```
            //
            // Select the HTML filter.
            //
            filechooser.setFileFilter( filter );

            filechooser.showSaveDialog( null );
            System.exit(0);

        } // main

    } // FileChooserTest



/**
 * A file filter that matches file name extensions.
 * These is to be a filter like this in the standard
 * JFC classes, making this obsolete. This filter is
 * based on the ExampleFileFilter in the JDK1.2 example
 * programs.
 *
 * @author Mike Foley
 **/
class ExtensionFileFilter extends FileFilter {

    /**
     * The description for this file filter.
     **/
    private String description;

    /**
     * The extensions that match this filter.
     **/
    private Hashtable filters = null;

    /**
     * ExtensionFileFilter, default Constructor.
     **/
    public ExtensionFileFilter() {
        filters = new Hashtable();
        setDescription( "undefined" );
    }

    /**
     * Add the given extension to the list of extensions
     * to match. The extension should not have a '.' in
     * it.
     * <p>
     * @param extension The extension to add to the list of mathing extensions.
     **/
    public void addExtension( String extension ) {
            filters.put(extension.toLowerCase(), this);
```

```
    }

    /**
     * @return The description of this file filter.
     **/
    public String getDescription() {
        return( description );
    }

    /**
     * Set the description of the filter. This
     * will be displayed in the file chooser's filter
     * selection box.
     * <p>
     * @param description The file filter's description.
     **/
    public void setDescription( String description ) {
        this.description = description;
    }

    /**
     * The file matches if its extension is contianed in our
     * filter hashtable.
     * <p>
     * @param f The File to test for matching the filter criteria.
     * @return True if the given File matches the filter criteria.
     *         False otherwise.
     **/
    public boolean accept(File f) {
        if( f != null ) {
            if( f.isDirectory() ) {
                return true;
            }
        String extension = getExtension( f );
            if( extension != null && filters.get( extension ) != null )
{

                return true;
            }
        }
        return false;
    }

    /**
     * Determine the extension of the given File.
     * <p>
     * @param f The File whose extension is desired.
     * @return The extension of the given File, in lower case.
     **/
    protected String getExtension( File f ) {
        if(f != null) {
            String filename = f.getName();
```

```
            int i = filename.lastIndexOf( '.' );
                if(i>0 && i<filename.length() - 1) {
                        return filename.substring( i + 1 ).toLowerCase();
            };
            }
        return null;
    }

}
```

FIGURE 19.4

File filters added to a JFileChooser *dialog box.*

> **NOTE**
>
> The ExtensionFileFilter class shown in the previous example is based on the demonstration applications in the 1.2 JDK. Standard file filters should be included with JFC, making this class obsolete. Until that time, it can be used with the JFileChooser class.

19

CHOICE DIALOG BOXES

Retrieving the Selected File or Directory

Up to this point, you have seen how to display a file chooser dialog box. If the file chooser is shown with any of the showDialog methods contained in the JFileChooser class, the resulting dialog box is modal. The showDialog method returns an integer containing the action selected by the user. Possible return values are the constants APPROVE_OPTION and CANCEL_OPTION, defined in the JFileChooser class. APPROVE_OPTION return type corresponds to the user choosing the button containing Open or Save in one of the default configurations. CANCEL_OPTION corresponds to the user choosing the Cancel button. When the file chooser dialog box is closed by an operation other than choosing one of the two buttons on the dialog box, the returned value is –1. This is consistent with the dialog boxes in the JOptionPane class seen in the previous chapter.

If `APPROVE_OPTION` is returned from the dialog box, the selected file or directory then needs to be queried from the file chooser. The `getCurrentDirectory` method returns the directory where the file chooser is displaying. The `getSelectedFile` and `getSelectedFiles` methods return the files selected in the chooser. When the file chooser is configured to display both files and directories, the `getSelectedFile` method returns `null` if a directory is selected or nothing is selected. If the file selection mode is `DIRECTORIES_ONLY`, the `getSelectedFile` method returns the selected directory.

The following example demonstrates typical usage of a file chooser dialog box. The `JFileChooser` instance is created and configured with the desired file filters. The appropriate `showDialog` method is called to display the modal dialog box. In this example, the `showSaveDialog` method is used to display a Save-type dialog box. After the dialog box is closed, the returned value is checked and acted upon. The `JFileChooser` class does not actually save the file. It simply gives the user a component to select a file. The `ExtensionFileFilter` class in this example is identical to that presented in the last example.

```java
package com.foley.test;

import java.io.File;
import java.util.Hashtable;

import javax.swing.*;
import javax.swing.filechooser.*;


/**
 * An application that displays a JFileChooser dialog box.
 *
 * @author Mike Foley
 **/
public class FileChooserTest extends Object {

    /**
     * Application entry point.
     * Display a dialog box from the JOptionPane class.
     *
     * @param args Command line parameter. Not used.
     **/
    public static void main( String args[] ) {

        JFileChooser filechooser = new JFileChooser();

        ExtensionFileFilter filter = new ExtensionFileFilter();
        filter.addExtension( "java" );
        filter.setDescription( "Java Source Files" );
        filechooser.addChoosableFileFilter( filter );
```

```
            filter = new ExtensionFileFilter();
            filter.addExtension( "html" );
            filter.addExtension( "htm" );
            filter.setDescription( "HTML Pages" );
            filechooser.addChoosableFileFilter( filter );
            filechooser.setFileFilter( filter );

            int selected = filechooser.showSaveDialog(null);

            switch( selected ) {
                case JFileChooser.APPROVE_OPTION:
                    File selectedFile = filechooser.getSelectedFile();
                    File directory = filechooser.getCurrentDirectory();
                    If( selectedFile != null ) {
                        // Save the file.
                    }
                    break;
                case JFileChooser.CANCEL_OPTION:
                    break;

                default:
                    // catches -1, the user closing the dialog without
                    // hitting a button.
                    break;
            }
            System.exit(0);

        } // main

} // FileChooserTest
```

The Accessory Component

The JFileChooser class provides methods to manage an accessory component. When added to a file chooser instance, the accessory component is displayed to the right of the file list. The accessory component must be an extension of the JComponent class and is set with the setAccessory method. The current accessory component can be queried with the getAccessory method.

The accessory component is often used to display a preview of the currently selected file. However, this component can be used for any purpose desired. Additionally, the accessory can be a complex component containing many child components to create an arbitrarily complex view.

The following example adds an image viewing accessory to a JFileChooser instance. The ImagePreviewer class extends the JLabel class and is used as an image viewer. The class listens for PropertyChangeEvents from the file chooser with which it is associated.

When the SELECTED_FILE_CHANGED_PROPERTY changes, the newly selected file is loaded. If the file contains an image, that image is set in the viewer. The image is then displayed in the file chooser dialog box. The resulting file chooser dialog box is shown in Figure 19.5.

```java
package com.foley.test;

import java.awt.*;
import java.io.File;
import java.util.Hashtable;
import java.beans.*;

import javax.swing.*;
import javax.swing.border.Border;
import javax.swing.filechooser.*;


/**
 * An application that displays a JFileChooser dialog box.
 *
 * @author Mike Foley
 **/
public class FileChooserTest extends Object {

    /**
     * Application entry point.
     * Display a dialog box from the JOptionPane class.
     *
     * @param args Command line parameter. Not used.
     **/
    public static void main( String args[] ) {

        try {
            UIManager.setLookAndFeel(
"com.sun.java.swing.plaf.windows.WindowsLookAndFeel" );
        } catch( Exception ex ) {
            System.err.println( "Exception: " + ex.getLocalizedMessage() );
        }


        JFileChooser filechooser = new JFileChooser();

        ExtensionFileFilter filter = new ExtensionFileFilter();
        filter.addExtension( "gif" );
        filter.setDescription( "GIF Images" );
        filechooser.setFileFilter( filter );

        filter = new ExtensionFileFilter();
        filter.addExtension( "jpeg" );
```

```
        filter.setDescription( "JPEG Images" );
        filechooser.addChoosableFileFilter( filter );

        ImagePreviewer accessory = new ImagePreviewer( filechooser );
        accessory.setBorder( BorderFactory.createLoweredBevelBorder() );
        accessory.setPreferredSize( new Dimension( 200, 200 ) );
        filechooser.setAccessory( accessory );

        int selected = filechooser.showOpenDialog(null);
        switch( selected ) {
            case JFileChooser.APPROVE_OPTION:
                File selectedFile = filechooser.getSelectedFile();
                File directory = filechooser.getCurrentDirectory();
                // Open the file
                break;
            case JFileChooser.CANCEL_OPTION:
                break;

            default:
                // Closed without hitting a button.
                break;
        }
        System.exit(0);

    } // main

} // FileChooserTest


/**
 * A class that gives a priview of gif or jpeg images.
 *
 * @author Mike Foley
 **/
class ImagePreviewer extends JLabel
    implements PropertyChangeListener {

    /**
     * ImagePreviewer, Constructor.
     * <p>
     * Register as a PropertyChangeListener to the
     * given JFileChooser instance. Center the icon
     * in our view area.
     * <p>
     * @param fileChooser The JFileChooser that we are previewing for.
     **/
    public ImagePreviewer( JFileChooser fileChooser ) {
        if( fileChooser == null ) {
            throw new IllegalArgumentException(
                    "fileChooser must be non-null" );
        }
```

```
        fileChooser.addPropertyChangeListener( this );
        setHorizontalAlignment( SwingConstants.CENTER );
        setVerticalAlignment( SwingConstants.CENTER );
    }

    /**
     * The the image in the given file.
     * <p>
     * @param f The file to load the image from.
     **/
    public void loadImageFromFile( File file ) {
        Icon icon = null;

        if( file != null ) {
            ImageIcon filesIcon =
                    new ImageIcon( file.getPath() );

            Dimension size = getSize();
            Insets insets = getInsets();
            if( insets != null ) {
                size.width -= insets.right + insets.left;
                size.height -= insets.top + insets.bottom;
            }

            //
            // Scale the image to our size.
            //
            if(filesIcon.getIconWidth() > size.width ) {

                icon = new ImageIcon(
                        filesIcon.getImage().getScaledInstance( size.
                                       ➥width,
                        size.height, Image.SCALE_DEFAULT ) );
            } else if(filesIcon.getIconWidth() < size.width ) {
                icon = new ImageIcon(
                        filesIcon.getImage().getScaledInstance( size.
                                       ➥width,
                        size.height, Image.SCALE_DEFAULT ) );
            } else {
                icon = filesIcon;
            }
        }
        setIcon( icon );
    }

    /**
     * propertyChange, from PropertyChangeListener
     * <p>
     * A property in the JFileChooser we are associated with
     * has changed. If it is the selected file property, try
     * to load the image in the file.
```

```
    *  <p>
    *  @param event The PropertyChangeEvent.
    **/
    public void propertyChange( PropertyChangeEvent event ) {

        String propertyName = event.getPropertyName();
        if( propertyName.equals( JFileChooser.
➡SELECTED_FILE_CHANGED_PROPERTY ) ) {
            File file = ( File )event.getNewValue();
            if(isShowing()) {
                loadImageFromFile( file );
                repaint();
            }
        }
    }

} // ImagePreviewer
```

FIGURE 19.5

Image viewer accessory added to a JFileChooser dialog box.

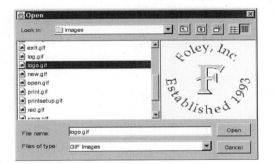

File Views

Adding a file view instance to a file chooser allows custom file user interface information to be displayed. The name, icon, and description associated with a file can be specified. A file view must be an extension of the abstract FileView class shown next. As with the FileFilter class, developers would have more options if the FileView class was an interface and a default implementation that returned null from each method was provided. This would allow developers to have any class implement the interface, rather than being required to inherit from the FileView class. The setFileView method is used to set the file view class. Similarly, the getFileView method returns the file view currently in use, or null if a file view has not been set for the file chooser. There can be only one user-specified file view for a file chooser. Thus the FileView class must be able to handle all file types for the file chooser.

```
public abstract class FileView {
    /**
```

19

CHOICE DIALOG BOXES

```
   * The name of the file. Normally this would be simply f.getName()
   */
  public abstract String getName(File f);

  /**
   * A human readable description of the file. For example,
   * a file named jag.jpg might have a description that read:
   * "A JPEG image file of James Gosling's face"
   */
  public abstract String getDescription(File f);

  /**
   * A human readable description of the type of the file. For
   * example, a jpg file might have a type description of:
   * "A JPEG Compressed Image File"
   */
  public abstract String getTypeDescription(File f);

  /**
   * The icon that represents this file in the JFileChooser.
   */
  public abstract Icon getIcon(File f);

  /**
   * Whether the directory is traversable or not. This might be
   * useful, for example, if you want a directory to represent
   * a compound document and don't want the user to descend into it.
   */
  public abstract Boolean isTraversable(File f);

}
```

When a `FileView` extension is asked for a piece of information, it can delegate to the
system default data by returning `null` from the query method. For example, if the
`getIcon` method in the `FileView` class returns `null`, the system default icon will be used
for the file or directory.

The `JavaFileView` class shown next when added to a `JFileChooser` instance displays
the familiar Java coffee cup icon for files with the extension of `.java`. For methods that
the class returns data for, it tests the given file's extension. If it is `.java`, the information
for the Java source file is returned. Otherwise, `null` is returned, allowing default processing for the file or directory.

```
package com.foley.utility;

import java.io.File;

import javax.swing.Icon;
import javax.swing.ImageIcon;
import javax.swing.filechooser.FileView;
```

```java
public class JavaFileView extends FileView {

    /**
     * The icon for Java source files.
     **/
    Icon cupIcon = null;


    /**
     * Allow default processing.
     * <p>
     * @param file The file whose name is requested.
     * @return The name for the file.
     **/
    public String getName( File file ) {
        return( null );
    }


    /**
     * @param file The file whose description is requested.
     * @return The description for the given file.
     **/
    public String getDescription( File file ) {
        String extension = getExtension( file );
        if( extension != null && extension.equals( "java" ) ) {
            return( "A Java source file" );
        } else {
            return( null );
        }
    }


    /**
     * @param file The file whose type description is requested.
     * @return The type description for the given file.
     **/
    public String getTypeDescription( File file ) {
        String extension = getExtension( file );
        if( extension != null && extension.equals( "java" ) ) {
            return( "Java source file" );
        } else {
            return( null );
        }
    }


    /**
     * @param file The file whose icon is requested.
     * @return The icon for the given file.
     **/
```

```
public Icon getIcon( File file ) {
    Icon icon = null;
    String extension = getExtension( file );
    if( extension != null && extension.equals( "java" ) ) {

        if( cupIcon == null )
            cupIcon = new ImageIcon( "javacup.gif" );

        icon = cupIcon;
    }
    return( icon );
}


/**
 * Allow default processing.
 * <p>
 * @param file The directory to test.
 * @return null to enable default processing.
 **/
public Boolean isTraversable( File file ) {
    return( null );
}

/**
 * Determine the extension of the given file.
 * <p>
 * @param f The File whose extension is desired.
 * @return The extension of the given File, in lower case.
 **/
protected String getExtension( File f ) {
        if(f != null) {
            String filename = f.getName();
        int i = filename.lastIndexOf( '.' );
            if(i>0 && i<filename.length() - 1) {
                    return filename.substring( i + 1 ).toLowerCase();
            };
            }
    return null;
}

} // JavaFileView
```

The `FileChooserTest` application was modified as shown next to use the `JavaFileView` class. The resulting dialog box is shown in Figure 19.6.

```
package com.foley.test;

import java.awt.*;
import java.io.File;
```

```
import javax.swing.*;
import javax.swing.filechooser.*;

import com.foley.utility.JavaFileView;


/**
 * An application that displays a JFileChooser dialog box
 * using a JavaFileView file view class.
 *
 * @author Mike Foley
 **/
public class FileChooserTest extends Object {

    /**
     * Application entry point.
     * Display a JFileChooser class.
     *
     * @param args Command line parameter. Not used.
     **/
    public static void main( String args[] ) {

        try {
            UIManager.setLookAndFeel(
"com.sun.java.swing.plaf.windows.WindowsLookAndFeel" );
        } catch( Exception ex ) {
            System.err.println( "Exception: " + ex.getLocalizedMessage()
);
        }


        JFileChooser filechooser = new JFileChooser();

        ExtensionFileFilter filter = new ExtensionFileFilter();
        filter.addExtension( "java" );
        filter.setDescription( "Java Source Files" );
        filechooser.addChoosableFileFilter( filter );
        filechooser.setFileFilter( filter );

        filechooser.setFileView( new JavaFileView() );

        int selected = filechooser.showOpenDialog(null);
        switch( selected ) {
            case JFileChooser.APPROVE_OPTION:
                File selectedFile = filechooser.getSelectedFile();
                File directory = filechooser.getCurrentDirectory();
                break;
            case JFileChooser.CANCEL_OPTION:
                break;

            default:
```

19

CHOICE DIALOG BOXES

```
            break;
        }
        System.exit(0);

    } // main

} // FileChooserTest
```

FIGURE 19.6

JavaFileView instance added to a JFileChooser dialog box.

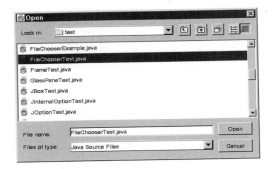

Customizing the `JFileChooser`

The `JFileChooser` dialog box contains predefined configurations for Save and Open modes. The dialog box can be used in other situations when a file is required. The text, mnemonic, and ToolTip for the Approve button can be queried and customized. The methods for customizing the Approve button are shown in Table 19.1.

TABLE 19.1 APPROVE BUTTON CUSTOMIZATION METHODS IN THE `JFileChooser` CLASS

Property	*Setter Method*	*Getter Method*
Mnemonic	setApproveButtonMnemonic	getApprovebuttonMnemonic
Text	setApproveButtonText	getApproveButtonText
ToolTip	setApproveButtonToolTip	getApproveButtonToolTip

Each of the string values shown in Table 19.1 is a bound property of the `JFileChooser` class. Listeners will receive notification when any of these properties are altered. The complete list of bound properties defined in the `JFileChooser` class is given in Table 19.2.

TABLE 19.2 JFileChooser **CLASS BOUND PROPERTIES**

Property	Setter Method	Getter Method
SELECTED_FILE CHANGED_PROPERTY	setSelectedFile	getSelectedFile
DIRECTORY_CHANGED PROPERTY	setCurrentDirectory	getCurrentDirectory
DIALOG_TYPE CHANGED_PROPERTY	setDialogType	getDialogType
APPROVE_BUTTON TOOL_TIP_TEXT CHANGED_PROPERTY	setApproveButton ToolTipText	getApproveButton ToolTipText
APPROVE_BUTTON MNEMONIC_CHANGED PROPERTY	setApproveButton Mnemonic	getApproveButton Mnemonic
APPROVE_BUTTON TEXT_CHANGED PROPERTY	setApproveButtonText	getApproveButtonText
CHOOSABLE_FILE FILTER_CHANGED PROPERTY	addChoosableFile Filter/remove ChoosableFileFilter	resetChoosableFile Filters/get ChoosableFileFilters
ACCESSORY_CHANGED PROPERTY	setAccessory	getAccessory
FILE_SELECTION MODE_CHANGED_ PROPERTY	setFileSelectionMode	getFileSelectionMode
MULTI_SELECTION ENABLED_CHANGED PROPERTY	setMultiSelection Enabled	isMultiSelection Enabled
FILE_HIDING CHANGED_PROPERTY	setFileHidingEnabled	isFileHidingEnabled
FILE_FILTER CHANGED_PROPERTY	setFileFilter	getFileFilter
FILE_VIEW CHANGED_PROPERTY	setFileView	getFileView
FILE_SYSTEM_VIEW CHANGED_PROPERTY	setFileSystemView	getFileSystemView

The title of the customized dialog box can be specified using the setDialogTitle method. The current title can be queried with the getDialogTitle method. The type of the dialog box can be queried using the getDialogType method. Possible dialog types are OPEN_DIALOG, SAVE_DIALOG, and CUSTOM_DIALOG. When the showOpenDialog or showSaveDialog method is called, the type is set appropriately. If any of the customization methods are called, the dialog is set to CUSTOM_DIALOG. An existing JFileChooser instance can be reset to one of the default configurations by using the setDialogType method.

The CustomFileChooserTest application shown next displays a custimized JFileChooser dialog box. Notice that the showDialog method is called instead of the showOpenDialog or showSaveDialog method. When the showDialog method is called, the current settings for the Approve button are used. Instead of calling in the setApproveButtonText, the showDialog box can be passed the text for the Approve button as its second parameter. In the example, null is passed as the second parameter, telling the JFileChooser class to use the current value of the Approve button text property. As with the other show methods, the first parameter is the parent component for the dialog box. The resulting dialog box is shown in Figure 19.7.

```java
package com.foley.test;

import java.io.File;

import javax.swing.*;


/**
 * An application that displays a customized
 * JFileChooser dialog box.
 *
 * @author Mike Foley
 **/
public class CustomFileChooserTest extends Object {

    /**
     * Application entry point.
     * Display a dialog box from the JOptionPane class.
     *
     * @param args Command line parameter. Not used.
     **/
    public static void main( String args[] ) {

        JFileChooser filechooser = new JFileChooser();

        filechooser.setApproveButtonText( "Attach" );
        filechooser.setApproveButtonMnemonic( 'A' );
```

```
        filechooser.setApproveButtonTool
➥TipText( "Attach the selected file" );
        filechooser.setDialogTitle( "Attach File Selection" );

        int selected = filechooser.showDialog( null, null );
        switch( selected ) {
            case JFileChooser.APPROVE_OPTION:
                File selectedFile = filechooser.getSelectedFile();
                File directory = filechooser.getCurrentDirectory();
                break;
            case JFileChooser.CANCEL_OPTION:
                break;

            default:
                break;
        }
        System.exit(0);

    } // main

} // CustomFileChooserTest
```

FIGURE 19.7

A customized JFileChooser dialog box.

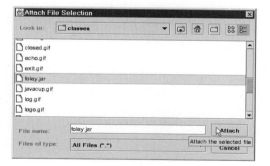

The JColorChooser Class

The JColorChooser class provides a control that can be used to visually select a color. The control can be used directly like any of the other JFC visual components, but the class also contains a convenient method that will display a color chooser in a modal dialog box. A color chooser dialog box is easily displayed. The following line of code will create and display a modal dialog box containing a JColorChooser instance. The resulting dialog box is shown in Figure 19.8. Three instances of the color chooser dialog box are shown in the figure to allow both tabs to be seen.

```
JColorChooser.showDialog( null, "Choose A Color", Color.red );
```

FIGURE **19.8**

Two
JColorChooser
dialog boxes.

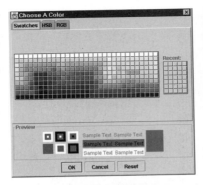

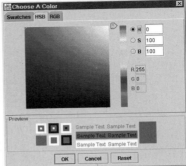

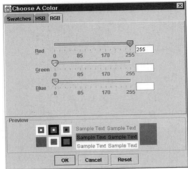

NOTE

The text for the buttons in the color chooser is read from a resource bundle. This may result in the text on the buttons to appear differently than shown in the figures in this chapter if a non-English version of the JDK is being used.

The JColorChooser class specifies the color as an RGB or HSB value. In the RGB color model three parameters define the color: the red, green, and blue portions of the color. The "Swatches" tab allows the user to select a color from a palette of existing colors. The box of colors on the right of the panel contains the most recently selected colors from the palette. The "RGB" tab allows the user to specify the exact red, blue, and green portions of the color via slider controls.

In the HSB color model the three parameters that define a color are hue, saturation, and brightness. The hue varies between 0 and 360 degrees, while the saturation and brightness vary between 0 and 100 percent. The vertical slider in the color chooser varies the parameter associated with the checked radio button. The range of the slider depends on the color property being varied. The color may also be selected by dragging the mouse in the color region. As the mouse is dragged in this region, the HSB and RGB values are updated.

Each panel contains a preview area where the current color in the chooser is shown in a variety of conditions.

Using the `JColorChooser` Dialog Box

The static `showDialog` method contained in the `JColorChooser` class creates and displays a modal dialog box used for selecting a color. The `ColorChooserTest` application shown next presents a simple application that demonstrates how this method is used. Notice how the code that creates and displays the dialog box is only one line of code. The resulting dialog box is shown in Figure 19.8. Once again, the power of the stock JFC dialog boxes is shown by this example. One line of code produces a very powerful dialog box for obtaining any color that can be used in Java.

```
package com.foley.test;

import java.awt.Color;
import javax.swing.*;


/**
 * An application that displays a JColorChooser dialog box.
 *
 * @author Mike Foley
 **/
public class ColorChooserTest extends Object {

    /**
     * Application entry point.
     * Display a dialog box from the JColorChooser class.
     *
     * @param args Command line parameter. Not used.
     **/
    public static void main( String args[] ) {
        Color selectedColor = JColorChooser.showDialog( null,
                                        "Choose A Color", Color.red );
        if( selectedColor != null ) {
            // selectedColor is the color the user specified.
        } else {
            // The user hit Cancel, or closed the dialog.
        }
        System.exit(0);
    } // main

} // ColorChooserTest
```

The first parameter to the `showDialog` method is the parent component. If the parent is `null`, as in the `ColorChooserTest` application, the dialog box is centered on the screen.

The second parameter is a string that will be used as the title of the dialog box. The final parameter is the initial color in the dialog box. Specifying `null` as the initial color will cause the dialog to use `Color.white` as the initial color.

When the OK button is selected, the dialog box is hidden, and the color defined in the `JColorChooser` is returned. If the user clicks the Cancel button or dismisses the dialog box by some other method, `null` is returned.

The Reset button is provided to allow the user the ability to restore the initial color that was displayed in the dialog box after making edits. The initial color is the color specified in the `showDialog` method call.

The `JColorChooser` class views the data defined by the `ColorSelectionModel` interface shown next. The interface defines methods to set and query the selected color as well as add and remove listeners. The `ChangeListener` is notified whenever the `Color` instance in the model changes. The current model being used by a color chooser can be queried with the `getSelectionModel` method. Similarly, the model can be set with the `setSelectionModel` method, or it can be specified in the `JColorChooser` class' constructor.

```
public interface ColorSelectionModel {
    /**
     * @return  the model's selection.
     * @see     #setSelectedColor
     */
    Color getSelectedColor();

    /**
     * Sets the model's selected color to <I>color</I>.
     *
     * Notifies any listeners if the model changes
     *
     * @see   #getSelectedColor
     * @see   #addChangeListener
     */
    void setSelectedColor(Color color);

    /**
     * Adds <I>listener</I> as a listener to changes in the model.
     */
    void addChangeListener(ChangeListener listener);

    /**
     * Removes <I>listener</I> as a listener to changes in the model.
     */
    void removeChangeListener(ChangeListener listener);
}
```

Using the `JColorChooser` as a Component

There are many situations where multiple colors need to be specified. Opening a separate dialog box for each color may not be convenient. One such example is a property sheet that allows multiple options to be specified. A simple example of such a display is shown in Figure 19.9. In this property sheet, the foreground and background colors can be specified with the `JColorChooser`. The radio buttons specify which color is being edited. A label is provided to show the current color combination. The remainder of this section will explore how the `JColorChooser` is used in this property sheet, named `ColorEditor`.

The `ColorEditor` acts as a mediator between the components on the panel. The three components are the radio group that specifies which property is being edited (foreground or background), the `JLabel` that shows the current color scheme, and the `JColorChooser` that allows the current property to be edited.

FIGURE 19.9

Foreground and background chooser.

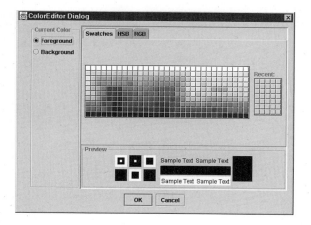

The `ColorEditor` constructor presented in the `ColorEditor` class's Listing 19.1 shows how the composite components and listeners are created. First, an `ActionListener` named `radioListener` is created. This is an anonymous inner class that will be added to each of the two radio buttons. When an `ActionEvent` is received, the listener determines which radio button was chosen. Then the `foreground` attribute, which is used to specify which property is being edited, is set. The color chooser is updated to the current value of the new property. The `setColor` method of `JColorChooser` is used for this purpose. This method is overloaded. There are also versions taking the RGB color definition. After this, the actual radio buttons and button group are created. The `ActionListener` is added to each radio button. The buttons are placed in a panel. This allows the border to be set on the panel and have it surround both radio buttons.

The final component created is the `JColorChooser` itself. This component is created with the current foreground color of the Color Editor and placed into the center portion of the panel. A `ChangeListener` is added to the color chooser's selection model to receive notification when the selected color changes. This allows the `ColorEditor` to fire a `PropertyChangeEvent` to listeners of the Color Editor itself when the color changes. The foreground color and background color are both bound properties of the `ColorEditor` class.

The `ColorEditor` also provides APIs that allow setting which property is being edited and setting and querying each property. See Listing 19.1 for these additional methods.

LISTING 19.1 THE `ColorEditor` CLASS

```
package com.foley.utility;

import java.awt.*;
import java.awt.event.*;

import java.io.Serializable;

import java.beans.*;

import javax.swing.*;
import javax.swing.event.*;
import javax.swing.colorchooser.*;


/**
 * A panel that allows colors to be specified
 * for a foreground and background.
 * <p>
 * @author Mike Foley
 **/
public class ColorEditor extends JPanel
    implements Serializable {

    /**
     * A radio button group for foreground, background
     * option.
     **/
    private ButtonGroup colorButtonGroup;
    private JRadioButton foregroundRadioButton;
    private JRadioButton backgroundRadioButton;

    /**
     * The color chooser.
     **/
    private JColorChooser colorChooser;
```

```
    /**
     * boolean used to decide which color is being changed.
     * true means foreground is being edited, false background.
     **/
    private boolean foregroundEditing = true;

    /**
     * Property change support.
     **/
    protected PropertyChangeSupport changeSupport = new PropertyChange
➥Support( this );

    /**
     * The current foreground and background Colors.
     **/
    private Color editForegroundColor;
    private Color editBackgroundColor;

    /**
     * This component contains two properties, foreground and
     * background color.
     **/
    public static final String EDITED_FOREGROUND_PROPERTY =
"ForegroundProperty";
    public static final String EDITED_BACKGROUND_PROPERTY =
"BackgroundProperty";

    /**
     * The default colors used in the editor.
     **/
    public static final Color DEFAULT_FOREGROUND_COLOR = Color.black;
    public static final Color DEFAULT_BACKGROUND_COLOR = Color.white;


    /**
     * ColorEditor, constructor.
     * <p>
     * Create a ColorEditor with the default foreground and
     * background colors.
     **/
    public ColorEditor() {
        this( DEFAULT_FOREGROUND_COLOR, DEFAULT_BACKGROUND_COLOR );
    } // ColorEditor


    /**
     * ColorEditor, constructor.
     * <p>
     * The ColorEditor may be thought of as a mediator between
     * the various components on the panel.  The radio buttons
     * choose which color is being edited.  Valid options are
```

19

CHOICE DIALOG BOXES

continues

LISTING 19.1   CONTINUED

```
 * foreground and background.  The JColorChooser allows visual
 * editing of these colors.
 * <p>
 * Create the components contained in the ColorEditor.
 * Create the listeners, and connect them to give the
 * component to component interactions.
 * <p>
 * @param foreground The initial foreground color for the editor.
 * @param background The initial background color for the editor.
 **/
public ColorEditor( Color foreground, Color background ) {

    super();

    //
    // If a color is null, use the default color.
    //
    if( foreground == null )
        foreground = DEFAULT_FOREGROUND_COLOR;
    if( background == null )
        background = DEFAULT_BACKGROUND_COLOR;

    this.editForegroundColor = foreground;
    this.editBackgroundColor = background;

    setLayout( new BorderLayout() );

    //
    // This action listener received messages when the radio
    // buttons change.  Set which property is being changed,
    // and update the color chooser to the current color
    // in that property.
    // A property change event doesn't need to be thrown here.
    // This only changes which property is being edited, not the
    // value of a property.
    //
    ActionListener radioListener = new ActionListener() {
        public void actionPerformed( ActionEvent event ) {
            if( event.getSource() == foregroundRadioButton ) {
                foregroundEditing = true;
                colorChooser.setColor( editForegroundColor );
            } else {
                foregroundEditing = false;
                colorChooser.setColor( editBackgroundColor );
            }
            colorChooser.repaint();
        }
    };

    //
    // Create a radio button group containing
```

```
        // two buttons, foreground and background color.
        //
        colorButtonGroup = new ButtonGroup();
        foregroundRadioButton = new JRadioButton( "Foreground" );
        foregroundRadioButton.setSelected( true );
        backgroundRadioButton = new JRadioButton( "Background" );
        colorButtonGroup.add( foregroundRadioButton );
        colorButtonGroup.add( backgroundRadioButton );
        foregroundRadioButton.addActionListener( radioListener );
        backgroundRadioButton.addActionListener( radioListener );

        //
        // The options panel contains the radio buttons
        //
        JPanel options = new JPanel();
        options.setLayout( new BorderLayout() );

        //
        // Place the radio buttons.
        //
        JPanel buttons = new JPanel();
        buttons.setLayout( new BoxLayout( buttons, BoxLayout.Y_AXIS ) );
        buttons.add( foregroundRadioButton );
        buttons.add( backgroundRadioButton );
        options.add( BorderLayout.NORTH, buttons );
        buttons.setBorder( BorderFactory.createTitledBorder(
                           BorderFactory.createEtchedBorder(), "Current
Color" ) );

        add( BorderLayout.WEST, buttons );

        //
        // Create the JColorChooser.
        //
        colorChooser = new JColorChooser( editForegroundColor );
        colorChooser.setBorder( BorderFactory.createLoweredBevelBorder
➥() );
        add( BorderLayout.CENTER, colorChooser );
        ColorSelectionModel model = colorChooser.getSelectionModel();
        model.addChangeListener( new ChangeListener() {
            public void stateChanged( ChangeEvent e ) {
                Color c = colorChooser.getColor();
                if( isEditingForeground() ) {
                    setEditedForegoundColor( c );
                } else {
                    setEditedBackgoundColor( c );
                }
            }
        } );
```

19

CHOICE DIALOG
BOXES

continues

LISTING 19.1   CONTINUED

```java
} // ColorEditor


/**
 * @return The current value of the foreground color.
 **/
public Color getEditedForegoundColor() {
    return( editForegroundColor );
}


/**
 * Provide an API to set the foreground color used in the editor.
 * If the foreground color is currently being edited, set the
 * value in the color chooser.  This will fire the property change
 * event, and the other components will update.
 * <p>
 * If the background is being edited, then set the color in the label.
 * The color chooser will update the next time foreground is edited.
 * <p>
 * This is a bound property.
 * <p>
 * @param c The new foreground color.
 **/
public void setEditedForegoundColor( Color c ) {

    if( foregroundEditing ) {
        colorChooser.setColor( c );
    }
    Color old = editForegroundColor;
    editForegroundColor = c;
    changeSupport.firePropertyChange( EDITED_FOREGROUND_PROPERTY,
                                                      old,
                                                      c );


} // setEditedForegoundColor


/**
 * @return The current value of the background color.
 **/
public Color getEditedBackgoundColor() {
    return( editBackgroundColor );
}


/**
 * Privide an API to set the background color used in the editor.
 * If the background color is currently being edited, set the
```

```
 * value in the color chooser.  This will fire the property change
 * event, and the other components will update.
 * <p>
 * If the foreground is being edited, then set the color in the label.
 * The color chooser will update the next time background is edited.
 * <p>
 * This is a bound property.
 * <p>
 * @param c The new background color.
 **/
public void setEditedBackgoundColor( Color c ) {

    if( !foregroundEditing ) {
        colorChooser.setColor( c );
    }
    Color old = editBackgroundColor;
    editBackgroundColor = c;
    changeSupport.firePropertyChange( EDITED_BACKGROUND_PROPERTY,
                                                          old,
                                                          c );

} // setEditedBackgoundColor


/**
 * Set which property is being edited.  These are in a radio
 * button, so selecting or unselecting the foreground button
 * will do the opposite to the background button.
 * <p>
 * Changing the selected state of the button will cause the proper
 * events to be fired which will update this object's state.
 * <p>
 * @param editForeground The new selected state for the foreground.
 **/
public void setEditingForeground( boolean editForeground ) {
    foregroundRadioButton.setSelected( true );
}


/**
 * Query which property is being edited.  Since there are
 * only two, this can be represented as a boolean.  The boolean
 * which was choosen is foreground radion button's selected state.
 * <p>
 * @return True if the foregound color is being edited. False is
   background.
 **/
public boolean isEditingForeground() {
    return( foregroundRadioButton.isSelected() );
}
```

continues

LISTING 19.1 CONTINUED

```
    public static Action getShowAction() {
        return( new ShowColorEditorAction() );
    }


    /**
        * addPropertyChangeListener
        *
      * The specified PropertyChangeListeners <b>propertyChange</b> method
      * will be called each time the value of any bound property is
changed.
        * The PropertyListener object is addded to a list of
PropertyChangeListeners
        * managed by this button, it can be removed with
removePropertyChangeListener.
        *
        * Note: the JavaBeans specification does not require
PropertyChangeListeners
        * to run in any particular order.
        *
        * @param l the PropertyChangeListener
        * @see #removePropertyChangeListener
        *
    **/
    public void addPropertyChangeListener( PropertyChangeListener l ) {
                changeSupport.addPropertyChangeListener( l );
    } // addPropertyChangeListener


    /**
        * removePropertyChangeListener
        *
      * Remove this PropertyChangeListener from the buttons internal list.
      * If the PropertyChangeListener isn't on the list, silently do
nothing.
        *
        * @param l the PropertyChangeListener
        * @see #addPropertyChangeListener
        *
    **/
    public void removePropertyChangeListener( PropertyChangeListener l ) {
                changeSupport.removePropertyChangeListener( l );
    } // removePropertyChangeListener

} // ColorEditor


/**
  * Class ShowColorEditorAction
```

```
 * <p>
 * An action which opens the ColorEditor dialog box.
 * <p>
 * @author Mike Foley
 * @version 1.2
 **/
class ShowColorEditorAction extends AbstractAction {

    /**
     * The default name used in a menu.
     **/
    private static final String DEFAULT_NAME = "Color Editor...";

    public ShowColorEditorAction() {
        this( DEFAULT_NAME, null );
    } // ShowColorEditorAction

    public ShowColorEditorAction( String name ) {
        this( name, null );
    } // ShowColorEditorAction

    public ShowColorEditorAction( String name, Icon icon ) {
        super( name, icon );
    } // ShowColorEditorAction


    /**
     * actionPerformed, from ActionListener
     * <p>
     * Perform the action.  Show the ColorEditor dialog box.
     * <p>
     * @param event The event causing the action to fire.
     **/
    public void actionPerformed( ActionEvent event ) {

        Frame parent = JOptionPane.getFrameForComponent( ( Component
)event.getSource() );
        JDialog dialog = new JDialog( parent );
        ColorEditor editor = new ColorEditor();
        dialog.getContentPane().add( BorderLayout.CENTER, editor );

        dialog.setModal( true );
        dialog.pack();
        dialog.setVisible( true );
        dialog.show();
    } // actionPerformed

} // ShowColorEditorAction
```

The JColorChooser class also contains the getColor method, which can be used to query the current color in the chooser. This method is used to store the current value in the color chooser when changing from foreground to background, and vice versa.

Summary

Canned components that allow the user to make a choice from possible values for a type are an important feature of any user interface toolkit. These components ensure that the choice is valid and provide a consistent look-and-feel between applications by using the chooser components. The current release of the JFC contains two such components: one for selecting files, and another for selecting colors. This chapter demonstrated how to use these classes in modal dialog boxes. This allows the application to receive the value entered by the user as the returned value from the method that displayed the dialog box. However, the chooser classes do not have to be used in the convenient dialog boxes created by the class. The components can be used to build displays in the same manner as any other JFC component. An example of using the JColorChooser class in a custom dialog box was presented.

In future releases of the JFC, the set of chooser components will continue to grow. The pending package contains example chooser components as well as preview components that should find their way into the JFC in an upcoming release. Choosers for dates and times, to name but a few, would be a welcome addition to the toolkit.

CHAPTER 20

JDialog

The JFC provides a rich collection of predefined dialog boxes that will meet most of your needs. However, there are cases where these dialog boxes will not address your needs. The JDialog class can be used in these situations; it provides an empty pane that you can configure in any way required. In this chapter, you will learn how to take advantage of the many features contained in the JDialog class. These include the following:

- The JDialog class configuration
- Using modal and non-modal dialog boxes
- Dialog box closing options
- Example JDialog dialog boxes

The JDialog class can be used to create modal and non-modal dialog boxes. If the application cannot continue before the information is queried from the user or a severe error has occurred, a modal dialog box may be most appropriate.

This chapter will show similarities between the JFrame and JDialog classes. This will be followed by an example of the use of the JDialog class.

JDialog Configuration

The JDialog class is an extension of the AWT java.awt.Dialog class. When shown, the JDialog will create a decorated window that can be moved and sized independently of other frames. A JDialog instance contains a single child, an instance of the JRootPane class. The JRootPane consists of many components. These are glassPane, layeredPane, optional menuBar, and contentPane. The contentPane provides the container where user components are to be added. The contentPane is guaranteed to be non-null. The contentPane comes configured with the BorderLayout layout manager by default. For a complete description of the JRootPane class, see the JFrame section of Chapter 8, "Frame Windows."

The JDialog class's configuration is similar to the JFrame class. Each class contains a single child that is an instance of the JRootPane class. Each is a descendant of the java.awt.Window class. However, the JDialog class extends the java.awt.Dialog class while the JFrame class extends the java.awt.Frame class.

When adding components to a JDialog instance, the component isn't added directly to the dialog box. Instead, the component is added to the contentPane, which is a child of the dialog box. A handle to the contentPane can be acquired by using the getContentPane method. If a layout manager other than the default BorderLayout is required, that needs to be set on the content pane as well.

A string can be given to the `JDialog` constructor to specify the title of the dialog box. The title can also be set and queried by using the `setTitle` and `getTitle` methods inherited from `java.awt.Dialog`.

The current `JDialog` class API does not contain a method to set the icon in the dialog box's title bar. This is an AWT omission and is promised for a future version of the JDK. When implemented, the dialog box will use the icon of its parent frame, if available. If the parent frame's icon is not appropriate, a method will be available to set a different icon for the dialog box.

JDialog Modality

A `JDialog` instance can be configured as modal or non-modal. When configured to be a modal dialog box, the `JDialog` instance will not allow input to other windows until the dialog box is dismissed. A modal dialog box is typically used for error conditions, or when user input is required before the application can continue. A non-modal dialog box allows the user to interact with other windows in the application while the dialog box is displayed.

Another consequence of the modality of the dialog box is whether or not the calling code blocks. When the `JDialog` instance is modal, the `show` method blocks until the dialog box is dismissed. This allows processing code to be placed immediately after the `show` method. However, if the dialog box is non-modal, the code continues to execute after the `show` method. This often requires the code that processes the user input to be placed in a listener or callback method.

The modality of a `JDialog` can be set by using the `setModal` method or at construction time. Passing a value of `true` to this method will cause the dialog box to be modal. The `setModal` method must be called before the `show` method is called to display the dialog box. If the `setModal` method is not called, the default mode for the dialog box will be non-modal. The modality of a dialog box can be queried with the `isModal` method. This will return the `boolean` modal state for the dialog box.

The `show` method is used to display the dialog box. If it is already visible when the `show` method is called, the dialog box is raised to the top of the window stack on the display. The `setVisible` method with a parameter of `false` will remove the dialog box from the display. The `setVisible` method with a parameter of `true` can also be used to display the dialog box. The `setVisible` method calls the `show` method. If the dialog box is to be modal, the protected `blockingShow` method of the `JDialog` class is called when the `show` method is invoked. This method mimics the functionality of the `EventDispatchThread` until the dialog box is no longer visible. It dispatches `AWTEvents` to components contained in the `JDialog` instance that is blocking.

Closing Options

The operation performed by the JDialog class when a WINDOW_CLOSING event is received can be configured using the setDefaultCloseOperation method. Possible operations are HIDE_ON_CLOSE, which will hide the dialog box but not dispose of it. DISPOSE_ON_CLOSE, which will hide the dialog box and then dispose of it. The final option is DO_NOTHING_ON_CLOSE. This option does not hide or dispose of the dialog box. Just as its name implies, it does nothing. The default value for this property is HIDE_ON_CLOSE. The current setting for this property can be queried with the getDefaultCloseOperation method.

The HIDE_ON_CLOSE option is typically used for dialog boxes that interact with the user but do not alter the application data until the dialog box is dismissed. The results of the user interaction are read from the dialog box after it has been hidden. The code that uses the dialog box is responsible for disposal of the dialog when it is no longer required. This mode can also be used if the same dialog box is reused multiple times.

The DISPOSE_ON_CLOSE option is useful for dialog boxes that update the application data as the user interacts with the dialog box. The updates can be performed via propertyChange notifications or by directly calling application methods. Using propertyChange events requires less knowledge of the application in the dialog box and makes dialog box reuse easier. In this situation, there is not any postmortem processing required, so the JDialog class can hide and dispose of the dialog box.

The DO_NOTHING_ON_CLOSE option can be used for dialog boxes that verify state information before allowing the dialog box to be closed. If the state is acceptable, the dialog box will be closed. If not, an error is reported to the user, and the dialog box remains open.

JDialog Class Usage Example

In the previous chapter, the ColorEditor component was presented. The ColorEditor contains components that allow the foreground and background colors to be visually specified. It would be useful to present this component in a dialog box to allow the user to change colors.

Depending on the required dialog box usage, the JFC provides multiple methods to present a ColorEditor instance in a dialog box. As was seen in Chapter 18, "JOptionPane," the JOptionPane can be used. For example, the following code will display the dialog box shown in Figure 20.1.

```
package com.foley.test;

import javax.swing.*;

/**
 * An application that displays a ColorEditor in a JOptionPane dialog box.
 *
 * @author Mike Foley
 **/
public class ColorEditorTest extends Object {

    /**
     * Application entry point.
     * Display a dialog box using the JOptionPane class.
     *
     * @param args Command line parameter. Not used.
     **/
    public static void main( String args[] ) {

        JOptionPane.showOptionDialog( parent,
                            new ColorEditor(),
                            "ColorEditor Dialog",
                            JOptionPane.OK_CANCEL_OPTION,
                            JOptionPane.PLAIN_MESSAGE,
                            null, null, null );

        System.exit(0);

    } // main

} // ColorEditorTest
```

FIGURE 20.1

ColorEditor *dialog box using* JOptionPane.

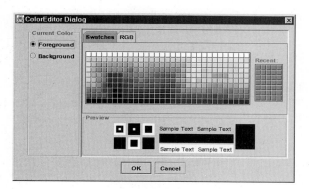

Using the JOptionPane to present a component in a dialog box is sufficient in many situations. However, when more control is desired, the JDialog class can be used. A primary reason is if you require a non-modal dialog box.

Non-Modal Dialog Box Using a PropertyChangeListener

This section presents a version of the `ColorEditor` dialog box using a non-modal dialog box. The dialog box contains an instance of the `ColorEditor` class created in Chapter 19, "Choice Dialog Boxes." The calling application listens for property change events occurring in the dialog box. When such an event occurs, the colors are updated in the application.

The `DialogColorEditorTest` application shown next produces the dialog box shown in Figure 20.2. The `ColorEditor` is created and placed in a border. An OK and Cancel button are added to a `JPanel` instance. Both panels are added to the content pane of the dialog box. If a component is added to the `JDialog` directly, a `RuntimeException` is thrown. Finally, the dialog box is packed and shown. It is important to call the `pack` method for the dialog box before showing it. The `pack` method will calculate the desired size for the dialog box. The default size is a width and height of 0. With this size, the dialog box will not be displayed. The dialog box in this example uses the default modality, which is non-modal. When the `show` method is called, the dialog box will not be modal and the code will not block.

```java
package com.foley.test;

import java.awt.*;

import javax.swing.*;

import com.foley.utility.ColorEditor;


/**
 * An application that displays a ColorEditor in a JDialog
 * dialog box.
 *
 * @author Mike Foley
 **/
public class DialogColorEditorTest extends Object {

    /**
     * Application entry point.
     * Display a dialog box using the JOptionPane class.
     *
     * @param args Command line parameter. Not used.
     **/
    public static void main( String args[] ) {

        ColorEditor colorEditor = new ColorEditor();
        colorEditor.setBorder( BorderFactory.createLoweredBevelBorder() );
```

```
            JDialog dialog = new JDialog( null, "ColorEditor Dialog" );
            dialog.getContentPane().add( BorderLayout.CENTER, colorEditor );

            JPanel buttonPanel = new JPanel();
            buttonPanel.add( new JButton( "OK" ) );
            buttonPanel.add( new JButton( "Cancel" ) );
            dialog.getContentPane().add( BorderLayout.SOUTH, buttonPanel );
            dialog.pack();
            dialog.show();

            // System.exit(0);

        } // main

    } // DialogColorEditorTest
```

FIGURE 20.2

ColorEditor *dialog box using the* JDialog *class.*

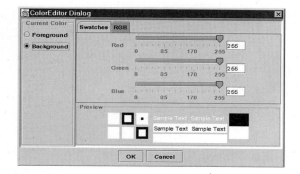

The code in the listing displays the dialog box, but doesn't contain any functionality. It may be desirable to have the color editor remain non-modal. To add functionality to the non-modal version of the ColorEditor, a PropertyChangeListener can be used. When colors are altered in the ColorEditor, EDITED_FOREGROUND_PROPERTY and EDITED_BACK-GROUND_PROPERTY property change events are fired.

The property change listener inner class is shown next. This code simply detects which property has changed, queries the new color from the event, and calls the appropriate method to alter the color. Notice that when checking the property name, the == operation can be used rather than the String.equals method. This is because the property names are defined as constants in the ColorEditor class, and the property name in the event will be the same instance as the constant defined in the ColorEditor class.

```
colorEditor.addPropertyChangeListener( new PropertyChangeListener() {
    public void propertyChange( PropertyChangeEvent event ) {
if( event.getPropertyName() ==
        ColorEditor.EDITED_FOREGROUND_PROPERTY ) {
        Color foreground = ( Color )event.getNewValue();
```

20

JDialog

```
        // Update foreground color
    } else if( event.getPropertyName() ==
        ColorEditor.EDITED_BACKGROUND_PROPERTY ) {
        Color background = ( Color )event.getNewValue();
        // Update background color.
    }
  }
} );
```

Using this property change listener, the dialog box updates colors from the ColorEditor. Unfortunately, the dialog box doesn't go away when the buttons are pressed. This is because you are not listening for action events from the buttons. Since the colors are continuously being updated from the property change events, the OK button only needs to close the dialog box. The Cancel button should also close the dialog box; however, it should also restore the original colors. A single ActionListener, shown in the following code, was created for this task. It hides and disposes of the dialog box. The action command is checked, and, if it is the Cancel button that fired the action, the original colors are restored. This example assumes that the application saves the original colors before the dialog box is opened, and provides a method to restore the saved colors. These methods are not presented in the example.

```
ActionListener actionListener = new ActionListener() {
    public void actionPerformed( ActionEvent event ) {
        dialog.setVisible( false );
        dialog.dispose();
        if( event.getActionCommand().equals( "Cancel" ) ) {
            // Reset Colors.
        }
    }
};
JButton ok = new JButton( "OK" );
JButton cancel = new JButton( "Cancel" );
ok.addActionListener( actionListener );
cancel.addActionListener( actionListener );

buttonPanel.add( ok );
buttonPanel.add( cancel );
```

Finally, since you are not caching this dialog box for reuse, the close operation should be set to dispose of the dialog box. This is done with the following line of code.

```
dialog.setDefaultCloseOperation( DISPOSE_ON_CLOSE );
```

These previous code examples are combined to create the complete ColorChooserDialog class shown in Listing 20.1.

LISTING 20.1 THE ColorChooserDialog APPLICATION

```java
package com.foley.test;

import java.awt.*;
import java.awt.event.*;
import java.beans.*;

import javax.swing.*;

import com.foley.utility.ColorEditor;


/**
 * An application that displays a ColorEditor in a JDialog
 * dialog box.
 *
 * @author Mike Foley
 **/
public class ColorChooserDialog extends Object {

    /**
     * Application entry point.
     * Display a dialog box using the JOptionPane class.
     *
     * @param args Command line parameter. Not used.
     **/
    public static void main( String args[] ) {

        ColorEditor colorEditor = new ColorEditor();
        colorEditor.setBorder( BorderFactory.createLoweredBevelBorder() );
        final JDialog dialog = new JDialog( null, "ColorEditor Dialog" );
        dialog.getContentPane().add( BorderLayout.CENTER, colorEditor );


        colorEditor.addPropertyChangeListener( new PropertyChangeListener
() {
            public void propertyChange( PropertyChangeEvent event ) {
                if( event.getPropertyName() ==
                    ColorEditor.EDITED_FOREGROUND_PROPERTY ) {
                    Color foreground = ( Color )event.getNewValue();
                    // Update foreground color
                } else if( event.getPropertyName() ==
                    ColorEditor.EDITED_BACKGROUND_PROPERTY ) {
                    Color background = ( Color )event.getNewValue();
                    // Update background color.
                }
            }
        } );
```

continues

20

JDialog

LISTING 20.1   CONTINUED

```
        JPanel buttonPanel = new JPanel();
        ActionListener actionListener = new ActionListener() {
            public void actionPerformed( ActionEvent event ) {
                dialog.setVisible( false );
                dialog.dispose();
                if( event.getActionCommand().equals( "Cancel" ) ) {
                    // Reset Colors.
                }
            }
        };
        JButton ok = new JButton( "OK" );
        JButton cancel = new JButton( "Cancel" );
        ok.addActionListener( actionListener );
        cancel.addActionListener( actionListener );

        buttonPanel.add( ok );
        buttonPanel.add( cancel );

        dialog.getContentPane().add( BorderLayout.SOUTH, buttonPanel );

        dialog.setDefaultCloseOperation( JDialog.DISPOSE_ON_CLOSE );
        dialog.pack();
        dialog.show();

    } // main

} // ColorChooserDialog
```

Non-Modal `ColorEditor` Dialog Box

The previous section presented a complete example of a non-modal dialog box where a property change listener was used to update the application as the colors were edited in the dialog box. Special processing had to be performed to allow the user to cancel the edits already performed. This is a useful dialog model for many situations, but not all. If the `ColorEditor` forces the entire application to be redrawn each time the color is changed in the editor, this could cause undesirable painting of the application. Also, if the operation being performed takes a significant amount of processing time, the dialog box will appear sluggish to the user.

Changing the `ColorEditor` dialog box to wait until the user chooses the OK button is a simple modification. The property change listener is not required, so it is not created or added to the `ColorEditor` component. The `ActionListener` has been modified as presented in the following code. In this version of the `ActionListener`, the dialog box is first hidden. If the OK button caused the action, the colors are retrieved from the dialog box and updated in the application. If the Cancel button caused the action event, the colors will not be modified. Finally, the dialog box is disposed of. The `dispose` method must be called after the colors have been retrieved from the dialog box, or the dialog box reference will not be valid for querying the colors selected by the user.

```
ActionListener actionListener = new ActionListener() {
    public void actionPerformed( ActionEvent event ) {
        dialog.setVisible( false );
        if( event.getActionCommand().equals( "OK" ) ) {
            Color foreground = colorEditor.getEditedForeground();
            Color background = colorEditor.getEditedBackground();
            // Set the colors.
        }
        dialog.dispose();
    }
};
```

Modal `ColorEditor` Dialog Box

There may be situations where it is desirable to have the `ColorEditor` instance dialog box be a modal. Changing the `ColorEditor` dialog box to be modal can be done by simply adding a call to the `setModal` method with a parameter of `true` before the non-modal dialog box in the previous section is displayed. For modal dialog boxes, the calling code is blocked by the `show` method. It is often convenient to have the dialog box return the action the user took rather than using an `ActionListener`. This allows the code that processes the results from the dialog box to be placed immediately after the call to the `show` method. This is similar to the show*XXX*Dialog methods provided by the `JOptionPane` class. It is easiest to create this type of dialog box by extending the `JDialog` class.

The `ColorEditorDialog` class is an extension of the `JDialog` class. Its visual appearance is identical to the dialog boxes presented in the previous sections and shown in Figure 20.2. The `ColorEditorDialog` class creates the content panel components in its constructor presented in Listing 20.2. The code is very similar to that used in the previous sections. The `buttonHit` attribute was added to allow the blocking `showDialog` method to return which button was used to dismiss the dialog box. This attribute is initialized to `JOptionPane.CLOSED_OPTION`. This constant will be returned if the dialog box is dismissed without hitting either the OK or Cancel button. The action listener for the buttons hide the dialog box and sets the `buttonHit` attribute to the appropriate button. The dialog box is not disposed of, because the calling code may need to query the edited colors from the dialog box. It is the responsibility of the client code to dispose of the dialog box.

Two versions of the constructor are provided. One that uses the default colors in the
ColorEditor, and another that allows the calling code to specify the initial foreground
and background colors in the editor. Either of these parameters can be null. If either
parameter is null, the default color will be used. The ColorEditorDialog constructors
specify the title to be used for the dialog box by specifying the title string in the call to
the JDialog constructor.

LISTING 20.2   THE ColorEditorDialog CLASS

```
package com.foley.dialogs;

import java.awt.*;
import java.awt.event.*;

import javax.swing.*;

import com.foley.utility.ColorEditor;


/**
 * The ColorEditorDialog is a class which implements a
 * modal dialog box allowing the visual editing of the
 * foreground and background colors.
 * <p>
 * The showDialog box is used to display the dialog.  This
 * method blocks until the dialog is dismissed.  The value
 * returned from this method specifies how the dialog was
 * dismissed.
 * <p>
 * Methods are provided to query the edited colors from the
 * dialog.
 **/
public class ColorEditorDialog extends JDialog {

    /**
     * The color editor used in the dialog.
     **/
    private ColorEditor colorEditor;

    /**
     * The code returned from the showDialog method.
     * This value is defined by the values defined in JOptionPane.
     **/
    private int buttonHit;

    /**
     * ColorEditorDialog, constructor
     * <p>
     * Create a ColorEditingDialog with default colors.
```

```
     * <p>
     * @param parent The Frame to use as the dialog's parent.
     **/
    public ColorEditorDialog( Frame parent ) {
        this( parent, null, null );
}


    /**
     * ColorEditorDialog, constructor
     * <p>
     * Create the contents of the ColorEditor dialog.
     * Add the action listeners to the buttons to close the dialog.
     * <p>
     * @param parent The Frame to use as the dialog's parent.
     * @param foreground The initial foreground color for the editor.
     * @param background The initial background color for the editor.
     **/
    public ColorEditorDialog( Frame parent,
            Color foreground, Color background ) {

        super( parent, "ColorEditor Dialog" );

        //
        // HIDE_ON_CLOSE is the default.
        // We rely on this functionality, as it is valid
        // to call methods on the dialog after it is closed.
        //
        setDefaultCloseOperation( JDialog.HIDE_ON_CLOSE );

        //
        // Default to CLOSED_OPTION.  If a button is hit,
        // then the return value will be set to the button.
        //
        buttonHit = JOptionPane.CLOSED_OPTION;

        //
        // Create the content of the dialog.
        //
        colorEditor = new ColorEditor( foreground, background );
        colorEditor.setBorder( BorderFactory.createLoweredBevelBorder());

        getContentPane().add( BorderLayout.CENTER, colorEditor );

        JPanel buttonPanel = new JPanel();

        //
        // The button action listener hides the dialog, and sets
        // the returned value attribute to which button was hit.
```

continues

LISTING 20.2   CONTINUED

```
        //
        ActionListener actionListener = new ActionListener() {
            public void actionPerformed( ActionEvent event ) {
                setVisible( false );
                if( event.getActionCommand().equals( "OK" ) ) {
                    buttonHit = JOptionPane.OK_OPTION;
                }
                if( event.getActionCommand().equals( "Cancel" ) ) {
                    buttonHit = JOptionPane.CANCEL_OPTION;
                }
            }
        };
        JButton ok = new JButton( "OK" );
        JButton cancel = new JButton( "Cancel" );
        ok.addActionListener( actionListener );
        cancel.addActionListener( actionListener );

        buttonPanel.add( ok );
        buttonPanel.add( cancel );
        getContentPane().add( BorderLayout.SOUTH, buttonPanel );

    } // ColorEditorDialog


    /**
     * @return The chosen foreground color.
     **/
    public Color getEditedForegoundColor() {
        return( colorEditor.getEditedForegoundColor() );
    }


    /**
     * @return The chosen background color.
     **/
    public Color getEditedBackgoundColor() {
        return( colorEditor.getEditedBackgoundColor() );
    }


    /**
     * show, overrides JDialog
     * <p>
     * We do not want the 'normal' show to be called.  Instead,
     * the showDialog should be used.
     **/
    public void show() {
        throw new RuntimeException( "show may not be called for "
                                    + ¦the ColorEditorDialog."
```

```
                                            + "  Use showDialog instead." );
    } // show


    /**
     * showDialog
     * <p>
     * The preferred method for displaying the dialog.
     * This method blocks until the dialog is dismissed, and
     * returns how the dialog was dismissed.
     * <p>
     * @return How the dialog was dismissed.  Valid return values are:
     *                JOptionPane.OK_OPTION;
     *                JOptionPane.CANCEL_OPTION;
     *                JOptionPane.CLOSED_OPTION;
     **/
    public int showDialog() {

        setModal( true );
        pack();
        super.show();

        return( buttonHit );

    } // showDialog

} // ColorEditorDialog
```

The showDialog method is provided to display the dialog box and return the operation that was used by the user to dismiss the dialog box. This method blocks the caller's code until the dialog box is dismissed. Setting the dialog box to modal and calling the show method in the JDialog class will implement this functionality. The buttonHit attribute can be returned to the calling program after the dialog box is dismissed. A common programming error when using the ColorEditorDialog class would be to call the show method instead of the showDialog method. To help programmers find this error, the show method is overridden from the show method in the JDialog class, and it throws a runtime exception explaining the error. The overridden show method and the showDialog methods are shown Listing 20.2.

Finally, a pair of methods are provided to determine which values the user specified in the ColorEditor. The getEditedForegroundColor and getEditedBackgroundColor methods are provided to return the colors selected by the user. Each of these methods simply calls the corresponding method in ColorEditor and returns the color.

20

JDialog

Summary

The JDialog class provides a frame in which any other components can be placed. The frame can be modal or non-modal. This provides the utmost in flexibility for dialog boxes.

This chapter presented an evolution of dialog boxes for a color editor. Various techniques for reporting the choices made in the dialog box to the calling application were explored. PropertyChangeEvents, ActionEvents, and blocking show methods where explored. The technique used in your dialog boxes will vary with the dialog boxes' functions.

Progress Monitor

CHAPTER 21

When a user-initiated operation may take a significant amount of time, visual feedback should be provided to the user. A common means for this visual feedback is by display-ing the wait cursor. If the operation can be run in a separate thread, the JFC provides the ProgressMonitor class as another mechanism to provide feedback to the user. The ProgressMonitor class contains methods that the operation can use to inform the user about the status of the operation. This makes the ProgressMonitor class superior to the wait cursor when it can be used. In this chapter, you will learn

- Timing considerations in the ProgressMonitor class
- How to customize a ProgressMonitor
- How to provide feedback with the ProgressMonitor
- See a complete ProgressMonitor example

The ProgressMonitor class provides a convenient mechanism to display a dialog box showing the progress of an operation. This class displays a dialog box that allows the operation to update its status and provide a note to inform the user as to what it is cur-rently doing. An example of the dialog box displayed by the ProgressMonitor class is shown in Figure 21.1. This chapter will present examples of using the ProgressMonitor class.

FIGURE 21.1

The
ProgressMonitor
dialog box.

Using the **ProgressMonitor**

When constructing a ProgressMonitor, the first parameter is the parent component. The second parameter is the message shown on the dialog. This message is processed the same way as the message parameter contained in the JOptionPane class. For a complete description of this parameter, see the discussion of the message parameter in Chapter 18, "JOptionPane."

The message that is given at construction is not changed for the lifetime of the dialog box. The third parameter is a String note. The note is to give the user feedback as to the current processing in the operation. The note can be changed as the operation progresses. The final parameters define a range that indicates the progress of the operation. Any inte-ger numeric range can be specified. However, a typical range will be from 0–100 percent completion.

The dialog box that the `ProgressMonitor` class creates is not immediately shown. Indeed, it is not immediately created. Instead, the progress of the operation is monitored and the dialog box is only created and displayed if deemed necessary by the `ProgressMonitor` class. Two parameters are used to determine if the dialog box should be displayed. These are the time to decide to pop-up parameter, and the time to pop-up parameter. These parameters work in conjunction with the operation updating the progress. After the time to decide has elapsed, the `ProgressMonitor` estimates how long the operation will take to complete. If the completion time of the operation is determined to be longer than the pop-up time, the dialog box is created and displayed. A simple linear approximation is used to estimate the duration of the action. The default values for these parameters are .5 seconds to decide to pop up, and the operation must be estimated to take more than 2 seconds for the dialog box to be displayed. However, these values can be changed by using the `setMillisToDecideToPopup` and `setMillisToPopup` methods. The time in each of these methods is specified in milliseconds. The values can be queried by using the `get` versions of the two methods.

The `setProgress` method is used to update the progress of the operation. The progress is an integer in the current operation range. The operation range is specified in the `ProgressMonitor`'s constructor and can be altered with the `setMinimum` and `setMaximum` methods. The `get` versions of each of these methods can be used to determine the current operation range. It is in the `setProgress` method that the `ProgressMonitor` determines if the dialog box is required. This implies that if there is a long delay between calls to this method around the decision time, there will be a delay before the dialog box is displayed. This class will work best if the operation can supply a consistent stream of calls to the `setProgress` method.

As the operation updates the progress, it can also update the `String` note presented to the user using the `setNote` method. For example, if the operation is processing a list of customers, the name of the customer being operated on could be presented in the note. A non-null note must be specified before the dialog box is created if the operation is going to update the note during the operation. If the note is `null` when the dialog box is created, a note will not be included in the dialog box. Subsequent calls to `setNote` will be ignored. To ensure that a note will be available if required by the operation, it is safest to specify a note during construction of the `ProgressMonitor` instance.

The `ProgressMonitor` class will close the dialog box when the progress is set to the maximum value of the operation range. The operation can also use the `close` method to tell the `ProgressMonitor` that the operation is complete, and the dialog box should be closed and disposed of.

The dialog box presented by the ProgressMonitor contains a Cancel button. The operation should periodically query the ProgressMonitor by using the isCancelled method to determine if the user wants to cancel the operation. This method returns true if the Cancel button has been clicked. The operation should stop if this is the case. To force the dialog box to be disposed of, the operation should set the progress to the maximum value, or call the close method of the ProgressMonitor during its cancel processing.

The final caveat to using the ProgressMonitor is that the operation should be executing in a thread other than the user interface thread. If this is not the case, the progress meter or note will not be updated when their values are set.

Example of ProgressMonitor Usage

The previous section gave the responsibilities of an operation to successfully use a ProgressMonitor. This section will present a working example of each of these responsibilities.

The example of ProgressMonitor usage is presented in Listing 21.1. The ProgressMonitor is created with an operation range of 0–100. A multiline message is specified. A note is given in the constructor because the sample operation will update the note as it progresses. The ProgressMonitor does not immediately show the dialog box. It waits for the progress to be set by the operation. It then estimates the duration of the operation, and, if this time is longer than the operation duration threshold, the dialog box will be displayed. In the example, the default values of 0.5 seconds and 2 seconds for the pop-up decision time and operation duration threshold times are used.

The operation in this example is a simple loop with a delay. Hopefully your programs will have more significant operations to perform. During each iteration through the loop, the progress and note of the ProgressMonitor are updated. Using the isCancelled method, the operation checks if the user has requested that the operation terminate. If so, the progress is set to the maximum value to dispose of the dialog box, and the operation terminates. If the user has not cancelled the operation, the operation sleeps. After the operation has iterated the desired number of times, the operation is complete and the close method is called to tell the ProgressMonitor that the operation has completed.

The example application creates a single button in a frame. When the button is pressed, a thread is created to run the operation. In this simple test application, a single progress monitor is shared between all operations. Thus, there will be multiple threads updating the progress monitor if the Start button is clicked when the progress meter is displayed.

From this example you will notice that there is a tight coupling between the progress monitor and the operation. The operation must update the progress monitor as it progresses, and ensure that the monitor is closed when the operation terminates. Also, the operation must periodically check if the user requested that the operation be cancelled. If it does not perform this check, when the Cancel button is clicked, the progress monitor will be removed from the screen but the operation will continue to execute, resulting in a condition that is obviously not what the user intended. It would enhance the design of the `ProgressMonitor` class if this coupling were defined in an interface. This would allow operations to interact with any class that implements the `Progress` interface rather than the concrete `ProgressMonitor` class. If this were the case, different types of progress monitors could be used without altering the operations that update the monitor. A progress monitor shown at the bottom of many frame windows comes to mind.

LISTING 21.1   `ProgressMonitor` EXAMPLE

```
package com.foley.test;

import java.awt.*;
import java.awt.event.*;
import javax.swing.*;



/**
 * An application that displays a ProgressMonitor
 * when the 'start' button is pressed. A simple
 * 'operation' to update the monitor
 *
 * @author Mike Foley
 **/
public class ProgressTest extends Object {

    /**
     * Application entry point.
     * Create the splash window, and display it.
     *
     * @param args Command line parameter. Not used.
     **/
    public static void main( String args[] ) {

        //
        // Create a frame with a single button in it.
        // When the button is pressed, a thread is spawned
        // to run out sample operation.
        //
        JFrame frame = new JFrame( "ProgressMonitor Test" );
```

continues

LISTING 21.1 CONTINUED

```java
        JButton button = new JButton( "Start" );
        frame.getContentPane().add( button, BorderLayout.CENTER );

        //
        // Create a ProgressMonitor. This will be started
        // when the button is pressed.
        //
        int min = 0;
        int max = 100;
        String[] message = new String[2];
        message[0] = "Performing Operation.";
        message[1] = "This may take some time...";
        final ProgressMonitor monitor = new  ProgressMonitor( frame,
                                                    message,
                                                    "Iteration",
                                                    min,
                                                    max );

        //
        // This is our sample operation.
        //
        final Runnable runnable = new Runnable() {
            public void run() {
                int sleepTime = 500;
                for( int i = 1; i < 100; i++ ) {
                    try {
                        monitor.setNote( "Iteration " + i );
                        monitor.setProgress( i );
                        if( monitor.isCancelled() ) {
                            monitor.setProgress( 100 );
                            break;
                        }
                        Thread.sleep( sleepTime );
                    } catch( InterruptedException dontcare ) {
                    }
                }
                monitor.close();
            }
        };

        button.addActionListener( new ActionListener() {
            public void actionPerformed( ActionEvent event ) {
                //
                // Run the operation in its own thread.
                //
                Thread thread = new Thread( runnable );
                thread.start();

            }
```

```
            } );

            //
            // Show the frame.
            //
            frame.pack();
            frame.setVisible( true );

        } // main

    } // ProgressTest
```

In this example, the progress is updated twice a second. This will cause the ProgressMonitor to determine that the operation should take approximately 50 seconds to complete, and the dialog box is required the first time the progress is set. The dialog box will be displayed at that time. The note and slider in the dialog box will be updated twice a second as the operation executes. If the user clicks the Cancel button, the dialog box will immediately be hidden. However, the operation will not terminate until the next time through the loop when the operation calls the isCancelled method. When the operation determines that the user cancelled the operation, it sets the progress to the maximum value to allow the dialog box to be disposed.

If the user doesn't click the Cancel button, the operation iterates through the loop. When the loop is finished, the close method is called to tell the ProgressMonitor that the operation has completed. The ProgressMonitor will close and dispose of the dialog box at that time.

Summary

The ProgressMonitor class provides a familiar visual feedback component for complex operations that meet its usage requirements. When the user initiates an operation that is going to take a substantial amount of time to complete, visual feedback should be provided to the user. If the operation can be divided into multiple processing chunks and be executed in a separate thread, it is an ideal candidate for ProgressMonitor usage. This allows the user to monitor the operations progress and cancel the operation if desired.

Extending JFC
Components

PART
V

Extending Existing Components

The pluggable look-and-feel architecture that Swing components are built on gives the developer many options when extending JFC components. A component can be extended in the traditional sense; extend the component and override selected methods. JFC components can also be extended by replacing their user-interface (UI) component. Finally, an entirely new look-and-feel implementation can be developed. As we will see in this chapter and the next two chapters, changing the "look" of JFC components is more common than changing their "feel."

In this chapter, you will learn

- About the pluggable look-and-feel (.plaf) architecture
- How UI delegates and Swing components are bound
- How to create your own UI delegate

The Pluggable Look-and-Feel (`.plaf`) Architecture

A common method for extending an AWT component was to override the paint and various size methods. For example, to create a multiline label, one approach was to extend the AWT Component class, override the getPreferredSize, getMinimumSize, and getMaximumSize methods to specify the size of the multiline label, and override the paint method to render the text to the display. The AWT Label class would probably be consulted as an example, or some may have extended this class directly. Coming from this background, developers may start down the same path with a JFC version of a multiline label. Imagine their surprise when they study the JLabel class and discover that it doesn't even contain a paint method! This seeming omission from the JLabel class is a fundamental difference between the AWT and JFC architectures.

"J" Component UI methods

Swing "J" components do not interact with the user or paint to the screen themselves. Instead, these operations are delegated to a UI object. Each "J" component contains four methods that manage its UI object. The getUI and setUI methods are simple JavaBean-compliant access methods. These methods cannot be inherited from JComponent, because the type of the UI object is specified. For example, these two methods in the JLabel class require a LabelUI instance. This is shown in the following code fragment from the JLabel class.

```
/**
 * Returns the L&F object that renders this component.
 *
```

```
 * @return LabelUI object
 */
public LabelUI getUI() {
    return (LabelUI)ui;
}


/**
 * Sets the L&F object that renders this component.
 *
 * @param ui  the LabelUI L&F object
 * @see UIDefaults#getUI
 * @beaninfo
 *       expert: true
 *  description: The L&F object that renders this component.
 */
public void setUI(LabelUI ui) {
    super.setUI(ui);
}
```

The `updateUI` method is called to set the UI for the instance. It is called from the class's constructor and by the `UIManager` if the look-and-feel for the instance changes. This method requests the current UI from the `UIManager` and sets it for the instance. The `updateUI` method from the `JLabel` class is shown next. The method is identical in the other Swing components except the cast is to the proper type for that component.

```
/**
 * Notification from the UIFactory that the L&F
 * has changed.
 *
 * @see JComponent#updateUI
 */
public void updateUI() {
    setUI((LabelUI)UIManager.getUI(this));
    invalidate();
}
```

Creating UI Objects

Looking at the `updateUI` method, the question comes to mind, "How does the `UIManager` know what UI class to use for the component?" The `UIManager` queries the component for its UI class by calling the `getUIClassID` method. Each "J" component defines a `String` constant, `uiClassID`, that defines the ID for the class. This constant is returned from the `getUIClassID` method. The class ID is used as the key into the `UIDefaults` dictionary. The value associated with the key is the key for the UI class for the component. Using reflection, an instance of the UI class is created with the parameter of the `getUI` method as the target for the newly created UI object. Finally, the UI object is returned to the component. There are three classes interacting to create the single UI instance for the

"J" component. The interaction between these objects for the JLabel class is shown in Figure 22.1. A complete description of the UIManager and UIDefaults classes is presented in Chapter 30, "Pluggable Look-and-Feel."

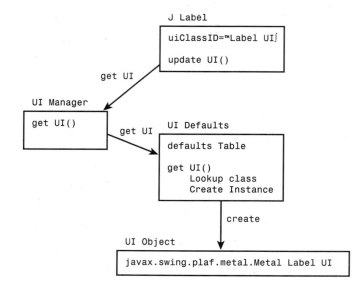

"J" Component and UI Object Interactions

Now you know how a UI object gets associated with a "J" component, but how do these objects interact and, more importantly, how does the UI object paint the "J" component? To answer this question, you need to first look at the pluggable look-and-feel package, abbreviated as plaf in the code, and its child packages.

The com.sun.java.swing.plaf Package Hierarchy

The plaf hierarchy is shown in Figure 22.2. The plaf package defines an abstract class, not an interface, for each user interface component in the JFC. Each of the classes associated with a non-abstract "J" class extends the ComponentUI class, also contained in the plaf package. The ComponentUI class is shown in Listing 22.1. A review of this class shows that many of the methods it defines are the familiar size and paint methods from the AWT Component class. Methods to install, uninstall, and create the UI object are also defined. The final methods query the accessibility information about this class. Also notice that these are method definitions, not abstract method declarations. Thus, extensions do not have to provide implementations for every method in the ComponentUI class. Most of the other classes in the plaf package are empty extensions of the ComponentUI class. However, a couple of the more complex UI classes, such as `ComboBoxUI` and `FileChooserUI`, define additional abstract methods in the `plaf` package.

FIGURE 22.2

The plaf *class hierarchy.*

```
javax.swing.plaf
    └─ javax.swing.plaf.basic
    └─ javax.swing.plaf.metal
    └─ javax.swing.plaf.multi
    └─ com.sun.java.swing.plaf.mac
    └─ com.sun.java.swing.plaf.motif
    └─ com.sun.java.swing.plaf.windows
```

LISTING 22.1 THE `ComponentUI` CLASS IN THE `plaf` PACKAGE

```java
public abstract class ComponentUI
{
    public void installUI(JComponent c) {
    }

    public void uninstallUI(JComponent c) {
    }

    public void paint(Graphics g, JComponent c) {
    }

    public void update(Graphics g, JComponent c) {
     if (c.isOpaque()) {
        g.setColor(c.getBackground());
        g.fillRect(0, 0, c.getWidth(),c.getHeight());
     }
     paint(g, c);
    }

    public Dimension getPreferredSize(JComponent c) {
     return null;
    }

    public Dimension getMinimumSize(JComponent c) {
     return getPreferredSize(c);
    }

    public Dimension getMaximumSize(JComponent c) {
     return getPreferredSize(c);
    }

    public boolean contains(JComponent c, int x, int y) {
```

continues

LISTING 22.1 CONTINUED

```
    return c.inside(x, y);
}

public static ComponentUI createUI(JComponent c) {
  throw new Error("ComponentUI.createUI not implemented.");
}

/**
 * Returns the number of accessible children in the object.  If all
 * of the children of this object implement Accessible, than this
 * method should return the number of children of this object.
 * UIs might wish to override this if they present areas on the
 * screen that can be viewed as components, but actual components
 * are not used for presenting those areas.
 *
 * @see #getAccessibleChild
 * @return the number of accessible children in the object.
 */
public int getAccessibleChildrenCount(JComponent c) {
    return SwingUtilities.getAccessibleChildrenCount(c);
}

/**
 * Return the nth Accessible child of the object.
 * UIs might wish to override this if they present areas on the
 * screen that can be viewed as components, but actual components
 * are not used for presenting those areas.
 *
 * @see #getAccessibleChildrenCount
 * @param i zero-based index of child
 * @return the nth Accessible child of the object
 */
public Accessible getAccessibleChild(JComponent c, int i) {
    return SwingUtilities.getAccessibleChild(c, i);
}
}
```

The javax.swing.plaf.basic contains concrete extensions of the leaf classes contained in the javax.swing.plaf package. The classes in the basic package provide common implementations for the methods in their parent class defined in the plaf package. The other child packages of the plaf package are the actual look-and-feel implementations. Each of these packages must also contain concrete implementations of the leaf classes defined in the plaf package that they customize. The classes contained in the basic package can be used directly if the look-and-feel does not need to alter the class. It is an instance of one of these packages that is instantiated in the getUI call in the UIManager. The classes in the look-and-feel implementations that are part of the JFC extend their counterparts in the basic package and override methods as required rather than extending the plaf class directly, and having to provide an implementation for every method that is required. This implies that there will be a separate UI class for every Swing component for each look-and-feel installed. The plaf package hierarchy extension model is similar to how AWT components are extended and is familiar to developers.

JComponent to the Rescue

Now you know where the UI objects live and how they are created, but you still have not seen how the UI object paints the component or how the UI object's sizing methods get called. There is really only one place where the UI object and "J" components can be bound, in the JComponent class. Recall from the discussion of the JComponent class in Chapter 3, "JComponent," that the JComponent class is the top of the visual component hierarchy in the JFC. As such, it is an ancestor of the AWT Component class. This ensures that JComponent class's sizing and painting methods will be called when required by layout managers or the repaint manager. Thus, the JComponent class can delegate to the UI object those methods defined in the ComponentUI class in the plaf package. As an example of this delegation, look at the getPreferredSize method contained in the JComponent class shown next.

```
public Dimension getPreferredSize() {
    if (preferredSize != null) {
        return preferredSize;
    }
    Dimension size = null;
    if (ui != null) {
        size = ui.getPreferredSize(this);
    }
    return (size != null) ? size : super.getPreferredSize();
}
```

Obviously, the method's signature has to match that contained in the AWT Component class to override that method. The method first checks to see if a preferred size has been set for the component that overrides the value specified by the component. If this is not the case, the UI object is called to calculate the preferred size. This is the size returned to the caller. There are similar implementations for the other methods that are delegated to the UI object.

The JComponent class's paint method does not follow the simple delegation pattern shown for the getPreferredSize method. Indeed, the paint method and its supporting methods are perhaps the most complex methods in the JComponent class. A simplified explanation of the methods is that they test for double buffering, and, if enabled, gets the offscreen image to which to draw. It then calls the paintComponent and paintBorder methods to paint the component, and finally calls the paintChildren method to paint any children of the component. (Recall that JComponent extends the AWT Container class and can contain children.) This still doesn't explain how the UI object's paint method gets called, but, if you dig deeper, you see that the paintComponent method calls the update method of its UI object. Another review of the ComponentUI class shown in Listing 22.1 shows that the update method paints the background if the component is opaque and then calls the paint method. There it is! Thus, the JComponent class provides the complete link between the "J" component and the UI object.

The strength of the pluggable look-and-feel architecture is that application code interacts with the "J" components. The application sets and queries properties and responds to events from these components to create its user interface. It is the "J" component that defines the API for the component. The UI object responds to property changes and acts accordingly. Changing the look-and-feel does not alter the application, because this type of change does not affect the "J" component, only the UI delegate object is replaced.

Example UI Class

The previous section explained how the pluggable look-and-feel architecture works. There are many components that work together to implement the architecture. You also saw that when you create a Swing component, you are actually creating the component itself and a UI delegate. The UIManager determines the class of the UI delegate and it is typically dependent on the current look-and-feel being used by the application. However, the UI delegate class can be overridden to provide your own implementation of the delegate. This is perhaps the easiest technique for extending a JFC component and will be presented in this section. More complex extension examples will be presented in the following chapters.

The MultiLineToolTipUI class shown in Listing 22.2 provides a UI class that will render ToolTips using multiple lines. The line breaks are determined by '\n' characters embedded in the ToolTip string registered for the component. The MultiLineToolTipUI class extends the BasicToolTipUI class from the javax.swing.plaf.basic package. It is very similar to that class and only overrides a few methods. As with the BasicToolTipUI class, a single instance of the class can be shared by all JToolTip instances. Thus, the MultiLineToolTipUI class is a singleton. The reference to the class is obtained by calling the createUI method. This method creates the UI object for the given JComponent. In this case, the singleton instance can be returned from this method. The other two methods that are overridden from the BasicToolTipUI class are the paint and getPreferredSize methods. These methods are similar in structure. A StringTokenizer is used to parse the ToolTip into multiple lines. The preferred size of the component is the number of lines times the height of each line, and the width of the widest line. The paint method simply loops through the ToolTip and renders each line on the ToolTip component. Notice how the font and colors are queried from the component, rather than being hard coded. The `paint` method renders single line ToolTips the same as the `BasicToolTipUI` component. (The margin was made a pixel smaller to conserve space; this could be changed to 3 pixels to exactly match the `BasicToolTipUI` class if wanted.) Thus, single-line ToolTips are unaffected by the change in the UI class.

LISTING 22.2 THE `MultiLineToolTipUI` CLASS

```
package com.foley.utility;

import java.awt.*;

import java.util.StringTokenizer;

import javax.swing.*;
import javax.swing.plaf.ComponentUI;
import javax.swing.plaf.basic.BasicToolTipUI;


/**
 * The MultiLineToolTipUI class may be registered with the UIManager
 * to replace the ToolTipUI for JToolTip instances. When used, it
 * divides the ToolTip into multiple lines. Each line is divided by
 * the '\n' character.
 * <p>
 * @author Mike Foley
 **/
public class MultiLineToolTipUI extends BasicToolTipUI {

    /**
     * The single shared UI instance.
     **/
    static MultiLineToolTipUI sharedInstance = new MultiLineToolTipUI();

    /**
     * The margin around the text.
     **/
    static final int MARGIN = 2;

    /**
     * The character to use in the StringTokenizer to
     * separate lines in the ToolTip. This could be the
     * system property end of line character.
     **/
    static final String lineSeparator = "\n";

    /**
```

continues

LISTING 22.2 CONTINUED

```java
 * MultiLineToolTipUI, constructor.
 * <p>
 * Have the constructor be protected so we can be subclassed,
 * but not created by client classes.
 **/
protected MultiLineToolTipUI() {
    super();
}


/**
 * Create the UI component for the given component.
 * The same UI can be shared for all components, so
 * return our shared instance.
 * <p>
 * @param c The component to create the UI for.
 * @return Our shared UI component instance.
 **/
public static ComponentUI createUI( JComponent c ) {
    return sharedInstance;
}


/**
 * Paint the ToolTip. Use the current font and colors
 * set for the given component.
 * <p>
 * @param g The graphics to paint with.
 * @param c The component to paint.
 **/
public void paint( Graphics g, JComponent c ) {

    //
    // Determine the size for each row.
    //
    Font font = c.getFont();
    FontMetrics fontMetrics = c.getFontMetrics( font );

    int fontHeight = fontMetrics.getHeight();
    int fontAscent = fontMetrics.getAscent();

    //
    // Paint the background in the tip color.
    //
    g.setColor( c.getBackground() );
    Dimension size = c.getSize();
    g.fillRect( 0, 0, size.width, size.height );

    //
```

```
        // Paint each line in the tip using the
        // foreground color. Use a StringTokenizer
        // to parse the ToolTip. Each line is left
        // justified, and the y coordinate is updated
        // through the loop.
        //
        g.setColor( c.getForeground() );
        int y = 2 + fontAscent;
        String tipText = ( ( JToolTip )c ).getTipText();
StringTokenizer tokenizer =
                    new StringTokenizer( tipText, lineSeparator );
        int numberOfLines = tokenizer.countTokens();
        for( int i = 0; i < numberOfLines; i++ ) {
            g.drawString( tokenizer.nextToken(), MARGIN, y );
            y += fontHeight;
        }

    } // paint


    /**
     * The preferred size for the ToolTip is the width of
     * the longest row in the tip, and the height of a
     * single row times the number of rows in the tip.
     *
     * @param c The component whose size is needed.
     * @return The preferred size for the component.
     **/
    public Dimension getPreferredSize( JComponent c ) {

        //
        // Determine the size for each row.
        //
        Font font = c.getFont();
        FontMetrics fontMetrics = c.getFontMetrics( font );

        int fontHeight = fontMetrics.getHeight();

        //
        // Get the tip text string.
        //
        String tipText = ( ( JToolTip )c ).getTipText();

        //
        // Empty tip, use a default size.
        //
        if( tipText == null )
            return new Dimension( 2 * MARGIN, 2 * MARGIN );

        //
```

22

EXTENDING
EXISTING
COMPONENTS

continues

LISTING 22.2   CONTINUED

```
        // Create a StringTokenizer to parse the ToolTip.
        //
StringTokenizer tokenizer =
                        new StringTokenizer( tipText, lineSeparator );
        int numberOfLines = tokenizer.countTokens();

        //
        // Height is number of lines times height of a single line.
        //
        int height = numberOfLines * fontHeight;

        //
        // Width is width of longest single line.
        //
        int width = 0;
        for( int i = 0; i < numberOfLines; i++ ) {
int thisWidth = fontMetrics.stringWidth(
➥                     tokenizer.nextToken() );
            width = Math.max( width, thisWidth );
        }

        //
        // Add the margin to the size, and return.
        //
return(new Dimension( width + 2 * MARGIN, height + 2 * MARGIN ));

   } // getPreferredSize

} // MultiLineToolTipUI
```

The `MultiLineToolTipTest` application shown in Listing 22.3 demonstrates how to register the `MultiLineToolTipUI` class with the `UIManager`. This enables the class to be used as the UI object for instances of the `JToolTip` class. Because the `MultiLineToolTipUI` class is registered as a user default, it will override the `ToolTipUI` registered by the look-and-feel. Thus, it will be used for all look-and-feels, even if the look-and-feel is changed at runtime. The resulting ToolTips for a multiline and single line ToolTip are shown in Figures 22.3 and 22.4.

LISTING 22.3   THE `MultiLineToolTipTest` APPLICATION

```
package com.foley.test;

import java.awt.*;

import javax.swing.*;

import com.foley.utility.ApplicationFrame;
```

```java
/**
 * An application that registers the MultiLineToolTip
 * class with the UIManager. Then a frame with some
 * components are created. MultiLineToolTips are added
 * to some of these components to test the class.
 *
 * @author Mike Foley
 **/
public class MultiLineToolTipTest extends Object {

    /**
     * Application entry point.
     * Register the MultiLineToolTip class.
     * Create the frame, and display it.
     *
     * @param args Command line parameter. Not used.
     **/
    public static void main( String args[] ) {

        //
        // Register the MultiLineToolTipUI class as the UI class
        // for the ToolTipUI key. This is the key used by the
        // JToolTip class.
        // There are two maps, one from the ToolTipUI key to the
        // key for the class of the UI object. The second is from
        // the key for the class of the UI object to an actual
        // Class for this key.
        //
        try {
            String multiLineToolTipUIClassName =
                        "com.foley.utility.MultiLineToolTipUI";
            UIManager.put( "ToolTipUI", multiLineToolTipUIClassName );
            UIManager.put( multiLineToolTipUIClassName,
                        Class.forName( multiLineToolTipUIClassName ) );
        } catch( ClassNotFoundException cnfe ) {
            System.err.println( "MultiLine ToolTip UI class not found" );
            System.err.println( cnfe );
        }

        JFrame frame = new ApplicationFrame( "MultiLineToolTipUI Test" );

        JToggleButton t1 = new JToggleButton( "Toggle" );
        t1.setToolTipText( "This is an example of\n"
                        + "a multiline ToolTip.\n"
                        + " \nIt can be very long\nif required.");
        JToggleButton t2 = new JToggleButton( "Toggle" );
        t2.setToolTipText( "Single line tips are unaltered" );

        JPanel center = new JPanel();
```

continues

LISTING 22.3   CONTINUED

```
        center.setBorder( BorderFactory.createCompoundBorder(
                    BorderFactory.createLoweredBevelBorder(),
                    BorderFactory.createEmptyBorder( 4, 4, 4, 4 ) ) );

        center.add( t1 );
        center.add( t2 );

        frame.getContentPane().add( center, BorderLayout.CENTER );
        frame.pack();
        frame.setVisible( true );

    } // main

} // MultiLineToolTipTest
```

FIGURE 22.3

A multiline ToolTip.

FIGURE 22.4

A single-line ToolTip.

The most interesting aspect of the `MultiLineToolTipTest` application is the block of code at the beginning of the `main` method that registers the `MultiLineToolTipUI` class with the `UIManager`. The registration is done with two `put` calls to the `UIManager`. The first call registers the class key for the `ToolTipUI` class. This is the `String` returned from the `getUIClassID` in the `JToolTip` class. The second registers the `Class` for the class key registered in the first call. In Listing 22.3, the class name of the `MultiLineToolTipUI` class is used as the key. However, any unique key can be used. For example, the following lines of code would also register the `MultiLineToolTipUI` class for the `ToolTipUI` key.

```
UIManager.put( "ToolTipUI", "fabcdesger" );
UIManager.put( "fabcdesger",
➥        Class.forName( multiLineToolTipUIClassName ) );
```

The application also demonstrates how to set a multi-line ToolTip for a `JComponent` instance. By embedding a `'\n'` character in the ToolTip string, the line will be broken at each occurrence of that character. Notice how two sequential `'\n'` characters cannot specify an empty line. Instead, at least one space must be provided for the line.

The choice of using the `'\n'` character as the line break character can be debated. It can be argued that the system `line.separator` property should be used instead. This could facilitate reading ToolTips from property files. The best solution may be to have the break character be a settable property in the `MultiLineToolTipUI` class.

Summary

This chapter introduced the JFC pluggable look-and-feel architecture. It demonstrated how a Swing component's UI object is created, and the responsibilities of the component to interact with the pluggable look-and-feel subsystem.

The `com.sun.java.swing.plaf` package hierarchy was presented. The `javax.swing.plaf` package contains abstract classes that define the methods that each UI object must implement for a Swing component. The `javax.swing.plaf.basic` package provides concrete classes containing default behavior for each Swing visual component. The remaining `com.sun.java.swing.plaf` child packages provide actual look-and-feel implementations. The specific look-and-feel classes tend to extend the `javax.swing.plaf.basic` package's implementation and override methods when required.

The first technique for extending a Swing component was presented. A new UI class was created and registered with the `UIManager` for the `ToolTipUI`. This is the UI used for the `JToolTip` class. The `MultiLineToolTipUI` class is an extension of the `BasicToolTipUI` class and provides a UI implementation that allows multiline ToolTips for Swing components. Once registered with the `UIManager`, this class is used as the UI object for `JToolTip` instances for all look-and-feels. The look-and-feel can even be changed at runtime, and the `MultiLineToolTipUI` class will still be used. This technique can be used for as many classes of UI objects as desired.

Creating a Custom Look-and-Feel

CHAPTER 23

Even though the JFC comes complete with look-and-feel implementations for popular windowing systems and a platform-neutral look-and-feel, you may still be required to create a custom look-and-feel. An example of such a requirement is a corporation that wants a company-branded application to be available on all platforms used by the company. This reduces the learning curve for users and reduces the dependency on hardware platforms. The Java look-and-feel can be used to meet the requirement of the same user interface on all platforms but does not meet the branding requirement.

Another requirement for a custom look-and-feel implementation is a UI designer who may want to implement a complete look-and-feel to demonstrate his or her design.

There are multiple levels of customizations that can be made to a look-and-feel. These range from changing colors and icons in an existing look-and-feel implementation to providing a custom user interface implementation for every component.

In this chapter, you will learn

- How to customize the look of existing look-and-feel implementations
- How to create custom themes
- How to change the feel of a component
- How to create a new look-and-feel

Customizing Existing Look-and-Feels

An amazing feature of the pluggable look-and-feel architecture the Swing components are built on is how much of the "look" can be customized without extending a single class. A look-and-feel implementation should not hard code its look into the source code. Instead, properties that define the look are registered with the UIManager. When the user interface delegate is to render a component, the properties are read from the UIManager and used appropriately for the component.

A client application can alter the UI properties to create a custom look. The set of properties that defines a look are often referred to as a theme. The Java look-and-feel has built-in support for installing custom themes. An ad hoc approach must be taken with other look-and-feel implementations.

Determining Available Properties

Setting properties in the UIManager provides a simple mechanism for altering the look of JFC components. However, you need to know the list of available properties to be able to change them. The available properties can be determined by examining the source code for the look-and-feel or by examining the properties defined in the UIManager at runtime. In this section, a combination of both techniques will be presented.

The PropertyViewer application shown in Listing 23.1 is an application that displays the properties of any of the registered look-and-feels. In the createComboBox method, the registered look-and-feels are queried from the UIManager by using the following line of code. An array of LookAndFeelInfo objects is returned from the getInstalled LookAndFeels method in the UIManager class. The LookAndFeelInfo class is defined in the UIManager class and contains information about a look-and-feel. This class contains two methods of interest: getName and getClassName. The name is a string suitable for use in menus or combo boxes, as shown here. The getClassName returns the name of the class that defines the look-and-feel. The result is a combo box containing the name of all the registered look-and-feels available in the JFC installation.

```
UIManager.LookAndFeelInfo[] info = UIManager.getInstalledLookAndFeels();
```

An ItemListener is added to the combo box. When the item is changed, the new look-and-feel is loaded and the properties are updated in the table. The setLookAndFeel method is used to update the look-and-feel for the application. The look-and-feel is set by passing the class name of the desired look-and-feel to the setLookAndFeel method contained in the UIManager class. The setLookAndFeel method updates the UIDefaults object that will cause the new look-and-feel to be used for newly created objects. However, it does not alter existing components. To change the UI object for existing components, call the updateComponenetTreeUI method in the SwingUtilities class. As its name implies, this method updates the UI object for the tree of components starting at the given component. If this method is called for each top-level window in an application, the look-and-feel can be totally changed at runtime. There is a single JFrame for this application, and that is passed to the updateComponenetTreeUI method. The following code fragment demonstrates this technique:

```
UIManager.setLookAndFeel( className );
SwingUtilities.updateComponentTreeUI(
             JOptionPane.getFrameForComponent( this ) );
```

The dumpLAFProperties method is used to query the UIDefaults instance from the UIManager and update the table model using these values. The following code performs this task:

```
UIDefaults defaults = UIManager.getDefaults();
Enumeration keys = defaults.keys();
Enumeration elements = defaults.elements();
tableModel.update( keys, elements );
```

The complete `PropertyViewer` application is in Listing 23.1. The executing application is shown in Figure 23.1.

LISTING 23.1   THE `PropertyViewer` APPLICATION

```
package com.foley.test;

import java.awt.*;
import java.awt.event.*;

import java.util.*;

import javax.swing.*;
import javax.swing.table.*;

import com.foley.utility.*;


/**
 * An application that displays the properties
 * of the installed look-and-feels
 *
 * @author Mike Foley
 **/
public class PropertyViewer extends JPanel
    implements ItemListener {

    JComboBox comboBox;
    JTable table;
    UITableModel tableModel;


    /**
     * PropertyViewer, constructor
     * <p>
     * Create the
     **/
    public PropertyViewer() {
        super();

        setLayout( new BorderLayout() );

        comboBox = createComboBox();
        tableModel = new UITableModel();
        sorter = new TableSorter( tableModel );
        table = new JTable( sorter );
```

```
        comboBox.addItemListener( this );

        add( comboBox, BorderLayout.NORTH );
        add( new JScrollPane( table ), BorderLayout.CENTER );

        dumpLAFProperties();
    }


    /**
     * Create a combo box containing the installed
     * look-and-feels.
     * <p>
     * @return A combo box containing the installed L&Fs.
     **/
    protected JComboBox createComboBox() {
        JComboBox comboBox = new JComboBox();

        UIManager.LookAndFeelInfo[] info =
            UIManager.getInstalledLookAndFeels();
        for( int i = 0; i < info.length; i++ ) {
            comboBox.addItem( info[i].getName() );
        }
        return( comboBox );
    }

    public void itemStateChanged( ItemEvent event ) {
        if( event.getStateChange() == ItemEvent.SELECTED ) {
            System.out.println( event.getItem() );
            String name = event.getItem().toString();
            UIManager.LookAndFeelInfo[] info =
                UIManager.getInstalledLookAndFeels();
            for( int i = 0; i < info.length; i++ ) {
                if( name.equals( info[i].getName() ) ) {
                    setLookAndFeel( info[i].getClassName() );
                    dumpLAFProperties();
                    break;
                }
            }
        }
    }


    /**
     * Set the look-and-feel to the given L&F.
     * Update your UI to the new look-and-feel.
     * <p>
     * @param className The class name of the L&F to set.
     **/
    private void setLookAndFeel( String className ) {
        try {
            UIManager.setLookAndFeel( className );
```

continues

LISTING 23.1 CONTINUED

```java
            SwingUtilities.updateComponentTreeUI(
                JOptionPane.getFrameForComponent( this ) );
        } catch( Exception e ) {
            System.err.println( "Cound not set look-and-feel" );
        }
    }


    /**
     * Print the properties of the current look-
     * and-feel to the text area component.
     **/
    public void dumpLAFProperties() {
        UIDefaults defaults = UIManager.getDefaults();
        Enumeration keys = defaults.keys();
        Enumeration elements = defaults.elements();
        tableModel.update( keys, elements );
    }


    /**
     * Application entry point.
     * Create a frame and a table and display them.
     *
     * @param args Command line parameter. Not used.
     **/
    public static void main( String args[] ) {

        JFrame frame = new ApplicationFrame( "PropertyViewer" );

        PropertyViewer propertyViewer = new PropertyViewer();
        propertyViewer.setBorder(
                BorderFactory.createLoweredBevelBorder() );

        Container content = frame.getContentPane();
        content.add( propertyViewer, BorderLayout.CENTER );

        frame.pack();
        frame.setVisible( true );

    } // main

} // PropertyViewer


class UITableModel extends AbstractTableModel {

    private Vector keyData;
```

```
    private Vector valueData;

    public UITableModel() {
        super();
        keyData = new Vector();
        valueData = new Vector();
    }


    public int getRowCount() {
        return( keyData.size() );
    }
    public int getColumnCount() {
        return( 2 );
    }

    public Class getColumnClass( int column ) {
        return( String.class );
    }

    public String getColumnName( int column ) {
        if( column == 0 ) {
            return( "Key" );
        } else {
            return( "Current Value" );
        }
    }

    public Object getValueAt(int row, int column) {
        if( column == 0 ) {
            return( keyData.elementAt( row ) );
        } else {
            return( valueData.elementAt( row ) );
        }
    }

    public void update( Enumeration keys, Enumeration values ) {
        keyData.removeAllElements();
        valueData.removeAllElements();
        while( keys.hasMoreElements() ) {
            keyData.addElement( keys.nextElement() );
            valueData.addElement( values.nextElement() );

        }
        fireTableStructureChanged();
    }

} // UITableModel
```

9780789714664

FIGURE 23.1

The PropertyViewer *application.*

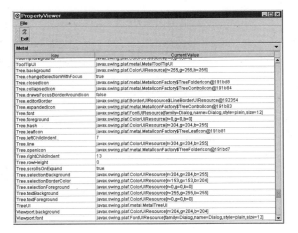

Using UI Properties

The previous section presented an application that displays the look-and-feel properties for any of the installed look-and-feels. Now that you know what properties are available for customizing Swing components, you can register your preferences with the UIManager.

As an example, customize the JTree class' UI object by altering some of its properties. Figure 23.1 displays the available properties for the JTree class and their default values for the Java look-and-feel. Properties range from the foreground and background colors to the icons used for the various tree node states. The main method of the TreeTest application presented in Chapter 11, "Tree Component," will be modified to register properties for the JTree class's UI object. The unmodified application is shown in Figure 23.2.

The following lines of code were added to the main method of the TreeTest application before the components were created. These lines of code set properties in the UIDefaults object. The put method in the UIManager class is a convenience method and is the equivalent of first getting the UIDefaults from the UIManager and then calling the put method of the UIDefaults object directly. The UIDefaults class is an extension of the Hashtable class, allowing the familiar Hashtable class's API to be used when modifying UI properties.

```
UIManager.put( "Tree.background", Color.lightGray );
UIManager.put( "Tree.textForeground", Color.blue );
UIManager.put( "Tree.textBackground", Color.yellow );
UIManager.put( "Tree.font", new Font( "Helvetica", Font.BOLD, 24 ) );
UIManager.put( "Tree.leftChildIndent", new Integer( 24 ) );
```

FIGURE 23.2

The unmodified `TreeTest` *application.*

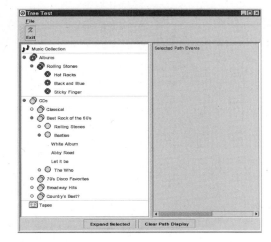

Setting the `"Tree.background"` property in the first line sets the tree's background color to black. Similarly, the text foreground and background color properties are set to blue and yellow, respectively. The font for the tree is set to an eye-popping 24-point Helvetica bold font. Because of the large font, the default indentation seemed too small, so the final line sets this property to 24 pixels. The resulting tree is shown in Figure 23.3. Any of the UI object's properties can be set by using this technique.

FIGURE 23.3

The modified `TreeTest` *application.*

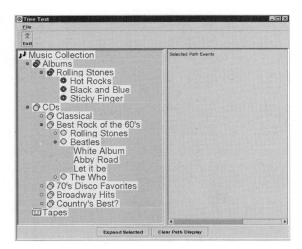

> **NOTE**
>
> Care must be taken when setting properties with the UIManager.put method. The keys are String instances. A typo in the key will execute without producing an error, but the property will not be used. The property will be added to the UIDefaults table but, since the key was not correct, when the UI object retrieves the property by using the correct key, your value will not be used. An interface containing all the keys defined as constants would eliminate this type of error.

The LookAndFeel Source Files

A look-and-feel is defined in a LookAndFeel class. The standard naming convention for this class is the look-and-feel implementation's name followed by LookAndFeel. For example, the MS Windows look-and-feel is defined in the WindowsLookAndFeel class. The LookAndFeel class contains methods to query the name, description, and ID for the look-and-feel. It also contains the initialization code for the UIDefaults properties. This file presents a valuable resource for property names and their default values.

Creating a Theme

When using the Java look-and-feel, also known as Metal, changing the theme can easily alter properties being used in an application. A theme consists of colors and fonts used by the look-and-feel.

The Java look-and-feel is designed by using three primary colors and three secondary colors for most components. The primary colors are the foreground colors, and the secondary colors are the background colors. Creating a theme class that specifies these six colors gives an easy method to change an application's look. Specifying fonts and colors in the theme can provide further customization.

The complete MetalTheme abstract class is shown in Listing 23.2. The listing shows the complete set of methods that a theme can override to customize the look-and-feel. The Metal look-and-feel defines the DefaultMetalTheme class, which is a concrete extension of the MetalTheme class. The DefaultMetalTheme class provides the default theme for the Metal look-and-feel and is also shown in Listing 23.2.

LISTING 23.2 THE MetalTheme AND DefaultMetalTheme CLASSES

```
public abstract class MetalTheme {

    private static ColorUIResource white =
                        new ColorUIResource( 255, 255, 255 );
    private static ColorUIResource black =
                        new ColorUIResource( 0, 0, 0 );

    public abstract String getName();

    // these are blue in Metal Default Theme
    protected abstract ColorUIResource getPrimary1();
    protected abstract ColorUIResource getPrimary2();
    protected abstract ColorUIResource getPrimary3();

    // these are gray in Metal Default Theme
    protected abstract ColorUIResource getSecondary1();
    protected abstract ColorUIResource getSecondary2();
    protected abstract ColorUIResource getSecondary3();

    public abstract FontUIResource getControlTextFont();
    public abstract FontUIResource getSystemTextFont();
    public abstract FontUIResource getUserTextFont();
    public abstract FontUIResource getMenuTextFont();
    public abstract FontUIResource getWindowTitleFont();
    public abstract FontUIResource getSubTextFont();

    protected ColorUIResource getWhite() { return white; }
    protected ColorUIResource getBlack() { return black; }

    public ColorUIResource getFocusColor() { return getPrimary2(); }

    public  ColorUIResource getDesktopColor() { return getPrimary2(); }

    public ColorUIResource getControl() { return getSecondary3(); }
    public ColorUIResource getControlShadow() {
      return getSecondary2();
    }
    public ColorUIResource getControlDarkShadow() {
        return getSecondary1();
    }
    public ColorUIResource getControlInfo() { return getBlack(); }
    public ColorUIResource getControlHighlight() { return getWhite(); }
    public ColorUIResource getControlDisabled() {
        return getSecondary2();
    }

    public ColorUIResource getPrimaryControl() { return getPrimary3(); }
    public ColorUIResource getPrimaryControlShadow() {
```

23

CREATING A CUSTOM LOOK-AND-FEEL

continues

LISTING 23.2 CONTINUED

```
            return getPrimary2();
    }
    public ColorUIResource getPrimaryControlDarkShadow() {
        return getPrimary1();
    }
    public ColorUIResource getPrimaryControlInfo() {
        return getBlack();
    }
    public ColorUIResource getPrimaryControlHighlight() {
        return getWhite();
    }

    public ColorUIResource getSystemTextColor() {
        return getPrimary1();
    }
    public ColorUIResource getControlTextColor() {
        return getControlInfo();
    }
    public ColorUIResource getInactiveControlTextColor() {
        return getControlDisabled();
    }
    public ColorUIResource getInactiveSystemTextColor() {
        return getSecondary2();
    }
    public ColorUIResource getUserTextColor() {
        return getBlack();
    }
    public ColorUIResource getTextHighlightColor() {
        return getPrimary3();
    }
    public ColorUIResource getHighlightedTextColor() {
        return getControlTextColor();
    }

    public ColorUIResource getWindowBackground() {
        return getWhite();
    }
    public ColorUIResource getWindowTitleBackground() {
        return getPrimary3();
    }
    public ColorUIResource getWindowTitleForeground() {
        return getBlack();
    }
    public ColorUIResource getWindowTitleInactiveBackground() {
        return getSecondary3();
    }
    public ColorUIResource getWindowTitleInactiveForeground() {
        return getBlack();
    }

    public ColorUIResource getMenuBackground() {
```

```
            return getSecondary3();
      }
      public ColorUIResource getMenuForeground() {
            return  getBlack();
      }
      public ColorUIResource getMenuSelectedBackground() {
            return getPrimary2();
      }
      public ColorUIResource getMenuSelectedForeground() {
            return getBlack();
      }
      public ColorUIResource getMenuDisabledForeground() {
            return getSecondary2();
      }
      public ColorUIResource getSeparatorBackground() {
            return getWhite();
      }
      public ColorUIResource getSeparatorForeground() {
          return getPrimary1();
      }
      public ColorUIResource getAcceleratorForeground() {
            return getPrimary1();
      }
      public ColorUIResource getAcceleratorSelectedForeground() {
            return getBlack();
      }

      public void addCustomEntriesToTable(UIDefaults table) {}
}

public class DefaultMetalTheme extends MetalTheme {

      private final ColorUIResource primary1 =
                        new ColorUIResource(102, 102, 153);
      private final ColorUIResource primary2 =
                        new ColorUIResource(153, 153, 204);
      private final ColorUIResource primary3 =
                        new ColorUIResource(204, 204, 255);

      private final ColorUIResource secondary1 =
                        new ColorUIResource(102, 102, 102);
      private final ColorUIResource secondary2 =
                        new ColorUIResource(153, 153, 153);
      private final ColorUIResource secondary3 =
                        new ColorUIResource(204, 204, 204);

      private final FontUIResource controlFont =
                      new FontUIResource("Dialog", Font.BOLD, 12);
      private final FontUIResource systemFont =
                      new FontUIResource("Dialog", Font.PLAIN, 12);
```

23

CREATING A
CUSTOM
LOOK-AND-FEEL

continues

LISTING 23.2 CONTINUED

```
    private final FontUIResource windowTitleFont =
                     new FontUIResource("SansSerif", Font.BOLD, 12);
    private final FontUIResource userFont =
                     new FontUIResource("Dialog", Font.PLAIN, 12);
    private final FontUIResource smallFont =
                     new FontUIResource("Dialog", Font.PLAIN, 10);

    public String getName() { return "Steel"; }

// these are blue in Metal Default Theme
    protected ColorUIResource getPrimary1() { return primary1; }
    protected ColorUIResource getPrimary2() { return primary2; }
    protected ColorUIResource getPrimary3() { return primary3; }

// these are gray in Metal Default Theme
    protected ColorUIResource getSecondary1() { return secondary1; }
    protected ColorUIResource getSecondary2() { return secondary2; }
    protected ColorUIResource getSecondary3() { return secondary3; }

    public FontUIResource getControlTextFont() { return controlFont;}
    public FontUIResource getSystemTextFont() { return systemFont;}
    public FontUIResource getUserTextFont() { return userFont;}
    public FontUIResource getMenuTextFont() { return controlFont;}
    public FontUIResource getWindowTitleFont() { return controlFont;}
    public FontUIResource getSubTextFont() { return smallFont;}
}
```

The `OutlandishTheme` class presented in Listing 23.3 shows an extension to the `DefaultMetalTheme` class that overrides the primary and secondary colors. When this theme is set for the `TreeTest` application, the result is the window shown in Figure 23.4. The window using the `DefaultMetalTheme` was shown in Figure 23.2.

LISTING 23.3 THE `OutlandishTheme` CLASS

```
package com.foley.utility;

import javax.swing.plaf.ColorUIResource;

import javax.swing.plaf.metal.DefaultMetalTheme;


/**
 * This class provides an outlandish color theme.
 * The primary and secondary colors are overridden.
 * The fonts and other theme properties are left unaltered.
 * <p>
 * @author Mike Foley
 **/
```

```
public class OutlandishTheme extends DefaultMetalTheme {

    public String getName() { return "OutlandishTheme"; }

    //
    // Primary Colors.
    //
    private final ColorUIResource primary1 =
                        new ColorUIResource( 255, 0, 0 );
    private final ColorUIResource primary2 =
                        new ColorUIResource(200, 25, 25);
    private final ColorUIResource primary3 =
                        new ColorUIResource(150, 150, 150);

    protected ColorUIResource getPrimary1() { return primary1; }
    protected ColorUIResource getPrimary2() { return primary2; }
    protected ColorUIResource getPrimary3() { return primary3; }

    //
    // Secondary Colors.
    //
    private final ColorUIResource secondary1 =
                        new ColorUIResource( 0,  255,  0);
    private final ColorUIResource secondary2 =
                        new ColorUIResource(25, 200, 25);
    private final ColorUIResource secondary3 =
                        new ColorUIResource(40, 180, 40);

    protected ColorUIResource getSecondary1() { return secondary1; }
    protected ColorUIResource getSecondary2() { return secondary2; }
    protected ColorUIResource getSecondary3() { return secondary3; }

} // OutlandishTheme
```

23

FIGURE 23.4

The OutlandishTheme *set for the* TreeTest *application.*

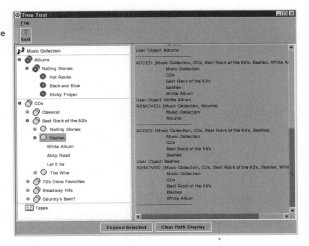

The theme is set for the application by calling the static `setCurrentTheme` method contained in the `MetalLookAndFeel` class. The following line of code was added to the `main` method in the `TreeTest` application to set `OutlandishTheme` for the application. The theme can be dynamically changed when the application is running. This allows themes to be selected from a menu or read from a property file while the application is executing.

```
MetalLookAndFeel.setCurrentTheme( new OutlandishTheme() );
```

> **NOTE**
>
> The `Metalworks` demonstration application that is part of the JDK distribution provides many custom themes that can be dynamically changed by selecting the desired theme from a menu. An example of reading a theme from a property file is also demonstrated.

The `OutlandishTheme` only customizes colors. However, other properties are just as easily specified in a theme. For example, adding the following lines of code to the `OutlandishTheme` class will set all the application's fonts to an 18-point sans serif bold font. Of course all the fonts don't have to be the same, and typically they aren't. The resulting window is shown in Figure 23.5. Creating a theme with large fonts is useful when giving demonstrations of an application.

```
//
// Fonts.
//
private final FontUIResource font = new FontUIResource("SansSerif",
Font.BOLD, 18);
public FontUIResource getControlTextFont() { return font;}
public FontUIResource getSystemTextFont() { return font;}
public FontUIResource getUserTextFont() { return font;}
public FontUIResource getMenuTextFont() { return font;}
public FontUIResource getWindowTitleFont() { return font;}
public FontUIResource getSubTextFont() { return font;}
```

The last method of interests in the `MetalTheme` class is the `addCustomEntriesToTable` method. This method is intended to provide the theme an opportunity to register custom properties in the `UIDefaults` table. These are the same UI properties that were identified and set in the previous section. Being able to set the properties in the theme class allows all customizations to be encapsulated in the same class. For example, the customizations to the `TreeUI` shown in the previous section would be specified in a theme by setting the properties in the `addCustomEntriesToTable` method. An example for this method that achieves the same customizations for the `TreeUI` object is shown next. Notice how the superclass' `addCustomEntriesToTable` method is called first to initialize the `UIDefaults` table with values inherited from the parent theme. (In the `DefaultMetalTheme` this method is empty.) After the table is initialized, the custom values can be specified in the table. The look-and-feel calls this method during initialization or when the theme is changed. After the method returns, the `UIDefaults` object is set in the `UIManager`.

```java
public void addCustomEntriesToTable(UIDefaults table) {
    super.addCustomEntriesToTable(table);

    table.put( "Tree.background", Color.black );
    table.put( "Tree.textForeground", Color.blue );
    table.put( "Tree.textBackground", Color.yellow );
    table.put( "Tree.font", new Font( "Helvetica", Font.BOLD, 24 ) );
    table.put( "Tree.leftChildIndent", new Integer( 24 ) );

}
```

FIGURE 23.5

Large fonts added to the TreeTest *application.*

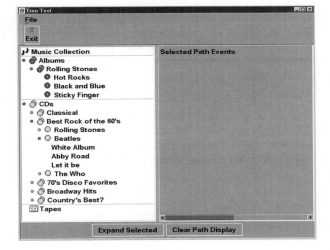

> **NOTE**
>
> Themes are an extremely powerful method for customizing an application. Reading the theme from a property file provides an easy mechanism that gives users the ability to customize an application. However, themes are only available when using the Java look-and-feel. This is unfortunate.

What About Feel?

To this point, all the customizations presented have to do with the look of an application, not its feel. This is for two reasons. First, there are not as many hooks in the JFC for customizing feel. The UIDefaults object does not contain properties that map user gestures to actions. However, this would be a welcome addition.

Secondly, more care must be used when altering the feel of an application. Changing the way an application responds to user gestures can make the program difficult to use. For example, if the feel of a button is changed to require a double-click instead of a single-click to perform the action, users will not know how to use the application and can become confused.

Changing colors, fonts, and icons can make an application look drastically different, but the standard components will still behave the way the user expects. This may not be the situation when the feel is changed. Moreover, there is no visual clue to the user that the feel has been changed. Thus, changing the feel of standard components must be performed with extreme caution and only for very good reasons.

When the situation does arise when the feel of a component needs to be changed, it is possible to do so. The technique is similar to that shown in the previous chapter when a new UI object was installed for the ToolTipUI.

Customizing the TreeUI

The TreeUI class expands and contracts a node when it is double-clicked with the mouse. I had an application that opened a dialog box when a node in the tree was double-clicked, and the tree expanding or contracting was a distraction to the user. The JTree class and the TreeUI implementations do not contain a property to control this action, so a new UI class was written and installed for the JTree class. The double-click causing the tree to expand and collapse was the only modification made to the tree's feel. Since the control immediately to the left on the node's text expands and collapses the tree, and the double-click performs another action that the user sees, changing this aspect of the tree's feel did not detract from the user's ability to use the application—instead, it enhanced it.

The NonExpandingTreeUI class shown in Listing 23.4 will prevent a JTree instance from expanding and collapsing when the user double-clicks a node. The createUI method is boilerplate look-and-feel code. It creates the UI object for the given component—in this case, a new instance of the NonExpandingTreeUI class. The isToggleEvent method is defined in the BasicTreeUI class to determine if the given mouse event should toggle the expansion state of a node. The BasicTreeUI class tests the click count in the event and returns true for a count of two and false for other counts. The NonExpandingTreeUI class always returns `false` from this method. Thus, no mouse event will toggle the node's expansion state.

LISTING 23.4   THE `NonExpandingTreeUI` CLASS

```
package com.foley.utility;

import java.awt.event.MouseEvent;

import javax.swing.JComponent;
import javax.swing.plaf.ComponentUI;
import javax.swing.plaf.basic.BasicTreeUI;


/**
 * A TreeUI that does not automatically expand or
 * collapse the tree on a double click event.
 * <p>
 * @author Mike Foley
 **/
public class NonExpandingTreeUI extends BasicTreeUI
{

    /**
     * Create the UI object for the given tree. This
     * is a new instance of this class.
     **/
    public static ComponentUI createUI( JComponent tree ) {
      return( new NonExpandingTreeUI() );
    }


    /**
     * NonExpandingTreeUI, constructor
     **/
    public NonExpandingTreeUI() {
        super();
    }


    /**
     * Returning true indicates the row under the mouse should be toggled
     * based on the event. This is invoked after
     * checkForClickInExpandControl, implying the location is not in the
     * expand (toggle) control
     * <p>
     * This is the behavior we want to stop, so always return false.
     * <p>
     * @return false
     **/
```

continues

LISTING 23.4   CONTINUED

```
    protected boolean isToggleEvent( MouseEvent event ) {
      return( false );
    }

} // NonExpandingTreeUI
```

Registering the UI Class

The code to register the `NonExpandingTreeUI` class is shown next. This code is the same
as that shown in the previous chapter when the `ToolTipUI` was replaced. Two keys in the
`UIDefaults` table define which UI class will be used for a component's UI object. The
first uses the `uiClassID`, defined in the component as the key, and maps to the class key.
The second uses the class key defined in the first entry to the name of the class to use for
that UI object. If there is not an entry in the `UIDefaults` table for the class key, the class
key is assumed to be the name of the class, and an instance of that class is instantiated.
Thus, if the value returned from the `uiClassID` key lookup is the name of the UI object's
class, the second entry in the table can be omitted. The following code will map all
`TreeUI` requests to the `NonExpandingTreeUI`.

```
try {
    String nonExpandingTreeUIClassName =
               "com.foley.utility.NonExpandingTreeUI";
    UIManager.put( "TreeUI", nonExpandingTreeUIClassName );
    UIManager.put( nonExpandingTreeUIClassName,
               Class.forName( nonExpandingTreeUIClassName ) );
} catch( ClassNotFoundException cnfe ) {
    System.err.println( "NonExpanding Tree UI class not found" );
    System.err.println( cnfe );
}
```

> **NOTE**
>
> The `NonExpandingTreeUI` class in the previous example extends the `BasicTreeUI`
> class and is registered for all look-and-feels. This has the side effect of losing the
> custom look-and-feel behavior defined in the specific look-and-feel `TreeUI`
> implementations. For example, the dividing lines available in the Java look-and-
> feel are not available when the `NonExpandingTreeUI` class is used.
>
> The workaround to this situation is to have a version of the
> `NonExpandingTreeUI` for each look-and-feel that your application supports. The
> `NonExpandingTreeUI` would extend the specific UI, rather than the UI in the

basic package. For example, a `WindowsNonExpandingTreeUI` extends the `WindowsTreeUI` class, `MetalNonExpandingTreeUI` extends the `MetalTreeUI` class, and `MacNonExpandingTreeUI` extends the `MacTreeUI` class if your application uses the native look-and-feel on Windows and the Macintosh, and the Java look-and-feel on UNIX platforms.

If multiple UI classes are supported, the registration process with the `UIManager` changes slightly. Instead of mapping the `TreeUI` key to the custom UI class key, the `TreeUI` mapping is left alone. Instead, the mapping from the look-and-feel class is altered to the customized class. The following code shows this:

```
try {
    UIManager.put( "javax.swing.plaf.metal.MetalTreeUI",
        Class.forName("com.foley.utility.MetalNonExpandingTreeUI"));
    UIManager.put( "com.sun.java.swing.plaf.windows.WindowsTreeUI",
        Class.forName("com.foley.utility.WindowsNonExpandingTreeUI"));
    UIManager.put( "com.sun.java.swing.plaf.windows.MacTreeUI",
        Class.forName( "com.foley.utility.MacNonExpandingTreeUI" ) );
} catch( ClassNotFoundException cnfe ) {
    System.err.println( "NonExpanding Tree UI classes not found" );
    System.err.println( cnfe );
}
```

General Customization Notes

In the previous section, a custom look-and-feel class was created and registered for the `TreeUI`. The customization was particularly easy because the behavior you wanted to alter was defined in a method that you could override. This is a good programming technique. Instead of burying implementation details deep in a method, define them in properties or query them from a "getter" method that can be overridden by extensions.

The classes in the basic package use this technique when creating the behavior of the look-and-feel. Instead of hard coding the listeners in the class, protected `create` methods are called. This allows an extension to override the `create` method and return a custom listener. If the `isToggleEvent` method was not defined in the `BasicTreeUI` class, you could have achieved the same result by changing the mouse listener for the tree. This would have been more complex, as the other existing behavior needs to remain. However, the hooks are in place to replace a listener. For example, in the `installUI` method in the `BasicTreeUI` class, the following lines appear:

```
// Boilerplate install block
installDefaults();
installListeners();
installKeyboardActions();
installComponents();
```

Any of these methods can be overridden to change the feel of the component with which the UI is used. Looking at the `installListeners` method shown next shows that a single class of listener can be changed by overriding the appropriate `create` method. For the previous example, the `createMouseListener` method would have to have been overridden to return the custom mouse listener. This listener would then have implemented the desired feel.

```java
protected void installListeners() {
    if((propertyChangeListener = createPropertyChangeListener())!= null){
        tree.addPropertyChangeListener(propertyChangeListener);
    }
    if ( (mouseListener = createMouseListener()) != null ) {
        tree.addMouseListener(mouseListener);
    }
    if ((focusListener = createFocusListener()) != null ) {
        tree.addFocusListener(focusListener);
    }
    if ((keyListener = createKeyListener()) != null) {
        tree.addKeyListener(keyListener);
    }
    if((treeExpansionListener = createTreeExpansionListener()) != null) {
        tree.addTreeExpansionListener(treeExpansionListener);
    }
    if((treeModelListener = createTreeModelListener()) != null &&
            treeModel != null) {
        treeModel.addTreeModelListener(treeModelListener);
    }
    if((selectionModelPropertyChangeListener =
        createSelectionModelPropertyChangeListener()) != null &&
        treeSelectionModel != null) {
        treeSelectionModel.addPropertyChangeListener
          (selectionModelPropertyChangeListener);
    }
    if((treeSelectionListener = createTreeSelectionListener()) != null &&
        treeSelectionModel != null) {

treeSelectionModel.addTreeSelectionListener(treeSelectionListener);
    }
}
```

The hooks are in place in the basic package to allow fine-grain customizations of the look-and-feel class. Creating the customized feel often involves looking at the UI to be customized in the basic package and determining the proper location to tie the custom code into the look-and-feel implementation.

Creating a Look-and-Feel

In the last chapter and previous sections in this chapter, you have seen many techniques for customizing the look-and-feel implementations delivered with the JFC. You have seen how to customize properties in the `UIDefaults` table maintained by the `UIManager`, how to register themes when using the Java look-and-feel, and how to selectively replace user interface implementations. If this level of customizing does not meet your requirements, an entire look-and-feel can be developed. You have already seen most of the techniques required to create a complete look-and-feel. In this section, the remaining pieces of the puzzle will be presented, and a look-and-feel will be implemented.

The `LookAndFeel` Class

The elements that comprise a look-and-feel are defined in the `look-and-feel` class. These elements include description and function methods, as well as a method to create the `UIDefaults` table for the look-and-feel. You have already seen examples of the user interface classes for the `ToolTipUI` and `TreeUI` objects.

The look-and-feel class must be an extension of the abstract `javax.swing.LookAndFeel` class. `LookAndFeel` is a class, not an interface, that defines the API for a look-and-feel. This class is shown in Listing 23.5. The class contains three types of methods. There are many `static` convenience methods that are used internally by Swing, and they are not overridden by extensions. These methods include the `installColors`, `installColorsAndFont`, `installBorder`, `uninstallBorder`, `parseKeyStroke`, `makeKeyBindings`, and `makeIcon` methods. The next type of methods are the informational methods. These are typically one-line or very small methods provided by extensions of the `LookAndFeel` class. The `getName`, `getID`, `getDescription`, `isNativeLookAndFeel`, and `isSupportedLookAndFeel` all fall into this category. The final type of methods in the `LookAndFeel` class are the functional methods. These are the methods that are called to install and uninstall a look-and-feel. The `initialize`, `uninitialize`, and `getDefaults` methods fall into this category.

LISTING 23.5 THE `LookAndFeel` CLASS

```
public abstract class LookAndFeel
{

    /**
     * Convenience method for initializing a component's foreground
     * and background color properties with values from the current
     * defaults table.  The properties are only set if the current
     * value is either null or a UIResource.
     *
```

continues

LISTING 23.5 CONTINUED

```
       * @param c the target component for installing default
       *           color/font properties
       * @param defaultBgName the key for the default background
       * @param defaultFgName the key for the default foreground
       *
       * @see #installColorsAndFont
       * @see UIManager#getColor
       */
      public static void installColors(JComponent c,
                            String defaultBgName,
                                      String defaultFgName)
      {
          Color bg = c.getBackground();
        if (bg == null ¦¦ bg instanceof UIResource) {
           c.setBackground(UIManager.getColor(defaultBgName));
        }

          Color fg = c.getForeground();
        if (fg == null ¦¦ fg instanceof UIResource) {
           c.setForeground(UIManager.getColor(defaultFgName));
        }
      }


      /**
       * Convenience method for initializing a components foreground
       * background and font properties with values from the current
       * defaults table.  The properties are only set if the current
       * value is either null or a UIResource.
       *
       * @param c the target component for installing default
       *           color/font properties
       * @param defaultBgName the key for the default background
       * @param defaultFgName the key for the default foreground
       * @param defaultFontName the key for the default font
       *
       * @see #installColors
       * @see UIManager#getColor
       * @see UIManager#getFont
       */
      public static void installColorsAndFont(JComponent c,
                                       String defaultBgName,
                                       String defaultFgName,
                                       String defaultFontName) {
          Font f = c.getFont();
        if (f == null ¦¦ f instanceof UIResource) {
           c.setFont(UIManager.getFont(defaultFontName));
        }
```

```
        installColors(c, defaultBgName, defaultFgName);
    }


    /**
     * Convenience method for installing a component's default Border
     * object on the specified component if either the border is
     * currently null or already an instance of UIResource.
     * @param c the target component for installing default border
     * @param defaultBorderName the key specifying the default border
     */
    public static void installBorder(JComponent c,
        String defaultBorderName) {
        Border b = c.getBorder();
        if (b == null || b instanceof UIResource) {
            c.setBorder(UIManager.getBorder(defaultBorderName));
        }
    }


    /**
     * Convenience method for un-installing a component's default
     * border on the specified component if the border is
     * currently an instance of UIResource.
     * @param c the target component for uninstalling default border
     */
    public static void uninstallBorder(JComponent c) {
        if (c.getBorder() instanceof UIResource) {
            c.setBorder(null);
        }
    }


    /**
     * @see parseKeyStroke
     */
    private static class ModifierKeyword {
      final String keyword;
      final int mask;
      ModifierKeyword(String keyword, int mask) {
          this.keyword = keyword;
          this.mask = mask;
      }
      int getModifierMask(String s) {
          return (s.equals(keyword)) ? mask : 0;
      }
    };


    /**
```

23

CREATING A
CUSTOM
LOOK-AND-FEEL

continues

LISTING 23.5 CONTINUED

```
     * @see parseKeyStroke
     */
    private static ModifierKeyword[] modifierKeywords = {
      new ModifierKeyword("shift", InputEvent.SHIFT_MASK),
      new ModifierKeyword("control", InputEvent.CTRL_MASK),
      new ModifierKeyword("meta", InputEvent.META_MASK),
      new ModifierKeyword("alt", InputEvent.ALT_MASK),
      new ModifierKeyword("button1", InputEvent.BUTTON1_MASK),
      new ModifierKeyword("button2", InputEvent.BUTTON2_MASK),
      new ModifierKeyword("button3", InputEvent.BUTTON3_MASK)
    };


    /**
     * Parse a string with the following syntax and return an
     * a KeyStroke:
     * <pre>
     *    "&lt;modifiers&gt;* &lt;key&gt;"
     *    modifiers := shift ¦ control ¦ meta ¦ alt ¦
     *                 button1 ¦ button2 ¦ button3
     *    key := KeyEvent keycode name, i.e. the name following "VK_".
     * </pre>
     * Here are some examples:
     * <pre>
     *     "INSERT" => new KeyStroke(0, KeyEvent.VK_INSERT);
     *     "control DELETE" => new KeyStroke(InputEvent.CTRL_MASK,
     *                                       KeyEvent.VK_DELETE);
     *     "alt shift X" => new KeyStroke(InputEvent.CTRL_MASK ¦
     *                        InputEvent.SHIFT_MASK, KeyEvent.VK_X);
     * </pre>
     */
    private static KeyStroke parseKeyStroke(String s)
    {
      StringTokenizer st = new StringTokenizer(s);
      String token;
      int mask = 0;

      while((token = st.nextToken()) != null) {
          int tokenMask = 0;

          /* if token matches a modifier keyword update mask and continue
    */

          for(int i = 0; (tokenMask == 0) &&
              (i < modifierKeywords.length); i++) {
            tokenMask = modifierKeywords[i].getModifierMask(token);
          }

          if (tokenMask != 0) {
```

```
          mask |= tokenMask;
          continue;
        }

        /* otherwise token is the keycode name less the "VK_" prefix */

        String keycodeName = "VK_" + token;
        int keycode;
        try {
          keycode =
KeyEvent.class.getField(keycodeName).getInt(KeyEvent.class);
        }
        catch (Exception e) {
          e.printStackTrace();
          throw new Error("Unrecognized keycode name: " + keycodeName);
        }

        return KeyStroke.getKeyStroke(keycode, mask);
    }

    throw new Error("Can't parse KeyStroke: \"" + s + "\"");
}


/**
 * Convenience method for building lists of KeyBindings.
 * <p>
 * Return an array of KeyBindings, one for each KeyStroke,Action pair
 * in <b>keyBindingList</b>.  A KeyStroke can either be a string in
 * the format specified by <code>parseKeyStroke</code> or a KeyStroke
 * object.  Actions are strings.  Here's an example:
 * <pre>
 *     JTextComponent.KeyBinding[] multilineBindings =
 *             makeKeyBindings( new Object[] {
 *          "UP", DefaultEditorKit.upAction,
 *        "DOWN", DefaultEditorKit.downAction,
 *     "PAGE_UP", DefaultEditorKit.pageUpAction,
 *   "PAGE_DOWN", DefaultEditorKit.pageDownAction,
 *       "ENTER", DefaultEditorKit.insertBreakAction,
 *         "TAB", DefaultEditorKit.insertTabAction
 *   });
 *
 * </pre>
 * @see #parseKeyStroke
 * @return an array of KeyBindings
 * @param keyBindingList an array of KeyStroke,Action pairs
 */
public static JTextComponent.KeyBinding[]
        makeKeyBindings(Object[] keyBindingList)
{
```

continues

LISTING 23.5 CONTINUED

```java
        JTextComponent.KeyBinding[] rv =
            new JTextComponent.KeyBinding[keyBindingList.length / 2];

    for(int i = 0; i < keyBindingList.length; i += 2) {
        KeyStroke keystroke = (keyBindingList[i] instanceof KeyStroke)
            ? (KeyStroke)keyBindingList[i]
            : parseKeyStroke((String)keyBindingList[i]);
        String action = (String)keyBindingList[i+1];
        rv[i / 2] = new JTextComponent.KeyBinding(keystroke, action);
    }

    return rv;
}


/**
 * Utility method that creates a UIDefaults.LazyValue that creates
 * an ImageIcon UIResource for the specified <code>gifFile</code>
 * filename.
 */
public static Object makeIcon(final Class baseClass,
                             final String gifFile) {
    return new UIDefaults.LazyValue() {
        public Object createValue(UIDefaults table) {
            byte[] buffer = null;
            try {
                /* Copy resource into a byte array.  This is
                 * necessary because several browsers consider
                 * Class.getResource a security risk because it
                 * can be used to load additional classes.
                 * Class.getResourceAsStream just returns raw
                 * bytes, which we can convert to an image.
                 */
                InputStream resource =
                    baseClass.getResourceAsStream(gifFile);
                if (resource == null) {
                    System.err.println(baseClass.getName() + "/" +
                                            gifFile + " not found.");
                    return null;
                }
                BufferedInputStream in =
                    new BufferedInputStream(resource);
                ByteArrayOutputStream out =
                    new ByteArrayOutputStream(1024);
                buffer = new byte[1024];
                int n;
                while ((n = in.read(buffer)) > 0) {
                    out.write(buffer, 0, n);
                }
                in.close();
```

```
                    out.flush();

                    buffer = out.toByteArray();
                    if (buffer.length == 0) {
                        System.err.println("warning: " + gifFile +
                                        " is zero-length");
                        return null;
                    }
                } catch (IOException ioe) {
                    System.err.println(ioe.toString());
                    return null;
                }

                return new IconUIResource(new ImageIcon(buffer));
            }
        };
    }

    /**
     * Return a short string that identifies this look and feel, e.g.
     * "CDE/Motif".  This string should be appropriate for a menu item.
     * Distinct look and feels should have different names, e.g.
     * a subclass of MotifLookAndFeel that changes the way a few
     * components are rendered should be called "CDE/Motif My Way";
     * something that would be useful to a user trying to select a
     * L&F from a list of names.
     */
    public abstract String getName();


    /**
     * Return a string that identifies this look and feel.  This string
     * will be used by applications/services that want to recognize
     * well known look and feel implementations.  Presently
     * the well known names are "Motif", "Windows", "Mac", "Metal".  Note
     * that a LookAndFeel derived from a well known superclass
     * that doesn't make any fundamental changes to the look or feel
     * shouldn't override this method.
     */
    public abstract String getID();


    /**
     * Return a one line description of this look and feel
     * implementation, e.g. "The CDE/Motif Look and Feel".
     * This string is intended for the user, e.g. in the title
     * of a window or in a ToolTip message.
     */
    public abstract String getDescription();
```

continues

LISTING 23.5 CONTINUED

```
/**
 * If the underlying platform has a "native" look and feel, and this
 * is an implementation of it, return true.  For example a CDE/Motif
 * look and implementation would return true when the underlying
 * platform was Solaris.
 */
public abstract boolean isNativeLookAndFeel();


/**
 * Return true if the underlying platform supports and or permits
 * this look and feel.  This method returns false if the look
 * and feel depends on special resources or legal agreements that
 * aren't defined for the current platform.
 *
 * @see UIManager#setLookAndFeel
 */
public abstract boolean isSupportedLookAndFeel();


/**
 * UIManager.setLookAndFeel calls this method before the first
 * call (and typically the only call) to getDefaults().  Subclasses
 * should do any one-time setup they need here, rather than
 * in a static initializer, because look and feel class objects
 * may be loaded just to discover that isSupportedLookAndFeel()
 * returns false.
 *
 * @see #uninitialize
 * @see UIManager#setLookAndFeel
 */
public void initialize() {
}


/**
 * UIManager.setLookAndFeel calls this method just before we're
 * replaced by a new default look and feel.  Subclasses may
 * choose to free up some resources here.
 *
 * @see #initialize
 */
public void uninitialize() {
}

/**
 * This method is called once by UIManager.setLookAndFeel to create
 * the look and feel specific defaults table.  Other applications,
```

```
     * for example an application builder, may also call this method.
     *
     * @see #initialize
     * @see #uninitialize
     * @see UIManager#setLookAndFeel
     */
    public UIDefaults getDefaults() {
        return null;
    }

    public String toString() {
        return "[" + getDescription() + " - " + getClass().getName() +
"]";
    }
}
```

Creating a `LookAndFeel` Class

The first decision to make when creating a `LookAndFeel` class is to determine which class to extend. As already pointed out, the class must be a descendant of the `LookAndFeel` class that can be extended directly. However, a more common approach is to extend the `BasicLookAndFeel` class in the `javax.swing.plaf.basic` package. Even if the `LookAndFeel` class is extended directly, the programming techniques in the `BasicLookAndFeel` class should be reviewed. This class provides a good example of a class that allows extensions to easily alter only the portions that they need to change. The look-and-feel implementations shipped with the JFC extend the `BasicLookAndFeel` class, as will be seen in the example in this section.

The Informational Methods

Regardless of which class your look-and-feel class extends, the informational methods must be provided. These methods are also easy to implement. For most custom look-and-feel implementations, these will be simple one-line methods. These methods for the `UnleashedLookAndFeel` are shown in Listing 23.6. Look-and-feel implementations that extend a concrete existing look-and-feel such as Metal should not override the `getID` method unless they make substantial changes to the look-and-feel. The `UnleashedLookAndFeel` look-and-feel does not fall into this category, so the `getID` method is overridden to return a unique ID for this look-and-feel. The name and description for the look-and-feel can be any strings that accurately describe the look-and-feel. The name should be unique from the collection of known look-and-feel implementations. Unless you are creating a better look-and-feel for one of the supported platforms, which really wouldn't be that difficult, your look-and-feel will return `false` from the `isNativeLookAndFeel` method. Finally, unless you want to restrict the platforms where your look-and-feel can execute, your `LookAndFeel` class should return `true` from the `isSupportedLookAndFeel` method.

LISTING 23.6 UnleashedLookAndFeel INFORMATIONAL METHODS

```java
/**
 * @return The name for this look-and-feel.
 **/
public String getName() {
    return "Unleashed";
}


/**
 * We are not a simple extension of an existing
 * look-and-feel, so provide our own ID.
 * <p>
 * @return The ID for this look-and-feel.
 **/
public String getID() {
    return "Unleashed";
}


/**
 * @return A short description of this look-and-feel.
 **/
public String getDescription() {
    return "The JFC Unleashed Look and Feel";
}


/**
 * This is not a native look and feel on any platform.
 * <p>
 * @return false, this isn't native on any platform.
 **/
public boolean isNativeLookAndFeel() {
    return false;
}


/**
 * This look and feel is supported on all platforms.
 * <p>
 * @return true, this L&F is supported on all platforms.
 **/
public boolean isSupportedLookAndFeel() {
    return true;
}
```

The Functional Methods

Recall that the LookAndFeel class defines three functional methods: initialize, unini-
tialize, and getDefaults. However, these are not abstract methods. Each contains an

empty implementation. The `initialize` method is a hook that allows the look-and-feel to perform any required initialization tasks. This method is called by the `UIManager` before the `getDefaults` method is called. The `uninitialize` method is called by the `UIManager` before a different look-and-feel replaces this look-and-feel and provides a hook to do any post-processing required by the look-and-feel. If any resources were allocated in the `initialize` method, they should be released in the `uninitialize` method. The current look-and-feel implementations that are part of the JFC do not perform any processing in these methods, nor will the Unleashed look-and-feel implementation. Thus these methods are not overridden.

That leaves the `getDefaults` methods. In this method the look-and-feel must create and initialize the `UIDefaults` object for the look-and-feel. Recall that the `UIDefaults` class is an extension of the `Hashtable` class. It maps component properties to values. The `UIDefaults` object is fundamental to the customizability features inherent in the JFC. You have seen how application code can change a property to alter the look of a component. This technique should be adhered to when creating your own look-and-feel. Under no circumstances should a developer hard code fonts, colors, or similar properties in a component.

As you saw earlier in this chapter, the standard look-and-feel implementations that are part of the Java platform define many properties for each component. Your look-and-feel implementation should use these properties whenever feasible. It is acceptable to define new properties that are specific to the new look-and-feel implementation. However, a new property that has the same meaning as an existing property should not be defined. Also, an existing property should not be redefined for a different use in your look-and-feel.

The `BasicLookAndFeel` class further divides the `getDefaults` method into class, system, and component defaults. This is shown in the `getDefaults` method contained in the `BasicLookAndFeel` class shown next. When extending the `BasicLookAndFeel` class, only the methods called from this method need to be overridden in the subclass.

```
public UIDefaults getDefaults() {
        UIDefaults table = new UIDefaults();

        initClassDefaults(table);
        initSystemColorDefaults(table);
        initComponentDefaults(table);

        return table;
}
```

The `BasicLookAndFeel` `initClassDefaults` Method

The `initClassDefaults` method registers the `uiClassID` strings to the class key. You previously saw how this table is used by the `UIManager` to determine which class to use as the UI object for a component. This method for the `BasicLookAndFeel` class is shown in Listing 23.7. To create a look-and-feel that provides an implementation for every UI class, an implementation is required for each entry in this table. This gives a graphic example of how much work is required to create a complete look-and-feel.

LISTING 23.7 THE `BasicLookAndFeel` CLASS' `initClassDefaults` METHOD

```
protected void initClassDefaults(UIDefaults table) {
    String basicPackageName = "com.sun.java.swing.plaf.basic.";
        Object[] uiDefaults = {
        "ButtonUI", basicPackageName + "BasicButtonUI",
        "CheckBoxUI", basicPackageName + "BasicCheckBoxUI",
        "ColorChooserUI", basicPackageName + "BasicColorChooserUI",
        "MenuBarUI", basicPackageName + "BasicMenuBarUI",
        "MenuUI", basicPackageName + "BasicMenuUI",
        "MenuItemUI", basicPackageName + "BasicMenuItemUI",
        "CheckBoxMenuItemUI",
                basicPackageName + "BasicCheckBoxMenuItemUI",
        "RadioButtonMenuItemUI",
                basicPackageName + "BasicRadioButtonMenuItemUI",
        "RadioButtonUI", basicPackageName + "BasicRadioButtonUI",
        "ToggleButtonUI", basicPackageName + "BasicToggleButtonUI",
        "PopupMenuUI", basicPackageName + "BasicPopupMenuUI",
        "ProgressBarUI", basicPackageName + "BasicProgressBarUI",
        "ScrollBarUI", basicPackageName + "BasicScrollBarUI",
        "ScrollPaneUI", basicPackageName + "BasicScrollPaneUI",
        "SplitPaneUI", basicPackageName + "BasicSplitPaneUI",
        "SliderUI", basicPackageName + "BasicSliderUI",
        "SeparatorUI", basicPackageName + "BasicSeparatorUI",
        "ToolBarSeparatorUI",
                basicPackageName + "BasicToolBarSeparatorUI",
        "PopupMenuSeparatorUI",
                basicPackageName + "BasicPopupMenuSeparatorUI",
        "TabbedPaneUI", basicPackageName + "BasicTabbedPaneUI",
        "TextAreaUI", basicPackageName + "BasicTextAreaUI",
        "TextFieldUI", basicPackageName + "BasicTextFieldUI",
        "PasswordFieldUI", basicPackageName + "BasicPasswordFieldUI",
        "TextPaneUI", basicPackageName + "BasicTextPaneUI",
        "EditorPaneUI", basicPackageName + "BasicEditorPaneUI",
        "TreeUI", basicPackageName + "BasicTreeUI",
        "LabelUI", basicPackageName + "BasicLabelUI",
        "ListUI", basicPackageName + "BasicListUI",
        "ToolBarUI", basicPackageName + "BasicToolBarUI",
        "ToolTipUI", basicPackageName + "BasicToolTipUI",
        "ComboBoxUI", basicPackageName + "BasicComboBoxUI",
```

```
            "TableUI", basicPackageName + "BasicTableUI",
            "TableHeaderUI", basicPackageName + "BasicTableHeaderUI",
            "InternalFrameUI", basicPackageName + "BasicInternalFrameUI",
            "StandardDialogUI", basicPackageName + "BasicStandardDialogUI",
            "DesktopPaneUI", basicPackageName + "BasicDesktopPaneUI",
            "DesktopIconUI", basicPackageName + "BasicDesktopIconUI",
            "OptionPaneUI", basicPackageName + "BasicOptionPaneUI",
            "PanelUI", basicPackageName + "BasicPanelUI",
            "ViewportUI", basicPackageName + "BasicViewportUI",
            };

        table.putDefaults(uiDefaults);
}
```

The `BasicLookAndFeel` `initSystemColorDefaults` Method

The `initSystemColorDefaults` method registers the system color default values. The `BasicLookAndFeel` class' implementation of this method is shown in Listing 23.8. When extending the `BasicLookAndFeel`, these colors can be used as is, selectively modified, or totally replaced. To change a color, register a new value with the same key shown in the `initSystemColorDefaults` method. UI objects that require a system color in your look-and-feel should obtain the color from the `UIDefaults` object to ensure that, when the value changes, the correct color is used.

LISTING 23.8 THE BasicLookAndFeel initSystemColorDefaults METHOD

```
protected void initSystemColorDefaults(UIDefaults table) {
    String[] defaultSystemColors = {
        /* Color of the desktop background */
        "desktop", "#005C5C",
        /* Color for captions (title bars) when they are active. */
        "activeCaption", "#000080",
        /* Text color for text in captions (title bars). */
        "activeCaptionText", "#FFFFFF",
        /* Border color for caption (title bar) window borders. */
        "activeCaptionBorder", "#C0C0C0",
        /* Color for captions (title bars) when not active. */
        "inactiveCaption", "#808080",
        /* Text color for text in inactive captions (title bars). */
        "inactiveCaptionText", "#C0C0C0",
        /*Border color for inactive caption (title bar) window borders.*/
        "inactiveCaptionBorder", "#C0C0C0",
        /* Default color for the interior of windows */
        "window", "#FFFFFF",
        /* ??? */
        "windowBorder", "#000000",
        /* ??? */
        "windowText", "#000000",
        /* Background color for menus */
```

continues

LISTING 23.8 CONTINUED

```
        "menu", "#C0C0C0",
        /* Text color for menus  */
        "menuText", "#000000",
        /* Text background color */
        "text", "#C0C0C0",
        /* Text foreground color */
        "textText", "#000000",
        /* Text background color when selected */
        "textHighlight", "#000080",
        /* Text color when selected */
        "textHighlightText", "#FFFFFF",
        /* Text color when disabled */
        "textInactiveText", "#808080",
        /* Default color for controls (buttons, sliders, etc) */
        "control", "#C0C0C0",
        /* Default color for text in controls */
        "controlText", "#000000",
        /* ??? */
        "controlHighlight", "#C0C0C0",
        /* Highlight color for controls */
        "controlLtHighlight", "#FFFFFF",
        /* Shadow color for controls */
        "controlShadow", "#808080",
        /* Dark shadow color for controls */
        "controlDkShadow", "#000000",
        /* Scrollbar background (usually the "track") */
        "scrollbar", "#E0E0E0",
        /* ??? */
        "info", "#FFFFE1",
        /* ??? */
        "infoText", "#000000"
    };

    loadSystemColors(table, defaultSystemColors, isNativeLookAndFeel());
}
```

The `BasicLookAndFeel` `initComponentDefaults` Method

The final method in the getDefaults method is the initComponentDefaults method. In this method, the properties for the components contained in the look-and-feel are registered with the UIDefaults object. It is in this method that the properties you modified earlier in this section get defined and are given default values. As with the other default properties, your look-and-feel should not redefine the standard properties defined in this method. For example, it would be a mistake to change the key CheckBox.font to CheckBox.Font to specify the font in a check box in a new look-and-feel. However, your look-and-feel may need to define additional keys to define properties that are new for your look-and-feel implementation. The initComponentDefaults method contained in the `BasicLookAndFeel` class is shown in Listing 23.9. The size of this method shows the number and depth of properties defined in a look-and-feel. It shows how many properties can be customized without creating a look-and-feel and may give pause to the decision to create a new look-and-feel.

LISTING 23.9 THE `BasicLookAndFeel` `initComponentDefaults` METHOD

```
protected void initComponentDefaults(UIDefaults table) {

    // *** Shared Fonts
    FontUIResource dialogPlain12 =
            new FontUIResource("Dialog", Font.PLAIN, 12);
    FontUIResource serifPlain12 =
            new FontUIResource("Serif", Font.PLAIN, 12);
    FontUIResource sansSerifPlain12 =
            new FontUIResource("SansSerif", Font.PLAIN, 12);
    FontUIResource monospacedPlain12 =
            new FontUIResource("Monospaced", Font.PLAIN, 12);
    FontUIResource dialogBold12 =
            new FontUIResource("Dialog", Font.BOLD, 12);

    // *** Shared Colors
    ColorUIResource red = new ColorUIResource(Color.red);
    ColorUIResource black = new ColorUIResource(Color.black);
    ColorUIResource white = new ColorUIResource(Color.white);
    ColorUIResource yellow = new ColorUIResource(Color.yellow);
    ColorUIResource gray = new ColorUIResource(Color.gray);
    ColorUIResource lightGray = new ColorUIResource(Color.lightGray);
    ColorUIResource darkGray = new ColorUIResource(Color.darkGray);
    ColorUIResource scrollBarTrack = new ColorUIResource(224, 224, 224);

    // *** Shared Insets
    InsetsUIResource zeroInsets = new InsetsUIResource(0,0,0,0);

    // *** Shared Borders
    Border zeroBorder =
            new BorderUIResource.EmptyBorderUIResource(0,0,0,0);
    Border marginBorder = new BasicBorders.MarginBorder();
    Border etchedBorder = BorderUIResource.getEtchedBorderUIResource();
    Border loweredBevelBorder =
            BorderUIResource.getLoweredBevelBorderUIResource();
    Border raisedBevelBorder =
            BorderUIResource.getRaisedBevelBorderUIResource();
    Border blackLineBorder =
            BorderUIResource.getBlackLineBorderUIResource();
    Border focusCellHighlightBorder =
            new BorderUIResource.LineBorderUIResource(yellow);
```

23

CREATING A CUSTOM LOOK-AND-FEEL

continues

LISTING 23.9 CONTINUED

```
// *** Button value objects

Object buttonBorder = new BorderUIResource.CompoundBorderUIResource(
                        new BasicBorders.ButtonBorder(
                                table.getColor("controlShadow"),
                                table.getColor("controlDkShadow"),
                                table.getColor("controlHighlight"),
                                table.getColor("controlLtHighlight")),
                        marginBorder);

Object buttonToggleBorder =
    new BorderUIResource.CompoundBorderUIResource(
                new BasicBorders.ToggleButtonBorder(
                        table.getColor("controlShadow"),
                        table.getColor("controlDkShadow"),
                        table.getColor("controlHighlight"),
                        table.getColor("controlLtHighlight")),
                marginBorder);

Object radioButtonBorder =
    new BorderUIResource.CompoundBorderUIResource(
                new BasicBorders.RadioButtonBorder(
                        table.getColor("controlShadow"),
                        table.getColor("controlDkShadow"),
                        table.getColor("controlHighlight"),
                        table.getColor("controlLtHighlight")),
                marginBorder);


// *** FileChooser / FileView value objects

Object newFolderIcon = LookAndFeel.makeIcon(getClass(),
                                "icons/NewFolder.gif");

Object upFolderIcon = LookAndFeel.makeIcon(getClass(),
                                "icons/UpFolder.gif");

Object homeFolderIcon = LookAndFeel.makeIcon(getClass(),
                                "icons/HomeFolder.gif");

Object detailsViewIcon = LookAndFeel.makeIcon(getClass(),
                                "icons/DetailsView.gif");

Object listViewIcon = LookAndFeel.makeIcon(getClass(),
                                "icons/ListView.gif");

Object directoryIcon = LookAndFeel.makeIcon(getClass(),
                                "icons/Directory.gif");
```

```
Object fileIcon = LookAndFeel.makeIcon(getClass(),
                                "icons/File.gif");

Object computerIcon = LookAndFeel.makeIcon(getClass(),
                                "icons/Computer.gif");

Object hardDriveIcon = LookAndFeel.makeIcon(getClass(),
                                "icons/HardDrive.gif");

Object floppyDriveIcon = LookAndFeel.makeIcon(getClass(),
                                "icons/FloppyDrive.gif");


// *** InternalFrame value objects

Object internalFrameBorder = new UIDefaults.LazyValue() {
  public Object createValue(UIDefaults table) {
    return new BorderUIResource.CompoundBorderUIResource(
            new BevelBorder(BevelBorder.RAISED,
                table.getColor("controlHighlight"),
                            table.getColor("controlLtHighlight"),
                            table.getColor("controlDkShadow"),
                            table.getColor("controlShadow")),
            BorderFactory.createLineBorder(
                table.getColor("control"), 1));
  }
};


// *** List value objects

Object listCellRendererActiveValue = new UIDefaults.ActiveValue() {
    public Object createValue(UIDefaults table) {
    return new DefaultListCellRenderer.UIResource();
    }
};


// *** Menus value objects

Object menuBarBorder = new BasicBorders.MenuBarBorder(
                            table.getColor("controlShadow"),
                            table.getColor("controlLtHighlight"));


Object menuItemCheckIcon = new UIDefaults.LazyValue() {
    public Object createValue(UIDefaults table) {
    return BasicIconFactory.getMenuItemCheckIcon();
    }
};
```

continues

LISTING 23.9   CONTINUED

```
Object menuItemArrowIcon = new UIDefaults.LazyValue() {
    public Object createValue(UIDefaults table) {
    return BasicIconFactory.getMenuItemArrowIcon();
    }
};

Object menuArrowIcon = new UIDefaults.LazyValue() {
    public Object createValue(UIDefaults table) {
    return BasicIconFactory.getMenuArrowIcon();
    }
};

Object checkBoxIcon = new UIDefaults.LazyValue() {
    public Object createValue(UIDefaults table) {
    return BasicIconFactory.getCheckBoxIcon();
    }
};

Object radioButtonIcon = new UIDefaults.LazyValue() {
    public Object createValue(UIDefaults table) {
    return BasicIconFactory.getRadioButtonIcon();
    }
};


Object checkBoxMenuItemIcon = new UIDefaults.LazyValue() {
    public Object createValue(UIDefaults table) {
    return BasicIconFactory.getCheckBoxMenuItemIcon();
    }
};

Object radioButtonMenuItemIcon = new UIDefaults.LazyValue() {
    public Object createValue(UIDefaults table) {
    return BasicIconFactory.getRadioButtonMenuItemIcon();
    }
};


// *** OptionPane value objects
Object optionPaneMinimumSize = new DimensionUIResource(262, 90);
Object optionPaneBorder =
    new BorderUIResource.EmptyBorderUIResource(10, 10, 12, 10);
Object optionPaneButtonAreaBorder =
    new BorderUIResource.EmptyBorderUIResource(6,0,0,0);

// *** ProgessBar value objects
Object progressBarBorder =
    new BorderUIResource.LineBorderUIResource(Color.green, 2);
```

```
// ** ScrollBar value objects
Object minimumThumbSize = new UIDefaults.LazyValue() {
  public Object createValue(UIDefaults table) {
    return new DimensionUIResource(8,8);
  };
};

Object maximumThumbSize = new UIDefaults.LazyValue() {
  public Object createValue(UIDefaults table) {
    return new DimensionUIResource(4096,4096);
  };
};


// ** Slider value objects
Object sliderFocusInsets = new InsetsUIResource( 2, 2, 2, 2 );
Object toolBarSeparatorSize = new DimensionUIResource( 10, 10 );

// *** SplitPane value objects
Object splitPaneBorder = new BasicBorders.SplitPaneBorder(
                           table.getColor("controlLtHighlight"),
                           table.getColor("controlDkShadow"));

// ** TabbedBane value objects
Object tabbedPaneTabInsets = new InsetsUIResource(2, 4, 2, 4);
Object tabbedPaneTabPadInsets = new InsetsUIResource(2, 2, 2, 1);
Object tabbedPaneTabAreaInsets = new InsetsUIResource(3, 2, 0, 2);
Object tabbedPaneContentBorderInsets =
               new InsetsUIResource(2, 2, 3, 3);


// *** Text value objects
Object textFieldBorder = new BasicBorders.FieldBorder(
                           table.getColor("controlShadow"),
                           table.getColor("controlDkShadow"),
                           table.getColor("controlHighlight"),
                           table.getColor("controlLtHighlight"));

Object editorMargin = new InsetsUIResource(3,3,3,3);

JTextComponent.KeyBinding[] fieldBindings = makeKeyBindings(
    new Object[]{
        "ENTER", JTextField.notifyAction
    }
);

JTextComponent.KeyBinding[] multilineBindings =
    makeKeyBindings( new Object[]{
      "UP", DefaultEditorKit.upAction,
      "DOWN", DefaultEditorKit.downAction,
```

continues

23

CREATING A
CUSTOM
LOOK-AND-FEEL

LISTING 23.9   CONTINUED

```
              "PAGE_UP", DefaultEditorKit.pageUpAction,
          "PAGE_DOWN", DefaultEditorKit.pageDownAction,
              "ENTER", DefaultEditorKit.insertBreakAction,
            "TAB", DefaultEditorKit.insertTabAction
        }
);

Object caretBlinkRate = new Integer(500);

// *** Component Defaults
Object[] defaults = {

    // *** Buttons
    "Button.font", dialogPlain12,
    "Button.background", table.get("control"),
    "Button.foreground", table.get("controlText"),
    "Button.border", buttonBorder,
    "Button.margin", new InsetsUIResource(2, 14, 2, 14),
    "Button.textIconGap", new Integer(4),
    "Button.textShiftOffset", new Integer(0),

    "ToggleButton.font", dialogPlain12,
    "ToggleButton.background", table.get("control"),
    "ToggleButton.foreground", table.get("controlText"),
    "ToggleButton.border", buttonToggleBorder,
    "ToggleButton.margin", new InsetsUIResource(2, 14, 2, 14),
    "ToggleButton.textIconGap", new Integer(4),
    "ToggleButton.textShiftOffset", new Integer(0),

    "RadioButton.font", dialogPlain12,
    "RadioButton.background", table.get("control"),
    "RadioButton.foreground", table.get("controlText"),
    "RadioButton.border", radioButtonBorder,
    "RadioButton.margin", new InsetsUIResource(2, 2, 2, 2),
    "RadioButton.textIconGap", new Integer(4),
    "RadioButton.textShiftOffset", new Integer(0),
    "RadioButton.icon", radioButtonIcon,

    "CheckBox.font", dialogPlain12,
    "CheckBox.background", table.get("control"),
    "CheckBox.foreground", table.get("controlText"),
    "CheckBox.border", radioButtonBorder,
    "CheckBox.margin", new InsetsUIResource(2, 2, 2, 2),
    "CheckBox.textIconGap", new Integer(4),
    "CheckBox.textShiftOffset", new Integer(0),
    "CheckBox.icon", checkBoxIcon,

    // *** ColorChooser
    "ColorChooser.font", dialogPlain12,
```

```
"ColorChooser.background", table.get("control"),
"ColorChooser.foreground", table.get("controlText"),
"ColorChooser.selectedColorBorder", loweredBevelBorder,

// *** ComboBox
"ComboBox.font", dialogPlain12,
"ComboBox.background", white,
"ComboBox.foreground", black,
"ComboBox.selectionBackground", table.get("textHighlight"),
"ComboBox.selectionForeground", table.get("textHighlightText"),
"ComboBox.disabledBackground", table.get("control"),
"ComboBox.disabledForeground", table.get("textInactiveText"),

// *** FileChooser
"FileChooser.acceptAllFileFilterText",
        new String ("All Files (*.*)"),
"FileChooser.cancelButtonText", new String("Cancel"),
"FileChooser.saveButtonText", new String("Save"),
"FileChooser.openButtonText", new String("Open"),
"FileChooser.updateButtonText", new String("Update"),
"FileChooser.helpButtonText", new String("Help"),
"FileChooser.cancelButtonToolTipText",
        new String("Abort file chooser dialog."),
"FileChooser.saveButtonToolTipText",
        new String("Save selected file."),
"FileChooser.openButtonToolTipText",
        new String("Open selected file."),
"FileChooser.updateButtonToolTipText",
        new String("Update directory listing."),
"FileChooser.helpButtonToolTipText",
        new String("FileChooser help."),
"FileChooser.newFolderIcon", newFolderIcon,
"FileChooser.upFolderIcon", upFolderIcon,
"FileChooser.homeFolderIcon", homeFolderIcon,
"FileChooser.detailsViewIcon", detailsViewIcon,
"FileChooser.listViewIcon", listViewIcon,
"FileView.directoryIcon", directoryIcon,
"FileView.fileIcon", fileIcon,
"FileView.computerIcon", computerIcon,
"FileView.hardDriveIcon", hardDriveIcon,
"FileView.floppyDriveIcon", floppyDriveIcon,

// *** InternalFrame
"InternalFrame.titleFont", dialogBold12,
"InternalFrame.border", internalFrameBorder,
"InternalFrame.icon",
        LookAndFeel.makeIcon(getClass(), "icons/JavaCup.gif"),

// Default frame icons are undefined for Basic.
"InternalFrame.maximizeIcon",
```

23

continues

LISTING 23.9 CONTINUED

```
                BasicIconFactory.createEmptyFrameIcon(),
        "InternalFrame.minimizeIcon",
                BasicIconFactory.createEmptyFrameIcon(),
        "InternalFrame.iconifyIcon",
                BasicIconFactory.createEmptyFrameIcon(),
        "InternalFrame.closeIcon",
                BasicIconFactory.createEmptyFrameIcon(),
        "InternalFrame.activeTitleBackground",
                table.get("activeCaption"),
        "InternalFrame.activeTitleForeground",
                table.get("activeCaptionText"),
        "InternalFrame.inactiveTitleBackground",
                table.get("inactiveCaption"),
        "InternalFrame.inactiveTitleForeground",
                table.get("inactiveCaptionText"),

        "DesktopIcon.border", internalFrameBorder,

        "Desktop.background", table.get("desktop"),

        // *** Label
        "Label.font", dialogPlain12,
        "Label.background", table.get("control"),
        "Label.foreground", table.get("controlText"),
        "Label.disabledForeground", white,
        "Label.disabledShadow", table.get("controlShadow"),
        "Label.border", null,

        // *** List
        "List.font", dialogPlain12,
        "List.background", table.get("window"),
        "List.foreground", table.get("textText"),
        "List.selectionBackground", table.get("textHighlight"),
        "List.selectionForeground", table.get("textHighlightText"),
        "List.focusCellHighlightBorder", focusCellHighlightBorder,
        "List.border", null,
        "List.cellRenderer", listCellRendererActiveValue,

        // *** Menus
        "MenuBar.font", dialogPlain12,
        "MenuBar.background", table.get("menu"),
        "MenuBar.foreground", table.get("menuText"),
        "MenuBar.border", menuBarBorder,

        "MenuItem.font", dialogPlain12,
        "MenuItem.acceleratorFont", dialogPlain12,
        "MenuItem.background", table.get("menu"),
        "MenuItem.foreground", table.get("menuText"),
        "MenuItem.selectionForeground", table.get("textHighlightText"),
```

```
"MenuItem.selectionBackground", table.get("textHighlight"),
"MenuItem.disabledForeground", null,
"MenuItem.acceleratorForeground", table.get("menuText"),
"MenuItem.acceleratorSelectionForeground",
        table.get("textHighlightText"),
"MenuItem.border", marginBorder,
"MenuItem.borderPainted", Boolean.FALSE,
"MenuItem.margin", new InsetsUIResource(2, 2, 2, 2),
"MenuItem.checkIcon", menuItemCheckIcon,
"MenuItem.arrowIcon", menuItemArrowIcon,

"RadioButtonMenuItem.font", dialogPlain12,
"RadioButtonMenuItem.acceleratorFont", dialogPlain12,
"RadioButtonMenuItem.background", table.get("menu"),
"RadioButtonMenuItem.foreground", table.get("menuText"),
"RadioButtonMenuItem.selectionForeground",
        table.get("textHighlightText"),
"RadioButtonMenuItem.selectionBackground",
        table.get("textHighlight"),
"RadioButtonMenuItem.disabledForeground", null,
"RadioButtonMenuItem.acceleratorForeground",
        table.get("menuText"),
"RadioButtonMenuItem.acceleratorSelectionForeground",
        table.get("textHighlightText"),
"RadioButtonMenuItem.border", marginBorder,
"RadioButtonMenuItem.borderPainted", Boolean.FALSE,
"RadioButtonMenuItem.margin", new InsetsUIResource(2, 2, 2, 2),
"RadioButtonMenuItem.checkIcon", radioButtonMenuItemIcon,
"RadioButtonMenuItem.arrowIcon", menuItemArrowIcon,

"CheckBoxMenuItem.font", dialogPlain12,
"CheckBoxMenuItem.acceleratorFont", dialogPlain12,
"CheckBoxMenuItem.background", table.get("menu"),
"CheckBoxMenuItem.foreground", table.get("menuText"),
"CheckBoxMenuItem.selectionForeground",
        table.get("textHighlightText"),
"CheckBoxMenuItem.selectionBackground",
        table.get("textHighlight"),
"CheckBoxMenuItem.disabledForeground", null,
"CheckBoxMenuItem.acceleratorForeground",
        table.get("menuText"),
"CheckBoxMenuItem.acceleratorSelectionForeground",
        table.get("textHighlightText"),
"CheckBoxMenuItem.border", marginBorder,
"CheckBoxMenuItem.borderPainted", Boolean.FALSE,
"CheckBoxMenuItem.margin", new InsetsUIResource(2, 2, 2, 2),
"CheckBoxMenuItem.checkIcon", checkBoxMenuItemIcon,
"CheckBoxMenuItem.arrowIcon", menuItemArrowIcon,

"Menu.font", dialogPlain12,
```

23

CREATING A
CUSTOM
LOOK-AND-FEEL

continues

LISTING 23.9 CONTINUED

```
            "Menu.acceleratorFont", dialogPlain12,
            "Menu.background", table.get("menu"),
            "Menu.foreground", table.get("menuText"),
            "Menu.selectionForeground", table.get("textHighlightText"),
            "Menu.selectionBackground", table.get("textHighlight"),
            "Menu.disabledForeground", null,
            "Menu.acceleratorForeground", table.get("menuText"),
            "Menu.acceleratorSelectionForeground",
                    table.get("textHighlightText"),
            "Menu.border", marginBorder,
            "Menu.borderPainted", Boolean.FALSE,
            "Menu.margin", new InsetsUIResource(2, 2, 2, 2),
            "Menu.checkIcon", menuItemCheckIcon,
            "Menu.arrowIcon", menuArrowIcon,

            "PopupMenu.font", dialogPlain12,
            "PopupMenu.background", table.get("menu"),
            "PopupMenu.foreground", table.get("menuText"),
            "PopupMenu.border", raisedBevelBorder,

            // *** OptionPane
            "OptionPane.font", dialogPlain12,
            "OptionPane.background", table.get("control"),
            "OptionPane.foreground", table.get("controlText"),
            "OptionPane.messageForeground", table.get("controlText"),
            "OptionPane.border", optionPaneBorder,
            "OptionPane.messageAreaBorder", zeroBorder,
            "OptionPane.buttonAreaBorder", optionPaneButtonAreaBorder,
            "OptionPane.minimumSize", optionPaneMinimumSize,
            "OptionPane.errorIcon", LookAndFeel.makeIcon(getClass(),
                    "icons/Error.gif"),
            "OptionPane.informationIcon",
                    LookAndFeel.makeIcon(getClass(), "icons/Inform.gif"),
            "OptionPane.warningIcon",
                    LookAndFeel.makeIcon(getClass(), "icons/Warn.gif"),
            "OptionPane.questionIcon",
                    LookAndFeel.makeIcon(getClass(), "icons/Question.gif"),

            // *** Panel
            "Panel.font", dialogPlain12,
            "Panel.background", table.get("control"),
            "Panel.foreground", table.get("textText"),

            // *** ProgressBar
            "ProgressBar.font", dialogPlain12,
            "ProgressBar.foreground", table.get("textHighlight"),
            "ProgressBar.background", table.get("control"),
            "ProgressBar.selectionForeground", table.get("control"),
            "ProgressBar.selectionBackground", table.get("textHighlight"),
```

```
"ProgressBar.border", progressBarBorder,
"ProgressBar.cellLength", new Integer(1),
"ProgressBar.cellSpacing", new Integer(0),

// *** Separator
"Separator.shadow", table.get("controlShadow"),
"Separator.highlight", table.get("controlLtHighlight"),

// *** ScrollBar/ScrollPane/Viewport
"ScrollBar.background", scrollBarTrack,
"ScrollBar.foreground", table.get("control"),
"ScrollBar.track", table.get("scrollbar"),
"ScrollBar.trackHighlight", table.get("controlDkShadow"),
"ScrollBar.thumb", table.get("control"),
"ScrollBar.thumbHighlight", table.get("controlLtHighlight"),
"ScrollBar.thumbDarkShadow", table.get("controlDkShadow"),
"ScrollBar.thumbLightShadow", table.get("controlShadow"),
"ScrollBar.border", null,
"ScrollBar.minimumThumbSize", minimumThumbSize,
"ScrollBar.maximumThumbSize", maximumThumbSize,

"ScrollPane.font", dialogPlain12,
"ScrollPane.background", table.get("control"),
"ScrollPane.foreground", table.get("controlText"),
"ScrollPane.border", etchedBorder,
"ScrollPane.viewportBorder", null,

"Viewport.font", dialogPlain12,
"Viewport.background", table.get("control"),
"Viewport.foreground", table.get("textText"),

// *** Slider
"Slider.foreground", table.get("control"),
"Slider.background", table.get("control"),
"Slider.highlight", table.get("controlLtHighlight"),
"Slider.shadow", table.get("controlShadow"),
"Slider.focus", table.get("controlDkShadow"),
"Slider.border", null,
"Slider.focusInsets", sliderFocusInsets,

// *** SplitPane
"SplitPane.background", table.get("control"),
"SplitPane.highlight", table.get("controlLtHighlight"),
"SplitPane.shadow", table.get("controlShadow"),
"SplitPane.border", splitPaneBorder,
"SplitPane.dividerSize", new Integer(5),

// *** TabbedPane
"TabbedPane.font", dialogPlain12,
"TabbedPane.background", table.get("control"),
```

continues

LISTING 23.9 CONTINUED

```
"TabbedPane.foreground", table.get("controlText"),
"TabbedPane.lightHighlight", table.get("controlLtHighlight"),
"TabbedPane.highlight", table.get("controlHighlight"),
"TabbedPane.shadow", table.get("controlShadow"),
"TabbedPane.darkShadow", table.get("controlDkShadow"),
"TabbedPane.focus", table.get("controlText"),
"TabbedPane.textIconGap", new Integer(4),
"TabbedPane.tabInsets", tabbedPaneTabInsets,
"TabbedPane.selectedTabPadInsets", tabbedPaneTabPadInsets,
"TabbedPane.tabAreaInsets", tabbedPaneTabAreaInsets,
"TabbedPane.contentBorderInsets", tabbedPaneContentBorderInsets,
"TabbedPane.tabRunOverlay", new Integer(2),

// *** Table
"Table.font", dialogPlain12,
"Table.foreground", table.get("controlText"),
"Table.background", table.get("window"),
"Table.selectionForeground", table.get("textHighlightText"),
"Table.selectionBackground", table.get("textHighlight"),
"Table.gridColor", gray,
"Table.focusCellBackground", table.get("window"),
"Table.focusCellForeground", table.get("controlText"),
"Table.focusCellHighlightBorder", focusCellHighlightBorder,
"Table.scrollPaneBorder", loweredBevelBorder,

"TableHeader.font", dialogPlain12,
"TableHeader.foreground", table.get("controlText"),
"TableHeader.background", table.get("control"),
"TableHeader.cellBorder", raisedBevelBorder,

// *** Text
"TextField.font", sansSerifPlain12,
"TextField.background", table.get("window"),
"TextField.foreground", table.get("textText"),
"TextField.inactiveForeground", table.get("textInactiveText"),
"TextField.selectionBackground", table.get("textHighlight"),
"TextField.selectionForeground", table.get("textHighlightText"),
"TextField.caretForeground", table.get("textText"),
"TextField.caretBlinkRate", caretBlinkRate,
"TextField.border", textFieldBorder,
"TextField.margin", zeroInsets,
"TextField.keyBindings", fieldBindings,

"PasswordField.font", monospacedPlain12,
"PasswordField.background", table.get("window"),
"PasswordField.foreground", table.get("textText"),
"PasswordField.inactiveForeground",
        table.get("textInactiveText"),
"PasswordField.selectionBackground",
```

```
        table.get("textHighlight"),
"PasswordField.selectionForeground",
        table.get("textHighlightText"),
"PasswordField.caretForeground", table.get("textText"),
"PasswordField.caretBlinkRate", caretBlinkRate,
"PasswordField.border", textFieldBorder,
"PasswordField.margin", zeroInsets,
"PasswordField.keyBindings", fieldBindings,

"TextArea.font", monospacedPlain12,
"TextArea.background", table.get("window"),
"TextArea.foreground", table.get("textText"),
"TextArea.inactiveForeground", table.get("textInactiveText"),
"TextArea.selectionBackground", table.get("textHighlight"),
"TextArea.selectionForeground", table.get("textHighlightText"),
"TextArea.caretForeground", table.get("textText"),
"TextArea.caretBlinkRate", caretBlinkRate,
"TextArea.border", marginBorder,
"TextArea.margin", zeroInsets,
"TextArea.keyBindings", multilineBindings,

"TextPane.font", serifPlain12,
"TextPane.background", white,
"TextPane.foreground", table.get("textText"),
"TextPane.selectionBackground", lightGray,
"TextPane.selectionForeground", table.get("textHighlightText"),
"TextPane.caretForeground", table.get("textText"),
"TextPane.inactiveForeground", table.get("textInactiveText"),
"TextPane.border", marginBorder,
"TextPane.margin", editorMargin,
"TextPane.keyBindings", multilineBindings,

"EditorPane.font", serifPlain12,
"EditorPane.background", white,
"EditorPane.foreground", table.get("textText"),
"EditorPane.selectionBackground", lightGray,
"EditorPane.selectionForeground", table.get("textHighlightText"),
"EditorPane.caretForeground", red,
"EditorPane.inactiveForeground", table.get("textInactiveText"),
"EditorPane.border", marginBorder,
"EditorPane.margin", editorMargin,
"EditorPane.keyBindings", multilineBindings,

// *** TitledBorder
"TitledBorder.font", dialogPlain12,
"TitledBorder.titleColor", table.get("controlText"),
"TitledBorder.border", etchedBorder,

// *** ToolBar
"ToolBar.font", dialogPlain12,
```

23

CREATING A
CUSTOM
LOOK-AND-FEEL

continues

LISTING 23.9   CONTINUED

```java
        "ToolBar.background", table.get("control"),
        "ToolBar.foreground", table.get("controlText"),
        "ToolBar.dockingBackground", table.get("control"),
        "ToolBar.dockingForeground", red,
        "ToolBar.floatingBackground", table.get("control"),
        "ToolBar.floatingForeground", darkGray,
        "ToolBar.border", etchedBorder,
        "ToolBar.separatorSize", toolBarSeparatorSize,

        // *** ToolTips
        "ToolTip.font", sansSerifPlain12,
        "ToolTip.background", table.get("info"),
        "ToolTip.foreground", table.get("infoText"),
        "ToolTip.border", blackLineBorder,

        // *** Tree
        "Tree.font", dialogPlain12,
        "Tree.background", table.get("window"),
        "Tree.foreground", table.get("textText"),
        "Tree.hash", gray,
        "Tree.textForeground", table.get("textText"),
        "Tree.textBackground", table.get("text"),
        "Tree.selectionForeground", table.get("textHighlightText"),
        "Tree.selectionBackground", table.get("textHighlight"),
        "Tree.selectionBorderColor", black,
        "Tree.editorBorder", blackLineBorder,
        "Tree.leftChildIndent", new Integer(7),
        "Tree.rightChildIndent", new Integer(13),
        "Tree.rowHeight", new Integer(16),
        "Tree.scrollsOnExpand", Boolean.TRUE,
        "Tree.openIcon",
            LookAndFeel.makeIcon(getClass(), "icons/TreeOpen.gif"),
        "Tree.closedIcon",
            LookAndFeel.makeIcon(getClass(), "icons/TreeClosed.gif"),
        "Tree.leafIcon",
            LookAndFeel.makeIcon(getClass(), "icons/TreeLeaf.gif"),
        "Tree.expandedIcon", null,
        "Tree.collapsedIcon", null,
    };

    table.putDefaults(defaults);
    }
```

The `UnleashedLookAndFeel` `initClassDefaults` Method

The `UnleashedLookAndFeel` class does not contain a `getDefaults` method. Instead, it inherits the method from its parent class, `BasicLookAndFeel`, and overrides the `initClassDefaults` and `initComponentDefaults` methods. It is in the initClassDefaults method that the UI classes comprising the new look-and-feel are registered. Looking at this method, you will quickly notice that the Unleashed look-and-feel does not provide UI classes for every component. When a UI class is not defined in this table, the implementation is inherited from the basic look-and-feel.

In this example, the UI object implementations are only being provided for a couple of classes. However, the technique for adding additional UI classes is the same. This points out a powerful aspect of extending an existing look-and-feel. Your implementation can start with a couple of UI classes and build from there. The look-and-feel is operational with a minimal set of UI classes as the complete set is being developed. This allows you to deploy the partial look-and-feel implementation with example applications that create components by using the completed UI classes and obtain feedback from users. This process can save you from developing a complete look-and-feel that users will not accept.

LISTING 23.10 THE UnleashedLookAndFeel initClassDefaults METHOD

```
/**
 * Initialize the uiClassID to UnleashedComponentUI mapping.
 * <p>
 * @see #getDefaults
 */
protected void initClassDefaults( UIDefaults table ) {
    //
    // Register the basic class defaults.
    //
    super.initClassDefaults( table );

    String basicPackageName = "com.foley.laf.";
    Object[] uiDefaults = {
        "ButtonUI", basicPackageName + "BasicButtonUI",
        "TreeUI", basicPackageName + "UnleashedTreeUI",
        "LabelUI", basicPackageName + "BasicLabelUI",
        "ToolTipUI", basicPackageName + "UnleashedToolTipUI",
    };

    table.putDefaults( uiDefaults );

} // initClassDefaults
```

The `UnleashedLookAndFeel initComponentDefaults` Method

The initClassDefaults method in the UnleashedLookAndFeel is similar to the initClassDefaults method. The parent class's initComponentDefaults method is used to register the bulk of the component default properties. Then the overridden properties are registered. In the UnleashedLookAndFeel, a UI is provided for the TreeUI key. There

23

CREATING A
CUSTOM
LOOK-AND-FEEL

are five icons associated with the component that are customized in the
`UnleashedLookAndFeel`. These need to be registered in the `UIDefaults` table in this
method. The `UnleashedLookAndFeel` class' `initComponentDefaults` method is shown in
Listing 23.11.

LISTING 23.11 THE `UnleashedLookAndFeel` initComponentDefaults METHOD

```
/**
 * Register the component defaults.
 * Let our parent do the real work, then update the defaults
 * to the icons used in this look-and-feel.
 * <p>
 * @param table The UIDefaults table to configure.
 **/
protected void initComponentDefaults( UIDefaults table ) {

    //
    // Register the basic component defaults.
    //
    super.initComponentDefaults( table );

    Object[] defaults = {

        "Tree.openIcon",
            LookAndFeel.makeIcon(getClass(), "images/TreeOpen.gif"),
        "Tree.closedIcon",
            LookAndFeel.makeIcon(getClass(), "images/TreeClosed.gif"),
        "Tree.leafIcon",
            LookAndFeel.makeIcon(getClass(), "images/TreeLeaf.gif"),
        "Tree.expandedIcon",
            LookAndFeel.makeIcon(getClass(), "images/TreeExpanded.gif"),
        "Tree.collapsedIcon",
            LookAndFeel.makeIcon(getClass(), "images/TreeCollapsed.gif"),
        "Tree.textBackground", table.get("window"),
    };

    table.putDefaults( defaults );

} // initComponentDefaults
```

The Complete `UnleashedLookAndFeel` Class

That's it! That's all there is to defining a look-and-feel. The Unleashed look-and-feel is a
first class look-and-feel that can be used in the same way as any of the stock look-and-
feel implementations that are part of the JFC. The complete listing for the
`UnleashedLookAndFeel` is shown in Listing 23.12.

LISTING 23.12 THE UnleashedLookAndFeel CLASS

```
package com.foley.laf;

import java.io.Serializable;

import javax.swing.*;
import javax.swing.plaf.basic.BasicLookAndFeel;


/**
 * @author MikeFoley
 */
public class UnleashedLookAndFeel extends BasicLookAndFeel
    implements Serializable {

    /**
     * @return The name for this look-and-feel.
     **/
    public String getName() {
        return "Unleashed";
    }


    /**
     * We are not a simple extension of an existing
     * look-and-feel, so provide our own ID.
     * <p>
     * @return The ID for this look-and-feel.
     **/
    public String getID() {
        return "Unleashed";
    }


    /**
     * @return A short description of this look-and-feel.
     **/
    public String getDescription() {
        return "The JFC Unleashed Look and Feel";
    }


    /**
     * This is not a native look and feel on any platform.
     * <p>
     * @return false, this isn't native on any platform.
     **/
    public boolean isNativeLookAndFeel() {
        return false;
    }
```

continues

LISTING 23.12 CONTINUED

```java
/**
 * This look and feel is supported on all platforms.
 * <p>
 * @return true, this L&F is supported on all platforms.
 **/
public boolean isSupportedLookAndFeel() {
    return true;
}


/**
 * Initialize the uiClassID to UnleashedComponentUI mapping.
 * <p>
 * @see #getDefaults
 */
protected void initClassDefaults( UIDefaults table )
{
    //
    // Register the basic class defaults.
    //
    super.initClassDefaults( table );

  String basicPackageName = "com.foley.plaf.unleashed.";
      Object[] uiDefaults = {
            "ButtonUI", basicPackageName + "BasicButtonUI",
             "TreeUI", basicPackageName + "UnleashedTreeUI",
             "LabelUI", basicPackageName + "BasicLabelUI",
           "ToolTipUI", basicPackageName + "UnleashedToolTipUI",
    };

        table.putDefaults( uiDefaults );

} // initClassDefaults


/**
 * Register the component defaults.
 * Let our parent do the real work, then update the defaults
 * to the icons used in this look-and-feel.
 * <p>
 * @param table The UIDefaults table to configure.
 **/
protected void initComponentDefaults( UIDefaults table ) {

    //
    // Register the basic component defaults.
    //
    super.initComponentDefaults( table );
```

```
        Object[] defaults = {

            "Tree.openIcon",
➡             LookAndFeel.makeIcon(getClass(), "images/TreeOpen.gif"),
            "Tree.closedIcon",
➡             LookAndFeel.makeIcon(getClass(), "images/TreeClosed.gif"),
            "Tree.leafIcon",
➡             LookAndFeel.makeIcon(getClass(), "images/TreeLeaf.gif"),
            "Tree.expandedIcon",
➡             LookAndFeel.makeIcon(getClass(), "images/TreeExpanded.gif"),
            "Tree.collapsedIcon",
➡             LookAndFeel.makeIcon(getClass(), "images/TreeCollapsed.gif"),
            "Tree.textBackground", table.get("window"),
            };

        table.putDefaults( defaults );

    } // initComponentDefaults


} // UnleashedLookAndFeel
```

Using the Unleashed Look-and-Feel

In the previous section the Unleashed look-and-feel was developed. Unleashed is an extension of the basic look-and-feel that adds a couple of UI classes. It can be registered and used just like any of the look-and-feels that are part of the JFC. The TestLookAndFeel application shown in Listing 23.13 registers the Unleashed look-and-feel, sets it as the current look-and-feel, and then creates a frame and components that have a UI class defined in this look-and-feel. This is a slightly modified version of the TreeTest application presented in Chapter 11. In the main method the UIManager's installLookAndFeel is called to install the Unleashed look-and-feel. The two parameters to this method are the look-and-feel's name and the fully qualified name of the class that defines the look-and-feel. Then the setLookAndFeel method is called to specify the Unleashed look-and-feel for the application. The single parameter to this method is the fully qualified class name of the Unleashed look-and-feel. There is also a version of this method that takes a reference to the LookAndFeel class that defines the look-and-feel. The resulting window is shown in Figure 23.6. In the figure, you can see that the UnleashedLabelUI implementation allows for multiple lines in a single label.

LISTING 23.13 THE TestLookAndFeel APPLICATION

```
package com.foley.test;

import java.awt.*;
import java.awt.event.*;
```

continues

23

CREATING A
CUSTOM
LOOK-AND-FEEL

LISTING 23.13 CONTINUED

```java
import java.util.*;

import javax.swing.*;
import javax.swing.event.*;
import javax.swing.tree.*;
import javax.swing.border.*;

import com.foley.utility.*;


/**
 * An application that registers the Unleashed
 * look-and-feel and displays a frame containing
 * some of the Swing components that have their
 * UI Object modified with this look-and-feel.
 *
 * @author Mike Foley
 **/
public class LookAndFeelTest
    implements ActionListener, TreeSelectionListener {

    /**
     * The tree used in the center of the dipslay.
     **/
    JTree tree;

    /**
     * The component where the selected path is displayed.
     **/
    JTextArea textArea;

    /**
     * The text contained in the JTextArea initially and after a clear.
     **/
    private static final String INITIAL_TEXT = "Selected Path Events\n";


    /**
     * Create the tree test component.
     * The display is a tree in the center of a BorderLayout.
     * The EAST region contains a JTextArea where selected
     * paths are displayed.
     * The bottom region contains buttons.
     * <p>
     * @return The component containing the tree.
     **/
    public JComponent createTreePanel() {

        JPanel treePanel = new JPanel();
```

```
    treePanel.setLayout( new BorderLayout() );

    JLabel title = new JLabel(
            "Tree Event Viewer\nSelect an item in the tree." );
    title.setHorizontalAlignment( SwingConstants.CENTER );
    treePanel.add( title, BorderLayout.NORTH );

    JSplitPane splitPane = new JSplitPane();
    splitPane.setOneTouchExpandable( true );
    treePanel.add( splitPane, BorderLayout.CENTER );

    tree = new JTree( createTreeModel() );
    tree.setEditable( true );
    tree.setCellEditor( new TreeLeafEditor( tree ) );
    tree.addTreeSelectionListener( this );
    tree.setBorder( BorderFactory.createLoweredBevelBorder() );
    splitPane.setLeftComponent( tree );

    JPanel buttonPanel = new JPanel();
    JButton expand = new JButton( "Expand Selected" );
    expand.addActionListener( this );
    expand.setToolTipText( "This button will expand\n" +
                    "the selected node in the tree." );

    JButton clear = new JButton( "Clear Path Display" );
    clear.addActionListener( new ActionListener() {
        public void actionPerformed( ActionEvent event ) {
            textArea.setText( INITIAL_TEXT );
        }
    } );
    clear.setToolTipText( "This button will clear\n" +
                    "the text in the event log." );
    buttonPanel.add( expand );
    buttonPanel.add( clear );
    treePanel.add( buttonPanel, BorderLayout.SOUTH );

    textArea = new JTextArea( INITIAL_TEXT, 16, 50 );
    textArea.setBackground( expand.getBackground() );
    textArea.setBorder( null );
    textArea.setBorder(
            BorderFactory.createEmptyBorder( 4, 4, 4, 4 ) );
    splitPane.setRightComponent( new JScrollPane( textArea ) );

    treePanel.setBorder( BorderFactory.createLoweredBevelBorder() );

    return( treePanel );
}


/**
```

continues

LISTING 23.13 CONTINUED

```
 * Create the data model used in the tree contained
 * in the application.
 * <p>
 * @return The data model for the tree.
 **/
protected TreeModel createTreeModel() {
    DefaultMutableTreeNode root =
        new DefaultMutableTreeNode( "Music Collection" );

    DefaultMutableTreeNode albums =
        new DefaultMutableTreeNode( "Albums" );
    DefaultMutableTreeNode cds =
        new DefaultMutableTreeNode( "CDs" );
    DefaultMutableTreeNode tapes =
        new DefaultMutableTreeNode( "Tapes" );

    root.add( albums );
    root.add( cds );
    root.add( tapes );

    DefaultMutableTreeNode stonesAlbums =
        new DefaultMutableTreeNode( "Rolling Stones" );
    albums.add( stonesAlbums );

    stonesAlbums.add( new DefaultMutableTreeNode( "Hot Rocks" ) );
    stonesAlbums.add(
        new DefaultMutableTreeNode( "Black and Blue" ) );
    stonesAlbums.add(
        new DefaultMutableTreeNode( "Sticky Finger" ) );

    DefaultMutableTreeNode c1 =
        new DefaultMutableTreeNode( "Classical" );
    DefaultMutableTreeNode c2 =
        new DefaultMutableTreeNode( "Best Rock of the 60's" );
    DefaultMutableTreeNode c3 =
        new DefaultMutableTreeNode( "70's Disco Favorites" );
    DefaultMutableTreeNode c4 =
        new DefaultMutableTreeNode( "Broadway Hits" );
    DefaultMutableTreeNode c5 =
        new DefaultMutableTreeNode( "Country's Best?" );

    cds.add( c1 );
    cds.add( c2 );
    cds.add( c3 );
    cds.add( c4 );
    cds.add( c5 );

    DefaultMutableTreeNode s1 =
        new DefaultMutableTreeNode( "Rolling Stones" );
```

```
        DefaultMutableTreeNode s2 =
            new DefaultMutableTreeNode( "Beatles" );
        DefaultMutableTreeNode s3 =
            new DefaultMutableTreeNode( "The Who" );

        c1.add( new DefaultMutableTreeNode( "Beethoven's Fifth" ) );

        c2.add( s1 );
        c2.add( s2 );
        c2.add( s3 );

        s1.add( new DefaultMutableTreeNode( "Gimmie Shelter" ) );
        s1.add( new DefaultMutableTreeNode( "Some Girls" ) );
        s1.add( new DefaultMutableTreeNode( "Emotional Rescue" ) );

        s2.add( new DefaultMutableTreeNode( "White Album" ) );
        s2.add( new DefaultMutableTreeNode( "Abby Road" ) );
        s2.add( new DefaultMutableTreeNode( "Let it be" ) );

        s3.add( new DefaultMutableTreeNode( "Tommy" ) );
        s3.add( new DefaultMutableTreeNode( "The Who" ) );

        c3.add( new DefaultMutableTreeNode( "Saturday Night Fever" ) );
        c3.add( new DefaultMutableTreeNode( "Earth Wind and Fire" ) );

        c4.add( new DefaultMutableTreeNode( "Cats Soundtrack" ) );

        c5.add( new DefaultMutableTreeNode( "Unknown" ) );

        return( new DefaultTreeModel( root ) );

    } // createTreeModel


    /**
     * actionEvent, from ActionListener.
     * <p>
     * The expand button was pressed. Expand the selected paths
     * in the tree.
     * <p>
     * @param event The actionEvent causing this method call.
     **/
    public void actionPerformed( ActionEvent event ) {
        TreePath[] paths = tree.getSelectionPaths();
        if( paths != null ) {
            for( int i = 0; i < paths.length; i++ ) {
                expandPath( paths[i] );
            }
        }
    }
```

continues

LISTING 23.13 CONTINUED

```java
/**
 * valueChanged, from TreeSelectionListener.
 * <p>
 * The selected state in the tree changed. Show the
 * selected path in the text area.
 * <p>
 * @param event The event causing this method to be called.
 **/
public void valueChanged( TreeSelectionEvent event ) {

    TreePath[] paths = event.getPaths();

    for( int i = 0; i < paths.length; i++ ) {
        //
        // Diplay the path and state.
        //
        Object[] path = paths[i].getPath();
        textArea.append( event.isAddedPath( paths[i] ) ?
                            "ADDED: " : "REMOVED: " );
        textArea.append( paths[i] + "\n" );
        for( int j = 0; j < path.length; j++ ) {
            textArea.append( "\t" + path[j] + "\n" );
        }
        if( event.isAddedPath( paths[i] ) ) {
            Object pathObject = paths[i].getLastPathComponent();

            //
            // This test is unfortunate. The MutableTreeNode
            // interface does not have a getUserObject method, so
            // we must test for a specific implementation.
            //
            if( pathObject instanceof DefaultMutableTreeNode ) {
                Object userObject = ( ( DefaultMutableTreeNode )
                    pathObject ).getUserObject();
                textArea.append( "User Object: "
                                    + userObject + "\n" );
            }
        }
    }
    textArea.append( "-------------------------------------\n" );

}


/**
 * Expand the node at the end of the given path.
 * This requires expanding all children node of the
 * path recursively until the entire subtree has been
 * expanded.
 **/
```

```
private void expandPath( TreePath path ) {
    Object o = path.getLastPathComponent();
    if( o instanceof TreeNode ) {
        for( Enumeration e = ( ( TreeNode )o ).children();
             e.hasMoreElements(); ) {
            TreeNode node = ( TreeNode )e.nextElement();
            expandChildren( node );
        }
    }
}


/**
 * Expand all the children of the given node.
 * <p>
 * @param expandNode The root of the subtree to expand.
 **/
private void expandChildren( TreeNode expandNode ) {

    if( expandNode.isLeaf() ) {

        Stack nodes = new Stack();

        //
        // Push the parents of the current node
        // until the root of the tree is reached.
        //
        TreeNode node = expandNode;
        nodes.push( node );
        while( ( node = node.getParent() ) != null )
            nodes.push( node );

        //
        // Create a path to the node passed into this
        // method by popping each element from the stack.
        //
        TreeNode[] path = new TreeNode[ nodes.size() ];
        for( int i = 0; i < path.length; i++ )
            path[i] = ( TreeNode )nodes.pop();
        TreePath treePath = new TreePath( path );

        //
        // Expand the path.
        //
        tree.expandPath( treePath );

    } else {

        //
        // Expand the children children of the
```

continues

LISTING 23.13   CONTINUED

```
➡              // node passed to the method.
               //
               for( Enumeration e = expandNode.children();
➡                    e.hasMoreElements(); ) {
                  expandChildren( ( DefaultMutableTreeNode )
➡                      e.nextElement() );
               }

          } // else

      } // expandChildren


      /**
       * Application entry point.
       * Create the frame, and place a tree into it.
       *
       * @param args Command line parameter. Not used.
       **/
      public static void main( String args[] ) {

          //
          // Set the look-and-feel to Unleashed.
          //
          try {
              String className =
                      "com.foley.plaf.unleashed.UnleashedLookAndFeel";
                                UIManager.installLookAndFeel( "Unleashed",
➡className );
              UIManager.setLookAndFeel( className );
          } catch( Exception ex ) {
              System.err.println( "Could not load look-and-feel" );
              System.err.println( ex );
              ex.printStackTrace();
          }

          LookAndFeelTest treeTest = new LookAndFeelTest();
          JFrame frame = new ApplicationFrame( "Tree Test" );
          frame.getContentPane().add( treeTest.createTreePanel(),
➡             BorderLayout.CENTER );
          frame.pack();
          frame.setVisible( true );

      } // main

} // LookAndFeelTest
```

> **NOTE**
>
> Notice that the portion of the code in the `LookAndFeelTest` application that creates and configures the user interface is identical to applications presented earlier in this book. The fact that the look-and-feel is different has no effect on the code that creates and configures the user interface. This is a fundamental concept of the pluggable look-and-feel architecture. Indeed, it is its biggest advantage.

FIGURE 23.6

The `LookAndFeelTest` *application.*

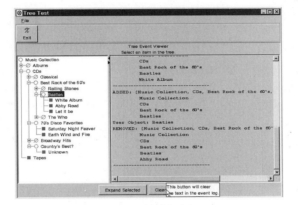

> **NOTE**
>
> In the `LookAndFeelTest` application shown in Listing 23.13, the `UnleashedLookAndFeel` is specified in the `main` method as the look-and-feel for this application. The default look-and-feel for a Java installation can be specified by setting the `swing.defaultlaf` property in the `swing.properties` file. The `UnleashedLookAndFeel` could be installed as the default look-and-feel for every Java application by adding the following line to the `swing.properties` file:
>
> ```
> swing.defaultlaf=com.foley.plaf.unleashed.UnleashedLookAndFeel
> ```

The Multiplexing Look-And-Feel

Up to this point, your focus has been on visual look-and-feels. However, the multiplexing look-and-feel allows multiple look-and-feels to be simultaneously active. However, only one of the look-and-feel implementations is visual. The others are known as auxiliary look-and-feels. The auxiliary look-and-feels can be used to interact with other devices such as sound cards or Braille readers.

If auxiliary look-and-feels are installed in the virtual machine, a multiplexing UI object is installed when a component's UI object is created. The multiplexing UI object passes a UI message to each look-and-feel registered. The visual look-and-feel is used without modification. In fact, each look-and-feel is unaware that the multiplexing is occurring.

The multiplexing UI object is guaranteed to contain the visual UI object as the first item in its multiplexed UI object array. This array is obtained by calling the `getUIs` method of the multiplexing UI object. This method is available in all classes in the `swing.plaf.multi` package.

Auxiliary Look-and-Feels

The intent of auxiliary look-and-feels is to augment the primary visual look-and-feel used by the application. For this reason, they tend to be nonvisual. However, there is nothing in the architecture that prevents an auxiliary look-and-feel from rendering to the display. This is both a good and a bad thing. This gives the developer of the auxiliary look-and-feel complete flexibility but also adds responsibilities. For example, the auxiliary look-and-feel should not compete with the default look-and-feel to paint a component.

When creating an auxiliary look-and-feel, you probably will not extend a visual look-and-feel. This is to avoid painting or processing input events that conflict with the default look-and-feel when your auxiliary look-and-feel is used. Instead, you can choose to extend the classes in the `swing.plaf` package or extend the `swing.LookAndFeel` class directly. Even when classes in the `swing.plaf` package are extended, care must be taken to override any methods that render to the screen. For example, the `update` method in the `ComponentUI` class clears the component's background if it is opaque. This behavior is undesirable in most auxiliary look-and-feels, because it will compete with the `update` method from the default visual look-and-feel being used for the application.

Registering Auxiliary Look-and-Feels

Before the multiplexing look-and-feel will be used, one or more auxiliary look-and-feel implementations must be registered with the Virtual Machine. This is done by adding entries to the `swing.auxiliarylaf` property in the `swing.properties` file or calling the `addAuxiliaryLookandFeel` method in the `UIManager`. The property file is located in the `$JDKHOME/lib` directory. Multiple auxiliary look-and-feel implementations can be specified for this property by separating each look-and-feel with a comma. Each property entry is the fully qualified class name of the look-and-feel class. The following line added to the `swing.properties` file would enable two auxiliary look-and-feel implementations in the Virtual Machine:

```
Swing.auxiliarylaf=com.foley.plaf.debug.DebugLookAndFeel,
                   com.foley.plaf.audio.AudioLookAndFeel
```

> **NOTE**
>
> The `swing.properties` file is only read at application startup. Changes in this file will not be used until the next time the Virtual Machine is started.

After auxiliary look-and-feel implementations are registered in the Virtual Machine, the multiplexing look-and-feel will be used without further programmer or user intervention when Swing components are created. The registered auxiliary look-and-feel implementations may be queried from the `UIManager` by calling the `getAuxiliaryLookAndFeels` method. Finally, an auxiliary look-and-feel may be removed from the Virtual Machine by passing the `removeAuxiliaryLookAndFeel` method the `LookAndFeel` instance to be removed.

Summary

A tremendous amount of material was presented in this chapter. The flexibility of the pluggable look-and-feel architecture that the Swing components are built on was explored. You saw that a "J" component is not a single object. Instead, it is two: the component that defines the API that the application programs to and the user interface object that renders the component on the display and interacts with the user. The separation of component class and UI object allows the UI object to be changed without affecting application code. This is the major strength of the pluggable look-and-feel architecture.

This chapter presented many options for configuring a look-and-feel. The look-and-feel implementations that are part of the JFC define a multitude of properties that define the characteristics of the look-and-feel. These properties include such items as colors, fonts, icons, and borders. An application can modify any or all of these properties to achieve an enormous amount of customization. The Java look-and-feel contains a theme mechanism. Changing the theme provides an easy alternative to changing properties for colors and fonts in the `UIManager`. A theme can be switched dynamically while the application is executing. Building a theme editor will give the user the ability to alter the colors in a theme while the application is executing. Alternatively, a theme can be read from a property file to allow the user to edit the theme file to easily configure the application.

Customizing the feel of an application isn't as easy as customizing its look. To customize the feel of a component, its UI object must be replaced with a customized version. The hooks in the basic UI implementations that facilitate this process were explored. A UI class that eliminates the double-click gesture from expanding or collapsing a node in a tree instance was presented.

If customizing an existing look-and-feel doesn't meet your requirements, an entirely new look-and-feel can be created and installed. In this chapter, the Unleashed look-and-feel was presented. This look-and-feel implementation, like the standard JFC look-and-feel implementations, extends the `BasicLookAndFeel` class. The Unleashed look-and-feel only provides UI classes for a few components. The other UI classes are those in the basic package. Adding additional UI classes and registering them in the `UnleashedLookAndFeel` class can expand the Unleashed look-and-feel. To develop a look-and-feel that provides a UI class for every component is a large undertaking. The ability to use existing implementations and adding classes as they are completed gives the developer a clear path for completing a look-and-feel. Also, the completed UI classes can be tested and reviewed as further classes are being developed. This is a nice way to develop a complete look-and-feel.

Auxiliary look-and-feels can be used to interface to devices such as sound cards and Braille readers. When an auxiliary look-and-feel is registered with the system, the JFC uses the multiplexing look-and-feel. When a UI object is created for a component, an instance of the appropriate multiplexing look-and-feel is created. This UI object manages the visual and auxiliary UI objects. When a UI method is to be called, the multiplexing UI object calls the corresponding methods in each look-and-feel. There should only be one visual look-and-feel being used at any given time.

Building a Custom Component

In the previous chapters, you learned how to customize existing Swing components via setting user interface properties, replacing the user interface object, and creating and installing a complete look-and-feel. What you have not seen is how to handle the situation when an existing Swing component doesn't meet your needs.

In this chapter, you will learn

- How to create a custom component
- How to implement the pluggable look-and-feel architecture for your component

Creating a Custom Component

There are many situations where an existing Swing component doesn't meet your needs. When this situation arises, you have many options: You can customize an existing Swing component; you can extend an existing Swing component's user interface object; or you can develop a new component. The previous chapters have discussed customizing existing Swing components. The level of customization ranges from setting UI properties to change the look of a component to replacing the user interface object for a component to change its feel. In this chapter, you will learn how to create a new component.

When developing any Java class, one of the first decisions to be made is where it fits into the existing class hierarchy. For a new component that is to coexist with Swing components, it is best that the component be a lightweight one. A new lightweight component must extend the AWT `Component` or `Container` class. However, as you saw in Chapter 22, "Extending Existing Components," the `JComponent` class is the foundation for the pluggable look-and-feel architecture on which the JFC is built. If your new component is to have a pluggable look-and-feel, it must be a descendant of the `JComponent` class. Where the new component fits into the Swing hierarchy depends on the nature of the component.

The other major architectural aspect of Swing components is the MVC separation of views and data. When creating a new component, the MVC architecture should be followed. This allows the new component to share data with other components and fit with the core Swing components. Thus, part of the design of a JFC-compliant component is the data model the component will view. This was not a concern when developing an AWT component. The model requirements for a new component is dependent on the data to be displayed in the view. However, if an existing Swing model can be used for the new component, it will be more interoperable with other components. The MVC architecture was discussed in Chapter 2, "MVC Architecture."

The existing library of Swing components is text based. There is a complete lack of graphical components. Many classes of graphical components can be created by extending the JComponent class and providing a custom paintComponent method to render the graphics for the component. This type of component tends to be very application/domain-specific and will not be addressed in this chapter. However, a general-purpose graphical component that is missing from the Swing component set is a chart component. In this chapter, a general-purpose charting component that displays numerical data contained in a TableModel will be developed.

A Swing-Compatible Chart Class

The Swing classes provide a rich set of textual components that can be used to build a user interface. However, there are not any graphical components. To help address this omission, the FChart class was developed. This class displays the numerical data contained in a TableModel. The first column in the model is defined to be the x coordinate data, and each subsequent column specifies the y coordinate for a single trace in the chart. The data in the model must be a descendant of the Number class. When an editable model is used with the FChart class, the points in the plot can be dragged to change the model's data. An example of the FChart class is shown in Figure 24.1.

FIGURE 24.1

The FChart *component.*

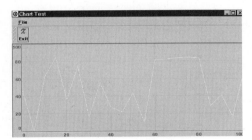

The FChart class supports the pluggable look-and-feel architecture on which the Swing components are built. A user interface implementation is provided for the Java and Windows look-and-feels, as well as a default implementation for other look-and-feel implementations. The component defines many user interface properties that an application can set to customize the component.

FChart Data Model

When designing the FChart class, one of the first decisions was what the data model should look like. If feasible, your component will be adaptable to more situations if its data model can be an existing JFC data model or an extension of an existing data model.

To meet this requirement for a chart left two options. The data model could be an array of `ListModel` instances, where each `ListModel` instance represents one trace in the chart, or the model could be a `TableModel` instance. Using an array of `ListModel` instances is more flexible than using a `TableModel` instance. The `ListModel` approach allows for traces of different lengths to easily be added to the chart. However, this approach was not taken. The benefit of using a `TableModel` was too great to pass up. This approach allows a `JTable` instance to display the same data as the chart. Changes to the data made in the table will be reflected in the chart and vice versa.

`TableModel` allows the data to be written back to the data model. The model defines the `isCellEditable` method that returns `true` if a cell is editable. Using this method, the `FChart` instance can determine if a data point is editable and, if so, allows the user to drag the data point to edit the data model.

FChart Class

The `FChart` class is the component class that is instantiated to create a chart. It extends the `JComponent` class and works within the pluggable look-and-feel architecture on which the core Swing components are built. This class provides the API available to users of the component.

The `FChart` class, shown in Listing 24.1, manages two axes: the x and the y axes. These are instances of the `FAxis` class, which is described later in this section. A custom layout manager, the `FChartLayoutManager` class, is used to size and position the axes on the chart. This class will also be presented later in this section.

The `FChart` class defines constants for its UI class and for bound property names. The `uiClassID` contains the name of the user interface class key to be used by the `UIManager` to create the UI object for the chart. This process was described in the previous chapter. This `String` is returned from the `getUIClassID` method. The `uiClassID` constant could be named anything, but the Swing class's convention is to use this name. Using the same name in your classes allows developers to easily identify the purpose of the constant.

The `FChart` contains two constructors: the default constructor and one taking a `TableModel` parameter. The default constructor is required to be JavaBean compliant and simply calls the second constructor with a `null` `TableModel` parameter. The second constructor is where the real work is performed. In this constructor, the layout manager and axis are created and set for the chart. The final method called in the constructor is very important. The `updateUI` method updates its UI by asking the `UIManager` to create the proper UI object for the chart. If this method is not called in the constructor, the UI object for the chart will not be created and the chart will not be drawn.

The missing piece in implementing the pluggable look-and-feel architecture is where the FChart UI object class keys are registered with the UIManager. In the previous chapter, you saw how the LookAndFeel implementations register the class keys for the core Swing components. However, the JFC look-and-feel implementations do not know about your custom components. When the updateUI method asks the UIManager to create its UI object by calling the getUI method, if the key returned from the getUIClassID method is not in the UIDefaults table, exceptions are thrown and your component is not created. The FChart class provides a static initialize method that registers the class keys for the FChart and FAxis classes with the UIManager. The process is further complicated by the fact that the class keys need to be updated when the LookAndFeel for the application changes. Once again, the keys for core Swing components are registered by the new LookAndFeel when it is activated. The FChart class's initialize method creates and registers a PropertyChangeListener to receive notifications from the UIManager when the look-and-feel changes. At that time, the class keys can be updated in the UIManager. In the FChart class, the keys are registered in the setLookAndFeelProperties method. This method checks for known look-and-feel class IDs and registers the proper class. If the look-and-feel is not known, the default UI object class is registered. The UI classes registered by setLookAndFeelProperties are presented later in this chapter.

> **NOTE**
>
> When creating a library of custom components, having a single initialize method that registers the UI objects for each component in the library will reduce the burden on users of the library. Also, isolating the properties in a single location will ease the maintenance of the library.

The updateUI, getUI, setUI, and getUIClassID methods are boilerplate methods required in a component to exist in the pluggable look-and-feel architecture. The methods must be implemented, rather than inherited, to provide methods taking and returning the proper types. In the getUIClassID method's case, the proper class ID String must be returned.

The writeObject method is required to conform to the Swing serialization policy. Before a JComponent class is written to the output stream, its UI object is temporarily removed. The test of the uiClassID being equal to the String returned from the getUIClassID method must be performed in the class where the uiClassID constant is defined. Thus, this method must be replicated in every class that conforms to the pluggable look-and-feel architecture and wants to be serialized.

The remaining methods in the FChart class are getter and setter methods that follow the JavaBean naming convention for manipulating the properties contained in the class. The setter methods fire PropertyChangeEvents for bound properties.

> **NOTE**
>
> Note that the method and property names for the model and grid properties are the same as those defined in the JTable class. Using the same API as core Swing classes that convey the same meaning makes your class easier to learn for developers familiar with the Swing classes.

LISTING 24.1 THE FChart CLASS

```java
package com.foley.chart;

import java.awt.*;
import java.beans.*;
import java.io.*;

import javax.swing.*;

import javax.swing.table.TableModel;


/**
 * Class FChart
 * A class that displays a chart containing
 * numerical data in a TableModel.
 * <p>
 * @beaninfo
 *      attribute: isContainer false
 *    description: A chart component
 * @author Mike Foley
 * @version 1.2
 **/
public class FChart extends JComponent
    implements Serializable {

    /**
     * @see #getUIClassID
     **/
    private static final String uiClassID = "FChartUI";

    /**
     * The X and Y Axis.
     **/
```

24

```java
private FAxis xAxis;
private FAxis yAxis;

/**
 * The color of the grid
 **/
protected Color gridColor;

/**
 * The table draws horizontal lines between cells
 * if showHorizontalLines is true
 **/
protected boolean showHorizontalLines;

/**
 * The table draws vertical lines between cells if
 * showVerticalLines is true
 **/
protected boolean showVerticalLines;

private TableModel model;

/**
 * Bound property names.
 **/
public static final String MODEL_PROPERTY = "model";
public static final String XAXIS_PROPERTY = "XAxis";
public static final String YAXIS_PROPERTY = "YAxis";
public static final String GRIDCOLOR_PROPERTY = "GridColor";
public static final String SHOWHORIZONTALLINES_PROPERTY =
            "ShowHorizontalLines";
public static final String SHOWVERTICALLINES_PROPERTY =
            "ShowVerticalLines";


/**
 * FChart, default constructor.
 **/
public FChart() {
    this( null );
}


/**
 * FChart, constructor.
 * <p>
 * Create a chart viewing the given model.
```

continues

LISTING 24.1   CONTINUED

```
 * <p>
 * @param model The model for the chart to view.
 **/
public FChart( TableModel model ) {

    setLayout( new FChartLayoutManager() );
    setXAxis( new FAxis( SwingConstants.HORIZONTAL ) );
    setYAxis( new FAxis( SwingConstants.VERTICAL ) );
    setModel( model );

    updateUI();

} // FChart


/**
 * Initialize this class with the UIManager.
 **/
public static void initialize() {

    setLookAndFeelProperties( UIManager.getLookAndFeel() );

    UIManager.addPropertyChangeListener(
        new PropertyChangeListener() {
        public void propertyChange( PropertyChangeEvent event ) {
            if( "lookAndFeel".equals( event.getPropertyName() ) ) {
                setLookAndFeelProperties(
                ( LookAndFeel )event.getNewValue() );
            }
        }
    } );

}


/**
 * Set the UI class properties for the given LookAndFeel class.
 *
 * @param lookAndFeel The look-and-feel to register ui classes for.
 **/
public static void setLookAndFeelProperties(
            LookAndFeel lookAndFeel ) {

    if( lookAndFeel == null )
        return;

    if( lookAndFeel.getID().equals( "Metal" ) ) {
        //
        // Metal, or Metal-compliant look-and-feel
```

```
         //
         UIManager.put( "FChartUI", "com.foley.chart.MetalFChartUI" );
         UIManager.put( "FAxisUI", "com.foley.chart.MetalFAxisUI" );
         UIManager.put( "FChart.gridColor",
                            new ColorUIResource( Color.lightGray ) );
      } else if( lookAndFeel.getID().equals( "Windows" ) ) {
         //
         // Windows, or Windows-compliant look-and-feel
         //
         UIManager.put("FChartUI", "com.foley.chart.WindowsFChartUI");
         UIManager.put( "FAxisUI", "com.foley.chart.WindowsFAxisUI" );
         UIManager.put( "FChart.gridColor",
                            new ColorUIResource( Color.darkGray ) );
      } else {
         //
         // Unsupported look-and-feel, use default
         //
         UIManager.put( "FChartUI", "com.foley.chart.FChartUI" );
         UIManager.put( "FAxisUI", "com.foley.chart.FAxisUI" );
         UIManager.put( "FChart.gridColor",
                            new ColorUIResource( Color.lightGray ) );
      }

   } // setLookAndFeelProperties


   /**
    * Returns the L&F object that renders this component.
    *
    * @return the FChartUI object that renders this component
    **/
   public FChartUI getUI() {
       return( FChartUI )ui;
   }


   /**
    * Sets the L&F object that renders this component.
    *
    * @param ui   the FChartUI L&F object
    * @see UIDefaults#getUI
    **/
   public void setUI( FChartUI ui ) {
       super.setUI( ui );
   }
```

continues

LISTING 24.1 CONTINUED

```
/**
 * Notification from the UIManager that the L&F has changed.
 * Replaces the current UI object with the latest version from the
 * UIManager.
 *
 * @see JComponent#updateUI
 **/
public void updateUI() {
    setUI( ( FChartUI )UIManager.getUI( this ) );
    invalidate();
}


/**
 * Returns the name of the L&F class that
 * renders this component.
 *
 * @return "FChartUI"
 * @see JComponent#getUIClassID
 * @see UIDefaults#getUI
 **/
public String getUIClassID() {
    return uiClassID;
}


/**
 * See readObject() and writeObject() in JComponent for more
 * information about serialization in Swing.
 * <p>
 * @exception IOException If the write can not be performed.
 **/
private void writeObject( ObjectOutputStream s )
    throws IOException {

    s.defaultWriteObject();
if( ( ui != null ) && ( getUIClassID().equals( uiClassID ) ) ) {
        ui.installUI( this );
    }
}


/**
 * Set the X Axis for the chart.
 * This is a bound property.
 * <p>
 * @param xAxis the new X Axis for the chart.
```

```
 * @see #getXAxis
 * @beaninfo
 *        bound: true
 * description: The X Axis for the chart.
 **/
public void setXAxis( FAxis xAxis ) {

    FAxis old = this.xAxis;

    if( this.xAxis != null )
        remove( this.xAxis );
    this.xAxis = xAxis;
    if( this.xAxis != null ) {
        add( xAxis );
        xAxis.setSize( xAxis.getPreferredSize() );
    }
    firePropertyChange( XAXIS_PROPERTY, old, xAxis );

}


/**
 * @return The current X Axis for the chart.
 * @see #setXAxis
 **/
public FAxis getXAxis() {
    return( this.xAxis );
}


/**
 * Set the Y Axis for the chart.
 * This is a bound property.
 * <p>
 * @param yAxis the new Y Axis for the chart.
 * @see #getYAxis
 * @beaninfo
 *        bound: true
 * description: The Y Axis for the chart.
 **/
public void setYAxis( FAxis yAxis ) {
    if( this.yAxis != null )
        remove( this.yAxis );
    this.yAxis = yAxis;
    if( this.yAxis != null ) {
        add( yAxis );
        yAxis.setSize( yAxis.getPreferredSize() );
    }
}
```

continues

LISTING 24.1   CONTINUED

```java
/**
 * @return The current Y Axis for the chart.
 * @see #setYAxis
 **/
public FAxis getYAxis() {
    return( this.yAxis );
}


/**
 * Set the model that the chart views.
 * The first column in the model specifies X
 * coordinate values. The remaining columns
 * specify y coordinates for each trace. This
 * implies that a model with four columns has
 * three traces in the chart.
 * <p>
 * This is a bound property.
 * <p>
 * @param model The new TableModel for the chart.
 * @see #getModel
 * @beaninfo
 *         bound: true
 * description: The data the chart contains.
 **/
public void setModel( TableModel model ) {
    TableModel old = this.model;
    this.model = model;
    firePropertyChange( MODEL_PROPERTY, old, model );
}


/**
 * @return The current data model for the chart.
 * @see #setModel
 **/
public TableModel getModel() {
    return( this.model );
}


/**
 * Sets the color used to draw grid lines to <I>color</I> and
 * redisplays the receiver. The default color is gray.
 *
 * @param gridColor The Color of the grid
 * @exception IllegalArgumentException if <I>color</I> is null
```

```
 * @see #getGridColor()
 * @beaninfo
 *        bound: true
 * description: The color for the grid in the chart.
 **/
public void setGridColor( Color gridColor ) {
    if( gridColor == null ) {
        throw new IllegalArgumentException(
            "The grid color may not be null." );
    }
    Color old = this.gridColor;
    this.gridColor = gridColor;

    firePropertyChange( GRIDCOLOR_PROPERTY, old, gridColor );

    repaint();

} // setGridColor


/**
 * Returns the color used to draw grid lines.
 * The default color is look-and-feel dependant.
 * <p>
 * @return  the color used to draw grid lines
 * @see     #setGridColor()
 **/
public Color getGridColor() {
    return gridColor;
}


/**
 * If true, the chart displays grid lines corresponding
 * to the major tick marks on the axis.
 * <p>
 * This is not a bound property. Instead the two component
 * lines are bound. I.e. horizontal lines and vertical lines
 * are bound properties.
 * <p>
 * @param showGrid If true draw grid lines, if false don't.
 * @see #setShowHorizontalLines
 * @see #setShowVerticalLines
 * @beaninfo
 *        bound: false
 * description: True to draw grid lines in the chart.
 **/
public void setShowGrid( boolean showGrid ) {
```

24

BUILDING A
CUSTOM
COMPONENT

continues

LISTING 24.1 CONTINUED

```java
        setShowHorizontalLines( showGrid );
        setShowVerticalLines( showGrid );

        repaint();
    }


    /**
     * If true, draw horizontal lines on the chart that correspond
     * to the Y axis major tick marks.
     *
     * @param showHorizontalLines If chart should draw horizontal lines.
     * @see #getShowHorizontalLines
     * @see #setShowGrid
     * @see #setShowVerticalLines
     * @beaninfo
     *         bound: true
     * description: If horizontal lines should be drawn on the chart.
     **/
    public void setShowHorizontalLines( boolean showHorizontalLines ) {

        boolean old = this.showHorizontalLines;
        this.showHorizontalLines = showHorizontalLines;

        firePropertyChange( SHOWHORIZONTALLINES_PROPERTY, old,
                    showHorizontalLines );

        repaint();
    }


    /**
     * Returns true if the chart draws horizontal lines on
     * the chart, and false if it doesn't.
     * <p>
     * @return true if the chart draws horizontal lines, false otherwise
     * @see #setShowHorizontalLines
     **/
    public boolean isShowHorizontalLines() {
        return( showHorizontalLines );
    }


    /**
     * Sets whether the chart draws vertical lines that correspond
     * to the major ticks on the X axis.
     * <p>
     * @param showVerticalLines If the chart should draw vertical lines.
     * @see #getShowVerticalLines
```

```
    * @see #setShowGrid
    * @see #setShowHorizontalLines
    * @beaninfo
    * description: If vertical lines should be drawn on the chart.
    **/
   public void setShowVerticalLines( boolean showVerticalLines ) {
       boolean old = this.showVerticalLines;
       this.showVerticalLines = showVerticalLines;

       firePropertyChange( SHOWVERTICALLINES_PROPERTY, old,
                          showVerticalLines );

       repaint();
   }


   /**
    * Returns true if the chart draws vertical lines on
    * the chart, and false if it doesn't.
    * <p>
    * @return true if the chart draws vertical lines, false otherwise
    * @see #setShowVerticalLines
    **/
   public boolean isShowVerticalLines() {
       return( showVerticalLines );
   }

   public Color getTraceColor( int trace ) {
       Color[] color = new Color[4];
       color[0] = java.awt.Color.yellow;
       color[1] = java.awt.Color.blue;
       color[2] = java.awt.Color.red;
       color[3] = java.awt.Color.black;
       return( color[ trace ] );
   }

} // FChart
```

FAxis Class

An instance of the FAxis class is used for the both the x and y axes contained in an FChart instance. The orientation property of the class specifies whether the axis should be rendered vertically or horizontally. The class uses a bounded range model to manage its minimum and maximum values. The current value in the model is not used by this class.

Like the FChart class, the FAxis class extends the JComponent class and implements the methods required to exist in the JFC pluggable look-and-feel architecture. The FAxis class keys are registered in the static initialize method contained in the FChart class.

The FAxis class's API is very similar to the JSlider class. Just as in the JSlider class, a label dictionary is used to specify the labels for the axis. If the user does not provide a dictionary, the class creates one. The major and minor tick properties are the same in these two classes. The FAxis class contains convenience methods for setting the minimum and maximum values in its model. Once again, the technique of using as many familiar property and API names makes the FAxis class very recognizable to developers familiar with the JSlider class.

The complete source listing for the FAxis class is not presented here but can be found in Appendix B, "com.foley.chart Package Source Code."

FChartLayoutManager Class

The FChartLayoutManager class is a layout manager dedicated to FChart instances. It implements the AWT LayoutManager interface to allow it to be used as a layout manager. A single instance of the class can be shared by all FChart instances. This is because the class does not maintain a reference to a single chart. The addLayoutComponent and removeLayoutComponent methods are not used. Instead, when the size for the layout is requested or the layout is to occur, the axes are queried from the given chart.

The algorithm used in the FChartLayoutManager is very simple. The preferred width of the layout is the sum of the preferred widths of the two axes and the left and right insets. Similarly, the preferred height is the sum of the preferred heights of the two axes and the top and bottom insets. The layout places the y-axis at the chart's origin and the x-axis at the point specified by (width, height) of the y-axis. (The proper insets are added to the placements.) This leaves the center of the chart for the traces to be drawn.

The complete listing for the FChartLayoutManager class is shown in Listing 24.2.

LISTING 24.2   THE FChartLayoutManager CLASS

```
package com.foley.chart;

import java.awt.*;


/**
 * A layout manager for the FChart Class.
 * <p>
 * The class lays out an X and a Y axis. The X axis
 * is along the bottom of the component, and the Y
 * along the left edge.
 * <p>
 * @author Mike Foley
 **/
```

```
public class FChartLayoutManager extends Object
    implements LayoutManager {

    /**
     * Adds the specified component with the specified name to
     * the layout.
     * @param name the component name
     * @param comp the component to be added
     */
    public void addLayoutComponent( String name, Component comp ) {
        // Not used.
    }


    /**
     * Removes the specified component from the layout.
     * @param comp the component to be removed
     */
    public void removeLayoutComponent( Component comp ) {
        // Not used.
    }


    /**
     * Calculates the preferred size dimensions for the specified
     * panel given the components in the specified parent container.
     * @param parent the component to be laid out
     *
     * @see #minimumLayoutSize
     */
    public Dimension preferredLayoutSize( Container parent ) {

        if( !( parent instanceof FChart ) )
            throw new RuntimeException(
                "FChartLayoutManager only valid for FChart instances" );

        FChart chart = ( FChart )parent;
        Insets insets = chart.getInsets();

        FAxis xAxis = chart.getXAxis();
        FAxis yAxis = chart.getYAxis();

        Dimension xAxisSize = xAxis.getPreferredSize();
        Dimension yAxisSize = yAxis.getPreferredSize();

        Dimension ourSize = new Dimension();
        ourSize.width = insets.right + insets.left +
                        xAxisSize.width + yAxisSize.width + 10;
        ourSize.height = insets.top + insets.bottom +
```

continues

24

BUILDING A
CUSTOM
COMPONENT

LISTING 24.2   CONTINUED

```
                              xAxisSize.height + yAxisSize.height + 10;

        return( ourSize );

    } // preferredLayoutSize


    /**
     * Calculates the minimum size dimensions for the specified
     * panel given the components in the specified parent container.
     * @param parent the component to be laid out
     * @see #preferredLayoutSize
     */
    public Dimension minimumLayoutSize( Container parent ) {

        if( !( parent instanceof FChart ) )
            throw new RuntimeException(
                "FChartLayoutManager only valid for FChart instances" );

        FChart chart = ( FChart )parent;
        Insets insets = chart.getInsets();

        FAxis xAxis = chart.getXAxis();
        FAxis yAxis = chart.getYAxis();

        Dimension xAxisSize = xAxis.getMinimumSize();
        Dimension yAxisSize = yAxis.getMinimumSize();

        Dimension ourSize = new Dimension();
        ourSize.width = insets.right + insets.left +
                        xAxisSize.width + yAxisSize.width;
        ourSize.height = insets.top + insets.bottom +
                        xAxisSize.height + yAxisSize.height;

        return( ourSize );

    } // minimumLayoutSize


    /**
     * Lays out the container in the specified panel.
     * @param parent the component which needs to be laid out
     */
    public void layoutContainer( Container parent ) {

        if( !( parent instanceof FChart ) )
            throw new RuntimeException(
                "FChartLayoutManager only valid for FChart instances" );
```

```
    FChart chart = ( FChart )parent;
    Dimension ourSize = chart.getSize();
    Insets insets = chart.getInsets();

    FAxis xAxis = chart.getXAxis();
    FAxis yAxis = chart.getYAxis();
    Dimension xAxisSize = xAxis.getPreferredSize();
    Dimension yAxisSize = yAxis.getPreferredSize();

    xAxis.setBounds( yAxisSize.width + insets.left - 1,
                ourSize.height - xAxisSize.height - insets.bottom,
                ourSize.width - yAxisSize.width ñ
                          insets.right - insets.left,
                xAxisSize.height );
    yAxis.setBounds( insets.top,
                insets.left,
                yAxisSize.width,
                ourSize.height - xAxisSize.height ñ
                          insets.top - insets.bottom );

  } // layoutContainer

} // FChartLayoutManager
```

24

BUILDING A
CUSTOM
COMPONENT

Pluggable Look-and-Feel Support

In the previous section, you saw the methods required by a component to exist in the pluggable look-and-feel architecture that the core Swing components implement. You saw how the component defines a UI object class key that the `UIManager` uses to create an instance of the UI class corresponding to the key. What you have not seen is a UI class itself. In this section, the UI classes for the `FChart` and `FAxis` classes will be presented.

As you saw in Chapter 22, a component's UI object is a descendant of the `ComponentUI` abstract class defined in the `.plaf` package. The complete listing for this class was presented in Listing 22.1. It is in this class that the responsibilities of a UI object are defined. The methods in this class will be familiar to those who have written AWT components. The `ComponentUI` class is `abstract`; however, it does not contain any `abstract` methods. This allows extensions to selectively choose which methods to implement. The most commonly implemented methods by extensions are the various size methods and the `paint` method. The `installUI` method will need to be implemented if the UI class is bound to a single component.

The `static` `createUI` method must be implemented by all concrete `ComponentUI` extensions. This method is called by the `UIDefaults` instance when the UI object is being set on a component. This method must return an instance of the class that is appropriate for the given JComponent instance. This is typically an instance of the UI class itself. If the UI object cannot be shared, this method generally creates a new instance of the class and returns that instance. If the UI object can be shared, the singleton instance of the class is returned from this method. The FChartUI class is bound to a single chart and cannot be shared. The FAxis class is not bound to a single axis and can be shared by any number of FAxis instances.

FChartUI Classes

The FChartUI class provides the basic UI functionality for the FChart class. There are look-and-feel–specific extensions available for the Windows and Metal look-and-feels. For any other look-and-feel being used, the FChartUI class itself is used as the UI object. The class is bound to the chart that it is the UI for, so a new instance of the FChartUI class is created for each FChart instance. The FChart component is shown in Figure 24.2 when the Windows look-and-feel is being used for the application. An FChart instance with the Metal look-and-feel was shown earlier in Figure 24.1.

FIGURE 24.2

The FChart *component with the* WindowsLookAnd-Feel.

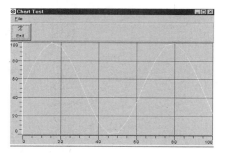

The FChartUI class is presented in Listing 24.3. As was mentioned earlier, FChartUI instances are not shared, so the createUI method creates a new instance each time it is called. In the installUI method, the FChartUI class adds itself as a propertyChangeListener for the chart in which it is being installed as the UI object. It also queries the model from the chart and, if the model is non-null, the UI object adds itself as a TableModelListener to the model. This allows for changes in the model to be detected. When a change is received, the chart is repainted, forcing the chart to be drawn with the new data. In the uninstallUI method, the UI object removes itself as a PropertyChangeListener from the chart and from being a TableModelListener to the model. When a PropertyChangeEvent is received in the propertyChange method, if the model has changed the UI object stops listening for changes from the old model and starts listening for changes in the new model.

24

NOTE

The `installUI` and `uninstallUI` methods are inverses of each other. Listeners, defaults, and keyboard actions that are added in the `installUI` method must be removed in the `uninstallUI` method. Many of the core Swing UI classes divide the `installUI` and `uninstallUI` methods into multiple methods, one for each specific task. These two methods from the `BasicLabelUI` class are shown next.

```
public void installUI(JComponent c) {
    installDefaults((JLabel)c);
    installComponents((JLabel)c);
    installListeners((JLabel)c);
    installKeyboardActions((JLabel)c);
}


public void uninstallUI(JComponent c) {
    uninstallDefaults((JLabel)c);
    uninstallComponents((JLabel)c);
    uninstallListeners((JLabel)c);
    uninstallKeyboardActions((JLabel)c);
}
```

The separation allows the code to be structured better by grouping related install and uninstall code together.

The remaining methods in the `FChartUI` class are the familiar `getPreferredSize` and `paint` methods. The preferred size is the summation of the widths and heights of the axes in the chart plus the insets of the component. The class inherits the `getMinimumSize` and `getMaximumSize` methods from the `ComponentUI` class, each of which calls the `getPreferredSize` method and returns the `Dimension` returned from that method. The `paint` method renders the chart's traces. Notice that the axes are not drawn here. Each axis is a component and, as such, it paints itself. Column 0 in the data model is considered the x coordinate for every other column. The other columns are the y coordinates, one trace per column. Thus, a data model with three columns will produce a chart with two traces. The `paint` method iterates through the data model and paints each trace. The `getLocationValue` method contained in the `FAxis` class is used to determine the coordinate in that direction. Simple lines are drawn between each point in the model.

LISTING 24.3 THE FChartUI CLASS

```java
package com.foley.chart;

import java.awt.*;
import java.beans.*;

import javax.swing.JComponent;
import javax.swing.table.TableModel;
import javax.swing.event.*;

import javax.swing.plaf.ComponentUI;


/**
 * Class FChartUI
 * <p>
 * The user-interface class for rendering FChart
 * instances.
 * <p>
 * @author Mike Foley
 * @version 1.2
 **/
public class FChartUI extends ComponentUI
    implements PropertyChangeListener, TableModelListener {

    /**
     * The FChart we are rendering.
     **/
    private FChart chart;


    /**
     * FChartUI, null constructor.
     **/
    public FChartUI() {
        chart = null;
    }


    /**
     * This UI may not be shared. Create a new
     * instance for each component.
     * <p>
     * @param c The component needing a UI.
     **/
    public static ComponentUI createUI(JComponent c) {
        return( new FChartUI() );
    }
```

```java
/**
 * Install ourselves as the UI for the given component.
 * We need to get property changes from the chart.
 * This way we can keep in sync with the chart's values.
 * <p>
 * @param c The component we are the UI for.
 **/
public void installUI( JComponent c ) {
    chart = ( FChart )c;
    TableModel model = chart.getModel();
    if( model != null )
        model.addTableModelListener( this );
    chart.addPropertyChangeListener( this );
}


/**
 * Uninstall ourselves as the UI for the given component.
 * Remove ourself as a PropertyChangeListener.
 * <p>
 * @param c The component we are uninstalling.
 **/
public void uninstallUI(JComponent c) {
    if( chart != c )
        throw new IllegalComponentStateException(
                    this + " was asked to uninstallUI for "
                + c + " that is not my chart " + chart + "." );

    chart.removePropertyChangeListener( this );
    TableModel model = chart.getModel();
    if( model != null )
        model.removeTableModelListener( this );
}


/**
 * tableChanged, from TableModelListener
 * <p>
 * The data in the table changed, repaint the chart.
 * <p>
 * @param event The change in the model.
 **/
public void tableChanged( TableModelEvent event ) {
    chart.repaint();
}


/**
```

continues

LISTING 24.3   CONTINUED

```
 * propertyChange, from PropertyChangeListener
 * <p>
 * If the change is a table model change start listening
 * to the new model.
 * <p>
 * @param event The change.
 **/
public void propertyChange( PropertyChangeEvent event ) {
    if( event.getPropertyName().equals( FChart.MODEL_PROPERTY ) ) {
        TableModel model = ( TableModel )event.getOldValue();
        if( model != null )
            model.removeTableModelListener( this );

        model = ( TableModel )event.getNewValue();
        if( model != null ) {
            model.addTableModelListener( this );
        }
    }
}


/**
 * @return The preferred size of this component.
 **/
public Dimension getPreferredSize( JComponent c ) {

    Insets insets = chart.getInsets();

    FAxis axis = chart.getXAxis();
    Dimension ourSize = new Dimension();
    Dimension x = axis.getPreferredSize();

    axis = chart.getYAxis();
    Dimension y = axis.getPreferredSize();

    ourSize.width = x.width + y.width + insets.right + insets.left;
    ourSize.height = x.height + y.height +
                          insets.top + insets.bottom;

    return( ourSize );
}


/**
 * Paint a representation of the <code>chart</code> instance
 * that was set in installUI().
 * <p>
 * @param g The graphics to paint with.
 * @param c The component to paint.
```

```
**/
public void paint( Graphics g, JComponent c ) {

    if( !( c instanceof FChart ) )
        return;

    TableModel model = chart.getModel();
    //
    // No data, no paint.
    //
    if( model == null )
        return;

    Dimension ourSize = c.getSize();

    FAxis xAxis = chart.getXAxis();
    FAxis yAxis = chart.getYAxis();
    Insets insets = chart.getInsets();
    Dimension yAxisSize = yAxis.getSize();

    g.translate( yAxisSize.width, insets.top + yAxisSize.height -1 );

    if( chart.isShowHorizontalLines() ) {
        paintHorizontalLines( g, xAxis, yAxis );
    }

    if( chart.isShowVerticalLines() ) {
        paintVerticalLines( g, xAxis, yAxis );
    }

    //
    // Now paint the traces.
    //
    for( int j = 1; j < model.getColumnCount(); j++ ) {

        g.setColor( chart.getTraceColor( j-1 ) );

        Number o0 = ( Number )model.getValueAt( 0, 0 );
        Number o1 = ( Number )model.getValueAt( 0, j );
        int x0 = xAxis.getLocationValue( o0.doubleValue() );
        int y0 = yAxis.getLocationValue( o1.doubleValue() );

        for( int i = 1; i < model.getRowCount(); i++ ) {

            o0 = ( Number )model.getValueAt( i, 0 );
            o1 = ( Number )model.getValueAt( i, j );
            int x1 = xAxis.getLocationValue( o0.doubleValue() );
            int y1 = yAxis.getLocationValue( o1.doubleValue() );
```

continues

LISTING 24.3 CONTINUED

```
                g.drawLine( x0, y0, x1, y1 );
                x0 = x1;
                y0 = y1;
            }
        }

        g.translate( -yAxisSize.width,
                -( insets.top + yAxisSize.height - 1 ) );

    } // paint


    /**
     * Paint the vertical grid lines in the chart.
     * <p>
     * @param g The Graphics to paint with.
     * @param xAxis The chart's X axis.
     * @param yAxis The chart's Y axis.
     **/
    protected void paintVerticalLines( Graphics g, FAxis xAxis,
                                        FAxis yAxis ) {

        g.setColor( chart.getGridColor() );

        int minimum = xAxis.getMinimum();
        int maximum = xAxis.getMaximum();
        int spacing = xAxis.getMajorTickSpacing();

        Insets insets = yAxis.getInsets();
        Dimension size = yAxis.getSize();
        int yAxisLength = size.height -
                    ( insets.top + insets.bottom ) - 2;

        for( int i = minimum + spacing; i <= maximum; i += spacing ) {
            int position = xAxis.getLocationValue( ( double )i );
            g.drawLine( position, 0, position, -yAxisLength );
        }

    }


    /**
     * Paint the horizontal grid lines in the chart.
     * <p>
     * @param g The Graphics to paint with.
     * @param xAxis The chart's X axis.
     * @param yAxis The chart's Y axis.
     **/
```

```
     protected void paintHorizontalLines( Graphics g,
                            FAxis xAxis, FAxis yAxis ) {

        g.setColor( chart.getGridColor() );

        int minimum = yAxis.getMinimum();
        int maximum = yAxis.getMaximum();
        int spacing = yAxis.getMajorTickSpacing();

        Insets insets = xAxis.getInsets();
        Dimension size = xAxis.getSize();
        int xAxisLength = size.width - (insets.left + insets.right) - 2;

        for( int i = minimum + spacing; i <= maximum; i += spacing ) {
            int position = yAxis.getLocationValue( ( double )i );
            g.drawLine( 0, position, xAxisLength, position );
        }

    }

} // FChartUI
```

The implementation of the FChartUI class is easy to understand, but not very efficient. Since an instance of the class is created for each chart, the property listener could be used more advantageously. For example, the preferred size is calculated each time it is requested. This value could be cached and updated when a change event is received from an axis in the chart. A bigger optimization would be to cache the translated coordinates returned from the getLocationValue method. Then when a tableChanged event is received, the altered cells in the model could be updated. At the least, the x coordinates should only be calculated once, rather then for each trace in the paint method.

Look-and-Feel Subclasses

The FChartUI class is the default UI object for the FChart class. However, there are two subclasses, WindowsFChartUI and MetalFChartUI, that are used with the Windows and Metal look-and-feels, respectively. These classes extend the FChartUI class and override the paint method. In this method, you attempt to make the look resemble other components in the corresponding look-and-feel implementation.

The complete source listings for these two classes are presented in Appendix C.

FAxisUI Class

The FAxisUI class provides the basic UI functionality for the FAxis class. There are look-and-feel–specific extensions available for the Windows and Metal look-and-feels. For any other look-and-feel being used, the FAxisUI class itself is used as the UI object. A single FAxisUI instance can be used as the UI object for all FAxis instances in an application. To implement the singleton pattern, a `static` reference is made to the one instance of the class. In the `createUI` method, a reference to this instance is returned. This technique is shown in Listing 24.4. The `FAxisUI` class does not need to perform any processing in the `installUI` or `uninstallUI` method, so these methods can be inherited from the `ComponentUI` class. Listing 24.4 presents only the UI-specific portion of the `FAxisUI` class. The complete source listing is presented in Appendix C.

LISTING 24.4 PARTIAL FAxisUI CLASS

```
/**
 * Class FAxisUI
 * <p>
 * The user-interface class for rendering FAxis
 * instances.
 * <p>
 * @author Mike Foley
 * @version 1.2
 **/
public class FAxisUI extends ComponentUI {

    /**
     * The singleton instance of this class.
     **/
    private static FAxisUI shared = new FAxisUI();

    /**
     * FAxis, default Constructor.
     **/
    public FAxisUI() {
        super();
    }


    /**
     * Create the UI object for the given component.
     * This class may share the same UI object for
     * all FAxis that are created.
     * <p>
     * @param c The component that needs a UI.
     * @return The singleton UI Object.
     **/
    public static ComponentUI createUI( JComponent c ) {
        return( shared );
    }
// Remainder of listing in Appendix C
```

The `FAxisUI` class calculates the preferred size each time this property is requested. It also performs many computations in its `paint` method. If the class was changed from a singleton to one UI object per component, many of these values can be cached and updated when a `PropertyChangeEvent` is received from the UI object's corresponding axes. This is a classic time versus space consideration. In this example, time was sacrificed for a less complex implementation that requires less memory.

Look-and-Feel Subclasses

The `FAxisUI` class is the default UI object for the `FAxis` class. However, there are two subclasses, `WindowsFAxisUI` and `MetalFAxisUI`, that are used with the Windows and Metal look-and-feels, respectively. These classes extend the `FAxisUI` class and override the `paint` method. In this method, you attempt to make the look resemble other components in the corresponding look-and-feel implementation.

The complete source listings for these two classes are presented in Appendix C.

Using the `FChart` Class

In the previous section, the `FChart` class and its support classes were presented. This class provides a chart view of the numerical data contained in a `TableModel` instance. The `ChartTest` application creates a chart and table that share the same data model. When a value is edited in the table, the chart will reflect the change. The two components are placed into a split pane to allow their sizes to be altered. The `TestDataModel` class, shown in Listing 24.5, is the shared data model. The model defines five columns resulting in four traces in the chart. The initial data contains linear, constant, sinusoidal, and random columns. The linear and constant data can be edited to alter the chart. When any value in the constant column is edited, all rows are changed to the new value. This ensures that the trace will always be constant. The resulting application is shown in Figure 24.3.

LISTING 24.5 THE `ChartTest` APPLICATION

```
package com.foley.test;

import java.awt.*;
import java.awt.event.*;
import java.beans.*;

import javax.swing.*;
import javax.swing.table.AbstractTableModel ;

import com.foley.chart.FChart;

import com.foley.utility.ApplicationFrame;
```

continues

LISTING 24.5   CONTINUED

```java
/**
 * An application that displays an FChart instance
 * and a JTable in a splitPane. The two components
 * share the same data model, so editing the table
 * will alter the chart.
 *
 * @author Mike Foley
 **/
public class ChartTest extends Object {

    /**
     * Application entry point.
     * Create a frame, the components, and display them.
     *
     * @param args Command line parameter. Not used.
     **/
    public static void main( String args[] ) {

        final JFrame frame = new ApplicationFrame( "Chart Test" );

        FChart.initialize();

        UIManager.addPropertyChangeListener(
                new PropertyChangeListener() {
            public void propertyChange( PropertyChangeEvent event ) {
                if( "lookAndFeel".equals( event.getPropertyName() ) ) {
                    SwingUtilities.updateComponentTreeUI( frame );
                }
            }
        } );

        //
        // Place the chart and table in a split pane.
        // The chart is on top.
        //
        JSplitPane splitPane = new JSplitPane(JSplitPane.VERTICAL_SPLIT);
        splitPane.setOneTouchExpandable( true );

        TestTableModel model = new TestTableModel();

        FChart chart = new FChart( model );
        JTable table = new JTable( model );

        splitPane.setTopComponent( chart );
        splitPane.setBottomComponent( new JScrollPane( table ) );
        splitPane.setBorder( BorderFactory.createLoweredBevelBorder() );
```

```
            frame.getContentPane().add( splitPane, BorderLayout.CENTER );

            frame.pack();
            frame.setVisible( true );

        } // main

} // ChartTest


/**
 * A simple model to test the FChart component.
 * The model has five column, resulting in four traces
 * being painted in the chart.
 * <p>
 * The first column defines the x coordinates for the data.
 * The second is a linear trace.
 * The third is a constant trace.
 * The four is a sine wave.
 * The fifth is random numbers.
 * <p>
 * Only two columns are editable. The linear may be changed to anything.
 * When any row in column three, the constant trace, is changed, all
 * values in that column are changed to the new value.
 * <p>
 * @author Mike Foley
 **/
class TestTableModel extends AbstractTableModel {

    double[] c0 = { 0, 5, 10, 15, 20, 25, 30, 35, 40, 45,
                    50, 55, 60, 65, 70, 75, 80, 85, 90, 95, 100 };
    double[] c1 = { 0, 5, 10, 15, 20, 25, 30, 35, 40, 45,
                    50, 55, 60, 65, 70, 75, 80, 85, 90, 95, 100 };
    double[] c2;
    Double[] c4;
    String[] columnNames = { "X-Value", "Y1", "Constant",
                             "Sin", "Random" };


    /**
     * TestTableModel, constructor.
     * <p>
     * Initialize the table model data.
     **/
    public TestTableModel() {
        c2 = new double[ c1.length ];
        c4 = new Double[ c1.length ];
        for( int i = 0; i < c2.length; i++ ) {
            c2[i] = 23.0;
```

continues

LISTING 24.5   CONTINUED

```
            c4[i] = new Double( 100 * Math.random() );
        }
    }


    /**
     * @return The number of rows in the model.
     **/
    public int getRowCount() {
        return( c1.length );
    }


    /**
     * @return The number of columns in the model.
     **/
    public int getColumnCount() {
        return( columnNames.length );
    }


    /**
     * @param column The column who's name is desired.
     * @return The column name of the given column.
     **/
    public String getColumnName(int column ) {
        return( columnNames[ column ] );
    }


    /**
     * Only columns 1 and 2 are editable.
     * The rows don't matter.
     * <p>
     * @param row The row of the cell in question.
     * @param column The column of the cell in question.
     * @return True if the cell is editable.
     **/
    public boolean isCellEditable( int row, int column ) {
        if( column == 1 || column == 2 )
            return( true );
        else
            return( false );
    }


    /**
     * The new value is assumed to be a string that can be
     * parsed by the Double class. If this is not the case,
```

```
 * there will be trouble.
 * <p>
 * @param value The new data.
 * @param row The row for the new data item.
 * @param column The column for the new data item.
 * @see #getValueAt
 **/
public void setValueAt( Object value, int row, int column ) {

    Double newValue = new Double( ( String )value );

    switch( column ) {
        case 1:
            c1[ row ] = newValue.doubleValue();
            fireTableCellUpdated( row, column );
            break;
        case 2:
            for( int i = 0; i < getRowCount(); i++ )
                c2[ i ] = newValue.doubleValue();
            fireTableRowsUpdated( 0, getRowCount() - 1 );
            break;
        default:
            throw new RuntimeException(
                "Unknown column in table model setValueAt" );
    }
}


/**
 * @param row The row of the requested data item.
 * @param column The column of the requested data item.
 * @return The value at the given row and column in the model.
 * @see #setValueAt
 **/
public Object getValueAt(int row, int column) {
    Object out;

    switch( column ) {
        case 0:
            out = new Double( c0[ row ] );
            break;
        case 1:
            out = new Double( c1[ row ] );
            break;
        case 2:
            out = new Double( c2[ row ] );
            break;
        case 3:
```

continues

24

BUILDING A
CUSTOM
COMPONENT

LISTING 24.5   CONTINUED

```
            out = new Double( 50 +  50 * Math.sin( 0.1 * c0[row] ) );
            break;
        case 4:
            out = c4[ row ];
            break;
        default:
            out = null;
    }
    return( out );

} // getValueAt

} // TestTableModel
```

FIGURE 24.3

The ChartTest *application.*

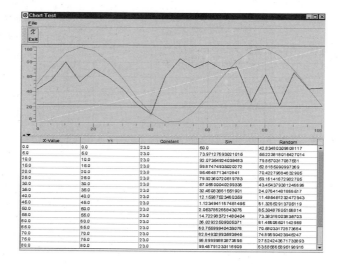

Summary

In this chapter, you created a custom Swing component extension. A component that is to work within the pluggable look-and-feel architecture is not a single class. Instead, it is a component class that defines the API for application interactions with the component and one or more user interface classes. A single UI class can be used with all look-and-feel implementations, or a class can be developed for each look-and-feel, or any combination in between.

Before the UI object can be used in the pluggable look-and-feel architecture, its class must be registered with the UIManager. The uiClassID key queried from the component class is used by the UIManager to determine the class to use for its UI object. There are no hooks in the JFC that allow the custom class to perform this initialization work. This forces the component to provide an initialization method or forces the user of the component to do this work. In this chapter's example, a static initialization method was provided that was called by the application before the first instance of the class was created. If the component supports different UI objects for different look-and-feel implementations, the component must also listen for LookAndFeel change messages from the UIManager so that the values in the UIManager can be kept current.

The FChart class and its helper class, FAxis, are two custom components that work together to display a chart. There are multiple UI classes for each component class. There are specific versions for the Windows and Metal look-and-feels and a generic version for any other look-and-feel that may be encountered. The component class is responsible for defining the API and properties available for the component. The UI class is responsible for interacting with the user. This includes calculating the size for the component, registering keystroke actions, responding to mouse gestures, and painting the component. The methods required by both the component class and the UI class to exist in the JFC's pluggable look-and-feel architecture were presented in these classes.

The FChart class displays numerical data contained in a TableModel instance. The FAxis class stores its range data in a BoundedRangeModel instance. Both the FChart and FAxis classes contain bound properties that are defined in other JFC components that represent similar properties. Leveraging existing models and properties from the core Swing components will make your custom components easier to use by experienced Swing developers. A developer who is familiar with the TableModel interface and the JSlider class will be familiar with the API defined by the FChart and FAxis classes. This will enable the developer to use the components with little expended effort.

24

BUILDING A
CUSTOM
COMPONENT

Advanced JFC Concepts

Part VI

IN THIS PART

ToolTips and Debug Graphics

CHAPTER 25

ToolTips are pop-up text labels that appear when the mouse cursor comes to rest over a component. They are also known as fly-over text or hover text. ToolTips can be used with any Swing component (JComponent), but are most commonly associated with user interface controls such as buttons.

All Swing components provide debug support for graphics-related operations. This feature can be useful for debugging drawing problems with components.

In this chapter, you will learn

- How to create basic and customized ToolTips.

  Implementing ToolTips with Swing components is really easy—it takes one line of code to create a basic ToolTip.

- How to use the ToolTipManager class to control the behavior of ToolTips.

  You can globally disable ToolTips for your application. You can also change various delay settings that control how ToolTips respond to mouse actions.

- How to use Swing's debug graphics capabilities.

  Debug graphic capabilities include logging drawing operations and drawing off-screen buffer operations to an external window.

ToolTips Basics

ToolTips are represented by the JToolTip class in the com.sun.java.swing package. However, unless you're interested in creating your own customized ToolTips, you don't need to directly use this class.

Any Swing component (including frames and panels as well as menus and tree controls) can have ToolTips by calling a single JComponent method, setToolTipText.

```
// Create a button with a ToolTip
JButton b = new JButton("Quit");
b.setToolTipText("Exits the application");
```

Calling the setToolTipText method is all you need to do to make use of the basic ToolTip capability of Swing components. Advanced use of ToolTips includes using custom ToolTips and using the ToolTip manager to control how ToolTips respond to mouse movement.

The ToolTipManager Class

You might want to alter the default behavior of ToolTips or even disable them altogether. Swing provides the ToolTipManager class (see Listing 25.1) to allow you to enable and disable ToolTips as well as set the characteristics of ToolTip behavior.

LISTING 25.1   `ToolTipManager` CLASS SIGNATURE

```
public class ToolTipManager extends MouseAdapter
                            implements MouseMotionListener {
  // Public class method
    public static ToolTipManager sharedInstance();
  // Public instance methods
    // methods to enable/disable and change response of ToolTips
    public void setEnabled(boolean enable);
    public void setDismissDelay(int delay);
    public void setInitialDelay(int delay);
    public void setReshowDelay(int delay);
    public boolean isEnabled();
    public int getDismissDelay();
    public int getInitialDelay();
    public int getReshowDelay();
    public void setLightWeightPopupEnabled(boolean enable);
    public boolean isLightWeightPopupEnabled();
    // overrides for mouse event handling
    public void mouseDragged(MouseEvent e);
    public void mouseEntered(MouseEvent e);
    public void mouseExited(MouseEvent e);
    public void mouseMoved(MouseEvent e);
    public void mousePressed(MouseEvent e);
    // methods called by components to register with ToolTip manager
    public void registerComponent(JComponent component);
    public void unregisterComponent(JComponent component);
}
```

Note that the `ToolTipManager` class does not have a public constructor. This is because an instance of the class already exists as a part of the system. Instead of calling a constructor to create an instance of the `ToolTipManager` class, you get a reference to the system's instance by calling the static class method `sharedInstance`. The following line of code uses `sharedInstance` to call the `setEnabled` method to disable ToolTips.

```
ToolTipManager.sharedInstance().setEnabled(false);
```

Controlling ToolTip Behavior

The methods you'll find most useful in this class are the methods that change ToolTip behavior: `setEnabled`, `setInitialDelay`, `setDismissDelay`, and `setReshowDelay`. `setEnabled` enables and disables ToolTips globally for an application. The delay-related functions change how ToolTips respond to the mouse.

- The *initial delay* determines how long the mouse must stop over a component before the ToolTip is made visible.
- The *dismiss delay* determines how long the ToolTip will remain visible.

25

TOOLTIPS AND DEBUG GRAPHICS

- The *reshow delay* determines the amount of time after the mouse exits a component with a visible ToolTip that the ToolTip will redisplay immediately (without waiting for the initial delay).

The `isEnabled`, `getInitialDelay`, `getDismissDelay`, and `getReshowDelay` methods return the current settings of the ToolTip manager. The remaining methods are methods the ToolTip manager overrides to handle mouse events.

Lightweight Versus Heavyweight ToolTips

The `ToolTipManager` class includes two methods, `setLightWeightPopupEnabled` and `isLightWeightPopupEnabled`, to control whether ToolTips are rendered as lightweight (Swing) or heavyweight (AWT) components. By default, ToolTips are rendered as lightweight components. If you are mixing Swing and AWT components in an application, you should disable lightweight ToolTips as shown in the following line of code.

```
ToolTipManager.sharedInstance().setLightWeightPopupEnabled(false);
```

The `JToolTip` Class

If for some reason you need more control over the appearance of ToolTips, you can supply your own implementation of ToolTips by extending the `JToolTip` class (see Listing 25.2).

LISTING 25.2   `JToolTip` CLASS SIGNATURE

```
public class JToolTip extends JComponent implements Accessible
{
  // Public constructor
    public JToolTip();
  // Public instance methods
    public ToolTipUI getUI();
    public void updateUI();
    public getUIClassID();
    public void setTipText(String string);
    public String getTipText();
    public void setComponent(JComponent component);
    public JComponent getComponent();
    public getAccessibleContext();
}
```

ToolTips are instantiated on-the-fly, at the time they need to be displayed. A listener (the `ToolTipManager`) listens for mouse movement within a component and instantiates a `JToolTip` object when it's time to display a ToolTip. To supply a customized ToolTip, you override the component's `createToolTip` method as shown in the following code fragment.

```
// Create a quit button with custom ToolTip
JButton b = new JButton("Quit") {
    // Override to use custom tooltip
    public JToolTip createToolTip() {return(new CustomToolTip(this));}
}
```

ToolTip objects extend JComponent which extends Component, one of the cornerstone objects of AWT. Thus, if you want to create more sophisticated customized ToolTips, you can override Component methods such as paint, setBackground, and setFont.

ToolTips Example

Listing 25.3 is the complete source for ToolTipsDemo, an application that illustrates basic and advanced capabilities of ToolTips. Figure 25.1 shows the completed ToolTipsDemo.

FIGURE 25.1

The ToolTipsDemo *example.*

LISTING 25.3 ToolTipsDemo.java

```
/* ToolTipsDemo.java
 *
 * Illustrates basic and customized ToolTips.
 */

import java.awt.*;
import java.awt.event.*;
import javax.swing.*;
import javax.swing.event.*;
import javax.swing.border.*;

/* App class
```

continues

LISTING 25.3   CONTINUED

```java
*/
public class ToolTipsDemo {
    // Main entry point
    public static void main(String s[]) {

        // create app panel
        ToolTipsDemoPanel panel = new ToolTipsDemoPanel();

        // create a frame for app
        JFrame frame = new JFrame("ToolTipsDemo");

        // add a window listener for window close events
        frame.addWindowListener(new WindowAdapter() {
            public void windowClosing(WindowEvent e) {System.exit(0);}
        });

        // add app panel to content pane
        frame.getContentPane().add(panel);

        // set initial frame size and make visible
        frame.setSize (250, 450);
        frame.setVisible(true);
    }
}

/* App panel class
 */
class ToolTipsDemoPanel extends JPanel {
    // Constructor
    public ToolTipsDemoPanel() {
        super();

        // create 2 radio buttons with custom ToolTips
        JRadioButton rb1 = new JRadioButton("Enable tool tips", true) {
            // override to use custom tooltip
            public JToolTip createToolTip() {
                return(new CustomToolTip(this));
            }
        };
        rb1.addActionListener(new ActionListener() {
            public void actionPerformed(ActionEvent e) {
                ToolTipManager.sharedInstance().setEnabled(true);
            }
        });
        rb1.setToolTipText("Enables tool tips for all components");
        JRadioButton rb2 = new JRadioButton("Disable tool tips", false) {
            // override to use custom tooltip
            public JToolTip createToolTip() {
                return(new CustomToolTip(this));
```

```
            }
        };
        rb2.addActionListener(new ActionListener() {
            public void actionPerformed(ActionEvent e) {
                ToolTipManager.sharedInstance().setEnabled(false);
            }
        });
        rb2.setToolTipText("Disables tool tips for all components");

        // add radio buttons to a button group
        ButtonGroup group = new ButtonGroup();
        group.add(rb1);
        group.add(rb2);

        // arrange radio buttons in box and panel(to provide label)
        MyBox box1 = new MyBox(BoxLayout.Y_AXIS);
        box1.add(rb1);
        box1.add(rb2);
        JPanel panel1 = new JPanel();
        panel1.setBorder(new TitledBorder("Tool Tips"));
        panel1.add(box1);

        // create 3 sliders with change listeners
        // each slider overrides createToolTip to use a custom ToolTip
        // slider 1
        final JSlider s1 = new JSlider(JSlider.HORIZONTAL, 0, 10000, 0) {
            // override to use custom tooltip
            public JToolTip createToolTip() {
                return(new CustomToolTip(this));
            }
        };
        s1.setPaintTicks(true);
        s1.setPaintLabels(true);
        s1.setMajorTickSpacing(5000);
        s1.setMinorTickSpacing(1000);
        s1.setSnapToTicks(true);
        s1.setValue(ToolTipManager.sharedInstance().getDismissDelay());
        s1.addChangeListener(new ChangeListener() {
            public void stateChanged(ChangeEvent e) {
                ToolTipManager.sharedInstance().setDismissDelay(
                ➥s1.getValue());
            }
        });
        s1.setToolTipText(
➥"Changes Tool Tip Manager's dismiss delay setting");
        // add slider to panel that has titled border
        JPanel panel2 = new JPanel();
        panel2.setBorder(new TitledBorder("Dismiss Delay"));
        panel2.add(s1);
```

continues

LISTING 25.3 CONTINUED

```
        // slider 2
        final JSlider s2 = new JSlider(JSlider.HORIZONTAL, 0, 10000, 0) {
            // override to use custom tooltip
            public JToolTip createToolTip() {
                return(new CustomToolTip(this));
            }
        };
        s2.setPaintTicks(true);
        s2.setPaintLabels(true);
        s2.setMajorTickSpacing(5000);
        s2.setMinorTickSpacing(1000);
        s2.setSnapToTicks(true);
        s2.setValue(ToolTipManager.sharedInstance().getInitialDelay());
        s2.addChangeListener(new ChangeListener() {
            public void stateChanged(ChangeEvent e) {
                ToolTipManager.sharedInstance().setInitialDelay(
➥s2.getValue());
            }
        });
        s2.setToolTipText(
            "Changes Tool Tip Manager's initial delay setting");
        // add slider to panel that has titled border
        JPanel panel3 = new JPanel();
        panel3.setBorder(new TitledBorder("Initial Delay"));
        panel3.add(s2);
        // slider 3
        final JSlider s3 = new JSlider(JSlider.HORIZONTAL, 0, 10000, 0) {
            // override to use custom tooltip
            public JToolTip createToolTip() {
                return(new CustomToolTip(this));
            }
        };
        s3.setPaintTicks(true);
        s3.setPaintLabels(true);
        s3.setMajorTickSpacing(5000);
        s3.setMinorTickSpacing(1000);
        s3.setSnapToTicks(true);
        s3.setValue(ToolTipManager.sharedInstance().getReshowDelay());
        s3.addChangeListener(new ChangeListener() {
            public void stateChanged(ChangeEvent e) {
                ToolTipManager.sharedInstance().setReshowDelay(
➥s3.getValue());
            }
        });
        s3.setToolTipText(
➥"Changes Tool Tip Manager's reshow delay setting");
        // add slider to panel that has titled border
        JPanel panel4 = new JPanel();
        panel4.setBorder(new TitledBorder("Reshow Delay"));
```

```
        panel4.add(s3);

        // add radio button and slider panels to vertical box
        MyBox box2 = new MyBox(BoxLayout.Y_AXIS);
        box2.add(panel1);    // radio buttons
        box2.add(panel2);    // sliders
        box2.add(panel3);    //
        box2.add(panel4);    //
        // put box in panel that has titled border
        JPanel panel5 = new JPanel();
        panel5.setBorder(new TitledBorder("Tool Tips Tweaks"));
        panel5.add(box2);
        add(panel5);

        // create a quit button with custom ToolTip
        JButton b = new JButton("Quit") {
            // override to use custom ToolTip
            public JToolTip createToolTip() {
                return(new CustomToolTip(this));
            }
        };
        b.setToolTipText("Exits the application");
        b.addActionListener(new ActionListener() {
            public void actionPerformed(ActionEvent e) {
                System.exit(0);
            }
        });
        add(b);
    }

    // Override to use custom ToolTip on panel
    public JToolTip createToolTip() { return(new CustomToolTip(this)); }
}


// A custom ToolTip class that simply changes the
// background color of the basic ToolTip.
class CustomToolTip extends JToolTip {
    // Constructor
    public CustomToolTip(JComponent component) {
        super();
        setComponent(component);
        setBackground(Color.yellow);
    }
}

// Workaround for problems with Box class
// Use JPanel with BoxLayout layout manager
class MyBox extends JPanel
```

continues

LISTING 25.3   CONTINUED

```
{
    public MyBox(int axis) {
        super();
        setLayout(new BoxLayout(this, axis));
    }
}
```

Overview of the `ToolTipsDemo` Example

The `ToolTipsDemo` example consists of three classes:

- `ToolTipsDemo` is a public class that contains the `main` entry point method.
- `ToolTipsDemoPanel` is a panel (`JPanel`) that contains the user interface for the application.
- `CustomToolTip` is an implementation of a custom ToolTip.

The `main` entry point creates a frame (`JFrame`) and an instance of `ToolTipsDemoPanel` that it adds to the frame.

The constructor for `ToolTipsDemoPanel` creates two radio buttons and three sliders to provide an interface for changing ToolTip manager settings. The radio buttons and sliders are contained in panels with titled borders used to identify the controls. Each component that uses a custom ToolTip overrides the `createToolTip` method and returns an instance of `CustomToolTip`.

Using the ToolTip Manager

The following fragment is the code that creates the radio button that enables ToolTips.

```
JRadioButton rb1 = new JRadioButton("Enable tool tips", true) {
    // override to use custom tooltip
    public JToolTip createToolTip() {return(new CustomToolTip(this));}
};
rb1.addActionListener(new ActionListener() {
    public void actionPerformed(ActionEvent e) {
        ToolTipManager.sharedInstance().setEnabled(true);
    }
});
rb1.setToolTipText("Enables tool tips for all components");
```

The radio button has an action listener implemented in an anonymous inner class. When an action event is received via the `actionPerformed` method, the listener gets a shared instance of the ToolTip manager and calls its `setEnabled` method to enable ToolTips.

The sliders are implemented like the radio buttons. The following code fragment creates the slider that controls the dismiss delay for ToolTips.

```
final JSlider s1 = new JSlider(JSlider.HORIZONTAL, 0, 10000, 0) {
    // override to use custom tooltip
    public JToolTip createToolTip() { return(new CustomToolTip(this)); }
};
s1.setPaintTicks(true);
s1.setPaintLabels(true);
s1.setMajorTickSpacing(5000);
s1.setMinorTickSpacing(1000);
s1.setSnapToTicks(true);
s1.setValue(ToolTipManager.sharedInstance().getDismissDelay());
s1.addChangeListener(new ChangeListener() {
    public void stateChanged(ChangeEvent e) {
        ToolTipManager.sharedInstance().setDismissDelay(s1.getValue());
    }
});
s1.setToolTipText("Changes Tool Tip Manager's dismiss delay setting");
```

One important difference between the slider and radio button implementation is that the slider variables are declared as `final`, to be accessed by the change listener because it is implemented in an inner class. (The radio button listeners were also implemented in an inner class, but they did not need to access the radio button instance.)

```
ToolTipManager.sharedInstance().setDismissDelay(s1.getValue());
```

The dismiss delay is set to the value returned by the slider's `getValue` method.

Using Custom ToolTips

The `ToolTipsDemo` example uses a very simple version of a customized ToolTip—it simply changes the background color of ToolTips to yellow. As shown earlier, each component that uses a custom ToolTip must override the `createToolTip` method and return an instance of the custom ToolTip. The following code fragment creates the Quit button, which uses a custom ToolTip.

```
// create a quit button with custom ToolTip
JButton b = new JButton("Quit") {
    // override to use custom ToolTip
    public JToolTip createToolTip() { return(new CustomToolTip(this)); }
};
b.setToolTipText("Exits the application");
```

To implement custom ToolTips, `ToolTipsDemo` simply extends the `JToolTip` class.

```
// A custom ToolTip class that simply changes the
// background color of the basic ToolTip.
class CustomToolTip extends JToolTip {
    // Constructor
```

```
public CustomToolTip(JComponent component) {
    super();
    setComponent(component);
    setBackground(Color.yellow);
}
}
```

The constructor for `CustomToolTip` takes a single parameter specifying the component with which the ToolTip is to be associated. The contents of this parameter are passed to the `JToolTip.setComponent` method. The constructor then sets the background color to yellow. You could also call `setFont` here to change the font used for custom ToolTips.

Using Debug Graphics

All Swing components come with built-in debug capability for graphics operations. This capability resides in the `DebugGraphics` class, which is an extension of the AWT `Graphics` class.

The `DebugGraphics` Class

`DebugGraphics` is a rather large class—it has more than 50 public methods. Fortunately, you only need to use a few of these methods to access the debug graphics capabilities of `JComponent` objects.

```
// Public constants (for getting and setting debug options)
public static final int LOG_OPTION;
public static final int FLASH_OPTION;
public static final int BUFFERED_OPTION;
public static final int NONE_OPTION;

// Public class methods to change debug options
public static void setFlashColor(Color color);
public static Color flashColor();
public static void setFlashTime(int time);
public static int flashTime();
public static void setFlashCount(int count);
public static int flashCount();
public static void setLogStream(PrintStream stream);
public static PrintStream logStream();
```

The remaining methods in the `DebugGraphics` class are `Graphics` method overrides that you normally won't need to use.

There are several static class methods you can use to change debug graphics options: `setFlashColor`, `setFlashTime`, `setFlashCount`, and `setLogStream`. Because these methods are static class methods, you don't need to create a DebugGraphics object to call them.

Enabling Debug Graphics Options

Debug graphics is enabled on a per-component basis. To enable debug graphics (by default it's disabled), you call the JComponent.setDebugGraphicsOptions method and specify one the following debug options:

- DebugGraphics.LOG_OPTION to specify that graphics operations be logged
- DebugGraphics.FLASH_OPTION to specify that drawing operations be performed slowly, and flash so you can observe the order and manner of component rendering
- DebugGraphics.BUFFERED_OPTION to specify that drawing operations be rendered in an external window

When you set debug graphic options with setDebugGraphicsOptions, the options you specify are combined with options that have been set previously. To disable all debug graphics options, call setDebugGraphicsOptions with the DebugGraphics.NONE_OPTION option.

> **NOTE**
>
> When you call a component's setDebugGraphicsOptions method, the settings also apply to components that are contained by the target component.

You must disable double buffering when using debug graphics. The following line of code shows how you can use the repaint manager to disable double buffering.

```
RepaintManager.currentManager(this).setDoubleBufferingEnabled(false);
```

Example Using Flash Option

Listing 25.4 is the complete source for FlashGraphicsDemo, an application that illustrates how to use the debug graphics flash option. Figure 25.2 shows the completed FlashGraphicsDemo.

FIGURE 25.2
The FlashGraphicsDemo *example.*

LISTING 25.4   FlashGraphicsDemo.java

```java
/* FlashGraphicsDemo.java
 *
 * Application illustrating use of debug graphics flash option.
 */

import java.awt.*;
import java.awt.event.*;
import javax.swing.*;

/* App class
 */
public class FlashGraphicsDemo {

    // Main entry point
    public static void main(String s[]) {
        // create app panel
        FlashGraphicsDemoPanel panel = new FlashGraphicsDemoPanel();

        // create a frame for app
        JFrame frame = new JFrame("FlashGraphicsDemo");

        // add a window listener for window close events
        frame.addWindowListener(new WindowAdapter() {
            public void windowClosing(WindowEvent e) {System.exit(0);}
        });

        // add app panel to content pane
        frame.getContentPane().add(panel);

        // set initial frame size and make visible
        frame.setSize (350, 120);
        frame.setVisible(true);
    }
}

/* App panel class
 */
class FlashGraphicsDemoPanel extends JPanel {
    // Constructor
    public FlashGraphicsDemoPanel () {
        // set flash option parameters
        DebugGraphics.setFlashCount(2);
        DebugGraphics.setFlashColor(Color.red);
        DebugGraphics.setFlashTime(25);

        // double buffering must be disabled
        // to use debug graphics options!!

RepaintManager.currentManager(this).setDoubleBufferingEnabled(false);
```

```
        // create a panel containing some debug objects
        final JPanel debugPanel = new JPanel();
        debugPanel.add(new JButton("Button"));
        debugPanel.add(new JSlider());

        // create a check box to turn debug on/off
        JCheckBox cb = new JCheckBox("Enable Flash Graphics Debug");
        cb.addItemListener(new ItemListener() {
            public void itemStateChanged(ItemEvent e) {
                if(e.getStateChange() == ItemEvent.SELECTED) {
                    // enable flash option

debugPanel.setDebugGraphicsOptions(DebugGraphics.FLASH_OPTION);
                    debugPanel.repaint();
                }
                else {
                    // disable flash option

debugPanel.setDebugGraphicsOptions(DebugGraphics.NONE_OPTION);
                }
            }
        });

        // create a repaint button
        JButton b = new JButton("Repaint");
        b.addActionListener (new ActionListener () {
            public void actionPerformed (ActionEvent e) {
                // repaint panel containing debug components
                debugPanel.repaint();
            }
        });

        // add components to panel
        add(cb);
        add(b);
        add(debugPanel);
    }
}
```

Overview of the `FlashGraphicsDemo` Example

The FlashGraphicsDemo example consists of two classes:

- FlashGraphicsDemo is a public class that contains the main entry point method.
- FlashGraphicsDemoPanel is a panel (JPanel) that contains the user interface for the application.

The main entry point creates a frame (JFrame) and an instance of FlashGraphicsDemoPanel that it adds to the frame.

The constructor for `FlashGraphicsDemoPanel` first sets parameters for the flash option by calling the `DebugGraphics` class methods `setFlashCount`, `setFlashColor`, and `setFlashTime`. It then disables double buffering and creates a debug panel containing a button and slider to illustrate how components are drawn when you enable the flash option. After creating a button that allows you to cause a repaint of the debug panel, the constructor creates a check box component that allows you to enable and disable the flash option. The following code fragment shows how the item listener for this check box enables and disables the flash option.

```
JCheckBox cb = new JCheckBox("Enable Flash Graphics Debug");
cb.addItemListener(new ItemListener() {
    public void itemStateChanged(ItemEvent e) {
        if(e.getStateChange() == ItemEvent.SELECTED) {
            // enable flash option

debugPanel.setDebugGraphicsOptions(DebugGraphics.FLASH_OPTION);
            debugPanel.repaint();
        }
        else {
            // disable flash option
            debugPanel.setDebugGraphicsOptions(DebugGraphics.NONE_OPTION);
        }
    }
});
```

After creating the check box and adding an item listener, the constructor adds the check box, the repaint button, and the debug panel to the main application panel.

The Logging Option

The debug graphics logging option (`DebugGraphics.LOG_OPTION`) will cause graphics operations to be logged on the standard output stream. If you wish, you can use the `DebugGraphics.setLogStream` method to specify a different stream for logging operations.

Logging operations can generate quite a bit of output. Listing 25.5 is the partial (about 15% of the total) debug output generated by drawing a basic `JButton` object.

LISTING 25.5   OUTPUT GENERATED BY ENABLING DEBUG GRAPHIC LOGGING (`LOG_OPTION`)

```
Graphics(0-1) Enabling debug
Graphics(0-1) Enabling debug
Graphics(1-1) Enabling debug
Graphics(1-1) Setting color: ColorUIResource[r=0,g=0,b=0]
Graphics(1-1) Setting font: FontUIResource[family=Dialog,name=Arial,
style=bold,size=12]
```

```
Graphics(2-1) Setting color: ColorUIResource[r=204,g=204,b=204]
Graphics(2-1) Filling rect: Rectangle[x=0,y=0,width=77,height=25]
Graphics(2-1) Setting font: FontUIResource[family=Dialog,name=Arial,
style=bold,size=12]
Graphics(2-1) Setting color: ColorUIResource[r=0,g=0,b=0]
Graphics(2-1) Drawing string: "Button" at: Point[x=17,y=16]
Graphics(1-1) Translating by: Point[x=0,y=0]
Graphics(1-1) Setting color: ColorUIResource[r=102,g=102,b=102]
Graphics(1-1) Drawing line: from (0, 0) to (74, 0)
Graphics(1-1) Drawing line: from (75, 0) to (75, 22)
Graphics(1-1) Drawing line: from (75, 23) to (1, 23)
Graphics(1-1) Drawing line: from (0, 23) to (0, 1)
Graphics(1-1) Setting color: ColorUIResource[r=255,g=255,b=255]
Graphics(1-1) Drawing line: from (1, 1) to (75, 1)
Graphics(1-1) Drawing line: from (76, 1) to (76, 23)
Graphics(1-1) Drawing line: from (76, 24) to (2, 24)
Graphics(1-1) Drawing line: from (1, 24) to (1, 2)
Graphics(1-1) Setting color: ColorUIResource[r=204,g=204,b=204]
Graphics(1-1) Drawing line: from (0, 24) to (1, 23)
Graphics(1-1) Drawing line: from (76, 0) to (75, 1)
Graphics(1-1) Translating by: Point[x=0,y=0]
Graphics(0-1) Setting new clipRect: Rectangle2D$Float[x=0.0,y=0.0,
w=87.0,h=35.0]
Graphics(0-1) Drawing image: BufferedImage@6fb03d9: type = 1
DirectColorModel: rmask=ff0000 gmask=ff00 bmask=ff amask=0
IntegerComponentRaster: width = 192 height = 173
#Bands = 3 #DataElements 1 xOff = 0 yOff = 0
dataOffset[0] 0 at: Point[x=0,y=0]
```

The Flash Option

The debug graphics flash option causes drawing operations to flash several times in a specified color before being rendered correctly. There are three DebugGraphics static class methods that allow you to control the number of times the drawing operations flash, the delay between the flashes, and the flash color.

```
public static void setFlashColor(Color color);
public static void setFlashTime(int time);
public static void setFlashCount(int count);
```

Using the flash option allows you to observe the order of drawing operations that occur when a component is rendered.

The Buffered Option

The buffered option will cause operations to the component's offscreen buffer to be rendered in an external frame window.

Summary

ToolTips can be a very effective way to provide information about a component when it's under the mouse cursor. All Swing components support ToolTips with the `setToolTipText` method. The `ToolTipsDemo` example shows how to use basic ToolTips as well as how to create and use customized ToolTips.

Swing components also provide several options of debug graphics capability. You can use these debug graphics options to better understand how components are rendered so you can correct drawing-related problems you may encounter in your code.

Focus Managers

CHAPTER 26

Focus management, coupled with keyboard accelerators and shortcuts, allows a GUI application to be navigated and operated with a keyboard. The 1.1 version of the JDK provided focus management services as a part of AWT, but did not allow applications much flexibility in modifying the default focus management behavior. JFC goes a step further by encapsulating focus management services for Swing components into public classes. This encapsulation allows JFC applications more control over managing focus changes—applications can even provide their own focus manager if necessary.

This chapter describes how to use the JFC's focus management capabilities. For details on how to use keyboard accelerators and shortcuts, see Chapter 29, "Keyboard Navigation."

In this chapter, you will learn

- About focus and focus managers

    For many applications, you won't really need to be concerned with focus management. However, if you're doing complicated dialog boxes or forms, you might want more control over how the focus manager moves the focus between your components.

- How Swing's focus management works

    Focus management comes "for free" with JFC, but even if you're content with the default focus management services, it helps to understand a bit about how the default focus management operates.

- How to explicitly set the focus to a component

    You can use this technique to implement "hot" components—components that grab the focus whenever they are under the mouse.

- How to detect when a component receives the focus

    You can use this technique to create components that change their appearance or make a sound when they get the focus.

- How to manage focus at the component level

    You can override the behavior of the default focus manager by creating components that manage focus changes.

- How to write a custom focus manager

    If you can't get the results you want with the default focus manager or by managing focus at the component level, you can write a custom focus manager for your application.

About Focus and Focus Managers

The term *focus* is shorthand for *input focus* or *current input focus*. The component that has the focus is the component that receives keyboard input events. For example, you can type text into a text field if and only if the text field has the focus. Likewise with button controls (JButton objects)—the button that has the focus will respond to the Return key by actuating and firing action events, just as if you had clicked the button with the mouse. Only one component can have the focus at a time. Focus is usually indicated visually so that it's clear to the user what component has the focus.

The focus order in AWT's focus manager is based on the order in which you add components to their container—you cannot change this behavior. JFC, however, abstracts and encapsulates focus management into the FocusManager and DefaultFocusManager classes. With JFC, you can create and use your own focus manager.

How Swing's Default Focus Manager Works

The default focus manager in Swing responds to the Tab key to advance the focus and the Shift+Tab key combination to move the focus back to the component that previously had the focus. The use of Tab and Shift+Tab for focus traversal is common to many operating environments.

> **NOTE**
>
> When a user interface control such as a button or menu has the focus, you can use the Return, Enter, or Spacebar key to actuate the control. You can also actuate the control with the mnemonic key, if one is set for the component. The focus manager does not control this behavior, however; it's controlled by the look-and-feel implementation. See Chapter 30, "Pluggable Look-and-Feel," for details on various look-and-feel implementations.

Swing's default focus manager determines which component will get the focus next with an algorithm that's based on the order in which the components were added to their container. This is the same algorithm as AWT used for focus management. Because most layout managers arrange components in the order in which they were added, this focus management algorithm generally works quite well. The focus proceeds from the upper-left area of a container to its lower-right area. In a grid of components, focus moves left-to-right across the first row and then down to the beginning of the next row and so on. Focus will traverse all focusable components in a container before passing to another container.

Managing Focus from Components

Focus management is a cooperative effort between components and the focus manager. Many focus-management operations can be handled at the component level, without having to create a custom focus manager. For example, components can request the focus and transfer the focus to the next focusable component in the component hierarchy. Components can also inform the focus manager that they will manage focus change operations.

The JComponent class provides several methods for controlling focus. A few of these methods are actually Component methods, but are presented here for the sake of completeness.

```
// Public instance methods
  public void addFocusListener(FocusListener listener);
  public void grabFocus();
  public boolean hasFocus();
  public boolean isRequestFocusEnabled();
  public void removeFocusListener(FocusListener listener);
  public void requestFocus();
  public void setRequestFocusEnabled(boolean enable);
  public void transferFocus();
// Overrides
  public boolean isFocusTraversable();
  public boolean isManagingFocus();
```

The hasFocus method can be used to determine if a component currently has the focus. If the component has the focus, hasFocus returns true.

The setRequestFocusEnabled method enables a component to accept focus change requests with the requestFocus method. You can use isRequestFocusEnabled to determine if a component is enabled for focus change requests.

> **NOTE**
>
> Disabling focus change requests will not prevent the component from getting focus from the focus manager. It will prevent the component from getting the focus when the focus is explicitly requested with the requestFocus method.

The `grabFocus` method will set the focus to a component, regardless of whether the component is enabled to receive explicit focus change requests. This method is meant to be used only by focus managers. Unless you're writing your own focus manager, you should use `requestFocus` to set the focus to a component.

The `transferFocus` method transfers the focus to the next focusable component in the component hierarchy.

The `requestDefaultFocus` method applies to containers—components that contain other focusable components. When called on a container, `requestDefaultFocus` will set the focus to the component that gets the focus by default. This is normally the first component that was added to the container.

The `addFocusListener` method allows components to listen for focus events. Components can use a focus listener to determine when they gain and lose the focus. `removeFocusListener` will remove a focus listener from a component.

The `isFocusTraversable` method is a method you can override to control whether a component can get the focus. Components that cannot normally receive the focus, like text labels and panels, should return `false` from `isFocusTraversable`. This override is also useful if you want to receive keystroke events in components that aren't normally focusable.

The `isManagingFocus` method is a method you can override for components that manage their own focus changes. If you override `isManagingFocus` and return `true`, the focus manager will send the component's key listener Tab and Shift+Tab keystrokes. See the "Example Using Component-Managed Focus" section later in this chapter for an example that overrides `isManagingFocus`.

Example Using `requestFocus` to Explicitly Set the Focus

Often, you'll want to override the default behavior of the focus manager and set the focus to a specific component. For example, when you instantiate a dialog box, you might want to set the focus to a user interface element that must be acted on before the dialog box can be closed. Or, if it's a dialog box that is presented mainly for user confirmation, you'll want to set the focus to the OK button so the user can easily dismiss it. To explicitly set the focus to a component, you simply call the component's `requestFocus` method.

Listing 26.1 is the complete source for `HotFocus`, an application that uses `requestFocus` to explicitly set the focus to the component that is under the mouse. See Figure 26.1 for the output of this code.

FIGURE 26.1

HotFocus *example.*

LISTING 26.1 HotFocus.java

```java
/* HotFocus.java
 *
 * Illustrates how to explicitly set the focus to a component.
 */

import java.awt.event.*;
import javax.swing.*;

/* App class
 */
public class HotFocus {

    // Main entry point
    public static void main(String s[]) {
        // create app panel
        HotFocusPanel panel = new HotFocusPanel();

        // create a frame for app
        JFrame frame = new JFrame("HotFocus");

        // add a window listener for window close events
        frame.addWindowListener(new WindowAdapter() {
            public void windowClosing(WindowEvent e) {System.exit(0);}
        });

        // add app panel to content pane
        frame.getContentPane().add(panel);

        // set initial frame size and make visible
        frame.setSize (150, 150);
        frame.setVisible(true);
    }
}

/* App panel class
 */
class HotFocusPanel extends JPanel {
    // Constructor
    public HotFocusPanel () {
        super();
```

```
        // create twelve buttons, arranged in four rows of three
        // use boxes to lay out to appear like a telephone keypad
        HotButton b0, b1, b2, b3, b4, b5, b6, b7, b8, b9,
                  bAsterisk, bPound;
        MyBox bx_h1 = new MyBox(BoxLayout.X_AXIS);   // row 1
        MyBox bx_h2 = new MyBox(BoxLayout.X_AXIS);   // row 2
        MyBox bx_h3 = new MyBox(BoxLayout.X_AXIS);   // row 3
        MyBox bx_h4 = new MyBox(BoxLayout.X_AXIS);   // row 4
        MyBox bx_v1 = new MyBox(BoxLayout.Y_AXIS);

        bx_h1.add(b1 = new HotButton("1"));
        bx_h1.add(b2 = new HotButton("2"));
        bx_h1.add(b3 = new HotButton("3"));
        bx_h2.add(b4 = new HotButton("4"));
        bx_h2.add(b5 = new HotButton("5"));
        bx_h2.add(b6 = new HotButton("6"));
        bx_h3.add(b7 = new HotButton("7"));
        bx_h3.add(b8 = new HotButton("8"));
        bx_h3.add(b9 = new HotButton("9"));
        bx_h4.add(bAsterisk = new HotButton("*"));
        bx_h4.add(b0 = new HotButton("0"));
        bx_h4.add(bPound = new HotButton("#"));

        // stack 4 row boxes in a vertical (column) box
        bx_v1.add(bx_h1);
        bx_v1.add(bx_h2);
        bx_v1.add(bx_h3);
        bx_v1.add(bx_h4);

        // add vertical box to panel
        add(bx_v1);
    }
}

// HotButton class
//
// An extension of JButton that requests the focus
// when the mouse enters the button.
class HotButton extends JButton {
    // Constructor
    public HotButton(String text) {
        super(text);

        // ensure that component can request focus
        // default is true, but just to be sure...
        setRequestFocusEnabled(true);

        // add a listener for mouse enter
        addMouseListener(new MouseAdapter() {
```

continues

LISTING 26.1   CONTINUED

```
            public void mouseEntered(MouseEvent event) {
                // Request the focus (if don't already have it)
                if(!hasFocus()) { requestFocus(); }
            }
        });
    }
}


// Workaround for problems with Box class
// Use JPanel with BoxLayout layout manager
class MyBox extends JPanel
{
    // Constructor
    public MyBox(int axis) {
        setLayout(new BoxLayout(this, axis));
    }
}
```

Overview of the `HotFocus` Example

The `HotFocus` example creates a panel containing twelve buttons in a layout designed to resemble a telephone keypad. The buttons are contained in boxes so they are arranged in four rows with three buttons in each row. The buttons are created from the `HotButton` class, an extension of `JButton`.

```
// HotButton class
//
// A simple extension of JButton that requests the focus
// when the mouse enters the button.
class HotButton extends JButton {
    // Constructor
    public HotButton(String text) {
        super(text);

        // ensure that component can request focus
        // default is true, but just to be sure...
        setRequestFocusEnabled(true);

        // add a listener for mouse enter
        addMouseListener(new MouseAdapter() {
            public void mouseEntered(MouseEvent event) {
                // request the focus (if don't already have it)
                if(!hasFocus()) { requestFocus(); }
            }
        });
    }
}
```

The HotButton constructor calls setRequestFocusEnabled to ensure that the component will respond to focus requests. The constructor then adds a mouse listener implemented in an anonymous inner class to detect when the mouse is over the button. When the mouseEntered event is received, the listener calls hasFocus to see if the button has the focus and, if not, it calls requestFocus to get the focus. The result is a button that gets the focus whenever it is under the mouse.

Getting Notification of Focus

Swing makes use of AWT's focus listener mechanism to notify components of focus changes. To get focus notification in a component, you must perform the following steps:

- Call the addFocusListener method to add a focus listener.
- Implement a focus listener by subclassing the FocusAdapter class.
- Override the focusGained and focusLost methods in the focus listener to process focus changes.

Example Using Focus Notification

Listing 26.2 is the complete source for HotFocus2, an example based on the previous HotFocus example. If you run the HotFocus example, you'll notice that the visual changes that occur when a component gets the focus are pretty subtle. HotFocus2 builds on HotFocus by detecting focus changes and altering the appearance of buttons when they have the focus (see Figure 26.2).

FIGURE 26.2

The HotFocus2
example.

LISTING 26.2   HotFocus2.java

```
/* HotFocus2.java
 *
 * Illustrates how to explicitly set the focus
 * and detect focus changes.
 */

import java.awt.Color;
import java.awt.event.*;
import javax.swing.*;
```

continues

LISTING 26.2 CONTINUED

```java
/* App class
 */
public class HotFocus2 {

    // Main entry point
    public static void main(String s[]) {
        // create app panel
        HotFocus2Panel panel = new HotFocus2Panel();

        // create a frame for app
        JFrame frame = new JFrame("HotFocus2");

        // add a window listener for window close events
        frame.addWindowListener(new WindowAdapter() {
            public void windowClosing(WindowEvent e) {System.exit(0);}
        });

        // add app panel to content pane
        frame.getContentPane().add(panel);

        // set initial frame size and make visible
        frame.setSize (150, 150);
        frame.setVisible(true);
    }
}

/* App panel class
 */
class HotFocus2Panel extends JPanel {
    // Constructor
    public HotFocus2Panel () {
        super();

        // create twelve buttons, arranged in four rows of three
        // use boxes to lay out to appear like a telephone keypad
        HotButton b0, b1, b2, b3, b4, b5, b6, b7, b8, b9,
                  bAsterisk, bPound;
        MyBox bx_h1 = new MyBox(BoxLayout.X_AXIS);   // row 1
        MyBox bx_h2 = new MyBox(BoxLayout.X_AXIS);   // row 2
        MyBox bx_h3 = new MyBox(BoxLayout.X_AXIS);   // row 3
        MyBox bx_h4 = new MyBox(BoxLayout.X_AXIS);   // row 4
        MyBox bx_v1 = new MyBox(BoxLayout.Y_AXIS);

        bx_h1.add(b1 = new HotButton("1"));
        bx_h1.add(b2 = new HotButton("2"));
        bx_h1.add(b3 = new HotButton("3"));
        bx_h2.add(b4 = new HotButton("4"));
        bx_h2.add(b5 = new HotButton("5"));
        bx_h2.add(b6 = new HotButton("6"));
```

```
        bx_h3.add(b7 = new HotButton("7"));
        bx_h3.add(b8 = new HotButton("8"));
        bx_h3.add(b9 = new HotButton("9"));
        bx_h4.add(bAsterisk = new HotButton("*"));
        bx_h4.add(b0 = new HotButton("0"));
        bx_h4.add(bPound = new HotButton("#"));

        // stack 4 row boxes in a vertical (column) box
        bx_v1.add(bx_h1);
        bx_v1.add(bx_h2);
        bx_v1.add(bx_h3);
        bx_v1.add(bx_h4);

        // add vertical box to panel
        add(bx_v1);
    }
}

// HotButton class
//
// An extension of JButton that requests the focus
// when the mouse enters the button. Also listens for
// focus changes and changes button appearance
// when button gets the focus.
class HotButton extends JButton {
    private boolean bFocusIndicated = false;
    private Color originalColor;

    // constructor
    public HotButton(String text) {
        super(text);

        // ensure that component can request focus
        // default is true, but just to be sure...
        setRequestFocusEnabled(true);

        // add a listener for mouse enter
        addMouseListener(new MouseAdapter() {
            public void mouseEntered(MouseEvent event) {
                // request the focus (if don't already have it)
                if(!hasFocus()) { requestFocus(); }
            }
        });
        // add a listener for focus events
        addFocusListener(new FocusAdapter() {
            public void focusGained(FocusEvent e) {
                if(!bFocusIndicated) {
                    // set background to a darker color to indicate focus
                    originalColor = getBackground();
```

continues

LISTING 26.2   CONTINUED

```
                        setBackground(originalColor.darker());
                        bFocusIndicated = true;
                    }
                }
                public void focusLost(FocusEvent e) {
                    // restore original background color
                    setBackground(originalColor);
                    bFocusIndicated = false;
                }
            });
        }
    }


// Workaround for problems with Box class
// Use JPanel with BoxLayout layout manager
class MyBox extends JPanel
{
    // Constructor
    public MyBox(int axis) {
        setLayout(new BoxLayout(this, axis));
    }
}
```

Overview of HotFocus2 Example

Like the previous HotFocus example, all of the focus-related functionality of HotFocus2 resides in the extension to the JButton class, HotButton. The following code fragment shows how the HotButton class implements a focus listener to handle focus changes.

```
// Add a listener for focus events
addFocusListener(new FocusAdapter() {
    public void focusGained(FocusEvent e) {
        if(!bFocusIndicated) {
            // Set background to a brighter color to indicate focus
            originalColor = getBackground();
            setBackground(originalColor.darker());
            bFocusIndicated = true;
        }
    }
    public void focusLost(FocusEvent e) {
        // Restore background color
        setBackground(originalColor);
        bFocusIndicated = false;
    }
});
```

When the button gets the focus, get and save the background color and then call the `Color.darker` method to make the background color darker. When the button loses the focus, restore the background to the original background color.

Since you can't be assured that a component with the focus won't receive additional `focusGained` events, you must keep track of whether a `HotButton` component has the focus or not. To accomplish this, use the `focusLost` and `focusGained` events to set the `bFocusIndicated` class member. You can't use the `hasFocus` method for this purpose because it will always return `true` when called while handling `focusGained` events.

Example Using Component-Managed Focus

The previous two examples show how a component can set the focus to itself and how a component can detect when it gains and loses the focus. You can also create components that manage focus traversal by listening for keystrokes and determining which components get the focus when the user presses the Tab and Shift+Tab keys. To create a component that manages focus traversal, you must implement the following steps:

- Override the `isManagingFocus` method to tell the focus manager that the component is managing focus traversal. The focus manager will then allow the Tab and Shift+Tab keystrokes to pass to the component.

- Add a key listener to listen for the Tab and Shift+Tab keystrokes.

- Implement some way of determining which component gets the focus when you detect a Tab or Shift+Tab keystroke.

Listing 26.3 is the complete source for `ComponentManagedFocus`, an example that overrides the focus manager and manages focus traversal at the component level. This example uses the same telephone keypad button arrangement as the `HotFocus` and `HotFocus2` examples, but manages focus changes so that the focus traverses vertically instead of horizontally. Note that the `ComponentManagedFocus` example does not change the focus to components under the mouse or indicate focus by darkening button colors (although you could easily add this capability to this example).

LISTING 26.3   ComponentManagedFocus.java

```
/* ComponentManagedFocus.java
 *
 * Illustrates how to implement component-managed
 * focus changes instead of using the focus manager.
 */

import java.awt.event.*;
```

continues

LISTING 26.3   CONTINUED

```java
import javax.swing.*;

/* App class
 */
public class ComponentManagedFocus {

    // Main entry point
    public static void main(String s[]) {
        // create app panel
        ComponentManagedFocusPanel panel =
new ComponentManagedFocusPanel();

        // create a frame for app
        JFrame frame = new JFrame("ComponentManagedFocus");

        // add a window listener for window close events
        frame.addWindowListener(new WindowAdapter() {
            public void windowClosing(WindowEvent e) {System.exit(0);}
        });

        // add app panel to content pane
        frame.getContentPane().add(panel);

        // set initial frame size and make visible
        frame.setSize (150, 150);
        frame.setVisible(true);
    }
}

/* App panel class
 */
class ComponentManagedFocusPanel extends JPanel {
    // Constructor
    public ComponentManagedFocusPanel () {
        super();

        // create twelve buttons, arranged in four rows of three.
        // use boxes to lay out to appear like a telephone keypad.
        MyButton b0, b1, b2, b3, b4, b5, b6, b7, b8, b9,
                    bAsterisk, bPound;
        MyBox bx_h1 = new MyBox(BoxLayout.X_AXIS);   // row 1
        MyBox bx_h2 = new MyBox(BoxLayout.X_AXIS);   // row 2
        MyBox bx_h3 = new MyBox(BoxLayout.X_AXIS);   // row 3
        MyBox bx_h4 = new MyBox(BoxLayout.X_AXIS);   // row 4
        MyBox bx_v1 = new MyBox(BoxLayout.Y_AXIS);

        bx_h1.add(b1 = new MyButton("1"));
        bx_h1.add(b2 = new MyButton("2"));
        bx_h1.add(b3 = new MyButton("3"));
```

```
        bx_h2.add(b4 = new MyButton("4"));
        bx_h2.add(b5 = new MyButton("5"));
        bx_h2.add(b6 = new MyButton("6"));
        bx_h3.add(b7 = new MyButton("7"));
        bx_h3.add(b8 = new MyButton("8"));
        bx_h3.add(b9 = new MyButton("9"));
        bx_h4.add(bAsterisk = new MyButton("*"));
        bx_h4.add(b0 = new MyButton("0"));
        bx_h4.add(bPound = new MyButton("#"));

        // set focus control such that focus traverses top to bottom,
        // left to right. For example, 1,4,7,*,2,5,8,0,3,6,9,#,1...
        b1.setFocusControl(b4, bPound);
        b2.setFocusControl(b5, bAsterisk);
        b3.setFocusControl(b6, b0);
        b4.setFocusControl(b7, b1);
        b5.setFocusControl(b8, b2);
        b6.setFocusControl(b9, b3);
        b7.setFocusControl(bAsterisk, b4);
        b8.setFocusControl(b0, b5);
        b9.setFocusControl(bPound, b6);
        bAsterisk.setFocusControl(b2, b7);
        b0.setFocusControl(b3, b8);
        bPound.setFocusControl(b1, b9);

        // stack 4 row boxes in a vertical (column) box
        bx_v1.add(bx_h1);
        bx_v1.add(bx_h2);
        bx_v1.add(bx_h3);
        bx_v1.add(bx_h4);

        // add vertical box to panel
        add(bx_v1);
    }
}

// MyButton class
//
// An extension of JButton that adds a new method, setFocusControl,
// that allows setting previous and next components to get the focus.
class MyButton extends JButton {
    private JComponent nextFocus = null;
    private JComponent prevFocus = null;

    // Constructor
    public MyButton(String text) {
        super(text);

        // add a listener for key events
```

continues

LISTING 26.3 CONTINUED

```java
        addKeyListener(new KeyAdapter() {
            public void keyPressed(KeyEvent event) {
                // look for tab key
                if(event.getKeyCode() == KeyEvent.VK_TAB
                || event.getKeyChar() == '\t') {
                    // is shift pressed?
                    if ((event.getModifiers()
                    & ActionEvent.SHIFT_MASK) == ActionEvent.SHIFT_MASK) {
                        // set previous focus
                        if (prevFocus != null) {
                            prevFocus.requestFocus();
                            event.consume();
                        }
                    }
                    else {
                        // set next focus
                        if (nextFocus != null) {
                            nextFocus.requestFocus();
                            event.consume();
                        }
                    }
                }
            }
        });
    }

    // Sets previous and next components to get the focus
    public void setFocusControl(JComponent nextFocus,
                                JComponent prevFocus) {
        this.nextFocus = nextFocus;
        this.prevFocus = prevFocus;
    }

// Override to inform focus manager that
    // component is managing focus changes
    public boolean isManagingFocus() {
        return true;
    }
}

// Workaround for problems with Box class
// Use JPanel with BoxLayout layout manager
class MyBox extends JPanel
{
    // Constructor
    public MyBox(int axis) {
        setLayout(new BoxLayout(this, axis));
    }
}
```

Overview of `ComponentManagedFocus` Example

The `ComponentManagedFocus` example is similar in structure to the `HotFocus` and `HotFocus2` examples. The constructor for the `ComponentManagedFocusPanel` class, an extension of `JPanel`, creates twelve instances of `MyButton` that it arranges in boxes to form four rows of three buttons each. The constructor then calls the `setFocusControl` method to specify which button gets the next and previous focus. This is a method added to the `MyButton` class that extends `JButton`.

NOTE

Instead of algorithmically determining focus traversal based on component location or position in the containment hierarchy, this example takes a hard-coded approach to solving the focus-traversal problem. This approach works well only when you have a fixed number of focusable components and do not want focus traversal to be dependent on component layout.

Take a look at `MyButton`, the class that extends `JButton` to implement component-managed focus traversal. `MyButton` adds two private data members, `nextFocus` and `prevFocus`, to store the next and previous components in the focus-traversal sequence. These data members are set by a public method added to `MyButton`, `setFocusControl`.

```
// Sets previous and next components to get the focus
public void setFocusControl(JComponent nextFocus, JComponent prevFocus) {
    this.nextFocus = nextFocus;
    this.prevFocus = prevFocus;
}
```

There is another method added to `MyButton`, `isManagingFocus`. This method is an override to tell the focus manager that the component is managing focus traversal. To receive Tab and Shift+Tab keystrokes, a component must override `isManagingFocus` and return true.

```
// Override to inform focus manager that
// component is managing focus changes
public boolean isManagingFocus() {
    return true;
}
```

The final element to managing focus traversal in `MyButton` is the key listener that listens for the Tab and Shift+Tab keystrokes. The constructor for `MyButton` adds a key listener that is implemented in an anonymous inner class.

```
// add a listener for key events
addKeyListener(new KeyAdapter() {
    public void keyPressed(KeyEvent event) {
        // look for tab key
        if(event.getKeyCode() == KeyEvent.VK_TAB
        || event.getKeyChar() == '\t') {
            // is shift pressed?
            if ((event.getModifiers()
            & ActionEvent.SHIFT_MASK) == ActionEvent.SHIFT_MASK) {
                // set previous focus
                if (prevFocus != null) {
                    prevFocus.requestFocus();
                    event.consume();
                }
            }
            else {
                // set next focus
                if (nextFocus != null) {
                    nextFocus.requestFocus();
                    event.consume();
                }
            }
        }
    }
});
```

If the key listener gets a `keyPressed` event, it checks to see if the keystroke is a Tab or Shift+Tab. If the keystroke is a Tab or Shift+Tab, the listener calls the `requestFocus` method on the component referenced by the appropriate `nextFocus` or `prevFocus` data member (the data members set with the `setFocusControl` method). Note that the listener calls `event.consume` to prevent Tab and Shift+Tab `keyPressed` events from propagating any further.

Using the Focus Manager

While most focus management can be handled at the component level, you may want to write your own focus manager or change the behavior of the default focus manager. JFC provides two classes that encapsulate focus management for Swing components: `FocusManager` and `DefaultFocusManager`. The `FocusManager` class is an abstract class that provides the basic underlying structure for supporting installable focus managers. The `DefaultFocusManager` class extends `FocusManager` and represents the implementation of the default focus manager.

The `FocusManager` Class

You use the `FocusManager` class (in the `com.sun.java.swing` package) when writing your own focus manager. Listing 26.4 gives the class signature for the `FocusManager` class.

LISTING 26.4   `FocusManager` CLASS SIGNATURE

```
public abstract class FocusManager extends Object {
  // Public class data
    public static String FOCUS_MANAGER_CLASS_PROPERTY;
    public static Hashtable managers;
  // Public class methods
    public static FocusManager getCurrentManager();
    public static void setCurrentManager(FocusManager focusManager);
    public static void disableSwingFocusManager();
    public static boolean isFocusManagerEnabled();
  // Public abstract instance methods
    public abstract void processKeyEvent(Component component,
                                         KeyEvent event);
    public abstract void focusNextComponent(Component component);
    public abstract void focusPreviousComponent(Component component);
}
```

The static class methods `getCurrentManager`, `setCurrentManager`, `disableSwingFocusManager`, and `isFocusManagerEnabled` give you access to the current focus manager and allow you to disable the Swing focus management services as well as install your own focus manager.

The abstract methods `processKeyEvent`, `focusNextComponent`, and `focusPreviousComponent` are methods you must override and implement if you are writing a focus manager.

Issues with Mixing AWT and Swing Components

There are actually two focus managers present in JFC. In addition to the Swing focus manager for managing focus with Swing components, JFC includes the AWT focus manager to manage focus for AWT components. If you are mixing AWT and Swing components in a component hierarchy, you need to disable the Swing focus manager by calling the static `FocusManager` method `disableSwingFocusManager`.

```
FocusManager.disableSwingFocusManager();
```

When you disable the Swing focus manager, your application will use the AWT focus manager for Swing components as well as AWT components.

Writing a Custom Focus Manager

If Swing's default focus manager is not adequate for the needs of your application, you can replace it with your own focus manager. To create a custom focus manager, you extend the abstract `FocusManager` class and implement the methods `processKeyEvent`, `focusNextComponent`, and `focusPreviousComponent`. The `processKeyEvent` method receives keystrokes from the component that currently has the focus. In the implementation for `processKeyEvent`, you listen for Tab and Shift+Tab keystrokes and use `grabFocus` to set the focus to the appropriate component. `focusNextComponent` and `focusPreviousComponent` are methods you must implement to change the focus to the previous or next component to get the focus after a given component. Creating the structure for a custom focus manager is fairly straight-forward—the challenge is in creating a general-purpose algorithm for determining focus traversal.

Example Using a Custom Focus Manager

Take a look at an example of a custom focus manager. The `CustomFocusManager` example is a different version of the focus-traversal implementation in the `ComponentManagedFocus` example. By all appearances, the applications operate identically—focus traverses vertically top-to-bottom instead of horizontally like the default focus manager.

The difference is in the implementation of focus management. While the `ComponentManagedFocus` example handles focus changes at the component level, `CustomFocusManager` implements the same algorithm in a custom focus manager. Listing 26.5 is the complete source for `CustomFocusManager`.

LISTING 26.5   `CustomFocusManager.java`

```
/* CustomFocusManager.java
 *
 * Illustrates how to implement a custom focus manager.
 */

import java.awt.*;
import java.awt.event.*;
import javax.swing.*;
import javax.swing.FocusManager;

/* App class
 */
public class CustomFocusManager {

    // Main entry point
```

```java
    public static void main(String s[]) {
        // create app panel
        CustomFocusManagerPanel panel = new CustomFocusManagerPanel();

        // create a frame for app
        JFrame frame = new JFrame("CustomFocusManager");

        // add a window listener for window close events
        frame.addWindowListener(new WindowAdapter() {
            public void windowClosing(WindowEvent e) {System.exit(0);}
        });

        // add app panel to content pane
        frame.getContentPane().add(panel);

        // create and install custom focus manager
        FocusManager fm = new MyFocusManager();
        FocusManager.setCurrentManager(fm);

        // set initial frame size and make visible
        frame.setSize (150, 150);
        frame.setVisible(true);
    }
}


/* App panel class
 */
class CustomFocusManagerPanel extends JPanel {
    // Constructor
    public CustomFocusManagerPanel () {
        super();

        // create twelve buttons, arranged in four rows of three.
        // use boxes to lay out to appear like a telephone keypad.
        MyButton b0, b1, b2, b3, b4, b5, b6, b7, b8, b9,
                 bAsterisk, bPound;
        MyBox bx_h1 = new MyBox(BoxLayout.X_AXIS);   // row 1
        MyBox bx_h2 = new MyBox(BoxLayout.X_AXIS);   // row 2
        MyBox bx_h3 = new MyBox(BoxLayout.X_AXIS);   // row 3
        MyBox bx_h4 = new MyBox(BoxLayout.X_AXIS);   // row 4
        MyBox bx_v1 = new MyBox(BoxLayout.Y_AXIS);

        bx_h1.add(b1 = new MyButton("1"));
        bx_h1.add(b2 = new MyButton("2"));
        bx_h1.add(b3 = new MyButton("3"));
        bx_h2.add(b4 = new MyButton("4"));
        bx_h2.add(b5 = new MyButton("5"));
        bx_h2.add(b6 = new MyButton("6"));
```

continues

LISTING 26.5   CONTINUED

```
        bx_h3.add(b7 = new MyButton("7"));
        bx_h3.add(b8 = new MyButton("8"));
        bx_h3.add(b9 = new MyButton("9"));
        bx_h4.add(bAsterisk = new MyButton("*"));
        bx_h4.add(b0 = new MyButton("0"));
        bx_h4.add(bPound = new MyButton("#"));

        // set focus control such that focus traverses top to bottom,
        // left to right. For example, 1,4,7,*,2,5,8,0,3,6,9,#,1...
        b1.setNextFocus(b4);          b1.setPreviousFocus(bPound);
        b2.setNextFocus(b5);          b2.setPreviousFocus(bAsterisk);
        b3.setNextFocus(b0);          b3.setPreviousFocus(b0);
        b4.setNextFocus(b7);          b4.setPreviousFocus(b1);
        b5.setNextFocus(b8);          b5.setPreviousFocus(b2);
        b6.setNextFocus(b9);          b6.setPreviousFocus(b3);
        b7.setNextFocus(bAsterisk);   b7.setPreviousFocus(b4);
        b8.setNextFocus(b0);          b8.setPreviousFocus(b5);
        b9.setNextFocus(bPound);      b9.setPreviousFocus(b6);
        bAsterisk.setNextFocus(b2);   bAsterisk.setPreviousFocus(b7);
        b0.setNextFocus(b3);          b0.setPreviousFocus(b8);
        bPound.setNextFocus(b1);      bPound.setPreviousFocus(b9);

        // stack 4 row boxes in a vertical (column) box
        bx_v1.add(bx_h1);
        bx_v1.add(bx_h2);
        bx_v1.add(bx_h3);
        bx_v1.add(bx_h4);

        // add vertical box to panel
        add(bx_v1);
    }
}

/* Interface that components must implement to
 * operate with custom focus manager in this example.
 */
interface MyFocusManagerSupport {
    // Sets next component to get the focus
    public void setNextFocus(JComponent component);
    // Sets previous component to get the focus
    public void setPreviousFocus(JComponent component);
    // Returns next component to get focus
    public JComponent getNextFocus();
    // Returns previous component to get focus
    public JComponent getPreviousFocus();
}

/* MyButton class
 *
```

```
 * An extension of JButton that implements
 * MyFocusManagerSupport interface.
 */
class MyButton extends JButton implements MyFocusManagerSupport {
    private JComponent nextFocus = null;
    private JComponent previousFocus = null;

    // Constructor
    public MyButton(String text) {
        super(text);
    }

    // Implementation of MyFocusManagerSupport interface

    public void setNextFocus(JComponent component) {
        nextFocus = component;
    }

    public void setPreviousFocus(JComponent component) {
        previousFocus = component;
    }

    public JComponent getPreviousFocus() { return (previousFocus); }

    public JComponent getNextFocus() { return (nextFocus); }
}

/* MyFocusManager class
 *
 * An implementation of a custom focus manager.
 *
 * Components managed by this focus manager must
 * implement the MyFocusManagerSupport interface.
 */
class MyFocusManager extends FocusManager {
    public MyFocusManager() {
        super();
    }

    // Implementations of abstract FocusManager methods

    // Handles key events on component with current focus
    public void processKeyEvent(Component component, KeyEvent event) {
        if(component instanceof MyFocusManagerSupport) {
            MyButton focusedButton = (MyButton) component;

            // look for tab key
            if(event.getKeyCode() == KeyEvent.VK_TAB
               || event.getKeyChar() == '\t') {
```

continues

LISTING 26.5 CONTINUED

```
                // change focus only on key pressed events
                if(event.getID() == KeyEvent.KEY_PRESSED) {
                    // is shift pressed?
                    if ((event.getModifiers()
➥& ActionEvent.SHIFT_MASK) == ActionEvent.SHIFT_MASK) {
                        // set previous focus
                        focusPreviousComponent(component);
                    }
                    else {
                        // set next focus
                        focusNextComponent(component);
                    }
                }
                // consume all tab key events
                event.consume();
            }
        }
    }

    // Changes focus to component that gets focus after given component
    public void focusNextComponent(Component component) {
        // ensure given component is one we can manage
        if(component instanceof MyFocusManagerSupport) {
            MyFocusManagerSupport focusedComponent
➥= (MyFocusManagerSupport) component;
            if (focusedComponent.getNextFocus() != null) {
                focusedComponent.getNextFocus().grabFocus();
            }
        }
    }

    // Changes focus to component that gets focus before given component
    public void focusPreviousComponent(Component component) {
        // ensure given component is one we can manage
        if(component instanceof MyFocusManagerSupport) {
            MyFocusManagerSupport focusedComponent
➥= (MyFocusManagerSupport) component;
            if (focusedComponent.getPreviousFocus() != null) {
                focusedComponent.getPreviousFocus().grabFocus();
            }
        }
    }
}

// Workaround for problems with Box class
// Use JPanel with BoxLayout layout manager
class MyBox extends JPanel
{
    // Constructor
```

```
    public MyBox(int axis) {
        setLayout(new BoxLayout(this, axis));
    }
}
```

Overview of `CustomFocusManager` Example

The focus traversal algorithm used by `CustomFocusManager` is simple—for each component, you must specify the previous and next components to get the focus. The example
defines an interface, `MyFocusManagerSupport`, that components must implement to be
managed by this custom focus manager.

```
/* Interface that components must implement to
 * operate with custom focus manager in this example.
 */
interface MyFocusManagerSupport {
    // Sets next component to get the focus
    public void setNextFocus(JComponent component);

    // Sets previous component to get the focus
    public void setPreviousFocus(JComponent component);

    // Returns next component to get focus
    public JComponent getNextFocus();

    // Returns previous component to get focus
    public JComponent getPreviousFocus();
}
```

The interface includes methods for setting and getting the previous and next components
to get the focus. The only focusable components in this example are the buttons represented by the `MyButton` class, an extension of `JButton`. `MyButton` simply provides a constructor for a textual button and implements the `MyFocusManagerSupport` interface by
adding two private data members to store the next and previous components to get the
focus.

Before looking at the implementation of the custom focus manager, consider how it is
installed. After creating the panel containing the application's user interface and adding it
to a frame, the main entry point in the `CustomFocusManager` class creates an instance of
`MyFocusManager` and installs it with the `FocusManager.setCurrentManager` static class
method.

```
// create and install custom focus manager
FocusManager fm = new MyFocusManager();
FocusManager.setCurrentManager(fm);
```

The custom focus manager is implemented in the MyFocusManager class, an extension of the abstract FocusManager class. In addition to a default constructor, MyFocusManager includes implementations of the three abstract FocusManager methods: processKeyEvent, focusNextComponent, and focusPreviousComponent.

The following code fragment is the implementation of the focusNextComponent method.

```
// Changes focus to component that gets focus after given component
public void focusNextComponent(Component component) {
    // ensure given component is one we can manage
    if(component instanceof MyFocusManagerSupport) {
    MyFocusManagerSupport focusedComponent
➥= (MyFocusManagerSupport) component;
        if (focusedComponent.getNextFocus() != null) {
            focusedComponent.getNextFocus().grabFocus();
        }
    }
}
```

The first thing focusNextComponent does is to check the given component to make sure it implements the MyFocusManagerSupport interface. The custom focus manager in this example can only manage focus traversal for components that implement this interface. focusNextComponent then calls the getNextFocus method on the given component to determine which component gets the next focus. If getNextFocus doesn't return null, the component's grabFocus method is called to give it the focus. The focusPreviousComponent method is implemented similarly to focusNextComponent.

The processKeyEvent method receives keystroke events for the component that currently has the focus. Its role is to listen for the keystrokes that change the focus (Tab and Shift+Tab) and call the focusNextComponent and focusPreviousComponent methods to change the focus.

```
// Handles key events on component with current focus
public void processKeyEvent(Component component, KeyEvent event) {
    if(component instanceof MyFocusManagerSupport) {
        MyButton focusedButton = (MyButton) component;

        // look for tab key
        if(event.getKeyCode() == KeyEvent.VK_TAB
➥|| event.getKeyChar() == '\t') {
            // change focus only on key pressed events
            if(event.getID() == KeyEvent.KEY_PRESSED){
                // is shift pressed?
                if ((event.getModifiers()
➥& ActionEvent.SHIFT_MASK) == ActionEvent.SHIFT_MASK) {
                    // set previous focus
                    focusPreviousComponent(component);
                }
```

```
        else {
            // set next focus
            focusNextComponent(component);
        }
    }
    // consume all tab key events
    event.consume();
    }
  }
}
```

Note that `processKeyEvent` changes focus only on `KEY_PRESSED` events and consumes `KEY_RELEASED` and `KEY_TYPED` events without taking any action. The result is that all Tab and Shift+Tab keystroke events are consumed by the focus manager and will never reach the component with the focus.

This implementation of a custom focus manager is useful if you want to control focus traversal for components, regardless of the order in which they are added to a container or how a layout manager arranges them. A more challenging exercise would be to write a focus manager that manages focus traversal with an algorithm based on component location.

Summary

Focus management is a collaborative effort between the focus manager and individual components. JFC enhances the focus management capabilities of AWT by making some of the classes that manage focus traversal public classes, and by adding to the focus-related methods in the `JComponent` class.

With JFC, you can explicitly set the focus to a component, manage focus changes from components, and detect when components gain and lose the focus. This chapter illustrates each of these techniques with examples. The `HotFocus` example shows you how to set the focus to a component whenever it is under the mouse. `HotFocus2` adds to this example by detecting when components gain the focus and indicating the focus visually. The `ComponentManagedFocus` example shows you how to manage focus from components by subclassing the `JButton` class and adding some methods to set the next and previous components to get the focus.

JFC also allows you to install a custom focus manager to replace the default focus manager for an application. Very few applications will actually need a custom focus manager though—most focus management needs can be handled with the default focus manager. The `CustomFocusManager` example illustrates how to implement a custom focus manager.

Custom Cursors

Applications, especially those that are user-interface intensive with many different types of interface elements, can benefit from the use of unique, custom cursors. Although previous versions of AWT allowed cursors to be changed, applications were limited to a collection of predefined cursors. The Java Foundation Classes include full support for custom cursors on any component.

In this chapter you will learn:

- How to use the `Toolkit` class to query for custom cursor support.

  Support for custom cursors is inherently dependent on the underlying platform. You may have to supply multiple images for each custom cursor if want to take full advantage of the various levels of support available on different platforms.

- How to create a custom cursor from an `Image` object and set a custom cursor for a component.

  After querying for custom cursor support, you can load the appropriate graphic file into an `Image` object and create a custom cursor from the image. You can then set this cursor to be the cursor for any AWT or Swing component.

Toolkit Methods for Custom Cursors

Support for custom cursors is manifested in the `java.awt.Toolkit` class. The `Toolkit` class includes three methods for custom cursors.

```
public Cursor createCustomCursor(Image cursor, Point hotSpot,
                                 String description);
public Dimension getBestCursorSize(int preferredWidth,
                                   int preferredHeight);
public int getMaximumCursorColors();
```

The `getBestCursorSize` and `getMaximumCursorColors` methods query the underlying operating system for the size and color depth that the system supports for cursors. `getBestCursorSize` returns the supported cursor dimension that is closest to the preferred size. If a system supports only a single cursor size, `getBestCursorSize` will return that size. If the underlying system doesn't support custom cursors, `getBestCursorSize` will return a (0, 0) dimension.

> **NOTE**
>
> The `Toolkit` class exists to bind the platform-independent portion of AWT with the native (peer) implementation on each platform. On many operating systems, cursor support is intertwined very closely with the hardware. This is the reason that custom cursor support must be somewhat platform-dependent.
>
> If you try to create a custom cursor from an image whose dimensions or number of colors aren't supported by the underlying operating system, the `Toolkit` implementation will attempt to resize the image and/or reduce the number of colors used by the image. It's best not to depend on `Toolkit` to convert images though—unless the conversion is a really simple one, you probably won't be satisfied with the results.

The `createCustomCursor` method creates a cursor from a given `Image` object, hot spot coordinate, and a localized description of the cursor for Java Accessibility purposes. If the hot spot coordinate is outside the bounds of the cursor, `createCustomCursor` throws an `IndexOutOfBoundsException` exception. Refer to Chapter 33, "Accessibility," for more information on Java accessibility.

Component Methods for Cursors

You use the `Component.setCursor` method to set a custom cursor for a component. This is not a new method—it was available in previous versions of the JDK to set predefined cursors (`WAIT_CURSOR`, `TEXT_CURSOR`, and so on). The `getCursor` method is provided to get the cursor that was previously set for a component.

Cursors are set on a per-component basis. If you want a container and all of its children to use a particular cursor (regardless of whether the cursor is a predefined or a custom cursor), you must call `setCursor` for the container and all of its children.

Example Using a Custom Cursor

Listing 27.1 is the complete source for `CustomCursorDemo`, an example that uses a custom cursor for a button component. To run this example, you will need to obtain or create a GIF file to represent the image used for the custom cursor. The image should be a 32×32 two-color image stored in GIF Format 89a. The filename for the image should be `"Cursor_X_32_32.gif"`.

LISTING 27.1   CustomCursorDemo.java

```java
/* CustomCursorDemo.java
 *
 * Illustrates how to use a custom cursor.
 */

import java.awt.*;
import java.awt.event.*;
import javax.swing.*;

/* App class
 */
public class CustomCursorDemo {

    // Main entry point
    public static void main(String s[]) {
        // Create app panel
        CustomCursorDemoPanel panel = new CustomCursorDemoPanel();

        // Create a frame for app
        JFrame frame = new JFrame("CustomCursorDemo");

        // Add a window listener for window close events
        frame.addWindowListener(new WindowAdapter() {
            public void windowClosing(WindowEvent e) {System.exit(0);}
        });

        // Add app panel to content pane
        frame.getContentPane().add(panel);

        // Set initial frame size and make visible
        frame.setSize (100, 100);
        frame.setVisible(true);
    }
}

/* App panel class
 */
class CustomCursorDemoPanel extends JPanel {
    // Constructor
    public CustomCursorDemoPanel() {
        super();

        // Create a quit button and add to panel
        JButton button = new JButton("Quit");
        button.addActionListener (new ActionListener () {
            public void actionPerformed (ActionEvent e) {
                System.exit (0);
            }
        });
        add(button);
```

```
        // Query for custom cursor support
        Toolkit tk = getToolkit();
        Dimension d = tk.getBestCursorSize(32, 32);
        int colors = tk.getMaximumCursorColors();
        if (!d.equals(new Dimension(0, 0)) && (colors != 0)) {
            // If getBestCursorSize returns a non-zero size and
            // getmaximumCursorColors returns a non-zero value,
            // then platform supports custom cursors

            // You can now load the appropriate image file (GIF or JPEG)
            // for the supported cursor size and number of colors
            // Most platforms will support 32x32, 2-color cursors
            // We assume here that Cursor_X_32_32.gif is a 32x32 2-color
            // gif file. For transparency, use 89a-format gifs.
            Image image = tk.getImage("Cursor_X_32_32.gif");

            if (image != null) {
                try {
                    // Create a custom cursor from the image
                    // Specify hot spot coordinates and a string
                    // containing a description of the cursor
                    // for use with Java Accessibility
                    Cursor cursor = tk.createCustomCursor(image, new
Point(16, 16),

                        "crosshair cursor");

                    // Set the custom cursor for button
                    button.setCursor(cursor);
                }
                catch(Exception exc) {
                    // Catch exceptions so that we
                    // don't try to set a null cursor
                    System.err.println("Unable to create custom cursor.");
                }
            }
        }
}
```

Overview of `CustomCursorDemo` Example

The `CustomCursorDemo` example consists of two classes.

- `CustomCursorDemo` is a public class that contains the `main` entry point method.
- `CustomCursorDemoPanel` is a panel that contains a button that uses a custom cursor.

The main entry point in `CustomCursorDemo` creates a frame (`JFrame`) to contain the application and an instance of `CustomCursorDemoPanel`. After adding the panel to the content pane of the frame, `main` sets the initial size of the frame and calls `setVisible` to make the frame visible.

The constructor for `CustomCursorDemoPanel` creates a button (`JButton`) with an action listener implemented in an anonymous inner class.

Querying for Custom Cursor Support

After adding the button to the panel, the constructor queries the `Toolkit` to determine the dimensions and color depth the platform supports for custom cursors.

```
// Query for custom cursor support
Toolkit tk = getToolkit();
Dimension d = tk.getBestCursorSize(32, 32);
int colors = tk.getMaximumCursorColors();
```

If you intend to create custom cursors that use colors or are a size other than 32×32 pixels, you should supply and load alternate images for platforms that do not support these features. You can then use `getBestCursorSize` and `getMaximumCursorColors` to determine which images to load.

Creating the Custom Cursor from an Image

After querying the `Toolkit` for custom cursor support, the code then tests the results of the queries to ensure that the platform supports custom cursors. If the queries return a non-zero size and non-zero number of colors, the constructor proceeds to load an image named `"Cursor_X_32_32.gif"`. If the image loads properly, the code calls `createCustomCursor` to create a custom cursor and then calls `setCursor` to set the cursor for the button created earlier.

```
if (!d.equals(new Dimension(0, 0)) && (colors != 0)) {
    // load cursor image
    Image image = tk.getImage("Cursor_X_32_32.gif");

    if (image != null) {
        try {
            // Create custom cursor from the image
            Cursor cursor = tk.createCustomCursor(image,
                                        new Point(16, 16),
                                        "crosshair cursor");

            // Set the custom cursor for button
            button.setCursor(cursor);
        }
        catch(Exception exc) {
```

```
            // Catch exceptions so that we don't try to set a null cursor
            System.err.println("Unable to create custom cursor.");
        }
    }
}
```

Note that the cursor is set for the button only if there is no exception when creating the custom cursor. This prevents the application from trying to set a null cursor.

Creating Images for Custom Cursors

Image objects are a platform-independent representation of displayable images. Although you can create Image objects from different types of graphics files, GIF files are probably the best choice to use for custom cursors because they are the most portable across the different platforms that support Java.

Transparency

Cursors require graphic images that use *transparency*, a technique in which a color is defined as the transparent color and pixels of that color are not painted onto the screen. The result is an image that can have any shape and can "float" above whatever image is in the background. In JFC, there is no provision for a mask image to define transparent pixels—you must load the image from a file or resource that is in a format that supports transparency. The GIF89a format is a commonly used format that supports transparency.

Hot Spots

In addition to transparency, another attribute of cursors is that they have a *hot spot*. A hot spot is a coordinate that you specify within the bounds of the cursor image to define precisely the position on the screen to which the cursor is pointing. For example, for an arrowhead-shaped cursor you would set the hot spot to be the point of the arrowhead. You must specify a hot spot coordinate when you call the createCustomCursor method to create a custom cursor. If you specify a hot spot that is outside the bounds of the image you supply, createCustomCursor will throw an IndexOutOfBoundsException exception.

FIGURE 27.1

A 32×32 cursor image.

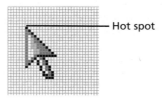

Hot spot

Summary

JFC enhances AWT cursor support by adding the ability to use custom cursors with components. Custom cursors are inherently platform-dependent and may not be supported on all platforms. Custom cursors require peer support—you create them with methods in the `Toolkit` class.

You can create a custom cursor from a GIF file or any other image file format that is supported by the toolkit on the platform running the application. GIF format 89a is one of the most widely supported image formats that supports transparency, an attribute essential to cursor images. Once you've created a custom cursor, you can install it using the same `Component.setCursor` method that you use to set predefined cursors. The `CustomCursorDemo` example illustrates how to create and set a custom cursor. Cursors are set on a component-by-component basis. If you want to use a custom cursor with an object and all of its children, you must explicitly set the cursor for each object that you want to use the custom cursor.

Undo and Redo

CHAPTER 28

The ability to undo and redo operations that change the state of a document (or any kind of data) is a powerful and useful feature. However, it's not the kind of feature that can be retrofitted to an application in the latter stages of development. It's much better to design the underlying data management to support undo from the beginning. The Java Foundation Classes make this task much easier by providing support for undo and redo operations in the javax.swing.undo package.

In this chapter you will learn

- How basic undo support works in JFC

  Implementing undo support in Java is much easier than in C or C++. You'll be surprised at how easy it is to add undo support to your editable objects.

- How to create and manage undoable objects

  To make an object undoable, you simply implement the StateEditable interface. Then you can use the UndoManager class to manage undoable edits represented by the StateEdit class.

Supporting Basic Undo Operations

The JFC javax.swing.undo package provides a complete framework for implementing and managing undoable edits to objects. Although the framework is a part of Swing, you're not restricted to using it with Swing components (components based on JComponent). You can use JFC's undo framework with any type of component, including AWT components.

There are several interfaces and classes you need to be familiar with to implement basic undo support:

- The UndoableEdit interface is an interface for edits that can be undone and redone.

- The AbstractUndoableEdit class is a minimal implementation of the UndoableEdit interface and is the base class for most of the classes in the javax.swing.undo package.

- The StateEditable interface is an interface for objects that are editable.

- The StateEdit class represents the state of an editable object.

- The UndoManager class represents an object that manages edits on a single editable object.

The `AbstractUndoableEdit` Class

The `AbstractUndoableEdit` class is an implementation of the `UndoableEdit` interface. Technically, `AbstractUndoableEdit` is not an abstract class. However, it is used much like an abstract class—you don't instantiate it directly, but instead instantiate subclasses of it. Most of the classes in the undo package are extensions of `AbstractUndoableEdit`.

```
public class AbstractUndoableEdit extends Object implements UndoableEdit
{
    public AbstractUndoableEdit();
    public void undo();
    public void redo();
    public void die();
    public boolean canUndo();
    public boolean canRedo();
    public boolean addEdit(UndoableEdit edit);
    public boolean replaceEdit(UndoableEdit edit);
    public boolean isSignificant();
    public String getPresentationName();
    public String getUndoPresentationName();
    public String getRedoPresentationName();
    public String toString();
}
```

You probably won't instantiate the `AbstractUndoableEdit` class directly, but you'll use its descendants like `StateEdit` and `UndoManager`. The `AbstractUndoableEdit` methods are discussed in the sections related to these classes.

The `StateEditable` Interface

The `StateEditable` interface is an interface that undoable objects must implement. It provides a mechanism for the undo manager to command objects to save and restore their state.

```
public interface StateEditable extends Object {
    public abstract void storeState(Hashtable hashtable);
    public abstract void restoreState(Hashtable hashtable);
}
```

`StateEditable` has only two methods, `storeState` and `restoreState`. Undoable edit objects implement these methods to save and restore their editable data to and from the given hash table.

The `StateEdit` Class

The `StateEdit` class, an extension of `AbstractUndoableEdit`, represents the state of an editable object. Each time you want to make an undoable change to editable data, you create a `StateEdit` object and pass it to the undo manager.

```
public class StateEdit extends AbstractUndoableEdit
{
  // Public constructors
    public StateEdit(StateEditable editableObject);
    public StateEdit(StateEditable editableObject, String
presentationName);
  // Public instance methods
    public void end();
    public String getPresentationName();
    public void redo();
    public void undo();
}
```

To construct a StateEdit, you supply an undoable object (an object that implements StateEditable) and, optionally, a *presentation name* for the edit. A presentation name is a String that can be presented to the user to identify the edit. For example, "delete text" or "paste image."

When you instantiate a StateEdit object, the undoable object associated with the edit will be requested to save its state (via the storeState method that the object must implement as part of the StateEditable interface). After you change the data in the undoable object, you call the StateEdit.end method to end the edit. The object will again be asked to save its state.

The undo method will cause the object to restore its state and the redo method will cause it to redo the changes. You don't normally call these methods directly from an application. Instead, the undo manager calls them when you call the undo manager to undo or redo the last edit.

The UndoManager Class

The UndoManager class represents a manager of undoable edit operations. Normally there is an undo manager for each undoable object. For example, each instance of an undoable text area would have an instance of an undo manager as would each instance of a document in a word processor.

```
public class UndoManager extends CompoundEdit
                          implements UndoableEditListener
{
  // Public constructor
    public UndoManager();
  // Public instance methods
    public synchronized boolean addEdit(UndoableEdit edit);
    public synchronized boolean canRedo();
    public synchronized boolean canUndo();
    public synchronized boolean canUndoOrRedo();
```

```
      public synchronized void discardAllEdits();
      public synchronized int getLimit();
      public synchronized String getUndoPresentationName();
      public synchronized String getUndoOrRedoPresentationName();
      public synchronized String getRedoPresentationName();
      public synchronized void redo();
      public synchronized void setLimit(int limit);
      public String toString();
      public synchronized void undo();
      public void undoableEditHappened(UndoableEditEvent event);
      public synchronized void undoOrRedo();
}
```

When you complete an edit operation, you call the `StateEdit.end` method and then add the completed edit (`StateEdit` object) to an undo manager with `UndoManager.addEdit`. The undo manager keeps the edits in a list in the order in which they occurred. When you call `undo`, the undo manager will undo the most recently added edit. `redo` will redo the most recently undone edit. `canUndo` and `canRedo` query to see if there are any edits to be undone or redone.

The `setLimit` and `getLimit` methods allow you to control the maximum number of edits that an undo manager will store. The default (if you don't call `setLimit`) is 100 edits. The `discardAllEdits` method will cause an undo manager to discard all of its edits.

The `getUndoPresentationName` and `getRedoPresentationName` methods will retrieve the presentation names of the next undoable and redoable edits. If you use `setLimit` to set the edit limit of an undo manager to be one, the edit becomes an undo/redo toggle. In this mode of operation, you use the `undoOrRedo` method to undo or redo the edit, whichever is appropriate in the context of the toggle. The other methods you use in the toggle mode are `getUndoOrRedoPresentationName` and `canUndoOrRedo`.

The `undoableEditHappened` method is present to implement the `UndoableEditListener` interface. You can use this interface to notify an undo manager whenever undoable edits occur.

A Basic Undo Example

Look at an example of a basic undo implementation to see how these classes are used. Listing 28.1 is the complete source for `TextAreaUndoDemo`, an example that extends AWT's `TextArea` class to be undoable. Figure 28.1 shows the completed demo.

FIGURE 28.1

TextAreaUndoDemo
example.

LISTING 28.1   TextAreaUndoDemo.java

```java
/* TextAreaUndoDemo.java
 *
 * Illustrates the basic concepts of supporting undo and redo
 * by adding this support to an extension of the TextArea class.
 */

import java.util.Hashtable;
import java.awt.*;
import java.awt.event.*;
import javax.swing.*;
import javax.swing.undo.*;

/* App class
 */
public class TextAreaUndoDemo {
    // Main entry point
    public static void main(String s[]) {
        // Create app panel
        TextAreaUndoDemoPanel panel = new TextAreaUndoDemoPanel();

        // Create a frame for app
        JFrame frame = new JFrame("TextAreaUndoDemo");

        // Add a window listener for window close events
        frame.addWindowListener(new WindowAdapter() {
            public void windowClosing(WindowEvent e) {System.exit(0);}
        });

        // Add app panel to content pane
        frame.getContentPane().add(panel);

        // Set initial frame size and make visible
        frame.setSize (300, 200);
        frame.setVisible(true);
    }
}


/* App panel class
 */
```

```
class TextAreaUndoDemoPanel extends JPanel {
    // Constructor
    public TextAreaUndoDemoPanel() {
        setLayout(new BorderLayout());

        // create an undoable text area
        // must be final to be accessed by
        // anonymous inner classes (listeners)
        final UndoableTextArea text
                = new UndoableTextArea("Your text here.");

        // create a toolbar for buttons
        JToolBar toolbar = new JToolBar();

        // create undo and redo buttons
        // add listeners for buttons
        JButton buttonUndo, buttonRedo;
        buttonUndo = new JButton("Undo");
        buttonUndo.addActionListener (new ActionListener () {
            public void actionPerformed (ActionEvent event) {
                text.undo ();
            }
        });
        buttonRedo = new JButton("Redo");
        buttonRedo.addActionListener (new ActionListener () {
            public void actionPerformed (ActionEvent event) {
                text.redo ();
            }
        });

        // add buttons to toolbar
        toolbar.add(buttonUndo);
        toolbar.add(buttonRedo);

        // add toolbar and text area to panel
        add(toolbar, "North");
        add(text, "Center");
    }
}

/* UndoableTextArea: An undoable extension of TextArea
 */
class UndoableTextArea extends TextArea implements StateEditable {
    private final static String KEY_STATE
    ➥= "UndoableTextAreaKey";  // hash key
    private boolean textChanged = false;
    private UndoManager undoManager;
    private StateEdit currentEdit;
```

continues

LISTING 28.1   CONTINUED

```java
// Constructors
//
// For all constructors, call corresponding superclass constructor
// and then do initialization to make TextArea undoable
public UndoableTextArea() {
    super();
    initUndoable();
}
public UndoableTextArea(String string) {
    super(string);
    initUndoable();
}
public UndoableTextArea(int rows, int columns) {
    super(rows, columns);
    initUndoable();
}
public UndoableTextArea(String string, int rows, int columns) {
    super(string, rows, columns);
    initUndoable();
}
public UndoableTextArea(String string, int rows,
                        int columns, int scrollbars) {
    super(string, rows, columns, scrollbars);
    initUndoable();
}


// Public methods
//

// method to undo last edit
public boolean undo() {
    try {
        undoManager.undo();
        return true;
    }
    catch (CannotUndoException exc) {
        System.out.println("Can't undo");
        return false;
    }
}

// method to redo last edit
public boolean redo() {
    try {
        undoManager.redo();
        return true;
    }
    catch (CannotRedoException ex) {
```

```
            System.out.println("Can't redo");
            return false;
        }
    }


    // Implementation of StateEditable interface
    //

    // save and restore data to/from hashtable
    public void storeState(Hashtable state) {
        state.put(KEY_STATE, getText());
    }
    public void restoreState(Hashtable state) {
        Object data = state.get(KEY_STATE);
        if (data != null) {
            setText((String)data);
        }
    }


    // Private methods
    //

    // Snapshots current edit state
    private void takeSnapshot() {
        // snapshot only if text changed
        if (textChanged) {
            // end current edit and notify undo manager
            currentEdit.end();
            undoManager.addEdit(currentEdit);

            // reset text changed semaphore and create a new current edit
            textChanged = false;
            currentEdit = new StateEdit(this);
        }
    }

    // Helper method to initialize object to be undoable
    private void initUndoable () {
        // create an undo manager to manage undo operations
        undoManager = new UndoManager();

        // create a StateEdit object to represent the current edit
        currentEdit = new StateEdit(this);

        // add listeners for various edit-related events
        // use these events to determine when to snapshot current edit
```

continues

LISTING 28.1   CONTINUED

```
        // key listener looks for action keys (non-character keys)
        addKeyListener(new KeyAdapter() {
            public void keyPressed(KeyEvent event) {
                if (event.isActionKey()) {
                    // snapshot on any action keys
                    takeSnapshot();
                }
            }
        });

        // focus listener looks for loss of focus
        addFocusListener(new FocusAdapter() {
            public void focusLost(FocusEvent event) {
                // snapshot when control loses focus
                takeSnapshot();
            }
        });

        // text listener looks for text changes
        addTextListener(new TextListener() {
            public void textValueChanged(TextEvent event) {
                textChanged = true;

                // snapshot on every change to text
                // might be too granular to be practical
                //
                // this will shapshot every keystroke when typing
                takeSnapshot();
            }
        });
    }
}
```

Overview of the `TextAreaUndoDemo` Example

The `TextAreaUndoDemo` example consists of three classes:

- `TextAreaUndoDemo` is a public class that contains the `main` entry point method.
- `TextAreaUndoDemoPanel` is a panel (`JPanel`) that contains the user interface for the application.
- `UndoableTextArea`, an extension of `TextArea`, is an implementation of an undoable text area.

The `main` entry point creates a frame (`JFrame`) and an instance of `TextAreaUndoDemoPanel` that it adds to the frame.

The constructor for `TextAreaUndoDemoPanel` creates a toolbar with two buttons (for "Undo" and "Redo"), and an undoable text area (instance of `UndoableTextArea`). The listeners for the buttons call the `undo` and `redo` methods of the undoable text area object. Note that the text variable representing the undoable text area must be declared as `final` so it can be accessed by the anonymous inner classes used to implement the button listeners.

The undo-related functionality of this example is contained in the implementation of the `UndoableTextArea` class, which is discussed in detail in the following section.

Overview of the `UndoableTextArea` Class

As stated earlier, the `UndoableTextArea` class extends the AWT `TextArea` class. In the constructors for this class, the `TextArea` constructors are overridden with constructors that call a helper method, called `initUndoable`, to handle initialization related to making the class undoable. The constructors then call the corresponding superclass constructor.

The `initUndoable` helper method creates an undo manager to manage edits and a `StateEdit` object to represent the current edit state. `initUndoable` then adds listeners for key, focus, and text events. These listeners are all implemented inline in anonymous inner classes. The purpose of the listeners is to detect significant edits to the text area contents so the edits can be registered with the undo manager. Each of these listeners call the `takeSnapshot` helper method to take a snapshot of the current edit state.

`takeSnapshot` checks the `textChanged` flag to see if the contents of the text area have changed since the last snapshot. It's possible, for example, to get a focus lost event when there have been no edits to the text area. The text listener sets the `textChanged` flag when the `textValueChanged` event occurs. If `textChanged` is true, `takeSnapshot` ends the current edit and adds it to the undo manager. It then resets the `textChanged` flag and creates a new `StateEdit` object to represent·the new edit state of the text area.

The final addition to the `TextArea` class is the implementation of the `StateEditable` interface. The two methods in this interface are `storeState` and `restoreState`. The undo manager calls these methods when you request an undo or redo operation. `TextAreaUndoDemo` implements these methods by using the `TextArea` `getText` and `setText` methods to save and restore the entire contents of the text area.

28

UNDO AND REDO

> **Note**
>
> The undo implementation in `TextAreaUndoDemo` is fine for relatively small amounts of text but would be impractical for an application such as a word processor. It would be too expensive (in terms of both performance and memory usage) to save the entire contents of a document each time an edit is made. This type of application requires an undo design that implements undo for lower-level objects such as text elements (paragraphs, words, and so on).

The following sections describe in detail how `TextAreaUndoDemo` implements the `StateEditable` interface and takes snapshots of its edit state.

Implementing the `StateEditable` Interface

Like all objects that are undoable, `UndoableTextArea` implements the `StateEditable` interface. There are only two methods in the `StateEditable` interface: `storeState` and `restoreState`.

```
public abstract void storeState(Hashtable);
public abstract void restoreState(Hashtable);
```

Undoable objects must provide an implementation of these two methods to save and restore the state of the object's editable data. From the following `TextAreaUndoDemo` code fragment, you can see that the `storeState` method simply puts the text area's text (its editable data) into the given hashtable. Likewise, `restoreState` pulls the text out of the hashtable and restores it to the text area.

```
// Implementation of StateEditable interface
//

// save and restore data to/from hashtable
public void storeState(Hashtable state) {
    state.put(KEY_STATE, getText());
}
public void restoreState(Hashtable state) {
    Object data = state.get(KEY_STATE);
    if (data != null) {
        setText((String)data);
    }
}
```

Taking Snapshots of Edits

In addition to implementing the `StateEditable` interface to store and restore edits, objects that support undoable edits must take *snapshots* of their data. Snapshots are representations of the object's editable data taken before and after undoable changes have been made to the data. Implementing a snapshot consists of ending the current edit (represented as a `StateEdit` object), adding it to the undo manager, and then creating a new object to represent the current edit. The following code fragment shows how the `TextAreaUndoDemo` example takes snapshots of its data.

```
// Snapshots current edit state
private void takeSnapshot() {
    // snapshot only if text changed
    if (textChanged) {
        // end current edit and notify undo manager
        currentEdit.end();
        undoManager.addEdit(currentEdit);

        // reset text changed semaphore and create a new current edit
        textChanged = false;
        currentEdit = new StateEdit(this);
    }
}
```

Note that when you end an edit by calling the `end` method, the corresponding object's `storeState` method will be called to store the object's data.

> **NOTE**
>
> The frequency with which you snapshot edits determines the granularity of changes to an undoable object's data. In the `TextAreaUndoDemo` example, the text listener in the `UndoableTextArea` class snapshots edits each time the `textValueChanged` method gets called. This a very granular undo implementation as this method is called on each keystroke.

Supporting Undo with Swing Text Components

The `TextAreaUndoDemo` example demonstrates how to add undo and redo support to an AWT `TextArea` component. To implement undo support in this example, you had to monitor edits made to the text and take snapshots of the text before and after undoable edits. The snapshots were passed to an undo manager that kept track of the edits and managed undo and redo operations. This example provides a good illustration of how to add undo support to AWT components and to your own objects, but is not directly applicable to Swing text components.

Swing text components are quite a bit more sophisticated than their AWT counterparts. They are based on a Model View Controller (MVC) architecture, where the model is represented by an object implementing the Document interface, and the view and controller are combined in a text component based on JTextComponent. See Chapter 7, "Text Components," for details on the architecture of Swing text components.

Much of the underlying plumbing required to support undo and redo is built into the Swing text components. There are only a couple of steps you need to take to provide basic undo support with components based on JTextComponent.

- Create an UndoManager object to manage undo operations.
- Register the UndoManager object as an undoable edit listener to the model (document).

You can then call the undo manager's undo and redo methods to undo and redo edits to the document. Listing 28.2 is the complete source for DocumentUndoDemo, an example that implements undo support on a JTextArea component. The appearance and operation of this example is identical to the previous TextAreaUndoDemo example.

LISTING 28.2   DocumentUndoDemo.java

```java
/* DocumentUndoDemo.java
 *
 * Illustrates how to support undo and redo in
 * components based on the JTextComponent class.
 */

import java.awt.BorderLayout;
import java.awt.event.*;
import javax.swing.*;
import javax.swing.undo.*;
import javax.swing.text.Document;

/* App class
 */
public class DocumentUndoDemo {
    // Main entry point
    public static void main(String s[]) {
        // Create app panel
        DocumentUndoDemoPanel panel = new DocumentUndoDemoPanel();

        // Create a frame for app
        JFrame frame = new JFrame("DocumentUndoDemo");

        // Add a window listener for window close events
        frame.addWindowListener(new WindowAdapter() {
            public void windowClosing(WindowEvent e) {System.exit(0);}
```

```
        });

        // Add app panel to content pane
        frame.getContentPane().add(panel);

        // Set initial frame size and make visible
        frame.setSize (300, 200);
        frame.setVisible(true);
    }
}


/* App panel class
 */
class DocumentUndoDemoPanel extends JPanel {
    // Constructor
    public DocumentUndoDemoPanel() {
        setLayout(new BorderLayout());

        // create a JTextArea component
        JTextArea text = new JTextArea("Your text here.");

        // create an undo manager to manage undo operations
        final UndoManager undoManager = new UndoManager();

        // install undo manager instance as listener for undoable edits
        text.getDocument().addUndoableEditListener(undoManager);

        // create a toolbar for undo/redo buttons
        JToolBar toolbar = new JToolBar();

        // create undo and redo buttons
        // add listeners for buttons
        JButton buttonUndo, buttonRedo;
        buttonUndo = new JButton("Undo");
        buttonUndo.addActionListener (new ActionListener () {
            public void actionPerformed (ActionEvent event) {
                try { undoManager.undo (); }
                catch (CannotUndoException ex) {
                    System.out.println("Can't undo");
                }
            }
        });
        buttonRedo = new JButton("Redo");
        buttonRedo.addActionListener (new ActionListener () {
            public void actionPerformed (ActionEvent event) {
                try { undoManager.redo (); }
                catch (CannotRedoException ex) {
                    System.out.println("Can't redo");
```

continues

28

UNDO AND REDO

LISTING 28.2   CONTINUED

```
                    }
              }
        });

        // add buttons to toolbar
        toolbar.add(buttonUndo);
        toolbar.add(buttonRedo);

        // add toolbar and text area to panel
        add(toolbar, "North");
        add(text, "Center");
    }
}
```

Overview of the `DocumentUndoDemo` Example

The `DocumentUndoDemo` example is quite a bit simpler than the previous
`TextAreaUndoDemo` example. There are only two classes: the main application class,
`DocumentUndoDemo`, and the `DocumentUndoDemoPanel` class, an extension of `JPanel`.

The constructor for the `DocumentUndoDemoPanel` class creates a `JTextArea` component
and an `UndoManager` instance to manage undo operations. The constructor then gets the
document associated with the text area and adds the `UndoManager` instance as an
undoable edit listener for the document.

```
// create a JTextArea component
JTextArea text = new JTextArea("Your text here.");

// create an undo manager to manage undo operations
final UndoManager undoManager = new UndoManager();

// install undo manager instance as listener for undoable edits
text.getDocument().addUndoableEditListener(undoManager);
```

This is all that you need to do to make a Swing text component support undo and redo
operations—everything else (maintaining current edit state, snapshotting edits, saving
and restoring state, and so on) is handled by the text component itself.

All that remains in this example is creating and hooking up the user interface. The
following code fragment creates two buttons with action listeners implemented in
anonymous inner classes. The listeners call the undo and redo methods in the previously
created undo manager to undo and redo edits.

```
// create undo and redo buttons
// add listeners for buttons
JButton buttonUndo, buttonRedo;
```

```
buttonUndo = new JButton("Undo");
buttonUndo.addActionListener (new ActionListener () {
    public void actionPerformed (ActionEvent event) {
        try { undoManager.undo (); }
        catch (CannotUndoException ex) {
            System.out.println("Can't undo");
        }
    }
});
buttonRedo = new JButton("Redo");
buttonRedo.addActionListener (new ActionListener () {
    public void actionPerformed (ActionEvent event) {
        try { undoManager.redo (); }
        catch (CannotRedoException ex) {
            System.out.println("Can't redo");
        }
    }
});
```

Note that you must catch the CannotUndoException and CannotRedoException exceptions when you call the undo manager's undo and redo methods.

A good exercise would be to add some code to this example to disable the undo and redo buttons when undo or redo operations are not available. You can use the undo manager's canUndo and canRedo methods to obtain this information. You could also access the presentation names of the edit associated with the next undo and redo operations and present these names to the user.

Summary

The javax.swing.undo package includes low-level support for adding undo and redo capability to any editable component. The TextAreaUndoDemo example illustrates how to use this package to add undo support to an AWT TextArea component. You can take the same approach and apply it to many different types of editable components. If you're using Swing text components, however, the task of implementing undo and redo is made much easier. Support for undo and redo is built in to all of the components based on JTextComponent. The second example, DocumentUndoDemo, illustrates how to use the undo support built in to Swing text components.

28

UNDO AND REDO

Keyboard
Navigation

29

CHAPTER

Even though you can count on almost any computer having a mouse or some other type of pointing device, it's important to design graphical user interfaces that can be navigated and operated with a keyboard. Accelerators, mnemonics, and shortcuts are user-interface techniques that enable common interface controls like buttons and menus to be navigated and operated with keystrokes. Swing supports all of these techniques, which, coupled with its focus management services, allow you to create graphical user interfaces that are easily navigable with keystrokes.

In this chapter, you will learn

- The difference between accelerators, mnemonics, and shortcuts

  These terms can be confusing—even JFC is sometimes inconsistent in its use of these terms.

- How to add keyboard navigation to menus and buttons

  Accelerators and mnemonics are keyboard navigation techniques associated with menu and button controls. These techniques provide a means of navigating and operating a user interface.

- How to create and use shortcuts

  Shortcuts (sometimes known as hot keys) directly associate a keystroke combination with an action—there are often no user-interface elements associated with shortcuts.

- How to add keyboard navigation to menus and buttons created from action objects

  Rather than explicitly creating menu items and buttons, you can create them by adding action objects to a menu or toolbar container. You can also add keyboard navigation to components created by using this powerful technique.

- How to use mnemonics with labels

  There are times when you may want to use a label to identify a component rather than including text within the component. The JLabel component allows you to specify a mnemonic for an associated component.

About Accelerators, Mnemonics, and Shortcuts

Accelerators, mnemonics, and shortcuts are similar (but not identical) mechanisms for navigating and operating user interfaces with keystrokes. These terms aren't always used consistently, which can lead to some confusion about their meaning. In this book, use the following definitions:

- *Mnemonics* (sometimes called keyboard equivalents) are associated with AbstractButton objects—objects such as JButton, JMenu, and JMenuItem. Mnemonics typically use the Alt key modifier, but modifier key usage depends on the look-and-feel implementation.

- *Shortcuts* (sometimes called hot keys) are associated with action listener objects (objects that implement the ActionListener interface). Shortcuts result in an immediate action, often with no visual changes to the corresponding interface elements (for example, the menus do not pop up on the execution of a shortcut-driven command). With shortcuts, you can specify the modifier key for the keystroke associated with the shortcut. Unlike the accelerator modifier key, the shortcut modifier key does not depend on the look-and-feel implementation.

- *Accelerators* are simply shortcuts that are associated with menu items. They have all of the same characteristics as shortcuts.

It's good design practice to use mnemonics on all menus and menu items, and to use accelerators on all frequently accessed menu items. You should also use mnemonics as much as possible on the user-interface components in dialog boxes. Reserve the use of shortcuts for heavily used, repetitive commands such as zooming in or out on a graphical view.

Using Mnemonics

As stated earlier, mnemonics are associated with textual menus and buttons. Mnemonic keys are often identified by underlining the letter corresponding to the mnemonic key. For example, in the File menu, the mnemonic is usually the "f" key, in which case the "F" in File appears with an underline.

The modifier key for mnemonics depends on the look-and-feel that is used. Most look-and-feel implementations use the Alt key as the modifier.

Adding Mnemonics to Buttons and Menus

The AbstractButton class, the class upon which all Swing buttons and menus are based, includes three methods for setting and getting key mnemonics:

```
public void setMnemonic(int keycode);
public void setMnemonic(char keychar);
public int getMnemonic();
```

The two setMnemonic methods allow you to set a mnemonic by specifying either a virtual key code or a character. The KeyEvent class includes constants for specifying virtual key codes. For example, the following code fragment creates an Exit button and sets its mnemonic to "x."

```
JButton button = new JButton("Exit");
button.setMnemonic(KeyEvent.VK_X);
```

Since the menu classes `JMenu` and `JMenuItem` are extensions of `AbstractButton`, you can use these same two `setMnemonic` methods to set mnemonics for menus.

> **NOTE**
>
> The `JMenuItem` class has a constructor that allows you to specify the mnemonic when you create a textual menu item. The `JMenu` class does not have a similar constructor—you must use the `setMnemonic` method to set a mnemonic with `JMenu` objects.

Example Using Mnemonics

Listing 29.1 is the complete source for `BasicMnemonicDemo`, an application illustrating how to implement a button and a menu with mnemonics. Figure 29.1 shows the output of this code.

FIGURE 29.1

`BasicMnemonicDemo` *example.*

LISTING 29.1   `BasicMnemonicDemo.java`

```
/* BasicMnemonicDemo.java
 *
 * A  basic JFC application with a button
 * and menu that use mnemonics.
 *
 * Illustrates how to set mnemonics for buttons and menus.
 */

import java.awt.BorderLayout;
import java.awt.event.*;
import javax.swing.*;


/* Application class
 */
```

```java
public class BasicMnemonicDemo extends JPanel {

    // Constructor
    public BasicMnemonicDemo() {
        setLayout(new BorderLayout());

        // create an action listener for use with exit button and menu
        ActionListener exitActionListener = new ActionListener() {
            public void actionPerformed(ActionEvent e) {
                System.exit(0);
            }
        };

        // create a non-floatable toolbar
        JToolBar toolbar = new JToolBar();
        toolbar.setFloatable(false);

        // create an exit button, add to toolbar
        JButton button = new JButton("Exit");
        button.addActionListener(exitActionListener);
        button.setMnemonic(KeyEvent.VK_X);
        toolbar.add(button);

        // create a menu bar with a File menu
        JMenuBar menubar = new JMenuBar();
        JMenu menuFile = new JMenu("File");
        menuFile.setMnemonic(KeyEvent.VK_F);
        menubar.add(menuFile);

        // create an Exit menu item, add to File menu
        JMenuItem itemExit = new JMenuItem("Exit",KeyEvent.VK_X);
        itemExit.addActionListener(exitActionListener);
        menuFile.add(itemExit);

        // add toolbar and menu bar to panel
        add(toolbar, BorderLayout.SOUTH);
        add(menubar, BorderLayout.NORTH);
    }

    // The main entry point
    public static void main(String s[]) {
        // create an instance of the app
        BasicMnemonicDemo appPanel = new BasicMnemonicDemo();

        // create a frame for app
        JFrame frame = new JFrame("BasicMnemonicDemo");

        // add a window listener for close events
        frame.addWindowListener(new WindowAdapter() {
```

29

KEYBOARD NAVIGATION

continues

LISTING 29.1   CONTINUED

```
                public void windowClosing(WindowEvent e) {System.exit(0);}
        });

        // add app panel to content frame
        frame.getContentPane().add(appPanel);

        // make frame visible, set initial size
        frame.setVisible(true);
        frame.setSize(200, 150);
    }
}
```

Overview of `BasicMnemonicDemo` Example

The `BasicMnemonicDemo` example consists of a single class, `BasicMnemonicDemo`, which extends `JPanel`. The `main` entry point method creates an instance of this panel and then creates a frame. After adding a window listener for `windowClosing` events, `main` adds the panel to the frame's content pane.

The constructor for the `BasicMnemonicDemo` class creates an action listener implemented in an inner class. This action listener is associated with both the Exit button and the Exit menu item. The action listener's `actionPerformed` method simply exits the application with a call to `System.exit`.

```
// create an action listener for use with exit button and menu
ActionListener exitActionListener = new ActionListener() {
    public void actionPerformed(ActionEvent e) {
        System.exit(0);
    }
};
```

The constructor goes on to create a toolbar, a button, a menu bar, a menu, and a menu item. The constructor uses `setMnemonic` to set mnemonics for the button, menu, and menu item. Note that there is no modifier key specified with mnemonics—the modifier key is determined by the look-and-feel implementation. Most implementations use the Alt key as the modifier key for mnemonics.

```
// create a non-floatable toolbar
JToolBar toolbar = new JToolBar();
toolbar.setFloatable(false);

// create an exit button, add to toolbar
JButton button = new JButton("Exit");
button.addActionListener(exitActionListener);
button.setMnemonic(KeyEvent.VK_X);
toolbar.add(button);
```

```
// create a menu bar with a File menu
JMenuBar menubar = new JMenuBar();
JMenu menuFile = new JMenu("File");
menuFile.setMnemonic(KeyEvent.VK_F);
menubar.add(menuFile);

// create an Exit menu item, add to File menu
JMenuItem itemExit = new JMenuItem("Exit", KeyEvent.VK_X);
itemExit.addActionListener(exitActionListener);
menuFile.add(itemExit);
```

After creating all of the button and menu components, the constructor adds the toolbar and the menu bar to the panel.

```
// add toolbar and menu bar to panel
add(toolbar, BorderLayout.SOUTH);
add(menubar, BorderLayout.NORTH);
```

The result is an application that exits (via the button's action listener) when you press the Alt+X key combination. If you press the Alt+F key combination, the File menu drops down and then if you press Alt+X, the menu's action listener exits the application. Note that this application uses the same action listener for both the button and the menu item, but you could use separate listeners.

> **NOTE**
>
> In addition to the modifier-key combination, some look-and-feel implementations, including the Metal look-and-feel, execute menu item actions when only the mnemonic key is pressed (with no modifier). For an illustration of this behavior, run the `BasicMnemonicDemo` example and press the Alt+F key combination, and then press the X key.

Using Menu Accelerators

In addition to a mnemonic, menu items can have an accelerator. An accelerator is a keystroke combination that immediately invokes the action associated with the menu item. For example, the Exit menu in the preceding example could have an accelerator, Ctrl+X, that quits the application. The keystroke combinations for menu accelerators appear in the right side of the menu item when it is displayed. See Figure 29.2 for an illustration of the appearance of a menu with an accelerator.

The `MenuItem` class has two methods for getting and setting accelerators.

```
public void setAccelerator(KeyStroke keyStroke);
public KeyStroke getAccelerator();
```

Unlike mnemonics, where modifier keys are determined by the look-and-feel implementation, accelerators allow you to specify a modifier key. The setAccelerator method uses the KeyStroke class to specify a keystroke combination that can (but is not required to) include a modifier key.

The KeyStroke Class

The following code gives the signature of the KeyStroke class. This class is used to specify shortcuts as well as menu accelerators. See the "Using Shortcuts (Hot Keys)" section later in this chapter for details on using shortcuts.

```
public class KeyStroke extends Object implements Serializable
{
    // Static methods to get a shared instance of a KeyStroke object
    public static KeyStroke getKeyStroke(char keychar);
    public static KeyStroke getKeyStroke(int keycode, int modifiers,
                                         boolean onRelease);
    public static KeyStroke getKeyStroke(int keycode, int modifiers);
    public static KeyStroke getKeyStrokeForEvent(KeyEvent event);

    public char getKeyChar();
    public int getKeyCode();
    public int getModifiers();
    public boolean isOnKeyRelease();
    public int hashCode();
    public boolean equals(Object);
}
```

The KeyStroke class doesn't have a public constructor—instead, the class provides four class methods to create KeyStroke objects. The following code fragment show how to use three of these class methods to create KeyStroke objects from a key character and a virtual key code combined with a key modifier (Shift, Alt, Ctrl, Meta). The third method creates a KeyStroke that triggers an action on key release—the default is to trigger the action on key press event.

```
// Create a "q" KeyStroke object from a key character
KeyStroke k1 = KeyStroke.getKeyStroke('q');

// Create a "Ctrl+Q" KeyStroke object that activates on key press event
KeyStroke k2 = KeyStroke.getKeyStroke(KeyEvent.VK_Q,
                                      InputEvent.CTRL_MASK);

// Create a "Ctrl+Q" KeyStroke object that activates on key release event
KeyStroke k3 = KeyStroke.getKeyStroke(KeyEvent.VK_Q,
                                      InputEvent.CTRL_MASK,
                                      true);
```

There is also a class method that creates a `KeyStroke` object from a `KeyEvent` object. The ID of the `KeyEvent` object can be either `KEY_PRESSED`, `KEY_RELEASED`, or `KEY_TYPED`.

You can specify any combination of the following constants (or none at all) for the modifier key combination when creating a `KeyStroke` object (see Table 29.1).

TABLE 29.1 Keystroke KEY MODIFIER CONSTANTS

Constant	Meaning
`Event.CTRL_MASK`	The Ctrl key
`Event.ALT_MASK`	The Alt key
`Event.SHIFT_MASK`	The Shift key
`Event.META_MASK`	The Meta key*

Note that the Meta key may not be present on all keyboards.

Example Using an Accelerator

Listing 29.2 is the complete source for `BasicAcceleratorDemo`, an application illustrating the implementation of a menu with a mnemonic and an accelerator. Figure 29.2 shows the output of this code.

FIGURE 29.2

BasicAccelerator Demo example.

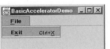

LISTING 29.2   `BasicAcceleratorDemo.java`

```
/* BasicAcceleratorDemo.java
 *
 * A basic JFC application with a menu
 * that has a mnemonic and an accelerator.
 *
 * Illustrates how to set a mnemonic
 * and accelerator for a menu item.
 */

import java.awt.*;
import java.awt.event.*;
import javax.swing.*;


/* Application class
```

29

KEYBOARD
NAVIGATION

continues

LISTING 29.2   CONTINUED

```java
*/
public class BasicAcceleratorDemo extends JPanel {

    // Constructor
    public BasicAcceleratorDemo() {
        setLayout(new BorderLayout());

        // create an action listener for use with exit menu
        ActionListener quitActionListener = new ActionListener() {
            public void actionPerformed(ActionEvent e) {
                System.exit(0);
            }
        };

        // create a menu bar with a File menu
        JMenuBar menubar = new JMenuBar();
        JMenu menuFile = new JMenu("File");
        menuFile.setMnemonic(KeyEvent.VK_F);
        menubar.add(menuFile);

        // create an Exit menu item with mnemonic,
        // set accelerator, action listener
        JMenuItem itemExit = new JMenuItem("Exit", KeyEvent.VK_X);
        itemExit.setAccelerator(KeyStroke.getKeyStroke(KeyEvent.VK_X,
                                                       Event.CTRL_MASK));
        itemExit.addActionListener(quitActionListener);

        // add menu item to menu, add menu bar to panel
        menuFile.add(itemExit);
        add(menubar, BorderLayout.NORTH);
    }

    // The main entry point
    public static void main(String s[]) {
        // create an instance of the app
        BasicAcceleratorDemo appPanel = new BasicAcceleratorDemo();

        // create a frame for app
        JFrame frame = new JFrame("BasicAcceleratorDemo");

        // add a window listener for close events
        frame.addWindowListener(new WindowAdapter() {
            public void windowClosing(WindowEvent e) {System.exit(0);}
        });

        // add app panel to content frame
        frame.getContentPane().add(appPanel);

        // make frame visible, set initial size
```

```
            frame.setVisible(true);
            frame.setSize(200, 100);
    }
}
```

Overview of `BasicAcceleratorDemo` Example

The `BasicAcceleratorDemo` example is structured very much like the previous `BasicMnemonicDemo` example. There is a single class, `BasicAcceleratorDemo`, that extends `JPanel`. The constructor creates an action listener with an `actionPerformed` method that calls `System.exit` to exit the application. This action listener is identical to the action listener in the previous `BasicMnemonicDemo` example.

```
// create an action listener for use with exit menu
ActionListener quitActionListener = new ActionListener() {
    public void actionPerformed(ActionEvent e) {
        System.exit(0);
    }
};
```

After creating a menu bar and menu, the constructor creates a menu item with a mnemonic specified as a virtual key code and calls the `setAccelerator` method to set the accelerator to the Ctrl+X key combination. The constructor then adds an action listener for the menu item.

```
// create an Exit menu item with mnemonic,
// set accelerator, action listener
JMenuItem itemExit = new JMenuItem("Exit", KeyEvent.VK_X);
itemExit.setAccelerator(KeyStroke.getKeyStroke(KeyEvent.VK_X,
                                               Event.CTRL_MASK));
itemExit.addActionListener(quitActionListener);
```

When you run the `BasicAcceleratorDemo` example and press the Ctrl+X key combination, the `actionPerformed` method in the menu item's action listener is called to exit the application.

Using Shortcuts (Hot Keys)

JFC provides a very flexible environment for implementing shortcuts. Unlike mnemonics and accelerators, shortcuts are not associated with a particular user interface control like a button or menu. Instead, shortcuts directly associate a keystroke combination with an action. The shortcut action can be any `ActionListener` object.

> **NOTE**
>
> The JMenu class implements accelerators by using a shortcut to associate a keystroke combination with the menu's action listener.

The JComponent.registerKeyboardAction Method

You can associate shortcuts with any JComponent object by calling the registerKeyboardAction method.

```
public void registerKeyboardAction(ActionListener action,
                                   KeyStroke keystroke,
                                   int condition);
```

The action parameter specifies the action listener whose actionPerformed method will be called when the shortcut is executed. The keystroke parameter specifies the keystroke that will trigger the shortcut. The keystroke is specified by use of a KeyStroke object (see the section on the KeyStroke class earlier in this chapter). The condition parameter specifies the focus conditions under which the shortcut will be triggered.

JComponent also provides the unregisterKeyboardAction and resetKeyboardActions methods to unregister shortcuts. unregisterKeyboardAction will unregister one specific shortcut and resetKeyboardActions will unregister all shortcuts registered for a component.

Focus Conditions for Shortcuts

The reason that the registerKeyboardAction method is a JComponent method is because shortcuts are controlled by the focus condition of the associated component. You must specify one (and only one) of the following JComponent-based constants to specify a focus condition when registering shortcuts:

- WHEN_FOCUSED   To indicate that the action be invoked when the specified keystroke is received while the component has the focus

- WHEN_IN_FOCUSED_WINDOW   To indicate that the action be invoked when the specified keystroke is received while any component in the component's window hierarchy has the focus

- WHEN_ANCESTOR_OF_FOCUSED_COMPONENT   To indicate that the action be invoked when the specified keystroke is received when the component has the focus or an ancestor of the component has the focus

Being able to specify a combination of a keystroke and a focus condition for a shortcut allows you to bind arbitrary key combinations to the appropriate component action in a hierarchical structure of components.

> **NOTE**
>
> It's not allowable to have the same keystroke registered under multiple focus conditions. When you register a keystroke that is already registered as a shortcut, you replace the original shortcut with a new shortcut.

More JComponent Shortcut Methods

The JComponent class has several methods that are useful for working with shortcuts in addition to the methods discussed earlier for registering and unregistering shortcuts:

```
public KeyStroke[] getRegisteredKeyStrokes();
public int getConditionForKeyStroke(KeyStroke keystroke);
public ActionListener getActionForKeyStroke(KeyStroke keystroke);
```

The getActionForKeyStroke method returns the object that will perform the action registered for a given shortcut (registered keystroke).

The getRegisteredKeyStrokes method returns an array of all registered shortcuts.

The getConditionForKeyStroke method returns the focus condition associated with a given shortcut.

A Simple Example Using a Shortcut

Listing 29.3 is the complete source for BasicShortcutDemo, an application illustrating the implementation of a keyboard shortcut. Figure 29.3 shows the output of this code.

FIGURE 29.3

BasicShortcutDemo *example.*

LISTING 29.3   BasicShortcutDemo.java

```
/* BasicShortcutDemo.java
 *
 * A basic JCF application with a Ctrl+Q keyboard shortcut.
 *
```

continues

LISTING 29.3 CONTINUED

```java
 * Illustrates how to create a KeyStroke object and
 * use the registerKeyboardAction method to register
 * the keystroke as a keyboard shortcut.
 */

import java.awt.event.*;
import javax.swing.*;


/* Application class
 */
public class BasicShortcutDemo extends JPanel {

    // App constructor
    public BasicShortcutDemo() {
        // Add some text to the app panel
        add(new JLabel("Press Ctrl+Q to quit."));

        // Create an action listener for registered keystrokes
        ActionListener actionQuit = new ActionListener() {
            public void actionPerformed(ActionEvent e) {
                System.exit(0);
            }
        };

        // Create a keystroke and register it as a shortcut
        KeyStroke keyStrokeQuit
= KeyStroke.getKeyStroke(KeyEvent.VK_Q, InputEvent.CTRL_MASK);
        registerKeyboardAction(actionQuit, keyStrokeQuit,
                             JComponent.WHEN_IN_FOCUSED_WINDOW);
    }

    // The main entry point
    public static void main(String s[]) {
        // Create an instance of the app
        BasicShortcutDemo appPanel = new BasicShortcutDemo();

        // Create a frame for app
        JFrame frame = new JFrame("BasicShortcutDemo");

        // Add a window listener for close events
        frame.addWindowListener(new WindowAdapter() {
            public void windowClosing(WindowEvent e) {System.exit(0);}
        });

        // Add app panel to content frame
        frame.getContentPane().add(appPanel);

        // Make frame visible, set initial size
```

```
        frame.setVisible(true);
        frame.setSize(200, 100);
    }
}
```

Overview of the `BasicShortcutDemo` Example

The `BasicShortcutDemo` example consists of a single class, `BasicShortcutDemo`, that extends `JPanel`. The constructor creates a label to display the text "Press Ctrl+Q to quit." It then creates an action listener for the shortcut, which is implemented in an inner class.

```
// Create an action for registered keystrokes
ActionListener actionQuit = new ActionListener() {
    public void actionPerformed(ActionEvent e) {
        System.exit(0);
    }
};
```

The action listener's `actionPerformed` method exits the application by calling `System.exit`.

After creating the action listener, the constructor creates a `KeyStroke` object and registers it as a keyboard action associated with the `actionQuit` action listener.

```
// Create a keystroke and register it as a shortcut
KeyStroke keyStrokeQuit = KeyStroke.getKeyStroke(KeyEvent.VK_Q,
                                        InputEvent.CTRL_MASK);
registerKeyboardAction(actionQuit, keyStrokeQuit,
                JComponent.WHEN_IN_FOCUSED_WINDOW);
```

This code registers the Ctrl+Q keystroke as a keyboard action that is valid whenever the `BasicShortcutDemo` panel is in a window with the focus; that is, whenever the application has the focus.

Keyboard Navigation with Action Objects

JFC allows you to add `Action` objects directly to menus and toolbars without having to create a menu item or button object. When you use this approach, JFC creates the menu item or button and associates it with the given action. This can be a powerful feature to use if you're designing a user interface that maps actions to more than one control because it allows you to centralize control of the interface in the code for the action object. When you disable an action by calling its `setEnabled` method, JFC will automatically change the state of the corresponding interface controls (buttons and menus) to be disabled.

AbstractButton does not use properties to implement mnemonics and accelerators, so you can't use the Action.putValue method to set these values. Instead, you take the objects returned from the add method you use to add the action to a container. The JToolbar.add method returns an object of type JButton, and the JMenu.add method returns an object of type JMenuItem. You can then call the setMnemonic and setAccelerator methods, as you would if you explicitly created the button or menu item.

Example Using Key Navigation with Action Object

Listing 29.4 is the complete source for KeyNavigationDemo, an example that creates a keyboard-navigable button and menu item from an Action object. Figure 29.4 shows the output of this code.

FIGURE 29.4

KeyNavigationDemo
example.

LISTING 29.4   KeyNavigationDemo.java

```
/* KeyNavigationDemo.java
 *
 * Illustrates how to set mnemonics and
 * key accelerators when implementing buttons
 * and menu items using Action objects.
 */

import java.awt.*;
import java.awt.event.*;
import javax.swing.*;

/* Application class
 */
public class KeyNavigationDemo extends JPanel {

    // Constructor
    public KeyNavigationDemo() {
        setLayout(new BorderLayout());

        // create action for exit command
        AbstractAction actionExit = new AbstractAction() {
            public void actionPerformed(ActionEvent e) {
                System.exit(0);
```

```
            }
        };
        actionExit.putValue(Action.NAME, "Exit");

        // create a non-floatable toolbar
        JToolBar toolbar = new JToolBar();
        toolbar.setFloatable(false);

        // add action to toolbar, set mnemonic for returned button
        JButton buttonExit = toolbar.add(actionExit);
        buttonExit.setMnemonic(KeyEvent.VK_X);

        // create a menu bar with a File menu
        JMenuBar menubar = new JMenuBar();
        JMenu menuFile = new JMenu("File");
        menuFile.setMnemonic(KeyEvent.VK_F);
        menubar.add(menuFile);

        // add action to menu, set mnemonic and
        // accelerator for returned menu item
        JMenuItem itemExit = menuFile.add(actionExit);
        itemExit.setMnemonic(KeyEvent.VK_X);
        itemExit.setAccelerator(KeyStroke.getKeyStroke(KeyEvent.VK_X,
                                                Event.CTRL_MASK));


        // add toolbar and menu bar to panel
        add(toolbar, BorderLayout.SOUTH);
        add(menubar, BorderLayout.NORTH);
    }

    // The main entry point
    public static void main(String s[]) {
        // create an instance of the app
        KeyNavigationDemo appPanel = new KeyNavigationDemo();

        // create a frame for app
        JFrame frame = new JFrame("KeyNavigationDemo");

        // add a window listener for close events
        frame.addWindowListener(new WindowAdapter() {
            public void windowClosing(WindowEvent e) {System.exit(0);}
        });

        // add app panel to content frame
        frame.getContentPane().add(appPanel);

        // make frame visible, set initial size
        frame.setVisible(true);
        frame.setSize(200, 150);
    }
}
```

Overview of the `KeyNavigationDemo` Example

Visually and functionally, the `KeyNavigationDemo` example is identical to the
`BasicShortcutDemo` example. The difference is in the implementation—the
`KeyNavigationDemo` example creates its button and menu item from an `Action` object.
The `KeyNavigation` example uses a single class, `KeyNavigationDemo`, that extends
`JPanel`. The constructor for this class creates an instance of an `AbstractAction` object
whose `actionPerformed` method calls `System.exit` to exit the application. One difference in this example is that it uses an `AbstractAction` object rather than an
`ActionListener` object to represent the exit action. After creating the action, you then
call the `putValue` method to set the name property of the action. This property determines the text that will appear on the button or menu item when the action is added to a
toolbar or menu.

```
// create action for exit command
AbstractAction actionExit = new AbstractAction() {
    public void actionPerformed(ActionEvent e) {
        System.exit(0);
    }
};
actionExit.putValue(Action.NAME, "Exit");
```

After creating a toolbar, the constructor adds the exit action to it and sets the mnemonic
on the returned button object. The following code fragment shows how the action is
added to the toolbar and how a mnemonic is set on the returned button object.

```
// add action to toolbar, set mnemonic for returned button
JButton buttonExit = toolbar.add(actionExit);
buttonExit.setMnemonic(KeyEvent.VK_X);
```

The constructor then creates a menu bar and adds a "File" menu to it. After adding the
exit action to the menu, the code goes on to set a mnemonic and accelerator for the
returned menu item. The following fragment shows how the action is added to the menu,
and how the mnemonic and accelerator are set on the returned menu item object.

```
// add action to menu, set mnemonic and accelerator for returned menu item
JMenuItem itemExit = menuFile.add(actionExit);
itemExit.setMnemonic(KeyEvent.VK_X);
itemExit.setAccelerator(KeyStroke.getKeyStroke(KeyEvent.VK_X,
                                               Event.CTRL_MASK));
```

The result is an application with a single "Exit" button in a toolbar and a "File" menu
with an "Exit" menu item. The mnemonic is Alt+Q for both the button and menu item.
The menu item also has an accelerator, Ctrl+Q.

Creating user interface controls from action objects is a powerful and efficient way to construct both simple and complex user interfaces. For more information on using this technique, see Chapter 4, "JFC Programming Techniques."

Using Mnemonics with Labels

The JLabel component allows you to display a mnemonic and associate it with another component. This technique can be useful if you have some graphical user-interface components that do not display any textual information. Labels are static controls and do not normally respond to user input. However, if you associate a label with a component and specify a mnemonic for the label, pressing the mnemonic key combination will transfer the focus to the associated component.

The following are the JLabel methods for working with mnemonics.:

```
void setDisplayedMnemonic(char character);
void setDisplayedMnemonic(int keycode);
int getDisplayedMnemonic();
void setLabelFor(Component component);
Component getLabelFor();
```

Like buttons and menus, label objects provide two methods that allow you to set a mnemonic by specifying the mnemonic as a character or a virtual key code. However, the names of the methods are different for labels. For buttons and menus, the methods to set and get mnemonics are setMnemonic and getMnemonic. For labels, the methods are setDisplayedMnemonic and getDisplayedMnemonic.

To use a mnemonic with a label, you must associate the label with a component by using the setLabelFor method. The associated component will get the focus whenever the mnemonic key combination is pressed.

Summary

An essential part of good user interface design is providing the ability for users to navigate and operate an application with a keyboard as well as a mouse. Swing components provide three types of keyboard navigation: accelerators, mnemonics, and shortcuts. These keyboard navigation devices are all similar in effect—they allow you to associate a keystroke with a component (or in the case of shortcuts, an action). Depending on the type of component and the current look-and-feel for the application, the associated keystroke will change the focus to the component and/or cause an action to be executed. The use of these keyboard navigation devices is illustrated with three examples: BasicAcceleratorDemo, BasicMnemonicDemo, and BasicShortcutDemo.

Pluggable
Look-and-Feel

CHAPTER 30

One feature of JFC that distinguishes it from other GUI tool kits is its pluggable look-and-feel that abstracts a component's look-and-feel from its implementation. This architecture allows you to dynamically change the look-and-feel of an application.

In this chapter, you will learn:

- About the pluggable look-and-feel architecture

  Pluggable look-and-feel is built on JFC's Model View Controller (MVC) architecture.

- How to use the UI manager

  In addition to allowing you to select a look-and-feel for your application, the UI manager allows you to query for information about installed look-and-feels.

- How to use UI defaults

  Many of the attributes describing how to render components are stored in a hashtable. By changing default attributes such as fonts, borders, and colors, you can change how all instances of a component type are rendered, regardless of the current look-and-feel.

- About themes and how to use them

  Themes allow you to specify attributes such as fonts and colors for a particular look-and-feel.

> **NOTE**
>
> This chapter presents pluggable look-and-feel from the perspective of an application. Chapter 22, "Extending Existing Components," describes how you can use the pluggable look-and-feel architecture to extend JFC components. Chapter 23, "Creating a Custom Look-and-Feel," describes how to create a custom look-and-feel to give all of your applications a distinct user interface. Chapter 24, "Building a Custom Component," describes how to implement the pluggable look-and-feel architecture in custom components.

Overview of Pluggable Look-and-Feel

Because AWT components are implemented by the use of peers, their look-and-feel is determined by the operating system on which the host application is running. JFC, however, implements components without the use of peers so the look-and-feel of its components are not determined by the underlying operating system. Peerless component implementation makes it possible to create applications with a look-and-feel that is consistent across all operating environments. JFC takes this concept one step further by providing an architecture that supports multiple look-and-feel implementations and allows applications to dynamically change their look-and-feel at runtime.

The pluggable look-and-feel implementation benefits from JFC's Model View Controller (MVC) component architecture. In the MVC architecture, a component's visual representation (the view) and response to user input (the controller) are abstracted from its implementation (the model). With JFC components, the view and controller elements of MVC are implemented by the pluggable look-and-feel modules.

The term *UI* and the JFC documentation to represent the view and controller elements of MVC are used throughout this chapter. The object that implements the UI is called the *UI delegate*.

Standard JFC Look-and-Feel Implementations

JFC includes the look-and-feels listed in the following table. In addition to the name of the look-and-feel, Table 30.1 gives the fully qualified class name corresponding to the implementation of each look-and-feel.

TABLE 30.1   LOOK-AND-FEEL CLASS NAMES

Name	Class Name
Metal (Java)	`javax.swing.plaf.metal.MetalLookAndFeel`
CDE/Motif	`com.sun.java.swing.plaf.motif.MotifLookAndFeel`
Windows	`com.sun.java.swing.plaf.windows.WindowsLookAndFeel`
Macintosh	`com.sun.java.swing.plaf.mac.MacLookAndFeel`

The Metal look-and-feel (also known as the Java look-and-feel) is the default look-and-feel implementation—applications that do not explicitly set a specific look-and-feel will run with the Metal look-and-feel. Metal is included as an integral part of JFC and will always be available on platforms that support JFC. The remaining look-and-feel implementations are considered optional parts of JFC and may or may not be present at runtime.

System Versus Cross-Platform Look-and-Feel Implementations

There are two types of look-and-feel implementations.

- *System look-and-feels* are designed to mimic the appearance of native components on a given operating system.

- *Cross-platform look-and-feels* are not designed to appear like native components—instead they are designed to provide a unique look-and-feel not associated with any particular operating system.

The Motif, Windows, and Macintosh look-and-feels are system look-and-feels. The Metal look-and-feel is a cross-platform look-and-feel.

> **NOTE**
>
> Because all look-and-feel implementations are based on a common architecture and constructed without the use of peer components, theoretically they can run on any platform. For example, the Windows look-and-feel should be able to run on a Macintosh. However, due to unresolved copyright issues with operating system vendors, certain system look-and-feels may be restricted to running only on their native operating systems.

Themes

Some look-and-feel implementations support *themes*, an easy way to change certain aspects of the look-and-feel without creating an entirely new look-and-feel implementation. Typically, themes allow you to specify attributes like fonts and color schemes. There is no common approach to implementing themes—each look-and-feel provides its own mechanism for creating and using themes.

UI Defaults

UI defaults are attributes that describe certain aspects of how a component UI is rendered. For example, the defaults for a button UI include the border, background and foreground colors, focus color, and font. JFC maintains the following three levels of defaults:

- *User defaults* are UI attributes defined by the application.
- *Look-and-feel defaults* are UI attributes defined by the current look-and-feel.
- *System defaults* are UI attributes defined in the abstract `BasicLookAndFeel` class, the class from which all look-and-feel implementations extend.

Look-and-feel implementations query the UI manager to get the attributes required to render the UI for components. The preceding list gives the levels of defaults in order of precedence as maintained by the UI manager. For example, user defaults take precedence over look-and-feel defaults, which take precedence over system defaults.

You can use the UI manager to set user defaults that override the defaults of the current look-and-feel. By setting user defaults, you can make minor changes to the appearance of an existing look-and-feel without having to actually create your own look-and-feel implementation. For example, you can use UI defaults to change the font size of menus in a JFC application.

Using the UI Manager

The UI manager provides applications with an interface for managing pluggable look-and-feels. It includes the ability to query for installed look-and-feels, install and uninstall look-and-feels, and set and get UI defaults. The UI manager is also used by look-and-feel implementations to get the UI defaults required to render a component UI. This section deals mainly with using the UI manager from the perspective of an application. Chapters 23 and 24 provide additional information on using the UI manager from the perspectives of a look-and-feel and a component.

The `UIManager` Class

Listing 30.1 gives the signature of the `UIManager` class.

LISTING 30.1 `UIManager` CLASS SIGNATURE

```
public class UIManager extends Object implements Serializable
{
  // Public class methods
    public static void addAuxiliaryLookAndFeel(LookAndFeel laf);
public static synchronized void addPropertyChangeListener(
➥PropertyChangeListener listener);
    public static Object get(Object key);
    public static LookAndFeel[] getAuxiliaryLookAndFeels();
    public static Border getBorder(Object key);
    public static Color getColor(Object key);
    public static String getCrossPlatformLookAndFeelClassName();
    public static UIDefaults getDefaults();
    public static Dimension getDimension(Object key);
    public static Font getFont(Object key);
    public static Icon getIcon(Object key);
    public static Insets getInsets(Object key);
```

continues

30

PLUGGABLE LOOK-AND-FEEL

LISTING 30.1 CONTINUED

```
    public static UIManager.LookAndFeelInfo[] getInstalledLookAndFeels();
    public static int getInt(Object key);
    public static LookAndFeel getLookAndFeel();
    public static UIDefaults getLookAndFeelDefaults();
    public static String getString(Object key);
    public static String getSystemLookAndFeelClassName();
    public static ComponentUI getUI(JComponent component);
public static void installLookAndFeel(
➥UIManager.LookAndFeelInfo info);
    public static void installLookAndFeel(String name, String className);
    public static Object put(Object key, Object value);
    public static boolean removeAuxiliaryLookAndFeel(LookAndFeel laf);
public static synchronized void removePropertyChangeListener(
➥PropertyChangeListener listener);
public static void setInstalledLookAndFeels(
➥UIManager.LookAndFeelInfo[] infos);
    public static void setLookAndFeel(LookAndFeel laf);
    public static void setLookAndFeel(String className);
  // Public inner classes
    public static class UIManager.LookAndFeelInfo extends Object {
        public LookAndFeelInfo(String name, String className);
        public String getClassName();
        public String getName();
        public String toString();
    }
}
```

There is no constructor for `UIManager` because all of its members are static. There are
two groups of methods in `UIManager`: methods for managing look-and-feels and methods
for managing UI defaults.

Methods to Manage Look-and-Feels

The `getInstalledLookAndFeels` method returns an array of `UIManager.`
`LookAndFeelInfo` objects that contains the name and class name of all installed look-
and-feel implementations, while the `getLookAndFeel` method returns the current look-
and-feel.

The `getSystemLookAndFeelClassName` returns the class name of the look-and-feel
associated with the system on which the application is running. For example, if the
application is running on Solaris, this method will return the class name of the Motif
look-and-feel. `getCrossPlatformLookAndFeel` returns the class name of the cross-
platform look-and-feel, which is the Metal look-and-feel.

UIManager includes two versions of the installLookAndFeel method to install a new look-and-feel. One of these methods allows you to describe the look-and-feel to install by specifying its name and class name. The other installLookAndFeel method allows you to specify the look-and-feel with a UIManager.LookAndFeelInfo object. Installing a look-and-feel makes it available to the UIManager—it does not set the current look-and-feel for the application. The setInstalledLookAndFeels method installs multiple look-and-feels with a single method call. The LookAndFeelInfo class is used by several ·UIManager methods to represent a user-presentable description of a look-and-feel.

The two setLookAndFeel methods are the methods that actually set the current look-and-feel. One method allows you to specify the look-and-feel by class name and the other allows you to specify it with a LookAndFeel object. Note that if you set a new look-and-feel after your components have been realized, you must call the updateUI method on all components before they can be redrawn with the new look-and-feel. The SwingUtilities class provides the updateComponentTreeUI method to update the UI on an entire component hierarchy.

There are two methods, addPropertyChangeListener and removeProperty-ChangeListener, that add and remove a property change listener for the UI manager. The UI manager fires a propertyChange event whenever you set a new look-and-feel.

Methods to Manage UI Defaults

The UIManager class includes the getDefaults method to return the current UI default settings. This method takes into account the three levels of defaults and returns the highest level default with a non-null key. getLookAndFeelDefaults returns the defaults from the look-and-feel level of UI defaults. Both methods return defaults in the form of a UIDefaults object, which is an extension of a hash table.

The get method is a general-purpose method to retrieve a specific default setting given a key. It returns an object of type Object. The getBorder, getColor, getDimension, getFont, getIcon, getInsets, getInt, and getString methods are special-purpose default retrieval methods that return objects of the appropriate type. There are corresponding put methods that will change UI default values.

The getUI method creates a look-and-feel–specific UI delegate (ComponentUI) for a given component. This method is used by component model implementations to render the visual representation of the component and to listen for user input gestures.

Example Querying for Look-and-Feel Information

Listing 30.2 is the complete source for LAFInfoDemo, an application that utilizes the UI manager to get and display information about the available look-and-feels (see Figure 30.1).

FIGURE 30.1

LAFInfoDemo
*example displays
information about
available look-
and-feels.*

LISTING 30.2   LAFInfoDemo.java

```java
/* LAFInfoDemo.java
 *
 * Illustrates how to query the UI manager
 * to get look and feel information.
 */

import java.awt.*;
import java.util.*;
import java.awt.event.*;
import javax.swing.*;

/* Application class
 */
public class LAFInfoDemo {

    // Main entry point
    public static void main(String s[]) {
        // Create app panel
        LAFInfoDemoPanel panel = new LAFInfoDemoPanel();

        // Create a frame for app
        JFrame frame = new JFrame("LAFInfoDemo");

        // Add a window listener for window close events
        frame.addWindowListener(new WindowAdapter() {
            public void windowClosing(WindowEvent e) {System.exit(0);}
        });
```

```
            // Add app panel to content pane
            frame.getContentPane().add(panel);

            // Set initial frame size and make visible
            frame.setSize (400, 300);
            frame.setVisible(true);
        }
    }

    /* App panel class
     */
    class LAFInfoDemoPanel extends JPanel {
        // Constructor
        public LAFInfoDemoPanel () {
            setLayout(new BorderLayout());

            // create and configure scrollable text area to display info
            JTextArea textArea = new JTextArea();
            textArea.setEditable(false);
            JScrollPane scrollpane = new JScrollPane();
            scrollpane.getViewport().add(textArea);
            add(scrollpane, BorderLayout.CENTER);

            // fill text area with look and feel info
            textArea.setText(getLAFInfo());
        }

    // Private method to get look and feel info,
        // which is returned in a String
        private String getLAFInfo() {
            String s = "";

            // Build string from headings and info from UI Manager

            s = s.concat("Current look and feel:\n");
            s = s.concat(UIManager.getLookAndFeel().getName());

            s = s.concat("\n\nInstalled look and feels:\n");
    UIManager.LookAndFeelInfo info[]
                = UIManager.getInstalledLookAndFeels();
            for(int i = 0; i < info.length; i++) {
                s = s.concat(info[i].getName() + "\n");
            }

            s = s.concat("\nAuxiliary look and feels:\n");
            LookAndFeel auxinfo[] = UIManager.getAuxiliaryLookAndFeels();
            if (auxinfo != null) {
                for(int i = 0; i < auxinfo.length; i++) {
                    s = s.concat(auxinfo[i].getName());
```

continues

30

**PLUGGABLE
LOOK-AND-FEEL**

LISTING 30.2   CONTINUED

```
            }
    }
    else {
        s = s.concat("None\n");
    }

    s = s.concat("\nCross-platform look and feel class name:\n");
    s = s.concat(UIManager.getCrossPlatformLookAndFeelClassName());

    s = s.concat("\n\nSystem look and feel class name:\n");
    s = s.concat(UIManager.getSystemLookAndFeelClassName());

    return(s);
    }
}
```

Overview of the `LAFInfoDemo` Example

The `LAFInfoDemo` example consists of two classes: `LAFInfoDemo` and `LAFInfoDemoPanel`. The `LAFInfoDemo` class is a public class containing the `main` entry point method. The `main` method creates a frame for the application and adds an instance of the `LAFInfoDemoPanel` class to the frame. The interesting part of the application is in the `LAFInfoDemoPanel` class.

The constructor `LAFInfoDemoPanel` class creates a scrollable text area to display the information obtained from the UI manager. It then calls a private method, `getLAFInfo`, to get a string containing the look-and-feel information. The `getLAFInfo` method builds a string by concatenating heading strings with strings obtained by calling static class methods in the `UIManager` class. For example, the following code fragment concatenates the name of the current look-and-feel to a string represented by variable s.

```
s = s.concat("Current look and feel:\n");
s = s.concat(UIManager.getLookAndFeel().getName());
```

To get a list of all installed look-and-feels, `LAFInfoDemo` uses the `UIManager` method `getInstalledLookAndFeels`, as shown in the following code fragment.

```
s = s.concat("\n\nInstalled look and feels:\n");
UIManager.LookAndFeelInfo info[] = UIManager.getInstalledLookAndFeels();
for(int i = 0; i < info.length; i++) {
    s = s.concat(info[i].getName() + "\n");
}
```

The `getInstalledLookAndFeels` method returns an array of `LookAndFeelInfo` objects (`LookAndFeelInfo` is an inner class of the `UIManager` class). This construction is useful for presenting a user with a menu of look-and-feels from which to choose, as illustrated by the next example, LAFInfoDemo2.

Setting the Look-and-Feel

The default look-and-feel for JFC applications is the Java look-and-feel (also known as the Metal look-and-feel). If you want to use a different look-and-feel in your application, you can call the UIManager.setLookAndFeel method to set the look-and-feel to any look-and-feel that is available on the platform on which the application is running.

To set a look-and-feel with setLookAndFeel, you specify the look-and-feel by its class name. For example, the following line of code sets the look-and-feel to the CDE/Motif look-and-feel.

```
UIManager.setLookAndFeel(
➥"com.sun.java.swing.plaf.motif.MotifLookAndFeel");
```

Instead of using a particular look-and-feel, you may want to set up your application to use the system look-and-feel—the look-and-feel corresponding to the platform on which the application is running. The following line of code sets the look-and-feel to the system look-and-feel.

```
UIManager.setLookAndFeel(UIManager.getSystemLookAndFeelClassName());
```

Ideally, you should set the look-and-feel before constructing any Swing components. If you set the look-and-feel after constructing Swing components, you must call the components' updateUI method to update the UI delegates to the delegates associated with the new look-and-feel.

> **NOTE**
>
> The SwingUtilities class provides a handy method, updateComponentTreeUI, for updating UI delegates on an entire component tree.

Example Setting the Look-and-Feel

Listing 30.3 is the complete source for LAFInfoDemo2, an example similar to the previous LAFInfoDemo example, with the addition of a menu that allows you to select a look-and-feel from a menu of installed look-and-feels (see Figure 30.2).

FIGURE 30.2

LAFInfoDemo2
*example allows
you to select a
look-and-feel.*

LISTING 30.3   LAFInfoDemo2.java

```java
/* LAFInfoDemo2.java
 *
 * Illustrates how to add a menu to an application
 * to allow user to select desired look and feel.
 */

import java.awt.*;
import java.util.*;
import java.awt.event.*;
import javax.swing.*;
import java.beans.PropertyChangeListener;
import java.beans.PropertyChangeEvent;

/* Application class
 */
public class LAFInfoDemo2 {

    // Main entry point
    public static void main(String s[]) {
        // Create app panel
        final LAFInfoDemo2Panel panel = new LAFInfoDemo2Panel();

        // Create a frame for app
        JFrame frame = new JFrame("LAFInfoDemo2");

        // Add a window listener for window close events
        frame.addWindowListener(new WindowAdapter() {
            public void windowClosing(WindowEvent e) {System.exit(0);}
        });

        // Add app panel to content pane
        frame.getContentPane().add(panel);

        // add listener for look and feel property changes
UIManager.addPropertyChangeListener(
➥new PropertyChangeListener() {
```

```
            public void propertyChange(PropertyChangeEvent event) {
                // update UI for all panel components
                SwingUtilities.updateComponentTreeUI(panel);
            }
        });

        // Set initial frame size and make visible
        frame.setSize (400, 300);
        frame.setVisible(true);
    }
}

/* App panel class
 */
class LAFInfoDemo2Panel extends JPanel {
    JTextArea textArea = null;

    // Constructor
    public LAFInfoDemo2Panel () {
        setLayout(new BorderLayout());

// create a menu bar with "Options" menu
        // and "Look and Feel" submenu
        JMenuBar menubar = new JMenuBar();
        JMenu menuOptions = new JMenu("Options");
        JMenu submenuLAF = new JMenu("Look and Feel");

        // create group for radio button menu items
        ButtonGroup group = new ButtonGroup();

        // construct menu items for each installed laf
        LAFMenuItem itemCurrentLAF = null;
String classnameCurrentLAF
            = UIManager.getLookAndFeel().getClass().getName();
        UIManager.LookAndFeelInfo info[]
            = UIManager.getInstalledLookAndFeels();
        for(int i = 0; i < info.length; i++) {
            // create menu item
            LAFMenuItem item = new LAFMenuItem(info[i].getName(),
                                        info[i].getClassName());

            // add to menu and group
            submenuLAF.add(item);
            group.add(item);

            // remember item that represents current look and feel
            if(info[i].getClassName().equals(classnameCurrentLAF)) {
                itemCurrentLAF = item;
            }
        }
```

continues

LISTING 30.3   CONTINUED

```java
// add submenu to menu, menu to menu bar, menu bar to panel
        menuOptions.add(submenuLAF);
        menubar.add(menuOptions);
        add(menubar, BorderLayout.NORTH);

        // create scrollable text area to display look and feel info
        textArea = new JTextArea();
        textArea.setEditable(false);
        JScrollPane scrollpane = new JScrollPane();
        scrollpane.getViewport().add(textArea);
        add(scrollpane, BorderLayout.CENTER);

        // update contents of text area with look and feel info
        updateLAFInfo();

        // select menu item representing current look and feel
        itemCurrentLAF.setSelected(true);
    }

    // JComponent override to detect look and feel changes
    // This is needed to update displayed look and feel info
    // when change to look and feel is detected.
    public void updateUI() {
        super.updateUI();

        // update displayed look and feel info
        updateLAFInfo();
    }

    // Private method to update look and feel info displayed in text area
    private void updateLAFInfo() {
        if(textArea != null) {
            // ensure setText is called on event-dispatch thread
            SwingUtilities.invokeLater(new Runnable() {
                public void run() {
                    textArea.setText(getLAFInfo());
                }
            });
        }
    }

// Private method to get look and feel info,
    // which is returned in a String
    private String getLAFInfo() {
        String s = "";

        // Build string from headings and info from UI Manager

        s = s.concat("Current look and feel:\n");
```

```
            s = s.concat(UIManager.getLookAndFeel().getName());

            s = s.concat("\n\nInstalled look and feels:\n");
    UIManager.LookAndFeelInfo info[]
            = UIManager.getInstalledLookAndFeels();
            for(int i = 0; i < info.length; i++) {
                s = s.concat(info[i].getName() + "\n");
            }

            s = s.concat("\nAuxiliary look and feels:\n");
            LookAndFeel auxinfo[] = UIManager.getAuxiliaryLookAndFeels();
            if (auxinfo != null) {
                for(int i = 0; i < auxinfo.length; i++) {
                    s = s.concat(auxinfo[i].getName());
                }
            }
            else {
                s = s.concat("None\n");
            }

            s = s.concat("\nCross-platform look and feel class name:\n");
            s = s.concat(UIManager.getCrossPlatformLookAndFeelClassName());

            s = s.concat("\n\nSystem look and feel class name:\n");
            s = s.concat(UIManager.getSystemLookAndFeelClassName());

            return(s);
        }
    }

    /* Class representing look and feel menu item
     *
     * Constructs a radio button menu item from a given look and feel name.
     * When item is selected, sets given look and feel.
     */
    class LAFMenuItem extends JRadioButtonMenuItem {
        private String lafClassName;

        // Constructor
        public LAFMenuItem(String name, String className) {
            super(name);

            // save look and feel class name in class data
            lafClassName = className;

            // add listener to detect menu selection
            addItemListener(new ItemListener() {
                public void itemStateChanged(ItemEvent event) {
                    if(event.getStateChange() == ItemEvent.SELECTED) {
```

continues

30

PLUGGABLE LOOK-AND-FEEL

LISTING 30.3   CONTINUED

```
                    try {
                        // set look and feel
                        UIManager.setLookAndFeel(lafClassName);
                    }
                    catch (Exception exc) {
System.out.println("Unable to set LAF");
                    }
                }
            }
        });
    }
}
```

Overview of the `LAFInfoDemo2` Example

The `LAFInfoDemo2` example is structured identically to the previous `LAFInfoDemo` example with the exception of an additional class, `LAFMenuItem`, that is used to represent a look-and-feel menu item. The interesting part of the example is contained in the `LAFInfoDemo2Panel` and `LAFMenuItem` classes.

The following code fragment from the `LAFInfoDemo2Panel` constructor creates a menu item for each installed look-and-feel and adds it to the "Look-and-Feel" menu.

```
// construct menu items for each installed laf
LAFMenuItem itemCurrentLAF = null;
String classnameCurrentLAF
    = UIManager.getLookAndFeel().getClass().getName();
UIManager.LookAndFeelInfo info[] = UIManager.getInstalledLookAndFeels();
for(int i = 0; i < info.length; i++) {
    // create menu item
    LAFMenuItem item = new LAFMenuItem(info[i].getName(),
                                       info[i].getClassName());

    // add to menu and group
    submenuLAF.add(item);
    group.add(item);

    // remember item that represents current look and feel
    if(info[i].getClassName().equals(classnameCurrentLAF)) {
        itemCurrentLAF = item;
    }
}
```

The first thing you do is get and save the class name of the current look-and-feel. This allows you to determine which menu item represents the current look-and-feel so you can show that item as selected when the application is run. Next, you get a list of the installed look-and-feels by calling the `UIManager` method `getInstalledLookAndFeels`.

This method returns an array of `LookAndFeelInfo` objects. Then you create a menu item for each `LookAndFeelInfo` object in the array.

Menu items are represented by the `LAFMenuItem` class, an extension of `JRadioButtonMenuItem`. The following fragment is the source for the `LAFMenuItem` class.

```
class LAFMenuItem extends JRadioButtonMenuItem {
    private String lafClassName;

    // Constructor
    public LAFMenuItem(String name, String className) {
        super(name);

        // save look and feel class name in class data
        lafClassName = className;

        // add listener to detect menu selection
        addItemListener(new ItemListener() {
            public void itemStateChanged(ItemEvent event) {
                if(event.getStateChange() == ItemEvent.SELECTED) {
                    try {
                        // set look and feel
                        UIManager.setLookAndFeel(lafClassName);
                    }
                    catch (Exception exc) {
System.out.println("Unable to set LAF");
                    }
                }
            }
        });
    }
}
```

Note that the class contains a single data member, `lafClassName`. This member is used to store the class name for the look-and-feel. This class name is passed to the constructor along with the user-presentable name of the look-and-feel. The item listener for the menu item uses this class name to set the look-and-feel when the menu item is selected.

If the item listener (implemented in an anonymous inner class) determines that the menu item has been selected, it calls the `UIManager` method `setLookAndFeel` to set the look-and-feel.

The `UIDefaults` Class

Listing 30.4 is the signature of the `UIDefaults` class, a class representing a complete set of UI defaults stored in a hash table. There can be several hundred entries in a typical `UIDefaults` hash table returned by the `getDefaults` method. Note that the `UIManager` class provides much of the same functionality as this class.

LISTING 30.4 UIDefaults CLASS SIGNATURE

```
public class UIDefaults extends Hashtable
{
  // Public constructors
    public UIDefaults();
    public UIDefaults(Object[] keyValueList);
  // Public class methods
    public Object get(Object key);
    public Object put(Object key, Object value);
    public void putDefaults(Object[] defaults keyValueList);
    public Font getFont(Object key);
    public Color getColor(Object key);
    public Icon getIcon(Object key);
    public Border getBorder(Object key);
    public String getString(Object key);
    public int getInt(Object key);
    public Insets getInsets(Object key);
    public Dimension getDimension(Object key);
    public Class getUIClass(String id, ClassLoader loader);
    public Class getUIClass(String id);
    public ComponentUI getUI(JComponent component);
public synchronized void addPropertyChangeListener(
➥PropertyChangeListener listener);
    public synchronized void removePropertyChangeListener(
➥PropertyChangeListener listener);
  // Public inner classes
    public abstract class UIDefaults.LazyValue extends Object {
        public abstract Object createValue(UIDefaults defaults);
    }
    public abstract class UIDefaults.ActiveValue extends Object {
        public abstract Object createValue(UIDefaults defaults);
    }
}
```

UIDefaults has two constructors—one constructor that creates an empty UI defaults object and another constructor that creates a UI defaults object with entries created from a given array of objects.

The class has the usual hashtable get and put methods as well as a host of methods to get specific types of defaults: getBorder, getColor, getFont, getIcon, and getString.

There is also a getUI method to create a look-and-feel–specific UI delegate (ComponentUI) for a given component.

The addPropertyChangeListener and removePropertyChangeListener methods allow you to add and remove a property change listener for changes to UI default settings.

Example Getting UI Defaults

Listing 30.5 is the complete source for `DumpDefaults`, an application that displays the current UI defaults settings in a text area (see Figure 30.3).

FIGURE 30.3

DumpDefaults
*example displays
current UI
defaults settings.*

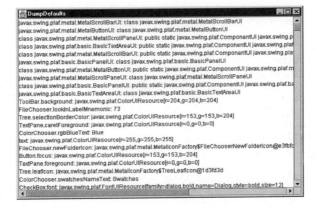

LISTING 30.5   DumpDefaults.java

```java
/* DumpDefaults.java
 *
 * Dumps the UI defaults settings to a text area.
 */

import java.awt.*;
import java.util.*;
import java.awt.event.*;
import javax.swing.*;

/* Application class
 */
public class DumpDefaults {

    // Main entry point
    public static void main(String s[]) {
        // Create app panel
        DumpDefaultsPanel panel = new DumpDefaultsPanel();

        // Create a frame for app
        JFrame frame = new JFrame("DumpDefaults");

        // Add a window listener for window close events
        frame.addWindowListener(new WindowAdapter() {
            public void windowClosing(WindowEvent e) {System.exit(0);}
        });
```

continues

LISTING 30.5 CONTINUED

```java
            // Add app panel to content pane
            frame.getContentPane().add(panel);

            // Set initial frame size and make visible
            frame.setSize (600, 400);
            frame.setVisible(true);
        }
    }

    /* App panel class
     */
    class DumpDefaultsPanel extends JPanel {
        // Constructor
        public DumpDefaultsPanel () {
            setLayout(new BorderLayout());

            // create and configure scrollable text area to display info
            JTextArea textArea = new JTextArea();
            textArea.setEditable(false);
            JScrollPane scrollpane = new JScrollPane();
            scrollpane.getViewport().add(textArea);
            add(scrollpane, BorderLayout.CENTER);

            // fill text area with look and feel info
            textArea.setText(getDefaults());
        }

        // Private method to get current ui defaults,
        // and return them in a String
        private String getDefaults() {
            String s = "";

            // get ui defaults
            UIDefaults defaults = UIManager.getDefaults();

            // enumerate contents of defaults,
            // concatenate to string in format "key: element"
            Enumeration keys = defaults.keys();
            Enumeration elements = defaults.elements();
            while(keys.hasMoreElements() && elements.hasMoreElements()) {
    s = s.concat(keys.nextElement()
                    + ": " + elements.nextElement() + "\n");
            }

            return(s);
        }
    }
```

The DumpDefaults example creates a text area and calls a private method, getDefaults, to get a string containing a description of the current UI default settings. The example then sets the text in the text area to the string containing the UI default settings. For a complete listing of all UI default settings, see UIManager.txt on the CD-ROM.

To get the defaults table, the private getDefaults method calls the static class method UIManager.getDefaults, which returns the defaults in a UIDefaults object. getDefaults then dumps the contents of the defaults table (which is a hashtable) to a string by enumerating all of the keys and elements in the table. It concatenates each key and a string representation of the associated element object to a single string that it returns to the caller.

Example Setting User Defaults

Listing 30.6 is the complete source for ChangeDefaultsDemo, an application that uses the UI defaults to change the font size of menus (see Figure 30.4).

FIGURE 30.4

ChangeDefaultsDemo *example uses UI defaults to change menu font sizes.*

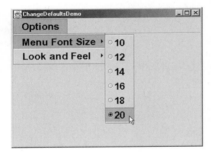

LISTING 30.6   ChangeDefaultsDemo.java

```
/* ChangeDefaultsDemo.java
 *
 * Illustrates how to change the UI default settings.
 * This example allows the user to change the menu font size
 * independently of the look and feel chosen.
 */

import java.util.*;
import java.awt.*;
import java.awt.event.*;
import javax.swing.*;
import javax.swing.plaf.FontUIResource;
import java.beans.PropertyChangeEvent;
import java.beans.PropertyChangeListener;
```

continues

LISTING 30.6   CONTINUED

```
/* Application class
 */
public class ChangeDefaultsDemo {

    // Main entry point
    public static void main(String s[]) {
        // create app panel
final ChangeDefaultsDemoPanel panel
            = new ChangeDefaultsDemoPanel();

        // create a frame for app
        JFrame frame = new JFrame("ChangeDefaultsDemo");

        // add a window listener for window close events
        frame.addWindowListener(new WindowAdapter() {
            public void windowClosing(WindowEvent e) {System.exit(0);}
        });

        // add app panel to content pane
        frame.getContentPane().add(panel);

        // implement listener for UI-releated property changes
        PropertyChangeListener lafChangeListener
➡= new PropertyChangeListener() {
            public void propertyChange(PropertyChangeEvent event) {
                // update UI for all panel components
                SwingUtilities.updateComponentTreeUI(panel);
            }
        };
        // add listener to UI manager and UI defaults
        UIManager.addPropertyChangeListener(lafChangeListener);
UIManager.getDefaults().addPropertyChangeListener
➡(lafChangeListener);

        // set initial frame size and make visible
        frame.setSize (400, 300);
        frame.setVisible(true);
    }
}

/* App panel class
 */
class ChangeDefaultsDemoPanel extends JPanel {
    // Constructor
    public ChangeDefaultsDemoPanel () {
        setLayout(new BorderLayout());

        // create a menu bar with "Options" menu
        JMenuBar menubar = new JMenuBar();
```

```
        JMenu menuOptions = new JMenu("Options");

        // create groups for radio button menu items
        ButtonGroup group1 = new ButtonGroup();
        ButtonGroup group2 = new ButtonGroup();

        // to keep track of which radio button menu items
        // should be selected when app is run
        JMenuItem itemSelected1 = null;
        JMenuItem itemSelected2 = null;

// create "Menu Font Size" submenu and
        // add to Options menu and group
        JMenu submenuFontSize = new JMenu("Menu Font Size");
        JRadioButtonMenuItem itemSize10 = new JRadioButtonMenuItem("10");
        JRadioButtonMenuItem itemSize12 = new JRadioButtonMenuItem("12");
        JRadioButtonMenuItem itemSize14 = new JRadioButtonMenuItem("14");
        JRadioButtonMenuItem itemSize16 = new JRadioButtonMenuItem("16");
        JRadioButtonMenuItem itemSize18 = new JRadioButtonMenuItem("18");
        JRadioButtonMenuItem itemSize20 = new JRadioButtonMenuItem("20");
        group1.add(itemSize10);
        group1.add(itemSize12);
        group1.add(itemSize14);
        group1.add(itemSize16);
        group1.add(itemSize18);
        group1.add(itemSize20);
        submenuFontSize.add(itemSize10);
        submenuFontSize.add(itemSize12);
        submenuFontSize.add(itemSize14);
        submenuFontSize.add(itemSize16);
        submenuFontSize.add(itemSize18);
        submenuFontSize.add(itemSize20);
        menuOptions.add(submenuFontSize);

        // implement font size item listener
        class FontSizeItemListener implements ItemListener {
            public FontSizeItemListener() {
                super();
            }
            public void itemStateChanged(ItemEvent event) {
                if(event.getStateChange() == ItemEvent.SELECTED) {
                    // get source of event
                    JMenuItem item = (JMenuItem) event.getSource();
                    // get new font size from menu item text
                    Integer temp = new Integer(item.getText());
                    // set new default
                    setMenuFontSizeDefault(temp.intValue());
                }
            }
        }
```

continues

30

PLUGGABLE LOOK-AND-FEEL

LISTING 30.6   CONTINUED

```
        // construct and add item listener for font size menu items
        FontSizeItemListener sizeListener = new FontSizeItemListener();
        itemSize10.addItemListener(sizeListener);
        itemSize12.addItemListener(sizeListener);
        itemSize14.addItemListener(sizeListener);
        itemSize16.addItemListener(sizeListener);
        itemSize18.addItemListener(sizeListener);
        itemSize20.addItemListener(sizeListener);

// create Look and Feel submenu and construct
        // menu items for each installed laf
        String classnameCurrentLAF =
UIManager.getLookAndFeel().getClass().getName();
        JMenu submenuLAF = new JMenu("Look and Feel");
UIManager.LookAndFeelInfo info[]
            = UIManager.getInstalledLookAndFeels();
        for(int i = 0; i < info.length; i++) {
            // create menu item
            LAFMenuItem item = new LAFMenuItem(info[i].getName(),
info[i].getClassName(),
                                                    this);
            // add to menu and group
            submenuLAF.add(item);
            group2.add(item);

            // remember item that represents current look and feel
            if(info[i].getClassName().equals(classnameCurrentLAF)) {
                itemSelected2 = item;
            }
        }

// add submenu to menu, menu to menu bar, menu bar to panel
        menuOptions.add(submenuLAF);
        menubar.add(menuOptions);
        add(menubar, BorderLayout.NORTH);

        // select menu item representing current font size, look and feel
        if(itemSelected1 != null)
            itemSelected1.setSelected(true);
        if(itemSelected2 != null)
            itemSelected2.setSelected(true);
    }

    // Private method to change default menu font size
    private void setMenuFontSizeDefault(int size) {
        // get font style and name from current menu font
        Font fontCurrent = UIManager.getFont("Menu.font");
        String name = fontCurrent.getName();
        int style = fontCurrent.getStyle();
```

```
            // create similar font with the specified size
FontUIResource fontResourceNew
            = new FontUIResource(name, style, size);

        // change UI defaults for all types of menu components
        UIManager.put("Menu.font", fontResourceNew);
        UIManager.put("MenuItem.font", fontResourceNew);
        UIManager.put("RadioButtonMenuItem.font", fontResourceNew);
        UIManager.put("PopupMenu.font", fontResourceNew);
    }
}


/* Class representing look and feel menu item
 *
 * Constructs a radio button menu item from a given look and feel name.
 * When item is selected, sets given look and feel and updates
 * the component tree beginning at the given root component.
 */
class LAFMenuItem extends JRadioButtonMenuItem {
    private String lafClassName;
    private Component rootComponent;

    // Constructor
    public LAFMenuItem(String name, String className, Component root) {
        super(name);

        // save look and feel class name and root component in class data
        lafClassName = className;
        rootComponent = root;

        // add listener to detect menu selection
        addItemListener(new ItemListener() {
            public void itemStateChanged(ItemEvent event) {
                if(event.getStateChange() == ItemEvent.SELECTED) {
                    try {
                        // set look and feel and update component tree
                        UIManager.setLookAndFeel(lafClassName);
                    }
                    catch (Exception exc) {
System.out.println("Unable to set LAF");
                    }
                }
            }
        });
    }
}
```

Overview of the `ChangeDefaultsDemo` Example

Although you can also change the font size of menus by calling the `setFont` method, you would have to call this method on each and every menu and menu item component. By changing the menu font in the UI defaults, you automatically change the font for every menu and menu item in the application.

Take a look at how `ChangeDefaultsDemo` changes the menu font size in the UI defaults. The following fragment is the code for a private method, `setMenuFontSizeDefault`, that sets the default font size for menu components to a specified size (specified in points).

```
private void setMenuFontSizeDefault(int size) {
    // get font style and name from current menu font
    Font fontCurrent = UIManager.getFont("Menu.font");
    String name = fontCurrent.getName();
    int style = fontCurrent.getStyle();

    // create similar font with the specified size
    FontUIResource fontResourceNew
            = new FontUIResource(name, style, size);

    // change UI defaults for all types of menu components
    UIManager.put("Menu.font", fontResourceNew);
    UIManager.put("MenuItem.font", fontResourceNew);
    UIManager.put("RadioButtonMenuItem.font", fontResourceNew);
    UIManager.put("PopupMenu.font", fontResourceNew);
}
```

The `setMenuFontSizeDefault` method first gets the current menu font by calling `UIManager.getFont` to get the `Menu.font` default setting. It then gets the name and style of the font and uses this information to create a new font of the specified size. The code then calls `UIManager.put` to change the default fonts for menus, menu items, radio button menu items, and pop-up menus. All instances of these types of components will now be drawn with the new font.

Summary

JFC's pluggable look-and-feel is made possible by the Model View Controller architecture used in components. This architecture abstracts the look-and-feel of components from the model or data the components represent. A UI manager, essentially a collection of static class methods, allows you to determine which look-and-feel implementations are available at runtime and to choose which look-and-feel to use in your application.

The pluggable look-and-feel architecture also supports the concept of UI defaults—default settings for various UI-rendering attributes such as font, borders, and colors. By changing the UI defaults, you can control aspects of how components are rendered, regardless of which look-and-feel you are using. In addition to several platform-specific look-and-feels, JFC includes a cross-platform look-and-feel known as the Metal or Java look-and-feel. The Metal look-and-feel is the default look-and-feel for JFC applications.

Timers

CHAPTER 31

General-purpose timers are often used in applications to periodically trigger actions and to monitor the progress of asynchronous operations. Until JFC, however, Java programmers had to develop their own timer classes or use timer objects provided with class libraries that accompany Java IDE products—this support was not previously available in the JDK.

In this chapter, you will learn

- How to create and use timers

    JFC timers are based on the `Timer` class. You can use this class to create both periodic and one-shot timers.

- How to ensure your timers are thread safe

    JFC places some restrictions on accessing Swing components from threads other than the event-dispatch thread. These restrictions apply to timers.

- About some issues related to timer resolution

    JFC timers are quite useful as general-purpose timers, but their resolution is not high enough for some demanding applications.

Timer Basics

There are two types of timers: *periodic* timers and *one-shot* timers. Periodic timers cause an action to occur periodically—they continue to run and cause actions until they are stopped. One-shot timers cause an action to happen only once, and then they must be restarted if they are to continue to operate. JFC timers can operate either as periodic or as one-shot timers.

In addition to the normal delay setting, JFC timers have an *initial delay* setting. The initial delay specifies the delay for the first timer period. Subsequent periods will be timed according the normal delay setting. For example, you can create a periodic timer with a delay of one second and an initial delay of five seconds. When started, the timer will generate an action event after five seconds and every second thereafter.

> **NOTE**
>
> JFC requires that Swing components be accessed by only one thread at a time, the event-dispatch thread. JFC timers are designed to execute on the event-dispatch thread, so there are no special requirements for accessing Swing components from timers.

The `Timer` Class

Take a look at the `Timer` class, the class that provides JFC's support for timers (see Listing 31.1).

LISTING 31.1   `Timer` CLASS SIGNATURE

```
public class Timer extends Object implements Serializable
{
  // Protected instance variable
    protected EventListenerList listenerList;
  // Public constructor
    public Timer(int delay, ActionListener listener);
  // Public class methods
    public static boolean getLogTimers();
    public static void setLogTimers(boolean enable);
  // Public instance methods
    public void addActionListener(ActionListener listener);
    public boolean doesCoalesce();
    public int getDelay();
    public int getInitialDelay();
    public boolean isRunning();
    public void removeActionListener(ActionListener listener);
    public boolean repeats();
    public void restart();
    public void setCoalesce(boolean enable);
    public void setDelay(int);
    public void setInitialDelay(int delay);
    public void setRepeats(boolean enable);
    public void start();
    public void stop();
  // Protected instance methods
    protected void fireActionPerformed(ActionEvent event);
}
```

There is a single public constructor for creating `Timer` objects. Although you must specify a delay value and an action listener when calling the constructor, you can change these values later with the `setDelay`, `setInitialDelay`, and `addActionListener` methods.

The `getDelay` and `getInitialDelay` methods return the current delay settings, and `removeActionListener` removes a specified action listener. Note that you can have multiple action listeners for a timer.

The `setRepeats` method determines whether a timer is a periodic or a one-shot timer. If you specify `true`, the timer will be a periodic timer. If you specify `false`, the timer will a one-shot timer. You don't have to call `setRepeats` if you want a periodic timer—timers are periodic by default. The repeats method queries a timer and returns true if it is set to be a periodic timer.

A timer won't begin operation until you call its start method. If you call a timer's stop method, the timer will stop operation without triggering an actionPerformed action. Note that calling stop and then start does not function like a pause/resume operation. When you start a timer after stopping it, the timer goes through its full delay cycle. To determine if a timer is started or stopped, you can call the isRunning method.

The restart method is the equivalent of calling stop and then start. This method is useful when you want to use a timer to detect the absence of some significant event for a period of time. For example, to detect when a user has not moved the mouse or pressed a key on the keyboard, you can start a one-shot timer and restart it each time you receive mouse movement or key press events. See the "Example Using Periodic and One-Shot Timers" section, later in this chapter, for an example illustrating this technique.

A busy application may not be able to keep up with the action events generated by a rapidly firing periodic timer. By default, timers coalesce multiple queued action events into a single event; this occurs when setCoalesce is set to true. You can change this behavior with the setCoalesce method. The doesCoalesce method will return true if a timer is coalescing queued events.

Creating and Using a Basic Timer

To create a timer, you call the Timer constructor, specify a delay value in milliseconds, and specify an action listener to be notified when the timer expires. To start the timer, you call the start method. Upon expiration, the timer will call the given action listener's actionPerformed method. For example, the following code fragment will create a periodic timer that will write "Tick" to the standard output stream every five seconds.

```
// Create a periodic timer with a delay of 5000 milliseconds
Timer timer = new Timer(5000, new ActionListener() {
    // Method called each time timer expires
    public void actionPerformed(ActionEvent event) {
        System.out.println("Tick");
    }
});
// Start timer
timer.start();
```

In this example, the timer's action listener is implemented as an anonymous inner class. Note that the default for a JFC timer is periodic. For a one-shot timer, you must call the setRepeats method with the enable parameter set to false to indicate that the timer should not repeat.

> **NOTE**
>
> When you create a timer, the normal delay *and* the initial delay are set to the specified delay value. However, if you use setDelay to change the delay of a timer, you must also call setInitialDelay to change the initial delay value.
>
> If a timer is set to be a one-shot timer, the timer uses only the initial delay setting. You must use the setInitialDelay method to set the delay of one-shot timers.

Example Using Periodic and One-Shot Timers

Listing 31.2 is the complete source for ActivityTimeout, an application that automatically shuts down after a period of 30 seconds of user inactivity. See Figure 31.1 for the output of this code. This example utilizes both periodic and one-shot timers.

FIGURE 31.1

ActivityTimeout-
Demo *example.*

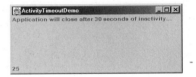

LISTING 31.2   ActivityTimeoutDemo.java

```
/* ActivityTimeoutDemo.java
 *
 * Application that shuts down after a
 * predetermined period of user inactivity.
 *
 * Illustrates the use of JFC timers (periodic and one-shot).
 */

import java.awt.*;
import java.awt.event.*;
import javax.swing.*;

/* App class
 */
public class ActivityTimeoutDemo {

    // Main entry point
```

continues

LISTING 31.2 CONTINUED

```java
    public static void main(String s[]) {
        // Create app panel
        ActivityTimeoutDemoPanel panel = new ActivityTimeoutDemoPanel();

        // Create a frame for app
        JFrame frame = new JFrame("ActivityTimeoutDemo");

        // Add a window listener for window close events
        frame.addWindowListener(new WindowAdapter() {
            public void windowClosing(WindowEvent e) {System.exit(0);}
        });

        // Add app panel to content pane
        frame.getContentPane().add(panel);

        // Set initial frame size and make visible
        frame.setSize (300, 150);
        frame.setVisible(true);
    }
}

/* App panel class
 *
 * All functionality of app resides here.
 */
class ActivityTimeoutDemoPanel extends JPanel {
    Timer timerActivity,        // input activity timer
          timerCountdown;       // countdown timer
    final int TIMEOUT = 30;                     // timeout period in seconds
    int countdownTicks = TIMEOUT;               // countdown value
    JLabel countdownDisplay;                    // countdown display component

    // Constructor
    public ActivityTimeoutDemoPanel () {

        setLayout(new BorderLayout());

        // request focus so that panel will get keyboard events
        // see also: isFocusTraversable override in this class
        requestFocus();

        // create label to display informational text
        String s = "Application will close after "
                + TIMEOUT + " seconds of inactivity...";
        add(new JLabel(s), "North");

        // create label to display countdown value
        add(countdownDisplay = new JLabel(Integer.toString(TIMEOUT)),
                                    "South");
```

```
        // add listeners to detect user activity
        // implement listeners in anonymous inner class
        addKeyListener(new KeyAdapter() {
            public void keyPressed(KeyEvent event) {
                handleUserActivity();
            }
        });
        addMouseListener(new MouseAdapter() {
            public void mouseClicked(MouseEvent event) {
                handleUserActivity();
            }
        });
        addMouseMotionListener(new MouseMotionAdapter() {
            public void mouseMoved(MouseEvent event) {
                handleUserActivity();
            }
        });

        // create periodic timer for countdown
        timerCountdown = new Timer(1000, new ActionListener() {
            public void actionPerformed(ActionEvent event) {
                serviceCountdownTimer();
            }
        });
        timerCountdown.setRepeats(true);

        // create one-shot timer for activity timeout
        timerActivity = new Timer(TIMEOUT*1000, new ActionListener() {
            public void actionPerformed(ActionEvent event) {
                serviceActivityTimer();
            }
        });
        timerActivity.setRepeats(false);

        // start both timers
        timerCountdown.start();
        timerActivity.start();
    }

    // Override so that panel can get input focus to receive keyboard
events
    // (by default, a panel will not get
    // the focus because it's not a UI component)
    public boolean isFocusTraversable () {
        return true;
    }

    // helper method called whenever user activity detected
    void handleUserActivity() {
```

continues

LISTING 31.2   CONTINUED

```
        // restart activity timeout
        timerActivity.restart();
        // reset countdown value and update display
        countdownTicks = TIMEOUT;
        updateDisplay();
    }

    // helper method called to service countdown timer
    void serviceCountdownTimer() {
        // decrement countdown value and update display
        —countdownTicks;
        updateDisplay();
    }

    // helper method called to update countdown display
    void updateDisplay() {
        countdownDisplay.setText(Integer.toString(countdownTicks));
    }

    // helper method to service activity timeout
    void serviceActivityTimer() {
        // Although this method is run in timer thread, it
        // does not make calls to Swing components. Therefore,
        // it's thread safe without use of invokeLater.

        // quit the app
        System.exit(0);
    }
}
```

Overview of the `ActivityTimeoutDemo` Example

ActivityTimeoutDemo uses a one-shot timer, timerActivity, to measure how much time has elapsed since the last user action. This timer is restarted whenever the application gets mouse, mouse movement, or keyboard events. If enough time elapses without activity, the timer fires and its listener calls the serviceActivityTimer helper method to exit the application.

Creating the Timers

The following is the code that creates the timerActivity timer. This code also includes the timer's listener that is implemented in an anonymous inner class.

```
// create one-shot timer for activity timeout
timerActivity = new Timer(TIMEOUT*1000, new ActionListener() {
    public void actionPerformed(ActionEvent event) {
        serviceActivityTimer();
```

```
    }
});
timerActivity.setRepeats(false);
```

The listener for this timer calls the `serviceActivityTimer` helper method that exits the application (because the timer has expired with no detected user input activity).

A second timer, `timerCountdown`, is a periodic timer used to provide a display of the number of seconds remaining before the application is shut down. Its delay is set to one second (1000 milliseconds). This timer is not restarted when user activity is detected—it continues to run until the application is exited.

```
// create periodic timer for countdown
timerCountdown = new Timer(1000, new ActionListener() {
    public void actionPerformed(ActionEvent event) {
        serviceCountdownTimer();
    }
});
timerCountdown.setRepeats(true);
```

The listener for the `timerCountdown` timer (again implemented in an anonymous inner class) calls the `serviceCountdownTimer` helper method. This helper method decrements the `countdownTicks` variable to keep track of the number of seconds that have elapsed since the most recent user activity. It also updates the countdown display, the value that appears in the lower-left corner of the application's window.

Updating the Countdown Display

The following code fragment is the `serviceCountdownTimer` helper method that is called each time the `timerCountdown` timer fires.

```
// helper method called to service countdown timer
void serviceCountdownTimer() {
    // decrement countdown value and update display
    --countdownTicks;
    updateDisplay();
}
```

The purpose of the `timerCountdown` timer is to provide a display indicating the number of seconds before the application automatically shuts down.

Detecting User Activity

To detect user activity, the example uses three listeners: a mouse listener, a mouse movement listener, and a key listener.

```
// add listeners to detect user activity
// implement listeners in anonymous inner class
addKeyListener(new KeyAdapter() {
```

```
    public void keyPressed(KeyEvent event) {
        handleUserActivity();
    }
});
addMouseListener(new MouseAdapter() {
    public void mouseClicked(MouseEvent event) {
        handleUserActivity();
    }
});
addMouseMotionListener(new MouseMotionAdapter() {
    public void mouseMoved(MouseEvent event) {
        handleUserActivity();
    }
});
```

All of these listeners call the `handleUserActivity` helper method. This method restarts
the one-shot `timerActivity` timer, resets the `countdownTicks` value, and updates the
countdown display.

```
// helper method called whenever user activity detected
void handleUserActivity() {
    // restart activity timeout
    timerActivity.restart();
    // reset countdown value and update display
    countdownTicks = TIMEOUT;
    updateCountdownDisplay();
}
```

In order to receive keyboard events, components must have the current input focus.
However, components that are not user-interface components, like panels, normally do
not get the focus. To receive keyboard events in the `ActivityTimeoutDemoPanel` class,
you must do two things:

- Override the `isFocusTraversable` method and return `true` to inform the focus
  manager that the component can get the focus.

- Call the `requestFocus` method to request the focus.

Another approach to detecting user activity (in lieu of using listeners) would be to override the panel's `processEvent` method. It's arguable whether this approach offers any
advantages over using listeners—it still requires the same approach to getting the focus
to receive keyboard events.

Example Illustrating Timer Resolution

JFC timers are fine for general-purpose use, but they are not designed to be used as high-precision timers. Examples of applications requiring high-precision timers include MIDI sequencers and high-performance animation engines. JFC timer implementation is based on a platform-dependent method in the System class currentTimeMillis. On the Windows platform, the resolution of currentTimeMillis is 55 milliseconds.

Listing 31.3 is the complete source for TimerResolutionDemo, an example that illustrates timer resolution. Figure 31.2 shows the output of this code.

FIGURE 31.2

TimerResolution-
Demo *example.*

LISTING 31.3   TimerResolutionDemo.java

```
/* TimerResolutionDemo.java
 *
 * Application measures timer periods and keeps
 * track of maximum, minimum, and average period.
 *
 * Illustrates basic use of JFC timers.
 */

import java.awt.*;
import java.awt.event.*;
import javax.swing.*;
import javax.swing.border.*;

/* App class
 */
public class TimerResolutionDemo {

    // Main entry point
    public static void main (String s[]) {
        // Create app panel
        TimerResolutionDemoPanel panel = new TimerResolutionDemoPanel();

        // Create a frame for app
        JFrame frame = new JFrame("TimerResolutionDemo");
```

continues

LISTING 31.3   CONTINUED

```java
        // Add a window listener for window close events
        frame.addWindowListener(new WindowAdapter() {
            public void windowClosing(WindowEvent e) {System.exit(0);}
        });

        // Add app panel to frame's content pane
        frame.getContentPane().add(panel);

        // Set size and make visible
        frame.setSize (350, 150);
        frame.setVisible (true);
    }
}

/* App panel class
 *
 * All functionality of app resides here.
 */
class TimerResolutionDemoPanel extends JPanel {
    Timer timer;
    int maxPeriod, minPeriod, avgPeriod, tickCount;
    long timeLastTick, timeStarted;

    // init string for display fields
    String sLabelInit = ("                   ");

    // max, min, avg period display fields
    JLabel labelMax = new JLabel(sLabelInit);
    JLabel labelMin = new JLabel(sLabelInit);
    JLabel labelAvg = new JLabel(sLabelInit);

    // constructor
    public TimerResolutionDemoPanel() {
        // create radio buttons to allow selection of timer period
        JRadioButton rb1 = new JRadioButton("1 msec");
        rb1.addActionListener(new ActionListener() {
            public void actionPerformed(ActionEvent e) {
                startTimer(1);
            }
        });
        JRadioButton rb2 = new JRadioButton("10 msec");
        rb2.addActionListener(new ActionListener() {
            public void actionPerformed(ActionEvent e) {
                startTimer(10);
            }
        });
        JRadioButton rb3 = new JRadioButton("100 msec");
        rb3.addActionListener(new ActionListener() {
            public void actionPerformed(ActionEvent e) {
```

```
                startTimer(100);
        }
    });
    JRadioButton rb4 = new JRadioButton("1000 msec");
    rb4.addActionListener(new ActionListener() {
        public void actionPerformed(ActionEvent e) {
            startTimer(1000);
        }
    });

    // create a button group for radio buttons
    ButtonGroup group = new ButtonGroup();
    group.add(rb1);
    group.add(rb2);
    group.add(rb3);
    group.add(rb4);

    // create a horizontal box to contain radio buttons
    MyBox box_h1 = new MyBox(BoxLayout.X_AXIS);
    box_h1.setBorder(new TitledBorder("Timer Period"));
    box_h1.add(rb1);
    box_h1.add(rb2);
    box_h1.add(rb3);
    box_h1.add(rb4);

    // create a vertical box and add labels for display fields
    MyBox box_v1 = new MyBox(BoxLayout.Y_AXIS);
    box_v1.add(new JLabel("Maximum Period:      "));
    box_v1.add(new JLabel("Minimum Period:      "));
    box_v1.add(new JLabel("Average Period:      "));

    // create a vertical box and add min, max, avg display fields
    MyBox box_v2 = new MyBox(BoxLayout.Y_AXIS);
    box_v2.add(labelMax);
    box_v2.add(labelMin);
    box_v2.add(labelAvg);

    // arrange the 2 vertical boxes side-by-side in a horizontal box
    MyBox box_h2 = new MyBox(BoxLayout.X_AXIS);
    box_h2.add(box_v1);
    box_h2.add(box_v2);

    // add the boxes to panel
    add(box_h1);
    add(box_h2);

    // create a periodic timer, don't coalesce events
    timer = new Timer(0, new TimerListener());
    timer.setRepeats(true);
```

continues

LISTING 31.3   CONTINUED

```
            timer.setCoalesce(false);
    }

    // helper function to restart timer with new delay
    void startTimer(int delay) {
        // reset min, max, avg values
        maxPeriod = 0;
        minPeriod = 100000;      // very large value
        avgPeriod = 0;
        tickCount = 0;

        // ensure timer is stopped
        if (timer.isRunning()) timer.stop();

        // change delay
        timer.setInitialDelay(delay);
        timer.setDelay(delay);

        // reset timestamps to current time and start timer
        timeStarted = timeLastTick = System.currentTimeMillis();
        timer.start();
    }

    // listener for timer
    class TimerListener implements ActionListener {
        public void actionPerformed(ActionEvent event) {
            // get current time
            long timeNow = System.currentTimeMillis();

            tickCount++;

            // calculate timer period
            int period = (int)(timeNow - timeLastTick);

            // calculate max, min, average
            if (period > maxPeriod) {
                maxPeriod = period;
            }
            if (period < minPeriod) {
                minPeriod = period;
            }
            avgPeriod = ((int)(timeNow - timeStarted)) / tickCount;

            // save time of this event to calculate next period
            timeLastTick = timeNow;

            // update display
            labelMax.setText(Integer.toString(maxPeriod));
            labelMin.setText(Integer.toString(minPeriod));
```

```
                    labelAvg.setText(Integer.toString(avgPeriod));
            }
        }
    }

// Workaround for problems with Box class
// Use JPanel with BoxLayout layout manager
class MyBox extends JPanel {
    public MyBox(int axis) {
        super();
        setLayout(new BoxLayout(this, axis));
    }
}
```

Overview of `TimerResolutionDemo` Example

A large portion of the `TimerResolutionDemo` example code is related to the user interface—four radio buttons and six labels. These components are grouped in boxes to create
the desired appearance. `TimerResolutionDemo` uses the `System.currentTimeMillis`
method to measure the delay of a periodic timer. Because JFC timers use
`currentTimeMillis` as their time source, this may seem like a dubious approach to mea-
suring timer resolution. However, `currentTimeMillis` is the only time source that is
available, and this approach actually works quite well to illustrate the resolution of JFC
timers.

The `TimerResolutionDemoPanel` constructor instantiates four radio buttons that use
anonymous inner classes to implement action listeners.

```
// create radio buttons to allow selection of timer period
JRadioButton rb1 = new JRadioButton("1 msec");
rb1.addActionListener(new ActionListener() {
        public void actionPerformed(ActionEvent e) {
                startTimer(1);
        }
});
JRadioButton rb2 = new JRadioButton("10 msec");
rb2.addActionListener(new ActionListener() {
        public void actionPerformed(ActionEvent e) {
                startTimer(10);
        }
});
JRadioButton rb3 = new JRadioButton("100 msec");
rb3.addActionListener(new ActionListener() {
        public void actionPerformed(ActionEvent e) {
                startTimer(100);
        }
});
JRadioButton rb4 = new JRadioButton("1000 msec");
```

```
rb4.addActionListener(new ActionListener() {
        public void actionPerformed(ActionEvent e) {
                startTimer(1000);
        }
});
```

The radio button listeners all call the `startTimer` helper method to initialize the timer to the specified delay in milliseconds and then start the timer.

Creating the Periodic Timer

After creating the remainder of the user interface, the constructor creates a periodic timer.

```
// create a periodic timer, don't coalesce events
timer = new Timer(0, new TimerListener());
timer.setRepeats(true);
timer.setCoalesce(false);
```

The `setCoalesce` method is called to inform the timer not to coalesce pending timer events. Since one of the tasks of the application is to calculate the average timer period, any coalesced events would affect the accuracy of this calculation. Note that the timer is created with a delay setting of zero. The proper delay value will be set before the timer is started.

Starting the Timer

The application doesn't begin operation until you select one of the radio buttons to specify a timer delay setting. The action listeners for the radio buttons call the `startTimer` helper method with a parameter specifying the chosen timer delay setting in milliseconds.

```
// helper function to restart timer with new delay
void startTimer(int delay) {
        // reset min, max, avg values
        maxPeriod = 0;
        minPeriod = 100000;        // very large value
        avgPeriod = 0;
        tickCount = 0;

        // ensure timer is stopped
        if (timer.isRunning()) timer.stop();

        // change delay
        timer.setInitialDelay(delay);
        timer.setDelay(delay);

        // reset timestamps to current time and start timer
```

```
        timeStarted = timeLastTick = System.currentTimeMillis();
        timer.start();
}
```

First, `startTimer` resets variables used to store the maximum, minimum, and average period and the tick count. The tick count is simply a count of the number of times the timer has fired. The method then ensures that the timer is stopped by querying with `isRunning` and, if necessary, calling `stop`. It then sets both the delay and the initial delay to the specified delay value. Remember, with periodic timers you must change both of these values (unless you actually want an initial delay that is different from the regular delay). After calling `currentTimeMillis` to get a new value for the `timeStarted` and `timeLastTick` variables, `startTimer` calls the `start` method to start the periodic timer.

Servicing the Timer

The listener for the periodic timer is implemented in a class named `TimerListener`. The following fragment is the source for `TimerListener`:

```java
// listener for timer
class TimerListener implements ActionListener {
    public void actionPerformed(ActionEvent event) {
        // get current time
        long timeNow = System.currentTimeMillis();

        tickCount++;

        // calculate timer period
        int period = (int)(timeNow - timeLastTick);

        // calculate max, min, average
        if (period > maxPeriod) {
            maxPeriod = period;
        }
        if (period < minPeriod) {
            minPeriod = period;
        }
        avgPeriod = ((int)(timeNow - timeStarted)) / tickCount;

        // save time of this event to calculate next period
        timeLastTick = timeNow;

        // update display
        labelMax.setText(Integer.toString(maxPeriod));
        labelMin.setText(Integer.toString(minPeriod));
        labelAvg.setText(Integer.toString(avgPeriod));
    }
}
```

Each time the timer fires, its listener receives an action event via the `actionPerformed` method. The first thing the timer listener does is call `currentTimeMillis` to get the current time in milliseconds. It then increments the tick count and determines the timer period from the difference in the current time and the time of the last timer action event (stored in the `timeLastTick` variable). After calculating the maximum, minimum, and average timer periods, the timer listener updates `timeLastTick` with the current time value.

Summary

JFC provides both periodic and one-shot timer services with the `javax.swing.Timer` class. The `ActivityTimeoutDemo` example illustrates how to create and use JFC timers by implementing an application that automatically quits after a certain period of time elapses with no detectable activity from the user.

The resolution of JFC timers depends on the platform that the application is running on—for the Windows platform, timer resolution is 55 milliseconds. The `TimerResolutionDemo` example explores timer resolution by comparing a periodic timer interval to an elapsed time obtained by using the `System.currentTimeMillis` method. You can use this example to observe how certain kinds of system activity affects timer accuracy.

CHAPTER 32

Swing Utilities

JFC provides a collection of miscellaneous utilities and constant definitions in the SwingUtilities and SwingConstants classes. This chapter provides an overview and summary of these classes.

In this chapter you will learn

- About the various utility methods in SwingUtilities

  This class includes utilities for converting coordinates, determining component bounds, navigating component hierarchies, invoking Runnable objects, working with mouse events, painting components, laying out complex menu items and labels, and working with accessibility.

- About the SwingConstants class

  This class includes constants used in several classes to specify the position of components or elements of components.

The SwingUtilities Class

The SwingUtilities class, included in the java.swing package, is a miscellaneous collection of utilities implemented as static class methods. Listing 32.1 gives the class signature for SwingUtilities.

LISTING 32.1   SwingUtilities CLASS SIGNATURE

```
public class SwingUtilities extends Object implements SwingConstants
{
   // Public class methods
     // coordinate system conversion utilities
     public static Point convertPoint(Component source, Point point,
                                      Component destination);
     public static Point convertPoint(Component source, int x, int y,
                                      Component destination);
public static void convertPointFromScreen(Point point,
                                                Component component);
     public static void convertPointToScreen(Point point,
                                              Component component);
     public static Rectangle convertRectangle(Component source,
                                              Rectangle rect,
                                              Component destination);
     // rectangle utilities
public static Rectangle[] computeDifference(Rectangle rect1,
                                                Rectangle rect2);
     public static Rectangle computeIntersection(int x, int y,
                                                 int width, int height,
                                                 Rectangle rect);
```

```
public static Rectangle computeUnion(int x, int y,
                                     int width, int height,
                                     Rectangle rect);
public static final boolean isRectangleContainingRectangle(
                                     Rectangle rect1,
                                     Rectangle rect2);

    // component bounds utilities
public static int computeStringWidth(FontMetrics metrics,
                                     String string);
    public static Rectangle getLocalBounds(Component component);

    // component containment hierarchy utilities
    public static Component findFocusOwner(Component component);
public static Container getAncestorNamed(String string,
                                     Component component);
    public static Container getAncestorOfClass(Class class,
                                     Component component);
    public static Component getDeepestComponentAt(Component component,
                                     int x, int y);
    public static JRootPane getRootPane(Component component);
public static boolean isDescendingFrom(Component component1,
                                     Component component2);
    public static Window windowForComponent(Component component);

    // utilities for invoking execution on the event-dispatch thread
    public static void invokeAndWait(Runnable runnable);
    public static void invokeLater(Runnable runnable);
    public static boolean isEventDispatchThread();

    // mouse event utilities
public static MouseEvent convertMouseEvent(Component source,
                                     MouseEvent event,
                                     Component destination);
    public static boolean isLeftMouseButton(MouseEvent event);
    public static boolean isMiddleMouseButton(MouseEvent event);
    public static boolean isRightMouseButton(MouseEvent event);

    // component layout utilities
public static String layoutCompoundLabel(FontMetrics metrics,
                                     String s, Icon icon,
                                     int vertAlign, int horiz
➥Align,
                                     int vertTextPos, int horiz
➥TextPos,
                                     Rectangle rect
➥View, Rectangle rectIcon,
                                     Rectangle rectText, int gap);
```

continues

32

SWING UTILITIES

LISTING 32.1 CONTINUED

```
      // paint utilities
public static void paintComponent(Graphics graphics,
                                  Component component,
                                  Container container,
                                  int x, int y,
                                  int width, int height);
public static void paintComponent(Graphics graphics,
                                  Component component,
                                  Container container,
                                  Rectangle rect);
    public static void updateComponentTreeUI(Component component);

    // accessibility utilities
public static Accessible getAccessibleAt(Component component,
                                         Point point);
    public static Accessible getAccessibleChild(Component component,
                                                int index);
    public static int getAccessibleChildrenCount(Component component);
    public static int getAccessibleIndexInParent(Component component);
public static AccessibleStateSet getAccessibleStateSet(
                                 Component component);
}
```

Note that there is no constructor for SwingUtilities as all of its methods because static class methods.

Coordinate System Conversion Utilities

The following SwingUtilities methods convert coordinates from the coordinate system of one component to the coordinate system of another component.

```
public static Point convertPoint(Component source, Point point,
                                 Component destination);
public static Point convertPoint(Component source, int x, int y,
                                 Component destination);
public static void convertPointToScreen(Point point,
                                        Component component);
public static void convertPointFromScreen(Point point,
                                          Component component);
public static Rectangle convertRectangle(Component source,
                                         Rectangle rect,
                                         Component destination);
```

The convertPoint methods convert a given coordinate from the coordinate system of a source component to the coordinate system of a destination component. The source and destination components must be members of a component tree hierarchy with a Window object at its root. `convertRectangle` works like the `convertPoint` methods, but converts the location of a given rectangle.

The `convertPointToScreen` and `convertPointFromScreen` methods convert component-based coordinates to and from screen-based coordinates.

Rectangle Utilities

The following `SwingUtilities` methods are useful for working with rectangles.

```
public static final boolean isRectangleContainingRectangle(
                            Rectangle rect1,
                            Rectangle rect2);
public static Rectangle computeIntersection(int x, int y,
                                    int width, int height,
                                    Rectangle rect);
public static Rectangle computeUnion(int x, int y,
                                int width, int height,
                                Rectangle rect);
public static Rectangle[] computeDifference(Rectangle rect1,
                                    Rectangle rect2);
```

`isRectangleContainingRectangle` takes two `Rectangle` objects and returns `true` if the first rectangle completely contains the second rectangle.

The `computeIntersection` and `computeUnion` methods allow you to calculate the intersection and union of two rectangles. In these two methods, you specify one rectangle as a `Rectangle` object and the other rectangle in terms of its origin and size (x, y, width, height). The `computeDifference` method takes two rectangles and returns an array of rectangles representing the regions of the first rectangle that do not overlap with the second rectangle. These three methods are useful for calculating dirty rectangle lists when batching repaint requests.

Component Bounds Utilities

`SwingUtilities` has two methods for determining the bounds of components.

```
public static Rectangle getLocalBounds(Component component);
public static int computeStringWidth(FontMetrics metrics, String string);
```

The `getLocalBounds` method returns the bounds of a component as a `Rectangle` object. The location of the returned rectangle is always (0, 0).

`computeStringWidth` returns the width (in pixels) of a given string when rendered with the given font metrics. This can be useful for determining the preferred and minimum sizes of components that contain text elements.

Utilities for Working with Component Containment Hierarchies

The following `SwingUtilities` methods are useful for obtaining information about component containment hierarchies.

```
public static Container getAncestorOfClass(Class class,
                                           Component component);
public static Container getAncestorNamed(String string,
                                          Component component);
public static Component getDeepestComponentAt(Component component,
                                              int x, int y);
public static boolean isDescendingFrom(Component component1,
                                       Component component2);
public static Window windowForComponent(Component component);
public static Component findFocusOwner(Component component);
public static JRootPane getRootPane(Component component);
```

The typical containment hierarchy for a JFC application begins with a `JFrame` (a `Window` object) or `JApplet` object. Each of these objects contains a single child, a `JRootPane` object, which contains the rest of the application's GUI objects. `SwingUtilities` has two methods that are useful for determining the window or root pane object associated with a given component. The `windowForComponent` method returns the `Window` object that contains a given component. The `getRootPane` method returns the root pane (`JRootPane` object) for a component.

There are several other utilities for working with component hierarchies. The `getAncestorOfClass` method walks up the component containment hierarchy beginning with the given component until it finds and returns a component that is an instance of the given class. `getAncestorNamed` walks up a component containment hierarchy, beginning with the given component, until it finds and returns a component with the given name. The `isDescendingFrom` method returns `true` if a given component is an ancestor of a second given component.

The `getDeepestComponentAt` method is useful for hit testing on component hierarchies. Given a component that may be a container, it returns the deepest child component at the given coordinates. If the given component is not a container, `getDeepestComponentAt` returns the given component.

The `findFocusOwner` method takes a component that is a parent in a component hierarchy and returns the child component (if any) that has the focus.

The getAccessibleChildrenCount method returns the number of accessible child objects contained by a given component. getAccessibleChild returns the nth accessible child contained by the given component.

For more information about accessibility, see Chapter 33, "Accessibility."

The SwingConstants Class

Many Swing classes include methods for positioning components or elements of components. For example, in JLabel objects, you can specify whether to put the icon to the left or to the right of the text. Because there are a number of classes that use positional information, there is a set of common constants defined in an interface class named SwingConstants. Listing 32.2 gives the class signature for this class.

LISTING 32.2   SwingConstants CLASS SIGNATURE

```
public interface SwingConstants extends Object {
    public static final int CENTER;
    public static final int TOP;
    public static final int LEFT;
    public static final int BOTTOM;
    public static final int RIGHT;
    public static final int NORTH;
    public static final int NORTH_EAST;
    public static final int EAST;
    public static final int SOUTH_EAST;
    public static final int SOUTH;
    public static final int SOUTH_WEST;
    public static final int WEST;
    public static final int NORTH_WEST;
    public static final int HORIZONTAL;
    public static final int VERTICAL;
}
```

All the classes that require you to specify positional information implement the SwingConstants interface, so you don't necessarily need to import the SwingConstants class. Instead, you can access the constants as members of the class you are using. For example, the following line of code uses the RIGHT constant to create a right-aligned label.

```
JLabel label = new JLabel("Label text goes here.", JLabel.RIGHT);
```

In this code, the RIGHT alignment constant is specified as a member of the JLabel class. If you want to access the constant value as a member of the SwingConstants class, you'll have to be sure to import the SwingConstants class.

> **NOTE**
>
> The SwingConstants members are not usable for specifying layout positions for the BorderLayout layout manager.

Summary

The SwingUtilities class contains a myriad of static class methods that the Swing developers found useful in implementing the classes in the javax.swing package. You may find some of these utilities useful when writing JFC applications. This chapter presents an overview of all of the methods in the SwingUtilities class—it's a good idea to familiarize yourself with what utilities are available so you don't end up spending time creating an already-available utility.

Accessibility

CHAPTER 33

As computers become more prevalent in the home and in the workplace, it becomes increasingly important to design applications with user interfaces that are accessible to everyone, including those people with limited abilities to view a display or manipulate a mouse or keyboard. The JDK provides built-in support for *assistive technologies*—technologies that provide accessibility to accommodate users with limited abilities.

In this chapter you will learn

- Why it is important to enable your applications to support assistive technologies

    Applications that are designed to be accessible can be used by a larger percentage of the general population. Some governments and universities are beginning to require that certain purchased software products meet accessibility requirements.

- About assistive technologies and how they operate

    There is a wide range of existing assistive technologies with new technologies being developed every year. Examples of existing assistive technologies include screen magnifiers and speech recognition systems.

- How to enable your applications to support assistive technologies

    All of the Swing components are implemented to support accessibility. If you're using Swing components, it's relatively easy to create accessible Java applets and applications.

About Accessibility and Assistive Technologies

In the general sense, assistive technologies include any technology that allows people with limited abilities to perform tasks they could not perform otherwise. Wheelchair ramps at curbs and closed-captioning on television programs are general examples of assistive technologies.

In the realm of computers, assistive technologies allow people with limited vision, hearing, or movement ability to operate the user interface of applications. Examples of assistive technologies on computers include screen readers and magnifiers, speech recognition systems, text-to-speech converters, and keyboard mnemonics.

The United States has passed legislation (Section 508 of the Federal Rehabilitation Act, the Americans with Disabilities Act, and the Telecommunications Act of 1996) to encourage support for accessibility in education and the workplace and in technology-related government purchases. There is strong sensitivity to accessibility in Europe and Japan as well.

Overview of JDK Support for Accessibility

JFC provides three areas of support for accessibility:

- The Java Accessibility API allows applications to operate with assistive technologies.
- Utility classes provide support for implementing assistive technologies.
- Pluggable look-and-feel also provides support for implementing certain types of assistive technologies.

The Java Accessibility API defines a contract between the user-interface components used by applications and the assistive technologies that provide access to accessible applications. To make your application accessible, you must fully implement this API in all of your user-interface components.

In addition to the Java Accessibility API, there is a collection of utility classes that support the implementation of assistive technologies. If you're not actually creating an assistive technology, you won't need to use these utility classes, but learning a bit about them will give you a better understanding of how assistive technologies operate.

JFC's pluggable look-and-feel provides a way to make applications accessible without the use of separate assistive technologies. For example, you could create a look-and-feel that uses large fonts or high-contrast colors for users with impaired vision. You could also create a look-and-feel that presents the user interface on devices other than a visual display. Examples of such alternate interface devices include tactile (Braille) and audio devices. For more information on using JFC's pluggable look-and-feel capabilities, see Chapter 30 "Pluggable Look-and-Feel."

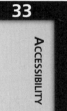

33

ACCESSIBILITY

> **NOTE**
>
> The Java Accessibility utility classes are not a part of the JDK. These classes, along with several examples of assistive technologies, are available in the Java Accessibility download available from JavaSoft.

Basic Accessibility Information

The following list describes the basic types of accessibility information that all accessible components provide through the AccessibleContext class.

- The name of the component
- A short description of the component's function
- The role of the component
- The state of the component

The *name* and *description* are specific to how you are using the component in your application. For example, for a File, Open menu item, the accessible name could be "Open" and the accessible description could be "Opens a file." Components, such as textual menus and buttons, will automatically generate an accessible name from the text supplied to the constructor or set with the setText method. Components with ToolTips will generate an accessible description from the ToolTip text. You should ensure that all of your user interface components have an accessible name and description.

The *role* is an intrinsic property of the component that describes its function. The role property is not set by applications. Examples of accessible roles for some of the Swing components include window, frame, list, menubar, and pushbutton. The AccessibleRole class defines role identifier constants for all of the Swing components. Assistive technologies can make use of these roles in a programmatic manner to navigate a user interface.

The *state* is also an intrinsic property of the component and is not directly set by applications (although applications can indirectly change a component's state by executing actions on the component). The AccessibleStateSet class, a collection of individual AccessibleState objects, is used to represent a component's state. Examples of component states include active, pressed, checked, editable, and focused.

Note that component role and state are programmatically accessed by the identifier constants defined in the AccessibleRole and AccessibleState classes. The examples presented in the previous two paragraphs present the human-readable forms of role and state that are also available through these classes.

Extended Accessibility Information

In addition to basic accessibility information, most components provide extended accessibility information. The following list describes the different types of extended accessibility information. The AccessibleContext class provides methods to get objects representing extended accessibility information.

- Actions that the component can perform
- Attributes of the component's graphical representation
- The current selection if the component contains selectable children

- Editable text contained by the component
- The numerical value represented by the component

Classes used to represent extended accessibility information in Swing components include `AccessibleAction`, `AccessibleComponent`, `AccessibleSelection`, `AccessibleText`, and `AccessibleValue`. Most of these classes are interface classes that are implemented by the components using them.

Support for extended accessibility information is fully implemented in all of the Swing components—you don't really need to be concerned with extended accessibility information unless you're creating a custom component by subclassing `JComponent` or creating an assistive technology application. See "Supporting Accessibility in Custom Components," later in this chapter, for a discussion of extended accessibility classes.

Supporting Accessibility in JFC Applications

To be accessible, user-interface components must fully implement the Java Accessibility API, a collection of interfaces and classes that allow components to be observed and operated by an assistive technology. All of the Swing components are designed to be accessible, and, as a result, it's relatively easy to create an accessible JFC application.

The basic Java Accessibility classes are the `Accessible` interface and the `AccessibleContext` class. All Swing components implement the `Accessible` interface to provide a method to get an `AccessibleContext` object containing the component's accessibility information.

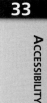

The `Accessible` Interface

The `Accessible` interface is an interface that all accessible components must implement.

```
public interface Accessible extends Object {
    public abstract AccessibleContext getAccessibleContext();
}
```

`Accessible` has a single method, `getAccessibleContext`, which returns an `AccessibleContext` object. The `AccessibleContext` object provides access to all of the accessibility information about a component. You should always check the return value from `getAccessibleContext` to ensure that it is not `null` and that the component is indeed accessible.

The `AccessibleContext` Class

The `AccessibleContext` class represents the basic accessibility information maintained by an accessible component (see Listing 33.1). The basic accessibility information includes the component's name, description, role, and state. `AccessibleContext` also provides methods to get the accessible parent and children of the component, as well as methods to access extended accessibility information contained in `AccessibleAction`, `AccessibleComponent`, `AccessibleSelection`, `AccessibleText`, and `AccessibleValue` objects.

LISTING 33.1   `AccessibleContext` CLASS SIGNATURE

```
public abstract class AccessibleContext extends Object
{
  // PropertyChangeEvent constants
    public static final String ACCESSIBLE_CARET_PROPERTY;
    public static final String ACCESSIBLE_DESCRIPTION_PROPERTY;
    public static final String ACCESSIBLE_NAME_PROPERTY;
    public static final String ACCESSIBLE_SELECTION_PROPERTY;
    public static final String ACCESSIBLE_STATE_PROPERTY;
    public static final String ACCESSIBLE_TEXT_PROPERTY;
    public static final String ACCESSIBLE_VALUE_PROPERTY;
    public static final String ACCESSIBLE_VISIBLE_DATA_PROPERTY;
  // Protected instance variables
    protected String accessibleDescription;
    protected String accessibleName;
    protected Accessible accessibleParent;
  // Public instance methods
public void addPropertyChangeListener(PropertyChangeListener
➥listener);
    public void firePropertyChange(String property,
                                   Object old, Object new);
    public abstract Accessible getAccessibleChild(int index);
    public abstract int getAccessibleChildrenCount();
    public String getAccessibleDescription();
    public abstract int getAccessibleIndexInParent();
    public String getAccessibleName();
    public Accessible getAccessibleParent();
    public abstract AccessibleRole getAccessibleRole();
    public abstract AccessibleStateSet getAccessibleStateSet();
    public AccessibleAction getAccessibleAction();
    public AccessibleComponent getAccessibleComponent();
    public AccessibleSelection getAccessibleSelection();
    public AccessibleText getAccessibleText();
    public AccessibleValue getAccessibleValue();
    public abstract Locale getLocale();
public void removePropertyChangeListener(PropertyChangeListener
➥listener);
    public void setAccessibleDescription(String description);
```

```
      public void setAccessibleName(String name);
      public void setAccessibleParent(Accessible parent);
}
```

There is no constructor provided for AccessibleContext. Instead, all accessible components implement the Accessible interface, which contains the getAccessibleContext method to return an AccessibleContext object. For example, the following code gets an AccessibleContext object and calls its setAccessibleName method to set a component's accessible name.

```
getAccessibleContext().setAccessibleName("First text field");
```

There are only two methods in AccessibleContext you need to use to make your applications accessible. setAccessibleName sets the accessible name for the component, and setAccessibleDescription sets the accessible description. All visible components should have an accessible name and accessible description. However, you don't always have to explicitly set these attributes. Components that display a name, such as textual buttons and menus, will use their name as the accessible name. Likewise, components with ToolTips will use the ToolTip text as the accessible description. For components that don't display a textual name or don't have a ToolTip, you'll have to explicitly set the accessible name or description by calling setAccessibleName or setAccessibleDescription.

The remaining members of AccessibleContext are used to make custom components accessible and to create assistive technologies. These methods are discussed later in this chapter in the "Supporting Accessibility in Custom Components" and "Creating Assistive Technologies" sections.

Guidelines for Creating Accessible Applications

The following is a list of guidelines to help you create accessible JFC applications:

- Use ToolTips on all user-interface components. See Chapter 25, "ToolTips and Debug Graphics," for details on using ToolTips. If you don't provide a ToolTip for a user-interface component, use AccessibleContext.setAccessibleDescription to provide a description of the component's purpose.

- Use keyboard mnemonics whenever possible. Ideally, your interface should be completely navigable using only the keyboard. See Chapter 29, "Keyboard Navigation," for details on using mnemonics.

- Whenever you use a JLabel object to label a component, use the setLabelFor method to associate the label with the component.

33

ACCESSIBILITY

- If you use `ImageIcon` objects as part of the user interface, construct the objects by using the constructor that allows you to specify a description or else use the `ImageIcon.setDescription` method to provide a short description of the object.

- Use the `AccessibleContext.setAccessibleName` method to provide a short name for user-interface components that don't display text identifying the component's function. Components such as textual buttons and menus will generate an accessible name from their identifying text.

- If you're designing your program so it can be internationalized, be sure to treat all accessible name and description text as you do other text that will be translated. Normally, text that will be translated for internationalization is stored in resource bundles.

Don't overlook testing your application's accessibility features.

Supporting Accessibility in Custom Components

If you're writing a custom component (a component that extends directly from the `JComponent` class), you should ensure the component is accessible by adhering to the following guidelines.

1. Create an `AccessibleContext` for your component. This is best handled by creating an inner class that extends from the `JComponent.AccessibleJComponent` class.

   `AccessibleJComponent` provides default implementations for many of the `AccessibleContext` methods. You should provide implementations for the basic `getAccessibleRole` and `getAccessibleStateSet` methods.

   The following code fragment illustrates the structure of a typical `AccessibleContext` implementation.

```
protected class AccessibleCustomComponent
        extends AccessibleJComponent {

    // Constructor
    AccessibleCustomComponent() { super();}

    // Accessible role info
    public AccessibleRole getAccessibleRole() {
        return AccessibleRole.CUSTOM_COMPONENT;
    }

    // Accessible state info
    public AccessibleStateSet getAccessibleStateSet() {
        // get basic JComponent state set
```

```
    AccessibleStateSet states =
➥super.getAccessibleStateSet();

        // add states for custom component

        return states;
    }

    // implement extended accessibility interfaces
    }
```

2. Override the component's `getAccessibleContext` method to create an instance of its `AccessibleContext` (if it doesn't exist already), store it in the protected instance variable `accessibleContext`, and return it to the caller.

   The following is an example of a typical implementation of `getAccessibleContext`. For this example, `AccessibleCustomComponent` is the name of the inner class that represents the component's `AccessibleContext`.

```
public AccessibleContext getAccessibleContext() {
    if (accessibleContext == null) {
        accessibleContext = new AccessibleCustomComponent();
    }
    return accessibleContext;
}
```

   Note that the `accessibleContext` variable used to store the `AccessibleContext` object in this example is a protected member of the `JComponent` class.

3. Implement each of the extended accessibility interfaces that your component requires in the inner class you created in step 1. The extended accessibility interfaces include `AccessibleAction`, `AccessibleComponent`, `AccessibleSelection`, `AccessibleText`, and `AccessibleValue`.

   For each extended accessibility interface you implement, override the corresponding `AccessibleContext` method to return the object providing extended accessibility support. For example, if your component supports the `AccessibleText` interface, override the `getAccessibleText` method to return an instance of the object implementing `AccessibleText`.

The following sections list and briefly describe each of the JFC extended accessibility classes.

The `AccessibleAction` Interface

The `AccessibleAction` interface provides a mechanism for assistive technologies to determine what actions an accessible component supports and to perform those actions. Examples of accessible actions include *clicking* a button and *closing* a window.

33

ACCESSIBILITY

You can determine if an object supports the `AccessibleAction` interface by getting the object's `AccessibleContext` and calling the `getAccessibleAction` method. A non-null return value indicates that the object supports the `AccessibleAction` interface.

Custom components that support actions should implement the `AccessibleAction` interface and override the `getAccessibleAction` method in the `AccessibleContext` to return an instance of the implementation.

Objects with accessible actions should maintain a list of actions that can be performed on the object. Actions are referenced by a zero-based index of their position in the list. The following code gives the class signature of the `AccessibleAction` class.

```
public interface AccessibleAction extends Object {
    public abstract int getAccessibleActionCount();
public abstract String getAccessibleActionDescription(int
➥indexAction);
    public abstract boolean doAccessibleAction(int indexAction);
}
```

The `getAccessibleActionCount` method returns the number of actions supported by the object. `getAccessibleActionDescription` retrieves a textual description of a given action. The `doAccessibleAction` method performs the given action.

The `AccessibleComponent` Interface

The `AccessibleComponent` interface is a core interface all visual components must implement to be accessible. You can determine if an object supports the `AccessibleComponent` interface by getting the object's `AccessibleContext` and calling the `getAccessibleComponent` method. A non-null return value indicates that the object supports the `AccessibleComponent` interface. `AccessibleComponent` provides standard methods that assistive technologies can use to work with visual components. Listing 33.2 gives the class signature of the `AccessibleComponent` interface.

LISTING 33.2   `AccessibleComponent` CLASS SIGNATURE

```
public interface AccessibleComponent extends Object {
    public abstract Color getBackground();
    public abstract void setBackground(Color color);
    public abstract Color getForeground();
    public abstract void setForeground(Color color);
    public abstract Cursor getCursor();
    public abstract void setCursor(Cursor cursor);
    public abstract Font getFont();
    public abstract void setFont(Font font);
    public abstract FontMetrics getFontMetrics(Font font);
    public abstract boolean isEnabled();
    public abstract void setEnabled(boolean enable);
```

```
    public abstract boolean isVisible();
    public abstract void setVisible(boolean visible);
    public abstract boolean isShowing();
    public abstract boolean contains(Point point);
    public abstract Point getLocationOnScreen();
    public abstract Point getLocation();
    public abstract void setLocation(Point location);
    public abstract Rectangle getBounds();
    public abstract void setBounds(Rectangle bounds);
    public abstract Dimension getSize();
    public abstract void setSize(Dimension );
    public abstract Accessible getAccessibleAt(Point point);
    public abstract boolean isFocusTraversable();
    public abstract void requestFocus();
    public abstract void addFocusListener(FocusListener listener);
    public abstract void removeFocusListener(FocusListener listener);
}
```

The `AccessibleJComponent` class (an inner class in `JComponent`) implements the `AccessibleComponent` interface and provides default implementations for all of its methods. Most of the `AccessibleComponent` methods map to a corresponding `JComponent` method of the same name.

The `AccessibleSelection` Interface

The `AccessibleSelection` interface provides a mechanism for determining the selected children of a component as well as for selecting and unselecting children.

You can determine if an object supports the `AccessibleSelection` interface by getting the object's `AccessibleContext` and calling the `getAccessibleSelection` method. A non-`null` return value indicates that the object supports the `AccessibleSelection` interface.

All components with selectable children should implement this interface and override the `getAccessibleSelection` method in the `AccessibleContext` to return an instance of the implementation. Listing 33.3 gives the class signature for the `AccessibleSelection` interface.

LISTING 33.3   `AccessibleSelection` CLASS SIGNATURE

```
public interface AccessibleSelection extends Object {
    public abstract int getAccessibleSelectionCount();
    public abstract Accessible getAccessibleSelection(int childIndex);
    public abstract boolean isAccessibleChildSelected(int childIndex);
    public abstract void addAccessibleSelection(int childIndex);
```

continues

LISTING 33.3   CONTINUED

```
        public abstract void removeAccessibleSelection(int childIndex);
        public abstract void clearAccessibleSelection();
        public abstract void selectAllAccessibleSelection();
}
```

The getAccessibleSelectionCount method returns the number of selected children. getAccessibleSelection returns a selected child, referenced by a zero-based index value. The index is based on the list of selected children, not the list of all children contained by the object. In all other AccessibleSelection methods, children are referenced by an index value based on the list of all children contained by the object.

The isAccessibleChildSelected method determines if a given child object is selected. If an object supports multiple selections, the addAccessibleSelection method adds the given child to the selection. If the object supports only a single selection, addAccessibleSelection replaces the current selection with the given selection. The removeAccessibleSelection method removes a given object from the selection. Finally, selectAllAccessibleSelection selects all of an object's children, and clearAccessibleSelection deselects all selected children.

The AccessibleText Interface

The AccessibleText interface provides a way for assistive technologies to work with objects that present textual information. You can determine if an object supports the AccessibleText interface by getting the object's AccessibleContext and calling the getAccessibleText method. A non-null return value indicates that the object supports the AccessibleText interface. Listing 33.4 gives the class signature for AccessibleText.

LISTING 33.4   AccessibleText CLASS SIGNATURE

```
public interface AccessibleText extends Object {
    public static final int CHARACTER;
    public static final int WORD;
    public static final int SENTENCE;
    public abstract int getIndexAtPoint(Point point);
    public abstract Rectangle getCharacterBounds(int index);
    public abstract int getCharCount();
    public abstract int getCaretPosition();
    public abstract String getAtIndex(int element, int index);
    public abstract String getAfterIndex(int element, int index);
    public abstract String getBeforeIndex(int element, int index);
    public abstract AttributeSet getCharacterAttribute(int index);
    public abstract int getSelectionStart();
    public abstract int getSelectionEnd();
```

```
    public abstract String getSelectedText();
}
```

Accessible text is represented as a single String object. The getCharCount method returns the number of characters in the text. The getAtIndex, getAfterIndex, and getBeforeIndex methods retrieve text by the sentence, by the word, or character-by-character. The getCaratPosition method gets the index of the character to the right of the carat.

Three methods allow you to work with a selection within the text object. getSelectionStart returns the index of the first character in the selection. getSelectionEnd returns the index of the character that follows the last character in the selection. If there is no selection, the start and end indexes will be equal. The getSelectedText method returns a String object containing the selected text.

AccessibleText includes two methods useful for working with the text from the perspective of the visual display of the text: getCharacterBounds retrieves a Rectangle corresponding to the bounds of the area occupied by the text, and getIndexAtPoint retrieves the index of the character under the given mouse coordinates.

The AccessibleValue Interface

The AccessibleValue interface provides a way for assistive technologies to manipulate numerical values that are associated with accessible objects. You can determine if an object supports the AccessibleValue interface by getting the object's AccessibleContext and calling the getAccessibleValue method. A non-null return value indicates that the object supports the AccessibleValue interface. Listing 33.5 gives the class signature for the AccessibleValue interface.

LISTING 33.5   AccessibleValue CLASS SIGNATURE

```
public interface AccessibleValue extends Object {
    public abstract Number getCurrentAccessibleValue();
    public abstract boolean setCurrentAccessibleValue(Number number);
    public abstract Number getMinimumAccessibleValue();
    public abstract Number getMaximumAccessibleValue();
}
```

The AccessibleValue interface has only four methods. Two methods, getCurrent-AccessibleValue and setCurrentAccessibleValue, get and set the current value. The getMinimumAccessibleValue and getMaximumAccessibleValue methods retrieve the

33

ACCESSIBILITY

minimum and maximum settings for the numerical value. If you try to set a value outside this range, `setCurrentAccessibleValue` will fail to set the value and will return `false`.

The `AccessibleBundle` Class

The `AccessibleBundle` class is a class designed to define a closely typed enumeration. It's used as the base class for the `AccessibleRole` and `AccessibleState` classes. Listing 33.6 gives the class signature for `AccessibleBundle`.

Listing 33.6   `AccessibleBundle` Class Signature

```
public abstract class AccessibleBundle extends Object
{
  // public constructor
    public AccessibleBundle();
  // public instance methods
public String toDisplayString(String resourceBundleName,
                                Locale locale);
    public String toDisplayString(Locale locale);
    public String toDisplayString();
    public String toString();
}
```

The `AccessibleBundle` class provides several methods to get localized human-readable string representations of enumeration elements.

The `AccessibleRole` Class

The `AccessibleRole` class provides a mechanism for describing the role of an accessible user interface component. Accessible technologies can determine the function of a user-interface component by getting the component's role. All accessible components must have a role. To get an object's role, first get its `AccessibleContext` and then call the `getAccessibleRole` method.

All of the public members of the `AccessibleRole` class are static final constants that define roles for Swing components. Listing 33.7 gives the class signature for this class.

Listing 33.7   `AccessibleRole` Class Signature

```
public class AccessibleRole extends AccessibleBundle
{
    public static final AccessibleRole ALERT;
    public static final AccessibleRole COLUMN_HEADER;
    public static final AccessibleRole COMBO_BOX;
    public static final AccessibleRole DESKTOP_ICON;
    public static final AccessibleRole INTERNAL_FRAME;
```

```
        public static final AccessibleRole DESKTOP_PANE;
        public static final AccessibleRole WINDOW;
        public static final AccessibleRole FRAME;
        public static final AccessibleRole DIALOG;
        public static final AccessibleRole DIRECTORY_PANE;
        public static final AccessibleRole FILE_CHOOSER;
        public static final AccessibleRole FILLER;
        public static final AccessibleRole LABEL;
        public static final AccessibleRole ROOT_PANE;
        public static final AccessibleRole GLASS_PANE;
        public static final AccessibleRole LAYERED_PANE;
        public static final AccessibleRole LIST;
        public static final AccessibleRole MENU_BAR;
        public static final AccessibleRole POPUP_MENU;
        public static final AccessibleRole MENU;
        public static final AccessibleRole MENU_ITEM;
        public static final AccessibleRole SEPARATOR;
        public static final AccessibleRole PAGE_TAB_LIST;
        public static final AccessibleRole PAGE_TAB;
        public static final AccessibleRole PANEL;
        public static final AccessibleRole PROGRESS_BAR;
        public static final AccessibleRole PASSWORD_TEXT;
        public static final AccessibleRole PUSH_BUTTON;
        public static final AccessibleRole TOGGLE_BUTTON;
        public static final AccessibleRole CHECK_BOX;
        public static final AccessibleRole RADIO_BUTTON;
        public static final AccessibleRole ROW_HEADER;
        public static final AccessibleRole SCROLL_PANE;
        public static final AccessibleRole SCROLL_BAR;
        public static final AccessibleRole VIEWPORT;
        public static final AccessibleRole SLIDER;
        public static final AccessibleRole SPLIT_PANE;
        public static final AccessibleRole TABLE;
        public static final AccessibleRole TEXT;
        public static final AccessibleRole TREE;
        public static final AccessibleRole TOOL_BAR;
        public static final AccessibleRole TOOL_TIP;
        public static final AccessibleRole AWT_COMPONENT;
        public static final AccessibleRole SWING_COMPONENT;
        public static final AccessibleRole UNKNOWN;
}
```

33

ACCESSIBILITY

If you need to define roles for your custom components, you should subclass `AccessibleRole` and add additional constant definitions as shown in the following code fragment that creates the DIALOG constant.

```
public static final AccessibleRole DIALOG = new AccessibleRole("dialog");
```

The `AccessibleState` Class

The `AccessibleState` class is used to describe a component's state. It's based on the `AccessibleBundle` class and is implemented to represent a closely typed enumeration. The actual state of a component is described by the `AccessibleStateSet` class, which contains an array of `AccessibleState` objects. Listing 33.8 gives the class signature of the `AccessibleState` class.

LISTING 33.8   `AccessibleState` CLASS SIGNATURE

```
public class AccessibleState extends AccessibleBundle
{
    public static final AccessibleState ACTIVE;
    public static final AccessibleState PRESSED;
    public static final AccessibleState ARMED;
    public static final AccessibleState BUSY;
    public static final AccessibleState CHECKED;
    public static final AccessibleState EDITABLE;
    public static final AccessibleState EXPANDABLE;
    public static final AccessibleState COLLAPSED;
    public static final AccessibleState EXPANDED;
    public static final AccessibleState ENABLED;
    public static final AccessibleState FOCUSABLE;
    public static final AccessibleState FOCUSED;
    public static final AccessibleState ICONIFIED;
    public static final AccessibleState MODAL;
    public static final AccessibleState OPAQUE;
    public static final AccessibleState RESIZABLE;
    public static final AccessibleState MULTISELECTABLE;
    public static final AccessibleState SELECTABLE;
    public static final AccessibleState SELECTED;
    public static final AccessibleState SHOWING;
    public static final AccessibleState VISIBLE;
    public static final AccessibleState VERTICAL;
    public static final AccessibleState HORIZONTAL;
    public static final AccessibleState SINGLE_LINE;
    public static final AccessibleState MULTI_LINE;
}
```

All the members of `AccessibleState` are static final constants. There is no public constructor for this class—if you need to define new constants to describe the state of your accessible objects, you should subclass `AccessibleState` and add your constants to the new class by using the technique shown in the following code fragment that creates the CHECKED state constant.

```
public static final AccessibleState CHECKED
                    = new AccessibleState("checked");
```

The basic states that are used with all types of Swing components include ENABLED, FOCUSABLE, VISIBLE, SHOWING, FOCUSED, SELECTABLE, SELECTED, and OPAQUE. Specific components can use additional states. For example, JButton objects also use the ARMED, PRESSED, and CHECKED states.

The AccessibleStateSet Class

The AccessibleStateSet class fully describes the state of an accessible component. You can determine an object's accessible state by getting the object's AccessibleContext and calling the getAccessibleStateSet method. Listing 33.9 gives the class signature of the AccessibleStateSet class.

LISTING 33.9   AccessibleStateSet CLASS SIGNATURE

```
public class AccessibleStateSet extends Object
{
    public AccessibleStateSet();
    public AccessibleStateSet(AccessibleState[] state);
    public boolean add(AccessibleState state);
    public void addAll(AccessibleState[] state);
    public boolean remove(AccessibleState state);
    public void clear();
    public boolean contains(AccessibleState state);
    public AccessibleState toArray()[];
    public String toString();
}
```

There are two public constructors for AccessibleStateSet. One constructor creates a state set containing the given array of AccessibleState objects. The other constructor creates an empty state set. The add and addAll methods add states to the state set. The remove method removes the given state from the state set. The clear method removes all states from the state set.

You can use the contains method to determine if a given state is in the state set. toArray returns an array of all AccessibleState objects in the state set. The toString method returns a localized string representing all of the states in the state set.

Creating Assistive Technologies

A full treatise on designing assistive technologies for Java Accessibility is beyond the scope of this book. If you're interested in creating assistive technologies, you should begin by downloading the latest Java Accessibility Utilities from the JavaSoft Web site at http:\\www.javasoft.com.

33

ACCESSIBILITY

The Java Accessibility Utilities

The Java Accessibility Utilities provide support for creating assistive technologies. The utilities include a small API that supports event monitoring and provides a mechanism for assistive technologies to be notified when top-level windows are created and destroyed.

The utilities include classes for monitoring events for all components that exist in applications running in the same Java Virtual Machine (JVM) as the assistive technology. The classes provide system-wide monitoring of all events for both AWT and Swing components.

Automatic Loading of Assistive Technologies

JDK 1.2 includes a mechanism for automatically loading assistive technologies. This is handled by putting a configuration line in the `accessibility.properties` file to specify which assistive technologies to load when launching an applet or application. Refer to the Java Accessibility Utilities documentation for details on automatic loading of assistive technologies.

Summary

Making applications accessible to users with limited abilities is becoming an important element of user-interface design. JFC facilitates the creation of accessible applications by providing components with built-in support for accessibility. It's relatively easy to write accessible JFC applications—the "Supporting Accessibility in JFC Applications" section gives some guidelines for what you need to do to accomplish this.

Drag and Drop

CHAPTER 34

Drag and Drop is a user interface gesture that allows users to request a data transfer between a source and a target. Drag and Drop can be used within an application as well as between applications. JFC provides a framework to support drag-and-drop gestures and to facilitate data transfer.

In this chapter you will learn

- About drag sources and drop targets.

  Drag sources and drop targets collaborate to facilitate drag-and-drop operations.

- How to implement a drag source

  Drag sources initiate drag-and-drop operations and are capable of transferring data to drop targets.

- How to implement a drop target

  One or more drop targets are required to complete the Drag and Drop mechanism. Drop targets are consumers of transferable data.

- How to transfer data from a drag source to a drop target

  Data can be MIME-based content such as plain text or serialized objects. The data transfer mechanism varies with different types of content.

Overview of JFC Drag and Drop

A drag-and-drop operation involves a *drag source* and multiple *drop targets*. The drag source is capable of producing certain types of transferable data, and the drop target is capable of consuming certain types of transferable data.

Since drag-and-drop operations are driven by user gestures, the drag source and the drop target are normally associated with components. For example, consider a user interface that allows the user to drag text labels and drop them on list boxes. The text label components would be drag sources and the list box components would be drop targets.

Source actions and *drop actions* describe types of operations on the content data. Examples of types of actions are copy, move, and link.

The Basic Protocol

Drag-and-drop operations are a collaborative effort between a drag source and multiple drop targets. The following sequence illustrates the basic procedural protocol of a drag-and-drop operation:

1. A drag source recognizes a user gesture (usually a click and drag with the mouse) and initiates a drag operation.

2. Drag sources and drop targets are notified whenever the cursor enters, exits, and moves over the target.

3. When notified of a drag enter event, the target can query the drag source to determine the drag action (copy or move) and the type of data associated with the drag operation and choose whether to accept or reject the drag.

4. When the user releases the mouse with the cursor over a valid drop target, the target is notified. The target must choose to either accept or reject the drop operation.

5. If the target accepts the drop action, it initiates a data transfer between the source and the target and then notifies the system that the drop is complete.

The operational protocol is actually a bit more complicated than this procedure illustrates. For one, drag sources can provide user interface feedback by changing cursors and drag images. Also, drop actions can change in the middle of an operation when the user presses or releases a key.

JFC Drag and Drop Implementation

JFC Drag and Drop operations involve two distinct mechanisms:

- The drag-and-drop mechanism
- The data transfer mechanism

The drag-and-drop mechanism consists of the GUI elements that make up the user interface for the drag-and-drop operation as well as the protocol that binds drag sources to drop targets. The java.awt.dnd package provides support for the drag-and-drop mechanism with classes for drag sources, drop targets, and various events to support the basic drag-and-drop protocol. The java.awt.dnd package is new with JDK 1.2.

The data transfer mechanism is based on the java.awt.datatransfer package. This package includes support for clipboards, data flavors based on MIME types, and transferable data. The java.awt.datatransfer package first appeared in JDK 1.1.

34

DRAG AND DROP

> **NOTE**
>
> In JDK 1.2, drag-and-drop is implemented by using peers and thus utilizes native platform drag-and-drop services. Drag-and-drop uses peers even when the drag source and drop target objects are owned by the same application.

Implementing a Drop Target

To implement a component that is a drop target, you must

- Implement a drop target listener (class `DropTargetListener`) to handle drag-and-drop events.
- Create a `DropTarget` object to manage drag-and-drop operations.

When you construct a `DropTarget` object, you associate it with the component that you want to be a drop target and with the component's drop target listener. You can do this by using one of the `DropTarget` constructors or after construction by using `public` instance methods.

The amount of overhead that you have to add to allow a component to be a drop target is minimal. The following code fragment illustrates this by showing what you need to add to a component to make it a drop target.

```
class DroppablePanel extends JPanel implements DropTargetListener {
    // Constructor
    public DroppablePanel() {
        super();

        // create a drop target for this component
        DropTarget dt = new DropTarget(this, this);
    }

    // DropTargetListener interface implementation
    public void dragEnter(DropTargetDragEvent dtde) { }
    public void dragExit(DropTargetEvent dte) { }
    public void dragOver(DropTargetDragEvent dtde) { }
    public void drop(DropTargetDropEvent dtde) { }
    public void dropActionChanged(DropTargetDragEvent dtde) { }
}
```

What this fragment does is define a `DroppablePanel` component that extends `JPanel` with a component that implements the `DropTargetListener` interface. `DroppablePanel` also instantiates a `DropTarget` object in the constructor. Bear in mind that this code doesn't really do very much—you have to add code to handle the various drop target events to make it useful.

Before getting into a working example, take a look at the classes that are used by drop targets: `DropTarget`, `DropTargetContext`, `DropTargetListener`, `DropTargetEvent`, `DropTargetDragEvent`, and `DropTargetDropEvent`.

The DropTarget Class

The DropTarget class represents a drop target. You must construct a DropTarget object for each component that you want to be a drop target.

```
public class DropTarget extends Object
                        implements DropTargetListener, Serializable
{
  // Public constructors
    public DropTarget();
    public DropTarget(Component component, int actions,
                  DropTargetListener listener);
    public DropTarget(Component component, int actions,
                  DropTargetListener listener, boolean active);
    public DropTarget(Component component, DropTargetListener listener);
    public DropTarget(Component component, int actions,
                  DropTargetListener listener, boolean active,
                  FlavorMap map)
  // Public instance methods
    public synchronized void addDropTargetListener(
          DropTargetListener listener);
    public void addNotify(ComponentPeer peer);
    public synchronized void dragEnter(DropTargetDragEvent event);
    public synchronized void dragExit(DropTargetEvent event);
    public synchronized void dragOver(DropTargetDragEvent event);
    public synchronized void drop(DropTargetDropEvent event);
    public void dropActionChanged(DropTargetDragEvent event);
    public synchronized Component getComponent();
    public synchronized int getDefaultActions();
    public DropTargetContext getDropTargetContext();
    public FlavorMap getFlavorMap();
    public synchronized boolean isActive();
    public synchronized void removeDropTargetListener(
          DropTargetListener listener);
    public void removeNotify(ComponentPeer peer);
    public synchronized void setActive(boolean active);
    public synchronized void setComponent(Component component);
    public synchronized void setDefaultActions(int actions);
    public void setFlavorMap(FlavorMap map)
}
```

34

DRAG AND DROP

In addition to a default constructor, DropTarget has several constructors that allow you to associate the target with a component and a drop target event listener. You can also specify the default drop actions, the data flavors the target supports, and whether the target is active or not. If you use the default constructor to instantiate a DropTarget, you must use the setComponent and addDropTargetListener methods to associate a component and a drop target event listener with the drop target.

The `DropTargetContext` Class

The `DropTargetContext` class represents the context of a drop target operation. JFC creates a drop target context whenever a drag operation enters the area occupied by a drop target.

```
public class DropTargetContext extends Object
{
  // Public instance methods
    public synchronized void addNotify(DropTargetContextPeer peer);
    public void dropComplete(boolean complete);
    public Component getComponent();
    public DropTarget getDropTarget();
    public synchronized void removeNotify();
}
```

There is no `public` constructor for the `DropTargetContext` class. You can obtain a drop target context when processing a drop target event by calling the event's `getDropTargetContext` method as shown in the following code fragment.

```
public void drop(DropTargetDropEvent dtde) {
    // get drop target context
    DropTargetContext dtc = dtde.getDropTargetContext();

    .
    .
    .


}
```

The most important method in this class is `dropComplete`. If you accept the drop operation while handling a `drop` event, you must call `dropComplete` after you complete the data transfer. The `getComponent` and `getDropTarget` methods get the component and drop target object that are associated with the drop target context.

There are a number of `protected` instance methods that are not shown in the `DropTargetContext` class signature. These methods are not normally used by applications and have been omitted for clarity.

> **NOTE**
>
> The `DropTargetDropEvent` class provides a `dropComplete` method that calls the drop target context's `dropComplete` method. You can implement a simple drop target without directly using the `DropTargetContext` class.

The `DropTargetListener` Interface

The `DropTargetListener` interface represents the event listener for drop target events. All drop targets must provide an implementation for `DropTargetListener` to handle drop target events.

```
public abstract interface DropTargetListener extends Object
                                      implements EventListener {
  // Abstract public instance methods
    public abstract void dragEnter(DropTargetDragEvent event);
    public abstract void dragExit(DropTargetEvent event);
    public abstract void dragOver(DropTargetDragEvent event);
    public abstract void drop(DropTargetDropEvent event);
    public abstract void dropActionChanged(DropTargetDragEvent event);
}
```

The `dragEnter` and `dragExit` methods notify a target when a drag operation enters and exits the area occupied by their associated components. The `dragOver` method is generated continually as the cursor is moved over the target.

The `drop` method notifies the target that the user has dropped data on the target. The target should then either accept or reject the drop operation by calling one of the `DropTargetDragEvent` methods, `acceptDrop` or `rejectDrop`. If the target accepts the drop, it must get the drop target context and call `dropComplete` after successfully or unsuccessfully transferring the drop data.

The `dropActionChanged` method notifies the target that the user has pressed or released keys on the keyboard to change the potential drop action.

The `DropTargetEvent` Class

The `DropTargetEvent` class is the base class for the drop target event classes `DropTargetDragEvent` and `DropTargetDropEvent`.

```
public class DropTargetEvent extends EventObject
{
  Public constructor
    public DropTargetEvent(DropTargetContext context);
  Public instance method
    public DropTargetContext getDropTargetContext();
}
```

The only method in the `DropTargetEvent` class is `getDropTargetContext`, which retrieves the context for the drop target associated with the event.

The `DropTargetDragEvent` Class

The `DropTargetDragEvent` class represents a drag event on a drop target. You can receive drop target drag events by implementing the `DropTargetListener` interface.

```
public class DropTargetDragEvent extends DropTargetEvent
{
  // Public constructor
    public DropTargetDragEvent(DropTargetContext context, Point location,
                               int dropActions, int sourceActions);
  // Public instance methods
    public void acceptDrag(int action);
    public DataFlavor[] getCurrentDataFlavors();
    public List getCurrentDataFlavorsAsList();
    public int getDropAction();
    public Point getLocation();
    public int getSourceActions();
    public boolean isDataFlavorSupported(DataFlavor flavor);
    public void rejectDrag();
}
```

Although there is a public constructor for this class, you don't normally need to construct objects of this type. The `dragEnter`, `dragOver`, `dragExit`, and `dropActionChanged` events in the `DropTargetListener` interface all have a `DropTargetDragEvent` as a parameter.

When a target receives a `dragEnter` event, the target should call the `getDropAction` and `getCurrentDataFlavors` methods to determine the current drop action and the types of data available. The target can then either accept or reject the drag operation by calling `acceptDrag` or `rejectDrag`. The `getSourceActions` method retrieves the types of drop actions (copy, move, link) that the source is capable of supporting.

The `DropTargetDropEvent` Class

The `DropTargetDropEvent` class represents a drop event on a drop target. You can receive drop target drop events by implementing the `DropTargetListener` interface.

```
public class DropTargetDropEvent extends DropTargetEvent
{
  // Public constructors
    public DropTargetDropEvent(DropTargetContext context, Point location,
                               int dropAction, int sourceActions);
    public DropTargetDropEvent(DropTargetContext context, Point location,
                               int dropAction, int sourceActions,
                               boolean isLocal);
  // Public instance methods
    public void acceptDrop(int action);
    public void dropComplete(boolean);
```

```
    public DataFlavor[] getCurrentDataFlavors();
    public List getCurrentDataFlavorsAsList();
    public int getDropAction();
    public Point getLocation();
    public int getSourceActions();
    public Transferable getTransferable();
    public boolean isDataFlavorSupported(DataFlavor flavor);
    public boolean isLocalTransfer();
    public void rejectDrop();
}
```

Although there are two `public` constructors for this class, you don't normally need to construct objects of this type. When data is dropped on a drop target, the target gets a drop event that has a `DropTargetDropEvent` object as a parameter. The target can use `getDropAction` and `getCurrentDataFlavors` to determine the current drop action and the types of data available. The target should then decide whether to accept or reject the drop operation and call either the `acceptDrop` or `rejectDrop` method. If the target accepts the drop, it should call `dropComplete` after completing the data transfer.

The `getLocation` method returns the coordinates of the cursor when the drop action occurred. The `getTransferable` method gets a `Transferable` object that is capable of transferring the dropped data.

Example of a Drop Target

Listing 34.1 is the complete source for `DropTargetDemo`, an application containing a drop target that displays information about drag operations. Figure 34.1 illustrates the appearance of `DropTargetDemo` when it's displaying information about a drag operation.

FIGURE 34.1

`DropTargetDemo`
example.

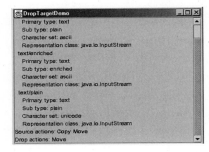

34

DRAG AND DROP

LISTING 34.1   `DropTargetDemo.java`

```
/* DropTargetDemo.java
 *
 * An example of a drop target implementation.
```

continues

LISTING 34.1   CONTINUED

```java
 * Creates an application that displays information
 * about drag operations over the target area.
 */

import java.awt.*;
import java.awt.event.*;
import javax.swing.*;
import java.awt.dnd.*;
import java.awt.datatransfer.Transferable;
import java.awt.datatransfer.DataFlavor;
import java.io.InputStream;
import java.io.InputStreamReader;
import java.io.BufferedReader;

/* App class
 */
public class DropTargetDemo {

    // Main entry point
    public static void main(String s[]) {
        // create app panel
        DropTargetDemoPanel panel = new DropTargetDemoPanel();

        // create a frame for app
        JFrame frame = new JFrame("DropTargetDemo");

        // add a window listener for window close events
        frame.addWindowListener(new WindowAdapter() {
            public void windowClosing(WindowEvent e) {System.exit(0);}
        });

        // add app panel to content pane
        frame.getContentPane().add(panel);

        // set initial frame size and make visible
        frame.setSize (400, 300);
        frame.setVisible(true);
    }
}

/* App panel class
 */
class DropTargetDemoPanel extends JPanel {
    // Constructor
    public DropTargetDemoPanel () {

        // use border layout to cause text area to fill window
        setLayout(new BorderLayout());
```

```
            // wrap drop target text area in scroll pane and add to panel
            add(new JScrollPane(new DropTargetTextArea()));
    }
}

/* DropTargetTextArea class
 *
 * Extends JTextArea class by making the text area a drop target.
 * Whenever a drag operation enters the text area, it changes
 * background color and displays information about the drag.
 */
class DropTargetTextArea extends JTextArea
                        implements DropTargetListener {
    // background colors for normal and under drag states
    private Color bkgNormal = Color.lightGray;
    private Color bkgUnderDrag = Color.yellow;

    // Constructor
    public DropTargetTextArea() {
        super();

        // set up text area
        setBackground(bkgNormal);
        setEditable(false);
        setText("Drag objects over this window!");

        // create a drop target for this component
        DropTarget dt = new DropTarget(this, this);
    }

    //
    // DropTargetListener interface implementation
    //
    public void dragEnter(DropTargetDragEvent dtde) {
        // display information about the drag operation
        setText(dumpDragEventToString(dtde));

        // accept all drags
        dtde.acceptDrag(dtde.getSourceActions());

        // visually indicate that drop target is under drag
        showUnderDrag(true);
    }

    public void dragExit(DropTargetEvent dte) {
        showUnderDrag(false);
    }

    public void dragOver(DropTargetDragEvent dtde) { }
```

34

DRAG AND DROP

continues

LISTING 34.1   CONTINUED

```java
public void drop(DropTargetDropEvent dtde) {
    // reject all drops in this demo
    dtde.rejectDrop();

    // need to indicate that drag operation is done
    showUnderDrag(false);
}

public void dropActionChanged(DropTargetDragEvent dtde) {
    // drop action has changed, update displayed
    // information about the drag operation
    setText(dumpDragEventToString(dtde));
}

//
// Private helper methods
//

// changes background to indicate that
// component is under drag operation
private void showUnderDrag(boolean underDrag) {
    if(underDrag) setBackground(bkgUnderDrag);
    else setBackground(bkgNormal);

    paintImmediately(0, 0, getWidth(), getHeight());
}

// dumps information about DropTargetDragEvent object to string
private String dumpDragEventToString(DropTargetDragEvent dtde) {
    DataFlavor[] flavors = dtde.getCurrentDataFlavors();

    String s = "";
    s += "MIME type(s):";
    for(int i = 0; i < flavors.length; i++) {
        s += ("\n  " + flavors[i].getHumanPresentableName());
        s += ("\n    Primary type: " + flavors[i].getPrimaryType());
        s += ("\n    Sub type: " + flavors[i].getSubType());
        if (flavors[i].getPrimaryType().equals("text")) {
            s += ("\n    Character set: "
                    + flavors[i].getParameter("charset"));
        }
        s += ("\n    Representation class: "
                + flavors[i].getRepresentationClass().getName());
    }
    s += ("\nSource actions: "
        + dumpActionsToString(dtde.getSourceActions()));
    s += ("\nDrop actions: "
        + dumpActionsToString(dtde.getDropAction()));
    return(s);
```

```
        }

        // takes bit field specifying drag/drop actions and
        // returns string containing corresponding action verbs
        private String dumpActionsToString (int actions) {
            String s = "";
            if ((actions & DnDConstants.ACTION_COPY) != 0)
                s += "Copy ";
            if ((actions & DnDConstants.ACTION_MOVE) != 0)
                s += "Move ";
            if ((actions & DnDConstants.ACTION_LINK) != 0)
                s += "Link ";

            return s;
        }
}
```

The `DropTargetDemo` example does not accept any drop operations or transfer any data—see "Transferring Data Between the Drag Source and Drop Target" later in this chapter for details on those topics.

Overview of the `DropTargetDemo` Example

`DropTargetDemo` consists of the following three classes:

- `DropTargetDemo`   The application class containing the main entry point
- `DropTargetDemoPanel`   A panel containing the user interface for the application
- `DropTargetTextArea`   An extension of `JTextArea` modified to be a drop target

All of the interesting code here is in the implementation of the `DropTargetTextArea` class. The following sections discuss how you extend the `JTextArea` class to be a drop target.

Creating a Drop Target Object

After setting up the text area to have a normal background and to be noneditable, the `DropTargetTextArea` constructor creates a `DropTarget` object for the component.

```
DropTarget dt = new DropTarget(this, this);
```

The arguments for the `DropTarget` constructor specify the component that you want to be a drop target and a drop target listener for drop target events. Because the `DropTargetTextArea` class implements the `DropTargetListener` class, you can specify this for both arguments.

Implementing the `DropTargetListener` Interface

The `DropTargetListener` interface consists of five methods: `dragEnter`, `dragExit`, `dragOver`, `drop`, and `dropActionChanged`. These methods notify the target when the user performs drag-and-drop operations over the target area.

The `dragEnter` method is called whenever a drag operation enters the drop target area.

```
public void dragEnter(DropTargetDragEvent dtde) {
    // display information about the drag operation
    setText(dumpDragEventToString(dtde));

    // accept all drags
    dtde.acceptDrag(dtde.getSourceActions());

    // visually indicate that drop target is under drag
    showUnderDrag(true);
}
```

The `DropTargetTextArea` implementation for `dragEnter` performs the following three operations:

- Displays information about the drag event by calling `setText` to display the string returned by the `dumpDragEventToString` helper method
- Calls `DropTargetDragEvent.acceptDrag` to accept the drag operation
- Calls the `showUnderDrag` helper method to visually indicate (by changing the background color of the target component) that the drop target is under a drag operation

> **NOTE**
>
> A more functional drop target implementation would get the data flavor and source actions before determining whether to accept or reject the drag.

The `dragExit` method is called whenever a drag operation exits the target area.

```
public void dragExit(DropTargetEvent dte) {
    showUnderDrag(false);
}
```

The `DropTargetTextArea` implementation for `dragExit` calls the `showUnderDrag` helper method with the `underDrag` parameter set to `false` to change the background of the target component back to its original color.

The `drop` method is called when the user releases the mouse button during a drag operation over a drop target. The target should respond by either accepting or rejecting the drop.

```
public void drop(DropTargetDropEvent dtde) {
    // reject all drops in this demo
    dtde.rejectDrop();

    // need to indicate that drag operation is done
    showUnderDrag(false);
}
```

The `DropTargetTextArea` implementation for drop calls `DropTargetDropEvent`
`.rejectDrop` to reject all drop operations. A fully functional drop target implementation
would get the available data flavors and drop action before deciding whether to accept or
reject the drop. Note that the drop code also calls `showUnderDrag` to reset the background color for the component—the `dragExit` method is not called if a drop operation
occurs.

The `dropActionChanged` method is called whenever the user changes the drop action
when a drag operation is over a target. An example of changing the drop action would be
pressing or releasing the Alt key to toggle between a copy and a move operation.

```
public void dropActionChanged(DropTargetDragEvent dtde) {
    // drop action has changed, update displayed
    // information about the drag operation
    setText(dumpDragEventToString(dtde));
}
```

The `DropTargetTextArea` implementation of `dropActionChanged` redisplays information
about the drag event by calling `setText` to display the string returned by the
`dumpDragEventToString` helper method.

Getting Information About the Drag Event

The `dumpDragEventToString` method is a private helper method that returns a string containing information about a given `DropTargetDragEvent` object. The method first gets
information about the data flavors that are available from the source by calling
`getCurrentDataFlavors` on the `DropTargetDragEvent` object.

```
DataFlavor[] flavors = dtde.getCurrentDataFlavors();
```

34

DRAG AND DROP

> **NOTE**
>
> The `DataFlavor` class is in the `java.awt.datatransfer` package, not the
> `java.awt.dnd` package.

After getting an array of `DataFlavor` objects, `dumpDragEventToString` dumps information about the data flavors to a local string. It then gets the source actions and current drop action and uses a second private helper method, `dumpActionsToString`, to concatenate information about the drop actions to the local string before returning it to the caller.

Implementing a Drag Source

To implement a component that is a drag source, you must do the following:

- Implement a drag source listener (class `DragSourceListener`) to handle drag source events.
- Implement a drag gesture listener (class `DragGestureListener`) to handle drag gesture events.
- Provide an implementation for the `Transferable` interface to handle the data transfer operation.
- Create a `DragSource` object to manage drag-and-drop operations.
- Create a `DragGestureRecognizer` object to recognize drag gestures.

The following code fragment illustrates what you need to add to a component to make it a drag source.

```
class DraggableLabel extends JLabel implements DragSourceListener,
                                                DragGestureListener,
                                                Transferable {
    // Constructor
    public DraggableLabel(String text) {
        super(text);

        // create a drag source
        DragSource ds = DragSource.getDefaultDragSource();

        // create a drag gesture recognizer
DragGestureRecognizer dgr = ds.createDefaultDragGestureRecognizer(
            this,                            // component
            DnDConstants.ACTION_COPY_OR_MOVE,  // actions
            this);                           // drag gesture listener
    }

    // DragGestureListener interface implementation
    public void dragGestureRecognized(DragGestureEvent event) {
        // start drag operation
        event.startDrag(null,        // drag cursor
                        this,        // transferable object
                        this);       // drag source listener
    }
```

```
    // Transferable interface implementation
    public Object getTransferData(DataFlavor flavor) {
        // return object capable of transferring data
    }

    public DataFlavor[] getTransferDataFlavors() {
        // return data flavors supported by drag source
    }

    public boolean isDataFlavorSupported(DataFlavor flavor) {
        // return boolean indicating if drag source
        // supports the specified data flavor
    }

    // DragSourceListener interface implementation
    public void dragDropEnd(DragSourceDropEvent dsde) { }
    public void dragEnter(DragSourceDragEvent dsde) { }
    public void dragExit(DragSourceEvent dse) { }
    public void dragOver(DragSourceDragEvent dsde) { }
    public void dropActionChanged(DragSourceDragEvent dsde) { }
}
```

What this fragment does is define a DraggableLabel component that extends JLabel by implementing the DragSourceListener, DragGestureListener, and Transferable interfaces. It also creates DragSource and DragGestureRecognizer objects in the constructor. Note that the dragGestureRecognized method, a member of the DragGestureListener class, actually begins the drag operation by calling DragGestureEvent.startDrag.

Remember that like the fragment presented earlier to illustrate the structure of a drop target, this code doesn't really do very much—you have to add some code to the methods to make it useful.

Before getting into a complete working example, take a look at the classes that are used by drop targets: DragSource, DragGestureListener, DragGestureEvent, DragSourceContext, and DragSourceListener.

34

DRAG AND DROP

NOTE

There are many similar methods implemented in multiple java.awt.dnd classes. In general, it's best to use methods on the objects that are closest in scope to the code you are writing. For example, both the DragSource and DragGestureEvent classes have a startDrag method. When a drag gesture

continues

listener's `dragGestureRecognized` method is called, you should call the `startDrag` method on the `DragGestureEvent` object passed to `dragGestureRecognized`, rather than getting the associated `DragSource` object and calling its `startDrag` method.

The **DragSource** Class

The `DragSource` class represents a source of drag-and-drop operations. Each component that will be a source of drag-and-drop operations requires a drag source object to manage drag-and-drop operations.

```
public class DragSource extends Object
{
  // Public constants
    public static final Cursor DefaultCopyDrop;
    public static final Cursor DefaultMoveDrop;
    public static final Cursor DefaultLinkDrop;
    public static final Cursor DefaultCopyNoDrop;
    public static final Cursor DefaultMoveNoDrop;
    public static final Cursor DefaultLinkNoDrop;
  // Public constructors
    public DragSource();
  // Public class methods
    public static DragSource getDefaultDragSource();
    public static boolean isDragImageSupported();
  // Public instance methods
    public DragGestureRecognizer createDefaultDragGestureRecognizer(
        Component component, int actions, DragGestureListener dsl);
    public DragGestureRecognizer createDragGestureRecognizer(
        Class recognizerClass, Component component, int actions,
        DragGestureListener dsl);
    public FlavorMap getFlavorMap();
    public void startDrag(DragGestureEvent trigger, Cursor dragCursor,
        Image dragImage, Point imageOffset, Transferable data,
        DragSourceListener dsl);
    public void startDrag(DragGestureEvent trigger, Cursor dragCursor,
        Image dragImage, Point imageOffset, Transferable data,
        DragSourceListener dsl, FlavorMap flavors);
    public void startDrag(DragGestureEvent trigger, Cursor dragCursor,
        Transferable data, DragSourceListener dsl);
    public void startDrag(DragGestureEvent trigger, Cursor dragCursor,
        Transferable data, DragSourceListener dsl, FlavorMap flavors);
}
```

Although there is a default constructor for `DragSource`, the recommended way to get a drag source is by calling the static class method `getDefaultDragSource`.

The only other `DragSource` method you'll need to use is
`createDefaultDragGestureRecognizer` to create a drag gesture recognizer. The remaining methods exist mainly to support the drag and drop infrastructure.

The `DragGestureListener` Interface

The `DragGestureListener` interface represents a listener for drag gesture events. Drag sources must provide a drag gesture listener to determine when to start a drag operation.

```
public abstract interface DragGestureListener extends Object
                                            implements EventListener {
    public abstract void dragGestureRecognized(DragGestureEvent event);
}
```

When a drag gesture listener's `dragGestureRecognized` event is called, the listener should start a drag operation by calling the `DragGestureEvent.startDrag` method.

The `DragGestureEvent` Class

The `DragGestureEvent` class represents a drag gesture event.

```
public class DragGestureEvent extends EventObject
{
  // Constructor
    public DragGestureEvent(DragGestureRecognizer dsl, int actions,
                            Point origin, List events);
  // Public instance methods
    public Component getComponent();
    public int getDragAction();
    public Point getDragOrigin();
    public DragSource getDragSource();
    public DragGestureRecognizer getSourceAsDragGestureRecognizer();
    public InputEvent getTriggerEvent();
    public Iterator iterator();
    public void startDrag(Cursor dragCursor, Image dragImage,
                          Point imageOffset, Transferable data,
                          DragSourceListener dsl);
    public void startDrag(Cursor dragCursor, Transferable data,
                          DragSourceListener dsl);
}
```

Although there is a constructor for `DragGestureEvent`, applications don't normally create instances of this class. Drag gesture events are sent to drag gesture listeners when the user attempts to initiate a drag operation.

The `DragGestureEvent` class includes two `startDrag` methods to start a drag-and-drop operation. Each method includes parameters to specify a cursor to represent the drag operation, a transferable data object, and a drag source listener. In addition, one of the

34

DRAG AND DROP

startDrag methods includes parameters to specify an image to represent the data being dragged.

The DragSourceContext Class

The DragSourceContext class represents the context of a drag operation. JFC creates a drag source context when you start a drag operation by calling the startDrag method in the DragSource or DragGestureEvent classes.

```
public class DragSourceContext extends Object
                                implements DragSourceListener
{
  // Public constructor
    public DragSourceContext(DragSourceContextPeer peer,
        DragGestureEvent trigger, Cursor dragCursor, Image dragImage,
        Point imageOffset, Transferable data, DragSourceListener dsl);
  // Public instance methods
    public synchronized void addDragSourceListener(
        DragSourceListener listener);
    public void cancelDrag();
    public synchronized void dragDropEnd(DragSourceDropEvent event);
    public synchronized void dragEnter(DragSourceDragEvent event);
    public synchronized void dragExit(DragSourceEvent event);
    public synchronized void dragOver(DragSourceDragEvent event);
public synchronized void dropActionChanged(
        DragSourceDragEvent event);
    public Component getComponent();
    public Cursor getCursor();
    public DragSource getDragSource();
    public int getSourceActions();
    public Transferable getTransferable();
    public DragGestureEvent getTrigger();
    public synchronized void removeDragSourceListener(
        DragSourceListener listener);
    public void setCursor(Cursor);
    public void transferablesFlavorsChanged();
}
```

Although there is a constructor for the DragSourceContext class, applications don't normally create instances of this class. You can obtain a drag source context when processing drag source events by calling the event's getDragSourceContext method.

The DragSourceListener Interface

The DragSourceListener interface represents a listener for drag source events. Drag sources must provide an implementation for this interface to handle drag source events.

```
public abstract interface DragSourceListener extends Object
                                implements EventListener {
```

```
    public abstract void dragDropEnd(DragSourceDropEvent event);
    public abstract void dragEnter(DragSourceDragEvent event);
    public abstract void dragExit(DragSourceEvent event);
    public abstract void dragOver(DragSourceDragEvent event);
    public abstract void dropActionChanged(DragSourceDragEvent event);
}
```

The `dragDropEnd` method is called when a drag-and-drop operation completes.
`dragEnter` and `dragExit` are called when a drag operation enters and exits the area occupied by a drop target. The `dragOver` method is called as the drag operation moves over a drop target. The `dropActionChanged` method is called to notify the source that the user has changed the drop action. An example of changing the drop action would be pressing or releasing the Alt key to toggle between a copy and a move operation.

Example of a Drag Source

Listing 34.2 is the complete source for `DndObjectsDemo`, an application that provides a window containing several drag sources and a separate window containing a drop target. Figure 34.2 illustrates the appearance of `DndObjectsDemo`.

FIGURE 34.2

`DndObjectsDemo`
example.

LISTING 34.2   `DndObjectsDemo.java`

```
/* DndObjectsDemo.java
 *
 * Illustrates drag and drop of Java object
 * between two frame windows in same Java VM.
 */

import java.awt.*;
import java.awt.event.*;
import javax.swing.*;
import java.awt.dnd.*;
import java.awt.datatransfer.Transferable;
import java.awt.datatransfer.DataFlavor;
import java.io.InputStream;
import java.io.InputStreamReader;
import java.io.BufferedReader;
```

continues

34

DRAG AND DROP

LISTING 34.2   CONTINUED

```
/* App class
 */
public class DndObjectsDemo {

    // Main entry point
    public static void main(String s[]) {
        // create two frame windows
        JFrame sourceFrame = new JFrame("Drag Sources");
        JFrame targetFrame = new JFrame("Drop Target");

        // add window listeners for window close events
        sourceFrame.addWindowListener(new WindowAdapter() {
            public void windowClosing(WindowEvent e) {System.exit(0);}
        });
        targetFrame.addWindowListener(new WindowAdapter() {
            public void windowClosing(WindowEvent e) {System.exit(0);}
        });

        // create panels for each window
        JPanel sourcePanel = new SourcePanel();
        JPanel targetPanel = new TargetPanel();

        // add panels to content panes
        sourceFrame.getContentPane().add(sourcePanel);
        targetFrame.getContentPane().add(targetPanel);

        // set initial frame size and make visible
        sourceFrame.setSize (300, 200);
        targetFrame.setSize (300, 200);
        targetFrame.setLocation(sourceFrame.getX()
                                + sourceFrame.getWidth(),
                                  sourceFrame.getY());
        sourceFrame.setVisible(true);
        targetFrame.setVisible(true);
    }
}

/* App panel class for source window
 */
class SourcePanel extends JPanel {
    // Constructor
    public SourcePanel() {
        super();
        setLayout(new BoxLayout(this, BoxLayout.Y_AXIS));

        // add some drag source components
        add(new DraggableLabel("Draggable Label 1"));
        add(new DraggableLabel("Draggable Label 2"));
        add(new DraggableLabel("Draggable Label 3"));
```

```
                add(new DraggableLabel("Draggable Label 4"));
                add(new DraggableLabel("Draggable Label 5"));
        }
}

/* App panel class for target window
 */
class TargetPanel extends JPanel {
        public TargetPanel() {
                super();
                setLayout(new BorderLayout());

                // add a drop target component
                DroppablePanel dropPanel = new DroppablePanel();
                dropPanel.setLayout(new BoxLayout(dropPanel, BoxLayout.Y_AXIS));
                add(dropPanel);
        }
}

/* Drag source component implementation
 */
class DraggableLabel extends JLabel implements DragSourceListener,
                                               DragGestureListener,
                                               Transferable {

        // Constructor
        public DraggableLabel(String text) {
                super(text);

                // create a drag source
                DragSource ds = DragSource.getDefaultDragSource();

                // create a drag gesture recognizer
DragGestureRecognizer dgr = ds.createDefaultDragGestureRecognizer(
                this,                                   // component
                DnDConstants.ACTION_COPY_OR_MOVE,       // actions
                this);                                  // drag gesture listener
        }

        // DragGestureListener interface implementation
        public void dragGestureRecognized(DragGestureEvent event) {
                event.startDrag(null,           // drag cursor
                        this,           // transferable object
                        this);          // drag source listener
        }

        // Transferable interface implementation
        public Object getTransferData(DataFlavor flavor) {
                // if we support requested data flavor,
```

continues

LISTING 34.2   CONTINUED

```java
            // return this object as transfer data
            if(flavor.equals(MyFlavors.draggableLabelFlavor)) {
                return(this);
            }
            else return null;
        }

    public DataFlavor[] getTransferDataFlavors() {
        // return suppported data flavors
        DataFlavor[] flavors = { MyFlavors.draggableLabelFlavor };
        return flavors;
    }

    public boolean isDataFlavorSupported(DataFlavor flavor) {
        if(flavor.equals(MyFlavors.draggableLabelFlavor))
            return true;
        else
            return false;
    }

    // DragSourceListener interface implementation
    public void dragDropEnd(DragSourceDropEvent dsde) { }
    public void dragEnter(DragSourceDragEvent dsde) { }
    public void dragExit(DragSourceEvent dse) { }
    public void dragOver(DragSourceDragEvent dsde) { }
    public void dropActionChanged(DragSourceDragEvent dsde) { }
}

/* Drop target component implementation
 */
class DroppablePanel extends JPanel implements DropTargetListener {
    // background colors for normal and under drag states
    private Color bkgNormal = Color.lightGray;
    private Color bkgUnderDrag = Color.yellow;

    // Constructor
    public DroppablePanel() {
        super();

        // create a drop target for this component
        DropTarget dt = new DropTarget(this, this);
    }

    //
    // DropTargetListener interface implementation
    //
    public void dragEnter(DropTargetDragEvent dtde) {
if(isValidDragDrop(dtde.getDropAction(),
                            dtde.getCurrentDataFlavors())) {
```

```
                // accept drag
                dtde.acceptDrag(DnDConstants.ACTION_COPY_OR_MOVE);

                // change background color to visually indicate
                // that drop target is under drag
                showUnderDrag(true);
            }
            else {
                dtde.rejectDrag();
            }
        }

    public void dragExit(DropTargetEvent dte) {
            // drop target no longer under drag, restore background color
            showUnderDrag(false);
        }

    public void dragOver(DropTargetDragEvent dtde) { }

    public void drop(DropTargetDropEvent dtde) {
            // validate drop action and data flavors
    if(isValidDragDrop(dtde.getDropAction(),
                            dtde.getCurrentDataFlavors())) {
                dtde.acceptDrop(dtde.getDropAction());

                try {
                    // get transfer data (DraggableLabel object)
                    Transferable xfer = dtde.getTransferable();
    Object obj = xfer.getTransferData(MyFlavors.draggableLabelFlavor);

                    // add object to panel and revalidate
                    if(obj instanceof JComponent) {
                        add((JComponent)obj);
                        revalidate();
                    }
                    // notify system that dnd completed successfully
                    dtde.dropComplete(true);
                }
                catch(Exception exc) {
                    System.err.println(exc);
                    exc.printStackTrace();
                    dtde.dropComplete(false);
                }

            }
            else {
                // invalid drop action or data flavor, reject drop
                dtde.rejectDrop();
            }
```

continues

LISTING 34.2   CONTINUED

```
            // drop operation complete, restore background color
            showUnderDrag(false);
        }

        public void dropActionChanged(DropTargetDragEvent dtde) { }

        //
        // Private helper methods
        //

        // validates given drop action and data flavor
        private boolean isValidDragDrop(int dropAction,
                                         DataFlavor flavors []) {
            if((dropAction & DnDConstants.ACTION_COPY_OR_MOVE) != 0) {
                for(int i=0; i<flavors.length; i++) {
                    if(flavors[i].getPrimaryType().equals("application")
        && flavors[i].getSubType().equals(
                        "x-java-serialized-object")) {
                        return true;
                    }
                }
            }
            return false;
        }

        // changes background color to indicate that
        // component is under drag operation
        private void showUnderDrag(boolean underDrag) {
            if(underDrag) setBackground(bkgUnderDrag);
            else setBackground(bkgNormal);

            paintImmediately(0, 0, getWidth(), getHeight());
        }
    }

/* Class containing predefined DataFlavor objects
 */
class MyFlavors extends Object {
    static public DataFlavor draggableLabelFlavor
        = createFlavor("DraggableLabel", "draggable Label object");

    // creates a DataFlavor object from
    // representation class name and description
    static private DataFlavor createFlavor(String className,
                                             String description) {
        Class cls;
        // create class from class name
        try {
            cls = Class.forName(className);
```

```
        }
        catch(Exception exc) {
            System.err.println(exc);
            cls = null;
        }
        // create and return data flavor
        return new DataFlavor(cls, description);
    }
}
```

Overview of `DndObjectsDemo` Example

`DndObjectsDemo` presents two windows. One window, titled Drag Sources, contains some draggable `JLabel` objects. The other window, titled Drop Target, contains a droppable `JPanel`. When you drag-and-drop one of the `JLabel` objects to the Drop Target window, the object is replicated and added to the panel in the Drop Target window. Take a look at the code for this example—you might be surprised at how easy it is to drag-and-drop Java objects between JFC applications (or within a JFC application). `DndObjectsDemo` contains six classes:

- The `DndObjectsDemo` class is the application class containing the `main` entry point.
- The `SourcePanel` class provides a panel for the Drag Sources window. The panel contains five `DraggableLabel` objects.
- The `TargetPanel` class provides a panel for the Drop Target window. The panel contains a single `DroppablePanel` object.
- The `DraggableLabel` class extends `JLabel` to be a drag source.
- The `DroppablePanel` class extends `JPanel` to be a drop target.
- The `MyFlavors` class is a convenience class used to define data flavors.

Implementation of the Drag Source

The `DraggableLabel` class extends `JLabel` by implementing the `DragSourceListener`, `DragGestureListener`, and `Transferable` interfaces. Note that although a drag source must provide implementations for these three interfaces, they don't all necessarily have to be implemented in the same class as they are in this example.

The `DraggableLabel` constructor gets the default platform drag source by calling a static class method in the `DragSource` class, `getDefaultDragSource`.

```
// Constructor
public DraggableLabel(String text) {
    super(text);

    // create a drag source
    DragSource ds = DragSource.getDefaultDragSource();
```

```
// create a drag gesture recognizer
DragGestureRecognizer dgr = ds.createDefaultDragGestureRecognizer(
        this,                             // component
        DnDConstants.ACTION_COPY_OR_MOVE, // actions
        this);                            // drag gesture listener
}
```

The constructor then uses this drag source object to create a drag gesture recognizer. The purpose of the drag gesture recognizer is to detect when the user initiates a drag operation and notify the drag source via its drag gesture listener.

The drag gesture listener consists of a single method, dragGestureRecognized.

```
// DragGestureListener interface implementation
public void dragGestureRecognized(DragGestureEvent event) {
    event.startDrag(null,      // drag cursor
                    this,      // transferable object
                    this);     // drag source listener
}
```

When the listener's dragGestureRecognized method is called, the listener starts a drag operation by calling DragGestureEvent.startDrag.

The Transferable interface implementation includes three methods: getTransferDataFlavors, isDataFlavorSupported, and getTransferData. The getTransferDataFlavors and isDataFlavorSupported methods make use of the draggableLabelFlavor object defined in the MyFlavors convenience class.

```
public DataFlavor[] getTransferDataFlavors() {
    // return supported data flavors
    DataFlavor[] flavors = { MyFlavors.draggableLabelFlavor };
    return flavors;
}

public boolean isDataFlavorSupported(DataFlavor flavor) {
    if(flavor.equals(MyFlavors.draggableLabelFlavor))
        return true;
    else
        return false;
}
```

The getTransferData method is where the actual data exchange takes place. See the "Transferring Data Between the Drag Source and Drop Target" section later in this chapter for a complete discussion of how data is transferred from a drag source to a drop target.

The remaining interface implementation, DragSourceListener, consists of five methods: dragEnter, dragOver, dragExit, dropActionChanged, and dragDropEnd. You'll notice that all of these methods in the DndObjectsDemo example are empty. Although you must provide an implementation for `DragSourceListener`, none of the methods in this interface are essential to the nuts and bolts of drag-and-drop.

> **NOTE**
>
> Although the `DndObjectsDemo` example supports both copy and move actions, for reasons of simplicity both types of actions are implemented as copy operations. A good exercise would be to modify `DndObjectsDemo` to differentiate between copy and move operations and behave appropriately.

Implementation of the Drop Target

The `DroppablePanel` class extends `JPanel` by implementing the `DropTargetListener` class. Much of the implementation is taken from the previous `DropTargetDemo` example. One difference is that the `DroppablePanel` class in `DndObjectsDemo` provides a complete implementation for the `DropTargetListener.drop` method.

```
public void drop(DropTargetDropEvent dtde) {
    // validate drop action and data flavors
if(isValidDragDrop(dtde.getDropAction(),
                    dtde.getCurrentDataFlavors())) {
        dtde.acceptDrop(dtde.getDropAction());

        try {
            // get transfer data (DraggableLabel object)
            Transferable xfer = dtde.getTransferable();
Object obj = xfer.getTransferData(MyFlavors.draggableLabelFlavor);

            // add object to panel and revalidate
            if(obj instanceof JComponent) {
                add((JComponent)obj);
                revalidate();
            }
            // notify system that dnd completed successfully
            dtde.dropComplete(true);
        }
        catch(Exception exc) {
            System.err.println(exc);
            exc.printStackTrace();
            dtde.dropComplete(false);
        }
    }
    else {
        // invalid drop action or data flavor, reject drop
        dtde.rejectDrop();
    }
```

```
    // drop operation complete, restore background color
    showUnderDrag(false);
}
```

The first thing the `drop` method does is call a private helper method, `isValidDragDrop`, to validate the given drop action and available data flavors.

```
private boolean isValidDragDrop(int dropAction, DataFlavor flavors []) {
    if((dropAction & DnDConstants.ACTION_COPY_OR_MOVE) != 0) {
        for(int i=0; i<flavors.length; i++) {
            if(flavors[i].getPrimaryType().equals("application")
&& flavors[i].getSubType().equals(
                    "x-java-serialized-object")) {
                return true;
            }
        }
    }
    return false;
}
```

The `isValidDragDrop` method verifies that the drop action is a copy or move action and checks the primary type and the subtype of the data flavor. Note that this implementation is written to accept any data flavor that represents a Java class. You could use the following code to validate only the `draggableLabelFlavor` data flavor:

```
if(flavors[i].equals(MyFlavors.draggableLabelFlavor)) {
    return true;
}
```

If the drop action and data flavor are valid for the drop target, the `drop` method calls `DropTargetDropEvent.acceptDrop` to accept the drop operation. It then gets the transferable data and, if the transferred object is a `JComponent`, it adds the component to the panel and revalidates the layout. Finally, the drop method completes the drop operation by calling `DropTargetDropEvent.dropComplete`. The following section discusses the details of getting the transferable data.

Transferring Data Between the Drag Source and Drop Target

Transferring data is a cooperative effort between a drag source and a drop target. In this example, the code required to transfer data from the drag source is quite simple. The following is the drag source's `getTransferData` method (from the `Transferable` interface).

```
public Object getTransferData(DataFlavor flavor) {
    // if we support requested data flavor,
    // return this object as transfer data
    if(flavor.equals(MyFlavors.draggableLabelFlavor)) {
        return(this);
    }
```

```
      else return null;
}
```

Note that the drag source object simply returns itself as the transfer data. The drag-and-drop system passes a serialized copy of this object to the drop target.

> **NOTE**
>
> To transfer types of data other than Java objects, you pass an instance of the representation class for the data type. For example, the representation class for transferring plain text is the `InputStream` class.

Now take a look at the code the drop target uses to get the data. Remember, this code is executed in the drop target listener's `drop` method after the drop action and data flavor are determined to be valid for the drop target.

```
// get transfer data (DraggableLabel object)
Transferable xfer = dtde.getTransferable();
Object obj = xfer.getTransferData(MyFlavors.draggableLabelFlavor);

// add object to panel and revalidate
if(obj instanceof JComponent) {
    add((JComponent)obj);
    revalidate();
}
```

The code first calls `DropTargetDropEvent.getTransferable` to get a transferable object. It then calls the transferable object's `getTransferData` method to get the data. In this example, the object returned by `getTransferData` should be a Java object (specifically, a `DraggableLabel` object). For most other types of transferable data, `getTransferData` will return an `InputStream` object capable of rendering the data.

Summary

JFC's Drag and Drop system is built on services provided by the native platform running the Java VM that hosts Java applications. This architecture allows you to drag-and-drop MIME-based content within a single JFC application, between two JFC applications, and between JFC applications and native applications. Drag-and-drop is a cooperative effort between a drag source and a drop target. Both the source and the target components must provide an implementation for certain drag-and-drop interfaces and follow the basic drag-and-drop protocol. This chapter gives two examples illustrating how to implement Drag and Drop. The first example, `DropTargetDemo`, implements a drop target that

34

DRAG AND DROP

identifies drag sources when they are moved over the target. The second example, DndObjectsDemo, is a complete drag-and-drop implementation that allows Java objects to be copied between two frame windows.

JFC Class Reference

by Luke Cassady-Dorion

IN THIS CHAPTER

Not too long ago, all computer programmers had to do was develop a powerful application and slap on a simple text-based interface, and they were ready to ship it. Those days are but a fading memory. Now that our job title has changed from "computer programmer" to "software engineer" or even "software architect," we're expected to develop powerful applications that are actually easy to use!

This means that not only do we have to agonize over every line of information-processing code, but also over all sorts of issues related to the user interface (UI). At every step along the development path, we must constantly consider whether the UI is as easy to use for engineers as it is for our grandparents. Fortunately, this hardship has arrived along with the popularity of object-oriented (OO) development languages, and with the advent of graphical screen-building tools. In the next few chapters, we will take a look at developing with the OO class libraries contained in the 1.1 and 1.2 releases of the JDK.

The Joys of Object-Oriented Class Libraries

If you close your eyes for a minute and think back to the first verse to the OO mantra that you learned so many years ago, you will no doubt have the words "software reuse" wedged in there somewhere. Having developed in OO languages for some period of time, I am sure that you have learned how to write code that can easily be reused not only within your current application, but also within other applications you develop. Now, due to component technologies such as Java Beans and ActiveX, it is even easier to develop reusable code.

> **NOTE**
>
> A component is basically a black box that you can stick in your application to serve a specific purpose. It has a defined set of input/output methods that you exploit to achieve a desired effect. If you use components that adhere to a standard (like Java Beans and ActiveX), it becomes very easy to integrate those third-party components directly into your code.

Although much of the "meat" (or internals) of an application is rather specific to that application, the various pieces of the UI are often easily reused from application to application. For this reason, developing a UI from off-the-shelf components is a simple task. However, deciding how the UI must come together is far from simple.

Developing with OO Class Libraries

In this chapter, we will take a look at the UI widgets contained in the `java.awt` package and those contained in the `javax.swing` package. The `java.awt` components were first introduced with the 1.0 release of the JDK, and were then changed to meet the new event model with the 1.1 release. These components are *peered* components, meaning that they exist as two halves: a Java half and a native half. The native half is actually displayed on the screen, and it gives components like `java.awt.Frame` a Mac look on a Mac and a Windows look on a Windows machine.

The components in the `javax.swing` (introduced in JDK 1.2) package are written totally in Java, and they manage to keep an OS-dependent look and feel through something called a "pluggable look and feel." What this means is that the components have an internal class that manages their onscreen representation, rendering them differently depending on the OS. This pluggable look and feel even gives developers the option of creating custom objects.

To begin your venture into development with UI class libraries, we will first take a look at two new concepts in the JDK 1.1: the delegation-based event model and the lightweight component model. Then we will cover the classes in the `java.awt` package, and then the `javax.swing` package.

New UI Developments in the JDK 1.1

Whereas the JDK 1.0.2 contained only a small subset of the features needed by professional developers, version 1.1 adds many of these important missing features. Of note are the improvements made in the `java.awt` packages and its new subpackages.

Added to the AWT in version 1.1 is a new event model, as well as support for lightweight components and component transparency. This means that developers can now develop applications with a look and feel very similar to a native-code application.

The Delegation-Based Event Model

The event model in the JDK 1.0.2 was lacking in many areas. First of all, it involved a lot of unnecessary message-passing due to its hierarchical nature. Whenever an event occurred, it had to propagate up the component hierarchy until it was absorbed; absorption occurred when a `handleEvent()` or `action()` method returned a `boolean` true.

A

The task of internationalization was a rather difficult one because the appropriate reaction to an event was often discovered using (language-dependent) string comparisons.

In an attempt to solve the problems created by a hierarchical-based event model, JavaSoft has introduced a completely new event model in their JDK 1.1 release. This new event model is delegation-based rather than hierarchical, which allows for the solution of these issues.

In a delegation-based event model, events propagate directly from the location where they occur (the source) to all interested parties (the listeners). For example, a button could be configured so that whenever it is clicked, the method that knows how to deal with that button will be directly invoked. To accomplish this change in event processing, a series of new classes and interfaces have been introduced.

The new classes and interfaces, contained in the package `java.awt.Event`, define a mechanism for receiving events and managing them. The interfaces are implemented by those objects that want to receive events generated by the component class associated with the interface. The classes in the `java.awt.event` package represent the different events themselves.

Fans of the JDK 1.0.2 class `java.awt.event` will notice that there is a fundamental change in the way events are represented. Under JDK 1.0.2, all instances of the class `java.awt.event`, and their source, are pinpointed using the `Event` object's `id` instance variable. Under the JDK 1.1, all event sources publish a unique event class (which extends from the base class `java.util.EventObject`). As you can guess, all event sources offer an interface that is implemented by listeners, and an event class that is instantiated and sent to all listeners when an event occurs.

As an example, we will build a simple application that builds a small screen and performs appropriate event handling. Listing 3.1 contains the code for the application. Pay specific attention to the methods `registerListeners()`, `itemStateChanged()`, and `actionPerformed()`. In `registerListeners()`, you notify all widgets that you want to receive notification when their states change. In `actionPerformed()` and `itemStateChanged()`, you receive notification when the associated event occurs.

LISTING 3.1 THE JDK 1.1 EVENT MODEL.

```
import java.awt.*;
import java.awt.event.*;


public class EventDemo extends   Frame
                  implements WindowListener,
                             ActionListener,
                             ItemListener {
```

```
    // some simple widgets
    private Button       demoButton;
    private Checkbox     demoCheckbox;
    private Choice       demoChoice;


    public EventDemo() {
        super("Event Demo");

        // instantiate the widgets
        demoButton = new Button("Click Me");
        demoCheckbox = new Checkbox("Check Me");
        demoChoice = new Choice();
        demoChoice.add("Option 1");
        demoChoice.add("Option 2");
        demoChoice.add("Option 3");
        demoChoice.add("Choose Me");

        // build the screen
        setLayout(new GridLayout(3,1));
        add(demoButton);
        add(demoCheckbox);
        add(demoChoice);

        registerListeners();
    }


    // register as listeners of all components
    private void registerListeners() {
        demoButton.addActionListener(this);
        demoCheckbox.addItemListener(this);
        demoChoice.addItemListener(this);
        this.addWindowListener(this);      }


    // as defined by ActionListener
    // called when the button is clicked
    public void actionPerformed(ActionEvent ae) {
        System.out.println("button clicked");
    }


    // as defined by ItemListener
    // called when the checkbox state is changed or when
    // the choice display option is changed
    public void itemStateChanged(ItemEvent ie) {
        // attempt to localize the event
        Object source = ie.getItemSelectable();
```

continues

A

JFC CLASS
REFERENCE

LISTING 3.1   CONTINUED

```
        if(source == demoCheckbox) {
            System.out.println("checkbox state changed");
        }
        else if(source == demoChoice) {
            System.out.println("choice display option changed");
        }
    }


            // as Defined by WindowListener
            // One of the following seven functions are called when
            // something happens to a window. We are only interested
            // in the windowClosing event, but all methods of the
            // interface must be implemented.
            public void windowActivated(WindowEvent we) {}
            public void windowClosed(WindowEvent we) {}
            public void windowClosing(WindowEvent we) {
                    // Exit the program when the Frame closes.
                    System.exit(0);
            }
            public void windowDeactivated(WindowEvent we) {}
            public void windowDeiconified(WindowEvent we) {}
            public void windowIconified(WindowEvent we) {}
            public void windowOpened(WindowEvent we) {}


    public static void main(String args[]) {
        EventDemo myDemo = new EventDemo();
        myDemo.pack();
        myDemo.setVisible(true);
    }

}
```

Although the delegation-based event model is probably different than the way you think about events in Java, this change is obviously for the better. As you will see during the development examples in this chapter, the new event model provides for more logical coding practices.

Lightweight Components

The lightweight component model, added to the JDK with release 1.1, allows for the creation of peerless components. Because instantiation of a native peer is a time-consuming task, this results in rapid instantiation of a component.

Added flexibility is present in the form of optional transparency. Component transparency is the capability to define an opaque portion of a component. This means that you can create a series of differently shaped components.

When you're building a custom component (a button, for example), the traditional process has been to build it as a child class of `java.awt.Canvas`. Then, in the `paint()` method of the `Canvas` object, you would perform the necessary drawing to create your component. A lot of time is wasted when the `Canvas` object is instantiated, because a peer class must also be instantiated.

To begin modeling your current custom components for the new lightweight component model, few code changes are needed. In fact, all you need to do is build your component as a child class of either `java.awt.Component` or `java.awt.Container`. Then, when your new lightweight component is instantiated, a peer class will not be associated with it.

Although speed of object instantiation is an obvious advantage of custom lightweight components, there are also other development advantages. As we all know, the 1.0.2 API has many drawbacks in terms of custom component development. Using the lightweight component model, your components can now possess the following features:

- Non-rectangular shape
- Transparency (you can see through part of the component)
- Overlapping (more than one component can draw in the same screen area)

Keep in mind that your component should implement methods that give it a similar programmatic feel to those components already in the AWT. This includes the following:

- Methods to allow the component state to be changed programmatically (for example, `setText()`).
- Methods to allow other components to add and remove themselves as event listeners (for example, `addActionListener()` and `removeActionListener()`).

In addition to giving your components a look and feel similar to existing AWT components, follow these tips to make your product much easier to use:

- In cases where events are to be received by the component, call the `enableEvents()` method in the constructor.
- After performing screen drawing in the `paint()` method, you must call `super.paint()` or the component will not appear onscreen.
- If your component will change size, call `invalidate()` before calling `repaint()`.
- If your component will only receive events in a portion of its visual representation, it must implement the `contains()` method.

A

JFC CLASS
REFERENCE

Now it's time to build a lightweight component. You will build a small button that takes on the shape of a triangle. In its default state, the triangle is black. When the button is clicked, it changes to pink. The button supports methods for adding and removing event listeners, and will notify all listeners whenever a button-click occurs.

The code for the `TriangleButton` class is contained in Listing 3.2, and a snapshot of the class in action is contained in Figure 3.1.

LISTING 3.2 TRANSPARENT COMPONENTS UNDER JDK 1.1

```
import java.awt.event.*;
import java.awt.*;
import java.util.*;


public class TriangleButton extends Component {
    private Polygon triangle;
    private Color   myColor;
    private Vector  listeners;
    private int     theID;


    public TriangleButton() {
        // enable the sending of mouse events
        enableEvents(AWTEvent.MOUSE_EVENT_MASK);

        // mark out the xpoints and ypoints
        int x[] = {0, 100, 50};
        int y[] = {0, 0, 100};

        triangle = new Polygon(x, y, 3);
        setSize(100,100);

        myColor = Color.black;
        listeners = new Vector();
    }


    public void paint(Graphics g) {
        g.setColor(myColor);
        g.fillPolygon(triangle);

        // super.paint() MUST be called, or your component
        // will NOT appear on screen.
        super.paint(g);
    }


    // called when the user clicks on the triangle
    public void processMouseEvent(MouseEvent me) {
```

```
        // make sure that the event occured over the triangle itself
        if(! triangle.contains(me.getPoint()) ) return;

        // if the mouse button was clicked change to alternate state
        if(me.getID() == MouseEvent.MOUSE_PRESSED) {
            theID = me.getID();
            myColor = Color.pink;
            repaint();
        }
        // if the mouse button was released change to initial state
        else if(me.getID() == MouseEvent.MOUSE_RELEASED) {
            theID = me.getID();
            myColor = Color.black;
            repaint();

            // send the event to all listeners
            sendEvents();
        }
    }


    public synchronized void addActionListener(ActionListener al) {
        listeners.addElement(al);
    }


    public synchronized void removeActionListener(ActionListener al) {
        listeners.removeElement(al);
    }


    private void sendEvents() {
        ActionEvent myEvent
        = new ActionEvent(this, theID, "button click occured");

        // create a clone of the listeners Vector.
        // This will place a "cut-off"
        // point after which new registrations
        // will not be considered for
// the current event being sent out.
        Vector listenerClone;
        synchronized(this) {
            listenerClone = (Vector)listeners.clone();
        }

        for(int i=0;i<listenerClone.size();i++) {
            ((ActionListener)listenerClone.elementAt(i))
             .actionPerformed(myEvent);
        }
    }
}
```

FIGURE 3.1

Creation of a triangle button using the light-weight component model.

PACKAGE # java.awt

The package java.awt contains the classes and interfaces used for interaction with the screen. This includes UI components and graphic primitives used for creating one's own components. Additionally, there are classes called LayoutManagers, used for describing screen layout information.

Note the concept of the container class in the AWT. A container class is one that has a visual screen representation and can display both itself and other components. A non-container class cannot display itself alone, and will need to be displayed within the confines of a container. For example, it is possible to create a generic window and display it onscreen. It is also possible to create a button and display it within the confines of a container. It is not possible, however, to create a button and simply display it by itself without some sort of container. Nor is it possible to create a Button object and place another component (like a Label object) within it.

In the java.awt package, most containers are created through a *peer* class. A peer class is implemented in native code and gives the native look and feel present when programming with Java. For example, when you create a window, a window peer is created that represents how a native window looks on the machine running the application. The problem with peer classes is that they are non-lightweight and instantiation time is rather long.

In addition to container classes, most other UI components are created using this peer approach. Again, this is what gives instances of the Button class a Solaris feel under Solaris, a Windows feel under Windows NT, and even a BeOS feel under BeOS. However, there is a category of AWT components and containers that are created using only Java code. These classes, called lightweight components, are new to the JDK with the 1.1 release and were covered earlier in this appendix in the "New UI Developments in the JDK 1.1" section.

Terms that appear in *italic monospaced font* are covered in more detail later in this appendix.

PACKAGE **java.awt: Summary**

Interfaces/Classes	Description
Interfaces	
ActiveEvent	Implemented by events that know how to dispatch themselves
Adjustable	Implemented by components that have a finite set of adjustable available values
Composite	Defines methods used to draw graphic primitives
CompositeContext	Defines an environment for compositing
ItemSelectable	Implemented by objects that contain a set of values, of which zero or more can be selected
LayoutManager	Implemented by layout manager classes
LayoutManager2	Implemented by constraint base layout manager classes
MenuContainer	Implemented by all menu containers
Paint	Defines color patterns used in 2D operations
PaintContext	Defines an environment used when working with 2D operations
PrintGraphics	Defines a mechanism for obtaining print graphics contexts
Shape	Implemented by any class wishing to be a polygon
Stroke	Models a graphical stroke
Transparency	Models behavior used by classes that support transparency
Classes	
AlphaComposite	Class that implements basic alpha compositing rules
AWTEvent	Abstract base class for all AWT events
AWTEventMulticaster	Class used to broadcast events

continues

Interfaces/Classes	Description
Classes	
AWTPermission	Class used to model an AWT permission
BasicStroke	Class that models basic rendering attributes for stroked graphics primitives
BorderLayout	Layout manager that allows components to be placed within a container at any of the following locations: North, South, East, West, Center
Button	Class used for creating a labeled button
Canvas	Basic class that may be drawn directly into
CardLayout	Layout manager that controls a series of components, no more than one of which may be visible at a given point in time
Checkbox	Class used to model a checkbox or radio button onscreen
CheckboxGroup	Class used to house a series of Checkbox objects, turning them into radio buttons; at most, one Checkbox object in a given CheckboxGroup may be checked at a given point in time
CheckboxMenuItem	Class that models a menu item that also displays a checkbox
Choice	Class that models a list of options, from which one may be selected at a given point in time
Color	Class that models an onscreen color
Component	Component is the base class for all objects that have a graphical presence and can be used for user interaction
ComponentOrientation	Class that models the orientation of elements and text of a Component

Interfaces/Classes	Description
	Classes
Container	Base class for all containers in the AWT
Cursor	Class that models an onscreen cursor
Dialog	Class used to build dialog boxes
Dimension	Class that allows the width and height of a component to be encapsulated into a single object
Event	Old JDK 1.0.n class used to model an event
EventQueue	Used to queue up events before they can be delivered
FileDialog	Class used when user interaction with the local file system is needed
FlowLayout	Layout manager that lays out components from left to right and top to bottom
Font	Class that models a unique font face
FontMetrics	Class used to model different attributes about a given font
Frame	Class that models a top-level window with a title bar and a menu bar
GradientPaint	Class used to fill a shape with a linear gradient pattern
Graphics	When rendering, components draw themselves directly into a Graphics object
Graphics2D	Class used for 2D rendering
GraphicsConfiguration	Class that models unique characteristics of a given graphics output device (monitor, printer, plotter, and so on)
GraphicsDevice	Class that models a unique graphics device (monitor, printer, plotter, and so on)
GraphicsEnvironment	Class that models a unique graphics environment

continues

A

JFC CLASS
REFERENCE

Interfaces/Classes	Description
Classes	
GridBagConstraints	Used with the `GridBagLayout` class to describe how a given component should be placed onscreen
GridBagLayout	Layout manager that allows for a high level of customization when building screens
GridLayout	Layout manager that breaks up the screen into a grid in which each block is of an equal size; a given grid block may contain exactly one component, and that component will be stretched to fill the block
Image	Abstract class that models an image
Insets	Class that models the amount of space separating the component border from the container border
Label	Class that displays a one-line `String` object
List	Class that displays a scrollable series of elements, one or more of which may be selected at a given point in time
MediaTracker	Class used to track the status of a series of `Image` objects; used to ensure that `Image` objects are fully loaded before they are shown
Menu	Class that models a menu (for example, File or Edit)
MenuBar	Class that houses and displays a collection of `Menu` objects and is bound to a `Frame`
MenuComponent	Abstract base class for all menu-related classes
MenuItem	`MenuItem` is the base class for all items that can appear in a `Menu`
MenuShortcut	Keyboard accelerator associated with a given menu item

Interfaces/Classes	Description
Classes	
`Panel`	A simple container class
`Point`	Class used to model a unique position in a 2D coordinate space
`Polygon`	Class used to model the collection of points that form a polygon
`PopupMenu`	Class used to create a pop-up menu
`PrintJob`	Abstract class used to model an active session with the printer
`Rectangle`	Class used to model the collection of points that form a rectangle
`Scrollbar`	Class used to model either a horizontal or vertical scrollbar
`ScrollPane`	Container that can house a series of components and, potentially, can scroll to show those components not currently visible
`SystemColor`	Class used to model the system-specific colors in use on the local machine
`TextArea`	Class used to model a multiline text area
`TextComponent`	Base class of both `TextArea` and `TextField` and any other Component that allows the editing of text
`TextField`	Class used to model a one-line text area
`TexturePaint`	Class used to fill a shape with a given texture
`Toolkit`	Abstract class for classes that are used to bind components to their native implementations
`Window`	Parent class to many containers

CLASS `java.awt.AWTEvent`

`public abstract class AWTEvent extends java.util.EventObject`

AWTEvent is the abstract base class for all AWT-related events. Because this class is abstract, you will never instantiate it directly, but you will often work with its child classes. Additionally, when you're developing your own UI components, any new event classes you may need should extend AWTEvent.

CLASS `java.awt.AWTEvent`: **Summary**

Fields/Methods	Description
`public static final long` `ACTION_EVENT_MASK`	Indicates an action event
`public static final long` `ADJUSTMENT_EVENT_MASK`	Indicates an adjustment event
`public static final long` `COMPONENT_EVENT_MASK`	Indicates a component event
`protected boolean consumed`	True if the event has been consumed
`public static final long` `CONTAINER_EVENT_MASK`	Indicates a container event
`public static final long` `FOCUS_EVENT_MASK`	Indicates a focus event
`protected int id`	Event ID
`public static final long` `INPUT_METHOD_EVENT_MASK`	Indicates an input method event
`public static final long` `ITEM_EVENT_MASK`	Indicates an item event
`public static final long` `KEY_EVENT_MASK`	Indicates a key event
`public static final long` `MOUSE_EVENT_MASK`	Indicates a mouse event
`public static final long` `MOUSE_MOTION_EVENT_MASK`	Indicates a mouse motion event
`public static final long` `RESERVED_ID_MAX`	Max reserved ID
`public static final long` `TEXT_EVENT_MASK`	Indicates a text event

Fields/Methods	Description
public static final long WINDOW_EVENT_MASK	Indicates a window event
protected void consume()	Invoked internally to consume an event
public int getID()	Obtains the event ID
protected boolean isConsumed()	Invoked internally to check if an event is consumed
public String paramString()	Obtains the parameter string associated with this event
public String toString()	Returns a string version of the object

CLASS
java.awt.BorderLayout

public class BorderLayout extends java.lang.Object implements
LayoutManager2, Serializable

The BorderLayout layout manager allows for positioning of up to five components in a container. Each component is assigned to either the north, south, east, west, or center of the container. When the container is resized, each of its components will automatically hold its relative position.

CLASS
java.awt.BorderLayout: Summary

Fields/Methods	Description
public static final String AFTER_LAST_LINE	Used to indicate that a component should be placed after the last line of the layout's content
public static final String AFTER_LINE_ENDS	Used to indicate that a component should be placed at the end of the line direction for the layout
public static final String BEFORE_FIRST_LINE	Used to indicate that a component should be placed before the first line of the layout's content
public static final String BEFORE_LINE_BEGINS	Used to indicate that a component should be placed at the beginning of the line direction for the layout

continues

Fields/Methods	Description
public static final String CENTER	Used to indicate that a component should be placed in the center region
public static final String EAST	Used to indicate that a component should be placed in the east region
public static final String NORTH	Used to indicate that a component should be placed in the north region
public static final String SOUTH	Used to indicate that a component should be placed in the south region
public static final String WEST	Used to indicate that a component should be placed in the west region
public void addLayoutComponent(Component, Object)	Adds the specified component to the screen using the specified constraints
public void addLayoutComponent (String, Component)	Adds the specified component to the container in region
public int getHgap()	Obtains the horizontal pixel gap
public int getLayoutAlignmentX(Container)	Obtains the alignment along the x-axis for the container using this layout
public int getLayoutAlignmentY(Container)	Obtains the alignment along the y-axis for the container using this layout
public int getVgap()	Obtains the vertical pixel gap
public void invalidateLayout(Container)	Invalidates the layout of the specified container
public void layoutContainer(Container)	Causes the specified container to be laid out
public Dimension maximumLayoutSize(Container)	Obtains the maximum size for the container using this layout
public Dimension minimumLayoutSize(Container)	Obtains the minimum size for the container using this layout
public Dimension preferredLayoutSize(Container)	Obtains the preferred size for the container using this layout
public void removeLayoutComponent(Component)	Removes the specified component from the screen

Fields/Methods	Description
`public void setHgap(int)`	Assigns the horizontal gap (in pixels)
`public void setVgap(int)`	Assigns the vertical gap (in pixels)
`public String toString()`	Obtains a string version of the object

CLASS java.awt.BorderLayout: Example

The `BorderLayout` layout manager allows components to be placed along the edges and center of a panel:

```java
import java.awt.*;

public class BorderLayoutDemo extends Frame {

    public BorderLayoutDemo() {
        Button northButton = new Button("North");
        Button westButton = new Button("West");
        Button eastButton = new Button("East");
        Button southButton = new Button("South");
        Button centerButton = new Button("Center");

        // Create a new BorderLayout object with 10 pixel gaps
        // between all components.
        BorderLayout borderLayout = new BorderLayout(10,10);

        // Set the layout.
        setLayout(borderLayout);

        // Add some components.
            add(northButton, BorderLayout.NORTH);
        add(westButton, BorderLayout.WEST);
        add(eastButton, BorderLayout.EAST);
        add(southButton, BorderLayout.SOUTH);
        add(centerButton, BorderLayout.CENTER);
            // Allow the program to be shut down by closing the
        // main window.
        addWindowListener(new WindowAdapter() {
          public void windowClosing(WindowEvent we) {
            System.exit(0);
          }
        });
    }


    public static void main(String args[]) {
        BorderLayoutDemo myDemo = new BorderLayoutDemo();
        myDemo.pack();
        myDemo.setVisible(true);
    }
}
```

A

CLASS **java.awt.Button**

`public class Button extends Component`

The `Button` class represents an onscreen button. Because this class is created using a native peer object, it will have the look and feel of a native button.

CLASS **java.awt.Button: Summary**

Methods	Description
`public void addActionListener(ActionListener)`	Adds an `ActionListener` to the collection of listeners; it is notified when the button is clicked on
`public void addNotify()`	Causes the button's peer to be created
`public String getActionCommand()`	Obtains the action command associated with this button
`public String getLabel()`	Obtains the label for this button
`public String paramString()`	Obtains the parameter string associated with this button
`protected void processActionEvent(ActionEvent)`	Invoked internally for event management
`protected void processEvent(AWTEvent)`	Invoked internally for event management
`public void removeActionListener(ActionListener)`	Removes an `ActionListener` from the collection of listeners
`public void setActionCommand(String)`	Sets the action command associated with this button
`public void setLabel(String)`	Sets the label associated with this button

CLASS **java.awt.Button: Example**

Creating and adding a `Button` object:

```
import java.awt.*;
import java.awt.event.*;

public class ButtonDemo extends Frame {

    public ButtonDemo() {
```

```
        // create a button
        Button demoButton = new Button("Demo Button");

        // add it to the screen
        add(demoButton);

        // Allow the program to be shut down by closing the
        // main window.
        addWindowListener(new WindowAdapter() {
                public void windowClosing(WindowEvent we) {
                        System.exit(0);
                }
        });
    }


    public static void main(String args[]) {
        ButtonDemo myDemo = new ButtonDemo();
        myDemo.pack();
        myDemo.setVisible(true);
    }
}
```

CLASS

java.awt.Canvas

`public class Canvas extends Component`

The `Canvas` class represents a peered component that can be drawn into. With the JDK 1.1, you will find that it is usually less expensive to directly subclass `Component` because that will allow you to draw into a peer-free piece of the screen.

If you do decide to subclass `Canvas`, all painting should occur in the `paint()` method. The JVM will automatically call this method when the `Canvas` object is shown on the screen.

CLASS

java.awt.Canvas: Summary

Methods	Description
`public void addNotify()`	Creates the component's peer
`public void paint(Graphics)`	Invoked when the component should draw itself into the specified `Graphics` object

A

java.awt.Canvas: Example

The Canvas class allows text and graphics primitives to be directly drawn onto it:

```java
import java.awt.*;
import java.awt.event.*;

class CanvasDemo extends Canvas {

    public CanvasDemo() {
        setSize(100,100);
    }


    public void paint(Graphics g) {
        g.setColor(Color.black);
        g.drawString("Canvas Demo", 20, 20);
    }

    public static void main(String[] args) {
        Frame myDemo = new Frame();

        myDemo.add(new CanvasDemo());

        myDemo.addWindowListener(new WindowAdapter() {
            public void windowClosing(WindowEvent we) {
                    System.exit(0);
                }
        });

        myDemo.pack();
        myDemo.setVisible(true);
    }
```

java.awt.CardLayout

public class CardLayout extends Object implements LayoutManager2, Serializable

The CardLayout layout manager allows for a series of components to be assigned to a unique container, with the understanding that only one component can be shown at a given time. This class is useful for instances where a "slide show" effect needs to be produced.

java.awt.CardLayout: Summary

Methods	Description
public void addLayoutComponent (Component, Object)	Adds the specified component to the container

Methods	Description
public void addLayoutComponent (String, Component)	Adds the specified component to the container. This function has been deprecated in deference to addLayoutComponent(Component, Object)
public void first(Container)	Shows the first component managed by the card layout
public void getHgap()	Obtains the horizontal gap (in pixels)
public int getLayoutAlignmentX(Container)	Obtains the alignment along the x-axis for the given container
public int getLayoutAlignmentY(Container)	Obtains the alignment along the y-axis for the given container
public int getVgap()	Obtains the vertical gap (in pixels)
public void invalidateLayout(Container)	Invalidates the specified container
public void last(Container)	Shows the last component managed by the card layout
public void layoutContainer(Container)	Lays out the specified container using card layout
public Dimension maximumLayoutSize(Container)	Obtains the maximum layout size for the specified container
public Dimension minimumLayoutSize(Container)	Obtains the minimum layout size for the specified container
public void next(Container)	Shows the next component managed by the card layout
public Dimension preferredLayoutSize(Container)	Obtains the preferred layout size for the specified container
public void previous(Container)	Shows the previous component managed by the card layout
public void removeLayoutComponent(Component)	Removes the specified component from the container

continues

Methods	Description
`public void setHgap(int)`	Sets the horizontal gap
`public void setVgap(int)`	Sets the vertical gap
`public void show(Container, String)`	Shows the given component
`public String toString()`	Returns a string describing this object

CLASS ## java.awt.Checkbox

`public class Checkbox extends Component implements ItemSelectable`

The `java.awt.Checkbox` class represents either an onscreen checkbox or a radio button. Because the `Checkbox` class is created using a native peer, it will have the look and feel of a native checkbox or radio button. Both a checkbox and a radio button serve a similar purpose, so JavaSoft engineers decided that they could be represented with the same class. Covered in the next section is the class `CheckboxGroup`. If you create a `Checkbox` object and add it to a `CheckboxGroup`, it will appear and act like a radio button. If you create a `Checkbox` object and do not add it to a `CheckboxGroup`, it will appear and act like a checkbox.

CLASS ## java.awt.Checkbox: Summary

Methods	Description
`public void addItemListener(ItemListener)`	Adds an `ItemListener` to the collection of listeners; an `ItemListener` is notified whenever the checkbox state changes
`public void addNotify()`	Causes the checkbox's peer to be created
`public void getCheckboxGroup()`	Obtains the `CheckboxGroup` associated with this object, or null if there is none
`public String getLabel()`	Obtains the label displayed with this checkbox
`public Object[] getSelectedObjects()`	Returns an array of length 1, with either the label of the checkbox if it is checked or null if it is not
`public boolean getState()`	Obtains the current state of the checkbox

Methods	Description
`protected String paramString()`	Obtains the parameter string associated with the checkbox
`protected void processEvent(AWTEvent)`	Used internally for event management
`protected void processItemEvent(ItemEvent)`	Used internally for event management
`public void removeItemListener(ItemListener)`	Removes an `ItemListener` from the collection of listeners
`public void setCheckboxGroup(CheckboxGroup)`	Associates this object with a `CheckboxGroup`
`public void setLabel(String)`	Sets the label displayed with the checkbox
`public void setState(boolean)`	Sets the current state of the checkbox

CLASS

`java.awt.Checkbox`: Example

Checkbox objects are used to represent an item with a binary state:

```java
import java.awt.*;
import java.awt.event.*;

public class CheckboxDemo extends Frame {

    public CheckboxDemo() {
        // create some widgets
        Label questionLabel
            = new Label("Check Off All Authors You Read:");
Checkbox demoCheckbox1 = new Checkbox("William Gibson");
        Checkbox demoCheckbox2 = new Checkbox("Larry Nevin");
        Checkbox demoCheckbox3 = new Checkbox("Irma S. Rombauer");
        Checkbox demoCheckbox4 = new Checkbox("Douglas Adams");
        Checkbox demoCheckbox5 = new Checkbox("Neal Stepenson");

        // set the layout
        setLayout( new GridLayout(6,1,10,10) );

        // add them to the screen
        add(questionLabel);
        add(demoCheckbox1);
        add(demoCheckbox2);
        add(demoCheckbox3);
        add(demoCheckbox4);
        add(demoCheckbox5);
    }
```

continues

A

```
public static void main(String args[]) {
    CheckboxDemo myDemo = new CheckboxDemo();

    // Allow the program to be shut down by closing the
    // main window.
    myDemo.addWindowListener(new WindowAdapter() {
        public void windowClosing(WindowEvent we) {
            System.exit(0);
        }
    });

    myDemo.pack();
    myDemo.setVisible(true);
}
}
```

CLASS # java.awt.CheckboxGroup

`public class CheckboxGroup extends Object`

Unlike the other classes in this section, `CheckboxGroup` is not a UI component itself. Rather, it is a utility class used with the `Checkbox` class.

To create radio buttons in Java, you instantiate a `CheckboxGroup` object and add to it a series of `Checkbox` objects. These `Checkbox` objects now appear onscreen as radio buttons, and only one `Checkbox` object in the `CheckboxGroup` may be true.

CLASS ## java.awt.CheckboxGroup: Summary

Methods/Events	Description
`public Checkbox getSelectedCheckbox()`	Obtains the currently selected checkbox
`public void setSelectedCheckbox(Checkbox)`	Sets the currently selected checkbox
`public String toString()`	Obtains a string representation of this object

CLASS ## java.awt.CheckboxGroup: Example

The `CheckboxGroup` class acts as an umbrella holding together `Checkbox` objects. A `Checkbox` object owned by a `CheckboxGroup` object is displayed as a radio button:

```
import java.awt.*;
import java.awt.event.*;

public class CheckboxGroupDemo extends Frame {

    public CheckboxGroupDemo() {
```

```
          // create some widgets
          Label questionLabel
          = new Label("Who is your favorite author?:");
CheckboxGroup demoGroup = new CheckboxGroup();
          Checkbox demoCheckbox1
           = new Checkbox("William Gibson", demoGroup, false);
          Checkbox demoCheckbox2
          = new Checkbox("Larry Nevin", demoGroup, false);
          Checkbox demoCheckbox3
          = new Checkbox("Irma S. Rombauer", demoGroup, true);
          Checkbox demoCheckbox4
          = new Checkbox("Douglas Adams", demoGroup, false);
          Checkbox demoCheckbox5
          = new Checkbox("Neal Stepenson", demoGroup, false);

          // set the layout
          setLayout( new GridLayout(6,1,10,10) );

          // add them to the screen
          add(questionLabel);
          add(demoCheckbox1);
          add(demoCheckbox2);
          add(demoCheckbox3);
          add(demoCheckbox4);
          add(demoCheckbox5);
     }


     public static void main(String args[]) {
          CheckboxGroupDemo myDemo = new CheckboxGroupDemo();

          // Allow the program to be shut down by closing the
          // main window.
          myDemo.addWindowListener(new WindowAdapter() {
              public void windowClosing(WindowEvent we) {
                   System.exit(0);
              }
          });
          myDemo.pack();
          myDemo.setVisible(true);
     }
}
```

CLASS   **`java.awt.CheckboxMenuItem`**

`public class CheckboxMenuItem extends MenuItem implements ItemSelectable`

Often a menu will simply allow the selection of a unique item. From time to time, however, a UI requires that a binary choice be placed in a pull-down menu. In such a situation, the CheckboxMenuItem class is used to place a checkbox next to a menu option in a pull-down menu.

java.awt.CheckboxMenuItem: Summary

Methods/Events	Description
public void addItemListener(ItemListener)	Adds an ItemListener to the collection of listeners; an ItemListener is notified whenever the checkbox state changes
public void addNotify()	Causes the CheckboxMenuItem's peer to be created
public Object[] getSelectedObjects()	Returns an array of length 1, with either the label of the checkbox if it is checked or null if it is not
public boolean getState()	Obtains the current state of the CheckboxMenuItem
protected String paramString()	Obtains the parameter string associated with the CheckboxMenuItem
protected void processEvent(AWTEvent)	Used internally for event management
protected void processItemEvent(ItemEvent)	Used internally for event management
public void removeItemListener(ItemListener)	Removes an ItemListener from the collection of listeners
public void setState(boolean)	Sets the current state of the CheckboxMenuItem

java.awt.CheckboxMenuItem: Example

The CheckboxMenuItem class allows for the displaying of a menu item that has a binary state:

```java
import java.awt.*;
import java.awt.event.*;

public class CheckboxMenuItemDemo extends Frame {

    public CheckboxMenuItemDemo() {
        MenuBar myMenuBar = new MenuBar();
        Menu options = new Menu("Options");
        CheckboxMenuItem toggle = new CheckboxMenuItem("Toggle");

        options.add(toggle);
        myMenuBar.add(options);
        setMenuBar(myMenuBar);
    }
```

```
    public static void main(String args[]) {
        CheckboxMenuItemDemo myDemo = new CheckboxMenuItemDemo();

        // Allow the program to be shut down by closing the
        // main window.
        myDemo.addWindowListener(new WindowAdapter() {
            public void windowClosing(WindowEvent we) {
                System.exit(0);
            }
        });
        myDemo.pack();
        myDemo.setVisible(true);
    }
}
```

java.awt.Choice

CLASS

public class Choice extends Component implements ItemSelectable

A Choice object is used to present the user with a list of options, from which he may select exactly one. Except during selection, the currently selected option only is displayed.

java.awt.Choice: Summary

CLASS

Methods/Events	Description
public void add(String)	Adds the String object to the Choice
public void addItem(String)	Adds the String object to the Choice
public void addItemListener(ItemListener)	Adds an ItemListener to the collection of listeners; an ItemListener is notified whenever the selected item changes
public void addNotify()	Creates the component's peer
public int countItems()	Obtains a count of items in the Choice. Deprecated, use getItemCount()
public String getItem(int)	Obtains the item at the specified index, or null if it does not exist
public int getItemCount()	Obtains a count of items in the Choice
public int getSelectedIndex()	Obtains the index of the selected item
public String getSelectedItem()	Obtains the selected item

A

**JFC CLASS
REFERENCE**

continues

Methods/Events	Description
public Object[] getSelectedObjects()	Obtains an array of length 1, where the first element is the selected item
public void insert(String, int)	Inserts the specified String at the specified index
protected String paramString()	Obtains the parameter string for this object
protected void processEvent(AWTEvent)	Used internally for event management
protected void processItemEvent(ItemEvent)	Used internally for event management
public void remove(int)	Removes the item at the specified index from the Choice
public void remove(String)	Removes the first occurrence of the specified item from the Choice
public void removeAll()	Removes all items from the Choice
public void removeItemListener(ItemListener)	Removes the specified ItemListener from the collection of listeners
public void select(int)	Selects the item at the specified index
public void select(String)	Selects the specified item

<img CLASS> ## java.awt.Choice: Example

The Choice class allows for a single item to be selected from a list containing many:

```java
import java.awt.*;
import java.awt.event.*;

public class ChoiceDemo extends Frame {

    public ChoiceDemo() {
        Label questionLabel
        = new Label("Who is your favorite author?:");

        Choice options = new Choice();
        options.add("William Gibson");
        options.add("Larry Nevin");
        options.add("Irma S. Rombauer");
        options.add("Douglas Adams");
        options.add("Neal Stepenson");

        setLayout(new FlowLayout(10));
        add(questionLabel);
        add(options);
```

```
        }

    public static void main(String args[]) {
        ChoiceDemo myDemo = new ChoiceDemo();

        // Allow the program to be shut down by closing the
        // main window.
        myDemo.addWindowListener(new WindowAdapter() {
            public void windowClosing(WindowEvent we) {
                System.exit(0);
            }
        });

        myDemo.pack();
        myDemo.setVisible(true);
    }
}
```

CLASS
java.awt.Color

`public class Color extends Object implements Serializable`

The class `Color` encapsulates RGB information for a given color. In addition to allowing user selection of red, green, and blue values, the class provides a series of static member variables representing commonly used colors.

CLASS
java.awt.Color: Summary

Fields/Methods	*Description*
`public static final Color black`	Represents the color black
`public static final Color blue`	Represents the color blue
`public static final Color cyan`	Represents the color cyan
`public static final Color darkGray`	Represents the color dark gray
`public static final Color gray`	Represents the color gray
`public static final Color green`	Represents the color green
`public static final Color lightGray`	Represents the color light gray
`public static final Color magenta`	Represents the color magenta
`public static final Color orange`	Represents the color orange
`public static final Color pink`	Represents the color pink
`public static final Color red`	Represents the color red
`public static final Color white`	Represents the color white
`public static final Color yellow`	Represents the color yellow

continues

A

JFC CLASS REFERENCE

Fields/Methods	Description
`public Color brighter()`	Returns a brighter version of the color represented by the active object
`public PaintContext createContext` `(ColorModel, Rectangle, Rectangle2D,` `AffineTransform, RenderingHints)`	Returns a `PaintContext` that can be used to generate a solid color pattern
`public Color darker()`	Returns a darker version of the color represented by the active object
`public static Color decode(String)`	Transforms the `String` object to an integer and returns the specified color
`public boolean equals(Object)`	Tests if the two objects reference the same color
`public int getAlpha()`	Returns the Alpha portion of the color
`public int getBlue()`	Obtains the blue portion of the color
`public static Color getColor(String)`	Obtains a color in the system properties identified by the specified string
`public static Color` `getColor(String, Color)`	Obtains a color in the system properties identified by the specified string; if the specified property cannot be found, the `Color` parameter is returned
`public static Color` `getColor(String, int)`	Obtains a color in the system properties identified by the specified string; if the specified property cannot be found, the `int` parameter is converted to a `Color` object and returned
`public float[] getColorComponents` `(ColorSpace, float[])`	Obtains an array containing the color components (no alpha) of the color, in the specified `ColorSpace`
`public float[]` `getColorComponents(float[])`	Obtains an array containing the color components (no alpha) of the color
`public ColorSpace getColorSpace()`	Obtains the `ColorSpace` of the `Color`

Fields/Methods	Description
`public float[] getComponents` `(ColorSpace, float[])`	Obtains an array containing the color components of the color, in the specified `ColorSpace`
`public float[] getComponents(float[])` and alpha components of the `Color`	Obtains an array containing the color
`public int getGreen()`	Obtains the green portion of the color
`public static Color` `getHSBColor(float, float, float)`	Creates a new `Color` object based on the hue, saturation, and brightness parameters
`public int getRed()`	Obtains the red portion of the color
`public int getRGB()`	Obtains an RGB code for the color
`public float[]` `getRGBColorComponents(float[])`	Obtains an array containing the color components (no alpha) of the color in the default `ColorSpace`
`public float[]` `getRGBComponents(float[])`	Obtains an array containing the color components of the color in the default `ColorSpace`
`public int hashCode()`	Obtains a hash code for the object
`public static int` `HSBtoRGB(float, float, float)`	Obtains an RGB value for the specified HSB value
`public static int` `RGBtoHSB(int, int, int, float[])`	Obtains an HSB value for the specified RGB value
`public String toString()`	Obtains a string representing this object

CLASS

`java.awt.Color`: Example

The `Color` object is used to represent a physical color:

```java
import java.awt.*;
import java.awt.event.*;

class ColorDemo extends Canvas implements Runnable {
    private Color myColor;
    private Thread myThread;
```

continues

```
    public ColorDemo() {
        setSize(100,100);
        myColor = Color.red;
    }


    public void paint(Graphics g) {
        // draw a square with the current color
        g.setColor(myColor);
        g.fillRect(0,0, getSize().width, getSize().height);
    }

public void start() {
        myThread = new Thread(this);
        myThread.start();
    }


    public void run() {
        while(true) {
            // get progressively brighter
            myColor = myColor.brighter();
            repaint();
        }
    }
}


public class DisplayFrameColor extends Frame {

    public DisplayFrameColor() {
        ColorDemo myDemo = new ColorDemo();
        myDemo.start();
        add(myDemo);
    }


    public static void main(String args[]) {
        DisplayFrameColor myDemo = new DisplayFrameColor();

        // Allow the program to be shut down by closing the
        // main window.
        myDemo.addWindowListener(new WindowAdapter() {
            public void windowClosing(WindowEvent we) {
                System.exit(0);
            }
        });

        myDemo.pack();
        myDemo.setVisible(true);
    }
}
```

CLASS   # `java.awt.Component`

`public class Component extends Object`

The class `Component` is the basic class that is extended by almost all UI classes in the package `java.awt`. If you understand its functionality, you'll understand all other UI components in the `java.awt` package.

CLASS   # `java.awt.Component`: **Summary**

Methods/Events	*Description*
`public void add(PopupMenu)`	Adds a pop-up menu to this component
`public void addComponentListener(ComponentListener)`	Adds a `ComponentListener` to the collection of listeners; a `ComponentListener` is notified whenever the component is hidden, shown, moved, or resized
`public void addFocusListener(FocusListener)`	Adds a `FocusListener` to the collection of listeners; a `FocusListener` is notified whenever focus is gained or lost
`Public void addInputMethodListener (InputMethodListener)`	Adds an `InputMethodListener` to the collection of listeners; an `InputMethodListener` is notified whenever a text editing event occurs
`public void addKeyListener(KeyListener)`	Adds a `KeyListener` to the collection of listeners; a `KeyListener` is notified every time a key is pressed on the keyboard
`public void addMouseListener(MouseListener)`	Adds a `MouseListener` to the collection of listeners; a `MouseListener` is notified every time the mouse is clicked, pressed, or released, or enters/exits the component

continues

Methods/Events	Description
public void addMouseMotionListener (MouseMotionListener)	Adds a MouseMotionListener to the collection of listeners; a MouseMotionListener is notified every time the mouse moves
public void addNotify()	Alerts the component that it is now part of a displayable containment hierarchy
public int checkImage(Image, ImageObserver)	Obtains the status of the image preparation for the specified image
public int checkImage (Image, int, int, ImageObserver)	Obtains the status of the image preparation for the specified image
protected AWTEvent coalesceEvents (AWTEvent, AWTEvent)	Potentially combines an existing event with a new event
public boolean contains(int, int)	Returns true if the specified component contains the specified coordinates
public boolean contains(Point)	Returns true if the specified component contains the specified coordinates
public Image createImage(ImageProducer)	Creates a new Image object using the data in the ImageProducer object
public Image createImage(int, int)	Creates a new Image object using the specified height and width; this method is usually used to create an offscreen image used in double-buffering
protected final void disableEvents(long)	Disables the events specified with the long parameter
public void dispatchEvent(AWTEvent)	Dispatches an event to this component, or one of its children
public void doLayout()	Lays out all components again
protected void enableEvents(long)	Enables the events specified with the long parameter
public void enableInputMethods(boolean)	Sets the enabled status of input method support
protected void firePropertyChange (String, Object, Object)	Report bound property changes
public float getAlignmentX()	Obtains the alignment along the x-axis for this component

Methods/Events	Description
public float getAlignmentY()	Obtains the alignment along the y-axis for this component
public Color getBackground()	Obtains the background color for this component
public Rectangle getBounds()	Obtains the bounding box for this component
public Rectangle getBounds(Rectangle)	Stores the bounding box for this component in the specified Rectangle, and returns the rectangle
public ColorModel getColorModel()	Obtains the color model in use for this component
public Component getComponentAt(int, int)	Obtains the child component at the specified coordinates
public Component getComponentAt(Point)	Obtains the child component at the specified coordinates
public ComponentOrientation getComponentOrientation()	Obtains the language-sensitive orientation that is used to order textual elements
public Cursor getCursor()	Obtains the current Cursor object in use
public DropTarget getDropTarget()	Obtains the DropTarget associated for this component
public Font getFont()	Obtains the current Font object in use
public FontMetrics getFontMetrics(Font)	Obtains the FontMetrics object corresponding to the current font in use
public Color getForeground()	Obtains the foreground color for this component
public Graphics getGraphics()	Obtains the Graphics object associated with this component
public int getHeight()	Obtains the height of this component
public InputContext getInputContext()	Obtains the InputContext for this component for text editing
public InputMethodRequests getInputMethodRequests()	Obtains the method request handler for this component
public Locale getLocale()	Obtains the locale of this component

continues

Methods/Events	Description
`public Point getLocation()`	Obtains the relative coordinates of the component's top-left corner
`public Point getLocation(Point)`	Stores the relative coordinates of the component's top left corner into the specified `Point` and returns that `Point`
`public Point getLocationOnScreen()`	Obtains the global coordinates of the component's top-left corner
`public Dimension getMaximumSize()`	Obtains the maximum size this component can take on
`public Dimension getMinimumSize()`	Obtains the minimum size this component can take on
`public String getName()`	Obtains the logical name describing this component
`public Object getParent()`	Obtains the parent component for this component
`public ComponentPeer getPeer()`	Obtains a reference to the component's `Peer`. Deprecated, use `isDisplayable()`
`public Dimension getPreferredSize()`	Obtains the preferred size for this component
`public Dimension getSize()`	Obtains the current size of this component
`public Dimension getSize(Dimension)`	Stores the current size of this component in the specified `Dimension` and returns that `Dimension`
`public Toolkit getToolkit()`	Obtains the `Toolkit` object associated with this component
`public final Object getTreeLock()`	Obtains the component tree locking object
`public int getWidth()`	Obtains the width of this component
`public int getX()`	Obtains the relative x coordinate of this component's top left corner
`public int getY()`	Obtains the relative y coordinate of this component's top left corner
`public boolean hasFocus()`	Determines whether this component has the keyboard focus or not

Methods/Events	Description
`public boolean imageUpdate (Image, int, int, int, int, int)`	Repaints the area bounded by the specified coordinates when the specified `Image` object has changed
`public void invalidate()`	Invalidates the component
`public boolean isDisplayable()`	Returns true if the component is displayable
`public boolean isDoubleBuffered()`	Returns true if the component uses double buffering
`public boolean isEnabled()`	Returns true if the component is enabled
`public boolean isFocusTraversable()`	Returns true if this component should receive focus when the user tabs through a screen
`public boolean isLightWeight()`	Returns true if the component does not have a toolkit peer
`public boolean isOpaque()`	Returns true if the component is completely opaque
`public boolean isShowing()`	Returns true if this component is currently showing
`public boolean isValid()`	Returns true if this component is currently valid
`public boolean isVisible()`	Returns true if this component is currently visible
`public void list()`	Prints a listing of this component to the output stream at `System.out`
`public void list(PrintStream)`	Prints a listing of this component to the specified output stream
`public void list(PrintStream, int)`	Prints a listing of this component to the specified output stream, starting at the specified indentation
`public void list(PrintWriter)`	Prints a listing of this component to the specified `PrintWriter` object
`public void list(PrintWriter, int)`	Prints a listing of this component to the specified `PrintWriter` object, starting at the specified indentation

continues

A

JFC CLASS REFERENCE

Methods/Events	Description
`public void paint(Graphics)`	Invoked when the component should paint itself into the specified `Graphics` object
`public void paintAll(Graphics)`	Invoked when the component should paint itself and all of its children into the specified `Graphics` object
`protected void paramString()`	Obtains the parameter string for this object
`public boolean prepareImage (Image, ImageObserver)`	Prepares the image for rendering into this component
`public boolean prepareImage (Image, int, int, ImageObserver)`	Prepares the image for rendering into this component
`public void print(Graphics)`	Invoked when the component should print itself into the specified `Graphics` object
`public void printAll(Graphics)`	Invoked when the component should print itself and all of its children into the specified `Graphics` object
`protected void processComponentEvent(ComponentEvent)`	Used internally to process component events
`protected void processEvent(AWTEvent)`	Used internally to process component events
`protected void processFocusEvent(FocusEvent)`	Used internally to process focus events
`protected void processInputMethodEvent (InputMethodEvent)`	Used internally to process text editing events
`protected void processKeyEvent(KeyEvent)`	Used internally to process key events
`protected void processMouseEvent(MouseEvent)`	Used internally to process mouse events
`protected void processMouseMotionEvent(MouseEvent)`	Used internally to process mouse motion events
`public void remove(MenuComponent)`	Removes the specified pop-up menu from the component
`public void removeComponentListener (ComponentListener)`	Removes the specified `ComponentListener` object from the collection of listeners

Methods/Events	Description
`public void removeFocusListener` `(FocusListener)`	Removes the specified `FocusListener` object from the collection of listeners
`public void removeInputMethodListener` `(InputMethodListener)`	Removes the specified `InputListener` object from the collections of listeners
`public void removeKeyListener` `(KeyListener)`	Removes the specified `KeyListener` object from the collection of listeners
`public void removeMouseListener` `(MouseListener)`	Removes the specified `MouseListener` object from the collection of listeners
`public void removeMouseMotionListener` `(MouseMotionListener)`	Removes the specified `MouseMotionListener` object from the collection of listeners
`public void removeNotify()`	Notifies the component that it has been removed from its peer, and destroys any existing peer objects
`public void` `removePropertyChangeListener` `(PropertyChangeListener)`	Removes the specified `PropertyChangeListener` from the collection of listeners
`public void` `removePropertyChangeListener` `(String, PropertyChangeListener)`	Removes the specified `PropertyChangeListener` for a specified property
`public void repaint()`	Method to call if you want the screen to repaint; invoking this method will cause the `paint()` method to be called
`public void repaint(int, int, int, int)`	Method to call if you want the screen to repaint for the specified coordinates
`public void repaint(long)`	Method to call if you want the screen to wait up to the specified number of milliseconds and before repainting
`public void repaint` `(long, int, int, int, int)`	Method to call if you want the screen to wait up to the specified number of milliseconds and before repainting the specified coordinates

continues

Methods/Events	Description
`public void requestFocus()`	Asks that focus be given to this component
`public void setBackground(Color)`	Sets the background color for this object
`public void setBounds(int, int, int, int)`	Sets the bounding box for this rectangle
`public void setBounds(Rectangle)`	Sets the bounding box for this rectangle
`public void setComponentOrientation (ComponentOrientation)`	Sets the orientation used to order the elements or text of the component
`public void setCursor(Cursor)`	Sets the cursor object currently in use
`public void setDropTarget (DropTarget)`	Sets the `DropTarget` associated with this component for drag and drop operations
`public void setEnabled(boolean)`	Sets the enabled status of this component
`public void setFont(Font)`	Sets the `Font` object currently in use
`public void setForeground(Color)`	Sets the foreground color currently in use by this component
`public void setLocale(Locale)`	Sets the locale for this component
`public void setLocation(int, int)`	Sets the location of this component
`public void setLocation(Point)`	Sets the location of this component
`public void setName(String)`	Sets the name of this component
`public void setSize(Dimension)`	Sets the dimensions of this component
`public void setSize(int, int)`	Sets the dimensions of this component
`public void setVisible(boolean)`	Sets the visible status of this component
`public String toString()`	Obtains a `String` object that represents this component
`public void transferFocus()`	Transfers focus to the next component waiting for it
`public void update(Graphics)`	Invoked immediately before a call to `paint()` is made
`public void validate()`	Validates the component

CLASS   **java.awt.Component: Example**

The Component class can be extended to create custom components:

```
import java.awt.*;
import_ java.awt.event.*;
import java.util.*;

public class ComponentDemo extends Component {
    private Polygon triangle;
    private Color   myColor;
    private Vector  listeners;
    private int     theID;


    public ComponentDemo() {
        // enable the sending of mouse events
        enableEvents(AWTEvent.MOUSE_EVENT_MASK);

        // mark out the xpoints and ypoints
        int x[] = {0, 100, 50};
        int y[] = {0, 0, 100};

        triangle = new Polygon(x, y, 3);
        setSize(100,100);

        myColor = Color.black;
        listeners = new Vector();
    }


    public void paint(Graphics g) {
        g.setColor(myColor);
        g.fillPolygon(triangle);

        // super.paint() MUST be called, or your component
        // will NOT appear on screen.
        super.paint(g);
    }


    // called when the user clicks on the triangle
    public void processMouseEvent(MouseEvent me) {
        // make sure that the event occured over the triangle itself
        if(! triangle.contains(me.getPoint()) ) return;

        // if the mouse button was clicked change to alternate state
        if(me.getID() == MouseEvent.MOUSE_PRESSED) {
```

```
            theID = me.getID();
            myColor = Color.pink;
            repaint();
        }
        // if the mouse button was released change to initial state
        else if(me.getID() == MouseEvent.MOUSE_RELEASED) {
            theID = me.getID();
            myColor = Color.black;
            repaint();

            // send the event to all listeners
            sendEvents();
        }
    }


    public Dimension getPreferredSize() {
        return new Dimension(200,200);
    }

    public Dimension getMinimumSize() {
        return new Dimension(200,200);
    }


    public synchronized void addActionListener(ActionListener al) {
        listeners.addElement(al);
    }


    public synchronized void removeActionListener(ActionListener al) {
        listeners.removeElement(al);
    }


    private void sendEvents() {
        ActionEvent myEvent
        = new ActionEvent(this, theID, "button click occured");

        // create a clone of the listeners Vector.
        // This will place a "cut-off"
        // point after which new registerations
        // will not be considered for
// the current event being sent out.
        Vector listenerClone;
        synchronized(this) {
            listenerClone = (Vector)listeners.clone();
        }
```

```
        for(int i=0;i<listenerClone.size();i++) {
            ((ActionListener)listenerClone.elementAt(i)).
            actionPerformed(myEvent);
    }
        }

    public static void main(String args[] ) {
        Frame myDemo = new Frame();

        myDemo.add(new ComponentDemo());

                // Allow the program to be shut down by closing the
        // main window.
        myDemo.addWindowListener(new WindowAdapter() {
            public void windowClosing(WindowEvent we) {
                System.exit(0);
            }
        });
        myDemo.pack();
        myDemo.setVisible(true);
    }
}
```

CLASS **java.awt.ComponentOrientation**

public final class ComponentOrientation extends Object implements
Serializable

The ComponentOrientation class encapsulates orientation for elements of a component
or text. It controls how characters are laid out into lines, how those lines are laid out into
blocks, and how items are laid out. For example, where the checkbox is laid out in rela-
tion to its text.

CLASS **java.awt.ComponentOrientation: Summary**

Fields/Methods	Description
public static final ComponentOrientation LEFT_TO_RIGHT	Indicates left to right, top to bottom flow
public static final ComponentOrientation RIGHT_TO_LEFT	Indicates right to left, top to bottom flow
public static final ComponentOrientation UNKNOWN	Indicates that orientation has not been set

continues

Fields/Methods	Description
`public static ComponentOrientation getOrientation(Locale)`	Obtains the appropriate orientation for the specified locale
`public static ComponentOrientation getOrientation(ResourceBundle)`	Obtains the appropriate orientation for the specified `ResourceBundle`'s localization
`public boolean isHorizontal()`	Returns true if the lines are laid out horizontally
`public boolean isLeftToRight()`	Returns true if items in horizontal lines flow left to right or if vertical lines flow left to right

CLASS `java.awt.Container`

`public abstract class Container extends Component`

As stated at the beginning of the section on the AWT, the `Container` class is used to visually group a series of components. Usually you will not subclass `Container`, but instead will work with one of its child classes like `Frame`. With the 1.1 release of the JDK, it is possible to create a child class of `Container` that becomes a peer-free container. This has the advantage of being very lightweight.

CLASS `java.awt.Container`: **Summary**

Methods/Events	Description
`public Component add(Component)`	Adds the specified component to the container
`public Component add(Component, int)`	Adds the specified component to the container at the specified index
`public void add(Component, Object)`	Adds the specified component to the container using the specified constraints

Methods/Events	Description
`public void add(Component, Object, int)`	Adds the specified component to the container at the specified index using the specified constraints
`public Component add(String, Component)`	Adds the specified component to the container at the specified position
`public void addContainerListener(ContainerListener)`	Adds a `ContainerListener` to the collection of listeners; a `ContainerListener` receives notification whenever a component is added or removed from the container
`protected void addImpl(Component, Object, int)`	Adds the specified component to the container at the specified index using the specified constraints
`public void addNotify()`	Causes the object's peer to be created
`public void doLayout()`	Lays out all components again
`public void Component findComponentAt (int, int)`	Searches children and their children (if necessary) to locate the visible component at the specified position
`public void Component findComponentAt (Point)`	Searches children and their children (if necessary) to locate the visible component at the specified `Point`
`public float getAlignmentX()`	Obtains the alignment along the x-axis for this component
`public float getAlignmentY()`	Obtains the alignment along the y-axis for this component
`public Component getComponent(int)`	Obtains the `Component` at the specified index
`public Component getComponentAt(int, int)`	Obtains the `Component` at the specified coordinates
`public Component getComponentAt(Point)`	Obtains the `Component` at the specified coordinates
`public int getComponentCount()`	Obtains a count of all components currently owned by the active container
`public Component[] getComponents()`	Obtains an array of all components currently owned by the container

continues

Methods/Events	Description
`public Insets getInsets()`	Obtains the insets for the container; insets for a given container specify the number of pixels that separate the container border from the first child component edge
`public LayoutManager getLayout()`	Obtains the active layout manager, or null if none is in use
`public Dimension getMaximumSize()`	Obtains the maximum size this component can take on
`public Dimension getMinimumSize()`	Obtains the minimum size this component can take on
`public Dimension getPreferredSize()`	Obtains the preferred size for this component
`public void invalidate()`	Invalidates the component
`public boolean isAncestorOf(Component)`	Returns true if the specified component is contained in the containment hierarchy of this component
`public void list(PrintStream, int)`	Prints a listing of this component to the specified output stream, starting at the specified indentation
`public void list(PrintWriter, int)`	Prints a listing of this component to the specified `PrintWriter` object, starting at the specified indentation
`public void paint(Graphics)`	Invoked when the component should paint itself into the specified `Graphics` object
`public void paintComponents(Graphics)`	Invoked when all child components should be painted to the specified `Graphics` object
`protected Sting paramString()`	Obtains a parameter string for this object
`public void print(Graphics)`	Invoked when the component should print itself into the specified `Graphics` object
`public void printComponents(Graphics)`	Invoked when all child components should be painted into the specified `Graphics` object

Methods/Events	Description
`protected void processContainerEvent(ContainerEvent)`	Used internally to handle events
`protected void processEvent(AWTEvent)`	Used internally to handle events
`public void remove(Component)`	Removes the specified component from the container
`public void remove(int)`	Removes the component at the specified index from the container
`public void removeAll()`	Removes all child components from the container
`public void removeContainerListener (ContainerListener)`	Removes the specified `ContainerListener` from the collection of listeners
`public void removeNotify()`	Notifies the component that has been removed from its peer, and destroys any existing peer objects
`public void setLayout(LayoutManager)`	Sets the active layout manager
`public void validate()`	Validates the component
`public void validateTree()`	Performs a layout on all child components that have been invalidated

CLASS

java.awt.Container: Example

The Container class is used to aggregate a collection of components:

```java
import java.awt.*;
import java.awt.event.*;

public class ContainerDemo extends Container {
    private ComponentDemo myComponent;

    public ContainerDemo() {
        myComponent = new ComponentDemo();
        add(myComponent);
    }

    public Dimension getPreferredSize() {
        return myComponent.getPreferredSize();
    }

    public Dimension getMinimumSize() {
```

continues

```
        return myComponent.getMinimumSize();
    }


    public static void main(String args[]) {
        Frame f = new Frame();
        f.add(new ContainerDemo());

        // Allow the program to be shut down by closing the
        // main window.
        f.addWindowListener(new WindowAdapter() {
            public void windowClosing(WindowEvent we) {
                System.exit(0);
            }
        });

        f.pack();
        f.setVisible(true);
    }
}
```

CLASS **java.awt.Cursor**

`public class Cursor extends Object implements Serializble`

The Cursor class encapsulates the bitmap representation of a screen cursor. Under normal circumstances, you will not need to create child classes of Cursor, but instead will work with its predefined forms. As noted in the next section, Cursor publishes a series of public member variables that represent commonly used cursors.

CLASS **java.awt.Cursor: Summary**

Fields/Methods	Description
`public static final int CROSSHAIR_CURSOR`	Cursor type for a crosshair cursor
`public static final int CUSTOM_CURSOR`	Cursor type for all custom cursors
`public static final int DEFAULT_CURSOR`	Cursor type for the default cursor
`public static final int E_RESIZE_CURSOR`	Cursor type for an east-facing resize cursor
`public static final int HAND_CURSOR`	Cursor type for a hand cursor
`public static final int MOVE_CURSOR`	Cursor type for a move cursor
`public static final int N_RESIZE_CURSOR`	Cursor type for a north-facing resize cursor

Fields/Methods	Description
`protected static String name`	Name given to the cursor
`public static final int NE_RESIZE_CURSOR`	Cursor type for a northeast-facing resize cursor
`public static final int NW_RESIZE_CURSOR`	Cursor type for a northwest-facing resize cursor
`protected static Cursor[] predefined`	Array of predefined cursors
`public static final int S_RESIZE_CURSOR`	Cursor type for a south-facing resize cursor
`public static final int SE_RESIZE_CURSOR`	Cursor type for a southeast-facing resize cursor
`public static final int SW_RESIZE_CURSOR`	Cursor type for a southwest-facing resize cursor
`public static final int TEXT_CURSOR`	Cursor type for a text cursor
`public static final int W_RESIZE_CURSOR`	Cursor type for a west-facing resize cursor
`public static final int WAIT_CURSOR`	Cursor type for a wait cursor
`public static Cursor getDefaultCursor()`	Obtains the default cursor
`public String getName()`	Obtains the name of this cursor
`public static Cursor getPredefinedCursor(int)`	Obtains a cursor object corresponding to one of the aforementioned types
`public static Cursor getSystemCustomCursor(String) throws AWTException`	Obtains a system specific custom cursor with the specified name
`public int getType()`	Obtains the type of the active cursor
`public String toString()`	Obtains a string representation of this cursor

CLASS

java.awt.Cursor: Example

The Cursor class is used to represent an onscreen cursor:

```
import java.awt.*;
import java.awt.event.*;
```

```java
public class CursorDemo extends Frame implements ActionListener {
    private Cursor defaultCursor;
    private Cursor waitCursor;
    private boolean currentCursorIsDefault;


    public CursorDemo() {
        defaultCursor = new Cursor(Cursor.DEFAULT_CURSOR);
        waitCursor = new Cursor(Cursor.WAIT_CURSOR);

        setCursor(defaultCursor);
        currentCursorIsDefault = true;

        Button toggleButton = new Button("Toggle Cursor");
        toggleButton.addActionListener(this);
        add(toggleButton);
    }


    public void actionPerformed(ActionEvent ae) {
        if(currentCursorIsDefault) setCursor(waitCursor);
        else setCursor(defaultCursor);

        currentCursorIsDefault = !currentCursorIsDefault;
    }


    public static void main(String args[]) {
        CursorDemo myDemo = new CursorDemo();

        // Allow the program to be shut down by closing the
        // main window.
        myDemo.addWindowListener(new WindowAdapter() {
            public void windowClosing(WindowEvent we) {
                System.exit(0);
            }
        });

        myDemo.pack();
        myDemo.setVisible(true);
    }

}
```

CLASS # java.awt.Dialog

```
public class Dialog extends Window
```

The Dialog class is used to prompt the user for an answer to some question. For example, a friendly box asks "Are You Sure You Want To Quit?" when you quit most applications. A dialog box can take on one of two forms: modal, which blocks access to all other UI components until the user dismisses the dialog; and modeless, which does not block access to other UI resources from which the user is deciding. In most traditional applications—like Microsoft Word—the Save As option produces a modal dialog prompting you to enter a filename and path.

A Dialog object is defined as either modal or modeless, and this parameter is specified through a boolean argument to the constructor. Additionally, modality may be specified through the use of the setModal(boolean) method.

CLASS ## java.awt.Dialog: Summary

Methods/Events	Description
`public void addNotify()`	Creates the dialog's peer
`public String getTitle()`	Obtains the title of the dialog
`public boolean isModal()`	Obtains the modal status of the dialog
`public boolean isResizable()`	Specifies whether or not the dialog can be resized
`protected String paramString()`	Obtains a parameter string for the dialog
`public void setModal(boolean)`	Sets the modal status of the dialog
`public void setResizable(boolean)`	Sets the resize status of the dialog
`public void setTitle(String)`	Sets the title of the dialog
`public void show()`	Displays the dialog on the screen

CLASS ## java.awt.Dialog: Example

A Dialog object can be used to prompt the user for input or to acknowledge an event:

```
import java.awt.*;
import java.awt.event.*;
```

A

```java
public class DialogDemo extends Dialog implements ActionListener {
    private Label questionLabel;
    private Button yesButton;
    private Button noButton;

    public DialogDemo(Frame parent) {
        super(parent, true);

        // add the components using the GridBagLayout
        GridBagLayout gridBagLayout;
        gridBagLayout = new GridBagLayout();
        setLayout(gridBagLayout);

        ssetSize(299,152);
        questionLabel = new Label
        ("Are You Sure You Want To Quit?",Label.CENTER);
questionLabel.setFont(new Font("Dialog", Font.BOLD, 16));

        GridBagConstraints gbc;
        gbc = new GridBagConstraints();
        gbc.gridx = 0;
        gbc.gridy = 1;
        gbc.gridwidth = 4;
        gbc.weightx = 1;
        gbc.weighty = 1;
        gbc.fill = GridBagConstraints.HORIZONTAL;
        gbc.insets = new Insets(0,0,0,0);
        gridBagLayout.setConstraints(questionLabel, gbc);
        add(questionLabel);

        yesButton = new Button("Yes");
        yesButton.addActionListener(this);

        gbc = new GridBagConstraints();
        gbc.gridx = 1;
        gbc.gridy = 2;
        gbc.weightx = 1;
        gbc.weighty = 1;
        gbc.fill = GridBagConstraints.HORIZONTAL;
        gbc.insets = new Insets(10,10,10,10);
        gbc.ipadx = 10;
        gbc.ipady = 10;
        gridBagLayout.setConstraints(yesButton, gbc);
        add(yesButton);

        noButton = new Button("No");
        noButton.addActionListener(this);
```

```
        gbc = new GridBagConstraints();
        gbc.gridx = 3;
        gbc.gridy = 2;
        gbc.weightx = 1;
        gbc.weighty = 1;
        gbc.fill = GridBagConstraints.HORIZONTAL;
        gbc.insets = new Insets(10,10,10,10);
        gbc.ipadx = 10;
        gbc.ipady = 10;
        gridBagLayout.setConstraints(noButton, gbc);
        add(noButton);
    }


    // As defined by ActionListener
    public void actionPerformed(ActionEvent ae) {
        if (ae.getActionCommand().toLowerCase().equals(ìyesî))
            System.exit(0);
        else {
            setVisible(false); // Hide the dialog
            this.dispose();        // release the dialogs resources
        }
    }

    public static void main(String args[]) {
        final Frame f = new Frame();

        // Allow the program to be shut down by closing the
        // main window.
        f.addWindowListener(new WindowAdapter() {
            public void windowClosing(WindowEvent we) {
                // Close if itís okay. . .
                DialogDemo d = new DialogDemo(f);
                d.setVisible(true);
            }
        });

        f.setSize(100,100);
        f.setVisible(true);
    }
}
```

CLASS **java.awt.Dimension**

```
public class Dimension extends Dimension2D implements Serializable
```

The Dimension class is a utility class used to encapsulate the height and width of a rectangular region. As an examination of many of the APIs listed in this book will show, this class is often a return value from many methods, including getPreferredSize(), getMinimumSize(), and getMaximumSize(). While Dimension provides getter and setter methods, its only two fields, height and width, are declared public. Therefore, access to the fields is usually done directly rather than through method calls.

CLASS `java.awt.Dimension`: **Summary**

Fields/Methods	Description
public int height	The height attribute
public int width	The width attribute
public boolean equals(Object)	Returns true if both Dimension objects have the same height and width fields
public Dimension getSize()	Obtains a copy of the object, added for consistency
public void setSize(Dimension)	Sets the height and width attributes
public void setSize(int, int)	Sets the height and width attributes
public String toString()	Obtains a string representation of the object

CLASS `java.awt.FileDialog`

public class FileDialog extends Dialog

The class FileDialog is a specialized Dialog class used for reading and writing files. Although it's a parameter to its constructor, it is possible to specify whether the FileDialog object is to be used for reading files (LOAD) or writing files (SAVE).

CLASS `java.awt.FileDialog`: **Summary**

Fields/Methods	Description
public static final int LOAD	Constant specifying that the FileDialog object is to be used for the loading of files
public static final int SAVE	Constant specifying that the FileDialog object is to be used for the saving of files

Fields/Methods	Description
`public void addNotify()`	Creates the component's peer
`public String getDirectory()`	Obtains the last directory referenced by this component
`public String getFile()`	Obtains the last filename referenced by this component
`public FilenameFilter getFilenameFilter()`	Obtains the `FilenameFilter` object (if any) used with this component; a `FilenameFilter` object is used to specify that only certain types of files appear in a file browser
`public int getMode()`	Obtains the current mode of the component (LOAD or SAVE)
`protected String paramString()`	Obtains the parameter string for this object
`public void setDirectory(String)`	Sets the default directory in which this component is to start browsing
`public void setFile(String)`	Sets a suggested filename
`public void setFilenameFilter(FilenameFilter)`	Sets the active `FilenameFilter` object
`public void setMode(int)`	Sets the current mode of the component (LOAD or SAVE)

CLASS

`java.awt.FileDialog`: Example

The `FileDialog` class allows a user to select a file for loading or saving:

```
import java.awt.*;
import java.awt.event.*;


public class FileDialogDemo extends Frame implements ActionListener {
    private Button openButton;
    private Button saveButton;
    private FileDialog openDialog;
    private FileDialog saveDialog;
```

continues

```
public FileDialogDemo() {
    openButton = new Button("Open");
    saveButton = new Button("Save");
    openDialog = new FileDialog
    (this, "Open File", FileDialog.LOAD);
    saveDialog = new FileDialog
    (this, "Save File", FileDialog.SAVE);

    openButton.addActionListener(this);
    saveButton.addActionListener(this);

    setLayout(new FlowLayout(10));
    add(openButton);
    add(saveButton);
}


public void actionPerformed(ActionEvent ae) {
    if(ae.getSource() == openButton) openDialog.setVisible(true);
    else saveDialog.setVisible(true);
}


public static void main(String args[]) {
    FileDialogDemo myDemo = new FileDialogDemo();

    // Allow the program to be shut down by closing the
    // main window.
    myDemo.addWindowListener(new WindowAdapter() {
        public void windowClosing(WindowEvent we) {
            System.exit(0);
        }
    });

    myDemo.pack();
    myDemo.setVisible(true);
}
}
```

CLASS # java.awt.FlowLayout

public class FlowLayout extends Object implements LayoutManager,
Serializable

The FlowLayout layout manager lays out all components from left to right until there is
no more space, and then continues down and to the right again.

CLASS `java.awt.FlowLayout:` **Summary**

Fields/Methods	*Description*
`public static final int CENTER`	Constant indicating that each row of components should be centered
`public static final int LEADING`	Constant indicating that each row of components should be justified to the leading edge of the container's orientation
`public static final int LEFT`	Constant indicating that each row of components should be left-justified
`public static final int RIGHT`	Constant indicating that each row of components should be right-justified
`public static final int TRAILING`	Constant indicating that each row of components should be justified to the trailing edge of the container's orientation
`public void` `addLayoutComponent(String, Component)`	Adds the specified component to the container with the specified name
`public int getAlignment()` `(LEADING, TRAILING, LEFT, CENTER, or RIGHT)`	Obtains the alignment for this container
`public int getHgap()`	Obtains the horizontal gap between each component owned by this container
`public int getVgap()`	Obtains the vertical gap between each component owned by this container
`public void layoutContainer(Container)`	Lays out the specified container
`public Dimension` `minimumLayoutSize(Container)`	Obtains the minimum dimensions needed to lay out the specified container
`public Dimension` `preferredLayoutSize(Container)`	Obtains the maximum dimensions needed to lay out the specified container
`public void` `removeLayoutComponent(Component)`	Implemented to fulfill interface requirements, but has no effect
`public void setAlignment(int)` `(LEFT, CENTER, or RIGHT)`	Sets the alignment for this container

continues

Fields/Methods	Description
`public void setHgap(int)`	Sets the horizontal gap between each component owned by this container
`public void setVgap(int)`	Sets the vertical gap between each component owned by this container
`public String toString()`	Obtains a `String` object representing the current state of this container

CLASS
`java.awt.FlowLayout`: Example

The `FlowLayout` class allows objects to be arranged either from left to right along a container or from top to bottom:

```java
import java.awt.*;
import java.awt.event.*;

public class FlowLayoutDemo extends Frame {

    public FlowLayoutDemo() {
        // Set the layout, use a 10 pixel gap between components
        setLayout(new FlowLayout(10));

        // Add some components
        add(new Label("Resize Me"));
        add(new Button("Flow"));
        add(new Label("Layout"));
    }


    public static void main(String args[]) {
        FlowLayoutDemo myDemo = new FlowLayoutDemo();

        // Allow the program to be shut down by closing the
        // main window.
        myDemo.addWindowListener(new WindowAdapter() {
            public void windowClosing(WindowEvent we) {
                System.exit(0);
            }
        });

        myDemo.pack();
        myDemo.setVisible(true);
    }
}
```

CLASS # java.awt.Font

`public class Font extends Object implements Serializable`

The `Font` class encapsulates information including typeface, style, and point size for a screen font. Each VM is in charge of implementing its own fonts, and a list of them can be obtained by calling the `Toolkit.getFontList()` method.

CLASS ## java.awt.Font: Summary

Fields/Methods	Description
`public static final int BOLD`	Constant used to specify the bold form of a font
`public static final int CENTER_BASELINE`	Specifies a center baseline
`public static final int HANGING_BASELINE`	Specifies a hanging baseline
`public static final int ITALIC`	Constant used to specify the italic form of a font
`protected String name`	The logical name of the current font
`public static final int PLAIN`	Constant used to specify the plain form of a font
`protected float pointSize`	The size of the font
`public static final byte ROMAN_BASELINE`	Location of roman baseline
`public int size`	Size of the current font
`public int style`	Style of the current font
`public boolean canDisplay(char)`	Returns true if the active `Font` object has a glyph for the specified character
`public int canDisplayUpTo(char[], int, int)`	Returns an index into the array that is an offset to the first character for which the font does not have a glyph. Returns −1 if the font has enough glyphs to display the string
`public int canDisplayUpTo (CharacterIterator, int, int)`	Returns an index into the array that is an offset to the first character for which the font does not have a glyph. Returns −1 if the font has enough glyphs to display the string

Fields/Methods	Description
`public int canDisplayUpTo(String)`	Returns true if the active `Font` object has sufficient glyphs to display the specified string
`public GlyphVector` `createGlyphVector(FontRenderContext, char[])`	Creates a `GlyphVector` for he specified tcharacter array using the specified context
`public GlyphVector createGlyphVector` `(FontRenderContext, CharacterIterator)`	Creates a `GlyphVector` for the specified string using the specified context
`public GlyphVector createGlyphVector` `(FontRenderContext, int[])`	Creates a `GlyphVector` for the specified glyph codes using the specified context
`public GlyphVector createGlyphVector` `(FontRenderContext, String)`	Creates a `GlyphVector` for the specified string using the specified context
`public static Font decode(String)`	Returns the `Font` object represented by the `String` object parameter
`public Font deriveFont(AffineTransform)`	Applies the specified transform to the current font and returns the new font
`public Font deriveFont(float)`	Creates a new `Font` object with all properties matching the original `Font` object except for the size, which is obtained from the parameter
`public Font deriveFont(int)`	Creates a new `Font` object with all properties matching the original `Font` object except for the style, which is obtained from the parameter
`public Font` `deriveFont(int, AffineTransform)`	Creates a new `Font` object with all properties matching the original `Font` object except for the style, which is obtained from the parameter; in addition to a modified style, the specified transform is applied
`public Font deriveFont(int, float)`	Creates a new `Font` object with all properties matching the original `Font` object except for the size and style, which are obtained from the parameters

Fields/Methods	Description
public Font deriveFont(Map)	Creates a new Font object with properties determined by both the original Font properties and the properties specified in the Map
public boolean equals(Object)	Returns true if the two Font objects have the same face, style, and point size
protected void finalize()	Invoked by the garbage collector when there are no longer any references to the active object
public Map getAttributes()	Obtains the attributes for the active font
public AttributedCharacterIterator.Attribute getAvailableAttributes()	Obtains all attribute names for the active font
public byte getBaselineFor(char)	Obtains the baseline used with this glyph
public String getFamily()	Obtains the font family
public String getFamily()	Obtains the font family localized for the specified locale
public static Font getFont(Map)	Obtains the font best suited to display glyphs, as specified in the Map object
public static Font getFont(String)	Obtains the Font object associated with the system property specified as a parameter, or null if none exist
public static Font getFont(String, Font)	Obtains the Font object associated with the system property specified as a parameter; if none exist, the Font object parameter is returned
public String getFontName()	Obtains a logical name for the font face
public String getFontName(Locale)	Obtains a logical name for the font face localized for the specified locale
public float getItalicAngle()	Obtains the angle applied to the font when it is in italic form

continues

Fields/Methods	Description
public LineMetrics getLineMetrics (char[], int, int, FontRenderContext)	Obtains the LineMetrics object for the specified character array
public LineMetrics getLineMetrics (CharacterIterator, int, int, FontRenderContext)	Obtains the LineMetrics object for the specified CharacterIterator
public LineMetrics getLineMetrics (String, FontRenderContext)	Obtains the LineMetrics object for the specified String
public LineMetrics getLineMetrics (String, int, int, FontRenderContext)	Obtains the LineMetrics object for the specified String
public Rectangle2D getMaxCharBounds(FontRenderContext)	Obtains the maximum bounding box for this font
public int getMissingGlyphCode()	Obtains the missing glyph code
public String getName()	Obtains the logical name for this font
public int getNumGlyphs()	Obtains the number of glyphs in this font
public FontPeer getPeer()	Obtains the peer associated with this font (deprecated; font rendering is now platform independent)
public String getPSName()	Obtains the postscript name for this font
public int getSize()	Obtains the point size of this font
public float getSize2D()	Obtains the point size of this font as a float
public Rectangle2D getStringBounds (char[], int, int, FontRenderContext)	Obtains the maximum bounding box for the specified character array
public Rectangle2D getStringBounds (CharacterIterator, int, int, FontRenderContext)	Obtains the maximum bounding box for the specified character iterator

Fields/Methods	Description
public Rectangle2D getStringBounds (String, FontRenderContext)	Obtains the maximum bounding box for the specified String
public Rectangle2D getStringBounds (String, int, int, FontRenderContext)	Obtains the maximum bounding box for the specified String
public int getStyle()	Obtains the style used with this font
public AffineTransform getTransform()	Obtains the transform associated with this font
public int hashCode()	Obtains a hash code for this font
public boolean hasUniformLineMetrics()	Returns true if the font has uniform line metrics
public boolean isBold()	Returns true if the font is bold
public boolean isItalic()	Returns true if the font is italic
public boolean isPlain()	Returns true if the font is plain
public String toString()	Obtains a String object that represents the current state of this object

CLASS

java.awt.Font: Example

The Font class is used to represent a unique screen or printer font:

```java
import java.awt.*;
import java.awt.event.*;

public class FontDemo extends Frame implements ActionListener {
    private MenuItem[]   fontItems;
    private Font         myFont;

    public FontDemo() {
        // Create a font menu
        Menu fontMenu = new Menu("Fonts");

        // Create menu items for each font,
        // and add the new item to the menu
String[] fontList = getToolkit().getFontList();
        fontItems = new MenuItem[fontList.length];
        for(int i=0;i<fontList.length; i++) {
```

continues

A

```
            // create the MenuItem
            fontItems[i] = new MenuItem(fontList[i]);
            // add the MenuItem to the Menu
            fontMenu.add(fontItems[i]);
            // register as a listener of the MenuItem
            fontItems[i].addActionListener(this);
        }

        MenuBar myMenuBar = new MenuBar();
        myMenuBar.add(fontMenu);
        setMenuBar(myMenuBar);

        setSize(200,200);

        myFont = new Font(fontList[0], Font.BOLD, 14);
    }


    public void paint(Graphics g) {
        g.setColor(Color.red);
        g.setFont(myFont);
        g.drawString("Font Demo", 50, 100);
    }


    public void actionPerformed(ActionEvent ae) {
        myFont = new Font
        (ae.getActionCommand().trim(), Font.BOLD, 14);
repaint();
    }


    public static void main(String args[]) {
        FontDemo myDemo = new FontDemo();

        // Allow the program to be shut down by closing the
        // main window.
        myDemo.addWindowListener(new WindowAdapter() {
            public void windowClosing(WindowEvent we) {
                System.exit(0);
            }
        });

        myDemo.setVisible(true);
    }
}
```

java.awt.FontMetrics

`public abstract class FontMetrics extends Object implements Serializable`

The `FontMetrics` class encapsulates information about a specific `Font` object, including leading, ascent, descent, and character width. The class is useful for determining screen position for something like a centered string, or for determining where to break words if text is to properly flow around an image.

java.awt.FontMetrics: Summary

Fields/Methods	Description
`public Font font`	The font being represented
`public int bytesWidth(byte[], int, int)`	Obtains the total width needed to show the specified characters
`public int charsWidth(char[], int, int)`	Obtains the total width needed to show the specified characters
`public int charWidth(char)`	Obtains the total width needed to show the specified character
`public int charWidth(int)`	Obtains the total width needed to show the specified character
`public int getAscent()`	Obtains the ascent in use for this font
`public int getDescent()`	Obtains the descent in use for this font
`public Font getFont()`	Obtains the font represented by the `FontMetrics` object
`public int getHeight()`	Obtains the height in use for this font
`public int getLeading()`	Obtains the leading in use for this font
`public LineMetrics getLineMetrics (char[], int, int, Graphics)`	Obtains the `LineMetrics` object for the specified character array
`public LineMetrics getLineMetrics (CharacterIterator, int, int, Graphics)`	Obtains the `LineMetrics` object for the specified `CharacterIterator`
`public LineMetrics getLineMetrics (String, Graphics)`	Obtains the `LineMetrics` object for the specified `String`

continues

Fields/Methods	Description
public LineMetrics getLineMetrics (String, int, int, Graphics)	Obtains the LineMetrics object for the specified String
public int getMaxAdvance()	Obtains the max advance in use for this font
public int getMaxAscent()	Obtains the max ascent in use for this font
public Rectangle2D getMaxCharBounds(Graphics)	Obtains the maximum bounding box
public int getMaxDescent()	Obtains the max descent in use for this font
public Rectangle2D getStringBounds (char[], int, int, Graphics)	Obtains the maximum bounding box for the specified character array
public Rectangle2D getStringBounds (CharacterIterator, int, int, Graphics)	Obtains the maximum bounding box for the specified character iterator
public Rectangle2D getStringBounds (String, Graphics)	Obtains the maximum bounding box for the specified String
public Rectangle2D getStringBounds (String, int, int, Graphics)	Obtains the maximum bounding box for the specified String
public int[] getWidths()	Obtains the widths of the first 256 glyphs
public int stringWidth(String)	Obtains the width of the specified string with the represented font applied
public String toString()	Obtains a String object representing the current state

CLASS `java.awt.FontMetrics`: Example

The FontMetrics class is used to represent parameters about a unique font object:

```
import java.awt.*;
import java.awt.event.*;
```

```java
public class FontMetricsDemo extends Frame {
    private Font       myFont;
    private String     displayString;
    private int        pointSize;

    public FontMetricsDemo() {
        setSize(200, 200);
        pointSize = 8;
        myFont = new Font("Helvetica", Font.BOLD, pointSize);
        displayString = new String("FontMetrics Demo");
    }


    public void paint(Graphics g) {
        // get the current FontMetrics
        FontMetrics myMetrics = getFontMetrics(myFont);

        // Keep increasing the point size until
        // displayString fills the window
        while(myMetrics.stringWidth(displayString) < getWidth()) {
            pointSize++;
            myFont = new Font("Helvetica", Font.BOLD, pointSize);
            myMetrics = getFontMetrics(myFont);
        }

        g.setFont(myFont);
        g.drawString(displayString, 0, 100);
    }


    public static void main(String args[]) {
        FontMetricsDemo myDemo = new FontMetricsDemo();

        // Allow the program to be shut down by closing the
        // main window.
        myDemo.addWindowListener(new WindowAdapter() {
            public void windowClosing(WindowEvent we) {
                System.exit(0);
            }
        });

        myDemo.setVisible(true);
    }
}
```

java.awt.Frame

`public class Frame extends Window implements MenuContainer`

The `Frame` class represents a top-level window with a title and possibly a menu bar. Anytime an application needs to create a window, it will usually create a `Frame` object. This class is implemented using peers, so it will have a native look and feel on each platform it runs on.

Unlike most classes covered in this section, we will not spend time on a coding example here. Flip to any other coding example because they are all implemented using a `Frame` object at some point.

java.awt.Frame: Summary

Fields/Methods	Description
`public static final int CROSSHAIR_CURSOR`	Cursor type for a crosshair cursor (deprecated, use `Cursor.CROSSHAIR_CURSOR`)
`public static final int DEFAULT_CURSOR`	Cursor type for the default cursor (deprecated, use `Cursor. DEFAULT_CURSOR`)
`public static final int E_RESIZE_CURSOR.`	Cursor type for an east-facing resize cursor (deprecated, use `Cursor. E_RESIZE_CURSOR`)
`public static final int HAND_CURSOR`	Cursor type for a hand cursor (deprecated, use `Cursor.HAND_CURSOR`)
`public static final int MOVE_CURSOR`	Cursor type for a move cursor (deprecated, use `Cursor.MOVE_CURSOR`)
`public static final int N_RESIZE_CURSOR`	Cursor type for a north-facing resize cursor (deprecated, use `Cursor. N_RESIZE_CURSOR`)
`public static final int NE_RESIZE_CURSOR`	Cursor type for a northeast-facing resize cursor (deprecated, use `Cursor.NE_RESIZE_CURSOR`)
`public static final int NW_RESIZE_CURSOR`	Cursor type for a northwest-facing resize cursor (deprecated, use `Cursor.NW_RESIZE_CURSOR`)
`public static final int S_RESIZE_CURSOR`	Cursor type for a south-facing resize cursor (deprecated, use `Cursor.S_RESIZE_CURSOR`)

Fields/Methods	Description
`public static final int SE_RESIZE_CURSOR`	Cursor type for a southeast-facing resize cursor (deprecated, use `Cursor.SE_RESIZE_CURSOR`)
`public static final int SW_RESIZE_CURSOR`	Cursor type for a southwest-facing resize cursor (deprecated, use `Cursor.SW_RESIZE_CURSOR`)
`public static final int TEXT_CURSOR`	Cursor type for a text cursor (deprecated, use `Cursor.TEXT_CURSOR`)
`public static final int W_RESIZE_CURSOR`	Cursor type for a west-facing resize cursor (deprecated, use `Cursor.W_RESIZE_CURSOR`)
`public static final int WAIT_CURSOR`	Cursor type for a wait cursor (deprecated, use `Cursor.WAIT_CURSOR`)
`public void addNotify()`	Creates the component's peer
`public void dispose()`	Frees any resources associated with the component and makes it a candidate for garbage collection
`protected void finalize()`	Internal use to prevent memory leak
`public static Frame getFrames()`	Obtains an array containing references to all frames created by the application
`public Image getIconImage()`	Obtains the icon image used to represent this component
`public MenuBar getMenuBar()`	Obtains the menu bar associated with this component
`public String getTitle()`	Obtains the title displayed in the title bar
`public boolean isResizable()`	Returns true if this window is resizable
`protected String paramString()`	Obtains the parameter string for this component
`public void remove(MenuComponent)`	Removes the specified menu bar from this component
`public void setIconImage(Image)`	Sets the icon image used to represent this component

continues

Fields/Methods	Description
`public void setMenuBar(MenuBar)`	Associates a menu bar with this component
`public void setResizable(boolean)`	Sets whether or not the frame can be resized
`public void setTitle(String)`	Sets the string displayed in the title bar

CLASS
java.awt.Graphics

`public abstract class Graphics extends Object`

When an application draws to either the screen or an off-screen `Image` object, all drawing is performed on a `Graphics` object. The `Graphics` object maintains state, indicating the component to draw into, the current color, the current font, the current logical pixel operation, the current color, and the current alternate color.

The class is abstract, so you will never instantiate it directly. However, you will receive a reference to an appropriate subclass either as a parameter to a `paint()` method or by calling the `Image.getGraphics()` method.

CLASS
java.awt.Graphics: Method/Event Summary

Methods/Events	Description
`public abstract void clearRect(int, int, int, int)`	Fills the area contained within the specified coordinates with the background color
`public abstract void clipRect(int, int, int, int)`	Intersects the current clip region with the area specified by the coordinates
`public abstract void copyArea(int, int, int, int, int, int)`	Copies an area of the component from one set of coordinates to the other
`public abstract Graphics create()`	Obtains a copy of the current Graphics object
`public Graphics create(int, int, int, int)`	Obtains a copy of the current Graphics object with the specified translation and clip area

Methods/Events	Description
`public abstract void dispose()`	Disposes of the `Graphics` object and makes it a candidate for garbage collection
`public void draw3DRect(int, int, int, int, boolean)`	Draws a 3D outline rectangle using the specified coordinates and raised status
`public void drawArc(int, int, int, int, int, int)`	Draws an outline arc using the specified coordinates and covering the given rectangle dimensions
`public void drawBytes(byte[], int, int, int, int)`	Draws the specified bytes at the specified location
`public void drawChars(char[], int, int, int, int)`	Draws the specified bytes at the specified location
`public abstract void drawImage(Image, int, int, Color, ImageObserver)`	Draws an image at the specified location with the specified background color
`public abstract void drawImage(Image, int, int, ImageObserver)`	Draws an image at the specified location
`public abstract void drawImage(Image, int, int, int, int, Color, ImageObserver)`	Draws an image at the specified location with the specified background color and height/width
`public abstract void drawImage(Image, int, int, int, int, ImageObserver)`	Draws an image at the specified location with the specified height/width
`public abstract void drawImage(Image, int, int, int, int, int, int, int, int, Color, ImageObserver)`	Draws an image at the specified location with the specified background color and scaling information

continues

Methods/Events	Description

`public abstract void`
`drawImage(Image, int, int,`
`int, int, int, int,`
`int, int, ImageObserver)`
	Draws an image at the specified location with the specified scaling information

`public abstract void` `drawLine(int, int, int, int)`	Draws a line from one point to the other
`public abstract void` `drawOval(int, int, int, int)`	Draws an outline oval using the specified coordinates
`public abstract void drawPolygon` `(int[], int[], int)`	Draws an outline polygon using the specified coordinates
`public void drawPolygon(Polygon)`	Draws an outline polygon using the specified coordinates
`public abstract void drawPolyline` `(int[], int[], int)`	Draws a sequence of lines as defined by the coordinates
`public void drawRect(int, int, int, int)`	Draws an outline rectangle using the specified coordinates
`public abstract void drawRoundRect` `(int, int, int, int, int, int)`	Draws an outline rounded rectangle using the specified coordinates and curve dimensions
`public abstract void drawString` `(AttributedCharacterIterator, int, int)`	Draws the specified text given by the specified iterator at the location specified
`public abstract void drawString` `(String, int, int)`	Draws the specified string at the location specified
`public void fill3DRect` `(int, int, int, int, boolean)`	Draws a 3D filled rectangle using the specified coordinates and raised status
`public abstract void fillArc` `(int, int, int, int, int, int)`	Draws a filled arc using the specified coordinates and arc dimensions

Methods/Events	Description
`public abstract void` `fillOval(int, int, int, int)`	Draws a filled oval using the specified coordinates
`public abstract void` `fillPolygon(int[], int[], int)`	Draws a filled polygon using the specified coordinates
`public void fillPolygon(Polygon)`	Draws a filled polygon using the specified coordinates
`public abstract void` `fillRect(int, int, int, int)`	Draws a filled rectangle using the specified coordinates
`public abstract void fillRoundRect` `(int, int, int, int, int, int)`	Draws a filled rectangle using the specified coordinates and curve dimensions
`public void finalize()`	Release resources during garbage collection
`public abstract Shape getClip()`	Obtains the active clipping area
`public abstract Rectangle getClipBounds()`	Obtains the bounding box for the active clipping area
`public abstract Rectangle` `getClipBounds(Rectangle)`	Stores the bounding box for the active clipping area in the specified `Rectangle` and returns it
`public abstract Color getColor()`	Obtains the current drawing color
`public abstract Font getFont()`	Obtains the current `Font` object in use
`public FontMetrics getFontMetrics()`	Obtains the current `FontMetrics` object
`public abstract FontMetrics` `getFontMetrics(Font)`	Obtains the `FontMetrics` object associated with the specified `Font` object
`public boolean hitClip(int, int, int, int)`	Returns true if the specified rectangular area intersects the active clipping region
`public abstract void` `setClip(int, int, int, int)`	Sets the active clipping area

continues

Methods/Events	Description
`public abstract void setClip(Shape)`	Sets the active clipping area
`public abstract void setColor(Color)`	Sets the active drawing color
`public abstract void setFont(Font)`	Sets the active font
`public abstract void setPaintMode()`	Sets the active paint mode
`public abstract void setXORMode(Color)`	Sets the XOR paint status
`public String toString()`	Obtains a String object representing the current state of this object
`public abstract void translate(int, int)`	Translates the active origin to the specified origin

CLASS   java.awt.Graphics: Example

Direct drawing of primitives and fonts is performed in a Graphics object:

```java
import java.awt.*;
import java.awt.event.*;


public class GraphicsDemo extends Frame implements MouseListener {
    private Point start = null;
    private Point stop = null;


    public GraphicsDemo() {
        setSize(300,300);
        addMouseListener(this);
    }

    // Keep the screen from updating
    public void update(Graphics g) {
        paint(g);
    }

    // Paint the screen
    public void paint(Graphics g) {
        // Make sure we are null free
        if( (start == null) || (stop == null) ) return;

        // Draw the line between two points
        g.drawLine(start.x, start.y, stop.x, stop.y);
    }
```

```
// Reset the start point
public void mousePressed(MouseEvent me) {
    start = me.getPoint();
    repaint();
}

// Reset the stop point
public void mouseReleased(MouseEvent me) {
    stop = me.getPoint();
    repaint();
}

public void mouseClicked(MouseEvent me ) {
}

public void mouseEntered(MouseEvent me) {
}

public void mouseExited(MouseEvent me) {
}


public static void main(String args[]) {
    GraphicsDemo myDemo = new GraphicsDemo();

    // Allow the program to be shut down by closing the
    // main window.
    myDemo.addWindowListener(new WindowAdapter() {
        public void windowClosing(WindowEvent we) {
            System.exit(0);
        }
    });

    myDemo.setVisible(true);
}
}
```

CLASS # java.awt.GridBagConstraints

public class GridBagConstraints extends Object implements Cloneable,
Serializable

When laying out screens using the GridBagLayout class, each component's screen position is set using a GridBagConstraints object. GridBagConstraints has fields for specifying relative screen location, relative screen size, and grow-on-resize parameters. As a side note, this class joins together with GridBagLayout to form both the most powerful and hardest to use layout manager.

Because GridBagLayout and GridBagConstraints are most assuredly bedfellows, we will hold off on a coding example until the section on GridBagLayout.

java.awt.GridBagConstraints: Summary

Fields/Methods	Description
public int anchor	Specifies where a component should be anchored
public static final int BOTH	Constant used with fill to specify that a component should stretch in a horizontal and vertical fashion
public static final int CENTER	Constant used with anchor to specify that a component should be anchored in the center of its region
public static final int EAST	Constant used with anchor to specify that a component should be anchored in the east of its region
public int fill	Specifies how a component is to be stretched to fill a region
public int gridheight	Specifies the relative grid height that a component is to take up
public int gridwidth	Specifies the relative grid width that a component is to take up
public int gridx	Specifies the relative x position for this component
public int gridy	Specifies the relative y position for this component
public static final int HORIZONTAL	Constant used with fill to specify that a component should stretch in a horizontal fashion
public Insets insets	Specifies the external padding of the component
public int ipadx	Specifies the internal padding along the x-axis

Fields/Methods	Description
`public int ipady`	Specifies the internal padding along the y-axis
`public static final int NONE`	Constant used with `fill` to specify that a component should not stretch
`public static final int NORTH`	Constant used with `anchor` to specify that a component should be anchored in the north of its region
`public static final int NORTHEAST`	Constant used with `anchor` to specify that a component should be anchored in the northeast of its region
`public static final int NORTHWEST`	Constant used with `anchor` to specify that a component should be anchored in the northwest of its region
`public static final int RELATIVE`	Constant that specifies relative positioning
`public static final int REMAINDER`	Constant that specifies this component is the last component in a given row
`public static final int SOUTH`	Constant used with `anchor` to specify that a component should be anchored in the south of its region
`public static final int SOUTHEAST`	Constant used with `anchor` to specify that a component should be anchored in the southeast of its region
`public static final int SOUTHWEST`	Constant used with `anchor` to specify that a component should be anchored in the southwest of its region
`public static final int VERTICAL`	Constant used with `fill` to specify that a component should stretch in a vertical fashion
`public int weightx`	Specifies the x grow factor
`public int weighty`	Specifies the y grow factor
`public static final int WEST`	Constant used with `anchor` to specify that a component should be anchored in the west of its region
`public Object clone()`	Clones the current object

A

CLASS # java.awt.GridBagLayout

public class GridBagLayout extends Object implements LayoutManger2, Serializable

GridBagLayout is, without a doubt, the most powerful layout manager in the JDK 1.1. It allows for very specific customization of the screens look and feel. However, it is also very hard to use. Having worked with Java since December of 1995, I have only begun to understand GridBagLayout, and still find tools like Visual Café invaluable when building screens using this class.

CLASS # java.awt.GridBagLayout: Summary

Fields/Methods	Description
public double[] columnWeights	Collection of column weights
public double[] columnWidths	Collection of column heights
public Hashtable comptable	Comptable information
protected GridBagConstraints defaultConstraints	
protected GridBagLayoutInfo layoutInfo	Screen meta-data
protected static final int MAXGRIDSIZE	Maximum number of available grid blocks
protected static final int MINSIZE	Minimum number of grid blocks
protected static final int PREFERREDSIZE	Preferred number of grid blocks
public double[] rowHeights	Collection of row heights
public double[] rowWeights	Collection of row weights
public void addLayoutComponent(Component, Object)	Adds the specified component using the specified constraints
public void addLayoutComponent(String, Component)	Adds the specified component using the specified name
protected void AdjustForGravity (GridBagConstraints, Rectangle)	Used internally to determine screen placing
protected void ArrangeGrid(Container)	Used internally to determine screen placing

Fields/Methods	Description
`public GridBagConstraints getConstraints(Component)`	Obtains the constraints applied to the specified component
`public float getLayoutAlignmentX(Container)`	Obtains the alignment along the x-axis
`public float getLayoutAlignmentY(Container)`	Obtains the alignment along the y-axis
`public int[][] getLayoutDimensions()`	Obtains all row widths and column heights
`protected GridBagLayoutInfo GetLayoutInfo(Container, int)`	Obtains `GridBagLayoutInfo` information used in debugging
`public Point getLayoutOrigin()`	Obtains the grid origin
`public double[][] getLayoutWeights()`	Obtains all row and column weights
`protected Dimension GetMinSize(Container, GridBagLayoutInfo)`	Used internally to determine screen placement
`public void invalidateLayout(Container)`	Invalidates the layout for the specified container
`public void layoutContainer(Container)`	Lays out the specified container
`public Point location(int, int)`	Determines the cell that owns the specified coordinates
`protected GridBagConstraints lookupConstraints(Component)`	Obtains the `GridBagConstraints` object used to lay out the specified component
`public Dimension maximumLayoutSize(Container)`	Obtains the maximum size the specified container can consume
`public Dimension minimumLayoutSize(Container)`	Obtains the minimum size the specified container can consume
`public Dimension preferredLayoutSize(Container)`	Obtains the preferred size the specified container can consume

continues

Fields/Methods	Description
`public void` `removeLayoutComponent(Component)`	Removes the specified component from the screen
`public void setConstraints` `(Component, GridBagConstraints)`	Applies the specified constraints to the specified component
`public String toString()`	Obtains a `String` object representing the current state of this object

CLASS

`java.awt.GridBagLayout`: Example

The `GridBagLayout` class allows complex screens to be built:

```
import java.awt.*;
import java.awt.event.*;

public class GridBagDemo extends Frame {
    private Choice  layoutChoice;
    private Label   questionLabel;


    public GridBagDemo() {
    GridBagLayout gridBagLayout;
    gridBagLayout = new GridBagLayout();
    setLayout(gridBagLayout);

    questionLabel = new Label("What Is Your Favorite Layout Manager");

    GridBagConstraints gbc;
    gbc = new GridBagConstraints();
    gbc.gridx = 0;
    gbc.gridy = 0;
    gbc.gridwidth = 3;
    gbc.weightx = 100;
    gbc.weighty = 100;
    gbc.fill = GridBagConstraints.HORIZONTAL;
    gbc.insets = new Insets(0,0,0,0);
    gridBagLayout.setConstraints(questionLabel, gbc);
    add(questionLabel);

    layoutChoice = new Choice();
    layoutChoice.add("GridBagLayout");
    layoutChoice.add("GridLayout");
    layoutChoice.add("BorderLayout");
    layoutChoice.add("FlowLayout");
```

```
    gbc = new GridBagConstraints();
    gbc.gridx = 4;
    gbc.gridy = 0;
    gbc.gridwidth = 2;
    gbc.weightx = 100;
    gbc.weighty = 100;
    gbc.fill = GridBagConstraints.HORIZONTAL;
    gbc.insets = new Insets(0,0,0,0);
    gridBagLayout.setConstraints(layoutChoice, gbc);
    add(layoutChoice);
    }


    public static void main(String args[]) {
        GridBagDemo myDemo = new GridBagDemo();

        // Allow the program to be shut down by closing the
        // main window.
        myDemo.addWindowListener(new WindowAdapter() {
            public void windowClosing(WindowEvent we) {
                System.exit(0);
            }
        });

        myDemo.pack();
        myDemo.setVisible(true);
    }
}
```

CLASS
java.awt.GridLayout

```
public class GridLayout extends Object implements LayoutManager,
Serializable
```

The GridLayout layout manager breaks up a container into a series of equally sized grid
squares. Each grid square must house exactly one component, and the size of all grid
squares defaults to the size of the largest component. This layout manager can be used to
build screens in certain situations, but it often produces undesirable results. GridLayout
is useful when each component is about the same size.

CLASS
java.awt.GridLayout: **Method/Event Summary**

Methods/Events	*Description*
public void addLayoutComponent(String, Component)	Adds the specified component using the specified name

continues

Methods/Events	Description
`public int getColumns()`	Obtains the number of columns
`public int getHgap()`	Obtains the horizontal gap between components
`public int getRows()`	Obtains the number of rows
`public int getVgap()`	Obtains the vertical gap between components
`public void layoutContainer(Container)`	Lays out the specified container
`public Dimension minimumLayoutSize(Container)`	Obtains the minimum size the specified container can consume
`public Dimension preferredLayoutSize(Container)`	Obtains the preferred size the specified container can consume
`public void removeLayoutComponent(Component)`	Removes the specified component from the screen
`public void setColumns(int)`	Sets the number of columns in use
`public void setHgap(int)`	Sets the horizontal gap between components
`public void setRows(int)`	Sets the number of rows in use
`public void setVgap(int)`	Sets the vertical gap between components
`public String toString()`	Obtains a `String` object representing the current state of the object

CLASS

java.awt.GridLayout: Example

The GridLayout class allows objects to be added to a container in a grid with equally sized partitions:

```java
import java.awt.*;
import java.awt.event.*;

public class GridLayoutDemo extends Frame {

    public GridLayoutDemo() {
        // Set the layout
        setLayout(new GridLayout(3,2));
```

```
            // add some components
            add(new Button("1"));
            add(new Button("2"));
            add(new Button("3"));
            add(new Button("4"));
            add(new Button("5"));
        }

    public static void main(String args[]) {
        GridLayoutDemo myDemo = new GridLayoutDemo();

            // Allow the program to be shut down by closing the
            // main window.
            myDemo.addWindowListener(new WindowAdapter() {
                public void windowClosing(WindowEvent we) {
                    System.exit(0);
                }
            });

            myDemo.pack();
            myDemo.setVisible(true);
        }
}
```

CLASS # java.awt.Image

`public abstract class Image extends Object`

The Image class represents a physical image. Images are inherently platform dependent, so this class contains a platform-dependent implementation and may not be directly instantiated. Instead, an instance of an appropriate subclass can be obtained by reading in a GIF or JPEG file or through the createImage() method.

CLASS ## java.awt.Image: Summary

Fields/Methods	Description
Fields	
`public static final int SCALE_AREA_AVERAGING`	Constant passed to getScaledInstance() specifying the AREA AVERAGING scaling algorithm
`public static final int SCALE_DEFAULT`	Constant passed to getScaledInstance() specifying the SCALE DEFAULT scaling algorithm

continues

Fields/Methods	Description
`public static final int SCALE_FAST`	Constant passed to `getScaledInstance()` specifying the `SCALE FAST` scaling algorithm
`public static final int SCALE_REPLICATE`	Constant passed to `getScaledInstance()` specifying the `SCALE REPLICATE` scaling algorithm
`public static final int SCALE_SMOOTH`	Constant passed to `getScaledInstance()` specifying the `SCALE SMOOTH` scaling algorithm
`public static final Object UndefinedProperty`	Returned from the `getProperty()` method whenever the requested property cannot be found
`public abstract void flush()`	Flushes all resources in use
`public abstract Graphics getGraphics()`	Obtains the `Graphics` object associated with this image
`public abstract int getHeight(ImageObserver)`	Obtains the height as viewed by `ImageObserver`
`public Object getProperty(String, ImageObserver)`	Obtains the named property from the image
`public Image getScaledInstance(int, int, int)`	Obtains a scaled version of the active image
`public abstract ImageProducer getSource()`	Obtains the `ImageProducer` associated with this image
`public abstract int getWidth(ImageObserver)`	Obtains the width as viewed by `ImageObserver`

CLASS

java.awt.Insets

`public class Insets extends Object implements Clonable, Serializable`

The Insets class represents the number of pixels that should be used for a container's borders. When the container is laying itself out, it will not place any components in the area specified by the Insets class. As a side note, when you're creating external views in an applet, you should allocate approximately 10 extra pixels along the bottom of a frame for the warning label.

CLASS ## java.awt.Insets: **Summary**

Fields/Methods	Description
public int bottom	The bottom inset in pixels
public int left	The left inset in pixels
public int right	The right inset in pixels
public int top	The top inset in pixels
public Object clone()	Obtains a copy of the current object
public boolean equals(Object)	Returns true if both Insets objects have the same values for all public member variables
public String toString()	Returns a String object representing the current state of this object

CLASS ## java.awt.Label

public class Label extends Component

The Label class is used to display a single line of read-only text. It is possible to write directly into a container using the Graphics.drawString() method, but this leaves all layout up to you and can be very time-consuming. Instead, the Label class is provided as a component that can display a string.

CLASS ## java.awt.Label: **Summary**

Fields/Methods	Description
public static final int CENTER	Constant used to specify that the label text should be center-justified
public static final int LEFT	Constant used to specify that the label text should be left-justified
public static final int RIGHT	Constant used to specify that the label text should be right-justified
public void addNotify()	Creates the label's peer
public int getAlignment()	Obtains the alignment of the label (CENTER, LEFT, or RIGHT)

continues

A

JFC CLASS
REFERENCE

Fields/Methods	Description
`public String getText()`	Obtains the text being displayed
`protected String paramString()`	Obtains the parameter string for this component
`public void setAlignment(int)`	Sets the alignment of the label (CENTER, LEFT, or RIGHT)
`public void setText(String)`	Sets the text being displayed

CLASS
java.awt.Label: Example

The Label class is used to represent a text identifier:

```java
import java.awt.*;
import java.awt.event.*;

public class LabelDemo extends Frame {

    public LabelDemo() {
        // Set the layout
        setLayout(new GridLayout(2,1));

        // add some labels
        add(new Label("Special Edition Using", Label.CENTER));
        add(new Label("Java Class Libraries", Label.CENTER));
    }

    public static void main(String args[]) {
        LabelDemo myDemo = new LabelDemo();

        // Allow the program to be shut down by closing the
        // main window.
        myDemo.addWindowListener(new WindowAdapter() {
            public void windowClosing(WindowEvent we) {
                System.exit(0);
            }
        });

        myDemo.pack();
        myDemo.setVisible(true);
    }
}
```

| CLASS | **java.awt.List** |

`public class List extends Component implements ItemSelectable`

Like the `Choice` object, the `List` object is used to display a series of choices to a user. By using the `List` object, however, the user can see and select more than one option at a time.

| CLASS | **java.awt.List: Summary** |

Methods/Events	*Description*
`public void add(String)`	Adds the string to the end of the list
`public void add(String, int)`	Adds the string at the specified index
`public void addActionListener(ActionListener)`	Adds an `ActionListener` to the collection of listeners; an `ActionListener` is notified whenever a user double-clicks on an item
`public void addItem(String)`	Adds the string to the end of the list (deprecated, use `add(String)`)
`public void addItem(String, int)`	Adds the string at the specified index (deprecated, use `add(String, int)`)
`public void addItemListener(ItemListener)`	Adds an `ItemListener` to the collection of listeners; an `ItemListener` is notified whenever the selected item changes
`public void addNotify()`	Creates the component's peer
`public void delItem(int)`	Removes the `String` at the specified index (deprecated, use `remove(int)`)
`public void deselect(int)`	Deselects the item at the index specified by the `int` parameter
`public String getItem(int)`	Obtains the item at the specified index
`public int getItemCount()`	Obtains a count of all items in the list
`public String[] getItems()`	Obtains an array containing all items in the list

continues

A

Methods/Events	Description
public Dimension getMinimumSize()	Obtains the minimum size of the list
public Dimension getMinimumSize(int)	Obtains the minimum size of a list with the specified number of rows
public Dimension getPreferredSize()	Obtains the preferred size of the list
public Dimension getPreferredSize(int)	Obtains the preferred size of a list with the specified number of rows
public int getRows()	Obtains the number of visible rows in the list
public int getSelectedIndex()	Obtains the index of the selected item
public int[] getSelectedIndexes()	Obtains an array containing all selected indices
public String getSelectedItem()	Obtains the selected item
public String[] getSelectedItems()	Obtains an array containing all selected items
public Object[] getSelectedObjects()	Obtains an array containing all selected items
public int getVisibleIndex()	Obtains the last index made visible with a call to makeVisible()
public boolean isIndexSelected(int)	Returns true if the specified index is currently selected
public boolean isMultipleMode()	Returns true if you are currently in multiple select mode
public void makeVisible(int)	Scrolls the list, ensuring that the item at the specified index is visible
protected void paramString()	Obtains a parameter string for the component
protected void processActionEvent(ActionEvent)	Used internally for event management
protected void processEvent(AWTEvent)	Used internally for event management
protected void processItemEvent(ItemEvent)	Used internally for event management
public void remove(int)	Removes the item at the specified index
public void remove(String)	Removes the first occurrence of the specified item

Methods/Events	Description
public void removeActionListener(ActionListener)	Removes the ActionListener from the collection of listeners
public void removeAll()	Removes all items from the list
public void removeItemListener(ItemListener)	Removes the ItemListener from the collection of listeners
public void removeNotify()	Separates the List object from its peer
public void replaceItem(String, int)	Replaces the item at the specified index with the String object
public void select(int)	Selects the item at the specified index
public void setMultipleMode(boolean)	Sets multiple select mode based on the parameter

· CLASS

java.awt.List: Example

The List class is used to represent a collection of items, from which either one or many can be selected:

```
import java.awt.*;
import java.awt.event.*;

public class ListDemo extends Frame {
    private List    layoutList;
    private Label   questionLabel;


    public ListDemo() {
        GridBagLayout gridBagLayout;
        gridBagLayout = new GridBagLayout();
        setLayout(gridBagLayout);

questionLabel = new Label("What Is Your Favorite" +
                            " Layout Manager");

        GridBagConstraints gbc;
        gbc = new GridBagConstraints();
        gbc.gridx = 0;
        gbc.gridy = 0;
        gbc.gridwidth = 3;
```

continues

A

```
        gbc.weightx = 100;
        gbc.weighty = 100;
        gbc.fill = GridBagConstraints.HORIZONTAL;
        gbc.insets = new Insets(0,0,0,0);
        gridBagLayout.setConstraints(questionLabel, gbc);
        add(questionLabel);

        // Create a new List object which allows multiple selections,
        // and displays up to 5 items at a time.
        layoutList = new List(5, true);
layoutList.add("GridBagLayout");
        layoutList.add("GridLayout");
        layoutList.add("BorderLayout");
        layoutList.add("FlowLayout");

        gbc = new GridBagConstraints();
        gbc.gridx = 4;
        gbc.gridy = 0;
        gbc.gridwidth = 2;
        gbc.gridheight = 4;
        gbc.weightx = 100;
        gbc.weighty = 100;
        gbc.fill = GridBagConstraints.HORIZONTAL;
        gbc.insets = new Insets(0,0,0,0);
        gridBagLayout.setConstraints(layoutList, gbc);
        add(layoutList);
    }


    public static void main(String args[]) {
        ListDemo myDemo = new ListDemo();

        // Allow the program to be shut down by closing the
        // main window.
        myDemo.addWindowListener(new WindowAdapter() {
            public void windowClosing(WindowEvent we) {
                System.exit(0);
            }
        });

        myDemo.pack();
        myDemo.setVisible(true);
    }
}
```

CLASS # java.awt.MediaTracker

```
public class MediaTracker extends Object implements Serializable
```

The MediaTracker class is a utility class provided to track the loading progress of Image objects. When an Image object is loaded from a file, a reference to the object is established. However, the Image is not actually loaded in until needed. Deferment of Image loading occurs to save time, but it also means a slowdown when the images are actually ready.

Using the MediaTracker class, it is possible to force the loading of a series of Image objects.

CLASS ## java.awt.MediaTracker: Summary

Fields/Methods	Description
`public static final int ABORTED`	Flag indicating that image loading was aborted
`public static final int COMPLETE`	Flag indicating that image loading is complete
`public static final int ERRORED`	Flag indicating that image loading received an error
`public static final int LOADING`	Flag indicating that image loading is in progress
`public void addImage(Image, int)`	Adds the specified image to the MediaTracker at the specified index
`public void addImage(Image, int, int, int)`	Adds a scaled version of the specified image to the MediaTracker at the specified index
`public boolean checkAll()`	Checks to see if all images being tracked have finished loading
`public boolean checkAll(boolean)`	Checks to see if all images being tracked have finished loading; if the boolean parameter is set to true, all unloaded images will be loaded
`public boolean checkID(int)`	Checks to see if the image(s) with the specified ID have finished loading

continues

A

Fields/Methods	*Description*
`public boolean checkID(int, boolean)`	Checks to see if the image(s) with the specified ID have finished loading; If the `boolean` parameter is set to true, all unloaded image(s) will be loaded
`public Object[] getErrorsAny()`	Obtains all `Image` objects that have generated an error-out while loading
`public Object[] getErrorsID(int)`	Obtains all `Image` objects with the specified ID that have generated an error-out while loading
`public boolean isErrorAny()`	Returns true if any objects being tracked have generated an error
`public boolean isErrorID(int)`	Returns true if any objects with the specified ID have generated an error
`public void removeImage(Image)`	Removes the specified image from the collection of images being tracked
`public void removeImage(Image, int)`	Removes the specified image with the specified ID from the collection of images being tracked
`public void removeImage(Image, int, int, int)`	Removes the specified image with the specified ID, width, and height from the collection of images being tracked
`public int statusAll(boolean)`	Returns the bitwise OR of all status codes; if the `boolean` parameter is true, all unloaded objects will be loaded
`public int statusID(int, boolean)`	Returns the bitwise OR of the status codes of all objects with the specified ID; if the `boolean` parameter is true, all unloaded objects will be loaded
`public boolean waitForAll()` `throws InterruptedException`	Waits for all objects to load
`public boolean waitForAll(long)` `throws InterruptedException`	Waits either for all objects to load or the amount of time specified as the `long` parameter (in milliseconds)

Fields/Methods	Description
`public boolean waitForID(int)` `throws InterruptedException`	Waits for all objects with the specified ID to load
`public boolean waitForID(int, long)` `throws InterruptedException`	Waits either for all objects with the specified ID to load or the amount of time specified as the `long` parameter (in milliseconds)

CLASS # java.awt.Menu

`public class Menu extends MenuItem implements MenuContainer`

The `Menu` class is used to create a pull-down menu. Used together with `MenuBar` and `MenuItem`, you can create the set of menus seen at the top of most windows.

Because the `Menu`, `MenuBar`, and `MenuItem` classes work together, the coding example for this class is included in the section on `MenuItem`.

CLASS # java.awt.Menu: Summary

Methods/Events	Description
`public MenuItem add(MenuItem)`	Adds the specified `MenuItem` to the end of the menu
`public void add(String)`	Adds the specified string to the end of the menu
`public void addNotify()`	Creates the `Menu` object's peer
`public void addSeparator()`	Adds a separator line to the end of the menu
`public MenuItem getItem(int)`	Obtains the `MenuItem` object at the specified index
`public int getItemCount()`	Obtains a count of all items in the menu
`public void insert(MenuItem, int)`	Inserts the specified `MenuItem` at the specified index

continues

Methods/Events	Description
`public void insert(String, int)`	Inserts the specified `MenuItem` at the specified index
`public void insertSeparator(int)`	Inserts a separator line to the menu at the specified index
`public boolean isTearOff()`	Returns true if this menu is a tear-off menu
`protected String paramString()`	Obtains the parameter string for this object
`public void remove(int)`	Removes the item at the specified index
`public void remove(MenuComponent)`	Removes the specified `MenuComponent`
`public void removeAll()`	Removes all items from the menu
`public void removeNotify()`	Detaches the `Menu` object from its peer

CLASS   **java.awt.MenuBar**

`public class MenuBar extends MenuComponent implements MenuContainer`

The `MenuBar` class represents the physical menu bar that rests at the top of most windows. Once a `MenuBar` object is ready for display, it can be placed on a frame using the `Frame.setMenuBar()` method.

Because the `Menu`, `MenuBar`, and `MenuItem` classes work together, the coding example for this class is included in the section on `MenuItem`.

CLASS   **java.awt.MenuBar: Summary**

Fields/Methods/Events	Description
`public Menu add(Menu)`	Adds the specified menu to the `MenuBar`
`public void addNotify()`	Creates the `MenuBar`'s peer
`public void deleteShortcut(MenuShortcut)`	Removes the specified `MenuShortcut`
`public Menu getHelpMenu()`	Obtains the Help menu, or null if none exists
`public Menu getMenu(int)`	Obtains the `Menu` object at the specified index
`public int getMenuCount()`	Obtains a count of all menus

Fields/Methods/Events	Description
public MenuItem getShortcutMenuItem(MenuShortcut)	Obtains the MenuItem associated with the specified MenuShortcut
public void remove(int)	Removes the menu at the specified index
public void remove(MenuComponent)	Removes the specified MenuComponent
public void removeNotify()	Detaches the MenuBar object from its peer
public void setHelpMenu(Menu)	Sets the Help menu
public Enumeration shortcuts()	Obtains a collection of all shortcuts

CLASS
java.awt.MenuComponent

public abstract class MenuComponent extends Object implements Serializable

MenuComponent is the abstract base class of all menu-related components. Like all other examples of abstract classes, there will obviously not be a code example for this section.

CLASS
java.awt.MenuComponent: Summary

Methods/Events	Description
protected void dispatchEvent(AWTEvent)	Used internally to send events
public Font getFont()	Obtains the font used to render the component
public String getName()	Obtains the logical name for this component
public MenuContainer getParent()	Obtains the parent component
protected String paramString()	Obtains a parameter string for this object
protected void processEvent(AWTEvent)	Used internally to send events
public void removeNotify()	Separates the component from its peer
public void setFont(Font)	Sets the font used to render the component
public void setName(String)	Set the logical name for this component
public String toString()	Obtains a String object representing the current state of this object

java.awt.MenuItem

public class MenuItem extends MenuComponent

MenuItem represents a choice in a pull-down menu. A MenuItem object consists of a logical name that is displayed in the pull-down menu, and an optional keyboard shortcut.

java.awt.MenuItem: Summary

Methods/Events	Description
public void addActionListener(ActionListener)	Adds the specified ActionListener to the collection of listeners; an ActionListener is notified whenever the MenuItem is selected
public void addNotify()	Creates the component's peer
public void deleteShortcut()	Removes the shortcut from this component
protected final void disableEvents(long)	Disables the events matching the specified event code
protected final void enableEvents(long)	Enables the events matching the specified event code
public void getActionCommand()	Obtains the action command associated with this object
public String getLabel()	Obtains the label used to render this component
public MenuShortcut getShortcut()	Obtains the menu shortcut associated with this component
public boolean isEnabled()	Returns true if this component is currently enabled
protected String paramString()	Obtains a parameter string representing the current state of this object
protected void processActionEvent(ActionEvent)	Used internally for event management
protected void processEvent(AWTEvent)	Used internally for event management
public void removeActionListener(ActionListener)	Removes the specified ActionListener from the collection of listeners

Methods/Events	Description
`public void setActionCommand(String)`	Sets the action command associated with this component
`public void setEnabled(boolean)`	Sets the enabled status of this component
`public void setLabel(String)`	Sets the label displayed with this component
`public void setShortcut(MenuShortcut)`	Sets the menu shortcut associated with this menu item

CLASS

`java.awt.MenuItem`: Example

The Menu class is used to represent an item on a menu bar.

```
import java.awt.*;
import java.awt.event.*;

public class MenuDemo extends Frame {

    public MenuDemo() {
        // Create a new Menu
        Menu demo = new Menu("Demo");

        // Create and add some MenuItems
        demo.add(new MenuItem("Demo Item"));
        demo.add(new CheckboxMenuItem("Demo Checkbox Item"));

        // Create a MenuBar
        MenuBar demoMB = new MenuBar();

        // Add the Menu to the MenuBar
        demoMB.add(demo);

        // Set the MenuBar
        setMenuBar(demoMB);
    }


    public static void main(String args[]) {
        MenuDemo myDemo = new MenuDemo();
        myDemo.setSize(200,200);
```

continues

```
        // Allow the program to be shut down by closing the
        // main window.
        myDemo.addWindowListener(new WindowAdapter() {
            public void windowClosing(WindowEvent we) {
                System.exit(0);
            }
        });

        myDemo.setVisible(true);
    }
}
```

CLASS

java.awt.MenuShortcut

public class MenuShortcut extends Object implements Serializable

Modern UIs contain keyboard shortcuts for popular menu choices. For example, when you save a document you don't want to have to move your hands off the keyboard, move the mouse to the File menu, and choose Save. Instead, you expect to hit Ctrl+S (or Command+S, or whatever your platform uses) and have your document saved instantly.

The class MenuShortcut is used in Java to associate a keyboard shortcut with a MenuItem object.

CLASS

java.awt.MenuShortcut: Summary

Methods/Events	Description
public boolean equals(MenuShortcut)	Returns true if the two MenuShortcut objects represent the same keyboard accelerator
public boolean equals(Object)	Returns true if the two MenuShortcut objects represent the same keyboard accelerator
public int getKey()	Obtains the key that one must press to activate this menu shortcut
public int hashCode()	Obtains the hashcode for the MenuShortcut
protected String paramString()	Obtains the parameter string for this object
public String toString()	Returns a String object representing the current state of this object
public boolean usesShiftModifier()	Returns true if the Shift key must be pressed to active this shortcut

java.awt.MenuShortcut: Example

The MenuShortcut class is used to represent a keyboard accelerator for a menu item.

The following example expands on the MenuItem example:

```java
import java.awt.*;
import java.awt.event.*;

public class MenuDemo extends Frame {

    public MenuDemo() {
        // Create a new Menu
        Menu demo = new Menu("Demo");

        // Create a MenuShortcut
        MenuShortcut demoShortcut = new MenuShortcut('q');

        // Create and add some MenuItems
        demo.add(new MenuItem("Demo Item"));
        demo.add(new CheckboxMenuItem("Demo Checkbox Item"));
        demo.add(new MenuItem("Quit", demoShortcut));

        // Create a MenuBar
        MenuBar demoMB = new MenuBar();

        // Add the Menu to the MenuBar
        demoMB.add(demo);

        // Set the MenuBar
        setMenuBar(demoMB);
    }


    public static void main(String args[]) {
        MenuDemo myDemo = new MenuDemo();

        // Allow the program to be shut down by closing the
        // main window.
        myDemo.addWindowListener(new WindowAdapter() {
            public void windowClosing(WindowEvent we) {
                System.exit(0);
            }
        });

        myDemo.setSize(200,200);
        myDemo.setVisible(true);
    }
}
```

java.awt.Panel

`public class Panel extends Container`

The `Panel` class is a peer-based container class.

java.awt.Panel: **Summary**

Methods/Events	Description
`public void addNotify()`	Creates the component's peer

java.awt.Point

`public class Point extends Object implements Serializable`

The `Point` class represents a physical location in a 2D coordinate space.

java.awt.Point: **Summary**

Fields/Methods	Description
`public int x`	The x coordinate of the point
`public int y`	The y coordinate of the point
`public boolean equals(Object)`	Returns true if the two `Point` objects have the same values for their x and y variables
`public Point getLocation()`	Returns a copy of the current object; this method is included for completeness
`public int hashCode()`	Obtains a hash code for this object
`public void move(int, int)`	Moves the point to the specified location
`public void setLocation(float, float)`	Sets the location of the point
`public void setLocation(int, int)`	Sets the location of the point
`public void setLocation(Point)`	Sets the location of the point
`public String toString()`	Obtains a `String` object representing the state of the current object
`public void translate(int, int)`	Translates the point using the specified deltas

java.awt.Polygon

`public class Polygon extends Object implements Shape, Serializable`

The `Polygon` class represents the physical coordinates of a polygon.

java.awt.Polygon: **Summary**

Fields/Methods	Description
`protected Rectangle bounds`	A bounding box for this component
`public int npoints`	Number of points specified
`public int[] xpoints`	Array of x points
`public int[] ypoints`	Array of y points
`public void addPoint(int, int)`	Adds a point to the polygon
`public boolean contains` `(double, double, double, double)`	Returns true if the specified rectangular region is wholly within the polygon
`public boolean contains(double, double)`	Returns true if the polygon contains the specified point
`public boolean contains(int, int)`	Returns true if the polygon contains the specified point
`public boolean contains(Point)`	Returns true if the polygon contains the specified point
`public boolean contains(Point2D)`	Returns true if the polygon contains the specified point
`public boolean contains(Rectangle2D)`	Returns true if the specified rectangle is wholly within the polygon
`public Rectangle getBounds()`	Returns the bounding box for this component
`public Rectangle2D getBounds2D()`	Returns the high precision bounding box for this component
`public PathIterator getPathIterator` `(AffineTransform, double)`	Obtains an iterator object that iterates along the boundary of the shape
`public PathIterator` `getPathIterator(AffineTransform)`	Obtains an iterator object that iterates along the boundary of the shape

continues

Fields/Methods	Description
public boolean intersects (double, double, double, double)	Returns true if the interior of the polygon intersects the interior of the specified rectangular region
public boolean intersects(Rectangle2D)	Returns true if the interior of the polygon intersects the interior of the specified rectangle
public void translate(int, int)	Translates all points using the specified deltas

CLASS

java.awt.Polygon: Example

The Polygon class is used to represent any form of polygon.

```java
import java.awt.*;
import java.awt.event.*;


public class PolygonDemo extends Frame {
    private Polygon triangle;

    public PolygonDemo() {
        // mark out the xpoints and ypoints
        int x[] = {0, 100, 50};
        int y[] = {0, 0, 100};

        // Create a triangle polygon
        triangle = new Polygon(x, y, 3);
    }

    public void paint(Graphics g) {
        g.setColor(Color.pink);
        g.fillPolygon(triangle);
    }


    public static void main(String args[]) {
        PolygonDemo myDemo = new PolygonDemo();
        myDemo.setSize(200,200);

        // Allow the program to be shut down by closing the
        // main window.
        myDemo.addWindowListener(new WindowAdapter() {
            public void windowClosing(WindowEvent we) {
```

```
                        System.exit(0);
                }
        });

        myDemo.setVisible(true);
    }
}
```

CLASS

java.awt.PopupMenu

```
public class PopupMenu extends Menu
```

The PopupMenu class, new to the JDK 1.1, represents a menu that can be dynamically popped up from any location within a component. It is useful for displaying context-sensitive speed menus.

CLASS

java.awt.PopupMenu: Summary

Methods/Events	Description
public void addNotify()	Creates the component's peer
public void show(Component, int, int)	Displays the menu at the specified point

CLASS

java.awt.PopupMenu: Example

A PopupMenu object can be spawned from any location on the screen:

```
import java.awt.*;
import java.awt.event.*;


public class PopupMenuDemo extends Frame implements ActionListener {
    private PopupMenu    myMenu;
    private Button       launchButton;


    public PopupMenuDemo() {
        myMenu = new PopupMenu();
        myMenu.add("Demo Option 1");
        myMenu.add("Demo Option 2");
        myMenu.add("Demo Option 3");

        launchButton = new Button("Launch Menu!");
        launchButton.addActionListener(this);
        setLayout(new FlowLayout(10));
        add(launchButton);
```

continues

A

```
        add(myMenu);
    }

    // Called when the launch button is clicked
    public void actionPerformed(ActionEvent ae) {
        myMenu.show(launchButton, 10, 10);
    }


    public static void main(String args[]) {
        PopupMenuDemo myDemo = new PopupMenuDemo();

        // Allow the program to be shut down by closing the
        // main window.
        myDemo.addWindowListener(new WindowAdapter() {
            public void windowClosing(WindowEvent we) {
                System.exit(0);
            }
        });

        myDemo.pack();
        myDemo.setVisible(true);
    }
}
```

CLASS

java.awt.PrintJob

`public abstract class PrintJob extends Object`

The PrintJob class initiates and executes a print job through native printing mechanisms. An instance of an appropriate subclass of PrintJob instance is obtained through the method Toolkit.getPrintJob(). To actually render the print image, you will obtain a PrintJob object, use its getGraphics() method, and then perform all drawing in the returned Graphics object.

CLASS

java.awt.PrintJob: Summary

Methods/Events	Description
`public abstract void end()`	Ends the print job
`public void finalize()`	Releases resources during garbage collection to prevent a memory leak
`public abstract Graphics getGraphics()`	Obtains the Graphics object associated with the print output device
`public abstract Dimension getPageDimension()`	Obtains the page dimensions; is not currently accurate

Methods/Events	Description
`public abstract int getPageResolution()`	Obtains the page resolutions
`public abstract boolean lastPageFirst()`	Returns true if the last page will be printed first

CLASS # java.awt.PrintJob: Example

The `PrintJob` class is used when an item needs to be sent to the printer:

```java
import java.awt.*;
import java.awt.event.*;


public class PrintJobDemo extends Frame implements ActionListener {
    private Panel printable;

    public PrintJobDemo() {
        // Add some components to the screen
        printable = new Panel();
        printable.setLayout(new GridLayout(2,2,10,10));
        add(new Button("Print"));
        add(new Button("Test"));
        add(new Label("java.awt."));
        add(new Label("PrintJob"));

        setLayout(new FlowLayout(10));
        add(printable);
        Button printButton = new Button("Print Above");
        add(printButton);
        printButton.addActionListener(this);
    }


    public void actionPerformed(ActionEvent ae) {
        // get a PrintJob object
        PrintJob pj = getToolkit().getPrintJob(this, "Luke", null);

        // obtain its graphics context
        Graphics printGraphics = pj.getGraphics();

        // draw to the graphics context
        printable.printAll(printGraphics);

        // finish up
        pj.end();
        pj.finalize();
```

continues

```
        }

    public static void main(String args[]) {
        PrintJobDemo myDemo = new PrintJobDemo();

        // Allow the program to be shut down by closing the
        // main window.
        myDemo.addWindowListener(new WindowAdapter() {
            public void windowClosing(WindowEvent we) {
                System.exit(0);
            }
        });

        myDemo.pack();
        myDemo.setVisible(true);
    }
}
```

CLASS   # java.awt.Rectangle

`public class Rectangle extends Rectangle2D implements Shape, Serializable`

The `Rectangle` object encapsulates information that represents a physical rectangle. This information includes height, width, x-position, and y-position.

CLASS   # java.awt.Rectangle: Summary

Fields/Methods	Description
`public int height`	Height of the rectangle
`public int width`	Width of the rectangle
`public int x`	x-position of the rectangle
`public int y`	y-position of the rectangle
`public void add(int, int)`	Adds the specified point to the rectangle
`public void add(Point)`	Adds the specified point to the rectangle
`public void add(Rectangle)`	Adds the specified rectangle to the rectangle; after this method executes, the rectangle will be the union of the `Rectangle` parameter and the original rectangle

Fields/Methods	Description
public boolean contains(int, int, int, int)	Returns true if the specified rectangular region is wholly contained in this rectangle
public boolean contains(int, int)	Returns true if the rectangle contains the specified point
public boolean contains(Point)	Returns true if the rectangle contains the specified point
public boolean contains(int, int, int, int)	Returns true if the specified rectangle is wholly contained in this rectangle
public Rectangle2D createIntersection(Rectangle2D)	Obtains a new rectangle that is the intersection of the specified rectangle with this rectangle
public Rectangle2D createUnion(Rectangle2D)	Obtains a new rectangle that is the smallest rectangle that will contain the specified rectangle and this rectangle
public boolean equals(Object)	Returns true if both rectangles have the same values for all fields
public Rectangle getBounds()	Returns a copy of the current object; provided for consistency
public double getHeight()	Obtains the height of this rectangle
public Point getLocation()	Obtains the location of the top left corner of this rectangle
public Dimension getSize()	Obtains the dimensions of this rectangle
public double getWidth()	Obtains the width of this rectangle
public void grow(int, int)	Grows the rectangle by the specified deltas
public void hashCode()	Obtains the hash code for the rectangle
public Rectangle intersection (Rectangle)	Obtains the intersection of the current rectangle and the one specified as a parameter

continues

Fields/Methods	Description
public boolean intersects(Rectangle)	Returns true if the current rectangle and the rectangle specified as a parameter intersect
public boolean isEmpty()	Returns true if this rectangle is empty, where "empty" is defined as having a width or height less than or equal to zero
public int outcode(double, double)	Indicates where the specified coordinates lie with respect to this rectangle
public void setBounds(int, int, int, int)	Sets the bounding box for this rectangle
public void setBounds(Rectangle)	Sets the bounding box for this rectangle
public void setLocation(int, int)	Sets the location of the top left corner of this rectangle
public void setLocation(Point)	Sets the location of the top left corner of this rectangle
public void setSize(Dimension)	Sets the size of this rectangle
public void setSize(int, int)	Sets the size of this rectangle
public String toString()	Obtains a String object that represents the current state of this object
public Rectangle translate(int, int)	Translates all points of the rectangle using the specified deltas
public Rectangle union(Rectangle)	Obtains the union of the current rectangle and the one specified as a parameter; the union is defined as the smallest rectangle that will contain both the specified rectangle and this rectangle

CLASS `java.awt.ScrollPane`

`public class ScrollPane extends Container`

The ScrollPane class, new to the JDK 1.1, is a container class with the added bonus of automatic scrolling for a single child component. A ScrollPane object can optionally display horizontal and vertical scrollbars. If it is not large enough to display its component, it will be logically shifted automatically when the user interacts with the scrollbars.

The most effective use of `ScrollPane` is to make its single component a `Container` object that can, in turn, contain other components. In that way, you can effectively have multiple components inside the `ScrollPane`.

java.awt.ScrollPane: Summary

Fields/Methods	Description
`public static final int SROLLBARS_ALWAYS`	Constant indicating that scrollbars should always appear
`public static final int SCROLLBARS_AS_NEEDED`	Constant indicating that scrollbars should appear only when required
`public static final int SCROLLBARS_NEVER`	Constant indicating that scrollbars should never appear
`protected void addImpl(Component, Object, int)`	Adds the specified component to the container
`public void addNotify()`	Creates the component's peer
`public void doLayout()`	Performs a layout on the container
`public Adjustable getHAdjustable()`	Obtains the active state of the horizontal scrollbar, or null if the scrollbar policy is never
`public int getHScrollbarHeight()`	Obtains the height potentially held by the horizontal scrollbar
`public int getScrollbarDisplayPolicy()`	Obtains the scrollbar display policy
`public Point getScrollPosition()`	Obtains the current relative position of the container's contents
`public Adjustable getVAdjustable()`	Obtains the active state of the vertical scrollbar, or null if the scrollbar policy is never
`public Dimension getViewportSize()`	Obtains the current size of the viewport
`public int getVScrollbarWidth()`	Obtains the width potentially held by the vertical scrollbar
`protected String paramString()`	Obtains the parameter string for this object
`public void printComponents(Graphics)`	Prints the child components

continues

Fields/Methods	Description
public void setLayout(LayoutManager)	Sets the internal layout manager
public void setScrollPosition(int, int)	Sets the current scroll position
public void setScrollPosition(Point)	Sets the current scroll position

CLASS

java.awt.TextArea

public class TextArea extends TextComponent

The TextArea class represents a multiline area where text may be entered. Although scrolling of the text is supported, stylized text (multifont, multicolor) is not.

CLASS

java.awt.TextArea: Summary

Fields/Methods	Description
Fields	
public static final int SCROLLBARS_BOTH	Constant specifying that scrollbars should appear along the horizontal and vertical axis
public static final int SCROLLBARS_HORIZONTAL_ONLY	Constant specifying that scrollbars should appear along the horizontal axis
public static final int SCROLLBARS_NONE	Constant specifying that scrollbars should not appear along either axis
public static final int SCROLLBARS_VERTICAL_ONLY	Constant specifying that scrollbars should appear along the vertical axes
Methods	
public void addNotify()	Creates the component's peer
public void append(String)	Adds the contents of the String parameter to the text area
public int getColumns()	Obtains the number of visible columns
public Dimension getMinimumSize()	Obtains the minimum size needed to display this component

Fields/Methods	Description
public Dimension getMinimumSize(int, int)	Obtains the minimum size needed to display a text area with the specified number of rows and columns
public Dimension getPreferredSize()	Obtains the preferred size of this component
public Dimension getPreferredSize(int, int)	Obtains the preferred size of a text area with the specified number of rows and columns
public int getRows()	Obtains the current number of visible rows
public int getScrollbarVisibility()	Obtains the current scrollbar visibility
public void insert(String, int)	Inserts the specified string at the specified index
protected String paramString()	Obtains the parameter string for this component
public void replaceRange(String, int, int)	Replaces the text between the specified indices with the contents of the string parameter
public void setColumns(int)	Sets the current number of visible columns
public void setRows(int)	Sets the current number of visible rows

CLASS
java.awt.TextArea: Example

The TextArea class is used to represent a multiline text entry field:

```
import java.awt.*;
import java.awt.event.*;

public class TextAreaDemo extends Frame {

    public TextAreaDemo() {
        setLayout(new BorderLayout());
```

continues

```
        // Create and add a text area
        add("Center", new TextArea("Demo Text Area"));
    }

    public static void main(String args[]) {
        TextAreaDemo myDemo = new TextAreaDemo();

        // Allow the program to be shut down by closing the
        // main window.
        myDemo.addWindowListener(new WindowAdapter() {
            public void windowClosing(WindowEvent we) {
                System.exit(0);
            }
        });

        myDemo.setSize(200,200);
        myDemo.show();
    }
}
```

CLASS

java.awt.TextComponent

```
public class TextComponent extends Component
```

The TextComponent class represents a UI component that contains some potentially editable text. Usually you will not work directly with this class, but instead will focus on TextArea and TextField.

CLASS

java.awt.TextComponent: Summary

Fields/Methods	Description
protected transient TextListener textListener	Reference to TextListener
public void addTextListener(TextListener)	Adds a TextListener to the collection of listeners; a TextListener is notified whenever the current text value changes
public int getCaretPosition()	Obtains the current position of the caret
public int getSelectedText()	Obtains the currently selected text
public int getSelectionEnd()	Obtains the index of the last selected character

Fields/Methods	Description
`public int getSelectionStart()`	Obtains the index of the first selected character
`public String getText()`	Obtains the contents of the text component
`public boolean isEditable()`	Returns true if this component is editable
`protected String paramString()`	Obtains a parameter string for this object
`protected void processEvent(AWTEvent)`	Used internally for event management
`protected void processTextEvent(TextEvent)`	Used internally for event management
`public void removeNotify()`	Separates this component from its peer
`public void removeTextListener(TextListener)`	Removes the specified `TextListener` from the collection of listeners
`public void select(int, int)`	Selects the text between the two indices
`public void selectAll()`	Selects all the text
`public void setCaretPosition(int)`	Sets the current caret position
`public void setEditable(boolean)`	Sets the current editable status
`public void setSelectionEnd(int)`	Sets the end of the text selection
`public void setSelectionStart(int)`	Sets the beginning of the text selection
`public void setText(String)`	Sets the contents of the text component

CLASS `java.awt.TextField`

`public class TextField extends TextComponent`

The `TextField` class represents a potentially editable one-line text component. It is usually used for creating forms and other screens that require creation of variable/data association.

CLASS ## java.awt.TextField: Summary

Methods/Events	Description
public void addActionListener(ActionListener)	Adds an ActionListener to the collection of listeners
public void addNotify()	Creates this component's peer
public boolean echoCharIsSet()	Returns true if there is currently an echo character set
public int getColumns()	Obtains the number of visible columns
public char getEchoChar()	Obtains the echo character
public Dimension getMinimumSize()	Obtains the minimum size this component can take up
public Dimension getMinimumSize(int)	Obtains the minimum size for a component with the specified number of visible columns
public Dimension getPreferredSize()	Obtains the preferred size for this component
public Dimension getPreferredSize(int)	Obtains the preferred size for a component with the specified number of visible columns
protected String paramString()	Obtains the parameter string for this object
protected void processActionEvent(ActionEvent)	Used internally for event management
protected void processEvent(AWTEvent)	Used internally for event management
public void removeActionListener(ActionListener)	Removes the specified ActionListener from the collection of listeners
public void setColumns(int)	Sets the current number of visible columns
public void setEchoChar(char)	Sets an echo character

CLASS ## java.awt.TextField: Example

The TextField class is used to represent a single-line text entry field:

```
import java.awt.*;
import java.awt.event.*;
```

```java
public class TextFieldDemo extends Frame {

    public TextFieldDemo() {
        setLayout(new BorderLayout());

        // Create and add a text area
        add("Center", new TextField("Demo Text Area"));
    }

    public static void main(String args[]) {
        TextFieldDemo myDemo = new TextFieldDemo();

        // Allow the program to be shut down by closing the
        // main window.
        myDemo.addWindowListener(new WindowAdapter() {
            public void windowClosing(WindowEvent we) {
                System.exit(0);
            }
        });

        myDemo.pack();
        myDemo.show();
    }
}
```

CLASS

java.awt.Toolkit

`public abstract class Toolkit extends Object`

The `Toolkit` is used by the AWT to obtain UI peers and other information associated with the native system. It is an abstract class. An instance of an appropriate subclass is obtained using the `Component.getToolkit()` method. Although there is a chance that your development efforts will require many of the `Toolkit` methods, usually you will only use `beep()`, `getFontList()`, `sync()`, `getPrintJob()`, and `getSystemClipboard()`.

CLASS

java.awt.Toolkit: Summary

Methods/Events	Description
`public void addPerperteyChangeListener` `(String, PropertyChangeListener)`	Adds the specified property change listener to the group of listeners for the named property
`public abstract beep()`	Causes a system beep
`public abstract int checkImage` `(Image, int, int, ImageObserver)`	Checks the loading status of the specified `Image` object

continues

A

Methods/Events	Description
`protected abstract ButtonPeer createButton(Button)`	Creates a `ButtonPeer` object
`protected abstract CanvasPeer createCanvas(Canvas)`	Creates a `CanvasPeer` object
`protected abstract CheckboxPeer createCheckbox(Checkbox)`	Creates a `CheckboxPeer` object
`protected abstract CheckboxMenuItemPeer createCheckboxMenuItem(CheckboxMenuItem)`	Creates a `CheckboxMenuItemPeer` object
`protected abstract ChoicePeer createChoice(Choice)`	Creates a `ChoicePeer` object
`protected abstract ComponentPeer createComponent(Component)`	Creates a `ComponentPeer` object
`protected abstract DialogPeer createDialog(Dialog)`	Creates a `DialogPeer` object
`public DragGestureRecognizer createDragGestureRecognizer (Class, DragSource, Component, DragGestureListener)`	Creates a `DragGestureListener` object
`public abstract DragSourceContextPeer createDragSourceContextPeer (DragGestureEvent)`	Creates a `DragSourceContextPeer` object
`protected abstract FileDialogPeer createFileDialog(FileDialog)`	Creates a `FileDialogPeer` object
`protected abstract FramePeer createFrame(Frame)`	Creates a `FramePeer` object
`public abstract Image createImage(byte[])`	Creates a new `Image` object using the source bytes
`public Image createImage(byte[], int, int)`	Creates a new `Image` object using the source bytes, and takes into account the specified offset/image length
`public abstract Image createImage(ImageProducer)`	Creates a new `Image` object using the image producer
`protected abstract LabelPeer createLabel(Label)`	Creates a `LabelPeer` object

Methods/Events	Description
protected abstract ListPeer createList(List)	Creates a ListPeer object
protected abstract MenuPeer createMenu(Menu)	Creates a MenuPeer object
protected abstract MenuBarPeer createMenuBar(MenuBar)	Creates a MenuBarPeer object
protected abstract MenuItemPeer createMenuItem(MenuItem)	Creates a MenuItemPeer object
protected abstract PanelPeer createPanel(Panel)	Creates a PanelPeer object
protected abstract PopupMenuPeer createPopupMenu(PopupMenu)	Creates a PopupMenuPeer object
protected abstract ScrollBarPeer createScrollbar(Scrollbar)	Creates a ScrollBarPeer object
protected abstract ScrollPanePeer createScrollPane(ScrollPane)	Creates a ScrollPanePeer object
protected abstract TextAreaPeer createTextArea(TextArea)	Creates a TextAreaPeer object
protected abstract TextFieldPeer createTextField(TextField)	Creates a TextFieldPeer object
protected abstract WindowPeer createWindow(Window)	Creates a WindowPeer object
public Dimension getBestCursorSize(int, int)	Obtains the supported cursor size that is closes to the desired sizes
public abstract ColorModel getColorModel()	Obtains the color model for this toolkit's screen
public static Toolkit getDefaultToolkit()	Obtains the default Toolkit object
public String[] getFontList()	Obtains an array of all font names (deprecated)
public FontMetrics getFontMetrics(Font)	Obtains the FontMetrics object for the specified font (deprecated)
protected abstract FontPeer getFontPeer(String, int)	Obtains the requested FontPeer object (deprecated)

continues

Methods/Events	Description
`public abstract Image getImage(String)`	Obtains the image from the file specified as a parameter
`public abstract Image getImage(URL)`	Obtains the image from the URL specified as a parameter
`public int getMaximumCursurColors()`	Obtains the maximum number of colors the toolit supports
`public int getMenuShortcutKeyMask()`	Determines the system dependent modifier key for menu shortcuts (Control, Command, and so on)
`protected static Container getNativeContainer(Component)`	Obtains a native `Container` object
`public abstract PrintJob getPrintJob(Frame, String, Properties)`	Obtains a `PrintJob` object and begins a dialog with the printer
`public static String getProperty(String, String)`	Obtains the property with the specified key and default value
`public abstract int getScreenResolution()`	Obtains the screen resolution
`public abstract Dimension getScreenSize()`	Obtains the screen size
`public abstract Clipboard getSystemClipboard()`	Obtains the system clipboard
`public final EventQueue getSystemEventQueue()`	Obtains the system event queue
`protected abstract EventQueue getSystemEventQueueImpl()`	Obtains the system event queue
`protected void initializeDesktopProperties()`	Initialize the desktop properties
`protected Object lazilyLoadDesktopProperty(String)`	Evaluate desktop property values
`public void loadSystemColors(int[])`	Fills the array with the current system color values
`public void prepareImage (Image, int, int, ImageObserver)`	Prepares the specified `Image` object for display

Methods/Events	Description
public void removePropertyChangeListener (String, PropertyChangeListener)	Removes the specified property change listener from the group of listeners for the specified property
protected final void setDesktopProperty(String, Object)	Sets the named property to the specified value and fires a property change event
public void sync()	Synchronizes the graphics state of this object

PACKAGE # `javax.swing`

The Swing class library (part of the Java Foundation Class library) from JavaSoft is an attempt to produce an all-Java windowing toolkit. As you will remember from the previous section on java.awt, the Abstract Windowing Toolkit (AWT) is JavaSoft's original approach to a windowing library and uses native code. In a nutshell, almost every AWT class is paired with a native class that takes care of drawing the UI widget on the screen. The fact that the native library draws to the screen gives each Java application the look and feel of the native platform that it is running under.

Applications produced with the Swing classes also maintain the native look and feel of the platform they are run under, but this is achieved through something called a *pluggable look-and-feel*. All Swing components are designed according to the Model-View-Controller (MVC) pattern, and each component provides a unique view for each platform it is run under. Taking this further, it is also possible to design custom views for use in producing interesting UIs.

As you examine the classes in the following table, you will note that in addition to providing a 100%-Java windowing toolkit, a series of new classes have been provided. With the 1.02 release of the JDK, JavaSoft provided only a bare minimum of the UI classes required by most applications. With the javax.swing classes, this is no longer the case. For example, the javax.swing package provides classes for creating combo boxes and color pickers.

`javax.swing`: Summary

Interfaces/Classes	Description
Interfaces	
Action	Used to model an interaction between the user of an application and the application itself
BoundedRangeModel	Model for a bounded range; useful for components like sliders and progress bars
ButtonModel	The default model used by `Button` objects
CellEditor	Interface implemented by cell editors
ComboBoxEditor	Interface implemented by all combo box editors
Interfaces	
ComboBoxModel	The default model used by `ComboBox` objects
DesktopManager	Class responsible for implementing look and feel behavior in the `JDesktopPane`
Icon	Implemented by classes that need to represent themselves as an onscreen icon
JComboBox.KeySelectionManager	Models the key selections in a combo box
ListCellRenderer	Implemented by classes that act as rubber stamps in a `JList`
ListModel	The default model for `JList`
ListSelectionModel	A model used to represent the state for any component that maintains an active list of values
MenuElement	Implemented by classes that can be placed into a menu
MutableComboBoxModel	A mutable version of the `ComboBoxModel`

Interfaces/Classes	Description
Interfaces	
Renderer	Interface implemented by renderers
Scrollable	Provides information to any component that can scroll
ScrollPaneConstants	Constants used when referring to anything that can scroll
SingleSelectionModel	A model used by components from which, at most, one item from a list may be selected
SwingConstants	Constants used by a variety of Swing classes
UIDefaults.ActiveValue	Used to store information
UIDefaults.LazyValue	Used to store information that is not created until the first time it is asked for
WindowConstants	Constants used by different classes that reference windows
Classes	
AbstractAction	Abstract parent class to all actions
AbstractButton	Abstract parent class to all buttons
AbstractListModel	Abstract list data model
BorderFactory	The BorderFactory singleton is responsible for passing out references to Border objects; through the use of a shared factory object, a shared instance will be returned when multiple objects request the same border
Box	A lightweight container that uses the BoxLayout layout manager by default; a series of methods are provided to facilitate building highly evolved screens
Box.Filler	Utility class used to take up space when building screens

continues

Interfaces/Classes	Description
Classes	
BoxLayout	A layout manager that will arrange all components either vertically or horizontally; in most situations, the Box class is used instead because it provides additional methods for component management
ButtonGroup	Used to create an aggregate of button objects in which only one object may have an "on" state at a given time
CellRendererPane	Sits between cell renderers and the components that use them; allows for desired view results
DebugGraphics	A development tool used when doing development with the java.awt.Graphics class; allows one to see exactly what is going on at a given point in time
DefaultBoundedRangeModel	Default implementation of the BoundedRangeModel interface
DefaultButtonModel	Default implementation of the ButtonModel interface
DefaultCellEditor	Default implementation of the TableCellEditor interface
DefaultCellEditor.EditorDelegate	Utility class used by DefaultCellEditor to manage events
DefaultListModel	Default implementation of the ListModel interface
DefaultListSelectionModel	Default implementation of the ListSelectionModel interface
DefaultSingleSelectionModel	Default implementation of the SingleSelectionModel interface
FocusManager	Manages focus for a series of components

Interfaces/Classes	Description
Classes	
GrayFilter	Used to display an image as "disabled"; GrayFilter turns an image into grayscale, and then brightens the pixels
ImageIcon	An implementation of the Icon interface, which allows Icon objects to be created from Image objects
JApplet	Subclass of the javaappletApplet class, which adds Swing UI advancements to the original Applet class
JButton	A generic Button class
JCheckBox	A generic CheckBox class
JCheckBoxMenuItem	A generic class used to place a checkbox next to a text string in a menu item
JColorChooser	A class used to prompt a user to select a color
JComboBox	A generic implementation of a combo box
JComponent	The base class for all Swing components
JdesktopPane	Container used to create MDI applications
JDialog	A generic class used to create dialog windows
JEditorPane	A text pane that can be used to edit various types of content, including HTML and RTF
JFileChooser	A generic file chooser class
JFrame	Subclass of the java.awt.Frame class that adds Swing UI advancements to the original Frame class
JInternalFrame	A lightweight object that provides features similar to a native window
JinternalFrame.JDesktopIcon	Provides an iconified view for a JinternalFrame

continues

Interfaces/Classes	Description
	Classes
JLabel	Used to display a read-only line of text, or a combination of a read-only line of text and an `Image` object
JLayeredPane	A generic container object that supports the definition of multiple layers within itself
JList	A generic implementation of a `List` class
JMenu	A generic implementation of a `Menu` class
JMenu.WinListener	Used by `JMenu` to listen for events
JMenuBar	A generic implementation of a `MenuBar` class
JMenuItem	A generic implementation of a `MenuItem` class
JOptionPane	A class used to create any number of different types of dialog boxes, including attention dialogs, yes/no dialogs, and input dialogs
JPanel	A generic implementation of a panel class; used in creating screens or for performing custom drawing
JPasswordField	A simple text field that masks all text entered into it
JPopupMenu	A generic pop-up menu class
JProgressBar	A generic progress bar class
JRadioButton	A generic radio button class
JRadioButtonMenuItem	A generic class used to place a radio button next to a text string in a menu item
JRootPane	The base pane used when laying out components

Interfaces/Classes	Description
Classes	
JRootPane.RootLayout	Layout manager used internally by JRootPane
JScrollBar	A generic implementation of a ScrollBar class
JScrollPane	A panel that scrolls over a view
JScrollPane.ScrollBar	Special type of JScrollBar used internally by JScrollPane
JSeparator	Used to place a separator line in a pull-down menu
JSlider	A generic slider class
JSlider.ModelListener	Used internally by JSlider to manage events
JSplitPane	A generic class used to display two and only two components, either side by side or on top of each other; the percentage of the screen given to each component can be determined programmatically or by having the user drag the bar between the components
JTabbedPane	A generic control that organizes a series of components in terms of tabbed folders
JTabbedPane.ModelListener	Used internally by JTabbedPane to manage events
JTable	A generic control that organizes data into a grid-like table
JTextArea	A generic text area class
JTextField	A generic text field class
JTextPane	A generic class that can display marked-up text
JToggleButton	A generic two-state button; JRadioButton and JCheckBox are both child classes of this class

continues

Interfaces/Classes	Description
Classes	
JToggleButton.ToggleButtonModel	Default toggle button model
JToolBar	A generic class used to model a toolbar
JToolBar.Separator	Used by JToolBar to separate data
JToolTip	A generic class used to represent a ToolTip
JTree	A generic control used to organize data in a hierarchical tree
JTree.DynamicUtilTreeNode	Used internally by JTree to create nodes
JTree.EmptySelectionModel	Used internally by JTree to model selection sets that can contain exactly zero elements
JTree.TreeSelectionRedirector	Used internally by JTree to manage events
JViewport	Container used by many other containers
JViewport.ViewListener	Used internally by JViewport to watch for component resizing
JWindow	A generic implementation of a Window component; usually, developers will work with one of JWindow's subclasses and not JWindow directly
KeyStroke	A class used to model a unique key-press by the application's user
LookAndFeel	A class that models a pluggable look-and-feel
MenuSelectionManager	
OverlayLayout	A layout manager class that allows components to be layered on top of each other
ProgressMonitor	A class used to monitor how long an operation takes, and to notify the user if the operation appears to be taking too long

Interfaces/Classes	Description
Classes	
ProgressMonitorInputStream	A class used to monitor how long reading from an input stream takes, and to notify the user if the operation appears to be taking too long
RepaintManager	Class used by Swing to determine which areas need to be repainted
ScrollPaneLayout	A layout manager used to lay out components in an area that will scroll to display anything not visible at a given point in time; usually you will use JScrollPane and not this class directly
SizeRequirements	Utility class used by layout managers to determine component sizes
SwingUtilities	A collection of static methods used to perform simple calculations
Timer	A utility class that is used to obtain notification at or after a certain time
ToolTipManager	Used internally by Swing to manage all tooltips
ToolTipManager.insideTimerAction	Used internally by ToolTipManager to handle display timing
ToolTipManager.outsideTimerAction	Used internally by ToolTipManager to handle display timing
ToolTipManager.stillInsideTimerAction	Used internally by ToolTipManager to handle display timing
TypedFile	TypedFile objects are returned by FileChooserModel after the user selects a file
UIDefaults	Collection of defaults used by Swing components
UIManager	Used internally by Swing to manage the UI
ViewportLayout	Layout manager used internally by JViewport

INTERFACE `javax.swing.Action`

`public interface javax.swing.Action`

The `Action` interface provides for the same functionality to be accessed by several controls.

INTERFACE `javax.swing.Action:` **Summary**

Fields/Methods	Description
`public static String DEFAULT`	Useful as a storage-retrieval key for setting or getting one of this objectís properties
`public static String LONG_DESCRIPTION`	Long description used to detail the `Action`
`public static String NAME`	Logical name associated with the `Action`
`public static String SHORT_DESCRIPTION`	Short description used to detail the `Action`
`public static String SMALL_ICON`	A small (often 16×16) icon used to represent the `Action` pictorially
`public void addProperty ChangeListener (PropertyChangeListener)`	Adds a `PropertyChangeListener` to the `Action`'s collection of listeners; these listeners will be notified when a change to a property occurs
`public boolean isEnabled()`	Obtains the enabled state of the `Action` object
`public void removePropertyChangeListener (PropertyChangeListener)`	Removes a `PropertyChangeListener` from the `Action`'s collection of listeners
`public void setEnabled(boolean)`	Sets the enabled state of the `Action`

INTERFACE `javax.swing.ButtonModel`

`public interface javax.swing.ButtonModel extends ItemSelectable`

The `ButtonModel` interface is implemented by any object wishing to act as a model to any of the `Button` objects that may be created from the Swing `Button` classes.

`javax.swing.ButtonModel`: **Summary**

Methods/Events	Description
`public void addActionListener` `(ActionListener)`	Adds an `ActionListener` to the button's collection of listeners; an `ActionListener` receives notification when the button is clicked
`public void addChangeListener` `(ChangeListener)`	Adds a `ChangeListener` to the button's collection of listeners
`public void addItemListener` `(ItemListener)`	Adds an `ItemListener` to the button's collection of listeners; an `ItemListener` receives notification when a multi-state button changes state
`public String getActionCommand()`	Obtains the action command sent with actions
`public int getMnemonic()`	Obtains the keyboard mnemonic for this model
`public boolean isArmed()`	Obtains the button's armed state
`public boolean isEnabled()`	Obtains the enabled state of the button
`public boolean isPressed()`	Obtains the pressed state of the button
`public boolean isRollover()`	Identifies whether the button is currently in a rollover state
`public boolean isSelected()`	Identifies that the mouse is over the button
`public void removeActionListener` `(ActionListener)`	Removes an `ActionListener` from the button's collection of listeners
`public void removeChangeListener` `(ChangeListener)`	Removes a `ChangeListener` from the button's collection of change listeners
`public void removeItemListener` `(ItemListener)`	Removes an `ItemListener` from the button's collection of item listeners

continues

A

JFC CLASS
REFERENCE

Methods/Events	Description
public void setActionCommand(String)	Sets the action command associated with button actions
public void setArmed(boolean)	Sets the button's armed state
public void setEnabled(boolean)	Sets the button's enabled state
public void setGroup(ButtonGroup)	Sets the button group to which the button belongs
public void setMnemonic(int)	Sets the keyboard shortcut associated with the button
public void setPressed(boolean)	Sets the current pressed state of the button
public void setRollover(boolean)	Sets the current rollover state of the button
public void setSelected(boolean)	Sets the current selected state of the button

INTERFACE **javax.swing.CellEditor**

public interface javax.swing.CellEditor

The CellEditor class is a default implementation of a cell editor.

INTERFACE **javax.swing.CellEditor: Summary**

Methods/Events	Description
public void addCellEditorListener (CellEditorListener)	Adds a CellEditorListener to the CellEditor's collection of listeners; a CellEditorListener is notified when editing is stopped or cancelled for a given cell
public void cancelCellEditing()	Cancels editing and rejects any partially edited value
public Object getCellEditorValue()	Obtains the current value present in the editor
public boolean isCellEditable (EventObject)	Obtains whether the cell is currently editable given the EventObject parameter

`public void removeCellEditorListener` `(CellEditorListener)`	Removes a `CellEditorListener` from the `CellEditor`'s collection of listeners
`public boolean shouldSelectCell` `(EventObject)`	Notifies the editor that, given the `EventObject` parameter, the `CellEditor` should begin editing
`public void stopCellEditing()`	Stops editing and accepts any partially edited value

INTERFACE

javax.swing.ComboBoxEditor

`public interface javax.swing.ComboBoxEditor`

The `ComboBoxEditor` interface is implemented by any object that wants to serve as a combo box editor. A default implementation of this interface is provided in `javax.swing.basic.BasicComboBoxEditor`.

INTERFACE

javax.swing.ComboBoxEditor: Summary

Methods/Events	*Description*
`public void addActionListener` `(ActionListener)`	Adds an action listener to the `ComboBoxEditor`'s collection of listeners
`public Component getEditorComponent()`	Obtains the component that should be added to the tree hierarchy for this editor
`public Object getItem()`	Obtains the item that should be edited
`public void removeActionListener` `(ActionListener)`	Removes an `ActionListener` from the `ComboBoxEditor`'s collection of listeners
`public void selectAll()`	Tells the editor to select everything
`public Object setItem(Object)`	Sets the item to be edited

INTERFACE

javax.swing.ComboBoxModel

`public interface javax.swing.ComboBoxModel extends ListModel`

A `ComboBox` model extends `ListModel` and adds the additional functionality of allowing a selected item.

INTERFACE `javax.swing.ComboBoxModel`: **Summary**

Methods/Events	Description
public Object getSelectedItem()	Obtains the selected item
public void setSelectedItem(Object)	Sets the selected item

INTERFACE `javax.swing.DesktopManager`

`public interface javax.swing.DesktopManager`

DesktopManager objects, owned by JDesktopPane objects, are charged with implementing look and feel behavior in a JDesktopPane object.

INTERFACE `javax.swing.DesktopManager`: **Summary**

Methods/Events	Description
public void activateFrame (JInternalFrame)	Displays the frame in its proper location relative to the JInternalFrame object
public void beginDraggingFrame (JComponent)	Invoked when a user begins dragging a frame
public void beginResizingFrame (JComponent, int)	Invoked when a user begins resizing a frame
public void closeFrame (JInternalFrame)	Removes a frame from its parent
public void deactivateFrame (JInternalFrame)	Deactivates (removes focus from) a frame
public void deiconifyFrame (JInternalFrame)	Deiconifies a frame and returns it to its size and location prior to the iconification
public void dragFrame (JComponent, int, int)	Invoked when the user has dragged the frame to a new location
public void endDraggingFrame (JComponent)	Invoked when a user completes the frame-dragging process
public void endResizingFrame (JComponent)	Invoked when a user completes the frame-resizing process

Methods/Events	Description
public void iconifyFrame (JInternalFrame)	Iconifies a frame
public void maximizeFrame (JInternalFrame)	Maximizes a frame
public void minimizeFrame (JInternalFrame)	Minimizes a frame
public void openFrame (JInternalFrame)	Tries to display the frame in a location relative to the JInternalFrame object
public void resizeFrame (JComponent, int, int, int, int)	Resizes a frame
public void setBoundsForFrame (JComponent, int, int, int, int)	Sets the frame's bounding box

INTERFACE javax.swing.Icon

public interface javax.swing.Icon

The Icon class is implemented by classes that need to represent themselves as an onscreen icon. An object that implements the Icon class has a fixed-size onscreen representation.

INTERFACE javax.swing.Icon: Summary

Methods/Events	Description
public int getIconHeight()	Obtains the Icon height
public int getIconWidth()	Obtains the Icon width
public void paintIcon (Component, Graphics, int, int)	Paints the Icon object into the Graphics object parameter

INTERFACE javax.swing.ListCellRenderer

public interface javax.swing.ListCellRenderer

The ListCellRenderer interface is implemented by objects that are to be used as rubber stamps in a JList.

A

JFC CLASS REFERENCE

INTERFACE **javax.swing.ListCellRenderer: Summary**

Methods/Events	Description
public Component getListCellRendererComponent (JList, Object, int, boolean, boolean)	Obtains a component configured to display the Object parameter

INTERFACE **javax.swing.ListModel**

public interface javax.swing.ListModel

The ListModel interface is implemented by objects that act as a model for a JList.

INTERFACE **javax.swing.ListModel: Summary**

Methods/Events	Description
public void addListDataListener (ListDataListener)	Adds a ListDataListener object to the collection of listeners that are notified when a List data model changes
public Object getElementAt(int)	Obtains the element at the specific index
public int getSize()	Obtains the length of the list
public void removeListDataListener (ListDataListener)	Removes a ListDataListener object from the collection of listeners that are notified when a List data model changes

INTERFACE **javax.swing.ListSelectionModel**

public interface javax.swing.ListSelectionModel

The ListSelectionModel interface is used by any class that maintains an active list of selectable values.

INTERFACE `javax.swing.ListSelectionModel`: **Summary**

Methods/Events	Description
`public void addListSelectionListener` `(ListSelectionListener)`	Adds a `ListSelectionListener` object to the `ListSelectionModel`'s collection of listeners; a `ListSelectionListener` receives notification every time the selected value changes
`public void addSelectionInterval` `(int, int)`	Changes the selection interval based on the parameters
`public void clearSelection()`	Modifies the set so that no item is selected
`public int getAnchorSelectionIndex()`	Obtains the selection interval (set by `addSelectionInterval()` or `setSelectionInterval()`)
`public int getLeadSelectionIndex()`	Obtains the lead selection index
`public int getMaxSelectionIndex()`	Obtains the maximum selection index or −1 if the selection is empty
`public int getMinSelectionIndex()`	Obtains the minimum selection index or −1 if the selection is empty
`public boolean getValueIsAdjusting()`	Obtains the active state of the model; true if changes are expected, false otherwise
`public void insertIndexInterval` `(int, int, boolean)`	Inserts additional values into the length indices
`public boolean isSelectedIndex(int)`	Returns true if the parameter is the index of the selected item
`public boolean isSelectionEmpty()`	Returns true if the selection is empty
`public void removeIndexInterval` `(int, int)`	Removes the indices identified by the parameters from the selection model
`public void removeListSelectionListener` `(ListSelectionListener)`	Removes a `ListSelectionListener` from the `ListSelectionModel`'s collection of listeners

continues

Methods/Events	Description
public void removeSelectionInterval (int, int)	Change the selection to be the difference of the current selection and the indices between (and including) the specified indices
public void setAnchorSelectionIndex(int)	Sets the anchor selection index
public void setLeadSelectionIndex(int)	Sets the lead selection index
public void setSelectionInterval (int, int)	Sets the active selection interval
public void setSelectionMode(int) (SINGLE_SELECTION, SINGLE_INTERVAL_SELECTION, MULTIPLE_INTERVAL_SELECTION)	Sets the selection mode
public void setValueIsAdjusting (boolean)	Returns true if upcoming changes to the state of the model should be considered a single event

INTERFACE javax.swing.Scrollable

public interface javax.swing.Scrollable

The Scrollable interface is implemented by objects that are to be controlled by an object such as JScrollPane. This interface tells JScrollPane how to move the Scrollable object when required.

INTERFACE javax.swing.Scrollable: Summary

Methods/Events	Description
public Dimension getPreferredScrollableViewportSize()	Obtains the preferred size of the Scrollable object
public int getScrollableBlockIncrement (Rectangle, int, int)	If the Scrollable object needs scrolling to occur in certain increments, that increment should be returned from this method

Methods/Events	Description
`public boolean` `getScrollableTracksViewportHeight()`	Returns true if the `Scrollable` object should have its height forced to match the height of the scrolling viewport
`public boolean` `getScrollableTracksViewportWidth()`	Returns true if the `Scrollable` object should have its width forced to match the width of the scrolling viewport
`public int getScrollableUnitIncrement` `(Rectangle, int, int)`	If the `Scrollable` object needs scrolling to occur in certain increments, these increments should be returned from this method

INTERFACE

javax.swing.SingleSelectionModel

`public interface javax.swing.SingleSelectionModel`

The `SingleSelectionModel` interface is used to model objects that support at most one indexed selection.

INTERFACE

javax.swing.SingleSelectionModel: Summary

Methods/Events	Description
`public void addChangeListener` `(ChangeListener)`	Adds a `ChangeListener` to the `SingleSelectionModel`'s collection of listeners; a `ChangeListener` is notified when the selected item changes
`public void clearSelection()`	Clears the active selection; further calls to `getSelectedIndex()` will return –1
`public int getSelectedIndex()`	Obtains the index of the selected index, or –1 if none is selected
`public boolean isSelected()`	Returns true if an item is currently selected

continues

Methods/Events	Description
public void removeChangeListener (ChangeListener)	Removes a ChangeListener from the SingleSelectionModel's collection of listeners
public void setSelectedIndex(int)	Sets the active selected index.kj

CLASS

javax.swing.BorderFactory

public class javax.swing.BorderFactory

The BorderFactory class is used to produce borders around objects. Through the use of the Factory pattern, it is possible for multiple objects to share the same border object.

CLASS

javax.swing.BorderFactory: Summary

Methods/Events	Description
public static Border createBevelBorder (int)	Obtains a beveled Border object in which the size of the bevel is specified by the parameter
public static Border createBevelBorder (int, Color, Color)	Obtains a beveled Border object in which the size of the bevel is specified by the int parameter, and the highlight and shadow colors are specified by the Color parameters
public static Border createBevelBorder (int, Color, Color, Color, Color)	Obtains a beveled Border object in which the size of the bevel is specified by the int parameter, and the highlight (inner and outer) and shadow (inner and outer) colors are specified by the Color parameters

Methods/Events	Description
`public static CompoundBorder` `createCompoundBorder()`	Obtains a blank `CompoundBorder` object
`public static CompoundBorder` `createCompoundBorder(Border, Border)`	Obtains a `CompoundBorder` object that is a composite of the two parameters
`public static Border` `createEmptyBorder()`	Obtains an empty `Border` object
`public static Border createEmptyBorder` `(int, int, int, int)`	Obtains an empty `Border` object with the dimensions specified by the parameters
`public static Border` `createEtchedBorder()`	Obtains a default `EtchedBorder` object
`public static Border createEtchedBorder` `(Color, Color)`	Obtains an `EtchedBorder` object with the highlight and shadow colors specified by the parameters
`public static Border createLineBorder` `(Color)`	Obtains a simple line `Border` object using the specified color
`public static Border createLineBorder` `(Color, int)`	Obtains a simple line `Border` object using the specified color and thickness
`public static Border` `createLoweredBevelBorder()`	Obtains a beveled `Border` object where the bevel is inset

`public static MatteBorder`
`createMatteBorder`
`(int, int, int, int, Color)`
	Obtains a `MatteBorder` object with the specified dimensions and color

`public static MatteBorder`
`createMatteBorder`
`(int, int, int, int, Icon)`
	Obtains a `MatteBorder` object with the specified dimensions and title icon

continues

Methods/Events	Description
`public static Border createRaisedBevelBorder()`	Obtains a beveled `Border` object where the border is raised
`public static TitledBorder createTitledBorder(Border)`	Obtains a `TitledBorder` object that is based on the specified Border object
`public static TitledBorder createTitledBorder(Border, String)`	Obtains a `TitledBorder` object that is a based on the specified `Border` object and bears a title specified by the `String` object
`public static TitledBorder createTitledBorder (Border, String, int, int)`	Obtains a `TitledBorder` object that is a based on the specified `Border` object and bears a title specified by the String object; the title is positioned according to the justification and position parameters
`public static TitledBorder createTitledBorder (Border, String, int, int, Font)`	Obtains a `TitledBorder` object that is a based on the specified `Border` object and bears a title specified by the `String` object; the title is positioned according to the justification and position parameters, and appears in the font specified by the `Font` parameter
public static TitledBorder createTitledBorder (Border, String, int, int, Font, Color)	Obtains a `TitledBorder` object that is a based on the specified `Border` object and bears a title

Methods/Events	Description
	specified by the `String` object; the title is positioned according to the justification and position parameters, appears in the font specified by the `Font` parameter, and is in the color specified by the `Color` parameter
`public static TitledBorder createTitledBorder(String)`	Obtains a `TitledBorder` object with the specified title

CLASS `javax.swing.BorderFactory`: **Example**

The `BorderFactory` class is used to obtain references to `Border` object singletons:

```
import java.awt.*;

import javax.swing.swing.*;
import javax.swing.swing.event.*;
import javax.swing.swing.tree.*;

public class BorderFactoryDemo extends JApplet {
    public void init() {
        resize(400, 400);

        // Create a new Grid Layout object with a 2x7 format and a
        // a 10 pixel gaps between all components.
        GridLayout gridLayout = new GridLayout(5, 2, 10,10);
          getContentPane().setLayout(gridLayout);

        //create components
        JPanel   jpnlLineBorder1 = new JPanel();
        JPanel   jpnlLineBorder2 = new JPanel();
        JPanel   jpnlRaisedBevelBorder = new JPanel();
        JPanel   jpnlLoweredBevelBorder = new JPanel();
        JPanel   jpnlBevelBorder = new JPanel();
        JPanel   jpnlEtchedBorder = new JPanel();
        JPanel   jpnlTitledBorder = new JPanel();
        JPanel   jpnlCompoundBorder = new JPanel();
        JPanel   jpnlMatteBorder = new JPanel();
```

```
JLabel  jlblLineBorder1 = new JLabel("Line Border 1");
JLabel  jlblLineBorder2
= new JLabel("Line Border 2 (specified width)");
JLabel  jlblRaisedBevelBorder
= new JLabel("Raised Bevel Border");
JLabel  jlblLoweredBevelBorder
= new JLabel("Lowered Bevel Border");
JLabel  jlblBevelBorder = new JLabel("Bevel Border");
JLabel  jlblEtchedBorder = new JLabel("Etched Border");
JLabel  jlblTitledBorder = new JLabel("Titled Border");
JLabel  jlblCompoundBorder = new JLabel("Compound Border");
JLabel  jlblMatteBorder = new JLabel("Matte Border");

//set borders
jpnlLineBorder1.setBorder
(BorderFactory.createLineBorder(java.awt.Color.blue));
jpnlLineBorder2.setBorder
(BorderFactory.createLineBorder(java.awt.Color.blue,5));
jpnlRaisedBevelBorder.setBorder
(BorderFactory.createRaisedBevelBorder());
jpnlLoweredBevelBorder.setBorder
(BorderFactory.createLoweredBevelBorder());
jpnlBevelBorder.setBorder
(BorderFactory.createBevelBorder(0));
jpnlEtchedBorder.setBorder
(BorderFactory.createEtchedBorder());
jpnlTitledBorder.setBorder
(BorderFactory.createTitledBorder("Title"));
jpnlCompoundBorder.setBorder
(BorderFactory.createCompoundBorder());
jpnlMatteBorder.setBorder
(BorderFactory.createMatteBorder(5,5,5,5,java.awt.Color.blue));

//add components
jpnlLineBorder1.setLayout(new BorderLayout());
jpnlLineBorder1.add(jlblLineBorder1,"Center");
jpnlLineBorder2.setLayout(new BorderLayout());
jpnlLineBorder2.add(jlblLineBorder2,"Center");
jpnlRaisedBevelBorder.setLayout(new BorderLayout());
jpnlRaisedBevelBorder.add(jlblRaisedBevelBorder,"Center");
jpnlLoweredBevelBorder.setLayout(new BorderLayout());
jpnlLoweredBevelBorder.add(jlblLoweredBevelBorder,"Center");
jpnlBevelBorder.setLayout(new BorderLayout());
jpnlBevelBorder.add(jlblBevelBorder,"Center");
jpnlEtchedBorder.setLayout(new BorderLayout());
jpnlEtchedBorder.add(jlblEtchedBorder,"Center");
jpnlTitledBorder.setLayout(new BorderLayout());
jpnlTitledBorder.add(jlblTitledBorder,"Center");
jpnlCompoundBorder.setLayout(new BorderLayout());
jpnlCompoundBorder.add(jlblCompoundBorder,"Center");
jpnlMatteBorder.setLayout(new BorderLayout());
```

```
        jpnlMatteBorder.add(jlblMatteBorder,"Center");

        getContentPane().add(jpnlLineBorder1, BorderLayout.CENTER);
        getContentPane().add(jpnlLineBorder2, BorderLayout.CENTER);
        getContentPane().add
        (jpnlRaisedBevelBorder, BorderLayout.CENTER);
        getContentPane().add
        (jpnlLoweredBevelBorder, BorderLayout.CENTER);
getContentPane().add
        (jpnlBevelBorder, BorderLayout.CENTER);
        getContentPane().add
        (jpnlEtchedBorder, BorderLayout.CENTER);
        getContentPane().add
        (jpnlTitledBorder, BorderLayout.CENTER);
        getContentPane().add
        (jpnlCompoundBorder, BorderLayout.CENTER);
getContentPane().add(jpnlMatteBorder, BorderLayout.CENTER);

    }

}
```

CLASS **javax.swing.Box**

`public class javax.swing.Box extends Container implements Accessible`

The Box class is a utility class used in building screens. The Box class uses the BoxLayout layout manager, and adds a series of useful methods that facilitate the building of screens. In general, you will be aided by the capability to create one of three invisible components: Glue, Strut, and Rigid. The Glue component allows you to control component position when all components are of the same size. A Strut (horizontal or vertical) places a fixed amount of space between two components. A Rigid simply takes up a preset amount of space.

CLASS **javax.swing.Box: Summary**

Methods/Events	Description
public static Component createGlue()	Obtains a Glue component for use in screen design
public static Box createHorizontalBox()	Obtains a Box object that displays objects from left to right
public static Component createHorizontalGlue()	Obtains a Glue object with a horizontal orientation

continues

Methods/Events	Description
`public static Component createHorizontalStrut(int)`	Obtains a `Strut` object with a horizontal representation
`public static Component createRigidArea(Dimension)`	Obtains a `Rigid` object with the specified dimensions
`public static Box createVerticalBox()`	Obtains a `Box` object that displays objects from top to bottom
`public static Component createVerticalGlue()`	Obtains a `Glue` object with a vertical orientation
`public static Component createVerticalStrut(int)`	Obtains a `Strut` object with a vertical orientation
`public AccessibleContext getAccessibleContext()`	Obtains an `Accessible Context` associated with the `JComponent`
`public void setLayout(LayoutManager)`	Sets the layout manager for the `Box`, because `Box` can only use `BoxLayout`, this method will throw an `AWTException` when invoked

CLASS
javax.swing.BoxLayout

`public class javax.swing.BoxLayout implements LayoutManager2, Serializable`

The `BoxLayout` layout manager will align components from either left to right or top to bottom. In general, this class is not used directly because the `Box` class provides additional methods used for screen design. In examining the following method listing, note that some methods, although implemented due to interface requirements, are not used by this class.

CLASS
javax.swing.BoxLayout: Summary

Fields/Methods	Description
`public static final int X_AXIS`	Used to specify that components should be laid out in a horizontal fashion
`public static final int Y_AXIS`	Used to specify that components should be laid out in a vertical fashion

Fields/Methods	*Description*
public void addLayoutComponent (Component, Object)	Unused in this class
public void addLayoutComponent (String, Component)	Unused in this class
public float getLayoutAlignmentX (Container)	Obtains the layout along the x-axis for the container passed as a parameter
public float getLayoutAlignmentY (Container)	Obtains the layout along the y-axis for the container passed as a parameter
public void invalidateLayout (Container)	Causes information about the layout to be recalculated
public void layoutContainer (Container)	Used by the AWT to make layout decisions when painting the screen
public Dimension maximumLayoutSize (Container)	Obtains the maximum dimensions that the given Container object can fill
public Dimension minimumLayoutSize (Container)	Obtains the minimum dimensions that the given Container object can comfortably fill
public Dimension preferredLayoutSize (Container)	Obtains the preferred dimensions that the given Container object can fill
public void removeLayoutComponent (Component)	Unused in this class

CLASS `javax.swing.ButtonGroup`

`public class javax.swing.ButtonGroup implements Serializable`

The ButtonGroup object is used to create an aggregate of button objects in which one and only one button may sport a selected state at a given point in time.

CLASS ## `javax.swing.ButtonGroup`: Summary

Methods/Events	Description
`public void add(AbstractButton)`	Adds a button to the `ButtonGroup`'s collection
`public Enumeration getElements()`	Obtains an enumeration of all objects in the `ButtonGroup`'s collection
`public ButtonModel getSelection()`	Obtains a reference to the currently selected object
`public boolean isSelected(ButtonModel)`	Returns true if the `ButtonModel` passed as a parameter is currently selected
`public void remove(AbstractButton)`	Removes the `AbstractButton` object passed as a parameter from the `ButtonGroup`'s collection
`public void setSelected (ButtonModel, boolean)`	Sets the selected state for the `ButtonModel` object passed as parameter

CLASS ## `javax.swing.GrayFilter`

`public class javax.swing.GrayFilter extends RGBImageFilter`

The `GrayFilter` class is used to create a "disabled" version of an `Image` by first turning it into a grayscale image and then brightening its pixels.

CLASS ## `javax.swing.GrayFilter`: Summary

Methods/Events	Description
`public static Image createDisabledImage(Image)`	Obtains a "disabled" version of the `Image` object specified as a parameter
`public int filterRGB(int, int, int)`	Used to change a single pixel from its original state to the "disabled" state; subclasses must override this method

CLASS ## `javax.swing.ImageIcon`

`public class javax.swing.ImageIcon implements Icon, Serializable`

The `ImageIcon` class implements the `Icon` interface and allows users to create `Icon` objects using an `Image` object.

CLASS **javax.swing.ImageIcon: Summary**

Constructors/Methods	Description
public ImageIcon()	Creates an empty ImageIcon object, the source image can be set using the setImage() method
public ImageIcon(Image)	Creates an ImageIcon object using the source Image specified as a parameter
public ImageIcon(Image, String)	Creates an ImageIcon object using the source Image specified as a parameter, and with a description specified as a String object parameter
public ImageIcon(String)	Creates an ImageIcon object using a source image in the location specified by the String object parameter; once created, the Image object will be preloaded using the MediaTracker class
public ImageIcon(String, String)	Creates an ImageIcon object using a source image in the location specified by the String object parameter, and bearing the description of the second String object parameter; once created, the Image object will be preloaded using the MediaTracker class
public ImageIcon(URL)	Creates an ImageIcon object using a source image in the location specified by the URL object parameter; once created, the Image object will be preloaded using the MediaTracker class
public ImageIcon(URL, String)	Creates an ImageIcon object using a source image in the location specified by the URL object parameter, and bearing the description of the String object parameter; once created, the Image object will be preloaded using the MediaTracker class

continues

A

Constructors/Methods	Description
public String getDescription()	Obtains a description of the ImageIcon object
public int getIconHeight()	Obtains the height of the ImageIcon object
public int getIconWidth()	Obtains the width of the ImageIcon object
public Image getImage()	Obtains the Image object used to produce the ImageIcon object
public ImageObserver getImageObserver()	Obtains the ImageObserver object associated with the source image
protected void loadImage(Image)	Utility method used to force Image loading
public void paintIcon(Component, Graphics, int, int)	Draws the Icon object into the specified Graphics object; the Component parameter is used to allow for discovery of default parameters like background color
public void setDescription(String)	Sets the description of the ImageIcon object to match the String parameter
public void setImage(Image)	Sets the source image object
public void setImageObserver(ImageObserver)	Sets the ImageObserver object

CLASS `javax.swing.JApplet`

public class javax.swing.JApplet extends Applet implements Accessible, RootPaneContainer

The JApplet class extends java.applet.Applet to add functionality unique to the Swing packages. When developing applets using Swing, developers should subclass JApplet and not Applet. In examining the methods and example associated with this class, a brief understanding of JFC views and panes is important. If you have not read the introduction at the beginning on the javax.swing section, please do so now.

CLASS `javax.swing.JApplet`: **Summary**

Fields/Methods	Description
protected String accessibleContext	String object representing the Accessible description of the object; external classes access this value through the getAccessibleDescription() method
protected JRootPane rootPane	The root pane for this object
protected boolean rootPaneCheckingEnabled	If true, causes calls to add() and setLayout() to throw exceptions
protected JRootPane createRootPane()	Creates the root pane for this object
getAccessibleContext()	Obtains a reference to the AccessibleContext object
public Container getContentPane()	Obtains a reference to the contentPane object
public Component getGlassPane()	Obtains a reference to the GlassPane object
public JMenuBar getJMenuBar()	Obtains a reference to the JMenuBar object owned by this object
public JLayeredPane getLayeredPane()	Obtains a reference to the JLayeredPane object
public JRootPane getRootPane()	Obtains a reference to this object's JRootPane object
protected boolean isRootPaneCheckingEnabled()	Returns the state of the isRootPaneCheckingEnabled field
protected void processKeyEvent(KeyEvent)	Catches and processes key events that occur over this object and sends them on to interested parties
public void setContentPane(Container)	Sets the active ContentPane
public void setGlassPane(Component)	Sets the active GlassPane
public void setJMenuBar(JMenuBar)	Sets the active JMenuBar object
public void setLayeredPane(JLayeredPane)	Sets the active JLayeredPane object
protected void setRootPane(JRootPane)	Sets the active JRootPane object

continues

Fields/Methods	Description
protected void setRootPaneCheckingEnabled(boolean)	Sets the value of the rootPaneCheckingEnabled field
public void update(Graphics g)	Causes the JApplet to paint itself

CLASS

javax.swing.JButton

public class javax.swing.JButton extends AbstractButton implements Accessible

The JButton class is a JFC version of a common button. The Swing libraries provide a richer collection of UI widgets than the AWT libraries, so this is not the only available button class. The JButton is a standard "push" type of button, but there are additional button classes, including a multi-state button class. JButtons also differ from the Button class in java.awt in that they can display an icon.

CLASS

javax.swing.JButton: Summary

Constructors/Methods	Description
public JButton()	Creates a default JButton object with no icon and no text
public JButton(Icon)	Creates a JButton object with an icon and no text
public JButton(String)	Creates a JButton object with text but no icon
public JButton(String, Icon)	Creates a JButton object with both an icon and text
public AccessibleContext getAccessibleContext()	Obtains a reference to the AccessibleContext object
public String getUIClassID()	Obtains the logical name identifying the look and feel characteristics of this object
public boolean isDefaultButton()	Returns true if this button is the default button for the root pane

Constructors/Methods	Description
`public boolean isDefaultCapable()`	Returns true if the button is capable of becoming the default button
`public void setDefaultCapable(boolean)`	Sets the ability of the button to be the default button
`public void updateUI()`	Invoked by the `UIFactory` when the look and feel of the application has changed

CLASS **`javax.swing.JButton`: Example**

The following code example demonstrates the `JButton` class, the `ImageButton` class, and the `JFrame` class.

```
import javax.swing.*;
import java.awt.event.*;

public class ButtonDemo extends JPanel {
    public ButtonDemo() {
        Icon iconLuke = new ImageIcon("luke.gif");
        JButton btnLuke = new JButton("Luke", iconLuke);
        add(btnLuke);
    }

    public static void main(String args[]) {
        JFrame frmMain = new JFrame("Button Demo!");
        frmMain.getContentPane().add(new ButtonDemo());

        // Allow the program to be shut down by closing the
        // main window.
        frmMain.addWindowListener(new WindowAdapter() {
            public void windowClosing(WindowEvent we) {
                System.exit(0);
            }
        });

        frmMain.pack();
        frmMain.setVisible(true);
    }
}
```

A

JFC CLASS REFERENCE

javax.swing.JCheckBox

```
public class javax.swing.JCheckBox extends JToggleButton implements
Accessible
```

The JCheckBox class is the JFC version of a standard checkbox. It's better than traditional AWT checkboxes because it can display an icon in addition to a text label.

CLASS # javax.swing.JCheckBox: Summary

Constructors/Methods	Description
public JCheckBox()	Creates a JCheckBox object with a false initial state, no icon, and no text label
public JCheckBox(Icon)	Creates a JCheckBox object with a false initial state, an icon, and no text label
public JCheckBox(Icon, boolean)	Creates a JCheckBox object with an initial state specified as a boolean parameter, an icon specified as an Icon parameter, and no text label
public JCheckBox(String)	Creates a JCheckBox object with a false initial state, no icon, and a text label specified as a parameter
public JCheckBox(String, boolean)	Creates a JCheckBox object with an initial state specified as a boolean parameter, no icon, and a text label specified as a String parameter
public JCheckBox(String, Icon)	Creates a JCheckBox object with a false initial state, an icon specified by the Icon parameter, and a label specified by the String parameter
public JCheckBox(String, Icon, boolean)	Creates a JCheckBox object with an initial state specified by the boolean parameter, an icon specified by the Icon parameter, and a label specified by the String parameter
public AccessibleContext getAccessibleContext()	Obtains a reference to the AccessibleContext object

Constructors/Methods	Description
`public String getUIClassID()`	Obtains the logical name identifying the look and feel characteristics of this object
`public void updateUI()`	Invoked by the `UIFactory` when the look and feel of the application have changed

CLASS

javax.swing.JCheckBox: Example

The following code example demonstrates the `JLabel` class, the `JCheckBox` class, and the `JFrame` class:

```
import javax.swing.*;
import java.awt.event.*;

public class CheckboxDemo extends JPanel {
    public CheckboxDemo() {
        JLabel lblOptions = new JLabel("Checkbox Demo");
        JCheckBox chkOn = new JCheckBox("Default Checked", true);
        JCheckBox chkOff = new JCheckBox("Default Unchecked", false);
        add(lblOptions);
        add(chkOn);
        add(chkOff);
    }
    public static void main(String args[]) {
        JFrame frmMain = new JFrame("Checkbox Demo!");
        frmMain.getContentPane().add(new CheckboxDemo());

        // Allow the program to be shut down by closing the
        // main window.
        frmMain.addWindowListener(new WindowAdapter() {
            public void windowClosing(WindowEvent we) {
                System.exit(0);
            }
        });

        frmMain.pack();
        frmMain.setVisible(true);
    }
}
```

A

JFC CLASS REFERENCE

CLASS

javax.swing.JCheckBoxMenuItem

public class javax.swing.ButtonGroup extends JMenuItem implements SwingConstants, Accessible

The JCheckBoxMenuItem class allows you to place an item in a pull-down menu that has a checkbox and optionally displays an icon or text label.

CLASS

javax.swing.JCheckBoxMenuItem: Summary

Constructors/Methods	Description
public JCheckBoxMenuItem()	Creates a JCheckBoxMenuItem object with a false initial state, no icon, and no text label
public JCheckBoxMenuItem(Icon)	Creates a JCheckBoxMenuItem object with a false initial state, an icon specified by the Icon parameter, and no text label
public JCheckBoxMenuItem(String)	Creates a JCheckBoxMenuItem object with a false initial state, no icon, and a text label specified by the String parameter
public JCheckBoxMenuItem(String, boolean)	Creates a JCheckBoxMenuItem object with an initial state specified by the boolean parameter, no icon, and a text label specified by the String parameter
public JCheckBoxMenuItem(String, Icon)	Creates a JCheckBoxMenuItem object with a false initial state, an icon specified by the Icon parameter, and a text label specified by the String parameter
public JCheckBoxMenuItem(String, Icon, boolean)	Creates a JCheckBoxMenuItem object with an initial state specified by the boolean parameter, an icon specified by the Icon parameter, and a text label specified by the String parameter

Constructors/Methods	Description
public AccessibleContext getAccessibleContext()	Obtains a reference to the AccessibleContext object
public Object[] getSelectedObjects()	Obtains all selected objects or null if the checkbox is not selected
public boolean getState()	Obtains the current state (checked or unchecked) of this object
public String getUIClassID()	Obtains a description of this object's UI; will always be CheckBoxMenuItemUI
protected void init(String, Icon)	Called during initialization
public void requestFocus()	Transfers focus to this object
public void setState(boolean)	Sets the current state of this object
public void updateUI()	Invoked when the look and feel parameters have been changed

CLASS `javax.swing.JColorChooser`

`public class javax.swing.JColorChooser extends Jcomponent implements Accessible`

The JColorChooser class allows a user to visually pick and configure a color for use in an application. In a painting program, for example, this class could be used to let the user select the active brush color.

CLASS `javax.swing.JColorChooser`: **Summary**

Constructors/Methods	Description
public JColorChooser()	Creates a new JColorChooser object with an initial color of white
public JColorChooser(Color)	Creates a new JColorChooser object with an initial color specified by the color parameter

continues

Constructors/Methods	Description
public JColorChooser (ColorSelectionModel)	Creates a new JColorChooser object with the specified ColorSelectionModel
public void addChooserPanel()	Adds a chooser panel to the ColorChooser
public static JColorChooser createDialog(Component, String, boolean, JColorChooser, ActionListener, ActionListener)	Creates and returns a new JColorChooser object that is optionally modal (as specified by the boolean parameter)
public Color getColor()	Obtains a reference to the currently selected color as a Color object
public AccessibleContext getAccessibleContext()	Obtains a reference to the AccessibleContext object
public AbstractColorChooserPanel[] getChooserPanels()	Obtains a reference to the available color panels
public int getColor()	Obtains the currently selected color as an int
public Jcomponent getPreviewPanel()	Obtains a reference to the getPreviewPanel
public ColorSelectionModel getSelectionModel()	Obtains a reference to the SelectionModel
public ColorChooserUI getUI()	Obtains a reference to the ColorChooserUI object
public String getUIClassID()	Obtains the name of the ColorChooserUI object
public AbstractColorChooserPanel removeChooserPanel (AbstractChooserPanel)	Removes the specified color panel
public void setChooserPanels (AbstractColorChooserPanel[])	Sets the available color panels
public void setColor(Color)	Sets the currently selected color using a Color object
public void setColor(int)	Sets the currently selected color using an int

Constructors/Methods	Description
public void setColor(int, int, int)	Sets the currently selected color using three ints as red, green, and blue values
public void setPreviewPanel(Jcomponent)	Sets the current preview panel
public void setSelectionModel (ColorSelectionModel)	Sets the model containing the selected color
public void setUI(ColorChooserUI)	Sets the look-and-feel object used to render this component
public static Color showDialog(Component, String, Color)	Creates and shows a new modal JColorChooser object; once showing, program flow will block and the selected color will be returned when the user clicks OK; if the user presses Cancel in the dialog, null will be returned
public void updateUI()	Notification that the look-and-feel has changed

CLASS

javax.swing.JComboBox

public class javax.swing.JComboBox extends JComponent implements ItemSelectable, ListDataListener, ActionListener, Accessible

The JComboBox class is a JFC version of a combo box UI widget.

CLASS

javax.swing.JComboBox: Summary

Methods/Events	Description
public void actionPerformed(ActionEvent)	Implemented to fulfill the requirements of the ActionListener interface; should never be invoked or overridden
public void addActionListener(ActionListener)	Adds an ActionListener to the combo box's collection of listeners; a ActionListener is notified whenever the selected item changes

continues

Methods/Events	Description
`public void addItem(Object)`	Adds an item to the collection of items displayed in the combo box
`public void addItemListener(ItemListener)`	Adds an `ItemListener` to the combo box's collection of listeners; a `ItemListener` is notified whenever the selected item changes
`public void configureEditor(ComboBoxEditor, Object)`	Allows for editing of the given object using the given editor
`public void contentsChanged(ListDataEvent)`	Implemented to fulfill interface requirements; should not be invoked or overridden
`protected JComboBox.KeySelectionManager createDefaultKeySelectionManager()`	Creates and returns a reference to the default `KeySelectionManager` object
`protected void fireActionEvent()`	Used to send action events to listeners
`protected void fireItemStateChanged(ItemEvent)`	Used to send item events to listeners
`public AccessibleContext getAccessibleContext()`	Obtains a reference to the `AccessibleContext` object
`protected String getActionCommand()`	Obtains the action command used when sending events
`public ComboBoxEditor getEditor()`	Obtains a reference to the ComboBoxEditor responsible for painting and editing the selected item
`public Object getItemAt(int)`	Obtains the item at the specified index
`public int getItemCount()`	Obtains a count of all items
`public JComboBox.KeySelectionManager getKeySelectionManager()`	Obtains the default `KeySelectionManager` object
`public int getMaximumRowCount()`	Obtains the maximum row count for this object
`public ComboBoxModel getModel()`	Obtains the model used to build this object

Methods/Events	Description
`public ListCellRenderer getRenderer()`	Obtains the renderer used to build this object
`public int getSelectedIndex()`	Obtains the index of the selected item
`public Object getSelectedItem()`	Obtains the selected item
`public Object[] getSelectedObjects()`	Obtains the selected item as the first element in an array; implemented due to interface requirements
`public ComboBoxUI getUI()`	Obtains a reference to the UI used when building this object
`public String getUIClassID()`	Obtains the logical name of the UI used to build this object; will always be `ComboBoxUI`
`public void hidePopup()`	Hides the pop-up portion of the combo box
`public void insertItemAt(Object, int)`	Inserts a new item at the index specified by the `int` parameter
`protected void installAncestorListener()`	
`public void intervalAdded(ListDataEvent)`	Invoked when a new interval is added
`public void intervalRemoved(ListDataEvent)`	Invoked when an interval is removed
`public boolean isEditable()`	Returns true if the elements in the combo box are editable
`public boolean isFocusTraversable()`	Returns true if the object can receive the focus
`public boolean isLightWeightPopupEnabled()`	Returns true if lightweight pop-ups are in use
`public boolean isPopupVisible()`	Returns true if the pop-up portion of the combo box is visible
`public void processKeyEvent(KeyEvent)`	Invoked when a key event occurs; should never be invoked or overridden
`public void removeActionListener(ActionListener)`	Removes an `ActionListener` from the collection of listeners
`public void removeAllItems()`	Removes all items from the combo box
`public void removeItem(Object)`	Removes the item specified as a parameter from the combo box

continues

Methods/Events	Description
public void removeItemAt(int)	Removes the item at the index specified as a parameter from the combo box
public void removeItemListener(ItemListener)	Removes an ItemListener from the collection of listeners
protected void selectedItemChanged()	Used to send item events
public boolean selectWithKeyChar(char)	Performs a select with the given char
public void setActionCommand(String)	Sets the action command sent with events
public void setEditable(boolean)	Sets whether this object is editable
public void setEditor(ComboBoxEditor)	Sets the active editor for this object
public void setEnabled(boolean)	Enables or disables this object
public void setKeySelectionManager (JComboBox.KeySelectionManager)	Sets the key selection manager for this object
public void setLightWeightPopupEnabled (boolean)	Sets whether or not to try to use a lightweight pop-up
public void setMaximumRowCount(int)	Sets the maximum row count for this object
public void setModel(ComboBoxModel)	Sets the model used to build this object
public void setPopupVisible(boolean)	Sets the visibility of the popup portion of the combo box
public void setRenderer(ListCellRenderer)	Sets the renderer used to build this object
public void setSelectedIndex(int)	Sets the currently selected item based on an index parameter
public void setSelectedItem(Object)	Sets the currently selected item based on the Object parameter
public void setUI(ComboBoxUI)	Sets the UI used to build this object
public void showPopup()	Forces the combo box pop-up to show
public void updateUI()	Invoked when the UI look-and-feel parameters are changed

CLASS **javax.swing.JComboBox: Example**

```java
import javax.swing.*;
import java.awt.event.*;

public class JComboBoxDemo extends JPanel {
        public JComboBoxDemo() {
            JLabel lblTitle = new JLabel
            ("Chose your favorite author, or entry your own");
            String[] sChoices
        = {"Rand", "Cassady-Dorion", "Gibson", "Stepenson"}
JComboBox jcCombo = new JComboBox();
int iLength = sChoices.length;
for (int i=0;i<iLength; jcCombo.addItem(sChoices[i++]));
        jcCombo.setEditable(true);
            add(lblTitle);
        add(jcCombo);
}
    public static void main(String args[]) {
        JFrame frmMain = new JFrame("JComboBox Demo!");
        frmMain.getContentPane().add(new JComboBoxDemo ());

        // Allow the program to be shut down by closing the
        // main window.
        frmMain.addWindowListener(new WindowAdapter() {
            public void windowClosing(WindowEvent we) {
                System.exit(0);
            }
        });

        frmMain.pack();
        frmMain.setVisible(true);
    }
}
```

CLASS **javax.swing.JComponent**

```java
public abstract class JComponent extends Container implements Serializable
```

The JComponent class is the base class for all Swing components. It implements basic functionality for a pluggable UI, ToolTips, Action object, borders, auto-scrolling, accessibility, simplified dialog construction, and internationalization.

javax.swing.JComponent: Summary

Fields/Methods	Description
protected AccessibleContext accessibleContext	Used for accessibility support
protected EventListenerList listenerList	Collection of EventListener objects
public static final String TOOL_TIP_TEXT_KEY	Text displayed in the ToolTip for this object
public static final int UNDEFINED_CONDITION	Constant used by certain classes to signify an undefined condition
public static final int WHEN_ANCESTOR_OF_FOCUSED_COMPONENT	Constant used by registerKeyboardAction() to mean that the component should receive events when it is the ancestor of a component that has focus
public static final int WHEN_FOCUSED	Constant used by registerKeyboardAction() to mean that the component should receive events when it has focus
public static final int WHEN_IN_FOCUSED_WINDOW	Constant used by registerKeyboardAction() to mean that the component should receive events when it is contained in a window that has focus
public void addAncestorListener(AncestorListener)	Adds an AncestorListener to the object's collection of listeners; an AncestorListener is notified whenever an ancestor of a given object is added, removed, hidden, or shown

Fields/Methods	Description
`public void addNotify()`	Notification to this component that it now has a parent component
`public void addPropertyChangeListener (PropertyChangeListener)`	Adds a `PropertyChangeListener` to the object's collection of listeners; a `PropertyChangeListener` is notified whenever a bound property value is changed
`public void addVetoableChangeListener (VetoableChangeListener)`	Adds a `VetoableChangeListener` to the object's collection of listeners; a `PropertyChangeListener` is notified whenever a constrained property value is changed
`public void computeVisibleRect(Rectangle)`	Places the value of the component's visible rectangle inside the `Rectangle` parameter
`public boolean contains(int, int)`	Returns true if the specified point is within the bounds of the component
`public JToolTip createToolTip()`	Creates and returns the `JToolTop` object that should be displayed for this object; to display context-sensitive tooltips, you would override this method
`public void firePropertyChange (String, boolean, boolean)`	Sends an event indicating a bound property change
`public void firePropertyChange (String, byte, byte)`	Sends an event indicating a bound property change
`public void firePropertyChange (String, char, char)`	Sends an event indicating a bound property change
`public void firePropertyChange (String, double, double)`	Sends an event indicating a bound property change
`public void firePropertyChange (String, float, float)`	Sends an event indicating a bound property change

continues

A

JFC CLASS
REFERENCE

Fields/Methods	Description
public void firePropertyChange (String, int, int)	Sends an event indicating a bound property change
public void firePropertyChange (String, long, long)	Sends an event indicating a bound property change
public void firePropertyChange (String, Object, Object)	Sends an event indicating a bound property change
public void firePropertyChange (String, short, short)	Sends an event indicating a bound property change
public void fireVetoableChange (String, Object, Object)	Sends an event indicating a constrained property change
public AccessibleContext getAccessibleContext()	Obtains a reference to the AccessibleContext object
public ActionListener getActionForKeyStroke(KeyStroke)	Obtains the ActionListener associated with the given keystroke
public float getAlignmentX()	Obtains this component's alignment along the x-axis
public float getAlignmentY()	Obtains this component's alignment along the y-axis
public boolean getAutoscrolls()	Returns true if this component scrolls automatically when its contents are adjusted
public Border getBorder()	Obtains the border associated with this object, or null if none exists
public Rectangle getBounds(Rectangle)	Places the bounds for this component in the Rectangle parameter and returns that value
public final Object getClientProperty(Object)	Obtains the property associated with the given key
protected Graphics getComponentGraphics(Graphics)	Obtains the Graphics object used to paint the component

Fields/Methods	Description
public int getConditionForKeyStroke(KeyStroke)	Obtains the execution condition associated with the given keystroke
public int getDebugGraphicsOptions()	Obtains the current debug graphics state
public Graphics getGraphics()	Obtains the Graphics object used to paint this component
public int getHeight()	Obtains the height of this component
public Insets getInsets()	Obtains the Insets object associated with this component
public Insets getInsets(Insets)	Stores the insets in the specified Insets object and returns that object
public Point getLocation(Point)	Places the current location of this component both in the Point object parameter and in the return value of this method
public Dimension getMaximumSize()	Obtains the maximum size this component can take on
public Dimension getMinimumSize()	Obtains the minimum size this component can fill
public Component getNextFocusableComponent()	Obtains the next component that should receive focus, or null if the focus manager is to determine the component
public Dimension getPreferredSize()	Obtains the preferred size for this component
public KeyStroke[] getRegisteredKeyStrokes()	Obtains all keystrokes that can initiate registered actions
public JrootPane getRootPane()	Obtains the JRootPane to which the component belongs
public Dimension getSize(Dimension)	Places the size of the component both in the Dimension parameter and in the method return value

continues

Fields/Methods	Description
`public Point getToolTipLocation(MouseEvent)`	Obtains the preferred location for the ToolTip associated with this component; if null is returned, a location will be chosen automatically
`public String getToolTipText()`	Obtains the text to be used in displaying the ToolTip for this component
`getToolTipText(MouseEvent)`	Obtains the text to be used in displaying the ToolTip for this component; if context-sensitive tooltips are used, this method is passed to the active location of the mouse
`public Container getTopLevelAncestor()`	Obtains the top level container or null if the component does not belong to another container
`public String getUIClassID()`	Obtains the logical name for this component's UI
`public Rectangle getVisibleRect()`	Obtains the visible rectangle for this component
`public int getWidth()`	Obtains the width of this component
`public int getX()`	Obtains the location of this component along the x-axis
`public int getY()`	Obtains the location of this component along the y-axis
`public void grabFocus()`	Used by the focus manager to obtain focus for this component; in general, it is a good practice to call `requestFocus()` instead
`public boolean hasFocus()`	Returns true if this component has focus, false otherwise
`public boolean isDoubleBuffered()`	Returns true if this component is using double-buffering to paint itself, false otherwise
`public boolean isFocusCycleRoot()`	If your component is part of a component tree with its own focus cycle, you will want to override this method and return true

Fields/Methods	Description
`public boolean isFocusTraversable()`	Returns true if this component can receive focus when the user tabs through the screen
`public static boolean isLightweightComponent(Component)`	Returns true if this component is lightweight, meaning that it does not have a native peer
`public boolean isManagingFocus()`	If your component is managing its own focus, override this method and return true
`public boolean isOpaque()`	Returns true if this component is completely opaque
`public boolean isOptimizedDrawingEnabled()`	Returns true if this component has optimized its drawing by ensuring that none of its children overlap
`public boolean isPaintingTile()`	Returns true if this component is currently in the process of painting a tile
`public boolean isRequestFocusEnabled()`	Returns true if the `requestFocus()` method will function properly for this component
`public void paint(Graphics)`	Invoked when this component should draw itself into the specified `Graphics` object
`protected void paintBorder (protected void paintBorder(Graphics)`	Invoked when this component should draw its border into the specified `Graphics` object
`public void paintChildren(Graphics)`	Invoked when this component should draw its children into the specified `Graphics` object
`public void paintComponent(Graphics)`	Method used to transfer the `Graphics` object to a UI-delegate, assuming one exists

continues

Fields/Methods	Description
public void paintImmediately(int, int, int, int)	Forces an immediate paint of the specified region
protected void processComponentKeyEvent (KeyEvent e)	Invoked when a key event occurs that the component itself recognizes
protected void processFocusEvent	Invoked when a focus event occurs
public void paintImmediately(Rectangle)	Forces an immediate paint of the specified region
protected void processKeyEvent(KeyEvent)	Invoked when a key event occurs
public protected processMouseMotionEvent(MouseEvent)	Invoked when a mouse motion event occurs
public void putClientProperty(Object, Object)	Adds the specified property and key to the client property collection
public void registerKeyboardAction (ActionListener, KeyStroke, int)	Registers an ActionListener object to receive events when the specified keystroke occurs
public void removeAncestorListener (AncestorListener)	Removes the AncestorListener specified as a parameter
public void removeNotify()	Invoked when this component no longer has a parent
public void removePropertyChangeListener (PropertyChangeListener)	Removes the specified PropertyChangeListener from the collection of listeners
public void removeVetoableChangeListener (VetoableChangeListener)	Removes the specified VetoableChangeListener from the collection of listeners
public void repaint(long, int, int, int, int)	Adds the area specified as a parameter to the list of regions that need to be repainted if the component is showing

Fields/Methods	Description
`public void repaint(Rectangle)`	Adds the area specified as a parameter to the list of regions that need to be repainted if the component is showing
`public void requestDefaultFocus()`	Requests that focus be given to the component that should have focus by default
`public void requestFocus()`	Requests that focus be given to this component
`public void resetKeyboardActions()`	Deletes all stored keyboard actions
`public void reshape(int, int, int, int)`	Resizes the component
`public void revalidate()`	Allows deferred automatic layout
`public void scrollRectToVisible(Rectangle)`	Attempts to show the region specified as a parameter
`public void setAlignmentX(float)`	Sets the x-alignment for this component
`public void setAlignmentY(float)`	Sets the y-alignment for this component
`public void setAutoscrolls(boolean)`	Sets whether this component can automatically scroll its contents
`public void setBorder(Border)`	Sets the border to be drawn with this component
`public void setBounds(int, int, int, int)`	Sets the bounding coordinates for the component
`public void setDebugGraphicsOptions(int)`	Either enables or disables debug graphics information
`public void setDoubleBuffered(boolean)`	Sets whether this component should buffer all drawing before moving it to the screen
`public void setEnabled(boolean)`	Sets the enabled state of the component
`public void setMaximumSize(Dimension)`	Sets the maximum size this component can fill

continues

Fields/Methods	Description
`public void setMinimumSize(Dimension)`	Sets the minimum size this component can use
`public void setNextFocusableComponent(Component)`	Sets the component that should receive focus after this component; focus is generally transferred when the Tab key is pressed
`public void setOpaque(boolean)`	Determines whether the components background is filled with the background color
`public void setPreferredSize(Dimension)`	Sets the preferred size for this component
`public void setRequestFocusEnabled(boolean)`	Sets whether this component can successfully obtain focus by invoking `requestFocus()`
`public void setToolTipText(String)`	Sets the ToolTip text to be displayed with this component
`protected void setUI(ComponentUI)`	Sets the UI associated with this component
`public void setVisible(boolean)`	Sets the visible state of the component
`public void unregisterKeyboardAction(KeyStroke)`	Removes a keyboard action from the list of registered actions
`public void update(Graphics)`	Updates this component; this method is called immediately before `paint()`
`public void updateUI()`	Invoked when the active look and feel parameters have changed

javax.swing.JDialog

`public class JDialog extends Dialog implements WindowConstants, Accessible, RootPaneContainer`

The JDialog class is used to display either a modal or modeless dialog to a user. When customizing the UI for a given dialog, children are not added directly to the JDialog object, but are added to its child obtained by invoking getContentPane().

CLASS `javax.swing.JDialog`: **Summary**

Methods/Events	Description
`protected JRootPane createRootPane()`	Invoked internally to create the root pane
`protected void dialogInit()`	Invoked internally to perform initialization tasks
`public AccessibleContext getAccessibleContext()`	Obtains a reference to the `AccessibleContext` object
`public Container getContentPane()`	Obtains the content pane for this object; when customizing the UI for a `JDialog` object, component additions must be made to the content pane and not the `JDialog` itself
`public int getDefaultCloseOperation()`	Obtains the default operation that is initiated when the window is closed
`public Component getGlassPane()`	Obtains the `GlassPane` object for this component
`public JmenuBar() getJMenuBar()`	Obtains the `JmenuBar` object for this component
`public JLayeredPane getLayeredPane()`	Obtains the `JLayeredPane` object associated with this object
`public JRootPane getRootPane()`	Obtains the `JRootPane` object associated with this object
`protected isRootPaneCheckingEnabled()`	Returns the state of the `RootPaneCheckingEnabled` variable
`public void setContentPane(Container)`	Sets the content pane for this object
`public void setDefaultCloseOperation(int)`	Sets the default operation that should execute when the window closes
`public void setGlassPane(Component)`	Sets the `GlassPane` used when displaying this object
`public void setJMenuBar(JmenuBar)`	Sets the `JDialog`'s menu bar to the specified `JmenuBar`
`public void setLayeredPane(JLayeredPane)`	Sets the `JLayeredPane` object associated with this object

continues

A

JFC CLASS REFERENCE

Methods/Events	Description
public void setLocationRelativeTo(Component)	Sets the location of the JDialog object near the Component parameter; if the Component is not showing, the JDialog object will be centered on the screen
protected void setRootPane(JRootPane)	Sets the JRootPane object associated with this object
protected void setRootPaneCheckingEnabled (boolean)	Sets the state of the rootPaneCheckingEnabled field
public void update(Graphics)	Causes the dialog to paint itself

CLASS # javax.swing.JEditorPane

public class JEditorPane extends JTextComponent

The JEditorPane class is used to display text in various rich formats, including RTF and HTML.

CLASS # javax.swing.JEditorPane: Summary

Methods/Events	Description
public void addHyperlinkListener (HyperlinkListener)	Adds a HyperlinkListener to the group of listener's objects; links are selected and entered, and so on
protected EditorKit createDefaultEditorKit()	Called during initialization to create the PlainEditorKit
public static EditorKit createEditorKitForContentType(String)	Create an EditorKit for the specified type from the registry of kits
public void fireHyperlinkUpdate (HyperlinkEvent)	Notify hyperlink listeners of a hyperlink event
public AccessibleContext getAccessibleContext()	Obtains a reference to the AccessibleContext object
public String getContentType()	Obtains the name of the content type that the editor pane handles

Methods/Events	Description
public EditorKit getEditorKit()	Obtains the current editor kit for handling content
public EditorKit getEditorKitForContentType(String)	Obtains the EditorKit to use for the specified content type
public URL getPage()	Obtains the URL used to supply the current text
public boolean getScrollableTracksViewportWidth()	Returns true if the width of the view port should always match the width of the scrollable
public String getUIClassID()	Obtains the class ID associated with this object
public boolean isManagingFocus()	Returns true if the component turns off tab traversal once it gains the focus
public static void registerEditorKitForContentType (String, String, ClassLoader)	Sets the default EditorKit to use for the specified content type
public static void registerEditorKitForContentType (String, String)	Sets the default EditorKit to use for the specified content type; uses the default ClassLoader
public void removeHyperlinkListener (HyperlinkListener)	Removes the specified HyperlinkListener from the group of listeners
protected void scrollToReference(String)	Scroll to the given reference
public void setContentType(String)	Sets the content type handled by this editor
public void setEditorKit(EditorKit)	Sets the EditorKit used to handle content
public void setEditorKit (String, EditorKit)	Sets the EditorKit used to handle the specified content type
public void setPage(String)	Sets the current URL being displayed
public void setPage(URL)	Sets the current URL being displayed

javax.swing.JFileChooser

public class JfileChooser extends Jcomponent implements Accessible

The JFileChooser class is a file-system browser that can be used to allow a user to select a file.

javax.swing.JFileChooser: Summary

Methods/Events	Description
public boolean accept(File)	Returns true if the specified file should be included in the list of files to choose from
public voi addActionListener(ActionListener)	Adds an ActionListener to the component's group of action listeners
public void addChooseableFileFilter(FileFilter)	Adds a file type to the list that the user can use to filter by
public void approveSelection()	Notification that the user has selected the approve button
public void changeToParentDirectory()	Set the new current directory to be the parent directory of the current directory
public void ensureFileIsVisible(File f)	Force the specified file to become visible
protected void fireActionPerformed(String)	Dispatch a notification to all action listeners
public FileFilter getAcceptAllFileFilter()	Obtains a reference to the AcceptAll file filter
public AccessibleContext getAccessibleContext()	Obtains a reference to the AccessibleContext object
public Component getAccessory()	Obtains the accessory component associated with this component
public int getApproveButtonMnemonic()	Obtains the mnemonic for the approve button
public String getApproveButtonText()	Obtains the text displayed by the approve button
public String getApproveButtonToolTipText()	Obtains the text displayed as a tool tip
public FileFilter[] getChoosableFileFilters()	Obtains a list of user-selectable file filters

Methods/Events	Description
public File getCurrentDirectory()	Obtains a reference to the current directory
public String getDescription(File)	Obtains a description of the specified file
public String getDialogTitle()	Obtains the text displayed in the dialog's title bar
public int getDialogType()	Obtains the mode of the dialog (open or save)
public FileFilter getFileFilter()	Obtains a reference to the currently selected file filter
public int getFileSelectionMode()	Obtains the mode of file selection
public FileSystemView getFileSystemView()	Obtains the current FileSystemView
public Icon getIcon(File f)	Obtains a reference to the icon used when displaying the specified file
public String getName(File f)	Obtains the name of the specified file
public File getSelectedFile()	Obtains a reference to the currently selected file
public File[] getSelectedFiles()	Obtains a list of all selected files
public String getTypeDescription(File)	Obtains a description of the current file's type
public FileChooserUI getUI()	Obtains the FileChooserUI object associated with this component
public String getUIClassID()	Obtains a logical description of the UI; will always return FileChooserUI
public boolean isDirectorySelectionEnabled()	Returns true if directories are selectable
public boolean isFileHidingEnabled()	Returns true if hidden files are not shown
public boolean isFileSelectionEnabled()	Returns true if files are selectable
public boolean isTraversable(File)	Returns true if the specified file is traversable
public void removeActionListener(ActionListener)	Remove the specified ActionListener from the group of listeners

continues

Methods/Events	Description
`public boolean` `removeChoosableFileFilter(FileFilter)`	Remove the specified filter from the group of user selectable file filters
`public void rescanCurrentDireactory()`	Force a rescan on the files of the current directory
`public void resetChoosableFileFilters()`	Return the user choosable file filter list to its default state
`public void setAccessory(Component)`	Assigns the accessory component
`public void setApprovedButtonMnemonic(char)`	Sets the keyboard shortcut for the approve button
`public void setApprovedButtonMnemonic(int)`	Sets the keyboard shortcut for the approve button
`public void setApprovedButtonText(String)`	Sets the text displayed by the approved button
`public void setApproveButtonToolTip(String)`	Sets the tooltip that will be displayed by the approve button
`public void setCurrentDirectory(File)`	Sets the current directory to the specified file
`public void setDialogTitle(String)`	Sets the text to be displayed in the dialog's title bar
`public void setDialogType(int)`	Sets the mode of the dialog
`public void setFileFilter(FileFilter)`	Sets the current file filter
`public void setFileHidingEnabled(boolean)`	Sets whether or not hidden files are displayed
`public void setFileSelectionMode(in)`	Sets what types of files may be selected (file, directory or both)
`public void setFileView()`	Sets the current view
`public void` `setMultiSelectionEnabled(boolean)`	Sets whether or not multiple files can be selected
`public void setSelectedFile(File)`	Sets the currently selected file
`public void setSelectedFiles(File[])`	Sets the currently selected files
`protected setup(FileSystemView)`	Called during initialization
`public int showDialog(Component)`	Shows the `JFileChooser` object relative to the `Component` object specified as a parameter

Methods/Events	Description
`public int showOpenDialog(Component)`	Shows the `JfileChooser` in the "Open File" mode
`public int showSaveDialog(Component)`	Shows the `JfileChooser` in the "Close File" mode
`public void updateUI()`	Invoked to indicate a UI look-and-feel change

CLASS

`javax.swing.JFrame`

`public class JFrame extends Frame implements WindowConstants, Accessible, RootPaneContainer`

The `JFrame` class extends `java.awt.Frame`, introducing a series of new features unique to Swing. The one major difference between this class and `Frame` is that children may not be added directly to the `JFrame` object. As an alternative, children must be added to the content pane that is obtained using the `getContentPane()` method.

CLASS

`javax.swing.JFrame`: Summary

Methods/Events	Description
`protected void addImpl(Component, Object, int)`	Adds the specified component to the `JFrame` object at the specified index
`protected JRootPane createRootPane()`	Invoked by the constructors to create the `JRootPane` object
`protected void frameInit()`	Invoked by the constructors to perform initialization tasks
`public AccessibleContext getAccessibleContext()`	Obtains a reference to the `AccessibleContext` object
`public Container getContentPane()`	Obtains the content pane for this object; when customizing the UI for a `JFrame` object, component additions must be made to the content pane and not the `JFrame` itself
`public int getDefaultCloseOperation()`	Obtains the default operation that is initiated when the window is closed

continues

A

Methods/Events	Description
public Component getGlassPane()	Obtains the GlassPane object for this component
public JMenuBar()	Obtains a reference to the JMenuBar for this JFrame
public JLayeredPane getLayeredPane()	Obtains the JLayeredPane object associated with this object
public JRootPane getRootPane()	Obtains the JRootPane object associated with this object
protected boolean isRootPaneCheckingEnabled()	Returns true if exceptions are thrown when add() or setLayout() is called
protected void processKeyEvent(KeyEvent)	Invoked when a key event occurs
protected void processWindowEvent(WindowEvent)	Invoked when a window event occurs
public void setContentPane(Container)	Sets the content pane for this object
public void setDefaultCloseOperation(int)	Sets the default operation that should execute when the window closes
public void setGlassPane(Component)	Sets the glass pane used when displaying this object
public void setJMenuBar(JmenuBar)	Sets the menu bar associated with this frame
public void setLayeredPane(JLayeredPane)	Sets the JLayeredPane object associated with this object
public void setRootPane(JRootPane)	Sets the JRootPane object associated with this object
protected void setRootPaneCheckingEnabled(boolean)	Sets whether or not calls to add() or setLayout() will throw exceptions
public void update(Graphics)	Invoked prior to calling paint()

CLASS **javax.swing.JInternalFrame**

public class JInternalFrame extends JComponent implements Accessible, WindowConstants, RootPaneContainer

The JInternalFrame class is a lightweight component that can often be used in place of a JFrame object. Like many Swing components, children are not added directly to a JInternalFrame object, but are added to its content pane.

CLASS   `javax.swing.JInternalFrame`: **Summary**

Methods/Events	Description
public void addInternalFrameListener (InternalFrameListener)	Adds the specified listener to the group of listeners
protected JRootPane createRootPane()	Invoked by the constructors to create the JRootPane object
public void dispose()	Frees resources associated with this frame
protected fireInternalFrameEvent(int)	Used for internal event handling
public AccessibleContext getAccessibleContext()	Obtains a reference to the AccessibleContext object
public Color getBackground()	Obtains the background color for the frame
public Container getContentPane()	Obtains the content pane for this object; when customizing the UI for a JInternalFrame object, component additions must be made to the content pane and not the JInternalFrame itself
public JInternalFrame.JDesktopIcon getDesktopIcon()	Obtains the JDesktopIcon used to display this window when iconified
public JDesktopPane getDesktopPane()	Searches the component hierarchy and returns the first JDesktopPane object that is found
public Color getForeground()	Obtains the foreground color for the frame
public JMenuBar getJMenuBar()	Obtains a reference to the menu bar for the frame
public Icon getFrameIcon()	Obtains an icon that can be used to represent this frame
public Component getGlassPane()	Obtains the glass pane object for this component

continues

Methods/Events	Description
`public int getLayer()`	Obtains the layer attribute for this component
`public JLayeredPane getLayeredPane()`	Obtains the `JLayeredPane` object associated with this object
`public JMenuBar getMenuBar()`	Obtains the `JMenuBar` object associated with this object
`public JRootPane getRootPane()`	Obtains the `JRootPane` object associated with this object
`public String getTitle()`	Obtains a title for this object
`public InternalFrameUI getUI()`	Obtains the active look and feel attributes for this object
`public String getUIClassID()`	Obtains a logical name associated with the UI; will always return `InternalFrameUI`
`public String getWarningString()`	Obtains the warning string that is associated with this window
`public boolean isClosable()`	Returns true if this object can be closed by the user
`public boolean isClosed()`	Returns true if this window is currently closed
`public boolean isIcon()`	Returns true if the `JInternalFrame` object is currently in icon form
`public boolean isIconifiable()`	Returns true if the `JInternalFrame` object can be iconified
`public boolean isMaximizable()`	Returns true if the `JInternalFrame` object can be maximized
`public boolean isMaximum()`	Returns true if the `JInternalFrame` object is currently maximized
`public boolean isResizable()`	Returns true if this component is resizable
`public boolean isSelected()`	Returns true if this component is currently selected
`public void moveToBack()`	Assuming the parent of this component is `JLayeredPane`, this method moves the `JInternalFrame` object to position −1

Methods/Events	Description
`public void moveToFront()`	Assuming the parent of this component is `JLayeredPane`, this method moves the `JInternalFrame` object to position 0
`public void pack()`	Causes the frame to be laid out at its preferred size
`public void removeInternalFrameListener` `(InternalFrameListener)`	Removes the specified listener from the group of listeners
`public void reshape(int, int, int, int)`	Sets the size and location of the top-left corner of the frame
`public void setBackground(Color)`	Set the background color for the frame
`public void setClosable(boolean)`	Sets whether this component can be closed by user action
`public void setClosed(boolean)`	An argument of true will close the frame
`public void setContentPane(Container)`	Sets the active content pane for this object
`public void setDesktopIcon(JDesktopIcon)`	Sets the active desktop icon for this object
`public void setForeground(Color)`	Sets the foreground color for the frame
`public void setFrameIcon(Icon)`	Sets the active frame icon for this object
`public void setGlassPane(Component)`	Sets the active glass pane for this object
`public void setIcon(boolean)`	Iconifies the frame
`public void setIconifiable(boolean)`	Sets whether this frame can be iconified
`public void setLayer(Integer)`	Assigns the layer attribute for this component
`public void setJMenuBar(JMenuBar)`	Associates the specified menu bar with the frame
`public void setLayeredPane(JLayeredPane)`	Sets the `JLayeredPane` object associated with this component
`public void setLayer(Integer)`	Sets the layer attribute of the frame
`public void setMaximizable(boolean)`	Sets whether this component can be maximized

continues

Methods/Events	Description
public void setMaximum(boolean)	Sets whether this component is currently maximized
public void setMenuBar(JMenuBar)	Associates this object with a JMenuBar object (deprecated, use setJMenuBar)
public void setResizable(boolean)	Sets whether this component can be resized
public void setRootPane(JRootPane)	Associates this component with a JRootPane object
protected void setRootPaneCheckingEnabled(boolean)	Sets whether or not calls to add() and setLayout() will throw an exception
public void setSelected(boolean)	Sets whether this component is currently selected
public void setTitle(String)	Sets the title for this component
public void setUI(InternalFrameUI)	Sets the pluggable look-and-feel attributes for this component
public void setVisible(boolean)	Set the visible state of the frame
public void show()	Shows the frame
public void toBack()	Sends the frame to the back
public void toFront()	Sends the frame to the front
public void updateUI()	Invoked to indicate a UI look-and-feel change

CLASS   # javax.swing.JInternalFrame.JDesktopIcon

public static class JInternalFrame.JDesktopIcon extends JComponent implements Accessible

The JDesktopIcon class is used to represent an iconified version of a JInternalFrame object.

CLASS   # javax.swing.JInternalFrame.JDesktopIcon: Summary

Methods/Events	Description
public AccessibleContext getAccessibleContext()	Obtains a reference to the AccessibleContext object

Methods/Events	Description
public JDesktopPane getDesktopPane()	Obtains the JDesktopPane associated with the JInternalFrame
public JInternalFrame getInternalFrame()	Obtains the JInternalFrame associated with this object
public DesktopIconUI getUI()	Obtains the DesktopIconUI object associated with this object
public String getUIClassID()	Obtains a logical name associated with this object; will always return DesktopIconUI
public void setInternalFrame(JInternalFrame)	Sets the JInternalFrame object associated with this object
public void setUI(DesktopIconUI)	Sets the DesktopIconUI object associated with this object
public void updateUI()	Invoked when the look and feel parameters have been updated

CLASS

javax.swing.JLabel

public class JLabel extends JComponent implements SwingConstants, Accessible

The JLabel class is used to display a read-only line of text, or a combination of a read-only line of text and an Image object.

CLASS

javax.swing.JLabel: Summary

Methods/Events	Description
public AccessibleContext getAccessibleContext()	Obtains a reference to the AccessibleContext object
public Icon getDisabledIcon()	If a disabled icon has been specified for this object, it is returned; otherwise, one is created using the default icon and the GrayFilter class
public int DisplayedMnemonic()	Obtains the keyboard accelerator for this component

continues

Methods/Events	Description
`public int getHorizontalAlignment()`	Obtains the alignment along the x-axis for this component; return value is either `SwingConstants.LEFT`, `SwingConstants.RIGHT`, or `SwingConstants.CENTER`
`public int getHorizontalTextPosition()`	Returns either `SwingConstants.LEFT`, `SwingConstants.RIGHT`, or `SwingConstants.CENTER` depending on horizontal alignment of the text relative to the icon
`public Icon getIcon()`	Obtains the icon (if any) associated with this component
`public int getIconTextGap()`	Obtains the number of pixels that separate the icon from the text label
`public Component getLabelFor()`	Obtains the component responsible for labeling
`public String getText()`	Obtains the text label associated with this component
`public LabelUI getUI()`	Obtains the current look and feel properties for this component
`public String getUIClassID()`	Obtains a logical name for the active UI; will always return `LabelUI`
`public int getVerticalAlignment()`	Obtains the alignment for this component along the y-axis; return value is either `SwingConstants.LEFT`, `SwingConstants.RIGHT`, or `SwingConstants.CENTER`
`public int getVerticalTextPosition()`	Returns either `SwingConstants.LEFT`, `SwingConstants.RIGHT`, or `SwingConstants.CENTER` depending on vertical alignment of the text relative to the icon
`public void setDisabledIcon(Icon)`	Sets the disabled icon for this component
`public void DisplayedMnemonic(char)`	Sets the keyboard accelerator for this component
`public void setDisplayedMnemonic(int)`	Sets the keyboard accelerator for this component

Methods/Events	Description
`public void setFont(Font)`	Sets the font to be used in this component
`public void setHorizontalAlignment(int)`	Sets the alignment along the x-axis for this component; parameter value is either `SwingConstants.LEFT`, `SwingConstants.RIGHT`, or `SwingConstants.CENTER`
`public int setHorizontalTextPosition(int)`	Sets the horizontal position of the text relative to the icon; parameter value is either `SwingConstants.LEFT`, `SwingConstants.RIGHT`, or `SwingConstants.CENTER`
`public void setIcon(Icon)`	Sets the icon to be used with this component
`public void setIconTextGap(int)`	Sets the number of pixels that separate the icon from the text label
`public void setLabelFor(Component)`	Sets the component responsible for labeling
`public void setText(String)`	Sets the text label for this component
`public void setUI(LabelUI)`	Sets the pluggable look and feel properties for this component
`public void setVerticalAlignment(int)`	Sets the vertical alignment of this component along the y-axis; parameter value is either `SwingConstants.TOP`, `SwingConstants.BOTTOM`, or `SwingConstants.CENTER`
`public void setVerticalTextPosition(int)`	Sets the vertical position of the text image relative to the icon; parameter value is either `SwingConstants.TOP`, `SwingConstants.BOTTOM`, or `SwingConstants.CENTER`
`public void updateUI()`	Invoked to indicate a change in the pluggable look and feel properties

javax.swing.JLayeredPane

`public class JLayeredPane extends JComponent implements Accessible`

The JLayeredPane container is used to lay out a series of components with the added bonus of being able to "layer" one component on top of another. Components on the same layer will behave just like a series of components in a normal container, and components on different layers will appear on top of each other. Each layer is assigned a number, and the layer with the highest number will appear first. In assigning layer numbers, you may use any of the constants that are defined or use your own numbering scheme.

javax.swing.JLayeredPane: Summary

Fields/Methods	Description
`public static final Integer DEFAULT_LAYER`	Used to add components to the default layer
`public static final Integer DRAG_LAYER`	Used to add components to the drag layer
`public static final Integer FRAME_CONTENT_LAYER`	Used to add components to the frame content layer
`public static final Integer MODAL_LAYER`	Used to add components to the default layer
`public static final Integer PALETTE_LAYER`	Used to add components to the default layer
`public static final Integer POPUP_LAYER`	Used to add components to the default layer
`protected void addImpl(Component, Object, int)`	Adds the specified component to the JLayeredPane object at the specified index
`public AccessibleContext getAccessibleContext()`	Obtains a reference to the AccessibleContext object
`public int getComponentCountInLayer(int)`	Obtains the number of components in the layer specified by the int parameter
`public Component[]getComponentsInLayer(int)`	Obtains the collection of components in the layer specified by the int parameter

Fields/Methods	Description
Methods	
`protected Hashtable getComponentToLayer()`	Obtains a hashtable that maps each component to its corresponding layer
`public int getIndexOf(Component)`	Obtains the absolute index of the `Component` object specified as a parameter
`public int getLayer(Component)`	Obtains the layer associated with the `Component` object parameter
`public static int getLayer(JComponent)`	Obtains the layer associated with the `Component` object parameter
`public static JLayeredPane getLayeredPaneAbove(Component)`	Obtains the first `JLayeredPane` object located up the hierarchy from the `Component` object parameter
`protected Integer getObjectForLayer(int)`	Used internally for layer management
`public int getPosition(Component)`	Obtains the relative position of the `Component` object parameter within its layer
`public int highestLayer()`	Obtains the highest layer currently in use, or 0 if there are none
`protected int insertIndexForLayer(int, int)`	Used internally to determine component positions
`public boolean isOptimizedDrawingEnabled()`	Returns true if this component has optimized its drawing by ensuring that none of its children overlap; will always return false, obviously
`public int lowestLayer()`	Obtains the lowest layer currently in use, or 0 if there are none
`public void moveToBack(Component)`	Moves the specified `Component` object to the back of its layer
`public void moveToFront(Component)`	Moves the specified `Component` object to the front of its layer
`public void paint(Graphics)`	Invoked when this component should draw itself into the specified `Graphics` object

continues

Fields/Methods	Description
`public static void putLayer(JComponent, int)`	Sets the layer property on the JComponent parameter
`public void remove(int)`	Removes the component specified by the `int` parameter from its container
`public void setLayer(Component, int)`	Sets the layer attribute for the specified Component object
`public void setLayer(Component, int, int)`	Sets the layer and position attributes for the specified Component object
`public void setPosition(Component, int)`	Sets the position attribute for the specified Component

CLASS ## `javax.swing.JList`

`public class JList extends JComponent implements Scrollable, Accessible`

The `JList` component allows a user to select one or (possibly) more items from a list. The data presented in the list is supplied by a `ListModel` object, and if scrolling is desired the `JList` object must be placed inside a `JScrollPane` object.

CLASS ## `javax.swing.JList`: Summary

Methods/Events	Description
`public void addListSelectionListener(ListSelectionListener)`	Adds a ListSelectionListener to the collection of listeners; a ListSelectionListener is notified every time the selected value changes
`public void addSelectionInterval(int, int)`	Changes the selection interval so that the new set of selected items is the union of the original selection interval and the selection interval formed by the two int parameters
`public void clearSelection()`	Alters the selection such that no items are currently selected

Methods/Events	*Description*
protected ListSelectionModel createSelectionModel()	Used internally to create a data model
public void ensureIndexIsVisible(int)	Ensures that the item identified by the int parameter is visible
protected void fireSelectionValueChanged (int, int, boolean)	Used internally to notify ListSelectionListeners
public AccessibleContext getAccessibleContext()	Obtains a reference to the AccessibleContext object
public int getAnchorSelectionIndex()	Obtains the most recent index (first parameter) used to modify the selection using either the addSelectionInterval() or setSelectionInterval() method
public Rectangle getCellBounds(int, int)	Assuming items exist at both parameters, the coordinates of their bounding box is returned
public ListCellRenderer getCellRenderer()	Obtains the ListCellRenderer object associated with this component
public int getFirstVisibleIndex()	Obtains the first visible index
public int getFixedCellHeight()	Obtains the fixed cell height property
public int getFixedCellWidth()	Obtains the fixed cell width property
public int getLastVisibleIndex()	Obtains the index of the last visible item
public int getLeadSelectionIndex()	Obtains the most recent index (second parameter) used to modify the selection using either the addSelectionInterval() or setSelectionInterval() methods
public int getMaxSelectionIndex()	Obtains the maximum cell index currently in use
public int getMinSelectionIndex()	Obtains the minimum cell index currently in use
public ListModel getModel()	Obtains the current data model
public Dimension getPreferredScrollableViewportSize()	Obtains the required dimensions to fully show the list

continues

Methods/Events	Description
`public Object getPrototypeCellValue()`	Obtains the prototype cell property
`public int getScrollableBlockIncrement (Rectangle, int, int)`	Obtains the desired block size to use when scrolling
`public boolean getScrollableTracksViewportHeight()`	Assuming the `JList` object is contained in a viewport, determines whether the height of the `JList` should change to match the changing height of the viewport
`public boolean getScrollableTracksViewportWidth()`	Assuming the `JList` object is contained in a viewport, determines whether the width of the `JList` should change to match the changing width of the viewport
`public int getScrollableUnitIncrement (Rectangle, int, int)`	Obtains the dimensions needed to fully show the next value while scrolling
`public int getSelectedIndex()`	Obtains the currently selected index
`public int[] getSelectedIndices()`	Obtains the currently selected indices
`public Object getSelectedValue()`	Obtains the currently selected value
`public Object[] getSelectedValues()`	Obtains all currently selected values
`public Color getSelectioinBackground()`	Obtains the background color of the selected cells
`public Color getSelectionForeground()`	Obtains the foreground color of the selected cells
`public int getSelectionMode()`	Obtains the selection mode
`public ListSelectionModel getSelectionModel()`	Obtains the active `ListSelectionModel` object
`public ListUI getUI()`	Obtains the current look and feel properties for this component
`public String getUIClassID()`	Obtains a logical name describing look and feel properties; always returns `ListUI`

Methods/Events	Description
public boolean getValueIsAdjusting(boolean)	Obtains the ValueIsAdjusting status
public int getVisibleRowCount()	Obtains the preferred number of rows that should be visible at a given point in time
public Point indexToLocation(int)	Obtains the physician location of the item at the specified index
public boolean isSelectedIndex(int)	Returns true if the selected index is currently selected
public Point isSelectionEmpty()	Returns true if there are currently no selected items
public int locationToIndex(Point)	Obtains the index of the item location at the specified coordinates
public void removeListSelectionListener (ListSelectionListener)	Removes a ListSelectionListener from the collection of listeners
public void removeSelectionInterval(int, int)	Sets the currently selected items to be the set difference of the currently selected items and the set created by the specified indices
public void setCellRenderer(ListCellRenderer)	Sets the ListCellRenderer object for this component
public void setFixedCellHeight(int)	Sets the fixed cell height property
public void setFixedCellWidth(int)	Sets the fixed cell width property
public void setListData(Object[])	Sets the elements that are to be displayed in the list; this method propagates the data change to the data model
public void setListData(Vector)	Sets the elements that are to be displayed in the list; this method propagates the data change to the data model
public void setModel(ListModel)	Sets the data model associated with this component
public void setPrototypeCellValue(Object)	Sets the fixed cell width and height properties based on the parameter

continues

Methods/Events	Description
public void setSelectedIndex(int)	Sets the currently selected item
public void setSelectedIndices(int[])	Sets the currently selected items
public void setSelectedValue(Object, boolean)	Sets the currently selected value to match that of the Object parameter; if the boolean parameter is set to true, the list will scroll to force the selected item into visibility
public void setSelectionInterval(int, int)	Sets the current selection interval
public void setSelectionModel(ListSelectionModel)	Sets the current selection model
public void setUI(ListUI)	Assigns pluggable look-and-feel parameters
public void setValueIsAdjusting(boolean)	Sets the ValueIsAdjusting parameter
public void setVisibleRowCount(int)	Sets the desired visible row count
public void updateUI()	Invoked to indicate a change in the pluggable look-and-feel

CLASS

javax.swing.JMenu

public class JMenu extends JMenuItem implements Accessible, MenuElement

The JMenu class is an implementation of a menu that can be used in a Swing environment. In most applications you will have a series of JMenu objects (File, Edit, and so on) that are all owned by a single JMenuBar object. The JMenuBar class is covered in the next section.

CLASS

javax.swing.Jmenu: Summary

Methods/Events	Description
public JMenuItem add(Action)	Adds the specified Action object to the bottom of the JMenu
public Component add(Component)	Adds the specified Component object to the bottom of the JMenu
public JMenuItem add(JMenuItem)	Adds the specified JMenuItem object to the bottom of the JMenu

Methods/Events	Description
`public JMenuItem add(String)`	Adds the specified `String` object to the bottom of the `JMenu`
`public void addMenuListener(MenuListener)`	Adds a `MenuListener` to the collection of listeners; a `MenuListener` is notified when a menu selection is made
`public void addSeparator()`	Adds a separator to the bottom of the `JMenu`
`protected PropertyChangeListener createActionChangeListener(JMenuItem)`	Used internally to create a new `PropertyChangeListener` object
`protected JMenu.WinListener createWinListener(JPopupMenu)`	Used internally to create a new `WinListener` object
`public void doClick(int pressTime)`	Causes a "click" programmatically
`protected void fireMenuCanceld()`	Used internally to send menu-canceled events
`protected void fireMenuDeselected()`	Used internally to send `MenuDeselected` events
`protected void fireMenuSelected()`	Used internally to send `MenuSelected` events
`public AccessibleContext getAccessibleContext()`	Obtains a reference to the `AccessibleContext` object
`public Component getComponent()`	Obtains a reference to the AWT component used to paint this item
`public int getDelay()`	Obtains the suggested delay (in milliseconds) that occurs between the time that the user selects a menu and the associated pop-up menu appears
`public JMenuItem getItem(int)`	Obtains the `JMenuItem` at the specified index
`public int getItemCount()`	Obtains a count of all items
`public Component getMenuComponent(int)`	Obtains the `Component` object at the specified index
`public int getMenuComponentCount()`	Obtains a count of all menu components

continues

Methods/Events	Description
`public Component[] getMenuComponents()`	Obtains an array containing all menu components
`public JPopupMenu getPopupMenu()`	Obtains the `JPopupMenu` object associated with this component
`public MenuElement[] getSubElements()`	Obtains an array of the sub-menu components
`public String getUIClassID()`	Obtains the logical name associated with the current look and feel; always returns `MenuUI`
`public JMenuItem insert(Action, int)`	Inserts the specified `Action` at the specified index
`public JMenuItem insert(JMenuItem, int)`	Inserts the specified `JMenuItem` at the specified index
`public void insert(String, int)`	Inserts the specified `String` at the specified index
`public void insertSeparator(int)`	Inserts a menu separator at the specified index
`public boolean isMenuComponent(Component)`	Returns true if the specified component is a menu component
`public boolean isPopupMenuVisible()`	Returns true if the pop-up menu is currently visible
`public boolean isSelected()`	Returns true if the menu is currently selected
`public boolean isTearOff()`	Returns true if the active `JMenu` object is a tear-off menu
`public boolean isTopLevelMenu()`	Returns true if the active `JMenu` object is a top-level menu
`public void menuSelectionChanged(boolean)`	Notifies if the menu selection changed
`public String paramString()`	Obtains a `String` object representing the state of the object; often used for debugging purposes
`protected void processKeyEvent(KeyEvent)`	Used internally for event handling
`public void remove(Component)`	Removes the specified `Component` object from the `JMenu`
`public void remove(int)`	Removes the object at the specified index from the `JMenu`

Methods/Events	Description
`public void remove(JMenuItem)`	Removes the specified `JMenuItem` object from the `JMenu`
`public void removeAll()`	Removes all objects from the `JMenu`
`public void removeMenuListener(MenuListener)`	Removes the specified `MenuListener` object from the `JMenu`
`public void setAccelerator(KeyStroke)`	Sets the keyboard accelerator associated with this menu
`public void setDelay(int)`	Sets the suggested delay (in milliseconds) that occurs between the time that the user selects a menu and the associated pop-up menu appears
`public void setMenuLocation(int, int)`	Sets the location of the `JMenu` object
`public void setModel(ButtonModel)`	Sets the data model
`public void setPopupMenuVisible(boolean)`	Sets whether the pop-up menu is currently visible
`public void setSelected(boolean)`	Sets whether the `JMenu` object is currently selected
`public void setUI(MenuUI)`	Sets the pluggable look-and-feel features for this component
`public void updateUI()`	Invoked to indicate a change in UI

CLASS   `javax.swing.JMenuBar`

`public class JMenuBar extends JComponent implements Accessible, MenuElement`

The `JMenuBar` class is used to represent a menu bar as owned by some container. A `JMenuBar` object will own a series of `JMenu` objects corresponding to each of the many menus (File, Edit, and so on) that a single application might sport.

CLASS   `javax.swing.JMenuBar`: **Summary**

Methods/Events	Description
`public JMenu add(JMenu)`	Adds the specified `JMenu` object to the `JMenu`
`public AccessibleContext getAccessibleContext()`	Obtains a reference to the `AccessibleContext` object

continues

A

JFC CLASS REFERENCE

Methods/Events	Description
public Component getComponent()	Implemented to meet MenuElement specification; returns this element
public Component getComponentAtIndex(int)	Obtains the Component object at the specified index
public int getComponentIndex(Component)	Obtains the index of the specified Component object
public JMenu getHelpMenu()	Obtains the JMenu object that is identified as a Help menu, or null if none exists; depending on the pluggable look-and-feel that is currently active, the Help menu may receive special treatment in the UI
public Insets getMargin()	Obtains the space separating the outline of the menu bar and its menus
public JMenu getMenu(int)	Obtains the JMenu object at the specified index
public int getMenuCount()	Obtains a count of all JMenu objects
public SingleSelectionModel getSelectionModel()	Obtains a reference to the selection model currently in use
public MenuElement[] getSubElements()	Obtains the collection of menu elements in this menu bar
public MenuBarUI getUI()	Obtains the current object responsible for the pluggable look-and-feel
public String getUIClassID()	Obtains a logical name describing the pluggable look-and-feel object; will always return MenuBarUI
public boolean isBorderPainted()	Returns true if the border has been painted
public boolean isManagingFocus()	Returns true if this component manages focus delegation for its children
public boolean isSelected()	Returns true if this component is currently selected
public void menuSelectionChanged(boolean)	Implemented to meet MenuElement specifications; does nothing
protected void paintBorder(Graphics)	Invoked to cause the border to be pained into the specified Graphics object

Methods/Events	Description
public void provessKeyEvent (KeyEvent, MenuElement[], MenuSelectionManager)	Used internally to process key events
public void processMouseEvent (MouseEvent, MenuElement[], MenuSelectionManager)	Used internally to process mouse events
public void setBorderPainted(boolean)	Sets whether the border has been painted
public void setHelpMenu(JMenu)	Associates a Help menu with the JMenuBar object
public void setMargin(Insets)	Sets the space between the outline of the menu bar and its menus
public void setSelected(Component)	Sets whether the specified Component object is currently selected
public void setSelectionModel(SingleSelectionModel)	Sets the selection model for this object
public void setUI(MenuBarUI)	Sets the pluggable look-and-feel object for this component
public void updateUI()	Invoked to indicate a pluggable look-and-feel change

CLASS   # `javax.swing.JMenuItem`

public class JMenuItem extends AbstractButton implements Accessible, MenuElement

A JMenuItem object represents an item in a JMenu. It can consist of any of the following properties: an icon identifier, a string identifier, or a keyboard shortcut.

CLASS   ## `javax.swing.JMenuItem`: Summary

Methods/Events	Description
public void addMenuDragMouseListener (MenuDragMouseListener)	Adds the specified listener to the appropriate group of listeners

continues

Methods/Events	Description
`public void addMenuKeyListener` `(MenuKeyListener)`	Adds the specified listener to the appropriate group of listeners
`protected void fireMenuDragMouseDragged` `(MenuDragMouseEvent)`	Used internally to notify appropriate listeners
`protected void fireMenuDragMouseEntered` `(MenuDragMouseEvent)`	Used internally to notify appropriate listeners
`protected void fireMenuDragMouseExited` `(MenuDragMouseEvent)`	Used internally to notify appropriate listeners
`protected void fireMenuDragMouseReleased` `(MenuDragMouseEvent)`	Used internally to notify appropriate listeners
`protected void fireMenuKeyPressed` `(MenuKeyEvent)`	Used internally to notify appropriate listeners
`protected void fireMenuKeyReleased` `(MenuKeyEvent)`	Used internally to notify appropriate listeners
`protected void fireMenuKeyTyped` `(MenuKeyEvent)`	Used internally to notify appropriate listeners
`public KeyStroke getAccelerator()`	Obtains the keyboard shortcut associated with this item
`public AccessibleContext` `getAccessibleContext()`	Obtains a reference to the `AccessibleContext` object
`public Component getComponent()`	Obtains the AWT component which draws this item
`public MenuElement[] getSubElements()`	Obtains an array of sub-menu components
`public String getUIClassID()`	Obtains a logical name describing the pluggable look and feel object; will always return `MenuItemUI`
`protected void init(String, Icon)`	Invoked internally to perform initialization
`public boolean isArmed()`	Returns true if the menu item is armed
`public void menuSelectioinChanged(boolean)`	Notification that the menu element's selected state has changed

Methods/Events	Description
public void processKeyEvent (KeyEvent, MenuElement[], MenuSelectionManager)	Processes key events
public void processMenuDragMouseEvent (MenuDrageMouseEvent)	Processes menu drag mouse events
public void processMouseEvent (MouseEvent, MenuElement[], MenuSelectionManager)	Processes mouse events
public void removeMenuDragMouseListener (MenuDragMouseListener)	Removes the specified listener from the group of listeners
public void removeMenuKeyListener (MenuKeyListener)	Removes the specified listener from the group of listeners
public void setAccelerator(KeyStroke)	Associates a keyboard shortcut with the menu item
public void setArmed(boolean)	Sets the armed status of this component
public void setEnabled(boolean)	Sets the enabled status of this component
public void setUI(MenuItemUI)	Sets the pluggable look-and-feel attributes of this object
public void updateUI()	Invoked to indicate a change in the pluggable look-and-feel properties

CLASS

javax.swing.JOptionPane

`public class JOptionPane extends JComponent implements Accessible`

During the pre-Swing UI dynasty, programmers had to either dynamically build a dialog's UI every time or build a collection of different dialog boxes. In fact, one of the first things I would do before beginning a project was collect the classes that act as message dialogs, Yes/No (confirmation) dialogs, and input dialogs. With the Swing dynasty, we can throw away the custom classes we wrote and use the JOptionPane class.

The JOptionPane class is used to create any number of different dialogs, including confirmation (Yes, No, Cancel), input, and message, as well as something called an option dialog, which is an amalgam of those three types.

CLASS **`javax.swing.JOptionPane`: Summary**

Fields/Constructors/Methods	Description
`public static final int CANCEL_OPTION`	Return value used to indicate that the Cancel button was chosen in a confirmation dialog
`public static final int CLOSED_OPTION`	Return value used if the user closes a window without clicking Yes/No/OK/Cancel
`public static final int DEFAULT_OPTION`	Used to indicate that look and feel properties should be supplied only by the `JOptionPane` object
`public static final int ERROR_MESSAGE`	Used by error messages
`public static final String ICON_PROPERTY`	Indicates the name of the icon; this is a bound property
`public static final int INFORMATION_MESSAGE`	Used by information messages
`public static final String INITIAL_SELECTION_VALUE_PROPERTY`	Indicates the `initialSelectionValue` variable; this property is bound
`public static final String INITIAL_VALUE_PROPERTY`	Indicates the `initialValue` variable; this property is bound
`protected transient Object initialSelectionValue`	Initial value used with the `initialValue` field
`protected transient Object initialValue`	Value that is initially selected in option dialogs will be painted opaque
`protected transient Object message`	Message displayed by the dialog
`public static final String MESSAGE_PROPERTY`	Indicates the message variable; this property is bound
`public static final String MESSAGE_TYPE_PROPERTY`	Indicates the message type; this property is bound
`protected int messageType`	The message type

Fields/Constructors/Methods	*Description*
`public static final int NO_OPTION`	Return value used to indicate that no option was selected in a dialog
`public static final int OK_CANCEL_OPTION`	Type used to indicate that a confirmation dialog is to be formed
`public static final int OK_OPTION`	Return value used to indicate that the OK button was clicked
`public static final String OPTION_TYPE_PROPERTY`	Type used to indicate the `optionType` variable; this property is bound
`protected transient Object[] options`	Array of options displayed to the user
`public static final String OPTIONS_PROPERTY`	Used to indicate the `options` variable; this property is bound
`protected int optionType`	The current option type; value will be one of the following: `DEFAULT_OPTION`, `YES_NO_OPTION`, `YES_NO_CANCEL_OPTION` or `OK_CANCEL_OPTION`
`public static final int PLAIN_MESSAGE`	Used to indicate that no icon is associated with the string
`public static final int QUESTION_MESSAGE`	Used to indicate a question message
`public static final String SELECTION_VALUES_PROPERTY`	Indicates the `selectionValues` variable; this property is bound
`protected transient Object[] selectionValues`	Array of values the user can choose from
`protected static Frame sharedFrame`	Frame used by the static methods that must present a UI
`public static final Object UNITIALIZED_VALUE`	Used to indicate that the user has yet to select a value
`protected transient Object value`	Currently selected value
`public static final String VALUE_PROPERTY`	Used to indicate the `value` variable; this property is bound
`public static final String WANTS_INPUT_PROPERTY`	Used to indicate the `wantsInput` variable; this property is bound

continues

A

Fields/Constructors/Methods	Description
`protected boolean wantsInput`	If true, the user will be prompted to input data
`public static final int WARNING_MESSAGE`	Used to indicate a warning message
`public static final int YES_NO_CANCEL_OPTION`	Used to indicate that a confirmation dialog with Yes/No/Cancel buttons should be created
`public static final int YES_NO_OPTION`	Used to indicate that a confirmation dialog with Yes/No buttons should be created
`public static final int YES_OPTION`	Return value used to indicate that the Yes button was clicked
`public JOptionPane()`	Creates a new `JOptionPane` dialog with a test message
`public JOptionPane(Object)`	Creates a new `JOptionPane` dialog using the specified object to populate the screen; if this object is a component, it will be added directly to the screen; if it is a icon or string, it will be placed in a `JLabel` object and added to the screen; finally, if the object is an array, each element will be tested as specified above
`public JOptionPane(Object, int)`	Creates a new `JOptionPane` object using the specified message and message type; the message is added to the screen according to the rules outlined in the `JOptionPane(Object)` constructor
`public JOptionPane(Object, int, int)`	Creates a new `JOptionPane` object using the specified message, message type, and option type; the message is added to the screen according to the rules outlined in the `JOptionPane(Object)` constructor

Fields/Constructors/Methods	Description
`public JOptionPane(Object, int, int, Icon)`	Creates a new `JOptionPane` object using the specified message, icon message type, and option type; the message is added to the screen according to the rules outlined in the `JOptionPane(Object)` constructor
`public JOptionPane` `(Object, int, int, Icon, Object[])`	Creates a new `JOptionPane` object using the specified message, icon message type, option type, and choice options; the message is added to the screen according to the rules outlined in the `JOptionPane(Object)` constructor

`public JOptionPane`
`(Object, int, int, Icon,`
`Object[], Object)`
	Creates a new `JOptionPane` object using the specified message, icon message type, option type, choice options, and initial value; the message is added to the screen according to the rules outlined in the `JOptionPane(Object)` constructor

`public JDialog` `createDialog(Component, String)`	Creates a new `JDialog` object with the specified owner and title
`public JInternalFrame` `createInternalFrame(Component, String)`	Creates a new `JInternalFrame` object with the specified owner and title

continues

A

JFC CLASS REFERENCE

Fields/Constructors/Methods	Description
Methods	
public AccessibleContext getAccessibleContext()	Obtains a reference to the AccessibleContext object
public static JDesktopPane getDesktopPaneForComponent(Component)	Returns the JDesktopPane object associated with the Component parameter, assuming one exists
public static Frame getFrameForComponent(Component)	Returns the Frame object associated with the Component parameter, assuming one exists
public Icon getIcon()	Obtains the Icon object associated with this object
public Object getInitialSelectionValue()	Obtains the initially selected value for this component
public Object getInitialValue()	Obtains the initial value for this component
public Object getInputValue()	Obtains the value input by the user
public int getMaxCharactersPerLineCount()	Obtains the maximum number of characters that can be input in a given line
public Object getMessage()	Obtains the message on display in this dialog
public int getMessageType()	Obtains the message type
public Object[] getOptions()	Obtains the choices that the user can select from
public int getOptionType()	Obtains the types of options that can be displayed
public static Frame getRootFrame()	Used by static methods to obtain a root frame
public Object[] getSelectionValues()	Obtains the selection values
public OptionPaneUI getUI()	Obtains the object that specifies look and feel properties
public String getUIClassID()	Obtains a logical name for the current look and feel object; will always return OptionPaneUI

Fields/Constructors/Methods	Description
	Methods
`public Object getValue()`	Obtains the value selected by the user
`public boolean getWantsInput()`	Returns true if this dialog is to prompt the user to enter data
`public void selectInitialValue()`	Selects the initial value for this component
`public void setIcon(Icon)`	Adds a display icon for this object
`public void setInitialSelectionValue(Object)`	Sets the initial selection value for this component
`public void setInitialValue(Object)`	Sets the initial value for this component
`public void setInputValue(Object)`	Sets the value input by the user
`public void setMessage(Object)`	Sets the message on display; see the constructor documentation for the rules on how this object is handled by the UI
`public void setMessageType(int)`	Sets the message type for this component
`public void setOptions(Object[])`	Sets the options the user can choose from
`public void setOptionType(int)`	Sets the option type for this component
`public static void setRootFrame(Frame)`	Sets the root frame for this component
`public void setSelectionValues(Object[])`	Sets the values the user has to select from
`public void setUI(OptionPaneUI)`	Sets the object responsible for the look and feel properties
`public void setValue(Object)`	Sets the value chosen by the user
`public void setWantsInput(boolean)`	Sets whether this dialog is to receive input from the user
`public static int showConfirmDialog(Component, Object)`	Shows a confirmation dialog constructed using the parameters, and returns the value chosen by the user

continues

Fields/Constructors/Methods	Description
Methods	

`public static int`
`showConfirmDialog`
`(Component, Object, String)`
	Shows a confirmation dialog constructed using the parameters, and returns the value chosen by the user

`public static int showConfirmDialog` `(Component, Object, String, int)`	Shows a confirmation dialog constructed using the parameters, and returns the value chosen by the user
`public static int showConfirmDialog` `(Component, Object, String, int, int)`	Shows a confirmation dialog constructed using the parameters, and returns the value chosen by the user
`public static int showConfirmDialog` `(Component, Object, String, int, int, Icon)`	Shows a confirmation dialog constructed using the parameters, and returns the value chosen by the user
`public static String showInputDialog` `(Component, Object)`	Shows an input dialog constructed using the parameters, and returns the value entered by the user
`public static String showInputDialog` `(Component, Object, String, int)`	Shows an input dialog constructed using the parameters, and returns the value entered by the user

`public static String showInputDialog`
`(Component, Object, String, int,`
`Icon, Object[],Object)`
	Shows an input dialog constructed using the parameters, and returns the value entered by the user

`public static String showInputDialog(Object)`	Shows an input dialog constructed using the parameters to build the UI; the return value is the value entered by the user

Fields/Constructors/Methods	Description
Methods	
`public static int showInternalConfirmDialog` `(Component, Object)`	Displays an internal confirm dialog using the parameters to build the UI; the return value is the choice as selected by the user
`public static int showInternalConfirmDialog` `(Component, Object, String, int)`	Displays an internal confirm dialog using the parameters to build the UI; the return value is the choice as selected by the user
`public static int showInternalConfirmDialog` `(Component, Object, String, int, int)`	Displays an internal confirm dialog using the parameters to build the UI; the return value is the choice as selected by the user
`public static int showInternalConfirmDialog` `(Component, Object, String, int, int, Icon)`	Displays an internal confirm dialog using the parameters to build the UI; the return value is the choice as selected by the user
`public static String showInternalInputDialog` `(Component, Object)`	Shows an internal input dialog constructed using the parameters to build the UI; the return value is the value entered by the user
`public static String showInternalInputDialog` `(Component, Object, String, int)`	Shows an input dialog constructed using the parameters to build the UI; the return value is the value entered by the user

continues

Fields/Constructors/Methods	Description
Methods	
`public static String showInternalInputDialog (Component, Object, String, int, Icon,Object[],Object)`	Shows an input dialog constructed using the parameters to build the UI; the return value is the value entered by the user
`public static void showInternalMessageDialog (Component, Object)`	Shows an internal message dialog with the UI built using the parameters
`public static void showInternalMessageDialog (Component, Object, String, int)`	Shows an internal message dialog with the UI built using the parameters
`public static void showInternalMessageDialog (Component, Object, String, int, Icon)`	Shows an internal message dialog with the UI built using the parameters
`public static int showInternalOptionDialog (Component, Object, String, int, int, Icon, Object[], Object)`	Shows an internal option dialog with the UI built using the parameters; the return value is the value as selected by the user
`public static void showMessageDialog(Component, Object)`	Shows a message dialog with the UI built using the parameters
`public static void showMessageDialog (Component, Object, String, int)`	Shows a message dialog with the UI built using the parameters
`public static void showMessageDialog (Component, Object, String, int, Icon)`	Shows a message dialog with the UI built using the parameters
`public static int showOptionDialog (Component, Object, String, int, int, Icon, Object[], Object)`	Shows an option dialog with the UI built using the parameters; the return value is the value as selected by the user
`public static void updateUI()`	Invoked to indicate a change to the pluggable look-and-feel features of the UI

CLASS # javax.swing.JPanel

`public class JPanel extends JComponent implements Accessible`

The `JPanel` class is a simple container that can be used to build a variety of screens. In many situations, you will build a series of `JPanel` objects that all house different portions of a screen, and then add each of those objects to a larger parent container.

CLASS ## javax.swing.JPanel: Summary

Methods/Events	Description
`public AccessibleContext getAccessibleContext()`	Obtains a reference to the `AccessibleContext` object
`public string getUIClassID()`	Obtains a string that specifies the name of the class that renders the panel
`public void updateUI()`	Invoked to indicate a change in the pluggable look and feel properties

CLASS # javax.swing.JPasswordField

`public class JPasswordField extends JTextField`

With most applications, fields in which one enters confidential data will not display the actual text being entered. For example, when you enter your PIN number at an ATM machine, a series of asterisks will usually appear instead of your actual PIN number. The `JPasswordField` class is a utility class that shows an "echo" character instead of the actual text entered into it.

CLASS ## javax.swing.JPasswordField: Summary

Methods/Events	Description
`public void copy()`	Copies the currently selected range in the text model to the clipboard without removing the contents
`public void cut()`	Cuts the currently selected range in the text model to the clipboard removing the contents
`public boolean echoCharIsSet()`	Returns true if the echo character for this component has been set

continues

Methods/Events	Description
public AccessibleContext getAccessibleContext()	Obtains a reference to the AccessibleContext object
public char getEchoChar()	Obtains the echo character for this component
public char[] getPassword()	Obtains the text contained in the component
public String getText()	Obtains the text contained in the component (deprecated, use getPassword())
public String getUIClassID()	Obtains a logical name describing the UI; always returns PasswordFieldUI
public void setEchoChar(char)	Sets the echo character for this component

CLASS

javax.swing.JPopupMenu

public class JPopupMenu extends JComponent implements Accessible, MenuElement

The JPopupMenu class allows a user to make a menu dynamically appear on the screen. In a text editor application, for example, a user could right-click on some highlighted text and a menu offering Cut, Copy, Paste choices would appear.

CLASS

javax.swing.JPopupMenu: Summary

Methods/Events	Description
public JMenuItem add(Action)	Adds the specified Action to the component
public JMenuItem add(String)	Adds the specified text to the component
public JMenuItem add(JMenuItem)	Adds the specified JMenuItem to the component
public void addPopupMenuListener (PopupMenuListener)	Adds the specified listener to the appropriate group of listeners

Methods/Events	Description
`public void addSeparator()`	Adds a separator to the end of the menu
`protected PropertyChangeListener createActionChangeListener(JMenuItem)`	Obtains a specific `PropertyChangeListener` for the specified menu item
`protected void firePopupMenuCanceled()`	Used internally for handling pop-up menu events
`protected void firePopupMenuWillBecomeInvisible()`	Used internally for handling pop-up menu events
`protected void firePopupMenuWillBecomeVisible()`	Used internally for handling pop-up menu events
`public AccessibleContext getAccessibleContext()`	Obtains a reference to the `AccessibleContext` object
`public Component getComponent()`	Obtains a reference to the AWT component responsible for drawing this item
`public Component getComponentAtIndex(int)`	Obtains the component at the specified index
`public int etComponentIndex(Component)`	Obtains the index of the specified component
`public static boolean getDefaultLightWeightPopupEnabled()`	Obtains the default value for the `LightWeightPopupEnabled` property
`public Component getInvoker()`	Obtains the object that spawned this menu
`public String getLabel()`	Obtains the pop-up's label
`public Insets getMargin()`	Obtains the margin between the border of the pop-up menu and its parent container
`public SingleSelectionModel getSelectionModel()`	Obtains the selection model for this component
`public PopupMenuUI getUI()`	Obtains the active pluggable look-and-feel properties

continues

Methods/Events	Description
`public String getUIClassID()`	Obtains a logical description of the UI; always returns `PopupMenuUI`
`public void insert(Action, int)`	Inserts the specified `Action` at the specified index
`public void insert(Component, int)`	Inserts the specified `Component` at the specified index
`public boolean isBorderPainted()`	Returns true if the border should be painted
`public boolean isLightWeightPopupEnabled()`	Returns true if lightweight pop-ups are in use
`public boolean isVisible()`	Returns true if this component is currently visible
`public void pack()`	Causes this component to take up only the space required by its children
`protected void paintBorder(protected void) paintBorder(Graphics)`	Invoked when the border should be painted into the specified `Graphics` object
`public void processKeyEvent(KeyEvent, MenuElement[], MenuSelectionManager)`	Processes key events
`public void processMouseEvent(MouseEvent, MenuElement[], MenuSelectionManager)`	Processes mouse events
`public void removePopupMenuListener (PopupMenuListener)`	Removes the specified listener from the group of listeners
`public void setBorderPainted(boolean)`	Sets whether the border should be painted
`public void setInvoker(Component)`	Sets the component responsible for spawning this component
`public void setLabel(String label)`	Sets the label of the pop-up
`public static void setDefaultLightWeightPopupEnabled(boolean)`	Set whether or not lightweight pop-ups are used

Methods/Events	Description
`public void setLocation(int, int)`	Sets the physical location of this component
`public void setPopupSize(Dimension)`	Sets the physical size of this component
`public void setPopupSize(int, int)`	Sets the physical size of this component
`public void setSelected(Component)`	Sets the active selection
`public void setSelectionModel(SingleSelectionModel)`	Sets the selection model
`public void setUI(PopupMenuUI)`	Sets the active pluggable look-and-feel properties
`public void setVisible(boolean)`	Sets the current visibility
`public void show(Component, int, int)`	Displays the pop-up menu with the specified parent at the specified location
`public void updateUI()`	Invoked to indicate a change in pluggable look-and-feel properties

CLASS ## `javax.swing.JProgressBar`

`public class JProgressBar extends JComponent implements SwingConstants, Accessible`

The `JProgressBar` class is used to visually report on the progress of an action. For example, when rendering a highly detailed screen, a progress bar might appear to report on the status of the rendering.

CLASS ## `javax.swing.JProgressBar`: Summary

Methods/Events	Description
`public void addChangeListener(ChangeListener)`	Adds a `ChangeListener` to the collection of listeners; a `ChangeListener` is notified whenever the state of the component changes

continues

Methods/Events	Description
protected ChangeListener createChangeListener()	Used internally for event management
protected void fireStateChanged()	Used internally for event management
public AccessibleContext getAccessibleContext()	Obtains a reference to the AccessibleContext object
public int getMaximum()	Obtains the maximum value for this component
public int getMinimum()	Obtains the minimum value for this component
public BoundedRangeModel getModel()	Sets the active model for this component
public int getOrientation()	Obtains the orientation of this component; return value is either JProgressBar.HORIZONTAL or JProgressBar.VERTICAL
public double getPercentComplete()	Obtains the percentage complete for the progress bar
public String getString()	Obtains the current progress string
public ProgressBarUI getUI()	Obtains the active pluggable look and feel properties
public String getUIClassID()	Obtains a logical name for the UI; always returns ProgressBarUI
public int getValue()	Obtains the current value of this component
public boolean isBorderPainted()	Returns true if the border should be painted for this component
protected void paintBorder(protected void paintBorder(Graphics)	Invoked when this component should paint its border into the specified Graphics object
public void removeChangeListener(ChangeListener)	Removes the specified ChangeListener from the collection of listeners
public void setBorderPainted(boolean)	Sets whether the border should be painted
public void setMaximum(int)	Sets the maximum value for this component

Methods/Events	Description
public void setMinimum(int)	Sets the minimum value for this component
public void setModel(BoundedRangeModel)	Sets the model for this component
public void setOrientation(int)	Sets the current orientation of this component (either JProgressBar. HORIZONTAL or JProgressBar. VERTICAL)
public void setString(String s)	Sets the value of the progress string
public void setUI(ProgressBarUI)	Sets the current pluggable look-and-feel properties for this component
public void setValue(int)	Sets the current value of this component
public void updateUI()	Invoked to indicate a change in pluggable look-and-feel properties

CLASS

javax.swing.JRadioButton

public class JRadioButton extends JToggleButton implements Accessible

The JRadioButton class is used when a series of choices are to be presented and only one may be selected. A radio button is not much use shown alone, and groups of radio buttons are logically held together using a ButtonGroup object.

CLASS

javax.swing.JRadioButton: Summary

Methods/Events	Description
public AccessibleContext getAccessibleContext()	Obtains a reference to the AccessibleContext object
public String getUIClassID()	Returns a logical description of the UI; always returns RadioButtonUI
public void updateUI()	Invoked to indicate a change in pluggable look-and-feel features

javax.swing.JRadioButton: Example

The JRadioButton is used to represent a binary state radio button.

```java
import java.awt.*;
import java.awt.event.*;
import javax.swing.*;
import javax.swing.*;
import javax.swing.event.*;

public class JRadioButtonDemo extends JApplet {

    JRadioButton    jradOption1;
    JRadioButton    jradOption2;
    ButtonGroup     group;

    public void init() {
        resize(400, 400);

        // Create a new 2x1 Grid Layout object with
        // a 10 pixel gaps between all components.
        GridLayout gridLayout = new GridLayout(1,2,10,10);

        // Set the layout.
        getContentPane().setLayout(gridLayout);

        //create components to add to layout
        jradOption1 = new JRadioButton
        ("Radio Button  1 is selected");
        jradOption1.setSelected(true);
        jradOption2 = new JRadioButton
        ("Radio Button  2 is not selected");
        group = new ButtonGroup();

        // Add components.
        getContentPane().add(jradOption1);
        getContentPane().add(jradOption2);

        //add radio buttons to button group
        group.add(jradOption1);
        group.add(jradOption2);

        Action action = new Action();
        jradOption1.addActionListener(action);
        jradOption2.addActionListener(action);
    }

    class Action implements java.awt.event.ActionListener {
        public final void actionPerformed(ActionEvent ae) {
            Object source = ae.getSource();
```

```
        if (source == jradOption1) {
            jradOption1.setText
            ("Radio Button  1 is selected");
            jradOption2.setText
            ("Radio Button  2 is not selected");
}

        else if (source == jradOption2) {
            jradOption2.setText
            ("Radio Button  2 is selected");
            jradOption1.setText
            ("Radio Button  1 is not selected");
}
    }
  }

}
```

CLASS   # javax.swing.JRadioButtonMenuItem

`public class JRadioButtonMenuItem extends JMenuItem implements Accessible`

The `JRadioButtonMenuItem` allows a radio button to be included as a menu item.

CLASS   ## javax.swing.JRadioButtonMenuItem: Summary

Methods/Events	Description
public AccessibleContext getAccessibleContext()	Obtains a reference to the AccessibleContext object
public String getUIClassID()	Obtains a logical description of the UI; always returns RadioButtonMenuItemUI
protected void init(String, Icon)	Used internally for initialization tasks
public void requestFocus()	Requests that focus be given to this object
public void setAction(Action)	Sets the Action object associated with this component
public void updateUI()	Invoked to indicate a change in plug-gable look-and-feel attributes

CLASS   # javax.swing.JRootPane

`public class JRootPane extends JComponent implements Accessible`

The `JRootPane` class is a container that always contains the following panes: GlassPane, ContentPane, and LayeredPane. The GlassPane is the first child owned by this

A

JFC CLASS
REFERENCE

component and can be optionally shown above all other components. The `ContentPane` is the area in which all additional child components should be added. For example, never add a child through a call like `JRootPane.add(foo)`, but instead use `JRootPane.getContentPane().add(foo)`. The `LayeredPane` can be used if component layering is needed.

`javax.swing.JRootPane`: Summary

Methods/Events	Description
`protected void addImpl(Component, Object, int)`	Adds the specified component to the container at the specified index
`public void addNotify()`	Registers root pane with the system event queue
`protected Container createContentPane()`	Used internally to create the content pane
`protected Component createGlassPane()`	Used internally to create the glass pane
`protected JLayeredPane createLayeredPane()`	Used internally to create the layered pane
`protected LayoutManager createRootLayout()`	Used internally to create the root layout manager
`public AccessibleContext getAccessibleContext()`	Obtains a reference to the `AccessibleContext` object
`public Container getContentPane()`	Obtains a reference to the content pane
`public JButton getDefaultButton()`	Obtains the default button for this root pane, or null if none exists
`public Component getGlassPane()`	Obtains a reference to the glass pane
`public Component getJMenuBar()`	Obtains a reference to the `JMenuBar` object
`public JLayeredPane getLayeredPane()`	Obtains a reference to the layered pane
`public JMenuBar getMenuBar()`	Obtains a reference to the `JMenuBar` object; deprecated, use `getJMenuBar`
`public boolean isValidateRoot()`	Returns true if validations on this component will cause all children to be validated as well
`public void setContentPane(Container)`	Sets the content pane

Methods/Events	Description
`public void setDefaultButton(JButton)`	Sets the default button for the root pane
`public void setGlassPane(Component)`	Sets the glass pane
`public setJMenuBar(JMenuBar)`	Associates the specified menu bar with this pane
`public void setLayeredPane(JLayeredPane)`	Sets the layered pane
`public void setMenuBar(JMenuBar)`	Sets the menu bar; deprecated, use `setJMenuBar(JMenuBar)`

CLASS | `javax.swing.JScrollBar`

`public class JScrollBar extends JComponent implements Adjustable, Accessible`

The `JScrollBar` class is used to model a physical scrollbar. In most situations, you will not deal directly with this class but instead will work with a class like `JScrollPane`.

CLASS | `javax.swing.JScrollBar`: **Summary**

Methods/Events	Description
`public void addAdjustmentListener (AdjustmentListener)`	Adds an `AdjustmentListener` to the collection of listeners; an `AdjustmentListener` is notified every time the scrollbar value changes
`protected void fireAdjustmentValueChanged (AdjustmentEvent)`	Used internally for event management
`public AccessibleContext getAccessibleContext()`	Obtains a reference to the `AccessibleContext` object
`public int getBlockIncrement()`	Obtains the delta for which each movement of the scrollbar is responsible
`public int getBlockIncrement(int)`	Obtains the delta for which each movement of a scrollbar with the specified direction is responsible

continues

Methods/Events	Description
`public int getMaximum()`	Obtains the maximum value this component can represent
`public Dimension getMaximumSize()`	Obtains the maximum size of this object
`public int getMinimum()`	Obtains the minimum value this component can represent
`public Dimension getMinimumSize()`	Obtains the minimum size this component can take up
`public BoundedRangeModel getModel()`	Obtains the value for this component
`public int getOrientation()`	Obtains the orientation of this component
`public ScrollBarUI getUI()`	Obtains the active pluggable look-and-feel features for this component
`public String getUIClassID()`	Obtains a logical description of the active UI; always returns `ScrollBarUI`
`public int getUnitIncrement()`	Obtains the increment value associated with this scrollbar
`public int getUnitIncrement(int)`	Obtains the increment value associated with a scrollbar that has the specified orientation
`public int getValue()`	Obtains the current value of this component
`public boolean getValueIsAdjusting()`	Returns true if an adjustment is in progress
`public int getVisibleAmount()`	Obtains the active visible amount
`public void removeAdjustmentListener (AdjustmentListener)`	Removes the specified `AdjustmentListener` from the collection of listeners
`public void setBlockIncrement(int)`	Sets the block increment associated with this object
`public void setEnabled(boolean)`	Sets the enabled status of this component
`public void setMaximum(int)`	Sets the maximum value this component can take on
`public void setMinimum(int)`	Sets the minimum value this component can take on

Methods/Events	Description
`public void setModel(BoundedRangeModel)`	Set the model associated with this component
`public void setOrientation(int)`	Sets the orientation of this component
`public void setUnitIncrement(int)`	Sets the unit increment of this component
`public void setValue(int)`	Sets the current value being displayed with this component
`public void setValueIsAdjusting(boolean)`	Sets the active `ValueIsAdjusting` status
`public void setValues(int, int, int, int)`	Sets the specified value properties
`public void setVisibleAmount(int)`	Sets the active visible amount
`public void updateUI()`	Invoked to indicate a change in pluggable look and feel features

CLASS   # javax.swing.JScrollPane

`public class JScrollPane extends JComponent implements ScrollPaneConstants, Accessible`

The `JScrollPane` component is a container that allows scrolling over a viewport. That portion of the view not currently visible will be placed offscreen, and the user can scroll to see it.

CLASS   ## javax.swing.JScrollPane: Summary

Methods/Events	Description
`public JScrollBar createHorizontalScrollBar()`	Used internally to build the UI
`public JScrollBar createVerticalScrollBar()`	Used internally to build the UI
`protected JViewport createViewport()`	Obtains a reference to the `JViewport` object
`public AccessibleContext getAccessibleContext()`	Obtains a reference to the `AccessibleContext` object
`public JViewport getColumnHeader()`	Obtains the column header
`public Component getCorner(String)`	Obtains the component with the specified key

continues

Methods/Events	Description
public JScrollBar getHorizontalScrollBar()	Obtains the horizontal scrollbar
public int getHorizontalScrollBarPolicy()	
public JViewport getRowHeader()	Obtains the row header
public ScrollPaneUI getUI()	Obtains the active pluggable look-and-feel properties
public String getUIClassID()	Obtains a logical description of the UI; always returns ScrollPaneUI
public JScrollBar getVerticalScrollBar()	Obtains the vertical scrollbar
public int getVerticalScrollBarPolicy()	Obtains the vertical scrollbar's policy
public JViewport getViewport()	Obtains the viewport associated with this object
public Border getViewportBorder()	Obtains the viewport border
public boolean isValidateRoot()	Returns true if validations on this component will cause all children to be validated as well
public void setColumnHeader(JViewport)	Sets the current column header
public void setColumnHeaderView(Component)	Sets the current column header view
public void setCorner(String, Component)	Sets the corner with the specified name
public void setHorizontalScrollBar(JScrollBar)	Set the scrollbar which controls horizontal scrolling
public void setLayout(LayoutManager)	Sets the layout manager for this container
public void setHorizontalScrollBarPolicy(int)	Sets the horizontal scrollbar's scroll policy
public void setRowHeader(JViewport)	Sets the row header
public void setRowHeaderView(Component)	Sets the row header view
public void setUI(ScrollPaneUI)	Sets the active pluggable look-and-feel properties
public void setVerticalScrollBar(JScrollBar)	Set the scrollbar which controls vertical scrolling
public void setVerticalScrollBarPolicy(int)	Sets the vertical scrollbar scroll policy
public void setViewport(JViewport)	Sets the active viewport

Methods/Events	Description
`public void setViewportBorder(Border)`	Sets the viewport border
`public void setViewportView(Component)`	Sets the viewport view
`public void updateUI()`	Invoked to indicate a change in pluggable look and feel properties

CLASS ## javax.swing.JSeparator

`public class JSeparator extends JComponent implements SwingConstants, Accessible`

The `JSeparator` class is a Swing implementation of a menu separator.

CLASS ## javax.swing.JSeparator: Summary

Methods/Events	Description
`public AccessibleContext getAccessibleContext()`	Obtains a reference to the `AccessibleContext` object
`public int getOrientation()`	Obtains the orientation of the separator
`public SeparatorUI getUI()`	Obtains the active pluggable look-and-feel properties
`public String getUIClassID()`	Obtains a logical description of the active UI; always returns `SeparatorUI`
`public void setOrientation(int)`	Sets the orientation of the component
`public void setUI(SeparatorUI)`	Sets the active pluggable look-and-feel properties
`public void updateUI()`	Invoked to indicate a change in pluggable look-and-feel properties

CLASS ## javax.swing.JSlider

`public class JSlider extends JComponent implements SwingConstants, Accessible`

The `JSlider` class represents a slider control. It has a minimum and maximum value, and also *n* number of ticks between each major number. Sliders are often used when a user can choose between a wide range of bounded values (for example, the amount of red, green, or blue in a color picker).

`javax.swing.JSlider`: **Summary**

Methods/Events	Description
`public void addChangeListener(ChangeListener)`	Adds a `ChangeListener` to the collection of listeners; a `ChangeListener` is notified whenever the value of the slider changes
`protected ChangeListener createChangeListener()`	Used internally for event management
`public Hashtable createStandardLables (int, int)`	Makes a hashtable of text labels starting with specified increments, starting from the specified position
`public Hashtable createStandardLables(int)`	Makes a hashtable of text labels starting with specified increments
`protected void fireStateChanged()`	Used internally for event management
`public AccessibleContext getAccessibleContext()`	Obtains a reference to the `AccessibleContext` object
`public int getExtent()`	Obtains the extent for this component
`public boolean getInverted()`	Returns true if the scale of the slider is inverted
`public Dictionary getLabelTable()`	Obtains a dictionary of labels to draw at different values
`public int getMajorTickSpacing()`	Obtains the major tick spacing for this component
`public int getMaximum()`	Obtains the maximum value displayed by this component
`public int getMinimum()`	Obtains the minimum value displayed by this component
`public int getMinorTickSpacing()`	Obtains the minor tick spacing displayed by this component

Methods/Events	Description
`public BoundedRangeModel getModel()`	Obtains the model for this component
`public int getOrientation()`	Obtains the orientation of this component
`public boolean getPaintLabels()`	Returns true if labels should be painted
`public boolean getPaintTicks()`	Returns true if ticks should be painted
`public boolean getPaintTrack()`	Returns true if the track should be painted
`public boolean getSnapToTicks()`	Returns true if the knob should only move in discreet increments
`public SliderUI getUI()`	Obtains the active pluggable look and feel attributes
`public String getUIClassID()`	Obtains a logical description of this component; always returns `SliderUI`
`public int getValue()`	Obtains the current value displayed by this component
`public boolean getValueIsAdjusting()`	Returns true if this component is currently adjusting
`public void removeChangeListener(ChangeListener)`	Removes the specified `ChangeListener` from the collection of listeners
`public void setExtent(int)`	Sets the extent for this component
`public void setInverted(boolean)`	Sets whether or not to invert the slider's scale
`public void setMajorTickSpacing(int)`	Sets the major tick spacing for this component
`public void setMaximum(int)`	Sets the maximum value this component can take on
`public void setMinimum(int)`	Sets the minimum value this component can take on
`public void setMinorTickSpacing(int)`	Sets the minor tick spacing
`public void setModel(BoundedRangeModel)`	Sets the model for this component
`public void setOrientation(int)`	Sets the orientation of this component
`public void setPaintLabels(boolean)`	Sets whether this component should paint labels

continues

Methods/Events	Description
`public void setPaintTicks(boolean)`	Sets whether this component should paint ticks
`public void setPainttrack(boolean)`	Sets whether this component should paint a track
`public void setSnapToTicks(boolean)`	Sets whether this component should only allow discreet values
`public void setUI(SliderUI)`	Sets the active pluggable look-and-feel attributes for this component
`public void setValue(int)`	Sets the active display value of this component
`public void setValueIsAdjusting(boolean)`	Sets whether the value is currently adjusting
`public String toString()`	Obtains a `String` object that represents the current state of this object
`protected void updateLabelUIs()`	Used internally to update the `Label` UI's
`public void updateUI()`	Invoked to indicate a change in pluggable look-and-feel features

CLASS

javax.swing.JSplitPane

`public class JSplitPane extends JComponent implements Accessible`

The `JSplitPane` class is used to split a single container into exactly two parts, each of which can independently house a series of components. The dividing line between the two containers can be moved by the user or can be done programmatically.

CLASS

javax.swing.JSplitPane: Summary

Fields/Methods	Description
`public static String BOTTOM`	Used to add a component below existing components
`public static final String CONTINUOUS_LAYOUT_PROPERTY`	Property associated with `continuousLayout`; this property is bound
`protected boolean continuousLayout`	True if views are actively redisplayed during a resize action

Fields/Methods	Description
public static String DIVIDER	Represents the component that acts as the physical divider
public static final String DIVIDER_SIZE_PROPERTY	Property associated with dividerSize; this property is bound
protected int dividerSize	Indicates the size of the divider
public static final int HORIZONTAL_SPLIT	Indicates that the divider should be horizontal
public static String LAST_DIVIDER_LOCATION_PROPERTY	Property associated with lastDividerLocation; this property is bound
protected int lastDividerLocation	Location of the split pane prior to the last move
public static String LEFT	Used to add a component to the left of the existing components
protected Component leftComponent	Depending on the orientation of the split, this represents the component in the top or left position
public static final String ONE_TOUCH_EXPANDABLE_PROPERTY	Property associated with oneTouchExpandable; this property is bound
protected boolean oneTouchExpandable	Indicates whether there is a widget to expand/collapse the split
protected int orientation	Indicates the split orientation
public static final String ORIENTATION_PROPERTY	Property associated with orientation; this property is bound
public static String RIGHT	Used to add a component to the right of existing components
protected Component rightComponent	Depending on the orientation of the split, this represents the component in the bottom or right position
public static String TOP	Used to add a component on top of existing components

continues

Fields/Methods	Description
`public static int VERTICAL_SPLIT`	Used to indicate that the screen should have a vertical split
`protected void addImpl(Component, Object, int)`	Adds the specified component to the pane specified by the `Object` parameter at the specified index; if a component already exists at that location, the new component will take its place
`public AccessibleContext getAccessibleContext()`	Obtains a reference to the `AccessibleContext` object
`public Component getBottomComponent()`	Depending on the orientation of the split, obtains the bottom or right component
`public int getDividerLocation()`	Obtains the current divider location
`public int getDividerSize()`	Obtains the current size of the divider
`public int getLastDividerLocation()`	Obtains the location of the divider before the last resize
`public Component getLeftComponent()`	Depending on the orientation of the split, obtains the top or left component
`public int getMaximumDividerLocation()`	Obtains the maximum location the divider can reach
`public int getMinimumDividerLocation()`	Obtains the minimum value the divider can take on
`public int getOrientation()`	Obtains the current orientation of the divider
`public Component getRightComponent()`	Depending on the orientation of the split, obtains the right or bottom component
`public Component getTopComponent()`	Depending on the orientation of the split, obtains the left or top component
`public SplitPaneUI getUI()`	Obtains the active pluggable look-and-feel properties
`public String getUIClassID()`	Obtains a logical description of the look-and-feel properties; always returns `SplitPaneUI`

Fields/Methods	Description
public boolean isContinuousLayout()	Returns true if views are actively redisplayed during a resize action
public boolean isOneTouchExpandable()	Returns true if a widget exists to dynamically collapse/expand the divider
public void paintChildren(Graphics)	Invoked when this component should paint its children into the specified Graphics object
public void remove(Component)	Removes the specified component from the view
public void remove(int)	Removes the component at the specified index from the view
public void removeAll()	Removes all components from the view
public void resetToPreferredSizes()	Lays out the screen again such that each component takes up the space returned by its getPreferredSize() method
public void setAccessibleValue(Number)	Sets the Accessible value for this component
public void setBottomComponent(Component)	Depending on the orientation of the split, sets either the bottom or right component
public void setDividerLocation(double)	Sets the location of the divider as a percentage
public void setContinuousLayout(boolean)	Sets whether this component should dynamically resize each container during a resize action
public void setDividerLocation(int)	Sets the current location of the divider
public void setDividerSize(int)	Sets the current size of the divider
public void setLastDividerLocation(int)	Sets the location of the divider prior to the last resize action
public void setLeftComponent(Component)	Depending on the orientation of the split, sets either the left or top component

continues

Fields/Methods	Description
`public void setOneTouchExpandable(boolean)`	Sets whether a widget exists to dynamically collapse/expand the split
`public void setOrientation(int)`	Sets the current orientation of the split
`public void setRightComponent(Component)`	Depending on the orientation of the split, sets either the right or bottom component
`public void setTopComponent(Component)`	Depending on the orientation of the split, sets either the left or top component
`public void setUI(SplitPaneUI)`	Sets the current look and feel properties for this component
`public void updateUI()`	Invoked to indicate a change in the pluggable look and feel properties

Class   `javax.swing.JTabbedPane`

`public class JTabbedPane extends JComponent implements Serializable, Accessible, SwingConstants`

The `JTabbedPane` class allows for switching between different components by clicking on a title tab. This class controls information according to a folder model, in which different bits of information are stored in each folder and users access a given folder by clicking on its tab.

Class   `javax.swing.JTabbedPane`: Summary

Methods/Events	Description
`publc Component add(Component, int)`	Adds component at the specified tab index
`public Component add(Component, Object)`	Adds a component with the specified constraints
`public Component add(Component)`	Adds a component to the tabbed pane
`public Component add(String, Component)`	Adds a component to the tabbed pane with the specified title

Methods/Events	Description
`public void addChangeListener(ChangeListener)`	Adds a `ChangeListener` to the collection of listeners; a `ChangeListener` is notified whenever the selected tab changes
`public void addTab(String, Component)`	Adds the specified tab with the specified name
`public void addTab(String, Icon, Component)`	Adds the specified tab with the specified name and icon
`public void addTab (String, Icon, Component, String)`	Adds the specified tab with the specified name, icon, and tooltip
`protected ChangeListener createChangeListener()`	Used internally for event management
`protected void fireStateChanged()`	Used internally for event management
`public AccessibleContext getAccessibleContext()`	Obtains a reference to the `AccessibleContext` object
`public Color getBackgroundAt(int)`	Obtains the background color of the specified tab
`public Rectangle getBoundsAt(int)`	Obtains the bounds of the specified tab
`public Component getComponentAt(int)`	Obtains the component at the specified index
`public Icon getDisabledIconAt(int)`	Obtains the icon used to represent the specified tab when it is disabled
`public Color getForegoundAt(int)`	Obtains the foreground color at the specified index
`public Icon getIconAt(int)`	Obtains the icon at the specified index
`public SingleSelectionModel getModel()`	Obtains the model associated with this object
`public Component getSelectedComponent()`	Obtains the currently selected component

continues

A

Methods/Events	Description
`public int getSelectedIndex()`	Obtains the index of the currently selected component
`public int getTabCount()`	Obtains the number of tabs currently in use
`public int getTabPlacement()`	Obtains the placement of tabs in the tab pane
`public int getTabRunCound()`	Obtains the number of rows of tabs
`public String getTitleAt(int)`	Obtains the title string at the specified index
`public String getToolTipText(MouseEvent)`	Obtains the tooltip text associated with the specified event
`public TabbedPaneUI getUI()`	Obtains the active pluggable look-and-feel properties
`public String getUIClassID()`	Obtains a logical description of the current UI; always returns `TabbedPaneUI`
`public int indexOfComponent(Component)`	Obtains the index of the first tab with the specified text
`public int indexOfTab(String)`	Obtains the index of the specified tab
`public int indexOfTab(Icon)`	Obtains the index of the first tab with the specified icon
`public void insertTab (String, Icon, Component, String, int)`	Inserts the specified tab at the specified index
`public boolean isEnabledAt(int)`	Returns true if the specified tab is enabled
`public void remove(Component)`	Removes the tab asscociated with the specified component
`public void removeAll()`	Removes all tabs from the pane
`public void removeChangeListener(ChangeListener)`	Removes the specified `ChangeListener` from the collection of listeners
`public void removeTabAt(int)`	Removes the tab at the specified index
`public void setBackgroundAt(int, Color)`	Sets background color of the specified tab to the specified color
`public void setComponentAt(int, Component)`	Replaces the component at the specified index with the specified component

Methods/Events	Description
`public void setDisabledIconAt(int, Icon)`	Replaces the disabled icon at the specified index with the specified icon
`public void setEnabledAt(int, boolean)`	Sets whether or not the specified tab is enabled
`public void setForegroundAt(int, Color)`	Sets foreground color of the specified tab to the specified color
`public void setIconAt(int, Icon)`	Replaces the icon at the specified index with the specified icon
`public void setModel(SingleSelectionModel)`	Sets the model for this component
`public void setSelectedComponent(Component)`	Selects the specified component
`public void setSelectedIndex(int)`	Selects the component at the specified index
`public void setTabPlacement(int)`	Sets the tab placement for the pane
`public void setTitleAt(int, String)`	Sets the title of the specified component
`public void setUI(TabbedPaneUI)`	Sets the active pluggable look-and-feel properties
`public void updateUI()`	Invoked to indicate a change in pluggable look-and-feel properties

CLASS

`javax.swing.JTabbedPane`: Example

The `JTabbedPane` class is used to create a screen that leverages the tab metaphor:

```
import java.awt.*;
import javax.swing.*;
import javax.swing.border.*;
import javax.swing.event.*;


public class JTabbedPaneDemo extends JApplet {
    JTabbedPane    tab;

    public void init() {
        resize(400, 400);

        // Create a new GridLayout object with a 2x2 format and
        // a 10 pixel gaps between all components.
        BorderLayout borderLayout = new BorderLayout();
```

A

```
        BorderLayout borderLayoutTab1 = new BorderLayout();
        BorderLayout borderLayoutTab2 = new BorderLayout();

        // Set the layout.
        getContentPane().setLayout(borderLayout);

        //create components to add to layout

        JPanel jpnlTab1 = new JPanel();
        jpnlTab1.setLayout(borderLayoutTab1);
        JLabel jlblTab1 = new JLabel
        ("This label appears in the panel on the first tab");

        JPanel jpnlTab2 = new JPanel();
        jpnlTab2.setLayout(borderLayoutTab2);
        JLabel jlblTab2 = new JLabel
        ("This label appears in the panel on the second tab");

        tab = new JTabbedPane();
        tab.addTab("Tab 1", jpnlTab1);
        tab.addTab("Tab 2", jpnlTab2);


        // Add components.
        jpnlTab1.add(jlblTab1, BorderLayout.CENTER);
        jpnlTab2.add(jlblTab2, BorderLayout.CENTER);
        getContentPane().add(tab,"Center");
        Change change = new Change();
        tab.addChangeListener(change);
    }

    class Change implements ChangeListener {
        public void stateChanged(ChangeEvent event) {
            Object object = event.getSource();
            if (object == tab) {
                if (tab.getTitleAt(tab.getSelectedIndex()).
                equals("Tab 1")) {
//Tab 1 stuff
                } else if (tab.getTitleAt(tab.getSelectedIndex()).
                  equals("Tab 2")) {
//Tab 2 stuff
                }
            }
        }
    }

}
```

javax.swing.JTable

```
public class JTable extends JComponent implements TableModelListener,
Scrollable, TableColumnModelListener, ListSelectionListener,
CellEditorListener, Accessible
```

The JTable class is used to model data best shown in a grid. A spreadsheet is the most obvious real-life example of an application that uses components similar to JTable.

javax.swing.JTable: Summary

Fields/Methods	Description
public static final int AUTO_RESIZE_ALL_COLUMNS	Indicates that a table resize should cause all columns to proportionally resize as well
public static final int AUTO_RESIZE_LAST_COLUMN	Indicates that a table resize should cause only the last column to resize
public static final int AUTO_RESIZE_NEXT_COLUMN	Indicates that a column resize causes the next column to resize in the opposite manner
public static final int AUTO_RESIZE_OFF	Indicates that a table resize should cause no columns to resize
public static final int AUTO_RESIZE_SUBSEQUENT_COLUMNS	Indicates that a table resize should cause columns to resize in order to preserve total width
protected boolean autoCreateColumnsFromModel	If true, the table model will provide the default column labels
protected int autoResizeMode	Current policy for table resizing
protected transient TableCellEditor cellEditor	Active cell editor
protected boolean cellSelectionEnabled	If true, then both row and column selection can be done at the same time

continues

Fields/Methods	Description
protected TableColumnModel columnModel	Active column model
protected TableModel dataModel	Active table model
protected Hashtable defaultEditorsByColumnClass	Table of content editors
protected Hashtable defaultRenderersByColumnClass	Table of content renderers
public int editingColumn	If you are currently editing the table, contains the column number of the cell; otherwise, contains −1
public int editingRow	If you are currently editing the table, contains the row number of the cell; otherwise, contains −1
protected transient Component editorComp	If you are currently editing the table, contains the editor component
protected Color gridColor	The color of the grid
protected Dimension preferredViewportSize	Preferred size
protected int rowHeight	Height of all rows
protected int rowMargin	Margin between rows
protected boolean rowSelectionAllowed	True if a user can select an entire row
protected Color selectionBackground	Background color for selected cells
protected Color selectionForeground	Foreround color for selected cells
protected ListSelectionModel selectionModel	ListSelectionModel object associated with this component
protected boolean showHorizontalLines	If true, table draws horizontal lines between components
protected boolean showVerticalLines	If true, table draws vertical lines between components
protected JTableHeader tableHeader	The JTableHeader object associated with this component
public void addColumn(TableColumn)	Adds the specified column
public void addColumnSelectionInterval(int, int)	Increases the current selection to include the specified column range

Fields/Methods	*Description*
`public void addNotify()`	Calls `configureEnclosingScrollPane()`
`public void addRowSelectionInterval(int, int)`	Increases the current selection to include the specified row range
`public void clearSelection()`	Clears the active selection
`public void columnAdded(TableColumnModelEvent)`	Invoked when a new column is added
`public int columnAtPoint(Point)`	Obtains the column at the specified coordinates, or −1 if there is none
`public void columnMarginChanged(ChangeEvent)`	Invoked when a column margin changes
`public void columnMoved(TableColumnModelEvent)`	Invoked when a column is moved
`public void columnRemoved(TableColumnModelEvent)`	Invoked when a column is removed
`protected void configureEnclosingScrollPane()`	If the table is a viewport for a `JScrollPane`, configure that `ScrollPane`
`public int convertColumnIndexToModel(int)`	Obtains the index of the column in the model which is being displayed in the `viewColumnIndex`
`public int convertColumnIndexToView(int)`	Obtains the index of the column in the model which is being displayed in the `modelColumnIndex`
`protected TableColumnModel createDefaultColumnModel()`	Used internally to create the `TableColumnModel` object
`public void createDefaultColumnsFromModel()`	Clears the current table and creates a new one using the default values in the mode
`protected TableModel createDefaultDataModel()`	Used internally to create the `TableModel` object
`protected void createDefaultEditors()`	Used internally to create the cell editor objects

continues

Fields/Methods	Description
`protected void createDefaultRenderers()`	Used internally to create the `cell rendering` objects
`protected ListSelectionModel createDefaultSelectionModel()`	Used internally to create the `ListSelectionModel` object
`protected JTableHeader createDefaultTableHeader()`	Used internally to create the `JTableHeader` object
`public static JScrollPane createScrollPaneForTable(JTable)`	Convenience method used to create a new `JScrollPane` object that houses the specified `JTable` object; deprecated, use new `JScrollPane(aTable)`
`public boolean editCellAt(int, int)`	Attempts to start editing the specified cell; returns false if editing is not possible or the cell does not exist
`public boolean editCellAt(int, int, EventObject)`	Attempts to start editing the specified cell; returns false if editing is not possible or the cell does not exist
`public void editingCanceled(ChangeEvent)`	Invoked when cell editing is cancelled
`public void editingStopped(ChangeEvent)`	Invoked when editing of a cell is stopped
`public AccessibleContext getAccessibleContext()`	Obtains a reference to the `AccessibleContext` object
`public boolean getAutoCreateColumnsFromModel()`	Returns true if the table model provides default columns
`public int getAutoResizeMode()`	Obtains the current resize policy
`public CellEditor getCellEditor()`	Obtains the cell editor for this component
`public CellEditor getCellEditor(int, int)`	Obtains the cell editor for the cell specified by row and column

Fields/Methods	*Description*
public int getCellRect(int, int, boolean)	Obtains the bounding box for the specified cell; if the boolean parameter is set to true, spacing is included
public TableCellRenderer getCellRenderer(int, int)	Obtain an appropriate renderer for the cell at the specified row and column
public boolean getCellSelectionEnabled()	Returns true if simultaneous row and column selections are allowed
public TableColumn getColumn(Object)	Obtains the column with the specified identifier
public Class getColumnClass(int)	Obtains the class associated with the specified column
public int getColumnCount()	Obtains the number of columns
public TableColumnModel getColumnModel()	Obtains table column information
public String getColumnName(int)	Obtains the name of the specified column
public boolean getColumnSelectionAllowed()	Returns true if column selection is allowed
public TableCellEditor getDefaultEditor(Class)	Obtains the default editor for a column
public int getEditingColumn()	Obtains the index of the editing column
public int getEditingRow()	Obtains the index of the editing row
public Component getEditorComponent()	If editing is currently active, returns the responsible component
public Color getGridColor()	Obtains the grid color
public Dimension getIntercellSpacing()	Obtains the horizontal and vertical spacing between cells
public TableModel getModel()	Obtains the table model associated with this component
public Dimension getPreferredScrollableViewportSize()	Obtains the preferred size of the table
public int getRowCount()	Obtains the number of rows

continues

Fields/Methods	Description
public int getRowHeight()	Obtains the total row height
public boolean getRowSelectionAllowed()	Returns true if row selection is allowed
public int getScrollableBlockIncrement (Rectangle, int, int)	Obtains the block increment for the specified data
public boolean getScrollableTracksViewportHeight()	Returns true if the scroll pane tracks the table height
public boolean getScrollableTracksViewportWidth()	Returns true if the scroll pane tracks the table width
public int getScrollableUnitIncrement (Rectangle, int, int)	Obtains the scrollable unit increment for the specified data
public int getSelectedColumn()	Obtains the selected column index, or −1 if there is none
public int getSelectedColumnCount()	Obtains the number of selected columns
public int[] getSelectedColumns()	Obtains an array containing the indices of all selected columns
public int getSelectedRow()	Obtains the index of the selected row, or −1 if there is none
public int getSelectedRowCount()	Obtains the number of selected columns
public int[] getSelectedRows()	Obtains an array containing the indices of all selected rows
public getSelectionBackground()	Obtains the background color of the selected cells
public getSelectionForeground()	Obtains the foreround color of the selected cells
public ListSelectionModel getSelectionModel()	Obtains the current selection model
public boolean getShowHorizontalLines()	Obtains true if horizontal lines are drawn between cells
public boolean getShowVerticalLines()	Obtains true if vertical lines are drawn between cells

Fields/Methods	Description
public JTableHeader getTableHeader()	Obtains the table header associated with this component
public String getToolTipText(MouseEvent)	Obtains the tooltip text associated with the specified event
public TableUI getUI()	Obtains the active pluggable look-and-feel properties
public String getUIClassID()	Obtains a logical name for the active look-and-feel properties; always returns TableUI
public Object getValueAt(int, int)	Obtains the value of the specified cell
protected void initializeLocalVars()	Invoked internally to initialize local variables
public boolean isCellEditable(int, int)	Returns true if the specified cell is editable
public boolean isCellSelected(int, int)	Returns true if the specified cell is selected
public boolean isColumnSelected(int)	Returns true if the specified column is selected
public boolean isEditing()	Returns true if editing is in progress
public boolean isRowSelected(int)	Returns true if the specified row is selected
public void moveColumn(int, int)	Moves the specified column from the original position to the target position
public Comment prepareEditor (TableCellEditor, int, int)	Prepares the specified editor for editing the specified cell
public Component prepareRenderer (TableCellEditor, int, int)	Prepares the specified renderer for rendering the specified cell
public void removeColumn(TableColumn)	Removes the specified column
public void removeColumnSelectionInterval (int, int)	Changes the active column selection to not include the specified interval

continues

Fields/Methods	Description
`public void removeEditor()`	Removes the cell editor
`public void removeRowSelectionInterval(int, int)`	Changes the active row selection to not include the specified interval
`protected void resizeAndRepaint()`	Performs a resize and marks the change area as needing a repaint
`public int rowAtPoint(Point)`	Obtains the index of the row at the specified point, or -1 if there is none
`public void selectAll()`	Selects as much of the table as its rules allow
`public void setAutoCreateColumnsFromModel(boolean)`	Sets whether the table model should provide default data to the columns
`public void setAutoResizeMode(int)`	Sets the auto resize policy
`public void setBounds(int, int, int, int)`	Sets the bounding box for this component
`public void setCellEditor(TableCellEditor)`	Sets the cell editor for this component
`public void setCellSelectionEnabled(boolean)`	Set whether row and column selection can be done simultaneously
`public void setColumnModel(TableColumnModel)`	Sets the column model for this component
`public void setColumnSelectionAllowed(boolean)`	Sets whether column selection is allowed
`public void setColumnSelectionInterval(int, int)`	Sets the selected set
`public void setDefaultEditor(Class, TableCellEditor)`	Sets the default editor
`public void setDefaultRenderer(Class, TableCellRenderer)`	Sets the default renderer
`public void setEditingColumn(int)`	Sets the column being edited
`public void setEditingRow(int)`	Sets the row being edited
`public void setGridColor(Color)`	Sets the grid color

Fields/Methods	Description
public void setIntercellSpacing(Dimension)	Sets the intercell spacing
public void setModel(TableModel)	Sets the table model
public void setPreferredScrollableViewportSize (Dimension)	Sets the preferred size of the viewport
public void setRowHeight(int)	Sets the total row height
public void setRowMargin(int)	Sets the number of pixels between rows
public void setRowSelectionAllowed(boolean)	Sets whether row selection is allowed
public void setRowSelectionInterval(int, int)	Sets the current selection set
public setSelectionBackground()	Sets the background color of the selected cells
public setSelectionForeground()	Sets the foreround color of the selected cells
public void setSelectionMode(int)	Sets the tables mode to allow for single selections, single contiguous selections, or multiple selections
public void setSelectionModel(ListSelectionModel)	Sets the selection model
public void setShowGrid(boolean)	Sets whether the grid is to be shown
public boolean setShowHorizontalLines()	Sets whether or not horizontal lines are drawn between cells
public boolean setShowVerticalLines()	Sets whether or not vertical lines are drawn between cells
public void setTableHeader(JTableHeader)	Sets the active table header
public void setUI(TableUI)	Sets the active pluggable look-and-feel properties
public void setValueAt(Object, Object, int)	Sets the value at the specified location
public void sizeColumnsToFit(boolean)	Sets whether columns should be sized to fit the viewable area

continues

Fields/Methods	Description
`public void sizeColumnsToFit(int)`	Resizes columns as necessary to make the total width of all columns equal to the width of the table
`public void tableChanged(TableModelEvent)`	Invoked when the table is changed
`public void updateUI()`	Invoked to indicate a change in pluggable look-and-feel properties
`public void valueChanged(ListSelectionEvent)`	Invoked when a value changes

CLASS   `javax.swing.JTextArea`: **Summary**

Methods/Events	Description
`public void append(String)`	Appends the specified text onto the current text
`protected Document createDefaultModel()`	Used internally to create the default data mode
`public AccessibleContext getAccessibleContext()`	Obtains a reference to the `AccessibleContext` object
`public int getColumns()`	Obtains the number of columns currently in place
`public int getColumnWidth()`	Obtains the width of all columns
`public int getLineCount()`	Obtains the number of lines of text
`public int getLineEndOffset(int)`	Obtains the offset to the end of the specified line
`public int getLineStartOffset(int)`	Obtains the offset to the start of the specified line
`public boolean getLineWrap()`	Returns true if lines are wrapped
`public Dimension getPreferredSize()`	Obtains the preferred size of this component
`public int getRowHeight()`	Obtains the height of all rows
`public int getRows()`	Obtains the number of rows in the component

Methods/Events	Description
`public int getScrollableUnitIncrement` `(Rectangle, int, int)`	Obtains the scrollable unit increment for the specified data
`public int getTabSize()`	Obtains the number of spaces consumed by a single tab press
`public String getUIClassID()`	Obtains a logical description of the UI; always returns `JTextAreaUI`
`public boolean getWrapStyleWord()`	Returns true if words are wrapped at word boundaries and false if wrapped at character boundaries
`public void insert(String, int)`	Inserts the specified text at the specified position
`public boolean isManagingFocus()`	Returns true if this component is managing focus internally; allows tabs pressed inside a text area to not change focus, but instead to tab across the text area
`protected String paramString()`	Obtains a parameter string for this object
`public void replaceRange(String, int, int)`	Replaces the text between the indices with the specified text
`public void setColumns(int)`	Sets the number of columns
`public void setFont(Font)`	Sets the current display font
`public void setLineWrap(boolean)`	Sets whether or not lines are wrapped
`public void setRows(int)`	Sets the number of rows
`public void setTabSize(int)`	Sets the number of spaces taken up when the Tab key is pressed
`public void setWrapStyleWord(boolean)`	Set to true if words are wrapped at word boundaries and false if wrapped at character boundaries

CLASS

`javax.swing.JTextArea`: Example

The `JTextArea` class allows for single-line input of text:

```
import java.awt.*;
import javax.swing.*;
```

```
import javax.swing.border.*;
import javax.swing.event.*;


public class JTextAreaDemo extends JApplet {

    JTextArea    jtxtaCenter;

    public void init() {
        resize(400, 400);

        // Create a new Border Layout object with
        // a 10 pixel gaps between all components.
        BorderLayout borderLayout = new BorderLayout(10,10);

        // Set the layout.
        getContentPane().setLayout(borderLayout);

        // create components to add to layout
        jtxtaCenter = new JTextArea
        ("The quick brown fox jumped over the lazy fox");
jtxtaCenter.setLineWrap(true);


        // Add components.
        getContentPane().add(jtxtaCenter,"Center");
    }

}
```

CLASS ## javax.swing.JTextField

```
public class JTextField extends JTextComponent implements SwingConstants
```

The JTextField class is used to display one line of potentially editable text.

CLASS ## javax.swing.JTextField: **Summary**

Methods/Events	Description
public void addActionListener(ActionListener)	Adds an ActionListener to the collection of listeners
protected Document createDefaultModel()	Used internally to create a default data model
protected void fireActionPerformed()	Used internally for event management
public AccessibleContext getAccessibleContext()	Obtains a reference to the AccessibleContext object

Methods/Events	Description
`public Action[] getActions()`	Obtains the list of available actions
`public int getColumns()`	Obtains the number of columns in this text field
`public int getColumnWidth()`	Obtains the total width of all columns
`public int getHorizontalAlignment()`	Obtains the horizontal alignment of the text
`public BoundedRangeModel getHorizontalVisibility()`	Obtains the horizontal visibility of the text
`public Dimension getPreferredSize()`	Obtains the preferred size of this component
`public int getScrollOffset()`	Obtains the scroll offset
`public boolean isValidateRoot()`	Returns true if validations on this component will cause all children to be validated as well
`public String getUIClassID()`	Obtains a logical description of the UI; always returns `JTextFieldUI`
`public void paint(Graphics)`	Invoked when the component should draw itself into the specified `Graphics` object
`protected String paramString()`	Obtains the parameter string for this object
`public void postActionEvent()`	Dispatches action events; you will usually have no need to invoke this method
`public void removeActionListener(ActionListener)`	Removes the specified `ActionListener` from the collection of listeners
`public void scrollRectToVisible(Rectangle)`	Scrolls to make the specified area visible
`public void setActionCommand(String)`	Sets the string that will be used in action events
`public void setColumns(int)`	Sets the number of columns
`public void setFont(Font)`	Sets the display font
`public void setHorizontalAlignment(int)`	Sets the alignment along the x-axis for this component; parameter value is either `SwingConstants.LEFT`, `SwingConstants.RIGHT`, or `SwingConstants.CENTER`
`public void setScrollOffset(int)`	Sets the scroll offset

CLASS | # javax.swing.JTextField: Example

The JTextField class allows for multi-line text entry:

```java
import java.awt.*;
import javax.swing.*;
import javax.swing.border.*;
import javax.swing.event.*;


public class JTextFieldDemo extends JApplet {

    JTextField    jtxtField;

    public void init() {
        resize(400, 400);

        // Create a new GridLayout object with a 2x2 format and
        // a 10 pixel gaps between all components.
        BorderLayout borderLayout = new BorderLayout();

        // Set the layout.
        getContentPane().setLayout(borderLayout);

        //create components to add to layout
        jtxtField = new JTextField();


        // Add components.
        getContentPane().add(jtxtField,"Center");
    }

}
```

CLASS | # javax.swing.JTextPane

```java
public class JTextPane extends JEditorPane
```

The JTextPane class is a text widget that has the capability to display rich text.

CLASS | # javax.swing.JTextPane: Summary

Methods/Events	Description
`public void addStyle(String, Style)`	Adds the specified style and style name to the collection of styles
`protected EditorKit createDefaultEditorKit()`	Called during initialization to create the default editor to use
`public AttributeSet getCharacterAttributes()`	Obtains the character attributes in effect at the current caret position

Methods/Events	Description
public MutableAttributeSet getInputAttributes()	Obtains the input attribute set
public Style getLogicalStyle()	Obtains the logical style in effect at the current caret position
public AttributeSet getParagraphAttributes()	Obtains the paragraph attributes in effect at the paragraph owned by the current caret position
public boolean getScrollableTracksViewportWidth()	Returns true if the width of the viewport should match the width of the scrollable
public String getStyle(String)	Obtains the style with the specified name
public StyledDocument getStyledDocument()	Obtains the active model
public StyledEditorKit getStyledEditorKit()	Obtains the active editor kit
public String getUIClassID()	Obtains a logical description of the UI; always returns TextUI
public void insertComponent(Component)	Inserts the specified component
public void insertIcon(Icon)	Inserts the specified icon
public void removeStyle(String)	Removes the style with the specified name
public void replaceSelection(String)	Replaces the highlighted text with the specified text
public void setCharacterAttributes (AttributeSet, boolean)	Sets the active character attributes for either the whole document, or the selected text if it exists
public void setDocument(Document)	Sets the active text document
public void setEditorKit(EditorKit)	Sets the active editor kit
public void setLogicalStyle(Style)	Sets the logical style for the paragraph containing the current caret position

continues

A

JFC CLASS REFERENCE

Methods/Events	Description
public void setParagraphAttributes (AttributeSet, boolean)	Sets the active character attributes for either the paragraph owned by the current caret position or the selected paragraph, if one exists
public void setStyledDocument(StyledDocument)	Sets the active styled document

CLASS # javax.swing.JToggleButton

public class JToggleButton extends AbstractButton implements Accessible

The JToggleButton represents a dual-state button. It is the parent class to both JRadioButton and JCheckBox.

CLASS # javax.swing.JToggleButton: Summary

Methods/Events	Description
public AccessibleContext getAccessibleContext()	Obtains a reference to the AccessibleContext object
public String getUIClassID()	Obtains a logical description of the pluggable look-and-feel attributes; always returns ToggleButtonUI
public void updateUI()	Invoked to indicate a change in pluggable look-and-feel attributes

CLASS # javax.swing.JToolBar

public class JToolBar extends JComponent implements SwingConstants, Accessible

The JToolBar class is an implementation of a toolbar class.

javax.swing.JToolBar: Summary

Methods/Events	Description
public void add(Action)	Adds the specified Action to the toolbar
protected void addImpl(Component, Object, int)	Adds the specified component to the container at the specified index using the specified constraints
public void addSeparator()	Adds a separator to the toolbar
public void addSeparator(Dimension)	Adds a separator to the toolbar
public AccessibleContext getAccessibleContext()	Obtains a reference to the AccessibleContext object
public Component getComponentAtIndex(int)	Obtains the index of the specified component
public int getComponentIndex(Component)	Obtains the index of the specified component
public Insets getMargin()	Obtains the margin between the toolbar's borders and its buttons
public ToolBarUI getUI()	Obtains the active pluggable look-and-feel properties
public String getUIClassID()	Obtains a logical name for the current UI; always returns ToolBarUI
public boolean isBorderPainted()	Checks whether a border should be painted for this component
protected void paintBorder(Graphics)	Causes the border to be painted for this component
public void setBorderPainted(boolean)	Sets whether a border is to be painted for this component
public void setFloatable(boolean)	Sets whether or not the toolbar can float
public void setMargin(Insets)	Sets the margin between the toolbar's borders and its buttons
public void setOrientation(int)	Sets the current orientation of this component

continues

A

JFC CLASS REFERENCE

Methods/Events	Description
`public void setUI(ToolBarUI)`	Sets the active pluggable look-and-feel properties
`public void updateUI()`	Invoked to indicate a change in pluggable look-and-feel properties

CLASS `javax.swing.JToolTip`

`public class JToolTip extends JComponent implements Accessible`

The `JToolTip` class is used to provide support for tooltips in Swing applications. A tooltip is a short description of a widget's function that is displayed when the mouse hovers over the widget for a certain period of time.

CLASS `javax.swing.JToolTip`: **Summary**

Methods/Events	Description
`getAccessibleContext()`	Obtains a reference to the `AccessibleContext` object
`public JComponent getComponent()`	Obtains the component described by this ToolTip
`public String getTipText()`	Obtains the text of this ToolTip
`public ToolTipUI getUI()`	Obtains the active pluggable look-and-feel properties
`public String getUIClassID()`	Obtains a logical description of the UI; always returns `ToolTipUI`
`public void setComponent(JComponent)`	Sets the component described by this ToolTip
`public void setTipText(String)`	Sets the text of this ToolTip
`public void updateUI()`	Invoked to indicate a change in pluggable look-and-feel properties

CLASS `javax.swing.JTree`

`public class JTree extends JComponent implements Scrollable, Accessible`

The `JTree` class is used to organize data in a hierarchical format. The obvious example of a practical application of this tool is in a file system browser. The top-level directory would be the root node, each folder beneath that would be its own node, and so on.

`javax.swing.JTree`: Summary

Fields/Methods	Description
`public static final String` `CELL_EDITOR_PROPERTY`	Bound property associated with the `cellEditor` variable
`public static final String` `CELL_RENDERER_PROPERTY`	Bound property associated with the `cellRenderer` variable
`protected transient TreeCellEditor` `cellEditor`	Editor associated with different nodes
`protected transient TreeCellRenderer` `cellRenderer`	Renderer used to draw nodes
`protected boolean editable`	If true, the tree is editable
`public static final String EDITABLE_PROPERTY`	Bound property associated with the editable variable
`public static final String` `INVOKES_STOP_CELL_EDITING_PROPERTY`	Bound property associated with stopping cell editing
`protected boolean invokesStopCellEditing`	True if, when editing is to be stopped, `stopCellEditing` is invoked and changes are made
`public static final String` `LARGE_MODEL_PROPERTY`	Bound property associated with the `largeModel` variable
`protected boolean largeModel`	True if the component is a large model
`public static final String` `ROOT_VISIBLE_PROPERTY`	Bound property associated with the `rootVisible` variable
`protected boolean rootVisible`	True if the root node should be displayed
`public static final String` `ROW_HEIGHT_PROPERTY`	Bound property associated with the `rowHeight` variable
`protected int rowHeight`	Height of each row

continues

Fields/Methods	Description
Fields	
public static final String SCROLLS_ON_EXPAND_PROPERTY	Bound property associated with the scrollsOnExpand variable
protected int scrollsOnExpand	True if scrolling occurs when a node is expanded
public static final String SELECTION_MODEL_PROPERTY	Bound property associated with the selectionModel variable
protected transient TreeSelectionModel selectionModel	Used to model actively selected nodes
protected JTree.TreeSelectionRedirector selectionRedirector	Used for event management
public static final String SHOWS_ROOT_HANDLES_PROPERTY	Bound property associated with the showsRootHandles variable
protected boolean showsRootHandles	True if there should be handles at the top level
public static final String TOGGLE_CLICK_COUNT_PROPERTY	Bound property associated with the toggleClickCount variable
protected transient toggleClickCount	Number of mouse clicks it takes to expand a node
public static final String TREE_MODEL_PROPERTY	Bound property associated with the treeModel variable
protected transient TreeModel treeModel	Models the active tree
public static final String VISIBLE_ROW_COUNT_PROPERTY	Bound property associated with the visibleRowCount variable
protected int visibleRowCount	Number of currently visible rows
public int addSelectionInterval(int, int)	Sets the selected set to include the specified rows
public void addSelectionPath(TreePath)	Sets the selected set to include the specified rows

Fields/Methods	Description
public void addSelectionPaths(TreePath[])	Sets the selected set to include the specified rows
public void addSelectionRow(int)	Sets the selected set to include the specified rows
public void addSelectionRows(int[])	Sets the selected set to include the specified rows
public void addTreeExpansionListener (TreeExpansionListener)	Adds the specified TreeExpansionListener to the collection of listeners; a TreeExpansionListener is notified whenever a tree node is expanded or collapsed
public void addTreeSelectionListener (TreeSelectionListener)	Adds the specified TreeSelectionListener to the collection of listeners; a TreeSelectionListener is notified whenever a node value changes
public void addTreeWillExpandListener (TreeWillExpandListener)	Adds the specified TreeWillExpandListener to the collection of listeners; a TreeWillExpandListener is notified whenever a branch is about to be expanded
public void cancelEditing()	Cancels the current editing
public void clearSelection()	Sets the selected set to include exactly zero rows
protected void clearToggledPaths()	Clears the toggled tree paths from the cache
public void collapsePath(TreePath)	Collapses the row at the specified path
public void collapseRow(int)	Collapses the specified row

continues

Fields/Methods	Description
public String convertValueToText (Object, boolean, boolean, boolean, int, boolean)	Used internally to convert added data into readable text
protected static TreeModel createTreeModel(Object)	Creates a tree model encasing the specified object
protected TreeModelListener createTreeModelListener()	Creates an instance of a TreeModelHandler
public void expandPath(TreePath)	Ensures that all nodes housed under the specified path are visible
public void expandRow(int)	Ensures that all nodes housed under the specified row are visible
public void fireTreeCollapsed(TreePath)	Used to dispatch events; you will rarely (if ever) need to invoke this method
public void fireTreeExpanded(TreePath)	Used to dispatch events; you will rarely (if ever) need to invoke this method
public void fireTreeWillCollapse(TreePath)	Used to dispatch events; you will rarely (if ever) need to invoke this method
public void fireTreeWillExpand(TreePath)	Used to dispatch events; you will rarely (if ever) need to invoke this method
public void fireValueChanged(TreeSelectionEvent)	Used to dispatch events; you will rarely (if ever) need to invoke this method
public AccessibleContext getAccessibleContext()	Obtains a reference to the AccessibleContext object
public TreeCellEditor getCellEditor()	Obtains the active cell editor
public TreeCellRenderer getCellRenderer()	Obtains the active cell renderer
public TreePath getClosestPathForLocation(int, int)	Obtains the closest path for the specified location
public int getClosestRowForLocation(int, int)	Obtains the closest row index for the specified location

Fields/Methods	Description
protected static TreeModel getDefaultTreeModel()	Obtains a default tree model
public TreePath getEditingPath()	Obtains the path to the node currently being edited
public Enumeration getExpandedDescendants(TreePath)	Obtains an enumeration of the children of the specified path that are expanded
public boolean getInvokesStopCellEditing()	Returns true if stopCellEditing is invoked when editing is interrupted
public Object getLastSelectedPathComponent()	Obtains the last path in the active selection
public TreePath getLeadSelectionPath()	Obtains the lead path in the active selection
public int getLeadSelectionRow()	Obtains the lead row index in the active selection
public int getMaxSelectionRow()	Obtains the maximum row index in the active selection
public int getMinSelectionRow()	Obtains the minimum row index in the active selection
public TreeModel getModel()	Obtains the model currently providing data
public TreePath getPathBetweenRows(int, int)	Obtains the path between the specified rows
public Rectangle getPathBounds(TreePath)	Obtains the bounding box for the specified selection
public TreePath getPathForLocation(int, int)	Obtains the path corresponding to the specified location
public TreePath getPathForRow(int)	Obtains the path corresponding to the specified row
public Dimension getPreferredScrollableViewportSize()	Obtains the preferred size of this component
public Rectangle getRowBounds(int)	Obtains the bounding box for the specified selection

continues

Fields/Methods	Description
`public int getRowCount()`	Obtains the number of rows currently being displayed
`public int getRowForLocation(int, int)`	Obtains the row index at the specified location
`public int getRowForPath(TreePath)`	Obtains the row index at the last location identified by the `TreePath` variable
`public int getRowHeight()`	Obtains the height of each row
`public int getScrollableBlockIncrement(Rectangle, int, int)`	Obtains the block increment for the specified region
`public boolean getScrollableTracksViewportHeight()`	Returns true if the tree height is tied to the scrollable height
`public boolean getScrollableTracksViewportWidth()`	Returns true if the tree width is tied to the scrollable width
`public int getScrollableUnitIncrement(Rectangle, int, int)`	Obtains the unit increment for the specified region
`public boolean getScrollsOnExpand()`	Returns true if scrolling occurs when a node is expanded
`public int getSelectionCount()`	Obtains a count of selected items
`public TreeSelectionModel getSelectionModel()`	Obtains the active selection model
`public TreePath getSelectionPath()`	Obtains the path to the first selected value
`public TreePath[] getSelectionPaths()`	Obtains the paths to all selected values
`public int[] getSelectionRows()`	Obtains the indices of all selected rows
`public boolean getShowsRootHandles()`	Returns true if root handles are shown
`public int getToggleClickCount()`	Obtains the number of clicks required to expand a node
`public String getToolTipText(MouseEvent)`	Obtains the ToolTip displayed
`public TreeUI getUI()`	Obtains the active pluggable look-and-feel model

Fields/Methods	Description
`public string getUIClassID()`	Obtains a logical description of the active UI; always returns `TreeUI`
`public int getVisibleRowCount()`	Obtains the number of visible rows
`public boolean hasBeenExpanded(TreePath)`	Returns true if the specified path has been expanded
`public boolean isCollapsed(int)`	Returns true if the specified row is collapsed
`public boolean isCollapsed(TreePath)`	Returns true if the specified path is collapsed
`public boolean isEditable()`	Returns true if the tree is editable
`public boolean isEditing()`	Returns true if the tree is currently being edited
`public boolean isExpanded(int)`	Returns true if the specified row is expanded
`public boolean isExpanded(TreePath)`	Returns true if the specified path is expanded
`public boolean isFixedRowHeight()`	Returns true if the row height is fixed
`public boolean isLargeModel()`	Returns true if this is a large data model
`public boolean isPathEditable(TreePath)`	Returns true if the specified path is editable
`public boolean isPathSelected(TreePath)`	Returns true if the specified path is selected
`public boolean isRootVisible()`	Returns true if the root is visible
`public boolean isRowSelected(int)`	Returns true if the specified row is selected
`public boolean isSelectionEmpty()`	Returns true if nothing is selected
`public boolean isVisible(TreePath)`	Returns true if the specified path is visible
`public void makeVisible(TreePath)`	Ensures that the specified path is visible
`protected void removeDescendantToggledPaths(Enumeration)`	Removes descendants of the specified `TreePaths` that have been expanded

continues

Fields/Methods	Description
`public void removeSelectionInterval(int, int)`	Modifies the selected set such that it does not contain any items in the specified interval
`public void removeSelectionPath(TreePath)`	Modifies the selected set such that it does not contain any items in the specified path
`public void removeSelectionPaths(TreePath[])`	Modifies the selected set such that it does not contain any items in the specified paths
`public void removeSelectionRow(int)`	Modifies the selected set such that it does not contain any items in the specified row
`public void removeSelectionRows(int[])`	Modifies the selected set such that it does not contain any items in the specified rows
`public void removeTreeExpansionListener (TreeExpansionListener)`	Removes the specified `TreeExpansionListener` from the collection of listeners
`public void removeTreeSelectionListener (TreeSelectionListener)`	Removes the specified `TreeSelectionListener` from the collection of listeners
`public void removeTreeWillExpandListener (TreeWillExpandListener)`	Removes the specified `TreeWillExpandListener` from the collection of listeners
`public void scrollPathToVisible(TreePath)`	Ensures that the specified path is visible
`public void scrollRowToVisible(int)`	Ensures that the specified row is visible
`public void setCellEditor(TreeCellEditor)`	Sets the editor
`public void setCellRenderer (TreeCellRenderer)`	Sets the renderer
`public void setEditable(boolean)`	Sets whether this tree is editable
`protected void setExpandedState(TreePath, boolean)`	Sets the expanded state

Fields/Methods	Description
Methods	
`public void setInvokesStopCellEditing()`	Set to true if `stopCellEditing` should be invoked when editing is interrupted
`public void setLargeModel(boolean)`	Sets whether this tree represents a large model
`public void setModel(TreeModel)`	Sets the model for this tree
`public void setRootVisible(boolean)`	Sets whether the root node is visible
`public void setRowHeight(int)`	Set the height of one row
`public boolean setScrollsOnExpand(boolean)`	Set to true if scrolling should occur when a node is expanded
`public void setSelectionInterval(int, int)`	Sets the selected set to be the specified interval
`public void setSelectionModel (TreeSelectionModel)`	Sets the selection model
`public void setSelectionPath(TreePath)`	Sets the selected set to be the specified path
`public void setSelectionPaths(TreePath[])`	Sets the selected set to be the specified paths
`public void setSelectionRow(int)`	Sets the selected set to be the specified row
`public void setSelectionRows(int[])`	Sets the selected set to be the specified rows
`public void setShowsRootHandles(boolean)`	Sets whether handles are shown at the root level
`public void setToggleClickCount(int)`	Sets the number of mouse clicks required to expand a node
`public void setUI(TreeUI)`	Sets the active pluggable look and feel attributes
`public void setVisibleRowCount(int)`	Set the number of currently visible rows
`public void startEditingAtPath(TreePath)`	Sets the location where editing is to start
`public void stopEditing()`	Stops editing

continues

A

JFC CLASS
REFERENCE

Fields/Methods	Description
`public void treeDidChange()`	Invoked when the tree has changed enough that a resize is needed
`public void updateUI()`	Invoked to indicate a change in plug-gable look-and-feel attributes

javax.swing.Jtree: Example

The JTree class allows for display of hierarchical information:

```java
import java.awt.*;

import javax.swing.*;
import javax.swing.event.*;
import javax.swing.tree.*;

public class JTreeDemo extends JApplet {

    JTree                   tree;
    DefaultMutableTreeNode  root;
    DefaultMutableTreeNode  folder;
    DefaultMutableTreeNode  node;


    public void init() {
        resize(400, 400);

        // Create a new Border Layout object with
        // a 10 pixel gaps between all components.
        BorderLayout borderLayout = new BorderLayout(10,10);
        getContentPane().setLayout(borderLayout);

        //create tree components
        root = new DefaultMutableTreeNode("Root");
        DefaultTreeModel treeModelData =
        new DefaultTreeModel(root);
        tree = new JTree(treeModelData);
        folder = new DefaultMutableTreeNode("Folder 1");
        treeModelData.insertNodeInto
            (folder, root, treeModelData.getChildCount(root));
        node = new DefaultMutableTreeNode("Leaf 1");
        treeModelData.insertNodeInto
            (node, folder, treeModelData.getChildCount(folder));
```

```
        folder = new DefaultMutableTreeNode("Folder 2");
        treeModelData.insertNodeInto
                (folder, root, treeModelData.getChildCount(root));
        node = new DefaultMutableTreeNode("Leaf 1");
        treeModelData.insertNodeInto
                (node, folder, treeModelData.getChildCount(folder));
        node = new DefaultMutableTreeNode("Leaf 2");
        treeModelData.insertNodeInto
                (node, folder, treeModelData.getChildCount(folder));
        node = new DefaultMutableTreeNode("Leaf 3");
        treeModelData.insertNodeInto
                (node, folder, treeModelData.getChildCount(folder));
        getContentPane().add
                (new JScrollPane(tree), BorderLayout.CENTER);
    }
}

import java.util.Vector;
```

CLASS

`javax.swing.KeyStroke`

`public class KeyStroke extends Object implements Serializable`

The `KeyStroke` class models a unique keypress on the keyboard. Included in the object is the key being pressed and any modifier keys pressed with it.

CLASS

`javax.swing.KeyStroke`: Summary

Methods/Events	Description
`public boolean equals(Object)`	Returns true if the two objects represent identical keystrokes
`public char getKeyChar()`	Obtains the key pressed
`public int getKeyCode()`	Obtains the key code associated with the key char
`public static KeyStroke getKeyStroke(char)`	Obtains the keystroke for the given char; note that this object is a shared instance
`public static KeyStroke getKeyStroke(int, int)`	Obtains the keystroke for the given key and modifier code; note that this object is a shared instance

continues

Methods/Events	Description
`public static KeyStroke getKeyStroke(int, int, boolean)`	Obtains the keystroke for the given key and modifier code; note that this object is a shared instance
`public static KeyStroke getKeyStroke(String)`	Obtains the keystroke for the given string; note that this object is a shared instance
`public static KeyStroke getKeyStrokeForEvent(KeyEvent)`	Obtains the key associated with the given event; note that this object is a shared instance
`public int getModifiers()`	Obtains any modifiers pressed with this key
`public int hashCode()`	Obtains the hash code for this object
`public boolean isOnKeyRelease()`	Returns true if this keystroke was sent on the key release
`public String toString()`	Obtains a `String` representation of the keystroke

CLASS

javax.swing.OverlayLayout

`public class OverlayLayout extends Object implements LayoutManager2, Serializable`

The `OverlayLayout` class is a layout manager that allows components to be physically placed on top of each other.

CLASS

javax.swing.OverlayLayout: Summary

Methods/Events	Description
`public void addLayoutComponent(Component, Object)`	Adds the specified component using the specified constraints
`public void addLayoutComponent(String, Component)`	Adds the specified component, associating it with the specified name

Methods/Events	Description
`public float getLayoutAlignmentX(Container)`	Obtains the alignment along the x-axis of the specified container
`public float getLayoutAlignmentY(Container)`	Obtains the alignment along the y-axis of the specified container
`public void invalidateLayout(Container)`	Invalidates the specified container
`public void layoutContainer(Container)`	Lays out the specified container
`public Dimension maximumLayoutSize(Container)`	Obtains the maximum size for the specified container
`public Dimension minimumLayoutSize(Container)`	Obtains the minimum size for the specified container
`public Dimension preferredLayoutSize(Container)`	Obtains the preferred size for the specified container
`public void removeLayoutComponent(Component)`	Removes the specified component

CLASS

javax.swing.ProgressMonitor

`public class ProgressMonitor extends Object`

The `ProgressMonitor` class is used to monitor the progress of an action that could potentially take a long time to complete. After a specified period of time has elapsed and the operation has not completed, the `ProgressMonitor` class will display a notification that the action is still in progress.

CLASS

javax.swing.ProgressMonitor: Summary

Methods/Events	Description
`public void close()`	To be invoked when the operation in question is complete
`public int getMaximum()`	Obtains the maximum amount of time the operation can take

continues

Methods/Events	Description
public int getMillisToDecideToPopup()	Obtains the number of milliseconds that must pass before you decide whether this operation could take a long time; once this number of milliseconds passes, you will wait the amount of time returned by getMillisToPopup() and then present a dialog
public int getMillisToPopup()	The amount of time after getMillisToDecideToPopup() until you display a dialog
public int getMinimum()	Obtains the minimum amount of time this operation can take
public String getNote()	Obtains the text of the dialog
public boolean isCancelled()	Returns true if this operation has been cancelled
public void setMaximum(int)	Sets the maximum amount of time this operation can take
public void setMillisToDecideToPopup(int)	Sets the number of milliseconds that must pass before you decide whether this operation could take a long time; once this number of milliseconds passes, you will wait the amount of time returned by getMillisToPopup() and then present a dialog
public void setMillisToPopup(int)	Sets amount of time after getMillisToDecideToPopup() until you display a dialog
public void setMinimum(int)	Sets the minimum amount of time this operation can take
public void setNote(String)	Sets the text to display in the dialog
public void setProgress(int)	Updates the progress of the operation

CLASS   **`javax.swing.ProgressMonitorInputStream`**

public class ProgressMonitorInputStream extends FilterInputStream

The ProgressMonitorInputStream class is similar to ProgressMonitor in that it monitors the progress of a potentially lengthy operation. The main difference is that this class monitor reads from an input stream. Because this class sits on top of the stream in question, users read directly from this stream.

javax.swing.ProgressMonitorInputStream: Summary

Methods/Events	Description
public void close()	Closes the input stream
public ProgressMonitor getProgressMonitor()	Obtains the ProgressMonitor class responsible for monitoring progress
public int read()	Reads the next byte from the stream
public int read(byte[])	Fills the specified array with data from the stream
public int read(byte[], int, int)	Fills the specified array between the specified indices with data from the stream
public void reset()	Moves the current stream reader position to the position of the last call to mark()
public void skip(long)	Skips over the specified number of bytes

APPENDIX B

com.foley.chart Package Source Code

The complete source listings for the classes contained in the com.foley.chart package presented in Chapter 24, "Building a Custom Component," are contained in this appendix.

FAxis Class

```java
package com.foley.chart;

import java.awt.*;
import java.io.*;
import java.util.*;

import javax.swing.*;
import javax.accessibility.*;


/**
 * Class FAxis.
 * FAxis is an axis component designed to work with the
 * FChart class, but could be used on any component that
 * needs an axis.
 * <p>
 * The Axis's range is defined in a BoundedRangeModel.
 * <p>
 * @beaninfo
 *       attribute: isContainer false
 *     description: An axis component
 * <p>
 * @version 1.2
 * @author Mike Foley
 **/
public class FAxis extends JComponent
    implements SwingConstants, Serializable, Accessible
{
    /**
     * @see #getUIClassID
     * @see #readObject
     **/
    private static final String uiClassID = "FAxisUI";

    private boolean paintTicks = true;
    private boolean paintLabels = true;

    /**
     * Bound property names.
     **/
```

com.foley.chart *Package Source Code*

APPENDIX B

1187

B

com.foley.chart
PACKAGE SOURCE
CODE

```java
private static String MODEL_PROPERTY = "model";
private static String ORIENTATION_PROPERTY = "orientation";
private static String MAJORTICKSPACING_PROPERTY = "majorTickSpacing";
private static String MINORTICKSPACING_PROPERTY = "minorTickSpacing";
private static String MAJORTICKSIZE_PROPERTY = "majorTickSize";
private static String MINORTICKSIZE_PROPERTY = "minorTickSize";
private static String PAINTTICKS_PROPERTY = "paintTicks";
private static String PAINTLABELS_PROPERTY = "paintLabels";
private static String PAINTLABELTABLE_PROPERTY = "labelTable";

/**
 * The data model that handles the numeric maximum value,
 * minimum value, and current-position value for the slider.
 */
protected BoundedRangeModel dataModel;

/**
 * The number of values between the major tick marks — the
 * larger marks that break up the minor tick marks.
 */
protected int majorTickSpacing = 20;

/**
 * The number of values between the minor tick marks — the
 * smaller marks that occur between the major tick marks.
 * @see #setMinorTickSpacing
 **/
protected int minorTickSpacing = 5;
private int majorTickSize = 10;
private int minorTickSize = 5;

/**
 * @see #setOrientation
 **/
protected int orientation;


/**
 * The labels for the axis.
 **/
private Dictionary labelTable;


/**
 * Ensure that the given orientation is valid for this
 * component. Using typed constants would be better, but
 * we want to use the constants defined in the SwingConstants
 * interface so our class works similiar to core classes.
 * <p>
 * @param orientation The required orientation for the axis.
 **/
```

```
    private void checkOrientation( int orientation ) {
        switch (orientation) {
        case VERTICAL:
        case HORIZONTAL:
            break;
        default:
throw new IllegalArgumentException(
            "orientation must be one of: VERTICAL, HORIZONTAL");
        }
    }


    /**
     * Creates a horizontal axis with the range 0 to 100.
     **/
    public FAxis() {
        this( HORIZONTAL, 0, 100 );
    }


    /**
     * Creates a slider using the specified orientation with the
     * range 0 to 100.
     **/
    public FAxis(int orientation) {
        this( orientation, 0, 100 );
    }


    /**
     * Creates a horizontal slider using the specified min and max.
     **/
    public FAxis( int min, int max ) {
        this( HORIZONTAL, min, max );
    }


    /**
     * Creates a slider with the specified orientation and the
     * specified mimimum, and maximum.
     *
     * @exception IllegalArgumentException
     *             if orientation is not one of VERTICAL, HORIZONTAL
     *
     * @see #setOrientation
     * @see #setMinimum
     * @see #setMaximum
     **/
    public FAxis( int orientation, int min, int max )
    {
```

```java
        checkOrientation( orientation );
        this.orientation = orientation;
        setModel( new DefaultBoundedRangeModel( 0, 0, min, max ) );
        updateUI();
    }


    /**
     * Creates a horizontal axis using the specified
     * BoundedRangeModel.
     **/
    public FAxis( BoundedRangeModel brm )
    {
        this.orientation = JSlider.HORIZONTAL;
        setModel( brm );
        updateUI();
    }


    /**
     * Gets the UI object which implements the L&F for this component.
     *
     * @return the FAxisUI object that implements the Slider L&F
     **/
    public FAxisUI getUI() {
        return( ( FAxisUI )ui );
    }


    /**
     * Sets the UI object which implements the L&F for this component.
     *
     * @param ui the FAxisUI L&F object
     * @see UIDefaults#getUI
     * @beaninfo
     *        bound: true
     *       hidden: true
     * description: The UI object that implements
     *                the slider's LookAndFeel.
     **/
    public void setUI( FAxisUI ui ) {
        super.setUI( ui );
    }


    /**
     * Notification from the UIFactory that the L&F has changed.
     * Called to replace the UI with the latest version from the
     * default UIFactory.
     *
```

```java
    * @see JComponent#updateUI
    **/
    public void updateUI() {
        updateLabelUIs();
        setUI((FAxisUI)UIManager.getUI(this));
    }


    /**
     * Returns the name of the L&F class that renders this component.
     *
     * @return "FAxisUI"
     * @see JComponent#getUIClassID
     * @see UIDefaults#getUI
     **/
    public String getUIClassID() {
        return uiClassID;
    }


    /**
 * Called internally to replace the label UIs with the latest
     * versions from the UIFactory when the UIFactory notifies us via
     * <code>updateUI</code> that the L&F has changed.
     *
     * @see JComponent#updateUI
     **/
    protected void updateLabelUIs() {
        if ( getLabelTable() == null ) {
            return;
        }
        Enumeration labels = getLabelTable().keys();
        while ( labels.hasMoreElements() ) {
            Object value = getLabelTable().get( labels.nextElement() );
            if ( value instanceof JComponent ) {
                JComponent component = (JComponent)value;
                component.updateUI();
                component.setSize( component.getPreferredSize()  );
            }
        }
    }


    /**
     * Returns data model that handles the sliders three
     * fundamental properties: minimum, maximum, value.
     *
     * @see #setModel
     **/
```

```java
public BoundedRangeModel getModel() {
    return dataModel;
}


/**
 * Sets the model that handles the sliders three
 * fundamental properties: minimum, maximum, value.
 *
 * @see #getModel
 * @beaninfo
 *        bound: true
 * description: The sliders BoundedRangeModel.
 **/
public void setModel(BoundedRangeModel newModel)
{
    BoundedRangeModel old = getModel();

    dataModel = newModel;

    if (newModel != null) {

        if (accessibleContext != null) {
            accessibleContext.firePropertyChange(
                    AccessibleContext.ACCESSIBLE_VALUE_PROPERTY,
                    (old == null
                     ? null : new Integer(old.getValue())),
                    (newModel == null
                     ? null : new Integer(newModel.getValue()))));
        }
    }

    firePropertyChange( MODEL_PROPERTY, old, dataModel );
}


/**
 * Returns the minimum value supported by the slider.
 *
 * @return the value of the models minimum property
 * @see #setMinimum
 **/
public int getMinimum() {
    return getModel().getMinimum();
}


/**
 * Sets the model's minimum property.
 *
```

```
    * @see #getMinimum
    * @see BoundedRangeModel#setMinimum
    * @beaninfo
    *    preferred: true
    * description: The slider's minimum value.
    **/
   public void setMinimum(int minimum) {
       getModel().setMinimum(minimum);
   }


   /**
    * Returns the maximum value supported by the slider.
    *
    * @return the value of the model's maximum property
    * @see #setMaximum
    **/
   public int getMaximum() {
       return getModel().getMaximum();
   }


   /**
    * Sets the model's maximum property.
    *
    * @see #getMaximum
    * @see BoundedRangeModel#setMaximum
    * @beaninfo
    *    preferred: true
    * description: The slider's maximum value.
    */
   public void setMaximum(int maximum) {
       getModel().setMaximum(maximum);
   }


   /**
    * @return VERTICAL or HORIZONTAL
    * @see #setOrientation
    */
   public int getOrientation() {
       return orientation;
   }


   /**
    * Set the scrollbar's orientation to either VERTICAL or HORIZONTAL.
    *
* @exception IllegalArgumentException
    *              if orientation is not one of VERTICAL, HORIZONTAL
    * @see #getOrientation
```

```
        *  @beaninfo
        *     preferred: true
        *         bound: true
    * description: Set the scrollbar's orientation to either
        *                 VERTICAL or HORIZONTAL.
        *             enum: VERTICAL SwingConstants.VERTICAL
        *                 HORIZONTAL SwingConstants.HORIZONTAL
        *
        */
    public void setOrientation(int orientation)
    {
        checkOrientation(orientation);
        int old = orientation;
        this.orientation = orientation;
        firePropertyChange( ORIENTATION_PROPERTY, old, orientation );

        if ((old != orientation) && (accessibleContext != null)) {
            accessibleContext.firePropertyChange(
                    AccessibleContext.ACCESSIBLE_STATE_PROPERTY,
                    ((old == VERTICAL)
                     ? AccessibleState.VERTICAL :
                       AccessibleState.HORIZONTAL),
                    ((orientation == VERTICAL)
                     ? AccessibleState.VERTICAL :
                       AccessibleState.HORIZONTAL));
        }
    }


    /**
    * This method returns the major tick spacing.  The number that is
    * returned represents the distance, measured in values, between
    * each major tick mark. If you have a slider with a range from 0
    * to 50 and the major tick spacing is set to 10, you will get
    * major ticks next to the following values: 0, 10, 20, 30, 40, 50.
    *
    * @return the number of values between major ticks
    * @see #setMajorTickSpacing
    */
    public int getMajorTickSpacing() {
        return majorTickSpacing;
    }


    /**
    * This method sets the major tick spacing.  The number that is
    * passed in represents the distance, measured in values, between
    * each major tick mark. If you have a slider with a range from 0
    * to 50 and the major tick spacing is set to 10, you will get major
    * ticks next to the following values: 0, 10, 20, 30, 40, 50.
    *
```

```
        * @see #getMajorTickSpacing
        * @beaninfo
        *        bound: true
        * description: Sets the number of values between major tick marks.
        *
        */
      public void setMajorTickSpacing(int n) {
          int old = majorTickSpacing;
          majorTickSpacing = n;
  firePropertyChange( MAJORTICKSPACING_PROPERTY,
                              old, majorTickSpacing);
      }



      /**
    * This method returns the minor tick spacing.  The number that is
        * returned represents the distance, measured in values, between each
        * minor tick mark. If you have a slider with a range from 0 to 50
        * and the minor tick spacing is set to 10, you will get minor ticks
        * next to the following values: 0, 10, 20, 30, 40, 50.
        *
        * @return the number of values between minor ticks
        * @see #getMinorTickSpacing
        */
      public int getMinorTickSpacing() {
          return minorTickSpacing;
      }



      /**
    * This method sets the minor tick spacing.  The number that is
        * passed in represents the distance, measured in values, between
        * each minor tick mark. If you have a slider with a range from 0 to
        * 50 and the minor tick spacing is set to 10, you will get minor
        * ticks next to the following values: 0, 10, 20, 30, 40, 50.
        *
        * @see #getMinorTickSpacing
        * @beaninfo
        *        bound: true
        * description: Sets the number of values between minor tick marks.
        */
      public void setMinorTickSpacing(int n) {
          int old = minorTickSpacing;
          minorTickSpacing = n;
          firePropertyChange( MINORTICKSPACING_PROPERTY,
                              old, minorTickSpacing);
      }


      /**
       *
```

com.foley.chart *Package Source Code*

APPENDIX B

1195

B

com.foley.chart
PACKAGE SOURCE
CODE

```
 * @return The size of major ticks, in pixels
 * @see #setMajorTickSpacing
 **/
public int getMajorTickSize() {
    return majorTickSize;
}


/**
 * @see #getMajorTickSize
 * @beaninfo
 *        bound: true
 * description: Sets the size of major tick marks.
 *
 **/
public void setMajorTickSize( int majorTickSize ) {
    int old = this.majorTickSize;
    this.majorTickSize = majorTickSize;
    firePropertyChange( MAJORTICKSIZE_PROPERTY, old, majorTickSize);
}


/**
 * @return The size of minor ticks, in pixels
 * @see #setMinorTickSpacing
 **/
public int getMinorTickSize() {
    return minorTickSize;
}


/**
 * @see #getMinorTickSize
 * @beaninfo
 *        bound: true
 * description: Sets the size of minor tick marks.
 *
 **/
public void setMinorTickSize( int minorTickSize ) {
    int old = this.minorTickSize;
    this.minorTickSize = minorTickSize;
    firePropertyChange( MINORTICKSIZE_PROPERTY, old, minorTickSize );
}


/**
 * @return true if tick marks are painted, else false
 * @see #setPaintTicks
 **/
```

```java
public boolean isPaintTicks() {
    return paintTicks;
}


/**
 * Determines whether tick marks are painted on the slider.
 * @see #getPaintTicks
 * @beaninfo
 *        bound: true
 * description: If true tick marks are painted on the slider.
 */
public void setPaintTicks( boolean b ) {
    boolean old = paintTicks;
    paintTicks = b;
    firePropertyChange( PAINTTICKS_PROPERTY, old, paintTicks);
}


/**
 * @return true if labels are painted, else false
 * @see #setPaintLabels
 */
public boolean isPaintLabels() {
    return paintLabels;
}


/**
 * Determines whether labels are painted on the slider.
 * @see #getPaintLabels
 * @beaninfo
 *        bound: true
 * description: If true labels are painted on the slider.
 */
public void setPaintLabels(boolean b) {
    boolean old = paintLabels;
    paintLabels = b;
    firePropertyChange( PAINTLABELS_PROPERTY, old, paintLabels);
}


/**
 * Returns the dictionary of what labels to draw at which values.
 *
 * @return the Dictionary containing labels and where to draw them
 */
public Dictionary getLabelTable() {

    if ( labelTable == null && getMajorTickSpacing() > 0 ) {
```

com.foley.chart *Package Source Code*

APPENDIX B

1197

B

com.foley.chart
PACKAGE SOURCE
CODE

```
        setLabelTable(createStandardLabels( getMajorTickSpacing() ));
            }

        return labelTable;
    }


    /**
     * Used to specify what label will be drawn at any given value.
* The key-value pairs are of this format:
     * <B>{ Integer value, java.awt.Component label }</B>
     *
     * @see #createStandardLabels
     * @see #getLabelTable
     * @beaninfo
     *       hidden: true
     *        bound: true
     * description: Specifies what labels will be drawn for
     *              any given value.
     */
    public void setLabelTable( Dictionary labels ) {
        Dictionary old = labelTable;
        labelTable = labels;
        updateLabelUIs();
        firePropertyChange( PAINTLABELTABLE_PROPERTY, old, labelTable );
    }


    /**
* Creates a hashtable that will draw text labels starting at the
     * slider minimum using the increment specified. If you call
     * createStandardLabels( 10 ) and the slider minimum is zero,
     * then it will make labels for the values 0, 10, 20, 30, and so on.
     * @see #setLabelTable
     */
    public Hashtable createStandardLabels( int increment ) {
        return createStandardLabels( increment, getMinimum() );
    }


    /**
* Creates a hashtable that will draw text labels starting at the
     * start point specified using the increment specified. If you call
     * createStandardLabels( 10, 2 ), then it will make labels for the
     * values 2, 12, 22, 32, and so on.
     * @see #setLabelTable
     */
    public Hashtable createStandardLabels( int increment, int start ) {
        if ( start > getMaximum() || start < getMinimum() ) {
throw new IllegalArgumentException(
```

```
➡                        "Slider label start point out of range." );
            }

        Hashtable table = new Hashtable();

for ( int labelIndex = start; labelIndex <= getMaximum();
➡                               labelIndex += increment ) {
            table.put( new Integer( labelIndex ),
                        new JLabel( ""+labelIndex, JLabel.CENTER ) );
        }

        return table;
    }


    /**
     * @param value The number to determine where it lies in the chart.
     * @return The pixel where the given value falls on this axis.
     **/
    public int getLocationValue( double value ) {

        Dimension size = getSize();
        Insets insets = getInsets();
        int minimum = getMinimum();
        int range = getMaximum() - minimum;
        int length;
        int start;
        int location;

        if( getOrientation() == VERTICAL ) {
            length = size.height - insets.top - insets.bottom - 1;
            start = insets.bottom;
location = ( int )Math.round( start -
➡                ( ( double )length / ( double )range ) * ( value - minimum
) );

            //
            // Range check the location.
            //
            int end = start - length + 1;
            location = Math.min( start, location );
            location = Math.max( end, location );
        } else {
            length = size.width - insets.right - insets.left - 1;
            start = insets.left;
location = ( int )Math.round( start +
➡        ( ( double )length / ( double )range ) * ( value - minimum ) );


        }
```

```
            return( location );
        }


    /**
     * Returns a string that displays and identifies this
     * object's properties.
     */
    public String toString()  {
        String containerString = "";

if (!isEnabled() && !isVisible())
            containerString = "(not Enabled, not Visible)";
        else if (!isEnabled()) containerString = "(not Enabled)";
        else if (!isVisible()) containerString = "(not Visible)";

        String sliderString =
            containerString +
            ((getOrientation() ==
              VERTICAL) ? "vertical" : "horizontal" ) + ", " +
            "min=" + getMinimum() + ", " +
            "max=" + getMaximum() + ", " +
            "majorTickSpacing=" + getMajorTickSpacing() + ", " +
            "minorTickSpacing=" + getMinorTickSpacing() + ", " +
            "majorTickSize=" + getMajorTickSize() + ", " +
            "paintLabels=" + isPaintLabels() + ", " +
            "paintTicks=" + isPaintTicks();

        return getClass().getName() + "[" + sliderString + "]";
    }


    /**
     * See readObject() and writeObject() in JComponent for more
     * information about serialization in Swing.
     */
    private void writeObject(ObjectOutputStream s) throws IOException {
        s.defaultWriteObject();
    if ((ui != null) && (getUIClassID().equals(uiClassID))) {
            ui.installUI(this);
        }
    }


///////////////////
// Accessibility support
///////////////////

    /**
     * Get the AccessibleContext associated with this JComponent
     *
```

```
         * @return the AccessibleContext of this JComponent
         */
        public AccessibleContext getAccessibleContext() {
            if (accessibleContext == null) {
                accessibleContext = new AccessibleFAxis();
            }
            return accessibleContext;
        }

        /**
         * The class used to obtain the accessible role for this object.
         * <p>
         **/
        protected class AccessibleFAxis extends AccessibleJComponent
            implements AccessibleValue {

            /**
             * Get the state set of this object.
             *
     * @return an instance of AccessibleState containing
             *             the current state
             * of the object
             * @see AccessibleState
             */
            public AccessibleStateSet getAccessibleStateSet() {
                AccessibleStateSet states = super.getAccessibleStateSet();
                if (getOrientation() == VERTICAL) {
                    states.add(AccessibleState.VERTICAL);
                } else {
                    states.add(AccessibleState.HORIZONTAL);
                }
                return states;
            }

            /**
             * Get the role of this object.
             *
     * @return an instance of AccessibleRole describing
             *             the role of the object
             */
            public AccessibleRole getAccessibleRole() {
                return AccessibleRole.SWING_COMPONENT;
            }

            /**
             * Get the AccessibleValue associated with this object if one
             * exists.  Otherwise return null.
             */
```

```java
        public AccessibleValue getAccessibleValue() {
            return this;
        }

        /**
         * Get the accessible value of this object.
         *
         * @return The current value of this object.
         */
        public Number getCurrentAccessibleValue() {
            return new Integer(0);
        }


        /**
         * Set the value of this object as a Number.
         *
         * @return True if the value was set.
         */
        public boolean setCurrentAccessibleValue(Number n) {
            return( false );
        }


        /**
         * Get the minimum accessible value of this object.
         *
         * @return The minimum value of this object.
         */
        public Number getMinimumAccessibleValue() {
            return new Integer(getMinimum());
        }

        /**
         * Get the maximum accessible value of this object.
         *
         * @return The maximum value of this object.
         */
        public Number getMaximumAccessibleValue() {
            return new Integer(getMaximum());
        }

    } // AccessibleFAxis
}
```

FAxisUI Class

```java
package com.foley.chart;

import java.awt.*;

import javax.swing.*;

import javax.swing.plaf.ComponentUI;

import java.util.*;


/**
 * Class FAxisUI
 * <p>
 * The user-interface class for rendering FAxis
 * instances.
 * <p>
 * @author Mike Foley
 * @version 1.2
 **/
public class FAxisUI extends ComponentUI {

    /**
     * The singleton instance of this class.
     **/
    private static FAxisUI shared = new FAxisUI();

    /**
     * FAxis, default Constructor.
     **/
    public FAxisUI() {
        super();
    }


    /**
     * Create the UI object for the given component.
     * This class may share the same UI object for
     * all FAxis that are created.
     * <p>
     * @param c The component that needs a UI.
     * @return The singleton UI Object.
     **/
    public static ComponentUI createUI( JComponent c ) {
        return( shared );
    }
```

```java
    public void installUI(JComponent c) {
//        axis = (FAxis)c;
/*

        rendererPane = new CellRendererPane();
        table.add(rendererPane);
*/

        installDefaults( ( FAxis )c );
/*

        installListeners();
        installKeyboardActions();
*/
    }




    /**
     * Determine the preferred size for the given FAxis.
     * <p>
     * @param c The component to calculate its preferred size.
     **/
    public Dimension getPreferredSize( JComponent c ) {

        if ( !( c instanceof FAxis ) )
            throw new IllegalComponentStateException(
                        this + " was asked to getPreferredSize for "
                        + c + " that is not an FAxis." );
        FAxis axis = ( FAxis )c;

        Dictionary labelTable = axis.getLabelTable();

        Dimension d = new Dimension();
        Insets insets = axis.getInsets();
        d.width = insets.left + insets.right;
        d.height = insets.top + insets.bottom;
        int tickSize = axis.getMajorTickSize();
        if( labelTable != null ) {

            //
            // Get the font information.
            //
            Font font = axis.getFont();
            if( font == null ) {
                font = ( Font )UIManager.get( "Label.font" );
            }
```

```
                    FontMetrics fontMetrics = axis.getToolkit().getFontMetrics(font);
                        int fontHeight = fontMetrics.getHeight();

                    if( axis.getOrientation() == SwingConstants.VERTICAL ) {

                        //
//'Add the label width and height. The width is the
                        // longest single label. The height is the sum of
                        // all labels.
                        //
                        int width = 0;
                        int height = 0;
                        int thisWidth;

for( Enumeration e = labelTable.elements();
➡           e.hasMoreElements(); ) {
                            Object o = e.nextElement();
                            if( o instanceof String ) {
thisWidth = fontMetrics.stringWidth((String)o);
                                height += fontHeight;
                            } else if( o instanceof Component ) {
Dimension cSize =
➡               ( ( Component )o ).getPreferredSize();
                                thisWidth = cSize.width;
                                height += cSize.height;
                            } else {
thisWidth =
➡               fontMetrics.stringWidth( o.toString() );
                                height += fontHeight;
                            }

                            width = Math.max( width, thisWidth );
                        }
                        d.width += width + tickSize;
                        d.height += height;

                    } else {
                        //
                        // Add the label width and height. The width is the sum
                        // of the labels. The height is the tallest label.
                        //
                        int width = 0;
                        int height = 0;
                        int thisWidth;
                        int thisHeight;

for( Enumeration e = labelTable.elements();
➡           e.hasMoreElements(); ) {
                            Object o = e.nextElement();
                            if( o instanceof String ) {
```

```java
                thisWidth = fontMetrics.stringWidth((String)o);
                            width += thisWidth;
                            thisHeight = fontHeight;
                        } else if( o instanceof Component ) {
Dimension cSize =
➡                        ( ( Component )o ).getPreferredSize();
                            thisWidth = cSize.width;
                            width += thisWidth;
                            thisHeight = cSize.height;
                        } else {
thisWidth =
➡                        fontMetrics.stringWidth( o.toString() );
                            width += thisWidth;
                            thisHeight = fontHeight;
                        }

                        height = Math.max( height, thisHeight );
                    }

                d.width += width;
                    d.height += height + tickSize;
                }
            }
        return d;
        }


    /**
     * Paint a representation of the <code>chart</code> instance
     * that was set in installUI().
     * <p>
     * @param g The graphics to paint with.
     * @param c The component to paint.
     **/
    public void paint( Graphics g, JComponent c ) {

        if( !( c instanceof FAxis ) )
            throw new IllegalComponentStateException(
                        this + " was asked to paint for "
                        + c + " that is not an FAxis." );
        FAxis axis = ( FAxis )c;

        g.setColor( axis.getForeground() );
        Insets insets = axis.getInsets();
        Dimension size = axis.getSize();
        if( axis.getOrientation() == SwingConstants.VERTICAL ) {
            int x = size.width - insets.right - 1;
            g.drawLine( x, insets.top,
                        x, size.height - insets.bottom );
            x -= 1;
            g.drawLine( x, insets.top,
```

```
                              x, size.height - insets.bottom );
        } else {
            int y = insets.top;
             g.drawLine( insets.left, y,
                        size.width - insets.right - 1, y );
            y += 1;
             g.drawLine( insets.left, y,
                        size.width - insets.right - 1, y );
        }

        if( axis.isPaintTicks() ) {
            paintMinorTicks( g, axis );
            paintMajorTicks( g, axis );
        }
        if( axis.isPaintLabels() ) {
            paintLabels( g, axis );
        }

    } // paint


    /**
     * Paint the minor tick marks on the axis.
     * <p>
     * @param g The Graphics to paint with.
     * @param axis The axis whose minor ticks need paints.
     **/
    protected void paintMinorTicks( Graphics g, FAxis axis ) {

        Insets insets = axis.getInsets();
        Dimension size = axis.getSize();
        BoundedRangeModel model = axis.getModel();
        int minimum = model.getMinimum();
        int maximum = model.getMaximum();
        int spacing = axis.getMinorTickSpacing();
        int tickSize = axis.getMinorTickSize();
        int axisHeight = size.height - (insets.top + insets.bottom) - 1;

        if( axis.getOrientation() == SwingConstants.VERTICAL ) {

                g.translate( 0, axisHeight );
            int x = size.width - insets.right - 1;
            for( int i = minimum; i <= maximum; i += spacing ) {
                int position = axis.getLocationValue( ( double )i );
                g.drawLine( x - tickSize, position, x, position );
            }
                g.translate( 0, -axisHeight );
        } else {
            int y = insets.top;
```

```
        for( int i = minimum; i <= maximum; i += spacing ) {
            int position = axis.getLocationValue( ( double )i );
            g.drawLine( position, y, position, y + tickSize );
        }
    }

} // paintMinorTicks


/**
 * Paint the major tick marks on the axis.
 * <p>
 * @param g The Graphics to paint with.
 * @param axis The axis whose major ticks need paints.
 **/
protected void paintMajorTicks( Graphics g, FAxis axis ) {

    Insets insets = axis.getInsets();
    Dimension size = axis.getSize();
    BoundedRangeModel model = axis.getModel();
    int minimum = model.getMinimum();
    int maximum = model.getMaximum();
    int spacing = axis.getMajorTickSpacing();
    int tickSize = axis.getMajorTickSize();
    int axisHeight = size.height - (insets.top + insets.bottom) - 1;

    if( axis.getOrientation() == SwingConstants.VERTICAL ) {

        g.translate( 0, axisHeight );
        int x = size.width - insets.right - 1;
        for( int i = minimum; i <= maximum; i += spacing ) {
            int position = axis.getLocationValue( ( double )i );
            g.drawLine( x - tickSize, position, x, position );
        }
        g.translate( 0, -axisHeight );
    } else {
        int y = insets.top;
        for( int i = minimum; i <= maximum; i += spacing ) {
            int position = axis.getLocationValue( ( double )i );
            g.drawLine( position, y, position, y + tickSize );
        }
    }

} // paintMajorTicks


/**
* Called for every label in the label table.
    * Used to draw the labels for horizontal axis.
    * The graphics have been translated to labelRect.y already.
```

```
      * @see JAxis#setLabelTable
      **/
    protected void paintHorizontalLabel( Graphics g, FAxis axis,
                                      int value, Component label ) {
        int tickSize = axis.getMajorTickSize();
        int labelCenter = axis.getLocationValue( ( double )value );
int labelLeft = labelCenter ñ
                    (label.getPreferredSize().width / 2);
        g.translate( labelLeft, tickSize );
        label.paint( g );
        g.translate( -labelLeft, -tickSize );
    }


    /**
 * Called for every label in the label table.
    * Used to draw the labels for vertical axis.
    * The graphics have been translated to labelRect.x already.
    * @see FAxis#setLabelTable
    */
    protected void paintVerticalLabel( Graphics g, FAxis axis,
                                      int value, Component label ) {
        int labelCenter = axis.getLocationValue( ( double )value );
int labelTop = labelCenter ñ
                    (label.getPreferredSize().height / 2);
        g.translate( 0, labelTop );
        label.paint( g );
        g.translate( 0, -labelTop );
    }


    /**
     * Paint the labels for the axis.
     * <p>
     * @param g The graphics to paint with.
     * @param axis The axis whose labels to print.
     **/
    public void paintLabels( Graphics g, FAxis axis ) {

        Insets insets = axis.getInsets();
        Dimension size = axis.getSize();
int axisHeight = size.height - (insets.top + insets.bottom) - 1;

        Dictionary dictionary = axis.getLabelTable();
        if ( dictionary != null ) {
            Enumeration keys = dictionary.keys();
            while( keys.hasMoreElements() ) {
```

```
                Integer key = ( Integer )keys.nextElement();
                Component label = ( Component )dictionary.get( key );

                if(axis.getOrientation() == SwingConstants.HORIZONTAL) {
                    g.translate( 0, insets.top );
paintHorizontalLabel(g, axis, key.intValue(), label);
                    g.translate( 0, -insets.top );
                } else {
                    g.translate( insets.right, axisHeight );
                    paintVerticalLabel( g, axis, key.intValue(), label );
                    g.translate( -insets.right, -axisHeight );
                }
            }
        }

    } // paintLabels

} // FAxisUI
```

FChart Class

```
package com.foley.chart;

import java.awt.*;
import java.beans.*;
import java.io.*;

import javax.swing.*;

import javax.swing.table.TableModel;


/**
 * Class FChart
 * A class that displays a chart containing
 * numerical data in a TableModel.
 * <p>
 * @beaninfo
 *       attribute: isContainer false
 *     description: A chart component
 * @author Mike Foley
 * @version 1.2
 **/
```

```java
public class FChart extends JComponent
    implements Serializable {

  /**
   * @see #getUIClassID
   **/
  private static final String uiClassID = "FChartUI";

  /**
   * The X and Y Axis.
   **/
  private FAxis xAxis;
  private FAxis yAxis;

  /**
   * The color of the grid
   **/
  protected Color gridColor = Color.lightGray;

  /**
* The table draws horizontal lines between cells if
   * showHorizontalLines is true
   **/
  protected boolean showHorizontalLines;

  /**
* The table draws vertical lines between cells if
   * showVerticalLines is true
   **/
  protected boolean showVerticalLines;

  private TableModel model;

  /**
   * Bound property names.
   **/
  public static final String MODEL_PROPERTY = "model";
  public static final String XAXIS_PROPERTY = "XAxis";
  public static final String YAXIS_PROPERTY = "YAxis";
  public static final String GRIDCOLOR_PROPERTY = "GridColor";
public static final String SHOWHORIZONTALLINES_PROPERTY =
➥                    "ShowHorizontalLines";
  public static final String SHOWVERTICALLINES_PROPERTY =
➥                    "ShowVerticalLines";


  /**
   * FChart, default constructor.
   **/
```

```java
    public FChart() {
        this( null );
    }


    /**
     * FChart, constructor.
     * <p>
     * Create a chart viewing the given model.
     * <p>
     * @param model The model for the chart to view.
     **/
    public FChart( TableModel model ) {

        setLayout( new FChartLayoutManager() );
        setXAxis( new FAxis( SwingConstants.HORIZONTAL ) );
        setYAxis( new FAxis( SwingConstants.VERTICAL ) );
        setModel( model );

        updateUI();

    } // FChart


    /**
     * Initialize this class with the UIManager.
     **/
    public static void initialize() {

        setLookAndFeelProperties( UIManager.getLookAndFeel() );

UIManager.addPropertyChangeListener(
            new PropertyChangeListener() {
            public void propertyChange( PropertyChangeEvent event ) {
                if( "lookAndFeel".equals( event.getPropertyName() ) ) {
setLookAndFeelProperties(
                ( LookAndFeel )event.getNewValue() );
                }
            }
        } );

    }


public static void setLookAndFeelProperties(
                LookAndFeel lookAndFeel ) {
```

```
            if( lookAndFeel == null )
                return;

            if( lookAndFeel.getID().equals( "Metal" ) ) {
                //
                // Metal, or Metal complient look-and-feel
                //
    UIManager.put( "FChartUI", "com.foley.chart.MetalFChartUI" );
                UIManager.put( "FAxisUI", "com.foley.chart.MetalFAxisUI" );
            } else if( lookAndFeel.getID().equals( "Windows" ) ) {
                //
                // Windows, or Windows complient look-and-feel
                //
    UIManager.put("FChartUI", "com.foley.chart.WindowsFChartUI");
                UIManager.put( "FAxisUI", "com.foley.chart.WindowsFAxisUI" );
            } else {
                //
                // Unsupported look-and-feel, use default
                //
                UIManager.put( "FChartUI", "com.foley.chart.FChartUI" );
                UIManager.put( "FAxisUI", "com.foley.chart.FAxisUI" );
            }.

    } // setLookAndFeelProperties


    /**
     * Returns the L&F object that renders this component.
     *
     * @return the FChartUI object that renders this component
     **/
    public FChartUI getUI() {
        return( FChartUI )ui;
    }


    /**
     * Sets the L&F object that renders this component.
     *
     * @param ui  the FChartUI L&F object
     * @see UIDefaults#getUI
     **/
    public void setUI( FChartUI ui ) {
        super.setUI( ui );
    }


    /**
     * Notification from the UIManager that the L&F has changed.
     * Replaces the current UI object with the latest version from the
```

```
 * UIManager.
 *
 * @see JComponent#updateUI
 **/
public void updateUI() {
    setUI( ( FChartUI )UIManager.getUI( this ) );
    invalidate();
}


/**
 * Returns the name of the L&F class that
 * renders this component.
 *
 * @return "FChartUI"
 * @see JComponent#getUIClassID
 * @see UIDefaults#getUI
 **/
public String getUIClassID() {
    return uiClassID;
}


/**
 * See readObject() and writeObject() in JComponent for more
 * information about serialization in Swing.
 * <p>
 * @exception IOException If the write cannot be performed.
 **/
private void writeObject( ObjectOutputStream s )
    throws IOException {

    s.defaultWriteObject();
    if( ( ui != null ) && ( getUIClassID().equals( uiClassID ) ) ) {
        ui.installUI( this );
    }
}


/**
 * Set the X Axis for the chart.
 * This is a bound property.
 * <p>
 * @param xAxis the new X Axis for the chart.
 * @see #getXAxis
 * @beaninfo
 *        bound: true
 * description: The X Axis for the chart.
 **/
```

```
public void setXAxis( FAxis xAxis ) {

    FAxis old = this.xAxis;

    if( this.xAxis != null )
        remove( this.xAxis );
    this.xAxis = xAxis;
    if( this.xAxis != null ) {
        add( xAxis );
        xAxis.setSize( xAxis.getPreferredSize() );
    }
    firePropertyChange( XAXIS_PROPERTY, old, xAxis );

}


/**
 * @return The current X Axis for the chart.
 * @see #setXAxis
 **/
public FAxis getXAxis() {
    return( this.xAxis );
}


/**
 * Set the Y Axis for the chart.
 * This is a bound property.
 * <p>
 * @param yAxis the new Y Axis for the chart.
 * @see #getYAxis
 * @beaninfo
 *        bound: true
 * description: The Y Axis for the chart.
 **/
public void setYAxis( FAxis yAxis ) {
    if( this.yAxis != null )
        remove( this.yAxis );
    this.yAxis = yAxis;
    if( this.yAxis != null ) {
        add( yAxis );
        yAxis.setSize( yAxis.getPreferredSize() );
    }
}


/**
 * @return the current Y axis for the chart.
 * @see #setYAxis
```

com.foley.chart *Package Source Code*

APPENDIX B

1215

B

com.foley.chart
PACKAGE SOURCE
CODE

```
    **/
public FAxis getYAxis() {
    return( this.yAxis );
}


/**
 * Set the model that the chart views.
 * The first column in the model specifies X
 * coordinate values. The remaining columns
 * specify y coordinates for each trace. This
 * implies that a model with four columns has
 * three traces in the chart.
 * <p>
 * This is a bound property.
 * <p>
 * @param model The new TableModel for the chart.
 * @see #getModel
 * @beaninfo
 *        bound: true
 * description: The data the chart contains.
 **/
public void setModel( TableModel model ) {
    TableModel old = this.model;
    this.model = model;
    firePropertyChange( MODEL_PROPERTY, old, model );
}


/**
 * @return The current data model for the chart.
 * @see #setModel
 **/
public TableModel getModel() {
    return( this.model );
}


/**
 * Sets the color used to draw grid lines to <I>color</I> and
 * redisplays the receiver. The default color is gray.
 *
 * @param gridColor The Color of the grid
 * @exception IllegalArgumentException if <I>color</I> is null
 * @see #getGridColor()
 * @beaninfo
 *        bound: true
 * description: The color for the grid in the chart.
 **/
```

```java
    public void setGridColor( Color gridColor ) {
        if( gridColor == null ) {
throw new IllegalArgumentException(
                "The grid color may not be null." );
        }
        Color old = this.gridColor;
        this.gridColor = gridColor;

        firePropertyChange( GRIDCOLOR_PROPERTY, old, gridColor );

        repaint();

    } // setGridColor


    /**
     * Returns the color used to draw grid lines.
     * The default color is look-and-feel dependent.
     * <p>
     * @return  the color used to draw grid lines
     * @see     #setGridColor()
     **/
    public Color getGridColor() {
        return gridColor;
    }


    /**
     * If true, the chart displays grid lines corresponding
     * to the major tick marks on the axis.
     * <p>
     * This is not a bound property. Instead the two component
     * lines are bound. I.e. horizontal lines and vertical lines
     * are bound properties.
     * <p>
     * @param showGrid If true draw grid lines, if false don't.
     * @see #setShowHorizontalLines
     * @see #setShowVerticalLines
     * @beaninfo
     *        bound: false
     * description: True to draw grid lines in the chart.
     **/
    public void setShowGrid( boolean showGrid ) {
        setShowHorizontalLines( showGrid );
        setShowVerticalLines( showGrid );

        repaint();
    }
```

```
    /**
     * If true, draw horizontal lines on the chart that correspond
     * to the Y axis major tick marks.
     *
 * @param showHorizontalLines true if chart should
     *                               draw horizontal lines.
     * @see #getShowHorizontalLines
     * @see #setShowGrid
     * @see #setShowVerticalLines
     * @beaninfo
     *       bound: true
 * description: Whether horizontal lines
     *                should be drawn on the chart.
     **/
    public void setShowHorizontalLines( boolean showHorizontalLines ) {

        boolean old = this.showHorizontalLines;
        this.showHorizontalLines = showHorizontalLines;

firePropertyChange( SHOWHORIZONTALLINES_PROPERTY,
                            old, showHorizontalLines );

        repaint();
    }


    /**
     * Returns true if the chart draws horizontal lines on
     * the chart, and false if it doesn't.
     * <p>
     * @return true if the chart draws horizontal lines, false otherwise
     * @see #setShowHorizontalLines
     **/
    public boolean isShowHorizontalLines() {
        return( showHorizontalLines );
    }


    /**
     * Sets whether the chart draws vertical lines that correspond
     * to the major ticks on the X axis.
     * <p>
 * @param showVerticalLines true if the chart should
     *                               draw vertical lines.
     * @see #getShowVerticalLines
     * @see #setShowGrid
     * @see #setShowHorizontalLines
     * @beaninfo
```

```
 * description: Whether vertical lines should be
 *                  drawn in between the cells.
 **/
    public void setShowVerticalLines( boolean showVerticalLines ) {
        boolean old = this.showVerticalLines;
        this.showVerticalLines = showVerticalLines;

firePropertyChange( SHOWVERTICALLINES_PROPERTY,
                            old, showVerticalLines );

        repaint();
    }


    /**
     * Returns true if the chart draws vertical lines on
     * the chart, and false if it doesn't.
     * <p>
     * @return true if the chart draws vertical lines, false otherwise
     * @see #setShowVerticalLines
     **/
    public boolean isShowVerticalLines() {
        return( showVerticalLines );
    }

    public Color getTraceColor( int trace ) {
        Color[] color = new Color[4];
        color[0] = java.awt.Color.yellow;
        color[1] = java.awt.Color.blue;
        color[2] = java.awt.Color.red;
        color[3] = java.awt.Color.black;
        return( color[ trace ] );
    }

} // FChart
```

FChartLayoutManager Class

```
package com.foley.chart;

import java.awt.*;


/**
 * A layout manager for the FChart Class.
 * <p>
 * The class lays out an X and Y axis. The X axis
 * is along the bottom of the component, and the Y
 * along the left edge.
 * <p>
```

```java
 * @author Mike Foley
 **/
public class FChartLayoutManager extends Object
    implements LayoutManager {

    /**
     * Adds the specified component with the specified name to
     * the layout.
     * @param name the component name
     * @param comp the component to be added
     */
    public void addLayoutComponent( String name, Component comp ) {
        // Not used.
    }


    /**
     * Removes the specified component from the layout.
     * @param comp the component to be removed
     */
    public void removeLayoutComponent( Component comp ) {
        // Not used.
    }


    /**
     * Calculates the preferred size dimensions for the specified
     * panel given the components in the specified parent container.
     * @param parent the component to be laid out
     *
     * @see #minimumLayoutSize
     */
    public Dimension preferredLayoutSize( Container parent ) {

        if( !( parent instanceof FChart ) )
            throw new RuntimeException(
                "FChartLayoutManager only valid for FChart instances" );

        FChart chart = ( FChart )parent;
        Insets insets = chart.getInsets();

        FAxis xAxis = chart.getXAxis();
        FAxis yAxis = chart.getYAxis();

        Dimension xAxisSize = xAxis.getPreferredSize();
        Dimension yAxisSize = yAxis.getPreferredSize();

        Dimension ourSize = new Dimension();
ourSize.width = insets.right + insets.left +
                    xAxisSize.width + yAxisSize.width + 10;
        ourSize.height = insets.top + insets.bottom +
```

```
➥                         xAxisSize.height + yAxisSize.height + 10;

        return( ourSize );

    } // preferredLayoutSize


    /**
     * Calculates the minimum size dimensions for the specified
     * panel given the components in the specified parent container.
     * @param parent the component to be laid out
     * @see #preferredLayoutSize
     */
    public Dimension minimumLayoutSize( Container parent ) {

        if( !( parent instanceof FChart ) )
            throw new RuntimeException(
                "FChartLayoutManager only valid for FChart instances" );

        FChart chart = ( FChart )parent;
        Insets insets = chart.getInsets();

        FAxis xAxis = chart.getXAxis();
        FAxis yAxis = chart.getYAxis();

        Dimension xAxisSize = xAxis.getMinimumSize();
        Dimension yAxisSize = yAxis.getMinimumSize();

        Dimension ourSize = new Dimension();
ourSize.width = insets.right + insets.left +
➥                 xAxisSize.width + yAxisSize.width;
        ourSize.height = insets.top + insets.bottom +
➥                   xAxisSize.height + yAxisSize.height;

        return( ourSize );

    } // minimumLayoutSize


    /**
     * Lays out the container in the specified panel.
     * @param parent the component which needs to be laid out
     */
    public void layoutContainer( Container parent ) {

        if( !( parent instanceof FChart ) )
            throw new RuntimeException(
                "FChartLayoutManager only valid for FChart instances" );
```

```
          FChart chart = ( FChart )parent;
          Dimension ourSize = chart.getSize();
          Insets insets = chart.getInsets();

          FAxis xAxis = chart.getXAxis();
          FAxis yAxis = chart.getYAxis();
          Dimension xAxisSize = xAxis.getPreferredSize();
          Dimension yAxisSize = yAxis.getPreferredSize();

          xAxis.setBounds( yAxisSize.width + insets.left,
                           ourSize.height - xAxisSize.height - insets.bottom,
                           ourSize.width - yAxisSize.width ñ
➡              insets.right - insets.left,
                           xAxisSize.height );
          yAxis.setBounds( insets.top,
                             insets.left,
                             yAxisSize.width,
ourSize.height - xAxisSize.height ñ
➡                  insets.top - insets.bottom );

     } // layoutContainer

} // FChartLayoutManager
```

FChartUI Class

```
package com.foley.chart;

import java.awt.*;
import java.beans.*;

import javax.swing.JComponent;
import javax.swing.table.TableModel;
import javax.swing.event.*;

import javax.swing.plaf.ComponentUI;


/**
 * Class FChartUI
 * <p>
 * The user-interface class for rendering FChart
 * instances.
 * <p>
 * @author Mike Foley
 * @version 1.2
 **/
```

```java
public class FChartUI extends ComponentUI
    implements PropertyChangeListener, TableModelListener {

    /**
     * The FChart we are rendering.
     **/
    private FChart chart;


    /**
     * FChartUI, null constructor.
     **/
    public FChartUI() {
        chart = null;
    }


    /**
     * This UI may not be shared. Create a new
     * instance for each component.
     * <p>
     * @param c The component needing a UI.
     **/
    public static ComponentUI createUI(JComponent c) {
        return( new FChartUI() );
    }


    /**
     * Install ourself as the UI for the given component.
     * We need to get property changes from the chart.
     * This way we can keep in sync with the chart's values.
     * <p>
     * @param c The component we are the UI for.
     **/
    public void installUI( JComponent c ) {
        chart = ( FChart )c;
        TableModel model = chart.getModel();
        if( model != null )
            model.addTableModelListener( this );
        chart.addPropertyChangeListener( this );
    }


    /**
     * Uninstall ourself as the UI for the given component.
     * Remove ourself as a PropertyChangeListener.
     * <p>
     * @param c The component we are uninstalling.
     **/
    public void uninstallUI(JComponent c) {
```

com.foley.chart *Package Source Code*

APPENDIX B

1223

B
com.foley.chart
PACKAGE SOURCE
CODE

```java
        if( chart != c )
            throw new IllegalComponentStateException(
                        this + " was asked to uninstallUI for "
                        + c + " that is not my chart " + chart + "." );

        chart.removePropertyChangeListener( this );
        TableModel model = chart.getModel();
        if( model != null )
            model.removeTableModelListener( this );
    }


    /**
     * tableChanged, from TableModelListener
     * <p>
     * The data in the table changed, repaint the chart.
     * <p>
     * @param event The change in the model.
     **/
    public void tableChanged( TableModelEvent event ) {
        chart.repaint();
    }


    /**
     * propertyChange, from PropertyChangeListener
     * <p>
     * If the change is a table model change start listening
     * to the new model.
     * <p>
     * @param event The change.
     **/
    public void propertyChange( PropertyChangeEvent event ) {
        if( event.getPropertyName().equals( FChart.MODEL_PROPERTY ) ) {
            TableModel model = ( TableModel )event.getOldValue();
            if( model != null )
                model.removeTableModelListener( this );

            model = ( TableModel )event.getNewValue();
            if( model != null ) {
                model.addTableModelListener( this );
            }
        }
    }


    /**
     * @return The preferred size of this component.
     **/
    public Dimension getPreferredSize( JComponent c ) {
```

```
        Insets insets = chart.getInsets();

        FAxis axis = chart.getXAxis();
        Dimension ourSize = new Dimension();
        Dimension x = axis.getPreferredSize();

        axis = chart.getYAxis();
        Dimension y = axis.getPreferredSize();

        ourSize.width = x.width + y.width + insets.right + insets.left;
        ourSize.height = x.height + y.height +
                    insets.top + insets.bottom;

        return( ourSize );
    }


    /**
     * Paint a representation of the <code>chart</code> instance
     * that was set in installUI().
     * <p>
     * @param g The graphics to paint with.
     * @param c The component to paint.
     **/
    public void paint( Graphics g, JComponent c ) {

        if( !( c instanceof FChart ) )
            return;

        TableModel model = chart.getModel();
        //
        // No data, no paint.
        //
        if( model == null )
            return;

        Dimension ourSize = c.getSize();

        FAxis xAxis = chart.getXAxis();
        FAxis yAxis = chart.getYAxis();
        Dimension yAxisSize = yAxis.getSize();

        g.translate( yAxisSize.width, yAxisSize.height - 1 );

        if( chart.isShowHorizontalLines() ) {
            paintHorizontalLines( g, xAxis, yAxis );
        }
```

```java
        if( chart.isShowVerticalLines() ) {
            paintVerticalLines( g, xAxis, yAxis );
        }

        //
        // Now paint the traces.
        //
        for( int j = 1; j < model.getColumnCount(); j++ ) {

            g.setColor( chart.getTraceColor( j-1 ) );

            Number o0 = ( Number )model.getValueAt( 0, 0 );
            Number o1 = ( Number )model.getValueAt( 0, j );
            int x0 = xAxis.getLocationValue( o0.doubleValue() );
            int y0 = yAxis.getLocationValue( o1.doubleValue() );

            for( int i = 1; i < model.getRowCount(); i++ ) {

                o0 = ( Number )model.getValueAt( i, 0 );
                o1 = ( Number )model.getValueAt( i, j );
                int x1 = xAxis.getLocationValue( o0.doubleValue() );
                int y1 = yAxis.getLocationValue( o1.doubleValue() );

                g.drawLine( x0, y0, x1, y1 );
                x0 = x1;
                y0 = y1;
            }
        }

        g.translate( -yAxisSize.width, -( yAxisSize.height - 1 ) );

    } // paint


    /**
     * Paint the vertical grid lines in the chart.
     * <p>
     * @param g The Graphics to paint with.
     * @param xAxis The chart's X axis.
     * @param yAxis The chart's Y axis.
     **/
    protected void paintVerticalLines( Graphics g,
                                       FAxis xAxis, FAxis yAxis ) {

        g.setColor( chart.getGridColor() );

        int minimum = xAxis.getMinimum();
        int maximum = xAxis.getMaximum();
        int spacing = xAxis.getMajorTickSpacing();
```

```
        Insets insets = yAxis.getInsets();
        Dimension size = yAxis.getSize();
        int yAxisLength = size.height - (insets.top + insets.bottom) - 1;

        for( int i = minimum + spacing; i <= maximum; i += spacing ) {
            int position = xAxis.getLocationValue( ( double )i );
            g.drawLine( position, 0, position, -yAxisLength );
        }

    }


    /**
     * Paint the horizontal grid lines in the chart.
     * <p>
     * @param g The Graphics to paint with.
     * @param xAxis The chart's X axis.
     * @param yAxis The chart's Y axis.
     **/
    protected void paintHorizontalLines( Graphics g,
                                   FAxis xAxis, FAxis yAxis ) {

        g.setColor( chart.getGridColor() );

        int minimum = yAxis.getMinimum();
        int maximum = yAxis.getMaximum();
        int spacing = yAxis.getMajorTickSpacing();

        Insets insets = xAxis.getInsets();
        Dimension size = xAxis.getSize();
        int xAxisLength = size.width - (insets.left + insets.right) - 1;

        for( int i = minimum + spacing; i <= maximum; i += spacing ) {
            int position = yAxis.getLocationValue( ( double )i );
            g.drawLine( 0, position, xAxisLength, position );
        }

    }

} // FChartUI
```

MetalFAxisUI Class

```
package com.foley.chart;

import java.awt.*;

import javax.swing.*;
```

```java
import javax.swing.plaf.ComponentUI;

import javax.swing.plaf.metal.MetalLookAndFeel;

import java.util.*;


/**
 * Class MetalFAxisUI
 * <p>
 * The Metal user-interface class for rendering FAxis
 * instances.
 * <p>
 * @author Mike Foley
 * @version 1.2
 **/
public class MetalFAxisUI extends FAxisUI {

    public MetalFAxisUI() {
    }


    public static ComponentUI createUI(JComponent c) {
        return( new MetalFAxisUI() );
    }


    /**
     * Paint a representation of the <code>chart</code> instance
     * that was set in installUI().
     * <p>
     * @param g The graphics to paint with.
     * @param c The component to paint.
     **/
    public void paint( Graphics g, JComponent c ) {

        if( !( c instanceof FAxis ) )
            throw new IllegalComponentStateException(
                        this + " was asked to paint for "
                        + c + " that is not an FAxis." );
        FAxis axis = ( FAxis )c;

        Insets insets = axis.getInsets();
        Dimension size = axis.getSize();
        if( axis.getOrientation() == SwingConstants.VERTICAL ) {
            g.setColor( MetalLookAndFeel.getControl() );
            int x = size.width - insets.right - 1;
            g.drawLine( x, insets.top,
                        x, size.height - insets.bottom );
            x -= 1;
```

```
            g.setColor( MetalLookAndFeel.getControlHighlight() );
             g.drawLine( x, insets.top,
                         x, size.height - insets.bottom );
             x -= 1;
            g.setColor( MetalLookAndFeel.getControlDarkShadow() );
             g.drawLine( x, insets.top,
                         x, size.height - insets.bottom );
        } else {
            g.setColor( MetalLookAndFeel.getControlDarkShadow() );
            int y = insets.top;
             g.drawLine( insets.left, y,
                         size.width - insets.right - 1, y );
             y += 1;
            g.setColor( MetalLookAndFeel.getControlHighlight() );
             g.drawLine( insets.left, y,
                         size.width - insets.right - 1, y );
             y += 1;
            g.setColor( MetalLookAndFeel.getControl() );
             g.drawLine( insets.left, y,
                         size.width - insets.right - 1, y );
        }

        if( axis.isPaintTicks() ) {
            paintMinorTicks( g, axis );
            paintMajorTicks( g, axis );
        }
        Color foreground = axis.getForeground();
        g.setColor( foreground );
        if( axis.isPaintLabels() ) {
            paintLabels( g, axis );
        }

    } // paint


    /**
     * Paint the minor tick marks on the axis.
     * <p>
     * @param g The Graphics to paint with.
     * @param axis The axis whose minor ticks need paints.
     **/
    protected void paintMinorTicks( Graphics g, FAxis axis ) {

        g.setColor( MetalLookAndFeel.getControlDarkShadow() );
        Insets insets = axis.getInsets();
        Dimension size = axis.getSize();
        BoundedRangeModel model = axis.getModel();
        int minimum = model.getMinimum();
        int maximum = model.getMaximum();
```

```
        int spacing = axis.getMinorTickSpacing();
        int tickSize = axis.getMinorTickSize();
        int axisHeight = size.height - (insets.top + insets.bottom) - 1;

        if( axis.getOrientation() == SwingConstants.VERTICAL ) {

                g.translate( 0, axisHeight );
            int x = size.width - insets.right - 4;
            for( int i = minimum; i <= maximum; i += spacing ) {
                int position = axis.getLocationValue( ( double )i );
                g.drawLine( x - tickSize, position, x, position );
            }
                g.translate( 0, -axisHeight );
        } else {
            int y = insets.top + 3;
            for( int i = minimum; i <= maximum; i += spacing ) {
                int position = axis.getLocationValue( ( double )i );
                g.drawLine( position, y, position, y + tickSize );
            }
        }

} // paintMinorTicks


/**
 * Paint the major tick marks on the axis.
 * <p>
 * @param g The Graphics to paint with.
 * @param axis The axis whose major ticks need paints.
 **/
protected void paintMajorTicks( Graphics g, FAxis axis ) {

    g.setColor( MetalLookAndFeel.getControlDarkShadow() );
    Insets insets = axis.getInsets();
    Dimension size = axis.getSize();
    BoundedRangeModel model = axis.getModel();
    int minimum = model.getMinimum();
    int maximum = model.getMaximum();
    int spacing = axis.getMajorTickSpacing();
    int tickSize = axis.getMajorTickSize();
    int axisHeight = size.height - (insets.top + insets.bottom) - 1;

    if( axis.getOrientation() == SwingConstants.VERTICAL ) {

            g.translate( 0, axisHeight );
        int x = size.width - insets.right - 4;
        for( int i = minimum; i <= maximum; i += spacing ) {
            int position = axis.getLocationValue( ( double )i );
            g.drawLine( x - tickSize, position, x, position );
        }
```

```
                    g.translate( 0, -axisHeight );
          } else {
              int y = insets.top + 3;
              for( int i = minimum; i <= maximum; i += spacing ) {
                  int position = axis.getLocationValue( ( double )i );
                  g.drawLine( position, y, position, y + tickSize );
              }
          }

      } // paintMajorTicks

} // MetalFAxisUI
```

MetalFChartUI Class

```java
package com.foley.chart;

import java.awt.*;
import java.beans.*;

import javax.swing.JComponent;
import javax.swing.table.TableModel;
import javax.swing.event.*;

import javax.swing.plaf.ComponentUI;


/**
 * Class MetalFChartUI
 * <p>
 * The Metal user-interface class for rendering FChart
 * instances.
 * <p>
 * @author Mike Foley
 * @version 1.2
 **/
public class MetalFChartUI extends FChartUI {

    public MetalFChartUI() {
    }

    public static ComponentUI createUI( JComponent c ) {
        return( new MetalFChartUI() );
    }

    public void paint( Graphics g, JComponent c ) {
        super.paint( g, c );
    }

} // MetalFChartUI
```

WindowsFAxisUI Class

```java
package com.foley.chart;

import java.awt.*;

import javax.swing.*;

import javax.swing.plaf.ComponentUI;

import java.util.*;


/**
 * Class WindowsFAxisUI
 * <p>
 * The Windows user-interface class for rendering FAxis
 * instances.
 * <p>
 * @author Mike Foley
 * @version 1.2
 **/
public class WindowsFAxisUI extends FAxisUI {


    public WindowsFAxisUI() {
    }


    public static ComponentUI createUI(JComponent c) {
        return( new WindowsFAxisUI() );
    }


    /**
     * Paint a representation of the <code>chart</code> instance
     * that was set in installUI().
     * <p>
     * @param g The graphics to paint with.
     * @param c The component to paint.
     **/
    public void paint( Graphics g, JComponent c ) {

        if( !( c instanceof FAxis ) )
            throw new IllegalComponentStateException(
                        this + " was asked to paint for "
```

```
                                   + c + " that is not an FAxis." );
            FAxis axis = ( FAxis )c;

            Insets insets = axis.getInsets();
            Dimension size = axis.getSize();
            if( axis.getOrientation() == SwingConstants.VERTICAL ) {
                g.setColor( UIManager.getColor("controlHighlight") );
                int x = size.width - insets.right - 1;
                 g.drawLine( x, insets.top,
                             x, size.height - insets.bottom );
                 x -= 1;
                g.setColor( UIManager.getColor("controlLtHighlight") );
                g.drawLine( x, insets.top,
                             x, size.height - insets.bottom );
                 x -= 1;
                g.setColor( UIManager.getColor("controlLtHighlight") );
                 g.drawLine( x, insets.top,
                             x, size.height - insets.bottom );
            } else {
                g.setColor( UIManager.getColor("controlShadow") );
                int y = insets.top;
                 g.drawLine( insets.left, y,
                             size.width - insets.right - 1, y );
                y += 1;
                g.setColor( UIManager.getColor("controlShadow") );
                 g.drawLine( insets.left, y,
                             size.width - insets.right - 1, y );
                y += 1;
                g.setColor( UIManager.getColor("controlDkShadow") );
                 g.drawLine( insets.left, y,
                             size.width - insets.right - 1, y );
            }

            if( axis.isPaintTicks() ) {
                paintMinorTicks( g, axis );
                paintMajorTicks( g, axis );
            }
            Color foreground = axis.getForeground();
            g.setColor( foreground );
            if( axis.isPaintLabels() ) {
                paintLabels( g, axis );
            }

        } // paint


        /**
         * Paint the minor tick marks on the axis.
         * <p>
         * @param g The Graphics to paint with.
```

com.foley.chart *Package Source Code*

APPENDIX B

1233

B

com.foley.chart
PACKAGE SOURCE
CODE

```java
 * @param axis The axis whose minor ticks need paints.
 **/
protected void paintMinorTicks( Graphics g, FAxis axis ) {

    g.setColor( UIManager.getColor("controlDkShadow") );
    Insets insets = axis.getInsets();
    Dimension size = axis.getSize();
    BoundedRangeModel model = axis.getModel();
    int minimum = model.getMinimum();
    int maximum = model.getMaximum();
    int spacing = axis.getMinorTickSpacing();
    int tickSize = axis.getMinorTickSize();
    int axisHeight = size.height - (insets.top + insets.bottom) - 1;

    if( axis.getOrientation() == SwingConstants.VERTICAL ) {

        g.translate( 0, axisHeight );
        int x = size.width - insets.right - 4;
        for( int i = minimum; i <= maximum; i += spacing ) {
            int position = axis.getLocationValue( ( double )i );
            g.drawLine( x - tickSize, position, x, position );
        }
        g.translate( 0, -axisHeight );
    } else {
        int y = insets.top + 3;
        for( int i = minimum; i <= maximum; i += spacing ) {
            int position = axis.getLocationValue( ( double )i );
            g.drawLine( position, y, position, y + tickSize );
        }
    }

} // paintMinorTicks


/**
 * Paint the major tick marks on the axis.
 * <p>
 * @param g The Graphics to paint with.
 * @param axis The axis whose major ticks need paints.
 **/
protected void paintMajorTicks( Graphics g, FAxis axis ) {

    g.setColor( UIManager.getColor("controlDkShadow") );
    Insets insets = axis.getInsets();
    Dimension size = axis.getSize();
    BoundedRangeModel model = axis.getModel();
    int minimum = model.getMinimum();
    int maximum = model.getMaximum();
    int spacing = axis.getMajorTickSpacing();
```

```
        int tickSize = axis.getMajorTickSize( );
        int axisHeight = size.height - (insets.top + insets.bottom) - 1;

        if( axis.getOrientation() == SwingConstants.VERTICAL ) {

                g.translate( 0, axisHeight );
            int x = size.width - insets.right - 4;
            for( int i = minimum; i <= maximum; i += spacing ) {
                int position = axis.getLocationValue( ( double )i );
                g.drawLine( x - tickSize, position, x, position );
            }
                g.translate( 0, -axisHeight );
        } else {
            int y = insets.top + 3;
            for( int i = minimum; i <= maximum; i += spacing ) {
                int position = axis.getLocationValue( ( double )i );
                g.drawLine( position, y, position, y + tickSize );
            }
        }

    } // paintMajorTicks

} // WindowsFAxisUI
```

WindowsFChartUI Class

```
package com.foley.chart;

import java.awt.*;
import java.beans.*;

import javax.swing.JComponent;
import javax.swing.table.TableModel;
import javax.swing.event.*;

import javax.swing.plaf.ComponentUI;


/**
 * Class WindowsFChartUI
 * <p>
 * The Windows user-interface class for rendering FChart
 * instances.
 * <p>
 * @author Mike Foley
```

```
 * @version 1.2
 **/
public class WindowsFChartUI extends FChartUI {

    public WindowsFChartUI() {
    }

    public static ComponentUI createUI(JComponent c) {
        return( new WindowsFChartUI() );
    }

} // WindowsFChartUI
```

APPENDIX C

com.foley.utility Source Code

Throughout this book, classes are developed for the `com.foley.utility` package. These are presented in context when they are introduced, and they are presented here for completeness.

AButton.java

```java
package com.foley.utility;

import java.beans.*;

import javax.swing.*;


/**
 * The AButton class is an Action aware button.
 * The button will configure itself to the Action set using
 * the setAction method.
 *
 * The class can be configured for only one Action at
 * a time. If a second Action is set using the setAction
 * method, the first Action will be removed. However, other
 * ActionListeners can be added as normal by using the
 * addActionListener method.
 *
 * @author Mike Foley
 **/
public class AButton extends JButton
    implements PropertyChangeListener {

    /**
     * The Action for which this button is configured.
     **/
    private Action action;

    /**
     * Bound property names.
     **/
    public static final String ACTION_PROPERTY = "action";


    /**
     * AButton, default constructor.
     * Creates a button with no set text or icon.
     **/
    public AButton() {
```

```java
        this( null );
    }

/**
 * AButton, constructor
 * Creates a button from the given Action.
 *
 * @see setAction
 * @param action—The Action to which to configure this button.
 **/
public AButton( Action action ) {

    super();

    //
    // The default placement is to set
    // the text below the Icon.
    //
    setHorizontalTextPosition( JButton.CENTER );
    setVerticalTextPosition( JButton.BOTTOM );

    setAction( action );
}


/**
 * Configure the button for the given Action.
 * If the button was already configured for
 * an Action, remove that Action from being
 * a listener to this button.
 * The Action is a bound property.
 *
 * @param action—The Action to which to configure this button.
 **/
public void setAction( Action action ) {

    Action oldAction = this.action;
    if( oldAction != null ) {
        //
        // Remove the bind between the button and the
        // old action.
        //
        oldAction.removePropertyChangeListener( this );
        removeActionListener( oldAction );
    }

    this.action = action;

    if( action != null ) {
```

```
        //
        // Update our appearance to that of the new action.
        //
        setText( ( String )action.getValue( Action.NAME ) );
        setIcon( ( Icon )action.getValue( Action.SMALL_ICON ) );

        setEnabled( action.isEnabled() );

        //
        // Bind ourself to the new Action.
        //
        action.addPropertyChangeListener( this );
        addActionListener( action );

    } else {

        //
        // null Action, set the button's view to 'empty'
        setText( "" );
        setIcon( null );

    } // else

    //
    // The Action is a bound property.
    //
    firePropertyChange( ACTION_PROPERTY, oldAction, this.action );

} // setAction


/**
 * propertyChange, from PropertyChangeListener.
 * Only handle changes from the Action for which we are configured.
 *
 * @param event—Property change event causing this method call.
 **/
public void propertyChange( PropertyChangeEvent event ) {
    if( event.getSource() == action ) {

        //
        // Get the name of the changed property, and
        // update ourself accordingly.
        //
        String propertyName = event.getPropertyName();

        if( propertyName.equals( Action.NAME ) ) {
            setText( ( String )event.getNewValue() );
        } else if( propertyName.equals(Action.SMALL_ICON)) {
            setIcon( ( Icon )event.getNewValue() );
            invalidate();
```

```
            } else if( propertyName.equals( "enabled" ) ) {
                Boolean enabled = ( Boolean )event.getNewValue();
                setEnabled( enabled.booleanValue() );
            }

            //
            // Update our display.
            //
            repaint();
        }

    } // propertyChange

} // AButton
```

ActionFocusListener.java

```java
package com.foley.utility;

import java.awt.event.ActionListener;
import java.awt.event.ActionEvent;
import java.awt.event.FocusListener;
import java.awt.event.FocusEvent;


/**
 * ActionFocusListener
 *
 * An action that takes an ActionListener.  When
 * the component that this action is listening on
 * loses focus, an ActionEvent is created and sent
 * to the action listener.
 *
 * @author Mike Foley
 * @version 1.1
 *
 **/
public class ActionFocusListener extends Object
        implements FocusListener
{
    private ActionListener actionListener;

    /**
     * ActionFocusListener
     *
     * Construction.  Takes the ActionListener who will
     * be notified when the focus is lost.
     *
     * @param actionListener Where actions are sent.
     *
```

```
   **/
   public ActionFocusListener( ActionListener actionListener ) {
       this.actionListener = actionListener;
   } // ActionFocusListener


   public void focusGained( FocusEvent e ) {
   } // focusGained

   public void focusLost( FocusEvent e ) {

       ActionEvent actionEvent = new ActionEvent(
                   e.getSource(), 0, "Focus", 0 );

       actionListener.actionPerformed( actionEvent );
   } // focusLost

} // ActionFocusListener
```

AlbumCollectionItem.java

```
package com.foley.utility;

import javax.swing.*;


/**
 * The AlbumCollectionItem class binds a name
 * and icon together.
 * <p>
 * @author Mike Foley
 **/
public class AlbumCollectionItem {
    String name;
    Icon icon;

    /**
     * AlbumCollectionItem, Constructor
     * <p>
     * @param name—The name of this item.
     * @param icon—The icon for this item.
     **/
    public AlbumCollectionItem( String name, Icon icon ) {
        this.name = name;
        this.icon = icon;
    }

    /**
     * @return—The name of this item.
     **/
```

```
    public String getName() {
        return( name );
    }

    /**
     * @return—The icon associated with this item.
     **/
    public Icon getIcon() {
        return( icon );
    }

    /**
     * @return—The String representation of this item.
     **/
    public String toString() {
        return( name );
    }

} // AlbumCollectionItem
```

AlbumTreeRenderer.java

```
package com.foley.utility;

import java.awt.Component;

import javax.swing.*;
import javax.swing.tree.*;


/**
 * A tree renderer that knows about the record
 * collection tree.
 * <p>
 * @author Mike Foley
 **/
public class AlbumTreeRenderer extends JLabel
    implements TreeCellRenderer, AlbumTypes {

    Icon albumIcon = new ImageIcon( "album.gif" );
    Icon albumsIcon = new ImageIcon( "albums.gif" );
    Icon cdsIcon = new ImageIcon( "cds.gif" );
    Icon tapesIcon = new ImageIcon( "tapes.gif" );


    /**
     * AlbumTreeRenderer, Constructor.
     * <p>
```

```
         * The renderer must be opaque so the background
         * color is painted.
         **/
        public AlbumTreeRenderer() {
            setFont( UIManager.getFont( "Tree.font" ) ) ;
            setOpaque( true );
        }


        /**
         * Configures the renderer based on the passed in components.
         * Text for the cell is obtained from the toString() method of
         * the value parameter.
         * <p>
         * Foreground and background colors are obtained from the
         * UIManager.
         * <p>
         * If the value is a DefaultMutableTreeNode, and its user object
         * is an AlbumCollectionItem, the icon is obtained from the item
         * and set for the cell.
         **/
        public Component getTreeCellRendererComponent( JTree tree,
                                  Object value,
                                  boolean selected,
                                  boolean expanded,
                                  boolean leaf,
                                  int row,
                                  boolean hasFocus ) {

            //
            // Set the text for the cell.
            //
            if( value != null )
                setText( value.toString() );
            else
                setText( "" );

            //
            // Set the colors for the cell.
            //
            if( selected ) {
                setBackground( UIManager.getColor(
                               "Tree.selectionBackground" ) );
                setForeground( UIManager.getColor(
                               "Tree.selectionForeground" ) );
            } else {
                setBackground( UIManager.getColor( "Tree.textBackground" ) );
```

```
            setForeground( UIManager.getColor( "Tree.textForeground" ) );
        } // else

        //
        // The type of the node is stored in the user object
        // in the mutable tree node.
        //
        setIcon( null );
        if( value instanceof DefaultMutableTreeNode ) {
            DefaultMutableTreeNode node = ( DefaultMutableTreeNode )value;
            Object o = node.getUserObject();
            if( o instanceof AlbumCollectionItem ) {
                AlbumCollectionItem albumItem = ( AlbumCollectionItem )o;
                setIcon( albumItem.getIcon() );
            }
        }

        return( this );
    }

} // AlbumTreeRenderer
```

AlbumTypes.java

```
package com.foley.utility;


public interface AlbumTypes {
    public static final int ALBUM = 1;
    public static final int ALBUMS = 2;
    public static final int CDS = 3;
    public static final int TAPES = 4;
}
```

ApplicationFrame.java

```
package com.foley.utility;

import java.awt.*;
import java.awt.event.*;
import java.util.Vector;
import java.io.Serializable;

import javax.swing.*;
import javax.swing.border.*;
import javax.swing.event.*;
```

```java
/**
 * A toplevel frame. The frame customizes the
 * Icon and content in the frameInit method.
 *
 * @author Mike Foley
 **/
public class ApplicationFrame extends JFrame implements Serializable {
    private MouseAdapter ourMouseAdapter;

    private static Icon exitIcon;
    private static Icon closeIcon;
    private static Icon saveIcon;
    private static Icon saveasIcon;
    private static Icon openIcon;
    private static Icon newIcon;
    private static Icon printIcon;
    private static Icon printsetupIcon;
    private static Icon logIcon;
    private static Icon echoIcon;
    private static Icon whiteIcon;
    private static Icon blackIcon;
    private static Icon redIcon;
    private static Icon blueIcon;

    /**
     * The MouseListener for content components. This will
     * pop up a menu and the popupTrigger is received.
     **/
    private MouseListener mouseListener;


    /**
     * Load images used in the frame.
     **/
    static {
        try {
            closeIcon = ImageLoader.loadIcon( "close.gif" );
            exitIcon = ImageLoader.loadIcon( "exit.gif" );
            saveIcon = ImageLoader.loadIcon( "save.gif" );
            saveasIcon = ImageLoader.loadIcon( "saveas.gif" );
            openIcon = ImageLoader.loadIcon( "open.gif" );
            newIcon = ImageLoader.loadIcon( "new.gif" );
            printIcon = ImageLoader.loadIcon( "print.gif" );
            printsetupIcon = ImageLoader.loadIcon( "printsetup.gif" );
            logIcon = ImageLoader.loadIcon( "log.gif" );
            echoIcon = ImageLoader.loadIcon( "echo.gif" );
            whiteIcon = ImageLoader.loadIcon( "white.gif" );
            blackIcon = ImageLoader.loadIcon( "black.gif" );
            redIcon = ImageLoader.loadIcon( "red.gif" );
            blueIcon = ImageLoader.loadIcon( "blue.gif" );
```

```
        } catch( InterruptedException ie ) {
        }

    }


    /**
     * ApplicationFrame, null constructor.
     **/
    public ApplicationFrame() {
        this( null );
    }


    /**
     * ApplicationFrame, constructor.
     *
     * @param title—The title for the frame.
     **/
    public ApplicationFrame( String title ) {
        super( title );
    }


    /**
     * Customize the frame for our application.
     **/
    protected void frameInit() {
        //
        // Let the super create the panes.
        super.frameInit();

        ourMouseAdapter = new MouseAdapter() {};

        Image bullseye = new ImageIcon( "bullseye.gif" ).getImage();
        setIconImage( bullseye );

        JMenuBar menuBar = createMenu();
        setJMenuBar( menuBar );

        JToolBar toolBar = createToolBar();
        Container content = getContentPane();
        content.add( BorderLayout.NORTH, toolBar );

        createApplicationContent();

    } // frameInit


    /**
     * Create the content for the applictaion
```

```
  **/
protected void createApplicationContent() {
} // createApplicationContent


/**
 * Create the menu for the frame.
 *
 * @return—The menu for the frame.
 **/
protected JMenuBar createMenu() {
    JMenuBar menuBar = new JMenuBar();

    JMenu file = new JMenu( "File" );
    file.setMnemonic( K eyEvent.VK_F );

    JMenuItem item;

    item = new JMenuItem( "Exit", exitIcon );
    item.setHorizontalTextPosition( SwingConstants.RIGHT );
    item.setMnemonic( KeyEvent.VK_X );
    item.setAccelerator( KeyStroke.getKeyStroke( KeyEvent.VK_X,
    Event.CTRL_MASK ) );
    item.addActionListener( new ActionListener() {
        public void actionPerformed( ActionEvent e ) {
            System.exit( 0 );
        }
    } );
    file.add( item );

    menuBar.add( file );



    return( menuBar );

} // createMenuBar


/**
 * Create the mouse listener for the frame.
 *
 * @return—The MouseListener for the content in the frame.
 **/
protected MouseListener createMouseListener() {
    return new ApplicationMouseListener();
}

protected JToolBar createToolBar() {
    final JToolBar toolBar = new JToolBar();
```

```
            toolBar.add( new ExitAction() );
            return( toolBar );
        }


        /**
         * Show or hide the wait cursor. The wait cursor
         * is set on the glass pane so input mouse events
         * are blocked from other componenets.
         * <p>
         * @param waitCursorVisible True to show the wait cursor,
         *                          False to hide the wait cursor.
         **/
        public void setWaitCursorVisible( boolean waitCursorVisible ) {
            Component glassPane = getGlassPane();
            if( waitCursorVisible ) {
                //
                // Show the wiat cursor.
                //
                glassPane.addMouseListener( ourMouseAdapter );
                glassPane.setCursor( Cursor.getPredefinedCursor(
                                     Cursor.WAIT_CURSOR ) );
                glassPane.setVisible( true );
            } else {
                //
                // Hide the wait cursor.
                //
                glassPane.removeMouseListener( ourMouseAdapter );
                glassPane.setCursor( Cursor.getPredefinedCursor(
                                     Cursor.DEFAULT_CURSOR ) );
                glassPane.setVisible( false );
            }
        }


        /**
         * Application entry point.
         * Create the frame, and display it.
         *
         * @param args Command line parameter. Not used.
         **/
        public static void main( String[] args ) {

            ApplicationFrame frame = new ApplicationFrame( "ApplicationFrame"
);
            frame.pack();
            frame.setVisible( true );

        }

} // ApplicationFrame
```

ApplicationMouseListener.java

```java
package com.foley.utility;

import java.awt.*;
import java.awt.event.*;

import javax.swing.*;


/**
 * Pop up the context sensitive menu when the pop-up
 * trigger event is delivered.
 **/
class ApplicationMouseListener extends MouseAdapter
    implements MouseListener {

    /**
     * See if the mouse event is the pop-up trigger. If so,
     * display the pop-up menu.
     *
     * @param e The mouse event causing this call.
     **/
    public void mouseReleased( MouseEvent e ) {
        if( e.isPopupTrigger() ) {
            showPopupMenu( ( Component )e.getSource(),
                        e.getX(), e.getY() );
        }
    }


    /**
     * See if the mouse event is the pop-up trigger. If so,
     * display the pop-up menu.
     *
     * @param e[em]The mouse event causing this call.
     **/
    public void mousePressed( MouseEvent e ) {
        if( e.isPopupTrigger() ) {
            showPopupMenu( ( Component )e.getSource(),
                        e.getX(), e.getY() );
        }
    }


    /**
     * Display the pop-up menu using the given invoker, and at the
     * specified location.
     *
     * @param invoker The component used as the menu's invoker.
```

```
         * @param x—The X coordinate for the pop-up menu.
         * @param y—The Y coordinate for the pop-up menu.
         **/
        private void showPopupMenu( Component invoker, int x, int y ) {
            Icon saveIcon = null;
            Icon saveasIcon = null;
            Icon printIcon = null;
            Icon printsetupIcon = null;

            try {
                //
                // Load the images used.
                //
                saveIcon = ImageLoader.loadIcon( "save.gif" );
                saveasIcon = ImageLoader.loadIcon( "saveas.gif" );
                printIcon = ImageLoader.loadIcon( "print.gif" );
                printsetupIcon = ImageLoader.loadIcon( "printsetup.gif" );
            } catch( InterruptedException ie ) {
                System.err.println( "Error loading images" );
                return;
            }

            JPopupMenu popup = new JPopupMenu( "Title" );

            JMenuItem item = new JMenuItem( "Save", saveIcon );
            item.setHorizontalTextPosition( SwingConstants.RIGHT );
            item.setMnemonic( KeyEvent.VK_S );
            popup.add( item );

            item = new JMenuItem( "Save As...", saveasIcon );
            item.setHorizontalTextPosition( SwingConstants.RIGHT );
            item.setMnemonic( KeyEvent.VK_A );
            popup.add( item );

            popup.addSeparator();

            item = new JMenuItem( "Print Setup...", printsetupIcon );
            item.setHorizontalTextPosition( SwingConstants.RIGHT );
            item.setMnemonic( KeyEvent.VK_U );
            popup.add( item );

            item = new JMenuItem( "Print", printIcon );
            item.setHorizontalTextPosition( SwingConstants.RIGHT );
            item.setMnemonic( KeyEvent.VK_P );
            popup.add( item );

            popup.show( invoker, x, y );

        }

    } // ApplicationMouseListener
```

ColorEditor.java

```java
package com.foley.utility;

import java.awt.*;
import java.awt.event.*;

import java.io.Serializable;

import java.beans.*;

import javax.swing.*;
import javax.swing.event.*;
import javax.swing.colorchooser.*;


/**
 * A panel that allows colors to be specified
 * for a foreground and background.
 * <p>
 * @author Mike Foley
 **/
public class ColorEditor extends JPanel
    implements Serializable {

    /**
     * A radio button group for foreground/background
     * option.
     **/
    private ButtonGroup colorButtonGroup;
    private JRadioButton foregroundRadioButton;
    private JRadioButton backgroundRadioButton;

    /**
     * The color chooser.
     **/
    private JColorChooser colorChooser;

    /**
     * boolean used to decide which color is being changed.
     * true means foreground is being edited, false background.
     **/
    private boolean foregroundEditing = true;

    /**
     * Property change support.
     **/
```

```
    protected PropertyChangeSupport changeSupport =
            new PropertyChangeSupport( this );

    /**
     * The current foreground and background Colors.
     **/
    private Color editForegroundColor;
    private Color editBackgroundColor;

    /**
     * This component contains two properties: foreground and
     * background color.
     **/
    public static final String EDITED_FOREGROUND_PROPERTY =
                            "ForegroundProperty";
    public static final String EDITED_BACKGROUND_PROPERTY =
                            "BackgroundProperty";

    /**
     * The default colors used in the editor.
     **/
    public static final Color DEFAULT_FOREGROUND_COLOR = Color.black;
    public static final Color DEFAULT_BACKGROUND_COLOR = Color.white;


    /**
     * ColorEditor, constructor.
     * <p>
     * Create a ColorEditor with the default foreground and
     * background colors.
     **/
    public ColorEditor() {
        this( DEFAULT_FOREGROUND_COLOR, DEFAULT_BACKGROUND_COLOR );
    } // ColorEditor


    /**
     * ColorEditor, constructor.
     * <p>
     * The ColorEditor can be thought of as a mediator between
     * the various components on the panel. The radio buttons
     * choose which color is being edited. Valid options are
     * foreground and background. The JColorChooser allows visual
     * editing of these colors.
     * <p>
     * Create the components contained in the ColorEditor.
     * Create the listeners and connects them to give the
     * component-to-component interactions.
     * <p>
```

```
 * @param foreground—The initial foreground color for the editor.
 * @param background—The initial background color for the editor.
 **/
public ColorEditor( Color foreground, Color background ) {

    super();

    //
    // If a color is null, use the default color.
    //
    if( foreground == null )
        foreground = DEFAULT_FOREGROUND_COLOR;
    if( background == null )
        background = DEFAULT_BACKGROUND_COLOR;

    this.editForegroundColor = foreground;
    this.editBackgroundColor = background;

    setLayout( new BorderLayout() );

    //
    // This action listener receives messages when the radio
    // buttons change. Set which property is being changed,
    // and update the color chooser to the current color
    // in that property.
    // A property change event doesn't need to be thrown here.
    // This only changes which property is being edited, not the
    // value of a property.
    //
    ActionListener radioListener = new ActionListener() {
        public void actionPerformed( ActionEvent event ) {
            if( event.getSource() == foregroundRadioButton ) {
                foregroundEditing = true;
                colorChooser.setColor( editForegroundColor );
            } else {
                foregroundEditing = false;
                colorChooser.setColor( editBackgroundColor );
            }
            colorChooser.repaint();
        }
    };

    //
    // Create a radio button group containing
    // two buttons: foreground and background color.
    //
    colorButtonGroup = new ButtonGroup();
    foregroundRadioButton = new JRadioButton( "Foreground" );
    foregroundRadioButton.setSelected( true );
    backgroundRadioButton = new JRadioButton( "Background" );
    colorButtonGroup.add( foregroundRadioButton );
```

```
            colorButtonGroup.add( backgroundRadioButton );
            foregroundRadioButton.addActionListener( radioListener );
            backgroundRadioButton.addActionListener( radioListener );

            //
            // The options panel contains the radio buttons.
            //
            JPanel options = new JPanel();
            options.setLayout( new BorderLayout() );

            //
            // Place the radio buttons.
            //
            JPanel buttons = new JPanel();
            buttons.setLayout( new BoxLayout( buttons, BoxLayout.Y_AXIS ) );
            buttons.add( foregroundRadioButton );
            buttons.add( backgroundRadioButton );
            options.add( BorderLayout.NORTH, buttons );
            buttons.setBorder( BorderFactory.createTitledBorder(
                            BorderFactory.createEtchedBorder(),
                        "Current Color" ) );

            add( BorderLayout.WEST, buttons );

            //
            // Create the JColorChooser.
            //
            colorChooser = new JColorChooser( editForegroundColor );
            colorChooser.setBorder( BorderFactory.createLoweredBevelBorder()
);
            add( BorderLayout.CENTER, colorChooser );
            ColorSelectionModel model = colorChooser.getSelectionModel();
            model.addChangeListener( new ChangeListener() {
                public void stateChanged( ChangeEvent e ) {
                    Color c = colorChooser.getColor();
                    if( isEditingForeground() ) {
                        setEditedForegoundColor( c );
                    } else {
                        setEditedBackgoundColor( c );
                    }
                }
            } );

        } // ColorEditor


    /**
     * @return The current value of the foreground color.
     **/
    public Color getEditedForegoundColor() {
```

```
            return( editForegroundColor );
        }


        /**
         * Provide an API to set the foreground color used in the editor.
         * If the foreground color is currently being edited, set the
         * value in the color chooser. This will fire the property change
         * event, and the other components will update.
         * <p>
         * If the background is being edited, set the color in the label.
         * The color chooser will update the next time foreground is edited.
         * <p>
         * This is a bound property.
         * <p>
         * @param c The new foreground color.
         **/
        public void setEditedForegoundColor( Color c ) {

            if( foregroundEditing ) {
                colorChooser.setColor( c );
            }
            Color old = editForegroundColor;
            editForegroundColor = c;
                changeSupport.firePropertyChange( EDITED_FOREGROUND_PROPERTY,
                                                  old,
                                                  c );

        } // setEditedForegoundColor


        /**
         * @return The current value of the background color.
         **/
        public Color getEditedBackgoundColor() {
            return( editBackgroundColor );
        }


        /**
         * Provide an API to set the background color used in the editor.
         * If the background color is currently being edited, set the
         * value in the color chooser. This will fire the property change
         * event, and the other components will update.
         * <p>
         * If the foreground is being edited, set the color in the label.
         * The color chooser will update the next time background is edited.
         * <p>
         * This is a bound property.
         * <p>
```

```java
     * @param c The new background color.
     **/
    public void setEditedBackgoundColor( Color c ) {

        if( !foregroundEditing ) {
            colorChooser.setColor( c );
        }
        Color old = editBackgroundColor;
        editBackgroundColor = c;
            changeSupport.firePropertyChange( EDITED_BACKGROUND_PROPERTY,
                                    old,
                                    c );

    } // setEditedBackgoundColor


    /**
     * Set which property is being edited. These are in a radio
     * button, so selecting or unselecting the foreground button
     * will do the opposite to the background button.
     * <p>
     * Changing the selected state of the button will cause the proper
     * events to be fired, which will update this object's state.
     * <p>
     * @param editForeground—The new state for the foreground.
     **/
    public void setEditingForeground( boolean editForeground ) {
        foregroundRadioButton.setSelected( true );
    }


    /**
     * Query which property is being edited. Because there are
     * only two, this can be represented as a Boolean. The Boolean
     * that was choosen is the foreground radio button's selected state.
     * <p>
     * @return true if the foregound color is being edited; false is
background.
     **/
    public boolean isEditingForeground() {
        return( foregroundRadioButton.isSelected() );
    }


    public static Action getShowAction() {
        return( new ShowColorEditorAction() );
    }


    /**
     * addPropertyChangeListener
```

```
     *
     * The specified PropertyChangeListeners <b>propertyChange</b> method
     * will be called each time the value of any bound property is
     * changed. The PropertyListener object is addded to a list of
     * PropertyChangeListener managed by this button, it can be removed
     * with removePropertyChangeListener.
     *
     * Note: the JavaBeans specification does not require
     * PropertyChangeListeners to run in any particular order.

     *
     * @param l—The PropertyChangeListener
     * @see #removePropertyChangeListener
      *
     **/
    public void addPropertyChangeListener( PropertyChangeListener l ) {
          changeSupport.addPropertyChangeListener( l );
    } // addPropertyChangeListener


    /**
     * removePropertyChangeListener
     *
     * Remove this PropertyChangeListener from the buttons internal list.
     * If the PropertyChangeListener isn't on the list, silently do
nothing.
     *
     * @param l the PropertyChangeListener
     * @see #addPropertyChangeListener
     *
     **/
    public void removePropertyChangeListener( PropertyChangeListener l ) {
          changeSupport.removePropertyChangeListener( l );
    } // removePropertyChangeListener

} // ColorEditor


/**
 * Class ShowColorEditorAction
 * <p>
 * An action that opens the ColorEditor dialog box.
 * <p>
 * @author Mike Foley
 * @version 1.2
 **/
class ShowColorEditorAction extends AbstractAction {

    /**
     * The default name used in a menu.
```

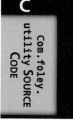

```
    **/
    private static final String DEFAULT_NAME = "Color Editor...";

    public ShowColorEditorAction() {
        this( DEFAULT_NAME, null );
    } // ShowColorEditorAction

    public ShowColorEditorAction( String name ) {
        this( name, null );
    } // ShowColorEditorAction

    public ShowColorEditorAction( String name, Icon icon ) {
        super( name, icon );
    } // ShowColorEditorAction


    /**
     * actionPerformed, from ActionListener
     * <p>
     * Perform the action. Show the ColorEditor dialog box.
     * <p>
     * @param event—The event causing the action to fire.
     **/
    public void actionPerformed( ActionEvent event ) {

        Frame parent = JOptionPane.getFrameForComponent(
                                 ( Component )event.getSource() );
        JDialog dialog = new JDialog( parent );
        ColorEditor editor = new ColorEditor();
        dialog.getContentPane().add( BorderLayout.CENTER, editor );

        dialog.setModal( true );
        dialog.pack();
        dialog.setVisible( true );
        dialog.show();
    } // actionPerformed

} // ShowColorEditorAction
```

ExitAction.java

```
package com.foley.utility;

import java.awt.event.ActionListener;
import java.awt.event.ActionEvent;

import javax.swing.AbstractAction;
import javax.swing.Icon;
```

```java
/**
 * Class ExitAction
 * <p>
 * An action that shuts down the java virtual machine.
 * <p>
 * @author Mike Foley
 * @version 1.2
 **/
public class ExitAction extends AbstractAction {

    /**
     * The default name and Icon for the Action.
     **/
    private static final String DEFAULT_NAME = "Exit";
    private static final String DEFAULT_ICON_NAME = "exit.gif";
    private static Icon DEFAULT_ICON;

    /**
     * ExitAction, default constructor.
     * Create the Action with the default name and Icon.
     **/
    public ExitAction() {
        this( DEFAULT_NAME, DEFAULT_ICON );
    } // ExitAction

    /**
     * ExitAction, constructor.
     * Create the Action with the given name and
     * default Icon.
     *
     * @param name The name for the Action.
     **/
    public ExitAction( String name ) {
        this( name, DEFAULT_ICON );
    } // ExitAction

    /**
     * ExitAction, constructor.
     * Create the Action with the given name and
     * Icon.
     *
     * @param name—The name for the Action.
     * @param icon—The small icon for the Action.
     **/
    public ExitAction( String name, Icon icon ) {
            super( name, icon );
    } // ExitAction

    /**
     * putValue, overriden from AbstractAction.
```

```
 * Guard against null values being added to the Action.
 *
 * @param key—The key for the value.
 * @param value—The value to be added to the Action.
 **/
public void putValue( String key, Object value ) {
    if( value != null )
        super.putValue( key, value );
}

/**
 * actionPerformed, from ActionListener
 * <p>
 * Perform the action. Exit the JVM.
 * <p>
 * @param event—The event causing the action to fire.
 **/
public void actionPerformed( ActionEvent event ) {
    System.exit(0);
} // actionPerformed

/**
 * static initialization. Load the default Icon.
 **/
static {
    try {
        DEFAULT_ICON = ImageLoader.loadIcon( DEFAULT_ICON_NAME );
    } catch( InterruptedException ie ) {
        System.err.println("Could not load ExitAction default Icon");
    }
}

} // ExitAction
```

FPartialEtchedBorder.java

```
package com.foley.utility;

import java.awt.Component;
import java.awt.Graphics;
import java.awt.Color;

import java.awt.event.ActionListener;
import java.awt.event.ActionEvent;

import javax.swing.border.AbstractBorder;

/**
 * Class FPartialEtchedBorder
```

```
 *  <p>
 *  A partial etched border.
 *  <p>
 *  @author Mike Foley
 *  @version 1.2
 **/
public class FPartialEtchedBorder extends AbstractBorder {

    Color highlight;
    Color shadow;

    public FPartialEtchedBorder() {
        super();
    } // FPartialEtchedBorder


    public FPartialEtchedBorder( Color highlight, Color shadow ) {
        super();
        this.highlight = highlight;
        this.shadow = shadow;

    } // FPartialEtchedBorder


    /**
     * @param c—The component for which this border is being painted
     * @param g—The paint graphics
     * @param x the x—Position of the painted border
     * @param y the y—Position of the painted border
     * @param width—The width of the painted border
     * @param height—The height of the painted border
     **/
    public void paintBorder( Component c, Graphics g,
                        int x, int y,
                        int width, int height ) {

        //
        // Save the graphics context. This will be
        // restored at the end of the method.
        // The original color and origin are what we change.
         // Translate to the corner of this component.
         // This way we can draw in a 0-width-1, 0-height-1 space.
        //
         Color oldColor = g.getColor();
         g.translate( x, y );

         int w = width;
         int h = height;
```

```
            g.setColor(shadow != null? shadow : c.getBackground().darker());
            g.drawLine( 0, 0, w-1, 0 );

            g.setColor( highlight != null ?
                        highlight : c.getBackground().brighter() );

            g.drawLine(1, 1, w-1, 1);

            //
            // Restore the graphic context.
            //
            g.translate( -x, -y );
            g.setColor( oldColor );

        } // paintBorder

} // FPartialEtchedBorder
```

ImageLoader.java

```
package com.foley.utility;

import java.awt.Component;
import java.awt.Toolkit;
import java.awt.Image;
import java.awt.MediaTracker;

import java.io.IOException;

import java.net.URL;

import javax.swing.Icon;
import javax.swing.ImageIcon;


/**
 * A class containing static methods that can
 * be used to load Images and Icons.
 * <p>
 * @author Mike Foley
 * @version 1.2
 **/
public class ImageLoader extends Component {
    private static ImageLoader imageLoader;

    /**
     * ImageLoader, constructor.
     * <p>
     * There should not be any instances of this
```

```
 * class created outside the private one used
 * in the class.
 **/
private ImageLoader() {
    super();
}


/**
 * loadImage
 * <p>
 * Load the image with the given name.
 * <p>
 * @param imageName—The name of the image to load.
 * @return—The Image for the image with the given name.
 * @see #loadIcon
 **/
public static Image loadImage( String imageName )
    throws java.lang.InterruptedException {

    //
    // get the image, and wait for it to be loaded.
    //
    URL url = Object.class.getResource( imageName );

    //
            // If the URL could not be located above, try
            // prepending a '/' to the image's ResourceName. This
            // will cause the search to begin at the top of the
            // CLASSPATH.
            //
        if( url == null )
                url = Object.class.getResource( "/" + imageName );
    if( url == null ) {
        RuntimeException e = new RuntimeException( "Image " +
                                    imageName + " not found" );
        e.printStackTrace();
        throw e;
    }


        //
        // Get the image and wait for it to be loaded.
        //
    Image image = Toolkit.getDefaultToolkit().getImage( url );
    MediaTracker tracker = new MediaTracker( imageLoader );
    tracker.addImage( image, 0 );
    tracker.waitForID( 0 );

    return( image );
```

```
    } // loadImage


    /**
     * loadIcon
     * <p>
     * Load the Icon with the given name.
     * <p>
     * @param imageName—The name of the image to load.
     * @return—The Icon for the image with the given name.
     * @see #loadImage
     **/
    public static Icon loadIcon( String imageName )
        throws java.lang.InterruptedException {

        Image image = loadImage( imageName );
        return( new ImageIcon( image ) );

    } // loadIcon


    /**
     * static initialization.
     * <p>
     * Create an instance of this class that can be
     * used as the parameter to the MediaTracker while
     * loading images.
     **/
    static {
        imageLoader = new ImageLoader();
    } // static

} // ImageLoader
```

JavaFileView.java

```
package com.foley.utility;

import java.io.File;

import javax.swing.Icon;
import javax.swing.ImageIcon;
import javax.swing.filechooser.FileView;


public class JavaFileView extends FileView {

    /**
     * The icon for Java source files.
```

```
   **/
   Icon cupIcon = null;


   /**
    * Allow default processing.
    * <p>
    * @param file—The file who's name is reqested.
    * @return—The name for the file.
    **/
   public String getName( File file ) {
       return( null );
   }


   /**
    * @param file—The file who's description is reqested.
    * @return—The description for the given file.
    **/
   public String getDescription( File file ) {
       String extension = getExtension( file );
       if( extension != null && extension.equals( "java" ) ) {
           return( "A Java source file" );
       } else {
           return( null );
       }
   }


   /**
    * @param file—The file who's type description is reqested.
    * @return—The type description for the given file.
    **/
   public String getTypeDescription( File file ) {
       String extension = getExtension( file );
       if( extension != null && extension.equals( "java" ) ) {
           return( "Java source file" );
       } else {
           return( null );
       }
   }


   /**
    * @param file—The file who's icon is reqested.
    * @return—The icon for the given file.
    **/
   public Icon getIcon( File file ) {
       Icon icon = null;
```

```java
        String extension = getExtension( file );
        if( extension != null && extension.equals( "java" ) ) {

            if( cupIcon == null )
                cupIcon = new ImageIcon( "javacup.gif" );

            icon = cupIcon;
        }
        return( icon );
    }


    /**
     * Allow default processing.
     * <p>
     * @param file—The directory to test.
     * @return null to enable default processing.
     **/
    public Boolean isTraversable( File file ) {
        return( null );
    }

    /**
     * Determine the extension of the given File.
     * <p>
     * @param f—The File whose extension is desired.
     * @return—The extension of the given File, in lower case.
     **/
    protected String getExtension( File f ) {
        if(f != null) {
            String filename = f.getName();
            int i = filename.lastIndexOf( '.' );
            if(i>0 && i<filename.length() - 1) {
                return filename.substring( i + 1 ).toLowerCase();
            };
        }
        return null;
    }

} // JavaFileView
```

JBox.java

```java
package com.foley.utility;

import javax.swing.*;


/**
 * The JBox class is a Box replacement that
```

```
 * is a descendent of the JComponent class.
 * It is a JPanel configured with a BoxLayout
 * layout manager.
 * <p>
 * @author Mike Foley
 **/
public class JBox extends JPanel {

    public JBox( int orientation ) {
        BoxLayout boxLayout = new BoxLayout( this, orientation );
        setLayout( boxLayout );
    }


    /**
     * Create a JBox configured along its X-axis.
     * <p>
     * @return—A JBox configured along its X-axis.
     **/
    public static JBox createHorizontalJBox() {
        return new JBox( BoxLayout.X_AXIS );
    }


    /**
     * Create a JBox configured along its Y-axis.
     * <p>
     * @return—A JBox configured along its Y-axis.
     **/
    public static JBox createVerticalJBox() {
        return new JBox( BoxLayout.Y_AXIS );
    }

} // JBox
```

MDIFrame.java

```
package com.foley.utility;

import java.awt.*;

import java.awt.event.*;
import java.io.Serializable;
import java.util.Vector;

import javax.swing.*;

import javax.swing.border.*;
```

```java
import javax.swing.event.*;


/**
 * A toplevel frame. The frame configures itself
 * with a JDesktopPane in its content pane.
 *
 * @author Mike Foley
 **/
public class MDIFrame extends JFrame implements Serializable {

    /**
     * The desktop pane in our content pane.
     **/
    private JDesktopPane desktopPane;


    /**
     * MDIFrame, null constructor.
     **/
    public MDIFrame() {
        this( null );
    }


    /**
     * MDIFrame, constructor.
     *
     * @param title—The title for the frame.
     **/
    public MDIFrame( String title ) {
        super( title );
    }


    /**
     * Customize the frame for our application.
     **/
    protected void frameInit() {
        //
        // Let the super create the panes.
        super.frameInit();

        JMenuBar menuBar = createMenu();
        setJMenuBar( menuBar );

        JToolBar toolBar = createToolBar();
        Container content = getContentPane();
        content.add( toolBar, BorderLayout.NORTH );
```

```java
        desktopPane = new JDesktopPane();
        desktopPane.setPreferredSize( new Dimension( 400, 300 ) );
        content.add( desktopPane, BorderLayout.CENTER );

    } // frameInit


    /**
     * Create the menu for the frame.
     * <p>
     * @return—The menu for the frame.
     **/
    protected JMenuBar createMenu() {
        JMenuBar menuBar = new JMenuBar();

        JMenu file = new JMenu( "File" );
        file.setMnemonic( KeyEvent.VK_F );

        file.add( new NewInternalFrameAction() );
        file.add( new ExitAction() );

        menuBar.add( file );

        JMenu options = new JMenu( "Options" );
        options.setMnemonic( KeyEvent.VK_O );
        Vector frames = new Vector();
        frames.add( this );
        options.add( new SetJavaLookAndFeelAction( frames ) );
        options.add( new SetWindowsLookAndFeelAction( frames ) );
        options.add( new SetMotifLookAndFeelAction( frames ) );
        menuBar.add( options );

        ( ( JComponent )getContentPane() ).registerKeyboardAction(
                    new SetJavaLookAndFeelAction(),
                    KeyStroke.getKeyStroke( 'm' ),
                    JComponent.WHEN_IN_FOCUSED_WINDOW );
        ( ( JComponent )getContentPane() ).registerKeyboardAction(
                    new SetMotifLookAndFeelAction(),
                    KeyStroke.getKeyStroke( 'u' ),
                    JComponent.WHEN_IN_FOCUSED_WINDOW );
        ( ( JComponent )getContentPane() ).registerKeyboardAction(
                    new SetWindowsLookAndFeelAction(),
                    KeyStroke.getKeyStroke( 'w' ),
                    JComponent.WHEN_IN_FOCUSED_WINDOW );
        return( menuBar );

    } // createMenuBar


    /**
     * Create the toolbar for this frame.
```

```
     * <p>
     * @return—The newly created toolbar.
     **/
    protected JToolBar createToolBar() {
        final JToolBar toolBar = new JToolBar();
        toolBar.setFloatable( false );

        toolBar.add( new NewInternalFrameAction() );
        toolBar.add( new ExitAction() );
        return( toolBar );
    }


    /**
     * Create an internal frame.
     * <p>
     * @return—The newly created internal frame.
     **/
    public JInternalFrame createInternalFrame() {

        final JInternalFrame internalFrame =
              new JInternalFrame( "Internal JLabel" );
        JMenuBar menuBar = new JMenuBar();

        JMenu file = new JMenu( "File" );
        file.setMnemonic( KeyEvent.VK_F );

        Action disposeAction =
              new DisposeInternalFrameAction( internalFrame );
        Action exitAction = new ExitAction();
        file.add( disposeAction );
        file.add( exitAction );

        menuBar.add( file );
        internalFrame.setJMenuBar( menuBar );

        JToolBar toolBar = new JToolBar();
        toolBar.add( disposeAction );
        toolBar.add( exitAction );

        internalFrame.getContentPane().add(toolBar, BorderLayout.NORTH);

        JComponent content = new JLabel( "Internal Frame Content" );
        content.setBorder( BorderFactory.createLoweredBevelBorder() );
        internalFrame.getContentPane().add(
                        content,
                        BorderLayout.CENTER );
        internalFrame.setResizable( true );
        internalFrame.setClosable( true );
        internalFrame.setIconifiable( true );
```

```
        internalFrame.setMaximizable( true );
        internalFrame.pack();

          return( internalFrame );
    }

/**
 * Create an internal frame.
 * <p>
 * @return—The newly created internal frame.
 **/
 /*
public JInternalFrame createInternalFrame() {

    JInternalFrame internalFrame =
                new JInternalFrame( "Internal JLabel" );
    internalFrame.getContentPane().add(
                new JLabel( "Internal Frame Content" ) );
    internalFrame.setResizable( true );
    internalFrame.setClosable( true );
    internalFrame.setIconifiable( true );
    internalFrame.setMaximizable( true );
    internalFrame.pack();

      return( internalFrame );
}
*/

/**
 * An Action that creates a new internal frame and
 * adds it to this frame's desktop pane.
 **/
public class NewInternalFrameAction extends AbstractAction {

    /**
     * NewInternalFrameAction, constructor.
     * Set the name and icon for this action.
     **/
    public NewInternalFrameAction() {
        super( "New", new ImageIcon( "new.gif" ) );
    }

    /**
     * Perform the action, create an internal frame and
     * add it to the desktop pane.
     * <p>
     * @param e—The event causing us to be called.
     **/
    public void actionPerformed( ActionEvent e ) {
        JInternalFrame internalFrame = createInternalFrame();
```

```
            desktopPane.add( internalFrame, JLayeredPane.DEFAULT_LAYER );
        }

    }


    /**
     * An Action that disposes of an internal frame.
     **/
    public class DisposeInternalFrameAction extends AbstractAction {

        /**
         * The internal pane to close.
         **/
        private JInternalFrame internalFrame;


        /**
         * CloseInternalFrameAction, constructor.
         * Set the name and icon for this action.
         * <p>
         * @param internalFrame—The internal frame that we dispose of.
         **/
        public DisposeInternalFrameAction(JInternalFrame internalFrame) {
            super( "Close", new ImageIcon( "close.gif" ) );
            this.internalFrame = internalFrame;
        }


        /**
         * Perform the action, dispose of the internal frame.
         * <p>
         * @param e—The event causing us to be called.
         **/
        public void actionPerformed( ActionEvent e ) {
            internalFrame.dispose();
        }

    }

} // MDIFrame
```

MetalNonExpandingTreeUI.java

```
package com.foley.utility;

import java.awt.event.MouseEvent;
```

```java
import javax.swing.JComponent;
import javax.swing.plaf.ComponentUI;
import javax.swing.plaf.basic.BasicTreeUI;


/**
 * A TreeUI that does not automatically expand or
 * collapse the tree on a double-click event.
 * <p>
 * @author Mike Foley
 **/
public class MetalNonExpandingTreeUI extends BasicTreeUI
{

    /**
     * Create the UI object for the given tree. This
     * is a new instance of this class.
     **/
    public static ComponentUI createUI( JComponent tree ) {
        return( new MetalNonExpandingTreeUI() );
    }


    /**
     * MetalNonExpandingTreeUI, constructor
     **/
    public MetalNonExpandingTreeUI() {
        super();
    }


    /**
     * Returning true indicates the row under the mouse should be toggled
     * based on the event. This is invoked after
     * checkForClickInExpandControl, implying the location is not in
     * the expand (toggle) control
     * <p>
     * This is the behavior we want to squish, so always return false.
     * <p>
     * @return false
     **/
    protected boolean isToggleEvent( MouseEvent event ) {
        return( false );
    }

} // MetalNonExpandingTreeUI
```

NonExpandingTreeUI.java

```java
package com.foley.utility;

import java.awt.event.MouseEvent;

import javax.swing.JComponent;
import javax.swing.plaf.ComponentUI;
import javax.swing.plaf.basic.BasicTreeUI;


/**
 * A TreeUI that does not automatically expand or
 * collapse the tree on a double click event.
 * <p>
 * @author Mike Foley
 **/
public class NonExpandingTreeUI extends BasicTreeUI
{

    /**
     * Create the UI object for the given tree. This
     * is a new instance of this class.
     **/
    public static ComponentUI createUI( JComponent tree ) {
        return( new NonExpandingTreeUI() );
    }


    /**
     * NonExpandingTreeUI, constructor
     **/
    public NonExpandingTreeUI() {
        super();
    }


    /**
     * Returning true indicates the row under the mouse should be toggled
     * based on the event. This is invoked after
     * checkForClickInExpandControl, implying the location is not in
     * the expand (toggle) control
     * <p>
     * This is the behavior we want to squish, so always return false.
     * <p>
     * @return false
     **/
```

```
    protected boolean isToggleEvent( MouseEvent event ) {
        return( false );
    }

} // NonExpandingTreeUI
```

NoOpAction.java

```
package com.foley.utility;

import java.awt.event.*;

import javax.swing.*;


/**
 * Class NoOpAction
 * <p>
 * An action that does nothing.
 * <p>
 * @author Mike Foley
 * @version 1.2
 **/
public class NoOpAction extends AbstractAction {

    /**
     * The default name used in a menu.
     **/
    private static final String DEFAULT_NAME = "NoOp";


    /**
     * NoOpAction, default constructor.
     * <p>
     * Create the action with the default name.
     **/
    public NoOpAction() {
        this( DEFAULT_NAME );
    } // NoOpAction


    /**
     * NoOpAction, constructor.
     * <p>
     * Create the action with the given name.
     * <p>
     * @param name The name for the Action.
     **/
```

```
    public NoOpAction( String name ) {
        super( name );
    } // NoOpAction


    /**
     * actionPerformed, from ActionListener
     * <p>
     * Do nothing.
     * <p>
     * @param event—The event causing the action to fire.
     **/
    public void actionPerformed( ActionEvent event ) {
    } // actionPerformed

} // NoOpAction
```

OutlandishTheme.java

```
package com.foley.utility;

import java.awt.Font;

import javax.swing.plaf.ColorUIResource;
import javax.swing.plaf.FontUIResource;

import javax.swing.plaf.metal.DefaultMetalTheme;


/**
 * This class provides an outlandish color theme.
 * The primary and secondary colors are overriden.
 * The fonts and other theme properties are left unaltered.
 * <p>
 * @author Mike Foley
 **/
public class OutlandishTheme extends DefaultMetalTheme {

    public String getName() { return "OutlandishTheme"; }


    //
    // Primary Colors.
    //
    private final ColorUIResource primary1 =
                new ColorUIResource( 255, 0, 0 );
    private final ColorUIResource primary2 =
                new ColorUIResource(200, 25, 25);
    private final ColorUIResource primary3 =
                new ColorUIResource(150, 150, 150);
```

```
      protected ColorUIResource getPrimary1() { return primary1; }
      protected ColorUIResource getPrimary2() { return primary2; }
      protected ColorUIResource getPrimary3() { return primary3; }

      //
      // Secondary Colors.
      //
      private final ColorUIResource secondary1 =
                 new ColorUIResource( 0,  255,   0);
      private final ColorUIResource secondary2 =
                 new ColorUIResource(25, 200, 25);
      private final ColorUIResource secondary3 =
                 new ColorUIResource(40, 180, 40);

      protected ColorUIResource getSecondary1() { return secondary1; }
      protected ColorUIResource getSecondary2() { return secondary2; }
      protected ColorUIResource getSecondary3() { return secondary3; }

      //
      // Fonts.
      //
      private final FontUIResource font =
                 new FontUIResource("SansSerif", Font.BOLD, 18);
   public FontUIResource getControlTextFont() { return font;}
   public FontUIResource getSystemTextFont() { return font;}
   public FontUIResource getUserTextFont() { return font;}
   public FontUIResource getMenuTextFont() { return font;}
   public FontUIResource getWindowTitleFont() { return font;}
   public FontUIResource getSubTextFont() { return font;}

} // OutlandishTheme
```

PercentSlider.java

```
package com.foley.utility;

import java.text.NumberFormat;
import java.util.Hashtable;

import javax.swing.*;


/**
 * The PercentSlider class is a slider that formats its
 * labels using the % sign.
 * <p>
 * @author Mike Foley
 **/
```

C

```java
public class PercentSlider extends JSlider
{
    /**
     * PercentSlider, constructor
     * <p>
     * Configure the slider for normal percent range,
     * 0-100 and a current value of 0. The default major
     * tick spacing is set to 25 and minor tick spacing
     * to 5. Both labels and ticks are painted.
     * <p>
     * These values can be changed by the client using the
     * public API.
     *
     * @see JSlider
     **/
    public PercentSlider() {
        setMinimum( 0 );
        setMaximum( 100 );
        setValue( 0 );
        setMajorTickSpacing( 25 );
        setMinorTickSpacing( 5 );
        setPaintTicks( true );
        setPaintLabels( true );

    }


    /**
     * Create labels for the slider. Format each label
     * to contain a percent sign. A label is created
     * for each value from:
     * <p>
     *      start + x * increment
     * <p>
     * until the maximum value is reached.
     * <p>
     * @param increment—The delta between labels.
     * @param start—The value of the first label.
     * @return—The table of labels for the slider.
     **/
    public Hashtable createStandardLabels( int increment, int start ) {
        if ( start > getMaximum() ¦¦ start < getMinimum() ) {
            throw new IllegalArgumentException(
                "Slider label start point out of range." );
        }

        NumberFormat percent = NumberFormat.getPercentInstance();

        Hashtable table = new Hashtable();
```

```
        for ( int i = start; i <= getMaximum(); i += increment ) {
            JLabel l = new JLabel( percent.format( ( double )i / 100.0 )
);
            table.put( new Integer( i ), l );
        }

        return table;
    }


    /**
     * The label table is created by this class. Do not
     * allow it to be set from the outside.
     * <p>
     * @exception—RuntimeException If this method is called.
     **/
    public void setLabelTable() {
        throw new RuntimeException(
            "Can not set the label table for the PercentSlider" );
    }


    /**
     * setMajorTickSpacing
     * <p>
     * This method in the JSlider class does not create
     * labels if the label table has been created once.
     * This may cause the labels to be drawn in areas that
     * do not correspond to the major ticks. This is fixed
     * here by creating the label table whenever a new
     * major tick spacing is specified.
     * <p>
     * @param n—The new major tick spacing.
     **/
    public void setMajorTickSpacing( int n ) {
        if( getMajorTickSpacing() != n )
            setLabelTable( createStandardLabels( n ) );
        super.setMajorTickSpacing( n );
    }
}

} // PercentSlider
```

PrintAction.java

```
package com.foley.utility;

import java.awt.Component;
```

```java
import java.awt.event.ActionListener;
import java.awt.event.ActionEvent;

import javax.swing.AbstractAction;
import javax.swing.Icon;


/**
 * Class PrintAction
 * <p>
 * An action that prints the source view.
 * <p>
 * @author Mike Foley
 * @version 1.2
 **/
public class PrintAction extends AbstractAction {

    /**
     * The default name and Icon for the Action.
     **/
    private static final String DEFAULT_NAME = "Print";
    private static final String DEFAULT_ICON_NAME = "print.gif";
    private static Icon DEFAULT_ICON;


    /**
     * PrintAction, constructor
     **/
    public PrintAction() {
        super( DEFAULT_NAME, DEFAULT_ICON );
    } // PrintAction


    /**
     * actionPerformed, from ActionListener
     * <p>
     * Perform the action. Print the view showing in the
     * tabbed panel in the frame where the event originated.
     * <p>
     * @param event—The event causing the action to fire.
     **/
    public void actionPerformed( ActionEvent event ) {
    } // actionPerformed


    /**
     * static initialization. Load the default Icon.
     **/
    static {
```

```
        try {
            DEFAULT_ICON = ImageLoader.loadIcon( DEFAULT_ICON_NAME );
        } catch( InterruptedException ie ) {
            System.err.println(
                    "Could not load PrintAction default Icon" );
        }
    }

} // PrintAction
```

SetJavaLookAndFeelAction.java

```
package com.foley.utility;

import java.util.Vector;

import javax.swing.Icon;


/**
 * Class SetJavaLookAndFeelAction
 * <p>
 * A convenience look-and-feel action that sets the Java look-and-feel.
 * <p>
 * @author Mike Foley
 * @version 1.2
 **/
public class SetJavaLookAndFeelAction extends SetLookAndFeelAction {

    /**
     * The default name used in a menu.
     **/
    private static final String DEFAULT_NAME = "Java";

    /**
     * The Java look-and-feel name.
     **/
    private static final String LOOKANDFEEL =
            "com.sun.java.swing.plaf.metal.MetalLookAndFeel";


    public SetJavaLookAndFeelAction() {
        this( null, null );
    } // SetJavaLookAndFeelAction

    public SetJavaLookAndFeelAction( Icon icon ) {
        this( icon, null );
    } // SetJavaLookAndFeelAction
```

```java
    public SetJavaLookAndFeelAction( Vector frames ) {
        this( null, frames );
    } // SetJavaLookAndFeelAction

    public SetJavaLookAndFeelAction( Icon icon, Vector frames ) {
        super( DEFAULT_NAME, icon, LOOKANDFEEL, frames );
    } // SetJavaLookAndFeelAction

    public SetJavaLookAndFeelAction( String name,
                                     Icon icon,
                                     Vector frames ) {
        super( name, icon, LOOKANDFEEL, frames );
    } // SetJavaLookAndFeelAction


    public String toString() {
        return( "Java" );
    }

} // SetJavaLookAndFeelAction
```

SetLookAndFeelAction.java

```java
package com.foley.utility;

import java.awt.*;
import java.awt.event.*;
import java.util.*;

import javax.swing.*;


/**
 * Class SetLookAndFeelAction
 * <p>
 * An action that sets the look-and-feel to the given
 * look-and-feel class name.
 * <p>
 * @author Mike Foley
 * @version 1.2
 **/
public class SetLookAndFeelAction extends AbstractAction {

    /**
     * The default name used in a menu.
     **/
    private static final String DEFAULT_NAME = "Set Look and Feel";
```

```
/**
 * The key into our property table of the name of the class
 * containing the look-and-feel.
 **/
private static final String LOOKANDFEELNAME_KEY =
                            "LookAndFeelNameKey";

/**
 * The key into our property table for the collection of Frames
 * to update when this action is invoked.
 **/
private static final String FRAMESTOUPDAT_KEY = "FramesToUpdateKey";

/**
 * Initialize the Action with the given name and look-and-feel name.
 * <p>
 * @param name—The name for the Action.
 * @param lookAndFeelName—The look-and-feel class name.
 **/
public SetLookAndFeelAction( String name, String lookAndFeelName ) {
    this( name, null, lookAndFeelName, null );
} // SetLookAndFeelAction

/**
 * Initialize the Action with the given name and look-and-feel name.
 * <p>
 * @param name—The name for the Action.
 * @param icon—The Icon for the Action.
 * @param lookAndFeelName—The look and feel class name.
 * @param framesToUpdate—Each Component in this array will have
 *         its component tree udpated when this action is invoked.
 **/
public SetLookAndFeelAction( String name,
                             Icon icon,
                             String lookAndFeelName,
                             Vector framesToUpdate ) {
    super( name );

    if( lookAndFeelName == null )
        throw new RuntimeException(
                "Look-and-feel name may not be null." );

    if( icon != null )
        putValue( SMALL_ICON, icon );
    putValue( LOOKANDFEELNAME_KEY, lookAndFeelName );
    if( framesToUpdate != null )
        putValue( FRAMESTOUPDAT_KEY, framesToUpdate );
```

```
} // SetLookAndFeelAction


/**
 * actionPerformed, from ActionListener
 * <p>
 * Perform the action. Set the look-and-feel
 * to that defined by the look-and-feel attribute.
 * Update the source frame and frames in the
 * frames Vector.
 * <p>
 * @param event—The event causing the action to fire.
 **/
public void actionPerformed( ActionEvent event ) {

    try {
        String lookAndFeelName = ( String )getValue(
                            LOOKANDFEELNAME_KEY );
        UIManager.setLookAndFeel( lookAndFeelName );

        //
        // Update component tree for the source of the event.
        //
        Object o = event.getSource();
        if( o instanceof Component ) {
            Frame frame = JOptionPane.getFrameForComponent(
                                ( Component )o );
            SwingUtilities.updateComponentTreeUI( frame );
        }

        //
        // See if there are any registered frames to update.
        //
        Vector framesToUpdate = (Vector)getValue(FRAMESTOUPDAT_KEY);
        if( framesToUpdate != null ) {
            for( Enumeration e = framesToUpdate.elements();
                 e.hasMoreElements(); ) {
                Object f = e.nextElement();
                if( f instanceof Component ) {
                    Frame frame = JOptionPane.getFrameForComponent(
                                        ( Component )f );
                    SwingUtilities.updateComponentTreeUI( frame );
                }
            }
        }
    } catch( ClassNotFoundException cnf ) {
        throw new RuntimeException( cnf.getLocalizedMessage() );
    } catch( InstantiationException ie ) {
        throw new RuntimeException( ie.getLocalizedMessage() );
```

```
            } catch( UnsupportedLookAndFeelException ulf ) {
                throw new RuntimeException( ulf.getLocalizedMessage() );
            } catch( IllegalAccessException ia ) {
                throw new RuntimeException( ia.getLocalizedMessage() );
            } // catch

        } // actionPerformed

    } // SetLookAndFeelAction
```

SetMotifLookAndFeelAction.java

```java
package com.foley.utility;

import java.util.Vector;

import javax.swing.Icon;


/**
 * Class SetMotifLookAndFeelAction
 * <p>
 * A convenience look-and-feel action that sets the motif look-and-feel.
 * <p>
 * @author Mike Foley
 * @version 1.2
 **/
public class SetMotifLookAndFeelAction extends SetLookAndFeelAction {

    /**
     * The default name used in a menu.
     **/
    private static final String DEFAULT_NAME = "Motif";

    /**
     * The motif look-and-feel name.
     **/
    private static final String LOOKANDFEEL =
                    "com.sun.java.swing.plaf.motif.MotifLookAndFeel";


    public SetMotifLookAndFeelAction() {
        this( null, null );
    } // SetMotifLookAndFeelAction
```

```
    public SetMotifLookAndFeelAction( Icon icon ) {
        this( icon, null );
    } // SetMotifLookAndFeelAction

    public SetMotifLookAndFeelAction( Vector frames ) {
        this( null, frames );
    } // SetJavaLookAndFeelAction

    public SetMotifLookAndFeelAction( Icon icon, Vector frames ) {
        super( DEFAULT_NAME, icon, LOOKANDFEEL, frames );
    } // SetMotifLookAndFeelAction

    public SetMotifLookAndFeelAction( String name,
                                      Icon icon,
                                      Vector frames ) {
        super( name, icon, LOOKANDFEEL, frames );
    } // SetMotifLookAndFeelAction


    public String toString() {
        return( "Motif" );
    }

} // SetMotifLookAndFeelAction
```

SetWindowsLookAndFeel.java

```
package com.foley.utility;

import java.util.Vector;

import javax.swing.Icon;


/**
 * Class SetWindowsLookAndFeelAction
 * <p>
 * A convenience look-and-feel action that sets the MS Windows look-and-
feel.
 * <p>
 * @author Mike Foley
 * @version 1.2
 **/
public class SetWindowsLookAndFeelAction extends SetLookAndFeelAction {

    /**
     * The default name used in a menu.
```

```
    **/
    private static final String DEFAULT_NAME = "Windows";

    /**
     * The Windows look-and-feel name.
     **/
    private static final String LOOKANDFEEL =
            "com.sun.java.swing.plaf.windows.WindowsLookAndFeel";


    public SetWindowsLookAndFeelAction() {
        this( null, null );
    } // SetWindowsLookAndFeelAction

    public SetWindowsLookAndFeelAction( Icon icon ) {
        this( icon, null );
    } // SetWindowsLookAndFeelAction

    public SetWindowsLookAndFeelAction( Vector frames ) {
        this( null, frames );
    } // SetJavaLookAndFeelAction

    public SetWindowsLookAndFeelAction( Icon icon, Vector frames ) {
        super( DEFAULT_NAME, icon, LOOKANDFEEL, frames );
    } // SetWindowsLookAndFeelAction

    public SetWindowsLookAndFeelAction( String name,
                                        Icon icon,
                                        Vector frames ) {
        super( name, icon, LOOKANDFEEL, frames );
    } // SetWindowsLookAndFeelAction


    public String toString() {
        return( "Windows" );
    }

} // SetWindowsLookAndFeelAction
```

SimpleListCellRenderer.java

```
package com.foley.utility;

import java.awt.*;
import java.io.*;

import javax.swing.*;
import javax.swing.border.*;
```

```
public class SimpleListCellRenderer extends JLabel
    implements ListCellRenderer, Serializable
{

    protected static Border emptyBorder;

    public SimpleListCellRenderer() {
        super();

            emptyBorder = BorderFactory.createEmptyBorder( 2, 2, 2, 2 );

            //
            // We change the background color, so need to be opaque.
            //
        setOpaque(true);
    }


    public Component getListCellRendererComponent(
        JList list,
         Object value,
        int index,
        boolean isSelected,
        boolean cellHasFocus)
    {

        if( isSelected ) {
            //
            // Draw like any other list when selected.
            //
            setBackground( list.getSelectionBackground() );
            setForeground( list.getSelectionForeground() );
        } else {
            //
            // Paint in the list's normal foreground and background
               colors.
            //
            setBackground( list.getBackground() );
            setForeground( list.getForeground() );
        } // else

        if( value instanceof Icon ) {
            setIcon( ( Icon )value);
            setText( "" );
        } else {
            setIcon( null );
            setText( (value == null ) ? "" : value.toString() );
        } // else

        setFont( list.getFont() );
        setBorder( ( cellHasFocus ) ?
```

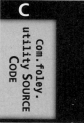

```
                    UIManager.getBorder( "List.focusCellHighlightBorder" ) :
                    emptyBorder );

            return this;
        }

    } // SimpleListRenderer
```

SliderValuePanel.java

```java
package com.foley.utility;

import java.awt.*;

import javax.swing.*;
import javax.swing.event.*;


/**
 * The SliderValuePanel class is a panel that contains a
 * slider and a label to dipslay the current value in the slider.
 * <p>
 * The current implementation requires the user to get the slider
 * to configure it. Wrapper methods for the BoundedRangeModel
 * method should be provided.
 * <p>
 * @author Mike Foley
 **/
public class SliderValuePanel extends JPanel
    implements ChangeListener {

    /**
     * Components in the panel.
     **/
    private JSlider slider;
    private JLabel label;

    /**
     * The String to which the current value is appended.
     **/
    private static final String labelBase = "Current Value: ";


    /**
     * SliderValuePanel, constructor
     * <p>
     * Create the JSlider instance and JLabel instance
     * and arrange them in the panel.
```

```
    **/
    public SliderValuePanel() {
        super();

        setLayout( new BorderLayout() );

        slider = new JSlider();
        slider.setMajorTickSpacing( 20 );
        slider.setMinorTickSpacing( 5 );
        slider.setPaintTicks( true );
        slider.setPaintLabels( true );

        label = new JLabel( labelBase + slider.getValue() );

        add( slider, BorderLayout.CENTER );
        add( label, BorderLayout.SOUTH );

        slider.addChangeListener( this );
    }


    /**
     * Return the slider in this panel. This allows
     * clients to get a handle to the slider and configure
     * it is required.
     * <p>
     * @return—The slider in this panel.
     **/
    public JSlider getSlider() {
        return( slider );
    }


    /**
     * stateChanged, from ChangeListener
     * <p>
     * The slider in the panel value has changed.
     * Update the label's text.
     * <p>
     * @param ChangeEvent event—The event causing this method to be
     *                                 called.
     **/
    public void stateChanged( ChangeEvent event ) {
        label.setText( labelBase + slider.getValue() );
    }

} // SliderValuePanel
```

SplashWindow.java

```java
package com.foley.utility;

import java.awt.*;
import java.beans.*;
import javax.swing.*;


/**
 * A window that contains an image.
 *
 * @author Mike Foley
 **/
public class SplashWindow extends JWindow {

    /**
     * The Icon displayed in the window.
     **/
    private Icon splashIcon;

    /**
     * A label used to display the Icon.
     **/
    private JLabel iconLabel;

    /**
     * Bound property support and name constants.
     **/
    private PropertyChangeSupport changeSupport;
    public static final String SPLASHICON_PROPERTY = "SplashIcon";


    /**
     * SplashWindow, null constructor.
     **/
    public SplashWindow() {
        this( null );
    }


    /**
     * SplashWindow, constructor.
     *
     * @param splashIcon—The Icon to view in the window.
     **/
    public SplashWindow( Icon splashIcon ) {
        super();
        iconLabel = new JLabel();
        iconLabel.setBorder( BorderFactory.createRaisedBevelBorder() );
        getContentPane().add( iconLabel, BorderLayout.CENTER );
```

```
        setSplashIcon( splashIcon );
    }


    /**
     * Set the image displayed in the window.
     * This is a bound property named SPLASHICON_PROPERTY.
     * If this property is changed when the window is
     * visible, the window is NOT re-centered on the screen.
     *
     * @param splashIcon—The icon to draw in the window.
     **/
    public void setSplashIcon( Icon splashIcon ) {
        Icon old = this.splashIcon;
        this.splashIcon = splashIcon;
        iconLabel.setIcon( splashIcon );
        pack();
        if( changeSupport != null ) {
            changeSupport.firePropertyChange( SPLASHICON_PROPERTY,
                                              old, splashIcon );
        }
    }


    /**
     * Extend the setVisible method to center this window
     * on the screen before being displayed.
     *
     * @param visible—True if showing the window, false if hiding.
     **/
    public void setVisible( boolean visible ) {

        if( visible ) {

            //
            // Display the window in the center of the screen.
            //
            Dimension screenSize =
                Toolkit.getDefaultToolkit().getScreenSize();
            Dimension size = getSize();
            int x;
            int y;

            x = screenSize.width / 2 - size.width / 2;
            y = screenSize.height / 2 - size.height / 2;

                setBounds( x, y, size.width, size.height);
        }

        //
        // Let super show or hide the window.
```

```
        //
        super.setVisible( visible );
    }


    /**
     * Need to handle PropertyChangeListeners here until this
     * type of code is moved from JComponent to Component.
     **/
    public synchronized void addPropertyChangeListener(
                        PropertyChangeListener listener) {
        if (changeSupport == null) {
            changeSupport = new PropertyChangeSupport(this);
        }
        changeSupport.addPropertyChangeListener(listener);
    }
    public synchronized void removePropertyChangeListener(
                        PropertyChangeListener listener) {
        if (changeSupport != null) {
            changeSupport.removePropertyChangeListener(listener);
        }
    }
}

} // SplashWindow
```

TableMap.java

```
package com.foley.utility;


import javax.swing.table.*;
import javax.swing.event.TableModelListener;
import javax.swing.event.TableModelEvent;


/**
 * Based on the example that comes with the Swing download.
 **/
public class TableMap extends AbstractTableModel
    implements TableModelListener {

    /**
     * The downstream model.
     **/
    protected TableModel model;

    /**
     * @return—Our table model.
     **/
```

```java
    public TableModel  getModel() {
        return model;
    }

    /**
     * Set our downstream table model.
     * If we already have a table model, stop listening
     * to that model and start listening to the new
     * model.
     * <p>
     * 2param The new model.
     **/
    public void  setModel(TableModel model) {
        if( this.model != null )
            this.model.removeTableModelListener(this);
        this.model = model;
        if( this.model != null )
            this.model.addTableModelListener(this);
    }

    public Object getValueAt(int aRow, int aColumn) {
        return model.getValueAt(aRow, aColumn);
    }

    public void setValueAt(Object aValue, int aRow, int aColumn) {
        model.setValueAt(aValue, aRow, aColumn);
    }

    public int getRowCount() {
        return (model == null) ? 0 : model.getRowCount();
    }

    public int getColumnCount() {
        return (model == null) ? 0 : model.getColumnCount();
    }

    public String getColumnName(int aColumn) {
        return model.getColumnName(aColumn);
    }

    public Class getColumnClass(int aColumn) {
        return model.getColumnClass(aColumn);
    }

    public boolean isCellEditable(int row, int column) {
        return model.isCellEditable(row, column);
    }
```

```
        public void tableChanged(TableModelEvent e) {
            fireTableChanged(e);
        }

} // TableMap
```

TableSorter.java

```java
package com.foley.utility;

import java.util.*;

import java.awt.event.MouseAdapter;
import java.awt.event.MouseEvent;
import java.awt.event.InputEvent;

import javax.swing.JTable;

import javax.swing.table.JTableHeader;
import javax.swing.table.TableColumn;
import javax.swing.table.TableColumnModel;
import javax.swing.table.TableModel;

import javax.swing.event.TableModelEvent;


/**
 * Based on the demo class that comes with the Swing package.
 **/
public class TableSorter extends TableMap
{
    int             indexes[];
    Vector          sortingColumns = new Vector();
    boolean         ascending = true;
    int compares;

    public TableSorter()
    {
        indexes = new int[0]; // For consistency.
    }

    public TableSorter(TableModel model)
    {
        setModel(model);
    }

    public void setModel(TableModel model) {
        super.setModel(model);
```

```
        reallocateIndexes();
}

public int compareRowsByColumn(int row1, int row2, int column)
{
    Class type = model.getColumnClass(column);
    TableModel data = model;

    // Check for nulls

    Object o1 = data.getValueAt(row1, column);
    Object o2 = data.getValueAt(row2, column);

    // If both values are null return 0
    if (o1 == null && o2 == null) {
        return 0;
    }
    else if (o1 == null) { // Define null less than everything.
        return -1;
    }
    else if (o2 == null) {
        return 1;
    }

    if (type.getSuperclass() == java.lang.Number.class)
        {
            Number n1 = (Number)data.getValueAt(row1, column);
            double d1 = n1.doubleValue();
            Number n2 = (Number)data.getValueAt(row2, column);
            double d2 = n2.doubleValue();

            if (d1 < d2)
                return -1;
            else if (d1 > d2)
                return 1;
            else
                return 0;
        }
    else if (type == java.util.Date.class)
        {
            Date d1 = (Date)data.getValueAt(row1, column);
            long n1 = d1.getTime();
            Date d2 = (Date)data.getValueAt(row2, column);
            long n2 = d2.getTime();

            if (n1 < n2)
                return -1;
            else if (n1 > n2)
                return 1;
```

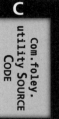

```
                    else return 0;
              }
        else if (type == String.class)
            {
                String s1 = ( (String)data.getValueAt(
                          row1, column) ).toUpperCase();
                String s2    = ( (String)data.getValueAt(
                          row2, column) ).toUpperCase();
                int result = s1.compareTo(s2);

                if (result < 0)
                    return -1;
                else if (result > 0)
                    return 1;
                else return 0;
            }
        else if (type == Boolean.class)
            {
                Boolean bool1 = (Boolean)data.getValueAt(row1, column);
                boolean b1 = bool1.booleanValue();
                Boolean bool2 = (Boolean)data.getValueAt(row2, column);
                boolean b2 = bool2.booleanValue();

                if (b1 == b2)
                    return 0;
                else if (b1) // Define false < true
                    return 1;
                else
                    return -1;
            }
        else
            {
                Object v1 = data.getValueAt(row1, column);
                String s1 = v1.toString();
                Object v2 = data.getValueAt(row2, column);
                String s2 = v2.toString();
                int result = s1.compareTo(s2);

                if (result < 0)
                    return -1;
                else if (result > 0)
                    return 1;
                else return 0;
            }
    }

    public int compare(int row1, int row2)
    {
        compares++;
```

```
        for(int level = 0; level < sortingColumns.size(); level++)
            {
                Integer column =
➡                       (Integer)sortingColumns.elementAt(level);
                int result = compareRowsByColumn(row1, row2,
➡                       column.intValue());
                if (result != 0)
                    return ascending ? result : -result;
            }
        return 0;
    }

    public void  reallocateIndexes()
    {
        int rowCount = model.getRowCount();

        // Set up a new array of indexes with the right number of
        // elements for the new data model.
        //
        indexes = new int[rowCount];

        // Initialise with the identity mapping.
        for(int row = 0; row < rowCount; row++)
            indexes[row] = row;
    }

    public void tableChanged(TableModelEvent e)
    {
        reallocateIndexes();
        sortByColumn(0);
        fireTableStructureChanged();
    }

    public void checkModel()
    {
        if (indexes.length != model.getRowCount()) {
            System.err.println(
                    "Sorter not informed of a change in model.");
        }
    }

    public void  sort(Object sender)
    {
        checkModel();

        compares = 0;
        shuttlesort((int[])indexes.clone(), indexes, 0, indexes.length);
    }
```

```java
public void shuttlesort(int from[], int to[], int low, int high) {
    if (high - low < 2) {
        return;
    }
    int middle = (low + high)/2;
    shuttlesort(to, from, low, middle);
    shuttlesort(to, from, middle, high);

    int p = low;
    int q = middle;

    if (high - low >= 4 &&
        compare(from[middle-1], from[middle]) <= 0) {
        for (int i = low; i < high; i++) {
            to[i] = from[i];
        }
        return;
    }

    for(int i = low; i < high; i++) {
        if (q >= high ||
            (p < middle && compare(from[p], from[q]) <= 0)) {
            to[i] = from[p++];
        }
        else {
            to[i] = from[q++];
        }
    }
}

public void swap(int i, int j) {
    int tmp = indexes[i];
    indexes[i] = indexes[j];
    indexes[j] = tmp;
}

public Object getValueAt(int aRow, int aColumn)
{
    checkModel();
    return model.getValueAt(indexes[aRow], aColumn);
}

public void setValueAt(Object aValue, int aRow, int aColumn)
{
    checkModel();
    model.setValueAt(aValue, indexes[aRow], aColumn);
}

public void sortByColumn(int column) {
    sortByColumn(column, true);
}
```

```
    public void sortByColumn(int column, boolean ascending) {
        this.ascending = ascending;
        sortingColumns.removeAllElements();
        sortingColumns.addElement(new Integer(column));
        sort(this);
        super.tableChanged(new TableModelEvent(this));
    }

} // TableSorter
```

TextFilterDocument.java

```
package com.foley.utility;

import java.awt.Toolkit;

import javax.swing.text.*;


/**
 * Document to only allow numbers.
 * <p>
 * @author Mike Foley
 **/
public class TextFilterDocument extends PlainDocument {

    /**
     * Valid number strings.
     **/
    public static final String NUMBERS = "0123456789";


    /**
     * TextFilterDocument, constructor
     **/
    public TextFilterDocument()
    {
        super();
    }


    /**
     * A String is being inserted into the document.
     * Ensure that all characters are in NUMBERS.
     *
     * @param offset—Where the new string goes.
     * @param string—The String to be inserted after check.
     * @param attributeSet—Attributes for the new string.
     **/
```

```java
        public void insertString( int offset, String string,
                                  AttributeSet attributeSet )
        throws BadLocationException {

            //
            // If nothing to insert, do nothing.
            //
            if( string == null )
                return;

            //
            // Ensure each character in the string is a number.
            //
            for( int i = 0; i < string.length(); i++ ) {
                if( NUMBERS.indexOf( string.valueOf(
                    string.charAt(i) ) ) == -1 ) {

                    //
                    // Not a number, don't insert the string.
                    // Beep to let the user know something is wrong.
                    //
                    Toolkit.getDefaultToolkit().beep();
                    return;
                }
            }

            //
            // Let our parent do the real work.
            //
            super.insertString( offset, string, attributeSet );

        } // insertString

} // TextFilterDocument
```

TreeLeafEditor.java

```java
package com.foley.utility;

import java.awt.event.*;
import java.util.*;

import javax.swing.*;
import javax.swing.tree.*;


/**
 * A tree editor that only allows editing of leaf nodes.
 * <p>
 * @author Mike Foley
```

```
**/
public class TreeLeafEditor extends DefaultCellEditor {

    /**
     * The tree we are editing.
     **/
    JTree tree;

    public TreeLeafEditor( JTree tree ) {
        super( new JTextField() );
        this.tree = tree;
    }


    /**
     * The cell is only editable if it is a leaf node and
     * the number of mouse clicks is equal to the value
     * returned from the getClickCountToStart method.
     * <p>
     * @param event—The event to test for cell editablity.
     * @return—True if the cell is editable given the current event.
     * @see—getClickCountToStart
     **/
    public boolean isCellEditable( EventObject event ) {

        if( event instanceof MouseEvent ) {
            MouseEvent mouseEvent = ( MouseEvent )event;
            if( mouseEvent.getClickCount() == getClickCountToStart() ) {
                TreePath hitPath = tree.getPathForLocation(
                                        mouseEvent.getX(),
                                        mouseEvent.getY() );
                Object hitObject = hitPath.getLastPathComponent();
                if( hitObject instanceof TreeNode )
                    return( ( ( TreeNode )hitObject ).isLeaf() );
            }
        }
        return( false );
    }

} // TreeLeafEditor
```

TwoStateInterface.java

```
//Title:       Utility Beans
//Version:     1.1
//Copyright:   Copyright (c) 1997
//Author:      Mike Foley
```

```
//Company:     Foley, Inc.
//Description:A collection of usefull beans.

package com.foley.utility;

import java.awt.AWTEvent;


/**
 * TwoStateInterface
 *
 * An interface for components that have two states.
 *
 * @author Mike Foley
 * @version 1.1
 *
 **/
public interface TwoStateInterface {
    public abstract boolean queryState();
    public abstract void stateOn();
    public abstract void stateOff();
} // TwoStateInterface
```

WindowsNonExpandingTreeUI.java

```
package com.foley.utility;

import java.awt.event.MouseEvent;

import javax.swing.JComponent;
import javax.swing.plaf.ComponentUI;
import javax.swing.plaf.basic.BasicTreeUI;


/**
 * A TreeUI that does not automatically expand or
 * collapse the tree on a double-click event.
 * <p>
 * @author Mike Foley
 **/
public class WindowsNonExpandingTreeUI extends BasicTreeUI
{

    /**
     * Create the UI object for the given tree. This
     * is a new instance of this class.
     **/
```

```
public static ComponentUI createUI( JComponent tree ) {
    return( new WindowsNonExpandingTreeUI() );
}


/**
 * WindowsNonExpandingTreeUI, constructor
 **/
public WindowsNonExpandingTreeUI() {
    super();
}


/**
 * Returning true indicates the row under the mouse should be toggled
 * based on the event. This is invoked after
 * checkForClickInExpandControl, implying the location is not in the
 * expand (toggle) control
 * <p>
 * This is the behavior we want to squish, so always return false.
 * <p>
 * @return false
 **/
protected boolean isToggleEvent( MouseEvent event ) {
    return( false );
}

} // WindowsNonExpandingTreeUI
```

INDEX

H

L

THE COMPREHENSIVE SOLUTION

Unleashed *takes you beyond the average technology discussions. It's the best resource for practical advice from experts and the most in-depth coverage of the latest information.* **Unleashed**—*the necessary tool for serious users.*

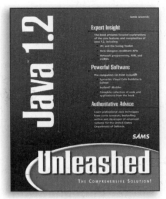

Java 1.2 Unleashed

Jamie Jaworski
ISBN: 1-57521-389-3
$49.99 U.S./$71.95 CAN

Other Unleashed Titles

Java 1.2 Unleashed
Jamie Jaworski
ISBN: 1-57521-389-3
$49.99 U.S./$71.95 CAN

Java 1.2 Class Libraries Unleashed
Krishan Sankar
ISBN: 0-7897-1292-x
$49.99 U.S./$71.95 CAN

Java 1.2 Class Libraries Unleashed

Krishan Sankar
ISBN: 0-7897-1292-x
$49.99 U.S./$71.95 CAN

SAMS

www.samspublishing.com

All prices are subject to change.

Other Related Titles

**Special Edition
Using Java 1.2**
Joseph L. Weber
ISBN: 0-7897-1529-5
$39.99 U.S./$57.95 CAN

Special Edition Using Java 1.2
Joseph L. Weber
ISBN: 0-7897-1529-5
$39.99 U.S./$57.95 CAN

**Data Structures and
Algorithms in Java (Mitchell
Waite Signature Series)**
*Mitchell Waite and
Robert Lafore*
ISBN: 0-57169-095-6
$49.99 U.S./$71.95 CAN

**Object-Oriented Programming
in Java (Mitchell Waite
Signature Series)**
*Stephen Gilbert and
Bill McCarty*
ISBN: 1-57169-086-7
$59.99 U.S./$85.95 CAN

Using Visual J++ 6
Scott Mulloy
ISBN: 0-7897-1400-0
$29.99 U.S./$42.95 CAN

**Sams Teach Yourself Visual
J++ 6 in 21 Days**
Rick Leinecker
ISBN: 0-672-31351-0
$29.99 U.S./$42.95 CAN

**Data Structures
and Algorithms in
Java (Mitchell
Waite Signature
Series)**
*Mitchell Waite and
Robert Lafore*
ISBN: 0-57169-095-6
$49.99 U.S./$71.95 CAN

**Object-Oriented
Programming in
Java (Mitchell
Waite Signature
Series)**
*Stephen Gilbert and
Bill McCarty*
ISBN: 1-57169-086-7
$59.99 U.S./$85.95 CAN

www.samspublishing.com

All prices are subject to change.

What's on the CD

Code

Complete code listings from the book.

3rd Party Products

- JBuilder Publisher's Edition—The most comprehensive set of visual development tools for creating Pure Java business and database applications.
- KAWA—A powerful and intuitive environment for Java development.
- Bluette—Compile and run source programs and browse class hierarchy and members.
- The Gamelet Toolkit—A framework of classes and interfaces used for developing arcade style video games and entertainment applets.
- Java Class Disassembler (JCD)—Win32 GUI program that allows you to view the contents of Java class files.
- CooCoo—Full Java chat and communications program.

Read This Before Opening Software

By opening this package, you are agreeing to be bound by the following:

This software is copyrighted and all rights are reserved by the publisher and its licensers. You are licensed to use this software on a single computer. You may copy the software for backup or archival purposes only. Making copies of the software for any other purpose is a violation of United States copyright laws. THIS SOFTWARE IS SOLD AS IS, WITHOUT WARRANTY OF ANY KIND, EITHER EXPRESSED OR IMPLIED, INCLUDING BUT NOT LIMITED TO THE IMPLIED WARRANTIES OF MERCHANTABILITY AND FITNESS FOR A PARTICULAR PURPOSE. Neither the publisher nor its dealers and distributors nor its licensers assume any liability for any alleged or actual damages arising from the use of this software. (Some states do not allow exclusion of implied warranties, so the exclusion may not apply to you.)

The entire contents of this disc and the compilation of the software are copyrighted and protected by United States copyright laws. The individual programs on the disc are copyrighted by the authors or owners of each program. Each program has its own use permissions and limitations. To use each program, you must follow the individual requirements and restrictions detailed for each. Do not use a program if you do not agree to follow its licensing agreement.